Wrestling Record Book:

Jim Crockett Promotions 1980-1988

Wrestling Record Book:

Jim Crockett Promotions 1980-1988

Mark James

Wrestling Record Book: Jim Crockett Promotions 1980-1988

Copyright @ 2014 by Mark James

All rights reserved. No part of this book may be reproduced or transmitted in any form or by any means, electronic or mechanical, including photocopying, recording, scanning, or by any information storage and retrieval system, without written permission from the author.

Published by Mark James www.memphiswrestlinghistory.com

Book layout by Mark James
Content Editing by Mark James
Covers created by Mark James
Cover photo by Mark James

James, Mark
Wrestling Record Book: Jim Crockett Promotions 1980-1988/by Mark James – 1st ed.

Printed in the United States of America

ISBN-13: 978-1500256593
ISBN-10: 1500256595

Table of Contents

Introduction

Dick Bourne

The 1980s were a decade of rapid and dramatic changes for the family run business of Jim Crockett Promotions.

While many territories began to struggle during this decade in the face of the WWF's aggressive and often hostile expansion, JCP steadily grew and became stronger, eventually becoming the only real challenger to Vince McMahon in the wrestling business in the mid-to-late 1980s.

Jim Crockett served as president of the National Wrestling Alliance for many of these years and his strong sponsorship of Ric Flair for the NWA world title led to the Nature Boy's ascension to the thrown in 1981. It was a spot Flair would occupy off and on for the next two decades.

In 1983, Crockett took the "super show" concept to a new level with the advent of Starrcade and the utilization of closed-circuit television. The success of these efforts led to further growth in the fledgling pay-per-view industry in the mid-to-late 1980s.

By 1985, Jim Crockett Promotions was in the middle of an aggressive expansion of its own, competing head to head for the first time with the WWF across the United States in the following years. They grabbed the national TV slots on Superstation WTBS and began to gobble up other struggling regional offices of the NWA to broaden their syndicated television network.

That rapid expansion came with a price, however, as payroll, programming, and travel costs ballooned and eventually JCP collapsed under a mountain of debt, resulting in the sale of the 53 year old company in 1988 to Ted Turner.

This collection of match listings and results is a huge snap-shot of the in-ring product of the company in its final decade, acting also as a talent roster over these years. As you browse these great shows, from the smallest venues to the largest, you are reminded of what a wonderful era the 1980s were for wrestling in Jim Crockett Promotions and the amazing amount of top talent who worked there. And you watch a company evolve from basically a three-state regional office to a national office.

Compiling results in this fashion requires a lot of work. Results collections, both in print and online, are always the result of collaborative efforts of many people going back over many years. We should thank all of them, named or unnamed, for what you now hold in your hand. And these things are never really complete. There is always one little spot show or television taping you discover down the road. But this collection is one of the most massive and comprehensive to date. There is no narrative provided here, no context for these listings except the great memories they conjure up when reading over them. The result is a lot of fun and a great deal of history recorded for older fans and the new generations alike.

The Mid-Atlantic Gateway's mission has always been to document the history of Jim Crockett Promotions in the 1970s and the 1980s. Mark James' *Jim Crockett Promotions Wrestling Record Book* for the 1980s shares in that effort in a big, big way.

Dick Bourne
Mid-Atlantic Gateway
www.midatlanticgateway.com

Foreword

Jim Cornette

My tag team partner Mark James, the royal researcher, the right reverend of results, has done it again! His newest book is the most comprehensive compendium of lineups and results from the glory days of Jim Crockett Promotions that I have ever seen. From 1980 to 1988, JCP was the Cadillac of wrestling territories, where every big name in the NWA wanted to go to show their skills. Mark has recaptured it all with an amazing amalgam of the date, city, arena, lineup and results of every match for every show held under the JCP banner. Whether you want to relive memories, settle bets, or just sit back and drool at the astonishing array of talent that was on parade every night in the Mid-Atlantic states, and as the decade progressed, the entire country, this is the book for you. My only suggestion is that it be placed in the next time capsule so that in case of nuclear war, future generations of mutated mammals are not deprived of this incredible historical masterwork. So what are you waiting for? Start turning the pages already!!

Jim Cornette
www.jimcornette.com

Acknowledgements

Mark James

When you hold this book in your hands and read through the many pages, it's easy to see what a feat it was. To undertake a project with such an enormous scope could not be more daunting. These pages contain all the cards and results for eight years for an entire promotion. That includes not just one city, but all the many cities Jim Crockett Promotions traveled to. The project was no small feat and nearly impossible to do. Look at the facts of it, decades have passed since these events took place and there is no wrestling museum to look all these materials up in.

When I decided to put this book together I went to several people who have taken it upon themselves to try and preserve as much wrestling history as possible. It goes without saying that their love of Mid-Atlantic Wrestling and Jim Crockett Promotions is unrivaled. Without these individuals there would have been no book.

First off I want to thank Dick Bourne. Dick runs the Mid-Atlantic Gateway which is one of my favorite wrestling related website ever. He also is an accomplished author and had released several wrestling books on his own. I'm glad to call Dick Bourne a friend. I went to Dick with my idea and test copy of the book and he was completely behind the project.

Dick Bourne then recommended I get in touch with Brian Rogers. Brian is a lifelong fan of Mid-Atlantic wrestling and was totally onboard with project. Within hours of emailing each other my inbox was full of hundreds of Jim Crockett Promotion cards and results for Greenville, SC and Atlanta, GA.

Through my own research I was able to find David Baker. The funny thing is David works on the Mid-Atlantic Gateway with Dick Bourne but I found him on my own. After exchanging a few emails we quickly got the ball rolling this book. David is a kindred spirit to me and lives and breathes the historical side of wrestling like I do. David's extensive collection of Jim Crockett Promotion cards and results comes from painstaking research from brick and mortar libraries, online newspaper archives, Google news, etc.

I want to thank David Williamson. To those of you who hit the Kayfabe Memories website, he's better known as "Tojo Mojo". David has helped me out since I became interested in documenting wrestling a decade ago. Over the years, "Tojo" would send me "care packages" that included photocopies of old wrestling newsletters from the 1960s, 1970s and 1980s. These newsletters included newspaper clippings of cards and results for wrestling that took place all over the country. When looking at the storage box it was deceptive, till I realized that the full box is around 10 inches tall. The reality is there are approximately 4000-5000 pages, (each page is

8.5"x11") of cards & results in those 30-40 year old papers. Thanks David for helping this process along.

There are several websites I looked at in my research and the one that was the most helpful was run by my buddy James Zordani, (also know online as Clawmaster). Jim's truly amazing website is a must-see and I highly recommend you check it out. It can be found at: http://sportsandwrestling.mywowbb.com

There are many people I'm leaving out and I apologize for that. With a project the size of this one, that covers decades in the making, I want to thank everyone involved any way with helping to document the glory days of JCP and Mid-Atlantic Wrestling.

While this book has all the cards and results we had, these are **not** all of the cards that took place for JCP. Even with this book now released, we are all dedicated to continuing to add to this information and every 12 to 18 months to release updated an edition of this book with the new discovered results included. If you have any cards or results from JCP and they are not in this book, please send me an email with them and we'll be sure to add them to the next book.

Mark James
www.memphiswrestlinghistory.com
mark@memphiswrestlinghistory.com

Chapter 1: 1980

1/1/80: Raleigh, NC @ Dorton Arena
Jimmy Snuka, John Studd & Ray Stevens beat Ric Flair, Blackjack Mulligan & Jim Brunzell
Rufus R. Jones beat Brute Bernard
Abe Jacobs beat Frank Monte
Don Kernodle(sub for Tony Garea) beat The Scorpion by DQ
Don Kernodle beat David Patterson

1/1/80: Greenville, SC @ Memorial Auditorium
Ricky Steamboat & Jay Youngblood beat Baron Von Raschke & Paul Jones
Johnny Weaver & Tim Woods beat Mr. X & Frankie Laine
Greg Valentine beat S.D. Jones
Bob Marcus beat Charlie Fulton
Billy Starr draw Doug Somers

1/2/80: Raleigh, NC @ WRAL Studios (TV)
Ric Flair & Blackjack Mulligan beat Frankie Laine & Doug Somers
Greg Valentine beat Abe Jacobs
Ricky Steamboat & Jay Youngblood beat Mr. X & Steve Travis
Ray Stevens beat Ron Sexton
Jimmy Snuka & Big John Studd beat Tony Garea & Bob Marcus

1/3/80: Norfolk, VA @ Scope
1/4/80: Winston-Salem, NC @ Coliseum
Ricky Steamboat & Jay Youngblood vs. Baron Von Raschke & Paul Jones in a Texas tornado match
Dewey Robertson vs. Tony Garea
Moose Morowski vs. Cocoa Samoa
Don Kernodle vs. Doug Somers
Luther Dargon & Leroy Dargon vs. Charlie Fulton & David Patterson

1/4/80: Charleston, SC @ County Hall
Gene Anderson beat Abe Jacobs
Plus other matches

1/4/80: Lynchburg, VA @ City Armory
Ric Flair & Blackjack Mulligan vs. Greg Valentine & John Studd
Rufus R. Jones vs. Frankie Laine
Rick McGraw vs. Mr. X
Bob Marcus vs. Ron Sexton
Frank Monte vs. Billy Starr

1/5/80: Spartanburg, SC @ Memorial Auditorium

1/5/80: Charlotte, NC @ Coliseum
Ric Flair beat Greg Valentine
Jimmy Snuka & John Studd beat Tony Garea & Bob Marcus
Greg Valentine beat Abe Jacobs
Plus other matches

1/6/80: Asheville, NC @ Civic Center
Jimmy Snuka vs. Ric Flair
Ricky Steamboat vs. Paul Jones
Greg Valentine vs. Rufus R. Jones
Tim Woods & Don Kernodle vs. Brute Bernard & Masked Scorpion
Plus 2 other matches

1/6/80: Savannah, GA @ Civic Center
Ric Flair beat Greg Valentine
Ricky Steamboat & Jay Youngblood vs. Paul Jones & Baron Von Raschke in a fence match
Dewey Robertson vs. S.D. Jones
Mr. X vs. Scott McGhee
Charlie Fulton vs. Abe Jacobs

1/6/80: Roanoke, VA @ Civic Center
Blackjack Mulligan beat John Studd Texas street fight
Tony Garea & Johnny Weaver beat Frankie Laine & Moose Morowski
Jim Brunzell beat Ray Stevens
Cocoa Samoa beat David Patterson
Doug Somers beat Rick McGraw
Ron Sexton beat Frank Monte

1/7/80: Fayetteville, NC
Jimmy Snuka vs. Tim Woods
Blackjack Mulligan vs. John Studd in a bounty match
Johnny Weaver & Rufus R. Jones vs. Brute Bernard & Doug Somers

1/7/80: Greenville, SC @ Memorial Auditorium
Ric Flair beat Greg Valentine
Jim Brunzell beat Jimmy Snuka by DQ
Don Kernodle & Rick McGraw beat Frankie Laine & Mr. X
Gene Lewis beat The Scorpion
Frank Monte draw Scott McGhee

1/8/80: Columbia, SC @ Township Auditorium
Blackjack Mulligan beat John Studd in a Texas death match
Mr. Wrestling beat Jimmy Snuka by countout
Rufus R. Jones & S.D. Jones beat Doug Somers & Brute Bernard
Dewey Robertson beat Rick McGraw
Billy Starr beat Frank Monte

1/8/80: Raleigh, NC @ Dorton Arena
Jim Brunzell vs. Ray Stevens
Ric Flair vs. Greg Valentine
Dewey Robertson vs. Tony Garea
Johnny Weaver & Don Kernodle vs. Frankie Laine & Mr. X

1/9/80: Raleigh, NC @ WRAL Studios (TV)
Ray Stevens, John Studd & Jimmy Snuka beat S.D. Jones, Billy Starr & Don Kernodle
Blackjack Mulligan & Ric Flair beat Brute Bernard & Frank Monte
Greg Valentine beat Bob Marcus
Dewey Robertson beat Cocoa Samoa
Jim Brunzell beat Steve Muslin

1/10/80: Norfolk, VA @ Scope

1/11/80: Richmond, VA @ Coliseum
Blackjack Mulligan beat John Studd in a Texas death match
Ray Stevens & Greg Valentine beat Rufus R. Jones & S.D. Jones
Ricky Steamboat beat Baron Von Raschke
Mr. Wrestling beat Dewey Robertson
Abe Jacobs beat Tony Russo
Tony Garea beat The Scorpion
Bob Marcus & Billy Starr beat Mr. X & Charlie Fulton
Cocoa Samoa beat Frank Monte

1/11/80: Charleston, SC @ County Hall
Jimmy Snuka beat Ric Flair
Jim Brunzell vs. Paul Jones
Johnny Weaver & Pedro Morales vs. Brute Bernard & Frankie Laine
Don Kernodle vs. Doug Somers
Ron Sexton vs. David Patterson

1/12/80: Cerro Gordo, NC
Ric Flair vs. Jimmy Snuka
Baron Von Raschke vs. Rufus R. Jones
Brute Bernard & The Scorpion vs. Pedro Morales & Tony Garea
Rick McGraw vs. Doug Somers
Abe Jacobs vs. Tony Russo

1/12/80: Spartanburg, SC @ Memorial Auditorium
Ricky Steamboat & Jay Youngblood beat Ray Stevens & Greg Valentine
Don Kernodle beat Toru Tanaka by DQ
S.D. Jones beat Mr. X
Bob Marcus beat Scott McGhee
Ron Sexton beat Frank Monte

1/13/80: Greensboro, NC @ Coliseum
Blackjack Mulligan beat John Studd(27:00) in a loser leaves town, cage match
Ricky Steamboat & Jay Youngblood beat Jack & Jerry Brisco via pinfall
Rufus R. Jones beat Baron Von Raschke
Jim Brunzell beat Paul Jones
S.D. Jones & Tony Garea beat Brute Bernard & Frankie Laine
Don Kernodle & Scott McGhee beat Doug Somers & The Scorpion
Mr. X I draw Ron Sexton(15:00)

1/13/80: Toronto, Ontario @ Maple Leaf Gardens
Dewey Robertson & Ric Flair beat Jimmy Snuka & Ray Stevens
WWF World Champion Bob Backlund DCO with The Destroyer
Greg Valentine beat Johnny Weaver
Pedro Morales beat David Patterson
Klondike Bill beat Joe Marcus
Sweet Daddy Siki draw Chris Tolos

1/14/80: Guelph, Ontario (TV)
Greg Valentine beat Big Mac
Pedro Morales beat John Forsythe
The Destroyer beat Joe Marcus
Greg Valentine & Jimmy Snuka beat Johnny Weaver & Tim Gerrard
Dewey Robertson beat John Forsythe & Tim Garrard
Jimmy Snuka & The Destroyer beat Johnny Weaver & Klondike Bill
Jimmy Snuka beat Earl Pinnock
Ric Flair & Dewey Robertson beat Tim Gerrard & David Patterson
Pedro Morales & Johnny Weaver beat John Forsythe & Big Mac
The Destroyer beat Earl Pinnock
Dewey Robertson beat David Patterson
Ric Flair beat Jimmy Snuka via pinfall
Dewey Robertson beat Ray Stevens by DQ

1/14/80: Greenville, SC @ Memorial Auditorium
Blackjack Mulligan beat Baron Von Raschke to win a 15- man battle royal
Jim Brunzell draw Jay Youngblood
John Studd beat S.D. Jones
Rufus R. Jones beat The Scorpion
Mr. Wrestling beat Mr. X

1/15/80: Columbia, SC @ Township Auditorium
Jimmy Snuka beat Mr. Wrestling in a lumberjack match
Greg Valentine & Ray Stevens beat Ric Flair & Jim Brunzell
Johnny Weaver beat Frankie Laine
Pedro Morales beat Mr. X
Bob Marcus beat Dave Patterson

1/15/80: Raleigh, NC
No Wrestling

1/16/80: Raleigh, NC @ WRAL Studios (TV)
Paul Jones & Baron Von Raschke beat Cocoa Samoa & Tony Garea
Ric Flair beat Doug Somers
Greg Valentine & Ray Stevens beat Ron Sexton & Billy Starr
Dewey Robertson beat Jacques Goulet
Ricky Steamboat & Jay Youngblood beat The Scorpion & David Patterson

1/17/80: Norfolk, VA @ Scope
Ray Stevens & Greg Valentine beat Ric Flair & Jim Brunzell
Ricky Steamboat & Jay Youngblood beat Paul Jones & Baron Von Raschke
S.D. Jones beat Frankie Laine
Pedro Morales & Tony Garea beat Brute Bernard & Mr. X
Don Kernodle beat Cocoa Samoa
Ricky Starr beat Frank Monte

1/18/80: Winston-Salem, NC @ Coliseum
Jimmy Snuka vs. Mr. Wrestling
Ricky Steamboat vs. Baron Von Raschke in a Texas death match
Jay Youngblood vs. Frankie Laine
Mr. X & David Patterson vs. Tony Garea & Klondike Bill
Geoff Portz vs. Ron Sexton

1/18/80: Charleston, SC @ County Hall
Blackjack Mulligan beat John Studd in a loser leaves town, street fight match
Dewey Robertson beat S.D. Jones
Johnny Weaver & Pedro Morales beat The Scorpion & Doug Somers
Rick McGraw beat Tony Russo
Leroy Dargon beat Dave Patterson

1/18/80: Lynchburg, VA @ City Armory
Greg Valentine & Ray Stevens beat Ric Flair & Jim Brunzell
Paul Jones vs. Rufus R. Jones
Plus 3 other matches

1/19/80: Asheville, NC @ Civic Center
Jimmy Snuka vs. Ric Flair
Ray Stevens & Greg Valentine vs. Pedro Morales & S.D. Jones
Fabulous Moolah vs. Candy Malloy
Frank Monte vs. Bob Marcus
Abe Jacobs vs. Luther Dargon

1/19/80: Roanoke, VA @ Civic Center
Ricky Steamboat & Jay Youngblood vs. Baron Von Raschke & Paul Jones in a steel cage match
Dewey Robertson vs. Rufus Jones
Leilani Kai vs. Wendi Richter
Plus 3 other matches

1/20/80: Charlotte, NC @ Coliseum
Jimmy Snuka beat Mr. Wrestling by DQ
Jim Brunzell beat Ray Stevens
Ric Flair & Blackjack Mulligan beat Greg Valentine & John Studd
Frankie Laine beat Bob Marcus
Pedro Morales beat The Scorpion
Johnny Weaver & S.D. Jones beat Tony Russo & Doug Somers
Dave Patterson beat Joe Furr

1/21/80: Greenville, SC @ Memorial Auditorium

1/21/80: Fayetteville, NC @ Cumberland County Civic Center
Ricky Steamboat & Jay Youngblood vs. Baron Von Raschke & Paul Jones in a fence match
Dewey Robertson vs. S.D. Jones
Don Kernodle vs. Mr. X
David Patterson vs. Bob Marcus

1/22/80: Sumter, SC @ Sumter County Exposition Center
Jimmy Snuka beat Blackjack Mulligan
Jay Youngblood beat Paul Jones by countout
Rufus R. Jones & Johnny Weaver double DQ The Scorpion & Dewey Robertson
Pedro Morales beat Doug Somers
Tony Garea beat Dave Patterson

1/22/80: Raleigh, NC @ Dorton Arena
Ricky Steamboat beat Baron Von Raschke in a Texas death match
Ric Flair & Jim Brunzell double DQ Greg Valentine & Ray Stevens
Frankie Laine beat Rick McGraw
S.D. Jones beat Brute Bernard
Bob Marcus beat Mr. X by DQ
Cocoa Samoa beat Frank Monte

1/23/80: Raleigh, NC @ WRAL Studios (TV)
John Studd beat Billy Starr
Rufus R. Jones & Mr. Wrestling beat Charlie Fulton & Ron Sexton
Jimmy Snuka beat Tony Russo
Jim Brunzell draw Johnny Weaver
Luther Dargon @ Leroy Dargon beat Ray Stevens & Greg Valentine by DQ

1/24/80: Norfolk, VA @ Scope

1/25/80: Charleston, SC @ County Hall
Ricky Steamboat & Jay Youngblood vs. Baron Von Raschke & Paul Jones in a no DQ, falls count anywhere match
Brute Bernard vs. S.D. Jones
Tony Garea vs. Doug Somers
Rick McGraw vs. Cocoa Samoa
Ron Sexton vs. Frank Monte

1/25/80: Richmond, VA @ Coliseum
Ric Flair beat Jimmy Snuka by DQ
Plus other matches

1/26/80: Spartanburg, SC

1/27/80: Columbia, SC @ Township Auditorium
Ricky Steamboat beat Baron Von Raschke in a Texas death match
Jimmy Snuka beat Jim Brunzell
Ric Flair beat Gene Anderson
Rick McGraw & Don Kernodle beat Doug Somers & Brute Bernard
Johnny Weaver beat Swede Hanson by DQ
The Scorpion beat Cocoa Samoa

1/27/80: Greensboro, NC @ Coliseum
Ricky Steamboat & Jay Youngblood beat Paul Jones & Baron Von Raschke in a falls count anywhere, no DQ match
Blackjack Mulligan beat Jimmy Snuka
Ric Flair beat Gene Anderson
Greg Valentine & Ray Stevens beat Rufus R. Jones & S.D. Jones
Tony Garea beat Dewey Robertson
Pedro Morales beat Mr. X
Frankie Laine beat Billy Starr
Abe Jacobs beat Tony Russo

1/28/80: Greenville, SC @ Memorial Auditorium

1/29/80: Raleigh, NC @ Dorton Arena

1/30/80: Raleigh, NC @ WRAL Studios (TV)
Baron Von Raschke & Paul Jones beat Cocoa Samoa & S.D. Jones
Ric Flair beat The Scorpion
Greg Valentine & Ray Stevens beat Rick McGraw & Scott McGhee
Johnny Weaver beat Brute Bernard
Ricky Steamboat & Jay Youngblood beat Doug Somers & Charlie Fulton

1/31/80: Norfolk, VA @ Scope

2/1/80: Winston-Salem, NC @ Coliseum
13-Man Battle Royal including Blackjack Mulligan, Tim Woods, Paul Jones, Johnny Weaver, Swede Hanson, Dewey Robertson, Jim Brunzell, Brute Bernard, Bob Marcus, Mr. X, S.D. Jones, Klondike Bill & Jimmy Snuka
Note: Last 2 wrestlers left in ring wrestle for $6500 purse
plus 5 other matches

2/1/80: Charleston, SC @ County Hall
Ric Flair beat Gene Anderson
Rufus R. Jones beat Baron Von Raschke
Frankie Laine & Doug Somers beat Pedro Morales & Ron Sexton
David Patterson beat Cocoa Samoa
Abe Jacobs beat Scott McGhee

2/2/80: Spartanburg, SC @ Memorial Auditorium
Paul Jones beat Ricky Steamboat
Jim Brunzell beat Greg Valentine by DQ
Don Kernodle & S.D. Jones beat Brute Bernard & Frankie Laine
Matt Borne beat Mr. X
Ron Sexton beat Tony Russo

2/2/80: Hampton, VA @ Coliseum
Ric Flair beat Gene Anderson
Ray Stevens beat Jay Youngblood
Bob Marcus beat David Patterson
Cocoa Samoa beat Joe Furr
Swede Hanson & Dewey Robertson beat Tony Garea & Mr. Wrestling
Fabulous Moolah beat Vivian St. John

2/3/80: Charlotte, NC @ Coliseum
Jimmy Snuka beat Ric Flair by DQ
Ray Stevens & Greg Valentine beat Ricky Steamboat & Jay Youngblood
Jim Brunzell & Rufus R. Jones beat Paul Jones & Baron Von Raschke
Fabulous Moolah beat Vivian St. John
Ox Baker beat Cocoa Samoa
Tony Garea beat The Scorpion
Matt Borne beat Billy Starr

2/3/80: Savannah, GA @ Civic Center
Ric Flair & Blackjack Mulligan double DQ Greg Valentine & Ray Stevens
Plus other matches

2/3/80: Roanoke, VA @ Civic Center
Ricky Steamboat & Jay Youngblood vs. Jimmy Snuka & Ray Stevens
Jim Brunzell vs. Johnny Weaver
Mr. Wrestling vs. Dewey Robertson
Plus 3 other matches

2/4/80: Fayetteville, NC @ Cumberland County Civic Center
Jimmy Snuka vs. Ric Flair
Jim Brunzell vs. Johnny Weaver
Dutch Mantell & Frankie Laine vs. Don Kernodle & Rick McGraw
Plus other matches

2/4/80: Greenville, SC @ Memorial Auditorium
Ray Stevens & Greg Valentine beat Ricky Steamboat & Jay Youngblood by DQ
Masked Superstar I & II beat Pedro Morales & S.D. Jones
Mr. Wrestling beat Dewey Robertson by referee's decision
Bob Marcus beat Doug Somers

2/5/80: Columbia, SC @ Township Auditorium
Ric Flair beat Jimmy Snuka by DQ
Plus other matches

2/5/80: Raleigh, NC @ Dorton Arena
Masked Superstar I(Bill Eadie) & Masked Superstar II(John Studd) beat lackjack Mulligan & Jim Brunzell
Frankie Laine & Ox Baker beat Bob Marcus & Johnny Weaver
Ox Baker beat S.D. Jones
David Patterson draw Ron Sexton

2/6/80: Raleigh, NC @ WRAL Studios (TV)
Dewey Robertson beat Frank Monte
Ray Stevens & Greg Valentine beat Ron Sexton & Cocoa Samoa
Jimmy Snuka beat Bob Marcus
Rufus R. Jones beat Baron Von Raschke by DQ
Blackjack Mulligan, Jim Brunzell & Ric Flair beat Brute Bernard, Doug Somers & The Scorpion

2/7/80: Norfolk, VA @ Scope

2/8/80: Richmond, VA @ Coliseum
Ric Flair beat Jimmy Snuka
Greg Valentine & Ray Stevens beat Ricky Steamboat & Jay Youngblood by DQ
Johnny Weaver & Rufus R. Jones beat Dewey Robertson & Swede Hanson
Frankie Laine & Doug Somers beat Abe Jacobs & Ron Sexton
Cocoa Samoa draw Scott McGhee
Matt Borne beat Bill Starr
Pedro Morales beat Brute Bernard

2/8/80: Charleston, SC @ County Hall
Masked Superstar I & II beat Blackjack Mulligan & Jim Brunzell
Paul Jones vs. S.D. Jones
Tony Garea beat The Scorpion
Don Kernodle beat David Patterson
Bob Marcus beat Tony Russo

2/9/80: Spartanburg, SC @ Memorial Auditorium

2/10/80: Greensboro, NC @ Coliseum (Afternoon Show)
Ricky Steamboat & Jay Youngblood beat Ray Stevens & Greg Valentine(27:40)
Jim Brunzell beat Johnny Weaver(22:15)
Mr. Wrestling II(sub for Tommy Rich) beat Masked Superstar I
Rufus R. Jones & S.D. Jones beat Swede Hanson & Frankie Laine
Bob Marcus beat Scott McGhee
Matt Borne beat Billy Starr
Ron Sexton draw David Patterson

2/10/80: Columbia, SC @ Township Auditorium
Ricky Steamboat & Jay Youngblood beat Ray Stevens & Greg Valentine by DQ
Paul Jones double DQ Jim Brunzell(sub for Tommy Rich)
Tony Garea draw Don Kernodle
Doug Somers & Masked Scorpion beat Abe Jacobs & Coco Samoa
Rick McGraw beat Tony Russo

2/10/80: Toronto, Ontario @ Maple Leaf Gardens
Dewey Robertson beat The Destroyer
Ric Flair beat Jimmy Snuka by DQ
Blackjack Mulligan beat John Studd in a Texas street fight
Pedro Morales beat Brute Bernard
The Blue Demons(Gene Anderson & Billy Red Lyons) beat Klondike Bill & Nick DeCarlo
Chris Tolos beat Ricky Johnson by submission

2/11/80: Greenville, SC @ Memorial Auditorium
Ricky Steamboat & Jay Youngblood beat Greg Valentine & Ray Stevens in match with 2 referees
S.D. Jones beat Swede Hanson
Rick McGraw beat Masked Scorpion
Matt Borne beat Billy Starr
Abe Jacobs beat David Patterson

2/11/1980: Amherst, VA
Johnny Weaver vs. Jim Brunzell
Paul Jones vs. Rufus R. Jones
Dutch Mantell & Frankie Laine vs. Tony Garea & Don Kernodle
plus 1 other match

2/11/80: Brantford, Ontario (TV)
John Studd beat Ricky Johnson & Earl Pinnock in a handicap match
Blackjack Mulligan beat Frank Marconi & Tim Gerrard in a handicap match
John Studd beat Klondike Bill & Ricky Johnson in a handicap match
Blackjack Mulligan & Dewey Robertson beat Brute Bernard & Tim Gerrard
Jimmy Snuka & John Studd beat Pedro Morales & Klondike Bill
Ric Flair & Dewey Robertson beat The Blue Demon & Frank Marconi
Nick DeCarlo beat Big Mac
Ric Flair & Blackjack Mulligan beat Brute Bernard & The Blue Demon
Dewey Robertson beat Earl Pinnock & Tim Gerrard in a handicap match
Ric Flair, Blackjack Mulligan & Dewey Robertson beat Jimmy Snuka, John Studd & Brute Bernard

2/12/80: Raleigh, NC @ Dorton Arena
Ric Flair beat Jimmy Snuka in a Texas death match
Ray Stevens beat Jay Youngblood
Rufus R. Jones & S.D. Jones beat Doug Somers & Swede Hanson
Rick McGraw beat Brute Bernard by DQ
Frankie Laine beat Coco Samoa

2/13/80: Raleigh, NC @ WRAL Studios (TV)
Ric Flair & Blackjack Mulligan beat David Patterson & Billy Starr

2/14/80: Richburg, SC @ Lewisville High School
Rufus R. Jones & Ric Flair vs. Paul Jones & Jimmy Snuka
Mr. Wrestling vs. Ox Baker
Brute Bernard vs. Tony Garea
Abe Jacobs vs. Doug Somers
Bob Marcus vs. David Patterson

2/15/80: Richmond, VA @ Coliseum
No Wrestling

2/15/80: Norfolk, VA @ Scope
Ricky Steamboat & Jay Youngblood beat Ray Stevens & Greg Valentine by DQ
Masked Superstar I beat Blackjack Mulligan
Rufus R. Jones & S.D. Jones beat Dewey Robertson & Swede Hanson
Ox Baker beat Pedro Morales
Matt Borne beat Masked Scorpion
Don Kernodle beat Billy Starr
Cocoa Samoa beat Tony Russo

2/15/80: Charleston, SC @ County Hall
Jimmy Snuka beat Ric Flair in a Texas death match
Jim Brunzell beat Masked Superstar II
Johnny Weaver & Tony Garea beat Frankie Laine & Brute Bernard
Bob Marcus beat Doug Somers
Ron Sexton beat David Patterson

2/16/80: Spartanburg, SC @ Memorial Auditorium

2/17/80: Charlotte, NC @ Coliseum
Paul Jones vs. Baron Von Raschke in a lights out match
Jimmy Snuka & Ray Stevens & Greg Valentine beat Ric Flair & Ricky Steamboat & Jay Youngblood
Masked Superstar I & II vs. S.D. Jones & Mr. Wrestling
Plus 3 other matches

2/17/80: Savannah, GA @ Civic Center
Ricky Steamboat & Jay Youngblood vs. Greg Valentine & Ray Stevens
Rufus R. Jones vs. Swede Hanson
Johnny Weaver vs. Brute Bernard
Bob Marcus vs. Doug Somers
Joe Furr vs. Ron Sexton

2/17/80: Roanoke, VA @ Civic Center
Ric Flair vs. Jimmy Snuka
Blackjack Mulligan vs. Masked Superstar I
Jim Brunzell vs. Ox Baker

2/18/80: Fayetteville, NC @ Cumberland County Civic Center
Blackjack Mulligan & Jim Brunzell vs. Masked Superstar I & II
Ox Baker vs. S.D. Jones
Dutch Mantell & Frankie Laine vs. Pedro Morales & Don Kernodle
plus other matches

2/18/80: Asheville, NC @ Civic Center
Ric Flair beat Jimmy Snuka in a Texas death match
Ray Stevens beat Jay Youngblood
Johnny Weaver & Tony Garea beat Swede Hanson & Dewey Robertson by DQ
Matt Borne beat The Scorpion
Brute Bernard beat Bob Marcus
Abe Jacobs beat Doug Somers

2/19/80: Raleigh, NC @ Dorton Arena
Ric Flair, Ricky Steamboat & Jay Youngblood beat Greg Valentine, Ray Stevens & Jimmy Snuka
S.D. Jones beat Swede Hanson
Matt Borne beat Tony Russo
Bob Marcus beat Billy Starr
Dewey Robertson beat Ron Sexton

2/19/80: Columbia, SC @ Township Auditorium
Jim Brunzell beat Paul Jones
Masked Superstar I & II beat Blackjack Mulligan & Rufus R. Jones
Ox Baker DCO with Pedro Morales
Tony Garea beat David Patterson
Doug Somers(sub for Dutch Mantell) & Frankie Laine beat Don Kernodle & Rick McGraw

2/20/80: Raleigh, NC @ WRAL Studios (TV)

2/21/80: Sumter, SC @ Sumter County Exposition Center
Jim Brunzell vs. Paul Jones
Greg Valentine vs. Jay Youngblood
Bob Marcus vs. Billy Starr
S.D. Jones & Tony Garea vs. Swede Hanson & David Patterson

2/21/80: Norfolk, VA @ Scope

2/22/80: Richmond, VA @ Coliseum
Ray Stevens, Greg Valentine & Jimmy Snuka beat Ric Flair, Ricky Steamboat & Jay Youngblood
Fabulous Moolah beat Vivian St. John
Dewey Robertson beat S.D. Jones
Johnny Weaver & Matt Borne beat Doug Somers & The Scorpion
Bob Marcus beat David Patterson
Billy Starr beat Ron Sexton

2/22/80: Winston-Salem, NC @ Coliseum
Blackjack Mulligan & Rufus R. Jones vs. Masked Superstar I & II
Frankie Laine vs. Tony Garea
Joyce Grable vs. Winona Little Heart
Rick McGraw vs. Abe Jacobs
Tony Russo vs. Cocoa Samoa

2/22/80: Charleston, SC @ County Hall
Scott McGhee draw Joe Furr
Pedro Morales & Don Kernodle beat Swede Hanson & Brute Bernard
Jim Brunzell beat Ox Baker
Baron Von Raschke beat Paul Jones in a lights out match

2/24/80: Columbia, SC @ Township Auditorium
Ric Flair beat Jimmy Snuka by DQ

2/24/80: Spartanburg, SC @ Memorial Auditorium
Blackjack Mulligan, Rufus R. Jones & Jim Brunzell beat Masked Superstars & Paul Jones
Ox Baker beat Pedro Morales
Tony Garea beat Brute Bernard by DQ
Doug Somers beat Ron Sexton

2/25/80: Greenville, SC @ Memorial Auditorium
Jimmy Snuka beat Ric Flair
Ricky Steamboat beat Greg Valentine
Swede Hanson & Dewey Robertson beat Johnny Weaver & S.D. Jones
Vivian St. John beat Joyce Grable
Bob Marcus draw Billy Starr
Don Kernodle beat David Patterson

2/25/80: Pembroke, NC @ High School
Jay Youngblood vs. Ray Stevens
Paul Jones vs. Rufus R. Jones
Brute Bernard & Frankie Laine vs. Matt Borne & Pedro Morales
The Scorpion vs. Ron Sexton

2/26/80: Raleigh, NC @ Dorton Arena
Ricky Steamboat & Jay Youngblood beat Greg Valentine & Ray Stevens
Matt Borne beat Doug Somers
Paul Jones beat Tony Garea

Dewey Robertson beat S.D. Jones
Winona Little Heart beat Joyce Grable

2/27/80: Raleigh, NC @ WRAL Studios (TV)
Masked Superstar I & II beat Cocoa Samoa & Scott McGhee
Winona Little Heart & Cindy Majors beat Joyce Grable & Vivian St. John
Johnny Weaver beat Paul Jones by DQ in NWA TV Title tournament
Blackjack Mulligan beat Ox Baker in a NWA TV Title tournament
Ricky Steamboat & Jay Youngblood beat Frankie Laine & Doug Somers

2/28/80: Mineral, VA
Ric Flair won a battle royal
Ric Flair beat Gene Anderson
Johnny Weaver beat Paul Jones by DQ
Johnny Weaver & Don Kernodle beat Frankie Laine & The Scorpion
The Scorpion beat Rick McGraw

2/29/80: Lynchburg, VA @ City Armory
Ric Flair beat Jimmy Snuka
Rufus R. Jones beat Paul Jones
Tony Garea beat Frankie Laine
Ric McGraw beat David Patterson

2/29/80: Charleston, SC @ County Hall
Ricky Steamboat & Jay Youngblood beat Ray Stevens & Greg Valentine
S.D. Jones beat Dewey Robertson
Swede Hanson beat Cocoa Samoa
Matt Borne beat Billy Starr
Ron Sexton beat Tony Russo

3/1/80: Spartanburg, SC @ Memorial Auditorium
Scott McGhee vs. Billy Starr
Rick McGraw vs. David Patterson
Ron Sexton vs. ??
Frankie Laine & Doug Somers vs. S.D. Jones & Don Kernodle
Jimmy Snuka vs. Ricky Steamboat

3/1/80: Charlotte, NC @ Coliseum
Paul Jones vs. Baron Von Raschke in a cage match
Ric Flair vs. Greg Valentine
Jay Youngblood vs. Ray Stevens
Dewey Robertson & Swede Hanson vs. Johnny Weaver & Rufus R. Jones
Plus 3 other matches

3/2/80: Asheville, NC @ Civic Center
Ricky Steamboat & Jay Youngblood vs. Greg Valentine & Ray Stevens
Jim Brunzell vs. Ox Baker
Brute Bernard vs. Tony Garea
Doug Somers vs. Don Kernodle
Abe Jacobs vs. Tony Russo

3/2/80: Savannah, GA @ Civic Center
Ricky Steamboat & Jay Youngblood vs. Ray Stevens & Greg Valentine
Ox Baker vs. Rufus R. Jones
Frankie Laine vs. Rick McGraw
David Patterson vs. Cocoa Samoa
Billy Starr vs. Ron Sexton

3/2/80: Greensboro, NC @ Coliseum
Paul Jones vs. Baron Von Raschke in a lights out match
Ric Flair vs. Jimmy Snuka
Blackjack Mulligan vs. Masked Superstar I
Dewey Robertson & Swede Hanson vs. Johnny Weaver & S.D. Jones

3/3/80: Greenville, SC @ Memorial Auditorium
Ricky Steamboat & Blackjack Mulligan beat Masked Superstar I & II by DQ
Johnny Weaver beat Swede Hanson
Dewey Robertson beat Don Kernodle
Matt Borne beat Doug Somers
Billy Starr beat Ron Sexton

3/3/80: Fayetteville, NC @ Cumberland County Civic Center
Greg Valentine vs. Jim Brunzell
Jimmy Snuka vs. Ric Flair
Ox Baker & Brute Bernard vs. Pedro Morales & S.D. Jones
Plus other matches

3/4/80: Raleigh, NC @ Dorton Arena

3/4/80: Columbia, SC @ Township Auditorium
Ricky Steamboat & Jay Youngblood beat Greg Valentine & Ray Stevens by DQ
S.D. Jones beat Ox Baker by DQ
Matt Borne beat Doug Somers
Billy Starr draw Abe Jacobs
Joe Furr beat Scott McGhee

3/5/80: Raleigh, NC @ WRAL Studios (TV)
Ric Flair & Blackjack Mulligan beat Ox Baker & Brute Bernard

3/6/80: Norfolk, VA @ Scope
Ricky Steamboat & Jay Youngblood vs. Greg Valentine & Ray Stevens
Ric Flair vs. Jimmy Snuka
Paul Jones vs. Jim Brunzell
Brute Bernard & Frankie Laine vs. Matt Borne & Abe Jacobs
Iron Sheik vs. S.D. Jones
Dewey Robertson vs. Tony Garea

3/6/80: Fairmont, NC @ High School
Blackjack Mulligan & Rufus R. Jones vs. Masked Superstar I & II
Ox Baker vs. Johnny Weaver
Pedro Morales vs. Swede Hanson
The Scorpion vs. Rick McGraw

3/7/80: Winston-Salem, NC @ Coliseum
Jim Brunzell beat Greg Valentine by DQ
Ricky Steamboat beat Jimmy Snuka
Swede Hanson & Dewey Robertson beat Tony Garea & S.D. Jones
Abe Jacobs beat Tony Russo
Matt Borne beat David Patterson

3/7/80: Charleston, SC @ County Hall
Blackjack Mulligan & Rufus R. Jones beat Masked Superstar I & II
Johnny Weaver beat Billy Starr(sub for Dewey Robertson)
Don Kernodle beat The Scorpion
Ron Sexton beat Scott McGhee
Billy Starr beat Joe Furr

3/8/80: Spartanburg, SC @ Memorial Auditorium
Blackjack Mulligan beat Masked Superstar I by DQ
S.D. Jones vs. Masked Superstar II
The Scorpion beat Cocoa Samoa
Ron Sexton beat Scott McGhee
Don Kernodle & Matt Borne beat Brute Bernard & The Scorpion(sub for Dewey Robertson)

3/9/80: Roanoke, VA @ Civic Center
$10,000 14 man battle royal
Masked Superstar I beat Jim Brunzell to win battle royal
Johnny Weaver beat Ox Baker by DQ
Jimmy Snuka beat S.D. Jones
Rufus R. Jones beat Brute Bernard
Tony Garea draw Swede Hanson
Others scheduled for the battle royal: Ricky Steamboat, Iron Sheik, Matt Borne

3/9/80: Toronto, Ontario @ Maple Leaf Gardens
Dewey Robertson beat Greg Valentine by DQ
Jay Youngblood beat Ray Stevens
Blackjack Mulligan beat John Studd
The Destroyer & Blue Demon beat Pedro Morales & Don Kernodle
Klondike Bill beat Tim Gerrard
Bob Marcus beat Bill White

3/10/80: Guelph, Ontario (TV)

3/10/80: Greenville, SC @ Memorial Auditorium
Ric Flair beat Jimmy Snuka by countout
Jim Brunzell beat Ox Baker
S.D. Jones & Tony Garea beat Swede Hansen & Frankie Laine
Abe Jacobs draw Rick McGraw

3/10/80: Lumberton, NC @ Recreation Center
Ricky Steamboat vs. Masked Superstar I
Rufus R. Jones & Johnny Weaver vs. Brute Bernard & Doug Somers
Matt Borne vs. Bob Marcus
Tony Russo vs. Ron Sexton

3/11/80: Raleigh, NC @ Dorton Arena
Jimmy Snuka beat Ric Flair
Blackjack Mulligan beat Ox Baker
Doug Somers beat Ron Sexton
Matt Borne beat David Patterson
Johnny Weaver & S.D. Jones beat Brute Bernard & Frankie Laine

3/11/80: Columbia, SC @ Township Auditorium
Ricky Steamboat & Jay Youngblood vs. Masked Superstar I & II
Rufus R. Jones vs. Dewey Robertson
Tony Garea vs. The Scorpion
Pedro Morales vs. Swede Hanson
Bob Marcus vs. Billy Starr

3/12/80: Raleigh, NC @ WRAL Studios (TV)

3/13/80: Norfolk, VA @ Scope

3/14/80: Charleston, SC @ County Hall
Jimmy Snuka beat Ric Flair
Blackjack Mulligan beat Masked Superstar II by DQ
Swede Hanson & Ox Baker beat Johnny Weaver & Don Kernodle
Bob Marcus beat David Patterson
Abe Jacobs beat Billy Starr

3/14/80: Richmond, VA @ Coliseum
Ricky Steamboat & Jay Youngblood beat Greg Valentine & Ray Stevens
Jim Brunzell beat Masked Superstar I
S.D. Jones, Rufus R. Jones & Pedro Morales beat Dewey Robertson, Frankie Laine & Brute Bernard
Rick McGraw beat ??
Matt Borne beat ??
Tony Garea beat ??
Tony Russo draw Cocoa Samoa

3/15/80: Spartanburg, SC @ Memorial Auditorium

3/15/80: Hampton, VA @ Coliseum
Masked Superstar I & II draw Ricky Steamboat & Jay Youngblood
Rufus Jones beat Ox Baker
Tony Garea beat Frankie Laine
Billy Starr beat Cocoa Samoa
Rick McGraw beat Tony Russo
Pedro Morales beat Brute Bernard

3/16/80: Columbia, SC @ Township Auditorium
Masked Superstar I won a 13-man battle royal
Masked Superstar I beat Rufus R. Jones
Swede Hanson beat Frankie Laine
Jay Youngblood draw Jim Brunzell
Tony Garea beat David Patterson
Don Kernodle beat Doug Somers

3/16/80: Greensboro, NC @ Coliseum
Paul Jones beat Baron Von Raschke in a fence match
Jimmy Snuka beat Ric Flair to win NWA United States Title
Ricky Steamboat beat Ray Stevens

Johnny Weaver & S.D. Jones beat Brute Bernard & Dewey Robertson
Ox Baker beat Pedro Morales
Matt Borne beat The Scorpion
Bob Marcus & Abe Jacobs beat Billy Starr & Tony Russo

3/17/80: Greenville, SC @ Memorial Auditorium
Ricky Steamboat & Jay Youngblood beat Greg Valentine & Ray Stevens
Dewey Robertson beat S.D. Jones
Matt Borne beat Billy Starr
Rick McGraw beat Scott McGhee
Masked Scorpion draw Bob Marcus

3/17/80: Fayetteville, NC @ Cumberland County Civic Center
Masked Superstar I & II vs. Blackjack Mulligan & Rufus R. Jones
Don Kernodle vs. Doug Somers
Johnny Weaver vs. Swede Hanson
David Patterson vs. Abe Jacobs
Joe Furr vs. Cocoa Samoa

3/18/80: Christiansburg, VA @ High School
Jim Brunzell vs. Ray Stevens
Blackjack Mulligan vs. Greg Valentine
Cocoa Samoa & S.D. Jones vs. The Scorpion & Brute Bernard
Billy Starr vs. Ron Sexton

3/18/80: Raleigh, NC @ Dorton Arena
Jimmy Snuka beat Ric Flair
Ox Baker vs. Rufus R. Jones
Plus other matches

3/19/80: Raleigh, NC @ WRAL Studios (TV)

3/20/80: Norfolk, VA @ Scope

3/21/80: Lynchburg, VA @ City Armory
Masked Superstar I & II beat Blackjack Mulligan & Rufus R. ones
Johnny Weaver beat Frankie Laine
Don Kernodle beat Bob Marcus
Rick McGraw beat Tony Russo

3/21/80: Charleston, SC @ County Hall
Ricky Steamboat & Jay Youngblood beat Ray Stevens & Greg Valentine
S.D. Jones beat Brute Bernard
Abe Jacobs beat David Patterson
Cocoa Samoa beat The Scorpion
Doug Somers beat Scott McGhee

3/21/80: Richmond, VA @ Coliseum
No Wrestling

3/22/80: Spartanburg, SC @ Memorial Auditorium

3/23/80: Asheville, NC @ Civic Center
Ric Flair & Ricky Steamboat & Jay Youngblood beat Greg Valentine & Jimmy Snuka & Ray Stevens
Ox Baker beat Johnny Weaver
Pedro Morales beat Billy Starr
Rick McGraw draw The Scorpion

3/23/80: Columbia, SC @ Township Auditorium
Jim Brunzell beat Masked Superstar II
Blackjack Mulligan beat Masked Superstar I by DQ
Rufus R. Jones & S.D. Jones beat Brute Bernard & Swede Hanson
Masked Scorpion beat Bob Marcus
Cocoa Samoa beat Tony Russo

3/23/80: Salem, VA
Jimmy Snuka beat Ric Flair
Ricky Steamboat beat Ray Stevens
Jay Youngblood beat Dewey Robertson
Matt Borne & Tony Garea beat Frankie Laine & Doug Somers
Don Kernodle beat Ron Sexton
Abe Jacobs beat David Patterson

3/24/80: Greenville, SC @ Memorial Auditorium
Masked Superstar I & II double DQ Blackjack Mulligan & Swede Hanson
Rufus R. Jones beat Dewey Robertson
Tony Garea beat The Scorpion
Don Kernodle draw Matt Borne
Abe Jacobs beat David Patterson

3/25/80: Raleigh, NC @ Dorton Arena
Masked Superstar I & II vs. Blackjack Mulligan & Rufus R. Jones
Dewey Robertson vs. Johnny Weaver
Matt Borne vs. Rick McGraw
The Scorpion vs. Bob Marcus
Plus other matches

3/26/80: Raleigh, NC @ WRAL Studios (TV)
The Masked Superstar I & II beat ?? & ?? to win vacant NWA Mid Atlantic Tag Title

3/27/80: Norfolk, VA @ Scope
Masked Superstar I & II beat Blackjack Mulligan & Swede Hanson
Ric Flair beat Jimmy Snuka by DQ
Frankie Laine beat Matt Borne
Ox Baker & Dewey Robertson beat Rufus R. Jones & Pedro Morales
Don Kernodle & Bob Marcus beat Tony Russo & Billy Starr

3/28/80: Richmond, VA @ Coliseum
Masked Superstar I & II vs. Blackjack Mulligan & Ricky Steamboat
Jim Brunzell vs. Ray Stevens
Dewey Robertson & Ox Baker vs. Pedro Morales & Tony Garea
Rick McGraw vs. Frankie Laine
Matt Borne vs. Don Kernodle

3/28/80: Charleston, SC @ County Hall
Jimmy Snuka beat Rufus R. Jones
Jay Youngblood beat Greg Valentine
Doug Somers beat Cocoa Samoa
The Scorpion beat Ron Sexton
Johnny Weaver & S.D. Jones beat Swede Hanson & Brute Bernard

3/29/80: Spartanburg, SC @ Memorial Auditorium
Ric Flair beat Jimmy Snuka by DQ
Jim Brunzell beat Masked Superstar II by DQ
Ox Baker & Brute Bernard beat Johnny Weaver & Don Kernodle
Abe Jacobs draw Billy Starr
Doug Somers beat Scott McGhee

3/29/80: Charlotte, NC @ Coliseum
Greg Valentine & Ray Stevens beat Ricky Steamboat & Jay Youngblood to win NWA World Tag Title
Blackjack Mulligan beat Masked Superstar I by DQ
Rufus R. Jones & S.D. Jones beat Dewey Robertson & Swede Hanson
Masked Superstar II beat Johnny Weaver
Matt Borne draw Tony Garea
Frankie Laine beat Ron Sexton

3/30/80: Columbia, SC @ Township Auditorium
Ric Flair & Blackjack Mulligan beat Masked Superstar I & II
Johnny Weaver beat Frankie Laine
S.D. Jones beat Swede Hanson
Tony Garea beat The Scorpion
Abe Jacobs draw Doug Somers

3/30/80: Toronto, Ontario @ Maple Leaf Gardens
Ricky Steamboat & Jay Youngblood beat Greg Valentine & Ray Stevens
Angelo Mosca beat Jimmy Snuka by DQ
Ox Baker beat Scott McGhee
Klondike Bill beat Brute Bernard by DQ
The Destroyer beat Billy Starr
Nick DeCarlo draw Chris Tolos

3/31/80: Greenville, SC @ Memorial Auditorium
Masked Superstar I & II beat Blackjack Mulligan & Swede Hansen
Rufus R. Jones beat Gene Lewis by DQ
Cocoa Samoa beat Tony Russo
Matt Borne beat Frankie Laine
Don Kernodle draw Bob Marcus

4/1/80: Raleigh, NC @ Dorton Arena
Masked Superstar I & II beat Blackjack Mulligan & Swede Hanson by DQ
Bob Marcus beat The Scorpion
Gene Lewis draw Tony Garea
Matt Borne beat Brute Bernard
S.D. Jones beat Ox Baker

4/2/80: Raleigh, NC @ WRAL Studios (TV)
Masked Superstar I beat Blackjack Mulligan in tournament final to win vacant NWA World Television Title in a tournament final

4/3/80: Norfolk, VA @ Scope
Jimmy Snuka beat Ric Flair
Blackjack Mulligan beat Masked Superstar I
Jim Brunzell, Tony Garea & S.D. Jones beat Ox Baker, Dewey Robertson & Brute Bernard
Masked Superstar II beat Matt Borne
Gene Lewis beat Abe Jacobs
Doug Somers draw Rick McGraw
Frankie Laine beat Ron Sexton

4/4/80: Winston-Salem, NC @ Coliseum
Ricky Steamboat & Jay Youngblood vs. Greg Valentine & Ray Stevens in a Texas tornado match
Johnny Weaver vs. Gene Lewis
The Scorpion vs. Rick McGraw
Bob Marcus vs. Doug Somers
Joe Furr vs. John Condrey

4/4/80: Lynchburg, VA @ City Armory
Ric Flair & Jim Brunzell beat Jimmy Snuka & Ox Baker
Matt Borne beat Brute Bernard
S.D. Jones beat Dewey Robertson
Tony Garea beat Ron Sexton
Frankie Laine draw Abe Jacobs

4/4/80: Charleston, SC @ County Hall
Blackjack Mulligan no contest with Swede Hanson
Joyce Grable & Wendi Richter beat Leilani Kai & Judy Martin
Cocoa Samoa beat Tony Russo
Don Kernodle beat Billy Starr

4/5/80: Savannah, GA @ Civic Center
Ric Flair beat Jimmy Snuka by DQ
Plus other matches

4/5/80: Spartanburg, SC @ Memorial Auditorium
Ricky Steamboat beat Ray Stevens
Fabulous Moolah beat Wenona Little Heart
Greg Valentine beat S.D. Jones
Gene Lewis & Doug Somers beat Bob Marcus & Cocoa Samoa

4/6/80: Roanoke, VA @ Civic Center
Ric Flair, Blackjack Mulligan & Andre The Giant vs. Jimmy Snuka & Masked Superstar I & II
Jim Brunzell vs. Dewey Robertson
Plus 3 other matches

4/6/80: Greensboro, NC @ Coliseum
Ric Flair beat Jimmy Snuka
Blackjack Mulligan & Andre The Giant beat Masked Superstar I & II
Matt Borne & Johnny Weaver & Jim Brunzell beat Dewey Robertson & Gene Lewis & Swede Hanson
Don Kernodle beat Brute Bernard
Billy Starr beat Bob Marcus

4/7/80: Greenville, SC @ Memorial Auditorium
Andre The Giant & Blackjack Mulligan beat Masked Superstar I & II
Dewey Robertson DCO with Johnny Weaver
Tony Garea beat Brute Bernard
Buzz Sawyer beat Doug Somers
Ron Ritchie draw Billy Starr

4/8/80: Raleigh, NC @ Dorton Arena
Ray Stevens & Greg Valentine beat Ricky Steamboat & Jay Youngblood
Ron Ritchie draw Doug Somers
Gene Lewis beat Bob Marcus
Matt Borne beat Dewey Robertson by DQ
Iron Sheik beat Johnny Weaver

4/8/80: Columbia, SC @ Township Auditorium
Blackjack Mulligan & Andre The Giant vs. Masked Superstar I & II
Ox Baker vs. S.D. Jones
Brute Bernard vs. Tony Garea
Frankie Laine vs. Buzz Sawyer
Billy Starr vs. Ron Sexton

4/9/80: Raleigh, NC @ WRAL Studios (TV)
Tony Russo & Swede Hanson vs. Rufus R. Jones & S.D. Jones
Ric Flair vs. The Scorpion
Ray Stevens & Greg Valentine vs. Matt Borne & Abe Jacobs
Ric Flair vs. Mike Miller

4/10/80: Norfolk, VA @ Scope

4/11/80: Charleston, SC @ County Hall
Ric Flair & Blackjack Mulligan beat Masked Superstar I & II
Rufus R. Jones beat Dewey Robertson
Matt Borne beat Billy Starr
Pedro Morales beat Doug Somers
Tony Russo draw Rick McGraw

4/12/80: Spartanburg, SC @ Memorial Auditorium
Don Kernodle beat Doug Somers
Dewey Robertson beat Pedro Morales
Matt Borne beat Billy Starr
Abe Jacobs beat Cocoa Samoa
Iron Sheik & Jimmy Snuka beat Ric Flair & Jim Brunzell

4/12/80: Hampton, VA @ Coliseum
Baron Von Raschke beat Paul Jones
Ricky Steamboat beat Ray Stevens by DQ
Jay Youngblood beat Greg Valentine by DQ
Tony Garea beat Frankie Laine
S.D. Jones & Johnny Weaver beat Brute Bernard & Ox Baker

4/13/80: Toronto, Ontario @ Maple Leaf Gardens
NWA World Champion Harley Race draw Dewey Robertson
Angelo Mosca beat Jimmy Snuka & Gene Anderson in a handicap match
Andre The Giant beat Ox Baker
Pedro Morales & Klondike Bill beat The Destroyer & The Scorpion
Hussein Arab(Iron Sheik) beat Ron Ritchie
Don Kernodle draw Nick DeCarlo

4/13/80: Charlotte, NC @ Coliseum
Ray Stevens & Greg Valentine vs. Jay Youngblood & Ricky Steamboat
Masked Superstar I & II vs. Blackjack Mulligan & Ric Flair
Jim Brunzell vs. Swede Hanson
Plus 3 other matches

4/14/80: Brantford, Ontario (TV)
Hussein Arab beat John Bonello
Andre The Giant beat John Forsythe & Tim Gerrard in a handicap match
Jimmy Snuka beat Don Kernodle via pinfall
Hussein Arab beat Joe Marcus
Dewey Robertson beat Bill White
The Destroyer & Ox Baker beat Joe Marcus & John Bonello
Angelo Mosca & Dewey Robertson beat John Forsythe & The Scorpion
Pedro Morales & Nick DeCarlo beat Tim Gerrard & John Forsthye
Jimmy Snuka & Hussein Arab beat Ron Ritchie & Klondike Bill
Angelo Mosca & Andre The Giant beat Ox Baker & Jimmy Snuka

4/14/80: Greenville, SC @ Memorial Auditorium

4/15/80: Raleigh, NC @ Dorton Arena
Ricky Steamboat & Jay Youngblood vs. Ray Stevens & Greg Valentine in match with 2 referees
Iron Sheik vs. Rufus R. Jones
Matt Borne vs. Dewey Robertson
Plus other matches

4/15/80: Columbia, SC @ Township Auditorium
Jimmy Snuka beat Ric Flair
Blackjack Mulligan double DQ Masked Superstar I
Masked Superstar II beat Jim Brunzell
Johnny Weaver & Tony Garea beat Swede Hanson & Brute Bernard
Rick McGraw draw Billy Starr

4/16/80: Raleigh, NC @ WRAL Studios (TV)

4/17/80: Norfolk, VA @ Scope

4/17/80: Walnut Cove, NC @ South Stokes High School
Including Swede Hanson, Masked Superstar I & II, Johnny Weaver & Blackjack Mulligan

4/18/80: Lynchburg, VA @ City Armory
Jim Brunzell beat Jimmy Snuka
Iron Sheik beat Rufus R. Jones

Tony Garea & Buzz Sawyer beat Swede Hanson & Gene Lewis
Ron Ritchie beat Ron Sexton

4/18/80: Charleston, SC @ County Hall
Ric Flair beat Masked Superstar I by DQ
Blackjack Mulligan beat Masked Superstar II
Ox Baker & Brute Bernard beat Pedro Morales & Don Kernodle
Doug Somers beat Rick McGraw
Billy Starr beat Cocoa Samoa

4/18/80: Richmond, VA @ Coliseum
No Wrestling

4/18/1980: Charlottesville, VA
Johnny Weaver vs. Dewey Robertson
Plus other matches

4/19/80: Bluefield, VA @ Brushfolk Armory

4/19/80: Spartanburg, SC @ Memorial Auditorium
Ricky Steamboat & Jay Youngblood beat Ray Stevens & Greg Valentine
Johnny Weaver beat Ox Baker
The Scorpion beat Ric McGraw
Doug Somers beat Abe Jacobs
Cocoa Samoa beat Bob Marcus

4/20/80: Roanoke, VA @ Civic Center
Ricky Steamboat & Jay Youngblood vs. Greg Valentine & Ray Stevens
Johnny Weaver vs. Gene Lewis
Rick McGraw vs. Swede Hanson
Plus 2 other matches

4/20/80: Greensboro, NC @ Coliseum
Ric Flair beat Jimmy Snuka to win NWA United States Title
Blackjack Mulligan beat Masked Superstar I
Jim Brunzell beat Iron Sheik
Rufus R. Jones & Buzz Sawyer beat Dewey Robertson & Ox Baker
Doug Somers & Gene Lewis beat Cocoa Samoa & Ron Ritchie
Pedro Morales beat Frankie Laine
Abe Jacobs draw Don Kernodle

4/21/80: Greenville, SC @ Memorial Auditorium
Ric Flair beat Jimmy Snuka
Masked Superstar I beat Rufus R. Jones
Iron Sheik beat Pedro Morales
Masked Superstar II beat Don Kernodle
Matt Borne & Buzz Sawyer beat Frankie Laine & Gene Lewis

4/21/80: Fayetteville, NC @ Cumberland County Civic Center
Blackjack Mulligan & Jim Brunzell vs. Greg Valentine & Ray Stevens
Abe Jacobs vs. Doug Somers
Ron Ritchie vs. Tony Russo
Dewey Robertson vs. Rick McGraw
S.D. Jones vs. Ox Baker

4/22/80: Columbia, SC @ Township Auditorium
Ricky Steamboat & Jay Youngblood beat Greg Valentine & Ray Stevens by DQ
Dewey Robertson beat Pedro Morales
S.D. Jones beat Gene Lewis by DQ
Cocoa Samoa beat Frankie Laine
Abe Jacobs draw Billy Starr

4/22/80: Raleigh, NC @ Dorton Arena
Johnny Weaver beat Ox Baker
Jimmy Snuka & Iron Sheik beat Ric Flair & Jim Brunzell
Plus other matches

4/23/80: Raleigh, NC @ WRAL Studios (TV)

4/24/80: Bakersville, NC @ Mitchell High School
Ricky Steamboat beat Masked Superstar by DQ
Jay Youngblood beat Dewey Robertson
Buzz Sawyer & Pedro Morales beat Brute Bernard & Gene Lewis
Billy Starr beat Bob Marcus

4/24/80: Pennington Gap, VA @ High School

4/25/80: Charleston, SC @ County Hall
Bob Marcus vs. Doug Somers
Brute Bernard vs. Don Kernodle
The Scorpion beat Ron Sexton
S.D. Jones beat Ox Baker
Greg Valentine & Ray Stevens beat Ricky Steamboat & Jay Youngblood

4/25/80: Richmond, VA @ Coliseum
Blackjack Mulligan beat Masked Superstar II
Matt Borne, Pedro Morales & Johnny Weaver beat Swede Hanson, Gene Lewis & Dewey Robertson
Jim Brunzell beat Iron Sheik by DQ
Masked Superstar I beat Rufus R. Jones
Tank Patton beat Cocoa Samoa
Ron Ritchie beat Frankie Laine
Buzz Sawyer beat Billy Starr

4/26/80: Spartanburg, SC @ Memorial Auditorium
Ron Ritchie vs. The Scorpion
Buzz Sawyer vs. Ron Sexton
S.D. Jones vs. Doug Somers
Gene Lewis vs. Johnny Weaver
Ric Flair & Jim Brunzell vs. Iron Sheik & Jimmy Snuka

4/27/80: Charlotte, NC @ Coliseum
Greg Valentine & Ray Stevens vs. Ricky Steamboat & Jay Youngblood in match with 2 referees
Blackjack Mulligan beat Masked Superstar II with Masked Superstar I locked in cage
Ox Baker vs. Rufus R. Jones
Plus 5 more matches

4/28/80: Greenville, SC @ Memorial Auditorium
Blackjack Mulligan beat Masked Superstar II
Masked Superstar I beat Johnny Weaver
Matt Borne & Buzz Sawyer beat Swede Hanson & Dewey Robertson
Gene Lewis beat Ron Ritchie
Masked Scorpion draw Bob Marcus

4/29/80: Columbia, SC @ Township Auditorium
Ric Flair beat Jimmy Snuka
Jim Brunzell beat Iron Sheik by DQ
Rufus R. Jones & Tony Garea beat Ox Baker & Swede Hanson
Matt Borne beat Frankie Laine
Doug Somers beat Cocoa Samoa

4/29/80: Raleigh, NC @ Dorton Arena
Blackjack Mulligan beat Masked Superstar II
Masked Superstar I beat Johnny Weaver
S.D. Jones & Buzz Sawyer beat Gene Lewis & Dewey Robertson

4/30/80: Raleigh, NC @ WRAL Studios (TV)
Iron Sheik beat Ron Ritchie
Rufus R. Jones & S.D. Jones beat Billy Starr & Brute Bernard
Jimmy Snuka beat Frankie Laine
Ric Flair beat Tank Patton

4/30/80: Greensboro, NC @ Coliseum
Jimmy Snuka beat Ric Flair in a lumberjack match
Plus other matches

5/1/80: Sumter, SC @ Sumter County Exposition Center
Blackjack Mulligan vs. Masked Superstar II
Masked Superstar I vs. Rufus R. Jones
Brute Bernard & Swede Hanson vs. Pedro Morales & Matt Borne
Abe Jacobs vs. Doug Somers
Ron Ritchie vs. Tony Russo

5/1/80: Norfolk, VA @ Scope
Greg Valentine & Ray Stevens beat Ricky Steamboat & Jay Youngblood
Ric Flair beat Jimmy Snuka
S.D. Jones & Johnny Weaver beat Ox Baker & Dewey Robertson
Iron Sheik beat Tony Garea
Buzz Sawyer beat Tank Patton
Don Kernodle beat Billy Starr
Gene Lewis beast Cocoa Samoa
The Scorpion beat Ron Sexton

5/2/80: Richmond, VA @ Coliseum
No Wrestling

5/2/80: Lexington, NC @ North Davidson Senior High School
Ric Flair & Jim Brunzell vs. Jimmy Snuka & Iron Sheik
Swede Hanson vs. Buzz Sawyer
Don Kernodle vs. Gene Lewis
Tony Russo vs. Ron Sexton

5/2/80: Lynchburg, VA @ City Armory
Ray Stevens & Greg Valentine double DQ Ricky Steamboat & Jay Youngblood
Johnny Weaver beat Tank Patton
S.D. Jones beat Ox Baker
Tony Garea beat The Scorpion
Billy Starr beat Cocoa Samoa

5/2/80: Charleston, SC @ County Hall
Blackjack Mulligan beat Masked Superstar II(unmasked as John Studd)
Masked Superstar I beat Rufus R. Jones
Brute Bernard & Dewey Robertson beat Matt Borne & Pedro Morales
Ron Ritchie beat Joe Furr
Abe Jacobs beat Doug Somers

5/3/80: Hampton, VA @ Coliseum
Blackjack Mulligan beat Masked Superstar II by DQ
Ricky Steamboat beat Masked Superstar I by DQ
S.D. Jones & Johnny Weaver beat Ox Baker & Tank Patton
Tony Garea beat Doug Somers
Abe Jacobs beat Billy Starr
Ron Ritchie beat Tony Russo

5/3/80: Spartanburg, SC @ Memorial Auditorium
Cocoa Samoa beat The Scorpion
Gene Lewis & Dewey Robertson beat Pedro Morales & Matt Borne
Rufus R. Jones beat Ray Stevens via DQ
Ric Flair beat Iron Sheik

5/4/80: Toronto, Ontario @ Maple Leaf Gardens
Ricky Steamboat & Jay Youngblood beat Ray Stevens & Greg Valentine by DQ
Blackjack Mulligan & Dewey Robertson beat Masked Superstar I & II
Pedro Morales beat The Destroyer by DQ
Billy Red Lyons beat Doug Somers
The Scorpion draw Bob Marcus
Frankie Laine beat Nick DeCarlo

5/5/80: Greenville, SC @ Memorial Auditorium
Ricky Steamboat & Jay Youngblood beat Ray Stevens & Greg Valentine by DQ
Rufus R. Jones beat Ox Baker
Johnny Weaver beat Tank Patton
Buzz Sawyer beat Ron Sexton
Len Denton beat Ron Ritchie

5/5/80: Fayetteville, NC @ Cumberland County Civic Center
Ric Flair & Jim Brunzell vs. Jimmy Snuka & Iron Sheik
Matt Borne vs. Brute Bernard
Tony Garea vs. Billy Starr
S.D. Jones vs. Gene Lewis
Tony Russo vs. Abe Jacobs

5/6/80: Columbia, SC @ Township Auditorium
Blackjack Mulligan vs. Masked Superstar II
Masked Superstar I vs. Rufus R. Jones
Dewey Robertson & Swede Hanson vs. Matt Borne & Tony Garea
Abe Jacobs vs. Doug Somers
Ron Sexton vs. Tony Russo

5/6/80: Raleigh, NC @ Dorton Arena
Jimmy Snuka beat Ric Flair by DQ
Jim Brunzell beat Iron Sheik
S.D. Jones & Buzz Sawyer beat Brute Bernard & Gene Lewis
Len Denton beat Joe Furr
Ron Ritchie draw The Scorpion

5/7/80: Raleigh, NC @ WRAL Studios (TV)

5/8/80: Norfolk, VA @ Scope

5/8/80: Niagara Falls, Ontario
Dewey Robertson beat Masked Superstar II by DQ
Blackjack Mulligan beat Masked Superstar I by DQ
Pedro Morales & Billy Red Lyons beat The Destroyer & The Scorpion
Nick DeCarlo beat Doug Somers
Frankie Laine draw Bob Marcus

5/9/80: Richmond, VA @ Coliseum
Ricky Steamboat & Jay Youngblood beat Ray Stevens & Greg Valentine with avid Crockett as special referee
Ric Flair beat Jimmy Snuka
Rufus R. Jones & S.D. Jones beat Ox Baker & Dewey Robertson
Pedro Morales beat Brute Bernard
Buzz Sawyer beat Tank Patton
Don Kernodle beat Doug Somers
Ron Sexton beat Abe Jacobs
Ron Ritchie beat Ken Timbs

5/9/80: Charleston, SC @ County Hall
Blackjack Mulligan beat Masked Superstar
Jim Brunzell beat Iron Sheik
Gene Lewis & Swede Hanson beat Johnny Weaver & Matt Borne
Tony Garea beat Billy Starr
Cocoa Samoa beat The Scorpion

5/10/80: Greensboro, NC @ Coliseum
Ricky Steamboat & Jay Youngblood beat Greg Valentine & Ray Stevens in a 2 of 3 falls match to win the NWA World Tag Title with David Crockett as special referee
Masked Superstar I vs. Blackjack Mulligan
Jimmy Snuka beat Ric Flair in a lumberjack match
14 Man, $5,000 Battle Royal, Winner to meet Ric Flair for United States Title at a later date
featuring Jimmy Snuka, Ox Baker, Gene Lewis, The Scorpion, Tank Patton, Len Denton, Swede Hanson, Johnny Weaver, Rufus R. Jones, Matt Borne, Buzz Sawyer, Tony Garea, Pedro Morales & Abe Jacobs
Plus 2 other matches

5/10/80: Spartanburg, SC @ Memorial Auditorium
Cocoa Samoa beat Billy Starr
Dewey Robertson & Brute Bernard beat Don Kernodle & S.D. Jones
Ric Flair double DQ Masked Superstar I
Blackjack Mulligan beat Masked Superstar II

5/11/80: Charlotte, NC @ Coliseum
Len Denton draw Ron Ritchie
Matt Borne & Buzz Sawyer beat Tank Patton & Doug Somers
Enforcer Luciano beat Cocoa Samoa
Gene Lewis & Dewey Robertson beat S.D. Jones & Pedro Morales
Ricky Steamboat beat Ray Stevens
Ric Flair draw Jimmy Snuka
Iron Sheik beat Jim Brunzell to win the NWA Mid Atlantic Title

5/12/80: Greenville, SC @ Memorial Auditorium
Ric Flair beat Iron Sheik
S.D. Jones & Tony Garea beat Swede Hansen & Gene Lewis
Abe Jacobs beat Masked Scorpion
Enforcer Luciano beat Cocoa Samoa
Jim Brunzell beat Dewey Robertson

5/12/1980: Lumberton, NC @ Recreation Center
Matt Borne vs. Billy Starr
Buzz Sawyer vs. Doug Somers
Tank Patton vs. Johnny Weaver
Ricky Steamboat & Jay Youngblood vs. Ray Stevens & Greg Valentine

5/13/80: Columbia, SC @ Township Auditorium

5/13/80: Raleigh, NC @ Dorton Arena
Ric Flair beat Jimmy Snuka
Rufus R. Jones & Johnny Weaver beat Swede Hanson & Gene Lewis
Enforcer Luciano beat Cocoa Samoa
Don Kernodle beat Billy Starr
Len Denton beat Ron Sexton

5/14/80: Raleigh, NC @ WRAL Studios (TV)

5/15/80: Norfolk, VA @ Scope
No Wrestling

5/16/80: Winston-Salem, NC @ Coliseum
Jimmy Snuka vs. Rufus R. Jones
Ric Flair vs. Iron Sheik
Swede Hanson & Doug Somers vs. Buzz Sawyer & Matt Borne
The Scorpion vs. Don Kernodle
Cocoa Samoa vs. Joe Furr

5/16/80: Charleston, SC @ County Hall
Masked Superstar I vs. Blackjack Mulligan in a lumberjack match
Jim Brunzell vs. Dewey Robertson

S.D. Jones & Pedro Morales vs. Brute Bernard & Ox Baker
Enforcer Luciano vs. Ron Sexton
Tony Russo vs. Abe Jacobs

5/16/80: Lynchburg, VA @ City Armory
Ricky Steamboat & Jay Youngblood beat Ray Stevens & Greg Valentine in a 2 of 3 falls match
Johnny Weaver beat Gene Lewis by DQ
Tony Garea beat Billy Starr
Len Denton beat Ron Ritchie

5/17/80: Spartanburg, SC @ Memorial Auditorium
Ron Ritchie draw Tony Russo
Doug Somers beat Joe Furr
Dewey Robertson & Swede Hanson beat Tony Garea & Abe Jacobs
Iron Sheik beat Johnny Weaver
Jimmy Snuka beat Ric Flair by countout

5/17/80: Wadesboro, NC
Ricky Steamboat & Jay Youngblood vs. Ray Stevens & Greg Valentine
S.D. Jones vs. Ox Baker
Don Kernodle vs. The Scorpion
Cocoa Samoa vs. Len Denton

5/18/80: Savannah, GA @ Civic Center
Jim Brunzell beat Iron Sheik
Ric Flair vs. Jimmy Snuka
Plus other matches

5/19/80: Greenville, SC @ Memorial Auditorium
Blackjack Mulligan beat Masked Superstar I by DQ
Doug Somers beat Ron Sexton
Len Denton beat Don Kernodle
Enforcer Luciano beat S.D. Jones
Gene Lewis & Dewey Robertson beat Buzz Sawyer & Don Kernodle(sub for Matt Borne)

5/19/80: Fayetteville, NC @ Cumberland County Civic Center
Ric Flair & Jim Brunzell vs. Jimmy Snuka, Iron Sheik & Gene Anderson in a handicap match
Swede Hanson vs. Tony Garea
Abe Jacobs vs. The Scorpion
Billy Starr vs. Joe Furr

5/20/80: Raleigh, NC
No Wrestling

5/20/80: Durham, NC
Ricky Steamboat & Jay Youngblood vs. Greg Valentine & Ray Stevens in a lumberjack match
Ox Baker vs. S.D. Jones
Don Kernodle vs. Tony Garea
The Scorpion vs. Ron Ritchie
Billy Starr vs. Abe Jacobs

5/20/80: Columbia, SC @ Township Auditorium

5/21/80: Raleigh, NC @ WRAL Studios (TV)
Masked Superstar & Enforcer Luciano beat Pedro Morales & Ron Sexton
Iron Sheik beat Joe Furr
Sweet Ebony Diamond beat The Demon
Blackjack Mulligan beat Ox Baker
Buzz Sawyer & Matt Borne beat Tony Russo & Doug Somers
Buzz Sawyer & Matt Borne beat Gene Lewis & The Scorpion
Iron Sheik beat Ron Ritchie
Tony Garea & Don Kernodle beat Masked Superstar & Enforcer Luciano by DQ
Sweet Ebony Diamond beat Billy Starr
Greg Valentine beat Ron Sexton

5/22/80: Norfolk, VA @ Scope
Ricky Steamboat vs. Greg Valentine
Ric Flair vs. Iron Sheik
Jim Brunzell vs. Jimmy Snuka
Dewey Robertson & Gene Lewis vs. Rufus R. Jones & S.D. Jones
Plus other matches

5/23/80: Richmond, VA @ Coliseum
Ricky Steamboat & Jay Youngblood beat Greg Valentine & Ray Stevens
Blackjack Mulligan beat Masked Superstar by DQ
Enforcer Luciano beat S.D. Jones
Buzz Sawyer & Matt Borne beat Dewey Robertson & Gene Lewis
Pedro Morales beat Brute Bernard by DQ
Len Denton & Doug Somers beat Abe Jacobs & Ron Ritchie
The Scorpion beat Billy Starr

5/23/80: Charleston, SC @ County Hall
Ric Flair beat Iron Sheik
Jim Brunzell beat Jimmy Snuka
Johnny Weaver & Tony Garea beat Ox Baker & Swede Hansen
Don Kernodle beat Cocoa Samoa
Tony Russo beat Ron Sexton

5/24/80: Spartanburg, SC @ Memorial Auditorium
Jimmy Snuka, Iron Sheik & Masked Superstar I beat Ric Flair, Blackjack Mulligan & Jim Brunzell
Enforcer Luciano beat Abe Jacobs
Ron Sexton beat Billy Starr
Tony Russo draw Cocoa Samoa

5/25/80: Toronto, Ontario @ Maple Leaf Gardens
Hussein Arab(Iron Sheik) beat Dewey Robertson to win Canadian Title
Blackjack Mulligan beat Masked Superstar II(unmasked as John Studd) in a Texas death match
Angelo Mosca beat Masked Superstar I by DQ
Tony Parisi beat Frankie Laine
Enforcer Luciano beat Don Kernodle
Bob Marcus & Nick DeCarlo beat Brute Bernard & Bill White

5/25/80: Greensboro, NC @ Coliseum
Ric Flair draw Greg Valentine(60:00)
Ray Stevens beat Ricky Steamboat
Jimmy Snuka beat Wahoo McDaniel
Sweet Ebony Diamond beat Ox Baker
Matt Borne & Buzz Sawyer beat Billy Starr & Len Denton
Johnny Weaver & Rufus R. Jones beat Gene Lewis & Swede Hanson
Tony Garea draw Abe Jacobs

5/25/80: Charlotte, NC @ Coliseum
Enforcer Luciano beat Johnny Weaver
Ric Flair beat Jimmy Snuka
Jim Brunzell beat Iron Sheik by DQ
Blackjack Mulligan beat Masked Superstar I by DQ

5/26/80: Dundas, Ontario
Dewey Robertson & Angelo Mosca vs. Hussein Arab & Masked Superstar I
Blackjack Mulligan vs. Masked Superstar II
Plus 8 other matches featuring Nick DeCarlo, Tony Parisi, Frankie Laine, londike Bill, Enforcer Luciano, Bob & Joe Marcus, Don Kernodle & The Scorpion

5/26/80: Greenville, SC @ Memorial Auditorium
Ric Flair beat Jimmy Snuka in a cage match
Jim Brunzell & Johnny Weaver beat Gene Lewis & Ox Baker
Abe Jacobs beat Tony Russo
Pedro Morales beat Ron Ritchie
S.D. Jones beat Doug Somers

5/27/80: Raleigh, NC @ Dorton Arena
Ric Flair beat Jimmy Snuka in a lumberjack match
Iron Sheik beat Jim Brunzell
Rufus R. Jones & S.D. Jones vs. Ox Baker(sub for Masked Superstar I) & nforcer Luciano
Abe Jacobs beat Doug Somers
Brute Bernard beat Ron Ritchie

5/27/80: Columbia, SC @ Township Auditorium
Ricky Steamboat & Jay Youngblood beat Greg Valentine & Ray Stevens in a cage match
Johnny Weaver beat Gene Lewis
Matt Borne & Buzz Sawyer beat Swede Hanson & Len Denton
The Scorpion draw Don Kernodle

5/28/80: Raleigh, NC @ WRAL Studios (TV)
Jimmy Snuka & Iron Sheik beat Abe Jacobs & Cocoa Samoa
Jim Brunzell beat The Scorpion
Masked Superstar & Enforcer Luciano beat Don Kernodle & Ron Ritchie
Ric Flair beat Billy Starr
Ricky Steamboat & Jay Youngblood beat Len Denton & Doug Somers
Masked Superstar & Enforcer Luciano beat Buzz Sawyer & Cocoa Samoa
Jim Brunzell beat Tony Russo
Jimmy Snuka & Iron Sheik beat Don Kernodle & Ron Ritchie
Ricky Steamboat & Jay Youngblood beat Len Denton & Doug Somers

5/29/80: Norfolk, VA @ Scope
No Wrestling

5/30/80: Charleston, SC @ County Hall

5/31/80: Spartanburg, SC @ Memorial Auditorium

6/1/80: Savannah, GA @ Civic Center
Jim Brunzell beat Iron Sheik by DQ
Jimmy Snuka beat Rufus R. Jones
Wendi Richter & Winona Little Heart beat Vivian St. John & Judy Martin
Buzz Sawyer & Matt Borne beat Len Denton & Doug Somers
Billy Starr beat Cocoa Samoa

6/2/80: Greenville, SC @ Memorial Auditorium
NWA Mid-Atlantic Tag Title tournament
1st Round
Johnny Weaver & Jim Brunzell vs. ?? & ??
Rufus R. Jones & S.D. Jones vs. ?? & ??
Ray Stevens & Greg Valentine vs. ?? & ??
Ox Baker & Brute Bernard vs. ?? & ??
Len Denton & Gene Lewis vs. ?? & ??
Matt Borne & Buzz Sawyer beat ?? & ??
Iron Sheik & Jimmy Snuka beat ?? & ??

Semifinals
Matt Borne & Buzz Sawyer beat ?? & ??
Iron Sheik & Jimmy Snuka beat ?? & ??

Finals
Matt Borne & Buzz Sawyer beat Jimmy Snuka & Iron Sheik in final to win
vacant NWA Mid Atlantic Tag Titles

6/3/80: Columbia, SC @ Township Auditorium
Ric Flair beat Jimmy Snuka
Jim Brunzell beat Iron sheik
Enforcer Luciano beat S.D. Jones
Pedro Morales & Tony Garea beat Ox Baker & Brute Bernard
Doug Somers beat Ron Sexton

6/3/80: Raleigh, NC @ Dorton Arena
Ricky Steamboat & Jay Youngblood beat Greg Valentine & Ray Stevens in a cage match
Johnny Weaver & Rufus R. Jones beat The Scorpion & Gene Lewis
Tony Russo draw Cocoa Samoa
Abe Jacobs beat Billy Starr by DQ

6/4/80: Raleigh, NC @ WRAL Studios (TV)
Rufus R. Jones & S.D. Jones beat Brute Bernard & Tony Russo
Blackjack Mulligan beat Tenryu
Jim Brunzell beat Doug Somers
Sweet Ebony Diamond beat Cocoa Samoa

Jimmy Snuka & Iron Sheik beat Tony Garea & Ron Ritchie
Masked Superstar & Enforcer Luciano beat Tony Garea & Ron Sexton
Sweet Ebony Diamond beat Doug Somers
Buzz Sawyer & Matt Borne beat Tenryu & Tony Russo
Blackjack Mulligan beat Brute Bernard
Jimmy Snuka & Iron Sheik beat S.D. Jones & Cocoa Samoa

6/5/80: Norfolk, VA @ Scope
Ric Flair vs. Jimmy Snuka in a Texas death match
Masked Superstar I & Enforcer Luciano vs. Blackjack Mulligan & Luke Mulligan(Killer Tim Brooks)
Sweet Ebony Diamond vs. Tenryu
Plus other matches

6/6/80: Asheville, NC @ Civic Center
Jimmy Snuka beat Ric Flair
Ricky Steamboat beat Paul Jones
Greg Valentine beat Rufus R. Jones
Mr. Wrestling & Don Kernodle beat The Scorpion & Brute Bernard
Bob Marcus draw Billy Starr
Tony Russo beat Joe Furr

6/6/80: Lynchburg, VA @ City Armory
Ric Flair & Sweet Ebony Diamond beat Jimmy Snuka & Iron Sheik
Johnny Weaver beat Tenryu
Pedro Morales beat Brute Bernard
Tony Garea beat Len Denton

6/6/80: Charleston, SC @ County Hall
Blackjack Mulligan & Luke Mulligan beat Masked Superstar & Enforcer Luciano by countout
S.D. Jones beat Gene Lewis
Don Kernodle beat Doug Somers
Abe Jacobs beat Ron Sexton
Tony Russo draw Ron Ritchie

6/6/80: Richmond, VA @ Coliseum
No Wrestling

6/7/80: Spartanburg, SC @ Memorial Auditorium
Masked Superstar I, Ray Stevens & Enforcer Luciano beat Blackjack Mulligan, Luke Mulligan & Jay Youngblood
S.D. Jones beat Gene Lewis
Pedro Morales beat Tenryu by DQ
Don Kernodle beat Masked Scorpion

6/7/80: Charlotte, NC @ Coliseum
Ric Flair draw Jimmy Snuka
Ricky Steamboat & Jay Youngblood beat Greg Valentine & Ray Stevens in a cage match
Blackjack Mulligan beat Masked Superstar by DQ
Enforcer Luciano beat S.D. Jones
Buzz Sawyer & Matt Borne beat Gene Lewis & Tenryu
Pedro Morales beat Doug Somers by DQ
Don Kernodle & Abe Jacobs beat The Scorpion & Billy Starr

6/7/80: Hampton, VA @ Coliseum
Iron Sheik beat Jim Brunzell
Sweet Ebony Diamond & Ric Flair beat Gene Anderson & Jimmy Snuka
Johnny Weaver & S.D. Jones beat Ox Baker & Len Denton
Tony Garea beat Brute Bernard by DQ
Ron Ritchie beat Ron Sexton
Cocoa Samoa draw Tony Russo

6/8/80: Roanoke, VA @ Civic Center
Ric Flair vs. Ray Stevens
Iron Sheik vs. Jim Brunzell
Plus other matches

6/8/80: Greensboro, NC @ Coliseum
Jimmy Snuka & Iron Sheik beat Greg Valentine(sub for Wahoo McDaniel) & Ric Flair in a cage match
Cousin Luke & Blackjack Mulligan DCO with Masked Superstar & Enforcer Luciano
Rufus R. Jones & S.D. Jones beat Ox Baker & Brute Bernard
Sweet Ebony Diamond beat Tenryu
Ray Stevens beat Pedro Morales
Don Kernodle beat Doug Somers
Ron Ritchie beat The Scorpion

6/9/80: Greenville, SC @ Memorial Auditorium
Blackjack Mulligan & Luke Mulligan beat Masked Superstar & Enforcer Luciano
Rufus R. Jones beat Gene Lewis
Pedro Morales & Tony Garea beat Len Denton & Tenryu
Steve Muslin beat Ron Sexton

6/9/80: Fayetteville, NC @ Cumberland County Civic Center
Iron Sheik vs. Jim Brunzell
Greg Valentine vs. Sweet Ebony Diamond
Doug Somers & Ox Baker vs. Johnny Weaver & S.D. Jones
Bill Starr vs. Don Kernodle
Tony Russo vs. Cocoa Samoa

6/10/80: Columbia, SC @ Township Auditorium
Steve Muslin beat Abe Jacobs
Tony Garea beat Doug Somers
Pedro Morales beat Ox Baker
Rufus R. Jones beat Gene Lewis
Ricky Steamboat & Jay Youngblood no contest with Iron Sheik & Jimmy Snuka

6/10/80: Raleigh, NC @ Dorton Arena
Ray Stevens, Enforcer Luciano & Masked Superstar beat Sweet Ebony Diamond, Blackjack Mulligan & Luke Mulligan by DQ
Johnny Weaver beat Tenryu
S.D. Jones beat Len Denton
Ron Ritchie beat Billy Starr

6/11/80: Raleigh, NC @ WRAL Studios (TV)

6/12/80: Madison, VA
Blackjack Mulligan & Luke Mulligan vs. Masked Superstar & Enforcer Luciano
Plus other matches

6/13/80: Richmond, VA @ Coliseum
Ric Flair beat Jimmy Snuka in a cage match
Masked Superstar & Enforcer Luciano beat Blackjack Mulligan & Cousin Luke Mulligan
Johnny Weaver beat Tenryu
Buzz Sawyer & Matt Borne beat Ox Baker & Gene Lewis
Swede Hansen & Brute Bernard beat Don Kernodle & Cocoa Samoa
Tony Garea beat Ron Ritchie
Joe Furr beat The Scorpion

6/13/80: Charleston, SC @ County Hall
Iron Sheik beat Jim Brunzell via pinfall
Ray Stevens & Greg Valentine beat S.D. Jones & Rufus R. Jones
Steve Muslin beat Ron Sexton
Doug Somers beat Pedro Morales
Abe Jacobs beat Billy Starr

6/14/80: Spartanburg, SC @ Memorial Auditorium

6/14/80: Niagara Falls, Ontario
Dewey Robertson & Angelo Mosca beat Ray Stevens & Jimmy Snuka by DQ
Ric Flair DCO with Hussein Arab
Pedro Morales beat Bob Marcus
Johnny Weaver beat Steve Muslin
Tony Parisi beat Doug Somers

6/15/80: Toronto, Ontario @ Maple Leaf Gardens
Hussein Arab beat Dewey Robertson
Ric Flair beat Jimmy Snuka
Angelo Mosca beat Ray Stevens by DQ
Tony Parisi beat Tim Gerrard
Pedro Morales & Johnny Weaver beat Steve Muslim & Doug Somers
Bob Marcus beat John Forsythe

6/16/80: Dundas, Ontario
Ric Flair, Dewey Robertson & Angelo Mosca vs. Jimmy Snuka, Ray Stevens & Hussein Arab
Johnny Weaver vs. ??
Tony Parisi vs. ??
Plus 7 other matches

6/16/80: Greenville, SC @ Memorial Auditorium
Blackjack Mulligan, Luke Mulligan & Sweet Ebony Diamond vs. Greg Valentine, Masked Superstar & Enforcer Luciano in a lumberjack match
Rufus R. Jones vs. Swede Hanson
Tony Garea vs. Masked Scorpion
Nick DeCarlo vs. Billy Starr
Ron Sexton vs. Tony Russo

6/17/80: Raleigh, NC @ Dorton Arena
Matt Borne & Buzz Sawyer beat Swede Hanson & Gene Lewis
Sweet Ebony Diamond beat Masked Superstar by DQ
Enforcer Luciano beat Blackjack Mulligan in a Detroit street fight match
Nick DeCarlo beat Tony Russo
Don Kernodle beat Doug Somers

6/17/80: Hampton, VA @ Coliseum

6/18/80: Raleigh, NC @ WRAL Studios (TV)

6/19/80: Norfolk, VA @ Scope
Greg Valentine double DQ Ric Flair
Enforcer Luciano beat Blackjack Mulligan
Iron Sheik beat Jim Brunzell
Sweet Ebony Diamond beat Masked Superstar by DQ
Buzz Sawyer & Matt Borne beat Gene Lewis & Dewey Robertson
Brute Bernard & Swede Hanson beat Pedro Morales & Tony Garea
Nick DeCarlo beat Ron Sexton
Abe Jacobs beat The Scorpion

6/19/80: Asheville, NC @ Civic Center
Abe Jacobs beat Blackjack Mulligan, Jr.
Bob Markus beat Frank Monte
Fabulous Moolah beat Judy Martin
Mr. Wrestling beat Mr. X
Ray Sevens & Greg Valentine beat S.D. Jones & Pedro Morales
Ric Flair beat Jimmy Snuka by DQ

6/20/80: Charleston, SC @ County Hall
Ricky Steamboat & Jay Youngblood beat Greg Valentine & Ray Stevens in a steel cage match
S.D. Jones beat Steve Muslin
Don Kernodle vs. Ben Alexander
Ron Ritchie beat Cocoa Samoa
Tony Russo vs. Joe Furr

6/20/80: Lynchburg, VA @ City Armory
Ric Flair beat Jimmy Snuka
Sweet Ebony Diamond beat Masked Superstar by DQ
Dewey Robertson & Gene Lewis beat Matt Borne & Buzz Sawyer
Abe Jacobs beat The Scorpion
Nick DeCarlo beat Doug Somers

6/21/80: Spartanburg, SC @ Memorial Auditorium
Ricky Steamboat, Jay Youngblood & Jim Brunzell beat Ray Stevens, Iron Sheik & Masked Superstar
Ron Ritchie beat Billy Starr
Don Kernodle beat Doug Somers
S.D. Jones beat Ox Baker

6/21/80: Charlotte, NC @ Coliseum
Ric Flair & Sweet Ebony Diamond beat Greg Valentine & Jimmy Snuka
Enforcer Luciano beat Blackjack Mulligan

Buzz Sawyer & Matt Borne beat Dewey Robertson & Swede Hanson
Gene Lewis & Steve Muslin beat Pedro Morales & Tony Garea
Johnny Weaver beat Scorpion
Ben Alexander beat Ron Sexton

6/22/80: Roanoke, VA @ Civic Center
Iron Sheik vs. Jim Brunzell in a match with 2 referees
12-man battle royal including Ric Flair, Sweet Ebony Diamond, Gene Lewis, Johnny Weaver, Greg Valentine, Jimmy Snuka, Ox Baker & others

6/22/80: Greensboro, NC @ Coliseum
Jimmy Snuka & Ray Stevens beat Ricky Steamboat & Jay Youngblood to win NWA World Tag Team Title
Ric Flair double DQ Greg Valentine
Matt Borne & Buzz Sawyer beat Dewey Robertson & Gene Lewis
S.D. Jones beat Ox Baker
Don Kernodle beat The Scorpion
Abe Jacobs beat Billy Starr
Nick DeCarlo beat Tony Russo

6/23/80: Greenville, SC @ Memorial Auditorium
Blackjack Mulligan vs. Enforcer Luciano in a Detroit street fight match
Iron Sheik vs. Jim Brunzell
Matt Borne & Buzz Sawyer vs. Dewey Robertson & Gene Lewis
David Patterson vs. Nick DeCarlo
Ricky Ferrara vs. Cocoa Samoa

6/23/80: Myrtle Beach, SC
Ricky Steamboat & Jay Youngblood beat Ray Stevens & Jimmy Snuka by DQ
Pedro Morales beat Ben Alexander
S.D. Jones beat Swede Hanson
Ron Ritchie beat Billy Starr

6/24/80: Columbia, SC @ Township Auditorium
Blackjack Mulligan vs. Enforcer Luciano in a Detroit street fight match
Masked Superstar vs. Sweet Ebony Diamond
Johnny Weaver & S.D. Jones vs. Dewey Robertson & Gene Lewis
Don Kernodle vs. Billy Starr
Ricky Ferrara vs. Cocoa Samoa

6/24/80: Raleigh, NC @ Dorton Arena
Ric Flair, Ricky Steamboat & Jay Youngblood beat Greg Valentine, Ray Stevens & Jimmy Snuka
Ben Alexander draw Nick DeCarlo
Tony Garea beat David Patterson
Steve Muslin beat Pedro Morales

6/25/80: Raleigh, NC @ WRAL Studios (TV)

6/26/80: Norfolk, VA @ Scope
No Wrestling

6/27/80: Charleston, SC @ County Hall
Enforcer Luciano beat Blackjack Mulligan in a Detroit street fight brawl
Sweet Ebony Diamond beat Masked Superstar by DQ
Dewey Robertson & Gene Lewis beat Matt Borne & Buzz Sawyer
Don Kernodle beat Ricky Ferrara
Nick DeCarlo beat Billy Starr

6/27/80: Fredericksburg, VA @ Stafford High School
Ricky Steamboat & Jay Youngblood beat Ray Stevens & Greg Valentine
Tony Garea beat Ox Baker via pinfall
S.D. Jones beat Steve Muslin
Abe Jacobs beat Ben Alexander

6/28/80: Richmond, VA @ Coliseum
No Wrestling

6/28/80: Spartanburg, SC @ Memorial Auditorium
Ray Stevens & Jimmy Snuka beat Ricky Steamboat & Jay Youngblood by DQ
Johnny Weaver beat Ox Baker
Don Kernodle beat Ricky Ferrara
Brett Wayne draw Tony Tosi

6/29/80: Roanoke, VA @ Civic Center
Sweet Ebony Diamond(Rocky Johnson) beat Masked Superstar by DQ
Plus other matches

6/29/80: Toronto, Ontario @ Maple Leaf Gardens
Hussein Arab beat Angelo Mosca by DQ
Ray Stevens & Jimmy Snuka draw Ricky Steamboat & Jay Youngblood
Giant Baba & Jumbo Tsuruta beat Bruiser Brody & Scott Irwin
Dory Funk, Jr. DCO with Abdullah The Butcher
Johnny Weaver & Tony Parisi beat David Patterson & Ben Alexander
The Destroyer beat Joe Marcus
Bob Marcus beat Brian Mackney

6/30/80: Niagara Falls, Ontario
Hussein Arab vs. Jay Youngblood
Angelo Mosca vs. Jimmy Snuka
Ricky Steamboat vs. Ray Stevens
Johnny Weaver & Tony Parisi beat Ben Alexander & David Patterson
The Destroyer vs. ??

6/30/80: Greenville, SC @ Memorial Auditorium
Ric Flair DCO with Greg Valentine
Sweet Ebony Diamond beat Masked Superstar by DQ
Gene Lewis & Swede Hanson beat S.D. Jones & Pedro Morales
Don Kernodle beat Doug Somers
Ron Ritchie beat Ricky Ferrara

7/1/80: Raleigh, NC @ Dorton Arena
Ray Stevens & Jimmy Snuka beat Ricky Steamboat & Jay Youngblood by DQ
Don Kernodle beat Ricky Ferrara
Don Kernodle(sub for Johnny Weaver) beat Ox Baker
Ron Ritchie beat David Patterson
Swede Hanson beat Tong Garea

7/1/80: Myrtle Beach, SC
Iron Sheik beat Jim Brunzell by DQ
Johnny Weaver beat Enforcer Luciano by countout
Buzz Sawyer & Matt Borne beat Gene Lewis & Ben Alexander
Abe Jacobs beat Billy Starr

7/2/80: Raleigh, NC @ WRAL Studios (TV)

7/3/80: Norfolk, VA @ Scope
Ricky Steamboat & Jay Youngblood vs. Ray Stevens & Jimmy Snuka
13-man Russian Roulette Battle royal including Andre The Giant, Enforcer Luciano, Blackjack Mulligan, S.D. Jones, Ox Baker, Steve Muslin, Tony Garea, Dewey Robertson, Don Kernodle & others
Plus 6 other matches

7/4/80: Shelby, NC
Masked Superstar vs. Andre The Giant
Plus other matches

7/4/80: Charleston, SC @ County Hall
No wrestling

7/4/80: Richmond, VA @ Coliseum
Ric Flair beat Greg Valentine
Jim Brunzell beat Iron Sheik by DQ
Cousin Luke Mulligan beat Enforcer Luciano
S.D. Jones beat Ox Baker
Dewey Robertson beat Pedro Morales
Gene Lewis & Swede Hanson beat Matt Borne & Buzz Sawyer
Don Kernodle & Ron Ritchie beat Tony Russo & Steve Muslin

7/4/80: Winston-Salem, NC @ Coliseum
Tony Garea & Johnny Weaver vs. Doug Somers & Ben Alexander
Andre The Giant vs. Masked Superstar
Plus other matches

7/5/80: Charlotte, NC @ Coliseum
Jimmy Snuka & Ray Stevens beat Ricky Steamboat & Jay Youngblood
Jim Brunzell beat Iron Sheik by DQ
Sweet Ebony Diamond beat Ox Baker
Johnny Weaver & Tony Garea beat Doug Somers & David Patterson
Swede Hanson beat Pedro Morales
Ricky Ferrara beat Cocoa Samoa
Ben Alexander draw Ron Ritchie

7/5/80: Hampton, VA @ Coliseum
Andre The Giant, Ric Flair & Blackjack Mulligan beat Greg Valentine, Masked Superstar & Enforcer Luciano
Buzz Sawyer & Matt Borne beat Dewey Robertson & Gene Lewis
S.D. Jones beat Steve Muslin
Don Kernodle beat Abe Jacobs
Nick DeCarlo beat Tony Russo

7/5/80: Spartanburg, SC @ Memorial Auditorium
Ricky Steamboat, Jay Youngblood & Jim Brunzell beat Ray Stevens, Jimmy Snuka & Iron Sheik
Johnny Weaver beat Swede Hanson by DQ
Tony Tosi beat Billy Starr
David Patterson beat Ron Ritchie

7/6/80: Greensboro, NC @ Coliseum
Ric Flair beat Greg Valentine
Blackjack Mulligan beat Enforcer Luciano
Ricky Steamboat beat Ray Stevens
Andre The Giant won a 15-man Battle Royal
Johnny Weaver beat Brute Bernard
Buzz Sawyer beat Billy Starr

7/6/80: Roanoke, VA @ Civic Center
Andre The Giant, Ric Flair & Blackjack Mulligan beat Greg Valentine, Masked Superstar & Enforcer Luciano
Buzz Sawyer & Matt Borne beat Dewey Robertson & Gene Lewis
S.D. Jones beat Steve Muslin
Don Kernodle beat Abe Jacobs
Nick DeCarlo beat Tony Russo

7/6/80: Asheville, NC @ Civic Center
Ray Stevens & Jimmy Snuka vs. Ricky Steamboat & Jay Youngblood
Sweet Ebony Diamond vs. Gene Lewis
Steven Muslin vs. Tony Garea
David Patterson vs. Ron Ritchie
Ricky Ferrara vs. Cocoa Samoa

7/7/80: Greenville, SC @ Memorial Auditorium
Ric Flair beat Greg Valentine
Blackjack Mulligan beat Enforcer Luciano
Buzz Sawyer & Matt Borne beat Gene Lewis & Dewey Robertson
Abe Jacobs beat Billy Starr
Brute Bernard beat Terry Yorkston

7/7/80: Richmond, VA @ Coliseum
Nick DeCarlo beat Tony Russo
Don Kernodle beat Abe Jacobs
S.D. Jones beat Steve Muslin
Matt Borne & Buzz Sawyer beat Gene Lewis & Dewey Robertson
Andre the Giant, Blackjack Mulligan & Ric Flair beat Enforcer Luciano, Masked Superstar & Greg Valentine

7/8/80: Raleigh, NC @ Dorton Arena
Ric Flair & Jim Brunzell beat Iron Sheik & Greg Valentine
S.D. Jones beat Dewey Robertson by DQ
Sweet Ebony Diamond beat Swede Hanson

Don Kernodle beat Tony Russo
Doug Somers draw Abe Jacobs

7/8/80: Columbia, SC @ Township Auditorium

7/9/80: Raleigh, NC @ WRAL Studios (TV)

7/10/80: Sumter, SC @ Sumter County Exposition Center
Andre The Giant & Sweet Ebony Diamond vs. Ray Stevens & Jimmy Snuka
Johnny Weaver vs. Bobby Duncum
Abe Jacobs vs. Tony Russo
Cocoa Samoa vs. Ricky Ferrara
Nick DeCarlo vs. Steve Muslin

7/10/80: Norfolk, VA @ Scope

7/11/80: Lynchburg, VA @ City Armory
Ray Stevens & Jimmy Snuka beat Ricky Steamboat & Jay Youngblood
Johnny Weaver beat Ox Baker
S.D. Jones beat Swede Hanson
Ron Ritchie draw Doug Somers
Cocoa Samoa beat Billy Starr

7/11/80: Charleston, SC @ County Hall
Ric Flair & Sweet Ebony Diamond beat Greg Valentine & Iron Sheik
Buzz Sawyer & Matt Borne beat Dewey Robertson & Gene Lewis
David Patterson vs. Don Kernodle
Tony Russo vs. Ben Alexander

7/11/80: Richmond, VA @ Coliseum
No Wrestling

7/12/80: Hampton, VA @ Coliseum
Cocoa Samoa draw Tony Russo
Ron Ritchie beat Ron Sexton
Tony Garea beat Brute Bernard by DQ
S.D. Jones & Johnny Weaver beat Ox Baker & Len Denton
Ric Flair & Sweet Ebony Diamond beat Gene Anderson & Jimmy Snuka
Iron Sheik beat Jim Brunzell

7/12/80: Spartanburg, SC @ Memorial Auditorium
Sweet Ebony Diamond & Jim Brunzell beat Greg Valentine & Iron Sheik
Johnny Weaver beat Swede Hanson
Cocoa Samoa beat David Patterson
Ron Ritchie beat Tony Russo

7/12/80: Kingsport, TN @ Dobyns-Bennett High School
Abe Jacobs vs. Billy Starr
Ricky Ferrara vs. Don Kernodle
Nick DeCarlo vs. Doug Somers
Bobby Duncum vs. Tony Garea
Andre the Giant & Blackjack Mulligan vs. Enforcer Luciano & Masked Superstar

7/14/80: Greenville, SC @ Memorial Auditorium
Ricky Steamboat & Jay Youngblood beat Ray Stevens & Jimmy Snuka countout
David Patterson beat Nick DeCarlo
Buzz Sawyer beat Dewey Robertson by DQ
Bobby Duncum beat S.D. Jones
Ben Alexander draw Abe Jacobs

7/15/80: Bakersville, NC @ Mitchell High School
Iron Sheik beat Jim Brunzell by DQ
Johnny Weaver beat Enforcer Luciano by DQ
Swede Hanson & Brute Bernard beat Tony Garea & Don Kernodle
Abe Jacobs beat Tony Russo

7/15/80: Raleigh, NC @ Dorton Arena
Ric Flair beat Greg Valentine
Sweet Ebony Diamond beat Masked Superstar by DQ
Steve Muslin beat Ox Baker
Dewey Robertson & Gene Lewis beat Matt Borne & Buzz Sawyer
Ron Ritchie beat Ricky Ferrara

7/16/80: Raleigh, NC @ WRAL Studios (TV)

7/17/80: Norfolk, VA @ Scope
Ric Flair beat Greg Valentine
Jim Brunzell beat Iron Sheik by DQ
Sweet Ebony Diamond beat Jimmy Snuka via pinfall
Swede Hanson & Dewey Robertson beat Matt Borne & Buzz Sawyer
Don Kernodle & Ron Ritchie beat Ox Baker & Ben Alexander
Steve Muslin beat Billy Starr
Cocoa Samoa draw Ricky Ferrara

7/18/80: Richmond, VA @ Coliseum
Ricky Steamboat & Jay Youngblood beat Jimmy Snuka & Ray Stevens by countout
Sweet Ebony Diamond beat Masked Superstar by DQ
Swede Hanson, Gene Lewis & Dewey Robertson beat Matt Borne, Johnny Weaver & Don Kernodle
Ron Ritchie & Don Kernodle beat David Patterson & Billy Starr
Steve Muslin beat Ben Alexander
Cocoa Samoa draw Ricky Ferrara

7/18/80: Charleston, SC @ County Hall
Ric Flair beat Greg Valentine
Iron Sheik beat Jim Brunzell
S.D. Jones & Tony Garea beat Ox Baker & Brute Bernard
Nick DeCarlo beat Tony Russo
Brute Bernard(sub for David Patterson) beat Abe Jacobs

7/19/80: Spartanburg, SC @ Memorial Auditorium

7/19/80: Buffalo, NY
Ric Flair & Sweet Ebony Diamond beat Greg Valentine & Iron Sheik
Angelo Mosca beat Masked Superstar by DQ
Dewey Robertson beat Swede Hanson via pinfall
Tony Parisi & Ron Ritchie beat The Destroyer & David Patterson
George Wells beat Don Kernodle via pinfall

7/20/80: Roanoke, VA @ Civic Center
Ray Stevens & Jimmy Snuka vs. Ricky Steamboat & Jay Youngblood
Blackjack Mulligan vs. Enforcer Luciano in a Texas street fight match
Plus other matches

7/20/80: Toronto, Ontario @ Maple Leaf Gardens
Angelo Mosca beat Hussein Arab wins Canadian Title
Ric Flair beat Greg Valentine
Dewey Robertson beat Masked Superstar by DQ
Sweet Ebony Diamond beat Swede Hanson
Don Kernodle beat Ron Ritchie
George Wells & Tony Parisi beat The Destroyer & David Patterson

7/21/80: Forest City, NC
Jim Brunzell beat Iron Sheik by countout
Blackjack Mulligan beat Enforcer Luciano
Ox Baker & Swede Hanson beat Pedro Morales & Johnny Weaver
Billy Starr beat Ron Sexton

7/21/80: Dundas, Ontario
Ric Flair, Dewey Robertson & Angelo Mosca beat Hussein Arab, Swede Hanson & Greg Valentine
plus 9 other matches

7/21/80: Greenville, SC @ Memorial Auditorium
Ray Stevens & Jimmy Snuka beat Ricky Steamboat & Jay Youngblood
Bobby Duncum beat Johnny Weaver
Ricky Ferrara beat Abe Jacobs
S.D. Jones beat Ox Baker
Steve Muslin beat Ricky Ferrara

7/22/80: Raleigh, NC @ Dorton Arena
NWA World Champion Harley Race beat Ric Flair by countout
Sweet Ebony Diamond beat Masked Superstar
Greg Valentine & Bobby Duncum beat Johnny Weaver & S.D. Jones
Enforcer Luciano beat Steve Muslin
David Patterson beat Cocoa Samoa

7/22/80: Columbia, SC @ Township Auditorium

7/23/80: Raleigh, NC @ WRAL Studios (TV)

7/24/80: Sumter, SC @ Sumter County Exposition Center
Blackjack Mulligan vs. Enforcer Luciano in a Texas street fight match
Jimmy Snuka vs. Sweet Ebony Diamond
Don Kernodle & Ron Ritchie vs. Dewey Robertson & Frankie Laine
Abe Jacobs vs. Ben Alexander
Cocoa Samoa vs. Doug Somers

7/24/80: Norfolk, VA @ Scope

7/25/80: Lynchburg, VA @ City Armory
Iron Sheik vs. Jim Brunzell
Jay Youngblood vs. Jimmy Snuka
Matt Borne & Buzz Sawyer vs. Swede Hanson & Gene Lewis
Ben Alexander vs. Abe Jacobs

7/25/80: Charleston, SC @ County Hall
Blackjack Mulligan beat Enforcer Luciano in a Texas street fight
Bobby Duncum beat S.D. Jones
Nick DeCarlo & Steve Muslin beat Ox Baker & Brute Bernard
Ricky Ferrara beat Billy Starr

7/25/80: Winston-Salem, NC @ Coliseum
Ric Flair & Sweet Ebony Diamond vs. Greg Valentine & Masked Superstar
Dewey Robertson vs. Johnny Weaver
David Patterson vs. Don Kernodle
Doug Somers vs. Cocoa Samoa
Ron Ritchie vs. Tony Russo

7/25/80: Richmond, VA @ Coliseum
No Wrestling

7/26/80: Spartanburg, SC @ Memorial Auditorium
Ric Flair & Sweet Ebony Diamond beat Greg Valentine & Harley Race
Johnny Weaver beat Enforcer Luciano
Steve Muslin beat Brute Bernard by DQ
David Patterson beat Nick DeCarlo
Ben Alexander draw Ron Ritchie

7/26/80: Charlotte, NC @ Coliseum
NWA World Champion Harley Race beat Sweet Ebony Diamond
Greg Valentine beat Ric Flair to win NWA United States Title
Iron Sheik beat Jim Brunzell
Masked Superstar & Bobby Duncum beat Matt Borne & Buzz Sawyer
David Patterson & Gene Lewis beat Cocoa Samoa & Abe Jacobs
Dewey Robertson beat Steve Muslin
Ricky Ferrara beat Tony Russo

7/27/80: Asheville, NC @ Civic Center
Ric Flair, Ricky Steamboat & Jay Youngblood beat Ray Stevens, Greg Valentine & Jimmy Snuka
Johnny Weaver beat Bobby Duncum
Ben Alexander beat Ron Ritchie
Frankie Laine beat Steve Muslin

7/28/80: Myrtle Beach, SC
Jay Youngblood beat Jimmy Snuka
Sweet Ebony Diamond beat Masked Superstar by DQ
Dewey Robertson & Gene Lewis beat Steve Muslin & Matt Borne
Joe Furr draw Billy Starr

7/28/80: Greenville, SC @ Memorial Auditorium
Ric Flair beat Greg Valentine by DQ
Ricky Steamboat beat Ray Stevens
Swede Hanson beat Cocoa Samoa
Bobby Duncum beat Buzz Sawyer
S.D. Jones & Don Kernodle beat Swede Hanson & Tony Russo

7/29/80: Raleigh, NC
No Wrestling

7/29/80: Hampton, VA @ Coliseum
Ray Stevens & Jimmy Snuka beat Jay Youngblood & Ricky Steamboat by DQ
Iron Sheik beat Jim Brunzell
Swede Hanson & Enforcer Luciano beat Johnny Weaver & S.D. Jones
Cocoa Samoa beat Tony Russo
Ron Ritchie beat David Patterson
David Patterson beat Steve Muslin

7/29/80: Columbia, SC @ Township Auditorium

7/30/80: Raleigh, NC @ WRAL Studios (TV)

7/30/80: ??
Greg Valentine DCO with Ric Flair
Sweet Ebony Diamond beat Masked Superstar by DQ
Gene Lewis & Swede Hanson beat Pedro Morales & S.D. Jones
Don Kernodle beat Doug Somers
Ron Ritchie beat Ricky Ferrara

7/31/80: Norfolk, VA @ Scope
No Wrestling

8/1/80: Richmond, VA @ Coliseum
Ray Stevens & Jimmy Snuka beat Ricky Steamboat & Jay Youngblood in a cage match
Blackjack Mulligan beat Enforcer Luciano in a Texas street fight
Bobby Duncum beat S.D. Jones
Johnny Weaver & Jim Brunzell vs. Dewey Robertson & Gene Lewis
Don Kernodle vs. Jim Nelson
David Patterson & Ben Alexander vs. Nick DeCarlo & Cocoa Samoa
Billy Starr vs. Abe Jacobs

8/1/80: Charleston, SC @ County Hall
Jim Brunzell(sub for Ric Flair) & Sweet Ebony Diamond beat Masked Superstar & Greg Valentine in an elimination match
Matt Borne & Buzz Sawyer beat Bill Calgary(sub for Brute Bernard) & Frankie Laine
Steve Muslin beat Brett Wayne(sub for Swede Hanson)
Ricky Ferrara beat Ron Ritchie

8/2/80: Spartanburg, SC @ Memorial Auditorium
Iron Sheik beat Jim Brunzell in a Texas death match
Frankie Laine & Enforcer Luciano beat Matt Borne & Buzz Sawyer
Ron Ritchie beat Ben Alexander
Ricky Ferrara beat Cocoa Samoa
Brett Wayne draw Tony Russo

8/3/80: Greensboro, NC @ Coliseum
Ricky Steamboat & Jay Youngblood beat Ray Stevens & Jimmy Snuka by CO
Iron Sheik beat Jim Brunzell
Sweet Ebony Diamond & S.D. Jones beat Enforcer Luciano & Masked Superstar
Bobby Duncum beat Frankie Laine
Matt Borne & Buzz Sawyer beat Swede Hanson & Gene Lewis
Dave Patterson draw Nick DeCarlo
Steve Muslin beat Ricky Ferrara

8/3/80: Roanoke, VA @ Civic Center
Ric Flair beat Greg Valentine by DQ
Ricky Steamboat beat Ray Stevens
Sweet Ebony Diamond beat Masked Superstar
Johnny Weaver & Billy Starr beat Ox Baker & Charlie Fulton
Jim Nelson vs. Nick DeCarlo
Ron Ritchie vs. Tony Russo

8/4/80: Greenville, SC @ Memorial Auditorium
Sweet Ebony Diamond beat Masked Superstar
Blackjack Mulligan beat Enforcer Luciano in a chain match
Abe Jacobs beat Billy Starr
Joe Furr beat Jim Nelson by DQ
S.D. Jones & Don Kernodle beat Frankie Laine & Tenryu

8/5/80: Raleigh, NC @ Dorton Arena
Iron Sheik vs. Jim Brunzell in a no DQ match
Blackjack Mulligan vs. Enforcer Luciano in a Texas street fight match
Bobby Duncum vs. S.D. Jones
Matt Borne & Buzz Sawyer vs. Swede Hanson & Brute Bernard
Billy Starr vs. Cocoa Samoa

8/5/80: Columbia, SC @ Township Auditorium

8/6/80: Raleigh, NC @ WRAL Studios (TV)

8/7/80: Norfolk, VA @ Scope
Ric Flair & Sweet Ebony Diamond beat Jimmy Snuka & Ray Stevens by DQ
Blackjack Mulligan vs. Enforcer Luciano in a Russian chain match
Bobby Duncum vs. Jim Brunzell
Plus other matches

8/8/80: Richmond, VA @ Coliseum
No Wrestling

8/8/80: Charleston, SC @ County Hall
Sweet Ebony Diamond beat Masked Superstar
Buzz Sawyer & Matt Borne vs. Dewey Robertson & Swede Hanson
Iron Sheik beat Jim Brunzell in a no DQ, falls count anywhere match
Brett Wayne beat Jim Nelson
Billy Starr draw Cocoa Samoa

8/8/80: Lynchburg, VA @ City Armory
Ric Flair & Blackjack Mulligan double DQ Bad Boy Duncum & Greg Valentine
Paul Jones beat Enforcer Luciano
Don Kernodle beat Ricky Ferrara
S.D. Jones beat Tenryu
Steve Muslin beat David Patterson

8/9/80: Buffalo, NY
Ricky Steamboat & Jay Youngblood vs. Ray Stevens & Jimmy Snuka
Hussein Arab vs. Sweet Ebony Diamond
Tony Parisi vs. ??
Angelo Mosca & Dewey Robertson vs. Swede Hanson & Billy Starr
Plus 1 other match

8/9/80: Charlotte, NC @ Coliseum
Greg Valentine & Bobby Duncum beat Ric Flair & Blackjack Mulligan
Paul Jones beat Masked Superstar
Jim Brunzell & Johnny Weaver beat Enforcer Luciano & Tenryu
Buzz Sawyer & Matt Borne beat Frankie Laine & Brute Bernard
S.D. Jones beat Ben Alexander
Nick DeCarlo beat Ricky Ferrara

8/10/80: Asheville, NC @ Civic Center
Jay Youngblood beat Jimmy Snuka
Masked Superstar draw Mr. Wrestling II
Bobby Duncum beat Jim Brunzell
Buzz Sawyer & Matt Borne beat Frankie Laine & Tenryu
Don Kernodle beat Cocoa Samoa

8/10/80: Toronto, Ontario @ Maple Leaf Gardens
Hussein Arab beat Angelo Mosca to win Canadian Title
Ric Flair beat Greg Valentine in a Texas death match
Blackjack Mulligan beat Enforcer Luciano
Dewey Robertson & Billy Red Lyons beat Swede Hansen & David Patterson
George Wells beat Billy Starr
Tony Parisi beat Ron Ritchie

8/11/80: Dundas, Ontario(TV)
Ric Flair beat Hussein Arab
Enforcer Luciano vs. Angelo Mosca
Ric Flair beat Billy Starr
Plus 6 other matches

8/11/80: Greenville, SC @ Memorial Auditorium
Greg Valentine beat Sweet Ebony Diamond
Blackjack Mulligan DCO with Bobby Duncum
Brute Bernard, Gene Lewis & Tenryu beat Johnny Weaver, Matt Borne & Buzz Sawyer
Ron Ritchie beat Tony Russo

8/12/80: Raleigh, NC @ Dorton Arena
Ric Flair & Blackjack Mulligan vs. Bobby Duncum & Greg Valentine
Billy Starr vs. Abe Jacobs
Nick DeCarlo vs. David Patterson
Johnny Weaver vs. Frankie Laine
Ron Ritchie vs. Tenryu

8/12/80: Columbia, SC @ Township Auditorium

8/13/80: Raleigh, NC @ WRAL Studios (TV)
Ric Flair & Blackjack Mulligan beat Frankie Laine & Jim Nelson

8/14/80: Norfolk, VA @ Scope

8/14/80: Sumter, SC @ Sumter County Exposition Center
Sweet Ebony Diamond beat Greg Valentine by DQ
Masked Superstar beat Johnny Weaver
S.D. Jones & Ron Ritchie beat Frankie Laine & Gene Lewis
Swede Hanson beat Nick DeCarlo
Abe Jacobs beat Billy Starr via pinfall

8/15/80: Charleston, SC @ County Hall
Sweet Ebony Diamond beat Iron Sheik by DQ
Johnny Weaver & S.D. Jones beat Swede Hanson & Enforcer Luciano
Jay Youngblood beat Jimmy Snuka
Tony Russo beat Cocoa Samoa
Nick DeCarlo beat Billy Starr

8/15/80: Richmond, VA @ Coliseum
Ric Flair & Blackjack Mulligan beat Masked Superstar(sub for Bobby Duncum) & Greg Valentine
Ricky Steamboat beat Ray Stevens
Paul Jones beat Dewey Robertson
Matt Borne & Buzz Sawyer beat Brute Bernard & Tenryu
Gene Lewis beat Abe Jacobs
George Wells beat Ben Alexander

8/16/80: Spartanburg, SC @ Memorial Auditorium
Ricky Steamboat & Jay Youngblood beat Ray Stevens & Jimmy Snuka by countout
George Wells beat Swede Hanson
Don Kernodle beat Brute Bernard by DQ
David Patterson beat Cocoa Samoa
Ricky Ferrara beat Joe Furr

8/17/80: Roanoke, VA @ Civic Center
Ric Flair & Blackjack Mulligan beat Greg Valentine & Masked Superstar

Matt Borne & Buzz Sawyer beat Frankie Laine & Gene Lewis
S.D. Jones beat David Patterson
Swede Hanson beat Ron Ritchie
Tenryu draw Steve Muslin

8/17/80: Greensboro, NC @ Coliseum
Jimmy Snuka & Ray Stevens beat Ricky Steamboat & Jay Youngblood
Ric Flair beat Greg Valentine
Sweet Ebony Diamond & Paul Jones beat Iron Sheik & Masked Superstar
Dewey Robertson beat Don Kernodle
Johnny Weaver beat Frankie Laine
George Wells beat Ben Alexander
Abe Jacobs & Cocoa Samoa beat Ricky Ferrara & Billy Starr

8/18/80: Greenville, SC @ Memorial Auditorium
Ric Flair beat Greg Valentine
Tenryu beat Matt Borne
Dewey Robertson beat Steve Muslin
George Wells beat Frankie Laine
Ron Ritchie beat Tony Russo

8/19/80: Raleigh, NC @ Dorton Arena
Paul Jones, Ricky Steamboat & Jay Youngblood beat Jimmy Snuka, Ray Stevens & Gene Anderson by countout
Nick DeCarlo beat Ricky Ferrara
Steve Muslin beat Ben Alexander
George Wells beat Dewey Robertson

8/19/80: Columbia, SC @ Township Auditorium

8/20/80: Raleigh, NC @ WRAL Studios (TV)

8/21/80: Norfolk, VA @ Scope
Ric Flair & Sweet Ebony Diamond vs. Bobby Duncum & Greg Valentine
Iron sheik vs. Paul Jones
Dewey Robertson & Swede Hanson vs. George Wells & S.D. Jones
Plus other matches

8/21/80: Harrisonburg, VA
Ricky Steamboat & Jay Youngblood vs. Ray Stevens & Jimmy Snuka
Johnny Weaver vs. Tenryu
Buzz Sawyer & Matt Borne vs. Frankie Laine & Gene Lewis
Steve Muslin vs. Ricky Ferrara

8/22/80: Richmond, VA @ Coliseum
No Wrestling

8/22/80: Elizabeth City, NC
Blackjack Mulligan & Sweet Ebony Diamond vs. Bobby Duncum & Iron Sheik
George Wells vs. Brute Bernard
Don Kernodle vs. David Patterson
Nick DeCarlo vs. Billy Starr

8/22/80: Culpeper, VA
Ric Flair beat Greg Valentine by DQ
Paul Jones beat Dewey Robertson
Ron Ritchie beat Tony Russo
S.D. Jones beat Gene Lewis

8/22/80: Charleston, SC @ County Hall
Ray Stevens & Jimmy Snuka beat Ricky Steamboat & Jay Youngblood
Steve Muslin beat Ricky Ferrara
Abe Jacobs beat Ben Alexander
Johnny Weaver beat Swede Hanson
Cocoa Samoa draw Tony Tosi

8/23/80: Spartanburg, SC @ Memorial Auditorium
Ricky Steamboat, Jay Youngblood & Paul Jones beat Jimmy Snuka, Ray Stevens & Gene Anderson
Johnny Weaver beat Dewey Robertson
Don Kernodle beat Frankie Laine
Ron Ritchie beat Ricky Ferrara

8/23/80: Charlotte, NC @ Coliseum
Ric Flair & Blackjack Mulligan beat Bobby Duncum & Greg Valentine
Sweet Ebony Diamond beat Iron Sheik by DQ
S.D. Jones & George Wells beat Swede Hanson & Gene Lewis
Buzz Sawyer & Matt Borne beat Tenryu & David Patterson
Steve Muslin beat Tony Russo
Ben Alexander beat Nick DeCarlo
Abe Jacobs beat Billy Starr

8/24/80: Toronto, Ontario @ Maple Leaf Gardens
Jimmy Snuka & Ray Stevens beat Ricky Steamboat & Jay Youngblood
Angelo Mosca beat Gene Anderson
Tiger Jeet Singh beat Gene Lewis
George Wells beat Ben Alexander
Tony Parisi beat Tim Gerrard
Bob Marcus beat Brian Mackney

8/25/80: Guelph, Ontario
Angelo Mosca, Ricky Steamboat & Jay Youngblood beat Jimmy Snuka, Ray Stevens & Gene Anderson
Tiger Jeet Singh beat Ben Alexander
George Wells beat Gene Lewis
Tony Parisi beat Bob Marcus

8/25/80: Greenville, SC @ Memorial Auditorium
NWA World Champion Harley Race beat Ric Flair by countout
Sweet Ebony Diamond beat Iron Sheik
Matt Borne & Buzz Sawyer beat Dewey Robertson & Tenryu
S.D. Jones beat David Patterson
Ron Ritchie draw Ricky Ferrara

8/26/80: Raleigh, NC @ Dorton Arena
NWA World Champion Harley Race draw Ric Flair in a no DQ match
Masked Superstar beat Johnny Weaver
S.D. Jones & George Wells vs. Swede Hanson & Gene Lewis
Don Kernodle beat Billy Starr
Tenryu draw Steve Muslin

8/26/80: Columbia, SC @ Township Auditorium

8/27/80: Raleigh, NC @ WRAL Studios (TV)
Ric Flair & Blackjack Mulligan beat Ben Alexander & Tenryu

8/28/80: Norfolk, VA @ Scope

8/29/80: Richmond, VA @ Coliseum
NWA World Champion Harley Race DCO with Ricky Steamboat
Ric Flair & Blackjack Mulligan beat Greg Valentine & Bobby Duncum
Johnny Weaver beat Brute Bernard
S.D. Jones & George Wells beat Tenryu & Frankie Laine
Swede Hanson & David Patterson draw Don Kernodle & Ron Ritchie
Ben Alexander beat Abe Jacobs
Nick DeCarlo beat Tony Russo

8/30/80: Spartanburg, SC @ Memorial Auditorium
Iron Sheik beat Johnny Weaver
Paul Jones beat Gene Anderson
Matt Borne & Buzz Sawyer beat Dewey Robertson & Swede Hanson
Cocoa Samoa beat Ben Alexander
Nick DeCarlo beat Tony Russo

8/30/80: Charlotte, NC @ Coliseum
Ric Flair DCO with Greg Valentine
Sweet Ebony Diamond beat Masked Superstar by DQ
Gene Lewis & Swede Hanson beat Pedro Morales & S.D. Jones
Don Kernodle beat Doug Somers
Ron Ritchie beat Ricky Ferrara by referee's decision

8/31/80: Asheville, NC @ Civic Center
Abe Jacobs beat Tony Russo
Ben Alexander draw Nick DeCarlo
Matt Borne, Buzz Sawyer & Johnny Weaver beat Brute Bernard, Gene Lewis & Tenryu
Ric Flair beat Bobby Duncum
Greg Valentine beat Paul Jones

8/31/80: Greensboro, NC @ Coliseum
Greg Valentine beat Ric Flair
Ricky Steamboat beat Jimmy Snuka
Blackjack Mulligan DCO with Bobby Duncum
Sweet Ebony Diamond & George Wells beat Dewey Robertson & Swede Hanson
S.D. Jones beat Frankie Laine
Don Kernodle draw David Patterson(20:00)
Steve Muslin & Ron Ritchie beat Billy Starr & Ricky Ferrara

9/1/80: Greenville, SC @ Memorial Auditorium
Ric Flair DCO with Greg Valentine
Blackjack Mulligan beat Bobby Duncum
Swede Hanson & Gene Lewis beat Don Kernodle & ??
Nick DeCarlo beat Billy Starr
Ben Alexander draw Ron Ritchie

9/2/80: Raleigh, NC @ Dorton Arena
Paul Jones, Ricky Steamboat & Jay Youngblood beat Jimmy Snuka, Ray Stevens & Gene Anderson in a fence match
Steve Muslin beat Tony Russo
Nick DeCarlo beat Ben Alexander
George Wells beat Gene Lewis

9/2/80: Columbia, SC @ Township Auditorium

9/3/80: Raleigh, NC @ WRAL Studios (TV)

9/4/80: Norfolk, VA @ Scope
Ray Stevens & Jimmy Snuka beat Ricky Steamboat & Jay Youngblood
Blackjack Mulligan vs. Bobby Duncum
Iron Sheik vs. Paul Jones
Swede Hanson & Tenryu vs. Johnny Weaver & George Wells
Ricky Ferrara & Billy Starr vs. Matt Borne & Buzz Sawyer
Tony Russo vs. Don Kernodle

9/4/80: Sumter, SC @ Sumter County Exposition Center
Ric Flair & Sweet Ebony Diamond beat Greg Valentine & Masked Superstar
S.D. Jones beat Gene Lewis
Dewey Robertson beat Steve Muslin
Brute Bernard beat Abe Jacobs via pinfall
Ron Ritchie draw David Patterson

9/5/80: Charleston, SC @ County Hall

9/5/80: Richmond, VA @ Coliseum
Greg Valentine vs. Ric Flair
Iron Sheik vs. Sweet Ebony Diamond
Ray Stevens vs. Paul Jones
Johnny Weaver & George Wells vs. Dewey Robertson & Swede Hanson
Tenryu vs. Nick DeCarlo
Matt Borne & Buzz Sawyer vs. Gene Lewis & Ricky Ferrara

9/6/80: Lovington, VA @ Nelson County High School
Blackjack Mulligan vs. Bobby Duncum
Johnny Weaver & George Wells vs. Brute Bernard & Ben Alexander
Billy Starr vs. Ron Ritchie
Tony Russo vs. Abe Jacobs

9/6/80: Toronto, Ontario @ Maple Leaf Gardens(Special Saturday Card)
Sweet Ebony Diamond beat Masked Superstar
Ric Flair & Angelo Mosca beat Hussein Arab & Greg Valentine
Tiger Jeet Singh beat Swede Hanson
Dewey Robertson beat Don Kernodle
Nick DeCarlo beat David Patterson
Frankie Laine draw Tony Parisi

9/7/80: Niagara Falls, Ontario
Ric Flair & Sweet Ebony Diamond beat Greg Valentine & Masked Superstar
Hussein Arab beat Dewey Robertson
Tony Parisi beat Swede Hanson
Frankie Laine beat David Patterson
Nick DeCarlo draw Don Kernodle

9/8/80: Brantford, Ontario(TV)
Ric Flair, Sweet Ebony Diamond & Dewey Robertson beat Greg Valentine,
Masked Superstar & Hussein Arab

9/8/80: Greenville, SC @ Memorial Auditorium
Paul Jones beat Gene Anderson in a lumberjack match
Bobby Duncum beat Luke Mulligan
Matt Borne & Buzz Sawyer beat Gene Lewis & Brute Bernard
Ron Ritchie beat Billy Starr
Abe Jacobs beat Tony Russo

9/9/80: Raleigh, NC @ Dorton Arena
Sweet Ebony Diamond beat Greg Valentine by countout
Ric Flair beat Bobby Duncum
Don Kernodle beat Ben Alexander
Gene Lewis beat Cocoa Samoa
Matt Borne & Buzz Sawyer beat Brute Bernard & Tenryu

9/9/80: Columbia, SC @ Township Auditorium

9/10/80: Raleigh, NC @ WRAL Studios (TV)

9/11/80: Forest City, NC
Sweet Ebony Diamond & Johnny Weaver beat Iron Sheik & Bobby Duncum DQ
George Wells beat Dewey Robertson
Steve Muslin beat Ricky Ferrara
Abe Jacobs beat Billy Starr

9/11/80: Norfolk, VA @ Scope

9/12/80: Lynchburg, VA @ City Armory
Iron Sheik vs. Sweet Ebony Diamond
Masked Superstar vs. Paul Jones
The Sheepherders vs. S.D. Jones & Don Kernodle
Cocoa Samoa vs. Tenryu
Ron Ritchie vs. David Patterson

9/12/80: Richmond, VA @ Coliseum
No Wrestling

9/12/80: Charleston, SC @ County Hall
No Wrestling

9/13/80: Spartanburg, SC @ Memorial Auditorium
Paul Jones beat Greg Valentine by DQ
Masked Superstar beat Jay Youngblood
George Wells & Johnny Weaver beat Tenryu & Brute Bernard
Steve Muslin draw Ben Alexander
Tony Tosi beat Billy Starr

9/13/80: Charlotte, NC @ Coliseum
Ray Stevens & Jimmy Snuka beat Sweet Ebony Diamond & Paul Jones
Greg Valentine beat Ric Flair by DQ
Matt Borne & Buzz Sawyer DDQ The Sheepherders (L. Williams & B. Miller)
Dewey Robertson beat Ron Ritchie
Tenryu beat Cocoa Samoa
Abe Jacobs beat David Patterson

9/14/80: Asheville, NC @ Civic Center
Masked Superstar & Paul Jones beat Ray Stevens & Jimmy Snuka by DQ
Bobby Duncum beat Jay Youngblood
George Wells & Johnny Weaver beat Swede Hanson & Gene Lewis
Ron Ritchie beat Ben Alexander
Don Kernodle beat Tony Russo

9/14/80: Savannah, GA @ Civic Center
Ray Stevens & Jimmy Snuka vs. Ricky Steamboat & Jay Youngblood
Blackjack Mulligan vs. Bobby Duncum
George Wells vs. Gene Lewis
Brute Bernard vs. Abe Jacobs
Ricky Ferrara vs. Ron Ritchie

9/15/80: Greenville, SC @ Memorial Auditorium
Greg Valentine draw Ric Flair
Paul Jones beat Tenryu
The Sheepherders beat George Wells & Johnny Weaver
Don Kernodle beat Swede Hanson by DQ
Ron Ritchie beat Tony Russo

9/16/80: Raleigh, NC
No Wrestling

9/16/80: Columbia, SC @ Township Auditorium

9/17/80: Raleigh, NC @ WRAL Studios (TV)

9/18/80: Sumter, SC @ Sumter County Exposition Center(Card Postponed)

9/18/80: Norfolk, VA @ Scope
Greg Valentine beat Ric Flair
Plus other matches

9/19/80: Charleston, SC @ County Hall
Greg Valentine beat Ric Flair
Plus other matches

9/19/80: Richmond, VA @ Coliseum
Masked Superstar & Paul Jones beat Ray Stevens & Jimmy Snuka
Sweet Ebony Diamond vs. Bobby Duncum
The Sheepherders beat Matt Borne & Buzz Sawyer
Jay Youngblood vs. Dewey Robertson
George Wells vs. Swede Hanson
Tenryu & David Patterson beat Nick DeCarlo & Abe Jacobs
Ricky Ferrara vs. Ron Ritchie

9/20/80: Spartanburg, SC @ Memorial Auditorium
Bobby Duncum beat Sweet Ebony Diamond
Ricky Steamboat beat Iron Sheik by DQ
Matt Borne & Buzz Sawyer beat David Patterson & Tenryu
Swede Hanson beat Abe Jacobs
Tony Russo beat Cocoa Samoa

9/20/80: Greensboro, NC @ Coliseum
Masked Superstar & Paul Jones beat Jimmy Snuka & Ray Stevens by DQ
Ric Flair beat Greg Valentine by countout
George Wells & Johnny Weaver beat Dewey Robertson & Gene Lewis
Sheepherders Luke Williams & Butch Miller beat Steve Muslin & S.D. Jones
Ron Ritchie beat Brute Bernard
Don Kernodle beat Ben Alexander
Nick DeCarlo beat Ricky Ferrara

9/21/80: Roanoke, VA @ Civic Center
Ricky Steamboat, Jay Youngblood & Paul Jones vs. Jimmy Snuka, Ray Stevens & Gene Anderson in a cage match
Johnny Weaver vs. Tenryu
The Sheepherders vs. S.D. Jones & George Wells

9/21/80: Hampton, VA @ Coliseum
Ric Flair, Masked Superstar & Sweet Ebony Diamond beat Bobby Duncum, Iron Sheik & Greg Valentine in a Texas tornado match
George Wells vs. Gene Lewis
Dewey Robertson vs. Steve Muslin
Brute Bernard vs. Nick DeCarlo
Ben Alexander vs. Abe Jacobs

9/22/80: Greenville, SC @ Memorial Auditorium
Masked Superstar vs. Jimmy Snuka
Ricky Steamboat vs. Bobby Duncum
Matt Borne & Buzz Sawyer vs. The Sheepherders
George Wells vs. Ben Alexander
Ricky Ferrara vs. Nick DeCarlo

9/23/80: Raleigh, NC @ Dorton Arena
Masked Superstar beat Greg Valentine by countout
Iron Sheik beat Sweet Ebony Diamond
Matt Borne & Buzz Sawyer beat The Sheepherders
Steve Muslin beat Tony Russo
Don Kernodle beat David Patterson
Dewey Robertson vs. Nick DeCarlo

9/23/80: Columbia, SC @ Township Auditorium

9/24/80: Raleigh, NC @ WRAL Studios (TV)

9/25/80: Norfolk, VA @ Scope

9/26/80: Charleston, SC @ County Hall
Ric Flair draw Greg Valentine(60:00) in match with 2 referees
Paul Jones beat Tenryu
George Wells & S.D. Jones beat Swede Hansen & Gene Lewis
Ron Ritchie beat Ricky Ferrara
Abe Jacobs beat Joe Furr

9/26/80: Lynchburg, VA @ City Armory
Iron Sheik beat Sweet Ebony Diamond
Masked Superstar beat Bad Boy Duncum
Matt Borne & Buzz Sawyer beat The Sheepherders
Steve Muslin beat David Patterson
Nick DeCarlo draw Ben Alexander

9/27/80: Spartanburg, SC @ Memorial Auditorium

9/27/80: Toronto, Ontario @ Maple Leaf Gardens (Special Saturday Card)
Greg Valentine beat Ric Flair
Tiger Jeet Singh beat Hussein Arab by DQ
Angelo Mosca no contest Bobby Duncum
Paul Jones & George Wells beat Swede Hanson & Gene Lewis
The Destroyer beat Don Kernodle
Frankie Laine beat Ron Ritchie

9/28/80: Kitchener, Ontario
Ric Flair beat Bobby Duncum
Angelo Mosca & Tiger Jeet Singh beat Greg Valentine & Hussein Arab
Paul Jones beat Swede Hanson
George Wells beat Gene Lewis
Tony Parisi beat Ron Ritchie
Frankie Laine draw Don Kernodle

9/28/80: Charlotte, NC @ Coliseum
Jimmy Snuka & Ray Stevens double DQ Masked Superstar & Blackjack Mulligan
The Sheepherders beat Matt Borne & Buzz Sawyer to win NWA Mid Atlantic Tag Titles
Sweet Ebony Diamond beat Gene Anderson
Johnny Weaver beat Tenryu
Steve Muslin beat Brute Bernard
Tony Tosi beat Ricky Ferrara

9/29/80: Buffalo, NY
Ric Flair & Blackjack Mulligan beat Bobby Duncum & Greg Valentine
Paul Jones beat Iron Sheik via pinfall
Angelo Mosca & George Wells beat Swede Hanson & Gene Lewis
The Destroyer beat Don Kernodle
Frankie Laine beat Ron Ritchie

9/29/80: Greenville, SC @ Memorial Auditorium
Masked Superstar & Sweet Ebony Diamond beat Jimmy Snuka & Ray Stevens by DQ
Jay Youngblood beat Dewey Robertson
S.D. Jones beat Tenryu
Steve Muslin beat David Patterson
Abe Jacobs beat Ricky Ferrara

9/30/80: Raleigh, NC @ Dorton Arena
Masked Superstar & Paul Jones beat Jimmy Snuka & Ray Stevens by DQ
Johnny Weaver beat Gene Lewis
Jay Youngblood beat Tenryu
Brute Bernard beat Cocoa Samoa
Don Kernodle beat Ricky Ferrara

9/30/80: Columbia, SC @ Township Auditorium

Note: Mid Atlantic Championship Wrestling ran cards in Knoxville from October 1980: until February 1981. The NWA Championship Wrestling Promotion (Mulligan/Flair) started in May 1981, & stopped running in 1982. Mid Atlantic Championship Wrestling then resumed hosting Knoxville cards.

10/1/80: Raleigh, NC @ WRAL Studios (TV)

10/2/80: Norfolk, VA @ Scope

10/3/80: Richmond, VA @ Coliseum
Ric Flair beat Greg Valentine by countout in match with 2 referees
Ricky Steamboat beat Iron Sheik
Bobby Duncum beat Blackjack Mulligan
Matt Borne & Buzz sawyer beat David Patterson & Tenryu
Johnny Weaver beat Gene Lewis
George Wells & Sweet Ebony Diamond beat The Sheepherders by DQ
Dewey Robertson beat Steve Muslin
Ricky Ferrara beat Cocoa Samoa

10/3/80: Charleston, SC @ County Hall
Jimmy Snuka & Ray Stevens vs. Masked Superstar & Paul Jones
Ivan Koloff beat S.D. Jones
Don Kernodle beat Swede Hanson
Nick DeCarlo draw Ben Alexander
Ron Ritchie beat Tony Russo

10/4/80: Spartanburg, SC @ Memorial Auditorium
Iron Sheik beat Ricky Steamboat
Ivan Koloff beat Buzz Sawyer
S.D. Jones & Don Kernodle beat Swede Hanson & Gene Lewis by DQ
Brute Bernard beat Nick DeCarlo
Tony Tosi beat Tony Russo

10/4/80: Hampton, VA @ Coliseum
Sweet Ebony Diamond, Blackjack Mulligan & Masked Superstar beat Jimmy Snuka, Ray Stevens & Gene Anderson
Matt Borne beat Dewey Robertson
Steve Muslin beat David Patterson
George Wells beat Tenryu
Cocoa Samoa draw Ricky Ferrara

10/5/80: Greensboro, NC @ Coliseum
Blackjack Mulligan & Masked Superstar beat Jimmy Snuka & Ray Stevens by DQ
Ric Flair beat Greg Valentine
Paul Jones beat Gene Anderson
Ivan Koloff beat S.D. Jones
The Sheepherders beat Matt Borne & Buzz Sawyer
Swede Hanson & Dewey Robertson beat Don Kernodle & Nick DeCarlo

10/5/80: Roanoke, VA @ Civic Center
Ricky Steamboat, Masked Superstar & Paul Jones vs. Jimmy Snuka, Ray Stevens & Bobby Duncum
Ivan Koloff vs. Johnny Weaver
George Wells vs. Brute Bernard

10/6/80: Greenville, SC @ Memorial Auditorium
Ric Flair beat Greg Valentine by countout
Sweet Ebony Diamond beat Ray Stevens
George Wells & Johnny Weaver beat The Sheepherders
Steve Muslin beat Brute Bernard by DQ
Jerry Caldwell draw Jim Nelson

10/7/80: Richburg, SC @ Lewisville High School
Ricky Steamboat vs. Iron Sheik
Ivan Koloff vs. Sweet Ebony Diamond
Matt Borne & Buzz Sawyer vs. Swede Hanson & Gene Lewis
Tony Russo vs. Cocoa Samoa

10/7/80: Raleigh, NC @ Dorton Arena
Masked Superstar & Paul Jones beat Jimmy Snuka & Ray Stevens by countout
Don Kernodle beat Jim Nelson
Dewey Robertson beat Nick DeCarlo
Roddy Piper beat S.D. Jones
Tenryu beat Ron Ritchie

10/8/80: Raleigh, NC @ WRAL Studios (TV)

10/9/80: Norfolk, VA @ Scope

10/9/80: Sumter, SC @ Sumter County Exposition Center
Ray Stevens & Jimmy Snuka vs. Masked Superstar & Sweet Ebony Diamond
Buzz Sawyer vs. Dewey Robertson
Matt Borne vs. Brute Bernard
Don Kernodle vs. David Patterson

10/10/80: Knoxville, TN @ Civic Coliseum
Ric Flair vs. Greg Valentine
Paul Jones vs. Ivan Koloff
The Sheepherders vs. Matt Borne & Buzz Sawyer
Ben Alexander vs. Don Kernodle
Tony Russo vs. Nick DeCarlo

10/10/80: Charleston, SC @ County Hall
Ray Stevens & Jimmy Snuka beat Blackjack Mulligan & Masked Superstar DQ
George Wells beat Dewey Robertson
Roddy Piper beat Cocoa Samoa
Brute Bernard beat Abe Jacobs
Swede Hanson beat Jerry Caldwell

10/10/80: Lynchburg, VA @ City Armory
Iron Sheik beat Sweet Ebony Diamond in a Texas death match
Ricky Steamboat beat Bad Boy Duncum by DQ
Johnny Weaver & S.D. Jones beat Tenryu & Gene Lewis
Steve Muslin beat Jim Nelson
Ron Ritchie beat Ricky Ferrara

10/11/80: Spartanburg, SC @ Memorial Auditorium

10/11/80: Charlotte, NC @ Coliseum
Ric Flair draw Greg Valentine(60:00)
Bobby Duncum beat Blackjack Mulligan by DQ
Masked Superstar beat Jimmy Snuka
Ivan Koloff beat S.D. Jones
Johnny Weaver & George Wells beat The Sheepherders
Dewey Robertson beat Don Kernodle
Swede Hanson beat Nick DeCarlo
Ben Alexander beat Jerry Caldwell

10/13/80: Greenville, SC @ Memorial Auditorium
Bobby Duncum beat Blackjack Mulligan
The Sheepherders beat Johnny Weaver & George Wells
Roddy Piper beat Don Kernodle
Gene Lewis beat Ron Ritchie
Steve Muslin beat Ricky Ferrara

10/14/80: Raleigh, NC @ Dorton Arena
Greg Valentine draw Ric Flair
Sheepherders beat Matt Borne & Buzz Sawyer
Blackjack Mulligan beat Bobby Duncum by DQ
Brute Bernard beat Jerry Caldwell
Roddy Piper beat Don Kernodle

10/14/80: Columbia, SC @ Township Auditorium

10/15/80: Raleigh, NC @ WRAL Studios (TV)

10/16/80: Norfolk, VA @ Scope
Ric Flair draw Greg Valentine in match with 2 referees
Ray Stevens & Jimmy Snuka vs. Masked Superstar & a mystery partner
The Sheepherders vs. Matt Borne & Buzz Sawyer
Roddy Piper vs. George Wells
Plus other matches

10/17/80: Winston-Salem, NC @ Coliseum
Sweet Ebony Diamond & Ricky Steamboat vs. Iron Sheik & Ivan Koloff
Roddy Piper vs. S.D. Jones
Jim Nelson vs. Matt Borne
Swede Hanson vs. Steve Muslin
Ric Ferrara vs. Abe Jacobs

10/17/80: Charleston, SC @ County Hall

10/18/80: Buffalo, NY
Blackjack Mulligan beat Bobby Duncum by DQ
Ric Flair beat Greg Valentine by DQ
Iron Sheik beat Paul Jones
Sweet Ebony Diamond & Matt Borne beat The Sheepherders by DQ
Angelo Mosca beat Frankie Laine
Dewey Robertson draw The Destroyer
Tony Parisi beat Ben Alexander

10/18/80: Hendersonville, NC
Ray Stevens, Jimmy Snuka & Gene Anderson vs. Johnny Weaver, Ricky Steamboat & Masked Superstar
Ivan Koloff vs. Buzz Sawyer
Brute Bernard vs. George Wells
Ricky Ferrara vs. Ron Ritchie

10/19/80: Roanoke, VA @ Civic Center
Ricky Steamboat & Masked Superstar vs. Jimmy Snuka & Ray Stevens
Ivan Koloff vs. Johnny Weaver in a no DQ match
Nick DeCarlo & Steve Muslin vs. Swede Hanson & Gene Lewis
Plus 2 other matches

10/19/80: Savannah, GA @ Civic Center
Ric Flair & Masked Superstar beat Jimmy Snuka & Ray Stevens
Ivan Koloff vs. S.D. Jones
Plus other matches

10/19/80: Toronto, Ontario @ Maple Leaf Gardens
Angelo Mosca beat Bobby Duncum
Greg Valentine beat Sweet Ebony Diamond
Hussein Arab beat Dewey Robertson
Matt Borne & Paul Jones beat The Sheepherders
Tony Parisi draw The Destroyer
Frankie Laine beat Ben Alexander

10/20/80: Fayetteville, NC @ Cumberland County Civic Center
Greg Valentine vs. Ric Flair
Ivan Koloff vs. Don Kernodle
Johnny Weaver & George Wells vs. Swede Hanson & Tenryu
Jim Nelson vs. Nick DeCarlo
Plus other matches

10/20/80: Greenville, SC @ Memorial Auditorium
Ricky Steamboat & Masked Superstar beat Gene Anderson(sub for Ray Stevens) & Jimmy Snuka
Roddy Piper beat S.D. Jones
Steve Muslin beat Gene Lewis
Ron Ritchie beat Brute Bernard
Abe Jacobs beat Tony Russo

10/21/80: Raleigh, NC @ Dorton Arena

10/21/80: Columbia, SC @ Township Auditorium

10/22/80: Raleigh, NC @ WRAL Studios (TV)

10/23/80: Norfolk, VA @ Scope

10/23/80: Sumter, SC @ Sumter County Exposition Center
Iron Sheik vs. Sweet Ebony Diamond
Tenryu & Swede Hanson vs. Matt Borne & Nick DeCarlo
Ivan Koloff vs. George Wells
Jerry Caldwell vs. Dewey Robertson
Tony Russo vs. Abe Jacobs

10/24/80: Richmond, VA @ Coliseum
Masked Superstar & Paul Jones beat Ray Stevens & Jimmy Snuka
Ricky Steamboat beat Iron Sheik by DQ
Roddy Piper beat S.D. Jones
Tenryu beat Nick DeCarlo
Johnny Weaver & George Wells beat The Sheepherders
Steve Muslin & Ron Ritchie beat Brute Bernard & Gene Lewis
Jim Nelson draw Wayne Rogers

10/24/80: Charleston, SC @ County Hall

10/25/80: Spartanburg, SC @ Memorial Auditorium
Ben Alexander beat Jerry Caldwell
Gene Lewis beat Wayne Rogers
Luke Williams & Butch Miller draw Johnny Weaver & S.D. Jones
Bobby Duncum DCO with Blackjack Mulligan
Iron Sheik beat Paul Jones

10/25/80: Charlotte, NC @ Coliseum
Ricky Steamboat & Masked Superstar beat Jimmy Snuka & Ray Stevens by DQ
Greg Valentine beat Ric Flair
George Wells beat Swede Hanson
Roddy Piper beat Matt Borne
Dewey Robertson & Tenryu beat Don Kernodle & Steve Muslin
Nick DeCarlo draw Ricky Ferrara

10/26/80: Asheville, NC @ Civic Center
Ricky Steamboat beat Jimmy Snuka
Masked Superstar beat Iron Sheik
Roddy Piper beat Matt Borne
Johnny Weaver & S.D. Jones beat Dewey Robertson & Tenryu
Jim Nelson draw Nick DeCarlo

10/27/80: Greenville, SC @ Memorial Auditorium
Ricky Steamboat & Masked Superstar beat Jimmy Snuka & Ray Stevens by DQ
Don Kernodle beat Jim Nelson
Swede Hanson beat Jerry Caldwell
George Wells beat Dewey Robertson
Roddy Piper beat Johnny Weaver

10/28/80: Raleigh, NC @ Dorton Arena
Ric Flair draw Greg Valentine
Ricky Steamboat beat Iron Sheik
George Wells & Johnny Weaver beat The Sheepherders by DQ
Tony Tosi beat Jim Nelson
Ben Alexander draw Abe Jacobs

10/28/80: Columbia, SC @ Township Auditorium

10/29/80: Raleigh, NC @ WRAL Studios (TV)

10/29/80: Knoxville, TN @ Civic Coliseum
Ray Stevens & Jimmy Snuka vs. Masked Superstar & Paul Jones
Sweet Ebony Diamond vs. Dewey Robertson
Johnny Weaver vs. Swede Hanson
Steve Travis vs. Tenryu
Nick DeCarlo vs. Ricky Ferrara

10/30/80: Norfolk, VA @ Scope

10/31/80: Charleston, SC @ County Hall

11/1/80: Richmond, VA @ Coliseum
Roddy Piper beat Paul Jones in tournament final of a one night tournament to win vacant NWA Mid Atlantic Television Title
Other participants included Bobby Duncum, Angelo Mosca, Ivan Koloff, The Sheepherders, Blackjack Mulligan, Sweet Ebony Diamond, Johnny Weaver, George Wells, Dewey Robertson & Matt Borne
Ricky Steamboat beat Iron Sheik to win NWA Mid Atlantic Title in a falls count anywhere match

11/1/80: Spartanburg, SC @ Memorial Auditorium
Ray Stevens & Jimmy Snuka beat Ric Flair & Masked Superstar by DQ
Swede Hanson beat Don Kernodle
Steve Muslin beat Tenryu by DQ
S.D. Jones beat Gene Lewis
Jim Nelson draw Wayne Rogers

11/2/80: Greensboro, NC @ Coliseum
Blackjack Mulligan beat Bobby Duncum in a Texas death match
Ricky Steamboat beat Ole Anderson in finals of 19-man, 2-ring battle royal which also included Terry Funk, Johnny Weaver, Ivan Koloff & others
Angelo Mosca beat Swede Hanson
The Sheepherders beat S.D. Jones & Nick DeCarlo
George Wells beat Gene Lewis
Matt Borne draw Tenryu

11/2/80: Toronto, Ontario @ Maple Leaf Gardens
Ray Stevens & Jimmy Snuka draw Masked Superstar & Paul Jones
Ric Flair beat Hussein Arab by countout
Roddy Piper beat Frankie Laine
Dewey Robertson beat Ben Alexander
The Destroyer beat John Bonello
Tony Parisi beat Bob Marcus

11/3/80: Charlotte, NC @ Coliseum
Gene Lewis beat Abe Jacobs
Don Kernodle beat Nick DeCarlo
Iron Sheik beat SD Jones
Matt Borne & George Wells beat The Sheepherders
Roddy Piper beat Paul Jones
Blackjack Mulligan beat Bobby Duncum in a Texas street fight match

11/3/80: Kitchener, Ontario
Ric Flair & Masked Superstar beat Ray Stevens & Jimmy Snuka
Hussein Arab vs. Dewey Robertson
Roddy Piper vs. Paul Jones
Tony Parisi vs. Frankie Laine
Brute Bernard vs. Bob Marcus

11/3/80: Greenville, SC @ Memorial Auditorium
Greg Valentine beat Ricky Steamboat
Blackjack Mulligan beat Bobby Duncum
Angelo Mosca & Don Kernodle beat Swede Hanson & Tenryu
S.D. Jones draw Ron Ritchie
Wayne Rogers vs. Ricky Ferrara

11/4/80: Raleigh, NC @ Dorton Arena

11/4/80: Columbia, SC @ Township Auditorium

11/5/80: Raleigh, NC @ WRAL Studios (TV)

11/6/80: Norfolk, VA @ Scope
Ric Flair beat Greg Valentine by countout
Plus other matches

11/6/80: Sumter, SC @ Sumter County Exposition Center
Ivan Koloff draw Sweet Ebony Diamond
Paul Jones beat Iron Sheik
Johnny Weaver & Don Kernodle beat Swede Hanson & Tenryu
Dewey Robertson draw Kim Duk(sub for Brute Bernard)
Ricky Ferrara beat Jerry Caldwell

11/7/80: Lynchburg, VA @ Armory
Nick DeCarlo vs. Ricky Ferrara
Ben Alexander vs. Ron Ritchie
The Sheepherders vs. Matt Borne & George Wells
Bobby Duncum vs. Sweet Ebony Diamond
Greg Valentine vs. Ric Flair

11/7/80: Shelby, NC
Blackjack Mulligan beat Iron Sheik
Paul Jones beat Roddy Piper by DQ
Don Kernodle & S.D. Jones beat Gene Lewis & Tenryu
Abe Jacobs draw Jim Nelson

11/7/80: Charleston, SC @ County Hall
Ricky Steamboat & Masked Superstar beat Jimmy Snuka & Ray Stevens by DQ
Wayne Rogers beat Tony Russo
Kim Duk beat Jerry Caldwell
Dewey Robertson beat Wayne Rogers
Ivan Koloff beat Johnny Weaver

11/8/80: Spartanburg, SC @ Memorial Auditorium

11/9/80: Asheville, NC @ Civic Center
Ric Flair beat Greg Valentine by countout
Blackjack Mulligan beat Bobby Duncum by DQ
Roddy Piper beat Paul Jones
The Sheepherders beat S.D. Jones & Johnny Weaver
Dewey Robertson double DQ Tenryu
Steve Muslin beat Jim Nelson

11/9/80: Hampton, VA @ Coliseum
Jimmy Snuka & Ray Stevens beat Ricky Steamboat & Masked Superstar
Matt Borne & George Wells beat Gene Lewis & Swede Hanson
Sweet Ebony Diamond beat Ivan Koloff
Don Kernodle beat Ben Alexander
Ricky Ferrara beat Wayne Rogers
Nick DeCarlo beat Tony Russo

11/10/80: Greenville, SC @ Memorial Auditorium
NWA World Champion Harley Race draw Ric Flair(60:00)
Ricky Steamboat beat Greg Valentine by DQ
The Sheepherders beat Matt Borne & George Wells
Johnny Weaver beat Dewey Robertson
Nick DeCarlo beat Tony Russo

11/11/80: Raleigh, NC @ Dorton Arena
Ricky Steamboat beat Roddy Piper by DQ
Sweet Ebony Diamond beat Ivan Koloff
The Sheepherders beat Matt Borne & S.D. Jones
Steve Muslin beat Ricky Ferrara
Kim Duk beat Abe Jacobs

11/11/80: Columbia, SC @ Township Auditorium

11/12/80: Raleigh, NC @ WRAL Studios (TV)

11/13/80: Fisherville, VA @ Augusta Expo Center
Blackjack Mulligan beat Bobby Duncum in a Texas death match
Sweet Ebony Diamond beat Ivan Koloff
Johnny Weaver & Steve Muslin beat The Sheepherders
Ricky Ferrara beat Wayne Rogers

11/13/80: Knoxville, TN @ Civic Coliseum
NWA World Champion Harley Race beat Ricky Steamboat
Paul Jones beat Iron Sheik
Roddy Piper beat Matt Borne
Swede Hanson & Dewey Robertson beat Don Kernodle & S.D. Jones
Nick DeCarlo draw Jim Nelson

11/14/80: Charleston, SC @ County Hall
Jimmy Snuka & Ray Stevens beat Ricky Steamboat & Masked Superstar in a Texas Tornado Match
Roddy Piper beat Matt Borne
Tenryu beat Abe Jacobs
Nick DeCarlo beat Ben Alexander
Gene Lewis beat Wayne Rogers

11/14/80: Richmond, VA @ Coliseum
NWA World Champion Harley Race beat Ric Flair by countout
Sweet Ebony Diamond beat Ivan Koloff
Blackjack Mulligan beat Bobby Duncum
Jerry Caldwell beat Tony Russo
Ron Ritchie beat Ricky Ferrara
Don Kernodle beat Jim Nelson
Johnny Weaver & George Wells beat Sheepherders

11/15/80: Savannah, GA @ Civic Center
Jimmy Snuka & Ray Stevens beat Masked Superstar & Paul Jones
Tenryu & Gene Lewis beat Matt Borne & S.D. Jones
Ivan Koloff beat Johnny Weaver via pinfall
Ben Alexander beat Jerry Caldwell

11/15/80: Spartanburg, SC @ Memorial Auditorium
NWA World Champion Harley Race beat Ricky Steamboat
Sweet Ebony Diamond, Ron Ritchie & Steve Muslin beat Kim Duk & The Sheepherders
Swede Hanson beat Abe Jacobs
Ricky Ferrara beat Wayne Rogers

11/16/80: Charlotte, NC @ Coliseum
Ray Stevens & Jimmy Snuka beat Ricky Steamboat & Masked Superstar
Sweet Ebony Diamond beat Ivan Koloff
Sheepherders beat S.D. Jones & Johnny Weaver
Matt Borne beat Gene Lewis
Ron Ritchie draw Ben Alexander
Ricky Ferrara beat Wayne Rogers
Cy Jernigan beat Tony Russo

11/16/80: Toronto, Ontario @ Maple Leaf Gardens
NWA World Champion Harley Race DCO with Ric Flair
Angelo Mosca beat Greg Valentine by DQ
Blackjack Mulligan beat Bobby Duncum
Roddy Piper beat Dewey Robertson
George Wells & Tony Parisi beat The Destroyer & Jim Nelson
Frankie Laine beat Don Kernodle

11/17/80: Greenville, SC @ Memorial Auditorium
Ricky Steamboat beat Iron Sheik
Sweet Ebony Diamond beat Ivan Koloff
Johnny Weaver & Matt Borne beat Sheepherders
Tenryu beat S.D. Jones
Steve Muslin draw Kim Duk

11/17/80: Niagara Falls, Ontario
Billy Red Lyons beat Frankie Laine
Nick DeCarlo beat Jim Nelson by DQ
Dewey Robertson beat Don Kernodle via pinfall
Tony Parisi & George Wells beat The Destroyer & Jim Nelson
Blackjack Mulligan & Angelo Mosca beat Roddy Piper & Bobby Duncum
Greg Valentine beat Ric Flair via pinfall

11/18/80: Raleigh, NC @ Dorton Arena
Ricky Steamboat beat Iron Sheik
Roddy Piper beat Ric Flair
Jim Nelson beat Jerry Caldwell
Gene Lewis beat Wayne Rogers
Johnny Weaver & George Wells beat Dewey Robertson & Tenryu

11/18/80: Columbia, SC @ Township Auditorium
Blackjack Mulligan vs. Bobby Duncum
Sweet Ebony Diamond vs. Iron Sheik
The Sheepherders vs. Don Kernodle & Matt Borne
Abe Jacobs vs. Swede Hanson
Ricky Ferrara vs. Ron Ritchie

11/19/80: Raleigh, NC @ WRAL Studios (TV)

11/20/80: Norfolk, VA @ Scope

11/20/80: Sumter, SC @ Sumter County Exposition Center
Johnny Weaver beat Roddy Piper by DQ
Blackjack Mulligan beat Bobby Duncum
The Sheepherders beat Matt Borne & S.D. Jones
Dewey Robertson beat Ben Alexander
Ricky Ferrara beat Wayne Rogers

11/21/80: Lynchburg, VA @ City Armory
Jimmy Snuka & Ray Stevens beat Masked Superstar & Paul Jones
The Sheepherders beat Johnny Weaver & S.D. Jones
Gene Lewis beat Steve Muslin
Cy Jernigan beat Jim Nelson

11/21/80: Charleston, SC @ County Hall
Blackjack Mulligan beat Bobby Duncum
Sweet Ebony Diamond beat Ivan Koloff
Dewey Robertson & Swede Hansen beat Nick DeCarlo & Tony Tosi
Abe Jacobs beat Ricky Ferrara
Mike Fever beat Jerry Caldwell

11/21/80: Winston-Salem, NC @ Coliseum
Ricky Steamboat vs. Iron Sheik
Roddy Pier vs. George Wells
Tenryu & Kim Duk vs. Don Kernodle & Ron Ritchie
Wayne Rogers vs. Ben Alexander
Tony Russo vs. Joe Furr

11/22/80: Culpeper, VA
Ric Flair beat Greg Valentine by DQ
Johnny Weaver beat Roddy Piper by DQ
The Sheepherders beat S.D. Jones & Don Kernodle
plus 2 other matches

11/22/80: Marion, NC
Ray Stevens, Jimmy Snuka & Gene Anderson beat Paul Jones, Masked Superstar & Sweet Ebony Diamond
Matt Borne beat Tenryu
Abe Jacobs draw Ben Alexander
Ricky Ferrara beat Jerry Caldwell

11/24/80: Greenville, SC @ Memorial Auditorium
Ric Flair beat Greg Valentine to win the NWA United States Title in a lumberjack match
Blackjack Mulligan beat Bobby Duncum
The Sheepherders beat Matt Borne & Johnny Weaver
Dewey Robertson beat Don Kernodle
Nick DeCarlo beat Ricky Ferrara

11/25/80: Raleigh, NC @ Dorton Arena
Bobby Duncum beat Blackjack Mulligan
George Wells & Sweet Ebony Diamond beat Ivan Koloff & Iron Sheik by DQ
Tenryu beat Wayne Rogers
Steve Muslin beat Butch Miller
Johnny Weaver beat Luke Williams

11/25/80: Columbia, SC @ Township Auditorium

11/26/80: Raleigh, NC @ WRAL Studios (TV)

11/27/80: Norfolk, VA @ Scope
Blackjack Mulligan vs. Bobby Duncum
Ivan Koloff vs. Sweet Ebony Diamond in a Russian chain match
Iron Sheik vs. George Wells
Plus other matches

11/27/80: Knoxville, TN @ Civic Coliseum
Ric Flair beat Greg Valentine

11/27/80: Greensboro, NC @ Coliseum
Masked Superstar & Paul Jones beat Jimmy Snuka & Ray Stevens in a cage match to win NWA World Tag Team Title
Ric Flair beat Greg Valentine in a cage match
The Sheepherders beat Matt Borne & Dewey Robertson
Roddy Piper beat Johnny Weaver
Candy Malloy beat Wendy Richter
S.D. Jones beat Ben Alexander
Ricky Ferrara draw Abe Jacobs

11/28/80: Charleston, SC @ County Hall
Bobby Duncum beat Blackjack Mulligan in a taped fist match
Johnny Weaver & Matt Borne beat The Sheepherders
Dewey Robertson beat Ben Alexander
S.D. Jones beat Ricky Ferrara
Jerry Caldwell beat Tony Russo

11/28/80: Richmond, VA @ Coliseum
Masked Superstar & Paul Jones beat Ray Stevens & Jimmy Snuka in a fence match
Roddy Piper beat Ric Flair
Ivan Koloff & Iron Sheik beat Don Kernodle & George Wells
Steve Muslin beat Tenryu by DQ
Swede Hanson beat Ron Ritchie
Kim Duk beat Nick DeCarlo
Cy Jernigan beat Gene Lewis
Jim Nelson draw Abe Jacobs

11/29/80: Spartanburg, SC @ Memorial Auditorium
Blackjack Mulligan & Sweet Ebony Diamond beat Bobby Duncum & Ivan Koloff
Iron Sheik beat Dewey Robertson
Tony Rosie beat Jim Nelson
Wayne Rogers beat Mike Fever
Ricky Ferrara beat Jerry Caldwell

11/29/80: Hampton, VA @ Coliseum
Greg Valentine vs. Ric Flair in a fence match
Masked Superstar vs. Gene Anderson
George Wells vs. Ray Stevens
Gene Lewis & Swede Hanson vs. Ron Ritchie & Don Kernodle
Tenryu vs. Steve Muslin
Kim Duk vs. Abe Jacobs
Cy Jernigan vs. Nick DeCarlo

11/30/80: Charlotte, NC @ Coliseum
Blackjack Mulligan beat Bobby Duncum in a Texas death match
Masked Superstar beat Ray Stevens by DQ
Roddy Piper beat Paul Jones
Matt Borne & George Wells beat The Sheepherders
Iron Sheik beat S.D. Jones
Don Kernodle beat Nick DeCarlo
Gene Lewis beat Abe Jacobs

11/30/80: Savannah, GA @ Civic Center
Ric Flair vs. Greg Valentine in a cage match
Ivan Koloff vs. Sweet Ebony Diamond
Tenryu & Kim Duk vs. Johnny Weaver & Dewey Robertson
Ben Alexander vs. Ron Ritchie
Ricky Ferrara vs. Wayne Rogers
Jim Nelson vs. Jerry Caldwell

12/1/80: Sumter, SC @ Sumter County Exposition Center
Ric Flair vs. Greg Valentine
Johnny Weaver vs. Roddy Piper in a no DQ match
The Sheepherders vs. Dewey Robertson & Matt Borne

Abe Jacobs vs. Ricky Ferrara

12/1/80: Greenville, SC @ Memorial Auditorium
Masked Superstar & Paul Jones beat Jimmy Snuka & Ray Stevens in a cage match
George Wells beat Iron Sheik by DQ
Steve Muslin beat Wayne Rogers
Gene Lewis beat Nick DeCarlo
Jim Nelson beat Jerry Caldwell

12/2/80: Raleigh, NC @ Dorton Arena
Ric Flair, Blackjack Mulligan & Sweet Ebony Diamond vs. Bobby Duncum, Roddy Piper & Greg Valentine

12/2/80: Columbia, SC @ Township Auditorium

12/3/80: Raleigh, NC @ WRAL Studios (TV)

12/4/80: Norfolk, VA @ Scope

12/5/80: Lynchburg, VA @ City Armory
Ric Flair beat Greg Valentine
Johnny Weaver beat Roddy Piper by DQ
George Wells & Steve Muslin beat The Sheepherders
Cy Jernigan beat Wayne Rogers

12/5/80: Charleston, SC @ County Hall
Masked Superstar & Paul Jones beat Gene Anderson & Ray Stevens
Ben Alexander beat Jerry Caldwell
Tenryu beat Nick DeCarlo
Matt Borne beat Gene Lewis
Dewey Robertson beat Swede Hanson

12/6/80: Knoxville, TN @ Chilhowee Park
Ric Flair vs. Roddy Piper
Plus other matches

12/6/80: Buffalo, NY
Bobby Duncum beat Blackjack Mulligan
Masked Superstar beat Iron Sheik
Ray Stevens beat Paul Jones
Angelo Mosca beat Jimmy Snuka by DQ
Tony Parisi & Steve Muslin beat The Destroyer & Gene Lewis
Billy Red Lyons draw Frankie Laine

12/6/80: Spartanburg, SC @ Memorial Auditorium
Ivan Koloff beat Sweet Ebony Diamond in a Russian chain match
Dewey Robertson & George Wells beat The Sheepherders
Nick DeCarlo beat Ben Alexander
Ron Ritchie beat Wayne Rogers
Abe Jacobs beat Jim Nelson

12/7/80: Asheville, NC @ Civic Center
Ric Flair beat Roddy Piper by DQ
Greg Valentine beat Sweet Ebony Diamond
Dewey Robertson beat Tenryu
Kim Duk & Swede Hanson beat Matt Borne & Don Kernodle
Nick DeCarlo beat Ben Alexander

12/7/80: Toronto, Ontario @ Maple Leaf Gardens
Masked Superstar & Paul Jones beat Ray Stevens & Jimmy Snuka
Hussein Arab beat Angelo Mosca
Ivan Koloff beat Steve Muslin
Destroyer beat John Bonello
Billy Red Lyons beat Frankie Laine
Tony Parisi beat Gene Lewis

12/7/80: Charlotte, NC @ Coliseum
Greg Valentine beat Ric Flair by DQ
Bobby Duncum beat Blackjack Mulligan
Roddy Piper beat Johnny Weaver
Sweet Ebony Diamond & Dewey Robertson beat The Sheepherders
Don Kernodle beat Ben Alexander
Kim Duk beat Nick DeCarlo

12/8/80: Greenville, SC @ Memorial Auditorium
Bobby Duncum beat Blackjack Mulligan
Roddy Piper & Greg Valentine beat Ric Flair & Johnny Weaver
Sweet Ebony Diamond beat Butch Miller
Dewey Robertson beat Luke Williams
Matt Borne beat Tenryu

12/9/80: Raleigh, NC @ Dorton Arena

12/9/80: Columbia, SC @ Township Auditorium

12/10/80: Raleigh, NC @ WRAL Studios (TV)

12/11/80: Raleigh, NC @ WRAL Studios (TV)

12/12/80: Richmond, VA @ Coliseum
Ric Flair beat Greg Valentine
Bobby Duncum beat Blackjack Mulligan in a brass knuckles, taped fist match
Ivan Koloff beat Sweet Ebony Diamond in a Russian chain match
George Wells & Dewey Robertson beat The Sheepherders to win NWA Mid Atlantic Tag Title
Iron Sheik beat Matt Borne
Swede Hanson & Gene Lewis beat Nick DeCarlo & Wayne Rogers
Ben Alexander beat Jerry Caldwell

12/12/80: Charleston, SC @ County Hall
Roddy Piper vs. Johnny Weaver
Masked Superstar vs. Ray Stevens
Kim Duk & Tenryu vs. Don Kernodle & Steve Muslin
Ron Ritchie vs. Jim Nelson
Abe Jacobs vs. Ricky Ferrara

12/13/80: Spartanburg, SC @ Memorial Auditorium
Roddy Piper & Greg Valentine beat Ric Flair & Ricky Steamboat
Johnny Weaver beat Tenryu
Don Kernodle beat Jim Nelson

Ron Ritchie beat S.D. Jones
Steve Muslin beat Ricky Ferrara

12/14/80: Roanoke, VA @ Civic Center
Ric Flair beat Roddy Piper
Blackjack Mulligan beat Bobby Duncum
Ricky Steamboat beat Iron Sheik
Ivan Koloff beat S.D. Jones
Cy Jernigan beat Ben Alexander
Ricky Ferrara beat Wayne Rogers

12/14/80: Greensboro, NC @ Coliseum
Greg Valentine & Roddy Piper beat Masked Superstar & Paul Jones by DQ
Bobby Duncum beat Blackjack Mulligan in a taped fist match
Johnny Weaver & George Wells beat Kim Duk & Tenryu
Peggy Lee & Candy Malloy beat Judy Martin & Joyce Grable
Abe Jacobs beat Ben Alexander
Ricky Ferrara beat Jerry Caldwell
Matt Borne beat Cy Jernigan

12/19/80: Richmond, VA @ Coliseum
No Wrestling

12/25/80: Greenville, SC @ Memorial Auditorium
Ric Flair beat Roddy Piper
Ricky Steamboat beat Greg Valentine
Bobby Duncum beat Sweet Ebony Diamond in a taped fist match
Tenryu & Kim Duk beat Johnny Weaver & Don Kernodle
Ron Ritchie beat Charlie Fulton
Abe Jacobs beat Bill White

12/25/80: Charlotte, NC @ Coliseum
Ric Flair beat Greg Valentine
Ricky Steamboat beat Roddy Piper by DQ
Blackjack Mulligan beat Bobby Duncum in a football match
Sweet Ebony Diamond & Johnny Weaver beat Kim Duk & Tenryu
Don Kernodle & Ron Ritchie beat Bill White & Charlie Fulton
Abe Jacobs beat Joe Furr
Ricky Ferrara draw Frank Monte

12/26/80: Richmond, VA @ Coliseum
Ric Flair beat Roddy Piper by DQ
Ricky Steamboat beat Greg Valentine
Blackjack Mulligan beat Bobby Duncum in a Texas street fight match
Dewey Robertson & George Wells beat Swede Hanson & Tenryu
Cy Jernigan beat Mike Fever
Bruno Sammartino, Jr. beat Gene Lewis
Jacques Goulet beat Steve Muslin

12/26/80: Charleston, SC @ County Hall
Ivan Koloff vs. Iron Sheik
Judy Martin & Leilani Kai vs. Betty Clarke & Peggy Lee
Johnny Weaver vs. Bill White
Plus 2 other matches

12/27/80: Spartanburg, SC @ Memorial Auditorium
Ric Flair & Ricky Steamboat beat Roddy Piper & Greg Valentine
Johnny Weaver beat Kim Duk
Ron Ritchie beat Bill White
Nick DeCarlo beat Jim Nelson by DQ
Ricky Ferrara draw Frank Monte

12/27/80: Knoxville, TN @ Chilhowee Park
Masked Superstar & Paul Jones vs. Jimmy Snuka & Ray Stevens
George Wells vs. Tenryu
Dewey Robertson vs. Gene Lewis
Judy Martin vs. Peggy Lee
Charlie Fulton vs. Abe Jacobs

12/28/80: Lynchburg, VA @ City Armory
Iron Sheik vs. Ivan Koloff
Sweet Ebony Diamond vs. Bobby Duncum
Leilani Kai vs. Betty Clark
Ben Alexander vs. Wayne Rogers

12/28/80: Asheville, NC @ Civic Center
Ric Flair beat Greg Valentine
Ricky Steamboat beat Roddy Piper by DQ
Betty Clark & Wendi Richter beat Judy Martin & Leilani Kai
Ron Ritchie beat Bill White
Nick DeCarlo beat Charlie Fulton

12/28/80: Toronto, Ontario @ Maple Leaf Gardens
Angelo Mosca beat Hussein Arab
Sweet Ebony Diamond beat Ivan Koloff
Paul Jones beat Ray Stevens by DQ
George Wells & Dewey Robertson beat Jacques Goulet & Ben Alexander
Tony Parisi beat Jim Nelson
Frankie Laine beat Bob Marcus

12/28/80: Greensboro, NC @ Coliseum
Ric Flair beat Roddy Piper
Ricky Steamboat beat Greg Valentine
Blackjack Mulligan beat Bobby Duncum
Masked Superstar beat Jimmy Snuka by DQ
Kim Duk & Tenryu beat Johnny Weaver & Don Kernodle
Swede Hansen & Gene Lewis beat Nick DeCarlo & Steve Muslin
Frank Monte draw Charlie Fulton

12/29/80: Greenville, SC @ Memorial Auditorium
Ric Flair beat Roddy Piper
Masked Superstar beat Jimmy Snuka
Blackjack Mulligan beat Bobby Duncum
Ricky Steamboat beat Greg Valentine

Swede Hansen & Gene Lewis beat Nick DeCarlo & Steve Muslin
Kim Duk & Tenryu beat Johnny Weaver & Don Kernodle
Charlie Fulton draw Frank Monte

12/29/80: Columbia, SC @ Township Auditorium(Special Monday Card)
Ricky Steamboat vs. Roddy Piper
Masked Superstar vs. Jimmy Snuka
Johnny Weaver, Don Kernodle & Steve Muslin vs. Kim Duk, Swede Hanson & Tenryu
Charlie Fulton vs. Frank Monte
Ron Ritchie vs. Gene Lewis

12/30/80: Raleigh, NC @ Dorton Arena
Ric Flair vs. Greg Valentine
18 man Russian Roulette Battle Royal featuring Roddy Piper, Bobby Duncum, Ric Flair, Greg Valentine, Ricky Steamboat, Ivan Koloff, The Superstar, Iron Sheik, Blackjack Mulligan, Paul Jones, Jimmy Snuka, Ray Stevens, Sweet Ebony Diamond, George Wells, Kim Duk, Sgt Goulet, Swede Hanson, Johnny Weaver
Plus 8 other matches

Chapter 2: 1981

1/1/81: Greenville, SC @ Memorial Auditorium
Iron Sheik double DQ Ivan Koloff
Blackjack Mulligan beat Bobby Duncum in a Texas street fight match
Dewey Robertson & George Wells beat Kim Duk & Tenryu
Nick DeCarlo beat Jacques Goulet
Ron Ritchie draw Charlie Fulton

1/2/81: Charleston, SC @ County Hall
Greg Valentine beat Ric Flair by DQ
Jimmy Snuka beat Paul Jones
Kim Duk & Tenryu beat Don Kernodle & Steve Muslin
Nick DeCarlo draw Charlie Fulton
Ricky Ferrara beat Mike Fever

1/3/81: Shelby, NC @ Recreation Center
Greg Valentine & Bobby Duncum beat Ric Flair & Blackjack Mulligan
Sweet Ebony Diamond beat Kim Duk
Don Kernodle beat Nick DeCarlo
Ron Ritchie beat Charlie Fulton

1/3/81: Sumter, SC @ Exposition Center
Ricky Steamboat beat Roddy Piper by DQ
Ivan Koloff double DQ Iron Sheik
Dewey Robertson & George Wells beat Swede Hanson & Tenryu
Abe Jacobs beat Jim Nelson

1/4/81: Roanoke VA @ Roanoke Civic Center
Masked Superstar & Paul Jones beat Greg Valentine & Roddy Piper
Ricky Steamboat beat Ray Stevens
Johnny Weaver & Sweet Ebony Diamond beat Swede Hanson & Jacques Goulet
Frank Monte beat Ricky Ferrara
Ron Ritchie beat Jim Nelson

1/5/81: Fayetteville, NC @ Cumberland County Memorial Auditorium
Ric Flair & Ricky Steamboat vs. Roddy Piper & Greg Valentine
Sweet Ebony Diamond vs. Swede Hanson
Don Kernodle vs. Gene Lewis

1/5/81: Greenville, SC @ Memorial Auditorium
Paul Jones & Masked Superstar beat Ray Stevens & Jimmy Snuka
Ivan Koloff beat Iron Sheik in a Russian chain match
Dewey Robertson & George Wells beat Kim Duk & Tenryu
Jacques Goulet beat Ron Ritchie
Nick DeCarlo beat Charlie Fulton

1/6/81: Columbia, SC @ Township Auditorium
Ric Flair & Ricky Steamboat DDQ Roddy Piper & Greg Valentine
Johnny Weaver beat Gene Lewis
Sweet Ebony Diamond beat Jacques Goulet
Don Kernodle beat Jim Nelson
Nick DeCarlo beat Ricky Ferrara

1/6/81: Raleigh NC @ Dorton Arena
Blackjack Mulligan beat Jimmy Snuka in a grudge match
Ivan Koloff no contest with Iron Sheik
Ray Stevens beat Paul Jones
George Wells & Dewey Robertson beat Kim Duk & Tenryu
Abe Jacobs beat Charlie Fulton

1/7/81: Raleigh, NC @ WRAL Studios (TV)

1/8/81: Norfolk, VA @ Scope
NWA World Champion Harley Race beat Ric Flair
Blackjack Mulligan beat Bobby Duncum in a Texas street fight match
Ray Stevens beat Paul Jones
Roddy Piper beat Johnny Weaver
Tenryu & Jacques Goulet beat Don Kernodle & Steve Muslin
Frank Monte draw Ricky Ferrara
Nick DeCarlo & Cy Jernigan beat Gene Lewis & Jim Nelson

1/8/81: Fisherville, VA @ Augusta Expo
Ricky Steamboat vs. Jimmy Snuka
Iron Sheik vs. Ivan Koloff
George Wells & Dewey Robertson vs. Swede Hanson & Kim Duk

1/9/81: Knoxville, TN @ Civic Coliseum
Ricky Steamboat draw Roddy Piper
Iron Sheik vs. Ivan Koloff in a lights out match
Swede Hanson & Kim Duk vs. Don Kernodle & Steve Muslin
Ron Ritchie vs. Charlie Fulton

1/9/81: Charleston, SC @ County Hall
NWA World Champion Harley Race double DQ Ric Flair
George Wells & Dewey Robertson beat Gene Lewis & Jim Nelson
Bobby Duncum beat Sweet Ebony Diamond
Jim Nelson(sub for Bill Irwin) beat Abe Jacobs
Frank Monte draw Tony Tosi

1/10/81: Spartanburg, SC @ Memorial Auditorium
Ricky Steamboat & Johnny Weaver beat Harley Race & Roddy Piper
Tenryu beat Steve Muslin
Jacques Goulet beat Nick DeCarlo
Tony Tosi beat Swede Hanson by DQ
Ricky Ferrara beat Joe Furr

1/10/81: Kitchener, Ontario @ Memorial Auditorium
Masked Superstar beat Ray Stevens
Bob Marcus beat Charlie Fulton
Don Kernodle draw Frankie Laine
Tony Parisi & George Wells beat Ivan Koloff & The Destroyer by DQ
Angelo Mosca & Blackjack Mulligan beat Bobby Duncum & Iron Sheik

1/11/81: Toronto, Ontario @ Maple Leaf Gardens
Ivan Koloff beat Angelo Mosca by DQ
Blackjack Mulligan beat Bobby Duncum in a Texas street fight match
Masked Superstar beat Ray Stevens
The Destroyer & Hossein Arab beat George Wells & Don Kernodle
Tony Parisi beat Charlie Fulton
Frankie Lane beat Bob Marcus

1/11/81: Asheville, NC @ Civic Center
NWA World Champion Harley Race beat Ric Flair by countout
Ricky Steamboat beat Greg Valentine
Johnny Weaver & Steve Muslin beat Jacques Goulet & Gene Lewis
Don Kernodle beat Jim Nelson
Charlie Fulton beat Joe Furr

1/11/81: Greensboro, NC @ Coliseum
NWA World Champion Harley Race beat Ric Flair
Mid Atlantic Champion Ricky Steamboat beat Jimmy Snuka
Roddy Piper beat Johnny Weaver
Dewey Robertson & Sweet Ebony Diamond beat Kim Duk & Tenryu
Swede Hanson beat Ron Ritchie
Jim Nelson draw Frank Monte

1/12/81: Lumberton NC @ Recreation Center
Ricky Steamboat vs. Greg Valentine
Masked Superstar vs. Jimmy Snuka
Mr. Fuji & Tenryu vs. Steve Muslin & Nick DeCarlo
Frank Monte vs. Ricky Ferrara

1/12/81: Greenville, SC @ Memorial Auditorium

1/13/81: Raleigh, NC @ Dorton Arena
Blackjack Mulligan beat Bobby Duncum in a Texas street fight match
Ricky Steamboat beat Greg Valentine
Gene Lewis beat Frank Monte
Abe Jacobs beat Kim Duk by DQ
Jacques Goulet & Swede Hanson beat Nick DeCarlo & Steve Muslin
Jimmy Snuka beat Dewey Robertson

1/13/81: Niagara Falls, Ontario(TV)
Ric Flair beat Charlie Fulton
Ric Flair & Angelo Mosca beat Roddy Piper & Ivan Koloff
Roddy Piper & Hossein Arab beat Frankie Laine & Earl Pinnock by DQ
Tony Parisi beat Iron Sheik
Ivan Koloff beat Don Kernodle
Angelo Mosca beat Brian Mackney & Charlie Fulton in a handicap match
Ivan Koloff beat Brian Mackney
Sweet Ebony Diamond beat Tim Gerard
Sweet Ebony Diamond & George Wells beat The Destroyer & Charlie Fulton
Joe Marcus & Bob Marcus beat Tim Gerard & Chris Jones
Iron Sheik beat Earl Pinnock & Alex Gerard in a handicap match

1/14/81: Raleigh, NC @ WRAL Studios (TV)

1/15/81: Sumter, SC @ Exposition Center
Ricky Steamboat double DQ Roddy Piper
Ivan Koloff vs. Iron Sheik in a Russian chain match
Charlie Fulton vs. Abe Jacobs
Jacques Goulet vs. Nick DeCarlo
Dewey Robertson & George Wells vs. Mr. Fuji & Tenryu

1/16/81: Richmond, VA @ Coliseum
Ricky Steamboat beat Jimmy Snuka
Roddy Piper beat Johnny Weaver
Ivan Koloff beat Iron Sheik
Sweet Ebony Diamond beat Mr. Fuji by DQ
Dewey Robertson & George Wells beat Tenryu & Kim Duk
Don Kernodle draw Cy Jernigan
Ron Ritchie beat Gene Lewis
Steve Muslin beat Ricky Ferrara

1/16/81: Charleston SC @ County Hall
Ric Flair beat Greg Valentine
Blackjack Mulligan beat Bobby Duncum in a Texas street fight match
Swede Hanson & Jacques Goulet beat Matt Borne & Frank Monte
Jim Nelson beat Nick DeCarlo
Abe Jacobs beat Charlie Fulton

1/17/81: Roanoke VA @ Civic Center
Ric Flair beat Greg Valentine
Roddy Piper double DQ Masked Superstar
Dewey Robertson & George Wells beat Kim Duk & Tenryu
Swede Hanson draw Don Kernodle
Cy Jernigan beat Ricky Ferrara

1/17/81: Newberry, SC
Ricky Steamboat vs. Jimmy Snuka
Ivan Koloff vs. Sweet Ebony Diamond
Mr. Fuji & Matt Borne vs. Swede Hanson & Steve Muslin
Ron Ritchie vs. Jim Nelson

1/18/81: Charlotte, NC @ Coliseum
Ric Flair beat Roddy Piper by DQ
Masked Superstar beat Jimmy Snuka

Ivan Koloff beat Iron Sheik
Blackjack Mulligan beat Bobby Duncum in a Texas street fight match
Dewey Robertson & George Wells beat Jacques Goulet & Kim Duk
Mr. Fuji beat Steve Muslin
Ron Ritchie beat Jim Nelson
Don Kernodle draw Gene Lewis

1/19/81: Greenville, SC @ Memorial Auditorium
Ric Flair beat Roddy Piper
Masked Superstar beat Jimmy Snuka
Greg Valentine beat Steve Muslin
Jacques Goulet & Swede Hanson beat Don Kernodle & Nick DeCarlo
Frank Monte beat Ricky Ferrara

1/20/81: Columbia, SC @ Township Auditorium
Ric Flair & Ricky Steamboat beat Roddy Piper & Greg Valentine in a match with George Scott as special ref
Iron Sheik beat Dewey Robertson
George Wells beat Swede Hanson by DQ
Mr. Fuji beat Ron Ritchie
Gene Lewis beat Frank Monte

1/20/81: Raleigh, NC @ Dorton Arena

1/21/81: Raleigh, NC @ WRAL Studios (TV)

1/22/81: Norfolk VA @ Scope
Ric Flair & Ricky Steamboat beat Greg Valentine & Roddy Piper in a match with George Scott as special referee
Blackjack Mulligan beat Bobby Duncum in a Texas street fight match
Dewey Robertson, George Wells & Don Kernodle beat Kim Duk, Tenryu & Mr. Fuji
Jacques Goulet beat Abe Jacobs
Bruno Sammartino, Jr. beat Charlie Fulton
Ron Ritchie beat Gene Lewis by DQ
Nick DeCarlo draw Jim Nelson

1/23/81: Lynchburg VA @ City Armory
Roddy Piper vs. Johnny Weaver
Ivan Koloff vs. Iron Sheik
Jacques Goulet & Mr. Fuji vs. Matt Borne & Don Kernodle
Gene Lewis vs. Ron Ritchie

1/23/81: Charleston, SC @ County Hall
Masked Superstar & Paul Jones beat Ray Stevens & Jimmy Snuka by DQ
Abe Jacobs beat Nick DeCarlo
Frank Monte beat Ricky Ferrara
Steve Muslin beat Jim Nelson
Sweet Ebony Diamond beat Swede Hanson

1/24/81: Spartanburg, SC @ Memorial Auditorium
Paul Jones, Masked Superstar & Sweet Ebony Diamond beat Ray Stevens, Jimmy Snuka & Gene Anderson
Johnny Weaver beat Jacques Goulet
Don Kernodle beat Nick DeCarlo
Ron Ritchie draw Jim Nelson

1/24/81: Greensboro, NC @ Coliseum
Ric Flair & Ricky Steamboat beat Roddy Piper & Greg Valentine
Blackjack Mulligan beat Bobby Duncum
Ivan Koloff beat Iron Sheik
George Wells & Dewey Robertson beat Mr. Fuji & Tenryu
Steve Muslin & Frank Monte beat Ricky Ferrara & Gene Lewis
Kim Duk beat Bruno Sammartino, Jr.
Abe Jacobs beat Charlie Fulton

1/26/81: Greenville, SC @ Memorial Auditorium
Roddy Piper & Greg Valentine beat Ric Flair & George Scott
Dewey Robertson & George Wells beat Swede Hanson & Jacques Goulet
Mr. Fuji beat Frank Monte
Bruno Sammartino, Jr. beat Charlie Fulton
Ron Ritchie beat Jim Nelson

1/26/81: Christiansburg VA @ High School
Masked Superstar, Paul Jones & Sweet Ebony Diamond vs. Jimmy Snuka, Ray Stevens & Gene Anderson
Johnny Weaver vs. Tenryu
Steve Muslin vs. Gene Lewis
Don Kernodle vs. Ricky Ferrara

1/27/81: Raleigh, NC @ Dorton Arena
Roddy Piper beat Ric Flair to win NWA United States Title
Masked Superstar & Paul Jones beat Jimmy Snuka & Ray Stevens by DQ
Bruno Sammartino, Jr. beat Ricky Ferrara
Swede Hanson beat Ron Ritchie
Mr. Fuji & Tenryu beat Don Kernodle & Steve Muslin

1/27/81: Columbia, SC @ Township Auditorium
Ricky Steamboat beat Greg Valentine by DQ
Blackjack Mulligan beat Bobby Duncum in a Texas street fight match
Ivan Koloff beat Iron Sheik
George Wells & Dewey Robertson beat Gene Lewis & Jacques Goulet
Charlie Fulton beat Abe Jacobs
Frank Monte beat Jim Nelson

1/28/81: Raleigh, NC @ WRAL Studios (TV)

1/30/81: Charleston, SC @ County Hall
Paul Jones & Masked Superstar beat Jimmy Snuka & Ray Stevens
Johnny Weaver beat Mr. Fuji
Swede Hanson beat Frank Monte
Ron Ritchie beat Charlie Fulton
Abe Jacobs draw Ricky Ferrara

1/30/81: Knoxville, TN @ Civic Coliseum
Ric Flair vs. Greg Valentine
Blackjack Mulligan vs. Bobby Duncum
George Wells & Dewey Robertson vs. Tenryu & Swede Hanson
Jim Nelson vs. Nick DeCarlo
Mike Fever vs. Tony Tosi

1/31/81: York, SC @ York Comprehensive High School
Ricky Steamboat vs. Roddy Piper
Sweet Ebony Diamond vs. Mr. Fuji
Dewey Robertson & Don Kernodle vs. Gene Lewis & Tenryu
Nick DeCarlo vs. Ron Ritchie
Charlie Fulton vs. Bruno Sammartino, Jr.

1/31/81: Cincinnati, OH @ Gardens
Jackie Ruffin beat Jim Nelson by DQ
Iron Sheik beat Frankie Laine
Ivan Koloff & Jimmy Snuka beat George Wells & Johnny Weaver
Blackjack Mulligan beat Bobby Duncum
Ric Flair beat Greg Valentine

2/1/81: Asheville, NC @ Civic Center
Roddy Piper draw Ricky Steamboat
Masked Superstar beat Ray Stevens
Sweet Ebony Diamond, Don Kernodle & Bruno Sammartino, Jr. beat Mr. Fuji, Tenryu & Jacques Goulet
Plus 2 other matches

2/1/81: Toronto, Ontario @ Maple Leaf Gardens
Angelo Mosca beat Ivan Koloff
Ric Flair beat Greg Valentine
Hossein Arab(Iron Sheik) beat George Wells
Jimmy Snuka beat Johnny Weaver
Billy Red Lyons & Tony Parisi beat Jim Nelson & Frankie Laine
The Destroyer draw Louis Lawrence

2/2/81: Greenville, SC @ Memorial Auditorium

2/2/81: Fayetteville, NC @ Cumberland County Memorial Auditorium
Paul Jones & Masked Superstar vs. Roddy Piper & Greg Valentine
Sweet Ebony Diamond vs. Ray Stevens
Mr. Fuji vs. Steve Muslin

2/2/81: Brantford, Ontario(TV)
Jimmy Snuka beat Joe Marcus
Angelo Mosca & Ric Flair beat Ivan Koloff & Jim Nelson
Tony Parisi & Johnny Weaver beat Tim Gerard & Jim Nelson
Jimmy Snuka & Iron Sheik beat Joe Marcus & Bob Marcus
George Wells & Frankie Laine beat Ivan Koloff & Tim Gerard
Jimmy Snuka beat Alex Girard & Brian Mackney in a handicap match
Tony Parisi & Johnny Weaver beat Joe Marcus & Bob Marcus
Ric Flair beat Jim Nelson
Jimmy Snuka beat Brian Mackney
Angelo Mosca double DQ Iron Sheik

2/3/81: Columbia, SC @ Township Auditorium
Ivan Koloff, Roddy Piper & Greg Valentine beat Ric Flair, Ricky Steamboat & George Scott
Bruno Sammartino, Jr. beat Charlie Fulton
George Wells beat Gene Lewis
Mr. Fuji beat Johnny Weaver

2/3/81: Raleigh, NC @ Dorton Arena

2/4/81: Raleigh, NC @ WRAL Studios (TV)
Johnny Weaver & Sweet Ebony Diamond beat Jacques Goulet & Ricky Ferrara
Ricky Steamboat beat Charlie Fulton
Ric Flair & Blackjack Mulligan beat Gene Lewis & Jim Nelson
Iron Sheik no contest with Frank Monte
Ray Stevens, Ivan Koloff & Jimmy Snuka beat Dewey Robertson, Steve Muslin & Don Kernodle
Mr. Fuji & Tenryu beat Frank Monte & Steve Muslin
Ric Flair beat Gene Lewis
Ivan Koloff & Ray Stevens beat Don Kernodle & Ron Ritchie
Iron Sheik beat Abe Jacobs
Roddy Piper & Greg Valentine beat Tony Tosi & Mike Fever

2/5/81: Norfolk, VA @ Scope
Roddy Piper, Greg Valentine & Ivan Koloff beat Ric Flair, Ricky Steamboat & George Scott
Iron Sheik beat Blackjack Mulligan
Dewey Robertson & George Wells beat Mr. Fuji & Tenryu
Bruno Sammartino, Jr. beat Gene Lewis
Don Kernodle beat Swede Hanson
Frank Monte beat Ricky Ferrara

2/5/81: Sumter, SC @ Exposition Center
Johnny Weaver beat Jacques Goulet
Jimmy Snuka, Ray Stevens & Gene Anderson beat Masked Superstar, Paul Jones & Sweet Ebony Diamond
Ron Ritchie beat Jim Nelson

2/6/81: Charleston, SC @ County Hall
Jimmy Snuka, Ray Stevens & Gene Anderson beat Ricky Steamboat, Masked Superstar & Paul Jones by DQ
Johnny Weaver beat Jacques Goulet
Ron Ritchie beat Jim Nelson
Charlie Fulton draw Abe Jacobs

2/6/81: Lynchburg VA @ City Armory
Ric Flair & Blackjack Mulligan beat Roddy Piper & Greg Valentine by DQ
Bruno Sammartino, Jr. beat Tenryu
Cy Jernigan beat Frank Monte
Steve Muslin beat Ricky Ferrara

2/7/81: Greensboro, NC @ Coliseum
Masked Superstar & Paul Jones beat Ivan Koloff & Ray Stevens by DQ
Roddy Piper beat Ric Flair
Blackjack Mulligan beat Iron Sheik
Mr. Fuji & Tenryu beat Dewey Robertson & George Wells to win NWA Mid Atlantic Tag Title
Steve Muslin & Frank Monte beat Jim Nelson & Ricky Ferrara
Bruno Sammartino, Jr. draw Jacques Goulet

2/8/81: Kingsport, TN
Roddy Piper & Greg Valentine beat Ric Flair & Blackjack Mulligan

2/9/81: Greenville, SC @ Memorial Auditorium
Roddy Piper beat Ric Flair by DQ
Ivan Koloff & Ray Stevens beat Masked Superstar & Paul Jones
Bruno Sammartino, Jr. beat Gene Lewis
Mr. Fuji beat Steve Muslin
Abe Jacobs beat Charlie Fulton

2/10/81: Raleigh, NC @ Dorton Arena
Ric Flair & Blackjack Mulligan beat Roddy Piper & Greg Valentine by DQ
Charlie Fulton draw Ron Ritchie
Don Kernodle beat Ben Alexander
Dewey Robertson beat Swede Hanson by DQ
Bruno Sammartino, Jr. beat Tenryu

2/10/81: Columbia, SC @ Township Auditorium
Ivan Koloff, Jimmy Snuka & Ray Stevens beat Sweet Ebony Diamond, Masked Superstar & Paul Jones
Johnny Weaver beat Mr. Fuji by DQ
Jacques Goulet beat Frank Monte
Abe Jacobs beat Jim Nelson

2/11/81: Raleigh, NC @ WRAL Studios (TV)
Ric Flair & Blackjack Mulligan beat Gene Lewis & Jim Nelson

2/12/81: Fishersville, VA @ Augusta Expo
Ric Flair & Johnny Weaver beat Roddy Piper & Greg Valentine
George Wells vs. Swede Hanson
Dewey Robertson vs. Mr. Fuji
Don Kernodle vs. Tenryu

2/13/81: Charleston, SC @ County Hall
Ricky Steamboat beat Jimmy Snuka
Blackjack Mulligan beat Ivan Koloff
Sweet Ebony Diamond & Johnny Weaver beat Mr. Fuji & Tenryu
Gene Lewis beat Steve Muslin
Ron Ritchie beat Ricky Ferrara

2/13/81: Richmond, VA @ Coliseum
Ric Flair beat Roddy Piper by DQ
Masked Superstar & Paul Jones beat Gene Anderson & Ole Anderson
Jim Nelson draw Frank Monte
Cy Jernigan beat Charlie Fulton
Dewey Robertson beat Swede Hanson
George Wells beat Greg Valentine by DQ
Jacques Goulet & Iron Sheik beat Don Kernodle & Bruno Sammartino, Jr.

2/14/81: Culpepper, VA @ High School
Ole Anderson beat Dewey Robertson
Blackjack Mulligan & Ric Flair beat Roddy Piper & Greg Valentine

2/14/81: Spartanburg, SC @ Memorial Auditorium
Ricky Steamboat beat Mr. Fuji
Ivan Koloff beat Iron Sheik in a Russian chain match
Don Kernodle & Steve Muslin beat Jacques Goulet & Gene Lewis
Tony Tosi beat Charlie Fulton
Abe Jacobs beat Ricky Harris by referee decision

2/15/81: Roanoke, VA @ Civic Center
Ric Flair beat Roddy Piper by DQ in a match with George Scott as special referee
Ricky Steamboat double DQ Jimmy Snuka
Blackjack Mulligan beat Greg Valentine
George Wells & Dewey Robertson beat Swede Hanson & Tenryu
Bruno Sammartino, Jr. draw Ron Ritchie
Abe Jacobs beat Charlie Fulton

2/15/81: Asheville, NC @ Civic Center
Masked Superstar & Paul Jones beat Gene Anderson & Ole Anderson
Sweet Ebony Diamond beat Mr. Fuji by DQ
Tony Tosi beat Frank Monte
Steve Muslin beat Ricky Harris
Jim Nelson double DQ Ben Alexander

2/16/81: Greenville, SC @ Memorial Auditorium
Steve Muslin draw Ricky Ferrara
Swede Hanson beat Ron Ritchie
George Wells beat Tenryu
Blackjack Mulligan beat Iron Sheik by countout
Masked Superstar & Paul Jones beat Ivan Koloff & Ray Stevens

2/17/81: Columbia, SC @ Township Auditorium
Sweet Ebony Diamond, Masked Superstar & Paul Jones beat Ivan Koloff, Jimmy Snuka & Ray Stevens
Johnny Weaver beat Jacques Goulet
Bruno Sammartino, Jr. beat Gene Lewis
Tenryu beat Abe Jacobs

2/17/81: Raleigh, NC @ Dorton Arena
Iron Sheik, Greg Valentine & Roddy Piper beat Blackjack Mulligan, Ric Flair & Ricky Steamboat
Jim Nelson beat Frank Monte
Don Kernodle draw Swede Hanson
George Wells beat Mr. Fuji

2/18/81: Raleigh, NC @ WRAL Studios (TV)

2/19/81: Norfolk, VA @ Scope
Ric Flair beat Roddy Piper by DQ
Ricky Steamboat beat Greg Valentine
Iron Sheik double DQ Blackjack Mulligan
Mr. Fuji & Tenryu beat Dewey Robertson & George Wells
Bruno Sammartino, Jr. beat Swede Hanson
Abe Jacobs beat Ricky Harris
Frank Monte & Ron Ritchie beat Charlie Fulton & Jim Nelson
Ben Alexander beat Ricky Ferrara

2/20/81: Winston-Salem, NC @ Memorial Coliseum
Ricky Steamboat vs. Jimmy Snuka
Bobby Duncum vs. Johnny Weaver
Swede Hanson & Tenryu vs. Bruno Sammartino, Jr. & George Wells
Frank Monte vs. Charlie Fulton
Ricky Ferrara vs. Tony Tosi

2/20/81: Charleston, SC @ County Hall
Roddy Piper beat Sweet Ebony Diamond
Blackjack Mulligan beat Iron Sheik
Don Kernodle & Steve Muslin beat Jacques Goulet & Gene Lewis
Susan Starr beat Joyce Grable
Hans Brauner beat Mike Fever

2/20/81: Lynchburg, VA @ City Armory
Masked Superstar & Paul Jones vs. Ray Stevens & Ivan Koloff
Dewey Robertson vs. Mr. Fuji
Plus 2 other matches

2/21/81: Cincinnati, OH @ Gardens
Frankie Laine draw Ron Ritchie
Jackie Ruffin beat Abe Jacobs via pinfall
Swede Hanson beat Dewey Robertson via pinfall
Sweet Ebony Diamond beat Ivan Koloff via pinfall
Paul Jones & Masked Superstar beat Jimmy Snuka & Ray Stevens

2/21/81: Charlotte, NC @ Coliseum
Roddy Piper beat Ric Flair by DQ
Ricky Steamboat beat Ole Anderson
Iron Sheik beat Blackjack Mulligan
George Wells & Johnny Weaver beat Mr. Fuji & Tenryu
Bruno Sammartino, Jr. beat Gene Lewis
Don Kernodle & Steve Muslin beat Jim Nelson & Jacques Goulet

2/21/81: Spartanburg, SC @ Memorial Auditorium
Ric Flair, Blackjack Mulligan & Ricky Steamboat beat Roddy Piper, Greg Valentine & Bobby Duncum
George Wells beat Mr. Fuji by DQ
Bruno Sammartino, Jr. beat Ricky Harris
Ricky Ferrara draw Tony Tosi

2/22/81: Toronto, Ontario @ Maple Leaf Gardens
Angelo Mosca beat Hossein Arab
Masked Superstar beat Ray Stevens by DQ
Jimmy Snuka beat Mad Dog Vachon
Bobby Duncum & Swede Hanson beat Sweet Ebony Diamond & Dewey Robertson
Frankie Laine beat Ron Ritchie
Tony Parisi draw Kurt Von Hess

2/22/81: Savannah, GA @ Civic Center
Jimmy Snuka beat Ricky Steamboat by DQ
Iron Sheik beat Blackjack Mulligan vs. Iron Sheik
Steve Muslin & Ron Ritchie beat Jacques Goulet & Swede Hanson
Sweet Ebony Diamond beat Greg Valentine
Jim Nelson beat Abe Jacobs

2/23/81: Buffalo, NY
Tony Parisi beat Ron Ritchie
Dewey Robertson beat Swede Hanson by DQ
Sweet Ebony Diamond beat Frankie Laine
Iron Sheik beat Mad Dog Vachon by submission
Blackjack Mulligan beat Bobby Duncum in a Texas street fight match
Masked Superstar & Paul Jones beat Jimmy Snuka & Ray Stevens

2/23/81: Greenville, SC @ Memorial Auditorium
Ric Flair beat Roddy Piper by reverse decision
George Wells beat Ivan Koloff by DQ
Mr. Fuji & Tenryu beat Johnny Weaver & Bruno Sammartino, Jr.
Ben Alexander beat Frank Monte
Tony Tosi beat Jim Nelson

2/23/81: Hillsville, VA @ Woodlawn Intermediate School
Ricky Steamboat vs. Greg Valentine
Jacques Goulet & Gene Lewis vs. Steve Muslin & Don Kernodle
Hans Brunner vs. Charlie Fulton
Abe Jacobs vs. Ricky Ferrara

2/24/81: Columbia, SC @ Township Auditorium
Ricky Steamboat beat Jimmy Snuka by DQ
Masked Superstar beat Ivan Koloff
Bruno Sammartino, Jr. & Don Kernodle beat Gene Lewis & Jacques Goulet
Frank Monte beat Charlie Fulton
Ben Alexander beat Ricky Ferrara

2/24/81: Raleigh, NC @ Dorton Arena
Ric Flair beat Roddy Piper by DQ
Blackjack Mulligan beat Greg Valentine
Johnny Weaver & George Wells beat Mr. Fuji & Tenryu
Jim Nelson beat Abe Jacobs
Steve Muslin beat Ricky Harris

2/24/81: Kitchener, Ontario @ Memorial Auditorium
Iron Sheik & Bobby Duncum beat Earl Pinnock & Ricky Johnson
Angelo Mosca beat John Orlick
Mad Dog Vachon & Dewey Robertson beat Iron Sheik & Bobby Duncum by DQ

Angelo Mosca beat Chris Jones & Tim Gerrard in a handicap match
Swede Hanson beat John Bonello
Frankie Laine draw Ron Ritchie
Sweet Ebony Diamond & Tony Parisi beat Kurt Von Hess & Brian Mackney
Swede Hanson beat Ron Ritchie
Iron Sheik beat Dewey Robertson
Angelo Mosca beat Bobby Duncum

2/25/81: Raleigh, NC @ WRAL Studios (TV)

2/25/81: London, Ontario @ Gardens
Tony Parisi draw Billy Red Lyons
Frankie Laine beat Ron Ritchie
Angelo Mosca beat Hossein Arab
Mad Dog Vachon & Dewey Robertson beat Bobby Duncum & Swede Hanson
Sweet Ebony Diamond beat Kurt Von Hess

2/26/81: Kingston, Ontario
Angelo Mosca beat Hossein Arab
Mad Dog Vachon & Dewey Robertson beat Bobby Duncum & Kurt Von Hess
Sweet Ebony Diamond beat Swede Hanson by CO
Frankie Laine beat Billy Red Lyons
Tony Parisi beat Ron Ritchie
2/26/81: Harrisonburg, VA @ High School
Ric Flair & Ricky Steamboat vs. Roddy Piper & Jimmy Snuka

2/27/81: Knoxville, TN @ Civic Coliseum
Paul Jones, Johnny Weaver(sub for Masked Superstar) & Sweet Ebony Diamond beat Ivan Koloff, Ray Stevens & Ole Anderson via pinfall
Mr. Fuji beat Frank Monte
Don Kernodle beat Gene Lewis
Ricky Harris draw Abe Jacobs

2/27/81: Richmond, VA @ Coliseum
Blackjack Mulligan beat Iron Sheik
Ric Flair & Ricky Steamboat beat Roddy Piper & Greg Valentine
Kurt Von Hess beat Ricky Ferrara
Ron Ritchie beat Jim Nelson
Cy Jernigan beat Ben Alexander
George Wells, Dewey Robertson & Bruno Sammartino, Jr. beat Jacques Goulet, Swede Hanson & Tenryu

2/28/81: Spartanburg, SC @ Memorial Auditorium
Ricky Steamboat DCO with Roddy Piper
Ivan Koloff beat Johnny Weaver
Mr. Fuji & Tenryu beat Don Kernodle & Bruno Sammartino, Jr.
Kurt Von Hess beat Ron Ritchie by referee decision
Ben Alexander beat Ricky Harris

2/28/81: Shelby, NC @ Recreation Center
Blackjack Mulligan & Sweet Ebony Diamond beat Iron Sheik & Bobby Duncum
Dewey Robertson beat Jacques Goulet
Steve Muslin beat Frank Monte
Abe Jacobs beat Charlie Fulton

3/1/81: Asheville, NC @ Civic Center
Jimmy Snuka beat Ricky Steamboat by DQ
Blackjack Mulligan beat Iron Sheik
Johnny Weaver & Bruno Sammartino, Jr. beat Kurt Von Hess & Gene Lewis
Susan Starr beat Betty Clark
Frank Monte beat Ricky Harris

3/1/81: Greensboro, NC @ Coliseum
Roddy Piper beat Ric Flair
Ivan Koloff & Ray Stevens beat Masked Superstar & Paul Jones to win NWA World Tag Title
Mr. Fuji & Tenryu beat Dewey Robertson & George Wells
Bobby Duncum beat Don Kernodle
Cy Jernigan beat Charlie Fulton
Tony Tosi beat Ricky Ferrara
Ben Alexander beat Ricky Harris

3/1/81: Savannah, GA @ Civic Center
Ricky Steamboat vs. Jimmy Snuka
Blackjack Mulligan vs. Iron Sheik
Greg Valentine vs. Sweet Ebony Diamond
Jacques Goulet & Swede Hanson vs. Steve Muslin & Ron Ritchie
Abe Jacobs vs. Jim Nelson

3/2/81: Fayetteville, NC @ Cumberland County Memorial Auditorium
Blackjack Mulligan vs. Iron Sheik
Bobby Duncum vs. Johnny Weaver
Mr. Fuji & Tenryu vs. Bruno Sammartino, Jr. & George Wells

3/2/81: Greenville, SC @ Memorial Auditorium
Paul Jones, Masked Superstar & Sweet Ebony Diamond beat Jimmy Snuka, Ivan Koloff & Ray Stevens
Dewey Robertson beat Swede Hanson by DQ
Don Kernodle beat Ben Alexander
Kurt Von Hess beat Ron Ritchie

3/3/81: Raleigh, NC @ Dorton Arena

3/4/81: Raleigh, NC @ WRAL Studios (TV)

3/5/81: Sumter, SC @ Exposition Center
Ricky Steamboat & Ric Flair vs. Roddy Piper & Greg Valentine
Jimmy Snuka vs. George Wells
Bruno Sammartino, Jr. vs. Tenryu
Ron Ritchie vs. Charlie Fulton
Steve Muslin vs. Ricky Ferrara

3/6/81: Charleston, SC @ County Hall
Ric Flair & Blackjack Mulligan beat Roddy Piper & Greg Valentine
Mr. Fuji beat Dewey Robertson
Kurt Von Hess beat Steve Muslin
Tony Tosi beat Jim Nelson
Ron Ritchie beat Charlie Fulton

3/7/81: Columbia, SC @ Township Auditorium(Special Saturday Card)
Ric Flair beat Roddy Piper by countout
Masked Superstar beat Ray Stevens
Mr. Fuji & Tenryu beat Dewey Robertson & George Wells
Bruno Sammartino, Jr. beat Ricky Harris
Tony Tosi beat Ricky Ferrara

3/7/81: Spartanburg, SC @ Memorial Auditorium
Rick Steamboat beat Ivan Koloff
Bobby Duncum beat Johnny Weaver
Kurt Von Hess & Ben Alexander beat Steve Muslin & Frank Monte
Charlie Fulton beat Abe Jacobs

3/7/81: Johnson City, TN
Blackjack Mulligan vs. Iron Sheik
Paul Jones vs. Jimmy Snuka
Don Kernodle & Ron Ritchie vs. Jim Nelson & Gene Lewis
Wayne Rogers vs. Mike Fever

3/8/81: Roanoke, VA
Ric Flair & Blackjack Mulligan beat Roddy Piper & Greg Valentine
Iron Sheik beat Dewey Robertson
Don Kernodle beat Gene Lewis
Steve Muslin beat Jim Nelson
Cy Jernigan beat Ricky Harris

3/8/81: Charlotte, NC @ Coliseum
Blackjack Mulligan beat Iron Sheik in a cage match
Ric Flair & Masked Superstar beat Roddy Piper & Greg Valentine
Paul Jones beat Ivan Koloff
Mr. Fuji & Tenryu beat Johnny Weaver & George Wells
Kurt Von Hess beat Frank Monte
Ron Ritchie beat Charlie Fulton
Abe Jacobs beat Ricky Ferrara

3/8/81: Toronto, Ontario @ Maple Leaf Gardens
Jimmy Snuka beat Angelo Mosca by countout
Bobby Duncum beat Sweet Ebony Diamond in a taped fist match
Ricky Steamboat beat Ray Stevens
Tony Parisi & David Sammartino beat Swede Hanson & Ben Alexander
The Destroyer beat John Bonello
Frankie Laine beat Tim Gerard

3/9/81: Greenville, SC @ Memorial Auditorium
Paul Jones & Masked Superstar beat Ray Stevens & Ivan Koloff by DQ
George Wells beat Greg Valentine
Steve Muslin beat Charlie Fulton
Don Kernodle beat Kurt Von Hess
Jim Nelson beat Frank Monte

3/9/81: Cincinnati, OH @ Gardens
Jose Martinez(aka El Bracero) draw Ben Alexander
Angelo Mosca beat Frankie Laine
Sweet Ebony Diamond & Bruno Sammartino, Jr. beat Swede Hanson & Bobby Duncum by DQ
Blackjack Mulligan beat Iron Sheik via pinfall
Ricky Steamboat beat Jimmy Snuka
Ric Flair beat Roddy Piper by DQ

3/10/81: Niagara Falls, Ontario(TV)
Bruno Sammartino, Jr. beat Ben Alexander
Jimmy Snuka & Bobby Duncum beat Joe Marcus & Bob Marcus
Swede Hanson beat Alex Gerrard & Steve Dugas in a handicap match
Bruno Sammartino, Jr. beat John Bonello
Bruno Sammartino, Jr. & Tony Parisi beat Tim Gerrard & Ben Alexander
Bobby Duncum & Swede Hanson beat Joe Marcus & Bob Marcus
Angelo Mosca beat Ben Alexander
Tony Parisi beat Bobby Duncum by DQ
Ricky Steamboat & Angelo Mosca beat Swede Hanson & Jimmy Snuka

3/10/81: Raleigh, NC @ Dorton Arena
No Wrestling

3/10/81: Columbia, SC @ Township Auditorium
No Wrestling

3/11/81: Raleigh, NC @ WRAL Studios (TV)

3/12/81: Fishersville, VA @ Augusta Expo
Ric Flair, Blackjack Mulligan & Sweet Ebony Diamond beat Roddy Piper, Bobby Duncum & Iron Sheik
Johnny Weaver vs. Mr. Fuji
Steve Muslin beat Jim Nelson
Bruno Sammartino, Jr. beat Gene Lewis

3/12/81: Portsmouth, VA
Kurt Von Hess beat Frank Monte
Dewey Robertson beat Ben Alexander
George Wells beat Tenryu
Ivan Koloff & Ray Stevens no contest with Masked Superstar & Paul Jones

3/13/81: Lynchburg, VA @ City Armory
Blackjack Mulligan vs. Iron Sheik
Masked Superstar vs. Greg Valentine
Mr. Fuji & Tenryu vs. Dewey Robertson & George Wells
Frank Monte vs. Jim Nelson

3/13/81: Charleston, SC @ County Hall
Roddy Piper beat Ric Flair
Sweet Ebony Diamond beat Ivan Koloff
Toni Tosi draw Ricky Ferrara
Bruno Sammartino, Jr. beat Ben Alexander
Kurt Von Hess & Swede Hanson beat Don Kernodle & Johnny Weaver

3/15/81: Savannah, GA @ Civic Center
Roddy Piper vs. Sweet Ebony Diamond
Ricky Steamboat vs. Jimmy Snuka

George Wells & Dewey Robertson vs. Mr. Fuji & Tenryu
Swede Hanson vs. Don Kernodle
Ron Ritchie vs. Ricky Harris

3/16/81: Greenville, SC @ Memorial Auditorium
Jim Nelson draw Ron Ritchie
Steve Muslin beat Ricky Harris
Sweet Ebony Diamond & George Wells beat Mr. Fuji & Tenryu
Masked Superstar beat Ivan Koloff
Blackjack Mulligan beat Roddy Piper by DQ

3/16/81: Lumberton, NC @ Recreation Center
Ricky Steamboat vs. Jimmy Snuka
Paul Jones vs. Greg Valentine
Bobby Duncum & Iron Sheik vs. Johnny Weaver & Dewey Robertson
Gene Lewis vs. Don Kernodle
Ricky Ferrara vs. Ben Alexander

3/17/81: Raleigh, NC @ Dorton Arena
Roddy Piper draw Ric Flair
Paul Jones beat Ivan Koloff
Jimmy Snuka beat Sweet Ebony Diamond
Kurt Von Hess beat Abe Jacobs
Johnny Weaver & George Wells beat Mr. Fuji & Tenryu by DQ

3/17/81: Columbia, SC @ Township Auditorium
No Wrestling

3/18/81: Raleigh, NC @ WRAL Studios (TV)

3/19/81: Sumter, SC @ Exposition Center
Blackjack Mulligan vs. Iron Sheik
Ricky Steamboat vs. Jimmy Snuka
Mr. Fuji & Tenryu vs. Johnny Weaver & George Wells
Swede Hanson vs. Steve Muslin
Ricky Ferrara vs. Frank Monte

3/20/81: Richmond, VA @ Coliseum
Ben Alexander beat Abe Jacobs
Ron Ritchie beat Charlie Fulton
Tenryu & Mr. Fuji beat Don Kernodle & Bruno Sammartino, Jr.
Jimmy Snuka beat Dewey Robertson
Sweet Ebony Diamond beat Bobby Duncum
Ric Flair draw Roddy Piper
Ivan Koloff & Ray Stevens beat Masked Superstar & Paul Jones by DQ

3/20/81: Charleston, SC @ County Hall
Blackjack Mulligan beat Iron Sheik in a cage match
Ricky Steamboat beat Greg Valentine
Steve Muslin beat Gene Lewis
Frank Monte beat Ricky Harris
Swede Hanson & Kurt Von Hess beat Johnny Weaver & George Wells

3/21/81: Forest City, NC
Rick Steamboat & Paul Jones beat Ivan Koloff & Ray Stevens
Dewey Robertson beat Tenryu
Ron Ritchie beat Gene Lewis
Frank Monte beat Ricky Harris

3/21/81: Chester, SC @ High School
Sweet Ebony Diamond vs. Greg Valentine
Ric Flair vs. Roddy Piper

3/22/81: Asheville, NC @ Civic Center
Ric Flair & Blackjack Mulligan beat Roddy Piper & Greg Valentine
Iron Sheik beat Johnny Weaver
Swede Hanson beat Steve Muslin
Dewey Robertson & Ron Ritchie beat Ben Alexander & Charlie Fulton

3/22/81: Greensboro, NC @ Coliseum
Paul Jones & Masked Superstar beat Ray Stevens & Ivan Koloff to win NWA World Tag Title
Ricky Steamboat beat Jimmy Snuka
WWF Champion Bob Backlund beat Bobby Duncum
Mr. Fuji & Tenryu beat Sweet Ebony Diamond & George Wells
Bruno Sammartino, Jr. beat Gene Lewis
Don Kernodle beat Kurt Von Hess
Jim Nelson beat Ricky Ferrara

3/23/81: Greenville, SC @ Memorial Auditorium
Ricky Ferrara beat Mike Fever
Charlie Fulton draw Abe Jacobs
Kurt Von Hess & Ricky Harris beat Frank Monte & Ron Ritchie
Dewey Robertson beat Tenryu
Paul Jones & Masked Superstar beat Ivan Koloff & Ray Stevens

3/24/81: Columbia, SC @ Township Auditorium
Masked Superstar & Paul Jones beat Ivan Koloff & Ray Stevens
Sweet Ebony Diamond beat Mr. Fuji
Tenryu beat Frank Monte
Abe Jacobs beat Gene Lewis
Abe Jacobs beat Charlie Fulton

3/24/81: Raleigh, NC @ Dorton Arena
Jimmy Snuka beat Ricky Steamboat by DQ
Ric Flair beat Roddy Piper by countout
Johnny Weaver, George Wells & Bruno Sammartino, Jr. beat Bobby Duncum, Iron Sheik & Kurt Von Hess
Ron Ritchie beat Ricky Harris

3/25/81: Raleigh, NC @ WRAL Studios (TV)

3/26/81: Harrisonburg, VA @ High School
Gene Lewis beat Mike Fever
Steve Muslin beat Swede Hanson
Johnny Weaver beat Kurt Von Hess
Masked Superstar & Paul Jones beat Ray Stevens & Ivan Koloff

3/26/81: Norfolk, VA @ Scope
Ric Flair beat Roddy Piper
Blackjack Mulligan beat Iron Sheik
Jimmy Snuka beat Ricky Steamboat
Bobby Duncum beat Dewey Robertson
Mr. Fuji & Tenryu beat George Wells & Sweet Ebony Diamond

3/27/81: Charleston, SC @ County Hall
Ray Stevens & Ivan Koloff beat Paul Jones & Masked Superstar by DQ
Johnny Weaver beat Kurt Von Hess
Swede Hanson beat Tony Tosi
Steve Muslin beat Ben Alexander
Gene Lewis beat Abe Jacobs

3/27/81: Lynchburg, VA @ City Armory
Ric Flair & Ricky Steamboat beat Roddy Piper & Greg Valentine
George Wells vs. Mr. Fuji

3/28/81: Buffalo, NY
The Destroyer draw Frankie Laine
Tony Parisi beat Johnny Weaver via pinfall
Sweet Ebony Diamond & George Wells beat Swede Hanson & Mr. Fuji by DQ
Angelo Mosca beat Bobby Duncum via pinfall
Ricky Steamboat beat Jimmy Snuka by DQ

3/28/81: Spartanburg, SC @ Memorial Auditorium
Masked Superstar & Paul Jones beat Ivan Koloff & Ray Stevens
Bruno Sammartino, Jr. beat Tenryu
Ron Ritchie beat Charlie Fulton
Frank Monte beat Jim Nelson
Ben Alexander beat Mike Fever

3/29/81: Charlotte, NC @ Coliseum
NWA World Champion Harley Race beat Ric Flair
Roddy Piper beat Ricky Steamboat
Masked Superstar beat Greg Valentine
Paul Jones beat Tenryu
Dewey Robertson & Bruno Sammartino, Jr. beat Gene Lewis & Kurt Von Hess
Charlie Fulton & Steve Muslin beat Jim Nelson & Ben Alexander
Ron Ritchie beat Ricky Ferrara
Frank Monte beat Ricky Harris

3/29/81: Toronto, Ontario @ Maple Leaf Gardens
Angelo Mosca beat Jimmy Snuka
Andre The Giant beat Hulk Hogan
Sweet Ebony Diamond beat Bobby Duncum in a Texas death match
Hossein Arab(Iron Sheik) & Swede Hanson beat George Wells & Johnny Weaver
Tony Parisi beat Mr. Fuji
Frankie Laine draw The Destroyer

3/30/81: Brantford, Ontario(TV)
George Wells beat Tim Gerard
Mr. Fuji beat Alex Girard
Jimmy Snuka & Swede Hanson beat Joe Marcus & Bob Marcus
Mr. Fuji beat Ricky Johnson
Angelo Mosca & Sweet Ebony Diamond beat Frankie Laine & Tim Gerard
Jimmy Snuka & Swede Hanson beat Johnny Weaver & John Bonello
Mr. Fuji beat John Bonello
Tony Parisi & Johnny Weaver beat Joe Marcus & Bob Marcus
George Wells beat Swede Hanson
Sweet Ebony Diamond & George Wells draw Mr. Fuji & Iron Sheik
Angelo Mosca draw Swede Hanson
Tony Parisi beat Tim Gerard
Angelo Mosca beat Iron Sheik in a lumberjack match

3/30/81: Richmond, VA @ Coliseum
Roddy Piper draw Ric Flair
Ivan Koloff & Ray Stevens beat Masked Superstar & Paul Jones by DQ
Sweet Ebony Diamond beat Bobby Duncum
Jimmy Snuka beat Dewey Robertson
Mr. Fuji & Tenryu beat Don Kernodle & Bruno Sammartino, Jr.
Ron Ritchie beat Charlie Fulton
Ben Alexander beat Abe Jacobs

3/30/81: Cincinnati, OH @ Gardens
Frank Monte beat Charlie Fulton(13:23) via pinfall
Ricky Jacobs beat Abe Jacobs(7:01) via pinfall
Dewey Robertson & Ron Ritchie beat Kurt Von Hess & Ben Alexander(14:20)
Andre The Giant beat Bobby Duncum(10:48) by DQ
Roddy Piper beat Ric Flair(19:08) via pinfall
NWA World Champion Harley Race beat Ricky Steamboat(15:08) via pinfall

3/31/81: London, Ontario @ Gardens
Angelo Mosca beat Bobby Duncum via pinfall
Andre The Giant beat Hossein Arab via pinfall
Sweet Ebony Diamond & George Wells beat Jimmy Snuka & Swede Hanson by DQ
Tony Parisi beat Johnny Weaver via pinfall
Frankie Laine draw Mr. Fuji

3/31/81: Columbia, SC @ Township Auditorium
NWA World Champion Harley Race beat Ricky Steamboat
Blackjack Mulligan beat Greg Valentine by DQ
Dewey Robertson & Frank Monte beat Kurt Von Hess & Gene Lewis
Jim Nelson beat Ron Ritchie
Frank Monte beat Ben Alexander

3/31/81: Raleigh, NC @ Dorton Arena
Masked Superstar & Paul Jones beat Ivan Koloff & Ray Stevens
Ricky Harris beat Abe Jacobs
Ricky Ferrara beat Mike Fever
Tony Tosi beat Charlie Fulton
Bruno Sammartino, Jr. beat Tenryu

4/1/81: Raleigh, NC @ WRAL Studios (TV)
Gene Anderson & Ole Anderson beat Frank Monte & Steve Muslin
Bruno Sammartino, Jr. beat Ricky Harris
Greg Valentine beat Mike Fever
Roddy Piper beat Ron Ritchie
Paul Jones & Masked Superstar beat Kurt Von Hess & Jim Nelson
Ricky Steamboat beat Charlie Fulton
Ivan Koloff beat Mike Fever
Ric Flair beat Ben Alexander
Gene Anderson & Ole Anderson beat Dewey Robertson & Ron Ritchie

4/1/81: Ottawa, Ontario @ Civic Centre
Jimmy Snuka beat Sweet Ebony Diamond via pinfall
Andre The Giant beat Bobby Duncum
Angelo Mosca beat Iron Sheik
Swede Hanson & Mr. Fuji beat Johnny Weaver & George Wells
Frankie Lane draw Tony Parisi

4/2/81: Niagara Falls, Ontario
Billy Red Lyons draw The Destroyer
Mr. Fuji beat Johnny Weaver
George Wells beat Swede Hanson by DQ
Sweet Ebony Diamond beat Bobby Duncum
Angelo Mosca & Tony Parisi beat Iron Sheik & Jimmy Snuka

4/2/81: Norfolk, VA @ Scope
Masked Superstar & Paul Jones beat Ivan Koloff & Ray Stevens
Roddy Piper beat Ricky Steamboat
Tenryu & Ricky Harris vs. Don Kernodle & Steve Muslin

4/3/81: Richmond, VA @ Coliseum
NWA World Champ Harley Race DDQ Roddy Piper
Blackjack Mulligan beat Iron Sheik in a cage match
Ricky Steamboat beat Jimmy Snuka
Greg Valentine beat Sweet Ebony Diamond
Mr. Fuji & Tenryu beat George Wells & Johnny Weaver
Kurt Von Hess beat Ben Alexander
Steve Muslin beat Ricky Ferrara

4/3/81: Charleston, SC @ County Hall
Masked Superstar & Paul Jones beat Ivan Koloff & Ray Stevens
Dewey Robertson beat Bobby Duncum
Bruno Sammartino, Jr. beat Gene Lewis
Frank Monte beat Jim Nelson
Ron Ritchie beat Charlie Fulton

4/4/81: Charlottesville, VA @ University Hall
Roddy Piper vs. Ricky Steamboat
Johnny Weaver & George Wells vs. Jimmy Snuka & Bobby Duncum in an elimination match
Mr. Fuji & Tenryu vs. Don Kernodle & Cy Jernigan

4/4/81: Greensboro, NC @ Coliseum
NWA World Champion Harley Race DCO with Blackjack Mulligan
Masked Superstar & Paul Jones beat Greg Valentine & Ray Stevens
Ric Flair beat Ivan Koloff
Gene Anderson & Ole Anderson beat Dewey Robertson & Steve Muslin
Bruno Sammartino, Jr. beat Jim Nelson
Swede Hanson beat Ron Ritchie
Ricky Ferrara beat Abe Jacobs

4/5/81: Johnson City, TN
Ric Flair & Ricky Steamboat vs. Roddy Piper & Jimmy Snuka
Sweet Ebony Diamond vs. Iron Sheik
Swede Hanson vs. George Wells
Don Kernodle vs. Dewey Robertson
Ricky Harris vs. Ben Alexander

4/5/81: Kingsport, TN
Ric Flair & Ricky Steamboat beat Greg Valentine & Roddy Piper
Tony Atlas beat Bobby Duncum
Mr. Wrestling II beat Ray Stevens
Steve Muslin beat Tenryu

4/5/81: Roanoke, VA @ Civic Center
NWA World Champion Harley Race beat Ric Flair
Blackjack Mulligan beat Iron Sheik
Mr. Fuji & Tenryu beat George Wells & Dewey Robertson
Kurt Von Hess beat Steve Muslin
Frank Monte beat Charlie Fulton
Jimmy Snuka beat Ricky Steamboat by DQ

4/5/81: Savannah, GA @ Civic Center
NWA World Champion Harley Race vs. Blackjack Mulligan
Ray Stevens & Ivan Koloff vs. Paul Jones & Masked Superstar
Bad Boy Bob Duncum vs. Johnny Weaver
Bruno Sammartino, Jr. vs. Gene Lewis
Jim Nelson vs. Ron Ritchie

4/6/81: Greenville, SC @ Memorial Auditorium
Roddy Piper beat Ric Flair
Paul Jones beat Ivan Koloff
Gene Anderson & Ole Anderson beat Dewey Robertson & Don Kernodle
Kurt Von Hess beat Steve Muslin
Charlie Fulton beat Ron Ritchie

4/6/81: Fayetteville, NC @ Cumberland County Memorial Auditorium
Ricky Steamboat vs. Greg Valentine
Sweet Ebony Diamond vs. Jimmy Snuka
Mr. Fuji & Tenryu vs. Johnny Weaver & George Wells
Swede Hanson vs. Bruno Sammartino, Jr.
Jim Nelson vs. Ben Alexander

4/7/81: Columbia, SC @ Township Auditorium
Roddy Piper beat Ric Flair
Blackjack Mulligan beat Iron Sheik
Mr. Fuji & Tenryu beat Dewey Robertson & Johnny Weaver
Bruno Sammartino, Jr. beat Jim Nelson
Frank Monte beat Gene Lewis

4/7/81: Raleigh, NC @ Dorton Arena
Jimmy Snuka beat Ricky Steamboat in a no DQ match
Sweet Ebony Diamond draw Greg Valentine
Paul Jones beat Ray Stevens
Ron Ritchie beat Ricky Ferrara
Bobby Duncum & Kurt Von Hess beat Ron Ritchie & George Wells

4/8/81: Raleigh, NC @ WRAL Studios (TV)
Sweet Ebony Diamond draw Greg Valentine
Frank Monte beat Charlie Fulton
Ivan Koloff beat Steve Muslin
Mr. Wrestling II beat Ricky Ferrara
Gene Anderson & Ole Anderson beat George Wells & Ron Ritchie
Bruno Sammartino, Jr. beat Ricky Harris
Ivan Koloff beat Ron Ritchie
Mr. Fuji beat Steve Muslin
Mr. Wrestling II beat Charlie Fulton
Gene Anderson & Ole Anderson beat Dewey Robertson & Mike Fever

4/9/81: Fishersville, VA @ Augusta Expo
Blackjack Mulligan DCO with Iron Sheik
Sweet Ebony Diamond beat Bobby Duncum
Swede Hanson & Ricky Harris beat Steve Muslin & Mike Fever
Dewey Robertson beat Charlie Fulton

4/9/81: Sumter, SC @ Exposition Center
Johnny Weaver vs. Kurt Von Hess
Roddy Piper vs. Masked Superstar
Paul Jones vs. Ivan Koloff
Mr. Fuji & Tenryu vs. Bruno Sammartino, Jr. & Ron Ritchie
Abe Jacobs vs. Gene Lewis

4/10/81: Charleston, SC @ County Hall
Ric Flair & Ricky Steamboat beat Gene Anderson & Ole Anderson
Ivan Koloff beat George Wells
Mr. Fuji & Tenryu beat Tony Tosi & Ron Ritchie
Ricky Ferrara beat Tony Russo

4/10/81: Lynchburg, VA @ City Armory
Masked Superstar, Paul Jones & Johnny Weaver beat Roddy Piper, Ray Stevens & Greg Valentine
Jimmy Snuka beat Cy Jernigan
Bruno Sammartino, Jr. beat Gene Lewis
Kurt Von Hess beat Abe Jacobs

4/11/81: Spartanburg, SC @ Memorial Auditorium
Paul Jones & Masked Superstar beat Jimmy Snuka & Greg Valentine
George Wells beat Gene Lewis
Johnny Weaver beat Ricky Harris
Abe Jacobs beat Ricky Ferrara
Ron Ritchie beat Jim Nelson

4/11/81: Charlotte, NC @ Coliseum
Paul Jones & Masked Superstar beat Ray Stevens & Greg Valentine
Ricky Steamboat beat Jimmy Snuka
Ric Flair & Tony Atlas beat Gene Anderson & Ole Anderson by DQ
Johnny Weaver beat Swede Hanson
George Wells beat Kurt Von Hess
Tony Tosi beat Charlie Fulton

4/11/81: Cincinnati, OH @ Gardens
Steve Muslin beat Mike Fever(9:59) via pinfall
Mr. Fuji & Tenryu beat Bruno Sammartino, Jr. & Frank Monte(17:34)
Dewey Robertson beat Bobby Duncum(18:41) via pinfall
Blackjack Mulligan beat Iron Sheik(8:15) in a Texas Street fight
Roddy Piper beat Sweet Ebony Diamond(11:40) via pinfall

4/12/81: Asheville, NC @ Civic Center
Blackjack Mulligan beat Iron Sheik in a Texas street fight
Gene Anderson & Ole Anderson vs. Blackjack Mulligan & Tony Atlas
Ricky Steamboat beat Ray Stevens
Sweet Ebony Diamond draw Greg Valentine
Bobby Duncum beat Dewey Robertson
Frank Monte vs. Ben Alexander
Jim Nelson vs. Steve Muslin

4/12/81: Toronto, Ontario @ Maple Leaf Gardens
John Bonello draw Charlie Fulton(15:00)
Tony Parisi beat Tim Gerrard(11:49)
Mr. Fuji & Swede Hanson beat Bruno Sammartino, Jr. & Bob Marcus(17:21)
Jimmy Snuka beat George Wells(18:05) via pinfall
Angelo Mosca DCO with Harley Race(12:13)
Ric Flair beat Roddy Piper(21:16) by DQ

4/13/81: Brantford, Ontario(TV)
Roddy Piper & Jimmy Snuka beat Ric Flair & Angelo Mosca by DQ
Mr. Fuji & Swede Hanson beat Bruno Sammartino, Jr. & John Bonello
Joe Marcus & Bob Marcus beat Tim Gerard & Charlie Fulton
Ric Flair & Angelo Mosca beat Frankie Lane & Charlie Fulton
George Wells & Tony Parisi beat Jimmy Snuka & Tim Gerard
Mr. Fuji & Swede Hanson beat Joe & Bob Marcus
Jimmy Snuka beat John Bonello
Roddy Piper beat Tim Gerard
Tony Parisi & Bruno Sammartino, Jr. beat Frankie Lane & Tim Gerard

Jimmy Snuka beat Tim Gerard

4/13/81: Greenville, SC @ Memorial Auditorium
Blackjack Mulligan & Tony Atlas beat Gene Anderson & Ole Anderson by DQ
Gene Anderson & Ole Anderson beat Paul Jones & Masked Superstar by DQ
Ron Ritchie beat Gene Lewis
Jim Nelson beat Toni Tosi
Kurt Von Hess beat Frank Monte

4/14/81: Columbia, SC @ Township Auditorium
Paul Jones & Masked Superstar double DQ Gene Anderson & Ole Anderson
Tommy Rich beat Bobby Duncum
Jim Duggan beat Ron Ritchie
Roberto Soto beat Ricky Harris
Toni Tosi beat Frank Monte

4/14/81: Kingston, Ontario
Roddy Piper beat Ric Flair
Angelo Mosca double DQ Jimmy Snuka
George Wells & Bruno Sammartino, Jr.(sub for Don Kernodle) beat Swede anson & Mr. Fuji
Bruno Sammartino, Jr. draw Frankie Laine
Tony Parisi beat Charlie Fulton

4/14/81: Raleigh, NC @ Dorton Arena
Blackjack Mulligan beat Iron Sheik
Greg Valentine draw Sweet Ebony Diamond
Cy Jernigan beat Jim Nelson
Gene Lewis beat Mike Fever
Johnny Weaver & Dewey Robertson beat Tenryu & Kurt Von Hess

4/15/81: Raleigh, NC @ WRAL Studios (TV)
Jimmy Snuka beat Frank Monte
Charlie Fulton beat Bruno Sammartino, Jr.
Mr. Wrestling II beat Ricky Harris
Mr. Fuji beat Steve Muslin
Gene Anderson & Ole Anderson beat Mike Fever & Ron Ritchie
Ivan Koloff beat Steve Muslin
Mr. Wrestling II beat Gene Lewis
Ron Ritchie beat Charlie Fulton
Masked Superstar & Paul Jones beat Jim Nelson & Ricky Harris
Bobby Duncum beat Dewey Robertson

4/16/81: Norfolk VA @ Scope
Gene Anderson & Ole Anderson beat Masked Superstar & Paul Jones by DQ
Sweet Ebony Diamond draw Greg Valentine
Blackjack Mulligan beat Iron Sheik in a Texas street fight match
Ivan Koloff beat Ricky Steamboat to win NWA Mid Atlantic Title
Tommy Rich beat Mr. Fuji
Tenryu beat Frank Monte
Steve Muslin beat Gene Lewis

4/17/81: Charleston, SC @ County Hall
Masked Superstar & Paul Jones beat Bobby Duncum & Greg Valentine
George Wells beat Jim Nelson
Kurt Von Hess beat Ron Ritchie
Frank Monte beat Charlie Fulton
Dewey Robertson beat Iron Sheik

4/17/81: Richmond, VA @ Coliseum
Roddy Piper beat Sweet Ebony Diamond
Cy Jernigan beat Gene Lewis
Tenryu beat Steve Muslin
Mr. Fuji beat Johnny Weaver
Ric Flair beat Jimmy Snuka
Ivan Koloff beat Ricky Steamboat
Gene Anderson & Ole Anderson double DQ Blackjack Mulligan, Sr. & Blackjack Mulligan, Jr.

4/18/81: Hampton, VA @ Coliseum
Ricky Steamboat beat Jimmy Snuka by DQ
Roddy Piper beat Masked Superstar
Paul Jones beat Bobby Duncum
Gene Lewis beat Steve Muslin
Cy Jernigan beat Charlie Fulton
Mr. Fuji & Tenryu beat George Wells & Johnny Weaver

4/18/81: Greensboro, NC @ Coliseum
Gene Anderson & Ole Anderson beat Blackjack Mulligan, Sr. & Blackjack Mulligan, Jr. by DQ
Ric Flair beat Ivan Koloff
Greg Valentine draw Sweet Ebony Diamond
Swede Hanson beat Dewey Robertson
Frank Monte beat Kurt Von Hess
Ron Ritchie beat Jim Nelson
Tony Tosi beat Ricky Harris

4/19/81: Kingsport, TN
Roddy Piper beat Ric Flair by DQ
Blackjack Mulligan beat Iron Sheik in a Texas street fight match
Masked Superstar beat Ray Stevens

4/19/81: Roanoke, VA @ Civic Center
Ric Flair beat Ivan Koloff
Blackjack Mulligan beat Iron Sheik in a Texas street fight match
Ricky Steamboat beat Jimmy Snuka in a no DQ match
Frank Monte beat Kurt Von Hess
Swede Hanson beat Steve Muslin
George Wells & Tony Tosi beat Charlie Fulton & Ricky Harris

4/20/81: Greenville, SC @ Memorial Auditorium
Paul Jones & Masked Superstar beat Greg Valentine & Jimmy Snuka
Andre The Giant beat Roddy Piper by DQ
George Wells beat Gene Lewis
Dewey Robertson beat Jim Nelson
Ron Ritchie beat Kurt Von Hess

4/21/81: Durham, NC @ High School
Gene Anderson & Ole Anderson vs. Masked Superstar & Paul Jones
Ivan Koloff vs. Ricky Steamboat
Gene Lewis vs. Tony Tosi
Swede Hanson vs. Abe Jacobs
Kurt Von Hess vs. Frank Monte

4/21/81: Columbia, SC @ Township Auditorium

4/22/81: Raleigh, NC @ WRAL Studios (TV)
Sweet Ebony Diamond draw Greg Valentine in tournament final for NWA World Television Title
Dewey Robertson beat Charlie Fulton
Ric Flair beat Kurt Von Hess
Mr. Fuji beat Frank Monte
Ivan Koloff beat Steve Muslin
Ricky Steamboat beat Kurt Von Hess
Greg Valentine beat Frank Monte
Gene Lewis beat Steve Muslin
Ivan Koloff beat Mike Fever
Gene Anderson & Ole Anderson beat Dewey Robertson & George Wells by forfeit

4/23/81: Harrisonburg, VA @ High School
Andre The Giant & Sweet Ebony Diamond beat Jimmy Snuka & Bobby Duncum
Cy Jernigan beat Charlie Fulton
Tenryu beat Steve Muslin
Mr. Fuji beat Dewey Robertson

4/24/81: Charleston, SC @ County Hall
Blackjack Mulligan vs. Iron Sheik in a Texas street fight match
Ricky Steamboat vs. Ivan Koloff
Kurt Von Hess vs. Bruno Sammartino, Jr.
Ricky Harris vs. Ron Ritchie
Abe Jacobs vs. Ricky Ferrara

4/24/81: Lynchburg, VA @ City Armory
Andre The Giant beat Roddy Piper via pinfall
Sweet Ebony Diamond beat Bobby Duncum
Mr. Fuji & Tenryu vs. Dewey Robertson & Steve Muslin

4/25/81: Spartanburg, SC @ Memorial Auditorium
Andre The Giant & Ricky Steamboat beat Gene Anderson & Ole Anderson by DQ
Sweet Ebony Diamond beat Greg Valentine
Dewey Robertson beat Mr. Fuji
Ron Ritchie beat Swede Hanson
Charlie Fulton beat Mike Fever by DQ

4/25/81: Charlotte, NC @ Coliseum
Ric Flair beat Ivan Koloff
Andre The Giant beat Roddy Piper by DQ
Blackjack Mulligan, Sr. & Blackjack Mulligan, Jr. beat Gene Anderson & Ole Anderson
Mr. Fuji beat George Wells
Steve Muslin beat Ricky Harris
Gene Lewis beat Mike Fever
Frank Monte beat Jim Nelson

4/26/81: Johnston City, TN
Andre The Giant beat Roddy Piper
Blackjack Mulligan, Sr. beat Iron Sheik in a Texas death match
Steve Muslin beat Mr. Fuji
Blackjack Mulligan, Jr. & George Wells vs. Tenryu & Jim Nelson
Bruno Sammartino, Jr. vs. Ricky Harris
Gene Lewis vs. Ron Ritchie

4/26/81: Asheville, NC @ Civic Center
Blackjack Mulligan, Sr. beat Iron Sheik
Ivan Koloff beat Ricky Steamboat
Andre The Giant & Paul Jones beat Roddy Piper & Greg Valentine
Sweet Ebony Diamond beat Kurt Von Hess
Dewey Robertson beat Ricky Harris
Swede Hanson beat Abe Jacobs

4/26/81: Savannah, GA @ Civic Center
Paul Jones & Masked Superstar vs. Jimmy Snuka & Mr. Fuji
Sweet Ebony Diamond vs. Greg Valentine
Ricky Steamboat vs. Ivan Koloff
Frank Monte vs. Charlie Fulton
Ricky Ferrara vs. Steve Muslin

4/27/81: Greenville, SC @ Memorial Auditorium
Ricky Steamboat beat Ivan Koloff by DQ
Ric Flair beat Jimmy Snuka
Blackjack Mulligan, Sr. & Blackjack Mulligan, Jr. beat Gene Anderson & Ole Anderson
George Wells beat Charlie Fulton
Jimmy Valiant beat Steve Muslin

4/28/81: Lexington, NC
Masked Superstar vs. Roddy Piper
Greg Valentine vs. Sweet Ebony Diamond

4/28/81: Columbia, SC @ Township Auditorium
Masked Superstar & Paul Jones beat Gene Anderson & Ole Anderson in a no DQ, no time limit match
Greg Valentine beat Sweet Ebony Diamond
Tommy Rich beat Mr. Fuji
Gene Anderson beat Steve Muslin
Ron Ritchie beat Charlie Fulton

4/28/81: Raleigh, NC @ Dorton Arena
Ricky Steamboat beat Roddy Piper by DQ
Ric Flair beat Jimmy Snuka
Ivan Koloff beat Dewey Robertson
Mike Fever beat Ricky Ferrara
Johnny Weaver & George Wells beat Gene Lewis & Jim Nelson

4/29/81: Raleigh, NC @ WRAL Studios (TV)
Sweet Ebony Diamond beat Ray Stevens
Ivan Koloff beat Bruno Sammartino, Jr.
George Wells beat Iron Sheik
Bobby Duncum beat Johnny Weaver
Blackjack Mulligan beat Swede Hanson
Jimmy Snuka beat Don Kernodle
Greg Valentine beat Dewey Robertson

Sweet Ebony Diamond beat Ivan Koloff
George Wells vs. Bobby Duncum
Blackjack Mulligan vs. Jimmy Snuka
Greg Valentine gets a bye
Sweet Ebony Diamond beat Greg Valentine to win vacant NWA Mid Atlantic television Title in tournament final
Ivan Koloff beat Frank Monte
Masked Superstar & Paul Jones beat Jim Nelson & Gene Lewis
Roddy Piper beat Steve Muslin
Charlie Fulton beat Ricky Ferrara
Ivan Koloff beat Tony Russo
Gene Anderson & Ole Anderson beat Ron Ritchie & Mike Fever

4/30/81: Norfolk, VA @ Scope
Gene Anderson & Ole Anderson double DQ Blackjack Mulligan, Sr. & Blackjack Mulligan, Jr.
Dusty Rhodes beat Roddy Piper by DQ
Ric Flair beat Jimmy Snuka
Ivan Koloff beat Ricky Steamboat
Angelo Mosca beat George Wells
Jimmy Valiant beat Dewey Robertson
Ron Ritchie beat Charlie Fulton

4/30/81: Sumter, SC @ Exposition Center
Ricky Steamboat & Ric Flair beat Gene Anderson & Ole Anderson by DQ
Masked Superstar beat Greg Valentine
Johnny Weaver beat Swede Hanson
Abe Jacobs beat Ricky Ferrara
Tony Tosi beat Jim Nelson

NWA Championship Wrestling Promotion(Mulligan/Flair) started in May 1981:, and stopped running in 1982. Mid Atlantic Championship Wrestling then resumed hosting Knoxville cards.

5/1/81: Richmond, VA @ Coliseum
Gene Anderson & Ole Anderson beat Masked Superstar & Paul Jones to win NWA World Tag Title
Dusty Rhodes beat Ivan Koloff by DQ
Sweet Ebony Diamond beat Greg Valentine by DQ
Ric Flair beat Angelo Mosca
Dewey Robertson beat Swede Hanson
Doug Sommers beat Frank Monte
Charlie Fulton beat Mike Fever

5/1/81: Winston-Salem, NC
Roddy Piper vs. Iron Sheik
Jimmy Snuka vs. Ricky Steamboat
Mr. Fuji & Tenryu vs. George Wells & Dewey Robertson
Fabulous Moolah & Terry Shane vs. Jill Fontaine & Angie Minelli
Jimmy Valiant vs. Johnny Weaver
Gene Lewis vs. Ricky Ferrara

5/2/81: Spartanburg, SC @ Memorial Auditorium
Sweet Ebony Diamond beat Greg Valentine
Paul Jones won an 8-man battle royal
Paul Jones beat Doug Sommers
Johnny Weaver beat Ricky Ferrara
Dewey Robertson beat Charlie Fulton

5/2/81: Roanoke, VA
Blackjack Mulligan, Sr. beat Angelo Mosca in a lights out match
Masked Superstar beat Jimmy Snuka
Roddy Piper double DQ Blackjack Milligan, Jr.
Fabulous Moolah & Brenda Van Hoffman beat Jill Fontaine & Angie Minelli
Swede Hanson beat Steve Muslin
Keith Larson draw Tony Russo

5/2/81: Charlotte, NC @ Coliseum
Ricky Steamboat beat Ivan Koloff by DQ
Ric Flair beat Jimmy Snuka
Gene Anderson & Ole Anderson beat Blackjack Mulligan, Sr. & Blackjack Mulligan, Jr.
George Wells beat Charlie Fulton
Jimmy Valiant beat Steve Muslin

5/3/81: Savannah, GA @ Civic Center
Paul Jones & Masked Superstar vs. The Assassins
Ricky Steamboat vs. Greg Valentine

5/3/81: Toronto, Ontario @ Maple Leaf Gardens
Angelo Mosca beat Jimmy Snuka
Roddy Piper beat Ric Flair
Dewey Robertson beat Swede Hanson
Tony Parisi & George Wells beat Ray Stevens & Kurt Von Hess
Bruno Sammartino, Jr. beat Ricky Harris
Billy Red Lyons draw Frankie Laine

5/4/81: Greenville, SC @ Memorial Auditorium
Paul Jones & Masked Superstar beat Gene Anderson & Ole Anderson
Sweet Ebony Diamond DCO with Greg Valentine
Mr. Wrestling II beat Tenryu
Jimmy Valiant beat Ron Ritchie
Mike Davis beat Ricky Ferrara

5/4/81: Brantford, Ontario(TV)
Ric Flair & Dewey Robertson beat Roddy Piper & Jimmy Snuka in a no DQ match
Ric Flair & Tony Parisi beat Jimmy Snuka & Ricky Harris
Roddy Piper & Ray Stevens beat Earl Pinnock & John Bonello
Roddy Piper beat John Bonello
Ray Stevens beat John Bonello
Ray Stevens beat Ricky Johnson
Dewey Robertson & George Wells beat Tim Gerard & Swede Hanson
Dewey Robertson & George Wells beat Ricky Harris & Chris Jones
Tony Parisi & Bruno Sammartino, Jr. beat Ricky Harris & Frankie Lane
Bruno Sammartino, Jr. beat Chris Jones
Kurt Von Hess beat Earl Pinnock

5/5/81: Ottawa, Ontario @ Civic Centre
Angelo Mosca beat Jimmy Snuka
Roddy Piper double DQ Ric Flair
Dewey Robertson & George Wells beat Ray Stevens & Kurt Von Hess
Billy Red Lyons beat Swede Hanson by DQ
Tony Parisi beat Ricky Harris
Bruno Sammartino, Jr. draw with Frankie Lane

5/5/81: Raleigh, NC @ Dorton Arena
Ivan Koloff beat Ricky Steamboat
Sweet Ebony Diamond beat Greg Valentine by DQ
Scott McGhee beat Jim Nelson
Mr. Wrestling II beat Tenryu
Johnny Weaver & Frank Monte beat Charlie Fulton & Ken Timbs

5/5/81: Columbia, SC @ Township Auditorium
Masked Superstar & Paul Jones beat Gene Anderson & Ole Anderson in a Texas tornado match
Tommy Rich beat Iron Sheik
Jimmy Valiant beat Ron Ritchie
Gene Lewis beat Mike Fever
Mike Davis beat Ricky Ferrara

5/6/81: Kingston, Ontario
Angelo Mosca & Dewey Robertson beat Jimmy Snuka & Ray Stevens
Tony Parisi beat Swede Hanson by DQ
Bruno Sammartino, Jr. DCO with Kurt Von Hess
George Wells beat Ricky Harris
Billy Red Lyons draw Frankie Lane

5/6/81: Raleigh, NC @ WRAL Studios (TV)
Ivan Koloff beat Mike Fever
Scott McGhee beat Ken Timbs
Sweet Ebony Diamond beat Tenryu
Mr. Wrestling II beat Jim Nelson
Gene Anderson & Ole Anderson beat Mike Davis & Tony Russo
Mr. Wrestling II beat Ken Timbs
Mike Davis beat Tony Russo
Paul Jones beat Jim Nelson
Greg Valentine beat Mike Fever
Ric Flair beat Tenryu

5/7/81: Oshawa, Ontario @ Civic Auditorium
Angelo Mosca & George Wells beat Jimmy Snuka & Ray Stevens
Dewey Robertson beat Kurt Von Hess
Billy Red Lyons beat Swede Hanson by DQ
Tony Parisi beat Ricky Harris
Bruno Sammartino, Jr. draw with Frankie Lane

5/7/81: Sumter, SC @ Exposition Center
Dusty Rhodes vs. ??
Mr. Wrestling II vs. The Assassin
Masked Superstar & Paul Jones vs. Gene Anderson & Ole Anderson

5/8/81: Lynchburg, VA @ City Armory
Ricky Ferrara beat Mike Fever
Cy Jernigan beat Frank Monte
Ron Ritchie beat Gene Lewis
Masked Superstar won a battle royal
Sweet Ebony Diamond beat Greg Valentine by DQ

5/8/81: Charleston, SC @ County Hall
Ric Flair beat Jimmy Snuka
Ivan Koloff beat Ricky Steamboat
Johnny Weaver & Dewey Robertson beat Tenryu & Jim Nelson
Scott McGhee beat Jim Nelson
Ron Ritchie beat Tony Tosi

5/8/81: Wilmington, NC @ Legion Stadium
Wahoo McDaniel vs. Assassin #1
Ole Anderson & Gene Anderson vs. Dusty Rhodes & Paul Jones
Mr. Wrestling II vs. Mr. Fuji

5/9/81: Knoxville, TN @ WBIR Studios (TV)
Iron Sheik beat Cowboy Young
Blackjack Mulligan, Jr. & Johnny Weaver beat Rick Connors & J.T. Jaggers
Mongolian Stomper beat Randy Miller
Super Destroyer I & Super Destroyer II beat Tim Horner & Kenny Hall
Blackjack Mulligan, Sr. beat Tony Peters

5/9/81: Spartanburg, SC @ Memorial Auditorium
Ivan Koloff double DQ Wahoo McDaniel
Ric Flair beat Greg Valentine by DQ
Jimmy Snuka beat Sweet Ebony Diamond
George Wells beat Tenryu
Dewey Robertson beat Gene Lewis
Mike Davis beat Ricky Ferrara

5/9/81: Greensboro, NC @ Coliseum
Wahoo McDaniel & Paul Jones beat Gene Anderson & Ole Anderson
Dusty Rhodes beat Ivan Koloff by DQ
Austin Idol beat Ricky Steamboat
Mr. Wrestling II beat Swede Hanson
Jimmy Valiant beat Ron Ritchie
Frank Monte beat Ken Timbs
Scott McGhee beat Charlie Fulton

5/10/81: Hampton, VA @ Coliseum
Dusty Rhodes & Paul Jones beat Gene Anderson & Ole Anderson
Ivan Koloff beat Wahoo McDaniel
Sweet Ebony Diamond beat Greg Valentine
Austin Idol beat Frank Monte
George Wells beat Ken Timbs
Ron Ritchie beat Ricky Harris
Gene Lewis beat Mike Fever

5/10/81: Asheville, NC @ Civic Center
Dusty Rhodes & Paul Jones beat Gene & Ole Anderson
Wahoo McDaniel beat Ivan Koloff
Sweet Ebony Diamond beat Greg Valentine
Austin Idol beat Johnny Weaver
Dewey Robertson beat Charlie Fulton
Jimmy Valiant beat Mike Davis
Scott McGhee beat Ricky Ferrara

5/10/81: Roanoke, VA @ Civic Center
Blackjack Mulligan won battle royal
Les Thornton double DQ Mr. Wrestling II
Blackjack Mulligan, Jr. double DQ Iron Sheik
Ricky Steamboat beat Jimmy Snuka
Masked Superstar beat Tenryu
Mr. Wrestling II beat Keith Larson
Keith Larson draw Tony Russo

5/11/81: Fayetteville, NC @ Cumberland County Memorial Auditorium
Ivan Koloff vs. Paul Jones
Ric Flair vs. Jimmy Snuka
George Wells vs. Gene Lewis
Fabulous Moolah vs. Jill Fontaine

5/11/81: Greenville, SC @ Memorial Auditorium
Gene Anderson & Ole Anderson beat Mr. Wrestling II & Masked Superstar
Roddy Piper beat Ricky Steamboat
Jimmy Valiant beat Frank Monte
Mike Reed draw Mike Fever
Scott McGhee beat Ricky Harris

5/11/81: Taylorsville NC @ Alexander H.S.
Sweet Ebony Diamond vs. Greg Valentine
Johnny Weaver & Dewey Robertson beat Mr. Fuji & Tenryu to win NWA Mid Atlantic Tag Title
Mike Davis vs. Ricky Ferrara
Jim Nelson vs. Tony Tosi
Suzette Ferreira vs. Angie Minelli

5/12/81: Raleigh, NC @ Dorton Arena
Roddy Piper beat Masked Superstar
Greg Valentine beat Sweet Ebony Diamond to win NWA Mid Atlantic Television Title
Paul Jones beat Gene Anderson
Mr. Fuji beat Ron Ritchie
Mike Davis & Scott McGhee beat Charlie Fulton & Ken Timbs

5/12/81: Columbia, SC @ Township Auditorium
Ivan Koloff beat Mr. Wrestling II by DQ
Ric Flair beat Jimmy Snuka
Jimmy Valiant beat Johnny Weaver
Frank Monte beat Ricky Harris
Dewey Robertson & George Wells beat Gene Lewis & Tenryu

5/13/81: Raleigh, NC @ WRAL Studios (TV)
Ricky Steamboat beat Jim Nelson
Roddy Piper beat Frank Monte
Scott McGhee beat Ricky Ferrara
Mr. Wrestling II & Masked Superstar beat Tenryu & Gene Lewis
Ivan Koloff beat Frank Monte
George Wells beat Gene Lewis
Ricky Steamboat beat Tenryu
Gene Anderson & Ole Anderson beat Johnny Reed & Mike Davis

5/14/81: Harrisonburg, VA @ High School
Jim Nelson vs. Abe Jacobs
Keith Larson vs. Tony Russo
Tim Horner draw Tony Anthony
Blackjack Mulligan, Jr. beat Super Destroyer I
Les Thornton beat Super Destroyer II
Blackjack Mulligan, Sr. beat Iron Sheik

5/14/81: Matthews, VA @ High School
Ivan Koloff vs. Paul Jones
Ric Flair vs. Jimmy Snuka
Jimmy Valiant vs. Ron Ritchie
Dewey Robertson & George Wells vs. Swede Hanson & Gene Lewis
Cy Jernigan vs. Charlie Fulton

5/15/81: Richmond, VA @ Coliseum

5/15/81: Charleston, SC @ County Hall
Paul Jones beat Ivan Koloff by DQ
Mr. Wrestling II beat Gene Anderson
George Wells beat Tenryu
Jimmy Valiant beat Frank Monte
Ron Ritchie beat Gene Lewis
Ricky Ferrara beat Mike Fever

5/16/81: Knoxville, TN @ WBIR Studios (TV)
Les Thornton beat Tim Horner
Ric Flair beat J.T. Jaggers
Blackjack Mulligan, Jr. beat Tony Anthony
Super Destroyer I & Super Destroyer II beat Cowboy Young & Johnny Meadows
Iron Sheik beat Danny Collins

5/16/81: Cincinnati, OH @ Gardens
Jimmy Valiant won a 10-man battle royal
Ivan Koloff beat Ricky Steamboat via pinfall
Sweet Ebony Diamond beat Greg Valentine via pinfall
Tommy Rich beat Jimmy Valiant by DQ
Ron Ritchie beat Ricky Harris
Scott McGhee beat Ricky Ferrara
Frank Monte beat Charlie Fulton

5/16/81: Spartanburg, SC @ Memorial Auditorium
Paul Jones beat Roddy Piper by DQ
Mr. Wrestling II beat Gene Anderson
Dewey Robertson beat Ken Timbs
George Wells beat Mike Reed
Johnny Weaver & George Wells beat Tenryu & Mr. Fuji by DQ
Mike Davis beat Gene Lewis

5/16/81: Charlotte, NC @ Coliseum
Wahoo McDaniel & Paul Jones beat Gene Anderson & Ole Anderson
Roddy Piper beat Masked Superstar by DQ
Ric Flair beat Ken Patera
Austin Idol beat Johnny Weaver
Mr. Wrestling II beat Swede Hanson
Dewey Robertson beat Gene Lewis
Mike Davis beat Ken Timbs

5/17/81: Wilmington, NC @ Legion Stadium
Gene Anderson & Ole Anderson vs. Sweet Ebony Diamond & George Wells
Roddy Piper vs. Dewey Robertson
12-man battle royal
Plus 4 other matches

5/17/81: Savannah, GA @ Civic Center
Paul Jones & Masked Superstar vs. The Assassins in a Texas tornado_match
Ivan Koloff vs. Ricky Steamboat
Jimmy Valiant vs. Johnny Weaver
Mr. Fuji vs. Abe Jacobs
Tenryu vs. Mike Fever

5/18/81: Monterey, VA @ Highland High School
Blackjack Mulligan, Sr. vs. Iron Sheik
Barbi Doll vs. Diamond Lil
Blackjack Mulligan, Jr. vs. Mongolian Stomper
Super Destroyers I(Don Kernodle) & II(Steve Muslin) vs. Terry Taylor & Keith Larson
Tony Peters vs. Tony Russo

5/18/81: Greenville, SC @ Memorial Auditorium
Gene Anderson & Ole Anderson beat Masked Superstar & Mr. Wrestling II
Sweet Ebony Diamond beat Greg Valentine
Jimmy Valiant beat Dewey Robertson
Ken Timbs beat Mike Fever
Ron Ritchie beat Gene Lewis

5/19/81: Durham, NC @ High School
Roddy Piper vs. Paul Jones
Sweet Ebony Diamond vs. Greg Valentine
Mr. Fuji & Ricky Harris vs. Johnny Weaver & George Wells
Mike Davis vs. Ricky Ferrara
Johnny Reed vs. Charlie Fulton

5/19/81: Raleigh, NC @ Dorton Arena
No Wrestling

5/19/81: Columbia, SC @ Township Auditorium
Gene Anderson & Ole Anderson beat Masked Superstar & Tommy Rich
Ivan Koloff beat Mr. Wrestling II in a no DQ Match
Jimmy Valiant beat Dewey Robertson
Scott McGhee beat Ken Timbs
Ron Ritchie beat Jim Nelson

5/19/81: Johnson City, TN
10 Man Battle Royal including Blackjack Mulligan Sr., Mongolian Stomper, lackjack Mulligan, Jr., Terry Taylor, Iron Sheik, Tony Peters, Keith Larson, Tony Russo, Super Destroyer I & Super Destroyer II

5/20/81: Raleigh, NC @ WRAL Studios (TV)
Greg Valentine beat Mike Fever
Ric Flair beat Jim Nelson
Austin Idol beat Ron Ritchie
Wahoo McDaniel & Jay Youngblood beat Charlie Fulton & Ken Timbs
Austin Idol beat Scott McGhee
Mr. Wrestling II beat Ken Timbs
Greg Valentine beat Mike Fever
Ivan Koloff beat Ron Ritchie
Wahoo McDaniel & Paul Jones beat Charlie Fulton & Jim Nelson

5/21/81: Norfolk VA @ Scope
Roddy Piper beat Masked Superstar
Sweet Ebony Diamond beat Greg Valentine
Gene Anderson & Ole Anderson beat Wahoo McDaniel & Paul Jones
Austin Idol beat Johnny Weaver
Jay Youngblood beat Jim Nelson
Mike Davis beat Ricky Ferrara
Frank Monte beat Ken Timbs

5/21/81: Sumter, SC @ Exposition Center
Ric Flair vs. Ivan Koloff
Mr. Wrestling II vs. Mr. Fuji
Jimmy Valiant vs. Dewey Robertson
George Wells & Scott McGhee vs. Ricky Harris & Charlie Fulton
Ron Ritchie vs. Johnny Reed

5/21/81: Fishersville, VA @ Augusta Expo
Blackjack Mulligan, Sr. beat Iron Sheik
Blackjack Mulligan, Jr. double DQ Mongolian Stomper
Barbi Doll beat Diamond Lil
Keith Larson & Terry Taylor beat Super Destroyer I & Super Destroyer II
Tony Peters draw Tony Russo

5/22/81: Charleston, SC @ County Hall
Sweet Ebony Diamond beat Greg Valentine
Mr. Fuji beat Mr. Wrestling II
Scott McGhee beat Ricky Harris
Jimmy Valiant beat Johnny Weaver
Charlie Fulton beat Mike Davis

5/22/81: Richmond, VA @ Coliseum
Frank Monte beat Ricky Ferrara
Ron Ritchie beat Ken Timbs
Jay Youngblood beat Jim Nelson
Austin Idol beat Dewey Robertson
Ric Flair beat Ivan Koloff by DQ
Masked Superstar & Wahoo McDaniel double DQ Gene Anderson & Ole Anderson

5/23/81: Knoxville, TN @ WBIR Studios (TV)
Blackjack Mulligan, Jr. & Terry Taylor beat Rick Connors & J.T. Jaggers
Mongolian Stomper beat Johnny Meadows
Super Destroyer I & Super Destroyer II beat Cowboy Young & Tony Anthony
Blackjack Mulligan, Sr. beat Ron Hunter & Danny Collins in a handicap match
Iron Sheik beat Randy Miller

5/23/81: Buffalo, NY
Frank Monte beat Charlie Fulton
Abe Jacobs beat John Bonello
Tony Parisi & George Wells beat Swede Hanson & Kurt Von Hess

Jimmy Valiant beat Dewey Robertson
Paul Jones beat Ken Patera by DQ
Rocky Johnson beat Greg Valentine
Jimmy Valiant won a 12-man battle royal

??5/23/81: Charlotte, NC @ Coliseum
Wahoo McDaniel & Jay Youngblood beat Gene Anderson & Ole Anderson by DQ

5/23/81: Greensboro, NC @ Coliseum
Ric Flair beat Roddy Piper(22:00) by countout
Wahoo McDaniel & Jay Youngblood beat Gene Anderson & Ole Anderson by DQ
Ivan Koloff beat Mr. Wrestling II
Austin Idol beat Masked Superstar
Mr. Fuji beat Mike Reed
Mike Davis beat Ricky Harris
Ron Ritchie beat Ken Timbs

5/24/81: Roanoke, VA @ Civic Center
Ric Flair & Wahoo McDaniel beat Ivan Koloff & Iron Sheik
Jay Youngblood beat Mongolian Stomper by countout
Blackjack Mulligan, Sr. & Blackjack Mulligan, Jr. beat Super Destroyer I & Super Destroyer II
Terry Taylor beat Tony Rossi
Tim Horner draw Keith Larsen
Barbi Doll beat Diamond Lil

5/24/81: Hampton, VA @ Coliseum
Paul Jones & Wahoo McDaniel beat Gene Anderson & Ole Anderson by DQ
Ivan Koloff beat Masked Superstar
Ric Flair beat Ken Patera
Jimmy Valiant beat Johnny Weaver
Mike Davis beat Jim Nelson
Scott McGhee beat Ricky Ferrara
Jay Youngblood double DQ Greg Valentine

5/24/81: Toronto, Ontario @ Maple Leaf Gardens
Angelo Mosca beat Roddy Piper by DQ
Ray Stevens beat Dewey Robertson
Mr. Fuji beat George Wells
Bruno Sammartino, Jr. & Tony Parisi beat Swede Hanson & Kurt Von Hess
Charlie Fulton beat Frank Monte
Frankie Lane beat Abe Jacobs
Billy Red Lyons draw Nick DeCarlo

5/25/81: Dundas, Ontario @ Arena(TV)
Bruno Sammartino, Jr. & Tony Parisi beat Charlie Fulton & Tim Gerard
Mr. Fuji beat Abe Jacobs
Dewey Robertson beat Charlie Fulton
John Bonello beat Alex Gerard
Mr. Fuji & Ray Stevens beat Frank Monte & Nick DeCarlo
Bruno Sammartino, Jr. & Tony Parisi beat Kurt Von Hess & Charlie Fulton
Roddy Piper beat Bob Marcus
Mr. Fuji beat Big Mac & Earl Pinnock in a handicap match
George Wells & Dewey Robertson beat Kurt Von Hess & Charlie Fulton
Ray Stevens beat Frank Monte
Roddy Piper beat Abe Jacobs by countout
Ray Stevens beat George Wells(6:36)
Dewey Robertson beat Roddy Piper by DQ

5/25/81: Greenville, SC @ Memorial Auditorium
Paul Jones & Wahoo McDaniel beat Gene Anderson & Ole Anderson by DQ
Johnny Weaver beat Jimmy Valiant
Jay Youngblood beat Ricky Harris
Donna Christianello beat Candi Malloy
Mike Reed beat Ken Timbs

5/25/81: Hillsville, VA @ Woodlawn Intermediate School
Blackjack Mulligan, Sr. vs. Iron Sheik in a Texas death match
Blackjack Mulligan, Jr. vs. Mongolian Stomper
Barbi Doll vs. Diamond Lil
Super Destroyer I & Super Destroyer II vs. Terry Taylor & Keith Larson
Tony Peters vs. Tony Russo

5/26/81: Columbia, SC @ Township Auditorium
Tommy Rich & Mr. Wrestling II beat Gene Anderson & Ole Anderson by DQ
Paul Jones beat Jimmy Valiant
Jay Youngblood beat Ricky Harris
George Wells beat Charlie Fulton
Mike Reed beat Ken Timbs

5/26/81: Raleigh, NC @ Dorton Arena
No Wrestling

5/27/81: Raleigh, NC @ WRAL Studios (TV)

5/28/81: Madison, VA
Blackjack Mulligan, Sr. & Blackjack Mulligan, Jr. vs. Mongolian Stomper & Iron Sheik

5/28/81: Bluefield, WV
Ric Flair & Blackjack Mulligan, Sr. vs. Super Destroyer I & Super Destroyer II

5/28/81: Lexington, NC
Sweet Ebony Diamond vs. Greg Valentine
Masked Superstar vs. Roddy Piper
George Wells & Dewey Robertson vs. Jim Nelson & Ricky Harris
Frank Monte vs. Ricky Ferrara
Ron Ritchie vs. Mike Fever

5/29/81: Charleston, SC @ County Hall
Mr. Wrestling II & Sweet Ebony Diamond beat Greg Valentine & Mr. Fuji
Jill Fontaine & Donna Christianello beat Diana Van Hoffman & Judy Martin
Scott McGhee beat Ricky Ferrara
Mike Davis beat Mike Reed

5/29/81: Knoxville, TN @ Chilhowee Park
Blackjack Mulligan vs. Iron Sheik in a Texas street fight match
Ron Fuller vs. Mongolian Stomper
Ric Flair & Blackjack Mulligan, Jr. vs. Super Destroyer I & Super Destroyer II
Terry Taylor vs. Tim Horner
Barbi Doll vs. Diamond Lil
Tony Russo vs. Keith Larson

5/29/81: Lynchburg, VA @ City Stadium
Roddy Piper vs. Masked Superstar
Gene Anderson & Ole Anderson vs. Paul Jones & Jay Youngblood
Leroy Brown vs. Jim Nelson

5/30/81: Knoxville, TN @ WBIR Studios (TV)
Blackjack Mulligan beat J.T. Jaggers

5/30/81: Greenville, SC @ Memorial Auditorium(Special Saturday Card)
Ric Flair beat Roddy Piper
Ivan Koloff DCO with Mr. Wrestling II
Mike Davis beat Mike Reed
Ron Ritchie beat Ricky Ferrara
Jimmy Valiant beat Johnny Weaver
George Wells & Dewey Robertson beat Charlie Fulton & Ricky Harris

5/30/81: Charlotte, NC @ Coliseum
Wahoo McDaniel & Paul Jones beat Gene Anderson & Ole Anderson by DQ
Sweet Ebony Diamond beat Greg Valentine to win NWA Mid Atlantic Television title in match with Leroy Brown as special referee
Austin Idol beat Masked Superstar
Jay Youngblood beat Mr. Fuji
Frank Monte beat Jim Nelson
Scott McGhee beat Ken Timbs

5/31/81: Savannah, GA @ Civic Center
Mr. Wrestling II won a 10-man battle royal
Ivan Koloff & Roddy Piper vs. Ric Flair & Masked Superstar
Austin Idol vs. Mr. Wrestling II
Jimmy Valiant vs. Dewey Robertson
Mr. Fuji vs. Bad Leroy Brown
Ricky Ferrara vs. Mike Davis
Jimmy Reed vs. Scott McGhee

5/31/81: Asheville, NC @ Civic Center
Ric Flair & Wahoo McDaniel beat Roddy Piper & Ivan Koloff
Paul Jones beat Greg Valentine by DQ
Austin Idol beat Masked Superstar
Jay Youngblood beat Charlie Fulton
Ron Ritchie beat Jim Nelson
Frank Monte beat Ricky Harris

6/1/81: Pulaski, VA @ Calfee Park
Blackjack Mulligan, Sr. vs. Iron Sheik Texas death match
Terry Taylor vs. Mongolian Stomper
Blackjack Mulligan, Jr. & Keith Larsen vs. Super Destroyer I & Super Destroyer II

6/1/81: Fayetteville, NC @ Cumberland County Memorial Auditorium
Wahoo McDaniel & Ric Flair vs. Ivan Koloff & Roddy Piper
Jay Youngblood vs. Charlie Fulton

6/2/81: Columbia, SC @ Township Auditorium
Ric Flair & Jay Youngblood beat Roddy Piper & Gene Anderson
George Wells beat Jimmy Valiant
El Toro beat Ron Ritchie
Charlie Fulton draw Mike Davis
Ron Sexton beat Ricky Harris

6/2/81: Raleigh, NC @ Dorton Arena
Sweet Ebony Diamond beat Greg Valentine with Leroy Brown as special referee
Mr. Wrestling II beat Ivan Koloff
Johnny Weaver & Dewey Robertson beat Bill White & Mr. Fuji
Scott McGhee beat Ricky Ferrara
Frank Monte beat Jim Nelson

6/2/81: Orange, VA
Blackjack Mulligan, Sr. & Blackjack Mulligan, Jr. vs. Mongolian Stomper & Iron Sheik
Super Destroyer II vs. Terry Taylor 2/3 falls match
Super Destroyer I vs. Keith Larson
Tim Horner vs. Tony Russo

6/3/81: Raleigh, NC @ WRAL Studios (TV)

6/4/81: Sumter, SC @ Exposition Center
Ric Flair & Don Kernodle(sub for Masked Superstar) beat Roddy Piper & Ivan Koloff
Don Kernodle beat El Toro
Donna Christianello beat Diana Von Hoffman
Frank Monte beat Jim Nelson
Scott McGhee beat Ken Timbs

6/4/81: Elizabeth City, NC
Gene Anderson & Ole Anderson vs. Paul Jones & Wahoo McDaniel
George Wells vs. Ricky Harris
Ron Sexton vs. Cy Jernigan
Charlie Fulton vs. Ron Ritchie
Ricky Ferrara vs. Mike Davis

6/5/81: Charleston, SC @ County Hall
Masked Superstar & Mr. Wrestling II beat Austin Idol & Jimmy Valiant
George Wells beat Ken Timbs
Ron Sexton draw Abe Jacobs
Scott McGhee beat Ken Timbs
Ricky Ferrara beat Mike Fever

6/5/81: Richmond, VA @ Coliseum
Ric Flair beat Ivan Koloff in a lumberjack match
Jay Youngblood & Leroy Brown beat Gene Anderson & Ole Anderson by DQ

Sweet Ebony Diamond beat Greg Valentine with Leroy Brown as special referee
Mike Davis beat Ricky Harris
Cy Jernigan beat Jim Nelson

6/5/81: Knoxville, TN @ Chilhowee Park
Blackjack Mulligan, Sr. vs. Iron Sheik in an Iranian strap match
Mongolian Stomper beat Blackjack Mulligan, Jr. to win vacant Southern Title in tournament final
Terry Taylor vs. Super Destroyer II
Keith Larson vs. Tony Peters
Tony Russo vs. Tim Horner
Rick Connors vs. Tony Anthony

6/6/81: Greensboro, NC @ Coliseum
Ric Flair beat Roddy Piper
Ivan Koloff beat Paul Jones(22:00) via pinfall
Jay Youngblood beat Gene Anderson
Leroy Brown beat Ole Anderson
Austin Idol beat Ron Ritchie(sub for Masked Superstar)
Ron Ritchie beat Jim Nelson
Frank Monte beat Ricky Harris
Scott McGhee beat Ricky Ferrara

6/6/81: Spartanburg, SC @ Memorial Auditorium
Ric Flair beat Roddy Piper by DQ
Greg Valentine & Jimmy Valiant beat Sweet Ebony Diamond & George Wells
Donna Christianello beat Diane Van Hoffman
Ron Sexton beat Mike Reed
Ken Timbs beat Mike Fever

6/7/81: Savannah, GA @ Civic Center
Ric Flair beat Roddy Piper by countout
Mr. Wrestling II beat Harley Race via pinfall
Jimmy Valiant beat Don Kernodle(sub for Masked Superstar)
Don Kernodle beat Charlie Fulton
Jay Youngblood beat Bill White

6/7/81: Roanoke, VA @ Civic Center
Terry Taylor beat Les Thornton to win NWA World Junior Title
Ivan Koloff double DQ Wahoo McDaniel
Greg Valentine beat Sweet Ebony Diamond
Mongolian Stomper beat Blackjack Mulligan, Jr.
Super Destroyer beat Dennis Brown
Tony Peters & Rick Connors beat Tony Anthony & Keith Larsen
Tim Horner beat Tony Russo

6/7/81: Wilmington, NC @ Legion Stadium
Wahoo McDaniel vs. Ivan Koloff
Gene Anderson & Ole Anderson vs. Tommy Rich & Paul Jones
Greg Valentine vs. Sweet Ebony Diamond

6/8/81: Lumberton, NC @ Recreation Center
Sweet Ebony Diamond & Leroy Brown vs. Greg Valentine & Jimmy Valiant
Jay Youngblood vs. Mr. Fuji
Dewey Robertson vs. Charlie Fulton
Ricky Harris vs. Ron Ritchie
Mike Davis vs. El Toro

6/8/81: Greenville, SC @ Memorial Auditorium
Wahoo McDaniel beat NWA World Champ Harley Race
Mr. Wrestling II & Paul Jones beat Roddy Piper & Ivan Koloff
Jacques Goulet beat Frank Monte
George Wells beat Jim Nelson
Scott McGhee beat Ricky Ferrara

6/9/81: Columbia, SC @ Township Auditorium
Gene Anderson & Ole Anderson no contest with Wahoo McDaniel & Jay Youngblood
Sweet Ebony Diamond beat Jimmy Valiant by DQ
Mr. Fuji beat Dewey Robertson
Don Kernodle beat Mike Fever
Scott McGhee beat Bill White

6/9/81: Raleigh, NC @ Dorton Arena
Paul Jones & Leroy Brown(sub for Ric Flair) beat Harley Race & Roddy Piper
Leroy Brown beat Ivan Koloff
Frank Monte beat El Toro
Tony Tosi beat Charlie Fulton
George Wells beat Ricky Harris

6/9/81: Johnson City, TN
Les Thornton vs. Terry Taylor
Blackjack Mulligan vs. Mongolian Stomper
Michael Hayes & Terry Gordy vs. Johnny Weaver & Ron Ritchie
Super Destroyer II vs. Keith Larson
Tim Horner vs. Tony Russo

6/10/81: Raleigh, NC(TV) @ WRAL Studios
Included Greg Valentine, Leroy Brown, Jay Youngblood, Mr. Wrestling II, Gene Anderson & Johnny Weaver

6/11/81: Fishersville, VA @ Augusta Expo
Blackjack Mulligan, Sr. & Blackjack Mulligan, Jr. vs. Mongolian Stomper & John tudd in a 2 of 3 falls match
Les Thornton vs. Terry Taylor
Tony Peters vs. Tim Horner

6/12/81: Knoxville, TN @ Chilhowee Park
Blackjack Mulligan vs. Iron Sheik in a cage match
Mongolian Stomper vs. Blackjack Mulligan, Jr. 2/3 falls
Terry Taylor beat Les Thornton wins NWA World Jr Title
Super Destroyer II vs. Tim Horner
Keith Larson vs. Rick Connors
Tony Anthony vs. Tony Russo

6/12/81: Richmond, VA @ Coliseum
Wahoo McDaniel & Jay Youngblood beat Gene Anderson & Ole Anderson by DQ
Leroy Brown beat Ivan Koloff
Don Kernodle beat Mike Fever
Cy Jernigan beat Ken Timbs
Jacques Goulet beat Ron Ritchie

6/12/81: Lynchburg, VA @ City Stadium
Roddy Piper beat Paul Jones
Greg Valentine beat George Wells
Johnny Weaver & Dewey Robertson beat Bill White & El Toro
Scott McGhee beat Ricky Ferrara
Mike Davis beat Mike Reed

6/12/81: Charleston, SC @ County Hall
Masked Superstar vs. Jimmy Valiant
Mr. Wrestling II vs. Mr. Fuji
Charlie Fulton vs. Frank Monte
Ricky Harris vs. Abe Jacobs
Jim Nelson vs. ?? McCombs

6/13/81: Spartanburg, SC @ Memorial Auditorium
Ric Flair & Mr. Wrestling II(sub for Masked Superstar) no contest with Harley Race & Ivan Koloff
Sweet Ebony Diamond beat Ricky Harris
Don Kernodle beat Mike Reed
Ron Ritchie beat El Toro
George Wells beat Jim Nelson

6/13/81: Charlotte, NC @ Coliseum
Ric Flair beat Ivan Koloff
Roddy Piper beat NWA World Champ Harley Race DQ
Austin Idol beat Paul Jones
Sweet Ebony Diamond & Mr. Wrestling II(sub for Masked Superstar) beat Jacques Goulet & El Toro
George Wells beat Ricky Harris
Frank Monte beat Ricky Ferrara
Don Kernodle beat Ken Timbs

6/13/81: Norfolk, VA @ Scope
Wahoo McDaniel & Jay Youngblood beat Gene Anderson & Ole Anderson
Leroy Brown beat Greg Valentine
Johnny Weaver beat Jimmy Valiant by DQ
Mr. Fuji beat Dewey Robertson(sub for Mr. Wrestling II)
Scott McGhee beat Bill White
Dewey Robertson beat Charlie Fulton

6/14/81: Asheville, NC @ Civic Center
Wahoo McDaniel & Paul Jones beat Gene Anderson & Ole Anderson
Jay Youngblood beat NWA World Champion Harley Race
Sweet Ebony Diamond beat Greg Valentine
Austin Idol beat Don Kernodle
Charlie Fulton beat Mike Reed
Don Kernodle beat Scott McGhee

6/14/81: Toronto, Ontario @ Maple Leaf Gardens
Angelo Mosca beat Mr. Fuji by DQ
Ric Flair beat Ivan Koloff
Ray Stevens beat Dewey Robertson
Bruno Sammartino, Jr. & Tony Parisi beat Tim Gerard & El Toro
Billy Red Lyons beat Brian Mackney
Nick DeCarlo draw Bob Marcus

6/14/81: Savannah, GA @ Civic Center
NWA World Champion Harley Race vs. Mr. Wrestling II
Sweet Ebony Diamond vs. Greg Valentine
Austin Idol & Jimmy Valiant vs. Johnny Weaver & George Wells
Jacques Goulet vs. Frank Monte
Jim Nelson vs. Ron Ritchie
Mike Davis vs. Ricky Harris

6/15/81: Dundas, Ontario @ Arena(TV)
Tony Parisi & Bruno Sammartino, Jr. beat Tim Gerard & Brian Mackney
Mr. Fuji beat Bob Marcus
Angelo Mosca beat El Toro
Ric Flair & Tony Parisi beat El Toro & Tim Gerard
Ivan Koloff beat John Bonello
Angelo Mosca beat Tim Gerard
Bruno Sammartino, Jr. beat Alex Gerard
Ivan Koloff & Mr. Fuji beat Nick DeCarlo & Bob Marcus
Dewey Robertson beat el Toro
Angelo Mosca & Tony Parisi beat Ivan Koloff & Tim Gerard
Ric Flair & Angelo Mosca beat Ivan Koloff & Mr. Fuji

6/15/81: Greenville, SC @ Memorial Auditorium
Wahoo McDaniel & Jay Youngblood beat Gene Anderson & Ole Anderson by DQ
Austin Idol beat Paul Jones
Scott McGhee beat Bill White
George Wells beat Charlie Fulton
Jacques Goulet beat Ron Ritchie

6/15/81: Fayetteville, NC @ Cumberland County Memorial Auditorium
Sweet Ebony Diamond vs. Greg Valentine in a match with Leroy Brown as special referee
Masked Superstar vs. Jimmy Valiant
Chris Markoff & Nikolai Volkoff vs. Johnny Weaver & Mr. Wrestling II
Don Kernodle vs. Ricky Harris
Ricky Ferrara vs. Frank Monte

6/16/81: Oshawa, Ontario @ Civic Auditorium
Ric Flair & Angelo Mosca draw Ivan Koloff & Mr. Fuji(sub for Ray Stevens)
Bruno Sammartino, Jr. beat El Toro
Tony Parisi beat Bob Marcus
Dewey Robertson beat John Bonello
Billy Red Lyons beat Nick DeCarlo

6/16/81: Raleigh, NC @ Dorton Arena
Wahoo McDaniel & Paul Jones beat Gene Anderson & Ole Anderson
Scott McGhee beat Bill White
Jacques Goulet beat George Wells
Jay Youngblood beat Jim Nelson
Nikolai Volkoff beat Ron Ritchie
Johnny Weaver beat Chris Markoff by DQ

6/17/81: Raleigh, NC @ WRAL Studios (TV)

6/18/81: Harrisonburg, VA @ High School
Ken Timbs beat Tony Russo
The Wolfman beat Keith Larson

Super Destroyer II beat Tony Anthony
Terry Taylor beat Les Thornton
Iron Sheik, Mongolian Stomper & John Studd beat Blackjack Mulligan, Sr., Blackjack Mulligan, Jr. & Ric Flair in an elimination match

6/18/81: Sumter, SC @ Exposition Center @ Sumter County Exhibition Center
Wahoo McDaniel & Jay Youngblood vs. Gene Anderson & Ole Anderson
Austin Idol vs. Paul Jones
Johnny Weaver vs. Ricky Harris
Bill White vs. Ken Timbs
Scott McGhee vs. Ricky Ferrara

6/19/81: Petersburg, VA
Scott McGhee beat Ricky Ferrara
Cy Jernigan beat Charlie Fulton
Jay Youngblood beat Iron Sheik
Johnny Weaver & Dewey Robertson beat Nikolai Volkoff & Chris Markoff by DQ
Ric Flair beat Ivan Koloff

6/19/81: Chesnee, SC @ High School
Gene Anderson & Ole Anderson vs. Paul Jones & Wahoo McDaniel
Austin Idol vs. Masked Superstar
Jim Nelson vs. Don Kernodle
Jacques Goulet vs. Mike Davis
Ricky Harris vs. Larry Miller

6/19/81: Charleston, SC @ County Hall
Mr. Wrestling II beat Mr. Fuji in a Texas death match
Leroy Brown & Sweet Ebony Diamond beat Jimmy Valiant & Greg Valentine
Ron Ritchie beat Bill White
Frank Monte beat El Toro
Terry Latham beat Ken Timbs

6/20/81: Roanoke, VA @ Civic Center
Les Thornton beat Terry Taylor to win NWA World Junior Title
John Studd beat Blackjack Mulligan, Sr.
Blackjack Mulligan, Jr. beat Mongolian Stomper by DQ
The Wolfman beat Tony Anthony
Super Destroyer beat Tim Horner
Rick Connors beat Dennis Brown
Keith Larsen draw Tony Russo

6/20/81: Buffalo, NY
Frankie Laine draw Nick DeCarlo(15:00)
Kurt Von Hess beat John Bonello(11:24) via pinfall
Mr. Fuji beat Ron Ritchie(14:42) via pinfall
Sweet Ebony Diamond beat Iron Sheik(13:10) by DQ
Jimmy Valiant beat Masked Superstar(13:18) via pinfall
Gene Anderson & Ole Anderson beat Paul Jones & Jay Youngblood(21:18) via pinfall

6/20/81: Greensboro, NC @ Coliseum
Ric Flair DCO with Ivan Koloff
Leroy Brown beat Greg Valentine via pinfall
Wahoo McDaniel beat Austin Idol by DQ
Johnny Weaver & Dewey Robertson beat Chris Markoff & Nikolai Volkoff by DQ
Mr. Wrestling II beat El Toro
Mike Davis beat Jacques Goulet
Frank Monte beat Charlie Fulton

6/21/81: Hampton, VA @ Coliseum
Wahoo McDaniel & Ric Flair DDQ Ivan Koloff & Roddy Piper
Jay Youngblood beat Charlie Fulton(sub for Austin Idol)
Chris Markoff & Nikolai Volkoff beat Paul Jones & Masked Superstar
Ron Ritchie beat El Toro
Larry Latham beat Charlie Fulton
Mike Miller beat Ken Timbs

6/21/81: Wilmington, NC @ Legion Stadium
Greg Valentine & Jimmy Valiant vs. Sweet Ebony Diamond & Leroy Brown
Iron Sheik vs. Ricky Steamboat
Mr. Wrestling II vs. Mr. Fuji

6/22/81: Greenville, SC @ Memorial Auditorium
Dusty Rhodes & Wahoo McDaniel beat Gene Anderson & Ole Anderson
Sweet Ebony Diamond beat Jimmy Valiant by DQ
Les Thornton beat Scott McGhee
Mr. Wrestling II beat Mr. Fuji
Dewey Robertson beat Jim Nelson
Ricky Harris draw Mike Miller

6/23/81: Raleigh, NC @ Dorton Arena
Ric Flair & Wahoo McDaniel DCO with Roddy Piper & Ivan Koloff
Terry Latham beat Ricky Ferrara
Tony Tosi draw El Toro
Don Kernodle beat Charlie Fulton
Les Thornton beat Scott McGhee

6/23/81: Columbia, SC @ Township Auditorium
Dusty Rhodes & Jay Youngblood vs. Gene & Ole Anderson
Mr. Wrestling II vs. Mr. Fuji
Johnny Weaver vs. Chris Markoff
Nikolai Volkoff vs. Ron Ritchie
Ricky Harris vs. Frank Monte
Bill White vs. Mike Miller

6/24/81: Raleigh, NC @ WRAL Studios (TV)
Sweet Ebony Diamond beat Greg Valentine in a match with Roddy Piper & Wahoo McDaniel as special res

6/26/81: Charleston, SC @ County Hall
Mr. Wrestling II beat Mr. Fuji in a lumberjack match
Chris Markoff & Nikolai Volkoff beat Johnny Weaver & Paul Jones
Les Thornton beat Scott McGhee
Frank Monte beat El Toro

6/26/81: Richmond, VA @ Coliseum
Dusty Rhodes & Wahoo McDaniel beat Austin Idol & Roddy Piper by DQ
Jay Youngblood beat Gene Anderson
Leroy Brown beat Ole Anderson
Jacques Goulet beat Mike Davis
Don Kernodle beat Jim Nelson
Ricky Ferrara beat Mike Reed

6/26/81: Lynchburg, VA @ City Stadium
Ric Flair beat Ivan Koloff in a lumberjack match
Greg Valentine draw Sweet Ebony Diamond
Ricky Steamboat beat Iron Sheik by DQ
Jimmy Valiant beat Dewey Robertson
Charlie Fulton beat Mike Miller
Terry Latham beat Ken Timbs
Ron Ritchie beat Ricky Harris

6/27/81: Knoxville, TN @ WBIR Studios (TV)
Blackjack Mulligan beat Jay Widener

6/27/81: Spartanburg, SC @ Memorial Auditorium
Ric Flair beat Ivan Koloff in a Texas death match
Chris Markoff & Nikolai Volkoff beat Johnny Weaver & Dewey Robertson
Ron Ritchie beat El Toro
Frank Monte beat Jim Nelson
Mike Davis beat Ricky Ferrara

6/27/81: Cincinnati, OH @ Gardens
Ole & Gene Anderson beat Paul Jones & Jay Youngblood
Masked Superstar beat Iron Sheik by DQ
Leroy Brown & Sweet Ebony Diamond beat Jimmy Valiant & Greg Valentine
Bill White beat Mike Miller
Terry Latham beat Charlie Fulton

6/27/81: Charlotte, NC @ Coliseum
Scott McGhee beat Ricky Harris
Jacques Goulet beat Don Kernodle
Mr. Wrestling II beat Mr. Fuji
Rick Steamboat beat Austin Idol by DQ
Chris Markoff & Nikolai Volkoff beat Johnny Weaver & Dewey Robertson to win NWA Mid Atlantic Tag Title
Ivan Koloff & Roddy Piper beat Ric Flair & Wahoo McDaniel

6/28/81: Toronto, Ontario @ Maple Leaf Gardens
Angelo Mosca beat Mr. Fuji
Ric Flair beat Roddy Piper by DQ
Ray Stevens beat Sweet Ebony Diamond
Billy Red Lyons beat John Bonello
Nick DeCarlo draw The Wolfman
Tony Parisi & David Sammartino beat Frankie Laine & Kurt Von Hess

6/28/81: Savannah, GA @ Civic Center
Les Thornton vs. Scott McGhee
Ivan Koloff vs. Ricky Steamboat
Greg Valentine & Jimmy Valiant vs. Leroy Brown & Mr. Wrestling II

6/29/81: St. Catherines, Ontario
Ric Flair & Angelo Mosca beat Roddy Piper & Mr. Fuji
Ray Stevens beat Tony Parisi by DQ
Sweet Ebony Diamond beat Nick DeCarlo
Bruno Sammartino, Jr. beat Kurt Von Hess
Billy Red Lyons beat Ricky Johnson

6/29/81: Greenville, SC @ Memorial Auditorium
Iron Sheik won a 10-man battle royal
Wahoo McDaniel & Leroy Brown beat Jimmy Valiant & Greg Valentine
Jay Youngblood beat the Iron Sheik
Don Kernodle beat Mike Miller
Ali Bey beat Frank Monte
Paul Jones beat Jacques Goulet
Tony Tosi beat El Toro

6/30/81: Columbia, SC @ Township Auditorium
El Toro draw Frank Monte
Scott McGhee beat Mike Miller
Jacques Goulet beat Mike Davis
Chris Markoff & Nikolai Volkoff beat Johnny Weaver & Dewey Robertson
Jay Youngblood beat Gene Anderson Texas death match

6/30/81: Raleigh, NC @ Dorton Arena
Jimmy Valiant won a 10 man battle royal
Wahoo McDaniel beat Ivan Koloff
Iron Sheik & Jimmy Valiant beat Paul Jones & Mr. Wrestling II
Ali Bey beat Toni Tosi
Don Kernodle beat Ricky Harris
Terry Latham beat Jim Nelson

6/30/81: Oshawa, Ontario @ Civic Auditorium
Roddy Piper & Ray Stevens beat Ric Flair & Tony Parisi by DQ
Mr. Fuji beat Sweet Ebony Diamond
Bruno Sammartino, Jr. beat Tim Gerard
Billy Red Lyons beat Kurt Von Hess
Frankie Lane draw John Bonello

6/30/81: Johnson City, TN
Blackjack Mulligan, Sr., Blackjack Mulligan, Jr. & Steve Muslin vs. John Studd, Don Carson & The Wolfman
Mongolian Stomper vs. Terry Taylor
Rick Connors vs. Tim Horner

7/1/81: Raleigh, NC @ WRAL Studios (TV)

7/2/81: Norfolk, VA @ Scope
Ric Flair beat Ivan Koloff by DQ
Ricky Steamboat beat Austin Idol by DQ
Sweet Ebony Diamond & Leroy Brown beat Ole Anderson & Ernie Ladd
Jacques Goulet beat Frank Monte
Mike Davis beat Mike Miller
Scott McGhee beat Ricky Ferrara

7/2/81: Sumter, SC @ Exposition Center
Wahoo McDaniel & Paul Jones beat Iron Sheik(sub for Roddy Piper) & Greg Valentine
Gene Anderson beat Jay Youngblood
Mr. Wrestling II beat Jimmy Valiant
Don Kernodle beat Jim Nelson
Terry Latham beat El Toro

7/3/81: Charleston, SC @ County Hall
Johnny Weaver & Dewey Robertson vs. Chris Markoff and Nikolai Volkoff
Iron Sheik vs. Mr. Wrestling II
Don Kernodle vs. Ricky Harris
Terry Latham vs. Jim Nelson
Ricky Ferrara vs. Mike Fever

7/3/81: Wilmington, NC @ Legion Stadium
Ric Flair & Sweet Ebony Diamond vs. Ivan Koloff & Greg Valentine
Paul Jones vs. Austin Idol
Plus 4 other matches

7/3/81: Knoxville, TN @ Chilhowee Park
Blackjack Mulligan, Sr. vs. Don Carson
Mongolian Stomper vs. Blackjack Mulligan, Jr. in a no DQ match with Sandy Scott as special referee
Terry Taylor vs. John Studd
Plus 2 other matches

7/4/81: Spartanburg, SC @ Memorial Auditorium
Terry Latham beat Ricky Harris
Mike Davis beat Charles Fulton
Scott McGhee beat Jim Nelson
Iron Sheik beat Dewey Robertson
Jay Youngblood & Johnny Weaver beat Chris Markoff & Nikolai Volkoff

7/4/81: Hampton, VA @ Coliseum
NWA World Champion Dusty Rhodes beat Roddy Piper in a match with Pat O'Connor as special referee
Wahoo McDaniel & Leroy Brown beat Gene Anderson & Ole Anderson
Sweet Ebony Diamond draw Austin Idol
Jimmy Valiant beat Mr. Wrestling II
Mr. Fuji beat Ron Ritchie
Ali Bey draw Frank Monte

7/5/81: Roanoke, VA @ Civic Center
Blackjack Mulligan, Jr. beat Mongolian Stomper by CO
John Studd & Don Carson beat Terry Taylor & Steve Muslin
Rick Connors beat Tim Horner
Abe Jacobs beat Tony Peters
Keith Larsen beat Tony Russo

7/5/81: Greensboro, NC @Coliseum
Roddy Piper beat Wahoo McDaniel
Ric Flair beat Ivan Koloff by DQ in a cage match
Ricky Steamboat beat Austin Idol by DQ
Gene Anderson & Ole Anderson beat Sweet Ebony Diamond & Leroy Brown
Jimmy Valiant beat Dewey Robertson
Ali Bey beat Ron Ritchie
Terry Latham beat Mike Miller

7/5/81: Asheville, NC @ Civic Center
Frank Monte beat Charlie Fulton
Scott McGhee beat Ricky Ferrara
Mr. Fuji beat Don Kernodle
Paul Jones beat Austin Idol by DQ
Ricky Steamboat beat Ivan Koloff
Leroy Brown & Wahoo McDaniel beat Gene Anderson & Ole Anderson
Ric Flair beat Roddy Piper in a lumberjack match

7/6/81: Greenville, SC @ Memorial Auditorium
Terry Latham beat Charlie Fulton
Don Kernodle beat Bill White
Sweet Ebony Diamond & Leroy Brown beat Jimmy Valiant & Greg Valentine
NWA World Champion Dusty Rhodes beat Iron Sheik by DQ
Wahoo McDaniel beat Roddy Piper by DQ

7/6/81: Fayetteville, NC @ Cumberland County Memorial Auditorium
Ric Flair vs. Ivan Koloff in a lumberjack match
Johnny Weaver & Mr. Wrestling II vs. Chris Markoff & Nikolai Volkoff
Jacques Goulet vs. Dewey Robertson
Ali Bey vs. Frank Monte

7/7/81: Columbia, SC @ Township Auditorium
Sweet Ebony Diamond vs. Greg Valentine in a match with Leroy Brown as Special referee
Johnny Weaver & Jay Youngblood vs. Chris Markoff & Nikolai Volkoff
Ali Bey vs. Frank Monte
Charlie Fulton vs. Scott McGhee
Jim Nelson vs. Mike Fever

7/7/81: Raleigh, NC @ Dorton Arena
NWA World Champion Dusty Rhodes beat Jimmy Valiant
Wahoo McDaniel beat Roddy Piper by DQ
Mr. Wrestling II beat Mr. Fuji
Don Kernodle beat Mike Miller
Ron Ritchie beat Bill White

7/8/81: Raleigh, NC @ WRAL Studios (TV)

7/9/81: Fishersville, VA @ Augusta Expo
Blackjack Mulligan, Jr. vs. Don Carson
Blackjack Mulligan, Sr. & Terry Taylor vs. Mongolian Stomper & John Studd
Luke Graham vs. Steve Muslin

7/10/81: Lynchburg, VA @ City Stadium
Ric Flair vs. Ivan Koloff in a lumberjack match
Gene Anderson vs. Jay Youngblood
Mr. Wrestling II vs. Mr. Fuji

7/10/81: Knoxville, TN @ Chilhowee Park
Blackjack Mulligan, Sr. DCO with Don Carson in a Texas street fight match
Blackjack Mulligan, Jr. beat Mongolian Stomper by DQ
John Studd beat Terry Taylor
Luke Graham beat Steve Muslin
Tim Horner beat Tony Russo
Rick Connors & Tony Anthony beat Dennis Brown & Keith Larson

7/10/81: Charleston, SC @ County Hall
Leroy Brown beat Jimmy Valiant
Chris Markoff & Nikolai Volkoff beat Johnny Weaver & Mike Davis(sub for Paul Jones)
Ali Bey beat Tony Tosi
Scott McGhee beat Ricky Ferrara
Ken Timbs beat Ricky Harris

7/10/81: Richmond, VA @ Coliseum
Frank Monte draw Jim Nelson
Cy Jernigan beat El Toro
Sweet Ebony Diamond beat Jacques Goulet
Ricky Steamboat beat Greg Valentine
Roddy Piper beat Wahoo McDaniel
NWA World Champion Dusty Rhodes beat Iron Sheik

7/11/81: Spartanburg, SC @ Memorial Auditorium
NWA World Champion Dusty Rhodes beat Gene Anderson
Leroy Brown beat Iron Sheik
Jay Youngblood beat Mike Miller
Ali Bey beat Ken Timbs
Bill White draw Mike Davis
Ron Ritchie beat Charlie Fulton

7/11/81: Charlotte, NC @ Coliseum
Ric Flair draw Roddy Piper in a Texas street fight match
Gene Anderson & Ole Anderson beat Ricky Steamboat & Leroy Brown
Wahoo McDaniel double DQ Greg Valentine
Mr. Wrestling II beat Mr. Fuji
Dewey Robertson beat Jacques Goulet
Ali Bey beat Ron Ritchie
Terry Latham beat Charlie Fulton
El Toro beat Mike Davis

7/12/81: Toronto, Ontario @ Maple Leaf Gardens
Mr. Fuji beat Angelo Mosca to win Canadian Title in a Texas death match
Ray Stevens & Roddy Piper beat Ric Flair & Tony Parisi
Ivan Koloff beat Jay Youngblood
Johnny Weaver beat El Toro
Frankie Laine beat Don Kernodle
Billy Red Lyons beat Kurt Von Hess
Charlie Fulton beat Goldie Rogers

7/12/81: Savannah, GA @ Civic Center
Mr. Wrestling II & Sweet Ebony Diamond beat Michael Hayes & Buddy Roberts
Chris Markoff & Nikolai Volkoff beat Ron Ritchie & Frank Monte
Leroy Brown beat Jimmy Valiant
Iron Sheik beat Dewey Robertson
Mike Davis beat Jim Nelson

7/13/81: Greenville, SC @ Memorial Auditorium
Ric Flair & Wahoo McDaniel beat Roddy Piper & Ivan Koloff
Dewey Robertson beat Mr. Fuji
Nikolai Volkoff beat Frank Monte
Chris Markoff beat Ron Ritchie
Terry Latham beat Charlie Fulton

7/14/81: Raleigh, NC @ Dorton Arena
Mike Davis beat El Toro
Terry Latham beat Charlie Fulton
Dewey Robertson draw Mr. Fuji
Jimmy Valiant beat Mr. Wrestling II
Wahoo McDaniel & Leroy Brown beat Roddy Piper & Greg Valentine

7/14/81: Columbia, SC @ Township Auditorium
Don Kernodle beat Ricky Harris
Scott McGhee beat Ricky Ferrara
Jacques Goulet beat Ron Ritchie
Sweet Ebony Diamond beat Iron Sheik
Nikolai Volkoff & Chris Markoff beat Jay Youngblood & Johnny Weaver
Ivan Koloff beat Ric Flair by DQ

7/15/81: Raleigh, NC @ WRAL Studios (TV)

7/16/81: Norfolk, VA @ Scope
Ric Flair beat Mr. Fuji(sub for Ivan Koloff) in a lumberjack match
Wahoo McDaniel double DQ Greg Valentine
Leroy Brown beat Ole Anderson
Sweet Ebony Diamond beat Jimmy Valiant
Mr. Fuji beat Don Kernodle
Terry Latham beat Charlie Fulton
Ali Bey beat Ron Ritchie
Scott McGhee beat Bill White

7/17/81: Charleston, SC @ County Hall
Mike Miller beat Mike Reed
Frank Monte beat Ricky Harris
Ali Bey beat Ron Ritchie
Nikolai Volkoff & Chris Markoff beat Johnny Weaver & Jay Youngblood
Mr. Wrestling II beat Mr. Fuji in a cage match

7/17/81: Winston-Salem, NC @ Memorial Coliseum
Gene Anderson & Ole Anderson vs. Terry Gordy & Michael Hayes
Ernie Ladd vs. Leroy Brown
Iron Sheik vs. Paul Jones
Jacques Goulet vs. Dewey Robertson
Bill White vs. Don Kernodle
Charlie Fulton vs. Larry Latham

7/17/81: Knoxville, TN @ Chilhowee Park
Mongolian Stomper beat Blackjack Mulligan, Jr. in a Texas death, cage match
Blackjack Mulligan, Sr. beat Don Carson in a cage match
John Studd & Luke Graham beat Terry Taylor & Sandy Scott
Tim Horner beat Tony Anthony
Tony Peters beat Keith Larson
Rick Connors beat Steve Muslin to win Tennessee Brass Knuckles Title
Tony Russo beat Denny Brown

7/18/81: Spartanburg, SC @ Memorial Auditorium
Paul Jones & Mr. Wrestling II beat Mr. Fuji & Jimmy Valiant
Iron Sheik beat Dewey Robertson
Ali Bey beat Frank Monte
Mike Davis beat Bill White
Terry Latham beat Jim Nelson

7/18/81: Buffalo, NY
Steve Bolus beat Goldie Rogers
The Destroyer draw Billy Red Lyons
Leroy Brown beat Ole Anderson by DQ
Gene Anderson beat Jay Youngblood in a Texas death match
Ric Flair beat Ernie Ladd
Ricky Steamboat beat Greg Valentine in a match with Leroy Brown as special referee

7/18/81: Roanoke, VA @ Civic Center
Blackjack Mulligan, Jr. beat Tony Peters(sub for Mongolian Stomper) in a chain match
Blackjack Mulligan, Sr. beat Don Carson
John Studd & Luke Graham beat Terry Taylor & Sandy Scott by DQ
Steve Muslin & Tim Horner beat Rick Connors & Tony Anthony
Dennis Brown draw Tony Russo

7/19/81: Asheville, NC @ Civic Center
Ricky Steamboat beat Ivan Koloff
Gene Anderson & Ole Anderson beat Ric Flair & Jay Youngblood
Iron Sheik beat Mr. Wrestling II
Jacques Goulet beat Don Kernodle
Scott McGhee beat Mike Miller
Ali Bey beat Frank Monte

7/19/81: Wilmington, NC @ Legion Stadium
Wahoo McDaniel vs. Roddy Piper
Leroy Brown vs. Greg Valentine
Paul Jones vs. Jimmy Valiant

7/20/81: Greenville, SC @ Memorial Auditorium
Ric Flair & Leroy Brown beat Gene Anderson & Jimmy Valiant by DQ
Iron Sheik beat Mr. Wrestling II
Scott McGhee beat Ricky Harris
Jacques Goulet beat Mike Davis
Terry Latham beat El Toro

7/20/81: Fayetteville, NC @ Cumberland County Memorial Auditorium
Wahoo McDaniel vs. Roddy Piper
Johnny Weaver & Jay Youngblood vs. Chris Markoff & Nikolai Volkoff
Sweet Ebony Diamond vs. Mr. Fuji
Ali Bey vs. Ron Ritchie

7/21/81: Raleigh, NC @ Dorton Arena
Ron Ritchie beat Rick Ferrara
Mike Davis beat Jim Nelson
Steve Muslin beat Bill White
Roddy Piper beat Wahoo McDaniel in a no DQ match
Leroy Brown beat Iron Sheik
Jay Youngblood beat Ali Bey

7/21/81: Columbia, SC @ Township Auditorium
Don Kernodle beat Mike Reed
El Toro beat Tony Tosi
Dewey Robertson draw Jacques Goulet
Ric Flair & Ricky Steamboat beat Ivan Koloff & Gene Anderson

7/22/81: Raleigh, NC @ WRAL Studios (TV)

7/22/81: Pulaski VA @ Calfee Park
Blackjack Mulligan, Jr. vs. John Studd
Blackjack Mulligan, Sr. vs. Don Carson
Mongolian Stomper & Luke Graham vs. Terry Taylor & Tim Horner
Keith Larson vs. Rick Connors
Tony Anthony vs. Tony Russo
Abe Jacobs vs. Dennis Brown

7/23/81: Sumter, SC @ Exposition Center
Ivan Koloff beat Ricky Steamboat
Leroy Brown beat Ole Anderson
Gene Anderson beat Mr. Wrestling II
Jacques Goulet beat Frank Monte
Ricky Ferrara beat Mike Reed
Terry Latham beat Charlie Fulton

7/23/81: Harrisonburg, VA @ High School
Tony Russo vs. Dennis Baker
Tony Anthony vs. Keith Larson
Tim Horner vs. Rick Connors
Sandy Scott & Terry Taylor vs. John Studd & Luke Graham
Blackjack Mulligan, Jr. vs. Mongolian Stomper in a Texas bullrope match
Blackjack Mulligan, Sr. vs. Don Carson

7/23/81: Hendersonville, NC
Ric Flair & Wahoo McDaniel beat Greg Valentine & Roddy Piper
Paul Jones beat Jimmy Valiant
Ali Bey draw Ron Ritchie
Scott McGhee beat El Toro
Jim Nelson vs. Mike Miller

7/24/81: Richmond, VA @ Coliseum
Ric Flair & Jay Youngblood vs. Gene & Ole Anderson
Wahoo McDaniel vs. Roddy Piper in a Texas street fight match
Ricky Steamboat vs. Ivan Koloff
Sweet Ebony Diamond vs. Iron Sheik

7/24/81: Knoxville, TN @ Chilhowee Park
John Studd beat Blackjack Mulligan, Jr.
Blackjack Mulligan, Sr. vs. Bruiser Brody
Terry Taylor vs. Kevin Sullivan
Tony Atlas vs. Luke Graham

7/24/81: Charleston, SC @ County Hall
Leroy Brown beat Greg Valentine by DQ
Chris Markoff & Nikolai Volkoff beat Mr. Wrestling II & Johnny Weaver
Dewey Robertson beat Ali Bey
Scott McGhee beat Bill White
Frank Monte beat Jim Nelson

7/25/81: Knoxville, TN @ WBIR Studios (TV)
Blackjack Mulligan, Sr. beat Masked Mr. X
John Studd beat Johnny Meadows & Jay Widener in a handicap match
Jay Strongbow beat Tony Russo
Terry Taylor & Blackjack Mulligan, Jr. beat Tony Anthony & Jimmy Lynn
Crazy Luke Graham beat Denny Brown

7/25/81: Cincinnati, OH @ Gardens
Frank Monte beat Mike Miller
Don Kernodle beat Jim Nelson
Sweet Ebony Diamond beat Mr. Fuji
Iron Sheik beat Mr. Wrestling II
Paul Jones & Johnny Weaver beat Michael Hayes & Terry Gordy
Paul Jones won 12-man battle royal
Ivan Koloff beat Ricky Steamboat

7/25/81: Greensboro, NC @ Coliseum
Gene & Ole Anderson beat Ric Flair & Jay Youngblood
Wahoo McDaniel beat Roddy Piper in an Indian strap match
Leroy Brown & Dewey Robertson beat Jimmy Valiant & Greg Valentine via pinfall

7/26/81: Toronto, Ontario @ Maple Leaf Gardens
Angelo Mosca beat Mr. Fuji(14:19) in a Texas street fight to win Canadian Title
Ric Flair & Andre The Giant beat Roddy Piper & Ray Stevens
Greg Valentine beat Sweet Ebony Diamond via pinfall
Tony Parisi beat Frankie Laine
Billy Red Lyons beat Bob Marcus
Nick DeCarlo beat Goldie Rogers

7/27/81: Greenville, SC @ Memorial Auditorium
Ric Flair beat Gene Anderson by DQ
Leroy Brown & Sweet Ebony Diamond beat Greg Valentine & Jimmy Valiant
Paul Jones beat Iron Sheik by DQ
Ali Bey beat Frank Monte
Don Kernodle beat The Blue Demon

7/28/81: Oshawa, Ontario @ Civic Auditorium
Angelo Mosca double DQ Ray Stevens
Andre The Giant beat Mr. Fuji
Tony Parisi & Billy Red Lyons beat Goldie Rogers & Bob Marcus
Nick DeCarlo beat Tim Gerard
Frankie Laine draw Steve Bolus

7/28/81: Durham, NC @ Durham Athletic Park
Wahoo McDaniel vs. Roddy Piper
Sweet Ebony Diamond vs. Iron Sheik

7/28/81: Columbia, SC @ Township Auditorium
Ivan Koloff beat Ric Flair in a lumberjack match
Ricky Steamboat & Jay Youngblood beat Jimmy Valiant & Gene Anderson
Dewey Robertson beat Jim Nelson
Dewey Robertson beat Mike Reed
Terry Latham beat Bill White

7/29/81: Raleigh, NC @ WRAL Studios (TV)
Wahoo McDaniel, Roddy Piper, Jay Youngblood appeared

Note: 7/29/81: was final television taping on Wednesdays at WRAL in Raleigh, NC. Starting the following Wednesday, the television tapings occurred at WPCQ in Charlotte, NC until 7/6/83 when mobile tapings started.

7/30/81: Norfolk, VA @ Scope
Gene Anderson & Ole Anderson double DQ Ric Flair & Jay Youngblood
Leroy Brown beat Greg Valentine by DQ
Ivan Koloff beat Mr. Wrestling II
Paul Jones beat Mr. Fuji
Terry Latham beat Ricky Ferrara
Don Kernodle beat Ricky Harris

7/31/81: Lynchburg, VA @ City Stadium
Ricky Steamboat & Jay Youngblood beat Ivan Koloff & Gene Anderson by countout
Paul Jones vs. Iron Sheik
Don Kernodle vs. Jacques Goulet
Jim Nelson vs. Cy Jernigan
Scott McGhee vs. Mike Miller

7/31/81: Knoxville, TN @ Chilhowee Park
Blackjack Mulligan, Sr. & Terry Taylor beat Ron Wright & Doug Vines(subs for Luke Graham & Tony Peters)
Blackjack Mulligan, Jr. beat John Studd by countout in a match where NWA Southern Title was held up
Ric Flair beat Tony Anthony
Wayne Farris beat Steve Muslin
Tony Atlas no contest with Kevin Sullivan
Rick Connors beat Doug Vines
Tony Russo beat Izzy Slapowitz
Tim Horner beat Keith Larsen

7/31/81: Charleston, SC @ County Hall
Leroy Brown & Sweet Ebony Diamond beat Greg Valentine & Jimmy Valiant
Charlie Fulton draw Tony Tosi
Frank Monte beat El Toro
Ricky Ferrara beat Mike Reed
Ali Bey beat Steve Muslin

8/1/81: Charlotte, NC @ Coliseum
Ric Flair & Leroy Brown beat Gene Anderson & Ole Anderson by DQ
Ivan Koloff beat Ricky Steamboat
Paul Jones beat Iron Sheik
Jimmy Valiant draw Mr. Wrestling II
Dewey Robertson beat Ali Bey
Jacques Goulet beat Frank Monte
Don Kernodle beat Mike Miller

8/1/81: Harlan, KY
Tim Horner beat Doug Vines
Tony Russo beat Izzy Slapowitz
Rick Connors beat Keith Larsen
Blackjack Mulligan, Sr. & Blackjack Mulligan, Jr. beat Wayne Farris & Tony Anthony
Terry Taylor beat Kevin Sullivan by countout

8/2/81: Hampton, VA @ Coliseum
Ric Flair & Wahoo McDaniel beat Roddy Piper & Gene Anderson
Sweet Ebony Diamond beat Iron Sheik
Jay Youngblood beat Jimmy Valiant
Don Kernodle beat Jim Nelson
Frank Monte beat Ricky Harris
Mike Davis beat Charlie Fulton

8/2/81: Roanoke, VA @ Civic Center
Ric Flair & Wahoo McDaniel beat Roddy Piper & Gene Anderson by DQ
John Studd double DQ Blackjack Mulligan, Jr.
Tony Atlas beat Wayne Farris(sub for Tony Peters)
Kevin Sullivan beat Keith Larsen
Terry Taylor beat Tony Anthony(sub for Luke Graham)
Tim Horner beat Tony Russo

8/3/81: Greenville, SC @ Memorial Auditorium
Ric Flair & Jay Youngblood beat Gene & Ole Anderson by DQ
Wahoo McDaniel vs. Roddy Piper in a no DQ match
Leroy Brown beat Greg Valentine by DQ
Don Kernodle beat Jim Nelson
Terry Latham beat Ricky Ferrara
Ron Ritchie beat Bill White

8/3/81: Fayetteville, NC @ Cumberland County Memorial Auditorium
Roddy Piper vs. Wahoo McDaniel in a no DQ match
Chris Markoff & Nikolai Volkoff vs. Johnny Weaver & Mr. Wrestling II in a Texas tornado match

8/3/81: Hazard, KY
Tim Horner beat Tony Russo
Rick Connors beat Izzy Slapowitz
Wayne Farris beat Keith Larsen
Blackjack Mulligan, Sr. & Blackjack Mulligan, Jr. beat Doug Vines & Tony Anthony
Kevin Sullivan no contest with Terry Taylor

8/4/81: Raleigh, NC @ Dorton Arena
Ric Flair & Sweet Ebony Diamond beat Greg Valentine & Gene Anderson by DQ
Wahoo McDaniel beat Roddy Piper by CO street fight match
Mr. Wrestling II beat Ali Bey
Terry Latham beat El Toro
Steve Muslin beat Mike Miller

8/4/81: Columbia, SC @ Township Auditorium
Mike Davis beat Bill White
Scott McGhee beat Ricky Harris
Don Kernodle beat Jim Nelson
Paul Jones & Leroy Brown beat Iron Sheik & Jacques Goulet
Ivan Koloff beat Ricky Steamboat

8/5/81: Charlotte, NC @ WPCQ Studios (TV)

8/5/81: Sandersville, VA
Tim Horner beat Rick Connors
Tony Russo beat Keith Larsen
Tim Horner & Keith Larsen beat Rick Connors & Tony Russo
Blackjack Mulligan, Sr. & Blackjack Mulligan, Jr. beat Doug Vines &Tony Anthony
Ric Flair beat John Studd by DQ

8/6/81: Sumter, SC @ Exposition Center
Gene Anderson & Ole Anderson vs. Leroy Brown & Sweet Ebony Diamond
Greg Valentine vs. Angelo Mosca
Jacques Goulet vs. Terry Latham
Jim Nelson vs. Steve Muslin
El Toro vs. Mike Davis

8/6/81: Spartanburg, SC @ Memorial Auditorium
Ricky Steamboat beat Ivan Koloff by DQ
Paul Jones & Jay Youngblood beat Ali Bey & Iron Sheik
Charlie Fulton beat Tony Tosi
Scott McGhee beat Ricky Harris
Don Kernodle beat Bill White

8/7/81: Charleston, SC @ County Hall
Mr. Wrestling II, Johnny Weaver & Dewey Robertson beat Nikolai Volkoff, Chris Markoff & Jimmy Valiant
Ali Bey beat Terry Latham
Scott McGhee beat Jim Nelson
Ron Ritchie beat Mike Miller
Ricky Ferrara beat Mike Davis

8/7/81: Richmond, VA @ Coliseum
Mr. Fuji beat Steve Muslin
Jacques Goulet beat Don Kernodle
Ron Bass beat Iron Sheik
Paul Jones beat Greg Valentine by DQ
Wahoo McDaniel beat Roddy Piper Indian strap match
Ricky Steamboat & Leroy Brown beat Gene & Ole Anderson by DQ

8/7/81: Knoxville, TN @ Chilwohee Park
John Studd beat Blackjack Mulligan, Jr.
Blackjack Mulligan beat Chris Canyon(sub for Bruiser Brody) by DQ
Terry Taylor DCO with Kevin Sullivan
Tony Anthony & Wayne Farris beat Tim Horner & Keith Larsen
Rick Connors beat Tony Russo
Chris Canyon beat Denny Brown

8/8/81: Knoxville, TN @ WBIR Studios (TV)
Wayne Farris beat Denny Brown
John Studd beat Keith Larsen
Jay Strongbow beat Jay Widener
Kevin Sullivan beat Kenny Hall
Terry Taylor & Blackjack Mulligan, Jr. beat Doug Vines & Jeff Sword

8/8/81: Greensboro, NC @ Coliseum
Wahoo McDaniel beat Roddy Piper to win NWA United States Title in a no time limit, no DQ match
Ric Flair & Blackjack Mulligan beat Ole & Gene Anderson by DQ
Ivan Koloff beat Ricky Steamboat
Ron Bass beat Iron Sheik
Ron Ritchie beat El Toro
Don Kernodle beat Mike Miller
Steve Muslin beat Charlie Fulton

8/9/81: Asheville, NC @ Civic Center
Ric Flair & Wahoo McDaniel double DQ Gene Anderson & Ole Anderson
Leroy Brown beat Greg Valentine by DQ
Ron Bass beat Iron Sheik
Paul Jones beat Jimmy Valiant
Terry Latham beat El Toro
Scott McGhee beat Ali Bey by referee decision

8/9/81: Dayton, OH @ Convention Center
Ivan Koloff vs. Ricky Steamboat
Roddy Piper vs. Jay Youngblood
Chris Markoff & Nikolai Volkoff vs. Johnny Weaver & Dewey Robertson

8/9/81: Toronto, Ontario @ Maple Leaf Gardens
Angelo Mosca beat Ray Stevens
Andre The Giant beat Roddy Piper
Ivan Koloff beat Ricky Steamboat
Johnny Weaver & Jay Youngblood beat Chris Markoff & Nikolai Volkoff by DQ
Tony Parisi beat Goldie Rogers
Billy Red Lyons beat The Destroyer by DQ
Frankie Laine draw John Bonello

8/10/81: Hamilton, Ontario
Andre The Giant & Angelo Mosca vs. Ivan Koloff & Ray Stevens
Jay Youngblood vs. Mr. Fuji

8/10/81: Covington, VA @ Casey Field
John Studd vs. Blackjack Mulligan, Jr.
Blackjack Mulligan, Sr. vs. Chris Canyon
Wayne Farris & Rick Connors vs. Dennis Brown & Keith Larsen
Izzy Slapowitz vs. Tony Russo

8/10/81: Greenville, SC @ Memorial Auditorium
Ric Flair, Ricky Steamboat & Leroy Brown beat Gene Anderson, Ole Anderson & Greg Valentine
Ron Bass beat The Iron Sheik
Laurent Soucie beat Charlie Fulton
Terry Latham beat Ricky Harris
Ron Ritchie beat El Toro

8/11/81: Pulaski, VA @ Calfee Park
John Studd vs. Blackjack Mulligan, Jr.
Blackjack Mulligan, Sr. vs. Chris Canyon
Terry Taylor vs. Kevin Sullivan

8/11/81: St. Catherine's, Ontario
Jay Youngblood beat Ivan Koloff by DQ
Andre the Giant beat Ray Stevens & The Destroyer in a handicap match
Tony Parisi & Steve Bolus beat Bob & Joe Marcus
Billy Red Lyons draw Frankie Laine
Nick DeCarlo beat Goldie Rogers

8/11/81: Columbia, SC @ Township Auditorium
Wahoo McDaniel beat Roddy Piper
Leroy Brown & Sweet Ebony Diamond beat Chris Markoff & Nikolai Volkoff
Scott McGhee beat Jim Nelson
Charlie Fulton draw Frank Monte
Mike Davis beat El Toro
Ali Bey beat Lawrence Soucie

8/11/81: Raleigh, NC @ Civic Center
Ric Flair & Ricky Steamboat beat Gene Anderson & Ole Anderson by DQ
Paul Jones beat Iron Sheik
Steve Muslin beat Bill White
Don Kernodle beat Ricky Harris
Dewey Robertson beat Jacques Goulet
Johnny Weaver beat Jimmy Valiant

8/12/81: Charlotte, NC @ WPCQ Studios (TV)

8/13/81: Fishersville, VA @ Augusta Expo
Tony Russo beat Izzy Slapowitz
Wayne Farris & Chris Canyon beat Tim Horner & Abe Jacobs
John Studd beat Blackjack Mulligan, Jr.
Blackjack Mulligan, Sr. beat Bruiser Brody in a Texas death match
Terry Taylor double DQ Kevin Sullivan

8/13/81: Spartanburg, SC @ Memorial Auditorium
Roddy Piper vs. Sweet Ebony Diamond
Greg Valentine vs. Jay Youngblood
Chris Markoff & Nikolai Volkoff vs. Johnny Weaver & Mr. Wrestling II
Ricky Harris vs. Dewey Robertson
Ali Bey vs. Terry Latham

8/14/81: Knoxville, TN @ Chilhowee Park
Dick The Bruiser double DQ John Studd
Blackjack Mulligan, Jr. & Terry Taylor beat Kevin Sullivan & Tony Anthony
Blackjack Mulligan, Sr. beat Bruiser Brody in a Texas death match
Wayne Farris beat Dennis Brown
Rick Connors beat Abe Jacobs
Chris Canyon beat Tim Horner
Keith Larson draw Tony Russo

8/14/81: Charleston, SC @ County Hall
Leroy Brown beat Greg Valentine
Iron Sheik beat Ron Bass
Dewey Robertson beat Mr. Fuji
Don Kernodle beat Ricky Harris
Mike Reed beat Charlie Fulton

8/14/81: Lynchburg, VA @ City Stadium
Ricky Steamboat beat Ivan Koloff by DQ
Ric Flair & Paul Jones beat Gene Anderson & Jimmy Valiant by DQ
Jim Nelson beat Cy Jernigan
Jacques Goulet beat Steve Muslin

8/14/81: Powhattan, VA
Frank Monte beat Mike Miller
Mike Davis beat El Toro
Scott McGhee beat Ali Bey
Jay Youngblood & Johnny Weaver beat Nikolai Volkoff & Chris Markoff
Sweet Ebony Diamond beat Roddy Piper by DQ

8/15/81: Knoxville, TN @ WBIR Studios (TV)
Bruiser Brody no contest with Blackjack Mulligan, Sr.
Terry Taylor & Blackjack Mulligan, Jr. beat Tony Anthony & Doug Vines
Jay Strongbow beat Masked Mr. X
Wayne Farris beat Kenny Hall
John Studd beat Deke Rivers & Johnny Meadows in a handicap match

8/15/81: Cincinnati, OH @ Gardens
Laurent Soucie beat Charlie Fulton
Ron Ritchie draw Scott McGhee
Jacques Goulet beat Steve Muslin
Chris Markoff & Nikolai Volkoff beat Johnny Weaver & Paul Jones
Jay Youngblood beat Jacques Goulet
Sweet Ebony Diamond beat Ivan Koloff by DQ

8/15/81: Spartanburg, SC @ Memorial Auditorium
Wahoo McDaniel vs. Ivan Koloff
Chris Markoff & Nikolai Volkoff vs. Johnny Weaver & Jim Nelson
Don Kernodle vs. Jim Nelson
El Toro vs. Frank Monte
Mike Miller vs. Ron Ritchie

8/15/81: Charlotte, NC @ Coliseum
Gene Anderson & Ole Anderson double DQ Ric Flair & Blackjack Mulligan
Leroy Brown beat Greg Valentine by DQ
Ricky Steamboat beat Roddy Piper
Ron Bass beat Iron Sheik
Mr. Fuji draw Dewey Robertson
Terry Latham beat Jim Nelson
Ali Bey beat Don Kernodle
Frank Monte beat Mike Miller

8/16/81: Wilmington, NC @ Legion Stadium
Ric Flair & Paul Jones vs. Gene Anderson & Ole Anderson
Greg Valentine vs. Leroy Brown
Don Carson vs. Iron Sheik

8/17/81: Fayetteville, NC @ Cumberland County Memorial Auditorium
Gene Anderson & Ole Anderson vs. Ric Flair & Jay Youngblood
Iron Sheik vs. Ron Bass

8/17/81: Greenville, SC @ Memorial Auditorium
Wahoo McDaniel beat Roddy Piper
Chris Markoff & Nikolai Volkoff beat Johnny Weaver & Dewey Robertson
Greg Valentine beat Ricky Steamboat
Frank Monte beat Mike Miller

8/18/81: Raleigh, NC @ Civic Center
Wahoo McDaniel beat Roddy Piper by DQ
Paul Jones beat Greg Valentine
Chris Markoff & Nikolai Volkoff beat Johnny Weaver & Dewey Robertson
Frank Monte beat Bill White

8/18/81: Columbia, SC @ Township Auditorium

8/19/81: Charlotte, NC @ WPCQ Studios (TV)

8/20/81: Orangeburg, SC
Leroy Brown & Paul Jones vs. Greg Valentine & Jimmy Valiant
Mr. Fuji vs. Steve Muslin
Ali Bey vs. Terry Latham
Bill White vs. Scott McGhee

8/20/81: Spartanburg, SC @ Memorial Auditorium
Wahoo McDaniel beat Ivan Koloff
Chris Markoff & Nikolai Volkoff beat Johnny Weaver & Dewey Robertson
Don Kernodle beat Jim Nelson
Frank Monte beat El Toro
Ron Ritchie beat Mike Miller

8/21/81: Richmond, VA @ Coliseum
Ric Flair & Ron Bass beat Ole Anderson & Mr. Fuji(sub for Gene Anderson)
Wahoo McDaniel beat Greg Valentine
Ivan Koloff beat Leroy Brown by DQ
Paul Jones beat Jimmy Valiant
Scott McGhee beat El Toro
Jacques Goulet beat Frank Monte
Austin Idol beat Siva Afi

8/21/81: Charleston, SC @ County Hall
Sweet Ebony Diamond beat Roddy Piper
Johnny Weaver beat Chris Markoff
Don Kernodle & Steve Muslin beat Jim Nelson & Mike Miller
Charlie Fulton draw Laurent Soucie

8/21/81: Knoxville, TN @ Chilhowee Park
John Studd no contest with Dick The Bruiser
Blackjack Mulligan, Sr. beat Bruiser Brody by DQ in a bullrope match
Terry Taylor beat Kevin Sullivan
Blackjack Mulligan, Jr. beat Chris Canyon
Jay Strongbow beat Wayne Farris
Doug Vines & Jeff Sword beat Tim Horner & Keith Larsen
Rick Connors beat Tony Anthony

8/22/81: Greensboro, NC @ Coliseum
Ron Bass beat Ivan Koloff by DQ
Ric Flair & Wahoo McDaniel beat Ole Anderson & Mr. Fuji (sub Gene Anderson)
Leroy Brown beat Greg Valentine(21:00)
Jake Roberts & Terry Latham beat Jacques Goulet & Jimmy Valiant

8/22/81: Morristown, TN
Rick Connors beat Tony Russo
Tony Anthony beat Izzy Slapowitz
Doug Vines beat Keith Larsen
Jay Strongbow beat Wayne Farris
Terry Taylor & Tim Horner beat John Studd & Kevin Sullivan
Blackjack Mulligan, Jr. beat Bruiser Brody

8/23/81: Asheville, NC @ Civic Center
Ric Flair & Wahoo McDaniel beat Ole Anderson & Mr. Fuji in a no DQ, falls count anywhere match
Leroy Brown beat Greg Valentine
Roddy Piper beat Jay Youngblood
Paul Jones beat Jacques Goulet
Don Kernodle beat Bill White
Ron Ritchie beat El Toro

8/23/81: Savannah, GA @ Civic Center
NWA World Champion Dusty Rhodes beat Ivan Koloff by DQ
Johnny Weaver & Dewey Robertson beat Chris Markoff & Nikolai Volkoff by DQ
Ron Bass beat Iron Sheik
Siva Afi beat Jim Nelson
Terry Latham beat Ali Bey
Sweet Ebony Diamond beat Jimmy Valiant via pinfall

8/23/81: Roanoke, VA @ Civic Center
Ric Flair & Wahoo McDaniel beat Ole Anderson & Mr. Fuji(sub for Gene Anderson)
Blackjack Mulligan, Sr. beat Bruiser Brody in a Texas death match
John Studd beat Blackjack Mulligan, Jr.
Kevin Sullivan double DQ Terry Taylor
Chief Jay Strongbow beat Wayne Farris
Tim Horner beat Rick Connors

8/24/81: Greenville, SC @ Memorial Auditorium
Ric Flair & Dusty Rhodes beat Ole Anderson & Mr. Fuji(sub for Gene Anderson)
Ivan Koloff beat Sweet Ebony Diamond
Siva Afi beat Mike Miller
Jacques Goulet beat Ron Ritchie
Jimmy Valiant beat Jay Youngblood by DQ

8/25/81: Raleigh, NC @ Civic Center
Steve Muslin beat Bill White
Laurent Soucie beat Charlie Fulton
Ali Bey beat Ron Ritchie
Jimmy Valiant beat Sweet Ebony Diamond
Ron Bass & Paul Jones beat Iron Sheik & Greg Valentine
Wahoo McDaniel beat Roddy Piper

8/25/81: Columbia, SC @ Township Auditorium
Mike Davis beat Mike Reed
Don Kernodle beat El Toro
Siva Afi beat Jim Nelson
Ric Flair beat Austin Idol by DQ
NWA World Champion Dusty Rhodes beat Ivan Koloff

8/25/81: Dublin, VA @ Dublin Fairgrounds
Blackjack Mulligan, Jr. & Tim Horner vs. Chris Canyon & Tony Anthony
Kevin Sullivan vs. Terry Taylor
Brass Knuckles Match
Rick Connors vs. Doug Vines
Izzy Slapowitz vs. Dennis Brown

8/26/81: Charlotte, NC @ WPCQ Studios (TV)
Ric Flair & Wahoo McDaniel beat Charlie Fulton & Ben Alexander

8/27/81: Spartanburg, SC @ Memorial Auditorium
Wahoo McDaniel beat Roddy Piper
Johnny Weaver & Jay Youngblood beat Chris Markoff & Nikolai Volkoff by DQ
Ron Bass beat Iron Sheik
Jacques Goulet draw Terry Latham
Ali Bey beat Frank Monte

8/27/81: Harrisonburg, VA @ High School
Blackjack Mulligan, Jr. vs. John Studd in a Texas death match

8/28/81: Lynchburg, VA @ City Armory
Leroy Brown beat Greg Valentine
Ric Flair beat Austin Idol by DQ
Dewey Robertson beat Ali Bey
Don Kernodle & Tony Anthony beat El Toro & Ali Bey
Mike Davis beat Charlie Fulton

8/28/81: Charleston, SC @ County Hall
NWA World Champion Dusty Rhodes beat Ivan Koloff
Sweet Ebony Diamond & Ron Bass beat Jimmy Valiant & Mr. Fuji
Frank Monte beat Mike Reed
Ron Ritchie beat Jim Nelson
Steve Muslin draw Laurent Soucie

8/28/81: Knoxville, TN @ Chilhowee Park
Dick The Bruiser beat John Studd by DQ with Otis Sistrunk as special referee
Terry Taylor beat Les Thornton by DQ
Blackjack Mulligan, Jr. beat Iron Sheik
Jay Strongbow beat Kevin Sullivan by DQ
Wayne Farris beat Jim Dalton by DQ
Ron Wright beat Rick Connors to win Tennessee Brass Knuckles Title
Jeff Sword & Doug Vines beat Tim Horner & Dennis Brown

8/29/81: Buffalo, NY
Billy Red Lyons beat Goldie Rogers
The Destroyer beat Frankie Laine
Austin Idol beat Steve Bolus
Ron Bass beat Iron Sheik
Leroy Brown beat Greg Valentine by DQ
Ric Flair & Jay Youngblood beat Ole Anderson & Mr. Fuji

8/30/81: Toronto, Ontario @ Maple Leaf Gardens
Frankie Laine draw Billy Red Lyons
The Destroyer beat Steve Bolus
Chris Markoff & Nikolai Volkoff beat Tony Parisi & Dewey Robertson
Angelo Mosca beat Greg Valentine
Ole Anderson & Mr. Fuji beat Ric Flair & Jay Youngblood
NWA World Champion Dusty Rhodes beat John Studd

8/31/81: Greenville, SC @ Memorial Auditorium
NWA World Champion Dusty Rhodes beat Ivan Koloff
Ric Flair & Wahoo McDaniel beat Roddy Piper & Ole Anderson
Ron Ritchie beat Jim Nelson
Siva Afi beat Charlie Fulton
Jake Roberts beat Ricky Harris
Paul Jones beat Les Thornton

8/31/81: St. Catherines, Ontario
Frankie Laine draw Nick DeCarlo
The Destroyer beat Steve Bolus
Billy Red Lyons beat Goldie Rogers
Chris Markoff & Nikolai Volkoff beat Dewey Robertson & Tony Parisi
Jay Youngblood beat Mr. Fuji in a Texas death match

9/1/81: Raleigh, NC @ Civic Center
NWA World Champion Dusty Rhodes beat Ivan Koloff
Wahoo McDaniel beat Jimmy Valiant
Jake Roberts beat Les Thornton
Johnny Weaver beat Ali Bey
Don Kernodle beat Jim Nelson
Steve Muslin beat Ricky Harris
Siva Afi beat Mike Miller

9/1/81: Columbia, SC @ Township Auditorium
Ric Flair & Leroy Brown beat Roddy Piper & Ole Anderson
Ron Bass beat Austin Idol
Frank Monte beat El Toro
Scott McGhee beat Mike Reed
Mike Davis beat Charlie Fulton

9/1/81: Hamilton, Ontario
Nick DeCarlo beat John Bonello
Frankie Laine beat Steve Bolus by DQ
Alfred Hayes beat Dewey Robertson
Tony Parisi & Jay Youngblood beat Chris Markoff & Nikolai Volkoff by DQ
Billy Red Lyons draw The Destroyer

9/2/81: Charlotte, NC @ WPCQ Studios (TV)
Ric Flair & Ron Bass beat Jacques Goulet & Jim Nelson

9/2/81: Maryville, TN
Tony Russo draw Keith Larsen
Wendi Richter beat Judy Martin
Jim Dalton beat Tony Anthony
Ron Wright beat Rick Connors
Blackjack Mulligan, Jr. & Wayne Farris beat Jeff Sword & Izzy Slapowitz
Kevin Sullivan beat Terry Taylor

9/3/81: Sumter, SC @ Exposition Center
Mike Davis beat El Toro
Jake Roberts beat Ricky Harris
Les Thornton beat Ron Ritchie
Leroy Brown beat Greg Valentine by DQ
Ron Bass beat Jacques Goulet
NWA World Champion Dusty Rhodes beat Ivan Koloff by DQ

9/3/81: Fishersville, VA @ Augusta Expo
Blackjack Mulligan, Jr. & Terry Taylor vs. Kevin Sullivan & John Studd
Judy Martin vs. Wendi Richter
Wayne Farris vs. Tony Anthony
Chris Canyon vs. Jim Dalton
Tim Horner vs. Izzy Slapowitz

9/3/81: Lawrenceville, VA
Wahoo McDaniel vs. Roddy Piper
Johnny Weaver & Dewey Robertson vs. Chris Markoff & Nikolai Volkoff

9/4/81: Knoxville, TN @ Chilhowee Park
John Studd & Kevin Sullivan vs. Dick The Bruiser & Terry Taylor
Ron Wright vs. Rick Connors
Doug Vines & Jeff Sword vs. Wayne Farris & Blackjack Mulligan, Jr.
Bobo Brazil vs. Tim Hampton
Jay Strongbow vs. Spike Huber

9/4/81: Charleston, SC @ County Hall
Alfred Hayes beat Johnny Weaver
Paul Jones & Jay Youngblood beat Chris Markoff & Nikolai Volkoff
Jimmy Valiant beat Sweet Ebony Diamond
Ron Ritchie beat Mr. Fuji
Mike Davis beat Mike Miller
Scott McGhee beat Ricky Harris

9/4/81: Richmond, VA @ Coliseum
Dewey Robertson beat Charlie Fulton
Steve Muslin beat Jim Nelson
Jacques Goulet beat Don Kernodle
Ron Bass beat Austin Idol
Wahoo McDaniel & Leroy Brown beat Greg Valentine & Roddy Piper
NWA World Champion Dusty Rhodes beat Ivan Koloff by DQ
Ric Flair beat Ole Anderson in a Texas bullrope match

9/5/81: Greensboro, NC @ Coliseum
Ric Flair beat Ole Anderson(17:00) in an Indian strap match
Abdullah The Butcher & Roddy Piper no contest with Ron Bass & Wahoo
McDaniel
The Grappler & Super Destroyer beat Jay Youngblood & Frank Monte
Leroy Brown beat Ivan Koloff by DQ
Jake Roberts beat Jacques Goulet
Mike Davis beat El Toro

9/6/81: Roanoke, VA @ Civic Center
Leroy Brown beat Austin Idol by DQ
Dick The Bruiser beat John Studd by DQ
Blackjack Mulligan, Jr. & Wayne Farris beat Ivan Koloff & Mr. Fuji
Kevin Sullivan beat Terry Taylor
Bobo Brazil beat Tim Hampton
Jay Strongbow beat spike Huber

9/6/81: Charlotte, NC @ Coliseum
Wahoo McDaniel & Ron Bass beat Roddy Piper & Abdullah The Butcher by DQ
NWA Champion Dusty Rhodes beat Greg Valentine by DQ
Ric Flair beat Ole Anderson in a Texas bullrope match
Paul Jones beat Jimmy Valiant
Jake Roberts beat Jacques Goulet
Ron Ritchie beat El Toro

9/6/81: Asheville, NC @ Civic Center
Ric Flair beat Ole Anderson in a strap match
Ron Bass beat Greg Valentine to win NWA Mid Atlantic Television Title
Wahoo McDaniel & Dusty Rhodes beat Roddy Piper & Abdullah The Butcher by DQ
Ali Bey beat Terry Latham
Mike Davis beat Jim Nelson
Scott McGhee beat Mike Miller
Siva Afi beat Frank Monte

9/6/81: Wilmington, NC @ Legion Stadium
Ricky Steamboat vs. Austin Idol
Jay Youngblood & Johnny Weaver vs. Chris Markoff & Nikolai Volkoff
Ivan Koloff vs. Leroy Brown

9/7/81: Greenville, SC @ Memorial Auditorium
Ivan Koloff vs. Ricky Steamboat
Ole Anderson vs. Ric Flair in a bullrope match
Chris Markoff & Nikolai Volkoff vs. Johnny Weaver & Leroy Brown
Jake Roberts vs. Jim Nelson
El Toro vs. Mike Davis
Ali Bey vs. Laurent Soucie

9/8/81: Pulaski, VA @ Calfee Park
John Studd vs. Otis Sistrunk
Blackjack Mulligan, Jr. & Wayne Farris vs. Jeff Sword & Doug Vines
Terry Taylor vs. Kevin Sullivan in a no DQ match

9/8/81: Columbia, SC @ Township Auditorium
Ron Ritchie beat El Toro
Mike Miller beat Frank Monte
Don Kernodle beat Ricky Harris
Paul Jones beat Mr. Fuji
Ricky Steamboat, Leroy Brown & Ron Bass beat Jimmy Valiant, Greg Valentine & Austin Idol

9/8/81: Raleigh, NC @ Civic Center
Wahoo McDaniel beat Ivan Koloff by DQ
Roddy Piper beat Jay Youngblood
Johnny Weaver beat Chris Markoff
The Grappler & Super Destroyer beat Scott McGhee & Terry Latham
Jake Roberts beat Charlie Fulton
Siva Afi beat Mike Reed

9/9/81: Charlotte, NC @ WPCQ Studios (TV)
Ricky Steamboat & Jake Roberts beat Mike Miller & Jim Nelson

9/10/81: Norfolk, VA @ Scope
Ric Flair vs. Ole Anderson
Wahoo McDaniel & Leroy Brown vs. Roddy Piper & Abdullah The Butcher
The Grappler & Super Destroyer vs. Jay Youngblood & Dewey Robertson
Austin Idol vs. Paul Jones
Jake Roberts vs. Jacques Goulet
Jim Nelson vs. Don Kernodle

9/11/81: Knoxville, TN @ Bill Meyer Stadium
Kevin Sullivan & John Studd vs. Jay Strongbow & Terry Taylor
Rick Connors vs. Ron Wright
Blackjack Mulligan, Jr. & Wayne Farris vs. Tony Anthony & Chris Canyon
Randy Rose vs. Mike Fever

9/11/81: Charleston, SC @ County Hall
Ricky Steamboat & Leroy Brown beat Greg Valentine & Ivan Koloff
Jake Roberts beat Les Thornton
The Grappler & Super Destroyer beat Mike Davis & Terry Latham
Mike Miller beat Frank Monte

9/11/81: Spartanburg, SC @ Memorial Auditorium
Scott McGhee beat El Toro
Jacques Goulet beat Ron Ritchie

Dewey Robinson beat Mr. Fuji
Chris Markoff, Nikolai Volkoff & Lord Alfred Hayes no contest with Johnny
Weaver, Ron Bass & Jay Youngblood
Ric Flair beat Roddy Piper

9/13/81: Kingsport, TN
Mike Fever beat Izzy Slapowitz
Tony Anthony draw Tim Horner
Chris Canyon beat Tony Russo
Jay Strongbow beat Wayne Farris
Rick Connors DCO with Ron Wright
Blackjack Mulligan, Jr. & Terry Taylor beat John Studd & Kevin Sullivan

9/13/81: Savannah, GA @ Civic Center
Ivan Koloff vs. Ricky Steamboat in a chain match
Johnny Weaver, Mr. Wrestling II & Sweet Ebony Diamond vs. Nikolai Volkoff, Chris Markoff & Alfred Hayes
Austin Idol vs. Jay Youngblood
Mr. Fuji vs. Ron Ritchie
Ricky Harris vs. Mike Davis
Ali Bey vs. Scott McGhee

9/13/81: Hampton, VA @ Coliseum
Wahoo McDaniel beat Abdullah The Butcher
Ric Flair & Leroy Brown beat Roddy Piper & Greg Valentine
The Grappler & Super Destroyer beat Dewey Robertson & Jake Roberts
Ron Bass beat Jimmy Valiant

9/14/81: Fayetteville, NC @ Cumberland County Memorial Auditorium
Ric Flair vs. Ole Anderson in a fence match
Ivan Koloff vs. Ricky Steamboat
Greg Valentine vs. Leroy Brown

9/14/81: Greenville, SC @ Memorial Auditorium
Wahoo McDaniel & Ron Bass beat Roddy Piper & Nikolai Volkoff
Jay Youngblood beat Austin Idol by DQ
Johnny Weaver beat Chris Markoff
Jacques Goulet beat Dewey Robertson
Scott McGhee beat Ricky Harris
Don Kernodle beat Charlie Fulton

9/15/81: Columbia, SC @ Township Auditorium
Leroy Brown beat Ole Anderson
Ricky Steamboat beat Ivan Koloff by DQ
Paul Jones beat Mike Miller
Siva Afi beat Laurent Soucie
Scott McGhee beat Ricky Harris
Terry Latham beat Charlie Fulton

9/15/81: Durham NC @ Durham Athletic Park
Wahoo McDaniel & Ric Flair vs. Roddy Piper & Greg Valentine
Ron Bass vs. ??
Jake Roberts vs. ??
The Grappler & Super Destroyer vs. ?? & ??

9/15/81: Mount Airy, NC @ Reeves Community Center
Chris Markoff & Nikolai Volkoff vs. Johnny Weaver & Jay Youngblood
Austin Idol vs. Sweet Ebony Diamond
Jacques Goulet vs. Steve Muslin
Ali Bey vs. Don Kernodle
El Toro vs. Mike Davis

9/16/81: Charlotte, NC @ WPCQ Studios (TV)
Ric Flair & Jake Roberts beat Mike Miller & Jim Nelson

9/17/81: Spartanburg, SC @ Memorial Auditorium
Johnny Weaver & Paul Jones beat Chris Markoff & Nikolai Volkoff by DQ in a Texas tornado match
Frank Monte beat Tony Tosi
Terry Latham beat Charlie Fulton
Dewey Robertson beat Jim Nelson
Austin Idol beat Jay Youngblood

9/17/81: Sumter, SC @ Exposition Center
Wahoo McDaniel & Leroy Brown beat Roddy Piper & Greg Valentine
Jake Roberts beat Ricky Harris
Don Kernodle beat Ali Bey
Scott McGhee beat Mike Miller
Steve Muslin beat Mike Reed

9/18/81: Charleston, SC @ County Hall
Leroy Brown beat Greg Valentine in a Lumberjack match
Jake Roberts, Paul Jones & Johnny Weaver beat Nikolai Volkoff, Chris Markoff & Austin Idol
Mike Davis beat Jacques Goulet
Don Kernodle beat Ricky Harris
Sivi Afi beat Mike Miller

9/18/81: Richmond, VA @ Coliseum
Ron Ritchie beat Charlie Fulton
Terry Latham beat Mike Reed
The Grappler & Super Destroyer beat Dewey Robertson & Steve Muslin
Ron Bass beat Ivan Koloff by DQ
Ricky Steamboat beat Ole Anderson
Wahoo McDaniel & Jay Youngblood(sub for Ric Flair) beat Abdullah The Butcher & Roddy Piper by DQ

9/18/81: Knoxville, TN @ Chilhowee Park
Blackjack Mulligan, Jr., Terry Taylor & Jay Strongbow beat Kevin Sullivan, John Studd & Chris Canyon
Wayne Farris beat Rick Connors
Jeff Sword & Doug Vines beat Tim Horner & Keith Larson
Don Carson beat Dennis Brown
Ron Wright beat Izzy Slapowitz
Mike Fever beat Tony Russo

9/19/81: Charlotte, NC @ Coliseum
Charlie Fulton beat Steve Muslin
Ron Ritchie beat Jim Nelson
Super Destroyer & Grappler beat Terry Latham & Dewey Robertson
Ivan Koloff beat Jay Youngblood
Wahoo McDaniel, Ricky Steamboat & Jake Roberts(sub for Ric Flair) beat Ole Anderson, Roddy Piper & Abdullah The Butcher

9/20/81: Asheville, NC @ Civic Center
Wahoo McDaniel & Ric Flair beat Ole Anderson & Roddy Piper in an Indian strap match
Leroy Brown beat Ivan Koloff
The Grappler & Super Destroyer beat Johnny Weaver & Dewey Robertson
Frank Monte beat Mike Reed
Scott McGhee beat Jim Nelson
Steve Muslin beat Mike Miller

9/20/81: Toronto, Ontario @ Maple Leaf Gardens
John Studd beat Angelo Mosca(15:10) to win Canadian Title
Ric Flair & Wahoo McDaniel beat Roddy Piper & Ole Anderson by DQ
Greg Valentine beat Jay Youngblood
Leroy Brown & Johnny Weaver beat Chris Markoff & Nikolai Volkoff
Ron Ritchie beat Goldie Rogers
Steve Bolus beat Kurt Von Hess
Frankie Laine beat Terry Latham

9/21/81: Guelph, Ontario(TV)
Johnny Weaver & Jay Youngblood beat Kurt Von Hess & Frank Marconi
Sgt. Slaughter beat Terry Latham
Nikolai Volkoff & Chris Markoff beat Ron Ritchie & John Bonello
Jay Youngblood beat Goldie Rogers
Jay Youngblood & Jake Roberts beat Frankie Laine & Tim Gerrard
Nikolai Volkoff & Chris Markoff beat Terry Latham & Brian Mackney
Jake Roberts beat Frank Marconi
John Studd beat Ron Ritchie
Sgt. Slaughter & Greg Valentine beat Johnny Weaver & Jay Youngblood

9/21/81: Greenville, SC @ Memorial Auditorium
Wahoo McDaniel & Ron Bass beat Roddy Piper & Abdullah The Butcher by DQ
Leroy Brown beat Austin Idol
The Grappler & Super Destroyer beat Don Kernodle & Paul Jones
Scott McGhee beat Tony Russo
Mike Davis beat Mike Miller

9/22/81: Harrisonburg, VA @ High School
included Blackjack Mulligan, Jr.

9/22/81: Hamilton, Ontario
Chris Markoff & Nikolai Volkoff beat Johnny Weaver & Tony Parisi
Jay Youngblood beat Alfred Hayes by countout
Billy Red Lyons beat Frankie Lane
Billy Red Lyons beat Kurt Von Hess
Goldie Rogers draw John Bonello

9/22/81: Raleigh, NC @ Dorton Arena
Wahoo McDaniel & Ron Bass beat Abdullah The Butcher & Roddy Piper by DQ
Terry Latham beat Charlie Fulton
Ricky Harris beat Frank Monte
Siva Afi beat Ali Bey
The Grappler & Super Destroyer beat Paul Jones & Ron Ritchie

9/22/81: Columbia, SC @ Township Auditorium
Don Kernodle beat Mike Miller
Jim Nelson beat Steve Muslin
Mike Davis beat Ricky Harris
Jake Roberts beat Jacques Goulet
Austin Idol beat Mike Davis
Wahoo McDaniel & Leroy Brown beat Ole Anderson & Ivan Koloff
Ivan Koloff won a 12-man battle royal

9/23/81: Charlotte, NC @ WPCQ Studios (TV)

9/24/81: Norfolk, VA @ Scope
Roddy Piper & Abdullah The Butcher beat Wahoo McDaniel & Jake Roberts(sub for Ric Flair) in a falls count anywhere match
Ricky Steamboat beat Ole Anderson
Ron Bass beat Ivan Koloff
The Grappler & Super Destroyer beat Mike Davis & Terry Latham
Jay Youngblood beat Jacques Goulet

9/24/81: Spartanburg, SC @ Memorial Auditorium
Johnny Weaver & Leroy Brown beat Chris Markoff & Nikolai Volkoff
Paul Jones beat Austin Idol
Sweet Ebony Diamond beat Ricky Harris
Don Kernodle beat Mike Miller
Ron Ritchie beat Jim Nelson

9/25/81: Charleston, SC @ County Hall
Leroy Brown beat Austin Idol
The Grappler & Super Destroyer beat Jay Youngblood & Paul Jones
Scott McGhee beat Charlie Fulton
Siva Afi beat Jim Nelson
Ali Bey beat Steve Muslin

9/25/81: Winston-Salem, NC @ Ernie Shore Field
Ivan Koloff vs. Ricky Steamboat
Chris Markoff & Nikolai Volkoff vs. Johnny Weaver & Ron Bass
Roddy Piper vs. Sweet Ebony Diamond
Jacques Goulet vs. Dewey Robertson

9/25/81: Knoxville, TN @ Chilhowee Park
Blackjack Mulligan, Sr. vs. John Studd
Blackjack Mulligan, Jr. vs. Wayne Farris
Kevin Sullivan vs. Jay Strongbow
Terry Taylor vs. Chris Canyon

9/26/81: Cincinnati, OH @ Gardens
Scott McGhee beat Ali Bey
Frank Monte beat Charlie Fulton
Jake Roberts beat Jacques Goulet
Ricky Steamboat beat Austin Idol by DQ
Roddy Piper beat Jay Youngblood
Sweet Ebony Diamond & Leroy Brown beat Ole Anderson & Ivan Koloff

9/27/81: Roanoke, VA @ Civic Center
John Studd & Kevin Sullivan beat Blackjack Mulligan, Sr. & Chief Jay Strongbow(sub for Bruiser Brody)
Dick The Bruiser beat Kevin Sullivan
Blackjack Mulligan, Jr. double DQ Wayne Farris
Terry Taylor beat Mike Fever
Bobby Eaton beat Tim Horner(sub for Rick Connors)
Bobby Eaton draw Jim Dalton

9/27/81: Savannah, GA @ Civic Center
NWA World Champion Ric Flair vs. ??
Ivan Koloff & Roddy Piper vs. Ricky Steamboat & Leroy Brown
The Grappler & Super Destroyer vs. Jay Youngblood & Terry Latham
Jake Roberts vs. Nikolai Volkoff

9/27/81: Wilmington, NC @ Legion Stadium
Ricky Steamboat, Ron Bass & Leroy Brown vs. Ole Anderson, Roddy Piper & Ivan Koloff
Johnny Weaver vs. Chris Markoff

9/28/81: Greenville, SC @ Memorial Auditorium
Ivan Koloff & Ole Anderson beat Ric Flair & Ricky Steamboat in a falls count anywhere match
The Grappler beat Sweet Ebony Diamond
Ron Bass beat Ricky Harris
Don Kernodle beat El Toro
Terry Latham & Ron Ritchie beat Charlie Fulton & Jim Nelson

9/29/81: Raleigh, NC @ Dorton Arena
NWA World Champion Ric Flair beat Ole Anderson
Leroy Brown beat Roddy Piper by countout
The Grappler & Super Destroyer beat Johnny Weaver & Paul Jones
Jacques Goulet beat Steve Muslin
Don Kernodle beat Ali Bey
Mike Davis beat Ricky Harris

9/29/81: Columbia, SC @ Township Auditorium
Dusty Rhodes beat Ivan Koloff by DQ
Jay Youngblood & Ricky Steamboat beat Chris Markoff & Nikolai Volkoff
Terry Latham beat Tony Russo
Scott McGhee beat Mike Miller
Jake Roberts beat Jim Nelson
Ron Ritchie beat Charlie Fulton

9/30/81: Charlotte, NC @ WPCQ Studios (TV)
Austin Idol beat Scott McGhee
Ron Bass beat Jim Nelson
Grappler & Super Destroyer beat Johnny Weaver & Ron Ritchie
Jake Roberts & Leroy Brown beat Ricky Harris & Mike Fever
Jay Youngblood beat Ole Anderson by DQ

10/1/81: Norfolk, VA @ Scope
Terry Latham beat Mike Miller
Don Kernodle beat Jim Nelson
Frank Monte beat Tony Russo
The Grappler & Super Destroyer beat Jake Roberts & Steve Muslin
Wahoo McDaniel beat Roddy Piper in an Indian strap match
Ivan Koloff DCO with Dusty Rhodes
NWA World Champion Ric Flair beat Ole Anderson cage match

10/1/81: Fishersville, VA @ Augusta Expo
Blackjack Mulligan, Sr. beat John Studd by DQ
Blackjack Mulligan, Jr. double DQ Wayne Farris
Kevin Sullivan, Jeff Sword & Doug Vines beat Terry Taylor, Tim Horner & Jay Strongbow
Bobby Eaton beat Keith Larson
Mike Fever draw Mike Reed

10/1/81: Spartanburg, SC @ Memorial Auditorium
Leroy Brown, Jay Youngblood & Johnny Weaver beat Nikolai Volkoff, Chris Markoff & Alfred Hayes by DQ
Ron Bass beat Jacques Goulet
Ali Bey beat Sivi Afi
Mike Davis beat El Toro
Ron Ritchie beat Charlie Fulton

10/2/81: Richmond, VA @ Coliseum
Don Kernodle beat Mike Miller
Scott McGhee beat Tony Russo
Johnny Weaver & Jay Youngblood beat Chris Markoff & Nikolai Volkoff
Leroy Brown beat Ole Anderson
Ivan Koloff beat Ricky Steamboat
Roddy Piper & Abdullah The Butcher beat Ron Bass & Wahoo McDaniel

10/2/81: Knoxville, TN @ Chilhowee park
Rick Connors beat Mike Fever
Bobby Eaton beat Tim Horner
Jeff Sword & Doug Vines beat Jim Dalton & Mike Reed
Jay Strongbow & Terry Taylor beat Kevin Sullivan & Don Carson
Blackjack Mulligan, Jr. DCO with Wayne Farris
Blackjack Mulligan, Sr. beat John Studd

10/4/81: Charlotte, NC @ Coliseum
Wahoo McDaniel beat Abdullah The Butcher in a lights out match
NWA United States Title Tournament
1st Round
Pat Patterson beat Mike Davis
Ricky Steamboat beat Nikolai Volkoff
Leroy Brown beat Super Destroyer
Ivan Koloff beat Ron Bass
Sgt. Slaughter beat Johnny Weaver
Jay Youngblood beat Steve Muslin
Jacques Goulet beat Dusty Rhodes
Ole Anderson beat Ron Ritchie

2nd Round
Ricky Steamboat beat Pat Patterson
Leroy Brown beat Ivan Koloff
Sgt. Slaughter beat Jay Youngblood
Ole Anderson double DQ Jacques Goulet

Semifinals
Ricky Steamboat beat Leroy Brown
Sgt. Slaughter received a bye

Finals
Sgt. Slaughter beat Ricky Steamboat to win vacant NWA United States Title

10/4/81: Toronto, Ontario @ Maple Leaf Gardens
Leroy Brown beat Ole Anderson
Wahoo McDaniel & Dusty Rhodes draw Roddy Piper & Abdullah The Butcher
Pat Patterson beat Ivan Koloff
Killer Khan beat Johnny Weaver
Sgt. Slaughter beat Jay Youngblood
Tony Parisi beat Goldie Rogers
Steve Bolus draw Frankie Laine
Lord Al Hayes beat Kurt Von Hess
Farmer Pete beat Little John (Ivan The Terrible)

10/4/81: Roanoke, VA @ Civic Center
Blackjack Mulligan, Sr. beat John Studd to win Southern Title
Blackjack Mulligan, Jr. DCO with Wayne Farris
Paul Jones beat Bobby Eaton by DQ
Bobby Eaton & Kevin Sullivan beat Jay Strongbow & Terry Taylor
Jim Dalton beat Rick Connors
Tim Horner beat Doug Vines
Terry Latham beat Ricky Harris

10/5/81: Brantford, Ontario(TV)
Sgt. Slaughter & Greg Valentine vs. Jay Youngblood & Pat Patterson
Ole Anderson & Ivan Koloff vs. Leroy Brown & Pat Patterson

10/5/81: Asheville, NC @ Civic Center
Tony Russo beat Frank Monte
Terry Latham beat Mike Miller
Ron Ritchie beat Jim Nelson
Siva Afi beat Ali Bey
Paul Jones & Jake Roberts beat Alexis Smirnoff & Nikolai Volkoff
Ron Bass beat Sgt. Jacques Goulet
Roddy Piper beat Wahoo McDaniel

10/5/81: Fayetteville, NC @ Cumberland County Memorial Auditorium
Ivan Koloff vs. Ricky Steamboat
Ole Anderson vs. Leroy Brown
Also included The Grappler, Super Destroyer, Sweet Ebony Diamond & others

10/6/81: Kingsport, TN
Dusty Rhodes, Ric Flair & Wahoo McDaniel beat Ole Anderson, Roddy Piper & Austin Idol
Blackjack Mulligan, Sr. beat John Studd
Jerry Brisco beat Les Thornton

10/6/81: Columbia, SC @ Township Auditorium
Wahoo McDaniel beat Roddy Piper
Jake Roberts & Ricky Steamboat beat Chris Markoff & Nikolai Volkoff
Don Kernodle beat Jacques Goulet
Tony Anthony beat Ricky Harris
Mike Davis beat Tony Russo
Frank Monte beat Ali Bey

10/7/81: Charlotte, NC @ WPCQ Studios (TV)
Wahoo McDaniel & Jay Youngblood beat Charlie Fulton & Jim Nelson
The Grappler & Super Destroyer beat Frank Monte & Siva Afi
Dusty Rhodes beat Ricky Harris
Ivan Koloff & Roddy Piper beat Steve Muslin & Ron Ritchie
Sgt. Slaughter beat Terry Latham
Ric Flair beat Billy Starr

10/8/81: Sumter, SC @ Exposition Center
Ricky Steamboat vs. Ivan Koloff
Leroy Brown & Jay Youngblood vs. Chris Markoff & Nikolai Volkoff
Ron Ritchie vs. Bob Scranton
Charlie Fulton vs. Mike Davis
Jim Nelson vs. Frank Monte

10/8/81: Spartanburg, SC @ Memorial Auditorium
Ron Ritchie beat Jim Nelson
Don Kernodle beat Mike Miller
Sweet Ebony Diamond beat Ricky Harris
Leroy Brown & Johnny Weaver beat Nikolai Volkoff & Chris Markoff
Paul Jones beat Austin Idol

10/9/81: Charleston, SC @ County Hall
Sweet Ebony Diamond & Jake Roberts beat The Grappler & Super Destroyer
Ron Bass beat Jacques Goulet
Leroy Brown beat Ricky Harris
Scott McGhee beat Tony Russo
Terry Latham beat Mike Miller

10/9/81: Lynchburg, VA @ City Armory
Wahoo McDaniel & Ricky Steamboat vs. Roddy Piper & Ivan Koloff
Chris Markoff & Nikolai Volkoff vs. Johnny Weaver & Jay Youngblood
Paul Jones vs. Sgt. Slaughter

10/9/81: Knoxville, TN @ Chilhowee Park
Blackjack Mulligan, Sr. & Blackjack Mulligan, Jr. vs. Kevin Sullivan & Wayne Farris
John Studd vs. Jay Strongbow
Bobby Eaton vs. Terry Taylor
Ron Wright vs. Rick Connors in a lights out match

10/10/81: Hampton, VA @ Coliseum
Wahoo McDaniel beat Roddy Piper in a Texas death match
Ricky Steamboat beat Ivan Koloff
Sgt. Slaughter beat Sweet Ebony Diamond
The Grappler & Super Destroyer beat Jay Youngblood & Jake Roberts
Frank Monte beat El Toro
Charlie Fulton beat Siva Afi
Tony Anthony beat Ali Bey

10/10/81: Greensboro, NC @ Coliseum
Wahoo McDaniel beat Roddy Piper
Ricky Steamboat beat Ivan Koloff to win NWA Mid Atlantic Title
Leroy Brown beat Ole Anderson
Sgt. Slaughter beat Sweet Ebony Diamond
Jacques Goulet beat Tony Anthony
Ron Ritchie beat Ricky Harris
Don Kernodle beat Mike Miller via pinfall
Mike Davis beat Tony Russo

10/11/81: Asheville, NC @ Civic Center
Buddy Landell beat Mike Miller
Jimmy Valiant beat Ricky Harris
Blackjack Mulligan, Jr. beat Jim Nelson
The Ninja beat Mike Davis
The Grappler beat Jay Youngblood
Gene Anderson & Ole Anderson beat Jake Roberts & Wahoo McDaniel
Leroy Brown beat Sgt. Slaughter by DQ
Roddy Piper beat Ricky Steamboat

10/11/81: Kingsport, TN
Rick Connors beat Izzy Slapowitz
Jim Dalton beat Mike Fever
Tim Horner beat Doug Vines
Jay Strongbow double DQ Kevin Sullivan
Paul Jones & Johnny Weaver beat Chris Markoff & Nikolai Volkoff
Blackjack Mulligan, Jr. beat Wayne Farris by DQ

10/12/81: Greenville, SC @ Memorial Auditorium
Ivan Koloff beat Ricky Steamboat in match where NWA Mid Atlantic Title was held up
Sgt. Slaughter beat Sweet Ebony Diamond
The Grappler & Super Destroyer beat Paul Jones & Jake Roberts
Vinnie Valentino beat Jim Nelson
Buddy Landell beat Charlie Fulton

10/13/81: Raleigh, NC @ Dorton Arena
Sgt. Slaughter vs. Sweet Ebony Diamond
Ricky Steamboat beat Ivan Koloff by DQ
Tony Anthony beat Charlie Fulton
Ricky Harris beat Ron Ritchie
Buddy Landell beat Tony Anthony
Johnny Weaver beat Alfred Hayes

10/13/81: Columbia, SC @ Township Auditorium
Wahoo McDaniel beat Roddy Piper
The Grappler & Super Destroyer beat Jay Youngblood & Jake Roberts
Mike Davis beat Mike Miller
Terry Latham beat Ali Bey
Tony Rossi beat Vinnie Valentino

10/14/81: Charlotte, NC @ WPCQ Studios (TV)
Roddy Piper vs. Jay Youngblood

10/15/81: Spartanburg, SC @ Memorial Auditorium
NWA World Champion Ric Flair beat Ole Anderson
Johnny Weaver beat Sgt. Slaughter by DQ
Jay Youngblood beat Roddy Piper
The Grappler & Super Destroyer beat Jake Roberts & Sweet Ebony Diamond
Tony Anthony beat Charlie Fulton
Mike Davis beat Ricky Harris

10/15/81: Fisherville, VA @ Augusta Expo
Blackjack Mulligan, Sr. & Blackjack Mulligan, Jr. vs. Wayne Farris & Kevin Sullivan
Jay Strongbow vs. John Studd

10/16/81: Charleston, SC @ County Hall
Jake Roberts & Sweet Ebony Diamond vs. The Grappler & Super Destroyer in a Texas tornado match
Ron Bass vs. Austin Idol
Chris Markoff & Nikolai Volkoff vs. Terry Latham & Ron Ritchie
Vinnie Valentino vs. Jim Nelson
Charlie Fulton vs. Buddy Landell

10/16/81: Cincinnati OH @ Gardens
Wahoo McDaniel vs. Roddy Piper
Mike Davis beat Jacques Goulet
Ricky Harris beat Tony Anthony
Leroy Brown & Jay Youngblood beat Ivan Koloff & Greg Valentine by DQ
Sgt. Slaughter beat Johnny Weaver
Jay Youngblood beat Roddy Piper
NWA World Champ Ric Flair beat Ole Anderson

10/16/81: Knoxville, TN @ Chilhowee Park
Blackjack Mulligan, Sr. & Blackjack Mulligan, Jr. & Jay Strongbow beat Wayne Farris, Kevin Sullivan & Bobby Eaton
Jerry Brisco beat Les Thornton by countout
Rick Connors draw Tony Anthony
Doug Vines & Jeff Sword beat Terry Taylor & Jim Dalton

10/17/81: Buffalo, NY
Frankie Laine beat John Bonello
Billy Red Lyons beat Goldie Rogers
Greg Valentine beat Steve Bolus
Sgt. Slaughter beat Jay Youngblood
Leroy Brown beat Ivan Koloff
Roddy Piper draw Wahoo McDaniel
NWA World Champion Ric Flair beat Ole Anderson in a strap match

10/17/81: Hendersonville, NC
The Grappler & Super Destroyer vs. Johnny Weaver & Jake Roberts
Ron Bass vs. Austin Idol
Chris Markoff & Nikolai Volkoff vs. Paul Jones & Sweet Ebony Diamond
El Toro vs. Ron Ritchie
Mike Miller vs. Mike Davis

10/18/81: Charlotte, NC @ Coliseum
Wahoo McDaniel beat Roddy Piper in a Texas death match
Sgt. Slaughter DCO with Ricky Steamboat
Jake Roberts beat Greg Valentine by DQ
Ole Anderson & Ivan Koloff beat Sweet Ebony Diamond & Leroy Brown
Ali Bey beat Frank Monte
Buddy Landell beat Tony Russo
Vinnie Valentino beat Mike Miller

10/18/81: Toronto, Ontario @ Maple Leaf Gardens
Angelo Mosca beat John Studd(14:19) by DQ
Bad Leroy Brown & Tony Parisi beat Ole Anderson & Ivan Koloff(20:36)
Roddy Piper DCO with Wahoo McDaniel(9:19)
Sgt. Slaughter beat Sweet Ebony Diamond(10:51)
Killer Kahn beat Jay Youngblood(7:19)
Greg Valentine beat Frankie Laine(6:10)
Steve Bolus beat Goldie Rogers

10/18/81: Salem, VA @ Civic Center
Paul Jones beat Gene Anderson by DQ
Chris Markoff & Nikolai Volkoff beat Johnny Weaver & Terry Taylor
Kevin Sullivan double DQ Chief Jay Strongbow
Jeff Sword & Doug Vines beat Blackjack Mulligan, Sr. & Blackjack Mulligan, Jr.
Rick Connors beat Tim Horner by DQ
Keith Larsen beat Mike Fever
Izzy Slapowitz beat Dennis Brown

10/18/81: Roanoke, VA @ Civic Center
Kevin Sullivan double DQ Jay Strongbow
Doug Vines & Jeff Sword beat Blackjack Mulligan Sr. & Blackjack Mulligan, Jr.
Chris Markoff & Nikolai Volkoff beat Johnny Weaver & Terry Taylor
Paul Jones beat Gene Anderson by DQ
Rick Connors beat Tim Horner by DQ
Keith Larson beat Mike Fever
Izzy Slapowitz beat Dennis Brown

10/19/81: Greenville, SC @ Memorial Auditorium
Ricky Steamboat beat Ivan Koloff to win held up NWA Mid Atlantic Title in a no DQ match
Leroy Brown beat Gene Anderson by DQ
Jake Roberts beat Austin Idol
The Grappler & Super Destroyer beat Johnny Weaver & Terry Latham
Don Kernodle beat Ricky Harris
Buddy Landell beat El Toro

10/19/81: Fayetteville, NC @ Cumberland County Memorial Auditorium
Wahoo McDaniel vs. Roddy Piper
Sgt. Slaughter vs. Sweet Ebony Diamond
Paul Jones & Jay Youngblood vs. Chris Markoff & Nikolai Volkoff

10/19/81: Jenkins, KY
Mike Fever draw Denny Brown
Don Carson no contest with Ron Wright
Rick Connors beat Keith Larsen
Jay Strongbow beat Doug Vines
Blackjack Mulligan, Jr. & Terry Taylor beat Kevin Sullivan & Wayne Farris

10/20/81: Kingsport, TN
NWA World Champion Ric Flair beat Roddy Piper
Blackjack Mulligan Sr. & Blackjack Mulligan, Jr. beat Ole Anderson & John Studd
Angelo Mosca draw Dick The Bruiser
Ron Wright beat Kevin Sullivan

10/20/81: Columbia, SC @ Township Auditorium
Ron Bass beat Carl Fergie
Sgt. Slaughter beat Sweet Ebony Diamond
Vinnie Valentino beat Mike Sharpe
Ken Timbs beat Buddy Landell
Johnny Weaver & Jake Roberts beat The Grappler & Super Destroyer

10/21/81: Charlotte, NC @ WPCQ Studios (TV)

10/22/81: Norfolk, VA @ Scope
Terry Latham beat Charlie Fulton
Vinnie Valentino beat Mike Miller
Johnny Weaver beat Lord Al Hayes
Paul Jones & Jimmy Valiant beat Chris Markoff & Ricky Harris
Jake Roberts beat Ole Anderson
Wahoo McDaniel beat Roddy Piper
Leroy Brown beat Sgt. Slaughter by DQ

10/23/81: Charleston, SC @ County Hall
Johnny Weaver beat Alfred Hayes in a Texas death match
Buddy Landell beat Tony Russo
Vinnie Valentino beat Ali Bey
Mike Miller draw Don Kernodle
Jake Roberts & Leroy Brown beat The Grappler & Super Destroyer

10/23/81: Richmond, VA @ Coliseum
Tournament for 1982 Cadillac featuring Ole Anderson, Roddy Piper, Ivan Koloff, Austin Idol, Ron Bass, Wahoo McDaniel, Ricky Steamboat, Paul Jones
Roddy Piper beat Wahoo McDaniel in tournament final.

10/23/81: Knoxville, TN @ Chilhowee Park
Kevin Sullivan vs. Jay Strongbow
Blackjack Mulligan, Sr. & Blackjack Mulligan, Jr. vs. Doug Vines & Jeff Sword
Ray Candy vs. Mike Fever
Rick Connors vs. Tim Horner
Terry Taylor vs. Izzy Slapowitz

10/25/81: Winston-Salem, NC @ Memorial Coliseum
Johnny Weaver beat Lord Alfred Hayes
Austin Idol beat Leroy Brown
The Grappler & Super Destroyer beat Jake Roberts & Jay Youngblood

10/25/81: Asheville, NC @ Civic Center
Wahoo McDaniel beat Roddy Piper Texas death match
Sgt. Slaughter beat Ricky Steamboat
Ole Anderson beat Jimmy Valiant
Johnny Weaver & Paul Jones beat Chris Markoff & Nikolai Volkoff
Don Kernodle beat Charlie Fulton
Buddy Landell beat El Toro
Keith Larson beat Mike Davis

10/26/81: Greenville, SC @ Memorial Auditorium
Wahoo McDaniel & Jimmy Valiant beat Gene Anderson & Ole Anderson by DQ
Sgt. Slaughter beat Jay Youngblood
Mike Davis beat Ricky Harris
Vinnie Valentino beat Charlie Fulton
Tony Russo beat Don Gilbert

10/26/81: Hillsville, VA @ Woodlawn Intermediate School
Kevin Sullivan vs. Jay Strongbow
Blackjack Mulligan, Sr. & Blackjack Mulligan, Jr. vs. Wayne Farris & Bobby Eaton
Ray Candy vs. Doug Vines
Terry Taylor vs. Jeff Sword
Rick Connors vs. Tim Horner

10/27/81: Raleigh, NC @ Dorton Arena
Jimmy Valiant & Ricky Steamboat beat Ivan Koloff & Roddy Piper by DQ
Jay Youngblood beat Austin Idol
Scott McGhee beat Charlie Fulton
Vinnie Valentino beat Ricky Harris
Mike Davis beat Jim Nelson

10/27/81: Columbia, SC @ Township Auditorium

10/28/81: Charlotte, NC @ WPCQ Studios (TV)
included Roddy Piper, Ole Anderson, Ivan Koloff & Ron Bass

10/29/81: Harrisonburg, VA @ High School
Ron Bass vs. Carl Fergie
Ricky Steamboat vs. Austin Idol
Wahoo McDaniel vs. Roddy Piper
Charlie Fulton vs. Scott McGhee
Tony Anthony vs. Ali Bey

10/29/81: Spartanburg, SC @ Memorial Auditorium
Sgt. Slaughter beat Johnny Weaver
Jake Roberts & Jimmy Valiant beat The Grappler & Super Destroyer
Vinnie Valentino beat Tony Russo
Buddy Landell beat Jim Nelson
Mike Davis draw Keith Larson

10/30/81: Charleston, SC @ County Hall
Chris Markoff & Nikolai Volkoff beat The Grappler & Super Destroyer
Jake Roberts beat Alfred Hayes
Vinnie Valentino beat Tony Russo
Don Kernodle beat Mike Miller
Mike Davis beat Jim Nelson

10/30/81: Lynchburg, VA @ City Armory
Sgt. Slaughter vs. Johnny Weaver
Wahoo McDaniel vs. Roddy Piper
Leroy Brown vs. Ivan Koloff

10/30/81: Knoxville, TN @ Chilhowee Park
Izzy Slapowitz beat Jackie Lakin
Rock Connors beat Tim Horner
Ray Candy beat Jim Dalton
Ox Baker beat Mike Fever
Kevin Sullivan no contest with Jay Strongbow
Terry Taylor, Blackjack Mulligan, Sr. & Blackjack Mulligan, Jr. beat Jeff Sword, Doug Vines & Jimmy Holiday

11/1/81: Roanoke, VA @ Civic Center
Ray Candy beat Blackjack Mulligan, Sr. by DQ in a special challenge match
Blackjack Mulligan, Sr. & Blackjack Mulligan, Jr. beat Jeff Sword & Doug Vines
Chief Jay Strongbow beat Kevin Sullivan by DQ
Ox Baker beat Tim Horner
Ray Candy beat Dennis Brown
Rick Connors draw Izzy Slapowitz
Ricky Steamboat & Jake Roberts vs. Roddy Piper & The Grappler(both teams no showed)

11/1/81: Toronto, Ontario @ Maple Leaf Gardens
John Studd beat Angelo Mosca
Ron Bass & Tony Parisi beat Greg Valentine & Ivan Koloff by DQ in a Texas tornado match
Killer Khan beat Paul Jones
Chris Markoff & Nikolai Volkoff beat Billy Red Lyons & Steve Bolus
Johnny Weaver beat Jim Dalton
Frankie Laine beat Deke Rivers
Goldie Rogers beat ken Hill

11/1/81: Greensboro, NC @ Coliseum
Sgt. Slaughter beat Leroy Brown
Roddy Piper beat Ricky Steamboat to win NWA Mid Atlantic Title
Gene Anderson & Ole Anderson beat Wahoo McDaniel & Jake Roberts
The Grappler beat Jay Youngblood
Jimmy Valiant beat Ricky Harris
The Ninja beat Mike Davis
Blackjack Mulligan, Jr. beat Jim Nelson
Buddy Landell beat Mike Miller

11/2/81: Fayetteville, NC @ Cumberland County Memorial Auditorium
Wahoo McDaniel vs. Sgt. Slaughter
Ricky Steamboat vs. Austin Idol
Ron Bass vs. Ivan Koloff
Also including The Ninja & others

11/2/81: Greenville, SC @ Memorial Auditorium
Roddy Piper beat NWA World Champ Ric Flair by DQ
Jimmy Valiant & Leroy Brown beat Gene Anderson & Ole Anderson by DQ
Jake Roberts beat Grappler
Ali Bey beat Keith Larson
Vinnie Valentino beat El Toro

11/3/81: Charlotte, NC @ Coliseum
Ivan Koloff beat Ron Bass to win NWA Mid Atlantic Television Title

11/3/81: Columbia, SC @ Township Auditorium
Leroy Brown beat Sgt. Slaughter by DQ
Jimmy Valiant & Jay Youngblood beat Gene Anderson & Super Destroyer
Jake Roberts beat The Grappler
Ninja beat Tony Anthony
Mike Davis beat Mike Miller by DQ

11/4/81: Orange, VA
Blackjack Mulligan, Sr. & Blackjack Mulligan, Jr. vs. Doug Vines & Jeff Sword in a Texas tornado match
Kevin Sullivan vs. Jim Dalton
Ox Baker vs. Dennis Brown
Ray Candy vs. Tim Horner
Ken Hall vs. Izzy Slapowitz

11/4/81: Charlotte, NC @ WPCQ Studios (TV)

11/5/81: Sumter, SC @ Exposition Center
NWA World Champion Ric Flair beat Sgt. Slaughter
Jimmy Valiant & Ricky Steamboat beat Gene Anderson & Roddy Piper
Terry Holiday beat Terry Latham
Jim Nelson beat Keith Larson
Don Kernodle beat Jim Nelson

11/6/81: Charleston, SC @ County Hall
Leroy Brown & Jake Roberts beat The Grappler & Super Destroyer
Jay Youngblood beat Austin Idol
The Ninja beat Terry Latham
Vinnie Valentino beat El Toro
Ricky Harris draw Keith Larson

11/6/81: Knoxville, TN @ Chilhowee Park
Tim Horner draw El Santo
Izzy Slapowitz beat Ted Allen
Rick Connors beat Jackie Lakin
Jim Dalton beat Jeff Sword by DQ
Blackjack Mulligan, Sr. & Blackjack Mulligan, Jr. beat Doug Vines & Ray Candy
Kevin Sullivan beat Jay Strongbow by DQ in a match with 2 referees
NWA World Champion Ric Flair beat Ivan Koloff

11/8/81: Greenville, SC @ Memorial Auditorium
Rick Steamboat won a Cadillac Tournament

11/8/81: Savannah, GA @ Civic Center
16-man battle royal featuring Johnny Weaver, Super Destroyer, The Grappler, Mr. Wrestling II, Roddy Piper, Leroy Brown, Jay Youngblood, Gene Anderson, Jake Roberts, Michael Hayes, Buddy Landell, Scott McGhee, Carl Fergie, Nikolai Volkoff & Jimmy Valiant
The Ninja vs. Tony Anthony

11/9/81: Weldon, NC
Keith Larsen beat Jim Nelson
Vinnie Valentino beat Mike Miller
Buddy Landell beat Charlie Fulton
Johnny Weaver & Jay Youngblood beat Chris Markoff & Nikolai Volkoff
Roddy Piper beat Wahoo McDaniel in a no DQ match

11/10/81: Columbia, SC @ Township Auditorium
Sgt. Slaughter beat Leroy Brown
Super Destroyer beat Jay Youngblood
Jake Roberts vs. The Grappler
The Ninja beat Terry Latham
Jim Nelson beat Vinnie Valentino
Mike Davis beat Ricky Harris

11/10/81: Raleigh, NC @ Dorton Arena
Ivan Koloff beat Ron Bass
Austin Idol beat Ricky Steamboat
Roddy Piper beat Jimmy Valiant by DQ
Buddy Landell & Scott McGhee beat Carl Fergie & Mike Miller
Don Kernodle beat El Toro
Tony Anthony beat Tony Russo

11/10/81: Christiansburg, VA @ Christiansburg High School
Johnny Weaver & Paul Jones vs. Chris Markoff & Nikolai Volkoff
Blackjack Mulligan, Jr. vs. Ray Candy
Jeff Sword vs. Tim Horner
Ox Baker vs. Dennis Brown
Doug Vines vs. Jim Dalton

11/11/81: Charlotte, NC @ WPCQ Studios (TV)

11/11/81: Marysville, TN
Jeff Sword draw Dennis Brown
Doug Vines beat Rick Connors by DQ

Doug Vines & Jeff Sword beat Rock Connors & Dennis Brown
Kevin Sullivan beat Jim Dalton
Ox Baker & Ray Candy beat Blackjack Mulligan, Jr. & Tim Horner

11/12/81: Norfolk, VA @ Scope
Gene & Ole Anderson vs. Ricky Steamboat & Jake Roberts
Sgt. Slaughter vs. Leroy Brown in a no DQ match
Nikolai Volkoff vs. Jimmy Valiant
The Ninja vs. ??

11/13/81: Knoxville, TN @ Chilhowee Park
Jim Duggan draw Rick Connors
Ray Candy beat Dennis Brown
Doug Vines & Jeff Sword beat Tim Horner & Jim Dalton
Blackjack Mulligan, Jr. beat Ox Baker by DQ
Jay Strongbow beat Kevin Sullivan by DQ in an Indian strap match
Blackjack Mulligan, Sr. beat Ray Stevens by DQ

11/13/81: Richmond, VA @ Coliseum
Johnny Weaver & Buddy Landell beat Carl Fergie & Mike Miller
Don Kernodle beat Charlie Fulton
The Ninja beat Terry Latham
Austin Idol beat Ron Bass
Ole Anderson & Jim Nelson beat Paul Jones & Jake Roberts
Roddy Piper beat Wahoo McDaniel
Ricky Steamboat beat Sgt. Slaughter by DQ

11/13/81: Charleston, SC @ County Hall
Ivan Koloff beat Leroy Brown
The Grappler & Super Destroyer beat Chris Markoff & Nikolai Volkoff
Jim Nelson vs. Scott McGhee
Tony Anthony vs. Ali Bey
El Toro vs. Tony Russo

11/14/81: Cincinnati, OH @ Gardens
Jim Dalton draw Jeff Sword
Tim Horner beat Doug Vines
Jake Roberts & Jimmy Valiant beat The Grappler & Super Destroyer
Wahoo McDaniel beat Roddy Piper by DQ
Ricky Steamboat beat Ivan Koloff
Sgt. Slaughter beat Leroy Brown

11/14/81: Pilot Mountain, NC
Chris Markoff, Nikolai Volkoff & Alfred Hayes vs. Blackjack Mulligan, Jr., Paul Jones & Jay Youngblood
Austin Idol vs. Ron Bass
The Ninja vs. Scott McGhee
Ali Bey vs. Dennis Brown

11/15/81: Asheville, NC @ Civic Center
Vinnie Valentino beat Ricky Harris
Jim Nelson beat Terry Latham
Michael Hayes beat Terry Gordy
Tommy Rich beat Roddy Piper
Blackjack Mulligan, Sr & Jr. beat Ole Anderson & Ivan Koloff
Blackjack Mulligan, Sr beat Sgt. Slaughter by DQ

11/15/81: Toronto, Ontario @ Maple Leaf Gardens(50th Anniversary Show)
NWA World Champion Ric Flair beat Harley Race
Andre The Giant double DQ Killer Khan
Angelo Mosca beat John Studd by countout
Ron Bass beat Mike Miller(sub for Kurt Von Hess)
Johnny Weaver beat Charlie Fulton
Tony Parisi & Mike Davis beat Doug Vines & Izzy Slapowitz

11/15/81: Greenville, SC @ Memorial Auditorium(Special Sunday Card)
Blackjack Mulligan, Sr. beat Sgt. Slaughter by DQ
Blackjack Mulligan, Sr. & Blackjack Mulligan, Jr. beat Ole Anderson & Ivan Koloff
Tommy Rich beat Roddy Piper
Michael Hayes beat Terry Gordy
Jim Nelson beat Terry Latham
Vinnie Valentino beat Ricky Harris

11/15/81: Hampton, VA @ Coliseum
Austin Idol beat Ricky Steamboat
Jimmy Valiant & Leroy Brown beat The Grappler & Super Destroyer
Jay Youngblood & Jake Roberts beat Chris Markoff & Nikolai Volkoff
The Ninja beat Tony Anthony
Buddy Landell beat Don Kernodle
Carl Fergie beat Keith Larson

11/16/81: Fayetteville, NC @ Cumberland County Memorial Auditorium
Blackjack Mulligan, Sr. & Blackjack Mulligan, Jr. vs. Chris Markoff & Nikolai Volkoff
Wahoo McDaniel vs. Sgt. Slaughter in a no DQ match
Roddy Piper vs. Ricky Steamboat
Paul Jones vs. Carl Fergie
Jim Nelson vs. Tony Anthony

11/16/81: Brantford, Ontario(TV)
Johnny Weaver beat Doug Vines
Harley Race beat Tim Horner
Johnny Weaver & Ron Bass beat Charlie Fulton & Doug Vines
Harley Race beat Mike Miller
Ron Bass beat Charlie Fulton
Harley Race beat Mike Davis
Tony Parisi beat Mike Miller
Harley Race beat Johnny Weaver
Mike Miller & Charlie Fulton beat Mike Davis & Tim Horner

11/17/81: Columbia, SC @ Township Auditorium
Sgt. Slaughter beat Wahoo McDaniel
Paul Jones & Jake Roberts beat The Grappler & Super Destroyer
Jay Youngblood beat The Ninja
Terry Latham beat Carl Fergie
Don Kernodle beat Jim Nelson

11/17/81: Raleigh, NC @ Dorton Arena
Roddy Piper & Austin Idol vs. Ricky Steamboat & Jimmy Valiant
Ivan Koloff vs. Leroy Brown
Chris Markoff vs. Ron Bass

11/18/81: Charlotte, NC @ WPCQ Studios (TV)
Jay Youngblood beat Ricky Harris
Sgt. Slaughter beat Ken Hall
Jimmy Valiant beat Deke Rivers
Ricky Steamboat & Jake Roberts beat The Grappler & Super Destroyer by DQ

11/19/81: Harrisonburg, VA @ High School
Paul Jones, Johnny Weaver & Blackjack Mulligan, Jr. vs. Nikolai Volkoff, Chris Markoff & Alfred Hayes
Ron Sexton vs. Kevin Sullivan
Jeff Sword vs. Jim Dalton
Doug Vines vs. Izzy Slapowitz

11/19/81: Sumter, SC @ Exposition Center
Sgt. Slaughter beat Ricky Steamboat
Jimmy Valiant & Ron Bass beat Austin Idol & Gene Anderson
Judy Martin beat Candy Malloy
Jake Roberts beat The Grappler
Tony Anthony beat Jim Nelson

11/19/81: Burlington, NC @ Cummings High School
Wahoo McDaniel vs. Roddy Piper
Jay Youngblood & Don Kernodle vs. Super Destroyer & Carl Fergie
Mike Davis vs. Ricky Harris
Keith Larsen vs. Tony Russo

11/20/81: Lynchburg, VA @ City Armory
Tony Anthony beat Tony Russo
Mike Davis beat Ricky Harris
Mike Miller beat Scott McGhee
Paul Jones, Johnny Weaver & Jimmy Valiant beat Nikolai Volkoff, Chris Markoff & Alfred Hayes

11/20/81: Winston-Salem, NC @ Memorial Coliseum
Roddy Piper vs. Wahoo McDaniel
Austin Idol vs. Jay Youngblood
The Grappler & Super Destroyer vs. Ron Bass & Buddy Landell

11/20/81: Knoxville, TN @ Chilhowee Park
El Santo beat Dennis Brown
Rick Connors beat Jim Dalton
Ron Sexton & Tim Horner beat Jeff Sword & Doug Vines
Kevin Sullivan beat Jay Strongbow in a Canadian lumberjack match
Michael Hayes beat Terry Gordy by DQ
Ray Candy beat Blackjack Mulligan, Jr.
Blackjack Mulligan, Sr. beat John Studd lights out match

11/20/81: Charleston, SC @ County Hall
Ivan Koloff vs. Ricky Steamboat
Judy Martin vs. Candi Malloy
Jake Roberts vs. Gene Anderson
The Ninja vs. Keith Larson
Vinnie Valentino & Don Kernodle vs. Charlie Fulton & Carl Fergie

11/22/81: Roanoke, VA @ Civic Center
Johnny Weaver & Jay Youngblood beat Chris Markoff & Nikolai Volkoff
Leroy Brown beat Ivan Koloff by DQ
Paul Jones & Jake Roberts beat The Grappler & Super Destroyer
The Ninja beat Scott McGhee(sub for Buddy Landell)
Kevin Sullivan beat Terry Latham
Carl Fergie beat Mike Davis
Dennis Brown beat Izzy Slapowitz

11/22/81: Kingsport, TN
Doug Vines & Jeff Sword beat Jim Dalton & Tim Horner
Super Destroyer beat Ron Sexton
Ray Candy beat Johnny Weaver
Paul Jones beat The Grappler
Leroy Brown beat Ivan Koloff by DQ

11/24/81: Columbia, SC @ Township Auditorium
Sgt. Slaughter beat Jay Youngblood
Leroy Brown & Jimmy Valiant beat The Grappler & Super Destroyer
Johnny Weaver beat The Ninja by DQ
Jim Nelson beat Mike Davis
Carl Fergie beat Vinnie Valentino

11/24/81: Raleigh, NC @ Dorton Arena
Ron Bass beat Ricky Harris
Buddy Landell beat Charlie Fulton
Don Kernodle beat Tony Russo
Chris Markoff & Nikolai Volkoff beat Paul Jones & Jake Roberts
Ricky Steamboat no contest with Roddy Piper
NWA World Champion Ric Flair beat Ivan Koloff by DQ

11/24/81: Somerset, KY @ National Guard Armory
Blackjack Mulligan, Sr. & Tim Horner vs. Ox Baker & Ray Candy
Kevin Sullivan vs. Ron Sexton
Jim Dalton vs. Jeff Sword
Denny Brown vs. Doug Vines

11/25/81: Charlotte, NC @ WPCQ Studios (TV)
Blackjack Mulligan & Jake Roberts beat Nikolai Volkoff & Charlie Fulton
The Ninja beat Vinnie Valentino
Ole Anderson & Roddy Piper beat Tony Anthony & Don Kernodle

11/26/81: Norfolk, VA @ Scope
Wahoo McDaniel vs. Sgt. Slaughter
Roddy Piper vs. Ricky Steamboat
Ole Anderson vs. Jake Roberts

Cadillac tournament featuring Jimmy Valiant, Ron Bass, Jay Youngblood, Leroy Brown, Jake Roberts, Roddy Piper, Ole Anderson and others

11/26/81: Knoxville, TN @ Chilhowee Park
El Santo draw Jackie Lakin
Rick Connors beat Jim Dalton
Blackjack Mulligan, Jr. beat Ray Candy by DQ
Doug Vines & Jeff Sword beat Ron Sexton & Tim Horner
Johnny Weaver beat Alfred Hayes
Blackjack Mulligan, Sr. DCO with Ox Baker
NWA World Champion Ric Flair beat Ivan Koloff

11/26/81: Greensboro, NC @ Coliseum
1982 Cadillac tournament
1st Round
Carl Fergie beat Mike Davis
Jake Roberts beat Mike Davis
Ivan Koloff beat Keith Larsen
Blackjack Mulligan Jr. beat Carl Fergie
Roddy Piper double DQ Ricky Steamboat
Angelo Mosca beat Buddy Landell
Greg Valentine beat Tony Anthony
Sgt. Slaughter beat Johnny Weaver

2nd Round
Ivan Koloff beat Jake Roberts
Blackjack Mulligan, Jr. beat Sgt. Slaughter by DQ
Greg Valentine double DQ Angelo Mosca

Finals
Blackjack Mulligan, Jr. beat Ivan Koloff via pinfall to win Cadillac tournament
Blackjack Mulligan Sr. DDQ John Studd lights out match
NWA World Champion Ric Flair beat Ole Anderson(26:00) in a cage match

11/27/81: Appalachia, VA
Johnny Weaver & Jay Youngblood beat Chris Markoff & Nikolai Volkoff to win NWA Mid Atlantic Tag Title

11/27/81: Richmond, VA @ Coliseum
Ole Anderson & Greg Valentine beat Ric Flair & Paul Jones
Blackjack Mulligan no contest with John Studd in a lights out match
Blackjack Mulligan, Jr.(sub for Wahoo McDaniel) beat Ivan Koloff
Blackjack Mulligan, Jr. beat Ricky Harris
Roddy Piper double DQ Ricky Steamboat
Don Kernodle beat The Ninja by DQ
Buddy Landell beat Charlie Fulton
Keith Larson beat Tony Russo
Vinnie Valentino beat Mike Miller

11/27/81: Charleston, SC @ County Hall
Jake Roberts vs. Gene Anderson
Leroy Brown & Jimmy Valiant vs. The Grappler & Austin Idol
Super Destroyer vs. Ron Bass
Jim Nelson vs. Mike Davis
Tony Anthony vs. Carl Fergie

11/28/81: Sumter, SC @ Exposition Center
Mike Miller vs. Vinnie Valentino
Don Gilbert vs. Jim Nelson
Paul Jones vs. The Ninja
The Grappler & Super Destroyer vs. Jake Roberts & Jimmy Valiant
Leroy Brown vs. Sgt. Slaughter

11/28/81: Knoxville, TN @ WBIR Studios (TV)

11/29/81: Savannah, GA @ Civic Center
Ivan Koloff vs. Mr. Wrestling II
Masked Superstar vs. Tommy Rich
Chris Markoff & Nikolai Volkoff vs. Johnny Weaver & Jay Youngblood
The Ninja vs. Steve O

11/29/81: Charlotte, NC @ Coliseum
Don Kernodle beat Mike Miller
Paul Jones beat The Angel
Buddy Landell & Ron Bass beat Ricky Harris & Carl Fergie
Ole Anderson & Roddy Piper beat Jake Roberts & Ricky Steamboat
Blackjack Mulligan, Jr. beat Sgt. Slaughter by DQ
Blackjack Mulligan, Sr. beat John Studd
NWA World Champion Ric Flair beat Ray Stevens via pinfall

11/29/81: Greenville, SC @ Memorial Auditorium
NWA World Champion Ric Flair beat Ole Anderson in a cage match
Blackjack Mulligan, Sr. & Blackjack Mulligan, Jr. beat Sgt. Slaughter & John Studd
Ricky Steamboat beat Roddy Piper
Ray Stevens draw Paul Jones
Jake Roberts beat Super Destroyer
Pvt. Nelson vs. Mike Davis
Vinnie Valentino beat Tony Anthony

11/30/81: Toronto, Ontario @ Maple Leaf Gardens
Leroy Brown beat John Studd by DQ
Ricky Steamboat & Ron Bass beat Greg Valentine & Ivan Koloff
Johnny Weaver beat Alfred Hayes by countout
Jay Youngblood beat Ricky Harris
Tony Parisi beat Frank Marconi
Steve Bolus beat Tim Gerard

12/1/81: Columbia, SC @ Township Auditorium
Blackjack Mulligan vs. Sgt. Slaughter
Johnny Weaver vs. The Ninja
Blackjack Mulligan, Jr. vs. Jim Nelson
Mike Miller vs. Tony Anthony
Leroy Brown & Jimmy Valiant vs. Axe Duggan & Carl Fergie

12/1/81: Raleigh, NC @ Dorton Arena
Ivan Koloff beat Ron Bass
Ricky Steamboat beat Roddy Piper by DQ
Mike Davis beat Charlie Fulton
Buddy Landell beat Ricky Harris
Don Kernodle beat Nikolai Volkoff
Paul Jones & Jake Roberts beat Austin Idol & Super Destroyer

12/2/81: Charlotte, NC @ WPCQ Studios (TV)
Blackjack Mulligan, Jr. & Jake Roberts beat Tony Russo & Mike Prater via pinfall
John Studd beat ??
Jim Nelson beat Tim Horner
Jay Youngblood beat Jeff Sword via pinfall
Ole Anderson & Ray Stevens beat Paul Jones & Buddy Landell via pinfall
Carl Fergie beat Larry Hamilton via pinfall

12/3/81: Charlotte, NC @ WPCQ Studios (TV)
Ricky Steamboat beat Charlie Fulton
Ivan Koloff beat Jim Gray
Ray Stevens beat Mike Prater
Jimmy Valiant beat ??
Sgt. Slaughter & Jim Nelson vs. ?? & ??

12/4/81: Knoxville, TN @ Chilhowee Park
Kevin Sullivan beat Blackjack Mulligan
Blackjack Mulligan, Jr. beat Ray Candy
Rick Connors DCO with Ron Sexton
Doug Vines & Jeff Sword beat Tim Horner & Jackie Lakin
Jim Dalton draw Dennis Brown

12/4/81: Lynchburg, VA @ City Armory
Tony Anthony beat Ricky Harris
Jim Nelson beat Don Kernodle
Paul Jones & Jay Youngblood beat Chris Markoff & Carl Fergie
Johnny Weaver beat Alfred Hayes by DQ
Ricky Steamboat double DQ Roddy Piper
Jimmy Valiant beat Ivan Koloff

12/4/81: Charleston, SC @ County Hall
Jake Roberts vs. Gene Anderson in a loser leaves town match
Leroy Brown & Ron Bass vs. Austin Idol & Super Destroyer
The Ninja vs. Mike Davis
Charlie Fulton vs. Buddy Landell
Vinnie Valentino vs. Mike Miller

12/5/81: Cincinnati, OH @ Gardens
Don Kernodle beat Ricky Harris
Jim Nelson beat Keith Larson
Jake Roberts & Paul Jones beat Chris Markoff & Alfred Hayes
Jimmy Valiant beat Super Destroyer via pinfall
Leroy Brown beat Sgt. Slaughter by DQ
Ricky Steamboat beat Roddy Piper via pinfall

12/5/81: Buffalo, NY
Ivan Koloff beat Ron Bass
Blackjack Mulligan Sr. & Blackjack Mulligan, Jr. beat Gene Anderson & Ole Anderson
NWA World Champion Ric Flair beat Ray Stevens

12/5/81: Spartanburg, SC @ Memorial Auditorium
No Wrestling

12/6/81: Roanoke, VA @ Civic Center
Ivan Koloff beat Leroy Brown in a no DQ match
Johnny Weaver beat Alfred Hayes in a Texas death match
Jimmy Valiant won a 12-man Battle Royal for 1982 Cadillac that also included Blackjack Mulligan, Jay Youngblood, Ron Bass, Ninja, Leroy Brown, Ivan Koloff, Johnny Weaver, Alfred Hayes

12/6/81: Asheville, NC @ Civic Center
Sgt. Slaughter beat Blackjack Mulligan, Jr.
Tommy Rich beat Roddy Piper by DQ
Ricky Steamboat beat Greg Valentine
Paul Jones & Jake Roberts beat Ole Anderson & Super Destroyer
Pvt. Nelson beat Keith Larson
Don Kernodle beat Ricky Harris

12/6/81: Charlotte, NC @ Coliseum
Cadillac battle royal including Ole Anderson, Roddy Piper, Paul Jones, Ricky Steamboat, Jake Roberts
Sgt. Slaughter vs. Blackjack Mulligan, Jr.

12/7/81: Greenville, SC @ Memorial Auditorium
Paul Jones & Jake Roberts beat Ole Anderson & Ivan Koloff by DQ
Blackjack Mulligan, Sr. draw John Studd
Jimmy Valiant beat Ivan Koloff
Tony Anthony beat Tony Russo
Buddy Landell beat Charlie Fulton
Vinnie Valentino beat Mike Miller

12/7/81: Fayetteville, NC @ Cumberland County Memorial Auditorium
Sgt. Slaughter vs. Jay Youngblood
Ricky Steamboat vs. Roddy Piper in a 2 of 3 falls match
Blackjack Mulligan, Jr. vs. Nikolai Volkoff
Ron Bass vs. The Ninja
Jim Duggan & Carl Fergie vs. Don Kernodle & Mike Davis

12/8/81: Raleigh, NC @ Civic Center
Blackjack Mulligan, Sr. beat John Studd
Leroy Brown beat Sgt. Slaughter by DQ
Jimmy Valiant & Jay Youngblood beat Austin Idol & Super Destroyer
Johnny Weaver beat Gene Anderson
Buddy Landell beat Chris Markoff
Tony Anthony beat Pvt. Nelson
Don Kernodle beat Vinnie Valentino

12/8/81: Columbia, SC @ Township Auditorium
Charlie Fulton beat Keith Larsen
Mike Davis beat Mike Miller
The Ninja beat Blackjack Mulligan, Jr.
Ox Baker & Carl Fergie beat Paul Jones & Jake Roberts
Ivan Koloff beat Ron Bass
Ricky Steamboat beat Roddy Piper by DQ

12/9/81: Charlotte, NC @ WPCQ Studios (TV)
Blackjack Mulligan, Jr. & Jake Roberts beat Charlie Fulton & Chris Markoff via pinfall
The Ninja beat Mike Davis via pinfall
Terry Taylor beat Mike Miller via pinfall
Jimmy Valiant beat Tony Russo via pinfall
Billy Robinson beat Don Kernodle via pinfall
Ox Baker & Carl Fergie beat Keith Larson & Jay Youngblood via pinfall

12/10/81: Charlotte, NC @ WPCQ Studios (TV)
Blackjack Mulligan, Jr. & Jake Roberts vs. Mike Miller & Charlie Fulton via pinfall
Billy Robinson beat Tony Anthony via pinfall
Ivan Koloff beat Keith Larsen via pinfall
Terry Taylor beat Tony Russo via pinfall
Ox Baker & Carl Fergie beat Vinnie Valentino & Don Kernodle

12/10/81: Harrisonburg, VA @ High School
Doug Vines & Jeff Sword vs. Tim Horner & Jim Dalton
Rick Connors vs. Denny Brown
Ray Candy vs. Ron Sexton
John Studd vs. Blackjack Mulligan
Roddy Piper vs. Ricky Steamboat

12/11/81: Richmond, VA @ Coliseum
NWA World Champion Ric Flair beat Ole Anderson
Blackjack Mulligan, Sr. beat John Studd
Jake Roberts beat Jim Nelson
Jimmy Valiant beat Chris Markoff
Sgt. Slaughter beat Paul Jones
Roddy Piper & Ivan Koloff beat Jay Youngblood & Ricky Steamboat in a Texas tornado match

12/11/81: Charleston, SC @ County Hall
Leroy Brown & Ron Bass vs. Ox Baker & Carl Fergie
Super Destroyer vs. Terry Taylor hair vs. mask match
The Ninja vs. Buddy Landell
Mike Miller vs. Mike Davis
Charlie Fulton vs. Tony Anthony

12/11/81: Knoxville, TN @ Chilhowee Park
Kevin Sullivan vs. Austin Idol
Terry Gordy vs. Michael Hayes in a Texas death match
Rick Connors vs. Ron Sexton in a boxing match
Doug Vines & Jeff Sword vs. Tim Horner & Jim Dalton

12/12/81: Hampton, VA @ Coliseum
Sgt. Slaughter(sub for Ivan Koloff) beat Ricky Steamboat
Sgt. Slaughter beat Blackjack Mulligan, Sr.
John Studd beat Blackjack Mulligan, Jr.
Jim Nelson beat Mike Davis
The Ninja beat Don Kernodle
Ox Baker & Carl Fergie beat Jimmy Valiant & Johnny Weaver

12/12/81: Spartanburg, SC @ Memorial Auditorium
Leroy Brown beat Roddy Piper by DQ
Gene Anderson beat Jay Youngblood
Jake Roberts & Paul Jones beat Chris Markoff & The Bounty Hunter
Ron Bass beat Mike Miller
Buddy Landell beat Charlie Fulton
Vinnie Valentino beat Keith Larson

12/13/81: Savannah, GA @ Civic Center
NWA World Champion Ric Flair vs. Ole Anderson
Sgt. Slaughter vs. Mr. Wrestling II
Johnny Weaver & Jay Youngblood vs. Jim Duggan & Carl Fergie
Buddy Landell vs. Charlie Fulton
Tony Russo vs. Mike Davis

12/13/81: Greensboro, NC @ Coliseum
Blackjack Mulligan, Sr. beat John Studd in a cage match
Ricky Steamboat & Ray Stevens beat Roddy Piper & Ole Anderson
Sgt. Slaughter beat Blackjack Mulligan, Jr. in title vs. Cadillac match
Jake Roberts beat Ivan Koloff
The Ninja beat Ron Bass
Paul Jones beat Mike Miller
Jim Nelson beat Don Kernodle

12/25/81: Charlotte, NC @ Coliseum
Sgt. Slaughter draw Blackjack Mulligan Jr.(60:00)
Blackjack Mulligan, Sr. beat Big John Studd
Roddy Piper & Gene Anderson beat Ricky Steamboat & Paul Jones
Ray Stevens beat Ole Anderson by DQ
Jake Roberts beat Greg Valentine
The Ninja beat Mike Davis
Buddy Landell draw Carl Fergie

12/25/81: Richmond, VA @ Coliseum(Afternoon Show)
Blackjack Mulligan, Sr. beat John Studd in a cage match
NWA World Champion Ric Flair beat Ole Anderson in a lumberjack match
Roddy Piper & Ivan Koloff beat Ricky Steamboat & Blackjack Mulligan, Jr.
The Ninja beat Jay Youngblood
Jimmy Valiant beat Alfred Hayes
Ray Stevens beat Gene Anderson
Johnny Weaver beat Charlie Fulton

12/26/81: Norfolk, VA @ Scope
Blackjack Mulligan vs. John Studd in a lights out match
Paul Jones vs. Gene Anderson in a loser leaves town match
Ivan Koloff vs. Jimmy Valiant
The Ninja vs. Johnny Weaver

12/26/81: Greenville, SC @ Memorial Auditorium
Blackjack Mulligan, Jr. beat Sgt. Slaughter
Ricky Steamboat beat Roddy Piper
Ray Stevens & Leroy Brown beat Ole Anderson & a mystery partner
Bill White beat Doug Vines
Abe Jacobs beat Izzy Slapowitz by referee decision
Carl Fergie beat Keith Larsen
Jim Nelson beat Tony Anthony

12/27/81: Asheville, NC @ Civic Center
Sgt. Slaughter vs. Blackjack Mulligan, Jr. in a match with 2 referees
Ivan Koloff & Ole Anderson vs. Paul Jones & Ray Stevens in a loser leaves town match
Ricky Steamboat beat Roddy Piper

12/27/81: Greensboro, NC @ Coliseum
Sgt. Slaughter beat Blackjack Mulligan
Ray Stevens, Jake Roberts & Blackjack Mulligan, Jr. beat Gene Anderson, Ole Anderson & Ivan Koloff by DQ in an elimination match
Ricky Steamboat beat Roddy Piper
The Ninja beat Paul Jones in a loser leaves town match
Jimmy Valiant beat Carl Fergie via pinfall
Terry Taylor beat Tony Russo
Keith Larson draw Tony Anthony

12/27/81: Toronto, Ontario @ Maple Leaf Gardens
Tony Parisi beat Tim Gerrard
Billy Red Lyons beat Kurt Von Hess by DQ
Farmer Pete beat Little John
Johnny Weaver & Jay Youngblood beat Kurt Von Hess & Frankie Laine
Blackjack Mulligan, Jr. & Jake Roberts beat The Grappler & Super Destroyer
Ivan Koloff beat Ron Bass
Big John Studd beat Leroy Brown
Andre The Giant beat Killer Khan in a Mongolian stretcher match

12/28/81: Lynchburg, VA @ City Armory
Mike Davis beat Tony Russo
Tony Anthony beat Charlie Fulton
Jay Youngblood beat Chris Markoff
Paul Jones beat The Ninja by DQ
Johnny Weaver beat Alfred Hayes in a lumberjack match
Leroy Brown & Jimmy Valiant beat Roddy Piper & Ivan Koloff

12/29/81: Raleigh, NC @ Dorton Arena
Blackjack Mulligan, Jr. beat Sgt. Slaughter by DQ
Johnny Weaver beat The Ninja by DQ in a bounty match
Jimmy Valiant & Leroy Brown beat Ivan Koloff & Jim Nelson
Jay Youngblood beat Mike Miller
Mike Davis beat Tony Russo
Tony Anthony beat Keith Larson

12/29/81: Columbia, SC @ Township Auditorium

12/30/81: Charlotte, NC @ WPCQ Studios (TV)
Jake Roberts & Jay Youngblood beat Mike Miller & Chris Markoff via pinfall
Ivan Koloff beat Ron Sexton via pinfall
Ray Stevens beat Tony Russo via pinfall
Blackjack Mulligan, Jr. beat Bill White
Sgt. Slaughter & Jim Nelson beat Mike Davis & Terry Taylor by submission

Chapter 3: 1982

1/1/82: Richmond, VA @ Coliseum
Don Kernodle beat Mike Miller
Jake Roberts beat Jim Nelson by DQ
Billy Robinson beat Johnny Weaver
Ray Stevens & Ricky Steamboat beat Ivan Koloff & Gene Anderson
Sgt. Slaughter beat Blackjack Mulligan, Jr.
Ole Anderson beat Paul Jones loser leaves town

1/1/82: Charleston, SC @ County Hall
Blackjack Mulligan, Sr. beat John Studd
Jay Youngblood & Jim Valiant beat Dr. X & Carl Fergie
The Ninja beat Buddy Landell
Terry Taylor beat Chris Markoff
Mike Davis beat Tony Russo
Tony Anthony draw Keith Larsen

1/2/82: Greenville, SC @ Memorial Auditorium
NWA World Champion Ric Flair beat John Studd
Ray Stevens beat Ole Anderson
Terry Taylor beat Jeff Sword
Johnny Weaver beat Doug Vines
Blackjack Mulligan, Jr. beat Chris Markoff
Michael Hayes beat Terry Gordy
Jake Roberts & Jay Youngblood beat Ox Baker & Carl Fergie

1/2/82: Hampton, VA @ Coliseum
Jim Nelson beat Don Kernodle
Billy Robinson beat Paul Jones
Jimmy Valiant beat Ivan Koloff to win NWA Mid Atlantic Television Title
Roddy Piper beat Ricky Steamboat
Sgt. Slaughter beat Blackjack Mulligan, Sr.

1/3/82: Roanoke, VA @ Civic Center
NWA World Champion Ric Flair beat Ole Anderson DQ
Sgt. Slaughter beat Blackjack Mulligan, Jr.
Jake Roberts & Jay Youngblood beat Ox Baker & Carl Fergie
Billy Robinson beat Don Kernodle
Alfred Hayes beat Keith Larsen
Tony Anthony beat Tony Russo

1/3/82: Greensboro, NC @ Coliseum
NWA World Champion Ric Flair beat John Studd(27:00) in a no DQ Match
Blackjack Mulligan, Sr. double DQ Sgt. Slaughter(16:00) in a match with 2 referees
Roddy Piper beat Ricky Steamboat
Ray Stevens beat Ole Anderson in a Texas street fight
The Ninja beat Johnny Weaver
Buddy Landell & Mike Davis beat Chris Markoff & Mike Miller
Terry Taylor beat Jim Nelson

1/5/82: Raleigh, NC @ Civic Center
Billy Robinson beat Johnny Weaver
Jimmy Valiant beat Ivan Koloff
Blackjack Mulligan, Sr. DCO with John Studd
Ricky Steamboat beat Roddy Piper by DQ
Tony Anthony beat Mike Miller
Buddy Landell & Mike Davis beat Jeff Sword & Doug Vines

1/5/82: Columbia, SC @ Township Auditorium
NWA World Champion Ric Flair vs. Ole Anderson in a Texas death match
The Ninja vs. Ray Stevens
Jake Roberts & Jay Youngblood vs. Ox Baker & Carl Fergie
Terry Taylor vs. Chris Markoff
Jim Nelson vs. Don Kernodle
Keith Larson vs. Tony Russo

1/6/82: Charlotte, NC @ WCPQ Studios (TV)
Blackjack Mulligan, Jr. & Jake Roberts beat Doug Vines & Mike Miller via pinfall
Billy Robinson beat Keith Larson via pinfall
Jimmy Valiant beat Jeff Sword
Terry Taylor beat Bill White
Ole Anderson & Ivan Koloff beat Tony Anthony & Buddy Landell

1/7/82: Sumter, SC @ Exposition Center
Blackjack Mulligan vs. John Studd lights out match
Ricky Steamboat & Jay Youngblood vs. Ox Baker & Carl Fergie
Johnny Weaver vs. Billy Robinson
Terry Taylor vs. Mike Miller
Alfred Hayes vs. Tony Anthony
Buddy Landell vs. Izzy Slapovitz

1/8/82: Charleston, SC @ County Hall
John Studd beat Blackjack Mulligan LA showdown
Mike Davis beat Jeff Sword
Buddy Landell beat Mike Miller
Terry Taylor beat The Ninja
Carl Fergie & Ox Baker beat Jay Youngblood & Jake Roberts

1/8/82: Cincinnati, OH @ Riverfront Coliseum
Ivan Koloff & Keith Larsen co-won a battle royal
Johnny Weaver beat Chris Markoff
Billy Robinson beat Tony Russo
Ivan Koloff beat Keith Larson
Roddy Piper beat Don Kernodle
Jimmy Valiant beat Alfred Hayes
Ricky Steamboat beat Jim Nelson
NWA World Champion Ric Flair beat Ole Anderson in a Texas death match
Johnny Weaver beat Roddy Piper by DQ
Ivan Koloff double DQ Ricky Steamboat
Billy Robinson beat Johnny Weaver
Leroy Brown beat Sgt. Slaughter by countout in a no DQ Match
Jimmy Valiant beat Billy Robinson via pinfall to win Cadillac in tournament final

1/10/82: Asheville, NC @ Civic Center
Ricky Steamboat beat Roddy Piper by DQ
Jake Roberts won a 15 man Cadillac Tournament that included Ray Stevens, Ole Anderson, John Studd, Blackjack Mulligan, Sr., Ox Baker, Jay Youngblood, Johnny Weaver, Carl Fergie, Billy Robinson, Jimmy Valiant, Don Kernodle, Terry Taylor, Blackjack Mulligan, Jr., Sgt. Slaughter & Ivan Koloff

1/10/82: Charlotte, NC @ Coliseum
Blackjack Mulligan beat John Studd in a steel cage match
Sgt. Slaughter beat Blackjack Mulligan, Jr.
Ricky Steamboat & Ray Stevens beat Roddy Piper & Ole Anderson in a Texas tornado match
Jake Roberts beat Carl Fergie
The Ninja beat Vinnie Valentino
Jim Nelson beat Buddy Landell
Chris Markoff beat Mike Davis
Tony Anthony beat Mike Miller

1/11/82: Greenville, SC @ Memorial Auditorium
Ray Stevens beat Ole Anderson
Blackjack Mulligan, Jr. beat Sgt. Slaughter by countout
Michael Hayes beat The Ninja(sub for Terry Gordy) via pinfall
Johnny Weaver beat Billy Robinson
Terry Taylor beat Jim Nelson
Alfred Hayes beat Vinnie Valentino

1/12/82: Columbia, SC @ Township Auditorium
Sgt. Slaughter beat Blackjack Mulligan, Jr.
Ray Stevens beat The Ninja
Terry Taylor & Buddy Landell beat Pvt. Nelson & Mike Miller
Johnny Weaver beat Billy Robinson
Mike Davis beat Tony Russo

1/12/82: Raleigh, NC @ Civic Center
Jimmy Valiant beat Austin Idol
Roddy Piper beat Ricky Steamboat
Ox Baker & Carl Fergie beat Jake Roberts & Jay Youngblood
Tony Anthony beat Jeff Sword
Vinnie Valentino beat Bill White
Chris Markoff beat Don Kernodle

1/13/82: Charlotte, NC @ WCPQ Studios (TV)
Terry Taylor vs. Ben Alexander
Austin Idol vs. Mike Davis
Blackjack Mulligan, Sr. & Blackjack Mulligan, Jr. vs. Ricky Harris & Jim Nelson
Jake Roberts vs. Bill White
Sgt. Slaughter vs. Buddy Landell
Sgt. Slaughter vs. Johnny Weaver

1/14/82: Norfolk, VA @ Scope
Sgt. Slaughter vs. Blackjack Mulligan, Jr.
Roddy Piper vs. Ricky Steamboat
Ray Stevens & Johnny Weaver vs. Gene Anderson & The Ninja
Don Kernodle vs. Billy Robinson

1/15/82: Charleston, SC @ County Hall
Blackjack Mulligan, Sr. beat John Studd in a Texas cage match
Ox Baker & Carl Fergie beat Jay Youngblood & Jake Roberts in a no DQ Match
Bill White vs. Don Kernodle
Vanessa McNeil vs. Leilani Kai
Vinnie Valentino vs. Jeff Sword

1/15/82: Richmond, VA @ Coliseum
Sgt. Slaughter vs. Blackjack Mulligan, Jr.
Roddy Piper vs. Ricky Steamboat
Ray Stevens & Leroy Brown vs. Ole Anderson & Masked Superstar
6-girl battle royal including Wendy Richter, Karen Sommer, Fabulous Moolah, Donna Christianello, Joyce Grable & Peggy Lee

1/17/82: Toronto, Ontario @ Maple Leaf Gardens
Angelo Mosca beat John Studd(10:11) to win Canadian Title in a cage match
Johnny Weaver beat Alfred Hayes in a cage match
WWF Champion Bob Backlund beat Greg Valentine
Adrian Adonis & Jesse Ventura beat Tony Parisi & Domenic DeNucci
Dino Bravo beat Frankie Lane(10:10)
Pat Patterson beat Kurt Von Hess(9:12)
John Bonello draw Tim Gerrard

1/17/82: Greensboro, NC @ Coliseum
NWA World Champion Ric Flair beat Sgt. Slaughter by DQ
Ricky Steamboat beat Billy Robinson(sub for Ivan Koloff)
Blackjack Mulligan, Jr. & Jake Roberts beat Ox Baker & Carl Fergie
Ray Stevens beat The Ninja to get 5 minutes with Gene Anderson
Ray Stevens beat Gene Anderson by DQ
Michael Hayes & Jimmy Valiant beat Terry Gordy & Austin Idol
Jim Nelson beat Jay Youngblood
Terry Taylor beat Chris Markoff

1/18/82: Greenville, SC @ Memorial Auditorium
Ole Anderson & Austin Idol beat Ray Stevens & Leroy Brown
Terry Gordy beat Michael Hayes
Terry Taylor beat The Ninja
Porkchop Cash beat Mike Miller

1/19/82: Columbia, SC @ Township Auditorium
Blackjack Mulligan, Sr. & Blackjack Mulligan, Jr. vs. Sgt. Slaughter & Jim Nelson
The Ninja vs. Ray Stevens
Terry Gordy vs. Jake Roberts
Tim Horner vs. Tony Russo
Porkchop Cash vs. Bill White

1/19/82: Raleigh, NC @ Civic Center
Roddy Piper & Austin Idol double DQ Jimmy Valiant & Leroy Brown

Jay Youngblood beat Carl Fergie in an Indian strap match
Buddy Landell beat Billy Robinson
Johnny Weaver beat Mike Miller
Terry Taylor beat Chris Markoff

1/20/82: Charlotte, NC @ WCPQ Studios (TV)
Austin Idol vs. Vinnie Valentino
Jay Youngblood & Jake Roberts vs. Chris Markoff & Ben Alexander
Porkchop Cash vs. Tony Russo
Terry Taylor vs. Steve Sybert
Sgt. Slaughter & Jim Nelson vs. Mike Davis & Don Gilbert

1/21/82: Harrisonburg, VA @ High School
Tony Anthony vs. Jim Nelson
Ox Baker & Carl Fergie vs. Johnny Weaver & Jay Youngblood
Roddy Piper vs. Jake Roberts
Sgt. Slaughter vs. Ricky Steamboat

1/22/82: Knoxville, TN @ Chilhowee Park
Keith Larsen beat Tony Russo
Jay Youngblood & Buddy Landell beat Doug Vines & Jeff Sword
Ivan Koloff beat Ron Sexton
Johnny Weaver beat Izzy Slapowitz by DQ
Kevin Sullivan beat Austin Idol in a no DQ Match
Jimmy Valiant beat Ox Baker
Roddy Piper beat Ricky Steamboat by DQ

1/22/82: Charleston, SC @ County Hall
The Ninja beat Ray Stevens in a bounty match
Cadillac Tournament including John Studd, Jake Roberts, Blackjack Mulligan, Jr., Terry Gordy, Carl Fergie, Don Kernodle, Jim Nelson, Chris Markoff, Tim Horner, Mike Davis, Vinnie Valentino, Steve Sybert
Blackjack Mulligan, Jr. beat John Studd in tournament final to win Cadillac

1/22/82: Cincinnati, OH @ Gardens
NWA World Champion Ric Flair beat Dick Slater

1/23/82: Spartanburg, SC @ Memorial Auditorium
Ricky Steamboat beat Roddy Piper by DQ
Sgt. Slaughter beat Jake Roberts
Porkchop Cash & Mike Davis beat Ox Baker & Carl Fergie
Don Kernodle beat Mike Miller
Tim Horner beat Bill White

1/24/82: Charlotte, NC @ Coliseum
NWA World Champion Ric Flair beat John Studd via pinfall
Blackjack Mulligan, Sr. & Blackjack Mulligan, Jr. beat Sgt. Slaughter & Pvt. Nelson
Johnny Weaver beat Alfred Hayes by countout
Leroy Brown & Porkchop Cash beat Ox Baker & Carl Fergie
Terry Taylor beat Chris Markoff
Tony Anthony beat Steve Sybert

1/25/82: Greenville, SC @ Memorial Auditorium
Blackjack Mulligan, Jr. beat Sgt. Slaughter by DQ
Ole Anderson beat Leroy Brown
The Ninja(sub for Terry Gordy) & Austin Idol beat Michael Hayes & Ray Stevens
Terry Taylor beat Mike Miller
Jim Nelson beat Tim Horner

1/26/82: Columbia, SC @ Township Auditorium
Sgt. Slaughter vs. Blackjack Mulligan, Jr.
Tommy Rich vs. Masked Superstar
Ox Baker vs. Jake Roberts in a loser leaves town match
Steve Sybert vs. Vinnie Valentino
Mike Miller vs. Mike Davis

1/26/82: Raleigh, NC @ Civic Center
Jim Nelson beat Buddy Landell
Terry Taylor beat Bill White
The Ninja beat Jay Youngblood
Johnny Weaver beat Lord Alfred Hayes by countout
Leroy Brown & Jimmy Valiant beat Austin Idol & Roddy Piper
Ray Stevens beat Ivan Koloff by DQ

1/27/82: Charlotte, NC @ WCPQ Studios (TV)
Black Jack Mulligan, Sr. & Jr. vs. Jeff Sword & Mike Miller
Ivan Koloff & Austin Idol vs. Keith Larson & Don Gilbert
Jim Nelson & Steve Sybert vs. Johnny Weaver & Don Kernodle
Ricky Steamboat & Jay Youngblood vs. Doug Vines & Bill White

1/28/82: Sumter, SC @ Exposition Center
Ivan Koloff vs. Jimmy Valiant
Jake Roberts vs. Austin Idol
Jay Youngblood & Don Kernodle vs. Carl Fergie & Eddie Mansfield
Johnny Weaver vs. Alfred Hayes
Mike Davis vs. Bill White

1/28/82: Norfolk, VA @ Scope
Blackjack Mulligan, Sr. & Blackjack Mulligan, Jr. beat Sgt. Slaughter & Jim Nelson
Ray Stevens beat The Ninja by DQ in a bounty match
Roddy Piper double DQ Bob Armstrong
Buddy Landell beat Mike Miller
Porkchop Cash beat Steve Sybert
Terry Taylor beat Chris Markoff

1/29/82: Charleston, SC @ County Hall
Blackjack Mulligan, Jr. beat John Studd in a match with 2 referees
Jake Roberts beat Jim Nelson
Porkchop Cash & Jay Youngblood beat Ox Baker & Carl Fergie to win NWA Mid Atlantic Tag Title
Don Kernodle beat Mike Miller

1/29/82: Richmond, VA @ Coliseum
Ricky Steamboat vs. Roddy Piper
Blackjack Mulligan vs. Sgt. Slaughter
Masked Superstar vs. Ole Anderson
Austin Idol & Ivan Koloff vs. Ray Stevens & Jimmy Valiant

1/31/82: Toronto, Ontario @ Maple Leaf Gardens(Cancelled snow)
Cadillac Tournament
Scheduled participants: Jay Youngblood, Johnny Weaver, Jimmy Valiant, Mr. Fuji, Jesse Ventura, Adrian Adonis, Sgt. Slaughter, Dino Bravo, Ricky Steamboat, Pvt. Nelson, Roddy Piper, John Bonello & Chris Markoff

1/31/82: Asheville, NC @ Civic Center
Ivan Koloff beat Jake Roberts in a title vs. Cadillac match
Blackjack Mulligan, Sr. & Ray Stevens beat Ole Anderson & Terry Gordy
Blackjack Mulligan, Jr. beat Ox Baker
The Ninja beat Don Kernodle
Porkchop Cash & Terry Taylor beat Carl Fergie & Ox Baker
Buddy Landell beat Mike Miller

2/1/82: Greenville, SC @ Memorial Auditorium
Ricky Steamboat beat Sgt. Slaughter by DQ
Jimmy Valiant beat Ivan Koloff
Austin Idol beat Don Kernodle(sub for Michael Hayes)
Blackjack Mulligan, Jr. beat Jim Nelson
Mike Davis & Don Kernodle beat Carl Fergie & Bill White

2/1/82: Guelph, Ontario @ Memorial Gardens (TV)
Johnny Weaver & Jay Youngblood beat Chris Markoff & Mike Miller
Roddy Piper beat John Bonello in a 2 of 3 falls match
Chris Markoff beat Big Mac via pinfall
Roddy Piper beat Keith Larsen via pinfall
Chris Markoff beat John Bonello via pinfall
Johnny Weaver & Jay Youngblood beat Mike Miller & Tim Gerrard
Johnny Weaver beat Tim Gerrard via pinfall
Roddy Piper & Chris Markoff beat Tony Anthony & Keith Larsen
Johnny Weaver beat Chris Markoff via pinfall
Roddy Piper DCO with Jay Youngblood

2/2/82: Raleigh, NC @ Civic Center
Blackjack Mulligan, Sr. beat Sgt. Slaughter by DQ
Blackjack Mulligan, Jr. beat John Studd
Mike Davis beat Steve Sybert
Terry Taylor beat Jim Nelson
Jay Youngblood beat The Ninja
Jake Roberts & Ray Stevens beat Bill White & Carl Fergie

2/2/82: Columbia, SC @ Township Auditorium
NWA World Champion Ric Flair beat Ole Anderson

2/3/82: Charlotte, NC @ WCPQ Studios (TV)
Ivan Koloff & Austin Idol vs. Don Gilbert & Vinnie Valentino
NWA World Champion Ric Flair draw Jay Youngblood
Blackjack Mulligan, Jr. vs. Jim Nelson
Jake Roberts vs. Buck Brannigan
Roddy Piper & ?? vs. Keith Larson & Tony Anthony

2/5/82: Charleston, SC @ County Hall
Blackjack Mulligan, Jr. beat John Studd
Jake Roberts beat Jim Nelson
Terry Taylor beat Bill White
Don Kernodle beat Steve Sybert
Porkchop Cash & Jay Youngblood beat Carl Fergie & David Patterson

2/5/82: Knoxville, TN @ Chilowee Park
Tommy Rich vs. Masked Superstar
Roddy Piper vs. Michael Hayes
Blackjack Mulligan & Johnny Weaver vs. Kevin Sullivan & Alfred Hayes
Buddy Landell vs. Jeff Sword

2/6/82: Cincinnati, OH @ Gardens
Jackie Lakin beat Tony Russo
Terry Taylor beat Mike Miller
Jake Roberts & Jay Youngblood beat Jeff Sword & Doug Vines
Ricky Steamboat beat Roddy Piper by DQ
Ivan Koloff DCO with Jimmy Valiant
NWA World Champion Ric Flair beat John Studd

2/6/82: Spartanburg, SC @ Memorial Auditorium
Ray Stevens & Porkchop Cash beat Gene Anderson & The Ninja
Blackjack Mulligan, Jr. beat Austin Idol by DQ
Carl Fergie & David Patterson beat Mike Davis & Don Kernodle
Tim Horner beat Steve Sybert

2/7/82: Roanoke, VA @ Civic Center
NWA World Champion Ric Flair beat Blackjack Mulligan, Jr.
Jimmy Valiant beat Ivan Koloff in a no DQ Match
Ray Stevens beat Austin Idol
Jay Youngblood & Jake Roberts beat Carl Fergie & Dave Patterson
Porkchop Cash beat Pvt. Nelson
Keith Larsen beat Jeff Sword

2/7/82: Greensboro, NC @ Coliseum
Ricky Steamboat beat NWA World Champion Ric Flair(38:34) by DQ
Sgt. Slaughter beat Blackjack Mulligan, Jr. via pinfall
Tag Team Tournament
1st Round
Adrian Adonis & Jesse Ventura beat Terry Taylor & Tim Horner
Ray Stevens & Pat Patterson beat Mr. Fuji & Mr. Saito
Jimmy Valiant & Johnny Weaver beat Ivan Koloff & Austin Idol by DQ
Ole Anderson & Stan Hansen beat Jay Youngblood & Jake Roberts

Semifinals
Ray Stevens & Pat Patterson beat Adrian Adonis & Jesse Ventura
Ole Anderson & Stan Hansen beat Jimmy Valiant & Johnny Weaver

Finals
Ole Anderson & Stan Hansen beat Ray Stevens & Pat Patterson in tournament final

2/8/82: Greenville, SC @ Memorial Auditorium
NWA World Champion Ric Flair beat Harley Race
Jimmy Valiant beat Ivan Koloff by DQ
The Ninja beat Ray Stevens
Jay Youngblood & Johnny Weaver beat Carl Fergie & David Patterson
Porkchop Cash beat Mike Miller
Tony Russo vs. Mike Davis

2/9/82: Columbia, SC @ Township Auditorium
Blackjack Mulligan, Jr. beat Sgt. Slaughter in a lumberjack match
Jake Roberts beat John Studd by DQ
Porkchop Cash & Jay Youngblood beat Carl Fergie & Jim Nelson
Mike Davis beat Chris Markoff
Don Kernodle beat Tim Horner
Keith Larson beat Mike Miller

2/9/82: Raleigh, NC @ Civic Center

2/10/82: Charlotte, NC @ WCPQ Studios (TV)

2/11/82: Winston-Salem, NC @ Memorial Coliseum
NWA World Champion Ric Flair vs. Leroy Brown
Roddy Piper vs. Ricky Steamboat
John Studd vs. Blackjack Mulligan in a bunkhouse match
Carl Fergie & Eddie Mansfield vs. Porkchop Cash & Jay Youngblood
Jim Nelson vs. Don Kernodle
Chris Markoff vs. Mike George

2/11/82: Sumter, SC @ Exposition Center
Jake Roberts & Jimmy Valiant vs. Austin Idol & Ivan Koloff
Johnny Weaver vs. Alfred Hayes in a lumberjack match
Leilani Kai vs. Velvet McIntyre
Jeff Sword vs. Tony Anthony
Mike Davis vs. Steve Sybert

2/12/82: Newberry, SC @ Junior High School
Roddy Piper vs. Ricky Steamboat
Porkchop Cash & Jay Youngblood vs. Carl Fergie & Eddie Mansfield
Mike Miller vs. Mike Davis
Don Kernodle vs. Steve Sybert
Chris Markoff vs. Tony Anthony

2/12/82: Charleston, SC @ County Hall
NWA World Champion Ric Flair beat Blackjack Mulligan, Jr.
Leroy Brown & Jake Roberts vs. Sgt. Slaughter & Jim Nelson

2/13/82: Hampton, VA @ Coliseum
Ricky Steamboat beat NWA World Champ Ric Flair DQ
Porkchop Cash beat Austin Idol
Porkchop Cash beat Sgt. Slaughter
Eddie Mansfield & Carl Fergie vs. Mike Davis & Tim Horner

2/13/82: Florence, SC
The Ninja beat Doug Gilbert
Chris Markoff draw Pvt. Kernodle
Velvet McIntyre beat Joyce Grable
Jay Youngblood & Terry Taylor beat The Ninja & Gene Anderson by DQ
Blackjack Mulligan, Sr. beat John Studd in a lumberjack match

2/14/82: Asheville, NC @ Civic Center
NWA World Champion Ric Flair DCO with Ricky Steamboat
Sgt. Slaughter beat Jack Brisco
Ole Anderson & Stan Hansen beat Ray Stevens & Tommy Rich
Austin Idol beat Jerry Brisco
Keith Larson beat Jeff Sword
Vinnie Valentino beat Bill White

2/14/82: Charlotte, NC @ Coliseum
Tag Team Tournament
1st Round
Jack & Jerry Brisco beat Sgt. Slaughter & Pvt. Nelson
Ole Anderson & Stan Hansen beat Jay Youngblood & Jake Roberts
Ray Stevens & Pat Patterson beat Ivan Koloff & Austin Idol
Roddy Piper & Greg Valentine beat Blackjack Mulligan, Sr. & Jr. by DQ

Semifinals
Jack & Jerry Brisco beat Roddy Piper & Greg Valentine
Ray Stevens & Pat Patterson beat Stan Hansen & Ole Anderson

Finals
Jack & Jerry Brisco beat Ray Stevens & Pat Patterson in tournament final
Ricky Steamboat beat Killer Kahn in a bounty match
NWA World Champion Ric Flair double DQ Tommy Rich

2/15/82: Greenville, SC @ Memorial Auditorium
Sgt. Slaughter beat Ricky Steamboat
Ole Anderson & Roddy Piper beat Blackjack Mulligan, Jr. & Jake Roberts
Ray Stevens beat Gene Anderson by DQ
Ray Stevens beat The Ninja
Johnny Weaver beat Carl Fergie by DQ
Pvt. Kernodle beat Tim Horner

2/16/82: Marion, VA
Roddy Piper vs. Ricky Steamboat
Ray Stevens & Johnny Weaver vs. The Ninja & Gene Anderson

2/16/82: Raleigh, NC @ Civic Center
Tommy Rich beat Super Destroyer
Blackjack Mulligan, Jr. & Jake Roberts beat Sgt. Slaughter & Pvt. Nelson
Pvt. Kernodle beat Abe Jacobs
Carl Fergie beat Vinnie Valentino
Terry Taylor beat David Patterson

2/17/82: Charlotte, NC @ WCPQ Studios (TV)
Blackjack Mulligan, Jr. & Jake Roberts vs. Buck Brannigan & Don Gilbert
Sgt. Slaughter vs. Vinnie Valentino
Porkchop Cash vs. Ben Alexander
Ivan Koloff vs. Rick Benefield
Steve Sybert vs. Mike George
Ole Anderson & Stan Hansen vs. Tony Anthony & Rick Benefield

2/18/82: Harrisonburg, VA @ High School
Ivan Koloff vs. Jimmy Valiant
Johnny Weaver vs. Alfred Hayes in a lumberjack match
Austin Idol vs. Terry Taylor in a lumberjack match
Carl Fergie & David Patterson vs. Keith Larsen & Vinnie Valentino
Mike Miller vs. Mike Davis

2/19/82: Charleston, SC @ County Hall
Blackjack Mulligan, Jr. & Jake Roberts beat Sgt. Slaughter & Pvt. Nelson

2/20/82: Roanoke, VA @ Civic Center
Pvt. Kernodle beat Tim Horner
Terry Taylor & Keith Larson beat Chris Markoff & Steve Sybert
Porkchop Cash DCO with Austin Idol
Jay Youngblood beat The Ninja by DQ
Ray Stevens beat Roddy Piper by DQ
Ivan Koloff beat Jimmy Valiant

2/21/82: Toronto, Ontario @ Maple Leaf Gardens
Blackjack Mulligan beat John Studd(13:45) by DQ
Ivan Koloff beat Jimmy Valiant(6:30) by DQ
Blackjack Mulligan, Jr. beat Austin Idol(17:50)
The Ninja & Gene Anderson beat Jay Youngblood & Johnny Weaver(19:10)
Tony Parisi beat Joe White(4:31)
John Bonello beat Louis Laurence(9:51)

2/21/82: Greensboro, NC @ Coliseum
NWA World Champion Ric Flair beat Ricky Steamboat via pinfall
Dusty Rhodes beat Sgt. Slaughter by DQ
Roddy Piper DCO with Bob Armstrong
Ole Anderson & Stan Hansen beat Leroy Brown & Ray Stevens
Jake Roberts beat Pvt. Nelson
Mike George beat Bill White
Porkchop Cash beat Chris Markoff
David Patterson beat Tony Anthony
Pvt. Kernodle beat Mike Davis

2/22/82: Greenville, SC @ Memorial Auditorium
Ricky Steamboat beat Sgt. Slaughter
Ole Anderson & Stan Hansen beat Ray Stevens & Jake Roberts
The Ninja beat Tony Anthony
Roddy Piper DCO with Bob Armstrong
Pvt. Nelson beat Vinnie Valentino
Kelly Kiniski beat Chris Markoff

2/22/82: Brantford, Ontario(TV)
Blackjack Mulligan, Jr. & Tony Parisi beat John White & Brian Mackney
Johnny Weaver beat Tim Gerrard
John Studd beat Louis Lawrence
Ivan Koloff beat John Bonello
John Studd beat Louis Lawrence
Johnny Weaver & Tony Parisi beat John White & Brian Mackney
John Studd beat John Bonello by DQ
Ivan Koloff beat Louis Lawrence
Blackjack Mulligan, Jr. & Tony Parisi beat Tim Gerrard & Brian Mackney
Ivan Koloff beat Louis Lawrence
John Studd & Ivan Koloff beat Johnny Weaver & Blackjack Mulligan, Jr. via pinfall

2/22/82: Lumberton, NC @ Recreation Center
Austin Idol vs. Porkchop Cash
Gene Anderson vs. Jimmy Valiant
Jake Roberts & Jay Youngblood vs. David Patterson & Carl Fergie
Keith Larson vs. Mike George
Bill White vs. Steve Sybert

2/23/82: Raleigh, NC @ Civic Center

2/23/82: Columbia, SC @ Township Auditorium

2/23/82: Hamilton, Ontario
Louis Lawrence draw Alex Gerrard
John Bonello beat Tim Gerrard
Billy Red Lyons beat John White
Tony Parisi beat Brian Mackney
Johnny Weaver & Blackjack Mulligan, Jr. beat Ivan Koloff & John Studd by DQ

2/24/82: Charlotte, NC @ WCPQ Studios (TV)
Terry Taylor vs. David Patterson
Pvt. Kernodle & Pvt. Nelson vs. Vinnie Valentino & Mike Davis
Mike George vs. Mike Miller
Bill White vs. Ron Ritchie
Ole Anderson & Stan Hansen vs. Don Gilbert & Kelly Kiniski

2/25/82: Elizabeth City, NC
12-man Battle royal
Austin Idol vs. Leroy Brown

Ricky Steamboat vs. Roddy Piper
Carl Fergie & David Patterson vs. Porkchop Cash & Mike Davis
Mike Miller vs. Keith Larson
Bill White vs. Vinnie Valentino

2/25/82: Sumter, SC @ Exposition Center
Ivan Koloff vs. Jimmy Valiant in a lumberjack match
Jay Youngblood & Ray Stevens vs. Gene Anderson & The Ninja
John Studd vs. Mike George
Jeff Sword vs. Tim Horner
Doug Vines vs. Tony Anthony

2/26/82: Richmond, VA @ Coliseum
Roddy Piper beat Ricky Steamboat via pinfall in a lumberjack match
Jerry Brisco beat Pvt. Nelson
NWA World Tag Title tournament
1st Round
Ray Stevens & Leroy Brown beat Austin Idol & John Studd by reverse decision
Sgt. Slaughter & Pvt. Nelson beat Kelly Kiniski & Ron Ritchie
Gene Anderson & Ole Anderson received a bye
Jack Brisco & Jerry Brisco received a bye
Semifinals
Sgt. Slaughter & Pvt. Nelson beat Ray Stevens & Leroy Brown by DQ
Jack & Jerry Brisco beat Gene Anderson & Ole Anderson
Finals
Sgt. Slaughter & Pvt. Nelson beat Jack Brisco & Jerry Brisco to win tournament

2/26/82: Charleston, SC @ County Hall
Tim Horner vs. Jeff Sword
Jay Youngblood & Terry Taylor vs. Carl Fergie & David Patterson
Porkchop Cash beat The Ninja(aka Mr. Pogo)
Ivan Koloff beat Jimmy Valiant
Johnny Weaver beat Alfred Hayes in a Texas death, steel cage match

2/27/82: Fredericksburg, VA @ Stafford High School(Cancelled due to weather)
Sgt. Slaughter vs. Blackjack Mulligan, Jr.
Ivan Koloff vs. Jimmy Valiant

2/28/82: Asheville, NC @ Civic Center
Ricky Steamboat beat John Studd(sub for Ric Flair)
Roddy Piper & Austin Idol beat Ray Stevens & Bob Armstrong
Jake Roberts beat John Studd by DQ
The Ninja beat Terry Taylor
Carl Fergie beat Mike Davis
David Patterson beat Keith Larsen

2/28/82: Atlanta, GA @ Omni
Jim Garvin beat Buzz Sawyer
Giant Baba beat Terry Gordy
Great Kabuki beat Dusty Rhodes in a Dragon Shi match
NWA World Champion Ric Flair double DQ Harley Race
East Coast" Tag Team Tournament
1st Round
Dory Jr & Terry Funk beat Buddy Rose & Rip Oliver
Jack & Jerry Brisco beat Ron Bass & Kevin Sullivan DQ
Ron Fuller & Leroy Brown beat Masked Superstar & Super Destroyer
Ole Anderson & Stan Hansen beat Brad Armstrong & Tommy Rogers

2nd Round
Jack & Jerry Brisco beat Dory Jr. & Terry Funk
Jumbo Tsuruta & Tenryu beat Ron Fuller & Leroy Brown
Ole Anderson & Stan Hansen received a bye

Semifinals
Ole Anderson & Stan Hansen beat Jumbo Tsuruta & Genichiro Tenryu
Jack Brisco & Jerry Brisco received a bye

Finals
Ole Anderson & Stan Hansen beat Jack & Jerry Brisco
Note: Anderson & Hansen eventually are awarded the NWA(Mid Atlantic) World Tag Titles due to break up of "West Coast" winners, Wahoo McDaniel & Don Muraco

3/1/82: Fayetteville, NC @ Cumberland County Memorial Auditorium
Pvt. Kernodle & Pvt. Nelson beat ?? win tag tournament. Also in the tournament were Stan Hanson & Ole Anderson, Jack & Jerry Brisco, Porkchop Cash & Jay Youngblood and other teams
Johnny Weaver vs. Alfred Hayes
Velvet McIntyre vs. Leilani Kai
Austin Idol vs. Jake Roberts

3/1/82: Greenville, SC @ Memorial Auditorium
Abe Jacobs draw Jeff Sword
Sgt. Slaughter beat Ricky Steamboat
Roddy Piper beat Bob Armstrong
Ron Ritchie beat Bill White
Ray Stevens beat The Ninja by countout
Carl Fergie & David Patterson beat Kelly Kiniski & Vinnie Valentino

3/2/82: Randleman, NC @ High School Gym
Ron Ritchie beat Chris Markoff
Abe Jacobs beat Tony Russo
Mike Davis beat Mike Miller
The Ninja beat Terry Taylor
Ricky Steamboat & Ray Stevens beat Roddy Piper & The Ninja

3/2/82: Columbia, SC @ Township Auditorium

3/3/82: Charlotte, NC @ WCPQ Studios (TV)
Austin Idol beat Vinnie Valentino
David Patterson beat Rick Benefield
Jack Brisco & Jerry Brisco beat Bill White & Bill Miller
Pvt. Kernodle & Pvt. Nelson beat Tony Anthony & Ron Ritchie

3/4/82: Hillsville, VA @ Woodlawn Intermediate School
Ron Ritchie vs. Jeff Sword
Vinnie Valentino vs. Doug Vines
Terry Taylor & Mike Davis vs. Pvt. Pvt. Nelson & Pvt. Pvt. Kernodle
Johnny Weaver vs. Alfred Hayes
Blackjack Mulligan, Jr. vs. Sgt. Slaughter

3/5/82: Charleston, SC @ County Hall
The Ninja beat Porkchop Cash by DQ
Velvet McIntyre won a battle royal to earn a shot at Woman's Champion Fabulous Moolah. The battle royal also included Donna Christianello, Leilani Kai, Joyce Grable, Princess Victoria & Wendi Richter
Fabulous Moolah beat Velvet McIntyre
Carl Fergie beat Ron Ritchie

3/5/82: Cincinnati, OH @ Gardens
Kelly Kiniski beat Steve Sybert
Mike George beat Jeff Sword
Walter Johnson beat Mike Miller
Jake Roberts beat Pvt. Nelson
Ole Anderson beat Ray Stevens
Roddy Piper DCO with Bob Armstrong
Tommy Rich beat Sgt. Slaughter by DQ
Ricky Steamboat beat Austin Idol

3/5/82: Knoxville, TN @ Chilhowee Park
Tony Anthony beat Rick Connors
Bill White beat Tim Horner
Kevin Sullivan beat Terry Taylor
Jay Youngblood beat Ivan Koloff by DQ
Jimmy Valiant beat Super Destroyer(unmasked as Don Kernodle)
Blackjack Mulligan, Jr. beat John Studd
Johnny Weaver beat Alfred Hayes

3/6/82: Florence, SC
Vinnie Valentino beat Steve Sybert
Mike George & Porkchop Cash beat David Patterson & Carl Fergie
Pvt. Nelson beat Kelly Kiniski
Porkchop Cash beat Austin Idol
Jake Roberts beat Sgt. Slaughter

3/6/82: Bluefield, WV @ Brushfork Armory
Super Destroyer(Don Kernodle) vs. Jay Youngblood in a mask vs. loser leaves town match
Johnny Weaver vs. Alfred Hayes in a lumberjack match
Ivan Koloff vs. Jimmy Valiant

3/7/82: Roanoke, VA @ Civic Center
Carl Fergie beat Vinnie Valentino
Pvt. Kernodle & Pvt. Nelson beat Terry Taylor & Tim Horner
Tommy Rich beat Ivan Koloff
Jack Brisco & Jerry Brisco beat Ole Anderson & Stan Hansen
Dusty Rhodes beat Sgt. Slaughter by DQ

3/7/82: Charlotte, NC @ Coliseum
Jerry Brisco beat David Patterson
Jumbo Tsuruta DCO with Tommy Rich
Alexis Smirnoff & Ivan Koloff beat Giant Baba & Genichiro Tenryu by DQ
Atsushi Onita beat Chavo Guerrero to win NWA World Junior Title
Dory Funk, Jr. draw Billy Robinson(30:00)
Ole Anderson & Stan Hansen beat Ray Stevens & Dusty Rhodes
Jack Brisco beat Sgt. Slaughter by DQ

3/7/82: Toronto, Ontario @ Maple Leaf Gardens
Cadillac tournament
1st Round
Jimmy Valiant beat Tim Gerrard(:52) via pinfall
Johnny Weaver beat Jay Youngblood
Jesse Ventura Mike Rotundo(2:57) via pinfall
John Studd beat John Bonello(3:04)
Blackjack Mulligan Jr. beat The Destroyer(9:10) by DQ
Ricky Steamboat beat Adrian Adonis(8:16)
Roddy Piper beat Dino Bravo(8:46)
Austin Idol beat Jake Roberts(8:26)

2nd Round
Jimmy Valiant beat Austin Idol(2:16)
Jesse Ventura beat Johnny Weaver(4:02)
Blackjack Mulligan, Jr. DCO with John Studd(12:27)
Ricky Steamboat beat Roddy Piper(12:27)
After the match, Piper attacked Steamboat & rammed him into the ring post, & steamboat was out of action for the night

Finals
Jimmy Valiant beat Jesse Ventura in tournament final to win Cadillac

3/8/82: Greenville, SC @ Memorial Auditorium
Dusty Rhodes beat Sgt. Slaughter by DQ
Ivan Koloff double DQ Jimmy Valiant
Ole Anderson & Stan Hansen beat Jack & Jerry Brisco
Kelly Kiniski beat Mike Miller
David Patterson beat Keith Larson
Mike George beat Bill White

3/8/82: Brantford, Ontario(TV)
John Studd vs. Jay Youngblood

3/9/82: Columbia, SC @ Township Auditorium
Keith Larsen beat Bill White
Ron Ritchie beat Jeff Sword
Mike George beat Chris Markoff
Leroy Brown beat John Studd
Ricky Steamboat & Ray Stevens beat Austin Idol & Roddy Piper

3/9/82: Christiansburg, VA

3/10/82: Charlotte, NC @ WCPQ Studios (TV)
Ron Ritchie beat Ivan Koloff by DQ
Jimmy Valiant beat Bill White
David Patterson & Carl Fergie beat Terry Taylor & Tim Horner

Ole Anderson & Stan Hansen beat ?? & ?? via pinfall

3/12/82: Charleston, SC @ County Hall
Blackjack Mulligan, Jr. & Jimmy Valiant beat John Studd & Ivan Koloff
Porkchop Cash beat The Ninja in a no DQ Match
Jay Youngblood & Johnny Weaver beat Carl Fergie & David Patterson
Kelly Kiniski beat Mike Miller

3/12/82: Richmond, VA @ Coliseum
Vinnie Valentino beat Steve Sybert
Mike Davis beat Jeff Sword
Ron Ritchie beat Bill White
Jake Roberts & Mike George beat Pvt. Kernodle & Pvt. Nelson
Roddy Piper & Stan Hansen beat Ray Stevens & Leroy Brown
Jack Brisco beat Sgt. Slaughter by DQ
Ricky Steamboat beat Austin Idol

3/13/82: Greensboro, NC @ Coliseum
NWA World Champion Ric Flair beat Wahoo McDaniel in an Indian strap match
Ricky Steamboat beat Sgt. Slaughter
Ole Anderson and Stan Hansen beat Dusty Rhodes and Ray Stevens by DQ
Jack Brisco beat Roddy Piper by DQ
Jake Roberts and Jerry Brisco beat John Studd and Austin Idol
Johnny Weaver beat Carl Fergie
David Patterson beat Tim Horner
Tony Anthony beat Bill White

3/15/82: Clover, SC @ High School
Roddy Piper vs. Ray Stevens
The Ninja vs. Jay Youngblood
Alfred Hayes vs. Johnny Weaver
Chris Markoff vs. Mike George
Bill White vs. Tony Anthony
Buck Brannigan vs. Don Gilbert

3/16/82: Wytheville, VA

3/16/82: Columbia, SC @ Township Auditorium
Mike George beat Steve Seibert
Ron Ritchie beat Tony Russo
The Ninja beat Keith Larsen
Porkchop Cash beat Mike Miller
Roddy Piper & John Studd beat Ricky Steamboat & Ray Stevens

3/17/82: Charlotte, NC @ WCPQ Studios (TV)
Jimmy Valiant vs. Steve Sybert
Sgt. Slaughter vs. Ron Ritchie
Terry Taylor vs. Mike Miller
Pvt. Kernodle & Pvt. Nelson vs. Tony Anthony & Vinnie Valentino
Jake Roberts vs. David Patterson
Ole Anderson & Stan Hansen vs. Kelly Kiniski & Mike Davis

3/18/82: Chester, SC @ High School
Roddy Piper vs. Ricky Steamboat
Alfred Hayes vs. Johnny Weaver
The Ninja vs. Porkchop Cash
Carl Fergie & David Patterson vs. Tony Anthony & Kelly Kiniski

3/19/82: Charleston, SC @ County Hall
Tim Horner beat Chris Markoff
Keith Larsen beat Mike Miller
Jay Youngblood & Blackjack Mulligan, Jr. beat Pvt. Kernodle & Pvt. Nelson
Porkchop Cash beat Austin Idol

3/20/82: Asheville, NC @ Civic Center
Jimmy Valiant beat Ivan Koloff
Ole Anderson & Stan Hansen beat Jack Brisco & Jerry Brisco
Austin Idol beat Ray Stevens by DQ
Mike Davis beat Chris Markoff
Tony Anthony beat Mike Miller
Tim Horner beat Steve Siebert

3/20/82: Charlotte, NC @ Coliseum
Sgt. Slaughter, Ole Anderson & Stan Hansen beat Ric Flair, Ricky Steamboat & Jake Roberts
Ivan Koloff double DQ Jimmy Valiant
Blackjack Mulligan, Jr. beat Austin Idol
Pvt. Nelson & Pvt. Kernodle beat Jay Youngblood & Porkchop Cash
The Ninja beat Ron Ritchie

3/21/82: Toronto, Ontario @ Maple Leaf Gardens
Tony Parisi beat Kurt Von Hess
Johnny Weaver beat Chris Markoff
Jay Youngblood beat Ninja by DQ
Ricky Steamboat beat Roddy Piper by DQ
Jimmy Valiant beat Ivan Koloff
Blackjack Mulligan, Sr. beat John Studd by DQ

3/21/82: Greensboro, NC @ Coliseum
Ole Anderson & Stan Hansen beat Dusty Rhodes & Ray Stevens
Wahoo McDaniel & Jake Roberts beat Sgt. Slaughter & Jim Nelson
Jack Brisco beat Austin Idol
Blackjack Mulligan, Jr. beat Don Kernodle
Jerry Brisco beat Steve Sybert
Mike George beat Ken Timbs
Kelly Kiniski draw Terry Taylor

3/22/82: Greenville, SC @ Memorial Auditorium
Bob Armstrong beat Roddy Piper by countout
Ray Stevens & Jimmy Valiant beat Ivan Koloff & John Studd
Ole Anderson draw Jay Youngblood
Les Thornton draw Terry Taylor
Kelly Kiniski beat Jeff Sword
Bill White beat Ken Timbs

3/23/82: Raleigh, NC @ Civic Center

3/23/82: Columbia, SC @ Township Auditorium
Tony Anthony beat Chris Markoff
Terry Taylor beat Jeff Sword
Les Thornton beat Ron Ritchie
Mike George beat Ken Timbs
Ricky Steamboat, Ray Stevens & Leroy Brown beat Roddy Piper, Austin Idol & John Studd

3/24/82: Charlotte, NC @ WCPQ Studios (TV)
Jake Roberts & Blackjack Mulligan, Jr. vs. Carl Fergie & Mike Miller
Jimmy Valiant vs. Bill White
Ron Ritchie vs. David Patterson
Jack Brisco vs. Steve Sybert
Pvt. Kernodle & Pvt. Nelson vs. Mike George & Tony Anthony

3/25/82: Winston-Salem, NC @ Memorial Coliseum
Tommy Rich vs. Ole Anderson
Roddy Piper vs. Leroy Brown
John Studd & Austin Idol vs. Blackjack Mulligan, Sr. & Jake Roberts
Chris Markoff vs. Kelly Kiniski
Tony Russo vs. Keith Larson
Vinnie Valentino vs. Steve Sybert

3/25/82: Harrisonburg, VA @ High School
Ivan Koloff vs. Jimmy Valiant
Johnny Weaver vs. Alfred Hayes lumberjack match
Jay Youngblood vs. The Ninja
Butcher Brannigan vs. Ron Ritchie
Carl Fergie & David Patterson vs. Terry Taylor & Mike Davis

3/25/82: Sumter SC @ Exposition Center
Sgt. Slaughter vs. Ricky Steamboat
Ray Stevens & Porkchop Cash vs. Pvt. Nelson & Pvt. Kernodle
Mike Miller vs. Mike George
Bill White vs. Tim Rogers
Jeff Sword vs. Tony Anthony

3/26/82: Richmond, VA @ Coliseum
Ricky Steamboat vs. Sgt. Slaughter
Stan Hansen & Ole Anderson vs. Ray Stevens & Blackjack Mulligan, Jr.
Jimmy Valiant vs. Ivan Koloff
Austin Idol vs. Mike Davis
Johnny Weaver vs. Carl Fergie
Peggy Lee vs. Leilani Kai

3/26/82: Lawrenceville, VA
Pvt. Kernodle & Pvt. Nelson beat Jay Youngblood & Porkchop Cash to win MWA Mid Atlantic Tag Title

3/27/82: Fredericksburg, VA @ Stafford High School
Ivan Koloff vs. Jimmy Valiant
Johnny Weaver vs. Alfred Hayes lumberjack match

3/28/82: Charlotte, NC @ Coliseum
Kelly Kiniski beat Tony Russo
Mike George beat Bill White
The Ninja beat Ron Ritchie
Les Thornton beat Steve Sybert
Pvt. Kernodle & Pvt. Nelson beat Jay Youngblood & Porkchop Cash
Jimmy Valiant DCO with Ivan Koloff
Blackjack Mulligan, Jr. beat Austin Idol by DQ
Ole Anderson, Stan Hansen & Sgt. Slaughter beat Ric Flair, Ricky Steamboat & Jake Roberts

3/29/82: Greenville, SC @ Memorial Auditorium
Bob Armstrong beat Roddy Piper in an Indian strap match
Jimmy Valiant beat Ivan Koloff in a match with Ole Anderson & Blackjack Mulligan, Jr. as special referees
Ole Anderson beat Blackjack Mulligan, Jr.
Carl Fergie & David Patterson beat Mike George & Kelly Kiniski
Mike Davis beat Steve Sybert

3/30/82: Raleigh, NC @ Civic Center

3/30/82: Columbia, SC @ Township Auditorium

3/31/82: Charlotte, NC @ WCPQ Studios (TV)
Jack & Jerry Brisco vs. Steve Sybert & Mike Miller
Tony Russo vs. Tim Horner
Jake Roberts vs. Bill White
Terry Taylor vs. Rick Benefield
Ole Anderson & Stan Hansen vs. Tony Anthony & Ron Ritchie
Ivan Koloff beat Vinnie Valentino
Jimmy Valiant beat Steve Sybert
Blackjack Mulligan, Jr. beat Mike Miller
Jack Brisco & Jerry Brisco beat Carl Fergie & Tony Russo

4/2/82: Charleston, SC @ County Hall
Tony Anthony beat Jeff Sword
Kelly Kiniski beat Chris Markoff
Judy Martin beat Princess Victoria
Pvt. Nelson & Pvt. Kernodle beat Porkchop Cash & Mike George
Sgt. Slaughter double DQ Jake Roberts

4/2/82: Knoxville, TN @ Civic Coliseum
Vinnie Valentino beat Mike Miller
Brad Armstrong beat Ken Timbs
Bill White beat Keith Larsen
Jay Youngblood beat The Ninja by DQ
Bob Armstrong beat Buzz Sawyer
Ivan Koloff beat Jimmy Valiant by DQ
Johnny Weaver beat Kevin Sullivan

4/3/82: Greensboro, NC @ Coliseum
Mike Davis beat Jeff Sword
Vinnie Valentino beat Bill White
Ron Ritchie beat Ben Alexander
Kelly Kiniski beat Chris Markoff
Jimmy Valiant beat Ivan Koloff
Gene & Ole Anderson & Stan Hansen beat Jack & Jerry Brisco & Ric Flair
Roddy Piper beat Bob Armstrong

4/4/82: Asheville, NC @ Civic Center
Ole Anderson, Stan Hansen & Sgt. Slaughter beat Ric Flair, Blackjack Mulligan, Jr. & Ray Stevens
Jack Brisco beat Roddy Piper
Jerry Brisco beat Bill White
Ron Ritchie beat Tony Russo
Terry Taylor beat Keith Larson

4/4/82: Charlotte, NC @ Coliseum
NWA World Champion Ric Flair beat Sgt. Slaughter DQ
Paul Jones beat Gene Anderson by DQ
Jack & Jerry Brisco beat Carl Fergie & David Patterson
Jake Roberts beat Alfred Hayes
Mike George beat Mike Miller
Kelly Kiniski beat Steve Sybert

4/4/82: Toronto, Ontario @ Maple Leaf Gardens
Tony Rocco beat Tito Senza
Johnny Weaver beat Jeff Sword
Pvt. Kernodle & Pvt. Nelson draw Tony Parisi & Jay Youngblood
Blackjack Mulligan beat The Ninja
Jimmy Valiant beat Ivan Koloff by DQ
Angelo Mosca beat Tarzan Tyler

4/5/82: Greenville, SC @ Memorial Auditorium
Ric Flair, Jack & Jerry Brisco beat Stan Hansen, Gene Anderson & Ole Anderson
Roddy Piper beat Ray Stevens
Porkchop Cash beat Jeff Sword
Ron Ritchie beat Ken Timbs
Vinnie Valentino beat Steve Sybert

4/6/82: Raleigh, NC @ Civic Center
Ric Flair & Paul Jones vs. Sgt. Slaughter & Pvt. Nelson
The Ninja vs. Jake Roberts

4/6/82: Columbia, SC @ Township Auditorium
Kelly Kiniski beat Jeff Sword
Mike George draw Pvt. Kernodle
Terry Taylor beat Steve Sybert
Jack Brisco beat Carl Fergie
Ray Stevens & Blackjack Mulligan, Jr. beat Roddy Piper & Gene Anderson by DQ

4/7/82: Charlotte, NC @ WCPQ Studios (TV)
Jimmy Valiant vs. Ben Alexander
Carl Fergie beat Keith Larson
Jack Brisco vs. Bill White
Ivan Koloff beat Tony Anthony
Tim Horner vs. Rusty Roberts
Terry Taylor & Kelly Kiniski vs. Pvt. Kernodle & Pvt. Nelson
Jack & Jerry Brisco beat Steve Sybert & Mike Miller
Tim Horner beat Tony Russo
Jake Roberts beat Bill White
Terry Taylor beat Rick Benefield
Stan Hansen & Ole Anderson beat Ron Ritchie & Tony Anthony
Jack Brisco beat Carl Fergie
Blackjack Mulligan, Jr. beat Rusty Roberts
Roddy Piper beat Vinnie Valentino
Jake Roberts beat Steve Sybert
Paul Jones beat Bill White
Wahoo McDaniel beat Ali Bey
Ron Ritchie beat Sgt. Slaughter

4/8/82: Sumter, SC @ Exposition Center
Vinnie Valentino draw Bill White
Mike George beat Steve Sybert
Jack Brisco beat Roddy Piper by countout
Jimmy Valiant & Jake Roberts beat The Ninja & Ivan Koloff by DQ
Terry Taylor beat Jeff Sword
Johnny Weaver beat Alfred Hayes in a lumberjack match

4/8/82: Fisherville, VA @ Augusta Expo
Ric Flair & Jake Roberts beat Sgt. Slaughter & Pvt. Nelson

4/9/82: Charleston, SC @ County Hall
Terry Taylor beat Bill White
Ron Ritchie & Mike Davis beat Steve Sybert & Rusty Roberts
Tony Russo beat Vinnie Valentino
Jimmy Valiant & Blackjack Mulligan, Jr. beat Ivan Koloff & Chris Markoff (sub for Austin Idol)
Ray Stevens beat The Ninja by DQ

4/9/82: Richmond, VA @ Coliseum
Sgt. Slaughter, Ole Anderson & Stan Hansen beat Ric Flair, Paul Jones & Jake Roberts
Jack Brisco beat Roddy Piper
Johnny Weaver beat Alfred Hayes
Pvt. Nelson & Pvt. Kernodle beat Tony Anthony & Tim Horner
Mike George draw Carl Fergie
Keith Larsen beat Ken Timbs
Jay Youngblood beat David Patterson

4/10/82: Cincinnati, OH @ Riverfront Coliseum
Tony Anthony beat Cowboy Young
Rick Conner beat Kenny Hall
Pvt. Nelson & Pvt. Kernodle beat Kelly Kiniski & Vinnie Valentino
Jack Brisco beat Ole Anderson via pinfall
Johnny Weaver beat Alfred Hayes in a lumberjack match
Leroy Brown beat Sgt. Slaughter in a Texas death match
Roddy Piper beat Bob Armstrong in a no DQ match

4/11/82: Roanoke, VA @ Civic Center
David Patterson beat Keith Larsen
David Patterson & Carl Fergie beat Mike Davis & Ron Ritchie
Blackjack Mulligan, Jr. beat The Ninja
Roddy Piper, Ivan Koloff & Sgt. Slaughter beat Jimmy Valiant, Jake Roberts & Paul Jones

4/12/82: Greenville, SC @ Memorial Auditorium
Angelo Mosca & Sgt. Slaughter double DQ Paul Jones & Jack Brisco
Johnny Weaver beat Alfred Hayes in a Texas death match
Blackjack Mulligan, Jr. beat The Ninja
Ron Ritchie beat Tony Russo
Terry Taylor beat Steve Sybert
David Patterson draw Kelly Kiniski

4/13/82: Raleigh, NC @ Civic Center
Keith Larsen beat Jeff Sword
Tim Horner beat Steve Sybert
Ron Ritchie beat Pvt. Nelson
Porkchop Cash beat Carl Fergie
Roddy Piper & Sgt. Slaughter beat Paul Jones & Jake Roberts

4/13/82: Columbia, SC @ Township Auditorium
Vinnie Valentino beat Ken Timbs
Kelly Kiniski beat Bill White
Mike George beat David Patterson
Jack Brisco, Ray Stevens & Blackjack Mulligan, Jr. beat Angelo Mosca, Pvt. Nelson & Gene Anderson

4/14/82: Charlotte, NC @ WCPQ Studios (TV)
Jack Brisco vs. Jim Dalton
Keith Larson beat Tony Russo
Angelo Mosca beat Vinnie Valentino
Mike George beat Steve Sybert
Pvt. Kernodle & Pvt. Nelson vs. Terry Taylor & Tony Antony
Jimmy Valiant beat Bill White
Carl Fergie beat Keith Larson
Ivan Koloff beat Tony Anthony
Tim Horner, Terry Taylor & Kelly Kiniski beat Rusty Roberts, Pvt. Kernodle & Pvt. Nelson
Jack Brisco beat Rusty Roberts
Sgt. Slaughter beat Vinnie Valentino
Angelo Mosca beat Mike Davis
Paul Jones & Blackjack Mulligan, Jr. beat Jeff Sword & Tony Russo

4/15/82: Norfolk, VA @ Scope
Kelly Kiniski beat Jeff Sword
Jim Dalton beat Mike Davis
Pvt. Kernodle & Pvt. Nelson beat Terry Taylor & Mike George
The Ninja beat Ray Stevens
Jack Brisco beat Roddy Piper
Sgt. Slaughter & Angelo Mosca beat Paul Jones & Jake Roberts

4/16/82: Knoxville, TN @ Chilhowee Park
Jimmy Valiant beat Ivan Koloff
Jay Youngblood beat The Ninja by DQ
Johnny Weaver double DQ Bill White
Tim Horner beat Jeff Sword
David Patterson beat Vinnie Valentino
Kelly Kiniski draw Rick Connors
Mike Davis beat Steve Sybert

4/16/82: Charleston, SC @ County Hall
Pvt. Nelson & Pvt. Kernodle beat Jake Roberts & Blackjack Mulligan, Jr.
Porkchop Cash beat Alfred Hayes
Mike George beat Carl Fergie
Keith Larsen beat Ken Timbs

4/17/82: Greensboro, NC @ Coliseum
Keith Larsen beat Ken Timbs
Jim Dalton beat Tony Anthony
Blackjack Mulligan, Jr. beat David Patterson
Jack Brisco & Jimmy Valiant beat Ivan Koloff & The Ninja
Sgt. Slaughter beat Jake Roberts
Wahoo McDaniel & Paul Jones beat Roddy Piper & Angelo Mosca

4/18/82: Asheville, NC @ Civic Center
NWA World Champion Ric Flair beat Ole Anderson
Roddy Piper & Angelo Mosca double DQ Wahoo McDaniel & Jack Brisco
Carl Fergie & David Patterson beat Jay Youngblood & Mike George
Kelly Kiniski beat Rick Connors
Tim Horner beat Jim Dalton

4/18/82: Charlotte, NC @ Coliseum
Ric Flair & Wahoo McDaniel double DQ Angelo Mosca & Sgt. Slaughter
Jack Brisco beat Ole Anderson
Jimmy Valiant & Jake Roberts beat The Ninja & Ivan Koloff
Terry Taylor beat David Patterson
Tony Anthony beat Jeff Sword
Vinnie Valentino beat Ken Timbs

4/19/82: Greenville, SC @ Memorial Auditorium
Bob Armstrong beat Roddy Piper in a Canadian lumberjack match
Jimmy Valiant & Blackjack Mulligan, Jr. beat The Ninja & Ivan Koloff by DQ
Angelo Mosca beat Paul Jones
Porkchop Cash beat Bill White
Terry Taylor beat Jim Dalton

4/20/82: Columbia, SC @ Township Auditorium
Jack Brisco beat Roddy Piper by DQ
Ivan Koloff & The Ninja beat Jimmy Valiant & Paul Jones
Porkchop Cash beat Pvt. Nelson
Ron Ritchie beat Jim Dalton
Kelly Kiniski draw Ken Timbs

4/20/82: Raleigh, NC @ Civic Center
Wahoo McDaniel & Jake Roberts beat Sgt. Slaughter & Angelo Mosca by DQ
Killer Kahn beat Paul Jones
Don Muraco beat Carl Fergie
Vinnie Valentino beat Jim Dalton
Mike Rotundo beat Ken Timbs

4/21/82: Charlotte, NC @ WCPQ Studios (TV)
Terry Taylor & Tim Horner beat Pvt. Kernodle & Pvt. Nelson by DQ
Paul Jones beat Jim Dalton
Sgt. Slaughter beat Tony Anthony
Wahoo McDaniel & Don Muraco beat David Patterson & Ken Timbs
Jack Brisco beat Jeff Sword
Keith Larson beat Tony Russo
Angelo Mosca beat Vinnie Valentino
Wahoo McDaniel beat Ali Bey
Mike George beat Steve Sybert
Terry Taylor & Jake Roberts beat Pvts. Kernodle & Nelson
Sgt. Slaughter beat Mike Davis
Jake Roberts beat Steve Sybert
Angelo Mosca beat Tony Anthony
Don Muraco beat Jim Dalton
NWA World Champion Ric Flair beat Pvt. Nelson
Ivan Koloff & Ninja beat Ron Ritchie & Keith Larson

4/22/82: Sumter, SC @ Exposition Center
Kelly Kiniski beat Jim Dalton
Ron Ritchie beat Jeff Sword
Porkchop Cash beat David Patterson
Blackjack Mulligan, Jr. double DQ Angelo Mosca
Jack Brisco & Ray Stevens beat Roddy Piper & Ivan Koloff

4/22/82: Portsmouth, VA
Mike Davis beat Tony Anthony
Terry Taylor beat Carl Fergie
Ron Ritchie draw David Patterson
Ray Stevens beat Gene Anderson
Jimmy Valiant & Porkchop Cash DDQ Ivan Koloff & Ninja

4/23/82: Charleston, SC @ County Hall
Kelly Kiniski beat Steve Sybert
Mike Davis beat Vinnie Valentino
Ron Ritchie beat Bill White
Mike George beat Jim Dalton
Ron Ritchie, Jake Roberts & Porkchop Cash NC with Pvt. Nelson, Pvt. Kernodle & The Ninja

4/23/82: Richmond, VA @ Coliseum
Terry Taylor beat Ken Timbs
Carl Fergie & David Patterson beat Ray Stevens & Tony Anthony
Angelo Mosca beat Jay Youngblood
Johnny Weaver & Alfred Hayes in a lumberjack match
Jimmy Valiant beat Ivan Koloff
Jack Brisco beat Roddy Piper by DQ
Wahoo McDaniel beat Sgt. Slaughter

4/24/82: Spartanburg, SC @ Memorial Auditorium
Wahoo McDaniel & Jake Roberts vs. Sgt. Slaughter & Pvt. Kernodle
Killer Kahn vs. Jay Youngblood
Pvt. Nelson vs. Mike Davis
Ken Timbs vs. Ron Ritchie
Steve Sybert vs. Vinnie Valentino

4/25/82: Buffalo, NY
Ray Stevens beat Ron Ritchie
Porkchop Cash & Johnny Weaver beat Pvt. Kernodle & Pvt. Nelson
Jim Valiant beat Ivan Koloff
Jay Youngblood & Ric Flair beat Ninja & Gene Anderson
Angelo Mosca beat John Studd by DQ

4/25/82: Toronto, Ontario @ Maple Leaf Gardens
NWA World Champion Ric Flair NC with Harley Race
Angelo Mosca beat Nick Bockwinkel by DQ
Jay Youngblood beat The Ninja Indian strap match
Ivan Koloff & Pvt. Kernodle beat Jimmy Valiant & Porkchop Cash
John Studd beat Ron Ritchie
Johnny Weaver beat Pvt. Nelson
Ray Stevens draw Tony Parisi

4/26/82: Ottawa, Ontario @ Civic Centre
Nick Bockwinkel beat Jay Youngblood
Angelo Mosca DCO with John Studd
Jimmy Valiant beat Ivan Koloff
Johnny Weaver beat The Ninja by DQ
Tony Parisi beat Tito Senza
Tarzan Tyler beat Tony Ricco

4/26/82: Greenville, SC @ Memorial Auditorium
Porkchop Cash beat Carl Fergie
David Patterson beat Keith Larson
Paul Jones beat Jim Dalton
Ron Ritchie beat David Patterson
Jack Brisco beat Roddy Piper
Wahoo McDaniel & Don Muraco beat Ole Anderson & Stan Hansen by DQ

4/27/82: Raleigh, NC @ Civic Center
Mike Rotundo beat Ken Timbs
Vinnie Valentino beat Jim Dalton
Don Muraco beat Carl Fergie
Killer Kahn beat Paul Jones
Jake Roberts & Wahoo McDaniel beat Sgt. Slaughter & Angelo Mosca by DQ

4/27/82: Columbia, SC @ Township Auditorium
Kelly Kiniski beat Tony Anthony
David Patterson beat Keith Larson
Johnny Weaver beat Alfred Hayes in a lumberjack match
Porkchop Cash beat Pvt. Kernodle
Jack Brisco & Jay Youngblood beat Gene Anderson & Ole Anderson

4/28/82: Charlotte, NC @ WCPQ Studios (TV)
Don Muraco & Wahoo McDaniel beat Carl Fergie & Bill White
Terry Taylor double DQ Pvt. Kernodle
Roddy Piper beat Keith Larson
Angelo Mosca & Killer Kahn beat Tony Anthony & Ron Ritchie

4/30/82: Charleston, SC @ County Hall
Jake Roberts & Terry Taylor(sub for Don Muraco) beat Pvt. Nelson & Pvt. Kernodle
Killer Kahn beat Porkchop Cash
Ron Ritchie vs. Jim Dalton
Terry Taylor vs. Steve Sybert
Ken Timbs vs. Tony Anthony

4/30/82: Knoxville, TN @ Chilhowee Park
Johnny Weaver beat Roddy Piper by DQ
Jimmy Valiant beat Ivan Koloff by DQ
Jay Youngblood beat The Ninja in an Indian strap match
Bill White beat Abe Jacobs
Keith Larsen beat Deke Rivers
Vinnie Valentino draw Rick Connors

5/2/82: Ashville, NC @ Civic Center
Wahoo McDaniel beat Roddy Piper
Jimmy Valiant & Paul Jones beat Ivan Koloff & The Ninja by DQ
Jim Dalton beat Tony Anthony
Kelly Kiniski beat Ken Timbs
Tim Horner beat Tony Russo

5/2/82: Roanoke, VA @ Civic Center
Ric Flair & Jake Roberts beat Angelo Mosca & Gene Anderson
Killer Kahn beat Johnny Weaver
Pvt. Kernodle & Pvt. Nelson beat Jay Youngblood & Porkchop Cash
Ron Ritchie beat Steve Sybert
Mike Davis beat Bill White

5/2/82: Greensboro, NC @ Coliseum
David Patterson draw Mike Rotundo
Killer Kahn beat Keith Larsen
Don Muraco beat Carl Fergie
Jack Brisco beat Gene Anderson
Ivan Koloff & The Ninja beat Jimmy Valiant & Ron Ritchie
Wahoo McDaniel beat Sgt. Slaughter
NWA World Champion Ric Flair beat Angelo Mosca by DQ

5/3/82: Greenville, SC @ Memorial Auditorium
NWA World Champion Ric Flair NC with Wahoo McDaniel
Sgt. Slaughter beat Don Muraco
Angelo Mosca beat Porkchop Cash
Carl Fergie draw Kelly Kiniski
Tony Anthony beat Vinnie Valentino
Mike Davis beat Rick Connors

5/4/82: Raleigh, NC @ Civic Center
NWA World Champion Ric Flair NC with Wahoo McDaniel
Don Muraco & Porkchop Cash beat Carl Fergie & David Patterson
Killer Kahn beat Ron Ritchie
Kelly Kiniski beat Jim Dalton
Tim Horner beat Ken Timbs

5/4/82: Columbia, SC @ Township Auditorium
Mike Rotundo beat Tony Russo
Bill White beat Keith Larson
Terry Taylor beat Ben Alexander
Jack Brisco beat Gene Anderson
Ivan Koloff & The Ninja beat Jimmy Valiant & Jake Roberts

5/5/82: Charlotte, NC @ WCPQ Studios (TV)
Jack Brisco vs. Roddy Piper
Killer Khan & Angelo Mosca beat Ron Ritchie & Don Gilbert
Ivan Koloff beat Keith Larson
Don Muraco & Wahoo McDaniel beat Jim Dalton & Steve Sybert
Jack Brisco beat Deke Rivers
Jake Roberts beat Ben Alexander

5/6/82: Norfolk, VA @ Scope
Mike Davis beat Ken Timbs
Kelly Kiniski beat Jim Dalton
Keith Larsen beat Bill White
Don Muraco & Johnny Weaver beat Pvt. Nelson & Pvt. Kernodle
Killer Kahn beat Ron Ritchie
Sgt. Slaughter & Angelo Mosca beta Porkchop Cash & Jake Roberts
NWA World Champion Ric Flair NC with Wahoo McDaniel

5/7/82: Midlothian, VA @ Clover Hill High School
Ric Flair vs. Angelo Mosca
Ivan Koloff & The Ninja vs. Jimmy Valiant & Paul Jones
Jay Youngblood vs. Ken Timbs

5/8/82: Lexington, NC @ North Davidson High School
Roddy Piper & Angelo Mosca vs. Jack Brisco & Wahoo McDaniel
Johnny Weaver vs. Michael Hayes
Carl Fergie vs. Terry Taylor
Tim Horner vs. Tony Russo
Mike Rotundo vs. Ken Timbs

5/9/82: Charlotte, NC @ Coliseum
Mike Rotundo beat Jim Dalton
Ron Ritchie draw Carl Fergie
Tommy Rich beat Roddy Piper by DQ
Don Muraco beat Sgt. Slaughter
Stan Hansen & Ole Anderson beat The Samoans
Jack & Jerry Brisco beat Killer Kahn & Angelo Mosca by DQ
Stan Hansen & Ole Anderson beat Jack & Jerry Brisco to win tournament

5/10/82: Greenville, SC @ Memorial Auditorium
Jack Brisco beat Roddy Piper to win NWA Mid Atlantic Title
Jake Roberts beat Sgt. Slaughter
Don Muraco beat Ole Anderson
Killer Kahn beat Kelly Kiniski
David Patterson beat Vinnie Valentino

5/11/82: Raleigh, NC @ Civic Center

5/11/82: Columbia, SC @ Township Auditorium
Tony Anthony beat Gary Moore
Vinnie Valentino beat Ken Timbs
Ron Ritchie beat Steve Sybert
Don Muraco beat David Patterson
Jack Brisco & Jimmy Valiant double DQ Ivan Koloff & The Ninja

5/12/82: Charlotte, NC @ WCPQ Studios (TV)
Ron Ritchie beat Jim Dalton via pinfall
Killer Kahn beat Vinnie Valentino via pinfall
King Parsons beat Tony Russo via pinfall
Angelo Mosca beat Kelly Kiniski via pinfall
Johnny Weaver & Jake Roberts NC with Pvt. Nelson & Pvt. Kernodle

5/13/82: Sumter, SC @ Exposition Center
Roddy Piper vs. Don Muraco
Johnny Weaver vs. Angelo Mosca
Bill White vs. Mike Rotundo
Gary Moore vs. Tony Anthony
Porkchop Cash & Ron Ritchie vs. Carl Fergie & David Patterson

5/14/82: Cincinnati, OH @ Gardens
Kelly Kiniski beat Ken Hall
Killer Kahn beat Mike Davis
Don Muraco beat Steve Sybert
Bob Armstrong beat Roddy Piper by countout
Jimmy Valiant & Leroy Brown beat Ivan Koloff & The Ninja

5/14/82: Hampton, VA @ Coliseum
Mike Rotundo beat Ken Timbs
Tim Horner beat Bill White
Ron Ritchie beat Jim Dalton
Pvt. Kernodle beat Terry Taylor
Porkchop Cash beat Pvt. Nelson
Sgt. Slaughter & Angelo Mosca beat Paul Jones & Jake Roberts

5/15/82: Spartanburg, SC @ Memorial Auditorium
Abe Jacobs beat Steve Sybert
Mike Rotundo beat Gary Moore(sub for Ben Alexander)
Mike Davis & Keith Larson beat Carl Fergie & Bill White
Killer Kahn beat Ken Hall
Jack Brisco beat Angelo Mosca
Angelo Mosca won a 12-man Battle Royal

5/15/82: Wilmington, NC @ Legion Stadium
Roddy Piper vs. Leroy Brown
Gene Anderson vs. Paul Jones
David Patterson vs. Vinnie Valentino
Tony Russo vs. Tony Anthony
Ivan Koloff & The Ninja vs. Jimmy Valiant & Jake Roberts

5/16/82: Asheville, NC @ Civic Center
Vinnie Valentino beat Tony Russo
Wahoo McDaniel beat Roddy Piper
Jack Brisco & Don Muraco beat Gene Anderson & Ole Anderson
Killer Kahn beat Ron Ritchie
Paul Jones & Porkchop Cash beat David Patterson & Carl Fergie

5/16/82: Toronto, Ontario @ Maple Leaf Gardens
Tim Horner draw Keith Larson
Kelly Kiniski beat Tito Senza
Johnny Weaver & Tony Parisi beat Tarzan Tyler & Pvt. Nelson
Jimmy Valiant beat Pvt. Kernodle
Jake Roberts beat Sgt. Slaughter by DQ
Ivan Koloff beat Ron Bass
Angelo Mosca & Jake Roberts beat Nick Bockwinkel & John Studd

5/17/82: Guelph, Ontario @ Memorial Gardens (TV)
Kelly Kiniski beat Tony Senza
Tarzan Tyler & John Studd beat Ron Bass & Tim Horner
Angelo Mosca beat Tito Senza
Kelly Kiniski beat Tito Senza & Tarzan Tyler
Pvt. Nelson beat Tim Horner
The Destroyer beat Tim Horner
Pvt. Nelson & Pvt. Kernodle beat Keith Larson & Kelly Kiniski
Johnny Weaver beat Pvt. Kernodle
Angelo Mosca beat John Studd by countout

5/17/82: Greenville, SC @ Memorial Auditorium
Mike Rotundo beat Tony Russo
King Parsons beat Bill White
Killer Kahn beat Mike Davis
Don Muraco & Jake Roberts beat Gene Anderson & Ole Anderson
Jimmy Valiant & Paul Jones beat Ivan Koloff & The Ninja

5/18/82: Oshawa, Ontario
Keith Larson beat Tito Senza
Kelly Kiniski beat Tim Horner
Tony Parisi beat Tarzan Tyler
Angelo Mosca beat John Studd by countout
Pvt. Nelson & Pvt. Kernodle beat Johnny Weaver & Billy Red Lyons

5/18/82: Raleigh, NC @ Civic Center
Don Muraco beat Sgt. Slaughter
Wahoo McDaniel beat Roddy Piper
King Parsons & Porkchop Cash beat Carl Fergie & David Patterson
Ron Ritchie beat Gary Moore

5/18/82: Columbia, SC @ Township Auditorium
Jack Brisco & Jimmy Valiant beat The Ninja & Ivan Koloff
Killer Kahn beat Paul Jones
Mike Rotundo beat Jim Dalton
Mike Davis beat Tony Russo
Abe Jacobs beat Steve Sybert

5/19/82: Niagara Falls, Ontario
Billy Red Lyons beat Tito Senza
Tim Horner draw Keith Larson
Kelly Kiniski beat Tarzan Tyler
John Studd beat Johnny Weaver
Angelo Mosca & Tony Parisi beat Pvt. Nelson & Pvt. Kernodle

5/19/82: Charlotte, NC @ WCPQ Studios (TV)
Wahoo McDaniel & Don Muraco beat Gary Moore & Steve Sybert
Jerry Brisco beat Tony Russo by submission
Carl Fergie beat Mike Davis
Killer Khan beat Ken Timbs
King Parsons beat Jim Dalton
Sgt. Slaughter beat Mike Rotundo

5/20/82: Harrisonburg, VA @ High School
Gene Anderson vs. Jack Brisco
Roddy Piper vs. Wahoo McDaniel

5/21/82: Richmond, VA @ Coliseum
Wahoo McDaniel beat Sgt. Slaughter to win the NWA United States Title
Jack Brisco beat Roddy Piper
Angelo Mosca & Killer Kahn beat Paul Jones & Don Muraco
Mike Rotundo beat Pvt. Kernodle
Mike Davis beat Gary Moore
Mike Rotundo beat Jim Dalton

5/22/82: Charlotte, NC @ Coliseum
Keith Larsen beat Ken Timbs
Kelly Kiniski beat Gary Moore
Porkchop Cash beat Bill White
Angelo Mosca beat Leroy Brown
Sgt. Slaughter beat Don Muraco
Gene Anderson & Ole Anderson beat Jack Brisco & Paul Jones
Wahoo McDaniel beat Roddy Piper

5/23/82: Greensboro, NC @ Coliseum
Mike Davis beat Bill White
Mike Rotundo beat Jim Dalton
Angelo Mosca beat Paul Jones
Jimmy Valiant & Jake Roberts beat Ivan Koloff & The Ninja
Roddy Piper beat Don Muraco
Wahoo McDaniel beat Sgt. Slaughter
NWA World Champion Ric Flair beat Jack Brisco

5/24/82: Greenville, SC @ Memorial Auditorium
NWA World Champion Ric Flair beat Wahoo McDaniel
Sgt. Slaughter beat Paul Jones
Ole Anderson beat King Parsons
The Samoans beat Carl Fergie & David Patterson
Ben Alexander beat Ken Hall

5/25/82: Raleigh, NC @ Civic Center
NWA World Champion Ric Flair beat Wahoo McDaniel
Mike Davis beat Bill White
King Parsons beat Jim Dalton
Paul Jones & Jake Roberts beat Killer Kahn & Angelo Mosca

5/25/82: Columbia, SC @ Township Auditorium
Keith Larson beat Ben Alexander
David Patterson beat Samoan #2
Carl Fergie beat Samoan #1
Don Muraco beat Sgt. Slaughter
Jack Brisco beat Roddy Piper

5/26/82: Charlotte, NC @ WCPQ Studios (TV)
Wahoo McDaniel & Don Muraco beat Bill White & Juan Reynosa
Terry Gibbs beat Ken Timbs
Pvt. Kernodle & Pvt. Nelson beat Johnny Weaver & Mike Davis(sub for Jake Roberts)
Ivan Koloff & The Ninja vs. The Samoans

5/27/82: Sumter, SC @ Exposition Center
NWA World Champion Ric Flair beat Wahoo McDaniel
Gene Anderson beat Abe Jacobs
Paul Jones beat Angelo Mosca
Killer Kahn beat Kelly Kiniski
The Samoans beat Steve Sybert & Jim Dalton

5/28/82: Charleston, SC @ County Hall
Samoan #2 beat Ken Timbs
King Parsons beat Abe Jacobs
Mike Rotundo beat Juan Reynosa
Porkchop Cash beat Jim Dalton
Angelo Mosca & Killer Kahn beat Don Muraco & Paul Jones
Wahoo McDaniel beat Sgt. Slaughter

5/28/82: Knoxville, TN @ Chilhowee Park
NWA World Champion Ric Flair beat Harley Race
Keith Larsen beat Carl Fergie
Dusty Rhodes beat Great Kabuki by DQ
Johnny Weaver & Tim Horner beat Bill White & Kevin Sullivan
David Patterson beat Kenny Hall

5/28/82: Lovington, VA @ Nelson County H.S.
Jimmy Valiant vs. The Ninja
Jack Brisco vs. Roddy Piper
Ivan Koloff vs. Jake Roberts
Pvt. Kernodle vs. Kelly Kiniski
Pvt. Nelson vs. Ron Ritchie
Steve Sybert vs. Mike Davis

5/29/82: Greenville, SC @ Memorial Auditorium(Special Saturday Card)
Terry Gibbs beat Jim Dalton
Carl Fergie & David Patterson beat the Samoans
King Parsons beat Gene Anderson
Paul Jones beat Sgt. Slaughter in a lumberjack match
Jimmy Valiant beat Ivan Koloff in a cage match

5/30/82: Asheville, NC @ Civic Center
NWA World Champion Ric Flair beat Jack Brisco
Wahoo McDaniel beat Sgt. Slaughter
Jimmy Valiant beat Ivan Koloff
Kelly Kiniski beat Killer Kahn

Terry Gibbs & Ron Ritchie beat Carl Fergie & David Patterson
Tim Horner beat Bill White

5/30/82: Roanoke, VA @ Civic Center
NWA World Champion Ric Flair beat Wahoo McDaniel
Sgt. Slaughter beat Don Muraco
Jack Brisco beat Angelo Mosca
Paul Jones & Johnny Weaver beat Pvt. Nelson & Pvt. Kernodle

5/31/82: Wilmington, NC @ Legion Stadium
Wahoo McDaniel vs. Sgt. Slaughter
Angelo Mosca vs. Don Muraco
Pvt. Kernodle & Pvt. Nelson vs. Porkchop Cash & King Parsons
Abe Jacobs vs. Mike Rotundo

6/1/82: Columbia, SC @ Township Auditorium
Samoan #2 beat Ali Bey
Samoan #1 beat Bill White
Paul Jones & King Parsons beat Pvt. Kernodle & Pvt. Nelson
Killer Kahn beat Johnny Weaver
Jack Brisco beat Roddy Piper

6/1/82: Wadesboro, NC @ Anson High School
Ivan Koloff & The Ninja vs. Jimmy Valiant & Jake Roberts
Carl Fergie vs. Ron Ritchie
Bill White vs. Kelly Kiniski

6/2/82: Charlotte, NC @ WCPQ Studios (TV)
Ivan Koloff & Steve Sybert beat Mike Rotundo & Jimmy Valiant(sub for Johnny Weaver)
Jack Brisco & Paul Jones beat David Patterson & Carl Fergie
Porkchop Cash & King Parsons beat Pvt. Kernodle & Pvt. Nelson
Angelo Mosca & Sgt. Slaughter beat The Samoans
Wahoo McDaniel beat Juan Reynosa

6/3/82: Norfolk, VA @ Scope
Terry Gibbs beat Juan Reynosa
Kelly Kiniski beat Bill White
Johnny Weaver & Mike Rotundo beat Pvt. Kernodle & Pvt. Nelson
Ivan Koloff & The Ninja beat Jimmy Valiant & King Parsons
Jack Brisco beat Roddy Piper

6/4/82: Charleston, SC @ County Hall
Samoan #2 beat Steve Sybert
Keith Larsen beat Ken Timbs
Mike Rotundo beat Bill White
King Parsons & Porkchop Cash beat Pvt. Kernodle & Pvt. Nelson
Jack Brisco beat Roddy Piper by CO

6/5/82: Charlotte, NC @ Coliseum
Ron Ritchie beat Keith Larsen
Jimmy Valiant beat Ivan Koloff in a Russian chain match
Wahoo McDaniel beat Sgt. Slaughter
Paul Jones beat Angelo Mosca
Kelly Kiniski & Mike Rotundo beat Carl Fergie & Dave Patterson
Jack Brisco & Don Muraco beat Roddy Piper & Ole Anderson

6/6/82: Greensboro, NC @ Coliseum
Wahoo McDaniel beat Sgt. Slaughter in a Canadian lumberjack match
Jack Brisco beat Roddy Piper
Paul Jones beat The Ninja
King Parsons & Mike Rotundo beat Gene Anderson & Iron Sheik
Juan Reynosa beat Tim Horner
Mike Rotundo beat Carl Fergie
Jim Dalton beat Keith Larson

6/6/82: Toronto, Ontario @ Maple Leaf Gardens
Angelo Mosca beat Gene Kiniski
Jimmy Valiant beat Ivan Koloff to win NWA Mid Atlantic Television Title(Only recognized in Toronto)
John Studd beat Jake Roberts
Johnny Weaver & Kelly Kiniski beat Pvt. Nelson & Pvt. Kernodle
The Destroyer beat Nick DeCarlo
Porkchop Cash beat Steve Siebert

6/7/82: Greenville, SC @ Memorial Auditorium
Bill White beat Jim Dalton
Mike Rotundo beat Ben Alexander
King Parsons beat Carl Fergie
Terry Gibbs beat David Patterson
Sgt. Slaughter beat Wahoo McDaniel(injured by Don Muraco) by forfeit to win NWA United States Title
Sgt. Slaughter beat Don Muraco
Terry Gibbs won a battle royal

6/7/82: Buffalo, NY
Mike Davis beat Steve Sybert
Kelly Kiniski beat Ken Timbs
Johnny Weaver & Jimmy Valiant beat Ivan Koloff & The Ninja
Pvt. Nelson & Pvt. Kernodle beat Porkchop Cash & Nick DeCarlo
Gene Kiniski beat Jake Roberts
Angelo Mosca beat John Studd

6/8/82: St. Catherines, Ontario @ Garden City Arena (TV)
Jimmy Valiant & Johnny Weaver beat Pvt. Nelson & Pvt. Kernodle
Pvt. Kernodle draw Johnny Weaver
Tony Parisi beat Pvt. Nelson
Tony Parisi beat The Destroyer by DQ
The Destroyer beat Mike Davis
Kelly Kiniski beat Steve Sybert
Kelly Kiniski beat Ken Timbs
Gene Kiniski beat Mike Davis
Gene Kiniski beat Chris Jones & Nick DeCarlo in a handicap match
Mike Davis beat Alex Girard

6/8/82: Columbia, SC @ Township Auditorium
Sgt. Slaughter beat Wahoo McDaniel
Don Muraco beat Angelo Mosca
King Parsons beat Gene Anderson
Mike Rotundo beat Jim Dalton
Ron Ritchie beat Bill White
Terry Gibbs beat Keith Larson

6/8/82: Raleigh, NC @ Civic Center
Tim Horner beat Carl Fergie
David Patterson beat Ali Bey
Keith Larson beat Juan Reynosa
Ivan Koloff & The Ninja beat Paul Jones & Porkchop Cash
Jack Brisco beat Roddy Piper

6/9/82: Charlotte, NC @ WCPQ Studios (TV)
Sgt. Slaughter beat Steve Sybert
Jack Brisco beat Don Muraco by DQ
Porkchop Cash & King Parsons beat Carl Fergie & Kurt Von Hess
Paul Jones beat Ken Timbs
The Ninja, Ivan Koloff & Angelo Mosca beat Kelly Kiniski, Mike Rotundo & Mike Davis
Sgt. Slaughter beat Porkchop Cash
Kelly Kiniski & Mike Rotundo beat David Patterson & Ali Bey
Don Muraco & Roddy Piper beat Mike Davis & Abe Jacobs
Ivan Koloff beat Keith Larsen
Paul Jones & Jimmy Valiant beat Bill White & Steve Sybert

6/10/82: Sumter, SC @ Exposition Center
David Patterson beat Mike Moore
Ken Timbs beat Abe Jacobs
Bill White beat Terry Gibbs
Johnny Weaver beat Jim Dalton
Sgt. Slaughter beat Mike Rotundo(sub for Wahoo McDaniel)
Paul Jones beat Angelo Mosca

6/11/82: Cincinnati, OH @ Gardens
Kelly Kiniski beat The Monk
Porkchop Cash beat Juan Reynosa
Roddy Piper beat Bob Armstrong in a Canadian lumberjack match
King Parsons beat Jim Dalton
Sgt. Slaughter beat Don Muraco

6/11/82: Knoxville, TN @ Chilhowee Park

6/12/82: Richmond, VA @ Coliseum
Kelly Kiniski beat The Monk
Jim Dalton beat Juan Reynosa
Gene Kiniski beat Porkchop Cash
Sgt. Slaughter beat King Parsons
Jack Brisco & Paul Jones beat Roddy Piper & Don Muraco

6/13/82: Roanoke, VA @ Civic Center
Sgt. Slaughter beat Jay Youngblood
Jack Brisco beat Roddy Piper
Jimmy Valiant beat The Ninja
Angelo Mosca beat Ron Ritchie
Pvt. Kernodle & Pvt. Nelson beat Porkchop Cash & King Parsons to win NWA Mid Atlantic Tag Title
Terry Gibbs beat Jim Dalton

6/13/82: Asheville, NC @ Civic Center
Jack Brisco beat Roddy Piper
Jimmy Valiant, Jay Youngblood & Paul Jones beat Ivan Koloff, Angelo Mosca & Gene Anderson
Johnny Weaver beat Bill White
Kelly Kiniski beat Juan Reynosa
Mike Rotundo beat The Monk
Tim Horner beat David Patterson

6/14/82: Greenville, SC @ Memorial Auditorium
King Parsons beat Ben Alexander
Terry Gibbs beat Pvt. Nelson
Jim Dalton beat Mike Davis
The Monk beat Keith Larson
Ron Ritchie beat Ali Bey
The Ninja & Roddy Piper beat Jack Brisco & Jimmy Valiant

6/15/82: Columbia, SC @ Township Auditorium
Jack Brisco beat Roddy Piper
Johnny Weaver beat Gene Anderson
Mike Rotundo beat Ron Ritchie
Keith Larsen beat Jim Dalton

6/15/82: Raleigh, NC @ Civic Center
No Wrestling

6/16/82: Charlotte, NC @ WCPQ Studios (TV)
Angelo Mosca beat King Parsons
Jack Brisco beat Juan Reynosa
Ivan Koloff & The Ninja beat Ron Ritchie & Rusty Roberts
David Patterson beat Keith Larsen
Jay Youngblood, Jake Roberts & Paul Jones beat Pvt. Kernodle, Pvt. Nelson & the Monk
Jack Brisco & Jay Youngblood beat Juan Reynosa & David Patterson
Ivan Koloff & The Ninja beat Terry Gibbs & Rusty Roberts
Roddy Piper beat Bill White
Angelo Mosca beat Ron Ritchie
Paul Jones & Jake Roberts beat The Monk & Ben Alexander

6/17/82: Harrisonburg, VA @ High School
Keith Larson vs. Bill White
Tim Horner vs. The Monk
Ron Ritchie vs. David Patterson
Kelly Kiniski vs. Matt Borne
Jay Youngblood & Paul Jones vs. Angelo Mosca & The Ninja

6/18/82: Charleston, SC @ County Hall
Bill White beat Keith Larson
Tim Horner beat David Patterson
Johnny Weaver beat The Monk

Angelo Mosca & The Ninja beat King Parsons & Porkchop Cash
Wahoo McDaniel beat Sgt. Slaughter in a Canadian lumberjack match

6/18/82: Wilmington, NC @ Legion Stadium
Jack Brisco vs. Roddy Piper
Jimmy Valiant vs. Ivan Koloff in a chain match
Jay Youngblood & Paul Jones vs. Pvt. Kernodle & Pvt. Nelson
Kelly Kiniski vs. Matt Borne
Mike Rotundo vs. Juan Reynosa
Mike Davis vs. Jim Dalton

6/19/82: Greensboro, NC @ Coliseum
Jimmy Valiant beat Ivan Koloff via DQ
Don Muraco & Roddy Piper beat Jack Brisco & Wahoo McDaniel by DQ
Paul Jones & Jake Roberts beat The Ninja & Gene Anderson
Angelo Mosca beat Johnny Weaver
Jay Youngblood beat The Monk
Mike Davis beat The Monk
Kelly Kiniski beat Jim Dalton
Ron Ritchie beat Juan Reynosa

6/21/82: Greenville, SC @ Memorial Auditorium
Jack Brisco beat Roddy Piper
The Ninja beat Paul Jones
Jake Roberts beat Gene Anderson
Pvt. Nelson & Pvt. Kernodle beat Porkchop Cash & King Parsons
Bill White beat Terry Gibbs
Ron Ritchie beat The Monk

6/22/82: Raleigh, NC @ Civic Center
Jack Brisco beat Roddy Piper
Paul Jones beat The Ninja by DQ
Jim Dalton beat Keith Larson
Steve Sybert beat Terry Gibbs
Ron Ritchie beat Ali Bey
Pvt. Nelson & Pvt. Kernodle beat Porkchop Cash & King Parsons

6/22/82: Sumter, SC @ Exposition Center
Jimmy Valiant beat Sgt. Slaughter by DQ
Jake Roberts beat Ivan Koloff
Jay Youngblood beat Angelo Mosca
Mike Rotundo beat Dave Patterson
Mike Davis beat Ken Timbs
Tim Horner beat Juan Reynosa

6/23/82: Charlotte, NC @ WCPQ Studios (TV)
Ricky Steamboat & Jack Brisco beat Matt Borne & Steve Sybert
Jake Roberts beat Roddy Piper by DQ
Jimmy Valiant beat Bill White
Sgt. Slaughter, Pvt. Nelson & Pvt. Kernodle beat Kelly Kiniski, Mike Rotundo & Mike Davis
Wahoo McDaniel & Jay Youngblood beat Ken Timbs & Ali Bey
Ivan Koloff beat Kelly Kiniski
Roddy Piper & Sgt. Slaughter beat Mike Rotundo & Mike Davis
Paul Jones & Jake Roberts beat Ken Timbs & Steve Sybert
Jack Brisco beat Pvt. Nelson
Wahoo McDaniel & Ricky Steamboat beat David Patterson & Bill White

6/25/82: Charleston, SC @ County Hall
Sgt. Slaughter beat Wahoo McDaniel
Jack Brisco NC with Roddy Piper
Jimmy Valiant beat Ivan Koloff by CO
Mike Rotundo & Kelly Kiniski beat Steve Sybert & David Patterson
Matt Borne beat Mike Davis
Ali Bey beat Keith Larsen
Ron Ritchie beat Bill White

6/26/82: Charlotte, NC @ Coliseum
Jack Brisco beat Roddy Piper
Angelo Mosca beat Paul Jones
Jimmy Valiant beat The Ninja by DQ
Pvt. Nelson & Pvt. Kernodle beat King Parsons & Porkchop Cash
Juan Reynosa beat Terry Gibbs
Ron Ritchie beat The Monk
Tim Horner beat Ali Bey

6/27/82: Asheville, NC @ Civic Center
Jack Brisco beat NWA World Champion Ric Flair by DQ
Jimmy Valiant beat Ivan Koloff in a Russian chain match
Wahoo McDaniel beat Sgt. Slaughter
Jake Roberts & Paul Jones beat The Ninja & Gene Anderson
Ali Bey beat Terry Gibbs
Kelly Kiniski beat Juan Reynosa
Mike Rotundo beat Jim Dalton

6/27/82: Toronto, Ontario @ Maple Leaf Gardens
Porkchop Cash beat Pvt. Nelson
Pvt. Kernodle beat King Parsons
Jay Youngblood beat David Patterson
The Destroyer beat Johnny Weaver
Porkchop Cash draw Pvt. Kernodle
Jay Youngblood beat The Destroyer in a tournament final to win vacant NWA Canadian Television Title
Angelo Mosca beat Gene Kiniski in a Texas death match
Wahoo McDaniel beat Sgt. Slaughter
NWA World Champion Ric Flair beat Jack Brisco(18:02) via pinfall

6/28/82: Kingston, Ontario
King Parsons beat Jerry Bryant
Tony Parisi beat David Patterson
The Destroyer beat Nick DeCarlo
Johnny Weaver & Porkchop Cash beat Pvt. Nelson & Pvt. Kernodle by DQ
Gene Kiniski beat Jay Youngblood

6/28/82: Greenville, SC @ Memorial Auditorium
Jack Brisco & Ricky Steamboat beat Ric Flair & Roddy Piper
Wahoo McDaniel beat Sgt. Slaughter by DQ in an Indian strap match
Mike Rotundo & Kelly Kiniski beat Juan Reynosa & Bill White
Ron Ritchie draw Matt Borne
Keith Larsen beat The Monk

6/29/82: Columbia, SC @ Township Auditorium
NWA World Champion Ric Flair beat Jack Brisco by DQ
Jimmy Valiant beat Ivan Koloff in a cage match
Paul Jones beat The Ninja by DQ
Matt Borne beat Ron Ritchie
Jim Dalton beat Abe Jacobs
Tim Horner beat Juan Reynosa
Bill White beat Ken Timbs

6/29/82: St. Catherines, Ontario @ Garden City Arena(TV)
Gene Kiniski beat Porkchop Cash
Pvt. Nelson & Pvt. Kernodle draw Jay Youngblood & Johnny Weaver
Jay Youngblood beat David Patterson
The Destroyer beat Nick DeCarlo
Gene Kiniski beat King Parsons
Porkchop Cash beat Pvt. Nelson
Tony Parisi beat David Patterson
Johnny Weaver beat Jay Youngblood by DQ
Porkchop Cash beat David Patterson
Tony Parisi beat Jerry Bryant
Porkchop Cash beat David Patterson
Pvt. Nelson & Pvt. Kernodle beat Johnny Weaver & Nick DeCarlo
King Parsons beat Jerry Bryant

6/29/82: Raleigh, NC @ Civic Center
No Wrestling

6/30/82: Charlotte, NC @ WCPQ Studios (TV)
Jay Youngblood beat Angelo Mosca by DQ
Greg Valentine beat Brock Wood
Wahoo McDaniel & Paul Jones beat David Patterson & Steve Sybert
Roddy Piper beat Jimmy Ventor
Ricky Steamboat beat Bill White
Paul Jones & Jake Roberts beat The Monk & David Patterson
Roddy Piper & The Ninja beat Mike Davis & Brock wood
Wahoo McDaniel beat Pvt. Kernodle by DQ
Sgt. Slaughter beat Jimmy Ventor
Ricky Steamboat & Jay Youngblood beat Bill White & Ben Alexander

7/1/82: Norfolk, VA @ Scope
King Parsons beat Jim Dalton
Matt Borne beat Ron Ritchie
Kelly Kiniski & Mike Rotundo beat David Patterson & Juan Reynosa
Porkchop Cash beat Gene Anderson
Wahoo McDaniel beat Sgt. Slaughter
Jack Brisco beat Roddy Piper
NWA World Champion Ric Flair beat Jay Youngblood

7/2/82: Fredericksburg, VA @ Stafford High School
Paul Jones & Jay Youngblood beat The Ninja & Angelo Mosca
Tim Horner beat Juan Reynosa
Ron Ritchie beat Bill White
Mike Davis beat Steve Sybert

7/2/82: Charleston, SC @ County Hall
Jimmy Valiant beat Ivan Koloff Russian chain match
Ricky Steamboat beat Greg Valentine
Johnny Weaver beat Gene Anderson
Pvt. Nelson & Pvt. Kernodle beat Porkchop Cash & King Parsons
David Patterson beat Keith Larson
Abe Jacobs vs. Jim Dalton

7/2/82: Richmond, VA @ Coliseum
NWA World Champion Ric Flair beat Jake Roberts
Sgt. Slaughter beat Wahoo McDaniel
Jack Brisco draw Roddy Piper
Jim Dalton beat The Monk
Kelly Kiniski beat Ken Timbs
Matt Borne drew Mike Rotundo

7/3/82: Salem, VA @ Civic Center
Wahoo McDaniel beat Sgt. Slaughter in a Canadian lumberjack match
Jack Brisco beat Angelo Mosca(sub for Roddy Piper)
Jimmy Valiant beat The Ninja
King Parsons beat Pvt. Nelson
Ron Ritchie beat Bill White
Johnny Weaver, Jay Youngblood & Jake Roberts beat Angelo Mosca, Pvt. Kernodle & Gene Anderson

7/3/82: Greensboro, NC @ Coliseum
NWA Champion Ric Flair beat Wahoo McDaniel by DQ
Ivan Koloff beat Jimmy Valiant in a cage match
Jack Brisco beat Roddy Piper
Paul Jones & Jake Roberts beat Gene Anderson & The Ninja
Matt Borne beat Ron Ritchie
Mike Rotundo beat Jim Dalton
David Patterson beat Kelly Kiniski
Tim Horner beat Bill White by DQ

7/4/82: Roanoke, VA @ Civic Center
Jimmy Valiant beat The Ninja
King Parsons beat Pvt. Nelson
Ron Ritchie beat Bill White
Jack Brisco beat Angelo Mosca
Wahoo McDaniel beat Sgt. Slaughter in a Canadian lumberjack latch
Johnny Weaver, Jake Roberts & Jay Youngblood beat Pvt. Kernodle, Angelo Mosca & Gene Anderson

7/5/82: Greenville, SC @ Memorial Auditorium
Sgt. Slaughter beat Wahoo McDaniel
Ricky Steamboat beat Angelo Mosca by DQ
The Ninja beat Jake Roberts

Jay Youngblood beat Gene Anderson
Ron Ritchie beat Jim Dalton
Tim Horner beat Juan Reynosa
Pvt. Kernodle & Pvt. Nelson beat Porkchop Cash & King Parsons

7/6/82: Raleigh, NC @ Civic Center
Ron Ritchie beat Juan Reynosa
Tim Horner beat Bill White
The Monk beat Mike Davis
Jimmy Valiant beat Ivan Koloff in a Russian chain match
The Ninja beat Jake Roberts
Ricky Steamboat beat Greg Valentine
Pvt. Nelson & Pvt. Kernodle beat Porkchop Cash & King Parsons

7/6/82: Columbia, SC @ Township Auditorium
Wahoo McDaniel beat Sgt. Slaughter
Keith Larson beat Ali Bey
Matt Borne draw Mike Rotundo
Kelly Kiniski beat Jim Dalton
Jack Brisco beat Roddy Piper
Paul Jones & Jay Youngblood beat Angelo Mosca & Gene Anderson

7/7/82: Charlotte, NC @ WCPQ Studios (TV)
Roddy Piper beat Jack Brisco wins Mid Atlantic Title
Sgt. Slaughter beat King Parsons
Greg Valentine beat Keith Larsen
Ricky Steamboat & Jay Youngblood beat Ali Bey & Bill White
King Parsons & Porkchop Cash beat Ali Bey & Ken Timbs
Jimmy Valiant & Jake Roberts beat Ben Alexander & Steve Sybert
Sgt Slaughter & Ninja beat Kelly Kiniski & Mike Rotundo
Ricky Steamboat & Paul Jones beat Matt Borne & Juan Reynosa

7/8/82: Hendersonville, NC @ E.L. Justus Field
Jack Brisco beat Roddy Piper
Ricky Steamboat beat Greg Valentine
Paul Jones & Jake Roberts vs. Gene Anderson & Ninja
Kelly Kiniski vs. Jim Dalton
Mike Rotundo vs. David Patterson
Tim Horner vs. The Monk

7/8/82: Sumter, SC @ Exposition Center
Jimmy Valiant vs. Ivan Koloff in a cage match
Wahoo McDaniel vs. Sgt. Slaughter
Kernodle & Nelson vs. Porkchop Cash & King Parsons
Evelyn Stevens vs. Winona Little Heart
Jay Youngblood vs. Angelo Mosca
Ron Ritchie vs. Matt Borne
Keith Larsen vs. Ken Timbs

7/9/82: Lovington, VA
Johnny Weaver vs. Matt Borne

7/9/82: Charleston, SC @ County Hall
Keith Larsen beat Ken Timbs
Mike Rotundo beat Bill White
Ron Ritchie beat Jim Dalton
Angelo Mosca beat Jay Youngblood
Ricky Steamboat beat Sgt. Slaughter by DQ
Jack Brisco beat Roddy Piper by CO

7/10/82: Charlotte, NC @ Coliseum
Jack Brisco & Ricky Steamboat beat Roddy Piper & Don Muraco in a cage match
Sgt. Slaughter beat Wahoo McDaniel
Jay Youngblood beat Greg Valentine by DQ
Matt Borne draw Mike Rotundo
Kelly Kiniski beat Ken Timbs
Ron Ritchie beat Juan Reynosa

7/11/82: Toronto, Ontario @ Maple Leaf Gardens
Ivan Koloff beat Jimmy Valiant
Jake Roberts beat The Ninja by DQ
Johnny Weaver beat Tim Gerrard
Sgt. Slaughter beat Wahoo McDaniel
Jack Brisco beat Roddy Piper
Tony Parisi beat Bob Marcus
WWF Champion Bob Backlund beat Greg Valentine

7/12/82: Greenville, SC @ Memorial Auditorium
Jimmy Valiant beat Ivan Koloff in a NY street fight
Ricky Steamboat beat Angelo Mosca
Jake Roberts beat The Ninja
Evelyn Stevens beat Winona Little Heart
Mike Davis beat Ben Alexander
Kelly Kiniski beat Ken Timbs
Mike Rotundo beat Bill White

7/13/82: Columbia, SC @ Township Auditorium
Mike Davis beat Ken Timbs
Jimmy Valiant beat Ivan Koloff by DQ NY street fight
Paul Jones beat Matt Borne by DQ
Pvt. Nelson & Pvt. Kernodle beat Porkchop Cash & King Parsons
Mike Rotundo beat Ali Bey

7/13/82: Raleigh, NC @ Civic Center

7/14/82: Charlotte, NC @ WCPQ Studios (TV)
Jake Roberts & Jimmy Valiant beat Jim Dalton & Juan Reynosa
Pvt. Nelson & Pvt. Kernodle beat Mike Davis & Porkchop Cash
Ivan Koloff, Sgt. Slaughter & Matt Borne beat Ron Ritchie, Abe Jacobs & King Parsons
Ricky Steamboat & Jay Youngblood beat Bill White & The Monk
Jack Brisco & Wahoo McDaniel beat David Patterson & Ben Alexander
Paul Jones, Jake Roberts & Jack Brisco beat Matt Borne, David Patterson & Bill White
Wahoo McDaniel beat Juan Reynosa
Jay Youngblood & Winona Little Heart beat Jim Dalton & Evelyn Stevens
Kelly Kiniski & Mike Rotundo beat Gene Anderson & The Ninja by DQ

7/17/82: Greensboro, NC @ Coliseum
Jack & Jerry Brisco beat Don Muraco & Roddy Piper
Sgt. Slaughter beat Wahoo McDaniel by DQ
Paul Jones beat Angelo Mosca
Winona Little Heart beat Evelyn Stevens
Pvt. Nelson & Pvt. Kernodle beat King Parsons & Porkchop Cash
Gene Anderson beat Johnny Weaver
Mike Rotundo beat Juan Reynosa
Ron Ritchie beat The Monk

7/17/82: Wilmington, NC @ Legion Stadium
Jimmy Valiant vs. Ivan Koloff in a steel cage match
Leroy Brown vs. The Ninja
Jake Roberts vs. Matt Borne
Johnny Weaver vs. David Patterson
Kelly Kiniski vs. Jim Dalton
Tim Horner vs. Steve Sybert
Keith Larson vs. Ken Timbs
Mike Davis vs. Ali Bey

7/18/82: Kingsport, TN
Wahoo McDaniel beat Sgt. Slaughter
Jimmy Valiant beat Ivan Koloff
Ricky Steamboat beat Gene Anderson
Tim Horner beat The Monk
Keith Larson beat Bill White
Jay Youngblood & Jake Roberts beat Pvt. Nelson & Pvt. Kernodle by DQ

7/18/82: Roanoke, VA @ Civic Center
Wahoo McDaniel vs. Sgt. Slaughter
Jimmy Valiant vs. Ivan Koloff in a Russian chain match
Leroy Brown vs. The Ninja

7/19/82: Greenville, SC @ Memorial Auditorium
Mike Davis beat Ali Bey
Mike Rotundo beat Ken Timbs
Kelly Kiniski draw David Patterson
Matt Borne beat Johnny Weaver
Angelo Mosca, Masked Superstar & Ivan Koloff beat Jimmy Valiant, Jack Brisco & Ricky Steamboat

7/20/82: Columbia, SC @ Township Auditorium
Johnny Weaver beat David Patterson
Kelly Kiniski beat Bill White
Sgt. Slaughter beat Wahoo McDaniel
Mike Davis beat Ken Timbs
Tim Horner beat Juan Reynosa
Ricky Steamboat & Jack Brisco beat Angelo Mosca & Gene Anderson

7/20/82: Raleigh, NC @ Civic Center
Keith Larsen beat Ali Bey
Ron Ritchie beat The Monk
Mike Rotundo beat Jim Dalton
Jimmy Valiant beat Ivan Koloff in a cage match
Leroy Brown beat The Ninja by DQ
Jay Youngblood beat Matt Borne
Pvt. Nelson & Pvt. Kernodle beat Paul Jones & Jake Roberts

7/21/82: Charlotte, NC @ WCPQ Studios (TV)
Roddy Piper & Don Muraco vs. Mike Davis & Abe Jacobs
Leroy Brown beat Keith Larson
Jimmy Valiant beat Jeff Sword
Sgt. Slaughter beat Tim Horner
Ricky Steamboat & Jack Brisco beat David Patterson & Ken Timbs
Angelo Mosca & Gene Anderson beat Jay Youngblood & Johnny Weaver
Matt Borne beat Mike Davis
King Parsons & Porkchop Cash beat Ali Bey & Ken Timbs
Ricky Steamboat, Jack Brisco & Mike Rotundo beat David Patterson, Bill White & Jim Dalton

7/23/82: Charleston, SC @ County Hall
Jimmy Valiant beat Ivan Koloff in a steel cage match
Pvt. Nelson & Pvt. Kernodle beat Jay Youngblood & Jake Roberts
Leroy Brown beat The Ninja
Gene Anderson beat Porkchop Cash
Mike Rotundo beat David Patterson
Tim Horner beat Bill White

7/23/82: Richmond, VA @ Coliseum
King Parsons beat Juan Reynosa
Paul Jones beat Matt Borne
Johnny Weaver beat Jim Dalton
Ricky Steamboat draw Don Muraco
Jack Brisco beat Roddy Piper by CO
Sgt. Slaughter beat Wahoo McDaniel in a lumberjack, strap match

7/24/82: Charlotte, NC @ Coliseum
Wahoo McDaniel beat Sgt. Slaughter in a lumberjack match
Jimmy Valiant beat Ivan Koloff in a New York street fight
Jack & Jerry Brisco beat Roddy Piper & Don Muraco in a Texas death match
Paul Jones & Jake Roberts beat Pvt. Nelson & Pvt. Kernodle
Mike Rotundo beat Bill White
Tim Horner draw David Patterson

7/25/82: Toronto, Ontario @ Maple Leaf Gardens
The Destroyer beat Nick DeCarlo
Tony Parisi beat Tim Gerrard
Ricky Steamboat & Jay Youngblood beat Pvt. Nelson & Pvt. Kernodle
Jimmy Snuka beat WWF Champion Bob Backlund by CO
The Ninja beat Johnny Weaver
Andre The Giant beat John Studd by DQ
Angelo Mosca beat Gene Kiniski in a lumberjack match

7/25/82: Asheville, NC @ Civic Center
Jack Brisco & Wahoo McDaniel beat Roddy Piper & Sgt. Slaughter
Jimmy Valiant beat Ivan Koloff
Jake Roberts beat Matt Borne

Paul Jones beat Gene Anderson
Kelly Kiniski draw David Patterson
Ron Ritchie beat Juan Reynosa
Mike Rotundo beat Jim Dalton

7/26/82: Greenville, SC @ Memorial Auditorium
Kelly Kiniski beat Jim Dalton
Mike Rotundo beat Billy White
Tim Horner beat Ben Alexander
Keith Larson beat Ken Timbs
Paul Jones & Jake Roberts beat Matt Borne & Gene Anderson
Jimmy Valiant beat Ivan Koloff Siberian salt match

7/26/82: Kingston, Ontario
Pvt. Nelson beat Nick DeCarlo
The Destroyer beat Tim Gerrard
Pvt. Kernodle draw Johnny Weaver
Gene Kiniski & John Studd beat Angelo Mosca & Jay Youngblood
Ricky Steamboat beat The Ninja

7/27/82: Columbia, SC @ Township Auditorium
Jack Brisco beat Leroy Brown by DQ
Wahoo McDaniel beat Sgt. Slaughter in a Canadian lumberjack match
David Patterson draw Kelly Kiniski
Matt Borne beat Mike Rotundo
Mike Davis beat The Monk
Ron Ritchie beat Ben Alexander

7/27/82: Raleigh, NC @ Civic Center
No Wrestling

7/27/82: Ottawa, Ontario @ Civic Centre
The Destroyer beat Tim Gerrard
Gene Kiniski beat Nick DeCarlo
NWA World Champion Ric Flair beat Ricky Steamboat
Angelo Mosca beat John Studd in a lumberjack match
Jay Youngblood beat The Ninja Indian strap match
Pvt. Nelson & Pvt. Kernodle beat Johnny Weaver & Tony Parisi

7/28/82: Charlotte, NC @ WCPQ Studios (TV)
Ricky Steamboat beat Juan Reynosa
Paul Jones & Jake Roberts beat Ken Timbs & Dave Patterson
Leroy Brown beat King Parsons
Sgt. Slaughter, Gene Anderson & Matt Borne beat Mike Rotundo, Mike Davis & Ron Ritchie
Jack Brisco & Wahoo McDaniel beat Bill White & Jim Dalton
Jay Youngblood & Johnny Weaver beat Pvt. Kernodle & Bill White
Ricky Steamboat beat Pvt. Nelson
Wahoo McDaniel beat David Patterson
Leroy Brown & The Ninja beat Mike Davis & Keith Larson

7/29/82: Harrisonburg, VA @ High School
Jimmy Valiant beat Ivan Koloff in a chain match
Porkchop Cash & King Parsons beat Matt Borne & David Patterson
Mike Davis beat Ali Bey
Matt Borne beat Keith Larson
Tim Horner beat Juan Reynosa
Jay Youngblood & Jake Roberts beat The Ninja & Gene Anderson by DQ

7/30/82: Richmond, VA @ Coliseum
Mike Rotundo beat Juan Reynosa
Kelly Kiniski beat David Patterson
Pvt. Kernodle & Pvt. Nelson beat Jake Roberts & Tim Horner
Angelo Mosca beat Jay Youngblood
Ricky Steamboat beat Leroy Brown by DQ
Roddy Piper beat Jack Brisco
Wahoo McDaniel beat Sgt. Slaughter in a strap match

7/31/82: Spartanburg, SC @ Memorial Auditorium
Ricky Steamboat & Jay Youngblood beat Angelo Mosca & The Ninja
Johnny Weaver beat Jim Dalton
Paul Jones beat David Patterson
Tim Horner beat Ken Timbs
Ron Ritchie beat Juan Reynosa
Mike Davis beat The Monk

8/1/82: Columbia, SC @ Township Auditorium
Tim Horner beat Jim Dalton
Ron Ritchie beat David Patterson
Gene Anderson beat Kelly Kiniski
Jake Roberts beat Angelo Mosca by DQ
Jack Brisco & Wahoo McDaniel beat Roddy Piper & Sgt. Slaughter
Jimmy Valiant beat Ivan Koloff

8/1/82: Savannah, GA @ Civic Center
Jimmy Valiant beat Ivan Koloff in a NY street fight
Mike Rotundo beat Juan Reynosa
Jay Youngblood beat Matt Borne
King Parsons & Porkchop Cash beat Pvt. Nelson & Pvt. Kernodle
Sgt. Slaughter beat Wahoo McDaniel
Roddy Piper beat Jack Brisco

8/2/82: Greenville, SC @ Memorial Auditorium
Roddy Piper beat Jack Brisco
Tim Horner beat David Patterson
Jim Dalton beat Keith Larson
Ricky Steamboat beat Leroy Brown
Gene Anderson & Angelo Mosca beat Johnny Weaver & Jay Youngblood
Matt Borne beat Mike Rotundo

8/2/82: Fayetteville, NC @ Cumberland County Memorial Auditorium
Ron Ritchie beat Ken Timbs
Kelly Kiniski beat Juan Reynosa
Mike Davis beat The Monk
Porkchop Cash & King Parsons beat Pvt. Nelson & Pvt. Kernodle
Paul Jones & Jake Roberts beat Ivan Koloff & Ninja
Wahoo McDaniel draw Sgt. Slaughter

8/3/82: Raleigh, NC @ Civic Center
Jim Valiant beat Ivan Koloff
Sgt. Slaughter beat Wahoo McDaniel
Mike Davis beat Ali Bey
Keith Larson beat Juan Reynosa
Tim Horner beat Dave Patterson
Matt Borne beat Ron Ritchie
Jack Brisco beat Roddy Piper to win Mid Atlantic Title
Note: Piper is stabbed in chest by a fan after this match

8/4/82: Charlotte, NC @ WCPQ Studios (TV)
Jack Brisco & Wahoo McDaniel beat Ben Alexander & David Patterson
Leroy Brown beat Ron Ritchie
Ricky Steamboat beat Juan Reynosa
King Parsons & Porkchop Cash beat Ali Bey & Ken Timbs
Matt Borne & The Ninja beat Tim Horner & Jay Youngblood
Jake Roberts, Jack Brisco & Wahoo McDaniel beat Pvt. Nelson, Pvt. Kernodle & Juan Reynosa
Jay Youngblood beat Ben Alexander
Ivan Koloff & Leroy Brown beat Leroy Dargon & Kelly Kiniski
Ricky Steamboat beat David Patterson
Gene Anderson, Matt Borne & The Ninja beat Ron Ritchie, Mike Davis & Tim Horner
Jake Roberts, Jack Brisco & Wahoo McDaniel beat Pvt. Nelson, Pvt. Kernodle & Juan Reynosa
Jay Youngblood beat Ben Alexander

8/6/82: Laurinburg, NC
Tim Horner beat Ben Alexander
Abe Jacobs beat Ken Timbs
Porkchop Cash beat Matt Bourne
Jack Brisco beat Roddy Piper
Wahoo McDaniel beat The Ninja

8/6/82: Charleston, SC @ County Hall
Mike Davis beat Ken Timbs
Ricky Steamboat beat Leroy Brown by DQ
Jay Youngblood & Johnny Weaver beat Angelo Mosca & Gene Anderson
Ron Ritchie beat Bill White
King Parsons beat Dave Patterson

8/7/82: Greensboro, NC @ Coliseum
Wahoo McDaniel beat NWA World Champion Ric Flair by DQ
Jimmy Valiant beat Ivan Koloff by DQ in a New York street fight match
Ricky Steamboat beat Leroy Brown
Angelo Mosca & Gene Anderson beat Johnny Weaver & Jay Youngblood
Mike Rotundo beat Dave Patterson
Kelly Kiniski beat Juan Reynosa
Ron Ritchie beat Ken Timbs
Bill White beat Mike Davis

8/8/82: Toronto, Ontario @ Maple Leaf Gardens
Tony Parisi draw Pvt. Nelson
Johnny Weaver beat Juan Reynosa
Kelly Kiniski & Mike Rotundo beat Bill White & Jim Dalton
Angelo Mosca beat Sgt. Slaughter by DQ
Jimmy Snuka beat WWF Champion Bob Backlund by CO
Paul Jones beat The Ninja
Pvt. Kernodle beat Jay Youngblood

8/8/82: Charlotte, NC @ Coliseum
Mike Davis beat Ken Timbs
Porkchop Cash & King Parsons beat Matt Borne & Dave Patterson
Ole Anderson beat Jake Roberts
Ricky Steamboat beat Leroy Brown by DQ
Jimmy Valiant beat Ivan Koloff
Wahoo McDaniel & Jack Brisco beat Roddy Piper & Ric Flair

8/9/82: Oshawa, Ontario
Mike Rotundo beat Juan Reynosa
Kelly Kiniski beat Jim Dalton
Paul Jones beat Bill White
Pvt. Kernodle & Pvt. Nelson beat Johnny Weaver & Billy Red Lyons
Jay Youngblood beat Gene Anderson

8/9/82: Greenville, SC @ Memorial Auditorium
Wahoo McDaniel beat Sgt. Slaughter in a lumberjack match
Keith Larson beat Tim Horner
Ron Ritchie beat Ali Bey
King Parsons & Porkchop Cash beat Ken Timbs & Matt Borne
Jake Roberts beat Angelo Mosca
Jimmy Valiant & Jack Brisco beat Ivan Koloff & Leroy Brown

8/10/82: Columbia, SC @ Township Auditorium
Mike Davis beat Ali Bey
Ivan Koloff & Leroy Brown beat Ricky Steamboat & Jimmy Valiant
Candi Malloy & Ron Ritchie beat Ben Alexander & Donna Christianello
King Parsons beat Ken Timbs
Keith Larson beat Tim Horner

8/10/82: Raleigh, NC @ Civic Center
Wahoo McDaniel beat Sgt. Slaughter in a lumberjack strap match
Jack Brisco beat Angelo Mosca
Jake Roberts beat Ole Anderson
Matt Borne beat Porkchop Cash
Leilani Kai & Joyce Grable beat Velvet McIntyre & Sabrina

8/10/82: St. Catherines, Ontario @ Garden City Arena(TV)
Jay Youngblood beat Pvt. Nelson
Tony Parisi beat Pvt. Kernodle by DQ
Johnny Weaver & Paul Jones beat Juan Reynosa & Bill White
Pvt. Kernodle beat Nick DeCarlo

Paul Jones & Johnny Weaver beat Pvt. Nelson & Pvt. Kernodle
Kelly Kiniski beat Jim Dalton
Tony Parisi beat Juan Reynosa
Mike Rotundo beat Bill White
Pvt. Nelson beat Nick DeCarlo
Jay Youngblood & Johnny Weaver beat Jim Dalton & Juan Reynosa
Pvt. Nelson & Pvt. Kernodle beat Kelly Kiniski & Mike Rotundo
Jay Youngblood beat Bill White
Paul Jones beat Juan Reynosa

8/11/82: Charlotte, NC @ WCPQ Studios (TV)
Ricky Steamboat & Jay Youngblood beat Pvt. Nelson & Jim Dalton
Ivan Koloff & Leroy Brown beat Mike Davis & Tim Horner
Jack Brisco & Jake Roberts beat Ken Timbs & Juan Reynosa
Pvt. Kernodle beat Leroy Dargon
Paul Jones & Gene Anderson beat Keith Larson & Abe Jacobs
Jack Brisco beat Matt Borne
Paul Jones beat Tim Horner
Ivan Koloff beat Leroy Dargon
Kelly Kiniski & Mike Rotundo beat Pvt. Nelson & Pvt. Kernodle by DQ
Ricky Steamboat, Jay Youngblood & Jake Roberts beat Jim Dalton, Ben Alexander & Juan Reynosa

8/12/82: Sumter, SC @ Exposition Center
Jimmy Valiant beat Ivan Koloff in a New York street fight match
Ricky Steamboat beat The Ninja by DQ
Jake Roberts & Jay Youngblood beat Angelo Mosca & Matt Borne
Ron Ritchie beat Bill White
Tim Horner beat Juan Reynosa
Keith Larsen beat Ben Alexander

8/12/82: Rocky Mount, NC
Ken Timbs beat Mike Davis
Mike Rotundo beat Ali Bey
Kelly Kiniski beat Jim Dalton
Porkchop Cash & King Parsons beat Pvt. Nelson & Pvt. Kernodle
Gene Anderson beat Johnny Weaver
Jack Brisco beat Leroy Brown
Wahoo McDaniel beat Sgt. Slaughter

8/13/82: Charleston, SC @ County Hall
Fabulous Moolah beat Peggy Lee
Wahoo McDaniel & Jack Brisco beat Sgt. Slaughter & Leroy Brown
Jake Roberts beat Matt Borne
Kelly Kiniski beat Jim Dalton
Bill White draw Keith Larson

8/13/82: Wilmington, NC @ Legion Stadium
Jimmy Valiant vs. Ivan Koloff in a New York street fight match
Paul Jones vs. Angelo Mosca
Pvt. Kernodle & Pvt. Nelson vs. Porkchop Cash & King Parsons
Mike Rotundo vs. David Patterson
Juan Reynosa vs. Tim Horner

8/14/82: Collinsville, VA @ Patrick Henry Community College
Jimmy Valiant & Jack Brisco vs. Ivan Koloff & Angelo Mosca
Johnny Weaver vs. Matt Borne
Fabulous Moolah & Donna Christianello vs. Penny Mitchell & Sherri Martel
Keith Larson vs. Ali Bey
King Parsons vs. David Patterson

8/15/82: Asheville, NC @ Civic Center
Jimmy Valiant beat Ivan Koloff in a New York street fight match
Jack Brisco & Paul Jones beat Sgt. Slaughter & Leroy Brown by DQ
Porkchop Cash & King Parsons beat Juan Reynosa & The Ninja
Gene Anderson beat Johnny Weaver
Ron Ritchie beat Jim Dalton
Keith Larson beat Ken Timbs

8/15/82: Roanoke, VA @ Civic Center
Ricky Steamboat beat Matt Borne
Pvt. Nelson & Pvt. Kernodle beat Jake Roberts & Jay Youngblood
Mike Rotundo beat Ben Alexander
Kelly Kiniski beat Bill White
Mike Davis beat Ali Bey
Jack Brisco beat Sgt. Slaughter by DQ
Jimmy Valiant beat Ivan Koloff in a cage match

8/16/82: Greenville, SC @ Memorial Auditorium
Judy Martin beat Candi Malloy
Porkchop Cash beat Bill White
King Parsons draw Juan Reynosa
Jack Brisco & Wahoo McDaniel beat Roddy Piper & Sgt. Slaughter by DQ
NWA World Champion Ric Flair beat Jake Roberts

8/17/82: Raleigh, NC @ Civic Center
NWA World Champion Ric Flair beat Jimmy Valiant
Ricky Steamboat beat Leroy Brown by DQ
Ron Ritchie beat Juan Reynosa
Gene Anderson beat Johnny Weaver
Jay Youngblood beat The Ninja by DQ
Jim Dalton & Bill White beat Mike Davis & Keith Larson

8/17/82: Columbia, SC @ Township Auditorium
Wahoo McDaniel, Jerry Brisco & Jake Roberts beat Ivan Koloff, Roddy Piper & Sgt. Slaughter by DQ
Paul Jones beat Abe Jacobs
Porkchop Cash & King Parsons draw Pvt. Nelson & Pvt. Kernodle
Kelly Kiniski beat Ken Timbs
Mike Rotundo beat Ali Bey

8/18/82: Charlotte, NC @ WCPQ Studios (TV)
Jack Brisco beat NWA World Champion Ric Flair
Roddy Piper & Jimmy Valiant beat Ken Timbs & Jim Dalton
Paul Jones beat Keith Larson
Sgt. Slaughter beat Jake Roberts
Wahoo McDaniel beat Gene Anderson by DQ
Gen Anderson & Leroy Brown beat Kelly Kiniski & Mike Rotundo
Sgt. Slaughter beat Keith Larson
Roddy Piper & Wahoo McDaniel beat Ken Timbs & Jim Dalton
Paul Jones beat Abe Jacobs
Jimmy Valiant beat Ivan Koloff by DQ

8/18/82: Wadesboro, NC
Ron Ritchie beat The Scorpion
Juan Reynosa beat Mike Davis
Jay Youngblood beat The Ninja by DQ
Pvt. Nelson & Pvt. Kernodle beat Porkchop Cash & King Parsons
NWA World Champion Ric Flair beat Jack Brisco

8/19/82: Winston-Salem, NC @ Memorial Coliseum
NWA World Champion Ric Flair beat Roddy Piper(sub for Jack Brisco) by DQ
Paul Jones & Sgt. Slaughter beat Wahoo McDaniel & Jake Roberts
Gene Anderson beat Ron Ritchie
Kelly Kiniski beat Juan Reynosa
Mike Davis & Ron Ritchie beat Ken Timbs & Ali Bey

8/19/82: Harrisonburg, VA @ High School
Bill White beat King Parsons
Mike Rotundo beat Jim Dalton
Pvt. Nelson & Pvt. Kernodle beat Porkchop Cash & King Parsons
Jay Youngblood beat Ninja by DQ
Ricky Steamboat beat Leroy Brown by DQ
Jimmy Valiant beat Ivan Koloff in a cage match

8/20/82: Charleston, SC @ County Hall
NWA World Champion Ric Flair DCO with Wahoo McDaniel
Ole Anderson beat Glenn Lane
Kelly Kiniski beat The Scorpion
Ron Ritchie draw Juan Reynosa
Johnny Weaver beat Ole Anderson
Sgt. Slaughter beat Jake Roberts

8/21/82: Dillon, SC
Mike Davis beat Jim Dalton
Ken Timbs beat Bill White
Pvt. Nelson & Pvt. Kernodle beat Porkchop Cash & King Parsons
Johnny Weaver & Jay Youngblood beat Gene Anderson & The Ninja
Ricky Steamboat beat Leroy Brown by DQ

8/21/82: Greensboro, NC @ Coliseum
Wahoo McDaniel beat Sgt. Slaughter in a lumberjack match
Jimmy Valiant beat Ivan Koloff in a Siberian glove match
Mike Rotundo, Roddy Piper & Jerry Brisco beat Ric Flair, Paul Jones & Oliver Humperdink
Kelly Kiniski beat Juan Reynosa
Ron Ritchie beat Ben Alexander
Ali Bey beat Keith Larson

8/22/82: Toronto, Ontario @ Maple Leaf Gardens
Tony Parisi beat Ken Timbs
Johnny Weaver beat Alex Girard
Paul Jones beat The Ninja
Ricky Steamboat & Jay Youngblood beat Pvt. Kernodle & Pvt. Nelson in a 2 of 3 falls match to win NWA Mid Atlantic Tag Title
Andre The Giant beat John Studd
WWF Champion Bob Backlund beat Jimmy Snuka

8/22/82: Charlotte, NC @ Coliseum
Wahoo McDaniel beat Sgt. Slaughter in a hair vs. title match to win NWA United States Title
Roddy Piper, Jerry Brisco & Jimmy Valiant beat Ivan Koloff, Leroy Brown & Ole Anderson
Mike Rotundo beat Bill White
Kelly Kiniski draw Jim Dalton
Ron Ritchie beat Juan Reynosa
Mike Davis beat Ali Bey

8/23/82: Greenville, SC @ Memorial Auditorium
Wahoo McDaniel beat Sgt. Slaughter
Mike Davis draw Juan Reynosa
Bill White beat Jerry Bright
Kelly Kiniski beat Jim Dalton
Pvt. Kernodle beat King Parsons
Roddy Piper & Jerry Brisco beat Ivan Koloff & Paul Jones

8/24/82: Columbia, SC @ Township Auditorium
Ron Ritchie beat Ali Bey
Jimmy Valiant & Ricky Steamboat beat Greg Valentine & Ivan Koloff
Jay Youngblood beat The Ninja by DQ
Kelly Kiniski beat Juan Reynosa
Mike Rotundo beat Jim Dalton

8/24/82: Raleigh, NC @ Civic Center
Leroy Brown & Paul Jones beat Roddy Piper & Johnny Weaver
Pvt. Nelson & Pvt. Kernodle beat Porkchop Cash & King Parsons
Johnny Weaver beat Gene Anderson
Mike Davis beat Ken Timbs
Bill White beat Keith Larson

8/25/82: Charlotte, NC @ WCPQ Studios (TV)
Paul Jones beat King Parsons
Jos LeDuc beat Mike Davis
Roddy Piper & Ricky Steamboat beat Juan Reynosa & The Ninja
Jay Youngblood beat Pvt. Nelson
Greg Valentine & Leroy Brown beat Keith Larson & Ron Ritchie

Greg Valentine beat Gary Black
King Parsons & Porkchop Cash beat Bill White & The Ninja
Jos LeDuc beat Ron Ritchie
Kelly Kiniski beat Paul Jones DQ
Ricky Steamboat & Jay Youngblood beat Jim Dalton & Juan Reynosa

8/26/82: Sumter, SC @ Exposition Center
Roddy Piper, Wahoo McDaniel & Jay Youngblood beat Paul Jones, Leroy Brown & Oliver Humperdink
Pvt. Kernodle & Pvt. Nelson beat Porkchop Cash & King Parsons
Ron Ritchie beat Juan Reynosa
Mike Davis beat Ben Alexander

8/26/82: Newberry, SC
Keith Larson beat Ali Bey
Vivian St. John beat Leilani Kai
Mike Rotundo beat Bill White
Kelly Kiniski beat Jim Dalton
The Gladiator beat Keith Larson
Johnny Weaver beat The Ninja by DQ
Ricky Steamboat beat Ivan Koloff

8/27/82: Richmond, VA @ Coliseum
Kelly Kiniski draw Ken Timbs
Mike Rotundo beat Jim Dalton
Porkchop Cash & King Parsons beat Pvt. Nelson & Pvt. Kernodle
Jay Youngblood beat The Ninja by reverse decision
Ricky Steamboat(sub for Wahoo McDaniel) & Roddy Piper beat Paul Jones & Leroy Brown by DQ
Wahoo McDaniel(sub for Jimmy Valiant) beat Ivan Koloff in a Russian chain match

8/28/82: Hampton, VA @ Coliseum
Kelly Kiniski beat Juan Reynosa
Wahoo McDaniel, Roddy Piper & Johnny Weaver beat Leroy Brown, Paul Jones & Oliver Humperdink
Mike Rotundo beat The Scorpion
Ron Ritchie beat Ken Timbs

8/29/82: Roanoke, VA @ Civic Center
Jimmy Valiant beat Ivan Koloff in a cage match
Ricky Steamboat beat Matt Borne
Pvt. Nelson & Pvt. Kernodle beat Jake Roberts & Jay Youngblood
Mike Rotundo beat Ben Alexander
Kelly Kiniski beat Bill White
Jack Brisco beat Sgt. Slaughter by DQ

8/29/82: Asheville, NC @ Civic Center
Wahoo McDaniel & Roddy Piper beat Leroy Brown & Paul Jones by DQ
Jay Youngblood beat The Ninja
Kelly Kiniski beat Juan Reynosa
Mike Rotundo beat The Gladiator
Ron Ritchie draw The Scorpion
Mike Davis beat Keith Larson

8/30/82: Fayetteville, NC @ Cumberland County Memorial Auditorium
Dennis Albert beat Keith Larsen
Ron Ritchie beat The Gladiator
Jay Youngblood beat Pvt. Kernodle
Kelly Kiniski beat Juan Reynosa
Wahoo McDaniel & Ricky Steamboat beat Leroy Brown & Oliver Humperdink

8/30/82: Greenville, SC @ Memorial Auditorium
Jimmy Valiant beat Ivan Koloff
Jerry Brisco & Roddy Piper beat The Ninja & Greg Valentine
Mike Davis draw Jim Dalton
Mike Rotundo beat Pvt. Nelson by DQ
Johnny Weaver beat The Spoiler
Porkchop Cash draw Pvt. Nelson

8/31/82: Raleigh, NC @ Civic Center
Jimmy Valiant beat Ivan Koloff in a cole miner's glove match
Jack Brisco beat Paul Jones by DQ
The Ninja beat Johnny Weaver
Kelly Kiniski beat Pvt. Nelson
Mike Rotundo beat Ali Bey
Keith Larson beat The Scorpion

8/31/82: Columbia, SC @ Township Auditorium
Ron Ritchie beat The Gladiator
Porkchop Cash & King Parsons beat Jim Dalton & Juan Reynosa
Pvt. Kernodle beat Jay Youngblood
Wahoo McDaniel, Roddy Pier & Ricky Steamboat beat Leroy Brown, Pvt. Kernodle & Oliver Humperdink

9/1/82: Charlotte, NC @ WCPQ Studios (TV)
Paul Jones beat Jack Brisco to win Mid Atlantic Title
Jos LeDuc beat Kelly Kiniski
Abdullah The Butcher beat Ron Ritchie
Greg Valentine beat Mike Rotundo
Roddy Piper & Wahoo McDaniel beat The Medic & The Gladiator
Jerry Brisco & Wahoo McDaniel beat Jim Dalton & Ben Alexander
Jay Youngblood beat The Gladiator
Roddy Piper beat The Medic
Paul Jones & Greg Valentine beat Ron Ritchie & Kelly Kiniski

9/2/82: Strasburg, VA
Jim Dalton draw Mike Davis
Johnny Weaver beat The Gladiator
Pvt. Kernodle & Pvt. Nelson beat Porkchop Cash & King Parsons
Paul Jones beat Jack Brisco

9/2/82: Norfolk, VA @ Scope
Ricky Steamboat beat Leroy Brown
Wahoo McDaniel & Roddy Piper beat Ivan Koloff & Greg Valentine
Juan Reynosa beat Kelly Kiniski
Mike Rotundo beat Ali Bey
Keith Larson draw The Scorpion

9/3/82: Charleston, SC @ County Hall
Ron Ritchie draw Mike Davis
Glenn Lane beat The Inferno
Jay Youngblood beat Jim Dalton
Johnny Weaver beat Gene Anderson
Pvt. Kernodle & Pvt. Nelson beat Porkchop Cash & King Parsons
Jimmy Valiant beat Ivan Koloff

9/3/82: Richmond, VA @ Coliseum
Wahoo McDaniel double DQ Greg Valentine
Paul Jones beat Jack Brisco
Ricky Steamboat & Roddy Piper beat Leroy Brown, The Ninja & Oliver Humperdink in a handicap match
Kelly Kiniski beat Juan Reynosa
Mike Rotundo beat The Gladiator
Keith Larsen beat Ali Bey

9/4/82: Greensboro, NC @ Coliseum
Kelly Kiniski draw Juan Reynosa
Mike Rotundo beat The Inferno
Porkchop Cash & King Parsons beat Pvt. Nelson & Pvt. Kernodle
Ricky Steamboat beat Leroy Brown
Paul Jones beat Jack Brisco
Wahoo McDaniel double DQ Greg Valentine

9/6/82: Greenville, SC @ Memorial Auditorium
Mike Davis draw King Parsons
Juan Reynosa beat Kelly Kiniski
Mike Rotundo beat Jim Dalton
Jack Brisco beat Paul Jones
Wahoo McDaniel beat Leroy Brown
Roddy Piper beat NWA World Champion Ric Flair by DQ

9/6/82: Wilmington, NC @ Legion Stadium
Jimmy Valiant vs. Ivan Koloff in a Siberian salt mine glove match
Ricky Steamboat & Jay Youngblood vs. Pvt. Kernodle & Pvt. Nelson
The Scorpion vs. Porkchop Cash
Keith Larson vs. Glenn Lane
Ali Bey vs. Mike Davis

9/7/82: Columbia, SC @ Township Auditorium
Jack Brisco beat NWA World Champion Ric Flair by DQ
Wahoo McDaniel double DQ Greg Valentine
Johnny Weaver beat The Ninja
Porkchop Cash & King Parsons beat Pvt. Nelson & Pvt. Kernodle
Keith Larson beat Bill White
Mike Davis beat Ken Timbs

9/7/82: Raleigh, NC @ Civic Center

9/8/82: Charlotte, NC @ WCPQ Studios (TV)
Jack Brisco & Wahoo McDaniel beat Paul Jones & Greg Valentine by DQ
Ricky Steamboat beat The Gladiator
Gene Anderson beat Keith Larson
Jimmy Valiant beat Juan Reynosa
Jos LeDuc & Leroy Brown beat Kelly Kiniski & Mike Rotundo
Mike Rotundo & Jay Youngblood beat Jim Dalton & Ben Alexander
Greg Valentine beat Kelly Kiniski
Pvt. Kernodle beat King Parsons
Paul Jones beat Johnny Weaver
Ricky Steamboat, Jack Brisco & Wahoo McDaniel beat Juan Reynosa, Bill White & Ken Timbs

9/9/82: Sumter, SC @ Exposition Center
Wahoo McDaniel double DQ Greg Valentine
Paul Jones beat Jack Brisco
Johnny Weaver beat Jerry Brisco by DQ
Mike Rotundo beat Ken Timbs
Bill White draw Mike Davis
King Parsons & Porkchop Cash beat Juan Reynosa & Jim Dalton

9/9/82: Fisherville, VA @ Augusta Expo
Ron Ritchie beat Ali Bey
Kelly Kiniski beat The Ninja by DQ
Keith Larsen beat Pvt. Nelson
Pvt. Kernodle beat Jay Youngblood
Ricky Steamboat beat Leroy Brown by DQ
Jimmy Valiant beat Ivan Koloff in a cage match

9/10/82: Charleston, SC @ County Hall
Mike Davis beat Pvt. Nelson
Mike Rotundo beat Bill White
Porkchop Cash & King Parsons beat Jim Dalton & Juan Reynosa
Jay Youngblood beat Gene Anderson
Leroy Brown beat Ricky Steamboat
Jimmy Valiant beat Ivan Koloff

9/10/82: Kenansville, NC
Keith Larsen beat Ali Bey
Keith Larsen beat Ken Timbs
Pvt. Kernodle beat Ron Ritchie
Jack Brisco beat The Ninja
Wahoo McDaniel double DQ Greg Valentine

9/11/82:Lumberton, NC @ Recreation Center
Jim Dalton vs. Kelly Kiniski
Juan Reynosa vs. Ron Ritchie
Porkchop Cash & King Parsons vs. Don Kernodle & Jim Nelson
Jack Brisco vs. The Ninja
Wahoo McDaniel vs. Greg Valentine

9/12/82: Asheville, NC @ Civic Center
Keith Larsen draw Bill White
Mike Davis beat Ali Bey
Pvt. Nelson beat Kelly Kiniski
Ricky Steamboat & Jack Brisco beat Leroy Brown & Jos LeDuc by DQ
Wahoo McDaniel double DQ Greg Valentine
Jimmy Valiant beat Ivan Koloff coal miner's glove match

9/12/82: Kingsport, TN
Jimmy Valiant beat Ivan Koloff in cage match
Rick Steamboat beat Leroy Brown by DQ
Wahoo McDaniel double DQ Greg Valentine

Jack Brisco beat Jos LeDuc by DQ
Porkchop Cash beat Jim Dalton
Mike Rotundo beat Ken Timbs
Ron Ritchie beat Juan Reynosa

9/13/82: Greenville, SC @ Memorial Auditorium
Jimmy Valiant beat Jos Leduc by DQ
Leroy Brown beat Ricky Steamboat
Jay Youngblood & Johnny Weaver beat Pvt. Nelson & Pvt. Kernodle
Ron Ritchie drew Juan Reynosa

9/14/82: Raleigh, NC @ Civic Center
Paul Jones beat Jack Brisco
Johnny Weaver beat Pvt. Kernodle
Inferno beat Glen Lane
Ron Ritchie beat Juan Reynosa
Keith Larson beat Ali Bey

9/14/82: Columbia, SC @ Township Auditorium
Jimmy Valiant beat Ivan Koloff in a loser leaves town match
Paul Jones beat Jack Brisco
Pvt. Kernodle beat Johnny Weaver
Ron Ritchie beat Juan Reynosa
Keith Larson beat Ali Bey
Glen Lane beat The Inferno
Jim Dalton beat Mike Davis

9/14/82: Rocky Mount, NC
King Parsons draw Bill White
Porkchop Cash & King Parsons beat Pvt. Nelson & Gene Anderson
Ricky Steamboat beat Leroy Brown
Jay Youngblood beat Jos LeDuc by DQ
Wahoo McDaniel beat Greg Valentine

9/15/82: Charlotte, NC @ WCPQ Studios (TV)
Ricky Steamboat & Jay Youngblood beat Jim Dalton & Juan Reynosa
Paul Jones & Greg Valentine beat Keith Larson & Porkchop Cash
Jack Brisco & Wahoo McDaniel beat Ken Timbs & Pvt. Kernodle
Mike Rotundo beat Ben Alexander
Jos LeDuc & Leroy Brown beat Mike Davis & King Parsons
Jos LeDuc beat King Parsons
Leroy Brown beat Porkchop Cash
Mike Rotundo & Ricky Steamboat beat Ali Bey & Juan Reynosa
Jack Brisco & Wahoo McDaniel beat Jim Dalton & Ben Alexander
Paul Jones & Greg Valentine beat Ron Ritchie & Mike Davis

9/16/82: Norfolk, VA @ Scope
Mike Rotundo beat The Gladiator
Johnny Weaver beat Jim Dalton
Ron Ritchie draw Juan Reynosa
Jack & Jerry Brisco beat Paul Jones & Greg Valentine
Leroy Brown beat Ricky Steamboat
Wahoo McDaniel beat Abdullah The Butcher by DQ

9/17/82: Richmond, VA @ Coliseum
Wahoo McDaniel beat Abdullah the Butcher
Paul Jones & Greg Valentine beat Jack Brisco & Jerry Brisco
Gene Anderson beat Jay Youngblood
Porkchop Cash & King Parsons beat Jim Dalton & Juan Reynosa
Mike Rotundo beat Pvt. Nelson

9/17/82: Charleston, SC @ County Hall
Mike Davis beat Abe Jacobs
Keith Larsen beat Mr. Pro
Ron Ritchie beat Glenn Lane
Pvt. Kernodle beat Johnny Weaver
Jimmy Valiant beat Jos LeDuc by DQ
Ricky Steamboat beat Leroy Brown

9/18/82: Greensboro, NC @ Coliseum
Wahoo McDaniel beat Abdullah The Butcher & Oliver Humperdink in a handicap match
Greg Valentine & Paul Jones beat Jack & Jerry Brisco
Ricky Steamboat beat Leroy Brown
Ron Ritchie beat Pvt. Nelson
Mike Rotundo beat Ben Alexander
King Parsons beat Juan Reynosa
Keith Larson beat Mr. Pro

9/18/82: Spartanburg, SC @ Memorial Auditorium
Jimmy Valiant beat Jos Leduc
Jay Youngblood beat Gene Anderson by reverse decision
Pvt. Kernodle beat Johnny Weaver
Porkchop Cash beat Jim Dalton
Mike Davis draw Bill White

9/19/82: Charlotte, NC @ Coliseum
Mike Davis beat Ken Timbs
Mike Rotundo beat Juan Reynosa
Ron Ritchie beat Jim Dalton
Jay Youngblood beat Gene Anderson
Jos LeDuc beat Jimmy Valiant to win NWA Mid Atlantic Television Title
Ricky Steamboat beat Leroy Brown
Wahoo McDaniel beat Abdullah The Butcher

9/20/82: Greenville, SC @ Memorial Auditorium
Dory Funk, Jr. beat Johnny Weaver
Paul Jones beat Jack Brisco
Wahoo McDaniel beat Greg Valentine
Abe Jacobs draw Ben Alexander
Mike Davis beat Jim Dalton
Ron Ritchie beat Mr. Pro
Mike Rotundo beat Juan Reynosa

9/20/82: South Hill, VA
Keith Larsen beat Ali Bey
Jay Youngblood beat Blue Shark
Porkchop Cash & King Parsons beat Pvt. Kernodle & Pvt. Nelson
Jimmy Valiant beat Jos LeDuc
Ricky Steamboat beat Leroy Brown by DQ

9/21/82: Columbia, SC @ Township Auditorium
Wahoo McDaniel beat Greg Valentine
Jack Brisco beat Paul Jones
Mike Rotundo beat Dory Funk, Jr.
Porkchop Cash & King Parsons beat Juan Reynosa & Jim Dalton
Ron Ritchie beat Ken Timbs

9/21/82: Raleigh, NC @ Civic Center
Bill White beat Keith Larsen
Mike Davis beat Ali Bey
Johnny Weaver & Jay Youngblood beat Pvt. Nelson & Pvt. Kernodle
Jimmy Valiant beat Jos LeDuc
Ricky Steamboat beat Leroy Brown

9/22/82: Charlotte, NC @ WCPQ Studios (TV)
Jay Youngblood beat Pvt. Nelson
Greg Valentine beat Keith Larson
Mike Rotundo beat Ali Bey
Jack Brisco & Wahoo McDaniel beat Bill White & Ken Timbs
Dory Funk, Jr. beat Mike Davis
Jimmy Valiant beat Jim Dalton
Mike Rotundo & Jack Brisco beat Ken Timbs & Bill White
Dory Funk, Jr. & Jos LeDuc beat Ron Ritchie & Mike Davis
Jay Youngblood beat Ali Bey
Paul Jones beat Rick Benefield
Greg Valentine & Leroy Brown beat Mike Reed & King Parsons

9/23/82: Union, SC
Ron Ritchie beat Tom Stanton
Porkchop Cash & King Parsons beat Jim Dalton & Juan Reynosa
Johnny Weaver beat Pvt. Nelson
Wahoo McDaniel & Jack Brisco beat Paul Jones & Greg Valentine

9/23/82: Winston-Salem, NC @ Memorial Coliseum
Mike Davis draw Ali Bey
Keith Larsen beat Bill White
Jerry Brisco, Jay Youngblood & Mike Rotundo beat Pvt. Kernodle, Leroy Brown & Gene Anderson
Jimmy Valiant beat Jos LeDuc

9/25/82: Roanoke, VA @ Civic Center
Jack & Jerry Brisco vs. Paul Jones & Leroy Brown
Jimmy Valiant vs. Jos LeDuc
Johnny Weaver vs. The Inferno

9/26/82: Hampton, VA @ Coliseum
Jack & Jerry Brisco beat Paul Jones & Greg Valentine
Ricky Steamboat beat Leroy Brown
Jimmy Valiant beat Jos Leduc
Jay Youngblood beat Gene Anderson
King Parsons & Porkchop Cash beat Jim Dalton & Juan Reynosa

9/27/82: Fayetteville, NC @ Cumberland County Memorial Auditorium
Mike Davis beat Glenn Lane
Keith Larsen beat Ali Bey
Johnny Weaver draw Jim Dalton
Jay Youngblood beat Gene Anderson
Jos LeDuc & Leroy Brown beat Ricky Steamboat & Jimmy Valiant

9/27/82: Greenville, SC @ Memorial Auditorium
Porkchop Cash & King Parsons beat The Medic & Ken Timbs
Ron Ritchie beat Juan Reynosa
Mike Rotundo beat Pvt. Nelson
Jack Brisco beat Paul Jones
Wahoo McDaniel beat Greg Valentine

9/28/82: Raleigh, NC @ Civic Center
Ron Ritchie beat Ken Timbs
Keith Larsen beat Ali Bey
Jay Youngblood & Mike Rotundo beat Gene Anderson & Juan Reynosa
Jos LeDuc beat Jimmy Valiant by DQ
Wahoo McDaniel beat Greg Valentine

9/28/82: Columbia, SC @ Township Auditorium

9/29/82: Charlotte, NC @ WCPQ Studios (TV)
Jack Brisco & Mike Rotundo beat Jim Dalton & Juan Reynosa
Dory Funk, Jr. beat Keith Larson
Jos LeDuc & Greg Valentine beat Porkchop Cash & Ron Ritchie
Sgt. Slaughter & Pvt. Kernodle beat King Parsons & Ali Bey
Ricky Steamboat & Jay Youngblood beat Ben Alexander & Ken Timbs
Mike Rotundo beat Juan Reynosa
Dory Funk, Jr. beat Porkchop Cash
Greg Valentine beat Mike Davis
Sgt. Slaughter & Pvt. Kernodle beat King Parsons & Ron Ritchie
Ricky Steamboat & Jay Youngblood beat Pvt. Nelson & Jim Dalton
Jack Brisco beat Bill White

9/30/82: Harrisonburg, VA @ High School
Mike Rotundo beat Bill White
Mike Davis beat Juan Reynosa
Ali Bey beat Keith Larsen
King Parsons & Ron Ritchie beat Pvt. Nelson & Pvt. Kernodle
Rocky Steamboat beat Leroy Brown
Jos LeDuc beat Jimmy Valiant by DQ

9/30/82: Weldon, NC
Mike Davis beat Ken Timbs
Porkchop Cash beat Tom Stanton
Johnny Weaver draw Gene Anderson
Jay Youngblood & Mike Rotundo beat Sgt. Slaughter & Greg Valentine by DQ
Jack Brisco beat Paul Jones

10/1/82: Charleston, SC @ County Hall
Paul Jones beat Jack Brisco
Sgt. Slaughter & Pvt. Kernodle beat Jay Youngblood & Johnny Weaver
Porkchop Cash beat Pvt. Nelson
Keith Larsen draw The Scorpion
Ken Timbs beat Ali Bey

10/1/82: Richmond, VA @ Coliseum
Wahoo McDaniel beat Greg Valentine
Ricky Steamboat beat Leroy Brown
Jos LeDuc beat Jimmy Valiant by DQ
Mike Rotundo beat Gene Anderson
King Parsons beat Red Dog Lane
Ron Ritchie draw Jim Dalton
Mike Davis beat Juan Reynosa

10/2/82: Culpeper, VA
Ricky Steamboat beat Leroy Brown by DQ
Paul Jones beat Jack Brisco
King Parsons & Mike Rotundo beat Jim Dalton & Juan Reynosa
Ron Ritchie beat Tom Stanton
Mike Davis beat ??
10/3/82: Greensboro, NC @ Coliseum
Wahoo McDaniel beat Sgt. Slaughter by DQ
Paul Jones beat Jack Brisco
Mike Rotundo beat Jos LeDuc
Ricky Steamboat DCO with Greg Valentine
Jay Youngblood beat Jim Dalton
Ken Timbs beat Red Dog Lane

10/3/82: Toronto, Ontario @ Maple Leaf Gardens
Abe Jacobs beat Kenny Hall
Tony Parisi & Nick DeCarlo beat The Destroyer & Rick Connors
Buddy Rose beat Tony Garea
Pvt. Kernodle & Pvt. Nelson beat Leo Burke & Johnny Weaver
WWF Champion Bob Backlund beat Bob Orton, Jr.
Jimmy Valiant beat Ivan Koloff

10/4/82: Greenville, SC @ Memorial Auditorium
Glenn Lane beat Jim Dalton
Mike Rotundo beat Dory Funk, Jr. by DQ
Ken Timbs draw Keith Larsen
Jay Youngblood beat Jos LeDuc by DQ
Wahoo McDaniel beat Sgt. Slaughter

10/5/82: Raleigh, NC @ Civic Center
Mike Davis beat Ali Bey
Ken Timbs beat Abe Jacobs
Porkchop Cash & King Parsons beat Jim Dalton & The Inferno(Bill White)
Mike Rotundo beat Dory Funk, Jr. by reverse decision
Pvt. Kernodle & Sgt. Slaughter draw Ricky Steamboat & Jay Youngblood

10/5/82: Columbia, SC @ Township Auditorium
Keith Larsen beat Juan Reynosa
Ron Ritchie beat Pvt. Nelson
Leroy Brown beat Johnny Weaver
Jimmy Valiant beat Jos LeDuc
Jack & Jerry Brisco beat Paul Jones & Greg Valentine

10/6/82: Charlotte, NC @ WCPQ Studios (TV)
Mike Rotundo beat Mike Reed
Jos LeDuc & Dory Funk, Jr. beat King Parsons & Abe Jacobs by DQ
Sgt. Slaughter & Pvt. Kernodle beat Ron Ritchie & Porkchop Cash
Ricky Steamboat & Jay Youngblood beat Juan Reynosa & Bill White
Roddy Piper & Wahoo McDaniel beat Ken Timbs & Jim Dalton
Paul Jones beat Keith Larson
Ricky Steamboat & Jay Youngblood beat Pvt. Nelson & Mike Reed
Paul Jones beat Abe Jacobs
Jos LeDuc beat Ron Ritchie by DQ
Dory Funk, Jr. & Greg Valentine beat Keith Larson & Ric Benfield
Jack Brisco beat Ken Timbs
Sgt. Slaughter & Pvt. Kernodle beat King Parsons & Porkchop Cash

10/7/82: Fisherville, VA @ Augusta Expo
Mike Rotundo beat Ali Bey
Keith Larsen beat The Medic
Johnny Weaver draw Pvt. Nelson
Jay Youngblood beat Gene Anderson
Ricky Steamboat beat Leroy Brown
Jimmy Valiant double DQ Jos LeDuc

10/7/82: Sumter, SC @ Exposition Center
Jack & Jerry Brisco beat Paul Jones & Greg valentine
Dory Funk, Jr. beat Ron Ritchie(sub for Mike Rotundo)
Pvt. Kernodle beat Porkchop Cash
King Parsons beat Juan Reynosa
Ron Ritchie beat Ken Timbs

10/8/82: Charleston, SC @ County Hall
Ron Ritchie beat Ken Timbs
Mike Rotundo beat Pvt. Kernodle
Jerry Brisco beat Jim Dalton
Paul Jones beat Jack Brisco
Wahoo McDaniel beat Sgt. Slaughter

10/9/82: Spartanburg, SC @ Memorial Auditorium
Pvt. Nelson beat David Pyle
Ron Ritchie beat Juan Reynosa
Gene Anderson & The Ninja draw King Parsons & Porkchop Cash
Ricky Steamboat beat Leroy Brown by DQ
Sgt. Slaughter & Pvt. Kernodle beat Jay Youngblood & Johnny Weaver

10/9/82: Roanoke, VA @ Civic Center
Jimmy Valiant beat Jos LeDuc by DQ
Jack & Jerry Brisco beat Paul Jones & Greg Valentine
Dory Funk, Jr. vs. Mike Rotundo
Keith Larsen draw Bill White
Mike Davis beat Ken Timbs

10/10/82: Asheville, NC @ Civic Center
Mike Davis beat Ken Timbs
Keith Larsen beat Juan Reynosa
Jay Youngblood beat Gene Anderson
Jack & Jerry Brisco beat Greg Valentine & Paul Jones
Wahoo McDaniel beat Sgt. Slaughter
Jos LeDuc beat Jimmy Valiant by DQ
Ricky Steamboat beat Leroy Brown

10/11/82: Greenville, SC @ Memorial Auditorium
Mike Davis beat Ben Alexander
Keith Larsen beat Ken Timbs
Ron Ritchie beat Juan Reynosa
Jimmy Valiant beat Greg Valentine
Jack Brisco draw Paul Jones
NWA World Champion Ric Flair beat Wahoo McDaniel

10/11/82: Fayetteville, NC @ Cumberland County Memorial Auditorium
Sgt. Slaughter & Pvt. Kernodle beat Ricky Steamboat & Jay Youngblood
Jack Brisco beat Paul Jones
Jimmy Valiant beat Jos LeDuc
Leroy Brown beat Mike Rotundo
Ron Ritchie beat Jim Dalton
Mike Rotundo beat Juan Reynosa
King Parson beat Ken Timbs

10/12/82: Tarboro, NC
Ali Bey beat Pvt. Nelson
Jim Dalton beat Mike Davis
Dory Funk, Jr. beat King Parsons
Porkchop Cash beat Leroy Brown by DQ
Greg Valentine beat Mike Rotundo
Jimmy Valiant beat Jos LeDuc by DQ

10/12/82: Columbia, SC @ Township Auditorium
Keith Larsen beat Ken Timbs
Gene Anderson beat Ron Ritchie
Johnny Weaver beat Juan Reynosa
Jack Brisco beat Paul Jones by DQ
Sgt. Slaughter & Pvt. Kernodle beat Ricky Steamboat & Jay Youngblood
NWA World Champion Ric Flair beat Wahoo McDaniel

10/12/82: Raleigh, NC @ Civic Center
No Wrestling

10/13/82: Charlotte, NC @ WCPQ Studios (TV)
Dory Funk Jr. beat Jay Youngblood
Ricky Steamboat beat Jos LeDuc by DQ
Mike Rotundo beat Gene Anderson
Pvt. Kernodle beat Glenn Lane
Johnny Weaver beat Pvt. Nelson
Ricky Steamboat & Jay Youngblood beat Jim Dalton & Jim Nelson
Mike Rotundo beat Leroy Brown by DQ
Jos LeDuc beat Glenn Lane

10/14/82: Winston-Salem, NC @ Memorial Coliseum
Princess Victoria & Velvet McIntyre beat Leilani Kai & Peggy Lee
Keith Larsen beat Ali Bey
Leroy Brown beat Johnny Weaver
Paul Jones beat Mike Rotundo
Pvt. Nelson beat Ron Ritchie
Jimmy Valiant beat Jos LeDuc by DQ

10/14/82: Norfolk, VA @ Scope
Porkchop Cash & King Parsons beat Jim Dalton & Ken Timbs
Sgt. Slaughter & Pvt. Kernodle beat Ricky Steamboat & Jay Youngblood
Wahoo McDaniel beat Dory Funk, Jr.
NWA World Champion Ric Flair beat Jack Brisco

10/15/82: Richmond, VA @ Coliseum
Mike Davis beat Ken Timbs
Bill White beat Abe Jacobs
Ron Ritchie beat Juan Reynosa
Greg Valentine beat Mike Rotundo
Jack Brisco beat Paul Jones
Sgt. Slaughter & Pvt. Kernodle beat Ricky Steamboat & Jay Youngblood
NWA World Champion Ric Flair beat Wahoo McDaniel by DQ

10/15/82: Charleston, SC @ County Hall
Jimmy Valiant vs. Jos Leduc
Porkchop Cash, King Parsons & Johnny Weaver vs. Leroy Brown, Gene Anderson & Oliver Humperdink
Princess Victoria vs. Leilani Kai
Pvt. Nelson vs. Glenn Lane
Keith Larsen vs. Jim Dalton

10/16/82: Hampton, VA @ Coliseum
Mike Davis beat Ken Timbs
Abe Jacobs beat Jim Nelson
Juan Reynosa beat Keith Larsen
Jimmy Valiant beat Jos LeDuc
Wahoo McDaniel beat Greg Valentine
Leroy Brown & Gene Anderson beat Porkchop Cash & King Parsons

10/17/82: Toronto, Ontario @ Maple Leaf Gardens
Rudy Kay draw Pvt. Nelson
Terry Kay beat Ken Timbs
Buddy Rose beat Nick DeCarlo
Johnny Weaver beat Leo Burke
Sal Bellomo beat Charlie Fulton
Swede Hansen beat Tim Gerrard
Jimmy Valiant beat Ivan Koloff in a New York street fight to win the NWA Mid Atlantic Television Title(Only recognized in Toronto)
NWA World Champion Ric Flair beat Dory Funk, Jr.

10/17/82: Charlotte, NC @ Coliseum
Wahoo McDaniel beat Sgt. Slaughter
Paul Jones beat Jack Brisco
Roddy Piper beat NWA World Champion Ric Flair by DQ
Jimmy Valiant beat Jos Leduc

Dory Funk, Jr. beat Mike Rotundo
Gene Anderson beat King Parsons
Mike Davis beat Bill White

10/18/82: Greenville, SC @ Memorial Auditorium
Wahoo McDaniel beat Greg Valentine
Jim Dalton beat Ron Ritchie
Gene Anderson beat Porkchop Cash
King Parsons beat Bill White
Sgt. Slaughter & Pvt. Kernodle beat Ricky Steamboat & Jay Youngblood by DQ
Jack Brisco beat Paul Jones wins Mid Atlantic Title

10/19/82: Raleigh, NC @ Civic Center
Ricky Steamboat & Jay Youngblood beat Sgt. Slaughter & Pvt. Kernodle in a Texas death match
Mike Rotundo beat Gene Anderson
Johnny Weaver & King Parsons beat Pvt. Nelson & Juan Reynosa
Jim Dalton beat Mike Davis
Keith Larson beat The Medic

10/19/82: Columbia, SC @ Township Auditorium
Abe Jacobs beat Ben Alexander
Leroy Brown beat Porkchop Cash
Jerry Brisco beat Greg Valentine
Jack Brisco beat Paul Jones
Jimmy Valiant beat Jos LeDuc

10/20/82: Charlotte, NC @ WCPQ Studios (TV)
Greg Valentine beat Ron Ritchie
Jerry Brisco beat Bill White
Jack Brisco beat Paul Jones
Jimmy Valiant beat Ken Timbs
Ricky Steamboat & Jay Youngblood beat Ben Alexander & Jim Dalton
Mike Rotundo & Jerry Brisco beat Ben Alexander & Ken Timbs
Greg Valentine beat Mike Davis
Paul Jones beat Keith Larson
Ricky Steamboat & Jay Youngblood beat Dalton & White

10/21/82: Sumter, SC @ Exposition Center
Wahoo McDaniel, Jimmy Valiant & Jack Brisco beat Greg Valentine, Leroy Brown & Jos Leduc
Jay Youngblood beat Sgt. Slaughter
Jerry Brisco beat Pvt. Nelson
Gene Anderson beat King Parsons
Mike Davis beat Juan Reynosa

10/22/82: Charleston, SC @ County Hall
Wahoo McDaniel beat Leroy Brown
Jimmy Valiant beat Jos Leduc by DQ
Johnny Weaver & Jerry Brisco beat Pvt. Nelson & Gene Anderson
Mike Davis beat Ron Ritchie
Abe Jacobs beat Juan Reynosa

10/22/82: Spotsylvania, VA
Ricky Steamboat, Jay Youngblood & Jack Brisco beat Sgt. Slaughter, Pvt. Kernodle & Paul Jones
Porkchop Cash beat The Medic

10/23/82: Greensboro, NC @ Coliseum
Sgt. Slaughter & Don Kernodle beat Ricky Steamboat & Jay Youngblood
Wahoo McDaniel beat Greg Valentine
Jimmy Valiant double DQ Jos LeDuc
Jerry Brisco beat Jim Dalton
Johnny Weaver beat Bill White
Mike Davis beat Keith Larsen
Ben Alexander beat Abe Jacobs

10/23/82: Shelby, NC @ Recreation Center
Ron Ritchie beat Ken Timbs
Porkchop Cash beat Juan Reynosa
Leroy Brown beat Mike Rotundo
King Parsons beat Pvt. Nelson
Jack Brisco beat Paul Jones

10/24/82: Roanoke, VA @ Civic Center
Sgt. Slaughter & Pvt. Kernodle beat Jay Youngblood & Jerry Brisco
Jack Brisco beat Paul Jones
Jimmy Valiant beat Jos LeDuc
Mike Rotundo beat Leroy Brown by DQ
Jim Dalton beat Keith Larsen
Mike Davis beat Juan Reynosa
King Parsons beat Bill White

10/25/82: Greenville, NC @ Memorial Auditorium
Keith Larsen beat Ben Alexander
Jim Dalton beat King Parsons
Johnny Weaver beat Ken Timbs
Wahoo McDaniel beat Greg Valentine
Jay Youngblood & Ricky Steamboat beat Sgt. Slaughter & Pvt. Kernodle by CO

10/25/82: Fayetteville, NC @ Cumberland County Memorial Auditorium
Bill White beat Porkchop Cash
Mike Davis beat Jim Dalton
Leroy Brown beat Mike Rotundo
Jimmy Valiant beat Leroy Brown(sub for Jos LeDuc)
Paul Jones beat Jack Brisco to win NWA Mid Atlantic Title

10/26/82: Raleigh, NC @ Civic Center
Jack Brisco beat Jos Leduc
Greg Valentine beat Jimmy Valiant by DQ
Paul Jones beat Johnny Weaver
Pvt. Nelson beat King Parsons
Porkchop Cash beat Jim Dalton
Keith Larson beat Ken Timbs

10/26/82: Columbia, SC @ Township Auditorium
Ben Alexander beat Abe Jacobs
Ron Ritchie beat Bill White
Gene Anderson beat Mike Davis
Mike Rotundo beat Leroy Brown
Sgt. Slaughter & Pvt. Kernodle beat Ricky Steamboat & Jay Youngblood by DQ

10/27/82: Charlotte, NC @ WCPQ Studios (TV)
Mike Rotundo beat Leroy Brown by DQ
Jack Brisco beat Jim Dalton
Jimmy Valiant beat Bill White
Wahoo McDaniel beat Ken Timbs
Ricky Steamboat & Jay Youngblood beat Pvt. Nelson & Ben Alexander
Jos LeDuc double DQ Jack Brisco
Ricky Steamboat & Jay Youngblood beat Ken Timbs & Bill White
Leroy Brown beat Ron Ritchie
Wahoo McDaniel beat Ricky Harris
Johnny Weaver beat Jim Dalton

10/29/82: Charleston, SC @ County Hall
NWA World Champion Ric Flair NC with Wahoo McDaniel
Sgt. Slaughter & Pvt. Kernodle beat Ricky Steamboat & Jay Youngblood
Greg Valentine vs. Johnny Weaver
Keith Larsen vs. Bill White
Mike Davis vs. Ken Timbs

10/31/82: Asheville, NC @ Civic Center
Ron Ritchie beat Jim Dalton
Mike Davis beat Ken Timbs
King Parsons beat Gene Anderson
Leroy Brown beat Mike Rotundo
Jimmy Valiant beat Jos LeDuc
Sgt. Slaughter & Pvt. Kernodle beat Ricky Steamboat & Wahoo McDaniel

10/31/82: Toronto, Ontario @ Maple Leaf Gardens
Jimmy Valiant beat Ivan Koloff
Buddy Rose beat WWF Champion Bob Backlund by CO
Leo Burke beat Johnny Weaver by DQ
Leroy Brown beat King Parsons
Salvatore Bellomo beat Swede Hansen
Rudy & Terry Kay beat Bill White & Pvt. Nelson
The Destroyer beat Mike Davis
Keith Larson draw John Bonello

11/1/82: Brantford, Ontario(TV)
Johnny Weaver beat Bobby Bass
Leroy Brown & Leo Burke beat Mike Davis & Keith Larsen
Rudy Kay & Terry Kay beat Bill White & Bill Armstrong
Pvt. Nelson beat John Bonello
Leroy Brown beat Keith Larsen
Rudy Kay beat Pvt. Nelson by DQ
Terry Kay beat Bill White
King Parsons beat Bobby Bass
Leroy Brown beat Keith Larsen & John Bonello in a handicap match
Mike Davis beat Bill Armstrong
Terry Kay beat Bobby Bass
Leroy Brown beat King Parsons
Jimmy Valiant beat Pvt. Nelson

11/1/82: Greenville, SC @ Memorial Auditorium
NWA World Champion Ric Flair NC with Wahoo McDaniel
Jack Brisco & Mike Rotundo beat Paul Jones & Greg Valentine
Porkchop Cash beat Jim Dalton
Ricky Harris beat Gary Black
Frank Monte beat Abe Jacobs
Rick Rudd draw Joe Lauren

11/2/82: Raleigh, NC @ Civic Center
Paul Jones beat Jack Brisco
Frank Monte beat Abe Jacobs
Bill White beat Gary Black
Keith Larson beat Gene Anderson by DQ
Jimmy Valiant & Mike Rotundo beat Greg Valentine & Oliver Humperdink

11/2/82: Columbia, SC @ Township Auditorium
NWA World Champion Ric Flair beat Wahoo McDaniel
Joe Lauren beat Rick Rudd
King Parsons beat Ken Timbs
Porkchop Cash beat Ben Alexander
Jerry Brisco beat Jos LeDuc

11/3/82: Charlotte, NC @ WCPQ Studios (TV)
Jos LeDuc beat Gary Black
Jack & Jerry Brisco beat Gene Anderson & Joe Lauren
Mike Rotundo beat Ben Alexander
Paul Jones beat Rick Rood
Ricky Steamboat & Jay Youngblood beat Ricky Harris & Masa Fuchi
Roddy Piper beat Ken Timbs
Sweet Brown Sugar beat Frank Monte
Ricky Steamboat & Jay Youngblood beat Frank Monte & Joe Lauren
Jack & Jerry Brisco beat Masa Fuchi & Ben Alexander
Jos LeDuc beat Rick Rood
Paul Jones beat Gary Black
Roddy Piper beat Ricky Harris
Sweet Brown Sugar beat Ken Timbs

11/3/82: Sumter, SC @ Exposition Center
Mike Davis beat Bill White
Jim Dalton beat Abe Jacobs
Pvt. Nelson beat Ron Ritchie
Jimmy Valiant beat Pvt. Kernodle
Wahoo McDaniel beat Greg Valentine

11/4/82: Norfolk, VA @ Scope
King Parsons beat Jim Dalton
Johnny Weaver beat Bill White
Gene Anderson beat Porkchop Cash
Jerry Brisco beat Ken Timbs
Mike Rotundo beat Pvt. Nelson
Greg Valentine beat Wahoo McDaniel to win NWA United States Title
Jay Youngblood & Ricky Steamboat beat Pvt. Kernodle & Sgt. Slaughter
NWA World Champion Ric Flair beat Jack Brisco

11/5/82: Richmond, VA @ Coliseum
NWA World Champion Ric Flair beat Wahoo McDaniel
Dusty Rhodes beat Leroy Brown
Paul Jones beat Jack Brisco

Ricky Steamboat & Jay Youngblood beat Sgt. Slaughter & Pvt. Kernodle
Mike Rotundo beat Gene Anderson
Porkchop Cash beat Bill White
Mike Davis beat Pvt. Nelson
Masa Fuchi beat Ken Timbs
Rick Rudd beat Joe Lauren

11/5/82: Charleston, SC @ County Hall
Jimmy Valiant beat Jos LeDuc NY street fight match
Dory Funk, Jr. vs. Sweet Brown Sugar
Johnny Weaver beat Jim Dalton
King Parsons beat Frank Monte
Abe Jacobs beat Keith Larson

11/6/82: Hampton, VA @ Coliseum
Wahoo McDaniel beat Greg Valentine by DQ
Dory Funk, Jr. draw Sweet Brown Sugar
Porkchop Cash beat Pvt. Nelson
Ken Timbs beat Abe Jacobs
Rick Rood beat Joe Lauren
Gene Anderson beat Mike Davis
Leroy Brown beat Mike Rotundo

11/6/82: Greensboro, NC @ Coliseum
Masa Fuchi beat Gary Black
King Parsons beat Frank Monte
Johnny Weaver beat Ricky Harris
Keith Larsen beat Bill White
Ron Ritchie beat Jim Dalton
Paul Jones beat Jack Brisco
Jimmy Valiant beat Jos LeDuc
Ricky Steamboat & Jay Youngblood beat Pvt. Kernodle & Sgt. Slaughter
NWA World Champion Ric Flair beat Dusty Rhodes DQ

11/7/82: Roanoke, VA @ Civic Center
NWA World Champion Ric Flair beat Jack Brisco
Johnny Weaver beat Pvt. Nelson
Sweet Brown Sugar beat Dory Funk, Jr. by DQ
Jimmy Valiant beat Jos Leduc
Wahoo McDaniel beat Greg Valentine
Sgt. Slaughter & Pvt. Kernodle beat Ricky Steamboat & Jay Youngblood

11/8/82: Greenville, SC @ Memorial Auditorium
Paul Jones beat Jack Brisco
Ricky Steamboat beat Jos LeDuc
Jimmy Valiant beat Greg Valentine
Masa Fuchi & Ricky Harris beat Ron Ritchie & Keith Larsen
Sweet Brown Sugar beat Ken Timbs
Mike Davis beat Frank Monte

11/9/82: Raleigh, NC @ Civic Center
Ricky Harris beat Ron Ritchie
Mike Davis beat Jim Dalton
King Parsons beat Keith Larsen
Wahoo McDaniel beat Greg Valentine by DQ
Sgt. Slaughter & Pvt. Kernodle beat Ricky Steamboat & Jay Youngblood

11/9/82: Columbia, SC @ Township Auditorium
Paul Jones beat Jack Brisco
Roddy Piper beat Jos Leduc
Johnny Weaver & Porkchop Cash beat Masa Fuchi & Bill White
Ben Alexander beat Gary Black
Frank Monte beat Abe Jacobs

11/10/82: Charlotte, NC @ WCPQ Studios (TV)
Sgt. Slaughter & Pvt. Kernodle beat King Parsons & Gary Black
Leroy Brown beat Mike Rotundo by DQ
Jack & Jerry Brisco & Jimmy Valiant beat Pvt. Nelson, Ken Timbs & Gene Anderson
Roddy Piper beat Frank Monte
Wahoo McDaniel beat Masa Fuchi
Jos LeDuc beat Rick Rood
Greg Valentine beat Ron Ritchie
Paul Jones beat Rick Rood
Jimmy Valiant beat Ricky Harris
Jack & Jerry Brisco beat Bill White & Ken Timbs
Sgt. Slaughter & Pvt. Kernodle beat Ron Ritchie & Mike Davis
Roddy Piper beat Masa Fuchi
Wahoo McDaniel beat Frank Monte

11/12/82: Charlotte, NC @ Coliseum
Ricky Harris beat Ron Ritchie
Sweet Brown Sugar beat Frank Monte
Johnny Weaver beat Masa Fuchi
Jerry Brisco beat Pvt. Nelson
Dusty Rhodes beat Leroy Brown via pinfall
Paul Jones beat Jack Brisco by DQ
Sgt. Slaughter & Pvt. Kernodle NC with Ricky Steamboat & Jay Youngblood
Roddy Piper & Wahoo McDaniel beat Ric Flair & Greg Valentine in a cage match

11/13/82: Spartanburg, SC @ Memorial Auditorium
Paul Jones beat Jack Brisco
Ricky Steamboat(sub for Jay Youngblood) beat Greg Valentine
Sweet Brown Sugar beat Leroy Brown by DQ
Johnny Weaver & Jerry Brisco beat Frank Monte & Ricky Harris
Mike Davis beat Jim Dalton

11/13/82: Lumberton, NC @ Recreation Center
Wahoo McDaniel & Roddy Piper beat Sgt. Slaughter & Pvt. Kernodle by DQ
Ron Ritchie beat Pvt. Nelson
Gene Anderson beat Keith Larsen
Rick Rudd beat Joe Lauren
Ben Alexander beat Gary Black

11/13/82: Fredericksburg, VA @ Stafford High School
Jos LeDuc & Oliver Humperdink beat Jimmy Valiant & Mike Rotundo
Fabulous Moolah beat Sabrina
King Parsons beat Ken Timbs
Porkchop Cash beat Bill White

11/14/82: Asheville, NC @ Civic Center
Frank Monte beat Abe Jacobs
Rick Rood beat Ken Timbs
Keith Larsen beat Joe Lauren
Ricky Harris beat Mike Davis
Jack Brisco beat Paul Jones
Sgt. Slaughter & Don Kernodle beat Ricky Steamboat & Johnny Weaver
Roddy Piper beat Greg Valentine

11/15/82: Greenville, SC @ Memorial Auditorium
Abe Jacobs draw Ricky Harris
Porkchop Cash & King Parsons beat Ken Timbs & Bill White
Jimmy Valiant beat Greg Valentine by DQ
Sweet Brown Sugar beat Leroy Brown
Jack Brisco beat Dory Funk, Jr.
Rick Rude beat Pvt. Nelson

11/16/82: Columbia, SC @ Township Auditorium

11/16/82: Raleigh, NC @ Civic Center
No Wrestling

11/17/82: Charlotte, NC @ WCPQ Studios (TV)
Bob Orton, Jr. beat Jim Dalton
Dory Funk, Jr. draw Sweet Brown Sugar
Paul Jones beat Jack Brisco by DQ
Pvt. Kernodle beat Ron Ritchie
Roddy Piper beat Ben Alexander

11/18/82: Sumter, SC @ Exposition Center
Jack Brisco(sub for Wahoo McDaniel) & Sweet Brown Sugar beat Sgt._Slaughter & Pvt. Kernodle
Jack Brisco beat Dory Funk, Jr.
Mike Rotundo(sub for Jay Youngblood) beat Paul Jones
Gene Anderson beat Frank Monte
Porkchop Cash beat Ricky Harris
Keith Larsen beat Ben Alexander

11/18/82: Harrisonburg, VA @ High School
Candi Malloy vs. Donna Christianello
Jimmy Valiant vs. Jos LeDuc in a cage match

11/19/82: Charleston, SC @ County Hall
Greg Valentine vs. Wahoo McDaniel
Porkchop Cash vs. Gene Anderson
Pvt. Nelson vs. Keith Larsen
Frank Monte vs. Rick Rudd
Gary Black vs. Masa Fuchi
Ricky Harris vs. Abe Jacobs

11/21/82: Roanoke, VA @ Civic Center
King Parsons beat Pvt. Nelson
Sweet Brown Sugar beat Gene Anderson
Leroy Brown beat Johnny Weaver
Dory Funk, Jr. beat Mike Rotundo
Roddy Piper & Ricky Steamboat beat Sgt. Slaughter & Pvt. Kernodle in a boot camp match
Greg Valentine beat Wahoo McDaniel
Ric Flair beat Jack Brisco in a no DQ Match

11/22/82: Greenville, SC @ Memorial Auditorium
Porkchop Cash beat Joe Lauren
Ken Timbs beat Rick Rude
Ron Ritchie & Mike Davis beat Masa Fuchi & Bill White
Jerry Brisco beat Pvt. Nelson
Bob Orton, Jr., Abdullah the Butcher & Jimmy Valiant beat Oliver Humperdink, Paul Jones & Jos LeDuc
Roddy Piper beat Greg Valentine
NWA World Champion Ric Flair beat Ricky Steamboat

11/23/82: Raleigh, NC @ Civic Center
NWA Champion Ric Flair beat Roddy Piper by DQ
Jack Brisco, Jimmy Valiant & Abdullah the Butcher beat Paul Jones, Jos Leduc & Leroy Brown
Keith Larsen beat Jim Dalton
Bill White beat Rick Rudd
Mike Davis beat Frank Monte

11/23/82: Columbia, SC @ Township Auditorium

11/24/82: Charlotte, NC @ WCPQ Studios (TV)
Mike Rotundo beat Ricky Harris
Paul Jones beat Masa Fuchi
Jack Brisco & Bob Orton, Jr. beat Bill White & Ken Timbs
Greg Valentine beat King Parsons
Jack Brisco beat Ken Timbs
Paul Jones beat King Parsons
Mike Rotundo beat Bill White
Bob Orton, Jr. beat Masa Fuchi

11/25/82: Greensboro, NC @ Coliseum
Mike Davis beat Masa Fuchi
Johnny Weaver beat Ken Timbs
Frank Monte beat Ron Ritchie
Bob Orton, Jr. beat Pvt. Nelson
Leroy Brown won a 20-man battle royal for $10,000 & vacant NWA Mid Atlantic Television Title
Other participants included Bob Orton, Jr., Keith Larsen, Jerry Black, Masa Fuchi, Jerry Brisco, Frank Monte, Ricky Rudd, Mike Rotundo, Mike Davis, Porkchop Cash, Ken Timbs, Pvt. Nelson, Ron Ritchie, Pvt. Kernodle,
King Parsons, Jim Dalton, Gene Anderson, Ricky Harris, Bill White, Sergeant Slaughter, & Johnny Weaver
Jack Brisco beat Greg Valentine
NWA World Champion Ric Flair beat Roddy Piper
Jimmy Valiant & Abdullah The Butcher beat Oliver Humperdink, Paul Jones & Jos LeDuc in a handicap, steel cage match

11/26/82: Charleston, SC @ County Hall
Jimmy Valiant & Abdullah The Butcher vs. Jos Leduc, Paul Jones & Oliver Humperdink in a handicap, steel cage match
Sweet Brown Sugar & Porkchop Cash vs. Pvt. Nelson & Bill White

11/26/82: Richmond, VA @ Coliseum
Masa Fuchi beat Ron Ritchie
Mike Davis beat Joe Lauren

Mike Rotundo beat Jim Dalton
Gene Anderson & Frank Monte beat Johnny Weaver & Gary Black
Sgt. Slaughter & Pvt. Kernodle beat Jack & Jerry Brisco
Dusty Rhodes beat Leroy Brown in a bullrope match
Roddy Piper & Bob Orton, Jr. beat Ric Flair & Greg Valentine by CO

11/27/82: Norfolk, VA @ Scope

Jim Dalton beat Ron Ritchie
Mike Rotundo beat Gene Anderson
Johnny Weaver beat Road Warrior(Joe Lauren)
Frank Monte & Masa Fuchi beat Mike Davis & Ron Ritchie
Paul Jones beat Sweet Brown Sugar
Bob Orton, Jr. beat Greg Valentine
Jimmy Valiant & Abdullah The Butcher beat Leroy Brown, Jos LeDuc & Oliver Humperdink in a handicap match

11/27/82: Greenville, SC @ Memorial Auditorium(Special Saturday Card)

NWA World Champ Ric Flair beat Roddy Piper by DQ
Sgt. Slaughter & Pvt. Kernodle beat Jack & Jerry Brisco
Porkchop Cash & King Parsons beat Pvt. Nelson & Bill White
Ricky Harris beat Keith Larsen
Ken Timbs beat Abe Jacobs
Rick Rudd beat Ben Alexander

11/28/82: Charlotte, NC @ Coliseum

Jack Brisco beat Paul Jones to win NWA Mid Atlantic Title in a no DQ Match
NWA World Champion Ric Flair double DQ Jimmy Valiant
Bob Orton, Jr. beat Greg Valentine
Roddy Piper & Abdullah The Butcher beat Sgt Slaughter & Pvt. Kernodle
Sweet Brown Sugar beat Leroy Brown by CO
Jos LeDuc beat Jerry Brisco
Porkchop Cash & King Parsons beat Bill White & Ken Timbs
Gene Anderson beat Mike Davis
Pvt. Nelson beat Keith Larsen

11/30/82: Columbia, SC @ Township Auditorium

Jack Brisco beat Paul Jones

11/30/82: Raleigh, NC @ Civic Center

Mike Davis beat Rick Connors
Frank Monte beat Ken Hall
Ricky Harris & Ken Timbs beat Keith Larson & Ron Ritchie
Greg Valentine beat Bob Orton, Jr.
Sgt. Slaughter & Pvt. Kernodle beat Jimmy Valiant & Sweet Brown Sugar by DQ

12/1/82: Charlotte, NC @ WCPQ Studios (TV)

Bob Orton, Jr. beat Rick Connors
Leroy Brown beat Mike Davis
Gene Anderson, Paul Jones & Jos LeDuc beat Ron Ritchie, Johnny Weaver & King Parsons
Sgt. Slaughter & Pvt. Kernodle beat Gary Black & Ken Hall
Greg Valentine double DQ Rick Rood
Sweet Brown Sugar beat Joe Lauren
Paul Jones, Jos LeDuc & Leroy Brown beat Ken Hall, King Parsons & Keith Larson
Sgt. Slaughter & Pvt. Kernodle beat Rick Rood & Mike Davis
Bob Orton, Jr. beat Ricky Harris
Greg Valentine double DQ Gary Black
Mike Rotundo & Sweet Brown Sugar beat Ken Timbs & Masa Fuchi

12/2/82: Sumter, SC @ Exposition Center

Sgt. Slaughter & Pvt. Kernodle beat Jerry Brisco & Sweet Brown Sugar
Jimmy Valiant beat Jos LeDuc in a NY street fight
Jimmy Valiant beat Oliver Humperdink via pinfall
Johnny Weaver beat Rick Connors
Bill White & Ken Timbs beat Mike Davis & Ron Ritchie
Pvt. Nelson beat Kenny Hall
Jim Dalton beat Rick Hudson

12/3/82: Charleston, SC @ County Hall

Sgt. Slaughter & Pvt. Kernodle vs. Jimmy Valiant & Sweet Brown Sugar
King Parsons, Jerry Brisco & Johnny Weaver vs. Jos Leduc, Gene Anderson & Pvt. Nelson
Jim Dalton vs. Ken Hall
Rick Rudd vs. Bill White
Mike Davis vs. Rick Connors

12/4/82: Hampton, VA @ Coliseum

Jack Brisco beat Roddy Piper by DQ
Jimmy Valiant beat Greg Valentine
Sgt. Slaughter & Pvt. Kernodle beat Jerry Brisco & Sweet Brown Sugar
Leroy Brown beat Mike Rotundo
Jos Leduc beat Johnny Weaver

12/5/82: Roanoke, VA @ Civic Center

Bill White beat Ken Hall
Jim Dalton beat Keith Larsen
Johnny Weaver beat Rick Connors
Gene Anderson & Pvt. Nelson beat Ron Ritchie & Mike Davis
Leroy Brown beat Mike Rotundo
Sgt. Slaughter & Pvt. Kernodle beat Jack & Jerry Brisco
Roddy Piper, Jimmy Valiant & Sweet Brown Sugar beat Jos LeDuc, Greg Valentine & Oliver Humperdink

12/6/82: Greenville, SC @ Memorial Auditorium

Ricky Harris beat Ken Hall
Joe Lauren beat Mike Davis
Johnny Weaver beat Pvt. Nelson
Porkchop Cash & King Parsons beat Masa Fuchi & Rick Connors
Sweet Brown Sugar beat Paul Jones
Roddy Piper & Bob Orton, Jr. beat Ric Flair & Greg Valentine

12/6/82: Fayetteville, NC @ Cumberland County Memorial Auditorium
Jim Dalton beat Abe Jacobs
Gene Anderson beat Ron Ritchie
Mike Rotundo beat Leroy Brown
Sgt. Slaughter & Pvt. Kernodle beat Jack & Jerry Brisco
Jimmy Valiant beat Jos LeDuc

12/7/82: Raleigh, NC @ Civic Center
Porkchop Cash & King Parsons beat Ricky Harris & Frank Monte
Jim Dalton beat Mark Fleming
Mike Davis beat Joe Lauren
Jack Brisco beat Paul Jones
Bob Orton, Jr. beat Greg Valentine in a Texas death match
Pvt. Kernodle & Sgt. Slaughter beat Sweet Brown Sugar & Jimmy Valiant

12/7/82: Columbia, SC @ Township Auditorium
Rick Rood beat Bill White
Ron Ritchie beat Masa Fuchi
Ken Timbs beat Abe Jacobs
Gene Anderson & Jim Nelson beat Keith Larsen & Johnny Weaver
Leroy Brown beat Mike Rotundo
NWA World Champion Ric Flair beat Roddy Piper

12/8/82: Charlotte, NC @ WCPQ Studios (TV)
Sgt. Slaughter & Pvt. Kernodle beat Mark Fleming & Ron Ritchie
Bob Orton, Jr. beat Ken Timbs
Jack Brisco beat Rick Connors
Paul Jones beat Ken Hall
Ric Flair & Greg Valentine beat Mike Davis & Keith Larson
Sgt. Slaughter & Pvt. Kernodle beat Ron Ritchie & Mike Davis
Paul Jones beat Mark Fleming
Bob Orton, Jr. beat Rick Connors
Jack Brisco beat Ken Timbs
Ric Flair & Greg Valentine beat Ken Hall & Keith Larson

12/9/82: Norfolk, VA @ Scope
Pvt. Nelson beat Mike Davis
Johnny Weaver beat Jim Dalton
Gene Anderson & Bill White beat Porkchop Cash & King Parsons
Paul Jones beat Mike Rotundo
Sweet Brown Sugar beat Jos LeDuc by DQ
Jimmy Valiant beat Leroy Brown by DQ
Greg Valentine beat Bob Orton, Jr.
Sgt. Slaughter & Pvt. Kernodle beat Jack & Jerry Brisco
NWA World Champion Ric Flair beat Roddy Piper by DQ

12/10/82: Charleston, SC @ County Hall
Sgt. Slaughter & Pvt. Kernodle beat Jack Brisco & Brad Armstrong
Johnny Weaver & King Parsons beat Gene Anderson & Pvt. Nelson
Mike Davis beat Jim Dalton
Porkchop Cash beat Bill White

12/10/82: Richmond, VA @ Coliseum
Ricky Harris & Ken Timbs beat Keith Larsen & Ron Ritchie
Frank Monte beat Joe Lauren
Jimmy Valiant, Mike Rotundo & Sweet Brown Sugar beat Jos LeDuc, Paul Jones & Oliver Humperdink
Dusty Rhodes beat Leroy Brown
Bob Orton, Jr. & Roddy Piper beat Ric Flair & Greg Valentine in a steel cage match

12/11/82: Asheville, NC @ Civic Center
Ken Timbs beat Keith Larsen
Ricky Harris beat Ron Ritchie
Mike Rotundo beat Gene Anderson
Paul Jones beat Johnny Weaver
Sweet Brown Sugar beat Leroy Brown by DQ
Jimmy Valiant beat Jos LeDuc
Roddy Piper beat Greg Valentine by DQ
Sgt. Slaughter & Pvt. Kernodle beat Bob Orton, Jr. & Jack Brisco

12/12/82: Toronto, Ontario @ Maple Leaf Gardens
WWF Champion Bob Backlund beat Buddy Rose in a Texas death match
Leo Burke beat Johnny Weaver by DQ
Salvatore Bellomo beat Mr. Fuji by DQ
Terry Kay beat Pvt. Nelson by DQ
Leroy Brown beat Porkchop Cash
Rudy Kay & Tony Parisi beat The Destroyer & Frank Monte
Billy Red Lyons beat Bobby Bass

12/12/82: Greensboro, NC @ Coliseum
Sgt. Slaughter & Don Kernodle beat Bob Orton, Jr. & Jimmy Valiant(23:00)
Jack Brisco beat Paul Jones(18:00) via pinfall
Roddy Piper beat Greg Valentine(21:00) by DQ
Sweet Brown Sugar beat Jos LeDuc by DQ
King Parsons beat Ben Alexander
Mike Rotundo beat Bill White
Ken Timbs beat Ron Ritchie

12/13/82: Greenville, SC @ Memorial Auditorium
Mike Davis beat Joe Lauren
Ben Alexander beat Abe Jacobs
Jim Dalton & Ricky Harris beat Keith Larsen & Ron Ritchie
Masa Fuchi draw Keith Larsen
Dusty Rhodes beat Leroy Brown
Roddy Piper beat Greg Valentine by DQ

12/14/82: Raleigh, NC @ Civic Center
Ben Alexander beat Ken Timbs
King Parsons beat Bill White
Paul Jones beat Porkchop Cash
Jack Brisco beat Jos LeDuc

Roddy Piper beat Greg Valentine

12/14/82: Columbia, SC @ Township Auditorium
Porkchop Cash beat Ben Alexander
King Parsons beat Bill White
Paul Jones beat Porkchop Cash
Jack Brisco beat Jos LeDuc
Roddy Piper beat Greg Valentine

12/15/82: Charlotte, NC @ WCPQ Studios (TV)
Sgt. Slaughter & Pvt. Kernodle beat Mike Davis & Abe Jacobs
Jimmy Valiant & Bob Orton, Jr. beat Ricky Harris & Jim Dalton
One Man Gang beat Keith Larson
Dory Funk, Jr. beat Ron Ritchie
Mike Rotundo beat Ken Timbs
Ricky Steamboat & Jay Youngblood beat Ricky Harris & Pvt. Nelson
Jimmy Valiant & Bob Orton, Jr. beat Masa Fuchi & Joe Lauren
One Man Gang beat Mike Davis
Dory Funk, Jr. beat Keith Larson
Sgt. Slaughter & Pvt. Kernodle beat Ron Ritchie & ??

12/15/82: Sumter, SC @ Exposition Center
Jimmy Valiant beat Jos LeDuc in a cage match
Mike Rotundo beat Leroy Brown by CO
Pvt. Nelson beat Ben Alexander
Ricky Harris beat Abe Jacobs
King Parsons beat Jim Dalton

12/25/82: Charlotte, NC @ Coliseum
Roddy Piper beat Greg Valentine
Ricky Steamboat & Jay Youngblood beat Sgt. Slaughter & Pvt. Kernodle
Jimmy Valiant, Bob Orton & Jerry Brisco beat Jos Leduc, Bruiser Brody & Oliver Humperdink
Jack Brisco beat Paul Jones
Mike Rotundo beat Leroy Brown to win NWA Mid Atlantic Television Title
Johnny Weaver & Sweet Brown Sugar beat Gene Anderson & Dory Funk, Jr.
Bill White beat Mike Davis

12/26/82: Greensboro, NC @ Coliseum
Ricky Steamboat & Jay Youngblood beat Sgt. Slaughter & Pvt. Kernodle
Roddy Piper beat Greg Valentine in a Texas death match
Sweet Brown Sugar beat Dory Funk, Jr. in a match with Ernie Shavers as special referee
Jack Brisco beat Bruiser Brody by DQ
Mike Rotundo beat Paul Jones
Jerry Brisco & Bob Orton, Jr. beat Gene Anderson & Masa Fuchi
One Man Gang beat Mike Davis

12/26/82: Richmond, VA @ Coliseum
King Parsons beat Frank Monte
Masa Fuchi beat Ben Alexander
Abe Jacobs beat Ken Timbs
Porkchop Cash beat Jim Dalton
Roddy Piper beat Greg Valentine
Sweet Brown Sugar beat Dory Funk, Jr.
Ricky Steamboat & Jay Youngblood beat Sgt. Slaughter & Pvt. Kernodle

12/26/82: Toronto, Ontario @ Maple Leaf Gardens
Angelo Mosca beat Leroy Brown by DQ
Andre The Giant & Salvatore Bellomo beat Mr. Fuji & Mr. Saito
Johnny Weaver beat Leo Burke by CO
Terry Kay beat Pvt. Nelson(10:58) to win NWA Canadian Television Title
Tony Parisi & Rudy Kay beat Bobby Bass & Bill White
Billy Red Lyons beat Ricky Harris
Farmer Pete beat Little John

12/27/82: Greenville, SC @ Memorial Auditorium
Mark Fleming beat Ken Timbs
Keith Larsen beat Jim Dalton
Jack & Jerry Brisco beat Bruiser Brody & Gene Anderson
Jimmy Valiant beat One Man Gang by DQ
Ricky Steamboat & Jay Youngblood beat Sgt. Slaughter & Pvt. Kernodle

12/27/82: Brantford, Ontario(TV)
Rudy Kay beat Leroy Brown by DQ
Angelo Mosca beat Ricky Harris
Johnny Weaver & Terry Kay beat Jerry Bryant & Bobby Bass
Angelo Mosca beat Bill White
Leroy Brown beat Nick DeCarlo
Leo Burke beat Bill Armstrong
Johnny Weaver beat Ricky Harris
Rudy Kay & Terry Kay beat Bill White & Bobby Bass
Leo Burke & Pvt. Nelson beat Nick DeCarlo beat Bill Armstrong
Rudy Kay beat Bobby Bass
Nick DeCarlo beat Jerry Bryant
Leo Burke & Pvt. Nelson beat Terry Kay & Johnny Weaver
Farmer Pete beat Little John

12/28/82: Raleigh, NC @ Civic Center
Jack Brisco beat One Man Gang(sub for Jos LeDuc)
Mike Davis beat Ricky Harris
Bruiser Brody beat Porkchop Cash
Jimmy Valiant beat One Man Gang
Paul Jones beat Jerry Brisco
Ricky Steamboat & Jay Youngblood beat Sgt. Slaughter & Pvt. Kernodle

12/28/82: Columbia, SC @ Township Auditorium
King Parsons beat Jim Dalton by referee's decision
Ben Alexander beat Frank Monte
Mark Fleming beat Ken Timbs
Johnny Weaver draw Tommy Gilbert
Mike Rotundo beat Gene Anderson
Sweet Brown Sugar beat Dory Funk, Jr.
Roddy Piper & Bob Orton, Jr. beat Ric Flair & Greg Valentine

12/29/82: Charlotte, NC @ WCPQ Studios (TV)
Paul Jones & One Man Gang beat Jimmy Valiant & Mike Rotundo
Bruiser Brody beat Vinnie Valentino
Tommy Gilbert beat Pvt. Kernodle by DQ
Jack & Jerry Brisco beat Jim Dalton & Ken Timbs
Ricky Steamboat beat Masa Fuchi
Ricky Steamboat beat Frank Monte
Tommy Gilbert beat Ken Timbs
Mike Rotundo beat Masa Fuchi
Bruiser Brody beat Mark Fleming
Jack & Jerry Brisco beat Ben Alexander & Jim Dalton

12/29/82: Sumter, SC @ Exposition Center

12/30/82: Norfolk, VA @ Scope
King Parson beat Bill White
Pvt. Nelson beat Porkchop Cash
One Man Gang beat Johnny Weaver
Sweet Brown Sugar & Jimmy Valiant beat Bruiser Brody & Dory Funk, Jr.
Sgt. Slaughter beat Ricky Steamboat by DQ
Jimmy Valiant beat Jos LeDuc by CO
Roddy Piper & Bob Orton, Jr. beat Ric Flair & Greg Valentine

Chapter 4: 1983

1/1/83: Charlotte, NC @ Coliseum
NWA World Champ Ric Flair beat Roddy Piper
Sgt. Slaughter & Pvt. Kernodle beat Ricky Steamboat & Jay Youngblood
Greg Valentine beat Bob Orton, Jr.
Johnny Weaver, Jack & Jerry Brisco beat Pvt. Nelson, Paul Jones & Gene Anderson
Abdullah the Butcher & Jimmy Valiant beat Jos Leduc & One Man Gang
Sweet Brown Sugar beat Dory Funk, Jr.
Tommy Gilbert beat Ricky Harris

1/2/83: Roanoke, VA @ Civic Center
Tommy Gilbert beat Ricky Harris
King Parsons & Porkchop Cash beat Masa Fuchi & Gene Anderson
Jimmy Valiant, Sweet Brown Sugar & Abdullah the Butcher beat Dory Funk, Jr., Paul Jones & One Man Gang
Roddy Piper & Bob Orton, Jr. beat Ric Flair & Greg Valentine

1/2/83: Asheville, NC @ Civic Center
Mike Davis beat Ken Timbs
Johnny Weaver & Jerry Brisco beat Nelson & Dalton
Mike Rotundo beat Dizzy Hogan
Jack Brisco beat Paul Jones
Jay Youngblood beat Pvt. Kernodle
Ricky Steamboat beat Sgt. Slaughter by DQ

1/2/83: Greensboro, NC @ Coliseum
Frank Monte beat Ricky Harris
Vinnie Valentino beat Bill White
Tommy Gilbert beat Masa Fuchi
Jimmy Valiant & Abdullah the Butcher beat Gene Anderson & One Man Gang
Greg Valentine beat Bob Orton, Jr.
Ricky Steamboat & Jay Youngblood beat Sgt. Slaughter & Pvt. Kernodle by DQ
NWA World Champ Ric Flair DDQ Roddy Piper

1/3/83: Fayetteville, NC @ Civic Center
Tommy Gilbert & Abe Jacobs beat RedDog Lane & Jim Dalton
One Man Gang beat Johnny Weaver
Bob Orton, Jr. beat Bruiser Brody
Dory Funk, Jr. beat Sweet Brown Sugar
Roddy Piper beat Greg Valentine
Ricky Steamboat & Jay Youngblood beat Sgt. Slaughter & Pvt. Kernodle by DQ

1/4/83: Raleigh, NC @ Civic Center
Vinnie Valentino beat Ken Timbs
Sweet Brown Sugar beat Pvt. Nelson
Mike Rotundo beat Jim Dalton
Jimmy Valiant, Jack & Jerry Brisco beat Dory Funk, Jr., Paul Jones & One Man Gang
Roddy Piper beat Greg Valentine

1/4/83: Columbia, SC @ Township Auditorium
Dizzy Hogan beat Mike Davis
Porkchop Cash & King Parsons beat Masa Fuchi & Frank Monte
Gene Anderson beat Tommy Gilbert
Bob Orton, Jr. beat Bruiser Brody by DQ
Abdullah the Butcher beat Jos LeDuc
Ricky Steamboat & Jay Youngblood beat Sgt. Slaughter & Pvt. Kernodle

1/5/83: Charlotte, NC @ WCPQ Studios (TV)
Mike Rotundo beat Ken Timbs
Jerry Brisco, Bob Orton, Jr. & Dick Slater beat Red Dog Lane, Dory Funk, Jr. & Greg Valentine by DQ
Jay Youngblood beat Ricky Harris
Johnny Weaver beat Pvt. Kernodle by DQ
Tommy Gilbert beat Ben Alexander
Roddy Piper beat Ken Timbs
Ricky Steamboat & Jay Youngblood beat Ricky Harris & Masa Fuchi
Dick Slater & Greg Valentine beat Tommy Gilbert & Mark Fleming
Bob Orton, Jr. beat Frank Monte
Mike Rotundo beat Red Dog Lane

1/5/83: Sumter, SC @ Exhibition Center
Abdullah The Butcher, Jimmy Valiant & Sweet Brown Sugar beat Bruiser Brody, Paul Jones & One Man Gang
Jack Brisco beat Pvt. Nelson
Mike Davis beat Dizzy Hogan
King Parsons beat Jim Dalton

1/6/83: Shelby, NC
Tommy Gilbert beat Ben Alexander
Jerry Bryant beat Red Dog Lane
Johnny Weaver beat Ricky Harris
Jack Brisco beat Dizzy Hogan
Abdullah The Butcher & Bob Orton, Jr. beat Paul Jones & One Man Gang

1/6/83: Norfolk, VA @ Scope
Pvt. Nelson beat Vinnie Valentino
One Man Gang beat Mike Davis
Tommy Gilbert & Johnny Weaver beat Red Dog Lane & Ken Timbs
Abdullah the Butcher, Sweet Brown Sugar & Jimmy Valiant beat Gene Anderson, Dory Funk, Jr. & Greg Valentine
Mike Rotundo beat Rufus R. Jones
Ricky Steamboat & Jay Youngblood DCO with Pvt. Kernodle & Sgt. Slaughter

1/7/83: Richmond, VA @ Coliseum
Mike Davis beat Masa Fuchi
Jim Nelson beat King Parsons
Vinnie Valentino & Johnny Weaver beat Gene Anderson & Red Dog Lane
Abdullah the Butcher & Bob Orton, Jr. beat Jos LeDuc & One Man Gang
Jimmy Valiant beat Greg Valentine
Ricky Steamboat & Jay Youngblood DCO with Don Kernodle & Sgt. Slaughter

1/7/83: Charleston, SC @ County Hall
Ricky Harris beat Abe Jacobs
Frank Monte beat Mark Fleming
Tommy Gilbert draw Dizzy Hogan
Porkchop Cash beat Bill White
Sweet Brown Sugar beat Paul Jones
Dory Funk, Jr. beat Mike Rotundo

1/9/83: Toronto, Ontario @ Maple Leaf Gardens
King Parsons beat Jerry Bryant(8:12)
Pvt. Nelson beat Nick DeCarlo(9:56)
Rudy Kay & Terry Kay beat Ken Timbs & Frank Monte(16:04)
Salvatore Bellomo beat Buddy Rose(14:06) by DQ
Leo Burke beat Johnny Weaver(13:36)
Ray Stevens beat Jimmy Snuka(10:24) by CO
Angelo Mosca beat Leroy Brown(7:17) in a steel cage match

1/9/83: Savannah, GA @ Civic Center
Abe Jacobs beat Bill White
Red Dog Lane beat Mike Davis
Porkchop Cash beat Ricky Harris by DQ
Jack Brisco, Mike Rotundo & Abdullah the Butcher beat Red Dog Lane, Gene Anderson & Paul Jones
Ricky Steamboat & Jay Youngblood beat Sgt. Slaughter & Pvt. Kernodle

1/9/83: Hampton, VA @ Coliseum
Tommy Gilbert beat Jim Dalton
Masa Fuchi beat Vinnie Valentino
Sweet Brown Sugar beat Dizzy Hogan
Jimmy Valiant beat One Man Gang
Bob Orton, Jr. beat Greg Valentine by DQ
Jack Brisco draw Dory Funk, Jr.

1/10/83: Greenville, SC @ Memorial Auditorium
Abe Jacobs beat Ben Alexander
Dizzy Hogan beat Porkchop Cash
Mike Rotundo beat Paul Jones
Jack Brisco beat Dory Funk, Jr.
Jerry Brisco beat Greg Valentine
Ricky Steamboat & Jay Youngblood beat Sgt. Slaughter & Pvt. Kernodle

1/11/83: Columbia, SC @ Township Auditorium
Vinnie Valentino beat Jim Dalton
Johnny Weaver beat Masa Fuchi
Tommy Gilbert beat Bill White
Bob Orton, Jr., Jack & Jerry Brisco beat Gene Anderson, Pvt. Nelson & Red Dog Lane
Greg Valentine beat Roddy Piper
Jimmy Valiant beat One Man Gang by DQ

1/11/83: Raleigh, NC @ Dorton Arena
Mike Davis beat Frank Monte
Sweet Brown Sugar beat Dizzy Hogan
Ricky Harris & Ken Timbs beat Porkchop Cash & King Parsons
Mike Rotundo beat Paul Jones
Abdullah the Butcher beat Dory Funk, Jr. by DQ
Ricky Steamboat & Jay Youngblood beat Sgt. Slaughter & Pvt. Kernodle by CO

1/12/83: Charlotte, NC @ WCPQ Studios (TV)
Sgt. Slaughter & Pvt. Kernodle beat Tommy Gilbert & Vinnie Valentino
Mike Rotundo, Jimmy Valiant & Bob Orton, Jr. beat Pvt. Nelson, Ricky Harris & Bill White
Jerry Brisco & Sweet Brown Sugar beat Dory Funk, Jr. & Dick Slater
Johnny Weaver beat Ken Timbs
Dick Slater beat Mike Davis
Ricky Steamboat & Jay Youngblood beat Red Dog Lane & Ken Timbs
Dory Funk, Jr., Dick Slater & Greg Valentine beat King Parsons, Tommy Gilbert & Vinnie Valentino
Mike Rotundo beat Ricky Harris
Bob Orton, Jr. beat Bill White
Johnny Weaver & Sweet Brown Sugar beat Jim Dalton & Masa Fuchi

1/13/83: York, SC @ High School
Jack Brisco vs. Greg Valentine
Jimmy Valiant, Bob Orton, Jr. & Jay Youngblood vs. Jos LeDuc, Paul Jones & One Man Gang
Sweet Brown Sugar vs. Dick Slater
Mike Rotundo vs. Red Dog Lane
Tommy Gilbert vs. Pvt. Nelson

1/14/83: Charleston, SC @ County Hall
Dizzy Hogan draw Ricky Harris
Sweet Brown Sugar beat Pvt. Nelson
One Man Gang beat Tommy Gilbert
Dory Funk, Jr. beat Mike Rotundo
Roddy Piper beat Greg Valentine

1/15/83: Kinston, NC
Ricky Harris beat Vinnie Valentino
Porkchop Cash & King Parsons beat Masa Fuchi & Jim Dalton
Mike Rotundo beat Pvt. Nelson
Mike Rotundo beat Paul Jones by DQ
Sgt. Slaughter & Pvt. Kernodle beat Porkchop Cash & King Parsons

1/15/83: Spartanburg, SC @ Memorial Auditorium
Jack Brisco, Jerry Brisco & Bob Orton, Jr. beat Greg Valentine, Dick Slater & One Man Gang
Dory Funk, Jr. draw Sweet Brown Sugar
Johnny Weaver & Mike Davis beat Gene Anderson & Bill White
Dizzy Hogan beat Ken Timbs
Red Dog Lane pinned Tommy Gilbert

1/16/83: Asheville, NC @ Civic Center
Tiny Tom beat Little Tokyo
Mark Fleming beat Ken Timbs
Tommy Gilbert beat Red Dog Lane
Johnny Weaver beat Gene Anderson
Jack Brisco beat Paul Jones
Greg Valentine & Dick Slater beat Bob Orton, Jr. & Jerry Brisco
Ricky Steamboat & Jay Youngblood beat Sgt. Slaughter & Pvt. Kernodle by CO

1/16/83: Hampton, VA @ Coliseum
Sweet Brown Sugar beat Dizzy Hogan
Jimmy Valiant beat One Man Gang
Dory Funk, Jr. beat Jack Brisco
Greg Valentine beat Bob Orton, Jr.

1/17/83: Iva, NC
Ricky Steamboat beat Greg Valentine
Jerry Brisco beat Sgt. Slaughter by DQ
Johnny Weaver & Tommy Gilbert beat Red Dog Lane & Gene Anderson
King Parsons beat Bill White
Ricky Harris beat Frank Monte

1/17/83: Lumberton, NC @ Recreation Center
Jack Brisco vs. Dory Funk, Jr.
Jimmy Valiant & Paul Jones vs. Sweet Brown Sugar & One Man Gang
Jerry Brisco vs. Pvt. Nelson

1/18/83: Columbia, SC @ Township Auditorium
Vinnie Valentino beat Frank Monte
Bill White beat Mike Davis
Sweet Brown Sugar beat Paul Jones
Jimmy Valiant beat One Man Gang
Dick Slater beat Bob Orton, Jr.
Jack Brisco beat Dory Funk, Jr.
Tiny Tom beat Little Tokyo
Ricky Steamboat & Jay Youngblood beat Sgt. Slaughter & Pvt. Kernodle by DQ

1/19/83: Charlotte, NC @ WCPQ Studios (TV)
Sgt. Slaughter & Pvt. Kernodle beat King Parsons & Mark Fleming
Jerry Brisco beat Red Dog Lane
Dory Funk, Jr. beat Dizzy Hogan
One Man Gang beat Vinnie Valentino
Jack Brisco beat Ken Timbs
Greg Valentine & Dick Slater beat Mike Davis & Tommy Gilbert

1/20/83: Norfolk, VA @ Scope
Tiny Tom beat Little Tokyo
Tommy Gilbert beat Red Dog Lane
Jack Brisco beat Paul Jones
Dick Slater beat Jerry Brisco
Johnny Weaver, Jimmy Valiant & Sweet Brown Sugar beat Greg Valentine, Dory Funk, Jr. & Oliver Humperdink
Ricky Steamboat & Jay Youngblood beat Sgt. Slaughter & Pvt. Kernodle

1/21/83: Richmond, VA @ Coliseum
King Parsons & Porkchop Cash beat Masa Fuchi & Ken Timbs
Mike Rotundo beat Dizzy Hogan
Tiny Tom beat Little Tokyo
Roddy Piper no contest with Dick Slater
Jimmy Valiant beat Oliver Humperdink by CO
Ricky Steamboat & Jay Youngblood beat Sgt. Slaughter & Pvt. Kernodle

1/21/83: Charleston, SC @ County Hall
Mike David & Vinnie Valentino beat Jim Dalton & Bill White
Tommy Gilbert beat Ricky Harris
Gene Anderson & Red Dog Lane beat Johnny Weaver & Mike Davis
Paul Jones beat Tommy Gilbert
Dory Funk, Jr. beat Sweet Brown Sugar

1/23/83: Greensboro, NC @ Coliseum
One Man Gang beat Jimmy Valiant
Tiny Tom beat Little Tokyo
Jack Brisco, Sweet Sugar Brown & Mike Rotundo beat Dory Funk, Jr., Paul Jones & Red Dog Lane
Roddy Piper & Jerry Brisco beat Greg Valentine & Dick Slater
Sgt. Slaughter & Pvt. Kernodle beat Ricky Steamboat & Jay Youngblood

1/23/83: Toronto, Ontario @ Maple Leaf Gardens
Billy Red Lyons beat Jerry Bryant(13:52)
Johnny Weaver beat Tim Gerrard(10:21)
The Destroyer & Bobby Bass beat Rudy & Terry Kay(22:46)
Leo Burke draw Tony Parisi(20:00)
Big John Studd beat Tony Garea(15:02)
Ricky Steamboat & Jay Youngblood beat Sgt. Slaughter & Pvt. Kernodle by DQ
Jimmy Snuka beat Ray Stevens(8:56)

1/24/83: Fayetteville, NC @ Cumberland County Civic Center
Masa Fuchi beat Vinnie Valentino
King Parsons beat Ricky Harris
Johnny Weaver beat Paul Jones
Gene Anderson & Red Dog Lane beat Tommy Gilbert & Sweet Brown Sugar
Jack Brisco beat Dory Funk, Jr.
Ricky Steamboat & Jay Youngblood beat Sgt. Slaughter & Pvt. Kernodle

1/24/83: Greenville, SC @ Memorial Auditorium
Mike Davis beat Ken Timbs
Dizzy Hogan beat Porkchop Cash
Tiny Tom beat Little Tokyo
Mike Rotundo beat Pvt. Nelson(sub for Jos LeDuc)
Jimmy Valiant beat One Man Gang by DQ
Roddy Piper & Jack Brisco beat Greg Valentine & Dick Slater

1/25/83: Columbia, SC @ Township Auditorium
King Parsons beat Jim Dalton
Gene Anderson & Pvt. Nelson beat Mike Davis & Tommy Gilbert
Jack Brisco beat Red Dog Lane
Jimmy Valiant beat One Man Gang
Roddy Piper, Jerry Brisco & Johnny Weaver beat Greg Valentine, Dory Funk, Jr. & Dick Slater

1/26/83: Charlotte, NC @ WCPQ Studios (TV)
Greg Valentine beat Mike Davis
Dick Slater beat Rick Benfield
Ric Flair beat Pat Rose
Sgt. Slaughter & Pvt. Kernodle beat Gary Black & Ken Hall
Dizzy Hogan & Sweet Brown Sugar beat Ricky Harris & Ken Timbs
Jerry Brisco beat Frank Monte
Dick Slater & Greg Valentine beat Mike Davis & King Parsons
Dory Funk, Jr. beat Vinnie Valentino
One Man Gang beat Rick Benfield
Dizzy Hogan, Sweet Brown Sugar & Jimmy Valiant beat Ricky Harris, Ken Timbs & Ben Alexander
Ricky Steamboat & Jay Youngblood beat Frank Monte & Jim Dalton

1/26/83: Sumter, SC @ Exhibition Center
Tiny Tom beat Little Tokyo
Porkchop Cash beat Masa Fuchi
Tommy Gilbert beat Red Dog Lane
Mike Rotundo beat Paul Jones
Ricky Steamboat & Jay Youngblood beat Sgt. Slaughter & Pvt. Kernodle

1/27/83: Harrisonburg, VA @ High School
Roddy Piper vs. Greg Valentine
Bob Orton, Jr. vs. Dick Slater
Johnny Weaver, Jerry Brisco & Abdullah The Butcher vs. Paul Jones, Jos LeDuc & Oliver Humperdink

1/28/83: Charleston, SC @ County Hall
Tiny Tom beat Little Tokyo
Ken Timbs beat King Parsons
Pvt. Nelson beat Mike Davis
Sweet Brown Sugar beat Red Dog Lane
One Man Gang beat Jimmy Valiant by DQ
Jack Brisco beat Dory Funk, Jr.
Ricky Steamboat & Jay Youngblood beat Sgt. Slaughter & Pvt. Kernodle

1/29/83: Asheville, NC @ Civic Center
Don Kernodle & Sgt. Slaughter beat Gary Black & Ken Hall
Dick Slater beat Pat Rose
Greg Valentine beat Mike Davis
Dizzy Hogan & Sweet Brown Sugar beat Ricky Harris & Ken Timbs

1/30/83: Charlotte, NC @ Coliseum
Mike Rotundo won an 18-man battle royal
Dick Slater beat Jerry Brisco by DQ
Jimmy Valiant beat One Man Gang
Roddy Piper & Dusty Rhodes beat Paul Jones & Red Dog Lane
Dory Funk, Jr. beat Jack Brisco to win NWA Mid Atlantic Title
Greg Valentine beat Masked Man
Ricky Steamboat & Jay Youngblood DDQ Sgt. Slaughter & Pvt. Kernodle

1/30/83: Savannah, GA @ Civic Center
Abe Jacobs beat Bill White
Red Dog Lane beat Mike Davis
Porkchop Cash beat Ricky Harris by DQ
Abdullah The Butcher, Jack Brisco & Mike Rotundo beat Paul Jones, Red Dog Lane & Gene Anderson
Ricky Steamboat & Jay Youngblood beat Sgt. Slaughter & Pvt. Kernodle

1/31/83: Greenville, SC @ Memorial Auditorium
Porkchop Cash & King Parsons beat Ken Timbs(sub for Ricky Harris) & Jim Dalton
Dizzy Hogan beat Ricky Harris
Johnny Weaver beat Gene Anderson
Jimmy Valiant beat One Man Gang in a no DQ match
Jack Brisco beat Dick Slater by DQ
Sgt. Slaughter & Pvt. Kernodle beat Ricky Steamboat & Jay Youngblood in a lumberjack match

2/1/83: Columbia, SC @ Township Auditorium
Bill White beat Mike Davis
Vinnie Valentino beat Ken Timbs
Johnny Weaver & Tommy Gilbert beat Gene Anderson & Red Dog Lane
Jerry Brisco draw Dory Funk, Jr.
Roddy Piper beat Dick Slater by DQ
Ricky Steamboat & Jay Youngblood beat Sgt. Slaughter & Pvt. Kernodle in a boot camp match

2/1/83: Raleigh, NC @ Dorton Arena
Porkchop Cash & King Parsons beat Masa Fuchi & Ricky Harris
Dizzy Hogan beat The Champ(Brian Blair)
Sweet Brown Sugar beat Paul Jones
Mike Rotundo beat Pvt. Nelson
Jack Brisco beat Greg Valentine
One Man Gang beat Jimmy Valiant by DQ

2/2/83: Charlotte, NC @ WCPQ Studios (TV)
Ricky Steamboat & Jay Youngblood beat Ricky Harris & Ken Timbs
Dory Funk, Jr. beat Tommy Gilbert
One Man Gang beat Mike Davis
Mike Rotundo beat Frank Monte
Sgt. Slaughter & Pvt. Kernodle beat Dizzy Hogan & Mike Davis
The Champ beat Ricky Harris
Mike Rotundo beat Ken Timbs
Sweet Brown Sugar beat Frank Monte

2/3/83: Sumter, SC @ Exhibition Center
Abe Jacobs beat Ken Timbs
Ricky Harris beat Mike Davis
Mike Rotundo beat Dizzy Hogan
Jack Brisco beat Paul Jones
Ricky Steamboat & Jay Youngblood beat Sgt. Slaughter & Pvt. Kernodle by DQ

2/3/83: Norfolk, VA @ Scope
Frank Monte beat Mark Fleming
Porkchop Cash beat Masa Fuchi
Johnny Weaver, Tommy Gilbert & King Parsons beat Pvt. Nelson, Gene Anderson & Red Dog Lane

Dory Funk, Jr. beat Sweet Brown Sugar
Jimmy Valiant beat One Man Gang
Greg Valentine beat The Champ
Roddy Piper beat Dick Slater

2/4/83: Charleston SC @ County Hall
Sgt. Slaughter & Pvt. Kernodle vs. Ricky Steamboat & Jay Youngblood in a lumberjack match
Jack Brisco vs. Dizzy Hogan
Sweet Brown Sugar vs. Ricky Harris
Pvt. Nelson vs. Mike Davis
Porkchop Cash & King Parsons vs. Ken Timbs & Masa Fuchi

2/4/83: Richmond, VA @ Coliseum
Abe Jacobs & Mark Fleming beat Frank Monte & Jim Dalton
Johnny Weaver beat Paul Jones by DQ
One Man Gang beat Jimmy Valiant by DQ
Mike Rotundo beat Dory Funk, Jr.
Roddy Piper & The Champ beat Greg Valentine & Dick Slater

2/5/83: Greensboro, NC @ Coliseum
Greg Valentine & King Parsons beat Masa Fuchi & Ken Timbs
Dizzy Hogan beat Bill White
Dusty Rhodes beat Gene Anderson
Jimmy Valiant beat One Man Gang
Dick Slater beat Jerry Brisco
Ricky Steamboat & Jay Youngblood no contest with Sgt. Slaughter & Pvt. Kernodle

2/6/83: Fayetteville, NC @ Cumberland County Civic Center
Tommy Gilbert beat The Champ
Mike Rotundo beat Red Dog Lane
Jimmy Valiant beat One Man Gang
Sgt. Slaughter & Pvt. Kernodle beat Dizzy Hogan & Sweet Brown Sugar
Jay Youngblood beat Dory Funk, Jr. in a bounty match
Greg Valentine & Dick Slater beat Mike Rotundo & Jack Brisco
NWA World Champ Ric Flair beat Ricky Steamboat

2/7/83: Greenville, SC @ Memorial Auditorium
Jack Brisco beat Dory Funk, Jr.
Johnny Weaver & Jerry Brisco beat Gene Anderson & Masa Fuchi
Dick Slater beat ??
Ricky Steamboat & Jay Youngblood beat Sgt. Slaughter & Pvt. Kernodle in a boot camp match
NWA World Champ Ric Flair beat Mike Rotundo

2/8/83: Columbia, SC @ Township Auditorium
Porkchop Cash & Vinnie Valentino beat Ken Timbs & Jim Dalton
Johnny Weaver beat Gene Anderson
Jay Youngblood beat Dory Funk, Jr.
Dick Slater beat The Champ
Jack & Jerry Brisco beat Sgt. Slaughter & Pvt. Kernodle by DQ
NWA World Champ Ric Flair beat Ricky Steamboat

2/9/83: Charlotte, NC @ WCPQ Studios (TV)
Jack Brisco beat Ricky Harris
Jerry Brisco & Mike Rotundo beat Dick Slater & Dory Funk, Jr. by DQ
Dizzy Hogan & Sweet Brown Sugar beat Jim Dalton & Ken Timbs
Dizzy Hogan & Sweet Brown Sugar beat Ricky Harris & Red Dog Lane
Dory Funk, Jr. beat Frank Monte
Dick Slater beat Mike Thompson
Mike Rotundo beat Ken Timbs

2/10/83: Norfolk, VA @ Scope
Dizzy Hogan beat Ricky Harris
Mike Rotundo beat Red Dog Lane
Roddy Piper & Jerry Brisco beat Greg Valentine & Dick Slater
Jack Brisco won a battle royal
NWA World Champ Ric Flair beat Ricky Steamboat

2/11/83: Charleston, SC @ County Hall
Frank Monte beat Ricky Harris
Tommy Gilbert draw Red Dog Lane
Sweet Brown Sugar beat The Ninja
Dick Slater beat Jerry Brisco
Jack Brisco beat Dory Funk, Jr. by DQ

2/12/83: Sumter, SC @ Exhibition Center
Frank Monte & Vinnie Valentino beat Ken Timbs & Masa Fuchi
Sweet Brown Sugar beat One Man Gang
Sgt. Slaughter & Pvt. Kernodle beat Mike Rotundo & Jerry Brisco
NWA World Champ Ric Flair beat Jimmy Valiant

2/13/83: Asheville, NC @ Civic Center
Bill White beat Masa Fuchi
The Ninja beat Vinnie Valentino
One Man Gang beat Dizzy Hogan
Ricky Steamboat & Jay Youngblood beat Greg Valentine & Dick Slater
Jimmy Valiant beat Terry Funk
Jack & Jerry Brisco beat Sgt. Slaughter & Pvt. Kernodle by DQ

2/13/83: Charlotte, NC @ Coliseum
Abe Jacobs beat Jim Dalton
Tommy Gilbert & Johnny Weaver beat Gene Anderson & Red Dog Lane
Pvt. Kernodle & Sgt. Slaughter beat Jack Brisco & Jerry Brisco
Dory Funk, Jr. beat Mike Rotundo
Ricky Steamboat & Jay Youngblood beat Dick Slater & Greg Valentine
Jimmy Valiant beat Terry Funk

2/14/83: Piedmont, SC @ Wren High School
Frank Monte beat Jim Dalton
Dizzy Hogan beat Ricky Harris
Jay Youngblood beat Red Dog Lane
Ricky Steamboat beat Greg Valentine
Pvt. Kernodle & Sgt. Slaughter beat Mike Rotundo & Sweet Brown Sugar

2/14/83: Lumberton, NC @ Recreation Center
Dory Funk, Jr. vs. Jack Brisco

2/15/83: Columbia, SC @ Township Auditorium
Jack Brisco beat Dory Funk, Jr. in a Texas death match

2/16/83: Charlotte, NC @ WCPQ Studios (TV)
Jack Brisco beat Ken Timbs
Mike Rotundo beat Ricky Harris
Dick Slater & Dory Funk, Jr. beat Frank Monte & Ricky Morton
Dory Funk, Jr. draw Ricky Morton
One Man Gang beat Frank Monte
Jack Brisco beat Bill White
Mike Rotundo beat Johnny Weaver
Dick Slater & Dory Funk, Jr. beat Ron Rossi & Ricky Morton

2/18/83: Richmond, VA @ Coliseum
The Ninja beat Ricky Morton
Jim Nelson beat Jim Dalton
Jack & Jerry Brisco beat Sgt. Slaughter & Pvt. Kernodle by DQ
Jimmy Valiant beat One Man Gang
Roddy Piper beat Dick Slater

2/18/83: Charleston, SC @ County Hall
Frank Monte beat Ken Timbs
Johnny Weaver & Tommy Gilbert beat Gene Anderson & Red Dog Lane
Dory Funk, Jr. no contest with Sweet Brown Sugar
Ricky Steamboat & Jay Youngblood beat Greg Valentine & Terry Funk

2/19/83: Newberry, SC
Jack & Jerry Brisco vs. Ricky Steamboat & Jay Youngblood
Greg Valentine vs. Sweet Brown Sugar
Ken Timbs vs. Frank Monte
Vinnie Valentino vs. Masa Fuchi

2/20/83: Greensboro, NC @ Coliseum
Red Dog Lane beat Ricky Morton
Dizzy Hogan & Red Dog Lane beat Ricky Harris & Bill White
Jack Brisco beat Paul Jones
Dick Slater beat Jerry Brisco
Jimmy Valiant beat One Man Gang in a New York street fight
Ricky Steamboat & Jay Youngblood beat Ric Flair & Greg Valentine
Sgt. Slaughter & Pvt. Kernodle beat Terry Funk & Dory Funk, Jr.

2/20/83: Toronto, Ontario @ Maple Leaf Gardens
Rudy Kay & Nick DeCarlo draw Jim Nelson & Tim Gerrard
Johnny Weaver beat Bobby Bass
The Destroyer beat Terry Kay
Leo Burke DCO with Tony Parisi
Sal Bellomo beat Ray Stevens by DQ
Jay Youngblood & Ricky Steamboat beat Sgt. Slaughter & Pvt Kernodle in a boot camp match
NWA World Champ Ric Flair beat Terry Funk(sub for Roddy Piper)

2/21/83: Hillsville, VA @ Woodlawn Intermediate School
Abe Jacobs beat Masa Fuchi
Tommy Gilbert beat The Ninja
Dizzy Hogan & Johnny Weaver beat Gene Anderson & Red Dog Lane
Dory Funk, Jr. beat Sweet Brown Sugar
Greg Valentine beat Mike Rotundo

2/22/83: Columbia, SC @ Township Auditorium
Jack & Jerry Brisco beat Dory Funk, Jr. & Red Dog Lane(sub for Terry Funk)
Dick Slater beat Mike Rotundo to win NWA Mid Atlantic Television Title
Jimmy Valiant beat Oliver Humperdink
Greg Valentine beat Sweet Brown Sugar
Gene Anderson beat Dizzy Hogan
Tommy Gilbert beat The Ninja
Frank Monte beat Masa Fuchi

2/23/83: Charlotte, NC @ WCPQ Studios (TV)
Greg Valentine beat Vinnie Valentino
Sgt. Slaughter & Pvt. Kernodle beat Frank Monte & Dizzy Hogan
Sweet Brown Sugar beat Ricky Harris
Jack Brisco beat Red Dog Lane
Dick Slater beat Mike Rotundo
Jack & Jerry Brisco beat Masa Fuchi & Ricky Harris
Dory Funk, Jr. beat Bill White
One Man Gang beat Vinnie Valentino
Sgt. Slaughter & Pvt. Kernodle beat Ben Alexander & Frank Monte
Greg Valentine beat Dizzy Hogan
Dick Slater beat Ron Rossi
Sweet Brown Sugar beat Ken Timbs

2/24/83: Harrisonburg, VA @ High School
Jimmy Valiant vs. One Man Gang
Jack Brisco vs. Dory Funk, Jr.

2/25/83: Charleston SC @ County Hall
Ricky Steamboat beat Dick Slater
Sweet Brown Sugar beat Dory Funk, Jr. by DQ
Jay Youngblood beat The Ninja
Mike George beat Ken Timbs
Bill White beat Frank Monte

2/26/83: Spartanburg, SC @ Memorial Auditorium
Masa Fuchi beat Vinnie Valentino
Mike George beat Ricky Harris
Dizzy Hogan beat Jim Nelson
Sgt. Slaughter & Pvt. Kernodle beat Mike Rotundo & Jerry Brisco
Jimmy Valiant beat One Man Gang in a New York street fight match

2/27/83: Winston-Salem, NC @ Memorial Coliseum
Mike George beat Frank Monte
Johnny Weaver & Jim Nelson beat Gene Anderson & Red Dog Lane
Ricky Steamboat & Jay Youngblood beat Dick Slater & One Man Gang
Sgt. Slaughter & Pvt. Kernodle beat Mike Rotundo & Jerry Brisco

2/28/83: Greenville, SC @ Memorial Auditorium
Masa Fuchi beat Vinnie Valentino
Dory Funk, Jr. beat Mike Rotundo
One Man Gang beat Johnny Weaver
Gene Anderson & Red Dog Lane beat Dizzy Hogan & Mike George
Greg Valentine beat Jimmy Valiant in a match with Roddy Piper as special referee

3/1/83: Columbia, SC @ Township Auditorium
Gene Anderson & Red Dog Lane beat Tom Prichard & Joe Lightfoot
Sweet Brown Sugar & Dizzy Hogan beat The Moondogs
Dory Funk, Jr. beat Jack Brisco
Jimmy Valiant beat Greg Valentine by DQ

3/2/83: Charlotte, NC @ WCPQ Studios (TV)
Mike Rotundo beat Dick Slater DQ
Jim Nelson & Johnny Weaver beat Masa Fuchi & Ricky Harris
One Man Gang beat Joe Lightfoot
Greg Valentine beat Tom Prichard
Ricky Steamboat & Jay Youngblood beat Ben Alexander & Ken Timbs
Sgt. Slaughter & Pvt. Kernodle beat Mark Fleming & Ron Rossi
Ricky Steamboat & Jay Youngblood beat Ben Alexander & Masa Fuchi
Sgt. Slaughter & Pvt. Kernodle beat Vinnie Valentino & Ron Rossi
One Man Gang beat Ken Timbs
Greg Valentine beat Joe Lightfoot
Dory Funk, Jr. beat Tom Prichard
Jack & Jerry Brisco beat Ricky Harris & Red Dog Lane

3/3/83: Sumter, SC @ Exhibition Center
Joe Lightfoot beat Ricky Harris
Velvet McIntyre beat Donna Christianello
Mike George & Chick Donovan beat The Moondogs
Dory Funk, Jr. beat Sweet Brown Sugar
Jimmy Valiant beat One Man Gang in a New York street fight match

3/4/83: Charleston, SC @ County Hall
Ricky Harris beat Vinnie Valentino
Dizzy Hogan beat Ken Timbs
Jimmy Valiant beat Greg Valentine
Ricky Steamboat & Jay Youngblood beat Dick Slater & One Man Gang
Sweet Brown Sugar beat Dory Funk, Jr. in a Texas death match

3/5/83: Charlotte, NC @ Coliseum
Masa Fuchi beat Bill White
Sweet Brown Sugar beat The Ninja
Mike George beat Ricky Harris
Jim Nelson beat Sgt. Slaughter by DQ
Dory Funk, Jr. beat Jack Brisco
Ricky Steamboat, Jay Youngblood & Jimmy Valiant beat Greg Valentine, Terry Funk & Oliver Humperdink

3/6/83: Savannah, GA @ Civic Center
Gene Anderson beat Dizzy Hogan
Mike George beat Masa Fuchi
One Man Gang beat Sweet Brown Sugar
Greg Valentine beat Mike Rotundo
Jimmy Valiant beat Dick Slater by DQ
Jack & Jerry Brisco beat Dory Funk, Jr. & Terry Funk

3/6/83: Toronto, Ontario @ Maple Leaf Gardens
Billy Red Lyons beat Bobby Bass
Johnny Weaver & Terry Kay beat the Destroyer & Red Dog Lane
Jim Nelson beat Rudy Kay via pinfall
Leo Burke beat Vinnie Valentino
Tiger Jeet Singh beat Kurt Von Hess
Big John Studd beat Salvatore Bellomo
Ricky Steamboat & Jay Youngblood beat Sgt. Slaughter & Pvt. Kernodle by CO

3/7/83: Greenville, SC @ Memorial Auditorium
Gene Anderson & Masa Fuchi beat Mike Davis & Mike George
Bugsy McGraw beat The Ninja
Jimmy Valiant beat Oliver Humperdink in a lights out match
Jimmy Valiant beat One Man Gang
Roddy Piper beat Dick Slater

3/8/83: Columbia, SC @ Township Auditorium
Bill White beat Dale Barnett
Johnny Weaver beat Chick Donovan
Ricky Steamboat & Jay Youngblood beat Gene Anderson & Red Dog Lane
Jimmy Valiant & Bugsy McGraw beat Dick Slater & One Man Gang
Jack Brisco beat Dory Funk, Jr. by DQ

3/9/83: Charlotte, NC @ WCPQ Studios (TV)
Jim Nelson & Johnny Weaver beat Ben Alexander & Chick Donovan
Dory Funk, Jr. beat Ken Timbs
Ric Flair beat Masa Fuchi
Greg Valentine beat Jim Burnett
One Man Gang & Dick Slater beat Vinnie Valentino & Ron Rossi
Mike Rotundo & Sweet Brown Sugar beat Bill White & Ricky Harris
Greg Valentine beat Ken Timbs
One Man Gang & Dick Slater beat Mike George & Vinnie Valentino
Dory Funk, Jr. beat Jim Burnett
Ric Flair beat Ron Rossi
Jim Nelson, Johnny Weaver & Sweet Brown Sugar beat Bill White, Masa Fuchi & Ben Alexander

3/9/83: Sumter, SC @ Exhibition Center
Sgt. Slaughter & Pvt. Kernodle vs. Jimmy Valiant & Bugsy McGraw
Ricky Steamboat & Jay Youngblood vs. Jack Brisco & Jerry Brisco
Dizzy Hogan vs. The Ninja
Masa Fuchi vs. Mike Davis

3/9/83: Fisherville, VA @ Augusta Expo
Tommy Gilbert beat Bill White
Frank Monte beat Ken Timbs
Masa Fuchi beat Mark Fleming
Johnny Weaver & Jim Nelson beat Red Dog Lane & Gene Anderson
Sweet Brown Sugar beat The Ninja by DQ
Dick Slater beat Jerry Brisco
Jimmy Valiant beat Greg Valentine

3/10/83: Chester, SC @ High School
Jimmy Valiant vs. Oliver Humperdink
Bugsy McGraw vs. Gene Anderson
The Moondogs vs. Chick Donovan & Mike George
Ricky Harris vs. Vinnie Valentino
Red Dog Lane vs. Tom Pritchard

3/10/83: Sumter, SC @ Exhibition Center
Mike Davis vs. Masa Fuchi
Dizzy Hogan vs. The Ninja
Jack & Jerry Brisco vs. Ricky Steamboat & Jay Youngblood
Pvt. Kernodle & Sgt. Slaughter vs. Bugsy McGraw & Jimmy Valiant

3/11/83: Hampton, VA @ Coliseum
Terri Shane & Joyce Grable beat Judy Martin & Liz Chase
Mike George beat Ken Timbs
Mike Rotundo beat Mark Fleming
Ricky Steamboat & Jay Youngblood beat One Man Gang & Red Dog Lane
Roddy Piper beat Dick Slater
NWA World Champ Ric Flair beat Dory Funk, Jr.

3/11/83: Charleston, SC @ County Hall
Bugsy McGraw beat Masa Fuchi
Sweet Brown Sugar beat Ricky Harris
Sgt. Slaughter & Pvt. Kernodle beat Johnny Weaver & Jim Nelson by DQ
Jimmy Valiant beat Gene Anderson
Jimmy Valiant beat Oliver Humperdink in a lights out match

3/12/83: Greensboro, NC @ Coliseum
Jim Nelson & Johnny Weaver beat Red Dog Lane & Gene Anderson
Jerry Brisco beat Ken Timbs
Mike Rotundo beat Ricky Harris
Roddy Piper beat Dick Slater
NWA World Champ Ric Flair draw Greg Valentine(60:00)
Ricky Steamboat & Jay Youngblood beat Sgt. Slaughter & Pvt. Kernodle in a steel cage match to win NWA World Tag Title

3/13/83: Roanoke, VA @ Civic Center
Mike George beat Bill White
Liz Chase beat Judy Martin
Sweet Brown Sugar & Dizzy Hogan beat Masa Fuchi & Jos LeDuc
Jimmy Valiant beat One Man Gang in a chain match
Bugsy McGraw beat Dick Slater
Jimmy Valiant beat Oliver Humperdink lightsout match

3/14/83: Greenville, SC @ Memorial Auditorium
Gene Anderson beat Vinnie Valentino
Jerry Brisco beat Lenny Lane
Sgt. Slaughter & Pvt. Kernodle beat Johnny Weaver & Jim Nelson
Jack Brisco beat Dory Funk, Jr. by DQ
Greg Valentine beat Roddy Piper

3/14/83: Newton, NC
Mike Rotundo beat Ken Timbs
Liz Chase beat Judy Martin
Ricky Steamboat & Jay Youngblood beat Gene Anderson & Red Dog Lane
Jerry Brisco beat Dory Funk, Jr. by DQ

3/15/83: Raleigh, NC @ Dorton Arena
Dizzy Hogan beat Bill White
Jos LeDuc beat Ricky Harris
Bugsy McGraw beat Masa Fuchi
Jimmy Valiant beat One Man Gang in a street fight match
Greg Valentine beat Sweet Brown Sugar

3/15/83: Columbia, SC @ Township Auditorium
Mike George beat Ken Timbs
Mike Rotundo beat Red Dog Lane
Jerry Brisco beat Gene Anderson
Sgt. Slaughter & Pvt. Kernodle beat Jim Nelson & Johnny Weaver
Jack Brisco beat Dory Funk, Jr. Texas death match

3/16/83: Charlotte, NC @ WCPQ Studios (TV)
Great Kabuki beat Mike Davis
One Man Gang beat Ken Timbs
Dory Funk, Jr. beat Masa Fuchi
Sgt. Slaughter & Pvt. Kernodle beat Vinnie Valentino & Ron Rossi
Wayne Jones, Sweet Brown Sugar & Mike Rotundo beat Ricky Harris, Ben Alexander & Red Dog Lane
Greg Valentine beat Bill White
Greg Valentine beat Mike Davis
One Man Gang beat Ron Rossi
Dory Funk, Jr. beat Ben Alexander
Great Kabuki beat Vinnie Valentino
Wayne Jones & Sweet Brown Sugar beat Masa Fuchi & Ricky Harris
Sgt. Slaughter & Pvt. Kernodle beat Ken Timbs & Bill White

3/17/83: Norfolk, VA @ Scope
Vinnie Valentino beat Mark Fleming
Jerry Brisco beat Masa Fuchi
Greg Valentine & Dick Slater beat Mike Rotundo & Bugsy McGraw

Dory Funk, Jr. beat Jack Brisco
Jimmy Valiant beat One Man Gang in a no DQ match
Jimmy Valiant beat Oliver Humperdink in a lights out match

3/18/83: Richmond, VA @ Coliseum
Mike George beat Mark Fleming
Mike Rotundo beat Masa Fuchi
Jack & Jerry Brisco beat Gene Anderson & Red Dog Lane
Mike Rotundo won a battle royal
Jimmy Valiant, Ricky Steamboat & Bugsy McGraw beat Dick Slater, One Man Gang & Oliver Humperdink
NWA World Champ Ric Flair draw Greg Valentine

3/18/83: Charleston, SC @ County Hall
Wayne Jones beat Bill White
Mike Davis beat Ken Timbs
Jos LeDuc beat Ricky Harris
Dory Funk, Jr. beat Sweet Brown Sugar in a Texas death match
Sgt. Slaughter & Pvt. Kernodle beat Johnny Weaver & Jim Nelson

3/19/83: Spartanburg, SC @ Memorial Auditorium
Bugsy McGraw beat Ricky Harris
Dizzy Hogan beat Bill White
Jake Roberts(sub for Masa Fuchi) beat Mike Davis
Sgt. Slaughter & Pvt. Kernodle beat Johnny Weaver & Jim Nelson
Jimmy Valiant beat Greg Valentine by DQ

3/20/83: Savannah, GA @ Civic Center
Jerry Brisco beat Ken Timbs
Jos LeDuc beat Ricky Harris
Mike George & Mike Davis beat Bill White & Masa Fuchi
Jimmy Valiant beat Oliver Humperdink
Sweet Brown Sugar beat Jake Roberts by DQ
Jimmy Valiant & Bugsy McGraw beat Greg Valentine & Dick Slater

3/20/83: Asheville, NC @ Civic Center
Ben Alexander beat Wayne Jones
Mike Rotundo beat Red Dog Lane
Johnny Weaver beat Gene Anderson
Sgt. Slaughter, Pvt. Kernodle & One Man Gang beat Jim Nelson, Ricky Steamboat & Jay Youngblood
Jack Brisco beat Dory Funk, Jr. by DQ

3/21/83: Greenville, SC @ Memorial Auditorium
Ricky Harris vs. Mike George
Jerry Brisco vs. Gene Anderson
Sweet Sugar Brown vs. Red Dog Lane
Johnny Weaver & Jim Nelson beat Jake Roberts & One Man Gang
Ricky Steamboat & Jay Youngblood vs. Sgt. Slaughter & Pvt. Kernodle in a steel cage match

3/22/83: Columbia, SC @ Township Auditorium
Ken Timbs beat Paul Jones
Vinnie Valentino beat Masa Fuchi
Gene Anderson beat Mike Davis
Jos LeDuc beat Dick Slater
Sgt. Slaughter & Pvt. Kernodle beat Ricky Steamboat & Jay Youngblood

3/23/83: Charlotte, NC @ WCPQ Studios (TV)
Jimmy Valiant beat Great Kabuki(:23)
Sgt. Slaughter & Pvt. Kernodle beat Mike George & Mike Davis
Jake Roberts & Dory Funk, Jr. beat Vinnie Valentino & Sweet Brown Sugar
Jos LeDuc beat Dick Slater(9:25) by DQ
Jack & Jerry Brisco beat Masa Fuchi & Ricky Harris
Sgt. Slaughter & Pvt. Kernodle beat Mike Davis & Bill White
Jake Roberts & Dory Funk, Jr. beat Mike Rotundo & Vinnie Valentino
Jack & Jerry Brisco beat Red Dog Lane & Ken Timbs

3/24/83: Harrisonburg, VA @ High School
Jos LeDuc vs. Ricky Harris
Bugsy McGraw vs. The Ninja
Dory Funk, Jr. vs. Jack Brisco
Greg Valentine vs. Mike Rotundo
Dick Slater vs. Jimmy Valiant

3/25/83: Fredericksburg, VA @ Stafford High School
Jimmy Valiant vs. One Man Gang
Jerry Brisco vs. The Ninja

3/25/83: Charleston, SC @ County Hall
Bill White beat Mike Davis
Sweet Brown Sugar beat Ken Timbs
Johnny Weaver beat Ricky Harris
Jim Nelson, Ricky Steamboat & Jay Youngblood beat Great Kabuki, Sgt. Slaughter & Pvt. Kernodle

3/26/83: Charlotte, NC @ Coliseum
Mike Davis beat Ken Timbs
Bill White draw Abe Jacobs
Wayne Jones beat Ben Alexander
Dick Slater fought Jos LeDuc
Jack & Jerry Brisco beat Dory Funk, Jr. & Paul Jones
Greg Valentine, Sgt. Slaughter & Pvt. Kernodle vs. Jim Nelson, Ricky Steamboat & Jay Youngblood

3/27/83: Roanoke, VA @ Civic Center
Jake Roberts & Gene Anderson beat Mike Davis & Mark Fleming
Bugsy McGraw beat Ricky Harris
Roddy Piper beat Dick Slater
Sgt. Slaughter & Pvt. Kernodle beat Ricky Steamboat & Jay Youngblood
Jimmy Valiant beat Greg Valentine by DQ

3/27/83: Asheville, NC @ Civic Center
Roddy Piper beat Dick Slater to win NWA Mid Atlantic Television Title

3/27/83: Toronto, Ontario @ Maple Leaf Gardens
Rudy Kay draw Billy Red Lyons
The Destroyer beat Nick DeCarlo
Tony Parisi beat Kurt Von Hess
Bobby Bass beat Brian Mackney
Tiger Jeet Singh beat Frankie Lane
Jim Nelson beat Terry Kay(13:31) to win NWA Canadian Television Title
Mike Rotundo beat Leo Burke by DQ
Ricky Steamboat & Jay Youngblood beat Sgt. Slaughter & Pvt. Kernodle in a steel cage match
NWA World Champ Ric Flair beat Roddy Piper

3/28/83: Greenville, SC @ Memorial Auditorium
Ben Alexander beat Vinnie Valentino
Ricky Harris beat Wayne Jones
Dick Slater beat Jos LeDuc in a taped fist match
Ricky Steamboat & Jay Youngblood beat Dory Funk, Jr. & Jake Roberts
Greg Valentine beat Roddy Piper in a match with 2 referees

3/29/83: Columbia, SC @ Township Auditorium
Vinnie Valentino beat Ben Alexander
Masa Fuchi beat Wayne Jones
Bill White beat Mark Fleming
Great Kabuki beat Sweet Brown Sugar
Dick Slater beat Jos LeDuc by DQ
Roddy Piper beat Greg Valentine by DQ

3/29/83: Wytheville, VA
Abe Jacobs beat Ricky Harris
Johnny Weaver beat Gene Anderson
Pvt. Kernodle beat Jim Nelson
Jimmy Valiant beat One Man Gang
Jimmy Valiant beat Oliver Humperdink

3/30/83: Charlotte, NC @ WCPQ Studios (TV)
Roddy Piper beat Ricky Harris
Great Kabuki beat Bill White
Jos LeDuc, Jimmy Valiant & Bugsy McGraw beat Ben Alexander, Ken Timbs & Masa Fuchi
Jake Roberts & Dory Funk, Jr. beat Mike Davis & Johnny Weaver
Mike Rotundo & Sweet Brown Sugar beat Bill White & Red Dog Lane
Jake Roberts & Dory Funk, Jr. beat Mike Davis & Vinnie Valentino
Roddy Piper beat Ken Timbs
Jos LeDuc, Jimmy Valiant & Bugsy McGraw beat Ben Alexander, Bill White & Ricky Harris
One Man Gang beat Ron Rossi

4/1/83: Charleston SC @ County Hall
Masa Fuchi beat Bill White
Roddy Piper beat Greg Valentine by DQ
Jake Roberts & Dory Funk, Jr. beat Sweet Brown Sugar & Wayne Jones
Mike Rotundo beat Gene Anderson
Johnny Weaver beat Bill White

4/2/83: Charlottesville, VA @ University Hall
Ricky Steamboat & Jay Youngblood beat Sgt. Slaughter & Pvt. Kernodle
Also including Bugsy McGraw & Great Kabuki

4/3/83: Greensboro, NC @ Coliseum
Red Dog Lane beat Mike Davis
Jake Roberts beat Vinnie Valentino
Mike Rotundo beat Gene Anderson
Great Kabuki, Sgt. Slaughter & Pvt. Kernodle beat Jim Nelson, Ricky Steamboat & Jay Youngblood
Jack & Jerry Brisco beat Dory Funk, Jr. & Paul Jones
Dick Slater beat Roddy Piper to win NWA Mid Atlantic Television Title
Andre the Giant, Jimmy Valiant & Bugsy McGraw beat Greg Valentine, One Man Gang & Oliver Humperdink

4/4/83: Greenville, SC @ Memorial Auditorium
Mike Davis beat Masa Fuchi
Great Kabuki beat Jim Nelson
Jake Roberts beat Johnny Weaver
Jack Brisco beat Red Dog Lane
Andre the Giant, Jimmy Valiant & Bugsy McGraw beat Greg Valentine, One Man Gang & Oliver Humperdink

4/5/83: Columbia, SC @ Township Auditorium
Greg Valentine beat Roddy Piper
Bugsy McGraw, Jerry Brisco & Jos Leduc beat One Man Gang, Dick Slater & Oliver Humperdink
Jimmy Valiant beat One Man Gang
Red Dog Lane beat Wayne Jones
Vinnie Valentino beat Bill White

4/6/83: Charlotte, NC @ WCPQ Studios (TV)
Jack Brisco beat Ken Timbs
Jim Nelson & Mike Rotundo beat Sgt. Slaughter & Pvt. Kernodle by DQ
Jake Roberts beat Vinnie Valentino
Great Kabuki beat Mike Davis & Abe Jacobs
Ricky Steamboat & Jay Youngblood beat Masa Fuchi & Ben Alexander

4/7/83: Norfolk, VA @ Scope
Andre The Giant, Bugsy McGraw & Jimmy Valiant beat Dick Slater, One Man Gang & Oliver Humperdink
Sgt. Slaughter & Pvt. Kernodle beat Ricky Steamboat & Jay Youngblood
Greg Valentine beat Roddy Piper
Ken Timbs beat Wayne Jones
Vinnie Valentino beat Mark Fleming

4/7/83: Sumter, SC @ Exhibition Center
Jack & Jerry Brisco vs. Dory Funk, Jr. & Paul Jones
Johnny Weaver vs. Great Kabuki
Sweet Brown Sugar vs. Jake Roberts
Jos LeDuc vs. Ricky Harris
Mike Rotundo vs. Paul Ellering

4/8/83: Charlotte, NC @ Coliseum
Mike Rotundo beat Masa Fuchi
Red Dog Lane beat Sweet Sugar Brown
Jos LeDuc beat Gene Anderson
Jack & Jerry Brisco beat Jake Roberts & Great Kabuki

Greg Valentine draw Roddy Piper
Andre the Giant, Jimmy Valiant & Bugsy McGraw beat Dick Slater, One Man Gang & Oliver Humperdink
Sgt. Slaughter & Pvt. Kernodle beat Ricky Steamboat & Jay Youngblood in a steel cage match

4/10/83: Asheville, NC @ Civic Center
Mike Davis & Vinnie Valentino beat Gene Anderson & Masa Fuchi
Bugsy McGraw beat Ken Timbs
Bugsy McGraw beat Gene Anderson
Roddy Piper beat Dick Slater
Jimmy Valiant beat Sir Oliver Humperdink no DQ match with Valiant having one hand tied behind back
Pvt. Kernodle & Sgt. Slaughter beat Ricky Steamboat & Jay Youngblood in a steel cage match
NWA World Champ Ric Flair beat Greg Valentine DQ

4/10/83: Toronto, Ontario @ Maple Leaf Gardens
Nick DeCarlo & Bob Marcus beat Kurt Von Hess & Bobby Bass
Jim Nelson draw Sweet Brown Sugar
Johnny Weaver beat Leo Burke wins North American Title
Jimmy Valiant & Tony Parisi beat One Man Gang & Oliver Humperdink
Andre the Giant beat The Destroyer & The Executioner
Jimmy Snuka beat Ray Stevens by CO Texas death match
NWA World Champ Ric Flair beat Roddy Piper by DQ

4/11/83: Greenville, SC @ Memorial Auditorium
Keith Larson beat Ken Timbs
Gene Anderson beat Vinnie Valentino
Great Kabuki beat Mike Davis
Roddy Piper beat Greg Valentine
Dick Slater beat Jos LeDuc in a taped fist match
Sgt. Slaughter & Pvt. Kernodle beat Ricky Steamboat & Jay Youngblood by DQ

4/12/83: Columbia, SC @ Township Auditorium
Sgt. Slaughter & Pvt. Kernodle beat Jay Youngblood & Ricky Steamboat by DQ
Jos Leduc beat Dick Slater
Kabuki beat Mike Rotundo
Jack Brisco beat Jake Roberts
Jerry Brisco beat Ricky Harris
Red Dog Lane beat Bill White

4/13/83: Charlotte, NC @ WCPQ Studios (TV)
Mike Rotundo beat Masa Fuchi
Jimmy Valiant beat Great Kabuki
Jos LeDuc beat Ricky Harris
One Man Gang beat Wayne Jones
Dick Slater & Greg Valentine beat Keith Larson & Sweet Brown Sugar
Jack & Jerry Brisco beat Bill White & Ben Alexander
Jos LeDuc beat Ken Timbs
One Man Gang beat Mike Davis
Bugsy McGraw beat Bill White
Mike Rotundo beat Red Dog Lane
Jake Roberts beat Wayne Jones
Dick Slater & Greg Valentine beat Vinnie Valentino & Sweet Brown Sugar

4/15/83: Charleston SC @ County Hall
Sgt. Slaughter & Pvt. Kernodle beat Ricky Steamboat & Jay Youngblood
Liz Chase beat Leilani Kai
Johnny Weaver beat Ricky Harris
Jim Nelson beat Bill White
Ken Timbs beat Wayne Jones
Mike Davis beat Vinnie Valentino

4/16/83: Spartanburg, SC @ Memorial Auditorium
Bugsy McGraw beat One Man Gang in a tug of war match
Jos LeDuc beat Dick Slater
Mike Rotundo beat Jake Roberts by DQ
Johnny Weaver & Sweet Brown Sugar beat Ricky Harris & Ben Alexander
Keith Larsen beat Vinnie Valentino

4/16/83: Greensboro, NC @ Coliseum
Bill White beat Wayne Jones
Jim Nelson beat Ken Timbs
Gene Anderson beat Mike Davis
Jack & Jerry Brisco beat Red Dog Lane & Masa Fuchi
Jimmy Valiant beat Great Kabuki
Roddy Piper beat Greg Valentine to win NWA US Title
Sgt. Slaughter & Pvt. Kernodle beat Ricky Steamboat & Jay Youngblood by DQ

4/18/83: Greenville, SC @ Memorial Auditorium
Sweet Brown Sugar beat Jacques Goulet
Keith Larson beat Bill White
Pvt. Kernodle beat Jim Nelson in a boot camp match
Jack & Jerry Brisco beat Paul Jones & Jake Roberts
Jimmy Valiant beat Greg Valentine

4/19/83: Columbia, SC @ Township Auditorium
Ricky Steamboat & Jay Youngblood beat Jake Roberts & Red Dog Lane
Pvt. Kernodle beat Jim Nelson
Jake Roberts beat Sweet Brown Sugar
Gene Anderson & Red Dog Lane beat Keith Larsen & Mark Fleming
Bill White beat Vinnie Valentino

4/20/83: Charlotte, NC @ WCPQ Studios (TV)
Jake Roberts beat Wayne Jones
One Man Gang beat Ron Rossi
Magic Dragon & Great Kabuki beat Keith Larson & Mark Fleming
Ricky Steamboat & Jay Youngblood beat Red Dog Lane & Bill White

4/21/83: Harrisonburg, VA @ High School
Magic Dragon vs. Keith Larson
Red Dog Lane vs. Mike Davis
Jos LeDuc vs. Ken Timbs
Great Kabuki vs. Mike Rotundo
Ricky Steamboat & Jay Youngblood vs. Sgt. Slaughter & One Man Gang

4/22/83: Charleston SC @ County Hall
Great Kabuki vs. Mike Rotundo in a Kendo stick match
Sgt. Slaughter vs. Jim Nelson in a boot camp match
Johnny Weaver vs. Magic Dragon

4/24/83: Asheville, NC @ Civic Center
Mike Davis beat Bill White
Jacques Goulet beat Vinnie Valentino
Jack & Jerry Brisco beat Gene Anderson & Red Dog Lane
Jos LeDuc beat One Man Gang
Jimmy Valiant & Bugsy McGraw beat Great Kabuki & Magic Dragon
Roddy Piper beat Dick Slater
NWA World Champ Ric Flair beat Greg Valentine

4/24/83: Charlotte, NC @ Coliseum
Ricky Harris beat Keith Larson
Johnny Weaver beat Masa Fuchi
Magic Dragon beat Jim Nelson
Jake Roberts beat Sweet Brown Sugar
Jimmy Valiant beat Great Kabuki
Roddy Piper beat Dick Slater
Sgt. Slaughter & Pvt. Kernodle beat NWA Tag Team Champs Ricky Steamboat & Jay Youngblood by DQ
NWA World Champ Ric Flair beat Greg Valentine DQ

4/25/83: Greenville, SC @ Memorial Auditorium
Vinnie Valentino beat Masa Fuchi
Johnny Weaver beat Ricky Harris
Jake Roberts beat Sweet Brown Sugar
Jack & Jerry Brisco beat Great Kabuki & Magic Dragon
Roddy Piper beat Greg Valentine in a no DQ match
NWA World Champ Ric Flair beat Dick Slater by DQ

4/25/83: Elizabethton, NC
Jay Youngblood, Jimmy Valiant & Bugsy McGraw beat One Man Gang, Pvt. Kernodle & Oliver Humperdink
Mike Rotundo beat Bill White
Mike Rotundo beat Red Dog Lane
Jim Nelson beat Ken Timbs
Jos LeDuc vs. Gene Anderson

4/26/83: Columbia, SC @ Township Auditorium
Red Dog Lane beat Ricky Harris
Keith Larsen beat Ken Timbs
Roddy Piper, Jos Leduc & Bugsy McGraw beat Greg Valentine, One Man Gang & Oliver Humperdink
NWA World Champ Ric Flair no contest with Jimmy Valiant

4/27/83: Charlotte, NC @ WCPQ Studios (TV)
Johnny Weaver & Mike Rotundo beat Masa Fuchi & Red Dog Lane
Roddy Piper beat Ben Alexander
Rufus R. Jones beat Bill White
Jos LeDuc beat Snake Brown
Magic Dragon & Great Kabuki beat Vinnie Valentino & Ron Rossi
Johnny Weaver & Mike Rotundo beat Ben Alexander & Snake Brown
Rufus R. Jones beat Masa Fuchi
Roddy Piper beat Red Dog Lane
Jack & Jerry Brisco beat Gene Anderson & Bill White
Magic Dragon & Great Kabuki beat Jim Nelson & Keith Larson

4/27/83: Sumter, SC @ Exhibition Center
NWA World Champ Ric Flair vs. Dick Slater
Andre The Giant, Bugsy McGraw & Jimmy Valiant vs. Jake Roberts, One Man Gang & Oliver Humperdink
Sweet Brown Sugar vs. Ricky Harris
Ken Timbs vs. Mike Davis

4/28/83: Norfolk, VA @ Scope
NWA World Champ Ric Flair beat Dick Slater
Jimmy Valiant beat Great Kabuki
Jack & Jerry Brisco beat Jake Roberts & Magic Dragon
Bugsy McGraw beat One Man Gang
Jos Leduc beat Bill White
Gene Anderson beat Sweet Brown Sugar
Ricky Harris beat Mark Fleming
Keith Larsen beat Massa Fuchi

4/29/83: Wilmington, NC
Ricky Steamboat & Jay Youngblood vs. Sgt. Slaughter & Pvt. Kernodle in a steel cage match
Jack & Jerry Brisco vs. Great Kabuki & Magic Dragon
Red Dog Lane vs. Sweet Brown Sugar
Johnny Weaver vs. Ricky Harris
Mike Davis vs. Keith Larson
Wayne Jones vs. Masa Fuchi

4/29/83: Charleston SC @ County Hall
Jos Leduc beat Dick Slater
Jimmy Valiant, Bugsy McGraw & Mike Rotundo beat One Man Gang, Jake Roberts & Oliver Humperdink
Jim Nelson beat Bill White
Vinnie Valentino beat Ken Timbs

4/30/83: Richmond, VA @ Coliseum
Ricky Steamboat & Jay Youngblood beat Sgt. Slaughter & Pvt. Kernodle in a cage match
Roddy Piper beat Greg Valentine
Jimmy Valiant beat Great Kabuki in a New York street fightmatch
Jos Leduc beat Dick Slater to win NWA Mid Atlantic Television Title in a lumberjack match
Jake Roberts beat Mike Graham
Bugsy McGraw beat One Man Gang
Jack & Jerry Brisco beat Gene Anderson & Angelo Mosca
Rufus R. Jones beat Ricky Harris
Mike Rotundo beat Bill White

5/1/83: Greensboro, NC @ Coliseum
Keith Larson beat Ken Timbs
Jos LeDuc beat Ricky Harris
Bugsy McGraw beat One Man Gang
Jake Roberts beat Mike Graham
Dick Slater beat Sweet Brown Sugar
Jack & Jerry Brisco beat Angelo Mosca & Gene Anderson
Jimmy Valiant beat Great Kabuki in a NY street fight
Greg Valentine beat Roddy Piper to win NWA US Title

Ricky Steamboat & Jay Youngblood beat Sgt. Slaughter & Pvt. Kernodle in a no DQ, steel cage match

5/2/83: Greenville, SC @ Memorial Auditorium
Magic Dragon beat Mike Davis
Kelly Kiniski beat Keith Larson
Mike Rotundo beat Jake Roberts
Greg Valentine beat Rufus R. Jones
Jimmy Valiant beat Great Kabuki
Ricky Steamboat & Jay Youngblood DDQ Jack & Jerry Brisco

5/3/83: Columbia, SC @ Township Auditorium
Vinnie Valentino beat Ken Timbs
Kelly Kiniski beat Keith Larson
Johnny Weaver beat Dick Slater by DQ
Pvt. Kernodle beat Jim Nelson in a boot camp match
Greg Valentine beat Rufus R. Jones
Ricky Steamboat & Jay Youngblood DDQ Jack & Jerry Brisco

5/3/83: Raleigh, NC @ Dorton Arena
Vinnie Valentino beat Ken Timbs
Kelly Kiniski beat Keith Larson
Pvt. Kernodle beat Jim Nelson in a boot camp match
Johnny Weaver beat Dick Slater by DQ
Greg Valentine beat Rufus R. Jones
Ricky Steamboat & Jay Youngblood no contest with Jack & Jerry Brisco

5/5/83: Sumter, SC @ Exhibition Center
Ricky Steamboat & Jay Youngblood vs. Greg Valentine & Dick Slater
Jos LeDuc vs. One Man Gang
Jake Roberts vs. Mike Rotundo
Rufus R. Jones vs. Ricky Harris
Wayne Jones vs. Masa Fuchi

5/6/83: Lenoir, NC
Ben Alexander beat Mike Davis
Masa Fuchi beat Abe Jacobs
Mike Rotundo draw Johnny Weaver
Jos LeDuc, Bugsy McGraw & Jimmy Valiant beat Gene Anderson, One Man Gang & Sir Oliver Humperdink

5/6/83: Charleston, SC @ County Hall
Ricky Steamboat & Jay Youngblood beat Greg Valentine & Dick Slater
Jim Nelson beat Jake Roberts
Liz Chase & Susan Starr beat Donna Christianello & Leilani Kai
Ricky Harris beat Vinnie Valentino

5/7/83: Hampton, VA @ Coliseum
Rufus R. Jones & Jimmy Valiant beat Great Kabuki, Magic Dragon & Gary Hart in a handicap match
Dory Funk, Jr. & Jake Roberts beat Dick Slater & Greg Valentine
One Man Gang beat Jos Leduc
Bugsy McGraw beat Bill White
Keith Larson beat Ken Timbs

5/8/83: Savannah, GA @ Civic Center
Tag Tournament(Winner faces NWA World Tag Champs)
1st Round
Jack & Jerry Brisco beat Kelly Kiniski & One Man Gang
Great Kabuki & Magic Dragon beat Jimmy Valiant & Bugsy McGraw
Mike Rotundo & Rufus R. Jones beat Gene Anderson & Greg Valentine
Jake Roberts & Dory Funk, Jr., beat Johnny Weaver & Jim Nelson

Semifinals
Jack & Jerry Brisco beat Great Kabuki & Magic Dragon
Jake Roberts & Dory Funk, Jr., beat Mike Rotundo & Rufus R. Jones

Finals
Jack & Jerry Brisco beat Jake Roberts & Dory Funk, Jr.

5/9/83: Greenville, SC @ Memorial Auditorium
Vinnie Valentino beat Bill White
Jim Nelson beat Ken Timbs
Dory Funk, Jr. & Jake Roberts beat Mike Rotundo & Johnny Weaver
One Man Gang beat Jos LeDuc
Ricky Steamboat & Jay Youngblood DCO with Jack & Jerry Brisco

5/10/83:: Columbia, SC @ Township Auditorium
Kelly Kiniski beat Keith Larsen
Magic Dragon beat Mark Fleming
Jimmy Valiant beat Great Kabuki
Bugsy McGraw beat Greg Valentine by CO
Jos LeDuc beat One Man Gang by DQ

5/11/83:: Charlotte, NC @ WCPQ Studios (TV)
Great Kabuki & Magic Dragon beat Keith Larsen & Ric McCord
Ricky Steamboat & Jay Youngblood beat Jack & Jerry Brisco by DQ
Mike Rotundo & Rufus R. Jones beat Dory Funk, Jr. & Jake Roberts
Dory Funk, Jr. & Jake Roberts beat Keith Larsen & Ric McCord

5/12/83: Norfolk, VA @ Scope
Magic Dragon beat Keith Larsen
Gene Anderson beat Rick McCord
Rufus R. Jones & Mike Rotundo beat Dory Funk, Jr. & Jake Roberts
Greg Valentine beat Johnny Weaver
Ricky Steamboat & Jay Youngblood beat Jack& Jerry Brisco
Jimmy Valiant beat Great Kabuki

5/13/83: Charleston SC @ County Hall
One Man Gang beat Jos Leduc
Jimmy Valiant & Bugsy McGraw beat Great Kabuki & Magic Dragon
Rufus R. Jones beat Ron Cheatham
Kelly Kiniski beat Abe Jacobs
Vinnie Valentino beat Ken Timbs

5/14/83: Roanoke, VA @ Civic Center
Ricky Steamboat & Jay Youngblood no contest with Jack Brisco & Jerry Brisco
Dory Funk, Jr. & Jake Roberts beat Johnny Weaver & Mike Rotundo
Jim Nelson beat Ron Cheatham
Keith Larson beat Jack Brown
Ric McCord beat Bill White
Ricky Harris beat Ken Timbs

5/14/83: Wilmington, NC @ Legion Stadium
Greg Valentine vs. Jimmy Valiant
Bugsy McGraw & Rufus R. Jones vs. Great Kabuki & Magic Dragon
Jos LeDuc vs. One Man Gang
Gene Anderson vs. Vinnie Valentino
Ken Timbs vs. Wayne Jones
Masa Fuchi vs. Abe Jacobs

5/15/83: Charlotte, NC @ Coliseum
Kelly Kiniski & One Man Gang beat Rick McCord & Vinnie Valentino
Dory Funk, Jr. beat Mike Rotundo
Jimmy Valiant, Rufus R. Jones & Bugsy McGraw beat Great Kabuki, Gary Hart & Magic Dragon
Greg Valentine beat Jos LeDuc
Jack & Jerry Brisco beat Sgt. Slaughter & Pvt. Kernodle
Ricky Steamboat & Jay Youngblood beat Sgt. Slaughter & Pvt. Kernodle
Jack & Jerry Brisco beat Ricky Steamboat & Jay Youngblood by DQ in finals of round robin tournament

5/15/83: Asheville, NC @ Civic Center
Bill White beat Ken Timbs
Kelly Kiniski beat Abe Jacobs
Jos LeDuc & Rufus R. Jones beat Kelly Kiniski & One Man Gang
Dory Funk, Jr. beat Mike Rotundo
Greg Valentine beat Bugsy McGraw
Jack & Jerry Brisco beat Ricky Steamboat & Jay Youngblood

5/15/83: Toronto, Ontario @ Maple Leaf Gardens
Bob Marcus beat Ricky Harris(9:21)
Mike Sharpe beat Joe Marcus(8:09)
Gene Kiniski & The Executioner beat Salvatore Bellomo & Nick DeCarlo(15:04)
Jim Nelson beat Keith Larson(14:06) via pinfall
Johnny Weaver beat Leo Burke(18:52)
Rocky Johnson beat Don Muraco(11:21) by CO
Roddy Piper beat Terry Funk(11:14) by CO
Angelo Mosca beat Bob Orton, Jr.(10:12)

5/16/83: Fayetteville, NC @ Cumberland County Civic Center
Mike Rotundo draw Jake Roberts

5/16/83: Greenville, SC @ Memorial Auditorium
Kelly Kiniski beat Vinnie Valentino
Rufus R. Jones beat Magic Dragon
Jimmy Valiant beat Great Kabuki
Greg Valentine beat Dory Funk, Jr.
Jos LeDuc beat One Man Gang

5/17/83: Raleigh, NC @ Dorton Arena
Rick McCord beat Masa Fuchi
Mike Rotundo beat Gene Anderson
Jimmy Valiant & Bugsy McGraw beat Great Kabuki & Magic Dragon
Rufus R. Jones beat Jake Roberts by DQ
Greg Valentine beat Dory Funk, Jr.

5/17/83: Columbia, SC @ Township Auditorium
Jack & Jerry Brisco beat Jay Youngblood & Ricky Steamboat by DQ
Jos Leduc & Johnny Weaver beat One Man Gang & Oliver Humperdink
Kelly Kiniski beat Vinnie Valentino
Bill White beat Abe Jacobs
Keith Larson beat Ricky Harris
Ken Timbs beat Ken Hall

5/18/83: Charlotte, NC @ WCPQ Studios (TV)
Greg Valentine beat Ken Hall
One Man Gang & Kelly Kiniski beat Rick McCord & Vinnie Valentino
Jim Nelson beat Jack Brisco by DQ
Jos LeDuc beat Rick Connors
Jake Roberts & Dory Funk, Jr. beat Keith Larson & Masa Fuchi

5/19/83: Sumter, SC @ Exhibition Center
Jimmy Valiant & Bugsy McGraw vs. Great Kabuki & Magic Dragon
One Man Gang & Kelly Kiniski vs. Jack Brisco & Jerry Brisco
Jos LeDuc vs. Ron Cheatham
Johnny Weaver vs. Masa Fuchi
Vinnie Valentino vs. Ken Timbs

5/20/83: Charleston, SC @ County Hall
Jack & Jerry Brisco beat Ricky Steamboat & Jay Youngblood by DQ
Dory Funk, Jr. beat Jack Brown
Jake Roberts beat Rick Connors
Ricky Harris beat Ken Hall
Vinnie Valentino beat Red Dog Lane

5/21/83: Spartanburg, SC @ Memorial Auditorium
Dory Funk, Jr. beat Mike Rotundo
Bugsy McGraw beat One Man Gang via pinfall
Johnny Weaver & Rick McCord beat Kelly Kiniski & Jack Brown(sub for Ron Cheatham)
Liz Chase beat Peggy Lee(sub for Terri Shane)
Abe Jacobs beat Ricky Harris
Ken Timbs beat Ben Alexander

5/21/83: Greensboro, NC @ Coliseum
Keith Larson beat Masa Fuchi
Bill White beat Ken Hall
Gene Anderson & Magic Dragon beat Rick Connors & Vinnie Valentino
Johnny Weaver beat Ricky Harris
Rufus R. Jones beat Jake Roberts

Great Kabuki beat Jimmy Valiant
Greg Valentine beat Jos LeDuc
Jack & Jerry Brisco beat Ricky Steamboat & Jay Youngblood by DQ

5/22/83: Roanoke, VA @ Civic Center
Ricky Steamboat & Jay Youngblood beat Jack Brisco & Jerry Brisco
Rufus R. Jones beat Gene Anderson
Bob Orton, Jr. beat Masa Fuchi
Abe Jacobs beat Kenny Hall
Wahoo McDaniel, Jimmy Valiant & Bugsy McGraw beat Great Kabuki, Magic Dragon & Gary Hart

5/23/83: Greenville, SC @ Memorial Auditorium
One Man Gang & Kelly Kiniski beat Jimmy Valiant & Bugsy McGraw in NWA Mid Atlantic Tag Title tournament
Mike Rotundo & Rufus R. Jones beat Dory Funk, Jr. & Jake Roberts in NWA Mid Atlantic Tag Title tournament
Keith Larson beat Jacques Goulet
Rick McCord beat Magic Dragon
Great Kabuki beat Jos LeDuc to win NWA Mid Atlantic Television Title
One Man Gang & Kelly Kiniski beat Mike Rotundo & Rufus R. Jones to win NWA Mid Atlantic Tag Title in tournament final
Jack & Jerry Brisco beat Ricky Steamboat & Jay Youngblood by DQ

5/24/83: Columbia, SC @ Township Auditorium
Dory Funk, Jr. & Jake Roberts beat Mike Rotundo & Rufus R. Jones

5/24/83: Raleigh, NC @ Dorton Arena
Masa Fuchi & Ricky Harris beat Red Dog Lane & Abe Jacobs
Vinnie Valentino beat Bill White
Jacques Goulet beat Ken Hall
Rick McCord beat Gene Anderson
One Man Gang beat Jos LeDuc
Jack & Jerry Brisco beat Ricky Steamboat & Jay Youngblood by DQ

5/25/83: Charlotte, NC @ WCPQ Studios (TV)
Bob Orton, Jr. beat Ricky Harris
Greg Valentine beat Keith Larson
One Man Gang & Kelly Kiniski beat Ken Hall & Vinnie Valentino
Jimmy Valiant & Rufus R. Jones beat Jack & Jerry Brisco
Jake Roberts beat Rick McCord

5/26/83: Norfolk, VA @ Scope
Rufus R. Jones beat Jake Roberts
NWA World Champ Ric Flair beat Greg Valentine

5/27/83: Charleston, SC @ County Hall
Jimmy Valiant beat Great Kabuki
Rufus R. Jones beat Jake Roberts
Bugsy McGraw beat Magic Dragon
Ricky Harris & Masa Fuchi beat Abe Jacobs & Red Dog Lane

5/27/83: Richmond, VA @ Coliseum
Johnny Weaver vs. Jacques Goulet
Mike Rotundo vs. Kelly Kiniski
Bob Orton, Jr. vs. Gene Anderson
Jos LeDuc vs. One Man Gang
Ricky Steamboat & Jay Youngblood vs. Jack Brisco & Jerry Brisco
NWA World Champ Ric Flair beat Greg Valentine

5/28/83: Charlotte, NC @ Coliseum
Gene Anderson & Jacques Goulet beat Mike Davis & Keith Larson
Vinnie Valentino beat Masa Fuchi
Bob Orton, Jr. beat Bill White
Wahoo McDaniel beat Magic Dragon
Great Kabuki beat Jimmy Valiant by CO
Ricky Steamboat & Jay Youngblood beat Jack Brisco & Jerry Brisco
Greg Valentine beat NWA World Champ Ric Flair by DQ

5/29/83: Asheville, NC @ Civic Center
Vinnie Valentino beat Bill White
Keith Larson & Mike Davis beat Jacques Goulet & Ricky Harris
Wahoo McDaniel beat Jake Roberts
Dory Funk, Jr. beat Mike Rotundo
Ricky Steamboat & Jay Youngblood beat Jack Brisco & Jerry Brisco
Greg Valentine beat NWA World Champ Ric Flair

5/29/83: Toronto, Ontario @ Maple Leaf Gardens
NWA World Champ Ric Flair beat Greg Valentine
Don Muraco beat Rocky Johnson
Mike Rotundo beat Dory Funk, Jr. in a $100,000 challenge match
Leo Burke beat Johnny Weaver
Kelly Kiniski beat Nick DeCarlo
The Executioner beat Joe Marcus
Billy Red Lyons beat Tim Gerrard
Bob Marcus beat Alex Gerrard

5/30/83: Wilmington, NC
Wahoo McDaniel vs. Greg Valentine
Ricky Steamboat & Jay Youngblood vs. Jack Brisco & Jerry Brisco
Jos LeDuc vs. Great Kabuki
Magic Dragon vs. Mike Davis
Ricky Harris vs. Vinnie Valentino

5/31/83: Columbia, SC @ Township Auditorium
Mike Rotundo & Rufus R. Jones beat Dory Funk, Jr. & Jake Roberts

6/??/83: Rocky Mount, NC
Greg Valentine beat Wahoo McDaniel
Jos Leduc beat Great Kabuki
One Man Gang beat Jimmy Valiant by DQ
Bugsy McGraw beat Magic Dragon
Johnny Weaver beat Rick McCord
Keith Larsen beat Bill White

6/1/83: Charlotte, NC @ WCPQ Studios (TV)
Jimmy Valiant & Rufus R. Jones beat Jacques Goulet & Bill White
Greg Valentine beat Vinnie Valentino
Dory Funk, Jr. beat Brett Hart(Barry Horowitz)
Great Kabuki beat Keith Larson
Greg Valentine beat Brett Hart
Bob Orton, Jr. beat Bill White
Bugsy McGraw beat Ben Alexander
Dory Funk, Jr. beat Vinnie Valentino
Keith Larson beat Great Kabuki by DQ

6/2/83: Sumter, SC @ Exhibition Center
Greg Valentine beat Wahoo McDaniel
Rufus R. Jones beat Great Kabuki
Bugsy McGraw & Bob Orton, Jr. beat Gene Anderson & Kelly Kiniski
Magic Dragon beat Abe Jacobs
Bill White beat Jacques Goulet

6/3/83: Charleston, SC @ County Hall
Greg Valentine beat Wahoo McDaniel
Johnny Weaver & Rufus R. Jones beat Great Kabuki & Magic Dragon
Bob Orton, Jr. beat Kelly Kiniski
Gene Anderson beat Brett Hart
Jacques Goulet beat Bill White

6/4/83: Greensboro, NC @ Coliseum
Greg Valentine vs. Wahoo McDaniel
Jimmy Valiant vs. Great Kabuki
Ricky Steamboat & Jay Youngblood vs. Jack Brisco & Jerry Brisco

6/5/83: Hampton, VA @ Coliseum
Mike Rotundo beat Kelly Kiniski
Bob Orton, Jr. beat Jacques Goulet
Rufus R. Jones beat Great Kabuki
Ricky Steamboat & Jay Youngblood beat Jack Brisco & Jerry Brisco
Wahoo McDaniel beat Greg Valentine by DQ

6/6/83: Greenville, SC @ Memorial Auditorium
Abe Jacobs beat Ben Alexander
Gene Anderson beat Brett Hart
Magic Dragon beat Vinnie Valentino
Jimmy Valiant & Johnny Weaver beat One Man Gang & Kelly Kiniski by DQ
Great Kabuki beat Jos LeDuc
Greg Valentine beat Bob Orton, Jr.

6/8/83: Charlotte, NC @ WCPQ Studios (TV)
Ricky Steamboat & Jay Youngblood beat Bill White & Masa Fuchi
Greg Valentine beat Mark Fleming
Magic Dragon & Great Kabuki beat Rick McCord & Brett Hart
Jake Roberts beat Mike Davis
Bob Orton, Jr. beat Ben Alexander
Ricky Steamboat & Jay Youngblood beat Brett Hart & Rick McCord
Greg Valentine beat Mike Davis
Bob Orton, Jr. beat Masa Fuchi
Jake Roberts beat Vinnie Valentino
Magic Dragon & Great Kabuki beat Mark Fleming & Keith Larson

6/9/83: Harrisonburg, VA @ High School
Jos LeDuc & Bugsy McGraw vs. One Man Gang & Oliver Humperdink in a cage match
Great Kabuki vs. Johnny Weaver

6/10/83: Charleston SC @ County Hall
Dory Funk, Jr. DDQ Great Kabuki
Jake Roberts beat Mike Rotundo
Magic Dragon beat Ric McCord
Bill White beat Brett Hart
Masa Fuchi beat Abe Jacobs

6/11/83: Roanoke, VA @ Civic Center
Greg Valentine beat Ric Flair by DQ

6/11/83: Spartanburg, SC @ Memorial Auditorium
Keith Larson & Rick McCord beat Masa Fuchi & Bill White
Jos LeDuc(sub for Johnny Weaver) beat Kelly Kiniski
Johnny Weaver(sub for Jay Youngblood) beat Magic Dragon
Dick Slater vs. Jos LeDuc
Rufus R. Jones beat Great Kabuki

6/12/83: Columbia, SC @ Township Auditorium
Vinnie Valentino beat Abe Jacobs
Magic Dragon beat Brett Hart
Jake Roberts beat Mike Davis
Keith Larsen & Rick McCord beat Ben Alexander & Gene Anderson
Rufus R. Jones & Jimmy Valiant beat Jack & Jerry Brisco
Greg Valentine beat Ric Flair by DQ

6/12/83: Toronto, Ontario @ Maple Leaf Gardens
Kelly Kiniski & Jacques Goulet beat John Bonello & Don Kolov
Bob Marcus beat Bill White
Nick DeCarlo beat Joe Marcus
Dick Slater beat Jos LeDuc
Johnny Weaver beat Leo Burke
Great Kabuki beat Mike Rotundo
Sgt. Slaughter beat Jay Youngblood
Don Muraco beat Angelo Mosca by DQ

6/12/83: Savannah, GA @ Civic Center
Chavo Guerrero DCO with Masa Fuchi(9:51)
Giant Baba & Genichiro Tenryu beat Jake Roberts & Jerry Grey(6:47) via pinfall
Terry Funk beat Bret Hart(5:47) by submission
Rufus R. Jones beat Dory Funk, Jr. by DQ
Jack & Jerry Brisco beat Jimmy Valiant & Bob Orton, Jr. via pinfall
Bruiser Brody DCO with Jumbo Tsuruta(15:56)
Greg Valentine beat Ric Flair(12:17) by DQ

6/13/83: Greenville, SC @ Memorial Auditorium
Vinnie Valentino vs. Masa Fuchi
One Man Gang vs. Cy Jernigan
Rick McCord vs. Magic Dragon
Jack & Jerry Brisco vs. Jimmy Valiant & Bob Orton, Jr.
Ric Flair beat Greg Valentine

6/14/83: Raleigh, NC @ Dorton Arena
Ric Flair beat Greg Valentine by DQ

6/15/83: Charlotte, NC @ WCPQ Studios (TV)
Bob Orton, Jr. beat Bill Howard
Jake Roberts & Dory Funk, Jr. beat Mike Davis & Mark Fleming
Great Kabuki beat John Bonello
Dick Slater beat Keith Larson
Bob Orton, Jr. beat Jerry Gray
Jake Roberts & Dory Funk, Jr. beat Mark Fleming & Brett Hart
Great Kabuki beat Keith Larson
Dick Slater beat Mike Davis

6/15/83: Sumter, SC @ Exhibition Center
Greg Valentine vs. Ric Flair
Rufus R. Jones & Jimmy Valiant vs. Jack Brisco & Jerry Brisco
Kim Duk vs. Cy Jernigan
Jacques Goulet vs. Abe Jacobs
Rick McCord vs. Bill White

6/16/83: Norfolk, VA @ Scope
Ric Flair beat Greg Valentine by DQ
Ricky Steamboat & Jay Youngblood beat Jack Brisco & Jerry Brisco
Jimmy Valiant beat Dory Funk, Jr. by DQ
Dick Slater beat Johnny Weaver
Jake Roberts beat Vinnie Valentino
Mike Davis beat Masa Fuchi
Keith Larson beat Bill Howard

6/17/83: Charleston, SC @ County Hall
Greg Valentine beat Rufus R. Jones
Jerry Gray beat Vinnie Valentino
Bill White beat Red Dog Lane
Kelly Kiniski beat Ric McCord
Jacques Goulet beat Brett Hart
Dick Slater beat Johnny Weaver

6/18/83: Greenville, SC @ Memorial Auditorium
Vinnie Valentino beat Bill White
Kelly Kiniski beat Brett Hart
Bob Orton, Jr. beat Kim Duk
Dick Slater beat Johnny Weaver
Jack & Jerry Brisco beat Ricky Steamboat & Jay Youngblood to win NWA World Tag Title
Greg Valentine & Dory Funk, Jr. beat Ric Flair & Roddy Piper by DQ

6/19/83: Wilmington, NC
Ric Flair & Roddy Piper vs. Greg Valentine & Dick Slater
Jack & Jerry Brisco vs. Rufus R. Jones & Jimmy Valiant
OMG & Kelly Kiniski vs. Bob Orton, Jr. & Jos LeDuc

6/20/83: Burlington, NC
Johnny Weaver vs. Dick Slater

6/21/83: Columbia, SC @ Township Auditorium
Ric Flair beat Greg Valentine by DQ
Dory Funk, Jr. beat Johnny Weaver
One Man Gang & Kelly Kiniski beat Jos LeDuc & Bob Orton, Jr.
Mike Davis beat Bill White
Gene Anderson beat John Bonello

6/22/83: Charlotte, NC @ WCPQ Studios (TV)
Dory Funk, Jr. beat John Bonello
Ricky Steamboat & Jay Youngblood beat Bill Howard & Masa Fuchi
Jimmy Valiant & Bob Orton, Jr. beat Magic Dragon & Great Kabuki
Jake Roberts beat Rick McCord
Greg Valentine DDQ Mike Rotundo
Jake Roberts beat Mike Davis
Ricky Steamboat & Jay Youngblood beat Jerry Gray & Masa Fuchi
Jimmy Valiant & Bob Orton, Jr. beat Ben Alexander & Bill White
Jos LeDuc beat Bill Howard

6/24/83: Richmond, VA @ Coliseum
Bob Orton, Jr. vs. Jake Roberts
Rufus R. Jones vs. Dick Slater
Dick Slater vs. Jos LeDuc
Jack & Jerry Brisco vs. Ricky Steamboat & Jay Youngblood
Ric Flair beat Greg Valentine by DQ

6/24/83: Charleston SC @ County Hall
Great Kabuki beat Jimmy Valiant
One Man Gang & Kelly Kiniski beat Mike Rotundo & Johnny Weaver
Magic Dragon beat Mike Davis
Gene Anderson beat Keith Larsen

6/25/83: Charlotte, NC @ Coliseum
Mike Rotundo beat Kelly Kiniski
Jos LeDuc beat One Man Gang
Jake Roberts beat Bob Orton, Jr.
Rufus R. Jones beat Magic Dragon
Great Kabuki beat Jimmy Valiant
Ric Flair & Roddy Piper beat Greg Valentine & Dory Funk, Jr.
Jack & Jerry Brisco beat Ricky Steamboat & Jay Youngblood

6/26/83: Asheville, NC @ Civic Center
Masa Fuchi beat Mark Fleming
Jacques Goulet beat Rick McCord
Gene Anderson beat John Bonello
Keith Larson beat Ben Alexander
Ric Flair & Roddy Piper beat Greg Valentine & Jake Roberts
Jack & Jerry Brisco beat Ricky Steamboat & Jay Youngblood

6/27/83: Greenville, SC @ Memorial Auditorium
Gene Anderson beat Jacques Goulet
Keith Larson beat Rick McCord
Kelly Kiniski beat John Bonello
Bob Orton, Jr. beat Magic Dragon
Rufus R. Jones beat Bill White
Ric Flair beat Dory Funk, Jr.
Jack & Jerry Brisco beat Ricky Steamboat & Jay Youngblood

6/28/83: Columbia, SC @ Township Auditorium
Ric Flair & Roddy Piper beat Greg Valentine & Dory Funk, Jr.

6/29/83: Charlotte, NC @ WPCQ Studios (TV)
Greg Valentine beat John Bonello
Jack & Jerry Brisco beat Rick McCord & Keith Larson
Jimmy Valiant & Bob Orton, Jr. beat Joel Deaton & Bill Howard
Dick Slater beat Vinnie Valentino
Jake Roberts & Dory Funk, Jr. beat Brett Hart & Mike Davis
Bob Orton, Jr. beat Bill Howard
One Man Gang & Kelly Kiniski beat Rick McCord & Keith Larson
Dick Slater & Greg Valentine beat Jerry Gray & Masa Fuchi
Jack & Jerry Brisco beat Mike Davis & Brett Hart
Note: 6/29/83: was the final television taping at WPCQ in Charlotte, NC
Starting on 7/6/83:, the taping were mobile at different locations, the first being in Greenville, SC on 7/4/83:

7/1/83: Charleston SC @ County Hall
Ric Flair & Roddy Piper beat Greg Valentine & One Man Gang
Mike Rotundo beat Kelly Kiniski
Johnny Weaver beat Bill White
Mark Fleming beat Bill Howard
Mike Davis beat Red Dog Lane

7/1/83: Lovington, VA
Cy Jernigan beat Joel Deaton
Ricky Steamboat & Jay Youngblood beat Jack & Jerry Brisco
Princess Victoria & Susan Starr beat Terry Shane & Leilani Kai
Keith Larsen beat Vinnie Valentino
Ric McCord beat Masa Fuchi

7/2/83: Greensboro, NC @ Coliseum
NWA World Champ Harley Race beat Ric Flair by DQ
Jack & Jerry Brisco beat Ricky Steamboat & Jay Youngblood
Roddy Piper & Wahoo McDaniel no contest with Greg Valentine & Dory Funk, Jr.
Jimmy Valiant & Rufus R. Jones beat Gary Hart & Great Kabuki
Dick Slater beat John Bonello
Susan Starr beat Leilani Kai
Gene Anderson beat Joel Deaton

7/3/83: Wilmington, NC
Jack & Jerry Brisco vs. Ricky Steamboat & Jay Youngblood
Jimmy Valiant vs. Great Kabuki
Jake Roberts vs. Mike Rotundo
Bob Orton, Jr. vs. Kelly Kiniski
Masa Fuchi vs. Vinnie Valentino
Mark Fleming vs. Jerry Gray

7/3/83: Savannah, GA @ Civic Center
NWA World Champ Harley Race beat Ric Flair by DQ
Wahoo McDaniel & Roddy Piper beat Greg Valentine & Dory Funk, Jr.
One Man Gang beat Jos Leduc
Dick Slater beat Johnny Weaver
Keith Larson & Ric McCord beat Jacques Goulet & Bill White
John Bonello beat Bill Howard

7/4/83: Greenville, SC @ Memorial Auditorium (TV)
NWA World Champ Harley Race DDQ Ric Flair
Jimmy Valiant beat Bill Howard
Mike Rotundo beat Bill White
The Assassin(Ray Hernandez) beat Mike Davis
Note: Ray Hernandez came in initially without partner Jody Hamilton. When Hamilton arrived, Ray Hernandez became Assassin # 2
Great Kabuki beat Gary Royal
Dick Slater & Jake Roberts beat Rick McCord & Keith Larson
Bob Orton, Jr. beat Jerry Gray
Mike Rotundo beat Bill Howard
Dick Slater & Jake Roberts beat Mike Davis & Keith Larson
Armand Hussein beat Red Dog Lane
The Assassin beat Gary Royal
Great Kabuki beat Joel Deaton

7/4/83: Columbia, SC @ Township Auditorium
Bob Orton, Jr. draw Dick Slater
Jack & Jerry Brisco beat Ricky Steamboat & Jay Youngblood
Ric Flair beat NWA World Champ Harley Race by DQ

7/5/83: Raleigh, NC @ Dorton Arena
Jos LeDuc beat Armand Hussein
Bugsy McGraw beat Magic Dragon
One Man Gang beat Mike Rotundo
Jake Roberts beat Rufus R. Jones
Roddy Piper & Jimmy Valiant beat Dory Funk, Jr. & Greg Valentine
NWA World Champ Harley Race DCO with Ric Flair

7/6/83: Sumter, SC @ Exhibition Center
NWA World Champ Harley Race DDQ Ric Flair
Roddy Piper & Bob Orton, Jr. vs. Greg Valentine & Jake Roberts

7/7/83: Norfolk, VA @ Scope
NWA World Champ Harley Race beat Wahoo McDaniel
Jake Roberts & Greg Valentine beat Ric Flair & Roddy Piper by DQ

Great Kabuki beat Jimmy Valiant
Dick Slater beat Johnny Weaver
Rufus R. Jones beat Magic Dragon
Jos Leduc beat Armand Hussein
Bugsy McGraw beat Bill Howard

7/8/83: Charleston, SC @ County Hall
Jimmy Valiant & Rufus R. Jones vs. Great Kabuki & Gary Hart
Bugsy McGraw vs. Magic Dragon
Johnny Weaver vs. Armand Hussein
Jacques Goulet vs. John Bonello
Keith Larsen vs. Jerry Gray

7/8/83: Richmond, VA @ Coliseum
One Man Gang beat Mike Rotundo
Bob Orton, Jr. beat Jake Roberts
Wahoo McDaniel & Roddy Piper beat Dory Funk, Jr. & Greg Valentine
Jack & Jerry Brisco beat Ricky Steamboat & Jay Youngblood
Ric Flair beat NWA World Champ Harley Race by DQ

7/9/83: Charlotte, NC @ Coliseum
Keith Larson & Rick McCord beat Gene Anderson & Bill Howard
The Assassin beat John Bonello
Jake Roberts beat Mike Davis
Dick Slater beat Jos LeDuc
Greg Valentine beat Roddy Piper by DQ
Jack & Jerry Brisco beat Ricky Steamboat & Jay Youngblood
Ric Flair beat NWA World Champ Harley Race by DQ

7/10/83: Asheville, NC @ Civic Center
Rick McCord & Keith Larson beat Gene Anderson & Bill White
Keith Larson beat Jerry Gray
The Assassin beat Brett Hart
Wahoo McDaniel beat Magic Dragon
Greg Valentine beat Roddy Piper by DQ
NWA World Champ Harley Race NC with Ric Flair
Jack & Jerry Brisco beat Bob Orton, Jr. & Rufus R. Jones

7/10/83: Toronto, Ontario @ Exhibition Stadium
Nick DeCarlo & Billy Red Lyons beat The Executioner & Bill Armstrong
Kelly Kiniski & Jacques Goulet beat Bob Marcus & Joe Marcus
Johnny Weaver & Mike Rotundo beat Alec Gerrard & Tim Gerrard
Fabulous Moolah beat Princess Victoria
Dick Slater beat Nick DeCarlo(sub for Jos LeDuc)
Great Kabuki beat Jimmy Valiant
Ricky Steamboat & Jay Youngblood beat Jake Roberts & Dory Funk, Jr.
Angelo Mosca beat One Man Gang
Greg Valentine NC with Wahoo McDaniel
Ric Flair beat NWA World Champ Harley Race by DQ

7/11/83: Greenville, SC @ Memorial Auditorium
Roddy Piper beat Greg Valentine by DQ
Dory Funk, Jr. beat Rufus R. Jones
Mike Rotundo beat Jake Roberts
Bugsy McGraw beat Magic Dragon
John Bonello beat Gary Royal
Brett Hart beat Joel Deaton

7/12/83: Raleigh, NC @ Dorton Arena
Ric Flair & Rufus R. Jones beat Dory Funk, Jr. & Jake Roberts

7/14/83: Harrisonburg, VA @ High School
Cy Jernigan beat Tom Lentz
Masa Fuchi beat Jerry Grey
The Assassin beat Keith Larsen
Mike Davis beat Jake Roberts
Jack & Jerry Brisco beat Ricky Steamboat & Jay Youngblood

7/15/83: Hampton, VA @ Civic Center
The Assassin beat Masa Fuchi
Keith Larsen beat Gene Anderson
Armand Hussein & Jake Roberts beat Mike Davis & Vinnie Valentino
Dory Funk, Jr. beat Johnny Weaver
Roddy Piper beat Greg Valentine
Jack & Jerry Brisco beat Ricky Steamboat & Jay Youngblood

7/15/83: Charleston, SC @ County Hall
Jimmy Valiant & Rufus R. Jones vs. Great Kabuki & Gary Hart in a steel cage match
Dick Slater vs. Ric McCord
Magic Dragon vs. Brett Hart
Joel Deaton vs. Abe Jacobs
Red Dog Lane vs. Jerry Gray

7/16/83: Spartanburg, SC @ Memorial Auditorium
Masa Fuchi vs. Cy Jernigan
Bill Howard beat Mark Fleming
Kelly Kiniski beat Mike Davis(sub for Johnny Weaver)
Bugsy McGraw beat One Man Gang
Jimmy Valiant, Bob Orton, Jr. & Johnny Weaver(sub for Jos LeDuc) beat Great Kabuki, Magic Dragon & Gary Hart

7/17/83: Greensboro, NC @ Coliseum
Ric Flair beat NWA World Champ Harley Race by DQ

7/18/83: Greenville, SC @ Memorial Auditorium
Ricky Steamboat & Jay Youngblood beat Jack & Jerry Brisco by DQ
Bugsy McGraw beat One Man Gang
Keith Larsen & Rick McCord beat Magic Dragon & Masa Fuchi
Mike Davis beat Tom Lentz
Jimmy Valiant & Bob Orton, Jr. beat Great Kabuki & Gary Hart by CO

7/19/83: Columbia, SC @ Township Auditorium
Ric Flair beat NWA World Champ Harley Race by DQ
Jack & Jerry Brisco beat Ricky Steamboat & Jay Youngblood
Bob Orton, Jr. draw Dick Slater
The Assassin beat Mike Davis
Vinnie Valentino & John Bonello beat Gene Anderson & Masa Fuchi

7/20/83: Emporia, VA
Rufus R. Jones & Bugsy McGraw beat One Man Gang & Kelly Kiniski to win NWA Mid Atlantic Tag Title

7/20/83: Winston-Salem, NC @ Memorial Coliseum (TV)
Dory Funk, Jr. vs. Rufus R. Jones
NWA World Champ Harley Race vs. Ric Flair
Jerry Gray beat Ric Flair
Jack & Jerry Brisco beat John Bonello & Vinnie Valentino by DQ
Great Kabuki beat Brett Hart
The Assassins beat Rick McCord & Keith Larson
Dick Slater beat Mike Davis
also included Jimmy Valiant, Greg Valentine, Roddy Piper, Ricky Steamboat & Jay Youngblood & Jos LeDuc

7/21/83: Norfolk, VA @ Scope
Keith Larsen beat Bill Howard
Mike Davis beat Gene Anderson
Dick Slater beat Cy Jernigan
The Assassin beat Barry Hart
Ric Flair & Rufus R. Jones beat Dory Funk, Jr. & Jake Roberts
Jack & Jerry Brisco beat Mike Rotundo & Ricky Steamboat
NWA World Champ Harley Race beat Bob Orton, Jr.

7/21/83: Sumter, SC @ Exhibition Center
Armand Hussein beat Rick McCord
Kelly Kiniski beat John Bonello
Bugsy McGraw, Jimmy Valiant & Johnny Weaver beat Great Kabuki, Magic Dragon & Gary Hart
Roddy Piper beat Greg Valentine by DQ

7/22/83: Charleston, SC @ County Hall
Jack & Jerry Brisco beat Johnny Weaver(sub for Ricky Steamboat) & Jay Youngblood
Bugsy McGraw beat Jake Roberts
Kelly Kiniski beat Ric McCord
Vinnie Valentino & Brett Hart beat Magic Dragon & Masa Fuchi
Tom Lentz beat John Bonello

7/22/83: Richmond, VA @ Coliseum
Keith Larson & Cy Jernigan beat Gene Anderson & Bill Howard
The Assassin beat Mike Davis
Dick Slater DCO with Bob Orton, Jr.
Great Kabuki beat Mike Rotundo
Dory Funk, Jr. beat Rufus R. Jones
Roddy Piper beat Greg Valentine by DQ
NWA World Champ Harley Race beat Ric Flair by DQ
Jimmy Valiant beat One Man Gang & Oliver Humperdink in a handicap hair vs. hair, loser leaves town, steel cage match

7/23/83: Charlotte, NC @ Coliseum
Jacques Goulet beat John Bonello
Vinnie Valentino beat Jerry Gray
Dick Slater & Jake Roberts beat Johnny Weaver & Brett Hart
Dory Funk, Jr. beat Rufus R. Jones
Jimmy Valiant & Bob Orton, Jr. beat Great Kabuki & Gary Hart in a steel cage match
Ric Flair beat NWA World Champ Harley Race by DQ

7/24/83: Asheville, NC @ Civic Center
Brett Hart beat Tom Lentz
The Assassin beat Keith Larson
Magic Dragon beat John Bonello
Dick Slater beat Bugsy McGraw
Jack & Jerry Brisco beat Ric Flair & Roddy Piper
NWA World Champ Harley Race beat Ricky Steamboat by DQ

7/24/83: Toronto, Ontario @ Exhibition Stadium
Rufus R. Jones beat Jake Roberts
Greg Valentine beat Cy Jernigan
Dory Funk, Jr. beat Mike Rotundo
Jimmy Valiant & Bob Orton, Jr. beat Great Kabuki & Gary Hart in a steel cage match
Jack & Jerry Brisco beat Ricky Steamboat & Jay Youngblood by DQ
Sgt. Slaughter beat Angelo Mosca(22:18) to win NWA Canadian Title
NWA World Champ Harley Race beat Ric Flair by DQ

7/25/83: Greenville, SC @ Memorial Auditorium
Roddy Piper beat Greg Valentine
Ric Flair beat Dick Slater
Bob Orton, Jr. & Jimmy Valiant beat Kabuki & Gary Hart
Magic Dragon beat Gary Hart
Keith Larson beat Joel Deaton

7/26/83: Columbia, SC @ Township Auditorium
Ric Flair & Ricky Steamboat beat Jack & Jerry Brisco by DQ
Roddy Piper beat Greg Valentine

7/27/83: Spartanburg, SC @ Memorial Auditorium (TV)
Jack & Jerry Brisco beat Ric Flair & Roddy Piper by DQ
Ricky Steamboat & Jay Youngblood beat Jack & Jerry Brisco by DQ
Greg Valentine beat Brett Hart
Great Kabuki beat Keith Larson
Bob Orton, Jr. beat Joel Deaton
Rufus R. Jones beat Dory Funk, Jr.
Jimmy Valiant & Roddy Piper & Mike Rotundo beat Masa Fuchi & Kelly Kiniski & Bill Howard
Greg Valentine beat Mike Davis
Dick Slater beat Ben Alexander
The Assassins beat Rick McCord & Brett Hart
Ric Flair beat NWA World Champ Harley Race

7/27/83: Lumberton, NC @ Recreation Center
Jimmy Valiant & Rufus R. Jones vs. Dory Funk, Jr. & Jake Roberts
Kelly Kiniski vs. Vinnie Valentino
Jacques Goulet vs. Mark Fleming
Cy Jernigan vs. Abe Jacobs

7/29/83: Culpeper, VA
Jimmy Valiant & Bob Orton, Jr. beat Great Kabuki & Gary Hart

7/29/83: Charleston, SC @ County Hall
Rufus R. Jones beat Dory Funk, Jr. by DQ
One Man Gang beat Bugsy McGraw
Mike Rotundo beat Kelly Kiniski
Jake Roberts beat Brett Hart
Gene Anderson beat Vinnie Valentino
Abe Jacobs beat Masa Fuchi

7/30/83: Wilmington, NC
Jimmy Valiant & Bob Orton, Jr. vs. Great Kabuki & Gary Hart in a steel cage match
Greg Valentine vs. Roddy Piper
Keith Larson & Rick McCord vs. Bill Howard & Jacques Goulet
Gene Anderson vs. Vinnie Valentino
Mike Davis vs. Joel Deaton

7/30/83: North Wilkesboro, NC @Wilkes Memorial Park
Ric Flair vs. Dory Funk, Jr.
Jos LeDuc vs. Armand Hussein
Mike Rotundo vs. The Assassin
Johnny Weaver vs. Jerry Gray
Abe Jacobs vs. Masa Fuchi

8/1/83: Greenville, SC @ Memorial Auditorium
Ric Flair & Ricky Steamboat beat Jack & Jerry Brisco by DQ
Bob Orton, Jr. beat Dory Funk, Jr.
Jake Roberts beat Rufus R. Jones
Mike Rotundo beat The Assassin
Gene Anderson beat Mike Davis
Vinnie Valentino beat Tom Lentz

8/2/83: Columbia, SC @ Township Auditorium
Ric Flair & Roddy Piper beat Jack & Jerry Brisco by DQ

8/3/83: Spartanburg, SC @ Memorial Auditorium (TV)
Ric Flair, Roddy Piper & Jimmy Valiant beat Greg Valentine, Dick Slater & Great Kabuki
Bob Orton, Jr. beat Jerry Grey
Roddy Piper beat Masa Fuchi
Great Kabuki beat Ric McCord
The Assassins beat Brett Hart & John Bonello
Bugsy McGraw beat Jerry Grey
Bob Orton, Jr. beat Ben Alexander
The Assassins beat Mike Rotundo & Mike Davis
Kabuki & Magic Dragon beat John Bonello & Ric McCord
Greg Valentine beat Brett Hart

8/4/83: Sumter, SC @ Exhibition Center
Ric Flair & Ricky Steamboat beat Jack & Jerry Brisco by DQ
Mike Rotundo vs. Dick Slater
The Assassin vs. Brett Hart
Rick McCord vs. Jacques Goulet
Keith Larsen vs. Joel Deaton

8/5/83: Charleston, SC @ County Hall
Jimmy Valiant vs. One Man Gang & Oliver Humperdink in a loser leaves town match
Great Kabuki vs. Bugsy McGraw
The Assassin vs. Keith Larsen
Jacques Goulet vs. Brett Hart
Kelly Kiniski vs. Joel Deaton

8/5/83: Richmond, VA @ Coliseum
Wahoo McDaniel & Ricky Steamboat beat Jack Brisco & Jerry Brisco
Greg Valentine beat Roddy Piper
Rufus R. Jones beat Dory Funk, Jr. to win NWA Mid Atlantic Title
Dick Slater beat Mike Rotundo
Johnny Weaver beat Mike Davis
Gene Anderson beat Cy Jernigan

8/6/83: Charlotte, NC @ Coliseum
The Assassin beat Jerry Gray
Gene Anderson beat Vinnie Valentino
One Man Gang & Kelly Kiniski beat Johnny Weaver & Mike Davis
Bob Orton, Jr., Rufus R. Jones & Bugsy McGraw beat Dory Funk, Jr., Paul Jones & Jake Roberts
Wahoo McDaniel beat Dick Slater by CO
Ric Flair & Ricky Steamboat beat Jack & Jerry Brisco by DQ

8/7/83: Asheville, NC @ Civic Center
Vinnie Valentino beat Tom Lentz
Brett Hart beat Jerry Gray
Joel Deaton beat Cy Jernigan
Ric Flair, Roddy Piper & Ricky Steamboat beat Dick Slater, Jack & Jerry Brisco
NWA World Champ Harley Race beat Wahoo McDaniel by DQ

8/7/83: Greensboro, NC @ Coliseum
Rick McGraw beat Billy Howard
Gene Anderson beat Keith Larson
The Assassin beat Steve Muslin
Jimmy Valiant beat Great Kabuki
Rufus R. Jones & Bugsy McGraw beat Dory Funk, Jr. & Jake Roberts
Roddy Piper & Wahoo McDaniel beat Greg Valentine & Dick Slater in an Indian strap match
NWA World Champ Harley Race beat Bob Orton, Jr.
Ric Flair & Ricky Steamboat beat Jack & Jerry Brisco by DQ

8/7/83: Toronto, Ontario @ Maple Leaf Gardens
Sgt. Slaughter NC with Angelo Mosca
Andre The Giant beat One Man Gang

Tournament for vacant NWA Canadian TV Title 1st Round
Don Kernodle beat Joe Marcus
Johnny Weaver DCO with Kelly Kiniski
Jacques Goulet beat Nick DeCarlo
Mike Rotundo beat Magic Dragon

Semifinals
Don Kernodle received a bye
Mike Rotundo beat Jacques Goulet

Finals
Mike Rotundo beat Don Kernodle to win vacant NWA Canadian Television Title in tournament final

8/8/83: Greenville, SC @ Memorial Auditorium
Ric Flair & Ricky Steamboat beat Jack & Jerry Brisco by DQ

8/8/83: Oshawa, Ontario @ Civic Centre
Johnny Weaver & Mike Rotundo beat One Man Gang & Don Kernodle
Little Beaver beat Little Brutus
Billy Red Lyons draw Jacques Goulet
Kelly Kiniski beat Bob Marcus
Joe Marcus beat Magic Dragon by DQ
The Executioner beat Nick DeCarlo

8/9/83: Raleigh, NC @ Dorton Arena
Ric Flair & Ricky Steamboat beat Jack & Jerry Brisco by DQ
Bob Orton, Jr. beat Jake Roberts
Dick Slater beat Mike Rotundo
Bret Hart beat Joel Deaton
Bill Howard beat Cy Jernigan
Vinnie Valentino beat Jerry Gray

8/10/83: Spartanburg, SC @ Memorial Auditorium (TV)
Ricky Steamboat & Jay Youngblood vs. Jack Brisco & Jerry Brisco
Jimmy Valiant beat Bill Howard
Jake Roberts beat Tracy Store
Dick Slater beat Keith Larsen
Mike Rotundo & Rufus R. Jones beat Jerry Grey & Bob Brown
Assassin #2(Ray Hernandez) beat Mike Davis
Kabuki beat Joel Deaton
Jimmy Valiant beat Bob Brown
Assassin #2 beat Vinnie Valentino
Jake Roberts beat Brett Hart
Dick Slater beat Red Dog Lane
Mike Rotundo & Rufus R. Jones beat Ben Alexander & Bill Howard
Great Kabuki beat Tracy Store

8/11/83: Fredericksburg, VA @ Stafford High School
Mike Davis beat Jerry Gray
The Assassin beat Mike Davis
Jacques Goulet beat Mark Fleming
Bugsy McGraw beat One Man Gang
Ric Flair & Ricky Steamboat beat Jack Brisco & Jerry Brisco

8/12/83: Charleston, SC @ County Hall
Gene Anderson beat Brett Hart
Keith Larson beat Rick McCord(sub for Rick McCord & Keith Larson vs. Bill Howard & Tom Lentz)
Princess Victoria beat Peggy Lee
Bob Orton, Jr. beat Jake Roberts
Roddy Piper beat Greg Valentine

8/12/83: Hampton, VA @ Coliseum
Ric Flair beat Dick Slater

8/13/83: Roanoke, VA @ Civic Center
Ric Flair & Ricky Steamboat beat Jack & Jerry Brisco by DQ

8/15/83: Greenville, SC @ Memorial Auditorium
Roddy Piper beat Greg Valentine by reverse decision
The Assassins beat Mike Rotundo & Johnny Weaver
Rufus R. Jones beat Jake Roberts
Dick Slater beat Bugsy McGraw
Gene Anderson beat Keith Larsen
Jacques Goulet beat Cy Jernigan

8/16/83: Raleigh, NC @ Dorton Arena
Jack & Jerry Brisco beat Ric Flair & Ricky Steamboat

8/16/83: Columbia, SC @ Township Auditorium

8/17/83: Winston-Salem NC @ Memorial Coliseum (TV)
Ric Flair, Roddy Piper & Ricky Steamboat vs. Jack & Jerry Brisco & Dick Slater
Ricky Steamboat & Roddy Piper beat Joel Deaton & Bill Howard
Greg Valentine & Dick Slater beat Vinnie Valentino & Mike Davis
Bugsy McGraw beat Jerry Grey
The Assassins beat Bret Hart & Keith Larsen
Bob Orton, Jr., Mike Rotundo & Rufus R. Jones beat Magic Dragon, Jacques Goulet & Tom Lentz
The Assassins beat Mike Davis & Rick McCord
Ric Flair & Bob Orton, Jr. beat Jerry Grey & Bill Howard
Bugsy McGraw beat Tom Lentz
Jake Roberts & Dory Funk, Jr. beat Red Dog Lane & Keith Larsen
Mike Rotundo & Rufus R. Jones beat Kelly Kiniski & Joel Deaton

8/18/83: Sumter, SC @ Exhibition Center
Great Kabuki vs. Jimmy Valiant
Jake Roberts vs. Bob Orton, Jr.
Magic Dragon vs. Brett Hart
Jacques Goulet & Bill Howard vs. Rick McCord & Steve Muslin
Jerry Grey vs. Mike Davis
Joel Deaton vs. Abe Jacobs

8/19/83: Charleston, SC @ County Hall
Greg Valentine beat Roddy Piper via pinfall
Bob Orton, Jr. & Mike Rotundo draw The Assassins
Mike Davis beat Magic Dragon
Jacques Goulet beat Vinnie Valentino
Brett Hart beat Bill Howard

8/19/83: Richmond, VA @ Coliseum
Mark Fleming beat Tom Lentz
Gene Anderson & Kelly Kiniski beat Johnny Weaver & Cy Jernigan
Dick Slater beat Bugsy McGraw
Dory Funk, Jr. beat Rufus R. Jones
Jimmy Valiant beat Great Kabuki
Jack & Jerry Brisco beat Ric Flair & Ricky Steamboat

8/21/83: Asheville, NC @ Civic Center
Mike Davis beat Billy Howard
Magic Dragon beat Vinnie Valentino
Johnny Weaver beat Kelly Kiniski
Wahoo McDaniel & Roddy Piper beat Greg Valentine & Dick Slater in a double Indian strap match
Jack & Jerry Brisco beat Ric Flair & Ricky Steamboat

8/21/83: Greensboro, NC @ Coliseum
Jack & Jerry Brisco beat Ricky Steamboat & Wahoo McDaniel by DQ
Great Kabuki beat Jimmy Valiant in a loser leaves town match
Roddy Piper beat Greg Valentine
Rufus R. Jones beat Jake Roberts
Gene Anderson beat Cy Jernigan
Bugsy McGraw beat Jerry Gray
The Assassins beat Mike Rotundo & Bob Orton, Jr.

8/22/83: Greenville, SC @ Memorial Auditorium
Jack & Jerry Brisco beat Ricky Steamboat & Wahoo McDaniel by DQ
Roddy Piper beat Greg Valentine
Dick Slater beat Johnny Weaver
Mike Davis beat Kelly Kiniski
Brett Hart beat Bill Howard
Vinnie Valentino beat Jerry Gray

8/23/83: Columbia, SC @ Township Auditorium

8/24/83: Spartanburg, SC @ Memorial Auditorium (TV)
Ricky Steamboat & Jay Youngblood beat Bill Howard & Jerry Grey
Ric Flair beat Ben Alexander
The Assassins beat Gene Ligon & Keith Larsen
Dick Slater & Jake Roberts beat Steve Muslim & Vinnie Valentino
Roddy Piper & Bob Orton, Jr. beat Bill Howard & Kelly Kiniski
Greg Valentine beat Vinnie Valentino
Bugsy McGraw beat Ben Alexander
The Assassins beat Rick McCord & Steve Muslim
Ric Flair beat Jerry Grey

8/25/83: Harrisonburg, VA @ High School
Jerry Gray vs. Cy Jernigan
Joel Deaton vs. Vinnie Valentino
Kelly Kiniski vs. Mike Davis
Dick Slater vs. Bugsy McGraw
Greg Valentine vs. Roddy Piper

8/25/83: Newberry, SC @ Hedgepath Stadium
Great Kabuki vs. Jay Youngblood
Johnny Weaver & Rufus R. Jones vs. The Assassins
Magic Dragon vs. Mike Rotundo
Tom Lentz vs. Ric McCord
Ben Alexander vs. Abe Jacobs

8/26/83: Charleston, SC @ County Hall
Jake Roberts beat Rufus R. Jones
The Assassins beat Mike Rotundo & Johnny Weaver
Jay Youngblood beat Great Kabuki
Jacques Goulet beat Ric McCord
Keith Larsen beat Tom Lentz

8/27/83: Charlottesville, VA @ Scott Stadium
Jimmy Valiant & Rufus R. Jones beat Kabuki & Gary Hart in a steel cage match
Dick Slater beat Jay Youngblood
The Assassins beat Bugsy McGraw & Cy Jernigan
Kelly Kiniski beat Brett Hart
Mike Davis beat Tom Lentz
Vinnie Valentino beat Bill Howard

8/28/83: Toronto, Ontario @ Maple Leaf Gardens
Nick DeCarlo beat Tim Gerrard
Bob Marcus beat Jerry Gray
Jacques Goulet beat Brett Hart
Billy Red Lyons beat Bill Howard
Johnny Weaver beat Kelly Kiniski
Mike Rotundo beat Don Kernodle
Greg Valentine & Jake Roberts beat Roddy Piper & Jimmy Valiant by DQ
Sgt. Slaughter beat Angelo Mosca by CO

8/29/83: Greenville, SC @ Memorial Auditorium
Ric Flair & Roddy Piper beat Greg Valentine & Dick Slater
Bob Orton, Jr. beat Great Kabuki by DQ
The Assassins beat Mike Rotundo & Johnny Weaver
Gene Anderson beat Steve Muslin

8/30/83: Columbia, SC @ Township Auditorium
Roddy Piper beat Greg Valentine in a Canadian lumberjack match
Ric Flair beat Dick Slater by CO
Rufus R. Jones beat Jake Roberts
The Assassins beat Bugsy McGraw & Johnny Weaver
Kelly Kiniski beat Mike Davis
Vinnie Valentino beat Bill Howard

8/31/83: Spartanburg, SC @ Memorial Auditorium (TV)
Ric Flair beat NWA World Champ Harley Race by DQ
Greg Valentine beat Keith Larson
Charlie Brown beat Jerry Gray
Ric Flair & Wahoo McDaniel beat Ron Rossi & Bill Howard
The Assassins beat Steve Muslin & Mark Fleming
Ricky Steamboat & Jay Youngblood beat Ben Alexander & Tom Lentz
Charlie Brown beat Ben Alexander
Jack & Jerry Brisco beat Rick McCord & Keith Larson
Dick Slater & Jake Roberts beat Gene Ligon & Brett Hart
Ric Flair & Wahoo McDaniel beat Tom Lentz & Jerry Gray
Greg Valentine beat Steve Muslin

9/1/83: Norfolk, VA @ Scope
Jack & Jerry Brisco beat Roddy Piper & Ricky Steamboat
Greg Valentine beat Rufus R. Jones
Wahoo McDaniel & Bob Orton, Jr. beat Dick Slater & Jake Roberts
Gene Anderson beat Mike Davis
Ric McCord beat Jacques Goulet
Keith Larsen beat Tom Lentz

9/1/83: Sumter, SC @ Exhibition Center
Bugsy McGraw & Charlie Brown vs. Great Kabuki & Gary Hart in a steel cage match
The Assassins vs. Johnny Weaver & Mike Rotundo
Brett Hart vs. Bill Howard
Magic Dragon vs. Vinnie Valentino
Kelly Kiniski vs. Steve Muslin

9/2/83: Charleston, SC @ County Hall
Charlie Brown(Jimmy Valiant) & Bugsy McGraw beat Great Kabuki & Gary Hart
The Assassins beat Mike Rotundo & Johnny Weaver
Brett Hart beat Kelly Kiniski
Magic Dragon beat Jerry Gray
Bill Howard beat Vinnie Valentino

9/2/83: Richmond, VA @ Coliseum
Ricky Steamboat & Jay Youngblood beat Jack Brisco & Jerry Brisco
Wahoo McDaniel & Roddy Piper beat Greg Valentine & Dick Slater
Rufus R. Jones beat Jake Roberts
Bob Orton, Jr. beat Jacques Goulet
Gene Anderson beat Ric McCord
Keith Larsen beat Steve Muslim
Tom Lentz beat Mike Davis

9/3/83: Greensboro, NC @ Coliseum
Ricky Steamboat & Jay Youngblood beat Jack & Jerry Brisco by DQ
Roddy Piper beat Greg Valentine lumberjack match
Wahoo McDaniel & Rufus R. Jones beat Dick Slater & Jake Roberts
Kelly Kiniski beat Mike Rotundo
Gene Anderson beat Vinnie Valentino

9/4/83: Asheville, NC @ Civic Center
Billy Howard beat Mark Fleming
Bugsy McGraw beat Jacques Goulet
Wahoo McDaniel NC with Dick Slater
Charlie Brown & Rufus R. Jones beat Great Kabuki & Gary Hart
Roddy Piper beat Greg Valentine

9/4/83: Savannah, GA @ Civic Center
Wahoo McDaniel beat Dick Slater in a lumberjack match
Greg Valentine beat Roddy Piper by DQ
Charlie Brown & Rufus R. Jones beat Kabuki & Gary Hart in a steel cage match
The Assassins beat Mike Rotundo & Johnny Weaver
Kelly Kiniski beat Vinnie Valentino
Magic Dragon beat Ric McCord
Brett Hart beat Jerry Grey

9/5/83: Greenville, SC @ Memorial Auditorium
Ricky Steamboat & Jay Youngblood beat Jack Brisco & Jerry Brisco
Charlie Brown beat Great Kabuki
The Assassins beat Mike Rotundo & Johnny Weaver
Magic Dragon beat Mike Davis
Brett Hart beat Bill White

9/6/83: Columbia, SC @ Township Auditorium

9/7/83: Spartanburg, SC @ Memorial Auditorium (TV)
Charlie Brown beat Bill Howard
Bob Orton, Jr. beat The Beastmaster
Rufus R. Jones & Wahoo McDaniel beat Bill White & Ben Alexander
Ricky Steamboat & Jay Youngblood beat Bill Howard & Jerry Gray
Jack & Jerry Brisco beat Mike Davis & Mark Fleming
Charlie Brown & Rufus R. Jones beat Tom Lentz & Ben Alexander
The Assassins beat Vinnie Valentino & Brett Hart
Charlie Brown beat Jerry Gray
The Assassins beat Brett Hart & Rick McCord
Roddy Piper & Wahoo McDaniel beat Dick Slater & Greg Valentine by DQ
Charlie Brown & Rufus R. Jones beat Magic Dragon & Jerry Gray
Mark Youngblood & Jay Youngblood & Ricky Steamboat beat Tom Lentz, Bill Howard & The Beastmaster
Dick Slater & Bob Orton, Jr. beat Gene Ligon & Rick McCord
The Assassins beat Mark Fleming & Keith Larson
Roddy Piper & Wahoo McDaniel beat Kelly Kiniski & Ben Alexander

9/9/83: Charleston, SC @ County Hall
Ricky Steamboat & Jay Youngblood beat Jack & Jerry Brisco in a no DQ match
Wahoo McDaniel beat Dick Slater
Mark Youngblood & Ric McCord beat Jacques Goulet & Bill Howard
Keith Larsen beat Jerry Gray

9/10/83: Greensboro, NC @ Coliseum
Ricky Steamboat & Jay Youngblood vs. Jack Brisco & Jerry Brisco
Charlie Brown vs. Great Kabuki
Wahoo McDaniel vs. Dick Slater
Johnny Weaver & Bugsy McGraw vs. The Assassins
Rick McCord vs. Gene Anderson
Vinnie Valentino vs. Magic Dragon
Steve Muslin vs. Jerry Gray

9/12/83: Greenville, SC @ Memorial Auditorium
Dory Funk, Jr., Bugsy McGraw & Rufus R. Jones beat The Assassins & Paul Jones
Great Kabuki beat Mark Youngblood
Brickhouse Brown beat Magic Dragon
John Bonello beat Gary Royal
Terry Gibbs beat Bill Howard

9/13/83: Columbia, SC @ Township Auditorium

9/14/83: Spartanburg, SC @ Memorial Auditorium (TV)
Mark Youngblood & Jay Youngblood beat Kelly Kiniski & Tom Lentz
Bob Orton, Jr. beat John Bonello
Bugsy McGraw beat Assassin #2 by DQ
Dory Funk, Jr. beat Scott McGhee
Greg Valentine beat Steve Muslin
Greg Valentine beat John Bonello
Mark Youngblood & Jay Youngblood beat Kelly Kiniski & Jerry Grey
Wahoo McDaniel beat Bill Howard
Bob Orton, Jr. beat Ric McCord
The Assassins beat Vinnie Valentino & Steve Muslin
Wahoo McDaniel, Charlie Brown, Mark Youngblood beat Greg Valentine, Jake Roberts & Great Kabuki

9/15/83: Sumter, SC @ Exhibition Center
Greg Valentine beat Mark Youngblood(sub for Roddy Piper)
Charlie Brown & Rufus R. Jones beat Kabuki & Jake Roberts
The Assassins beat Johnny Weaver & Mike Rotundo
Scott McGhee beat Bill Howard
Kelly Kiniski beat John Bonello
Magic Dragon beat Vinnie Valentino

9/16/83: Charleston, SC @ County Hall
Ricky Steamboat & Jay Youngblood beat Jack & Jerry Brisco by DQ
Charlie Brown beat Great Kabuki
Magic Dragon beat Vinnie Valentino
Gene Anderson beat Keith Larsen
John Bonello beat Tom Lentz
Ric McCord beat Jerry Gray

9/17/83: Charlotte, NC @ Coliseum
Ricky Steamboat & Jay Youngblood beat Jack Brisco & Jerry Brisco
Greg Valentine beat Mark Youngblood
Charlie Brown beat Great Kabuki
Bob Orton, Jr. beat Johnny Weaver
The Assassins beat Ric McCord & Keith Larsen
Scott McGhee beat Kelly Kiniski
Brett Hart beat Jerry Grey

9/17/83: Conway, SC
The Ninja beat Mark Fleming
John Bonello beat Tom Lentz
Vinnie Valentine beat Bill Howard
Dory Funk, Jr. beat Bugsy McGraw
Wahoo McDaniel beat Dick Slater by CO
Rufus R. Jones beat Jake Roberts

9/18/83: Asheville, NC @ Civic Center
Roddy Piper DDQ Greg Valentine in a lumberjack match
Jack & Jerry Brisco beat Ricky Steamboat & Jay Youngblood
Wahoo McDaniel & Charlie Brown beat Dick Slater & Great Kabuki
Bugsy McGraw beat Dory Funk, Jr.
Gene Anderson beat Vinnie Valentino
Magic Dragon beat Brett Hart

9/18/83: Greensboro, NC @ Coliseum
The Ninja beat Brett Hart
Gene Anderson beat Vinnie Valentino
Bugsy McGraw & Charlie Brown beat Great Kabuki & Dick Slater
Wahoo McDaniel beat Greg Valentine in a lumberjack match
Ricky Steamboat & Jay Youngblood beat Jack & Jerry Brisco

9/18/83: Toronto, Ontario @ Maple Leaf Gardens
Nick DeCarlo beat Jerry Grey
Don Kolov beat Joe Marcus
Bob Marcus beat Tom Lentz
Don Kernodle beat Rick McCord
Johnny Weaver & Keith Larson beat Kelly Kiniski & The Executioner
Greg Valentine beat Bob Orton, Jr.
Angelo Mosca beat Sgt. Slaughter by CO
NWA World Champ Harley Race beat Mike Rotundo

9/19/83: Greenville, SC @ Memorial Auditorium
Wahoo McDaniel & Mark Youngblood beat Greg Valentine & Dick Slater by DQ
Vinnie Valentine & Scott McGhee beat Gene Anderson & The Ninja
Bob Orton, Jr. beat Bugsy McGraw
Rufus R. Jones beat Jake Roberts
John Bonello beat Abe Jacobs

9/19/83: Fayetteville, NC @ Cumberland County Civic Center
Ricky Steamboat & Jay Youngblood beat Jack Brisco & Jerry Brisco
Charlie Brown beat Great Kabuki in a bounty match
The Assassins beat Steve Muslim & Mark Fleming

9/20/83: Columbia, SC @ Township Auditorium
Ricky Steamboat & Jay Youngblood beat Jack & Jerry Brisco
Charlie Brown beat Baron Von Raschke
Rufus R. Jones beat Jake Roberts in a Texas death match
Gene Anderson & Kelly Kiniski beat Scott McGhee & John Bonello

9/21/83: Shelby, NC(TV)
Jimmy Valiant beat Baron Von Raschke
Mark Youngblood & Jay Youngblood beat Jerry Grey & Ben Alexander
Mark Lewin & Kevin Sullivan beat Ric McCord & Keith Larsen
Baron Von Raschke beat Barry Hart
Dick Slater & Bob Orton, Jr. NC with Scott McGhee & Steve Muslin
The Assassins beat Vinnie Valentino & John Bonello
Mark Youngblood & Jay Youngblood beat Tom Lentz & Kelly Kiniski
Bob Orton, Jr. beat John Bonello
Bugsy McGraw beat Assassin # 2 by DQ
Dory Funk, Jr. beat Scott McGee
Greg Valentine beat Steve Muslin
Greg Valentine beat John Bonello
Mark Youngblood & Jay Youngblood beat Jerry Gray & Kelly Kiniski
Wahoo McDaniel beat Bill Howard
Bob Orton, Jr. beat Rick McCord
The Assassins beat Vinnie Valentino & Steve Muslin

9/22/83: Harrisonburg, VA @ High School
Dick Slater, Jack & Jerry Brisco vs. Ricky Steamboat, Wahoo McDaniel & Jay Youngblood
Johnny Weaver vs. Bob Orton, Jr.
Gene Anderson vs. Brett Hart
Kelly Kiniski vs. Vinnie Valentino
Jerry Gray vs. Cy Jernigan

9/23/83: Charleston, SC @ County Hall
Rufus R. Jones & Bugsy McGraw beat Dory Funk, Jr. & Jake Roberts
Baron Von Raschke beat Charlie Brown
Mark Youngblood & Scott McGhee beat Magic Dragon & The Ninja
Gene Ligon beat Tom Lentz
John Bonello beat Jerry Gray

9/23/83: Richmond, VA @ Coliseum
Brett Hart beat Kelly Kiniski
Gene Anderson beat Vinnie Valentino
The Assassins beat Keith Larson & Ric McCord
Bob Orton, Jr. beat Johnny Weaver
Wahoo McDaniel beat Dick Slater
Wahoo McDaniel beat Greg Valentine lumberjack match
Ricky Steamboat & Jay Youngblood beat Jack & Jerry Brisco by DQ

9/24/83: Greensboro, NC @ Coliseum
Ricky Steamboat & Jay Youngblood beat Jack Brisco & Jerry Brisco
Baron Von Raschke beat Charlie Brown in a bounty match
Wahoo McDaniel beat Dick Slater in a taped fist match
Bob Orton, Jr. beat Johnny Weaver
The Assassins beat Scott McGhee & Steve Muslim
Gene Anderson beat John Bonello
Brett Hart beat Tom Lentz

9/25/83: Hampton, VA @ Coliseum
Wahoo McDaniel & Mark Youngblood beat Dick Slater & Greg Valentine
Baron Von Raschke beat Charlie Brown
The Assassins beat Bugsy McGraw & Johnny Weaver
Rufus R. Jones beat Jake Roberts
Dory Funk, Jr. beat Scott McGhee
Brett Hart beat Jerry Grey

9/25/83: Roanoke, VA @ Civic Center
Jack & Jerry Brisco DDQ Ricky Steamboat & Jay Youngblood
Wahoo McDaniel beat Greg Valentine in a lumberjack match
Baron Von Raschke beat Charlie Brown
Bob Orton, Jr. beat Steve Muslim
Vinnie Valentino & John Bonello beat Kelly Kiniski & Tom Lentz
Gene Anderson beat Ric McCord

9/26/83: Greenville, SC @ Memorial Auditorium
Wahoo McDaniel & Mark Youngblood beat Dick Slater & Greg Valentine in a double Indian strap match
Baron Von Raschke beat Charlie Brown
Bob Orton, Jr. beat Steve Muslim
Scott McGhee beat Magic Dragon
Gene Anderson beat Vinnie Valentino
Kelly Kiniski beat Jerry Grey

9/27/83: Raleigh, NC @ Dorton Arena
Wahoo McDaniel & Mark Youngblood beat Dick Slater & Greg Valentine in a double Indian strap match
Baron Von Raschke beat Charlie Brown
Bob Orton, Jr. beat Johnny Weaver
Magic Dragon beat Brett Hart
Ric McCord beat The Ninja
John Bonello Beat Tom Lentz

9/27/83: Columbia, SC @ Township Auditorium

9/28/83: Spartanburg, SC @ Memorial Auditorium (TV)
Bob Orton, Jr. & Dick Slater NC with Keith Larson & Rick McCord(1:30)
Greg Valentine vs. Steve Travis
Jack & Jerry Brisco beat Vinnie Valentino & John Bonello
The Assassins vs. Mark Youngblood & Scott McGhee
Wahoo McDaniel & Chavo Guerrero vs. Jerry Gray & Magic Dragon
Bob Orton, Jr. & Dick Slater beat Rick McCord & Gene Ligon(6:15) via pinfall
Terry Gibbs, Charlie Brown & Brickhouse Brown vs. Jerry Gray, Tom Lynch & Kelly Kiniski
Jack & Jerry Brisco beat Barry Horowitz & Gene Ligon

Mark Youngblood & Jay Youngblood beat Jerry Gray & Ben Alexander
Kevin Sullivan & Mark Lewin beat Rick McCord & Keith Larson
Baron Von Raschke beat Brett Hart
Dick Slater & Bob Orton, Jr. beat Steve Muslin & Scott McGhee by DQ
The Assassins beat John Bonello & Vinnie Valentino
Charlie Brown beat Jerry Gray
Kevin Sullivan & Mark Lewin beat John Bonello & Vinnie Valentino
The Assassins beat Rick McCord & Keith Larson
Mark Youngblood & Jay Youngblood beat Magic Dragon & The Ninja

9/29/83: Roswell, VA
Mark Youngblood & Jay Youngblood beat Jack Brisco & Jerry Brisco
Ricky Steamboat beat Dick Slater by DQ
Bob Orton, Jr. beat Steve Muslim
Brett Hart beat The Ninja
Vinnie Valentino beat Cy Jernigan

9/30/83: Charlottesville, VA
Ricky Steamboat & Jay Youngblood beat Jack Brisco & Jerry Brisco
Dick Slater & Greg Valentine beat Wahoo McDaniel & Mark Youngblood
Bob Orton, Jr. beat Brett Hart
Vinnie Valentino beat The Ninja
Magic Dragon beat Cy Jernigan

9/30/83: Charleston, SC @ County Hall
Charlie Brown beat Baron Von Raschke in a steel cage, bounty match
The Assassins beat Johnny Weaver & Scott McGhee
Mark Lewin beat John Bonello
Kevin Sullivan beat Mark Fleming
Tom Lentz beat Gene Ligon

10/1/83: Morganton, NC
Baron Von Raschke beat Charlie Brown in a bounty match
The Assassins beat Johnny Weaver & Bugsy McGraw
Ric McCord beat Kelly Kiniski

10/1/83: Conway, SC
Joel Deaton beat Abe Jacobs
Vinnie Valentino beat Jerry Grey
Scott McGhee beat Tom Lentz
Rufus R. Jones beat Dory Funk, Jr.
Wahoo McDaniel beat Dick Slater in a lumberjack match
Liz Chase beat Donna Christianello

10/2/83: Asheville, NC @ Civic Center
Terry Gibbs beat Magic Dragon
Kevin Sullivan beat Rick McCord
Mark Lewin beat John Bonello
Ric Flair & Wahoo McDaniel DDQ Bob Orton, Jr. & Dick Slater
Jack & Jerry Brisco beat Ricky Steamboat & Jay Youngblood

10/2/83: Charlotte, NC @ Coliseum
Dick Slater & Bob Orton, Jr. beat Ric Flair & Wahoo McDaniel by DQ
Baron Von Raschke beat Charlie Brown
Gene Anderson beat Rufus R. Jones
Mark Youngblood beat Magic Dragon
Scott McGhee beat Jerry Grey
Vinnie Valentino beat Tom Lentz

10/2/83: Greensboro, NC @ Coliseum
Rick Steamboat & Jay Youngblood beat Jack & Jerry Brisco to win NWA World Tag Title

10/3/83: Fayetteville, NC @ Cumberland County Civic Center
Dick Slater & Bob Orton, Jr. beat Ric Flair & Wahoo McDaniel by DQ
Roddy Piper beat Greg Valentine
Dory Funk, Jr. beat Rufus R. Jones
Kevin Sullivan & Mark Lewin beat Keith Larsen & Ric McCord
Terry Gibbs beat Jerry Grey

10/3/83: Greenville, SC @ Memorial Auditorium
Ricky Steamboat & Jay Youngblood beat Jack Brisco & Jerry Brisco
Charlie Brown beat Baron Von Raschke
The Assassins beat Bugsy McGraw & Mark Youngblood
Scott McGhee beat Kelly Kiniski
Brickhouse Brown beat Bill Howard

10/4/83: Columbia, SC @ Township Auditorium
Bob Orton, Jr. & Dick Slater beat Ric Flair & Wahoo McDaniel by DQ
Greg Valentine beat Bugsy McGraw
Kevin Sullivan beat Brett Hart
Gene Anderson beat John Bonello
Terry Gibbs beat Tom Lentz
Magic Dragon draw Vinnie Valentino

10/4/83: Raleigh, NC @ Dorton Arena
Ricky Steamboat & Jay Youngblood beat Jack Brisco & Jerry Brisco
Charlie Brown beat Baron Von Raschke in a steel cage, bounty match
Johnny Weaver beat Steve Muslim
Brickhouse Brown beat Bill Howard
Ric McCord beat Gene Ligon
Kelly Kiniski beat Mark Fleming

10/5/83: Winston-Salem, NC @ Memorial Coliseum
Wahoo McDaniel beat The Ninja
The Assassins beat Mark Youngblood & Scott McGhee
Kevin Sullivan & Mark Lewin beat Brett Hart & Steve Muslim
Ricky Steamboat & Jay Youngblood beat Kelly Kiniski & Ben Alexander
Wahoo McDaniel vs. The Ninja(aka Mr. Pogo)
The Assassins vs. Mark Youngblood & Scott McGhee
Kevin Sullivan & Mark Lewin vs. Steve Travis & Barry Horowitz

Ricky Steamboat & Jay Youngblood vs. Ben Alexander & Kelly Kiniski
Scott McGhee & Mark Youngblood vs. The Ninja & Kelly Kiniski
Greg Valentine vs. Barry Horowitz
Bugsy McGraw & Rufus R. Jones vs. Tom Lentz & Jerry Gray
Baron Von Raschke vs. John Bonello

10/6/83: Sumter, SC @ Exhibition Center
Andre The Giant, Charlie Brown & Bugsy McGraw beat Baron Von Raschke & The Assassins
Rufus R. Jones beat Dory Funk, Jr. by DQ
Mark Youngblood beat Magic Dragon
Scott McGhee beat Kelly Kiniski

10/6/83: Norfolk, VA @ Scope
Ric Flair & Wahoo McDaniel beat Dick Slater & Bob Orton, Jr.
Roddy Piper beat Greg Valentine in a lumberjack match
Ricky Steamboat & Jay Youngblood beat Jack Brisco & Jerry Brisco
Kevin Sullivan beat Johnny Weaver
Mark Lewin beat Brett Hart
Gene Anderson beat Terry Gibbs
Brickhouse Brown beat Bill Howard

10/7/83: Richmond, VA @ Coliseum
Johnny Weaver beat Dory Funk, Jr. in a 2-ring Battle Royal
Baron Von Raschke beat Charlie Brown in a steel cage, bounty match
Dory Funk, Jr. beat Johnny Weaver
Kevin Sullivan & Mark Lewin beat Vinnie Valentino & John Bonello
Terry Gibbs beat Tom Lentz
Brickhouse Brown beat Jerry Grey

10/7/83: Charleston, SC @ County Hall
Ricky Steamboat & Jay Youngblood beat Jack & Jerry Brisco in a no DQ match
Roddy Piper beat Greg Valentine in a lumberjack strap match
Mark Youngblood vs. Assassin #1
Scott McGhee vs. Assassin #2
Kelly Kiniski vs. Ric McCord

10/8/83: Greensboro, NC @ Coliseum
Rick McCord beat Tom Lentz
Mark Lewin & Kevin Sullivan beat Vinnie Valentino & John Bonello
Rufus R. Jones beat Dory Funk, Jr.
Bugsy McGraw & Mark Youngblood beat The Assassins
Roddy Piper & Charlie Brown beat Baron Von Raschke & Gary Hart
Ric Flair & Wahoo McDaniel DDQ Bob Orton, Jr. & Dick Slater

10/8/83: Burlington, NC
Ricky Steamboat & Jay Youngblood beat Jack Brisco & Jerry Brisco
Greg Valentine beat Johnny Weaver
Scott McGhee beat Magic Dragon
Kelly Kiniski beat Steve Muslim
Brickhouse Brown beat Jerry Grey

10/10/83: Greenville, SC @ Memorial Auditorium
Ric Flair & Roddy Piper beat Bob Orton, Jr. & Dick Slater by DQ
Wahoo McDaniel beat Greg Valentine by CO
Kevin Sullivan & Mark Lewin beat Johnny Weaver & Ric McCord
Chavo Guerrero beat The Ninja
Gene Anderson beat Keith Larsen

10/11/83: Columbia, SC @ Township Auditorium
Ric Flair & Wahoo McDaniel beat Dick Slater & Bob Orton, Jr.
Charlie Brown beat Baron Von Raschke in a steel cage, bounty match
The Assassins beat Rufus R. Jones & Mark Youngblood
Kevin Sullivan beat Steve Muslim
Mark Lewin beat Brett Hart
Magic Dragon beat Brickhouse Brown

10/12/83: Spartanburg, SC @ Memorial Auditorium (TV)
Ric Flair, Wahoo McDaniel & Mark Youngblood beat Dick Slater, Dory Funk, Jr. & Mark Lewin
Greg Valentine beat Steve Muslim
Jack & Jerry Brisco beat Vinnie Valentino & John Bonello
The Assassins beat Mark Youngblood & Scott McGhee
Wahoo McDaniel & Chavo Guerrero beat Magic Dragon & Jerry Grey
Bob Orton, Jr. & Dick Slater beat Keith Larsen & Ric McCord
Charlie Brown, Brickhouse Brown & Terry Gibbs beat Kelly Kiniski, Jerry Grey & Tom Lentz
Jack & Jerry Brisco beat Brett Hart & Gene Ligon
Chavo Guerrero beat Ben Alexander
The Assassins beat Steve Muslim & John Bonello
Kevin Sullivan & Mark Lewin beat Mark Fleming & Vinnie Valentino

10/13/83: Orange, VA
Ric Flair beat Dory Funk, Jr.
Jimmy Valiant & Johnny Weaver beat Bob Orton, Jr. & Baron Von Raschke by DQ
Chavo Guerrero beat The ninja
Mark Lewin beat Steve Muslin
Kevin Sullivan beat Vinnie Valentino

10/13/83: Marion, NC
Wahoo McDaniel beat Dick Slater by CO
The Assassins beat Mark Youngblood & Bugsy McGraw
Scott McGhee beat Bill White

10/14/83: Hampton, VA @ Coliseum
Ric Flair & Roddy Piper beat Bob Orton, Jr. & Dory Funk, Jr.
Charlie Brown beat Baron Von Raschke
Kevin Sullivan & Mark Lewin beat Johnny Weaver & Terry Gibbs

Chavo Guerrero beat The Ninja
Magic Dragon beat Brett Hart
Vinnie Valentino beat Jerry Grey

10/14/83: Charleston, SC @ County Hall
Wahoo McDaniel beat Dick Slater
The Assassin beat Mark Youngblood & Bugsy McGraw
Brickhouse Brown vs. Bill Howard
Scott McGhee beat Bill Howard(sub for Gene Anderson)
Keith Larsen beat Tom Lentz

10/15/83: Culpeper, VA
Vinnie Valentino beat The Ninja
Brett Hart beat Jerry Gray
Chavo Guerrero beat Magic Dragon
Kevin Sullivan & Mark Lewin beat Johnny Weaver & Terry Gibbs
Ric Flair beat Bob Orton, Jr. by CO

10/15/83: Roanoke, VA @ Civic Center
Charlie Brown & Mark Youngblood beat Baron Von Raschke & Gary Hart
Dick Slater beat Dory Funk, Jr.
The Assassins beat Bugsy McGraw & Brickhouse Brown
Scott McGhee beat Kelly Kiniski
Gene Anderson beat Keith Larsen

10/16/83: Toronto, Ontario @ Maple Leaf Gardens
Nick DeCarlo beat Scrap Iron Sheppard
Rudy & Terry Kay beat Bob Marcus & Joe Marcus
Kelly Kiniski beat Big Mac
Johnny Weaver beat Bill Howard
Leo Burke beat Bret Hart
Don Kernodle beat Mike Rotundo(13:02) to win NWA Canadian Television Title
Angelo Mosca beat Sgt. Slaughter
Roddy Piper beat Greg Valentine

10/16/83: Fayetteville, NC @ Cumberland County Civic Center
Ric Flair & Wahoo McDaniel beat Dick Slater & Bob Orton, Jr.
Charlie Brown beat Baron Von Raschke in a street fight match
Dory Funk, Jr. beat Chavo Guerrero
Kevin Sullivan & Mark Lewin beat Scott McGhee & John Bonello
Vinnie Valentino beat The Ninja

10/16/83: Greensboro, NC @ Coliseum
Ric Flair beat Bob Orton, Jr.
Baron Von Raschke vs. Charlie Brown in a cage match
Wahoo McDaniel beat Dick Slater by DQ
Jack & Jerry Brisco vs. Ricky Steamboat & Jay Youngblood
Gene Anderson beat Keith Larsen
Terry Gibbs beat Tom Lentz
Scott McGhee beat Magic Dragon
Dory Funk, Jr., Bugsy McGraw & Mark Youngblood beat The Assassins & Paul Jones

10/17/83: Greenville, SC @ Memorial Auditorium
Dick Slater & Bob Orton, Jr. beat Ric Flair & Wahoo McDaniel
Jerry Brisco beat Ricky Steamboat
The Assassins beat Mark Youngblood & Terry Gibbs
Chavo Guerrero beat Magic Dragon
Mark Lewin beat Vinnie Valentino
John Bonello beat Jerry Grey

10/18/83: Columbia, SC @ Township Auditorium
Ricky Steamboat & Jay Youngblood beat Jack Brisco & Jerry Brisco
The Assassins beat Charlie Brown & Mark Youngblood
Kevin Sullivan beat Terry Gibbs
Keith Larsen beat Bill Howard
Gene Anderson beat Steve Muslim

10/19/83: Shelby, NC(TV)
Ricky Steamboat & Jay Youngblood beat Magic Dragon & Bill Howard
Dick Slater beat Steve Muslim
Kevin Sullivan & Mark Lewin beat Brett Hart & Vinnie Valentino
Charlie Brown & Bugsy McGraw beat Kelly Kiniski & Tom Lentz
Mark Youngblood & Scott McGhee beat The Assassins
Chavo Guerrero beat Magic Dragon
Kevin Sullivan & Mark Lewin beat Brett Hart & John Bonello
Dick Slater beat Keith Larsen
Ricky Steamboat & Jay Youngblood beat Bill Howard & Tom Lentz
The Assassins beat Terry Gibbs & Steve Muslim

10/20/83: Norfolk, VA @ Scope
Ric Flair & Wahoo McDaniel NC with Dick Slater & Bob Orton, Jr.
Charlie Brown beat Great Kabuki
The Assassins beat Johnny Weaver & Terry Gibbs
Mark Lewin beat Bugsy McGraw
Mark Youngblood beat Gene Anderson
Scott McGhee beat Kelly Kiniski

10/20/83: Sumter, SC @ Exhibition Center
Ricky Steamboat & Jay Youngblood beat Jack Brisco & Jerry Brisco
Rufus R. Jones beat Dory Funk, Jr.
Kevin Sullivan beat Keith Larsen
Chavo Guerrero beat The Ninja
Gary Royal beat Ric McCord
Vinnie Valentino beat Tim Gerrard

10/21/83: Charleston, SC @ County Hall
Greg Valentine beat Roddy Piper
Dory Funk, Jr. beat Rufus R. Jones
Kevin Sullivan beat Keith Larsen
The Ninja beat Chavo Guerrero
Magic Dragon beat John Bonello
Brett Hart beat Tom Lentz

10/21/83: Richmond, VA @ Coliseum
The Assassins beat Charlie Brown & Mark Youngblood
Kabuki beat Scott McGhee
Bugsy McGraw beat Gene Anderson
Mark Lewin beat Johnny Weaver
Terry Gibbs beat Kelly Kiniski
Jack & Jerry Brisco beat Ricky Steamboat & Jay Youngblood to win NWA World Tag Title
Ric Flair & Wahoo McDaniel beat Bob Orton, Jr. & Dick Slater

10/23/83: Asheville, NC @ Civic Center
Kelly Kiniski beat John Bonello
Vinnie Valentino beat Jerry Gray
Bugsy McGraw beat Magic Dragon
The Assassins beat Rufus R. Jones & Mark Youngblood
Charlie Brown beat Great Kabuki
Jack & Jerry Brisco beat Ricky Steamboat & Jay Youngblood by DQ

10/23/83: Roanoke, VA @ Civic Center
Ric Flair & Roddy Piper NC with Dick Slater & Bob Orton, Jr.
Wahoo McDaniel beat Greg Valentine by CO
Kevin Sullivan & Mark Lewin beat Johnny Weaver & Terry Gibbs
Brett Hart beat Tom Lentz
Keith Larsen beat Tim Gerrard
Ric McCord beat ??

10/23/83: Charlotte, NC @ Coliseum
Ric Flair & Wahoo McDaniel NC with Dick Slater & Bob Orton, Jr.
Jack & Jerry Brisco beat Ricky Steamboat & Jay Youngblood
Greg Valentine beat Roddy Piper
Rufus R. Jones & Bugsy McGraw beat The Assassins
Dory Funk, Jr. beat Mark Youngblood
Angelo Mosca beat Gene Anderson
Scott McGhee beat The Ninja
Brickhouse Brown beat Gary Royal

10/24/83: Greenville, SC @ Memorial Auditorium
Ric Flair & Wahoo McDaniel NC with Bob Orton, Jr. & Dick Slater
Jack & Jerry Brisco beat Ricky Steamboat & Jay Youngblood
Mark Lewin beat Johnny Weaver
Scott McGhee beat The Ninja
Vinnie Valentino beat Tom Lentz
Angelo Mosca vs. Gene Anderson

10/25/83: Columbia, SC @ Township Auditorium
Ric Flair, Roddy Piper & Wahoo McDaniel beat Greg Valentine, Bob Orton, Jr. & Dick Slater via pinfall
Dory Funk, Jr. beat Scott McGhee
Kevin Sullivan & Mark Lewin beat Johnny Weaver & Terry Gibbs
Angelo Mosca beat Tom Lentz
Vinnie Valentino beat Magic Dragon

10/26/83: Winston-Salem, NC @ Memorial Coliseum (TV)
Ric Flair, Roddy Piper & Wahoo McDaniel vs. Bob Orton, Jr., Dick Slater & Dory Funk, Jr.
Chavo Guerrero beat Gary Royal
The Assassins DDQ Charlie Brown & Bugsy McGraw
Great Kabuki beat Steve Muslim
Bob Orton, Jr. beat Ric McCord
Kevin Sullivan beat Tim Gerrard
Great Kabuki beat Keith Larsen
Wahoo McDaniel & Chavo Guerrero beat Kelly Kiniski & Tom Lentz
Mark Youngblood & Rufus R. Jones beat Bill Howard & Gary Royal
The Assassins beat Steve Muslim & Tim Gerrard

10/28/83: Charleston, SC @ County Hall
The Assassins beat Scott McGhee & Mark Youngblood
Ric Flair & Wahoo McDaniel DDQ Bob Orton, Jr. & Dick Slater
Gene Anderson beat Keith Larson
Dory Funk, Jr. beat Steve Muslin
Brickhouse Brown beat Gary Royal

10/30/83: Toronto, Ontario @ Maple Leaf Gardens
Blackjack Mulligan beat Sgt. Slaughter by DQ
Charlie Brown beat Baron Von Raschke
Tito Santana beat Leo Burke
Don Kernodle beat Johnny Weaver
Rudy & Terry Kay beat Nick DeCarlo & Mark Fleming
Kelly Kiniski beat Vinnie Valentino(7:06)
Kurt Von Hess draw Bob Marcus
Joe Marcus beat Tom Lentz

10/30/83: Charlotte, NC @ Coliseum
Ric Flair beat Bob Orton, Jr.

10/31/83: Greenville, SC @ Memorial Auditorium
Dory Funk, Jr. Rufus R. Jones & Bugsy McGraw beat The Assassins & Paul Jones
Great Kabuki beat Mark Youngblood
John Bonello beat Gary Royal
Brickhouse Brown beat Magic Dragon
Terry Gibbs beat Bill Howard

11/1/83: Raleigh, NC @ Dorton Arena
Ric Flair & Wahoo McDaniel beat Dick Slater & Bob Orton, Jr. by CO
Mark Lewin & Greg Valentine beat Roddy Piper & Mark Youngblood
Dory Funk, Jr. beat Scott McGhee
Johnny Weaver beat Gary Royal
John Bonello beat Tom Lentz

11/2/83: Spartanburg, SC @ Memorial Auditorium (TV)
Greg Valentine beat Gary Royal
Dick Slater & Bob Orton, Jr. beat Scott McGee & Steve Muslin
Great Kabuki beat John Bonello

Charlie Brown, Rufus R. Jones & Dory Funk, Jr. beat Bill Howard, Kelly Kiniski & Tom Lentz
Wahoo McDaniel beat Magic Dragon
Dick Slater & Bob Orton, Jr. beat John Bonello & Vinnie Valentino
Great Kabuki beat Gary Royal
Kevin Sullivan & Mark Lewin beat Brett Hart & Steve Muslin
Charlie Brown, Bugsy McGraw & Rufus R. Jones beat Jerry Gray, Bill Howard & Ben Alexander

11/3/83: Norfolk, VA @ Scope
Ric Flair, Roddy Piper & Wahoo McDaniel beat Greg Valentine, Dick Slater & Bob Orton, Jr.
Jack & Jerry Brisco beat Ricky Steamboat & Jay Youngblood
Angelo Mosca beat Gene Anderson
Mark Lewin beat Rufus R. Jones
Kevin Sullivan beat Vinnie Valentino
Scott McGhee beat Magic Dragon

11/4/83: Charleston, SC @ County Hall
Wahoo McDaniel beat Dick Slater in taped fist match
Roddy Piper & Angelo Mosca beat Greg Valentine & Dory Funk, Jr.
Johnny Weaver beat The Ninja
John Bonello beat Tom Lentz
Terry Gibbs beat Keith Larsen

11/4/83: Spotsylvania, VA @ High School
Ricky Steamboat & Jay Youngblood vs. Jack Brisco & Jerry Brisco
Kevin Sullivan vs. Scott McGhee
Mark Lewin vs. Vinnie Valentino
Rufus R. Jones vs. Gene Anderson
Magic Dragon vs. Mark Fleming

11/6/83: Rock Hill, SC @ Winthrop Coliseum (TV)
Ric Flair beat Bob Orton, Jr. in a lumberjack match
Jack & Jerry Brisco beat Roddy Piper & Wahoo McDaniel
The Assassins & Paul Jones beat Charlie Brown, Dory Funk, Jr. & Bugsy McGraw
John Bonello & Steve Muslin beat Dick Slater & Bob Orton, Jr. by DQ
Wahoo McDaniel beat Gary Royal
Jack & Jerry Brisco beat Brett Hart & Ric McCord
The Cobra beat Magic Dragon
Ricky Steamboat & Jay Youngblood beat Gary Royal & Bill Howard
Great Kabuki beat Steve Muslin
Dick Slater & Bob Orton, Jr. beat Vinnie Valentino & Gene Ligon

11/6/83: Columbia, SC @ Township Auditorium
Ric Flair beat Bob Orton, Jr. by DQ
Dory Funk, Jr. beat Scott McGhee

11/7/83: Greenville, SC @ Memorial Auditorium
Great Kabuki beat Charlie Brown
Dory Funk, Jr. & Rufus R. Jones beat The Assassins
Mark Youngblood beat Kelly Kiniski
Keith Larsen & Rick McCord beat Jerry Grey & Gary Royal
Brett Hart beat Tom Lentz

11/9/83: Spartanburg, SC @ Memorial Auditorium (TV)
Charlie Brown & Wahoo McDaniel beat Tom Lentz & Kelly Kiniski
Kevin Sullivan & Mark Lewin beat Scott McGee & Terry Gibbs
Greg Valentine beat John Bonello
The Assassins DDQ Charlie Brown & Wahoo McDaniel
Ricky Steamboat & Jay Youngblood beat Ben Alexander & Jerry Gray
Dick Slater & Bob Orton, Jr. beat Terry Gibbs & Brett Hart
Angelo Mosca beat Bill Howard
Kevin Sullivan & Mark Lewin beat Scott McGee & Rick McCord
Great Kabuki beat John Bonello
Mark Youngblood beat Gary Royal

11/11/83: Charleston, SC @ County Hall
The Assassins & Paul Jones beat Charlie Brown, Dory Funk, Jr. & Bugsy McGraw
Rufus R. Jones beat Great Kabuki
Vinnie Valentino beat Bill Howard
John Bonello beat Jerry Gray
Terry Gibbs beat Magic Dragon

11/11/83: Richmond, VA @ Coliseum
Johnny Weaver beat Gary Royal
Scott McGhee beat Gene Anderson
Kevin Sullivan beat Keith Larson
Angelo Mosca beat Kelly Kiniski
Ricky Steamboat beat Mark Lewin
Dick Slater & Greg Valentine beat Roddy Piper & Wahoo McDaniel
Ric Flair beat Bob Orton, Jr.

11/12/83: Hampton, VA @ Coliseum
Ric Flair beat Bob Orton, Jr.

11/13/83: Asheville, NC @ Civic Center
John Bonello beat Tom Lentz
Vinnie Valentino beat Keith Larson
Magic Dragon beat Bret Hart
Brickhouse Brown beat Gene Anderson
Mark Lewin & Kevin Sullivan beat Mark Youngblood & Jay Youngblood
Ricky Steamboat beat Great Kabuki
Ric Flair & Wahoo McDaniel beat Bob Orton, Jr. & Dick Slater in a steel cage match

11/13/83: Columbia, SC @ Township Auditorium
Ric Flair beat Bob Orton, Jr. in a steel cage match

11/13/83: Toronto, Ontario @ Maple Leaf Gardens
Bob Marcus beat Tim Gerrard
Nick DeCarlo beat Scrap Iron Sheppard
Leo Burke beat Herb Gallant
The Destroyer & Kurt Von Hess beat Johnny Weaver & Billy Red Lyons
Angelo Mosca & Jimmy Valiant beat Leo Burke & The Destroyer(subs for Jack Brisco & Jerry Brisco)
Blackjack Mulligan NC with Masked Superstar
Roddy Piper beat Greg Valentine by DQ

11/14/83: Kitchener, Ontario
Nick DeCarlo beat Kurt Von Hess
Kelly Kiniski beat Tim Gerrard
Billy Red Lyons draw The Destroyer
Ric Flair & Angelo Mosca beat Bob Orton, Jr. & Dick Slater by DQ
Leo Burke beat Johnny Weaver
Jimmy Valiant beat Great Kabuki

11/14/83: Greenville, SC @ Memorial Auditorium
Ric Flair beat Bob Orton, Jr.
Wahoo McDaniel & Roddy Piper beat Greg Valentine & Dick Slater
Kevin Sullivan & Mark Lewin beat Bugsy McGraw & Johnny Weaver
Vinnie Valentino beat Gene Anderson
Terry Gibbs beat Magic Dragon
John Bonello beat Bill Howard

11/15/83: Hampton, VA @ Coliseum
Ric Flair beat Bob Orton, Jr.
Wahoo McDaniel beat Greg Valentine by DQ
Roddy Piper beat Dick Slater
Kabuki beat Scott McGhee
Angelo Mosca beat Gene Anderson
Johnny Weaver & Mark Fleming beat Tom Lentz & Kelly Kiniski
Keith Larsen beat Jerry Grey
Bill Howard beat Ric McCord

11/16/83: Spartanburg, SC @ Memorial Auditorium (TV)
Wahoo McDaniel beat Gary Royal
Dick Slater & Bob Orton, Jr. beat John Bonello & Steve Muslin
Jack & Jerry Brisco beat Brett Hart & Rick McCord
King Cobra beat Magic Dragon
Angelo Mosca beat Tom Lentz

11/17/83: Sumter, SC @ Exhibition Center
Ric Flair beat Bob Orton, Jr. in a lumberjack match

11/17/83: Fredericksburg, VA @ Stafford High School
Wahoo McDaniel & Roddy Piper vs. Jack Brisco & Jerry Brisco
Jay Youngblood vs. Dick Slater
Magic Dragon vs. Terry Gibbs
Scott McGhee vs. Bill Howard
The Ninja vs. Vinnie Valentino

11/18/83: Charleston, SC @ County Hall
Ric Flair beat Bob Orton, Jr. in a steel cage match
Greg Valentine beat Ricky Steamboat
Kevin Sullivan & Mark Lewin beat Johnny Weaver & Rick McGraw
Angelo Mosca beat Gene Anderson
Brickhouse Brown beat Jerry Gray

11/18/83: Colonial Heights, VA @ High School
Roddy Piper & Wahoo McDaniel vs. Jack Brisco & Jerry Brisco
Dick Slater vs. Jay Youngblood
Bill Howard vs. Vinnie Valentino
The Ninja vs. Terry Gibbs
Magic Dragon vs. Scott McGhee

11/19/83: Hendersonville, NC @ West Henderson High School
Rufus R. Jones, Charlie Brown & Ricky Steamboat vs. The Assassins & Paul Jones
Mark Lewin vs. Mark Youngblood
Kevin Sullivan vs. Keith Larsen
Tom Lentz vs. Brett Hart
Jerry Gray vs. John Bonello

11/19/83: Front Royal, VA
Ric Flair & Wahoo McDaniel beat Dick Slater & Bob Orton, Jr.
Terry Gibbs beat Magic Dragon
Scott McGhee beat Mark Fleming
Vinnie Valentino beat Bill Howard

11/19/83: Charlotte, NC @ Coliseum
Brett Hart beat Jerry Gray
Kelly Kiniski beat Scott McGhee
Bob Orton, Jr. beat Johnny Weaver
The Assassins beat Keith Larson & Rick McCord
Jimmy Valiant beat Great Kabuki
Greg Valentine beat Mark Youngblood(sub for Roddy Piper)
Ricky Steamboat & Jay Youngblood beat Jack & Jerry Brisco in a no DQ match

11/20/83: Kitchener, Ontario
Ric Flair & Angelo Mosca beat Dick Slater & Bob Orton, Jr. by DQ
Charlie Brown beat Great Kabuki
Leo Burke beat Johnny Weaver
Billy Red Lyons beat The Destroyer
Kelly Kiniski beat Tim Gerrard
Nick DeCarlo beat Kurt Von Hess

11/21/83: Greenville, SC @ Memorial Auditorium
Dick Slater beat Roddy Piper
Greg Valentine beat Ricky Steamboat
The Assassins beat Jay Youngblood & Rufus R. Jones
Tommy Rich beat Magic Dragon

11/21/83: Kingston, Ontario
Kelly Kiniski beat Tim Gerrard
Nick DeCarlo beat Kurt Von Hess
The Destroyer draw Billy Red Lyons

Johnny Weaver beat Leo Burke by DQ
Jimmy Valiant beat Great Kabuki

11/22/83: Goldsboro, NC
John Bonello beat Magic Dragon
Bill Howard beat Vinnie Valentino
Kelly Kiniski beat Terry Gibbs
Rufus R. Jones & Mark Youngblood beat Paul Jones & The Assassin
Charlie Brown & Angelo Mosca beat Kevin Sullivan & Mark Lewin

11/23/83: Winston-Salem, NC @ Memorial Coliseum (TV)
Tommy Rich beat Jerry Gray(2:46) via pinfall
Rufus R. Jones beat Bill Howard(3:23)
Dick Slater beat John Bonello(2:59)
Kevin Sullivan & Mark Lewin beat Vinnie Valentino & Rick McCord(5:04) by submission
Bob Orton, Jr. beat Brett Hart(4:38) via pinfall
Wahoo McDaniel beat Tom Lentz(4:22) via pinfall

11/24/83: Greensboro, NC @ Coliseum
Starrcade 83: A Flair for the Gold
The Assassins beat Rufus R. Jones & Bugsy McGraw(8:12) via pinfall
Kevin Sullivan & Mark Lewin beat Scott McGhee & Johnny Weaver(6:42)
Abdullah the Butcher beat Carlos Colon(4:29) via pinfall
Dick Slater & Bob Orton, Jr. beat Wahoo McDaniel & Mark Youngblood(14:46)
Charlie Brown (Jimmy Valiant) beat Great Kabuki(10:35) wins NWA Mid Atlantic Television Title in a no DQ, no time limit mask vs. title match
Ricky Steamboat & Jay Youngblood beat Jack Brisco & Jerry Brisco (12:59) via pinfall to NWA World Tag Title
Roddy Piper beat Greg Valentine (16:08) in a dog collar match
Ric Flair beat Harley Race (23:49) via pinfall to win NWA World Title in a steel cage match with Gene Kiniski as special referee

11/25/83: Charleston, SC @ County Hall
No Wrestling

11/30/83: Spartanburg, SC @ Memorial Auditorium (TV)
Jimmy Valiant beat Magic Dragon
Kevin Sullivan & Mark Lewin beat Rick McCord & John Bonello
Ricky Steamboat & Jay Youngblood beat Gary Royal & Kelly Kiniski
Greg Valentine beat Keith Larson
Mark Youngblood beat Bill Howard
Dick Slater beat Vinnie Valentino
Ricky Steamboat & Jay Youngblood beat Bill Howard & Jerry Gray
Dick Slater beat Keith Larson
Jimmy Valiant beat Ben Alexander
The Assassins beat Gene Ligon & John Bonello
Mark Youngblood beat Magic Dragon
Bob Orton, Jr. beat Vinnie Valentino

12/1/83: Sumter, SC @ Exhibition Center
Kelly Kiniski beat Rick McCord
Brickhouse Brown beat Magic Dragon
Bugsy McGraw beat Terry Gibbs
Bob Orton, Jr. beat Johnny Weaver
Greg Valentine beat Ricky Steamboat
Wahoo McDaniel beat Dick Slater

12/1/83: Chester, SC @ High School
Great Kabuki vs. Jay Youngblood
Charlie Brown & Rufus R. Jones vs. The Assassins
Mark Lewin vs. Mark Youngblood
Angelo Mosca vs. Gene Anderson
Jerry Gray vs. John Bonello
Vinnie Valentino vs. Bill Howard

12/2/83: Lynchburg, VA @ Armory
Roddy Piper & Jimmy Valiant vs. The Assassins
Rufus R. Jones vs. Greg Valentine

12/2/83: Charleston, SC @ County Hall
Dick Slater & Bob Orton, Jr. beat Ricky Steamboat & Jay Youngblood
Greg Valentine beat Great Kabuki
Mark Youngblood & Bugsy McGraw beat Gene Anderson & Jerry Grey
Angelo Mosca beat Kelly Kiniski
Brett Hart beat Steve Muslin

12/3/83: Newton, NC
Rick McCord beat Gary Royal
Brett Hart beat Jerry Grey
Kelly Kiniski beat Vinnie Valentino
Johnny Weaver beat Gene Anderson
Mark Youngblood beat Great Kabuki
Wahoo McDaniel & Roddy Piper beat Greg Valentine & Bob Orton, Jr.

12/3/83: Hampton, VA @ Coliseum
The Assassins beat Jimmy Valiant & Brickhouse Brown
Keith Larsen beat Bill Howard
John Bonello beat Steve Muslin
Terry Gibbs beat Mark Fleming
Angelo Mosca beat Don Kernodle
Dick Slater beat Rufus R. Jones to win NWA Mid Atlantic Title
Ricky Steamboat & Jay Youngblood beat Jack & Jerry Brisco in a cage match

12/4/83: Roanoke, VA @ Civic Center
John Bonello beat Bill Howard
Terry Gibbs beat Rick McCord
Jerry Grey beat Brickhouse Brown
Gene Anderson beat Vinnie Valentino
The Assassins beat Jimmy Valiant & Wahoo McDaniel
Ricky Steamboat & Jay Youngblood beat Jack & Jerry Brisco in a cage match

12/4/83: Toronto, Ontario @ Maple Leaf Gardens
Rudy Kay beat Nick DeCarlo
Terry Kay draw Billy Red Lyons
The Destroyer beat Joe Marcus
Johnny Weaver beat Kelly Kiniski
Leo Burke beat Keith Larson
Buddy Hart(aka Bret Hart) beat Great Kabuki
Angelo Mosca & Blackjack Mulligan beat Sgt. Slaughter & Don Kernodle
Roddy Piper beat Greg Valentine in a dog collar match

12/5/83: Greenville, SC @ Memorial Auditorium
Terry Gibbs beat Gary Royal
Kelly Kiniski beat John Bonello
Bob Orton, Jr. beat Johnny Weaver
The Assassins beat Jimmy Valiant & Wahoo McDaniel
Angelo Mosca beat Don Kernodle by DQ

12/5/83: Fayetteville, NC @ Cumberland County Civic Center
Brickhouse Brown beat Jerry Grey
Vinnie Valentino beat Bill Howard
Mark Youngblood beat Gene Anderson
Rufus R. Jones beat Dick Slater by DQ
Roddy Piper beat Greg Valentine
Ricky Steamboat & Jay Youngblood beat Jack Brisco & Jerry Brisco

12/6/83: Raleigh, NC @ Dorton Arena
John Bonello beat Jerry Grey
Keith Larsen beat Brett Hart
Terry Gibbs beat Rick McCord
Greg Valentine & Bob Orton, Jr. beat Ricky Steamboat & Jay Youngblood
The Assassins beat Jimmy Valiant & Mark Youngblood

12/6/83: Columbia, SC @ Township Auditorium
Vinnie Valentino beat Bill Howard
Brickhouse Brown beat Kelly Kiniski
Johnny Weaver beat Gene Anderson
Roddy Piper beat Dick Slater
Angelo Mosca & Rufus R. Jones beat Gary Hart & Don Kernodle

12/7/83: Spartanburg, SC @ Memorial Auditorium (TV)
Ricky Steamboat & Jay Youngblood beat Greg Valentine & Bob Orton, Jr.
Roddy Piper beat Dick Slater
Jimmy Valiant & Rufus R. Jones vs. Ben Alexander & Kelly Kiniski
Great Kabuki vs. Ric McCord
Tommy Rich & Mark Youngblood vs. Jerry Grey & Bill Howard
The Assassins vs. Vinnie Valentino & Keith Larsen
The Road Warriors vs. Ric McCord & Steve Muslim
Ricky Steamboat & Jay Youngblood vs. Terry Gibbs & Magic Dragon

12/8/83: Norfolk, VA @ Scope
Mark Fleming beat Kelly Kiniski
Brett Hart beat Jerry Grey
Johnny Weaver beat Gene Anderson
Angelo Mosca beat Don Kernodle
The Assassins beat Jimmy Valiant & Rufus R. Jones
Dick Slater & Bob Orton, Jr. beat Ricky Steamboat & Jay Youngblood
Roddy Piper beat Greg Valentine

12/9/83: Charleston, SC @ County Hall
Roddy Piper beat Greg Valentine in a dog collar match
Mark Youngblood & Abe Jacobs beat Terry Gibbs & Bill Howard
Keith Larsen beat Vinnie Valentino
Brickhouse Brown beat Gary Royal
John Bonello beat Ben Alexander

12/9/83: Richmond, VA @ Coliseum
Jerry Grey beat Mark Fleming
Kelly Kiniski beat Brett Hart
Gene Anderson beat Ric McCord
Dick Slater beat Johnny Weaver
The Assassins beat Jimmy Valiant & Jay Youngblood
Ricky Steamboat & Angelo Mosca beat Don Kernodle & Gary Hart by DQ

12/12/83: Asheville, NC @ Civic Center
Rick McCord beat Jerry Gray
Gene Anderson beat John Bonello
Bob Orton, Jr. beat Johnny Weaver
Dick Slater beat Rufus R. Jones
Jimmy Valiant & Mark Youngblood beat The Assassins
Angelo Mosca beat Don Kernodle by DQ
Ricky Steamboat & Jay Youngblood beat Jack & Jerry Brisco

12/13/83: Shelby, NC(TV)
Dick Slater beat Greg Valentine to win NWA United States Title
Mark Youngblood & Rufus R. Jones beat Bill Howard & Tony Russo
Don Kernodle beat Rick McCord
The Assassins beat Keith Larson & John Bonello
Dick Slater beat Mark Fleming
Tommy Rich beat Jerry Gray
Ricky Steamboat & Jay Youngblood beat Hans Schroeder & Gary Royal
Ricky Steamboat & Jay Youngblood beat Bill Howard & Kelly Kiniski
Don Kernodle beat Mark Fleming
Bob Orton, Jr. beat Vinnie Valentino
Angelo Mosca beat Ben Alexander
Rufus R. Jones & Mark Youngblood beat Terry Gibbs & Gary Royal

12/14/83: Charlotte, NC @ Coliseum (TV)
Note: NWA United States Champ Dick Slater gave up his NWA Mid Atlantic Title by giving it to Ivan Koloff
Don Kernodle beat Pete Martin
Tommy Rich beat Magic Dragon
Ivan Koloff beat Brett Hart
The Road Warriors beat Rick McCord & Keith Larson
Ricky Steamboat & Jay Youngblood beat Ben Alexander & Kelly Kiniski

Ricky Steamboat & Jay Youngblood beat Terry Gibbs & Gary Royal
The Road Warriors beat Rick McCord & Keith Larson
Ivan Koloff beat Gene Ligon
Dick Slater & Bob Orton, Jr. beat John Bonello & Brickhouse Brown
Angelo Mosca & Rufus R. Jones beat Bill Howard & Kelly Kiniski

12/25/83: Greenville, SC @ Memorial Auditorium
Ricky Steamboat & Jay Youngblood beat Bob Orton, Jr. & Dick Slater
Greg Valentine beat Roddy Piper
Wahoo McDaniel, Jimmy Valiant & Rufus R. Jones beat The Assassins & Paul Jones in a lumberjack match
Johnny Weaver won a battle royal

12/25/83: Charlotte, NC @ Coliseum
Ricky Steamboat & Jay Youngblood beat Jack & Jerry Brisco in a steel cage match
Roddy Piper beat Greg Valentine in a dog collar match
Jimmy Valiant beat Great Kabuki
The Assassins beat Dory Funk, Jr. & Rufus R. Jones by DQ
Angelo Mosca beat Don Kernodle
Bob Orton, Jr. beat Mark Youngblood
Wahoo McDaniel beat Barry Orton
Vinnie Valentino beat Gene Anderson
John Bonello beat Tony Russo

12/26/83: Greensboro, NC @ Coliseum
Ricky Steamboat & Jay Youngblood beat Jack & Jerry Brisco in a steel cage match
Roddy Piper beat Greg Valentine in a dog collar match
Jimmy Valiant beat Great Kabuki
Dick Slater beat Rufus R. Jones
Wahoo McDaniel & Angelo Mosca beat Bob Orton, Jr. & Don Kernodle
The Assassins beat Dory Funk, Jr. & Johnny Weaver
Gene Anderson beat John Bonello
Keith Larsen beat Jerry Grey

12/26/83: Toronto, Ontario @ Maple Leaf Gardens
Terry Kay beat Nick DeCarlo
Rudy Kay beat Joe Marcus
Billy Red Lyons beat The Destroyer by DQ
Leo Burke beat Bob Marcus
Little Beaver beat Pancho Boy
Fabulous Moolah beat Leilani Kai
Jimmy Valiant & Johnny Weaver beat Baron von Raschke & Gary Hart
Roddy Piper & Dory Funk, Jr. beat The Assassins

12/27/83: Raleigh, NC @ Dorton Arena
Rick McCord beat Tony Russo
Vinnie Valentino beat Hans Schroeder
The Assassins beat Rufus R. Jones & Dory Funk, Jr.
Wahoo McDaniel & Angelo Mosca beat Don Kernodle & Gary Hart
Charlie Brown beat Great Kabuki via forfeit
Dick Slater beat Mark Youngblood

12/27/83: Columbia, SC @ Township Auditorium
Johnny Weaver & Ricky Steamboat beat Jack & Jerry Brisco in a steel cage match
Roddy Piper beat Greg Valentine in a dog collar match
Gene Anderson beat Barry Hart
Brickhouse Brown beat Jerry Grey
John Bonello beat Gary Royal

12/28/83: Charlotte, NC @ Coliseum (TV)
Rufus R. Jones beat Jerry Gray
Jimmy Valiant beat Don Herbert
Bob Orton, Jr. beat Brett Hart
Ivan Koloff beat Vinnie Valentino
The Road Warriors beat Rick McCord & Steve Muslin
Mark Youngblood & Dory Funk, Jr. beat Bill Howard & Terry Gibbs
Mark Youngblood & Jay Youngblood beat Tony Russo & Hans Schroeder
Angelo Mosca beat Ivan Koloff by DQ
The Road Warriors beat Keith Larson & Gene Ligon
Dick Slater beat Mark Fleming
Dory Funk, Jr. beat Bill Howard

12/29/83: Lynchburg, VA
Ricky Steamboat & Jay Youngblood vs. Jack & Jerry Brisco in a Lumberjack match
Greg Valentine vs. Roddy Piper in a dog collar match

12/30/83: Charleston, SC @ County Hall
Angelo Mosca beat Don Kernodle
Brickhouse Brown & Keith Larsen beat Gary Royal & Tony Russo
Brett Hart beat Don Herbert
Red Dog Lane beat Jerry Gray
Barry Orton beat John Bonello

12/30/83: Richmond, VA @ Coliseum
Ricky Steamboat & Jimmy Valiant(sub for Jay Youngblood) beat Jack & Jerry Brisco in steel cage match
Roddy Piper beat Greg Valentine in a dog collar match
Dick Slater beat Wahoo McDaniel
The Assassins beat Dory Funk, Jr. & Rufus R. Jones
Bob Orton, Jr. beat Mark Youngblood
Johnny Weaver beat Gene Anderson
Hans Schroeder beat Barry Buckley

Chapter 5: 1984

1/2/84: Greenville, SC @ Memorial Auditorium
Ricky Steamboat beat Ivan Koloff
Roddy Piper beat Bob Orton, Jr.
Angelo Mosca, Sr. & Angelo Mosca, Jr. beat Don Kernodle & Gary Hart
Mark Youngblood beat Gene Anderson
Brickhouse Brown beat Barry Orton
Bubba Smith(aka Bubba Douglas) beat Tony Russo

1/2/84: Fayetteville, NC @ Cumberland County Civic Center
Dick Slater beat Wahoo McDaniel
The Assassins & Paul Jones beat Jimmy Valiant, Dory Funk, Jr. & Rufus R. Jones
Johnny Weaver beat Hans Schroeder
Sam Houston & Keith Larsen beat Don Herbert & Don Kernodle
John Bonello beat Gary Royal

1/3/84: Raleigh, NC @ Dorton Arena
The Assassins beat Jimmy Valiant & Dory Funk, Jr.
Ricky Steamboat beat Ivan Koloff
Rufus R. Jones beat Gene Anderson
Johnny Weaver & Bubba Smith beat Hans Schroeder & Don Herbert
Brett Hart(aka Barry Horowitz) beat Gary Royal

1/3/84: Columbia, SC @ Township Auditorium
NWA World Champ Ric Flair beat Dick Slater
Bob Orton, Jr. beat Wahoo McDaniel by DQ
Angelo Mosca, Sr. & Angelo Mosca, Jr. beat Don Kernodle & Gary Hart
Barry Orton beat Keith Larsen
Sam Houston beat Tony Russo

1/4/84: Spartanburg, SC @ Memorial Auditorium (TV)
Angelo Mosca, Jr. beat John Bonello
Wahoo McDaniel & Dory Funk, Jr. beat Hans Schroeder & Jerry Grey
Rufus R. Jones beat Tony Russo
Ivan Koloff & Don Kernodle beat Vinnie Valentino & Keith Larsen
NWA World Champ Ric Flair beat Dick Slater via by DQ

1/5/84: Sumter, SC @ Exhibition Center
Keith Larsen beat Gary Royal
John Bonello beat Ali Bey
Barry Orton beat Sam Houston
Roddy Piper & Mark Youngblood beat The Assassins
NWA World Champ Ric Flair beat Bob Orton, Jr.

1/6/84: Newberry, SC
Barry Hart beat Ben Alexander
Bubba Smith beat Gary Royal
Fabulous Moolah beat Princess Victoria
Mark Youngblood beat Gene Anderson
Rufus R. Jones & Jimmy Valiant beat The Assassins

1/6/84: Charleston, SC @ County Hall
Brickhouse Brown beat Ali Bey
Mark Fleming beat Hans Schroeder
Penny Mitchell & Peggy Patterson beat Donna Christianello & Leilani Kai
Don Kernodle & Ernie Ladd beat Angelo Mosca, Sr. & Angelo Mosca, Jr.

1/7/84: Jacksonville, NC @ White Oak High School
NWA World Champ Ric Flair vs. Dory Funk, Jr.
Dick Slater vs. Greg Valentine
Rufus R. Jones vs. Don Kernodle
Ali Bey vs. Brett Hart
Jeff Sword vs. Sam Houston
Brickhouse Brown & Bubba Smith vs. Barry Orton & Hans Schroeder

1/8/84: Charlotte, NC @ Coliseum
Ricky Steamboat beat Sgt. Slaughter in his farewell match
Greg Valentine beat Dick Slater by DQ
NWA World Tag Title Tournament
1st Round
The Assassins beat Mark Youngblood & Jay Youngblood
Jimmy Valiant & Dory Funk, Jr. beat Ivan Koloff & Ernie Ladd
The Road Warriors DDQ Buzz Sawyer & Wahoo McDaniel
David Von Erich & Kevin Von Erich beat Bubba Smith & Rufus R. Jones
Angelo Mosca, Sr. & Angelo Mosca, Jr. received a bye
Bob Orton, Jr. & Don Kernodle received a bye

2nd Round
The Assassins beat Angelo Mosca, Sr. & Angelo Mosca, Jr.
Dory Funk, Jr. & Jimmy Valiant received a bye
Bob Orton, Jr. & Don Kernodle beat David Von Erich & Kevin Von Erich

Semifinals
Dory Funk, Jr. & Jimmy Valiant beat The Assassins
Don Kernodle & Bob Orton, Jr. received a bye

Finals
Bob Orton, Jr. & Don Kernodle beat Dory Funk, Jr. & Jimmy Valiant to win vacant NWA World Tag Title in tournament final

1/8/84: Asheville, NC @ Civic Center
Ricky Steamboat beat Dory Funk, Jr.
Dick Slater beat Mark Youngblood
Wahoo McDaniel & Jimmy Valiant beat The Assassins
Greg Valentine beat Bob Orton, Jr.
Gene Anderson & Hans Schroeder beat Brett Hart & Keith Larsen
Bubba Smith beat Ali Bey

1/8/84: Toronto, Ontario @ Maple Leaf Gardens
Angelo Mosca, Sr. beat Sgt. Slaughter by CO
Tito Santana beat Leo Burke
Roddy Piper beat Kurt Von Hess(sub for Buzz Sawyer) in a dog collar match
Rudy Kay & Terry Kay beat Johnny Weaver & Sam Houston
Vic Rossitani beat John Bonello
Nick DeCarlo & Brickhouse Brown beat Gary Royal & Tim Gerrard
The Destroyer draw Billy Red Lyons

1/9/84: Greenville, SC @ Memorial Auditorium
Ric Flair & Angelo Mosca, Sr. beat Bob Orton, Jr. & Don Kernodle
Greg Valentine beat Dick Slater by DQ
Jimmy Valiant & Baron Von Raschke beat The Assassins
Angelo Mosca, Jr. beat Gene Anderson
Brett Hart beat Ali Bey

1/10/84: Columbia, SC @ Township Auditorium
Greg Valentine beat Dick Slater by DQ
Wahoo McDaniel beat Bob Orton, Jr.
Ivan Koloff beat Mark Youngblood
Brett Hart beat Gary Royal
Sam Houston & Bubba Smith beat Barry Orton & Hans Schroeder

1/10/84: Raleigh, NC @ Dorton Arena
Jimmy Valiant, Dory Funk, Jr., & Baron Von Raschke beat The Assassins & Paul Jones
Angelo Mosca, Sr. & Angelo Mosca, Jr. beat Ernie Ladd & Don Kernodle
Rufus R. Jones beat Ali Bey
Keith Larsen beat Bill White

1/11/84: Spartanburg, SC @ Memorial Auditorium (TV)
Dick Slater beat Keith Larsen
Ivan Koloff beat Bubba Smith
Greg Valentine beat John Bonello
The Assassins beat Bubba Smith & Sam Houston
Angelo Mosca, Jr. beat Tony Russo
Wahoo McDaniel beat Ben Alexander

1/12/84: Norfolk, VA @ Scope
Dory Funk, Jr., Jimmy Valiant & Dusty Rhodes beat Paul Jones & The Assassins
Dory Funk, Jr. beat Dick Slater by DQ
Johnny Weaver beat Hans Schroeder
John Bonello beat Ali Bey
Gene Anderson beat Sam Houston
Ivan Koloff beat Johnny Weaver

1/13/84: Charleston, SC @ County Hall
Angelo Mosca, Sr., Angelo Mosca, Jr. & Baron Von Raschke vs. Ernie Ladd, Don Kernodle & Gary Hart

1/14/84: North Wilkesboro, NC
Jimmy Valiant, Dory Funk, Jr. & Baron Von Raschke beat The Assassins & Paul Jones
Greg Valentine beat Bob Orton, Jr.
Gene Anderson beat John Bonello
Barry Orton beat Sam Houston
Brickhouse Brown beat John Bonello

1/15/84: Fayetteville, NC @ Cumberland County Civic Center
Greg Valentine beat Dick Slater by DQ
Keith Larsen beat Ali Bey
Vinnie Valentino beat Bill White
Wahoo McDaniel & Dory Funk, Jr. beat Don Kernodle & Bob Orton, Jr.
Dusty Rhodes & Jimmy Valiant beat The Assassins
Rufus R. Jones won a battle royal

1/15/84: Greensboro, NC @ Coliseum
Greg Valentine beat Dick Slater
Jimmy Valiant & Dusty Rhodes & Baron Von Raschke beat Paul Jones & The Assassins
Ricky Steamboat beat Ivan Koloff
Don Kernodle & Bob Orton, Jr. beat Wahoo McDaniel & Mark Youngblood
Ernie Ladd beat Angelo Mosca, Sr.
Angelo Mosca, Jr. beat Gene Anderson
Barry Orton beat Sam Houston

1/16/84: Greenville, SC @ Memorial Auditorium
Baron Von Raschke & Dusty Rhodes & Jimmy Valiant beat Paul Jones & The Assassins
Vinnie Valentino beat Gary Royal
Johnny Weaver beat Hans Schroeder
Rufus R. Jones beat Gene Anderson
Dory Funk, Jr. beat Bob Orton, Jr.

1/17/84: Raleigh, NC @ Dorton Arena
Angelo Mosca, Sr. & Angelo Mosca, Jr. beat Ernie Ladd & Don Kernodle
Ivan Koloff beat Dory Funk, Jr.
Dick Slater DCO with Wahoo McDaniel
Greg Valentine beat Bob Orton, Jr.
Sam Houston beat John Bonello
Bubba Smith beat Gary Royal

1/18/84: Spartanburg, SC @ Memorial Auditorium (TV)
Bob Orton, Jr. & Don Kernodle beat Brett Hart & Brickhouse Brown
Ernie Ladd beat Sam Houston
Assassins beat Dory Funk, Jr. & Rufus R. Jones DQ
Angelo Mosca, Sr. & Angelo Mosca, Jr. beat Bill White & Tony Russo
NWA World Champ Ric Flair vs. Dick Slater

1/19/84: Harrisonburg, VA @ High School
Gary Royal vs. Keith Larsen
Sam Houston & Johnny Weaver vs. Barry Orton & Gene Anderson
Ivan Koloff vs. Mark Youngblood
Wahoo McDaniel vs. Dick Slater
Bob Orton, Jr. vs. Greg Valentine

1/19/84: Sumter, SC @ Exhibition Center
Jimmy Valiant, Dory Funk, Jr. & Baron Von Raschke vs. The Assassins & Paul Jones

Angelo Mosca, Sr. & Angelo Mosca, Jr. vs. Ernie Ladd & Don Kernodle
Rufus R. Jones vs. Ali Bey
Buddy Landell vs. Brett Hart
Bubba Douglas vs. Hans Schroeder

1/20/84: Winston-Salem, NC @ Memorial Coliseum
NWA World Champ Ric Flair beat Dick Slater by reverse decision

1/20/84: Charleston, SC @ County Hall
Vinnie Valentino beat Ali Bey
Bubba Smith draw Brett Hart
John Bonello beat Tony Russo
Rufus R. Jones beat Hans Schroeder
Angelo Mosca, Sr., Angelo Mosca, Jr. & Baron Von Raschke beat Ernie Ladd, Don Kernodle & Gary Hart in a cage match

1/20/84: Richmond, VA @ Coliseum
Greg Valentine beat Dick Slater by DQ
Wahoo McDaniel beat Bob Orton, Jr.
Ricky Steamboat beat Dory Funk, Jr.
The Assassins beat Dusty Rhodes & Jimmy Valiant
Ivan Koloff beat Mark Youngblood
Gene Anderson beat Keith Larsen
Johnny Weaver beat Barry Orton
Sam Houston beat Gary Royal

1/21/84: Rock Hill, SC @ Winthrop Coliseum
The Assassins vs. Dory Funk, Jr. & Jimmy Valiant
Greg Valentine vs. Dick Slater
Rufus R. Jones vs. Ernie Ladd
Johnny Weaver vs. Gene Anderson
Brickhouse Brown vs. Vinnie Valentino
John Bonello vs. Buddy Landell

1/22/84: Roanoke, VA @ Civic Center
Jimmy Valiant & Wahoo McDaniel beat The Assassins; then Jimmy Valiant beat Paul Jones by DQ in a special 5-minute match
Greg Valentine beat Dick Slater by DQ
Ricky Steamboat beat Ivan Koloff via pinfall
Ernie Ladd won a 10-man $4,500 battle royal
Mark Youngblood beat Ali Bey Ali Bey
Vinnie Valentino beat Bill White via pinfall

1/22/84: Brantford, Ontario (TV)
Leo Burke beat Bobby Bas
Terry Kay beat Joe Marcus
Johnny Weaver beat Lynn Denton
Bob Marcus beat Kurt Von Hess by DQ
Leo Burke beat Nick DeCarlo
Don Kernodle beat Joe Marcus
Terry Kay & Rudy Kay beat Keith Larsen & Bob Marcus
Don Kernodle beat Nick DeCarlo
Johnny Weaver beat Goldie Rogers
Leo Burke draw Joe Marcus
Roddy Piper & Johnny Weaver beat Rudy Kay & Terry Kay by DQ
Leo Burke beat Keith Larsen

1/22/84: Toronto, Ontario @ Maple Leaf Gardens
Angelo Mosca beat Sgt. Slaughte win Canadian Title
Leo Burke beat Roddy Piper by DQ
Tito Santana beat Don Kernodle
Rudy & Terry Kay beat Johnny Weaver & Keith Larsen
Len Denton beat Nick DeCarlo
Keith Larsen beat Kurt Von Hess
Bob Marcus & Joe Marcus beat Bobby Bass & Ben Alexander

1/23/84: Greenville, SC @ Memorial Auditorium
Dick Slater & Bob Orton, Jr. beat Wahoo McDaniel & Greg Valentine by DQ
Ivan Koloff beat Angelo Mosca, Jr.
Johnny Weaver & Tim Horner beat Len Denton & Tony Anthony
Brickhouse Brown draw Bill White
Sam Houston beat Tony Russo

1/24/84: Raleigh, NC @ Dorton Arena
Dick Slater beat Wahoo McDaniel
Ivan Koloff beat Johnny Weaver
Vinnie Valentino & Tim Horner beat Len Denton & Tony Anthony
Mark Fleming beat Ben Alexander

1/25/84: Shelby, NC @ Rec Center (TV)
Wahoo McDaniel, Dory Funk, Jr. & Rufus R. Jones beat Bill White, Gary Royal & Hans Schroeder(2:00)
Angelo Mosca, Jr. beat Ivan Koloff(11:53) via pinfall to win NWA Mid Atlantic Title
Assassins beat Mark Fleming & Brett Hart via pinfall
Mark Youngblood beat Barry Orton(5:36) via pinfall in NWA World Television Title tournament
Tim Horner beat Tony Russo(5:36) via pinfall
Dick Slater beat Vinnie Valentino(5:00) via pinfall
Jimmy Valiant & Dory Funk, Jr. beat Bill White & Ben Alexander
The Assassins beat Brickhouse Brown & Sam Houston
Angelo Mosca, Jr. draw Ivan Koloff
Rufus R. Jones beat Gary Royal
Mark Youngblood beat Tony Russo
Ernie Ladd beat John Bonello

1/30/84: Spencer, NC @ North Rowan High School
Angelo Mosca, Jr. beat Ivan Koloff

2/1/84: Spartanburg, SC @ Memorial Auditorium (TV)
Don Kernodle & Bob Orton, Jr. vs. Angelo Mosca, Sr. & Angelo Mosca, Jr.
Dick Slater vs. Wahoo McDaniel

2/2/84: Sumter, SC @ Exhibition Center
Don Kernodle & Bob Orton, Jr. vs. Angelo Mosca, Sr. & Angelo Mosca, Jr.
Ernie Ladd vs. Dory Funk, Jr.
Johnny Weaver vs. Gene Anderson
Sam Houston vs. Tony Russo
Bubba Smith vs. Ben Alexander

2/2/84: Norfolk, VA @ Scope
Dick Slater beat Greg Valentine
The Assassins beat Wahoo McDaniel & Jimmy Valiant
Ivan Koloff beat Rufus R. Jones
Bob Orton, Jr. beat Brickhouse Brown
Vinnie Valentino beat Gary Royal
Keith Larsen beat Jeff Brower
Tim Horner beat ??

2/3/84: Charleston, SC @ County Hall
Ernie Ladd vs. Johnny Weaver
Angelo Mosca, Jr. vs. Ivan Koloff
Jimmy Valiant & Rufus R. Jones vs. The Assassins

2/5/84: Greensboro, NC @ Coliseum
Bruiser Brody & Stan Hansen beat Dory Funk, Jr. & Terry Gibbs

2/5/84: Greenville, SC @ Memorial Auditorium
Dick Slater beat NWA World Champ Ric Flair

2/6/84: Newberry, SC
Brett Hart beat Ben Alexander
Bubba Smith beat Nelson Royal
Fabulous Moolah beat Princess Victoria
Mark Youngblood beat Gene Anderson
Rufus R. Jones & Jimmy Valiant beat The Assassins

2/7/84: Raleigh, NC @ Dorton Arena
Ric Flair & Wahoo McDaniel beat Bob Orton, Jr. & Don Kernodle
Angelo Mosca, Jr. beat Ivan Koloff
Jay Youngblood beat Great Kabuki by DQ
Angelo Mosca, Jr. beat Bill White
Keith Larsen beat Ali Bey
Mark Fleming beat Jeff Sword

2/7/84: Columbia, SC @ Township Auditorium
Vinnie Valentino beat Tony Russo
Tim Horner beat Gary Royal
Mark Youngblood beat Hans Schroeder
Johnny Weaver beat Ernie Ladd
Assassins beat Dory Funk Jr. & Jimmy Valiant by DQ

2/8/84: Spartanburg, SC @ Memorial Auditorium (TV)
Wahoo McDaniel & Mark Youngblood beat Tony Russo & Bill White
Dick Slater beat Tim Horner
Jimmy Valiant & Dory Funk, Jr. beat The Assassins by DQ
Rufus R. Jones beat Jeff Sword
Greg Valentine beat Ernie Ladd by DQ in NWA World Television Title tournament
Angelo Mosca, Sr. & Angelo Mosca, Jr. vs. Hans Schroeder & Gary Royal

2/9/84: Fisherville, VA @ Augusta Expo
Donna Christianello vs. Peggy Patterson
Including Wahoo McDaniel, Dory Funk, Jr., Jimmy Valiant, The Assassins & Paul Jones, Johnny Weaver, Barry Orton

2/9/84: Lynchburg, VA @ City Armory
Angelo Mosca, Jr. vs. Ivan Koloff
Greg Valentine vs. Dick Slater
Also including Rufus R. Jones & Angelo Mosca, Sr.

2/10/84: Charleston, SC @ County Hall
Sam Houston beat Danny Brower
Tim Horner beat Ali Bey
Vinnie Valentino beat Tony Russo
Mark Youngblood & Jay Youngblood beat Barry Orton & Gene Anderson
Ernie Ladd DDQ Greg Valentine
Dick Slater beat NWA World Champ Ric Flair in a lights out match

2/10/84: Richmond, VA @ Coliseum
Jimmy Valiant & Angelo Mosca, Sr. beat The Assassins
Don Kernodle & Bob Orton, Jr. beat Angelo Mosca & Wahoo McDaniel
Angelo Mosca, Jr. beat Ivan Koloff
Rufus R. Jones beat Great Kabuki by DQ
Donna Christianello beat Peggy Patterson
Keith Larsen beat Bill White
Bret Hart beat Jeff Sword
Ben Alexander beat Bubba Smith

2/11/84: Hampton, VA @ Coliseum
NWA World Champ Ric Flair draw Dick Slater
Ivan Koloff beat Angelo Mosca, Jr.
Bob Orton, Jr. & Don Kernodle beat Wahoo McDaniel & Greg Valentine
Brickhouse Brown beat Mark Fleming
Rufus R. Jones beat Gary Royal
Ali Bey beat Bubba Smith
Barry Hart beat Ben Alexander

2/12/84: Roanoke, VA @ Civic Center
Sam Houston draw Gary Royal
Rufus R. Jones beat Mark Fleming
Brett Hart beat Brickhouse Brown
Angelo Mosca, Jr. beat Hans Schroder
Wahoo McDaniel & Jimmy Valiant & Dusty Rhodes beat Paul Jones & The Assassins
Angelo Mosca, Sr. beat Ivan Koloff by DQ

2/12/84: Brantford, Ontario (TV)
Swede Hanson & Bobby Bass beat Vinnie Valentino & John Bonello
Johnny Weaver & Buddy Hart beat Terry Kay & Rudy Kay by CO
Leo Burke beat Bob Marcus
James J. Dillon beat Joe Marcus
Leo Burke beat Vinnie Valentino
Buddy Hart beat Goldie Rogers
Johnny Weaver beat Swede Hanson by DQ
Buddy Hart beat Kurt Von Hess
Rudy Kay beat Joe Marcus
Tony Parisi & Johnny Weaver beat Kurt Von Hess & Goldie Rogers
Buddy Hart beat Bobby bass
Terry Kay beat Vinnie Valentino
Johnny Weaver & Buddy Hart beat James J. Dillon & Leo Burke

2/12/84: Toronto, Ontario @ Maple Leaf Gardens
NWA World Champ Ric Flair beat Harley Race in a cage match
Jimmy Valiant & Dusty Rhodes beat Assassins by CO
Leo Burke beat Vinnie Valentino
Bret Hart beat James J. Dillon
Rudy Kay & Terry Kay beat Johnny Weaver & Billy Red Lyons
Swede Hansen beat John Bonello
Kurt Von Hess draw Joe Marcus

2/12/84: Greenville, SC @ Memorial Auditorium
Bill White beat Ali Bey
Keith Larsen beat Dan Brower
Gene Anderson beat Bubba Smith
Tim Horner beat Ben Alexander
Dory Funk, Jr. beat Ernie Ladd
Mark Youngblood & Jay Youngblood beat Don Kernodle & Bob Orton, Jr. by DQ
Greg Valentine beat Dick Slater in a taped fist match

2/13/84: Asheville, NC @ Civic Center
Dick Slater beat Greg Valentine
Jimmy Valiant, Mark Youngblood & Jay Youngblood beat Paul Jones & The Assassins
Rufus R. Jones beat Gene Anderson
Johnny Weaver beat Hans Schroeder
Vinnie Valentine beat Gary Royal
Bubba Smith beat Tony Russo

2/13/84: Fayetteville, NC @ Cumberland County Civic Center
Bob Orton, Jr. & Don Kernodle beat Dory Funk, Jr. & Wahoo McDaniel
Denny Brown beat Mark Fleming
Tim Horner beat Ali Bey
Keith Larsen draw Barry Orton
Angelo Mosca, Jr. beat Bill White
Ivan Koloff beat Angelo Mosca, Sr.

2/14/84: Columbia, SC @ Township Auditorium
Wahoo McDaniel beat Dick Slater
Mark Youngblood beat Ernie Ladd
The Assassins beat Jimmy Valiant & Dory Funk, Jr.
Tim Horner beat Barry Orton
Sam Houston beat Tony Russo
Brett Hart beat Gary Royal

2/15/84: Rockingham, NC @ Richmond High School (TV)
Assassin #2 beat Johnny Weaver(8:41) via pinfall in NWA World Television Title tournament
Ernie Ladd vs. Keith Larsen
Angelo Mosca, Sr.. & Angelo Mosca, Jr. vs. ?? & ??
Mark Youngblood, Angelo Mosca, Jr. & Tim Horner vs. Tony Russo, Gary Royal & Bill White
Ivan Koloff beat Dave McCoy
Dick Slater beat Dory Funk, Jr. in NWA World Television Title tournament
Ernie Ladd beat Bubba Smith
Tully Blanchard beat Vinnie Valentino

2/16/84: Sumter, SC @ Exhibition Center
Ivan Koloff beat Keith Larsen
Vinnie Valentino beat Jeff Sword
Tim Horner beat Ali Bey
Ernie Ladd beat Denny Brown
Greg Valentine beat Dick Slater in a taped fist match
Bob Orton, Jr. & Don Kernodle beat Angelo Mosca, Sr. & Angelo Mosca, Jr.

2/16/84: Powhatan, VA @ High School

2/17/84: Lynchburg, VA @ City Armory
Hans Schroder beat Sam Houston
Mark Fleming beat Tony Russo
Tully Blanchard beat Brett Hart
Johnny Weaver beat Barry Orton
The Assassins beat Dory Funk, Jr. & Rufus R. Jones
Jimmy Valiant beat Ivan Koloff

2/17/84: Charleston, SC @ County Hall
Greg Valentine beat Ernie Ladd
Angelo Mosca, Sr. & Angelo Mosca, Jr. beat Don Kernodle & Bob Orton, Jr.

2/18/84: Greensboro, NC @ Coliseum
Jimmy Valiant & Dusty Rhodes beat The Assassins
Greg Valentine beat Dick Slater by DQ
Wahoo McDaniel & Mark Youngblood beat Bob Orton, Jr. & Don Kernodle by DQ
Angelo Mosca, Jr. beat Ivan Koloff
Bubba Smith beat Tony Russo
Tully Blanchard beat Mark Fleming
Tim Horner beat Bill White
Barry Orton beat Keith Larsen

2/19/84: Fayetteville, NC @ Cumberland County Civic Center
Tully Blanchard beat Sam Houston
Brett Hart beat Gary Royal
Greg Valentine & Wahoo McDaniel beat Bob Orton, Jr. & Dick Slater in a Texas tornado match
Rufus R. Jones & Dory Funk, Jr. & Jimmy Valiant beat Paul Jones & The Assassins
Angelo Mosca, Jr. beat Great Kabuki

2/19/84: Charlotte, NC @ Coliseum
Jimmy Valiant & Greg Valentine & Dory Funk, Jr. beat The Assassins & Paul Jones
Wahoo McDaniel beat Dick Slater by CO
Johnny Weaver beat Jeff Sword
Tim Horner beat Barry Orton
Mark Youngblood & Jay Youngblood beat Jack & Jerry Brisco
Angelo Mosca, Sr. & Angelo Mosca, Jr. beat Ivan Koloff & Ernie Ladd

2/20/84: Greenville, SC @ Memorial Auditorium
Mark Youngblood & Jay Youngblood beat Jack & Jerry Brisco
Wahoo McDaniel & Jimmy Valiant beat The Assassins
Angelo Mosca, Jr. beat Ernie Ladd
Tim Horner beat Gary Royal
Vinnie Valentino beat Bobby Bass

2/21/84: Columbia, SC @ Township Auditorium
Keith Larsen beat Ali Bey
Paul Jones & The Assassins beat Jimmy Valiant, Tully Blanchard & Dory Funk, Jr. in an elimination match
Dick Slater beat Wahoo McDaniel
Mark Youngblood & Jay Youngblood beat Jack & Jerry Brisco
Tim Horner beat Bobby Bass

2/21/84: Raleigh, NC @ Dorton Arena
Greg Valentine beat Great Kabuki
Ivan Koloff beat Rufus R. Jones
Johnny Weaver beat Ben Alexander
Sam Houston beat Hans Schroeder
Brett Hart beat Gary Royal
Bob Orton, Jr. & Don Kernodle beat Angelo Mosca, Sr. & Angelo Mosca, Jr.

2/22/84: Spartanburg, SC @ Memorial Auditorium (TV)
The Assassins beat Keith Larsen & Brett Hart
Dick Slater beat Greg Valentine(7:29) by CO in NWA World Television title tournament
Bob Orton, Jr. & Don Kernodle beat Tim Horner & Vinnie Valentino via pinfall
Great Kabuki beat Brickhouse Brown
Tully Blanchard beat Sam Houston

2/23/84: Elizabethtown, NC @ East Bladen High School
Jimmy Valiant, Rufus R. Jones & Jay Youngblood vs. The Assassins & Paul Jones
Dick Slater vs. Dory Funk, Jr.
Tully Blanchard vs. Johnny Weaver
Brickhouse Brown vs. Jeff Sword
Buddy Lane vs. Hans Schroder

2/24/84: Richmond, VA @ Coliseum
Bob Orton, Jr. & Don Kernodle beat Mark Youngblood & Wahoo McDaniel
Greg Valentine beat Dick Slater by DQ
Sam Houston beat Ben Alexander
Denny Brown beat Gary Royal
Tully Blanchard beat Johnny Weaver
Angelo Mosca, Sr., Dusty Rhodes & Jimmy Valiant beat The Assassins & Paul Jones

2/25/84: Fredericksburg, VA @ Stafford High School
Wahoo McDaniel & Greg Valentine vs. Dick Slater & Bob Orton, Jr.
Angelo Mosca, Sr. vs. Don Kernodle
Tully Blanchard vs. Brickhouse Brown
Johnny Weaver vs. Gene Anderson
Gary Royal vs. Sam Houston

2/25/84: Conway, SC
Brett Hart beat Ali Bey
Tim Horner beat Bill White
Great Kabuki beat Rufus R. Jones
Angelo Mosca, Jr. beat Ivan Koloff
The Assassins & Paul Jones beat Dory Funk, Jr., Mark Youngblood & Jimmy Valiant

2/26/84: Asheville, NC @ Civic Center
Greg Valentine beat Jeff Sword
Mark Fleming beat Bobby Bass
Great Kabuki beat Tim Horner
Jay Youngblood beat Ivan Koloff
Don Kernodle & Bob Orton, Jr. beat Angelo Mosca, Jr. & Mark Youngblood
The Road Warriors NC with Angelo Mosca, Sr. & Wahoo McDaniel

2/26/84: Columbia, SC @ Township Auditorium
Dick Slater beat Greg Valentine
Brett Hart beat Gary Royal
Barry Orton beat Gene Ligon
Ernie Ladd beat Johnny Weaver
Jimmy Valiant beat Tully Blanchard
The Assassins beat Dory Funk, Jr. & Rufus R. Jones

2/26/84: Savannah, GA @ Civic Center
Keith Larsen beat Ali Bey
Sam Houston beat Ben Alexander
Tully Blanchard beat Brett Hart
Denny Brown beat Hans Schroeder
Rufus R. Jones beat Ernie Ladd
Greg Valentine beat Dick Slater
Dory Funk, Jr. & Jimmy Valiant beat The Assassins

2/27/84: Greenville, SC @ Memorial Auditorium
Dory Funk, Jr., Jimmy Valiant & Rufus R. Jones beat The Assassins & Paul Jones
Mark Youngblood & Jay Youngblood draw Bob Orton, Jr. & Don Kernodle(60:00)
Barry Orton beat Sam Houston
Tim Horner beat Jeff Sword
Ernie Ladd beat Brickhouse Brown

2/27/84: Fayetteville, NC @ Cumberland County Civic Center
NWA World Champ Ric Flair beat Dick Slater
The Road Warriors beat Wahoo McDaniel & Greg Valentine
Angelo Mosca, Sr. & Angelo Mosca, Jr. beat Ivan Koloff & Great Kabuki
Tully Blanchard beat Johnny Weaver
Keith Larsen beat Ali Bey
Mark Fleming beat Bobby Bass

2/28/84: York, SC @ High School
The Assassins vs. Jimmy Valiant & Dory Funk, Jr.
Dick Slater vs. Rufus R. Jones
Ernie Ladd vs. Wahoo McDaniel
Tully Blanchard vs. Vinnie Valentino
Gary Royal vs. Tim Horner
Jeff Sword vs. Brett Hart

2/29/84: Winston-Salem, NC @ Memorial Coliseum (TV)
NWA World Champ Ric Flair vs. Dick Slater
Greg Valentine & Wahoo McDaniel vs. The Road Warriors
Jimmy Valiant vs. Great Kabuki
Mark Youngblood & Jay Youngblood beat Gary Royal & Barry Orton

Angelo Mosca, Jr. beat Ivan Koloff by DQ
Brickhouse Brown beat Ernie Ladd
Dick Slater beat Gene Ligon
Stan Hansen beat Brett Hart
Tully Blanchard beat Keith Larsen

3/1/84: Norfolk, VA @ Scope
NWA World Champ Ric Flair beat Angelo Mosca, Jr.
Wahoo McDaniel & Greg Valentine beat Bob Orton, Jr. & Don Kernodle
Mark Fleming beat Bobby Bass
Johnny Weaver beat Barry Orton
Tully Blanchard beat Denny Brown
Angelo Mosca, Sr. beat Great Kabuki
Jimmy Valiant beat Paul Jones by DQ
Rufus R. Jones & Jimmy Valiant beat The Assassins

3/1/84: Manning, SC @ High School
Dick Slater vs. Dory Funk, Jr.
Mark Youngblood & Jay Youngblood vs. Ivan Koloff & Ernie Ladd
Angelo Mosca, Jr. vs. Tully Blanchard
Gary Royal vs. Sam Houston
Ali Bey vs. Vinnie Valentino
Bill White vs. Tim Horner

3/2/84: Lynchburg, VA @ City Armory
Bob Orton, Jr. & Don Kernodle vs. Wahoo McDaniel & Greg Valentine
also including Johnny Weaver, Tim Horner & Barry Orton

3/2/84: Charleston, SC @ County Hall
Brett Hart beat Ali Bey
Tully Blanchard beat Sam Houston
Great Kabuki beat Jay Youngblood
Jimmy Valiant, Rufus R. Jones & Mark Youngblood beat The Assassins & Paul Jones in an elimination match
NWA World Champ Ric Flair beat Dory Funk, Jr.

3/4/84: Charlotte, NC @ Coliseum
Jimmy Valiant, Rufus R. Jones & Dory Funk, Jr. beat Paul Jones & The Assassins in a cage match
Wahoo McDaniel & Mark Youngblood beat Bob Orton, Jr. & Don Kernodle to win NWA World Tag Title
Dick Slater beat Greg Valentine in a taped fist match
Angelo Mosca, Sr. & Angelo Mosca, Jr. beat Great Kabuki & Ivan Koloff
Denny Brown beat Ali Bey
Keith Larsen beat Gary Royal

3/5/84: Greenville, SC @ Memorial Auditorium
Mark Youngblood & Jay Youngblood beat Bob Orton, Jr. & Don Kernodle
Wahoo McDaniel beat Dick Slater in an Indian strap match
Angelo Mosca, Sr. & Angelo Mosca, Jr. beat Ivan Koloff & Great Kabuki
Ernie Ladd beat Rufus R. Jones by DQ
Brickhouse Brown beat Hans Schroeder
Keith Larsen beat Doug Vines

3/6/84: Columbia, SC @ Township Auditorium
Keith Larsen beat Doug Vines
Brett Hart beat Ben Alexander
Ernie Ladd beat Denny Brown
Jimmy Valiant beat Paul Jones
The Assassins beat Jimmy Valiant & Rufus R. Jones
Jay Youngblood beat Tully Blanchard

3/6/84: Raleigh, NC @ Dorton Arena
Jeff Sword beat Mark Fleming
Sam Houston beat Bobby Bass
Johnny Weaver beat Barry Orton
Great Kabuki beat Tim Horner
Angelo Mosca, Jr. beat Dory Funk, Jr.
Angelo Mosca, Sr. beat Ivan Koloff
Bob Orton, Jr. & Don Kernodle beat Mark Youngblood & Wahoo McDaniel by DQ

3/7/84: Spartanburg, SC @ Memorial Auditorium (TV)
Jimmy Valiant & Rufus R. Jones beat The Assassins
Mark Youngblood beat Dick Slater(7:00) via pinfall to win vacant NWA Mid Atlantic Television Title in tournament final
Ernie Ladd beat Wahoo McDaniel
The Assassins beat Tim Horner & Keith Larsen
Dory Funk, Jr. & Angelo Mosca beat Doug Vines & Bobby Bass
Stan Hansen beat Steve Brinson
Stan Hansen beat Don Herbert
Tully Blanchard beat Mark Fleming

3/8/84: Rocky Mount, VA @ Franklin City Gym
Including Wahoo McDaniel, Greg Valentine, Dick Slater, Bob Orton, Jr. & Tully Blanchard

3/9/84: Charleston, SC @ County Hall
Angelo Mosca, Sr. & Angelo Mosca, Jr. beat Ivan Koloff & Great Kabuki
Rufus R. Jones beat Ernie Ladd

3/9/84: Richmond, VA @ Coliseum
Wahoo McDaniel & Mark Youngblood beat Bob Orton, Jr. & Don Kernodle
Greg Valentine beat Dick Slater in a taped fist match
The Assassins beat Jimmy Valiant & Jay Youngblood
Jimmy Valiant beat Paul Jones
Dory Funk, Jr. beat Tully Blanchard
Tim Horner beat Jeff Sword
Barry Orton beat Denny Brown
Bobby Bass beat Keith Larsen

3/10/84: Roanoke, VA @ Civic Center
Dick Slater beat Greg Valentine
Doug Vines beat Gary Hart
Mark Fleming beat Ali Bey
Gary Royal beat Sam Houston
Great Kabuki beat Johnny Weaver
Angelo Mosca, Jr. beat Tully Blanchard by DQ
Bob Orton, Jr. & Don Kernodle beat Mark Youngblood & Jay Youngblood

3/11/84: Sumter, SC @ Exhibition Center
Brett Hart beat Jeff Sword
Barry Orton beat Hans Schroeder
Denny Brown beat Gary Royal
Dick Slater beat Greg Valentine
Angelo Mosca, Sr., Rufus R. Jones & Jimmy Valiant beat Paul Jones & The Assassins
Angelo Mosca, Jr. beat Great Kabuki

3/11/84: Savannah, GA @ Civic Center
Keith Larsen beat Ben Alexander
Vinnie Valentino beat Bobby Bass
Ernie Ladd beat Rufus R. Jones by DQ
Bob Orton, Jr. & Don Kernodle beat Johnny Weaver & Mark Youngblood
Dick Slater beat Greg Valentine in a cage match
Jimmy Valiant beat Assassin #2 in a hair vs. mask match

3/12/84: Greenville, SC @ Memorial Auditorium
Dick Slater beat Greg Valentine
Angelo Mosca, Sr. & King Kong Bundy beat The Road Warriors
Rufus R. Jones beat Ernie Ladd
Johnny Weaver beat Doug Vines
Barry Orton beat Tim Horner
Brickhouse Brown beat Bobby Bass

3/12/84: Fayetteville, NC @ Cumberland County Civic Center
Tully Blanchard beat Jeff Sword
Gary Royal beat Sam Houston
Wahoo McDaniel & Mark Youngblood beat Bob Orton, Jr. & Don Kernodle
Ivan Koloff beat Dory Funk, Jr.
Great Kabuki beat Angelo Mosca, Jr. by CO
Jimmy Valiant beat Paul Jones
The Assassins beat Jay Youngblood & Jimmy Valiant

3/13/84: Columbia, SC @ Township Auditorium
Kurt Von Hess beat Vinnie Valentino
Denny Brown beat Doug Vines
Keith Larsen beat Barry Orton
Ernie Ladd beat Rufus R. Jones by DQ
Tully Blanchard beat Johnny Weaver
Ivan Koloff & Great Kabuki beat Angelo Mosca, Sr. & Angelo Mosca, Jr.
Dick Slater beat Greg Valentine in a cage match

3/13/84: Raleigh, NC @ Dorton Arena
Wahoo McDaniel & Mark Youngblood beat Bob Orton, Jr. & Don Kernodle in a Texas tornado match
Jay Youngblood & Dory Funk, Jr. & Jimmy Valiant beat Paul Jones & The Assassins
Tim Horner beat Brett Hart
Tim Horner beat Bobby Bass

3/15/84: Norfolk, VA @ Scope
Mark Fleming beat Ali Bey
Denny Brown beat Gary Royal
Great Kabuki beat Angelo Mosca, Jr.
Angelo Mosca, Sr. beat Ivan Koloff
Tully Blanchard beat Johnny Weaver
Jimmy Valiant beat Paul Jones
Wahoo McDaniel & Mark Youngblood beat Bob Orton, Jr. & Don Kernodle

3/16/84: Charleston, SC @ County Hall
Keith Larsen beat Jeff Sword
Bobby Bass beat Gene Ligon
Kurt Von Hess beat Tim Horner
Penny Patterson beat Peggy Lee
Rufus R. Jones beat Ernie Ladd
Dick Slater beat Greg Valentine in a no DQ, cage match

3/16/84: Lynchburg, VA @ City Armory
Wahoo McDaniel & Mark Youngblood vs. Bob Orton, Jr. & Don Kernodle
Johnny Weaver vs. Doug Vines
Also including Mark Youngblood, Jay Youngblood & Tully Blanchard

3/17/84: Greensboro, NC @ Coliseum
Tully Blanchard beat Dory Funk, Jr.
Rufus R. Jones beat Ernie Ladd
Wahoo McDaniel & Mark Youngblood beat Don Kernodle & Bob Orton, Jr.
Angelo Mosca, Jr., Angelo Mosca, Sr. & Junkyard Dog beat Gary Hart, Great Kabuki & Ivan Koloff
Dick Slater beat Greg Valentine no DQ, cage match
NWA World Champ Ric Flair draw Ricky Steamboat(60:00)
Paul Jones tied with a bullrope to Dusty Rhodes
Jimmy Valiant beat Assassin #2 (unmasked as Ray Hernandez) in a hair vs. mask match

3/18/84: Columbia, SC @ Township Auditorium
Denny Brown beat Hans Schroeder
Doug Vines beat Sam Houston
Tully Blanchard beat Dory Funk, Jr.
Kurt Von Hess beat Tim Horner
Rufus R. Jones beat Ernie Ladd
Junkyard Dog, Angelo Mosca, Sr. & Angelo Mosca, Jr. beat Ivan Koloff & Great Kabuki & Gary Hart

3/18/84: Asheville, NC @ Civic Center
Keith Larsen beat Barry Orton
Johnny Weaver beat Brett Hart
Vinnie Valentino beat Ali Bey
Don Kernodle beat Mark Youngblood
Jimmy Valiant beat Assassin #2 hair vs. mask match
Greg Valentine & Wahoo McDaniel beat Don Kernodle & Bob Orton, Jr. in a Texas tornado match

3/18/84: Charlotte, NC @ Coliseum
Mark Fleming beat Bobby Bass
Keith Larsen beat Jeff Sword
Gary Royal beat Brett Hart
Angelo Mosca, Sr. beat Great Kabuki
Ivan Koloff beat Angelo Mosca, Jr. To win NWA Mid Atlantic Title
Wahoo McDaniel & Greg Valentine beat Tully Blanchard & Don Kernodle in a Texas tornado match
Dory Funk, Jr., Jimmy Valiant & Junkyard Dog beat The Assassins & Paul Jones in an elimination match

3/19/84: Appomattox, VA @ High School Gym
Including Ernie Ladd, The Assassins & Paul Jones, Jimmy Valiant, Dory Funk, Jr. & Rufus R. Jones

3/19/84: Greenville, SC @ Municipal Auditorium
Mark Youngblood & Jay Youngblood beat Jack & Jerry Brisco
Jimmy Valiant & Wahoo McDaniel beat The Assassins
Angelo Mosca, Jr. beat Ernie Ladd
Tim Horner beat Gary Royal
Vinnie Valentino beat Bobby Bass

3/20/84: Raleigh, NC @ Dorton Arena
Jimmy Valiant & Dory Funk, Jr. beat The Assassins
Great Kabuki & Ivan Koloff beat Angelo Mosca, sr. & Angelo Mosca, Jr.
Jimmy Valiant beat Paul Jones
Barry Orton beat Brett Hart
Mark Fleming beat Kurt Von Hess
Tully Blanchard beat Johnny Weaver

3/21/84: Spartanburg, SC @ Memorial Auditorium (TV)
Great Kabuki beat Tim Horner
Assassin #1(Jody Hamilton) beat Vinnie Valentino via pinfall
Ivan Koloff & Don Kernodle beat Gene Ligon & Brickhouse Brown via pinfall
Junkyard Dog & Jimmy Valiant beat Gary Royal & Barry Orton
Brian Adidas beat Ali Bey
Tully Blanchard beat Brett Hart

3/22/84: Harrisonburg, VA @ High School
Barry Orton & Doug Vines vs. Vinnie Valentino & Mark Fleming
Assassin #1 vs. Tony Charles
Tully Blanchard vs. Johnny Weaver
If Youngblood can beat Assassin #2, he would get 5 minutes with Paul Jones
Assassin #2 vs. Mark Youngblood
Dick Slater vs. Dory Funk, Jr.

3/23/84: Hampton, VA @ Coliseum
Dick Slater beat Greg Valentine
Junkyard Dog, Jimmy Valiant & Mark Youngblood beat Paul Jones & The Assassins
Keith Larsen beat Gary Royal
Sam Houston beat Ali Bey
Rufus R. Jones beat Ernie Ladd
Don Kernodle & Barry Orton beat Larry Hamilton & Vinnie Valentino

3/23/84: Charleston, SC @ County Hall
Brett Hart beat Bobby Bass
Brian Adidas beat Doug Vines
Barry Orton beat Brickhouse Brown
Tully Blanchard beat Johnny Weaver
Angelo Mosca, Sr., Angelo Mosca, Jr. & Dory Funk, Jr. beat Ivan Koloff, Great Kabuki & Gary Hart

3/24/84: Lenoir, NC
Sam Houston beat Ali Bey
Jeff Sword beat Denny Brown
Angelo Mosca, Jr. beat Tully Blanchard
Assassin #1 beat Johnny Weaver
Dory Funk, Jr. & Jay Youngblood beat Bob Orton, Jr. & Don Kernodle
Rufus R. Jones beat Ernie Ladd

3/24/84: Richmond, VA @ Coliseum
Larry Hamilton beat Bobby Bass
Vinnie Valentino beat Kurt Von Hess
Brian Adidas beat Barry Orton
Junkyard Dog beat Great Kabuki
Ivan Koloff beat Angelo Mosca, Sr. in a chain match
Wahoo McDaniel & Mark Youngblood beat The Road Warriors
Dick Slater beat Greg Valentine in a cage match
Jimmy Valiant beat Assassin #2 in a hair vs. mask match

3/25/84: Roanoke, VA @ Civic Center
Jeff Sword beat Keith Larsen
Kurt Von Hess & Hans Schroeder beat Keith Larsen & Denny Brown
Rufus R. Jones beat Ernie Ladd
Jimmy Valiant beat Assassin #2
Angelo Mosca, Sr., Angelo Mosca, Jr. & Junkyard Dog beat Gary Hart & Ivan Koloff & Great Kabuki

3/25/84: Greensboro, NC @ Coliseum
Dick Slater beat Junkyard Dog
Wahoo McDaniel & Mark Youngblood beat Bob Orton, Jr. & Don Kernodle
Paul Jones beat Jimmy Valiant
Assassin #1 beat Jimmy Valiant
Angelo Mosca, Sr. beat Ivan Koloff
Angelo Mosca, Jr. beat Great Kabuki
Jay Youngblood beat Tully Blanchard
Johnny Weaver beat Doug Vines
Brian Adidas beat Bobby Bass
Brett Hart beat Ali Bey

3/26/84: Fayetteville, NC @ Cumberland County Civic Center
Mark Fleming beat Ali Bey
Johnny Weaver beat Doug Vines
Wahoo McDaniel & Mark Youngblood beat Tully Blanchard & Don Kernodle
Ernie Ladd beat Jay Youngblood
Angelo Mosca, Jr. beat Great Kabuki
Ivan Koloff beat Angelo Mosca

3/26/84: Greenville, SC @ Memorial Auditorium
Junkyard Dog beat Dick Slater by CO
Vinnie Valentino & Larry Hamilton beat Kurt Von Hess & Hans Schroeder
Brett Hart beat Bobby Bass
Dory Funk, Jr. draw Brian Adidas
Jimmy Valiant beat Paul Jones
Rufus R. Jones & Jimmy Valiant beat The Assassins

3/27/84: Columbia, SC @ Township Auditorium
Doug Vines beat Mark Fleming
Barry Orton beat Brett Hart
Keith Larsen beat Kurt Von Hess
Rufus R. Jones & Jay Youngblood beat Ernie Ladd & Assassin #1
Junkyard Dog beat Dick Slater by DQ
Jimmy Valiant beat Assassin #2 in a hair vs. mask match

3/27/84: Raleigh, NC @ Dorton Arena
Brian Adidas draw Dory Funk, Jr.
Jeff Sword beat Denny Brown
Sam Houston beat Gary Royal
Mark Youngblood beat Tully Blanchard
Wahoo McDaniel beat Don Kernodle
Angelo Mosca, Sr. & Angelo Mosca, Jr. beat Ivan Koloff & Great Kabuki

3/28/84: Spartanburg, SC @ Memorial Auditorium (TV)
Jimmy Valiant & Brian Adidas beat Jeff Sword & Kurt Von Hess
Tully Blanchard beat Mark Youngblood(6:30) via pinfall to win NWA Mid Atlantic Television Title
Junkyard Dog DDQ Dick Slater
Angelo Mosca, Sr. & Angelo Mosca, Jr. beat Gary Royal & Bobby Bass

3/29/84: Sumter, SC @ Exhibition Center
Brian Adidas beat Ali Bey
Doug Vines beat Brett Hart
Keith Larsen beat Jeff Sword
Rufus R. Jones beat Ernie Ladd
Jimmy Valiant beat Paul Jones
Jimmy Valiant & Junkyard Dog beat The Assassins

3/30/84: Charleston, SC @ County Hall
Larry Hamilton beat Ben Alexander
Jeff Sword beat Vinnie Valentino
Brett Hart beat Gary Royal
Brian Adidas beat Hans Schroeder
Jimmy Valiant & Junkyard Dog beat The Assassins

3/30/84: Lynchburg, VA @ City Armory
Tully Blanchard vs. Jay Youngblood
Mark Youngblood vs. Don Kernodle
Ernie Ladd vs. Rufus R. Jones

3/31/84: Hickory, NC
Greek Goddess(aka Despina Montagues) beat Donna Christianello
Gene Ligon beat Jeff Sword
Keith Larsen beat Gary Royal
Keith Larsen beat Hans Schroeder
Junkyard Dog, Angelo Mosca, Sr. & Angelo Mosca, Jr. beat Great Kabuki & Ivan Koloff & Gary Hart

4/1/84: Fayetteville, NC @ Cumberland County Civic Center
Brett Hart beat Ali Bey
Ben Alexander beat Kurt Von Hess
Adrian Street beat Brian Adidas
Tully Blanchard beat Larry Hamilton
Junkyard Dog beat Ernie Ladd
Angelo Mosca, Sr. & Angelo Mosca, Jr. beat Ivan Koloff & Gary Hart
Jack & Jerry Brisco beat Junkyard Dog & Mark Youngblood

4/1/84: Greensboro, NC @ Coliseum
Larry Hamilton beat Jeff Sword
Doug Vines beat Sam Houston
Barry Orton beat Mark Fleming
Adrian Street beat Keith Larsen
Tully Blanchard beat Brian Adidas
Tully Blanchard beat Larry Hamilton
Junkyard Dog beat Ernie Ladd
Angelo Mosca, Sr. & Angelo Mosca, Jr. beat Ivan Koloff & Gary Hart
Jack & Jerry Brisco beat Junkyard Dog & Mark Youngblood

4/1/84: Toronto, Ontario @ Maple Leaf Gardens
Jimmy Valiant, Dory Funk, Jr. & Rufus R .Jones beat The Assassins & Paul Jones
Bret Hart beat Leo Burke by DQ
Jay Youngblood & Johnny Weaver beat Rudy Kay & Terry Kay by CO
Great Kabuki beat Brickhouse Brown
The Grapplers beat Bob Marcus & Vinnie Valentino
Pez Whatley beat Gary Royal
The Destroyer beat Goldie Rogers

4/2/84: Greenville, SC @ Memorial Auditorium
Keith Larsen beat Doug Vines
Kurt Von Hess beat Brett Hart
Tully Blanchard beat Sam Houston
Adrian Street beat Larry Hamilton
Ivan Koloff beat Angelo Mosca, Jr.
Junkyard Dog beat Dick Slater in a lumberjack match
Jack & Jerry Brisco beat Mark Youngblood & Wahoo McDaniel

4/3/84: Natural Bridge, VA @ High School
Keith Larsen beat Bobby Bass
Barry Orton beat Brett Hart
Mark Fleming beat Jeff Sword
Brian Adidas beat Barry Orton
Wahoo McDaniel, Jimmy Valiant & Angelo Mosca, Jr. beat Assassin #1, Paul Jones & Ron Bass

4/3/84: Raleigh, NC @ Dorton Arena
Ivan Koloff beat Angelo Mosca, Sr. in a chain match
Mark Youngblood & Jay Youngblood beat Jack & Jerry Brisco
Vinnie Valentino beat Kurt Von Hess
Tully Blanchard beat Larry Hamilton
Great Kabuki beat Rufus R. Jones
Pez Whatley beat Adrian Street by DQ

4/4/84: Spartanburg, SC @ Memorial Auditorium (TV)
Adrian Street beat Brian Adidas
Pez Whatley(sub for Junkyard Dog) beat Tully Blanchard

Jack & Jerry Brisco beat Wahoo McDaniel & Mark Youngblood to win NWA World Tag Title
Wahoo McDaniel & Mark Youngblood beat Jeff Sword & Kurt Von Hess
Tully Blanchard beat Larry Hamilton
Ivan Koloff & Don Kernodle beat Vinnie Valentino & Brett Hart
Junkyard Dog vs. Great Kabuki
Angelo Mosca, Jr. beat Ben Alexander

4/6/84: Charleston, SC @ County Hall
Vinnie Valentino beat Bobby Bass
Doug Vines beat Mark Fleming
Rufus R. Jones beat Barry Orton
Don Kernodle beat Pez Whatley
Tully Blanchard beat Brian Adidas
Jimmy Valiant beat Paul Jones
Assassin #1 beat Jimmy Valiant

4/6/84: Norfolk, VA @ Scope
Jeff Sword beat Keith Larsen
Sam Houston beat Gary Royal
Kurt Von Hess beat Brett Hart
Angelo Mosca, Sr. & Angelo Mosca, Jr. beat Ivan Koloff & Great Kabuki
Wahoo McDaniel beat Adrian Street
Mark Youngblood & Jay Youngblood beat Jack & Jerry Brisco
Dick Slater beat Junkyard Dog

4/8/84: Roanoke, VA @ Civic Center
Keith Larsen beat Gary Royal
Kurt Von Hess beat Italian Stallion
Tully Blanchard & Don Kernodle beat Pez Whatley & Vinnie Valentino
Brian Adidas beat Tully Blanchard
Assassin #1 beat Jimmy Valiant
Jimmy Valiant beat Paul Jones
Jack & Jerry Brisco beat Wahoo McDaniel & Mark Youngblood

4/8/84: Savannah, GA @ Civic Center
Mark Fleming beat Ali Bey
Gene Ligon beat Ben Alexander
Brett Hart beat Doug Vines
Adrian Street beat Jay Youngblood
Rufus R. Jones beat Ernie Ladd
Angelo Mosca, Sr. & Angelo Mosca, Jr. beat Ivan Koloff & Great Kabuki
Dick Slater beat Junkyard Dog

4/8/84: Charlotte, NC @ Coliseum
Larry Hamilton beat Bobby Bass
Sam Houston beat Hans Schroeder
Cowboy Lang beat Little Tokyo
Jack & Jerry Brisco beat Mark Youngblood & Jay Youngblood
Ivan Koloff beat Angelo Mosca, Jr.
Wahoo McDaniel beat Adrian Street
Dick Slater beat Junkyard Dog
Jimmy Valiant beat Assassin #2 hair vs. mask matc0h

4/9/84: Greenville, SC @ Memorial Auditorium
Adrian Street beat Sam Houston
Angelo Mosca, Sr. beat Great Kabuki by DQ
Brian Adidas beat Kurt Von Hess
Wahoo McDaniel & Mark Youngblood beat Ivan Koloff & Don Kernodle
Junkyard Dog & Jay Youngblood beat Dick Slater & Tully Blanchard

4/10/84: Columbia, SC @ Township Auditorium
Mark Fleming beat Ali Bey
Pez Whatley beat Bobby Bass
Assassin #1 beat Larry Hamilton
Ernie Ladd beat Rufus R. Jones by DQ
Tully Blanchard & Don Kernodle beat Wahoo McDaniel & Mark Youngblood
Jimmy Valiant beat Paul Jones in a street fight match

4/10/84: Raleigh, NC @ Dorton Arena
Keith Larsen beat Kurt Von Hess
Doug Vines beat Brett Hart
Cowboy Lang beat Little Tokyo
Adrian Street beat Sam Houston
Great Kabuki beat Brian Adidas
Angelo Mosca, Sr. & Angelo Mosca, Jr. beat Gary Hart & Ivan Koloff in a double Russian chain match
Angelo Mosca, Jr. beat Ivan Koloff in a Russian chain match

4/11/84: ?? (TV)
Brian Adidas & Pez Whatley beat Ali Bey & Kurt Von Hess via pinfall
Ivan Koloff & Don Kernodle beat Gene Ligon & Vinnie Valentino via pinfall
Adrian Street beat Keith Larsen
Assassin #1 beat Sam Houston
Angelo Mosca, Jr. beat Barry Orton
Great Kabuki beat Brett Hart
Mark Youngblood & Jay Youngblood beat Jeff Sword & Doug Vines

4/12/84: Amherst, VA @ County Gym
Cowboy Lang vs. Little Tokyo
Including Great Kabuki, Ivan Koloff, Angelo Mosca, Sr. & Angelo Mosca, Jr.

4/12/84: Sumter, SC @ Exhibition Center
Jeff Sword beat Sam Houston
Ben Alexander beat Ali Bey
Larry Hamilton beat Hans Schroeder
Brian Adidas beat Jeff Sword
Assassin #1 & Ernie Ladd beat Jimmy Valiant & Jay Youngblood by DQ

4/13/84: Charleston, SC @ County Hall
Italian Stallion beat Bobby Bass
Jeff Sword beat Gary Royal
Kurt Von Hess draw Sam Houston
Don Kernodle & Hans Schroeder(sub for Bob Orton, Jr.) beat Johnny Weaver & Larry Hamilton
Ernie Ladd beat Jay Youngblood
Mark Youngblood beat Tully Blanchard

4/13/84: Richmond, VA @ Coliseum
Brett Hart beat Ali Bey
Gene Legion beat Ben Alexander
Mark Fleming beat Doug Vines
Cowboy Lang beat Little Tokyo
Adrian Street beat Brian Adidas
Pez Whatley beat Great Kabuki by DQ
Dick Slater beat Jimmy Valiant
Angelo Mosca, Sr. & Angelo Mosca, Jr. beat Ivan Koloff & Gary Hart in a double Russian chain match

4/14/84: Fredericksburg, VA @ Stafford High School
Jimmy Valiant vs. Paul Jones in a special 5 minute challenge match
Jimmy Valiant vs. The Masked Assassin
Angelo Mosca, Jr. vs. Ivan Koloff
Little Tokyo vs. Cowboy Lang
Adrian Street vs. Brian Adidas

4/14/84: Conway, SC
Keith Larsen beat Gary Royal
Sam Houston beat Kurt Von Hess
Mark Youngblood & Jay Youngblood beat Ernie Ladd & Don Kernodle
Angelo Mosca & Pez Whatley beat Great Kabuki & Gary Hart
Dick Slater beat Pez Whatley

4/15/84: Toronto, Ontario @ Maple Leaf Gardens
Jimmy Valiant beat Assassin #2 in a hair vs. mask match(unmasked as Ray Hernandez)
Jay Youngblood & Johnny Weaver beat Rudy Kay & Terry Kay in a lumberjack match
Leo Burke beat Buddy Hart(aka Bret Hart)
Great Kabuki beat Keith Larsen
Pez Whatley beat Ben Alexander
The Destroyer & Goldie Rogers beat Sam Houston & John Bonello
Nick DeCarlo draw Bob Marcus

4/15/84: Asheville, NC @ Civic Center
Larry Hamilton beat Kurt Von Hess
Don Kernodle beat Gene Ligon
Cowboy Lang beat Little Tokyo
Dick Slater beat Wahoo McDaniel
Adrian Street beat Brian Adidas
Angelo Mosca, Sr. beat Ernie Ladd
Angelo Mosca, Jr. beat Ivan Koloff by DQ
Mark Youngblood beat Tully Blanchard

4/16/84: Greenville, SC @ Memorial Auditorium
Gary Royal beat Ali Bey
Ernie Ladd beat Jay Youngblood by DQ
Brett Hart beat Jeff Sword
Mark Fleming beat Gary Royal
The Road Warriors beat King Kong Bundy & Wahoo McDaniel

4/16/84: Fayetteville, NC @ Cumberland County Civic Center
Cowboy Lang beat Little Tokyo
Brian Adidas beat Doug Vines
Kurt Von Hess beat Gene Ligon
Don Kernodle beat Larry Hamilton
Mark Youngblood beat Adrian Street
Ivan Koloff beat Angelo Mosca, Jr.
Angelo Mosca, Sr. beat Tully Blanchard

4/17/84: Raleigh, NC @ Dorton Arena
Brian Adidas & Larry Hamilton beat Gary Royal & Doug Vines
Pez Whatley beat Great Kabuki by DQ
Assassin #1 beat Angelo Mosca, Sr.
Keith Larsen beat Ali Bey
Mark Fleming beat Bobby Bass
Jimmy Valiant beat Paul Jones in a street fight match

4/17/84: Columbia, SC @ Township Auditorium
Cowboy Lang beat Little Tokyo
Jeff Sword beat Brett Hart
Sam Houston beat Kurt Von Hess
Adrian Street beat Jay Youngblood by DQ
Ivan Koloff beat Angelo Mosca, Jr.
Wahoo McDaniel & Mark Youngblood beat Tully Blanchard & Don Kernodle in a Texas tornado match

4/18/84: Spartanburg, SC @ Memorial Auditorium (TV)
Jimmy Valiant & Brian Adidas beat Gary Royal & Doug Vines
Rufus R. Jones beat Jeff Sword
Pez Whatley beat Adrian Street by DQ
Dick Slater beat Sam Houston
Wahoo McDaniel & Mark Youngblood beat Ben Alexander & Kurt Von Hess
Ivan Koloff & Don Kernodle beat Larry Hamilton & Brett Hart via pinfall
Pez Whatley beat Jeff Sword
Ivan Koloff & Don Kernodle beat Brett Hart & Larry Hamilton
Brian Adidas beat Ben Alexander
Little Tokyo beat Cowboy Lang
Ernie Ladd beat Sam Houston
Mark Youngblood & Jay Youngblood beat Gary Royal & Kurt Von Hess via pinfall

4/19/84: Harrisonburg, VA @ High School
Paul Jones vs. Jimmy Valiant in a New York street fight match
Brian Adidas vs. Ernie Ladd
Angelo Mosca, Jr. vs. Assassin #1
Larry Hamilton & Johnny Weaver vs. Bobby Bass & Doug Vines
Keith Larsen vs. Jeff Sword

4/19/84: Hampton, VA @ Coliseum
Brett Hart beat Ali Bey
Sam Houston beat Kurt Von Hess
Cowboy Lang beat Little Tokyo
Pez Whatley beat Great Kabuki
Angelo Mosca, Jr. beat Adrian Street
Tully Blanchard beat Jay Youngblood
Mark Youngblood & Wahoo McDaniel beat Ivan Koloff & Don Kernodle

4/20/84: Lynchburg, VA @ City Armory
Gary Royal beat Brett Hart
Dick Slater beat Jay Youngblood
Ivan Koloff & Don Kernodle beat Wahoo McDaniel & Mark Youngblood
Larry Hamilton beat Ali Bey
Brian Adidas beat Kurt Von Hess
Pez Whatley beat Doug Vines

4/21/84: Greensboro, NC @ Coliseum
Ricky Steamboat beat Dick Slater to win NWA United States Title
Jimmy Valiant beat Paul Jones in a cage match
Jack & Jerry Brisco beat Pez Whatley & Jay Youngblood
Dusty Rhodes beat Adrian Street by DQ
Assassin #1 beat Angelo Mosca, Sr.
Great Kabuki beat Johnny Weaver
Brian Adidas beat Kurt Von Hess
Larry Hamilton & Sam Houston beat Gary Royal & Doug Vines

4/21/84: Charleston, SC @ County Hall
Keith Larsen beat Ali Bey
Brett Hart beat Jeff Sword
Angelo Mosca, Jr. beat Bobby Bass
Cowboy Lang beat Little Tokyo
Ernie Ladd beat Rufus R. Jones
Wahoo McDaniel & Mark Youngblood beat Ivan Koloff & Don Kernodle

4/22/84: Roanoke, VA @ Civic Center
Keith Larsen beat Bobby Bass
Hamilton beat Ben Alexander
Pez Whatley beat Kurt Von Hess
Cowboy Lang beat Little Tokyo
Ernie Ladd beat Rufus R. Jones
Adrian Street beat Jay Youngblood by DQ
Jack & Jerry Brisco beat Wahoo McDaniel & Jay Youngblood

4/22/84: Savannah, GA @ Civic Center
Sam Houston beat Ali Bey
Brett Hart beat Gene Ligon
Gary Royal beat Italian Stallion
Johnny Weaver & Brian Adidas beat Great Kabuki & Don Kernodle
Assassin #1 beat Angelo Mosca, Sr.
Jimmy Valiant beat Paul Jones in a cage match
NWA World Champ Ric Flair beat Dick Slater

4/22/84: Charlotte, NC @ Coliseum
Doug Vines beat Mark Fleming
Vinnie Valentino beat Jeff Sword
Dick Slater beat Johnny Weaver
Angelo Mosca, Sr. beat Assassin #1
Dusty Rhodes beat Adrian Street
Angelo Mosca, Jr. beat Ivan Koloff to win the NWA Mid Atlantic Title
Wahoo McDaniel & Mark Youngblood beat Jack & Jerry Brisco by DQ
Jimmy Valiant beat Paul Jones
NWA World Champ Ric Flair draw Ricky Steamboat

4/23/84: Greenville, SC @ Memorial Auditorium
Dusty Rhodes beat Adrian Street by DQ
Sam Houston beat Bobby Bass
Don Kernodle beat Johnny Weaver
Pez Whatley beat Kurt Von Hess
Tully Blanchard beat Brian Adidas
NWA World Champ Ric Flair draw Ricky Steamboat(60:00)
Jack & Jerry Brisco beat Mark & Jay Youngblood by DQ

4/24/84: Columbia, SC @ Township Auditorium
Vinnie Valentino beat Gary Royal
Brett Hart beat Ben Alexander
Don Kernodle beat Johnny Weaver
Adrian Street beat Pez Whatley
Jimmy Valiant beat Assassin #1
Jack & Jerry Brisco beat Wahoo McDaniel & Mark Youngblood by DQ
NWA World Champ Ric Flair beat Dick Slater

4/25/84: Myrtle Beach, SC (TV)
NWA World Champ Ric Flair beat Dick Slater
Jack & Jerry Brisco beat Mark & Jay Youngblood
Dusty Rhodes beat Adrian Street
Wahoo McDaniel beat Barry Orton
Ivan Koloff & Don Kernodle beat Mark Fleming & Vinnie Valentino
Jimmy Valiant & Rufus R. Jones beat Kurt Von Hess & Gary Royal
Brian Adidas beat Jeff Sword
Pez Whatley beat Don Kernodle by DQ
Angelo Mosca, Jr. beat Doug Vines
Wahoo McDaniel & Brian Adidas beat Gary Royal & Bobby Bass
Vinnie Valentino beat Ernie Ladd by DQ
Adrian Street beat Mark Fleming
Penny Mitchell beat Leilani Kai
Angelo Mosca, Jr. beat Barry Orton
Ivan Koloff & Don Kernodle beat Brett Hart & Italian Stallion

4/26/84: Norfolk, VA @ Scope
Vinnie Valentino beat Ben Alexander
Keith Larsen beat Kurt Von Hess
Don Kernodle beat Johnny Weaver
Dusty Rhodes beat Adrian Street by DQ
Wahoo McDaniel beat Tully Blanchard
Jimmy Valiant beat Paul Jones
Jack & Jerry Brisco beat Wahoo McDaniel & Mark Youngblood
NWA World Champ Ric Flair beat Dick Slater

4/27/84: Richmond, VA @ Coliseum
Keith Larsen beat Ben Alexander
Vinnie Valentino beat Kurt Von Hess
Don Kernodle & Ivan Koloff beat Johnny Waver & Hamilton
Assassin #1 beat Angelo Mosca, Sr.
Dick Slater beat Angelo Mosca, Jr.
Mark Youngblood & Wahoo McDaniel beat Jack & Jerry Brisco
Jimmy Valiant beat Paul Jones
NWA World Champ Ric Flair draw Ricky Steamboat

4/28/84: Bassett, VA @ High School Gym

4/29/84: Toronto, Ontario @ Maple Leaf Gardens
NWA Canadian Title tournament
1st Round
Dick Slater beat Johnny Weaver
Buddy Hart beat Leo Burke
(Leo injured Bret after the match & Hart was eliminated)
Brian Adidas beat Tully Blanchard by referee decision
Great Kabuki beat Carlos Colon
Angelo Mosca, Jr. beat Terry Kay
Grappler #1 beat Jay Youngblood
Mark Youngblood beat Grappler #2
Pez Whatley beat Jake Roberts by referee decision
Ivan Koloff beat Vinnie Valentino

2nd Round
Brian Adidas beat Dick Slater by DQ
Angelo Mosca, Jr. beat Great Kabuki(:38)
(Great Kabuki sprayed Mosca with his mist afterwards & Mosca could not continue)
Mark Youngblood DDQ Grappler #2
Ivan Koloff beat Pez Whatley

Finals
Ivan Koloff beat Brian Adidas to win vacant NWA Canadian Title in tournament final

4/29/84: Rock Hill, SC @ Winthrop Coliseum
Keith Larsen beat Gary Royal
Kurt Von Hess & Don Kernodle beat Larry Hamilton & Sam Houston
Wahoo McDaniel & Brad Armstrong beat Jack & Jerry Brisco
Ernie Ladd beat Rufus R. Jones
Adrian Street beat Jimmy Valiant by DQ
Despina Montages beat Leilani Kai

4/30/84: Greenville, SC @ Memorial Auditorium
Keith Larsen beat Ben Alexander
Jesse Barr beat Doug Vines
Ernie Ladd beat Rufus R. Jones
Wahoo McDaniel beat Tully Blanchard
Ivan Koloff & Don Kernodle beat Angelo Mosca, Sr. & Angelo Mosca, Jr.

4/30/84: Fayetteville, NC @ Cumberland County Civic Center
Larry Hamilton draw Gary Royal
Mark Fleming beat Ali Bey
Jay Youngblood beat Kurt Von Hess
Jimmy Valiant beat Adrian Street
Dick Slater beat Mark Youngblood

5/1/84: Raleigh, NC @ Dorton Arena
Jesse Barr beat Jeff Sword
Keith Larsen beat Doug Vines
Brian Adidas beat Kurt Von Hess
Ernie Ladd beat Rufus R. Jones
Dick Slater beat Jay Youngblood by DQ
Wahoo McDaniel beat Tully Blanchard

5/1/84: Columbia, SC @ Township Auditorium
Brett Hart beat Ali Bey
Larry Hamilton beat Barry Orton
Ivan Koloff & Don Kernodle beat Angelo Mosca, Sr. & Angelo Mosca, Jr.
Pez Whatley beat Great Kabuki
Jimmy Valiant beat Adrian Street

5/2/84: Spartanburg, SC @ Memorial Auditorium (TV)
Jimmy Valiant beat Bobby Bass
Ivan Koloff & Don Kernodle beat Mike Jackson & Joshua Stroud
Pez Whatley beat Randy Barber
Wahoo McDaniel, King Kong Bundy & Brian Adidas beat Doug Vines, Jeff Sword & Gary Royal
Wahoo McDaniel & King Kong Bundy beat The Road Warriors
Wahoo McDaniel & Brian Adidas vs. Gary Royal & Bobby Bass
Ernie Ladd vs. Vinnie Valentino
Leilani Kai vs. Penny Mitchell
Angelo Mosca, Jr. vs. Barry Orton
Ivan Koloff & Don Kernodle vs. Sam Houston & Italian Stallion
Jimmy Valiant, Rufus R. Jones, & Pez Whatley vs. Doug Vines, Ben Alexander, & Kurt Von Hess

5/4/84: Lynchburg, VA @ City Armory
Tully Blanchard vs. Jimmy Valiant
Ivan Koloff & Don Kernodle vs. Angelo Mosca, Sr. & Angelo Mosca, Jr
Judy Martin vs. Desiree Peterson

5/4/84: Hampton, VA @ Coliseum
Brett Hart beat Jeff Sword
Jesse Barr beat Bobby Bass
Brian Adidas beat Doug Vines
Junkyard Dog beat Gary Hart
Ernie Ladd beat Rufus R. Jones
Junkyard Dog beat Adrian Street
Dick Slater beat Jay Youngblood
Wahoo McDaniel & Mark Youngblood beat Jack & Jerry Brisco

5/5/84: Greensboro, NC @ Coliseum
Mark Fleming beat Bobby Bass
Johnny Weaver beat Barry Orton
Brian Adidas beat Doug Vines
Pez Whatley beat Jeff Sword
Ernie Ladd beat Rufus R. Jones
Wahoo McDaniel beat Tully Blanchard
Ricky Steamboat beat Dick Slater
Wahoo McDaniel & Mark Youngblood beat Jack & Jerry Brisco to win NWA World Tag Title

5/6/84: Savannah, GA @ Civic Center
Mark Fleming beat Chuck Marbary
Jeff Sword beat Gene Ligon
Johnny Weaver & Larry Hamilton beat Kurt Von Hess & Bobby Bass
Pez Whatley beat Tully Blanchard
Ernie Ladd beat Rufus R. Jones

Jimmy Valiant beat Adrian Street

5/6/84: Asheville, NC @ Civic Center
Vinnie Valentino beat Doug Vines
Sam Houston beat Ali Bey
Jesse Barr beat Barry Orton
Ivan Koloff & Don Kernodle beat Angelo Mosca, Sr. & Angelo Mosca, Jr.
Dick Slater beat Brian Adidas
Wahoo McDaniel & Mark Youngblood beat Jack & Jerry Brisco

5/6/84: Charlotte, NC @ Coliseum
Sam Houston beat Barry Orton
Doug Vines beat Brett Hart
Keith Larsen beat Gary Royal
Adrian Street beat Brian Adidas
Jimmy Valiant beat Tully Blanchard
Angelo Mosca, Jr. beat Ivan Koloff
Ricky Steamboat beat Dick Slater
Wahoo McDaniel & Mark Youngblood beat Jack & Jerry Brisco

5/7/84: Kinston, NC
Kurt Von Hess draw Doug Vines
Jesse Barr beat Vinnie Valentino
Pez Whatley beat Barry Orton
Wahoo McDaniel & Mark Youngblood beat Tully Blanchard & Jesse Barr
Jimmy Valiant beat Adrian Street

5/7/84: South Hill, VA @ Parkview High School
Including Ernie Ladd, Ivan Koloff, Don Kernodle, Rufus R. Jones & Brian Adidas

5/8/84: Raleigh, NC @ Dorton Arena
Sam Houston beat Ben Alexander
Brian Adidas beat Barry Orton
Adrian Street beat Rufus R. Jones
Jimmy Valiant beat Tully Blanchard by DQ
Don Kernodle & Ivan Koloff beat Wahoo McDaniel & Mark Youngblood to win NWA World Tag Title

5/8/84: Columbia, SC @ Township Auditorium
Vinnie Valentino beat Jeff Sword
Gary Royal beat Doug Vines
Jesse Barr beat Brett Hart
Johnny Weaver beat Kurt Von Hess
Wahoo McDaniel beat Ernie Ladd
Ricky Steamboat beat Dick Slater by DQ

5/9/84: Spencer, NC @ North Rowan High School (TV)
Jimmy Valiant & King Kong Bundy beat Doug Vines & Randy Barber
Mark & Jay Youngblood beat Ivan Koloff & Don Kernodle by DQ
The Road Warriors beat Mike Jackson & Steve Brinson
Ricky Steamboat beat Barry Orton
Masked Outlaw (Dory Funk, Jr.) beat Angelo Mosca, Jr. to win NWA Mid Atlantic Title

5/10/84: Sumter, SC @ Exhibition Center
Johnny Weaver beat Doug Vines
Vinnie Valentino beat Bobby Bass by DQ
Brian Adidas beat Bobby Bass
Pez Whatley beat Barry Orton
Ivan Koloff & Don Kernodle beat Angelo Mosca, Sr. & Angelo Mosca, Jr.

5/10/84: Norfolk, VA @ Scope
Keith Larsen beat Gary Royal
Jesse Barr beat Kurt Von Hess
Mark Fleming beat Jeff Sword
Mark Youngblood beat Tully Blanchard
Dick Slater beat Jimmy Valiant
Rufus R. Jones beat Ernie Ladd
Dusty Rhodes beat Adrian Street

5/12/84: Charleston, SC @ County Hall
Rufus R. Jones beat Ernie Ladd in a lights out match
Jimmy Valiant beat Tully Blanchard by DQ
Pez Whatley beat Kurt Von Hess
Jesse Barr beat Glenn Lane
Doug Vines beat David Dillon
Sam Houston beat Pinky Graham

5/12/84: Winchester, VA @ James Wood High School
Mark & Jay Youngblood vs. Dick Slater & Masked Outlaw
Johnny Weaver vs. Gary Royal
Bobby Bass vs. Vinnie Valentino
Mark Fleming vs. Ben Alexander
Italian Stallion vs. Ali Bey

5/13/84: Roanoke, VA @ Civic Center
Brett Hart beat Barry Orton
Ben Alexander beat Italian Stallion
Junkyard Dog beat Tully Blanchard
Assassin #1 beat Jimmy Valiant
Mark Youngblood beat Adrian Street
Rufus R. Jones beat Ernie Ladd

5/13/84: Richmond, VA @ Coliseum
Gary Royal beat Jeff Sword
Jesse Barr beat Kurt Von Hess
Masked Outlaw beat Keith Larsen
Adrian Street beat Sam Houston
Rufus R. Jones beat Ernie Ladd
Jimmy Valiant beat Assassin #1 by DQ
Junkyard Dog beat Tully Blanchard
Ricky Steamboat beat Dick Slater by DQ

5/13/84: Toronto, Ontario @ Maple Leaf Gardens
Angelo Mosca, Sr. & Angelo Mosca, Jr. beat Ivan Koloff & Great Kabuki
Leo Burke beat Buddy Hart
Tony Parisi beat Don Kernodle by DQ
Pez Whatley & Vinnie Valentino beat The Destroyer & Doug Vines
Brian Adidas beat Terry Kay
Don Kolov beat Goldie Rogers

5/14/84: St. Catherines, Ontario
Tony Parisi beat Leo Burke
Billy Red Lyons & Johnny Weaver beat Rudy Kay & Terry Kay
Terry Kay beat Don Kolov
John Bonello beat Goldie Rogers
Bobby Bass beat Nick DeCarlo

5/14/84: Greenville, SC @ Memorial Auditorium
Brett Hart beat Gary Royal
The Outlaw beat Vinnie Valentino
Jimmy Valiant beat Adrian Street
Ronnie Garvin beat Jake Roberts
Don Kernodle & Ivan Koloff DDQ Pez Whatley & Mark Youngblood

5/15/84: Raleigh, NC @ Dorton Arena
Tully Blanchard beat Vinnie Valentino
Dick Slater beat Brian Adidas
Masked Outlaw draw Angelo Mosca, Jr.
Adrian Street beat Jimmy Valiant

5/15/84: Columbia, SC @ Township Auditorium
Brett Hart draw Jeff Sword
Keith Larsen beat Doug Vines
Rufus R. Jones beat Great Kabuki
Ron Garvin beat Jake Roberts
Don Kernodle & Ivan Koloff beat Pez Whatley & Mark Youngblood

5/16/84: ?? (TV)
Masked Outlaw beat Keith Larsen
Ivan Koloff & Don Kernodle beat Dale Veasey & Brett Hart via pinfall
Angelo Mosca, Jr. beat Bob Brown
Dick Slater beat Jason Walker
Wahoo McDaniel beat Randy Barber
Rufus R. Jones beat Barry Orton

5/17/84: Chester, SC @ High School
Ernie Ladd vs. Rufus R. Jones
Wahoo McDaniel vs. Tully Blanchard
Johnny Weaver vs. Adrian Street
Kurt Von Hess vs. Pink Graham
Ali Bey vs. Keith Larsen
Jeff Sword vs. Brett Hart

5/17/84: Roxboro, NC @ Optimist Park

5/17/84: Fisherville, VA @ Augusta Expo
Including Ivan Koloff, Don Kernodle, Mark & Jay Youngblood, Assassin #1 & Paul Jones & Angelo Mosca, Jr.

5/17/84: Sumter, SC @ Exhibition Center
Kurt Von Hess beat Keith Larsen
Brian Adidas beat Jeff Sword
Rufus R. Jones & Pez Whatley beat Ernie Ladd & Jesse Barr
Angelo Mosca, Jr. beat Masked Outlaw
Jimmy Valiant beat Adrian Street

5/19/84: Greensboro, NC @ Coliseum
Doug Vines beat Keith Larsen
Kurt Von Hess beat Gary Royal
Paul Kelly beat Sam Houston
Dick Slater beat Brett Hart
Angelo Mosca, Sr. beat Assassin #1
Jimmy Valiant beat Adrian Street
Tully Blanchard beat Wahoo McDaniel
Ivan Koloff & Don Kernodle beat Mark Youngblood & Pez Whatley

5/20/84: Charlotte, NC @ Coliseum
Wahoo McDaniel & Dusty Rhodes beat Ivan Koloff & Don Kernodle by DQ
Ricky Steamboat beat Dick Slater
Jimmy Valiant beat Adrian Street
Assassin #1 beat Angelo Mosca, Sr.
Rufus R. Jones & Mark Youngblood beat Ernie Ladd & Jesse Barr
Johnny Weaver beat Bobby Bass
Vinnie Valentino beat Jeff Sword

5/21/84: Greenville, SC @ Memorial Auditorium
Brett Hart beat Bobby Bass
Keith Larsen beat Paul Kelly
Angelo Mosca beat Assassin #1
Angelo Mosca, Jr. beat Masked Outlaw by referee's decision
Ivan Koloff & Don Kernodle beat Pez Whatley & Mark Youngblood

5/22/84: Columbia, SC @ Township Auditorium
Ivan Koloff & Don Kernodle beat Pez Whatley & Mark Youngblood
Angelo Mosca, Jr. beat Assassin #1
Ernie Ladd beat Brett Hart
Great Kabuki beat Mark Fleming
Keith Larsen beat Kurt Von Hess

5/22/84: Raleigh, NC @ Dorton Arena
Sam Houston beat Gary Royal
Vinnie Valentino beat Doug Vines
Brian Adidas beat Jesse Barr
Rufus R. Jones beat Adrian Street
Dick Slater & Masked Outlaw beat Johnny Weaver & Angelo Mosca, Jr.
Wahoo McDaniel beat Tully Blanchard

5/23/84: Spartanburg, SC @ Memorial Auditorium (TV)
Angelo Mosca, Jr. beat Gary Royal
Ivan Koloff & Don Kernodle beat Sam Houston & Mark Fleming via pinfall
Pez Whatley beat Kurt Von Hess
Jesse Barr beat Brett Hart
Rufus R. Jones beat Assassin #1 by DQ
Mark Youngblood & Brian Adidas beat Doug Vines & Jeff Sword
Mark Youngblood beat Bob Owens(4:11) via pinfall
Masked Outlaw beat Mark Fleming(2:00)
Wahoo McDaniel beat Ben Alexander(4:09) via pinfall
Adrian Street beat Keith Larsen(3:49) via pinfall
Assassin #1 beat Al Scott(3:07) via pinfall

Ivan Koloff & Don Kernodle beat Randy Barber & Gerald Finley(4:07) via pinfall

5/24/84: Sumter, SC @ Exhibition Center
Jimmy Valiant beat Adrian Street
Keith Larsen beat Kurt Von Hess
Brian Adidas beat Paul Kelly
Angelo Mosca, Sr. draw Masked Outlaw
Pez Whatley & Rufus R. Jones beat Ernie Ladd & Jesse Barr

5/24/84: Norfolk, VA @ Scope
Dusty Rhodes & Wahoo McDaniel beat Ivan Koloff & Don Kernodle by DQ
Ricky Steamboat beat Dick Slater
Tully Blanchard beat Mark Youngblood
Vinnie Valentino beat Doug Vines
Johnny Weaver beat Jeff Sword
Junkyard Dog beat Great Kabuki
Assassin #1 beat Angelo Mosca, Sr.

5/25/84: Richmond, VA @ Coliseum
Keith Larsen beat Kurt Von Hess
Ron Bass beat Jeff Sword
Vinnie Valentino beat Doug Vines
Johnny Weaver beat Paul Kelly
Assassin beat Angelo Mosca, Sr.
Ricky Steamboat DCO with Dick Slater
Wahoo McDaniel & Dusty Rhodes beat Ivan Koloff & Don Kernodle

5/25/84: Charleston, SC @ County Hall
Adrian Street beat Pez Whatley
Brett Hart beat Gary Royal
Masked Outlaw beat Angelo Mosca, Jr.
Tully Blanchard beat Mark Youngblood
Rufus R. Jones & Brian Adidas beat Ernie Ladd & Jesse Barr

5/26/84: Greenville, SC @ Memorial Auditorium
Assassin #1 beat Angelo Mosca, Sr.
Tully Blanchard beat Dusty Rhodes
Jimmy Valiant beat Adrian Street
Ricky Steamboat beat Dick Slater

5/27/84: Toronto, Ontario @ Maple Leaf Gardens
NWA World Champ Ric Flair beat Dick Slater
Angelo Mosca, Sr. beat Ivan Koloff in a Russian chain match
Angelo Mosca, Jr. beat Great Kabuki
The Grapplers beat Pez Whatley & Vinnie Valentino
Buddy Hart & Johnny Weaver beat Leo Burke & Rudy Kay
Terry Kay beat Don Kolov
Brian Adidas beat Doug Vines
Tony Parisi beat Jeff Sword

5/28/84: Fayetteville, NC @ Cumberland County Civic Center
Wahoo McDaniel beat Tully Blanchard
Ron Garvin beat Jake Roberts
Jimmy Valiant beat Adrian Street
Angelo Mosca, Jr. beat Masked Outlaw
Jesse Barr beat Keith Larsen
Ivan Koloff & Don Kernodle beat Mark Youngblood & Rufus R. Jones

5/29/84: East Rutherford, NJ @ Meadowlands
Invader #1(Jose Gonzales) beat Great Kabuki via pinfall
Ron Garvin beat Jake Roberts
Les Thornton beat El Gran Apollo by CO
Dusty Rhodes beat The Assassin(Jesse Barr)(1:30) via pinfall
Ivan Koloff & Don Kernodle beat Pez Whatley & Mark Youngblood via pinfall
Wahoo McDaniel DDQ Stan Hansen
The Road Warriors beat Jimmy Valiant & King Kong Bundy via pinfall
Carlos Colon beat Tully Blanchard via pinfall
NWA World Champ Ric Flair beat Ricky Steamboat(32:00) via pinfall

5/30/84: ?? (TV)
The Road Warriors beat Brett Hart & ??
Invader #1 beat Doug Vines
Carlos Colon beat Jesse Barr
Stan Hansen beat Steve Brinson
Carlos Colon & Invader #1 beat Jeff Sword & Ben Alexander
Stan Hansen beat ??
Carlos Colon & Invader #1 beat Jesse Barr & Dale Veasey
The Road Warriors beat Joshua Stroud & Italian Stallion
Stan Hansen vs. ??

5/31/84: Emporia, VA
NWA World Champ Ric Flair vs. Dick Slater
Also including Wahoo McDaniel, Brian Adidas, Tully Blanchard, Adrian Street & others

5/31/84: Charlotte Courthouse, VA @ Randolph Henry Field
Including Ivan Koloff, Don Kernodle, Mark Youngblood, Rufus R. Jones & Johnny Weaver

6/2/84: Roanoke, VA @ Civic Center
NWA World Champ Ric Flair beat Dick Slater
The Road Warriors NC with Ivan Koloff & Don Kernodle
Angelo Mosca, Jr. draw Masked Outlaw
Pez Whatley beat Jeff Sword
Mark Youngblood beat Kurt Von Hess
Brett Hart beat Paul Kelly
Keith Larsen beat Italian Stallion
Mark Fleming beat Bobby Bass

6/3/84: Asheville, NC @ Civic Center
Tully Blanchard beat Ron Garvin
Jimmy Valiant beat Adrian Street
NWA World Champ Ric Flair beat Dick Slater by DQ
Jesse Barr beat Sam Houston
Assassin #1 beat Mark Fleming
Keith Larsen beat Doug Vines

6/3/84: Savannah, GA @ Civic Center
Gene Ligon beat Ben Alexander
Sam Houston beat Gary Royal
Brett Hart beat Kurt Von Hess
Angela Mosca, Jr. beat Masked Outlaw
Ivan Koloff & Don Kernodle beat Pez Whatley & Mark Youngblood

6/4/84: Greenville, SC @ Memorial Auditorium
NWA World Champ Ric Flair beat Tully Blanchard
Ricky Steamboat beat Dick Slater in a falls count anywhere match
Ivan Koloff & Don Kernodle beat Wahoo McDaniel & Brian Adidas
Angelo Mosca, Jr. beat Masked Outlaw
Jimmy Valiant beat Adrian Street
Sam Houston beat Kurt Von Hess
Brett Hart beat Paul Kelly
Keith Larsen beat Doug Vines

6/5/84: Columbia, SC @ Township Auditorium
NWA World Champ Ric Flair draw Ricky Steamboat
Sam Houston beat Kurt Von Hess
Brian Adidas beat Paul Kelly
Angelo Mosca, Jr. beat Masked Outlaw
Kimala won a battle royal
Wahoo McDaniel draw Tully Blanchard
Ivan Koloff & Don Kernodle beat Pez Whatley & Mark Youngblood

6/6/84: Raleigh, NC @ Dorton Arena (TV)
Michael Hayes & Terry Gordy beat Doug Vines & ??
King Kong Bundy beat Dale Veasey
Rufus R. Jones beat Assassin #1
Michael Hayes & Buddy Roberts beat Paul Kelly & Doug Vines
Terry Gordy & Buddy Roberts beat Jeff Sword & Ben Alexander
Nikita Koloff beat Brett Hart
King Kong Bundy beat Paul Kelly
The Road Warriors beat Keith Larsen & ??
Wahoo McDaniel beat Tully Blanchard by DQ
Michael Hayes, Terry Gordy & Buddy Roberts beat The Road Warriors & Paul Ellering
NWA World Champ Ric Flair NC with Harley Race in a cage match

6/7/84: Norfolk, VA @ Scope
Paul Kelly beat Keith Larsen
Johnny Weaver beat Bobby Bass
Pez Whatley beat Kurt Von Hess
Kimala beat Brett Hart
Stan Hansen beat Jesse Barr
Rufus R. Jones beat Assassin #1
Harley Race beat Angelo Mosca, Jr.
The Road Warriors NC with Junkyard Dog & King Kong Bundy
Wahoo McDaniel beat Tully Blanchard
Terry Gordy & Buddy Roberts beat Ivan Koloff & Don Kernodle by DQ
NWA World Champ Ric Flair draw Ricky Steamboat

6/8/84: Richmond, VA @ Coliseum
NWA World Champ Ric Flair beat Harley Race in a cage match
Ricky Steamboat beat Dick Slater in a falls count anywhere match
Tully Blanchard beat Wahoo McDaniel
Jimmy Valiant beat Adrian Street
Sam Houston beat Gary Royal
Vinnie Valentino beat Paul Kelly
Pez Whatley beat Doug Vines
Angelo Mosca, Jr. won a battle royal
Rufus R. Jones & Junkyard Dog beat Assassin #1 & Paul Jones by DQ

6/9/84: Greensboro, NC @ Coliseum
Ivan Koloff & Don Kernodle beat Mark Youngblood & The Renegade(Jay Youngblood)
Ricky Steamboat beat Masked Outlaw
Masked Outlaw beat Angelo Mosca, Jr.
Brett Hart beat Bobby Bass
Jeff Sword beat Sam Houston
Doug Vines beat Mark Fleming
Rufus R. Jones & Pez Whatley beat Paul Jones & Assassin #1 by DQ
Jesse Barr beat Keith Larsen

6/10/84: Toronto, Ontario @ Maple Leaf Gardens
Angelo Mosca, Jr. beat Ivan Koloff to win NWA Canadian Title
Angelo Mosca, Sr. beat Assassin #1 by DQ
Brian Adidas beat Don Kernodle to win NWA Canadian Television Title
Pez Whatley beat Leo Burke by DQ
The Grapplers beat Buddy Hart & Johnny Weaver
Terry Kay beat Nick DeCarlo
Don Kolov & Vinnie Valentino beat John White & George Guimond

6/11/84: Greenville, SC @ Memorial Auditorium
Ivan Koloff & Don Kernodle beat Mark Youngblood & The Renegade by DQ
Paul Jones & Assassin #1 beat Jimmy Valiant & Rufus R. Jones by DQ
Kimala beat Italian Stallion
Sam Houston beat Doug Vines
Mark Fleming beat Kurt Von Hess

6/12/84: Raleigh, NC @ Dorton Arena
Brett Hart beat Kurt Von Hess
Wahoo McDaniel beat Ernie Ladd
Jimmy Valiant beat Adrian Street
Don Kernodle & Ivan Koloff beat Mark Youngblood & The Renegade by DQ
Tully Blanchard beat Johnny Weaver

6/13/84: ?? (TV)
Jimmy Valiant beat Doug Vines
Assassin # 1 beat Keith Larsen
Brian Adidas vs. Gary Royal
The Road Warriors vs. Dale Veasey & Sam Houston
Ricky Steamboat vs. Dick Slater
Jesse Barr beat Paul Kelly

Angelo Mosca, Jr. beat Ben Alexander
Assassin #1 beat Italian Stallion
Pez Whatley & Brian Adidas beat Doug Vines & Paul Kelly
King Kong Bundy & Wahoo McDaniel vs. Dale Veasey & ?? Carpenter
Masked Outlaw beat Gene Ligon
Jimmy Valiant beat Adrian Street by CO
Dick Slater DCO with Ricky Steamboat

6/14/84: Hampton, VA @ Coliseum
Tully Blanchard beat Wahoo McDaniel
Ivan Koloff & Don Kernodle beat Mark Youngblood & The Renegade by DQ
Kimala beat Brett Hart
Mark Fleming beat Gary Royal
Vinnie Valentino draw Bobby Bass
Junkyard Dog & Rufus R. Jones beat Assassin & Paul Jones

6/14/84: Harrisonburg, VA @ High School
Paul Kelly vs. Keith Larsen
Pez Whatley & Brian Adidas vs. Ernie Ladd & Jesse Bass
Masked Outlaw vs. Angelo Mosca, Jr.
Jimmy Valiant vs. Adrian Street

6/15/84: Reidsville, NC @ Diamond I Arena

6/15/84: Charleston, SC @ County Hall
Bobby Bass beat Sam Houston
Brett Hart beat Jeff Sword
Vinnie Valentino beat Kurt Von Hess
Ivan Koloff & Don Kernodle beat Mark Youngblood & The Renegade by DQ
Jimmy Valiant beat Adrian Street

6/15/84: Lynchburg, VA @ City Armory
Tully Blanchard vs. Wahoo McDaniel
Masked Outlaw vs. Angelo Mosca, Jr.
Johnny Weaver, Pez Whatley & Brian Adidas vs. Ernie Ladd, Jesse Barr & Paul Kelly

6/16/84: Roanoke, VA @ Civic Center
Adrian Street beat Paul Jones by DQ
Tully Blanchard beat Johnny Weaver
Jimmy Valiant beat Buzz Sawyer by DQ
Assassin #1 & Assassin #3(Barry Orton) beat Brian Adidas & Keith Larsen
Nikita Koloff beat Paul Kelly
Brett Hart beat Mark Fleming
Keith Larsen beat Ali Bey

6/16/84: Conway, SC
Vinnie Valentino beat Doug Vines
Johnny Weaver beat Jesse Barr
Pez Whatley beat Ernie Ladd by DQ
Masked Outlaw beat Angelo Mosca, Jr.
Mark Youngblood & The Renegade beat Nikita Koloff & Don Kernodle

6/16/84: Charlotte, NC @ Coliseum
Paul Kelly beat Brett Hart
Brian Adidas beat Kurt Von Hess
Sam Houston & Keith Larsen beat Jeff Sword & Gary Royal
Kimala beat Mark Fleming
Jimmy Valiant beat Adrian Street
Jimmy Valiant & Rufus R. Jones beat Assassin #1 & Paul Jones
Tully Blanchard beat Wahoo McDaniel
Ricky Steamboat beat Ivan Koloff

6/17/84: Totowa, NJ
Bobby Bass beat Terry Dunne
Jesse Barr beat Paul Kelly
Invader #1 beat Doug Vines
Ted DiBiase beat Vinnie Valentino
Wahoo McDaniel & Pez Whatley beat Stan Hansen & Les Thornton by DQ
Carlos Colon beat Tully Blanchard

6/17/84: Columbia, SC @ Township Auditorium
Keith Larsen beat Ali Bey
Sam Houston beat Mark Fleming
Nikita Koloff beat Gene Ligon
Ivan Koloff & Don Kernodle beat Mark Youngblood & The Renegade by DQ
Rufus R. Jones, Sweet Brown Sugar & King Kong Bundy beat Kimala, Assassin I1 & Paul Jones

6/18/84: Morristown, NJ
Bobby Bass beat Angelo Gomez
Jody Shields beat Lady Adonis
Jesse Barr beat Doug Vines
Invader #1 beat Paul Kelly
Carlos Colon beat Les Thornton
Stan Hansen beat Vinnie Valentino
Wahoo McDaniel & Pez Whatley beat The Road Warriors by DQ

6/18/84: Greenville, SC @ Memorial Auditorium
Keith Larsen beat Jeff Sword
Gary Royal beat Mark Fleming
Brickhouse Brown beat Kurt Von Hess
Jimmy Valiant, Rufus R. Jones & Brian Adidas beat Kimala, Assassin #1 & Paul Jones

6/19/84: Danville, VA @ Tunstill High School
Jimmy Valiant vs. Adrian Street
Johnny Weaver & Pez Whatley vs. Ernie Ladd & Jesse Barr

6/19/84: Raleigh, NC @ Dorton Arena
Keith Larsen beat Paul Kelly
Nikita Koloff beat Brett Hart
Masked Outlaw beat Angelo Mosca, Jr.
Wahoo McDaniel & Rufus R. Jones beat Assassin #1 & Kimala
Mark Youngblood & The Renegade beat Ivan Koloff & Don Kernodle by DQ

6/20/84: Spartanburg, SC @ Memorial Auditorium (TV)
Ivan Koloff & Don Kernodle vs. Mark Youngblood & The Renegade
Tully Blanchard vs. Jimmy Valiant
Brian Adidas & Pez Whatley beat Gary Royal & Doug Vines
Angelo Mosca, Jr. beat Paul Kelly
Kamala beat Italian Stallion
Nikita Koloff, Ivan Koloff & Don Kernodle beat Sam Houston, Brett Hart & Mark Fleming

6/21/84: Norfolk, VA @ Scope
Vinnie Valentino beat Bobby Bass
Keith Larsen beat Gary Royal
Nikita Koloff beat Sam Houston
Jimmy Valiant beat Assassin #1
Angelo Mosca, Jr. beat Masked Outlaw to win NWA Mid Atlantic Title
Paul Jones & Kimala beat Angelo Mosca, Jr. & Rufus R. Jones
Ivan Koloff & Don Kernodle beat Mark Youngblood & The Renegade

6/21/84: Sumter, SC @ Exhibition Center
Mark Fleming beat Paul Kelly
Kurt Von Hess beat Italian Stallion
Ernie Ladd & Jesse Barr beat Johnny Weaver & Brian Adidas
Adrian Street beat Pez Whatley
Wahoo McDaniel beat Tully Blanchard by DQ

6/22/84: Charleston, SC @ County Hall
Italian Stallion beat Ali Bey
Mark Fleming beat Jeff Sword
Brett Hart & Sam Houston beat Gary Royal & Doug Vines
Kurt Von Hess beat Gene Ligon
Tully Blanchard beat Johnny Weaver

6/22/84: Richmond, VA @ Coliseum
Mark Youngblood & The Renegade beat Ivan Koloff & Don Kernodle by DQ
Keith Larsen beat Bobby Bass
Nikita Koloff beat Vinnie Valentino
Pez Whatley & Brian Adidas beat Jesse Barr & Paul Kelly
Angelo Mosca, Jr. beat Masked Outlaw
Rufus R. Jones, Jimmy Valiant & Adrian Street beat Assassin #1, Kimala & Paul Jones

6/23/84: Fredericksburg, VA @ Stafford High School
Nikita Koloff beat Mark Fleming
Vinnie Valentino & Keith Larsen beat Jesse Barr & Paul Kelly
Adrian Street beat Brickhouse Brown
Ivan Koloff & Don Kernodle beat Angelo Mosca, Jr. & Rufus R. Jones

6/24/84: Asheville, NC @ Civic Center
Ivan Koloff & Din Kernodle beat Mark Youngblood & The Renegade by DQ
Masked Outlaw beat Angelo Mosca, Jr.
Tully Blanchard beat Wahoo McDaniel
Gene Ligon beat Italian Stallion
Doug Vines beat Sam Houston
Keith Larsen beat Jeff Sword
Brett Hart beat Ali Bey

6/24/84: Greensboro, NC @ Coliseum
Wahoo McDaniel beat Ricky Steamboat to win NWA United States Title
Ivan Koloff & Don Kernodle beat Mark Youngblood & The Renegade
Masked Outlaw & Gary Hart beat Rufus R. Jones & Angelo Mosca, Jr.
Johnny Weaver beat Tully Blanchard
Nikita Koloff beat Brett Hart
Keith Larsen beat Kurt Von Hess
Mark Fleming beat Paul Kelly

6/24/84: Toronto, Ontario @ Maple Leaf Gardens
Angelo Mosca, Jimmy Valiant & Buzz Sawyer beat Kamala, Assassin #1 & Paul Jones
Pez Whatley & Vinnie Valentino beat The Grapplers by CO
Brian Adidas beat Bobby Bass
Tony Parisi beat Gary Royal
Nick DeCarlo beat Bob Marcus
Jesse Barr beat John Bonello

6/25/84: Welland, Ontario
Brian Adidas beat Jesse Barr
Buzz Sawyer & Pez Whatley draw The Grapplers
Billy Red Lyons beat John Bonello
Vinnie Valentino beat Gary Royal
Tony Parisi beat Bobby Bass

6/25/84: Greenville, SC @ Memorial Auditorium
Mark Youngblood & The Renegade beat Ivan Koloff & Don Kernodle
Nikita Koloff beat Brett Hart
Sam Houston beat Paul Kelly
Jeff Sword beat Gene Ligon
Wahoo McDaniel draw Tully Blanchard

6/25/84: Fayetteville, NC @ Cumberland County Civic Center
Kurt Von Hess beat Ben Alexander
Mark Fleming beat Ali Bey
Italian Stallion beat Kurt Von Hess
Masked Outlaw beat Keith Larsen
Assassin #1 & Kimala beat Rufus R. Jones & Angelo Mosca

6/26/84: Raleigh, NC @ Dorton Arena
Vinnie Valentino beat Doug Vines
Kimala beat Brett Hart
Adrian Street beat Johnny Weaver
Ron Garvin beat Jake Roberts
Pez Whatley beat Assassin #1 by DQ
Rufus R. Jones & Angelo Mosca, Jr. beat Masked Outlaw & Gary Hart by CO

6/26/84: Columbia, SC @ Township Auditorium
Paul Kelly beat Italian Stallion
Brian Adidas draw Jesse Barr
Nikita Koloff beat Keith Larsen
Tully Blanchard beat Wahoo McDaniel
Mark Youngblood & The Renegade beat Ivan Koloff & Don Kernodle by CO

6/27/84: Shelby, NC @ Rec Center (TV)
Pez Whatley beat Mike Jackson
Buddy Roberts & Terry Gordy beat Kurt Von Hess & Mike Bond
Kamala Keith Larsen & Roger Bond
Nikita Koloff beat Paul Kelly
Angelo Mosca, Jr. beat Doug Vines
Terry Gordy & Buddy Roberts beat Mike Bond & Gary Royal
Nikita Koloff beat Mike Jackson
Kimala beat Italian Stallion & Jason Walker
Brian Adidas, Pez Whatley & Angelo Mosca, Jr. beat Mike Starbuck, Ron Bass & Kurt Von Hess
Wahoo McDaniel beat Brett Hart(5:10) via pinfall
Angelo Mosca, Jr. beat Masked Outlaw NWA Mid Atlantic Title

6/29/84: Lynchburg, VA @ City Armory
Including Ivan Koloff, Don Kernodle, Mark Youngblood & The Renegade, Adrian Street & Pez Whatley

6/29/84: Charleston, SC @ County Hall
Keith Larsen(sub for Ken Dillinger) beat Ben Alexander
Paul Kelly beat Mark Fleming
Bobby Bass & Kurt Von Hess beat Brett Hart & Keith Larsen
Masked Outlaw beat Angelo Mosca, Jr. 2/3 falls match
Wahoo McDaniel beat Tully Blanchard

7/1/84: Sumter, SC @ Exhibition Center
NWA World Champ Ric Flair beat Wahoo McDaniel
Mark Youngblood & The Renegade beat Ivan Koloff & Don Kernodle
Pez Whatley & Angelo Mosca, Jr. beat Masked Outlaw & Gary Hart
Brian Adidas beat Kurt Von Hess
Johnny Weaver beat Doug Vines
Jeff Sword beat Sam Houston

7/1/84: Charlotte, NC @ Coliseum
Tully Blanchard beat NWA World Champ Ric Flair DQ
Wahoo McDaniel beat Ricky Steamboat
Adrian Street beat Paul Jones by DQ
Mark Youngblood & The Renegade beat Ivan Koloff & Don Kernodle
Kimala beat Italian Stallion
Buzz Sawyer beat Brett Hart
Nikita Koloff beat Mark Fleming
Midnight Express Twins(Luther Dargon & Leroy Dargon) beat Jesse Barr & Paul Kelly

7/2/84: Fayetteville, NC @ Cumberland County Civic Center
Ivan Koloff & Don Kernodle beat Mark Youngblood & The Renegade by DQ
Tully Blanchard NC with Jimmy Valiant
Buzz Sawyer beat Italian Stallion
Brian Adidas beat Paul Kelly
Nikita Koloff beat Gary Royal
Johnny Weaver & Angelo Mosca, Jr. beat Masked Outlaw & Gary Hart

7/2/84: Greenville, SC @ Memorial Auditorium
Vinnie Valentino beat Bobby Bass
The Assassins beat Rufus R. Jones & Pez Whatley
Adrian Street beat Paul Jones by DQ
Dusty Rhodes beat Kimala by CO
NWA World Champ Ric Flair beat Wahoo McDaniel

7/3/84: Columbia, SC @ Township Auditorium
Jimmy Valiant beat Kimala by DQ
Ivan Koloff & Don Kernodle beat Mark Youngblood & The Renegade in a lumberjack match
Adrian Street beat Assassin #1
Johnny Weaver beat Kurt Von Hess
Nikita Koloff beat Brett Hart
Assassin #3 beat Sam Houston
Keith Larsen beat Ali Bey

7/3/84: Raleigh, NC @ Dorton Arena
Masked Outlaw & Gary Hart beat Buzz Sawyer & Angela Mosca, Jr.
Rufus R. Jones beat Jesse Barr
Ricky Steamboat NC with Tully Blanchard
NWA World Champ Ric Flair beat Wahoo McDaniel

7/4/84: Myrtle Beach, SC (TV)
NWA World Champ Ric Flair beat Wahoo McDaniel DQ
Masked Outlaw beat Mark Fleming
The Renegade beat Ben Alexander
Jimmy Valiant, Adrian Street & Rufus R. Jones beat Bobby Bass, Paul Kelly & Kurt Von Hess
Buzz Sawyer beat Brett Hart
NWA World Champ Ric Flair beat Gary Royal
The Assassins beat Vinnie Valentino & Italian Stallion

7/5/84: Icard, NC
Sam Houston beat Kurt Von Hess
Pez Whatley & Brian Adidas beat Jesse Barr & Jeff Sword
Nikita Koloff beat Brett Hart
Angelo Mosca, Jr. beat Masked Outlaw
Mark Youngblood & The Renegade beat Ivan Koloff & Don Kernodle

7/5/84: Norfolk, VA @ Scope
NWA World Champ Ric Flair beat Wahoo McDaniel
Buzz Sawyer beat Keith Larsen
Mr. Olympia beat Gary Royal
Assassin #3 beat Vinnie Valentino
Tully Blanchard beat Johnny Weaver
Tom Shaft beat Paul Kelly
Jimmy Valiant, Dusty Rhodes & Adrian Street beat Assassin #1, Paul Jones & Kimala

7/6/84: Richmond, VA @ Coliseum
Tom Shaft beat Gary Royal
Nikita Koloff beat Vinnie Valentino
Buzz Sawyer beat Mark Fleming
Assassin #1 beat Keith Larsen
Mr. Olympia beat Paul Kelly
Adrian Street beat Paul Jones by DQ
Jimmy Valiant beat Assassin #3
Dusty Rhodes beat Kimala
Ivan Koloff & Don Kernodle beat Mark Youngblood & The Renegade
NWA World Champ Ric Flair beat Ricky Steamboat

7/6/84: Charleston, SC @ County Hall
Brett Hart beat Doug Vines
Brian Adidas beat Jesse Barr
Rufus R. Jones beat Bobby Bass
Johnny Weaver & Angela Mosca, Jr. beat Gary Hart & Masked Outlaw
Tully Blanchard draw Pez Whatley

7/7/84: Greensboro, NC @ Coliseum
Jimmy Valiant beat Kimala
Sam Houston beat Ali Bey
Tom Shaft beat Kurt Von Hess
Buzz Sawyer beat Johnny Weaver
Rufus R. Jones beat Jesse Barr
Adrian Street beat Paul Jones by DQ
Tully Blanchard beat Ricky Steamboat by DQ
NWA World Champ Ric Flair beat Wahoo McDaniel

7/8/84: Asheville, NC @ Civic Center
Gene Anderson & Ole Anderson beat Ivan Koloff & Don Kernodle by DQ
The Assassins beat Buzz Sawyer & Adrian Street
Nikita Koloff beat Gary Royal
Vinnie Valentino beat Italian Stallion
Mark Fleming beat Ali Bey
Brett Hart beat Bobby Bass

7/9/84: Greenville, SC @ Memorial Auditorium
Johnny Weaver & Angelo Mosca, Jr. beat Masked Outlaw & Gary Hart
Buzz Sawyer beat Vinnie Valentino
Jesse Barr beat Jeff Sword
Sam Houston beat Bobby Bass
Dusty Rhodes, Jimmy Valiant & Adrian Street beat The Assassins & Paul Jones

7/9/84: Kinston, NC
Keith Larsen beat Gary Royal
Brett Hart beat Doug Vines
Tom Shaft beat Paul Kelly
Tully Blanchard beat Brian Adidas
Pez Whatley, Mark Youngblood & The Renegade beat Ivan Koloff, Nikita Koloff & Don Kernodle

7/10/84: Raleigh, NC @ Dorton Arena
Mark Youngblood & The Renegade beat Ivan Koloff & Don Kernodle by CO
Keith Larsen beat Ali Bey
Nikita Koloff beat Gary Royal
Pez Whatley, Angelo Mosca, Jr. & Brian Adidas beat Gary Hart, Buzz Sawyer & Masked Outlaw

7/10/84: Columbia, SC @ Township Auditorium
Jimmy Valiant, Wahoo McDaniel & Adrian Street beat Paul Jones & The Assassins
Tully Blanchard beat Dusty Rhodes
Tom Shaft beat Paul Kelly
Sam Houston beat Jeff Sword
Vinnie Valentino beat Bobby Bass

7/11/84: Spartanburg, SC @ Memorial Auditorium (TV)
Wahoo McDaniel beat Ben Alexander
Brian Adidas & Pez Whatley beat Doug Vines & Paul Kelly
Buzz Sawyer beat Italian Stallion(aka Gary Quartinelli)
Ivan Koloff & Don Kernodle beat Luther Dargon & Leroy Dargon
Nikita Koloff beat Mark Fleming
Jimmy Valiant beat Bobby Bass

7/12/84: Harrisonburg, VA @ High School
Ivan Koloff & Don Kernodle vs. Mark Youngblood & The Renegade
Nikita Koloff vs. Gary Royal
Doug Vines vs. Vinnie Valentino
Italian Stallion vs. Ben Alexander

7/13/84: Lynchburg, VA @ City Armory
Ivan Koloff & Don Kernodle vs. Mark Youngblood & The Renegade
Including Nikita Koloff

7/13/84: Charleston, SC @ County Hall
Dusty Rhodes beat Buzz Sawyer
Johnny Weaver & Angelo Mosca, Jr. beat Gary Hart & Masked Outlaw
Brian Adidas draw Jesse Barr
Sam Houston beat Ali Bey
Marc Fleming beat Gene Ligon

7/14/84: Charlotte, NC @ Coliseum
Sam Houston beat Doug Vines
Italian Stallion beat Jeff Sword
Nikita Koloff beat Vinnie Valentino
Brian Adidas draw Buzz Sawyer
Jimmy Valiant & Adrian Street beat The Assassins
Ricky Steamboat beat Wahoo McDaniel by DQ
Mark Youngblood & The Renegade beat Ivan Koloff & Don Kernodle by DQ

7/15/84: Roanoke, VA @ Civic Center
The Assassins beat Brian Adidas & Keith Larsen
Keith Larsen beat Ali Bey
Brett Hart beat Mark Fleming
Nikita Koloff beat Paul Kelly
Jimmy Valiant beat Buzz Sawyer by DQ
Tully Blanchard beat Johnny Weaver
Adrian Street beat Paul Jones by DQ

7/15/84: Savannah, GA @ Civic Center
Sam Houston beat Jeff Sword

Bobby Bass beat Dave Dillinger
Ivan Koloff & Don Kernodle beat The Renegade & Pez Whatley by DQ
Pez Whatley & Angelo Mosca, Jr. beat Masked Outlaw & Gary Hart
Tom Shaft beat Jesse Barr

7/16/84: Greenville, SC @ Memorial Auditorium
The Renegade & Pez Whatley beat Ivan Koloff & Don Kernodle in a lumberjack match
Brett Hart beat Paul Kelly
Nikita Koloff beat Gary Royal
Angelo Mosca, Jr. beat Masked Outlaw via pinfall
Tully Blanchard beat Johnny Weaver
Rufus R. Jones beat Kurt Von Hess

7/16/84: Fayetteville, NC @ Cumberland County Civic Center
The Assassins beat Wahoo McDaniel & Adrian Street
Vinnie Valentino beat Jeff Sword
Jesse Barr beat Tom Shaft
Brian Adidas beat Doug Vines
Jimmy Valiant beat Buzz Sawyer by DQ

7/17/84: Raleigh, NC @ Dorton Arena
Keith Larsen beat Kurt Von Hess
The Renegade & Pez Whatley beat Ivan Koloff & Don Kernodle in a lumberjack match
Nikita Koloff beat Paul Kelly
Buzz Sawyer beat Brett Hart
Angelo Mosca, Jr. beat Masked Outlaw

7/17/84: Columbia, SC @ Township Auditorium
The Assassins beat Johnny Weaver & Brian Adidas
Adrian Street draw Paul Jones
Jimmy Valiant beat Tully Blanchard by DQ
Rufus R. Jones beat Jesse Barr
Tom Shaft beat Bobby Bass

7/18/84: Winston-Salem, NC @ Memorial Coliseum (TV)
Mark Youngblood & The Renegade beat Gary Royal & Doug Vines
Buzz Sawyer beat Keith Larsen
The Assassins beat Vinnie Valentino & Mark Fleming
Ivan Koloff & Don Kernodle beat Brett Hart & Sam Houston
Brian Adidas beat Jeff Sword
Jimmy Valiant & Adrian Street beat Bobby Bass & Ali Bey
Ivan Koloff, Nikita Koloff & Don Kernodle beat Angelo Mosca, Jr., Rufus R. Jones & Tom Shaft
Tully Blanchard beat Brett Hart
Buzz Sawyer beat Keith Larsen
Wahoo McDaniel beat Sam Houston
Jimmy Valiant beat Beach Boy Harper
Gene & Ole Anderson & Jimmy Valiant vs. The Assassins & Paul Jones
Masked Outlaw vs. Angelo Mosca, Jr. whipping match

7/19/84: Sumter, SC @ Exhibition Center
Rufus R. Jones, Pez Whatley & Adrian Street beat The Assassins & Paul Jones
Jesse Barr beat Mark Fleming
Johnny Weaver beat Kurt Von Hess
Paul Kelly beat Doug Vines
Keith Larsen beat Gary Royal

7/19/84: Norfolk, VA @ Scope
Tully Blanchard beat Brian Adidas
Ivan Koloff & Don Kernodle beat Mark Youngblood & The Renegade
Brett Hart & Sam Houston beat Bobby Bass & Jeff Sword
Nikita Koloff beat Vinnie Valentino
Buzz Sawyer beat Jimmy Valiant
Angelo Mosca, Jr. beat Masked Outlaw

7/20/84: Charleston, SC @ County Hall
Ben Alexander beat Italian Stallion
Johnny Weaver beat Paul Kelly
Jesse Barr beat Ken Dillinger
Rufus R. Jones beat Kurt Von Hess
The Assassins beat Pez Whatley & Adrian Street
Angelo Mosca, Jr. beat Masked Outlaw in a whipping match

7/20/84: Richmond, VA @ Coliseum
Ricky Steamboat beat Wahoo McDaniel
Ivan Koloff & Don Kernodle beat Mark Youngblood & The Renegade
Tully Blanchard draw Jimmy Valiant
Buzz Sawyer draw Brian Adidas
Nikita Koloff beat Gary Royal
Sam Houston beat Vinnie Valentino
Tom Shaft beat Ali Bey
Keith Larsen & Mark Fleming beat Bobby Bass & Jeff Sword

7/21/84: Greensboro, NC @ Coliseum
Rufus R. Jones, Jimmy Valiant & Adrian Street beat The Assassins & Paul Jones
Wahoo McDaniel beat Ricky Steamboat by DQ
Ivan Koloff & Don Kernodle beat Mark Youngblood & The Renegade
Tully Blanchard beat Pez Whatley
Nikita Koloff beat Vinnie Valentino
Buzz Sawyer beat Brett Hart
Sam Houston beat Jesse Barr

7/24/84: Columbia, SC @ Township Auditorium
Junkyard Dog beat Wahoo McDaniel by DQ
Mark Youngblood & The Renegade DDQ Don Kernodle & Ivan Koloff
Tully Blanchard beat Johnny Weaver
Brian Adidas beat Jeff Sword
Tom Shaft beat Doug Vines

7/25/84: ?? (TV)
Brian Adidas beat Paul Kelly
Ivan Koloff & Don Kernodle beat Italian Stallion & Mark Fleming
NWA World Champ Ric Flair beat Gary Royal
Jimmy Valiant beat Kurt Von Hess
The Renegade beat Jeff Sword
Buzz Sawyer beat Sam Houston

7/26/84: Rocky Mount, VA @ High School
Including Jimmy Valiant, Tully Blanchard & Pez Whatley

7/26/84: Wilson, NC
Jeff Sword beat Italian Stallion
Sam Houston beat Brett Hart
Nikita Koloff beat Gary Royal
Ivan Koloff & Don Kernodle draw Mark Youngblood & The Renegade
Angelo Mosca, Jr. beat Wahoo McDaniel by DQ

7/27/84: Hampton, VA @ Coliseum
Angelo Mosca, Jr. beat Buzz Sawyer
Jimmy Valiant & Dusty Rhodes beat The Assassins
Adrian Street beat Paul Jones
Pez Whatley beat Kurt Von Hess
Tully Blanchard beat Johnny Weaver
Brian Adidas beat Jeff Sword
Sam Houston beat Paul Kelly

7/27/84: Charleston, SC @ County Hall
Tom Shaft beat Jeff Sword
Vinnie Valentino beat Bobby Bass
Nikita Koloff beat Brett Hart
Junkyard Dog & Rufus R. Jones beat Gary Royal & Jesse Barr
Ivan Koloff & Don Kernodle beat Mark Youngblood & The Renegade

7/28/84: Charlotte, NC @ Coliseum
Brian Adidas beat Paul Kelly
Pez Whatley beat Gary Royal
Angelo Mosca, Jr. beat Buzz Sawyer
Dusty Rhodes beat Masked Outlaw
Junkyard Dog beat Wahoo McDaniel
Ricky Steamboat beat Tully Blanchard by DQ
Ivan Koloff & Don Kernodle beat Mark Youngblood & The Renegade

7/28/84: Lovington, VA @ Nelson County High School
Including Jimmy Valiant, Adrian Street, The Assassins & Paul Jones, Rufus R. Jones & Johnny Weaver

7/31/84: Raleigh, NC @ Dorton Arena
Tom Shaft beat Doug Vines
Johnny Weaver beat Bobby Bass
Rufus R. Jones beat Jesse Barr
Brian Adidas beat Buzz Sawyer
Assassin #3 beat Adrian Street
Jimmy Valiant beat Assassin #1 in a lumberjack match

7/31/84: Columbia, SC @ Township Auditorium
Ricky Steamboat beat Wahoo McDaniel by DQ
Don Kernodle & Ivan Koloff beat Mark Youngblood & The Renegade
Tully Blanchard beat Pez Whatley
Nikita Koloff beat Brett Hart
Vinnie Valentino beat Kurt Von Hess

8/1/84: Spartanburg, SC @ Memorial Auditorium (TV)
Tully Blanchard vs. Dusty Rhodes
Rufus R. Jones beat Kurt Von Hess
Mark Youngblood beat Doug Vines
Assassin #1 beat Sam Houston
Jimmy Valiant beat Jeff Sword
Nikita Koloff beat Gary Royal
Wahoo McDaniel & Tully Blanchard beat Brian Adidas & Pez Whatley via pinfall

8/2/84: Norfolk, VA @ Scope
Sam Houston beat Paul Kelly
Johnny Weaver & Brian Adidas beat Paul Kelly & Jesse Barr
Assassin #3 beat Adrian Street
Ivan Koloff, Nikita Koloff & Don Kernodle beat Mark Youngblood, The Renegade & Pez Whatley
Jimmy Valiant beat Assassin #1
Dusty Rhodes beat Tully Blanchard by DQ
Ricky Steamboat beat Wahoo McDaniel by reverse decision

8/3/84: Richmond, VA @ Coliseum
Keith Larsen beat Doug Vines
Assassin #3(Nick Patrick) beat Sam Houston
Johnny Weaver beat Gary Royal
Brian Adidas beat Paul Kelly
Nikita Koloff beat Pez Whatley
Mark Youngblood & The Renegade beat Ivan Koloff & Don Kernodle
Dusty Rhodes beat Assassin #1
Ricky Steamboat & Jimmy Valiant beat Wahoo McDaniel & Tully Blanchard by DQ

8/4/84: Greensboro, NC @ Coliseum
Wahoo McDaniel beat Ricky Steamboat(23:00) via pinfall
Tully Blanchard draw Jimmy Valiant(20:00)
Mark Youngblood & The Renegade beat Ivan Koloff & Don Kernodle by DQ
Assassin #1 beat Rufus R. Jones
Nikita Koloff beat Johnny Weaver
Brian Adidas beat Jeff Sword
Sam Houston beat Gary Royal

8/5/84: Charlotte, NC @ Coliseum
Brian Adidas beat Jeff Sword
Pez Whatley beat Jesse Barr
Assassin #3 beat Adrian Street
Jimmy Valiant beat Assassin #1
Dusty Rhodes, Mark Youngblood & The Renegade beat Ivan Koloff, Nikita Koloff & Don Kernodle
Ric Flair & Ricky Steamboat beat Tully Blanchard & Wahoo McDaniel

8/5/84: Sumter, SC @ Exhibition Center
NWA World Champ Ric Flair beat Wahoo McDaniel
Dusty Rhodes vs. Tully Blanchard
Jimmy Valiant & Adrian Street vs. The Assassins
Angelo Mosca, Jr. vs. Ivan Koloff
Johnny Weaver vs. Don Kernodle
Buzz Sawyer vs. Sam Houston

8/6/84: Fayetteville, NC @ Cumberland County Civic Center
NWA World Champ Ric Flair beat Wahoo McDaniel DQ

8/6/84: Greenville, SC @ Memorial Auditorium
Tully Blanchard beat Dusty Rhodes
Mark Youngblood & The Renegade beat Ivan Koloff & Don Kernodle by DQ
Nikita Koloff beat Brett Hart
Johnny Weaver beat Kurt Von Hess
Keith Larsen beat Jeff Sword
Sam Houston beat Gary Royal

8/7/84: Columbia, SC @ Township Auditorium
NWA World Champ Ric Flair beat Wahoo McDaniel DQ
Tully Blanchard beat Vinnie Valentino
Mark Youngblood & The Renegade beat Ivan Koloff & Don Kernodle
Nikita Koloff beat Sam Houston
Johnny Weaver beat Jeff Sword

8/7/84: Raleigh, NC @ Dorton Arena
Tom Shaft beat Bobby Bass
Brian Adidas beat Gary Royal
James J. Dillon beat Brett Hart
Assassin #3 beat Adrian Street
Assassin #1 beat Rufus R. Jones
Angelo Mosca, Jr. beat Kurt Von Hess

8/8/84: ?? (TV)
Angelo Mosca, Jr. beat Gary Royal
Brian Adidas beat Bobby Bass
Assassin #1 beat Doug Vines
Mark Youngblood & The Renegade beat Jesse Barr & Jeff Sword
Nikita Koloff & Ivan Koloff beat Sam Houston & Brett Hart

8/9/84: Rocky Mount, NC
NWA World Champ Ric Flair beat Wahoo McDaniel DQ

8/9/84: Fisherville, VA @ Augusta Expo
Johnny Weaver beat Gary Royal

8/10/84: Lynchburg, VA @ City Armory

8/10/84: Charleston, SC @ County Hall
Keith Larsen vs. Jeff Sword
Pez Whatley vs. Jesse Barr
Johnny Weaver vs. Buzz Sawyer
Tully Blanchard vs. Angelo Mosca, Jr.
NWA World Champ Ric Flair beat Wahoo McDaniel DQ

8/11/84: Wilmington, NC @ Legion Stadium
NWA World Champ Ric Flair vs. Wahoo McDaniel
Tully Blanchard vs. Angelo Mosca, Jr.
Rufus R. Jones vs. Assassin #1
Adrian Street vs. Assassin #3
Jesse Barr vs. Pez Whatley
Gary Royal vs. Vinnie Valentino
Doug Vines vs. Keith Larsen

8/14/84: Columbia, SC @ Township Auditorium
Ricky Steamboat draw Tully Blanchard
Angelo Mosca, Jr. beat Wahoo McDaniel by DQ
Ivan Koloff & Don Kernodle beat Mark Youngblood & The Renegade
Nikita Koloff beat Johnny Weaver
Ben Alexander beat Jesse Barr
Keith Larsen beat Paul Kelly

8/14/84: Raleigh, NC @ Dorton Arena
Assassin #1 beat Jimmy Valiant in a taped fist match
Adrian Street beat Gary Royal
Rufus R. Jones beat Assassin #3
Tom Shaft beat Kurt Von Hess
Brett Hart beat Bobby Bass
Brian Adidas beat Jeff Sword

8/15/84: Shelby, NC @ Rec Center (TV)
Brian Adidas beat Kurt Von Hess(3:00) via pinfall
Angelo Mosca, Jr. beat Doug Vines(5:07) via pinfall
Rufus R. Jones beat Gary Royal(5:00)
James J. Dillon beat Sam Houston via pinfall
Barry Windham beat ??(:30)
Wahoo McDaniel beat Keith Larsen(5:52) via pinfall

8/16/84: Sumter, SC @ Exhibition Center
Ivan Koloff & Don Kernodle beat Mark Youngblood & The Renegade
Nikita Koloff beat Johnny Weaver
Adrian Street beat Jeff Sword
Tom Shaft beat Kurt Von Hess
Paul Kelly beat Mike Golden

8/16/84: Norfolk, VA @ Scope
Wahoo McDaniel & Tully Blanchard beat Ric Flair & Ricky Steamboat
Brett Hart beat Doug Vines
Denny Brown beat Mike Fever
James J. Dillon beat Keith Larsen
Brian Adidas beat Gary Royal
Angelo Mosca, Jr. beat Assassin #3
Rufus R. Jones beat Assassin #1

8/17/84: Richmond, VA @ Coliseum
Denny Brown beat Paul Kelly
Angelo Mosca, Jr. beat Nikita Koloff by DQ
James J. Dillon beat Adrian Street
Ivan Koloff & Don Kernodle beat The Renegade & Brian Adidas
Assassin #1 beat Rufus R. Jones
Jimmy Valiant draw Tully Blanchard
NWA World Champ Ric Flair beat Wahoo McDaniel DQ

8/18/84: Greensboro, NC @ Coliseum
Denny Brown beat Paul Kelly
Ron Bass & Black Bart beat Rufus R. Jones & Brian Adidas
Dusty Rhodes beat Assassin #3
The Renegade beat Don Kernodle by DQ
Barry Windham beat Ivan Koloff
Assassin #1 beat Jimmy Valiant in a taped fist match
Ricky Steamboat draw Tully Blanchard
NWA World Champ Ric Flair beat Wahoo McDaniel DQ

8/19/84: Asheville, NC @ Civic Center
Dusty Rhodes & Blackjack Mulligan NC with Wahoo McDaniel & Tully Blanchard
Assassin #1 beat Jimmy Valiant in a taped fist match
Mark Youngblood, The Renegade & Angelo Mosca, Jr. beat Ivan Koloff, Nikita Koloff & Don Kernodle
James J. Dillon beat Denny Brown
Keith Larsen beat Jeff Sword
Keith Larsen beat Mike Fever

8/19/84: Charlotte, NC @ Coliseum
Denny Brown beat Gary Royal
Tom Shaft beat Jeff Sword
Ron Bass & Black Bart beat Johnny Weaver & Angelo Mosca, Jr.
Ivan Koloff & Nikita Koloff beat Rufus R. Jones & Brian Adidas
Assassin #1 beat Jimmy Valiant in a taped fist match
Dusty Rhodes beat Don Kernodle by DQ
Blackjack Mulligan NC with Wahoo McDaniel
Ricky Steamboat draw Tully Blanchard

8/20/84: Greenville, SC @ Memorial Auditorium
Ricky Steamboat draw Tully Blanchard
Blackjack Mulligan NC with Wahoo McDaniel
The Renegade beat Ivan Koloff by DQ
Nikita Koloff beat Mark Youngblood
Brian Adidas beat Paul Kelly
Sam Houston beat Mark Fever
Denny Brown beat Ben Alexander

8/20/84: East Rutherford, NJ(Show cancelled)
Dusty Rhodes vs. One Man Gang
The Freebirds vs. The Road Warriors
Ivan Koloff & Don Kernodle vs. Mark & Jay Youngblood

8/21/84: Columbia, SC @ Township Auditorium
Blackjack Mulligan NC with Wahoo McDaniel
The Renegade beat Ivan Koloff by DQ
Nikita Koloff beat Mark Youngblood
Brian Adidas beat Paul Kelly
Sam Houston beat Jeff Sword
Mike Fever beat Gary Royal

8/21/84: Raleigh, NC @ Dorton Arena
Jimmy Valiant beat Assassin #1 in a New York street fight match
Tully Blanchard beat Johnny Weaver
Ron Bass beat Rufus R. Jones
Black Bart beat Tom Shaft
Assassin #3 draw Denny Brown

8/22/84: Winston-Salem, NC @ Memorial Coliseum (TV)
Brian Adidas beat Paul Garner
James J. Dillon beat Brett Hart
NWA World Champ Ric Flair beat Kurt Von Hess
Wahoo McDaniel & Tully Blanchard beat Randy Barber & ?? Horton
Ivan Koloff & Don Kernodle vs. Mark Youngblood & The Renegade
Wahoo McDaniel vs. Jimmy Valiant
NWA World Champ Ric Flair vs. Assassin #1

8/23/84: Fredericksburg, VA @ Stafford High School
Jimmy Valiant beat Assassin #1
Mike Rotundo beat Assassin #3
Brian Adidas beat Jeff Sword
Bret Hart beat Paul Kelly
Bobby Bass beat Brett Hart

8/24/84: Hampton, VA @ Coliseum
Ivan Koloff & Don Kernodle beat Mark Youngblood & The Renegade
Tully Blanchard beat Johnny Weaver
Denny Brown beat Paul Kelly
James J. Dillon beat Brett Hart
Mike Rotundo beat Nikita Koloff by DQ
Black Bart & Ron Bass beat Brian Adidas & Sam Houston

8/25/84: Roanoke, VA @ Civic Center
Ivan Koloff & Don Kernodle beat Mark Youngblood & The Renegade
Ron Bass beat Rufus R. Jones
Black Bart beat Johnny Weaver
Nikita Koloff beat Mike Fever
Denny Brown draw Brett Hart

8/26/84: Sumter, SC @ Exhibition Center
Ivan Koloff & Don Kernodle beat Mark Youngblood & The Renegade
Angelo Mosca beat Nikita Koloff by DQ
Johnny Weaver beat James J. Dillon
Ron Bass & Black Bart beat Denny Brown & Mike Fever
Keith Larsen draw Black Bart

8/27/84: Kinston, NC
Angelo Mosca beat Assassin #3
Rufus R. Jones beat Nikita Koloff by DQ
Ivan Koloff & Don Kernodle beat Angelo Mosca, Jr. & The Renegade
Assassin #1 beat Jimmy Valiant in a taped fist match

8/27/84: Greenville, SC @ Memorial Auditorium
Tom Shaft beat Doug Vines
Mike Rotundo beat Jeff Sword
Ron Bass & Black Bart beat Johnny Weaver & Denny Brown
Brian Adidas beat Ben Alexander
Barry Windham beat Wahoo McDaniel
Tully Blanchard beat Dusty Rhodes

8/28/84: Raleigh, NC @ Dorton Arena
Assassin #1 beat Jimmy Valiant in a Texas death match
The Renegade & Mark Youngblood beat Ivan Koloff & Don Kernodle by DQ
Angelo Mosca, Jr. beat Jeff Sword
Nikita Koloff beat Sam Houston
Assassin #3 beat Keith Larsen
Brett Hart beat Doug Vines

8/28/84: Columbia, SC @ Township Auditorium
Wahoo McDaniel beat Dusty Rhodes by DQ

Tully Blanchard draw Barry Windham
Ron Bass & Black Bart beat Johnny Weaver & Rufus R. Jones
Mike Rotundo beat James J. Dillon
Brian Adidas beat Ben Alexander
Mike Fever beat Denny Brown

8/29/84: Spartanburg, SC @ Memorial Auditorium (TV)
Angelo Mosca, Jr. & Brian Adidas beat Jeff Sword & Doug Vines
Ivan Koloff beat Mike Fever
Barry Windham beat Gary Royal
Ron Bass & Black Bart beat Gene Ligon & Tom Shaft
Mike Rotundo beat Paul Kelly
The Zambui Express beat Sam Houston & Denny Brown

8/31/84: Charleston, SC @ County Hall
Gene Ligon vs. Ben Alexander
Denny Brown vs. Paul Kelly
Sam Houston & Angelo Mosca, Jr. vs. The Zambui Express
Wahoo McDaniel vs. Mike Rotundo
Tully Blanchard vs. Barry Windham

8/31/84: Lynchburg, VA @ City Armory

9/1/84: York, SC @ High School
Rufus R. Jones & Mark Youngblood vs. The Zambui Express
Johnny Weaver vs. Paul Kelly
Keith Larsen vs. Doug Vines
Ben Alexander vs. Gary Royal
Brett Hart vs. Gene Ligon

9/1/84: Greensboro, NC @ Coliseum
Ric Flair & Blackjack Mulligan NC with Wahoo McDaniel & Tully
Blanchard
Dusty Rhodes beat Don Kernodle
Assassin #1 beat Jimmy Valiant in a Texas death match
Barry Windham & Mike Rotundo beat Ivan Koloff & Nikita Koloff by DQ
Ron Bass & Black Bart beat Angelo Mosca & Brian Adidas
Denny Brown beat Mike Fever
Sam Houston beat Jeff Sword
Jay Youngblood beat Assassin #3

9/2/84: Asheville, NC @ Civic Center
NWA World Champ Ric Flair beat Wahoo McDaniel

9/3/84: Greenville, SC @ Memorial Auditorium
James J. Dillon beat Denny Brown
Mark Youngblood beat Paul Kelly
Jay Youngblood beat Jeff Sword
Black Bart beat Brian Adias
Ron Bass beat Angelo Mosca, Jr.
Dusty Rhodes & Ricky Steamboat beat Tully Blanchard & Wahoo McDaniel

9/3/84: Covington, VA @ Casey Field

9/4/84: Raleigh, NC @ Dorton Arena
Mike Fever beat Doug Vines
Nikita Koloff beat Rufus R. Jones
Mike Rotundo beat Assassin #1
The Zambui Express beat Mark Youngblood & The Renegade
Barry Windham beat Ivan Koloff by DQ

9/5/84: Spartanburg, SC @ Memorial Auditorium (TV)
Dusty Rhodes vs. Wahoo McDaniel
Barry Windham & Mike Rotundo beat Jeff Sword & Paul Kelly
Black Bart beat Mike Fever
The Zambui Express beat Mark Fleming & Brett Hart
Rob Bass beat Angelo Mosca, Jr. to win NWA Mid Atlantic Title
Assassin #1 beat Ron Rossi

9/6/84: Harrisonburg, VA @ High School
Mike Fever vs. Jeff Sword
Brett Hart vs. Doug Lyons
Denny Brown vs. Paul Kelly
Assassin #3 vs. Mark Youngblood
Brian Adias & The Renegade vs. The Zambui Express
Assassin #1 vs. Rufus R. Jones

9/6/84: Norfolk, VA @ Scope
Keith Larsen beat Gary Royal
Nikita Koloff beat Johnny Weaver
Tully Blanchard & Wahoo McDaniel beat Ric Flair & Dusty Rhodes by DQ
Barry Windham beat Ivan Koloff
Mike Rotundo beat Don Kernodle
Black Bart & Ron Bass beat Denny Brown & Sam Houston

9/7/84: Charleston, SC @ County Hall
Doug Vines beat Brett Hart
Mike Fever fought Jeff Sword to a draw
Johnny Weaver beat Assassin #3
The Zambui Express beat Mark & Jay Youngblood
Assassin #1 beat Jimmy Valiant in a taped fist match

9/7/84: Richmond, VA @ Coliseum
Denny Brown beat Gary Royal
Nikita Koloff beat Sam Houston
Rufus R. Jones beat Paul Kelly
Don Kernodle beat Angelo Mosca, Jr.
Blackjack Mulligan beat Wahoo McDaniel by DQ
Black Bart & Ron Bass beat Brian Adidas & Mike Rotundo
Barry Windham beat Ivan Koloff
Dusty Rhodes beat Tully Blanchard

9/8/84: Wilmington, NC @ Legion Stadium
Wahoo McDaniel vs. Blackjack Mulligan
Tully Blanchard vs. Dusty Rhodes
Jimmy Valiant vs. Assassin #1 in a NY street fight
Brian Adidas & Angelo Mosca, Jr. vs. Zambui Express
Assassin #3 vs. Denny Brown

9/9/84: Charlotte, NC @ Coliseum
Nikita Koloff beat Sam Houston & Brett Hart in a handicap match
Black Bart & Ron Bass beat Brian Adidas & Denny Brown
Gary Royal beat Doug Vines
Mike Rotundo beat Don Kernodle
Tully Blanchard beat Ricky Steamboat
Barry Windham beat Ivan Koloff
Barry Windham beat Wahoo McDaniel in a Texas death match

9/9/84: Asheville, NC @ Civic Center

9/10/84: Greenville, SC @ Memorial Auditorium
The Zambui Express beat Angelo Mosca, Jr. & Brian Adidas
Mike Rotundo beat Ron Bass by DQ
Tully Blanchard draw Barry Windham(20:00)
Dusty Rhodes beat Wahoo McDaniel via pinfall

9/11/84: Columbia, SC @ Township Auditorium
Paul Kelly beat Mike Fever
Denny Brown beat Gary Royal
Black Bart beat Rufus R. Jones
Don Kernodle beat Brian Adias
Mike Rotundo beat Ron Bass by DQ
Ricky Steamboat beat Wahoo McDaniel

9/12/84: ?? (TV)
Mark Youngblood beat Doug Vines
Assassin #1 beat Mike Fever
Barry Windham & Mike Rotundo beat Paul Kelly & Gary Royal
The Zambui Express beat Brett Hart & Keith Larsen
Don Kernodle beat Denny Brown
Black Bart beat Sam Houston

9/13/84: Roxboro, NC @ Optimist Park

9/14/84: Charleston, SC @ County Hall
Kareem Muhammad beat Denny Brown
Elijah Akeem beat Sam Houston
Nikita Koloff beat Johnny Weaver
Rufus R. Jones beat Doug Vines
Ron Bass & Black Bart beat Mike Rotundo & Brian Adidas
Ivan Koloff & Don Kernodle draw Barry Windham & Ricky Steamboat
Assassin #1 beat Jimmy Valiant in a taped fist match
Ole Anderson & Dusty Rhodes beat Tully Blanchard & Wahoo McDaniel

9/15/84: Greenville, SC @ Memorial Auditorium
Tully Blanchard beat Ricky Steamboat
Dusty Rhodes & Barry Windham beat Ivan Koloff & Don Kernodle by DQ
Mike Rotundo beat Nikita Koloff
Brian Adidas beat Assassin #1
Rufus R. Jones beat Paul Kelly
Doug Vines beat Denny Brown
Keith Larsen beat Gary Royal

9/16/84: Asheville, NC @ Civic Center
Sam Houston beat Doug Vines
Elijah Akeem beat Denny Brown
Rufus R. Jones beat Paul Kelly
Ron Bass & Black Bart beat Mike Rotundo & Angelo Mosca, Jr.
Jimmy Valiant beat Assassin #1 in a NY Street Fight
Dusty Rhodes & Barry Windham beat Ivan Koloff & Don Kernodle by DQ
Ricky Steamboat draw Tully Blanchard

9/18/84: Raleigh, NC @ Dorton Arena
Ultimate Assassin(J. Weaver) beat Assassin #1 by DQ
Dusty Rhodes & Ric Flair NC with Wahoo McDaniel & Tully Blanchard
Mike Davis beat Jeff Sword
Kareem Muhammad beat Denny Brown
Elijah Akeem beat Sam Houston

9/18/84: Columbia, SC @ Township Auditorium
Mike Rotundo & Barry Windham beat Ivan Koloff & Don Kernodle by DQ
Ron Bass beat Angelo Mosca
Brian Adidas beat Nikita Koloff by DQ
Black Bart beat Keith Larsen
Brett Hart beat Doug Vines
Gary Royal beat Mike Fever

9/19/84: Spartanburg, SC @ Memorial Auditorium (TV)
Manny Fernandez vs. Gary Royal

9/20/84: Norfolk, VA @ Scope
Nikita Koloff beat Denny Brown
Keith Larsen beat Jeff Sword
Black Bart beat Mike Davis
Ron Bass beat Sam Houston
Mike Rotundo beat Ivan Koloff
Barry Windham beat Don Kernodle
Ric Flair & Dusty Rhodes beat Wahoo McDaniel & Tully Blanchard

9/20/84: Orangeburg, SC
Mark Fleming draw Paul Kelly
Mike Fever beat Gary Royal
Johnny Weaver beat Doug Vines
The Zambui Express beat Keith Larsen & Brett Hart
Assassin #1 beat Jimmy Valiant in a taped fist match

9/21/84: Richmond, VA @ Coliseum
Nikita Koloff beat Denny Brown
Sam Houston beat Jeff Sword
Black Bart beat Keith Larsen
Ron Bass beat Mike Davis
Mike Rotundo & Dusty Rhodes beat Ivan Koloff & Don Kernodle by DQ
Barry Windham beat Wahoo McDaniel
Tully Blanchard draw Ricky Steamboat

9/21/84: Charleston, SC @ County Hall
Jimmy Valiant beat Assassin #1 in a NY Street Fight
Mark Youngblood beat Elijah Akeem
Ultimate Assassin beat Mike Fever

Kareem Muhammad beat Brett Hart
Paul Kelly beat Joel Deaton

9/22/84: Greensboro, NC @ Coliseum
Ricky Steamboat draw Tully Blanchard
Jimmy Valiant beat Assassin #1 in a NY Street Fight
Barry Windham beat Wahoo McDaniel
Briand Adidas beat Mike Fever
Mike Rotundo beat Don Kernodle
Jay Youngblood & Mike Davis beat Ron Bass & Black Bart
Johnny Weaver & Denny Brown beat The Zambui Express

9/23/84: Sumter, SC @ Exhibition Center
Dusty Rhodes & Barry Windham beat Wahoo McDaniel & Tully Blanchard by DQ
Jimmy Valiant beat Assassin #1 in a NY Street Fight
Ivan Koloff beat Brian Adidas
Mike Rotundo beat Don Kernodle by DQ
Black Bart & Ron Bass beat Brian Adidas & Mike Davis
Denny Brown beat Paul Kelly

9/24/84: Greenville, SC @ Memorial Auditorium
Jeff Sword beat Joel Deaton
Denny Brown beat Paul Kelly
James J. Dillon beat Keith Larsen
Barry Windham beat Jeff Sword
Ron Bass & Black Bart beat Sam Houston & Brian Adidas
Dusty Rhodes beat Nikita Koloff by DQ
Wahoo McDaniel beat Ricky Steamboat

9/25/84: Columbia, SC @ Township Auditorium
Wahoo McDaniel beat Barry Windham
Ultimate Assassin beat Assassin #1 by DQ
The Zambui beat Keith Larsen & Sam Houston
Black Bart beat Mike Davis
Jeff Sword beat Mike Fever
Brett Hart beat Doug Vines

9/26/84: Raleigh, NC @ Dorton Arena (TV)
Mike Rotundo vs. Paul Kelly
Nikita Koloff vs. Mark Fleming
Brian Adidas vs. Mike Jackson
Dusty Rhodes & Manny Fernandez vs. Horton & Randy Barber
Wahoo McDaniel & Tully Blanchard vs. Don Sanders & Mike Fever
Mark Youngblood vs. Joel Deaton
Mark Youngblood & The Renegade vs. Ivan Koloff & Don Kernodle
Ron Bass beat Mike Rotundo
Black Bart beat Brett Hart
Zambui Express beat Keith Larsen & Denny Brown
Manny Fernandez beat Mike Fever
Ivan Koloff, Nikita Koloff & Don Kernodle beat Brian Adidas, Mike Davis & Sam Houston
Assassin #1 beat Ultimate Assassin
Tully Blanchard beat Barry Windham by DQ
Wahoo McDaniel beat Dusty Rhodes

9/28/84: Hampton, VA @ Coliseum
Manny Fernandez beat Gary Royal
Zambui Express beat Brian Adidas & Keith Larsen
Black Bart beat Mark Youngblood
Ultimate Assassin beat Assassin #1 by DQ
Wahoo McDaniel NC with Barry Windham
Dusty Rhodes beat Tully Blanchard by DQ

9/29/84: Danville, VA @ George Washington High School
Tully Blanchard vs. Barry Windham
Mike Rotundo vs. Ron Bass

9/30/84: Asheville, NC @ Civic Center
Ric Flair & Dusty Rhodes beat Tully Blanchard & Wahoo McDaniel
Ultimate Assassin beat Assassin #1 by DQ
Ron Bass beat Mark Youngblood
Zambui Express beat Keith Larsen & Brett Hart
Manny Fernandez beat Doug Vines
Black Bart beat Denny Brown

10/1/84: Greenville, SC @ Memorial Auditorium
Dusty Rhodes beat Ivan Koloff in a lumberjack match
Barry Windham beat Nikita Koloff by DQ
Assassin #1 beat Ultimate Assassin
Manny Fernandez beat Don Kernodle
Zambui Express beat Joel Deaton & Sam Houston

10/1/84: Fayetteville, NC @ Cumberland County Civic Center
Mike Davis beat Paul Kelly
James J. Dillon beat Keith Larsen
Gary Royal beat Doug Vines
Ron Bass & Black Bart beat Brian Adidas & Mark Youngblood
Mike Rotundo draw Tully Blanchard
Ricky Steamboat NC with Wahoo McDaniel

10/2/84: Spartanburg, SC @ Memorial Auditorium (TV)
Tully Blanchard vs. Barry Windham
Nikita Koloff vs. Dusty Rhodes
Mike Rotundo vs. Mike Jackson
Ron Bass & Black Bart vs. Sam Houston & Rocky King
American Starship(Coyote[aka Scott Hall] & Eagle[aka Dan Spivey]) vs. Gary Royal & Don Sanders
Manny Fernandez vs. Jeff Sword
Barry Windham vs. Paul Kelly
Ivan Koloff vs. Bob Owens

10/2/84: Columbia, SC @ Township Auditorium
NWA World Champ Ric Flair NC with Wahoo McDaniel
Ultimate Assassin beat Assassin #1 by DQ in a mask vs. mask match
Zambui Express beat Mark Youngblood & Mike Davis
Joel Deaton beat Brett Hart
Keith Larsen beat Mike Fever
Denny Brown beat Doug Vines

10/3/84: Raleigh, NC @ Dorton Arena
NWA World Champ Ric Flair NC with Wahoo McDaniel
Ron Bass beat Brian Adidas
James J. Dillon beat Mike Brown
Assassin #1 & The Zambui Express beat Ultimate Assassin, Mark Youngblood & Mike Davis
Manny Fernandez beat Black Bart
Ricky Steamboat draw Tully Blanchard
Barry Windham & Mike Rotundo beat Nikita Koloff & Don Kernodle
Dusty Rhodes beat Ivan Koloff by DQ

10/5/84: Charleston, SC @ County Hall
Mike Fever beat Joel Deaton
Paul Kelly beat Brett Hart
Keith Larsen beat Gary Royal
Ultimate Assassin beat Paul Jones
Jimmy Valiant beat Assassin #1 Texas death match

10/5/84: Richmond, VA @ Coliseum
Dusty Rhodes beat Nikita Koloff
NWA World Champ Ric Flair beat Wahoo McDaniel
Sam Houston beat Jeff Sword
Black Bart beat Mike Davis
Ron Bass beat Mark Youngblood
Tully Blanchard beat Ricky Steamboat
Ivan Koloff & Don Kernodle beat Manny Fernandez & Brian Adidas

10/6/84: Greensboro, NC @ Coliseum
Nikita Koloff beat Mike Davis
Manny Fernandez beat Wahoo McDaniel by CO
Ron Bass beat The Renegade
Tully Blanchard beat Ricky Steamboat by DQ
Ivan Koloff & Don Kernodle beat Ole Anderson & Brian Adidas

10/7/84: Charlotte, NC @ Coliseum
NWA United States Title Tournament
1st Round
Mike Rotundo beat Assassin #1 by DQ
Manny Fernandez beat ??
Ivan Koloff beat Brian Adidas
Dusty Rhodes beat Don Kernodle
Ricky Steamboat draw Ron Bass
Billy Graham beat Carlos Colon by CO
Wahoo McDaniel beat Mark Youngblood
Tully Blanchard beat Jimmy Valiant

2nd Round
Manny Fernandez beat Billy Graham by DQ
Dusty Rhodes NC with Ivan Koloff
Wahoo McDaniel beat Mike Rotundo
Tully Blanchard received a bye

Semifinals
Manny Fernandez beat Tully Blanchard
Wahoo McDaniel received a bye

Finals
Wahoo McDaniel beat Manny Fernandez to win vacant NWA United States Title

10/8/84: Greenville, SC @ Memorial Auditorium
Dusty Rhodes & Manny Fernandez beat Tully Blanchard & Wahoo McDaniel in a lights out, Texas tornado match
Ron Bass beat Mike Rotundo by DQ
Ivan & Nikita Koloff beat Brian Adidas & Mark Youngblood
Ultimate Assassin beat Assassin #1 by DQ
Black Bart beat Sam Houston
Brian Adidas beat Don Kernodle by DQ
Sam Houston beat Denny Brown
Sam Bowie beat Mike Davis

10/10/84: Spartanburg, SC @ Memorial Auditorium (TV)
Brian Adidas vs. Jason Walker
Mike Rotundo vs. Rocky King
American Starship vs. Don Sanders & Randy Barber
Manny Fernandez vs. Doug Vines
The Zambui Express vs. Mike Jackson & Steve Miller

10/11/84: Kenansville, NC
Sam Houston beat Jeff Sword
Nikita Koloff beat Mike Fever
The Zambui Express beat Mike Davis & Keith Larsen
Brian Adidas beat Don Kernodle by DQ
Manny Fernandez beat Ivan Koloff

10/12/84: Hampton, VA @ Coliseum
Joel Deaton beat Paul Kelly
The Zambui Express beat Sam Houston & Denny Brown
Assassin #1 beat Jimmy Valiant
Ron Bass & Black Bart beat Manny Fernandez & Mike Rotundo
Don Kernodle beat Brian Adidas
Tully Blanchard draw Manny Fernandez
Dusty Rhodes beat Ivan Koloff

10/13/84: Richmond, VA @ Coliseum
Dusty Rhodes beat Nikita Koloff DQ lumberjack match
Jimmy Valiant beat Assassin #1 in a lights out, taped fist, cage match
Wahoo McDaniel NC with Manny Fernandez in a Texas death match
Tully Blanchard beat Mike Rotundo
Ivan Koloff & Don Kernodle beat Ultimate Assassin & Brian Adidas
Ron Bass beat Mike Davis
Black Bart beat Sam Houston
The Zambui Express beat Joel Deaton & Keith Larsen
Denny Brown beat Jeff Sword

10/14/84: Asheville, NC @ Civic Center
Denny Brown beat Doug Vines
James J. Dillon beat Keith Larsen
The Zambui Express beat Sam Houston & Joel Deaton
Don Kernodle beat Mike Davis
Assassin #1 beat Ultimate Assassin
Nikita Koloff beat Bret Hart & Mike Fever
Mike Rotundo & Brian Adidas beat Ron Bass & Black Bart by DQ
Wahoo McDaniel NC with Manny Fernandez

10/15/84: Fayetteville, NC @ Cumberland County Civic Center
Joel Deaton beat Mike Fever
Denny Brown beat Paul Kelly
Sam Houston beat Jeff Sword
Ron Bass & Black Bart beat Keith Larsen & Mike Davis
Don Kernodle beat Ultimate Assassin
Manny Fernandez beat Ivan Koloff
Dusty Rhodes beat Nikita Koloff by DQ

10/17/84: ?? (TV)
Mike Rotundo beat Doug Vines
Assassin #1 beat Ultimate Assassin
Manny Fernandez beat Mark Fleming
Ron Bass & Black Bart beat Sam Houston & Brett Hart
Wahoo McDaniel beat Joel Deaton
Tully Blanchard beat Brian Adidas
Mike Rotundo beat Mark Fleming
Manny Fernandez beat Jeff Sword
Ron Bass & Black Bart beat Denny Brown & Doug Vines
Wahoo McDaniel beat Brett Hart
The Zambui Express beat Mike Davis & Sam Houston
American Starship beat Joel Deaton & Doug Vines

10/20/84: Greensboro, NC @ Coliseum
Joel Deaton beat Jeff Sword
Black Bart beat Keith Larsen
The Zambui Express beat Mike Davis & Sam Houston
Nikita Koloff beat Brett Hart & Mark Fleming in a handicap match
Tully Blanchard beat Brian Adidas
Wahoo McDaniel beat Jimmy Valiant
Dusty Rhodes & Manny Fernandez beat Ivan Koloff & Don Kernodle in a cage match to win NWA World Tag Title

10/21/84: Charlotte, NC @ Coliseum
Black Bart beat Mike Davis
American Starship beat Gary Royal & Jeff Sword
Ron Bass beat Brian Adidas
Ultimate Assassin beat Assassin #1 by CO
Ivan Koloff beat Mike Rotundo
Dusty Rhodes beat Nikita Koloff by DQ in a Texas bullrope match
Manny Fernandez NC with Wahoo McDaniel
Ron Garvin draw Tully Blanchard

10/21/84: Sumter, SC @ Exhibition Center
Manny Fernandez draw Tully Blanchard
Ultimate Assassin & Jimmy Valiant draw Assassin #1 & Paul Jones
Ron Bass beat Brian Adidas
Starship beat Doug Vines & Mark Fleming
Black Bart beat Joel Deaton
Denny Brown beat Gary Royal

10/23/84: Spartanburg, SC @ Memorial Auditorium (PW USA TV Taping)
Jerry Lawler beat Randy Barber(3:25) via pinfall
Ivan Koloff & Nikita Koloff beat Rocky King & Don Sanders(4:51) via pinfall
Mr. Saito beat Jason Walker(6:12) via pinfall
Bob Backlund beat Mike Jackson(7:55) via pinfall
Ricky Steamboat beat Gary Royal(2:47)
The Road Warriors beat Steve Miller & Mark Fleming(3:09) by submission
Ricky Steamboat beat Bobby Bass(1:44) by submission
Bob Backlund beat Gary Royal(7:59) by submission
Nikita Koloff beat Mark Fleming(2:24)
Mr. Saito beat Gene Ligon(4:43) via pinfall
Jerry Lawler & Tommy Rich beat Randy Barber & Don Sanders(4:11) via pinfall
Carlos Colon beat Mike Jackson(5:09) via pinfall
Ivan & Nikita Koloff beat Mike Jackson & Jason Walker(5:10)
Bob Backlund beat Randy Barber(6:54) by submission
Mr. Saito beat Steve Miller(3;31) by submission
The Road Warriors beat Gene Ligon & Lee Ramsey(1:32) via pinfall

10/24/84: Raleigh, NC @ Dorton Arena (TV)
Buzz Tyler vs. ??
Black Bart vs. Gene Ligon
Dick Slater vs. Mike Fever
Mike Rotundo vs. Joel Deaton

10/25/84: Norfolk, VA @ Scope
Dick Slater beat Jeff Sword
Black Bart beat Denny Brown
Ron Bass beat Mike Davis
American Starship beat Zambui Express by DQ
Ultimate Assassin beat Assassin #1
Ivan Koloff beat Brian Adidas
Ole Anderson beat Tully Blanchard by DQ
Manny Fernandez NC Wahoo McDaniel
Dusty Rhodes beat Nikita Koloff Texas bullrope match

10/26/84: Charleston, SC @ County Hall
Wahoo McDaniel DDQ Manny Fernandez
Ron Bass & Black Bart beat Keith Larsen & Brian Adidas
The American Starship beat The Zambui Express
Mike Davis beat Joel Deaton
Gene Ligon beat David Deaton
Denny Brown beat Doug Vines

10/30/84: Columbia, SC @ Township Auditorium
Dusty Rhodes & Manny Fernandez vs. Ivan & Nikita Koloff
Wahoo McDaniel vs. Ricky Steamboat
Tully Blanchard vs. Mike Rotundo
Assassin #1 vs. Elijah Akeem
Ron Bass vs. Brian Adidas
American Starship vs. Black Bart & James J. Dillon
Buzz Tyler vs. Kareem Muhammad
Tommy Lane vs. Jeff Sword

10/31/84: ?? (TV)
Buzz Tyler vs. Ben Alexander
Elijah Akeem vs. Tommy Lee
Mike Davis vs. Gene Ligon
Ivan Koloff vs. Lee Ramsey
Ron Bass vs. Gerald Finley

11/2/84: Richmond, VA @ Coliseum
Black Bart beat Tommy Kay
American Starship beat Paul Kelly & Jeff Sword
Buzz Tyler beat Ivan Koloff
Wahoo McDaniel & Tully Blanchard beat Dick Slater & Brian Adidas
Assassin #1 beat Paul Jones
Ricky Steamboat beat Ron Bass by DQ
Dusty Rhodes & Manny Fernandez beat The Zambui Express

11/4/84: Asheville, NC @ Civic Center
Denny Brown beat Gary Royal
Buzz Tyler beat Black Bart
American Starship beat The Zambui Express by DQ
Ivan Koloff beat Brian Adidas
Assassin #1 beat Paul Jones by DQ
Ricky Steamboat beat Ron Bass by DQ
Dick Slater & Manny Fernandez beat Wahoo McDaniel & Tully Blanchard

11/5/84: Greenville, SC @ Memorial Auditorium
Tommy Lane beat Joel Deaton
Keith Larsen beat Mike Fever
Nikita Koloff beat Tyler
Assassin #1 beat Ivan Koloff by DQ
Dick Slater beat Wahoo McDaniel
Dusty Rhodes & Manny Fernandez beat The Zambui Express

11/6/84: Columbia, SC @ Township Auditorium
Tommy Lane beat Jeff Sword
Buzz Tyler beat Kareem Muhammad
American Starship beat Black Bart & James J. Dillon
Ron Bass beat Brian Adias
Assassin #1 beat Elijah Akeem by DQ
Tully Blanchard draw Dick Slater
Ricky Steamboat beat Wahoo McDaniel by DQ
Dusty Rhodes & Manny Fernandez beat Ivan & Nikita Koloff in a steel cage match

11/6/84: Spartanburg, SC @ Memorial Auditorium (TV)
Assassin #1 vs. Elijah Akeem
American Starship & Manny Fernandez vs. Ron Bass, Black Bart & James J. Dillon
Brian Adidas vs. Mark Fleming
Wahoo McDaniel & Tully Blanchard vs. Sam Houston & Brett Hart
Nikita Koloff vs. Joel Deaton
The Zambui Express vs. Tommy Lane & Gary Royal

11/7/84: Raleigh, NC @ Dorton Arena
American Starship beat Doug Vines & Joel Deaton
Ricky Steamboat beat Ron Bass by DQ
Assassin #1 beat Ivan Koloff
Nikita Koloff beat Brian Adidas
Dick Slater beat Black Bart
Buzz Tyler beat Jeff Sword
Dusty Rhodes & Manny Fernandez beat Wahoo McDaniel & Tully Blanchard

11/8/84: Norfolk, VA @ Scope
Jeff Sword beat Denny Brown
Keith Larsen beat Gary Royal
Buzz Tyler beat Mike Fever
Assassin #1 & American Starship beat Jeff Sword, Paul Jones & Kareem Muhammad
Ric Flair & Dick Slater beat Tully Blanchard & Wahoo McDaniel
Dusty Rhodes & Manny Fernandez beat Ivan & Nikita Koloff cage match

11/9/84: Huntington, WV
American Starship beat James J. Dillon & Joel Deaton
Buzz Tyler beat Black Bart
Nikita Koloff beat Brian Adidas
Assassin #1 & Dick Slater beat The Zambui Express
Ivan Koloff beat Johnny Weaver
Ricky Steamboat beat Ron Bass by DQ
Dusty Rhodes & Manny Fernandez beat Wahoo McDaniel & Tully Blanchard

11/10/84: Logan, WV @ Logan Memorial Fieldhouse
NWA World Champ Ric Flair vs. Ricky Steamboat
Wahoo McDaniel vs. Dusty Rhodes

11/12/84: Fayetteville, NC @ Cumberland County Civic Center
Denny Brown beat Brett Hart
Keith Larsen beat Sean Royal
Sam Houston beat Paul Kelly
Black Bart beat Mike Davis
Buzz Tyler beat Wahoo McDaniel by DQ
Dusty Rhodes & Manny Fernandez beat Ivan & Nikita Koloff

11/12/84: Greenville, SC @ Memorial Auditorium
American Starship beat Doug Vines & Joel Deaton
Tommy Lane beat Jeff Sword
Brian Adidas beat The Inferno
Elijah Akeem beat Johnny Weaver
Assassin #1 beat Kareem Muhammad
Ricky Steamboat beat Ron Bass by DQ
Dick Slater beat Tully Blanchard

11/14/84: Raleigh, NC @ Dorton Arena (TV)
Assassin #1 & Brian Adidas vs. Gary Royal & Paul Kelly
Manny Fernandez vs. Jeff Sword
Black Bart vs. Joel Deaton
Buzz Tyler vs. Mark Fleming
Ivan & Nikita Koloff vs. Denny Brown & Tommy Lane
Elijah Akeem vs. Sam Houston

11/15/84: Sumter, SC @ Exhibition Center(PWUSA TV Taping)
Ivan & Nikita Koloff beat Sam Houston & Bret Hart(4:44)
Manny Fernandez beat Paul Kelly(1:03) via pinfall
Brian Adidas beat Gary Royal(8:08) via pinfall
Harley Race beat Tommy Lane(6:10) via pinfall
Dick Slater beat Mike Feve(6:00) via pinfall

Ron Bass beat Joel Deaton(4:14) via pinfall
NWA World Champ Ric Flair beat Mike Davis
Billy Graham beat Brett Hart(1:24) by submission
Wahoo McDaniel beat Joel Deaton(4:56) via pinfall
Tully Blanchard beat Sam Houston(5:02) via pinfall
Ivan & Nikita Koloff beat Denny Brown & Tommy Lane(3:38)
Ron Bass beat Bob Backlund by DQ
Billy Graham beat Sam Houston(2:59) by submission
Mr. Saito beat Lee Ramsey(3:38) by submission
Harley Race beat Mike Davis(8:49) via pinfall
Carlos Colon beat Ben Alexander(3:54) by submission
Ivan & Nikita Koloff beat Mike Fever & Gene Ligon(4:27)
Jerry Lawler & Brian Adidas beat Joel Deaton & Paul Kelly(4:01) via pinfall
Dusty Rhodes & Manny Fernandez beat Doug Vines & Jeff Sword(1:11) via pinfall
Rick Martel beat Joel Deaton(5:20) via pinfall
Wahoo McDaniel beat Lee Ramsey(2:39) via pinfall
NWA World Champ Ric Flair beat Tommy Lane
Ron Bass & Black Bart beat Sam Houston & Brett Hart(2:53) via pinfall
Carlos Colon beat Tully Blanchard(8:28) by DQ
Dick Slater beat Gary Royal
Ron Bass & Black Bart beat Jerry Lawler & Brian Adidas
Mr. Saito beat Bob Backlund by DQ
Manny Fernandez beat Gary Royal
Jerry Lawler beat Mike Fever
Billy Graham beat Joel Deaton

11/16/84: Charleston, SC @ County Hall
Tommy Lane beat Paul Kelly
Black Bart beat Brian Adidas
American Starship beat Joel Deaton & Mike Fever
Ricky Steamboat beat Ron Bass by DQ
Ivan & Nikita Koloff beat Dusty Rhodes & Manny Fernandez

11/19/84: Greenville, SC @ Memorial Auditorium
Tommy Lane beat Paul Kelly
Denny Brown beat Gary Royal
Ron Bass & Black Bart beat Assassin #1 & Buzz Tyler
Ivan Koloff beat Manny Fernandez Texas death match
Dick Slater & Ricky Steamboat beat Wahoo McDaniel & Tully Blanchard

11/21/84: ?? (TV)
Manny Fernandez vs. Paul Kelly
Assassin #1 vs. Jeff Sword
Buzz Tyler vs. Joel Deaton
Ivan Koloff vs. Mike Fever
Ron Bass vs. Tommy Lane

11/22/84: Greensboro, NC @ Coliseum
Starrcade 84: The Millon Dollar Challenge
Denny Brown beat Mike Davis wins NWA World Jr Title
Brian Adidas beat Mr. Ito via pinfall
Jesse Barr beat Mike Graham via pinfall
Assassin #1 & Buzz Tyler beat The Zambui Express in an elimination match
Manny Fernandez beat Black Bart to win NWA Mid Atlantic Brass Knuckles Title
Paul Jones beat Jimmy Valiant loser leaves town, tuxedo street fight match
Ron Bass beat Dick Slater by DQ
Ivan & Nikita Koloff beat Ole Anderson & Keith Larsen
Tully Blanchard beat Ricky Steamboat(13:15)
Wahoo McDaniel beat Billy Graham
NWA World Champ Ric Flair beat Dusty Rhodes ref's decision at 12:09 (Joe Frazier as special ref).

11/23/84: Jacksonville, NC @ Onslow County High School
NWA World Champ Ric Flair vs. ??
Ivan & Nikita Koloff vs. ?? & ??

11/26/84: Greenville, SC @ Memorial Auditorium
Dusty Rhodes & Manny Fernandez beat Black Bart & Ron Bass
Wahoo McDaniel DCO with Dick Slater
Tully Blanchard beat Brian Adidas
Ole Anderson & Keith Larsen draw Ivan & Nikita Koloff
Denny Brown beat Sam Houston
Assassin #1 beat Kareem Muhammad taped fist match
Mike Davis & Tommy Lane beat Jeff Sword & Paul Kelly
Buzz Tyler beat Elijah Akeem

11/27/84: Misenheimer, NC @ Pfeiffer College Gym (TV)
Buzz Tyler beat George South(1:47) via pinfall
Ron Bass & Black Bart vs. ?? & ??

11/28/84: Raleigh, NC @ Dorton Arena
Mike Davis & Tommy Lane beat Gary Royal & Paul Kelly
Denny Brown beat Sam Houston
Assassin #1 beat Kareem Muhammad taped fist match
Buzz Tyler beat Elijah Akeem
Manny Fernandez beat Ivan Koloff by DQ
Dick Slater beat Tully Blanchard
Dusty Rhodes & Ricky Steamboat beat Ron Bass & Black Bart

11/29/84: Lawrenceville, VA
Keith Larsen beat Mark Fleming
Denny Brown beat Sam Houston
Tully Blanchard draw Manny Fernandez
Elijah Akeem beat Mike Davis
Ron Bass & Black Bart beat Buzz Tyler & Tommy Lane
Dick Slater beat Ivan Koloff

11/30/84: Shelby, NC @ Rec Center (TV)
Sam Houston, Mike Davis & Brian Adidas vs. Gary Royal, Joel Deaton & Doug Vines
Buzz Tyler vs. Ben Alexander
Wahoo McDaniel vs. Gene Ligon
Assassin #1 vs. ??
Ivan & Nikita Koloff vs. Lee Ramsey & ?? Diamond
Buzz Tyler vs. Joel Deaton
Manny Fernandez vs. Tommy Lane

Dick Slater, Dusty Rhodes & Manny Fernandez vs. Joel Deaton, Jeff Sword & Gary Royal
Black Bart vs. Lee Ramsey
Magnum TA vs. The Inferno
Tully Blanchard vs. Mike Davis
Ivan & Nikita Koloff vs. Keith Larsen & Sam Houston

12/1/84: Morganton, NC
Brett Hart beat The Inferno
Tommy Lane beat Doug Vines
American Starship beat James J. Dillon & Joel Deaton
Kareem Muhammad beat Johnny Weaver
Black Bart & Ron Bass beat Brett Hart & Brian Adidas
Dick Slater draw Tully Blanchard

12/2/84: Sumter, SC @ Exhibition Center
Denny Brown beat Mike Davis
Kareem Muhammad beat Sam Houston
Black Bart & Ron Bass beat Assassin #1 & Brian Adidas
Dick Slater draw Tully Blanchard
Buzz Tyler beat Elijah Akeem
Dusty Rhodes & Manny Fernandez beat Ivan & Nikita Koloff

12/4/84: Columbia, SC @ Township Auditorium
Denny Brown beat Mike Davis
Elijah Akeem beat Tommy Lane
Assassin #1 beat Kareem Muhammad
Tully Blanchard beat Brian Adidas
Wahoo McDaniel beat Buzz Tyler
Dick Slater, Manny Fernandez & Keith Larsen beat Ivan Koloff, Nikita Koloff & Black Bart
Ron Bass beat Ricky Steamboat in a Texas death match

12/5/84: Raleigh, NC @ Dorton Arena
Denny Brown, Mike Davis & Sam Houston beat Gary Royal, Jeff Sword & Doug Vines
Brian Adidas beat Kareem Muhammad
Assassin #1 beat Elijah Akeem in a taped fist match
Buzz Tyler beat Wahoo McDaniel by DQ
Tully Blanchard beat NWA World Champ Ric Flair by DQ
Manny Fernandez & Keith Larsen beat Ivan & Nikita Koloff
Dick Slater & Ricky Steamboat beat Black Bart & Ron Bass

12/6/84: Norfolk, VA @ Scope
Mike Davis & Sam Houston beat Gary Royal & Jeff Sword
Denny Brown beat Tommy Lane
The Zambui Express beat Brian Adidas in a handicap match
Assassin #1 beat Rufus R. Jones
Buzz Tyler beat Black Bart
Dusty Rhodes beat Tully Blanchard by DQ
Ivan Koloff, Nikita Koloff & Ron Bass beat Dick Slater, Manny Fernandez & Keith Larsen
NWA World Champ Ric Flair beat Wahoo McDaniel

12/7/84: Richmond, VA @ Coliseum
Keith Larsen beat Gary Royal
Tommy Lane beat Jeff Sword
Denny Brown draw Mike Davis
Assassin #1 & Brian Adidas beat The Zambui Express
Buzz Tyler NC with Black Bart
Ron Bass beat Ricky Steamboat in a Texas death match
Tully Blanchard beat Dick Slater by DQ
Dusty Rhodes & Manny Fernandez beat Ivan & Nikita Koloff

12/8/84: Greensboro, NC @ Coliseum
Denny Brown beat Sam Houston
American Starship beat Gary Royal & Doug Vines
Kareem Muhammad beat Brian Adidas
Assassin #1 beat Gary Royal
Dusty Rhodes, Manny Fernandez & Keith Larsen beat Ivan Koloff, Nikita Koloff & Khrusher Khruschev
Black Bart & Ron Bass beat Dick Slater & Ricky Steamboat by DQ
Wahoo McDaniel beat Buzz Tyler
NWA World Champ Ric Flair beat Tully Blanchard

12/9/84: Charlotte, NC @ Coliseum
Denny Brown beat Sam Houston
Kareem Muhammad beat Brian Adidas
Assassin #1 beat Elijah Akeem in a taped fist match
Dick Slater & Ricky Steamboat beat Black Bart & Ron Bass by DQ
Wahoo McDaniel beat Buzz Tyler
NWA World Champ Ric Flair beat Tully Blanchard
Dusty Rhodes & Manny Fernandez beat Ivan & Nikita Koloff cage match

12/9/84: Charleston, SC @ County Hall
NWA World Champ Ric Flair beat Tully Blanchard

12/10/84: Greenville, SC @ Memorial Auditorium
NWA World Champ Ric Flair beat Wahoo McDaniel

12/10/84: Fayetteville, NC @ Cumberland County Civic Center
Dusty Rhodes & Manny Fernandez vs. Ivan & Nikita Koloff in a double chain match
Ron Bass vs. Ricky Steamboat
Black Bart vs. Buzz Tyler
Denny Brown vs. Mike Davis
The Inferno vs. Keith Larsen
Jeff Sword vs. Sam Houston

12/11/84: Spartanburg, SC @ Memorial Auditorium (TV)
NWA World Champ Ric Flair vs. Ron Bass
The Road Warriors vs. Sam Houston & Dale Veasey
Ron Bass & Black Bart vs. Keith Larsen & Brett Hart
Wahoo McDaniel & Tully Blanchard vs. Randy Barber & Steve Brinson

12/14/84: Charleston, SC @ County Hall
Denny Brown beat Mike Davis
Sam Houston beat Gary Royal

Ivan & Nikita Koloff beat Brian Adidas & Assassin #1
Tully Blanchard beat Dick Slater by DQ
Dusty Rhodes & Manny Fernandez beat The Zambui Express
NWA World Champ Ric Flair beat Wahoo McDaniel

12/15/84: Hampton, VA @ Coliseum
NWA World Champ Ric Flair beat Tully Blanchard
Dick Slater & Manny Fernandez beat Ivan & Nikita Koloff
Black Bart beat Johnny Weaver
Brian Adidas beat The Inferno
Denny Brown beat Sam Houston
American Starship & Assassin #1 beat Rufus R. Jones, Jeff Sword & Masked Man

12/25/84: Charlotte, NC @ Coliseum (TV)
Steve Casey beat Joel Deaton
American Starship beat The Infernos
Denny Brown beat Tommy Lane
Billy Graham beat Brian Adidas
Magnum TA beat Super Destroyer
Nikita Koloff draw Manny Fernandez
Assassin #1 beat Kareem Muhammad
Buzz Tyler beat Inferno #1
The Barbarian beat Sam Houston
Magnum TA beat Ben Alexander
Steve Casey beat Gary Royal
Dusty Rhodes, Dick Slater & Ricky Steamboat beat Tully Blanchard, Ron Bass & Black Bart in a bunkhouse match
Don Kernodle beat Ivan Koloff

12/26/84: Raleigh, NC @ Dorton Arena
Don Kernodle beat Ivan Koloff in a flag match
Keith Larsen beat Joel Deaton
Steve Casey beat Mike Fever
Billy Graham beat Mike Davis
Nikita Koloff beat Johnny Weaver
Dick Slater beat Kareem Muhammad(sub for Wahoo McDaniel)
Magnum TA, Buzz Tyler & Manny Fernandez beat Ron Bass, Black Bart & James J. Dillon

12/27/84: Norfolk, VA @ Scope
Sam Houston & Keith Larsen beat Ben Alexander & Joel Deaton
Buzz Tyler beat The Inferno
Steve Casey beat Jeff Sword
Billy Graham beat Mike Davis
Magnum TA beat Kareem Muhammad
Don Kernodle beat Ivan Koloff
Dusty Rhodes, Dick Slater & Manny Fernandez beat Black Bart, Ron Bass & Tully Blanchard

12/28/84: Charleston, SC @ County Hall
Steve Casey vs. Joel Deaton
Sam Houston vs. Doug Vines
Billy Graham vs. Johnny Weaver
Magnum TA vs. Black Bart
Dick Slater vs. Nikita Koloff
Don Kernodle vs. Ivan Koloff in a flag match

12/29/84: Lynchburg, VA @ City Armory
James J. Dillon beat Gene Ligon
Tommy Lane beat Ben Alexander
Kareem Muhammad & Dr. Death beat Mike Davis & Keith Larsen
Manny Fernandez beat Tully Blanchard
Ron Bass beat Buzz Tyler

12/29/84: Greensboro, NC @ Coliseum
Ricky Steamboat, Dusty Rhodes & Dick Slater beat Tully Blanchard, Black Bart & Ron Bass in a bunkhouse match
Buzz Tyler beat Kareem Muhammad
Don Kernodle beat Ivan Koloff in a flag match
Nikita Koloff beat Manny Fernandez
Billy Graham beat Mike Davis
Magnum TA beat Doug Vines
Johnny Weaver & Tommy Lane beat Inferno #2 & Joel Deaton
Steve Casey beat Super Destroyer

12/30/84: Richmond, VA @ Coliseum
Ricky Steamboat, Dusty Rhodes & Dick Slater vs. Tully Blanchard, Black Bart & Ron Bass in a bunkhouse match
Buzz Tyler & Don Kernodle vs. Ivan & Nikita Koloff
Kareem Muhammad vs. Magnum TA

Chapter 6: 1985

1/2/85: Raleigh, NC @ Dorton Arena (TV)
Dusty Rhodes & Manny Fernandez beat Ron Bass & Black Bart
Don Kernodle beat Ivan Koloff in a flag match
Buzz Tyler beat Tully Blanchard by DQ
Dick Slater beat Billy Graham by CO
Magnum TA beat The Inferno
The Barbarian beat Sam Houston
Tully Blanchard, Black Bart & Ron Bass vs. Tommy Lane, Lee Ramsey & Paul Diamond
The Barbarian vs. Joel Deaton
Assassin #1 vs. Curt Henderson
Magnum TA vs. Doug Vines

1/3/85: Columbia, SC @ Township Auditorium
Magnum TA beat Kareem Muhammad
Buzz Tyler beat Billy Graham
Manny Fernandez beat Ivan Koloff by DQ
Dusty Rhodes, Dick Slater & Ricky Steamboat beat Ron Bass, Black Bart & Tully Blanchard bunkhouse match
Don Kernodle beat Nikita Koloff in a flag match

1/5/85: Richmond, VA @ Coliseum
Tommy Lane beat The Inferno
Johnny Weaver beat Jeff Sword
American Starship beat Mark Fleming & Doug Vines
Dick Slater beat Kareem Muhammad
Magnum TA DCO with Nikita Koloff
Tully Blanchard beat Ricky steamboat
Don Kernodle beat Ivan Koloff in a flag match

1/5/85: Conway, SC
Buzz Tyler won by COR over Superstar Billy Graham

1/6/85: Greensboro, NC @ Coliseum
Magnum TA won a 20-man battle royal by eliminating Wahoo McDaniel that also included Ole Anderson, Ricky Steamboat, The Barbarian, Nikita Koloff
NWA World Champ Ric Flair beat Harley Race
Don Kernodle beat Ivan Koloff in a lights out match
Dusty Rhodes & Manny Fernandez beat Road Warriors
Magnum TA beat Wahoo McDaniel
Tully Blanchard beat Dick Slater
Charlie Brown, Assassin #1 & Buzz Tyler beat Billy Graham, Ron Bass & James J. Dillon
Cowboy Lang beat Lord Littlebrook
Steve Casey beat Black Bart

1/7/85: Greenville, SC @ Memorial Auditorium
Ron Bass & Black Bart beat Ricky Steamboat & Dick Slater in a no DQ match
Buzz Tyler beat Tully Blanchard by DQ
Magnum TA beat Harley Race by DQ
Charlie Brown beat James J. Dillon
Denny Brown vs. Rocky Kernodle
Steve Casey beat Kareem Muhammad

1/7/85: Fayetteville, NC @ Cumberland County Civic Center
Don Kernodle beat Ivan Koloff in a flag match
Manny Fernandez beat Nikita Koloff
Assassin #1 beat Billy Graham by DQ
The Barbarian beat Mike Davis
Dusty Rhodes beat Super Destroyer(Jeff Sword)
Cowboy Lang beat Lord Littlebrook

1/8/85: ?? (TV)
Magnum TA & Manny Fernandez vs. Joel Deaton & Jeff Sword
Steve Casey vs. Ben Alexander
Ron Bass vs. Mike Davis
Buzz Tyler vs. Mike Fever
Nikita Koloff vs. Tommy Lane
Billy Graham & The Barbarian vs. ?? & ??

1/9/85: Raleigh, NC @ Dorton Arena
Dick Slater beat Wahoo McDaniel by DQ
Harley Race DCO with Dusty Rhodes
Manny Fernandez beat Black Bart
Magnum TA beat Ron Bass
Billy Graham beat Ricky Steamboat(sub for Charlie Brown)
Tully Blanchard draw Ricky Steamboat(20:00)
Cowboy Lang beat Lord Littlebrook

1/10/85: Charleston, SC @ County Hall
Denny Brown vs. Rocky Kernodle
Buzz Tyler beat Super Destroyer(sub for Wahoo McDaniel)
Magnum TA beat Kareem Muhammad(sub for Doug Vines)
Cowboy Lang beat Lord Littlebrook
Charlie Brown beat Billy Graham
Dusty Rhodes & Don Kernodle beat Ivan & Nikita Koloff in a flag match

1/12/85: Spartanburg, SC @ Memorial Auditorium
Wahoo McDaniel beat NWA World Champ Ric Flair by DQ
Dusty Rhodes beat Nikita Koloff by CO
Buzz Tyler beat Super Destroyer
Sam Houston & Cowboy Lang beat Jeff Sword & Ben Alexander
Mike Davis beat Gene Ligon

1/12/85 Bassett, VA @ H.S. Gym
Superstar Billy Graham vs ?

1/13/85: Asheville, NC @ Civic Center
Don Kernodle beat Ivan Koloff in a flag match
Buzz Tyler & Tom Able beat Wahoo McDaniel & Tully Blanchard
Charlie Brown beat Billy Graham
Assassin #1 beat The Barbarian
Denny Brown draw Rocky Kernodle
Cowboy Lang beat Lord Littlebrook

1/13/85: Charlotte, NC @ Coliseum
Dusty Rhodes & Don Kernodle beat Ivan & Nikita Koloff
Wahoo McDaniel beat Buzz Tyler
Ron Bass & Black Bart beat Dick Slater & Ricky Steamboat by CO
Magnum TA draw Harley Race
Manny Fernandez beat Tully Blanchard by DQ
Billy Graham & Barbarian beat Charlie Brown & Assassin
Cowboy Lang beat Lord Littlebrook
American Starship Eagle beat Joel Deaton

1/14/85: Greenville, SC @ Memorial Auditorium
Ricky Steamboat & Don Kernodle beat Ivan & Nikita Koloff
Dick Slater beat Ron Bass by DQ
Dusty Rhodes beat Super Destroyer
Magnum TA beat Kareem Muhammad
Manny Fernandez beat Billy Graham by DQ

1/15/85: ?? (TV)
Manny Fernandez vs. Doug Vines
Dick Slater vs. The Inferno
Assassin #1 & Steve Casey vs. Jeff Sword & Ben Alexander
Billy Graham beat American Starship Eagle in a full nelson challenge match
Black Bart & Ron Bass vs. Denny Brown & Tommy Lane
Tully Blanchard vs. Mike Davis
Buzz Tyler vs. Doug Vines
Magnum TA vs. Mike Fever
Ron Bass & Black Bart vs. Denny Brown & Frank Lang
Wahoo McDaniel vs. Sam Houston
Billy Graham & The Barbarian vs. American Starship
Ivan Koloff vs. Lee Ramsey

1/16/85: Raleigh, NC @ Dorton Arena
Black Bart beat Manny Fernandez to win NWA Mid Atlantic Brass Knuckles Title
Steve Casey draw Denny Brown
Magnum TA beat Kareem Muhammad
Assassin #1 & Buzz Tyler beat Billy Graham & The Barbarian
Ricky Steamboat & Don Kernodle beat Ivan & Nikita Koloff
Dick Slater beat Wahoo McDaniel by DQ

1/17/85: Pittsburgh, PA @ Civic Arena
NWA World Champ Ric Flair beat Tommy Rich
Don Kernodle & Manny Fernandez beat Ivan & Nikita Koloff
Magnum TA beat Kareem Muhammad
Ron Garvin draw Tully Blanchard
Dusty Rhodes beat Joel Deaton
Billy Graham beat Mike Davis
Dick Slater beat Ken Jugan

1/18/85: Charleston, SC @ County Hall
Steve Casey vs. The Inferno
Lord Littlebrook vs. Cowboy Lang
Denny Brown vs. Rocky Kernodle
Manny Fernandez vs. Black Bart
Ron Bass vs. Buzz Tyler

1/18/85: Richmond, VA @ Coliseum
Wahoo McDaniel beat NWA World Champ Ric Flair DQ
Ivan Koloff beat Don Kernodle lumberjack, flag match
Tully Blanchard beat Dusty Rhodes
Billy Graham & Barbarian beat Assassin1 & Dick Slater
Magnum TA beat Kareem Muhammad
Nikita Koloff beat Mike Davis
Johnny Weaver beat Doug Vines
Sam Houston beat Jeff Sword

1/19/85: Fredericksburg, VA @ Stafford H.S.
Mike Davis beat Sam Houston
Johnny Weaver beat Jeff Sword
Billy Graham beat Mike Davis
Assassin #1 beat The Barbarian by DQ
Dick Slater draw Tully Blanchard

1/19/85: Lumberton, NC @ Recreation Center
Don Kernodle & Manny Fernandez vs. Ivan & Nikita Koloff in a flag match
Buzz Tyler vs. Ron Bass
Magnum TA vs. Black Bart
Denny Brown vs. Rocky Kernodle
Cowboy Lang vs. Lord Littlebrook

1/22/85: Spartanburg, SC @ Memorial Auditorium (TV)
Buzz Tyler beat Joe Young
NWA World Champ Ric Flair NC with Wahoo McDaniel
Don Kernodle beat Ben Alexander
Ricky Steamboat beat Joel Deaton
Billy Graham & King Tonga beat Lee Ramsey & Ron Rossi
Manny Fernandez beat Tully Blanchard by DQ
Ricky Steamboat & Magnum TA beat Frank Lang & Joe Young
Don Kernodle & Rocky Kernodle beat Doug Vines & Ben Alexander by DQ
Billy Graham beat Ron Rossi
Manny Fernandez beat Joel Deaton
Dick Slater beat The Inferno
Ivan & Nikita Koloff beat Lee Ramsey & Gene Ligon

1/23/85: Raleigh, NC @ Dorton Arena
Manny Fernandez draw Tully Blanchard
Don Kernodle beat Ivan Koloff in a Texas death match
Magnum TA beat Super Destroyer
Buzz Tyler beat Ron Bass by DQ
Billy Graham & The Barbarian beat Dick Slater & Assassin #1
Black Bart beat American Starship Eagle

1/25/85: Charleston, SC @ County Hall
Billy Graham, Paul Jones & Barbarian beat Buzz Tyler, Assassin #1 & Manny Fernandez
Steve Casey beat Doug Vines
Sam Houston beat The Inferno
Johnny Weaver beat Ben Alexander
Frank Lang beat Tommy Lane

1/21/85: Fayetteville, NC
Dick Slater vs Superstar Billy Graham

1/25/85: Norfolk, VA @ Scope
Ricky Steamboat & Don Kernodle beat Ivan & Nikita Koloff in a chain match
Dusty Rhodes draw Tully Blanchard
Dick Slater beat Terry Funk
Magnum TA beat Black Bart
Mike Davis beat Joel Deaton
Denny Brown draw Rocky Kernodle

1/26/85: Greensboro, NC @ Coliseum
Dick Slater beat Terry Funk in a lights out, bunkhouse bounty match
Wahoo McDaniel beat Buzz Tyler
Tully Blanchard beat Dusty Rhodes
Manny Fernandez, Don Kernodle & Ricky Steamboat beat Ivan Koloff, Nikita Koloff & Krusher Khrushchev
Billy Graham & The Barbarian beat Assassin #1 & ??
Steve Casey & American Starship beat Masked Infernos
Magnum TA beat Cowboy Ron Bass
Black Bart beat Sam Houston

1/27/85: Roanoke, VA @ Civic Center
Wahoo McDaniel beat NWA World Champ Ric Flair by DQ
Magnum TA draw Tully Blanchard
Buzz Tyler NC with Black Bart
Billy Graham beat American Starship Coyote
Steve Casey beat Doug Vines
American Starship Eagle beat Joel Deaton

1/28/85: Greenville, SC @ Memorial Auditorium
NWA World Champ Ric Flair beat Wahoo McDaniel
Magnum TA draw Tully Blanchard
Buzz Tyler NC with Black Bart
Billy Graham beat American Starship Coyote
Johnny Weaver beat Doug Vines
Scott Casey beat Joel Deaton

1/29/85: Spartanburg, SC @ Memorial Auditorium (TV)
Don Kernodle vs. Ivan Koloff
Ricky Steamboat & Magnum TA vs. Frank Lang & Joe Young
Don Kernodle & Rocky Kernodle vs. Doug Vines & Ben Alexander
Billy Graham vs. Ron Rossi
Manny Fernandez vs. Joel Deaton
Dick Slater vs. The Inferno
Ivan & Nikita Koloff vs. Gene Ligon & Lee Ramsey
This was a television taping advertised to include Ric Flair, Dick Slater, The Barbarian, Manny Fernandez, Buzz Tyler, Magnum TA, Wahoo McDaniel, Tully Blanchard & Nikita Koloff.

1/31/85: Mineral, VA
Ric Flair vs. Tully Blanchard
Dick Slater & Assassin #1 vs. Billy Graham & The Barbarian

1/31/85: Sumter, SC @ Exhibition Center (TV)
Manny Fernandez beat Joel Deaton
Magnum TA beat Golden Terror
Ivan Koloff, Nikita Koloff & Krusher Khruschev beat Denny Brown, Mark Fleming & Frank Lang
Tully Blanchard beat Brian Adidas
Dory Funk, Jr. beat Brian Adidas
Ricky Steamboat & Don Kernodle beat Ivan & Nikita Koloff
Manny Fernandez beat Frank Lang

2/1/85: Norfolk, VA @ Scope
NWA World Champ Ric Flair beat Wahoo McDaniel
Magnum TA beat Tully Blanchard by DQ
Dusty Rhodes & Manny Fernandez beat Ivan & Nikita Koloff
Ron Bass beat Dick Slater by DQ
Denny Brown beat Sam Houston
Don Kernodle beat Frank Lang
Rocky Kernodle beat Mark Fleming

2/1/85: Charleston, SC @ County Hall
American Starship Coyote vs. Billy Graham
The Barbarian vs. Johnny Weaver
Buzz Tyler vs. Black Bart

2/2/85: Pilot Mountain, NC @ East Surrey H.S.
Ivan & Nikita Koloff vs. Manny Fernandez & Don Kernodle
Billy Graham vs. Dick Slater
The Barbarian vs. Steve Casey
Assassin #1 vs. Elijah Akeem
Denny Brown vs. Rocky Kernodle

2/3/85: Savannah, GA @ Civic Center
NWA World Champ Ric Flair beat Wahoo McDaniel
Magnum TA draw Tully Blanchard
Denny Brown beat Sam Houston
American Starship Coyote beat Frank Lang

2/3/85: Charlotte, NC @ Coliseum
Brian Adidas draw Doug Vines
Buzz Tyler beat Black Bart
Magnum TA beat Joel Deaton
Manny Fernandez beat The Barbarian
Dick Slater beat Ox Baker in a bounty match
Sheik Adnan beat Doug Vines
Dusty Rhodes draw Tully Blanchard
Ricky Steamboat & Don Kernodle beat Ivan & Nikita Koloff in a flag match
NWA World Champ Ric Flair beat Wahoo McDaniel DQ

2/4/85: Spartanburg, SC @ Memorial Auditorium (TV)
Manny Fernandez & Don Kernodle vs. Nikita Koloff & Krusher Khruschev
Black Bart vs. Buzz Tyler
Steve Casey vs. Golden Terror
Dory Funk Jr. vs. Brian Adidas
Ivan & Nikita Koloff vs. Ricky Steamboat & Don Kernodle in a flag match
Manny Fernandez vs. Frank Lang

2/5/85: Philadelphia, PA @ Civic Center
NWA World Champ Ric Flair beat Ricky Steamboat(34:12)
Ronnie Garvin NC with Wahoo McDaniel
Bob Backlund & Dusty Rhodes beat Ron Bass & Black Bart
Tully Blanchard beat Manny Fernandez
Ole Anderson & Thunderbolt Patterson beat The Hollywood Blondes(Ted Oates & Rip Rogers)
Billy Graham beat Brian Adidas
Dick Slater beat Joel Deaton
Magnum TA beat Super Destroyer

2/6/85: Raleigh, NC @ Dorton Arena
The Barbarian beat Denny Brown
Black Bart draw Steve Casey
Krusher Khruschev, Ivan & Nikita Koloff beat Rocky Kernodle, Don Kernodle & Ricky Steamboat
Ron Bass beat Dick Slater by DQ
Tully Blanchard beat Manny Fernandez
Magnum TA beat Wahoo McDaniel by DQ

2/7/85: Columbia, SC @ Township Auditorium
Sam Houston beat Doug Vines
Denny Brown beat Frank Lang
Sam Houston beat Mike Fever
Manny Fernandez beat The Barbarian
Dusty Rhodes draw Tully Blanchard
Magnum TA beat Wahoo McDaniel by DQ

2/8/85: Richmond, VA @ Coliseum
Buzz Tyler beat Black Bart
Krusher Khruschev, Ivan & Nikita Koloff beat Brian Adidas, Don Kernodle & Steve Casey
Dick Slater beat Ron Bass
Magnum TA draw Tully Blanchard
Wahoo McDaniel beat Ricky Steamboat
Dusty Rhodes & Manny Fernandez beat The Barbarian & Billy Graham

2/9/85: Culpeper, VA @ Junior H.S.
Black Bart beat Rocky Kernodle
Denny Brown beat Doug Vines
Steve Casey beat Ron Bass by DQ
Buzz Tyler beat Black Bart
Tully Blanchard draw Manny Fernandez

2/10/85: Asheville, NC @ Civic Center
Magnum TA beat Wahoo McDaniel by DQ
Tully Blanchard draw Dick Slater
Ivan Koloff, Nikita Koloff & Krusher Khruschev beat Ricky Steamboat, Manny Fernandez & Don Kernodle
Buzz Tyler beat Black Bart
The Barbarian beat Johnny Weaver

2/10/85: Charlotte, NC @ Coliseum
Magnum TA beat Wahoo McDaniel by CO

2/11/85: Greenville, SC @ Memorial Auditorium
Steve Casey beat Jeff Sword
Ron Bass & Black Bart beat Dick Slater & Buzz Tyler
Manny Fernandez beat The Barbarian
Wahoo McDaniel beat ??
Krusher Khruschev, Ivan & Nikita Koloff beat ??

2/12/85: Spartanburg, SC @ Memorial Auditorium (TV)
Don Kernodle & Manny Fernandez vs. Nikita Koloff & Krusher Khrushchev
Buzz Tyler vs. Black Bart
Nikita Koloff & Krusher Khruschev vs. Mark Fleming & Gene Ligon
Dory Funk Jr. vs. Denny Brown
Manny Fernandez vs. Joel Deaton
The Barbarian vs. Frank Lang
Tully Blanchard vs. Buzz Tyler

2/12/85: Allentown, PA @ Agricultural Hall
Billy Graham beat Johnny Weaver

2/13/85: Altoona, PA @ Jaffa Mosque
Sgt. Slaughter beat Ron Bass
Bob Backlund beat Ivan Koloff by DQ
James J. Dillon beat Sam Houston
Johnny Weaver beat Doug Vines
Billy Graham beat Steve Casey
Larry Zbyszko & Rocky Jones beat Joel Deaton & Super Destroyer

2/13/85: Raleigh, NC @ Dorton Arena
Denny Brown beat Rocky Kernodle
Manny Fernandez beat The Barbarian
Buzz Tyler beat Black Bart
Dick Slater & Don Kernodle beat Nikita Koloff & Krusher Khruschev by DQ
Tully Blanchard draw Magnum TA
Wahoo McDaniel beat Ricky Steamboat

2/14/85: Trenton, NJ @ CYO Building
Sgt. Slaughter & Bob Backlund vs. Ivan Koloff & Ron Bass
Billy Graham vs. Steve Casey
Samoan Afa vs. Super Destroyer
Samoan Sika vs. Joel Deaton
Brian Adidas vs. Doug Vines
James J. Dillon vs. Sam Houston

2/14/85: Sumter, SC @ Exhibition Center
The Barbarian beat Rocky Kernodle
Magnum TA beat Frank Lang
Buzz Tyler beat Black Bart
Dick Slater draw Tully Blanchard
Dusty Rhodes & Manny Fernandez beat Krusher Khruschev & Nikita Koloff

2/15/85: Hampton, VA @ Coliseum
Dusty Rhodes draw Tully Blanchard
Ivan & Nikita Koloff beat Don Kernodle & Magnum TA
Jimmy Valiant beat Billy Graham by DQ
Dick Slater beat Ron Bass
Manny Fernandez beat The Barbarian
Buzz Tyler beat Black Bart
Brian Adidas beat Scott Casey

2/16/85: Baltimore, MD @ Civic Center
NWA World Champ Ric Flair beat Sgt. Slaughter by DQ

Dusty Rhodes & Manny Fernandez beat Ivan & Nikita Koloff
Ole Anderson NC with Wahoo McDaniel
Dick Slater beat Dory Funk, Jr.
Jimmy Valiant & Bob Backlund beat Barbarian & Billy Graham by DQ
Magnum TA beat Doug Vines
Denny Brown beat Rocky Kernodle

2/17/85: Greensboro, NC @ Coliseum
Wahoo McDaniel beat Ricky Steamboat
Dusty Rhodes draw Tully Blanchard
Ivan Koloff beat Don Kernodle in a Russian chain match
Dick Slater & Manny Fernandez beat Dory Funk, Jr. & Black Bart
Magnum TA beat John Tatum
Khrusher Khrushchev beat Brian Adidas
Billy Graham beat American Starship Eagle
The Barbarian beat American Starship Coyote

2/18/85: Fayetteville, NC
Sam Houston vs Superstar Billy Graham

2/19/85: ?? (TV)
Steve Casey vs. Doug Vines
John Tatum vs. Sam Houston
The Barbarian vs. Mark Fleming
Ivan Koloff & Krusher Khruschev vs. Lee Ramsey & Joel Deaton
Tully Blanchard vs. Rocky Kernodle
Manny Fernandez & Buzz Tyler vs. Dory Funk Jr. & Black Bart

2/20/85: Pittsburgh, PA @ Civic Arena
Wahoo McDaniel beat Ricky Steamboat
Dusty Rhodes & Manny Fernandez beat Ivan & Nikita Koloff
Bob Backlund beat Black Bart
Buzz Tyler draw Ron Bass
Magnum TA beat Davey G
The Barbarian beat Sean O'Riley
Dick Slater beat Leopard Man
James J. Dillon beat Brian O'Riley

2/21/85: Norfolk, VA @ Scope
Sam Houston draw John Tatum
Barbarian beat American Starship Coyote
Billy Graham beat American Starship Eagle
Dick Slater & Buzz Tyler beat Ron Bass & Black Bart
Magnum TA draw Tully Blanchard
Manny Fernandez, Don Kernodle & Dusty Rhodes beat Ivan Koloff, Nikita Koloff & Krusher Khruschev by DQ

2/22/85: Richmond, VA @ Coliseum
Black Bart draw Steve Casey
The Barbarian beat Rocky Kernodle
Buzz Tyler beat Ron Bass by DQ
Dusty Rhodes, Don Kernodle & Jimmy Valiant beat Krusher Khruschev, Ivan & Nikita Koloff by DQ
Tully Blanchard beat Manny Fernandez
Magnum TA beat Wahoo McDaniel by DQ

2/24/85: Washington, DC
Wahoo McDaniel beat Ricky Steamboat
Dick Slater draw Tully Blanchard
Dusty Rhodes & Jimmy Valiant beat Ron Bass & Black Bart
Bob Backlund beat Ivan Koloff by DQ
Magnum TA beat James J. Dillon
Billy Graham beat ?? Walker
Dory Funk, Jr. beat Rocky Kernodle
Manny Fernandez beat Mark Fleming

2/24/85: East Rutherford, NJ @ Meadowlands
Jimmy Valiant, Chris Youngblood & Mark Youngblood draw Larry Zbyszko, Nick Bockwinkel & Dory Funk, Jr.
Kamala beat ?? & ?? in a handicap match
Bob Backlund beat Billy Robinson via pinfall
Jim Brunzell & Greg Gagne DCO with Mr. Saito & Masked Superstar
Ivan & Nikita Koloff beat Steve Keirn & Jimmy Valiant
Jimmy Garvin beat Rick Martel by DQ
The Road Warriors beat Jerry Lawler & Baron Von Raschke
NWA World Champ Ric Flair beat Harley Race
Sergeant Slaughter won a tag team battle royal by himself, (Slaughter's partner, Jerry Blackwell, was injured & could not compete.)
Also in the battle royal were: The Road Warriors, Ivan & Nikita Koloff, Greg Gagne & Jim Brunzell, Kamala & Billy Robinson, Mark Youngblood & Chris Youngblood, Jerry Lawler & Baron Von Raschke, Bob Backlund & Jimmy Valiant, Mr. Saito & Masked Superstar, Nick Bockwinkel & Dory Funk, Jr., Jimmy Garvin & Larry Zbyszko and Steve Keirn & Jerry Oski

2/24/85: Asheville, NC @ Civic Center
Billy Graham vs. Don Kernodle
Wahoo McDaniel vs. Magnum TA
Tully Blanchard vs. Manny Fernandez
Ron Bass & Black Bart vs. Dick Slater & Buzz Tyler
Steve Casey vs. The Barbarian
Denny Brown vs. Sam Houston

2/24/85: Charlotte, NC @ Coliseum
Billy Graham beat American Starship Eagle
Magnum TA beat John Tatum
Krusher Khruschev, Ivan & Nikita Koloff beat Rocky Kernodle, Ricky Steamboat & Don Kernodle
NWA World Champ Ric Flair beat Wahoo McDaniel
Tully Blanchard beat Dusty Rhodes by DQ
Dick Slater & Manny Fernandez beat Ron Bass & Black Bart in an elimination match
Buzz Tyler beat The Barbarian

2/25/85 Fayetteville, NC
Magnum TA & Manny Fernandez vs Superstar Graham & Barbarian

2/26/85: Altoona, PA @ Jaffa Mosque
Bob Backlund beat Ron Bass
Magnum TA beat Bob Roop
Billy Graham beat American Starship Eagle
Ronnie Garvin beat Ron Starr
American Starship Coyote draw John Tatum

2/26/85: ?? (TV)
Steve Casey vs. Joel Deaton
The Barbarian vs. Gary Quartinelli
Nikita Koloff & Krusher Khruschev vs. ?? & ??
Manny Fernandez vs. Chick Donovan
NWA World Champ Ric Flair vs. Doug Vines
Tully Blanchard vs. Denny Brown

2/27/85: Allentown, PA @ Agricultural Hall
Billy Graham vs. ??

2/28/85: Philadelphia, PA @ Civic Center
NWA World Champ Ric Flair beat Sgt. Slaughter by DQ
Tully Blanchard beat Dusty Rhodes by DQ
Wahoo McDaniel beat Dick Slater
Ricky Steamboat & Magnum TA draw with Ivan Koloff & Black Bart
Bob Backlund beat Ron Bass
Magnum TA beat John Tatum
Billy Graham beat American Starship Coyote

3/1/85: Columbia, SC @ Township Auditorium
The Barbarian beat Gene Ligon
Denny Brown beat Sam Houston
Billy Graham beat Frank Lang
Manny Fernandez, Don Kernodle & Magnum TA beat Ivan Koloff, Nikita Koloff & Krusher Khruschev by DQ
Tully Blanchard beat Dusty Rhodes

3/2/85: Greensboro, NC @ Coliseum
NWA World Champ Ric Flair beat Wahoo McDaniel
Dusty Rhodes & Manny Fernandez beat Billy Graham & The Barbarian
Dick Slater beat Dory Funk, Jr.
Tully Blanchard beat Frank Lang & Mark Fleming in a handicap match
Nikita Koloff & Krusher Khruschev beat Lee Ramsey & Gene Ligon
Magnum TA beat Joel Deaton
Johnny Weaver draw John Tatum

3/2/85: Greenville, SC @ Memorial Auditorium
John Tatum draw Johnny Weaver
Magnum TA beat Joel Deaton
Nikita Koloff & Krusher Khruschev beat Gene Ligon & Lee Ramsey
Tully Blanchard beat Mark Fleming & Frank Lang in a handicap match
Dick Slater beat Dory Funk, Jr.
Dusty Rhodes & Manny Fernandez beat The Barbarian & Billy Graham
NWA World Champ Ric Flair beat Wahoo McDaniel

3/5/85: Spartanburg, SC @ Memorial Auditorium
Manny Fernandez vs. The Barbarian
Black Bart & Ron Bass vs. Buzz Tyler & Jimmy Valiant
Krusher Khruschev vs. Mark Fleming
Magnum TA, Dick Slater & Buzz Tyler vs. Joel Deaton, Doug Vines & Golden Terror
Arn Anderson vs. Sam Houston
Billy Graham vs. Frank Lang
Great Kabuki vs. Mike Fever
Buddy Landell vs. Rocky Kernodle
Nikita Koloff & Krusher Khruschev vs. Joel Deaton & Frank Lang
Arn Anderson vs. Gene Ligon
Great Kabuki & The Barbarian vs. Jimmy Valiant & Buzz Tyler
Manny Fernandez vs. Doug Vines
Magnum TA vs. Golden Terror & The Inferno in a handicap match
Tully Blanchard vs. Steve Casey

3/6/85: Raleigh, NC @ Dorton Arena
Black Bart beat Sam Houston
Arn Anderson, Krusher Khruschev & Ivan Koloff beat Don Kernodle, Buzz Tyler & Manny Fernandez
Magnum TA NC with Wahoo McDaniel
Tully Blanchard beat Dusty Rhodes by DQ
Steve Casey beat Ron Bass by DQ
Buddy Landell beat Denny Brown

3/7/85 Charlestown, SC
Superstar Billy Graham, Barbarian vs Magnum TA, Jimmy Valiant
Ron Bass vs. Buzz Tyler
Pez Whatley vs. John Tatum
Black Bart vs. Jim Cayce

3/8/85: Richmond, VA @ Coliseum
Ron Bass beat Sam Houston
Magnum TA beat John Tatum
Jimmy Valiant beat Billy Graham
Tully Blanchard beat Dusty Rhodes by DQ
Manny Fernandez & Dick Slater beat Ron Bass & Black Bart

3/8/85: Charleston, SC @ County Hall
Steve Casey vs. Black Bart
Pez Whatley vs. John Tatum
Ron Bass vs. Buzz Tyler
The Barbarian & Billy Graham vs. Magnum TA & Jimmy Valiant

3/9/85: Charlotte, NC @ Coliseum
Buddy Landell beat Sam Houston
Manny Fernandez beat Black Bart
Steve Casey draw Mike Davis
Dick Slater beat Dory Funk, Jr. in a bounty match
Jimmy Valiant beat Billy Graham by DQ
Ivan Koloff beat Don Kernodle Russian chain match
Ric Flair & Magnum TA co-won a tag team battle royal

3/10/85: Sumter, SC @ Exhibition Center
Buddy Landell beat Sam Houston
Buzz Tyler & Steve Casey beat Tommy Lane & Mike Davis
Jimmy Valiant beat Billy Graham by DQ
Ivan Koloff beat Don Kernodle Russian chain match
Dick Slater & Magnum TA beat Wahoo McDaniel & Tully Blanchard

3/11/85: Greenville, SC @ Memorial Auditorium
Johnny Weaver beat Doug Vines
Denny Brown beat Joel Deaton
Black Bart beat Sam Houston

Magnum TA beat John Tatum
Jimmy Valiant beat The Barbarian
Tully Blanchard & Wahoo McDaniel beat Dusty Rhodes & Manny Fernandez DQ

3/11/85: Mount Holly, NJ
Sgt. Slaughter beat Ivan Koloff by CO
Bob Backlund beat Ron Bass
Billy Graham beat Manuel Soto
Larry Zbyszko beat Rocky Jones
Pez Whatley beat James J. Dillon
Pete Sanchez draw Davey O'Hannon

3/12/85: Winchester, VA @ Frederick County Middle School
Ivan & Nikita Koloff vs. Don Kernodle & Pez Whatley
Rocky Kernodle vs. Tommy Lane
Johnny Weaver vs. Joel Deaton
Gene Ligon vs. Doug Vines
Golden Terror vs. Rocky King

3/12/85: Allentown, PA @ Agricultural Hall
Sgt. Slaughter & Bob Backlund beat Ron Bass & Ivan Koloff by DQ
Larry Zbyszko beat Pete Sanchez
Billy Graham beat Steve King
Pez Whatley beat James J. Dillon
Davey O'Hannon draw Manny Soto

3/13/85: Altoona, PA @ Jaffa Mosque
Bob Backlund beat Nikita Koloff(29:00) by DQ
Pez Whatley draw Ron Bass(15;00)
Billy Graham(sub for Sgt. Slaughter) beat Ivan Koloff(15:00)
Luis Martinez beat Otto Von Mark(9:00)
Dominic DeNucci beat Bill Berger(11:00)
Pez Whatley(sub for Manuel Soto) beat James J. Dillon(:24)
Davey O'Hannon vs. Pete Sanchez(Match cancelled)

3/14/85: Baltimore, MD @ Civic Center
Ole Anderson, Dusty Rhodes & Sgt. Slaughter beat Ivan Koloff, Nikita Koloff & Krusher Khrushchev by DQ
Rick Martel beat Mr. Saito
Bob Backlund beat The Barbarian by DQ
Tommy Rich draw Tully Blanchard
Terry Gordy & Michael Hayes beat Tommy Lane & Mike Davis
Manny Fernandez draw Billy Graham
Tom Zenk beat Alaskan I

3/14/85: Norfolk, VA @ Scope
Arn Anderson beat Scott Casey
Pez Whatley beat John Tatum
Buddy Landell beat Sam Houston
Jimmy Valiant beat Black Bart
Ron Bass beat Buzz Tyler
Dick Slater beat Dory Funk, Jr.
Magnum TA NC with Wahoo McDaniel

3/15/85: Elizabethtown, NC @ East Bladen H.S.
Tully Blanchard vs. Manny Fernandez
Ivan & Nikita Koloff vs. Don Kernodle & Dick Slater
Arn Anderson vs. Sam Houston
Rocky Kernodle vs. Krusher Khrushchev
Tommy Lane & Mike Davis vs. Johnny Weaver & Frank Lang

3/16/85: Greensboro, NC @ Coliseum
NWA World Champ Ric Flair beat Wahoo McDaniel in an Indian strap match
Dusty Rhodes beat Tully Blanchard to win the NWA Mid Atlantic Television Title
Buzz Tyler beat Ron Bass wins NWA Mid Atlantic Title
Magnum TA, Don Kernodle & Sergeant Slaughter beat Ivan Koloff, Nikita Koloff & Krusher Khrushchev
Dick Slater beat The Barbarian in bounty match
Jimmy Valiant beat Black Bart
Sam Houston beat Arn Anderson
Manny Fernandez draw Buddy Landell
Arn Anderson beat Lee Ramsey(2:30) by submission
Arn Anderson beat Gene Ligon(4:11) via pinfall
Arn Anderson beat Rocky King
Dusty Rhodes beat ??
Pez Whatley vs. John Tatum
Arn Anderson vs. Steve Casey
Magnum TA & Manny Fernandez vs. Tommy Lane & Mike Davis
Jimmy Valiant vs. Billy Graham

3/17/85: Asheville, NC @ Civic Center
Wahoo McDaniel vs. Magnum TA
Tully Blanchard vs. Dusty Rhodes
Billy Graham vs. Jimmy Valiant
Johnny Weaver vs. The Barbarian
Denny Brown & Sam Houston vs. Tommy Lane & Mike Davis

3/18/85: Fayetteville, NC @ Cumberland County Civic Center
Pez Whatley draw Buddy Landell
Arn Anderson beat Sam Houston
Don Kernodle beat Krusher Khruschev
Buzz Tyler beat Tully Blanchard by DQ
Magnum TA NC with Wahoo McDaniel
Jimmy Valiant beat Great Kabuki
Ivan & Nikita Koloff beat Dusty Rhodes & Manny Fernandez to win NWA World Tag Title

3/19/85: Columbia, SC @ Township Auditorium
The Barbarian beat Gene Ligon
Denny Brown beat Sam Houston
Billy Graham beat Frank Lang
Magnum TA, Manny Fernandez & Don Kernodle beat Krusher Khrushchev, Ivan & Nikita Koloff by DQ
Tully Blanchard beat Dusty Rhodes by DQ

3/20/85: Raleigh, NC @ Dorton Arena
Dusty Rhodes beat Tully Blanchard
Buddy Landell beat Sam Houston
Don Kernodle beat Nikita Koloff
Arn Anderson beat Manny Fernandez by DQ
The Barbarian & Billy Graham beat Pez Whatley & Denny Brown
Jimmy Valiant beat Great Kabuki
Magnum TA beat Wahoo McDaniel by DQ

3/23/85: Charlotte, NC @ Coliseum
Buddy Landell beat Denny Brown
Pez Whatley beat Barbarian by DQ
Dick Slater & Don Kernodle beat Ivan & Nikita Koloff by DQ
Jimmy Valiant beat Great Kabuki
Dusty Rhodes draw Tully Blanchard
Billy Graham beat Steve Casey
Arn Anderson beat Manny Fernandez by DQ
Magnum TA beat Wahoo McDaniel in a cage match to win NWA United States Title

3/24/85: Atlanta, GA @ Omni
Brett Sawyer beat Doug Somers
Thunderbolt Patterson beat Kareem Muhammad
Ron Garvin beat Ron Starr by DQ
Magnum TA beat Chic Donovan
Jimmy Valiant beat Bob Roop by DQ
Gene & Ole Anderson NC Ivan & Nikita Koloff
Buzz Sawyer beat Bill Irwin in a lights out match
Rip Rogers beat Tommy Rich in a loser gets their hair painted white match

3/25/85: Steubenville, OH
Mike Davis beat Jimmy Jackson
Sam Houston beat John Tatum
Denny Brown & Pez Whatley beat Tommy Lane & Mike Davis
Jimmy Valiant beat The Barbarian
Manny Fernandez beat Ivan Koloff

3/26/85: Philadelphia, PA @ Civic Center
Buzz Tyler beat John Tatum
Buddy Landell beat Sam Houston
Jimmy Valiant beat The Barbarian
Pez Whatley & Denny Brown beat Tommy Lane & Mike Davis
Dusty Rhodes draw Tully Blanchard
Manny Fernandez beat Arn Anderson by DQ
Magnum TA beat Ivan Koloff

3/27/85: Altoona, PA @ Jaffa Mosque
Jimmy Jackson beat Super Assassin
Buddy Landell beat Denny Brown
Sam Houston beat John Tatum
Arn Anderson beat Sam Houston
Buzz Tyler & Pez Whatley beat Tommy Lane & Mike Davis
Manny Fernandez beat Ivan Koloff by DQ

3/28/85: Pittsburgh, PA @ Civic Arena
Tommy Lane & Mike Davis draw Denny Brown & Sam Houston
Jimmy Jackson beat Super Assassin
Magnum TA beat Ivan Koloff
Tully Blanchard beat Dusty Rhodes by DQ
Jimmy Valiant beat Barbarian by CO
Manny Fernandez, Buzz Tyler & Pez Whatley beat Buddy Landell, Arn Anderson & John Tatum

3/29/85: Richmond, VA @ Coliseum
Rocky Kernodle & Denny Brown draw Tommy Lane & Mike Davis
Pez Whatley beat John Tatum
Buzz Tyler beat Ivan Koloff by DQ
Magnum TA beat Buddy Landell
Manny Fernandez NC with Arn Anderson
Jimmy Valiant beat The Barbarian lumberjack match
Tully Blanchard beat Dusty Rhodes by DQ

3/30/85: Greensboro, NC @ Coliseum
Dusty Rhodes & Ric Flair beat Wahoo McDaniel & Tully Blanchard
Magnum TA beat Ivan Koloff
Buzz Tyler beat Buddy Landell
The Barbarian beat Jimmy Valiant
Manny Fernandez NC with Arn Anderson
Pez Whatley & Rocky Kernodle beat Tommy Lane & Mike Davis
Sam Houston draw Rocky King

3/31/85: Sumter, SC @ Exhibition Center
Jimmy Valiant vs. The Barbarian
Arn Anderson vs. Manny Fernandez
John Tatum vs. Rocky Kernodle
Johnny Weaver vs. Golden Terror
Frank Lang vs. Joel Deaton

4/2/85: Spartanburg, SC @ Memorial Auditorium (TV)
Buzz Tyler vs. Ivan Koloff
Manny Fernandez vs. Arn Anderson
Pez Whatley & Buzz Tyler vs. John Tatum & Joel Deaton
The Barbarian vs. Mark Fleming
Magnum TA vs. Buddy Landell
Manny Fernandez vs. David Dillinger
Arn Anderson & Buddy Landell vs. Sam Houston & Denny Brown
Dusty Rhodes vs. Doug Vines

4/3/85: Raleigh, NC @ Dorton Arena
Arn Anderson beat Manny Fernandez
Buzz Tyler beat Buddy Landell by DQ
Jimmy Valiant beat The Barbarian
Pez Whatley beat Doug Vines
Sam Houston & Denny Brown draw Tommy Lane & Mike Davis
Dusty Rhodes beat Tully Blanchard
Magnum TA beat Ivan Koloff

4/5/85: Columbia, SC @ Township Auditorium
Sam Houston beat Doug Vines
Joel Deaton draw Rocky King
Buddy Landell beat Sam Houston
Manny Fernandez NC with Arn Anderson
Barbarian beat Jimmy Valiant by DQ
Dusty Rhodes beat Tully Blanchard

4/6/85: Atlanta, GA @ WTBS Studios (TV)
Note: World Champship Wrestling - the first episode promoted by Jim Crockett Promotions
Ivan & Nikita Koloff beat George South & Greg Stone
Jimmy Valiant beat Mark Hill
Tully Blanchard beat Sam Houston
Billy Graham beat Rocky King

NWA World Champ Ric Flair beat Gene Ligon
Manny Fernandez beat Arn Anderson by DQ
Magnum TA beat Paul Barnett
The Barbarian beat Josh Stroud
Buddy Landell beat David Dillinger
Black Bart beat Ron Rossi
Don Kernodle beat Randy Barber
Black Bart beat George South
Ivan & Nikita Koloff beat David Dillinger & Ron Rossi
Tully Blanchard beat Rocky King
Magnum TA beat Joel Deaton
Ole & Arn Anderson beat Sam Houston & Greg Stone

4/6/85: Charlotte, NC @ Coliseum
John Tatum beat Rocky King
Black Bart beat Denny Brown
Billy Graham beat Pez Whatley
Arn Anderson beat Rocky Kernodle
Jimmy Valiant beat The Barbarian in a lumberjack match
Ron Garvin & Italian Stallion beat Blue Devil & Ron Starr
NWA World Champ Ric Flair beat Tommy Rich

4/??/85: Hampton, VA @ Coliseum
Buzz Tyler beat John Tatum
Pez Whatley & Rocky Kernodle beat Tommy Lane & Mike Davis
Johnny Weaver beat The Inferno
Denny Brown beat Mark Fleming
Magnum TA beat Ivan Koloff via pinfall

4/9/85: ?? (TV)
Jimmy Valiant & Pez Whatley beat Doug Vines & David Dillinger(2:40)
Black Bart beat Gene Ligon(7:12) via pinfall
Manny Fernandez beat Joel Deaton(2:58) via pinfall
Buddy Landell beat Lee Ramsey(2:48) by submission
Nikita Koloff beat Rocky King(1:22) by submission
Arn Anderson beat Ron Rossi(2:250 by submission

4/10/85: Raleigh, NC @ Dorton Arena
Arn Anderson beat Manny Fernandez
Buzz Tyler beat Buddy Landell by DQ
Jimmy Valiant beat The Barbarian
Pez Whatley beat Doug Vines
Denny Brown & Sam Houston draw Tommy Lane & Mike Davis
Dusty Rhodes beat Tully Blanchard
Magnum TA beat Ivan Koloff

4/10/85: Pittsburgh, PA @ Civic Center
Tommy Lane beat Jimmy Jackson
Mike Davis beat Irish Brad Walsh
Arn Anderson beat Sam Houston
Buddy Landell beat Denny Brown
Buzz Tyler beat Black Bart
Ivan & Nikita Koloff beat Manny Fernandez & Don Kernodle
Jimmy Valiant beat The Barbarian
Magnum TA beat Tully Blanchard

4/11/85: Fredericksburg, VA @ Stafford H.S.
Magnum TA beat Buddy Landell via pinfall
Arn Anderson draw Manny Fernandez
Jimmy Valiant beat The Barbarian via pinfall
Billy Graham beat Mark Fleming via pinfall

4/12/85: Winchester, VA @ Frederick County Middle School
Ivan & Nikita Koloff vs. Don Kernodle & Pez Whatley
Tommy Lane vs. Rocky Kernodle
Johnny Weaver vs. Joel Deaton
Doug Vines vs. Gene Ligon

4/12/85: Norfolk, VA @ Scope
Sam Houston draw Tommy Lane
Buddy Landell beat Denny Brown
John Tatum beat Mark Fleming
Buzz Tyler beat Black Bart
Jimmy Valiant beat Billy Graham in a lumberjack match
Manny Fernandez NC with Arn Anderson

4/13/85: Atlanta, GA @ WTBS Studios (TV)
Buddy Landell vs. Sam Houston
Michael Hayes vs. Joel Deaton
Thunderbolt Patterson & Manny Fernandez vs. Mike Jackson & Paul Garner
Tully Blanchard vs. Paul Diamond
Ole & Arn Anderson vs. Gene Ligon & Rocky King
Ivan Koloff vs. Buzz Sawyer
Nikita Koloff vs. Joshua Stroud
Billy Graham & The Barbarian vs. Mac Jeffers & Jim Jeffers
Magnum TA beat George South(:13)
Pez Whatley vs. Vernon Deaton
Krusher Khruschev vs. Mike Simani
Buzz Sawyer beat Joel Deaton
Ivan Koloff & Krusher Khruschev beat Sam Houston & Rocky King
The Barbarian & Billy Graham beat Paul Diamond & Mike Jackson
Manny Fernandez beat Paul Garner
Ole & Arn Anderson beat Mark Cooper & George South

4/13/85: Greensboro, NC @ Coliseum
The Barbarian beat Johnny Weaver
Tommy Lane & Mike Davis beat Sam Houston & Denny Brown
Jimmy Valiant beat Billy Graham
Manny Fernandez beat Arn Anderson
Buzz Tyler & Don Kernodle beat Ivan & Nikita Koloff
Magnum TA beat Buddy Landell
Dusty Rhodes beat Tully Blanchard

4/14/85: Richmond, VA @ Coliseum
NWA World Champ Ric Flair vs. Wahoo McDaniel in an Indian strap match
Dusty Rhodes vs. Tully Blanchard barbed wire match
Ivan Koloff, Nikita Koloff & Krusher Khruschev vs. Buzz Tyler, Pez Whatley & Don Kernodle

4/14/85: Atlanta, GA @ Omni
Ron Garvin beat Bob Roop
Tully Blanchard beat Italian Stallion
Magnum TA beat Buddy Landell
Dusty Rhodes, Jimmy Valiant & Buzz Sawyer beat Ivan Koloff, Nikita Koloff & Krusher Khruschev
Barbarian beat Pez Whatley
Thunderbolt Patterson & Manny Fernandez beat Ole & Arn Anderson by DQ
NWA World Champ Ric Flair beat Michael Hayes

4/14/85: Asheville, NC @ Civic Center
Magnum TA vs. Buddy Landell
Manny Fernandez vs. Arn Anderson in a no DQ match
Jimmy Valiant vs. Billy Graham
Dory Funk, Jr. vs. Johnny Weaver
Rocky King vs. The Barbarian
Gene Ligon vs. Joel Deaton

4/15/85: Altoona, PA @ Jaffa Mosque
Mike Davis beat Red Walsh
Johnny Weaver beat Tommy Lane
Mike Davis beat Yukon Bob
Krusher Khruschev beat Jimmy Jackson
Manny Fernandez NC with Arn Anderson

4/15/85 Fayetteville, NC
Jimmy Valiant vs Billy Graham (karate is legal)
Buzz Tyler vs. the Barbarian
Dusty Rhodes vs. Tully Blanchard Barbed Wire match

4/16/85: Allentown, PA @ Agricultural Hall
Manny Fernandez vs. Arn Anderson
Also included Pez Whatley, Krusher Khruschev, Tommy Lane & Mike Davis

4/16/85: Rock Hill, SC @ Winthrop Coliseum (TV)
Dusty Rhodes beat Tully Blanchard in a cage match
Ivan & Nikita Koloff beat Rocky King & Gene Ligon
Billy Graham beat Lee Ramsey
Buddy Landell beat David Dellinger
Don Kernodle beat Joel Deaton
Buzz Tyler beat Black Bart
Magnum TA, Jimmy Valiant & Buzz Tyler beat Joel Deaton, John Tatum & Doug Vines
Nikita Koloff beat Mark Fleming
Denny Brown beat Golden Terror
Dave Dellinger & Lee Ramsey beat Billy Graham & The Barbarian by DQ
Buddy Landell beat Gene Ligon by submission
Sam Houston beat Tully Blanchard by DQ

4/16/85: Talladega, AL @ H.S.
Italian Stallion beat Doug Sommers
Ron Garvin beat Ron Starr
Buzz & Brett Sawyer beat Bob Roop & Scott Irwin
Thunderbolt Patterson beat Kareem Muhammad
Pez Whatley beat Rip Rogers

4/17/85: Raleigh, NC @ Dorton Arena
Magnum TA beat Buddy Landell by DQ
Billy Graham beat Denny Brown
Black Bart beat Sam Houston
Ivan Koloff, Nikita Koloff & Krusher Khruschev beat ??, Don Kernodle & Johnny Weaver
Tully Blanchard & Arn Anderson beat Buzz Tyler & Manny Fernandez

4/17/85: Marietta, OH @ Ban Johnson Field

4/18/85: Columbia, SC @ Township Auditorium
Sam Houston beat Mike Davis
Denny Brown beat John Tatum
Black Bart beat Johnny Weaver
Billy Graham beat Denny Brown
Arn Anderson beat Manny Fernandez
Buzz Tyler beat Buddy Landell by DQ
Magnum TA beat Tully Blanchard

4/18/85: Washington, DC
The Wild Samoans beat Billy Graham & King Tonga

4/18/85: Williamson, WV @ Fieldhouse

4/18/85: Columbia, SC
Billy Graham vs. Denny Brown

4/19/85: Lenoir, NC
Rocky King beat Joel Deaton
Black Bart beat Sam Houston
Rocky King beat James J. Dillon
Buzz Tyler beat Barbarian by DQ
Magnum TA beat Tully Blanchard

4/19/85: Charleston, WV @ Civic Center

4/20/85: Atlanta, GA @ WTBS Studios (TV)
Buddy Landell vs. Mac Jeffers
Ivan Koloff vs. Joshua Stroud
Abdullah the Butcher vs. Gene Ligon
Tully Blanchard vs. T.J. Trippe
Dusty Rhodes beat Krusher Khruschev(7:24) via pinfall
Ole & Arn Anderson vs. Gerald Finley & George South
Black Bart vs. Ron Rossi
Thunderbolt Patterson & Manny Fernandez vs. Randy Barber & Jim Jeffers
Billy Graham & Barbarian beat Dave Dillinger & Ron Rossi

4/20/85: Cleveland, OH @ Convention Center
Bill Irwin beat Ben Alexander
Joel Deaton beat Paul Diamond
Thunderbolt Patterson beat Kareem Muhammad in a lumberjack match
Italian Stallion beat Ron Starr
Ron Garvin beat Bob Roop
Pez Whatley beat Rip Rogers loser leaves town match
The Road Warriors beat Buzz Sawyer & Brett Sawyer

4/21/85: Canton, OH @ Civic Center

4/21/85: Mansfield, OH
Joel Deaton beat Paul Diamond
Italian Stallion beat Ben Alexander

Thunderbolt Patterson beat Kareem Muhammad
Buzz & Brett Sawyer beat Bill Irwin & Bob Roop
Ron Garvin beat Ron Starr
Pez Whatley beat Rip Rogers loser leaves town match

4/21/85: Sumter, SC @ Exhibition Center
Doug Vines beat Rocky King
Rocky Kernodle draw John Tatum
Buzz Tyler beat Dory Funk, Jr.
Arn Anderson beat Denny Brown
Ivan & Nikita Koloff beat Don Kernodle & Manny Fernandez
Magnum TA beat Tully Blanchard by DQ

4/22/85: Saginaw, MI @ Civic Center

4/23/85: Toledo, OH @ Sports Arena
Rip Rogers vs. Tommy Rich loser leaves town match
Ron Starr vs. Ron Garvin
Scott Irwin & Bob Roop vs. Buzz & Brett Sawyer
Kareem Muhammad vs. Thunderbolt Patterson
Doug Sommers vs. Italian Stallion
Chic Donovan vs. Paul Diamond

4/23/85: ?? (TV)
Manny Fernandez vs. Mike Davis
Billy Graham & The Barbarian vs. Rocky King & Gene Ligon
Nikita Koloff vs. George South
Arn Anderson vs. Mark Fleming
Magnum TA vs. Black Bart

4/25/85: Norfolk, VA @ Scope
Mark Fleming draw Doug Vines
Sam Houston beat Joel Deaton
Rocky Kernodle beat John Tatum
The Barbarian beat Denny Brown
Magnum TA & Don Kernodle beat Ivan & Nikita Koloff
Jimmy Valiant beat Billy Graham
Dusty Rhodes beat Tully Blanchard bunkhouse match

4/27/85: Atlanta, GA @ WTBS Studios (TV)
Ole & Arn Anderson vs. Italian Stallion & Gerald Finlay
Manny Fernandez vs. Doug Vines
Bob Roop vs. Golden Terror
Tully Blanchard vs. Lee Ramsey
Ron Garvin vs. George South
Magnum TA vs. Scott Irwin
Ivan & Nikita Koloff vs. Mike Jackson & Paul Garner
Thunderbolt Patterson beat Randy Barber
Pez Whatley vs. Vernon Deaton
Ron Bass vs. Rocky King
Billy Graham, The Barbarian & Abdullah the Butcher vs. Gene Ligon, Ron Rossi & Mike Simani

4/27/85: Columbus, GA @ Municipal Auditorium
Barbarian beat Paul Diamond
Jimmy Valiant & Buzz Tyler beat Ivan & Nikita Koloff
Italian Stallion draw Ron Starr
Pez Whatley beat Scott Irwin
Ron Garvin beat Bob Roop
Thunderbolt Patterson NC with Arn Anderson

4/27/85: Richmond, VA @ Coliseum
Denny Brown draw John Tatum
Magnum TA beat Nikita Koloff
Jimmy Valiant beat Billy Graham by DQ
Buzz Tyler beat Ivan Koloff
Don Kernodle beat Krusher Khruschev
Buddy Landell beat Sam Houston
Black Bart beat Rocky Kernodle
Tully Blanchard beat Dusty Rhodes by DQ

4/28/85: Marietta, GA @ Cobb County Civic Center
Italian Stallion beat Kim Duk
Barbarian beat Johnny Weaver
Ron Starr beat Rocky King
Pez Whatley draw Bob Roop
Ron Garvin beat Scott Irwin
Buzz Tyler beat Khrusher Khruschev

4/28/85: Asheville, NC @ Civic Center
Jimmy Valiant vs. Billy Graham Texas death match
Magnum TA vs. Buddy Landell in a no DQ match
Manny Fernandez & Thunderbolt Patterson vs. Ole & Arn Anderson
Don Kernodle vs. Nikita Koloff
Pez Whatley vs. Black Bart
Buzz Tyler vs. Tommy Lane
Denny Brown vs. Mike Davis

4/28/85: Charlotte, NC @ Coliseum
Jimmy Valiant beat Billy Graham martial arts match
Don Kernodle beat Krusher Khruschev
Buzz Tyler draw Ron Bass
Ole & Arn Anderson beat Manny Fernandez & Thunderbolt Patterson to win NWA National Tag Title
Magnum TA & Dick Slater beat Ivan & Nikita Koloff DQ
Tully Blanchard beat Dusty Rhodes to win NWA World (Mid Atlantic) Television Title

4/29/85: Vineland, NJ @ H.S.

4/29/85: Fayetteville, NC
Jimmy Valiant vs. Superstar Billy Graham (Texas Death Match)
Ivan & Nikita Koloff vs Don & Rocky Kernodle
Black Bart vs. Mark Fleming
Ron Bass vs. Gene Ligon

4/29/85: Greenville, SC @ Memorial Auditorium
Stoney Burke beat Golden Terror
Ricky Reeves beat Doug Vines
Buddy Landell beat Sam Houston
Magnum TA beat Scott Irwin
Manny Fernandez & Thunderbolt Patterson beat Ole & Arn Anderson by DQ
Dusty Rhodes beat Tully Blanchard

4/30/85: ?? (TV)
Magnum TA vs. Doug Vines
The Barbarian vs. Gene Ligon
Ron Bass vs. Rocky King
Don Kernodle vs. Ben Alexander
Ivan & Nikita Koloff vs. Mark Fleming & Ron Rossi

4/30/85: Philadelphia, PA @ Civic Center
Denny Brown draw John Tatum
Buzz Tyler & Pez Whatley beat Tommy Lane & Mike Davis
Krusher Khruschev beat Denny Brown
Ron Garvin beat Bob Roop
Manny Fernandez & Thunderbolt Patterson beat Ole & Arn Anderson by DQ
Dusty Rhodes beat Tully Blanchard in a cage match

4/30/85: Spartanburg, SC
Magnum TA vs. Ivan Koloff
Also on the card: Superstar Billy Graham, Dusty Rhodes, Nikita Koloff, Tully Blanchard, Paul Jones, Jimmy Valiant, JJ Dillon, Thunderbolt Patterson.

5/1/85: Trenton, NJ @ CYO Building
Denny Brown beat Mike Davis
Stoney Burke draw John Tatum
Buzz Tyler beat Krusher Khruschev by DQ
Pez Whatley beat Bob Roop
Thunderbolt Patterson & Manny Fernandez beat Ole & Arn Anderson by DQ
Ron Garvin beat Tully Blanchard

5/2/85: Pittsburgh, PA @ Civic Center
Ron Garvin beat Tully Blanchard by DQ
Ole & Arn Anderson beat Thunderbolt Patterson & Manny Fernandez
Buzz Tyler draw Bob Roop
Krusher Khruschev beat Stoney Burke
Pez Whatley beat Mike Davis

5/2/85: Columbia, SC @ Township Auditorium
Sam Houston beat Doug Vines
Ron Starr draw Pat Tanaka
Black Bart beat Johnny Weaver
Ron Bass beat Rocky Kernodle
Nikita Koloff beat Don Kernodle
Magnum TA beat Buddy Landell

5/3/85: Columbus, OH @ Ohio Center
Dusty Rhodes beat Ivan Koloff
Thunderbolt Patterson & Manny Fernandez beat Ole & Arn Anderson by DQ
Dick Slater beat Bill Irwin
Buzz Sawyer beat Joel Deaton
Kim Duk beat Stoney Burke
Italian Stallion beat Rocky Reeves

5/4/85: Atlanta, GA @ WTBS Studios (TV)
Jimmy Valiant beat Randy Barber
Tully Blanchard beat Dale Williams
Black Bart beat Kent Glover
Magnum TA beat Golden Terror
NWA World Champ Ric Flair beat Rocky King
Ole & Arn Anderson beat Richard Dye & Gerald Finley
Nikita Koloff beat Alan Martin
Tully Blanchard beat Rocky King
Ivan & Nikita Koloff beat Gene Ligon & Dale Williams
Black Bart beat Gerald Finley
Pez Whatley beat Lee Ramsey
Arn & Ole Anderson beat Kent Glover & Ron Rossi

5/4/85: Cincinnati, OH @ Riverfront Coliseum
Ricky Reeves beat Kim Duk
Joel Deaton beat Stoney Burke
Scott Irwin beat Italian Stallion
Buzz Tyler beat Ivan Koloff
Manny Fernandez & Thunderbolt Patterson beat Ole & Arn Anderson

5/4/85: Greensboro, NC @ Coliseum
Magnum TA beat wahoo McDaniel
Dusty Rhodes beat Tully Blanchard
Buzz Tyler beat Ron Bass
Nikita Koloff beat Don Kernodle
Black Bart beat Rocky Kernodle
Buddy Landell beat Ron Starr
Pat Tanaka beat John Tatum

5/4/85: Columbus, GA @ Municipal Auditorium
Black Bart beat Sam Houston
Buzz Tyler draw Bob Roop
Nikita Koloff beat Sam Houston
Magnum TA NC with Buddy Landell
Ronnie Garvin beat Tully Blanchard by DQ
Dusty Rhodes & Dick Slater beat Barbarian & Billy Graham

5/5/85: Steubenville, OH
Ricky Reeves beat Kim Duk
Italian Stallion draw Scott Irwin
Krusher Khruschev beat Stoney Burke
Buzz Tyler beat Ivan Koloff
Manny Fernandez & Thunderbolt Patterson beat Ole & Arn Anderson by DQ

5/5/85: Marietta, GA @ Cobb County Civic Center
Black Bart beat Sam Houston
Buzz Tyler draw Bob Roop
Nikita Koloff beat Sam Houston
Magnum TA beat Buddy Landell
Ron Garvin beat Tully Blanchard by DQ
Dusty Rhodes & Dick Slater beat Billy Graham & Barbarian

5/6/85: Greenville, SC @ Memorial Auditorium
Black Bart beat Sam Houston
Ron Bass draw Buzz Tyler
Buddy Landell beat Pez Whatley
Dick Slater & Jimmy Valiant beat The Barbarian & Billy Graham
Tully Blanchard beat Ronnie Garvin
Magnum TA beat Nikita Koloff by DQ

5/6/85: Greensburg, PA
Italian Stallion beat Kim Duk
Stoney Burke draw Ricky Reeves
Italian Stallion beat Scott Irwin
Buzz Sawyer beat Krusher Khruschev
Manny Fernandez NC with Arn Anderson

5/7/85: Spartanburg, SC @ Memorial Auditorium (TV)
Magnum TA vs. Ivan Koloff
Dick Slater & Jimmy Valiant vs. Ron Rossi & Golden Terror
Billy Graham vs. Gene Ligon
Buddy Landell vs. Mark Fleming
Nikita Koloff vs. Rocky King
Tully Blanchard vs. Don Kernodle
Manny Fernandez vs. Gene Ligon

5/7/85: Allentown, PA @ Agricultural Hall
Ricky Reeves beat Stony Burke
Italian Stallion draw Scott Irwin
Joe Lightfoot beat Doug Vines
Buzz Sawyer beat Krusher Khruschev
Manny Fernandez beat Arn Anderson

5/8/85: Raleigh, NC @ Dorton Arena
Ivan & Nikita Koloff beat Dick Slater & Don Kernodle
Pat Tanaka draw Denny Brown
Pez Whatley beat Black Bart
Buddy Landell beat Sam Houston
Jimmy Valiant beat Billy Graham
Buzz Tyler beat Ron Bass by DQ
Magnum TA NC with Tully Blanchard

5/9/85: Norfolk, VA @ Scope
Pez Whatley beat Black Bart
Mark Fleming beat Mike Davis
Ron Bass beat Buzz Tyler
Magnum TA beat Buddy Landell
Dick Slater & Jimmy Valiant beat Billy Graham & The Barbarian
Ivan & Nikita Koloff beat Don Kernodle & Rocky Kernodle

5/11/85: Atlanta, GA @ WTBS Studios (TV)
Ronnie Garvin beat Larry Clark
Manny Fernandez beat Paul Garner
NWA World Champ Ric Flair beat Ron Rossi
Magnum TA beat George South
Nikita Koloff beat Kent Glover
Italian Stallion, Buzz Sawyer & Pez Whatley beat Arn & Ole Anderson & Bob Roop
Thunderbolt Patterson beat Randy Barber
Krusher Khruschev beat Alan Martin
Abdullah the Butcher beat Mac Jeffers
Tully Blanchard beat Jim Jeffers
Manny Fernandez beat Ron Rossi
Arn & Ole Anderson beat Jim & Mac Jeffers
Tully Blanchard beat Kent Glover
Ivan & Nikita Koloff & Krusher Khruschev beat Paul Garner, Alan Martin & George South
Buzz Sawyer & Pez Whatley beat Randy Barber & Dale Williams

5/10/85: Richmond, VA @ Coliseum
Jimmy Valiant beat Billy Graham in a cage match
Tully Blanchard beat Magnum TA
Dick Slater beat The Barbarian
Buddy Landell beat Don Kernodle
Mike Davis beat Stoney Burke

5/11/85: Charlotte, NC @ Coliseum
Dick Slater & Magnum TA draw Ivan & Nikita Koloff
Jimmy Valiant beat Billy Graham in a NY Street Fight
Tully Blanchard beat Manny Fernandez
Ole & Arn Anderson beat Buzz Sawyer & Pez Whatley
Dusty Rhodes beat Scott Irwin
Buddy Landell beat Johnny Weaver
Barbarian beat Sam Houston

5/12/85: Sumter, SC @ Exhibition Center
Buzz Tyler vs. Ron Bass
Tommy Lane & Mike Davis vs. Denny Brown & Stoney Burke
Buddy Landell vs. Don Kernodle
Rocky Kernodle vs. Black Bart
Pat Tanaka vs. Ricky Reeves
Rocky King vs. Joel Deaton

5/12/85: Atlanta, GA @ Omni
Dusty Rhodes & Dick Slater beat Ivan & Nikita Koloff
Manny Fernandez & Thunderbolt Patterson beat Ole & Arn Anderson
Jimmy Valiant NC with Abdullah The Butcher
Tully Blanchard beat Ronnie Garvin
Magnum TA beat John Tatum
Buzz Sawyer draw Krusher Khrushchev
Billy Graham beat Italian Stallion
Barbarian beat Sam Houston

5/13/85: Greenville, SC @ Memorial Auditorium
Rocky King beat Golden Terror
Stoney Burke beat Doug Vines
Krusher Khruschev beat Ricky Reeves
Ivan Koloff beat Joe Lightfoot
Dick Slater beat The Barbarian
Jimmy Valiant beat Billy Graham

5/14/85: ?? (TV)
Don Kernodle vs. Golden Terror
Buddy Landell vs. Pat Tanaka
Nikita Koloff vs. Mark Fleming
Jimmy Valliant vs. Ron Rossi
Tully Blanchard vs. Gene Ligon
Billy Graham vs. Rocky King
Billy Graham & The Barbarian vs. Pat Tanaka & Mark Fleming
Ron Bass vs. Ron Rossi
Jimmy Valiant vs. Ben Alexander
Buzz Tyler vs. Doug Vines
Krusher Khruschev, Ivan & Nikita Koloff vs. Sam Houston, Ricky Reeves & Stoney Burke

5/14/85: Saginaw, MI
Joel Deaton beat John Tatum
Italian Stallion beat Scott Irwin
Buzz Sawyer beat Tommy Lane
Pez Whatley beat Mike Davis by DQ
Ronnie Garvin beat Bob Roop
Thunderbolt Patterson beat Arn Anderson

5/15/85: Raleigh, NC @ Dorton Arena
Jimmy Valiant beat Billy Graham
Dusty Rhodes beat Tully Blanchard by DQ
Buddy Landell beat Gene Ligon
Buzz Tyler beat Ron Bass
Krusher Khruschev beat Sam Houston
Ivan & Nikita Koloff beat Dick Slater & Magnum TA

5/17/85: Wheeling, WV
Scott Irwin beat Joel Deaton
Italian Stallion beat Mike Davis by DQ
Buzz Sawyer beat Tommy Lane
Pez Whatley draw Bob Roop
Ron Garvin beat John Tatum
Manny Fernandez & Thunderbolt Patterson beat Ole & Arn Anderson

5/18/85: Atlanta, GA @ WTBS Studios (TV)
Ivan & Nikita Koloff vs. ?? & ??
Dick Slater vs. Golden Terror
Ron Bass vs. ??
Tully Blanchard vs. ??
NWA World Champ Ric Flair beat Sam Houston
Abdullah the Butcher vs. ??
Magnum TA vs. ??
Buddy Landell vs. ??
Jimmy Valiant vs. ??

5/18/85: Cleveland, OH @ Convention Center
Scott Irwin beat Italian Stallion
Mike Davis beat Joel Deaton
Pez Whatley draw Tommy Lane
Buzz Tyler beat John Tatum
Ron Garvin beat Bob Roop
Manny Fernandez & Thunderbolt Patterson beat Ole & Arn Anderson by DQ

5/18/85: Greensboro, NC @ Coliseum
Jimmy Valiant beat Billy Graham
Tully Blanchard beat Dusty Rhodes
Magnum TA beat Buddy Landell
Ron Bass beat Stoney Burke
Black Bart beat Sam Houston
Ricky Reeves beat Doug Vines
Pat Tanaka draw Denny Brown
Ivan & Nikita Koloff beat Dick Slater & Buzz Tyler

5/19/85: Asheville, NC @ Civic Center
Sam Houston beat Black Bart
Krusher Khrushchev beat Ricky Reeves
Ivan Koloff beat Rocky Kernodle
Buzz Tyler beat Ron Bass by DQ
The Barbarian beat Sam Houston
Jimmy Valiant beat Billy Graham in a NY Street Fight

5/19/85: Roanoke, VA @ Civic Center
Gene Ligon beat Mark Fleming
Golden Terror beat Gene Ligon
Buddy Landell beat Stoney Burke
Denny Brown draw Pat Tanaka
Dick Slater beat Nikita Koloff by DQ
Magnum TA NC with Tully Blanchard

5/19/85: Columbia, SC @ Township Auditorium
Buddy Landell beat Stoney Burke
Black Bart beat Ricky Reeves
Buzz Tyler beat Ron Bass
Dick Slater beat Ivan Koloff
Tully Blanchard beat Magnum TA
Dusty Rhodes beat Nikita Koloff
Jimmy Valiant beat Billy Graham in a lights out, NY Street Fight

5/19/85: Marietta, GA @ Cobb County Civic Center
Scott Irwin beat Joel Deaton
Buzz Tyler & Pez Whatley beat Tommy Lane & Mike Davis
Ron Garvin beat John Tatum
Arn Anderson beat Thunderbolt Patterson
Manny Fernandez beat Ole Anderson

5/20/85: Greenville, SC
Superstar Billy Graham vs Dick Slater

5/21/85: ?? (TV)
Ole & Arn Anderson vs. Gene Ligon & Stoney Burke
Buzz Sawyer vs. Golden Terror
The Barbarian vs. Rocky King
Nikita Koloff vs. Pat Tanaka
Jimmy Valliant, Manny Fernandez & Thunderbolt Patterson vs. Ron Rossi, Joel Deaton & Doug Vines
Buddy Landell, & Ron Bass vs. Buzz Tyler, & Sam Houston
Krusher Khruschev, Ivan & Nikita Koloff vs. Pat Tanaka, Stoney Burke & Gene Ligon
Manny Fernandez vs. Joel Deaton
Ole & Arn Anderson vs. Denny Brown & George South
Pez Whatley & Thunderbolt Patterson vs. Doug Vines & Ron Rossi
Buddy Landell vs. Ricky Reeves
Tully Blanchard vs. Buzz Sawyer

5/22/85: Raleigh, NC @ Dorton Arena
Buzz Tyler beat Ron Bass
Arn Anderson beat Pez Whatley
Jimmy Valiant beat The Barbarian
Manny Fernandez beat Ole Anderson by DQ
Dick Slater & Buzz Sawyer beat Ivan Koloff & Krusher Khruschev
Magnum TA beat Tully Blanchard by DQ

5/23/85: Norfolk, VA @ Scope
Sam Houston beat John Tatum
The Barbarian beat Mark Fleming
Jimmy Valiant beat Billy Graham in a NY Street Fight
Pat Tanaka draw Denny Brown
Ole & Arn Anderson beat Sam Houston & Manny Fernandez
Tully Blanchard beat Magnum TA by DQ

5/24/85: Richmond, VA @ Coliseum
Denny Brown beat John Tatum
Buddy Landell beat Rocky Kernodle
Ole & Arn Anderson beat Sam Houston & Manny Fernandez

Magnum TA beat Tully Blanchard
Dusty Rhodes & Jimmy Valiant beat Billy Graham & The Barbarian in a NY Street Fight

5/24/85: Albany, GA @ Civic Center
Ricky Reeves vs. Bob Roop
Joel Deaton vs. Scott Irwin
Stoney Burke vs. Krusher Khruschev
Black Bart vs. Italian Stallion
Ronnie Garvin vs. Ron Bass
Ivan & Nikita Koloff vs. Buzz Sawyer & Dick Slater

5/25/85: Atlanta, GA @ WTBS Studios (TV)
Ivan Koloff & Krusher Khruschev beat Richard Dye & Gerald Finley
Italian Stallion beat Terry Flynn
Tully Blanchard beat Stoney Burke
Thunderbolt Patterson beat Joel Deaton
Black Bart beat Ricky Reeves
Ronnie Garvin beat Ron Bass by DQ
Arn & Ole Anderson beat Vernon Deaton & Mike Simani
Magnum TA beat Paul Garner
Buzz Sawyer beat Randy Barber
Bob Roop beat Richard Dye
Thunderbolt Patterson beat Paul Garner
Arn & Ole Anderson beat Stoney Burke & Gerald Finley
Italian Stallion beat Joel Deaton
Black Bart beat Mike Simani
Ivan Koloff & Krusher Khruschev beat Vernon Deaton & Ricky Reeves

5/25/85: Columbus, GA @ Municipal Auditorium
Scott Irwin beat Ricky Reeves
Bob Roop beat Stoney Burke
Krusher Khruschev beat Italian Stallion
Buzz Tyler beat Nikita Koloff by DQ
Ron Garvin beat Ron Bass
Dick Slater beat Ivan Koloff

5/25/85: Wilson, NC
Ben Alexander beat Doug Vines
Denny Brown draw Pat Tanaka
Rocky Kernodle & Mark Fleming beat Tommy Lane & Mike Davis
Pez Whatley beat Barbarian
Jimmy Valiant beat Billy Graham

5/26/85: Marietta, GA @ Cobb County Civic Center
Pez Whatley beat John Tatum
Black Bart beat Italian Stallion
Ron Garvin beat Bob Roop
Buzz Sawyer beat Krusher Khruschev
Thunderbolt Patterson & Manny Fernandez NC with Ole & Arn Anderson

5/26/85: Fayetteville, NC @ Cumberland County Civic Center
Denny Brown draw Pat Tanaka
Buddy Landell beat Sam Houston
Ivan & Nikita Koloff beat Rocky Kernodle & Mark Fleming
Ric Flair & Jimmy Valiant beat The Barbarian & Billy Graham
Tully Blanchard beat Magnum TA by DQ

5/26/85: Greensboro, NC @ Coliseum
Sam Houston beat Joel Deaton
Buddy Landell beat Denny Brown
Buzz Tyler beat Ron Bass
Nikita Koloff beat Ricky Reeves & Stoney Burke in a handicap match
Dusty Rhodes & Jimmy Valiant beat Billy Graham & The Barbarian
Tully Blanchard beat Dick Slater by DQ
NWA World Champ Ric Flair draw Magnum TA(60:00)

5/27/85: Greenville, SC @ Memorial Auditorium
Ron Garvin beat Buddy Landell by DQ
Buzz sawyer beat Krusher Khruschev
Italian Stallion beat Bob Roop
Sam Houston beat John Tatum
Scott Irwin beat Rocky King
Denny Brown draw Pat Tanaka(20:00)
Buzz Tyler beat Ron Bass

5/27/85: Pittsburgh, PA @ Three Rivers Stadium
NWA World Champ Ric Flair beat Magnum TA
Dusty Rhodes draw Tully Blanchard
Jimmy Valiant beat Billy Graham
Dick Slater & Manny Fernandez beat Ivan & Nikita Koloff by DQ
Ole & Arn Anderson beat Pez Whatley & Thunderbolt Patterson

5/28/85: ?? (TV)
Buddy Landell vs. George South
Ivan Koloff vs. Pat Tanaka
Tully Blanchard vs. Rocky Kernodle
Buzz Sawyer vs. Doug Vines
Ron Bass vs. Gene Ligon
Nikita Koloff vs. Denny Brown
Magnum TA vs. Ron Rossi
Sam Houston vs. Ron Rossi
Ron Bass vs. David Diamond
Ivan & Nikita Koloff vs. Pat Tanaka & Rocky Kernodle
Magnum TA vs. George South
Buddy Landell vs. Denny Brown
Buzz Sawyer vs. Doug Vines
Abdullah the Butcher vs. Gene Ligon

5/28/85: Altoona, PA @ Jaffa Mosque
Scott Irwin beat Mike Donatelli
Ricky Reeves beat Tommy Lane
Mike Davis beat Stony Burke
Buzz Tyler beat The Barbarian by DQ
Jimmy Valiant beat Billy Graham

5/28/85: Lansing, MI @ Civic Center
Italian Stallion beat John Tatum
Pez Whatley draw Bob Roop
Buzz Sawyer beat Krusher Khruschev
Ron Garvin beat Black Bart by DQ
Ole & Arn Anderson beat Thunderbolt Patterson & Manny Fernandez

5/29/85: Grand Rapids, MI @ Stadium
Italian Stallion beat John Tatum
Pez Whatley draw Bob Roop
Buzz Sawyer beat Black Bart by DQ
Ron Garvin beat Krusher Khruschev
Manny Fernandez NC with Arn Anderson
Thunderbolt Patterson beat Ole Anderson

5/29/85: Raleigh, NC @ Dorton Arena
Sam Houston beat Joel Deaton
Pat Tanaka draw Denny Brown
Buddy Landell beat Rocky King
Ron Bass beat Rocky Kernodle
Dick Slater & Magnum TA beat Ivan & Nikita Koloff DQ
NWA World Champ Ric Flair beat Tully Blanchard

5/30/85: Columbia, SC @ Township Auditorium
The Barbarian vs. Jimmy Valiant
Ivan & Nikita Koloff vs. Dick Slater & Buzz Tyler
Tully Blanchard vs. Dusty Rhodes
NWA World Champ Ric Flair vs. Magnum TA

5/31/85: Charleston, SC @ County Hall
Tommy Lane & Mike Davis vs. Stoney Burke & Ricky Reeves
Denny Brown vs. Pat Tanaka
The Barbarian vs. Steve Keirn & Ole Anderson
Buzz Tyler vs. Ron Bass
Jimmy Valiant vs. Billy Graham in a NY Street Fight

6/1/85: Atlanta, GA @ WTBS Studios (TV)
Ronnie Garvin & Buzz Sawyer beat Randy Barber & Mike Simani
Magnum TA beat Larry Clark
NWA World Champ Ric Flair beat George South
Black Bart beat Mac Jeffers
Tully Blanchard beat Paul Garner
Arn & Ole Anderson beat Mark Cooper & Alan Martin
Black Bart beat Ronnie Garvin

6/1/85: Charlotte, NC @ Coliseum
Pat Tanaka beat Doug Vines
Kendo Nagasaki beat Ricky Reeves
Buddy Landell beat Gene Ligon
Buzz Tyler beat Ron Bass
Jimmy Valiant & Dick Slater beat Billy Graham & The Barbarian
Magnum TA draw Tully Blanchard
Dusty Rhodes beat Abdullah The Butcher

6/1/85: Cincinnati, OH @ Gardens
Nikita Koloff vs. Buzz Sawyer

6/2/85: Atlanta, GA @ Omni
Arn Anderson beat Italian Stallion
Bob Roop beat Gerald Finley
Ron Garvin, Jimmy Valiant & Buzz Sawyer beat Billy Graham, Abdullah The Butcher & The Barbarian
Tully Blanchard beat Pez Whatley
Thunderbolt Patterson beat Ole Anderson by DQ
Ivan Koloff & Krusher Khruschev beat Dusty Rhodes & Dick Slater by DQ
NWA World Champ Ric Flair draw Magnum TA

6/2/85: Asheville, NC @ Civic Center
NWA World Champ Ric Flair beat Magnum TA by DQ
Dusty Rhodes beat Tully Blanchard by DQ
Jimmy Valiant & Manny Fernandez vs. Billy Graham & The Barbarian
Buzz Tyler vs. Ron Bass
Denny Brown vs. Kendo Nagasaki
Sam Houston vs. The Eliminator

6/4/85: Spartanburg, SC @ Memorial Auditorium (TV)
Sam Houston, Jimmy Valliant & Magnum TA vs. Doug Vines, Ron Rossi & Joel Deaton
Buddy Landell vs. Ricky Reeves
Manny Fernandez vs. The Barbarian
Kendo Nagasaki vs. Gene Ligon
Abdullah The Butcher vs. Gerald Finley
Nikita Koloff vs. Stoney Burke
Ron Bass vs. Ricky Reeves
Nikita Koloff & Krusher Khruschev vs. Sam Houston & Gene Ligon
Magnum TA & Manny Fernandez vs. Joel Deaton & Ron Rossi
Ivan Koloff vs. Stoney Burke
Abdullah the Butcher vs. Pat Tanaka
Stoney Burke vs. Kendo Nagasaki
Nikita Koloff vs. Gene Ligon & Ricky Reeves in a handicap match
Sam Houston vs. Abdullah the Butcher
Rocky Kernodle vs. Ron Bass
Tully Blanchard vs. Buzz Tyler
Jimmy Valiant vs. Billy Graham steel cage match

6/5/85: Raleigh, NC @ Dorton Arena
Kendo Nagasaki beat Sam Houston
Denny Brown beat Joel Deaton
Jimmy Valiant NC with Abdullah The Butcher
Tully Blanchard beat Buzz Sawyer
Buzz Tyler beat Ron Bass in a taped fist match
Ivan Koloff & Krusher Khruschev draw Magnum TA & Manny Fernandez

6/6/85: Norfolk, VA @ Scope
Kendo Nagasaki beat Mark Fleming
Billy Graham beat Denny Brown
Ron Bass beat Sam Houston
Jimmy Valiant beat Barbarian in a lumberjack match
Manny Fernandez & Buzz Tyler beat Krusher Khruschev & Ivan Koloff by DQ
Dusty Rhodes & Magnum TA NC with Tully Blanchard & Abdullah The Butcher

6/7/85: Columbia, SC @ Township Auditorium
Denny Brown draw Pat Tanaka
Arn Anderson beat Stoney Burke
Billy Graham beat Sam Houston
Dusty Rhodes & Manny Fernandez beat Ivan & Nikita Koloff by DQ
Jimmy Valiant beat Barbarian NY street fight, cage match

6/7/85: Wilmington, NC @ Legion Stadium
Tully Blanchard beat Buzz Tyler by DQ

Buzz Tyler beat Ron Bass
Krusher Khrushchev beat Mark Fleming
Ricky Reeves beat Ron Bass
Mark Fleming beat Doug Vines
Note: Scheduled main event was Ric Flair vs. Magnum TA but they failed to appear

6/7/85: Albany, GA @ Civic Center
Rocky King vs. John Tatum
Thunderbolt Patterson vs. Bob Roop
Italian Stallion vs. Kevin Sullivan
Mike Davis & Tommy Lane vs. Buzz Sawyer & Pez Whatley
Scott Irwin vs. Dick Slater
Ronnie Garvin vs. Black Bart

6/8/85: Atlanta, GA @ WTBS Studios (TV)
Manny Fernandez beat George South
Magnum TA beat Mike Simani
Tully Blanchard beat Mark Hawk
Buzz Sawyer beat Joel Deaton
Arn Anderson beat Larry Clark
Nikita Koloff beat Rocky King
Black Bart beat Ron Garvin wins National Title loser leaves WTBS
Dick Slater beat Paul Garner
Italian Stallion, Thunderbolt Patterson & Pez Whatley beat Randy Barber, Tommy Lane & Mike Davis
Abdullah the Butcher beat Mike Nichols
Ivan Koloff beat The Green Shadow
Buddy Landell beat Gerald Finley
Ivan & Nikita Koloff beat Randy Beason & Larry Clark
Tully Blanchard beat Mike Nichols
Buzz Sawyer & Dick Slater beat Paul Garner & Mike Simani
Thunderbolt Patterson & Pez Whatley beat Randy Barber & George South
Arn Anderson beat Mark Hawk

6/8/85: Zanesville, OH
Yukon Eric beat Ken Jugan
Italian Stallion & Pez Whatley beat Tommy Lane & Mike Davis
Buzz Sawyer beat Joel Deaton
Dick Slater beat The Eliminator
Black Bart beat Brett Sawyer by DQ
Thunderbolt Patterson beat Ole Anderson

6/8/85: Greensboro, NC @ Coliseum
NWA World Champ Ric Flair beat Buddy Landell
Dusty Rhodes & Magnum TA beat Abdullah the Butcher & Tully Blanchard
Manny Fernandez beat Ivan Koloff
Arn Anderson beat Pat Tanaka
Kendo Nagasaki beat Ricky Reeves
Nikita Koloff beat Denny Brown
John Tatum beat Sam Houston

6/9/85: Wheeling, WV @ Civic Center
The Eliminator beat Yukon Eric
Italian Stallion beat Joel Deaton
Buzz Sawyer & Pez Whatley beat Tommy Lane & Mike Davis
Black Bart beat Brett Sawyer
Thunderbolt Patterson beat Ole Anderson by DQ
Dick Slater beat Ric Flair by DQ

6/9/85: Roanoke, VA @ Civic Center
Denny Brown beat Ron Rossi
Kendo Nagasaki beat Mark Fleming
The Barbarian beat George South
Buddy Landell beat Pat Tanaka
Buzz Tyler beat Ron Bass
Jimmy Valiant beat Billy Graham

6/10/85: Greenville, SC @ Memorial Auditorium
Magnum TA, Dusty Rhodes & Jimmy Valiant beat Billy Graham, The Barbarian & Paul Jones
Tully Blanchard beat Manny Fernandez by DQ
Buzz Tyler draw Ivan Koloff
Buddy Landell beat Sam Houston
Nikita Koloff beat Ricky Reeves & Stoney Burke
Ron Bass beat Denny Brown

6/11/85: ?? (TV)
Manny Fernandez vs. Lee Ramsey
Arn Anderson vs. Denny Brown
NWA World Champ Ric Flair vs. George South
Nikita Koloff vs. Mike Link
Ron Bass, Kendo Nagasaki & Buddy Landell vs. Ron Rossi, David Diamond, & Mark Fleming
Sam Houston vs. George South
Krusher Khruschev vs. Denny Brown
The Barbarian vs. Mike Lake
Ron Bass & Buddy Landell vs. Buzz Tyler & Manny Fernandez
Arn Anderson vs. Stoney Burke
Kendo Nagasaki vs. Ricky Reeves
Nikita Koloff vs. Mark Fleming

6/12/85: Philadelphia, PA @ Civic Center
Italian Stallion beat Joel Deaton
Pez Whatley & Buzz Tyler beat Tommy Lane & Mike Davis
Black Bart beat Brett Sawyer
Jimmy Valiant beat The Eliminator
Thunderbolt Patterson beat Ole Anderson
NWA World Champ Ric Flair draw Magnum TA
Ivan & Nikita Koloff beat Manny Fernandez & Dick Slater by DQ
Dusty Rhodes beat Tully Blanchard barbed wire match

6/14/85: Salisbury, MD
Krusher Khruschev beat Mark Fleming
Kendo Nagasaki beat Denny Brown
Ron Bass beat Stoney Burke
Krusher Khruschev beat Sam Houston
Ivan & Nikita Koloff beat Manny Fernandez & Buzz Sawyer
Magnum TA draw Tully Blanchard
NWA World Champ Ric Flair beat Dusty Rhodes by DQ

6/15/85: Atlanta, GA @ WTBS Studios (TV)
Buzz Sawyer & Dick Slater vs. Ron Rossi & ?? Hill
Manny Fernandez vs. Randy Barber
Kamala vs. Alan Martin
Ole & Arn Anderson vs. Italian Stallion & Joe Lightfoot
The Barbarian vs. Jason Walker
Tully Blanchard vs. Gerald Finlay
NWA World Champ Ric Flair draw Magnum TA(10:18)

6/15/85: Cleveland, OH @ Convention Center
Joel Deaton beat The Eliminator
Pez Whatley beat Mike Davis
John Tatum beat Yukon Eric
Ole Anderson beat Thunderbolt Patterson in a Texas death match
Black Bart beat Brett Sawyer
Jimmy Valiant beat Billy Graham

6/15/85: Richmond, VA @ Coliseum
Kendo Nagasaki beat Denny Brown
Ron Bass beat Mark Fleming
Ivan & Nikita Koloff & Krusher Khruschev beat Sam Houston & Buzz Tyler & Starship Eagle
Manny Fernandez NC with The Barbarian
NWA World Champ Ric Flair beat Buddy Landell by DQ
Dusty Rhodes & Magnum TA beat Tully Blanchard & Abdullah The Butcher in a cage match

6/16/85: Asheville, NC @ Civic Center
Dusty Rhodes & Magnum TA vs. Abdullah The Butcher & Tully Blanchard
Manny Fernandez vs. The Barbarian
Also including The Road Warriors, Ivan Koloff, Nikita Koloff, Billy Graham, Krusher Khruschev, Buddy Landell, Kendo Nagasaki, Jimmy Valiant, Buzz Tyler, Ron Bass & Sam Houston

6/16/85: Marietta, GA @ Cobb County Civic Center
Joe Lightfoot beat John Tatum
Thunderbolt Patterson beat Tommy Lane
Kevin Sullivan beat Pez Whatley
Dick Slater & Italian Stallion beat Bob Roop & The Eliminator
Black Bart beat Brett Sawyer
Buzz Sawyer NC with Arn Anderson

6/16/85: Sumter, SC @ Exhibition Center
Billy Graham vs. Jimmy Valiant in a NY Street Fight
Manny Fernandez vs. The Barbarian
Buzz Tyler vs. Ron Bass
Sam Houston vs. Krusher Khruschev
Denny Brown vs. Buddy Landell
Pat Tanaka vs. Kendo Nagasaki

6/17/85: Greenville, SC @ Memorial Auditorium
Krusher Khruschev beat Starship Eagle
Kendo Nagasaki beat Sam Houston
Manny Fernandez & Jimmy Valiant beat Billy Graham & The Barbarian
Buzz Tyler beat Ron Bass in a bullrope match
Magnum TA & Dusty Rhodes beat Tully Blanchard & Abdullah theButcher cage match

6/18/85: Hickory, NC
Buddy Landell beat Sam Houston
Billy Graham beat Ricky Reeves
Jimmy Valiant beat Barbarian by DQ
Magnum TA beat Tully Blanchard

6/19/85: Spartanburg, SC (TV)
Ivan Koloff & Krusher Khrushchev vs. Pat Tanaka & Mark Fleming
The Barbarian vs. Sam Houston
Abdullah The Butcher vs. David Dillinger
The Road Warriors vs. Ricky Reeves & ??
Buddy Landell vs. George South
The Road Warriors beat Ron Rossi and George South
Magnum TA beat Dave Dillinger
Tully Blanchard and Abdullah The Butcher beat Denny Brown and Pat Tanaka
Buddy Landell beat Joel Deaton with Figure Four
Starship Eagle beat Lee Ramsey with a Legdrop
Nikita Koloff beat Sam Houston with Russian Sickle

6/20/85: Columbia, SC @ Township Auditorium
Billy Graham beat Stoney Burke
Krusher Khruschev beat Sam Houston
Jimmy Valiant beat Buddy Landell
Manny Fernandez beat Barbarian
Buzz Tyler beat Ron Bass by knockout in a Texas death match
Dusty Rhodes & Magnum TA beat Abdullah The Butcher & Tully Blanchard

6/21/85: Charleston, SC @ County Hall
Gene Ligon vs. Doug Vines
Johnny Weaver vs. Joel Deaton
Denny Brown vs. Pat Tanaka in a 2 of 3 falls match
Ron Bass beat Buzz Tyler in a bullrope match
Jimmy Valiant beat The Barbarian steel cage match

6/21/85: Hampton, VA @ Coliseum
Buddy Landell beat Stoney Burke
Krusher Khruschev beat Sam Houston
Kendo Nagasaki beat Ricky Reeves
Ivan Koloff beat Starship Eagle(Dan Spivey)
Manny Fernandez beat Billy Graham
Magnum TA & Dusty Rhodes beat Abdullah The Butcher & Tully Blanchard

6/22/85: Atlanta, GA @ WTBS Studios (TV)
Brett & Buzz Sawyer beat Randy Barber & Larry Clark
Magnum TA beat Paul Garner
Jimmy Valiant beat Carl Styles
Tully Blanchard beat Terry Flynn
Ivan & Nikita Koloff beat Mark Cooper & Alan Martin
Ric Flair, Ole & Arn Anderson beat Italian Stallion, Pez Whatley & Rocky King(14:00) by submission
Buddy Landell beat Jason Walker
Thunderbolt Patterson beat Tommy Lane
Kevin Sullivan beat Gerald Finley
Billy Graham beat Mark Hill

6/22/85: Columbus GA @ Municipal Auditorium
Thunderbolt Patterson & Italian Stallion beat Tommy Lane & Mike Davis

Pez Whatley beat Ole Anderson
Kevin Sullivan beat Rocky King
Jimmy Valiant beat Billy Graham
Ivan & Nikita Koloff beat Buzz Sawyer & Brett Sawyer
NWA World Champ Ric Flair beat Dick Slater by DQ

6/23/85: Atlanta, GA @ Omni
Magnum TA beat NWA World Champ Ric Flair by DQ
Ole & Arn Anderson beat Dick Slater & Buzz Sawyer
Jimmy Valiant beat Billy Graham
Black Bart beat Starship Eagle
Thunderbolt Patterson beat Bob Roop
Pez Whatley & Italian Stallion beat Tommy Lane & Mike Davis
Kevin Sullivan beat Rocky King

6/23/85: Greensboro, NC @ Coliseum
Dusty Rhodes & Wahoo McDaniel beat Abdullah the Butcher & Tully Blanchard
Manny Fernandez beat The Barbarian
Buddy Landell beat Pat Tanaka
Nikita Koloff beat Sam Houston
Kendo Nagasaki beat Ricky Reeves
Ivan Koloff & Krusher Khrushchev beat Joe Lightfoot & Billy Thundercloud
Ron Bass DDQ Buzz Tyler in a Texas bullrope match

6/24/85: Greenville, SC @ Memorial Auditorium
Joel Deaton beat Lee Ramsey
Krusher Khruschev beat Ricky Reeves
Ivan Koloff beat Stoney Burke
Nikita Koloff beat Starship Eagle
Magnum TA beat Tully Blanchard
Dusty Rhodes beat Buddy Landell by DQ

6/25/85: Lansing, MI @ Civic Center
Italian Stallion beat Mike Davis
Joe Lightfoot draw Tommy Lane
Thunderbolt Patterson & Pez Whatley beat Kevin Sullivan & Bob Roop
Black Bart beat Brett Sawyer
Dick Salter & Buzz Sawyer beat Ole & Arn Anderson by DQ

6/25/85: ?? (TV)
Jimmy Valliant vs. Joel Deaton
Ivan Koloff & Krusher Khrushchev vs. Stoney Burke & Ricky Reeves
Nikita Koloff vs. Lee Ramsey
The Barbarian & Kendo Nagasaki vs. Sam Houston & Buzz Tyler
Dusty Rhodes & Manny Fernandez vs. Ron Rossi & David Dillinger
Buddy Landell vs. Mark Fleming
Ron Bass vs. Mark Fleming
Ivan Koloff & Krusher Khruschev vs. Sam Houston & Paul Diamond
Magnum TA & Manny Fernandez vs. Lee Ramsey & Joel Deaton
Jimmy Valiant vs. Ron Rossi
Billy Graham & The Barbarian vs. Ricky Reeves & Stoney Burke
Tully Blanchard vs. Gene Ligon

6/26/85: Raleigh, NC @ Dorton Arena
Sam Houston beat Mark Fleming
Ivan Koloff beat Ricky Reeves
Krusher Khruschev beat Starship Eagle
The Barbarian beat Manny Fernandez
Kendo Nagasaki & Buddy Landell beat Jimmy Valiant & Buzz Tyler by DQ

6/26/85: Steubenville, OH
Italian Stallion & Joe Lightfoot draw Tommy Lane & Mike Davis
Thunderbolt Patterson beat Bob Roop
Kevin Sullivan beat Pez Whatley
Black Bart beat Brett Sawyer
Dick Slater & Buzz Sawyer beat Ole & Arn Anderson

6/27/85: Norfolk, VA @ Scope
Krusher Khruschev beat Mark Fleming
Ivan Koloff beat Sam Houston
Nikita Koloff beat Starship Eagle
Ron Bass beat Stoney Burke
Manny Fernandez beat Kendo Nagasaki
Magnum TA beat Buddy Landell
Ric Flair & Jimmy Valiant beat Billy Graham & The Barbarian in a cage match
Dusty Rhodes beat Tully Blanchard in a cage match

6/28/85: Richmond, VA @ Coliseum
Buddy Landell beat Ricky Reeves
The Barbarian beat Manny Fernandez
Ivan Koloff, Nikita Koloff & Krusher Khruschev beat Starship Eagle, Jimmy Valiant & Buzz Tyler
Kendo Nagasaki beat Stoney Burke
Ron Bass beat Sam Houston
Denny Brown beat Mark Fleming
Dusty Rhodes beat Tully Blanchard

6/29/85: Atlanta, GA @ WTBS Studios (TV)
Arn & Ole Anderson beat Roy George & Alan Martin
Ivan Koloff beat Gerald Finley
Buzz Sawyer beat Jimmy Dill
The Midnight Express(Dennis Condrey & Bobby Eaton) beat Larry Clark & Dale Williams
Jimmy Valiant beat Carl Styles
Black Bart beat Italian Stallion
Manny Fernandez beat Kent Glover
Sam Houston beat Jason Walker
Denny Brown beat Paul Garner
Dick Slater beat Nick Busick

6/29/85: Los Angeles, CA @ Olympic Auditorium
Armando Guerrero & Jay York beat Budda Khan & Pistol Pete by DQ
Debbie The Killer Tomato beat Charlie The Golden Cat to win California Ladies Title
Jay Strongbow, Jr. draw Jack Armstrong
Manny Fernandez beat Krusher Khruschev
Dusty Rhodes beat Tully Blanchard
NWA World Champ Ric Flair beat Magnum TA by DQ

6/29/85: Augusta, GA @ Richmond County Civic Center
Denny Brown beat Stoney Burke
Starship Eagle beat John Tatum
The Barbarian beat Sam Houston
Ivan Koloff beat Italian Stallion
Dick Slater & Buzz Sawyer beat Ole & Arn Anderson by DQ
Jimmy Valiant beat Billy Graham

6/30/85: Marietta, GA @ Cobb County Civic Center
Denny Brown beat Mike Davis
Thunderbolt Patterson beat Bob Roop
Pez Whatley & Joe Lightfoot beat Tommy Lane & Mike Davis
Kevin Sullivan beat Italian Stallion
Black Bart beat Brett Sawyer
Dick Slater & Buzz Sawyer beat Ole & Arn Anderson by DQ

7/1/85: ?? (TV)
Tully Blanchard vs. Stoney Burke
Ron Bass vs. John Tatum
Buddy Landell vs. Ricky Reeves
Dusty Rhodes, Manny Fernandez & Magnum TA vs. Ivan Koloff, Nikita Koloff & Krusher Khruschev
Jimmy Valiant vs. Black Kat
Ole & Arn Anderson vs. Ricky Reeves & Stoney Burke
Buddy Landell vs. Sam Houston
Dick Slater vs. Tommy Lane
Krusher Khruschev, Ivan & Nikita Koloff vs. Starship Eagle, Buzz Tyler & Brett Sawyer
Manny Fernandez vs. John Tatum
NWA World Champ Ric Flair vs. Mike Davis

7/2/85: Columbia, SC @ Township Auditorium
Buzz Tyler beat John Tatum
Nikita Koloff beat Sam Houston & Denny Brown in a handicap match
Barbarian beat Manny Fernandez
Jimmy Valiant beat Kendo Nagasaki
Buddy Landell beat Ron Bass by DQ
Dusty Rhodes & Ric Flair beat Ivan Koloff & Krusher Khruschev
Magnum TA beat Tully Blanchard in a lumberjack match

7/3/85: Raleigh, NC @ Dorton Arena
Buddy Landell beat Sam Houston
Nikita Koloff beat Starship Eagle
Manny Fernandez beat The Barbarian by DQ
Magnum TA beat Kendo Nagasaki
Dick Slater & Buzz Sawyer draw Ole & Arn Anderson
Ivan Koloff & Krusher Khruschev won a tag team battle royal

7/4/85: Norfolk, VA @ Scope
Ricky Reeves draw Tommy Lane
Denny Brown beat Mike Davis
Kendo Nagasaki beat Stony Burke
Billy Graham beat Pat Tanaka
Buddy Landell beat Ron Bass
Jimmy Valiant, Manny Fernandez & Buzz Tyler beat The Barbarian, Abdullah The Butcher & Paul Jones

7/4/85: Atlanta, GA @ Omni
The Midnight Express beat Sam Houston & Italian Stallion
Thunderbolt Patterson beat Kevin Sullivan by DQ
Ole & Arn Anderson beat Buzz Sawyer & Brett Sawyer
Ron Garvin NC with Black Bart
Ivan Koloff, Nikita Koloff & Krusher Khruschev beat Dick Slater, Pez Whatley & Bill Watts
NWA World Champ Ric Flair beat Magnum TA

7/5/85: Talladega, AL
Midnight Express beat Brett Sawyer & Italian Stallion

7/5/85: Richmond VA @ Coliseum
Krusher Khruschev beat American Starship Eagle
Ron Bass & Buzz Tyler beat Joel Deaton & John Tatum
Ronnie Garvin beat Ole Anderson
Manny Fernandez & Jimmy Valiant beat The Barbarian & Billy Graham
Abdullah The Butcher DDQ Magnum TA
Ivan & Nikita Koloff won a 9-team battle royal

7/6/85: Atlanta, GA @ WTBS Studios (TV)
Brett Sawyer & Buzz Sawyer beat Larry Clark & Vernon Deaton
Ronnie Garvin beat Art Pritts
The Midnight Express beat Mark Cooper & Alan Martin
Kevin Sullivan beat Jason Walker
Magnum TA beat Ron Rossi
Ivan & Nikita Koloff, & Krusher Khruschev beat Black Cat, Tommy Lane & Mike Davis
Arn Anderson beat Gene Ligon
Jimmy Valiant vs. Randy Barber
Sam Houston vs. Roy George
Denny Brown beat Mike Simani
Black Bart beat Rocky King

7/6/85: Charlotte, NC @ Memorial Stadium
Ron Bass draw Buddy Landell(20:00)
Ole & Arn Anderson beat Buzz Sawyer & Dick Slater
Manny Fernandez, Sam Houston & Buzz Tyler beat Billy Graham, The Barbarian, & Abdullah the Butcher
Jimmy Valiant beat Paul Jones dog collar chain match
Road Warriors DDQ Krusher Khruschev & Ivan Koloff
Magnum TA beat Kamala(6:45) by DQ
NWA World Champ Ric Flair beat Nikita Koloff
Dusty Rhodes beat Tully Blanchard cage match to win NWA World Television Title

7/6/85: Columbus, GA @ Memorial Auditorium
Thunderbolt Patterson beat Mike Davis
Kevin Sullivan beat Pez Whatley
Brett Sawyer beat Kendo Nagasaki
The Midnight Express beat Joe Lightfoot & Italian Stallion
Ron Garvin NC with Black Bart in a lights out match
The Midnight Express won battle royal

7/7/85: Marietta, GA @ Cobb County Civic Center
Thunderbolt Patterson & Rocky King beat Tommy Lane & Mike Davis
Midnight Express beat Brett Sawyer & Italian Stallion
Kevin Sullivan beat Pez Whatley
Ronnie Garvin beat Black Bart by CO
Buzz Sawyer beat Arn Anderson lights out

7/7/85: Greenville, SC @ Memorial Auditorium
Pat Tanaka & Denny Brown draw Gene Ligon & John Tatum
The Barbarian beat Sam Houston
Ivan Koloff, Nikita Koloff & Krusher Khruschev beat Jimmy Valiant & Buzz Tyler & Manny Fernandez
Buddy Landell beat Ron Bass
Dusty Rhodes beat Abdullah The Butcher DQ bullrope match
NWA World Champ Ric Flair beat Magnum TA by DQ

7/8/85: Swainsboro, GA
The Midnight Express beat Rocky King & Pez Whatley

7/8/85: Oklahoma City, OK
NWA World Champ Ric Flair vs. Dusty Rhodes

7/8/85:, Shelby, NC @ Recreation Center (TV)
Ron Bass & Buzz Tyler beat Mark Fleming & Gene Ligon(3:59) via pinfall
Magnum TA beat Black Cat(:46) via pinfall
The Rock & Roll Express beat Joel Deaton & John Tatum(3:06) via pinfall
Abdullah the Butcher beat Stoney Burke(3:04)
The Barbarian vs. Ron Rossi
Buddy Landell beat Sam Houston(11:28) via pinfall
The Rock & Roll Express beat Ivan Koloff & Krusher Khruschev via pinfall to win NWA World Tag Titles

7/9/85: Blackshear, GA @ NFC Gym
Black Bart vs. Brett Sawyer
Kevin Sullivan vs. Arn Anderson
Dick Slater vs. Buzz Sawyer
The Midnight Express beat Italian Stallion & Pez Whatley
Bob Roop vs. Thunderbolt Patterson
Rocky King vs. Mike Davis
Gerald Finley vs. The Eliminator

7/10/85: Miami, FL
NWA World Champ Ric Flair vs. Dusty Rhodes

7/10/85: Raleigh, NC @ Dorton Arena
Kendo Nagasaki beat Gerald Finley
Ivan & Nikita Koloff beat Sam Houston & Jimmy Valiant
Billy Graham beat Mark Fleming
Buddy Landell beat Ron Bass
Manny Fernandez beat The Barbarian in a Mexican death match
Magnum TA & Dusty Rhodes NC with Tully Blanchard & Abdullah The Butcher

7/11/85: Columbia, SC @ Township Auditorium
Gene Ligon beat George South
John Tatum beat Lee Ramsey
Jimmy Valiant beat The Barbarian
Jimmy Valiant beat Paul Jones
Ron Bass beat Kendo Nagasaki
Magnum TA beat Nikita Koloff
Dusty Rhodes beat Buddy Landell

7/12/85: Dillwyn, VA @ Buckingham County H.S.
Billy Graham vs. Sam Houston
Ivan Koloff & Krusher Khruschev vs. Starship Eagle & Buzz Tyler
Tully Blanchard vs. Manny Fernandez

7/13/85: Atlanta, GA @ WTBS Studios (TV)
Buddy Landell beat Rocky King
Brett Sawyer & Buzz Sawyer beat Randy Barber & George South
The Midnight Express beat Terry Flynn & Jason Walker
Dick Slater beat Gerald Finley
Black Bart beat Gene Ligon
Jimmy Valiant beat The Barbarian by DQ
Terry Taylor beat Mike Nichols
Arn Anderson beat Adrian Bivins
The Rock & Roll Express beat Larry Clark & Chuck Levins

7/13/85: Greensboro, NC @ Coliseum
NWA World Champ Ric Flair beat Buddy Landell
Dusty Rhodes beat Nikita Koloff
Khrusher Khruschev beat Sam Houston
Ivan Koloff beat Starship Eagle
Rising Sun #2(Tatsutoshi Goto) beat Stoney Burke
Sam Houston beat Joel Deaton

7/13/85: Charlotte, NC @ Coliseum
NWA World Champ Ric Flair beat Buddy Landell

7/13/85: Cleveland, OH @ Convention Center
Brett Sawyer beat Mike Davis
Thunderbolt Patterson beat Bob Roop
Dick Slater NC with Kevin Sullivan
The Midnight Express beat Italian Stallion & Pez Whatley
Black Bart beat Ron Garvin
Buzz Sawyer beat Arn Anderson
Jimmy Valiant beat Barbarian by DQ
Jimmy Valiant beat Paul Jones by CO

7/14/85: Asheville, NC @ Civic Center
Gene Ligon beat Lee Ramsey
Ricky Reeves beat Tommy Lane
The Rising Suns(Kazao Sakurada[aka Kendo Nagasaki] & Tatsutoshi Goto) beat Starship Eagle & Sam Houston
Manny Fernandez beat Ivan Koloff
Magnum TA beat Nikita Koloff
Dusty Rhodes beat Buddy Landell

7/14/85: Charleston, WV @ Civic Center
Pez Whatley beat Bob Roop
Thunderbolt Patterson beat Mike Davis
Kevin Sullivan beat Italian Stallion
Dick Slater & Buzz Sawyer draw The Midnight Express
Brett Sawyer beat Arn Anderson
Black Bart beat Ron Garvin
Jimmy Valiant beat Barbarian
Jimmy Valiant beat Paul Jones by DQ

7/15/85: Greenville, SC @ Memorial Auditorium
The Rock & Roll Express beat Billy Graham & Kendo Nagasaki
Magnum TA beat Nikita Koloff by DQ
Dusty Rhodes draw Buddy Landell
Ron Bass beat Joel Deaton
Ivan Koloff & Krusher Khruschev beat Starship Eagle & Sam Houston
Abdullah The Butcher DCO with Manny Fernandez

7/15/85: Canton, OH @ Civic Center
The Midnight Express beat Pez Whatley & Italian Stallion

7/16/85: Gaffney, SC @ Timken Physical Education Center (TV)
Magnum TA vs. Ivan Koloff
Buddy Landell vs. Dusty Rhodes
Ivan Koloff, Nikita Koloff & Krusher Khruschev vs. Ricky Reeves, Sam Houston & Mark Fleming
Buddy Landell vs. George South
The Rock & Roll Express vs. Ron Rossi & Lee Ramsey
Jimmy Valliant & Manny Fernandez vs. The Barbarian & Billy Graham
Magnum TA vs. Joel Deaton
Ron Bass vs. Kendo Nagasaki
Jimmy Valiant vs. Joel Deaton
The Barbarian vs. Denny Brown
Rock & Roll Express vs. George South & Gene Ligon
Magnum TA vs. Kendo Nagasaki
Nikita Koloff & Krusher Khruschev vs. Starship Eagle & Lee Ramsey

7/16/85: Marion, OH
The Midnight Express beat Dick Slater & Brett Sawyer

7/17/85: Columbia, SC @ Township Auditorium
Manny Fernandez & Jimmy Valiant beat Billy Graham & The Barbarian by DQ

7/17/85: Cincinnati, OH
Dusty Rhodes beat Tully Blanchard
Magnum TA beat Ivan Koloff
Buzz Sawyer draw Arn Anderson
Dick Slater beat Abdullah The Butcher by DQ
The Midnight Express beat Pez Whatley & Brett Sawyer
Thunderbolt Patterson beat Mike Davis
Italian Stallion beat Bob Roop

7/18/85: Columbus, OH
Magnum TA beat NWA World Champ Ric Flair by DQ
Dusty Rhodes beat Tully Blanchard
Buzz Sawyer beat Arn Anderson in a Texas death match
Dick Slater NC with Kevin Sullivan
Black Bart beat Ronnie Garvin
The Midnight Express beat Italian Stallion & Pez Whatley
Thunderbolt Patterson beat Mike Davis
Brett Sawyer beat Bob Roop

7/18/85: Norfolk, VA @ Scope
The Rising Suns beat Sam Houston & Mark Fleming
Nikita Koloff beat Ricky Reeves
Buddy Landell beat Ron Bass
The Rock & Roll Express beat Billy Graham & The Barbarian
Manny Fernandez beat Abdullah The Butcher by DQ
Jimmy Valiant beat Paul Jones in a dog collar match

7/19/85: Richmond, VA @ Coliseum
James J. Dillon beat Ricky Reeves
Sam Houston beat Mark Fleming
The Rock & Roll Express beat The Rising Suns
Jimmy Valiant beat Paul Jones in a dog collar match
Magnum TA beat Tully Blanchard
Dusty Rhodes beat Buddy Landell

7/19/85: Wheeling, WV
Brett Sawyer beat Bob Roop
Thunderbolt Patterson beat Mike Davis
The Midnight Express beat Pez Whatley & Italian Stallion
Dick Slater beat Kevin Sullivan by DQ
Buzz Sawyer beat Arn Anderson Texas death match
Black Bart beat Ron Garvin

7/20/85: Atlanta, GA @ WTBS Studios (TV)

7/20/85: Columbus, GA @ Municipal Auditorium
The Midnight Express beat Pez Whatley & Italian Stallion

7/20/85: Philadelphia, PA @ Civic Center
Sam Houston beat James J. Dillon
Manny Fernandez beat Billy Graham
Buddy Landell beat Ron Bass
Dick Slater beat The Barbarian
Magnum TA beat Nikita Koloff by CO
Dusty Rhodes beat Tully Blanchard bullrope match
Jimmy Valiant beat Paul Jones in a dog collar match
The Rock & Roll Express beat Ivan Koloff & Krusher Khruschev by DQ

7/21/85: Charlotte, NC @ Coliseum
Thunderbolt Patterson beat Joel Deaton
Ron Bass beat Rising Sun #2
Jimmy Valiant beat Rising Sun #1
Dusty Rhodes beat Buddy Landell by DQ
Tully Blanchard beat Magnum TA to win NWA US Title
Manny Fernandez beat Barbarian Mexican death match
The Rock & Roll Express beat Ivan & Nikita Koloff DQ

7/21/85: Atlanta, GA @ Omni
Terry Taylor beat Bob Roop
Midnight Express beat Pez Whatley & Italian Stallion
Jimmy Valiant beat Paul Jones dog collar, chain match
Tully Blanchard beat Brett Sawyer
Dick Slater beat Kevin Sullivan
Dusty Rhodes & Magnum TA NC Ole & Arn Anderson
Black Bart beat Ron Garvin in a cage match

7/22/85: ?? (TV)
Ivan Koloff & Krusher Khruschev vs. Stoney Burke & Denny Brown
The Rising Suns vs. Pat Tanaka & Sam Houston
Nikita Koloff vs. Gerald Finley
Magnum TA vs. Ron Rossi
The Rock & Roll Express vs. Joel Deaton & Mark Fleming
Abdullah The Butcher vs. Lee Ramsey
The Rising Suns vs. Denny Brown & Stony Burke
Buddy Landell vs. Joel Deaton
The Midnight Express vs. Dale Williams & Carry Clarke
Ricky Morton & Robert Gibson vs. Mark Fleming & Lee Ramsey
Tully Blanchard vs. Starship Eagle
Abdullah the Butcher vs. Ron Bass
Krusher Khruschev, Ivan & Nikita Koloff vs. Sam Houston, Stoney Burke & Pat Tanaka

7/22/85: Saginaw, MI
Bob Roop beat Rocky King
Pez Whatley beat Mike Davis
Thunderbolt Patterson beat Tommy Lane
Black Bart beat Italian Stallion
Buzz & Brett Sawyer draw The Midnight Express
Dick Slater beat Kevin Sullivan by DQ
Jimmy Valiant beat The Barbarian
Jimmy Valiant draw Paul Jones

7/22/85: Greenville, SC @ Memorial Auditorium
Pat Tanaka beat Joel Deaton
Billy Graham beat Denny Brown
Arn Anderson beat Sam Houston
Magnum TA beat Tully Blanchard by DQ
Dusty Rhodes DDQ Nikita Koloff
NWA World Champ Ric Flair beat Buddy Landell

7/23/85: Lansing, MI
Tommy Lane beat Rocky King
Thunderbolt Patterson beat Mike Davis
Pez Whatley beat Bob Roop
Kevin Sullivan beat Italian Stallion
Black Bart beat Brett Sawyer
The Midnight Express beat Dick Slater & Buzz Sawyer
Jimmy Valiant beat The Barbarian
Jimmy Valiant beat Paul Jones by DQ

7/23/85: Columbia, SC @ Township Auditorium
Joel Deaton beat Ricky Reeves
Billy Graham beat Lee Ramsey
Jimmy Valiant beat Abdullah The Butcher
Manny Fernandez beat The Barbarian
The Rock & Roll Express beat Ivan Koloff & Krusher Khruschev

7/24/85: Newton, NC
Sam Houston draw Joel Deaton
Krusher Khruschev beat Starship Eagle
Manny Fernandez beat Billy Graham
Ron Bass beat Buddy Landell
The Rock & Roll Express beat Ivan & Nikita Koloff

7/25/85: Athens, GA @ J & J Center
Midnight Express beat Brett Sawyer & Italian Stallion

7/26/85: Albany, GA @ Civic Center
Joe Lightfoot vs. Bob Roop
Mike Davis vs. Rocky King
Black Bart vs. Pez Whatley
Midnight Express beat Italian Stallion & Brett Sawyer
Arn Anderson & Kevin Sullivan vs. Buzz Sawyer & Dick Slater in a steel cage
The Midnight Express co-won an 18-man $10,000 battle royal

7/26/85: Hampton, VA @ Coliseum
Denny Brown draw Pat Tanaka
The Rising Suns beat Starship Eagle & Sam Houston
Ron Bass beat Buddy Landell in a Texas death match
Magnum TA beat Nikita Koloff by DQ
Dusty Rhodes beat Tully Blanchard

7/27/85: Atlanta, GA @ WTBS Studios (TV)
Buddy Landell beat Pat Tanaka
Brett Sawyer & Buzz Sawyer beat Randy Barber & Vernon Deaton
Nikita Koloff beat Black Cat
Midnight Express beat Sam Houston & Joe Lightfoot
Terry Taylor beat Larry Clark
Dusty Rhodes beat Arn Anderson
Abdullah the Butcher beat George South
Jimmy Valiant & Pez Whatley beat Jim Jeffers & Donald Ross
Bob Roop beat Rocky King
Rock & Roll Express beat Terry Flynn & Mike Nichols
Tully Blanchard beat Mac Jeffers

7/27/85: Greensboro, NC @ Coliseum
NWA World Champ Ric Flair beat Nikita Koloff
Dusty Rhodes beat Buddy Landell
The Rock & Roll Express draw Ivan & Nikita Koloff
Jimmy Valiant beat Paul Jones in a dog collar match
Ron Bass beat Joel Deaton via pinfall
Sam Houston beat George South
Ricky Reeves beat Mark Fleming

7/27/85: Columbus, GA @ Municipal Auditorium
Bob Roop beat Joe Lightfoot
Tommy Lane & Mike Davis beat Gerald Finley & Rocky King
The Midnight Express beat Bret Sawyer & Italian Stallion
Black Bart beat Pez Whatley
Kevin Sullivan beat Dick Slater by DQ
Buzz Sawyer beat Arn Anderson in a cage match

7/28/85: Asheville, NC @ Civic Center
The Rock & Roll Express vs. Ivan Koloff & Krusher Khruschev
Magnum TA vs. Tully Blanchard
Jimmy Valiant vs. Paul Jones in a dog collar match
Manny Fernandez vs. The Barbarian
Billy Graham vs. Sam Houston
Denny Brown vs. Patrick Tanaka

7/28/85: Augusta, GA @ Richmond County Civic Center
Midnight Express beat Brett Sawyer & Italian Stallion

7/29/85: Greenville, SC @ Memorial Auditorium
The Rock & Roll Express draw Ivan Koloff & Krusher Khrushchev(60:00)
Ron Bass beat Buddy Landell by DQ
Jimmy Valiant beat Paul Jones
Abdullah the Butcher beat Ricky Reeves
Joel Deaton beat Lee Ramsey
Sam Houston beat George South

7/30/85: ?? (TV)
Manny Fernandez vs. Gerald Finley
Krusher Khruschev vs. Lee Ramsey
The Rock & Roll Express vs. Mac Jeffers & Jim Jeffers
Ron Bass vs. Mark Fleming
Magnum TA vs. George South
Jimmy Valliant vs. Tully Blanchard
Tully Blanchard & Abdullah the Butcher vs. Ricky Reeves & Stoney Burke
Buddy Landell vs. Pat Tanaka
Magnum TA vs. Gerald Finley
Dusty Rhodes vs. Joel Deaton
Nikita Koloff vs. Sam Houston
Jimmy Valiant, Manny Fernandez, Ricky Morton & Robert Gibson vs. Billy Graham, The Barbarian & The Rising Suns

7/30/85: Jasper, GA
Midnight Express beat Brett Sawyer & Italian Stallion

7/31/85: Raleigh, NC @ Dorton Arena
Rising Sun #2 beat Ricky Reeves
Rising Sun #1 beat Sam Houston
Krusher Khruschev beat Mark Fleming
The Rock & Roll Express beat Ivan & Nikita Koloff by DQ
Magnum TA NC with Tully Blanchard
Terry Taylor beat Black Bart

8/1/85: Mount Holly, NJ
Denny Brown draw Stoney Burke
Pat Tanaka beat Gerald Finley
Ron Bass beat The Barbarian by DQ
Manny Fernandez beat Billy Graham
Dusty Rhodes beat Abdullah The Butcher by CO

8/1/85: Huntington, WV @ Memorial Fieldhouse
NWA World Champ Ric Flair draw Magnum TA
The Rock & Roll Express beat Ivan & Nikita Koloff
Jimmy Valiant beat Paul Jones in a dog collar match
Tully Blanchard beat Starship Eagle
Ole & Arn Anderson beat Johnny Weaver & Sam Houston

8/2/85: Charleston, SC @ County Hall
Italian Stallion vs. Billy Graham
Black Bart vs. Terry Taylor
Thunderbolt Patterson & Pez Whatley vs. The Rising Suns
Dick Slater vs. Abdullah the Butcher
Manny Fernandez vs. The Barbarian in a Mexican death match
Jimmy Valiant vs. Paul Jones in a dog collar match

8/2/85: Charlotte, NC @ Coliseum
The Midnight Express beat Denny Brown & Pat Tanaka
Arn Anderson beat Starship Eagle
Ole Anderson beat Sam Houston
Ron Bass beat Buddy Landell in a Texas death match
The Rock & Roll Express beat Ivan Koloff & Krusher Khruschev by DQ
Dusty Rhodes NC with Nikita Koloff
Magnum TA beat Tully Blanchard by CO

8/3/85: Atlanta, GA @ WTBS Studios (TV)
Manny Fernandez beat Mike Thor
Terry Taylor beat El Geeko
Ivan & Nikita Koloff beat Jimmy Backlund & Steve Blackmon
Italian Stallion beat Kent Glover
Rock & Roll Express beat Randy Barber & Lee Ramsey
Billy Jack Haynes & Wahoo McDaniel vs. Jack Hart & Rick Rude
The Midnight Express beat Vernon Deaton & Mike Simani
Buddy Landell beat Pablo Crenshaw
Bob Roop beat Jason Walker

8/3/85: Macon, GA @ Coliseum
The Midnight Express beat Buzz & Brett Sawyer

8/3/85: Florence, SC
Billy Graham beat Sam Houston
Rising Sun #2 beat Denny Brown
Rising Sun #1 beat Stoney Burke
Jimmy Valiant beat Paul Jones in a dog collar match
Ron Bass beat Buddy Landell in a Texas death match
Rock & Roll Express beat Ole & Arn Anderson by DQ

8/4/85: Roanoke, VA @ Civic Center
Denny Brown & Sam Houston vs. The Rising Suns
Ron Bass vs. Buddy Landell in a Texas death match
Jimmy Valiant beat Paul Jones in a dog collar match

8/4/85: Sumter, SC @ Exhibition Center
Ricky Reeves beat Ron Rossi
Billy Graham beat Johnny Weaver
Ben Alexander beat Ken Ramsey
Starship Eagle beat Billy Graham by DQ
Rock & Roll Express beat Ole & Arn Anderson DQ

8/4/85: Marietta, GA @ Cobb County Civic Center
Italian Stallion beat Mike Davis

Thunderbolt Patterson beat Tommy Lane
Bob Roop beat Pez Whatley
Terry Taylor beat Italian Stallion
Dick Slater, Buzz & Brett Sawyer beat Bob Roop & The Midnight Express

8/5/85: Greenville, SC @ Memorial Auditorium
Rising Sun #1 beat Ricky Reeves
Denny Brown beat Joe Lightfoot
Abdullah the Butcher beat Starship Eagle
Tully Blanchard beat Manny Fernandez
Dusty Rhodes & Magnum TA beat Ole & Arn Anderson by DQ
NWA World Champ Ric Flair DCO with Nikita Koloff

8/6/85: Rock Hill, SC @ Winthrop Coliseum (TV)
Rock & Roll Express beat Ole & Arn Anderson by DQ
Tully Blanchard beat Manny Fernandez
Magnum TA beat Mark Fleming
Abdullah the Butcher & The Barbarian beat Ricky Reeves & Stoney Burke
Krusher Khrushchev & Nikita Koloff beat Denny Brown & George South
Buddy Landell beat Lee Ramsey by submission
Rock & Roll Express beat Golden Terror & Joel Deaton
Tully Blanchard, Arn & Ole Anderson beat Sam Houston, American Starship & Ron Bass
Manny Fernandez & Jimmy Valiant beat Rising Suns
Buddy Landell beat George South by submission
Rock & Roll Express beat Gerald Finley & Mark Fleming
Ole & Arn Anderson beat Ricky Reeves & Stoney Burke
Abdullah the Butcher beat Lee Ramsey
Jimmy Valiant & Manny Fernandez beat Golden Terror & Joel Deaton
Jimmy Valiant beat Tully Blanchard(3:10) by DQ

8/6/85: Gainesville, GA @ Georgia Mountain Center
Midnight Express beat Buzz & Brett Sawyer

8/7/85: Wheeling, WV @ Civic Center
Dick Slater beat Kevin Sullivan
Pez Whatley beat Mike Davis
Thunderbolt Patterson beat Tommy Lane
Italian Stallion beat Bob Roop
Midnight Express beat Buzz Sawyer & Brett Sawyer
Terry Taylor beat Black Bart

8/7/85: Raleigh, NC @ Dorton Arena
Tully Blanchard beat Manny Fernandez by DQ
Buddy Landell beat Sam Houston
Arn Anderson beat Starship Eagle
Jimmy Valiant beat The Barbarian
Ole Anderson beat Magnum TA
Rock & Roll Express beat Ivan Koloff & Krusher Khruschev

8/8/85: Canton, OH @ Civic Center
Midnight Express beat Buzz Sawyer & Brett Sawyer

8/8/85: Norfolk, VA @ Scope
Joel Deaton beat Mark Fleming
Ron Bass NC with Buddy Landell
Ole & Arn Anderson beat Sam Houston & Starship Eagle
Jimmy Valiant beat Billy Graham
Manny Fernandez beat The Barbarian
Magnum TA beat Tully Blanchard by DQ
Rock & Roll Express draw Ivan Koloff & Krusher Khruschev

8/9/85: Columbia, SC @ Township Auditorium
Rising Sun #1 beat Black Cat
Billy Graham beat Ben Alexander
The Barbarian beat Joe Lightfoot
Ron Bass beat Buddy Landell in a Texas death match
Nikita Koloff beat Sam Houston
The Rock & Roll Express beat Ivan Koloff & Krusher Khruschev

8/9/85: Charleston, WV @ Civic Center
Italian Stallion beat Tommy Lane
Pez Whatley draw Bob Roop
Thunderbolt Patterson beat Mike Davis
Black Bart beat Terry Taylor by DQ
Dick Slater beat Kevin Sullivan anything goes match
Midnight Express beat Buzz Sawyer & Brett Sawyer
Dusty Rhodes & Magnum beat Ole & Arn Anderson DQ

8/10/85: Atlanta, GA @ WTBS Studios (TV)
Ron Bass beat Gerald Finley
Tully Blanchard draw Terry Taylor(20:00)
Harley Race beat Jim Jeffers
Nikita Koloff beat Brodie Chase
The Rock & Roll Express beat Keith Eric & Alan Martin
Ron Bass beat Jim Jeffers
Harley Race beat George South
Rock & Roll Express beat Larry Clark & Terry Flynn
The Midnight Express beat Brodie Chase & Jim Jeffers
Brett & Buzz Sawyer beat Adrian Bivins & Alan Martin

8/10/85: Columbus, GA @ Municipal Auditorium
Tommy Lane beat Gerald Finley
Italian Stallion beat Bob Roop
Black Bart beat Terry Taylor by DQ
Jimmy Valiant beat Paul Jones dog collar, chain match
Kevin Sullivan beat Adrian Bivins
Buzz & Brett Sawyer NC The Midnight Express

8/10/85: Greensboro, NC @ Coliseum
Magnum TA NC with Tully Blanchard
The Rock & Roll Express & Dusty Rhodes beat Ivan Koloff, Nikita Koloff & Krusher Khrushchev
Manny Fernandez beat The Barbarian in a Mexican death match
Ole Anderson beat Starship Eagle
Arn Anderson beat Sam Houston
Denny Brown beat Joel Deaton via pinfall

8/11/85: Asheville, NC @ Civic Center
Joel Deaton beat Sam Houston
Manny Fernandez beat Krusher Khruschev
Jimmy Valiant beat The Barbarian
Ron Bass beat Buddy Landell
Magnum TA beat Tully Blanchard by CO
The Rock & Roll Express beat Ivan & Nikita Koloff

8/11/85: Atlanta, GA @ Omni
Terry Taylor beat Mike Davis
Italian Stallion beat Bob Roop
Jimmy Valiant beat Black Bart by DQ
The Midnight Express beat Buzz Sawyer & Manny Fernandez
Tully Blanchard beat Italian Stallion
Dusty Rhodes & Magnum TA beat Ole & Arn Anderson by DQ
NWA World Champ Ric Flair DCO with Nikita Koloff

8/12/85: Greenville, SC @ Memorial Auditorium
The Midnight Express beat Jim Jeffers & Gerald Finley
Magnum TA beat Buddy Landell by DQ
Rock & Roll Express beat The Barbarian & Billy Graham

8/13/85: Shelby, NC @ Recreation Center (TV)
The Midnight Express beat Ron Rossi & ??
Midnight Express beat Denny Brown & Starship Eagle
Jimmy Valiant & Manny Fernandez vs. Joel Deaton & Golden Terror
The Midnight Express vs. Ricky Reeves & Jim Jeffers
Ole & Arn Anderson vs. Mike Starr & Ron Rossi
Buddy Landell vs. Gerald Finley
Tully Blanchard vs. Vernon Deaton
Abdullah the Butcher & The Barbarian vs. Denny Brown & George South
Rock & Roll Express beat The Midnight Express DQ
Abdullah The Butcher & The Barbarian vs. David Deaton & Jim Jeffers
Midnight Express vs. Denny Brown & Gerald Finley
Manny Fernandez vs. Joel Deaton
The Rock & Roll Express vs. The Rising Suns
Billy Graham vs. George South
Ron Bass vs. Jim Jeffers
Harley Race vs. George South
The Rock & Roll Express vs. Terry Flynn & Larry Clark
The Midnight Express vs. Brody Chase & Mac Jeffers
Buzz & Brett Sawyer vs. Alan Martin & Adrian Bivins
Terry Taylor vs. Randy Barber

8/14/85: Raleigh, NC @ Dorton Arena
Tully Blanchard beat Manny Fernandez
Buddy Landell beat Denny Brown
Ron Bass NC with Abdullah The Butcher
Ole & Arn Anderson beat Sam Houston & Starship Eagle
The Rock & Roll Express & Jimmy Valiant beat Ivan Koloff, Nikita Koloff & Khrusher Khruschev by DQ

8/15/85: Athens, GA @ J & J Center
Midnight Express beat Pez Whatley & Brett Sawyer

8/16/85: Albany, GA @ Civic Center
Midnight Express beat Buzz Sawyer & Brett Sawyer

8/16/85: Richmond, VA @ Coliseum
Krusher Khruschev beat Sam Houston
Arn Anderson beat American Starship Eagle
Ron Bass beat Buddy Landell in a Texas death match
Tully Blanchard DDQ Magnum TA
Ivan & Nikita Koloff beat The Rock & Roll Express

8/16/85: East Rutherford, NJ @ Meadowlands
Brad Rheingans beat Boris Zhukov by DQ
Steve Regal beat Buck Zumhofe via pinfall
Greg Gagne & Curt Hennig beat Nick Bockwinkel & Ray Stevens(19:00)
Rick Martel beat Larry Zbyszko(19;00) via pinfall
Sgt. Slaughter beat NWA World Champ Ric Flair(34:00) by DQ
Road Warriors & Paul Ellering beat Michael Hayes, Buddy Roberts & Terry Gordy DQ

8/17/85: Landover, MD
Magnum TA beat NWA World Champ Ric Flair by DQ
Dusty Rhodes NC with Tully Blanchard
Rick Martel beat Larry Zbyszko
Jimmy Valiant beat Paul Jones
Bob Backlund beat Larry Sharpe

8/17/85: Atlanta, GA @ WTBS Studios (TV)
Terry Taylor vs. Tommy Lane
Arn Anderson vs. Rocky King
Tully Blanchard vs. Joel Deaton
Magnum TA vs. Golden Terror
The Barbarian vs. Lee Ramsey
The Rock & Roll Express vs. The Rising Suns
Ivan Koloff & Krusher Khruschev vs. Pez Whatley & Italian Stallion
Starship Eagle vs. Gerald Finley
The Midnight Express vs. Jim Jeffers & Mac Jeffers
Buddy Landell vs. Ron Rossi
Sam Houston vs. Black Bart

8/17/85: Columbus, GA @ Municipal Auditorium
Italian Stallion beat Tommy Lane
Krusher Khruschev beat Mike Davis
Pez Whatley beat Kevin Sullivan
Terry Taylor beat Black Bart
Midnight Express beat Buzz Sawyer & Brett Sawyer
The Rock & Roll Express beat Ivan & Nikita Koloff

8/18/85: Charlotte, NC @ Coliseum
Sam Houston beat Rising Sun #2
Denny Brown draw Rising Sun #1
Starship Eagle beat Golden Terror
The Rock & Roll Express beat Abdullah The Butcher & The Barbarian by DQ
Ron Bass beat Buddy Landell in a bunkhouse match
Wahoo McDaniel NC with Tully Blanchard
Dusty Rhodes & Magnum TA beat Ole & Arn Anderson

8/18/85: Cleveland, OH @ Convention Center
The Midnight Express beat Buzz & Brett Sawyer

8/20/85: ?? (TV)
Sam Houston vs. Golden Terror
The Midnight Express vs. American Eagle & Denny Brown
Buddy Landell vs. Ron Rossi
Tully Blanchard vs. Joel Deaton
Ole & Arn Anderson vs. Mark Fleming & Lee Ramsey
Rock & Roll Express vs. George South & Jim Jeffers
Buzz Sawyer vs. Mac Jeffers
Nikita Koloff vs. Ron Rossi

Abdullah The Butcher vs. Rocky King
Buddy Landell vs. Jim Jeffers
Ole & Arn Anderson vs. Joel Deaton & Tommy Lane
Sam Houston vs. Lee Ramsey
Ron Bass vs. Gerald Finley
The Midnight Express vs. Ron Rossi & Mark Fleming
The Rock & Roll Express vs. Joel Deaton & Golden Terror
Buddy Landell vs. Jim Jeffers
Abdullah the Butcher & The Barbarian vs. George South & Mac Jeffers
Tully Blanchard, Ole & Arn Anderson vs. Sam Houston, Starship Eagle & Denny Brown

8/22/85: Lovington, VA @ Nelson County H.S. Gymnasium
Jimmy Valiant vs. Paul Jones in a dog collar match
Manny Fernandez vs. The Barbarian in a Mexican death match
Abdullah The Butcher vs. Starship Eagle
Denny Brown & Rising Sun #1 vs. Stoney Burke & Ricky Reeves

8/22/85: Columbia, SC @ Township Auditorium
Arn Anderson beat Sam Houston
Ron Bass beat Buddy Landell in a bunkhouse match
Tully Blanchard beat Magnum TA
Dusty Rhodes beat Ole Anderson in a bullrope match
The Rock & Roll Express beat Krusher Khruschev & Ivan Koloff
NWA World Champ Ric Flair beat Nikita Koloff by DQ

8/23/85: Philadelphia, PA @ Civic Center
Krusher Khruschev beat Starship Eagle
Ole & Arn Anderson beat Pez Whatley & Jimmy Valiant
Ron Bass draw Buddy Landell
Magnum TA draw Tully Blanchard
NWA World Champ Ric Flair beat Dusty Rhodes by DQ
Manny Fernandez beat Barbarian in a Mexican death match
Rock & Roll Express beat Ivan & Nikita Koloff by DQ

8/24/85: Atlanta, GA @ WTBS Studios (TV)
Manny Fernandez beat Jim Jeffers
The Barbarian beat Lee Ramsey
Terry Taylor beat Mike Davis
Arn & Ole Anderson beat Brodie Chase & Jason Walker
Black Bart beat Ron Rossi
Ivan Koloff, Nikita Koloff & Krusher Khruschev vs. Ron Bass, Starship Eagle & Jimmy Valiant
Buzz & Brett Sawyer beat Randy Barber & George South
Buddy Landell beat Gerald Finley
The Rock & Roll Express beat Larry Clark & Mac Jeffers
The Rock & Roll Express beat Jim Jeffers & Jason Walker
Abdullah the Butcher & The Barbarian beat Brodie Chase & Vernon Deaton
Terry Taylor beat Mike Simani
Starship Eagle beat Adrian Bivins
Ron Bass beat Mac Jeffers
Buddy Landell beat Larry Clark

8/24/85: Macon, GA @ Coliseum
Terry Taylor, Buzz & Brett Sawyer beat Jim Cornette & The Midnight Express

8/24/85: Greensboro, NC @ Coliseum
NWA World Champ Ric Flair beat Nikita Koloff
Magnum TA beat Tully Blanchard
Dusty Rhodes beat Ole Anderson in the Texas bullrope match
Ivan Koloff & Khrusher Khruschev beat The Rock & Roll Express by DQ
Sam Houston beat Joel Deaton
Arn Anderson beat Starship Eagle
Stoney Burke beat George South

8/25/85: Atlanta, GA @ WTBS Studios (TV)
The Midnight Express beat Jimmy Backlund & Adrian Bivins
Arn & Ole Anderson beat Wayne Levinski & Mike Thorn
Ron Bass beat Black Bart by DQ
Nikita Koloff beat Jason Walker
The Rock & Roll Express beat Randy Barber & Kent Glover
Magnum TA beat Jim Jeffers
Ivan & Nikita Koloff beat Paul Garner & Ron Rossi
Sam Houston beat George South
Jimmy Valiant beat Lee Ramsey
Black Bart beat Mike Simani

8/25/85: College Park, GA @ Henderson's Arena
The Midnight Express beat Buzz & Brett Sawyer

8/26/85: Wildwood, NJ
The Midnight Express beat Buzz & Brett Sawyer

8/26/85: Greenville, SC @ Memorial Auditorium
Starship Eagle draw Rising Sun #1
Krusher Khruschev beat Sam Houston
Little Coco beat Cowboy Lang
Manny Fernandez NC with Abdullah The Butcher
Ivan & Nikita Koloff beat The Rock & Roll Express DQ
Dusty Rhodes, Magnum TA & Ron Bass beat Ole & Arn Anderson & Tully Blanchard

8/27/85: ?? (TV)
Ron Bass vs. Ron Rossi
Manny Fernandez vs. Tommy Lane
Ole & Arn Anderson vs. George South & Lee Ramsey
Buddy Landell vs. Joel Deaton
The Rock & Roll Express vs. Jim Jeffers & Mac Jeffers
Krusher Khruschev, Ivan & Nikita Koloff vs. Stoney Burke, Ricky Reeves & Denny Brown

8/27/85: Allentown, PA @ Agricultural Hall
The Midnight Express beat Buzz Sawyer & Italian Stallion
The Barbarian vs. Pez Whatley
Billy Graham vs. Jimmy Valiant
Dick Slater vs. Kevin Sullivan
Tully Blanchard vs. Magnum TA
Dusty Rhodes vs. Abdullah the Butcher in a steel cage match

8/28/85: Raleigh, NC @ Dorton Arena
Little Coco beat Cowboy Lang
Buddy Landell beat Starship Eagle
Manny Fernandez NC with Abdullah The Butcher
Tully Blanchard beat Jimmy Valiant
Magnum TA & Dusty Rhodes beat Ole & Arn Anderson by DQ
The Rock & Roll Express beat Ivan & Nikita Koloff

8/29/85: Athens, GA @ J & J Center
Jim Cornette & The Midnight Express beat Italian Stallion, Buzz & Brett Sawyer

8/29/85: Norfolk, VA @ Scope
The Barbarian beat Starship Eagle
Little Coco beat Cowboy Lang
Jimmy Valiant NC with Abdullah The Butcher
Buddy Landell beat Sam Houston
Ole & Arn Anderson beat Ron Bass & Manny Fernandez
Ivan Koloff & Krusher Khruschev beat The Rock & Roll Express by DQ
Tully Blanchard beat Magnum TA

8/30/85: Richmond, VA @ Coliseum
Little Coco beat Cowboy Lang
The Barbarian beat Sam Houston
Buddy Landell beat American Starship Eagle
The Rock & Roll Express beat Ivan Koloff & Krusher Khruschev
Dusty Rhodes, Magnum TA & Ron Bass beat Tully Blanchard, Ole Anderson & rn Anderson in a bunkhouse match
NWA World Champ Ric Flair beat Nikita Koloff

8/31/85: Charlotte, NC @ Coliseum
Joel Deaton beat Mark Fleming
Denny Brown draw Pat Tanaka
Arn Anderson beat Sam Houston
The Rock & Roll Express & Jimmy Valiant beat Ivan Koloff, Nikita Koloff & Krusher Khruschev by DQ
Dusty Rhodes beat Ole Anderson in a bunkhouse match
Tully Blanchard beat Magnum TA
NWA World Champ Ric Flair beat Buddy Landell

8/31/85: Columbus, GA @ Municipal Auditorium
Rocky King draw Mike Davis
Tommy Lane beat mike Simani
Pez Whatley beat Nick Busick
Pez Whatley beat Kevin Sullivan
Black Bart beat Terry Taylor
The Midnight Express beat Buzz Sawyer & Brett Sawyer

8/31/85: Atlanta, GA @ WTBS Studios (TV)
Ron Bass vs. Black Bart
Nikita Koloff vs. Jason Walker

9/1/85: Atlanta, GA @ WTBS Studios (TV)
Buddy Landell beat Paul Garner
The Midnight Express beat Nick Busick & Ron Rossi
Nikita Koloff beat Mike Nichols
Tully Blanchard beat Jim Jeffers
Ron Bass beat Kent Glover
Arn & Ole Anderson beat Terry Taylor & Buzz Sawyer
Denny Brown beat George South
Jimmy Valliant vs. Joel Deaton
Sam Houston, Italian Stallion & Starship Eagle beat Randy Barber, Pablo Crenshaw & Larry Clark
The Rock & Roll Express beat Tommy Lane & Mike Davis

9/1/85: Greensboro, NC @ Coliseum
The Rock & Roll Express beat Ivan Koloff & Krusher Khruschev
Tully Blanchard beat Terry Taylor
Manny Fernandez draw Abdullah the Butcher
Little Coco beat Cowboy Lang
Joel Deaton beat Ricky Reeves
The Rising Suns beat Stoney Burke & Pez Whatley

9/1/85: Atlanta, GA @ Omni
Billy Graham beat Sam Houston
The Barbarian beat Starship Eagle
Buddy Landell beat Italian Stallion
Ron Bass beat Black Bart by DQ
The Midnight Express & Jim Cornette beat Jimmy Valiant, Buzz Sawyer & Brett Sawyer
Dusty Rhodes & Magnum TA beat Ole & Arn Anderson
NWA World Champ Ric Flair beat Nikita Koloff in a lumberjack match

9/2/85: Greenville, SC @ Memorial Auditorium
Pez Whatley beat Joel Deaton
Terry Taylor draw Krusher Khruschev
The Midnight Express beat Buzz Sawyer & Brett Sawyer
Jimmy Valiant beat Black Bart by DQ
Manny Fernandez beat Abdullah The Butcher
The Rock & Roll Express beat Ivan & Nikita Koloff

9/3/85: Gaffney, SC (TV)
Jimmy Valiant & Manny Fernandez vs. the Rising Sun & Golden Terror
Billy Graham vs. George South
Magnum TA vs. Tommy Lane
The Midnight Express vs. Gerald Finley & Lee Ramsey
Sam Houston beat Arn Anderson(4:48) via pinfall
Tully Blanchard vs. Rocky King
The Barbarian & Abdullah the Butcher vs. Starship Eagle & Mark Fleming

9/4/85: Raleigh, NC @ Dorton Arena
Arn Anderson beat Sam Houston
Ron Bass beat Buddy Landell
Manny Fernandez beat Abdullah The Butcher
Jimmy Valiant & The Rock & Roll Express beat Ivan Koloff, The Barbarian & Krusher Khruschev
Starship Eagle & Little Coco beat Joel Deaton & Cowboy Lang
Magnum TA NC with Tully Blanchard
NWA World Champ Ric Flair NC with Nikita Koloff

9/5/85: Lexington, KY @ Rupp Arena
Ron Bass fought Buddy Landell to a draw

Koko Ware beat Tom Branch
Dog Collar: Jimmy Valiant beat Paul Jones
The Rock & Roll Express beat The Midnight Express
Manny Fernandez beat Tully Blanchard by DQ
Southern Tag Titles: The Fabulous Ones beat The Sheepherders (c)
The Road Warriors beat Ivan & Nikita Koloff by DQ
NWA World Champ Ric Flair beat Jerry Lawler by DQ
Steel Cage: America's Team beat Ole & Arn Anderson

9/6/85: Hampton, VA @ Coliseum
Joel Deaton beat Stoney Burke
Billy Graham beat Starship Eagle
Italian Stallion & Denny Brown beat The Rising Suns
Manny Fernandez NC with Abdullah The Butcher
The Rock & Roll Express beat Ivan Koloff & Krusher Khruschev
NWA World Champ Ric Flair beat Buddy Landell

9/7/85: Philadelphia, PA @ Civic Center
Rocky King draw Mike Davis
Little Coco beat Cowboy Lang
Arn Anderson beat Starship Eagle
Ole Anderson beat Sam Houston
NWA World Champ Ric Flair beat Dusty Rhodes
The Road Warriors beat Ivan & Nikita Koloff
Tully Blanchard beat Magnum TA

9/7/85: Springfield, MA
Manny Fernandez vs. The Barbarian
Billy Graham vs. Brett Sawyer
Abdullah The Butcher vs. Buzz Sawyer
Black Bart vs. Terry Taylor
Tim O'Reilly vs. Tony Ulyses
Comanche Kid vs. Prince of Pain

9/8/85: Atlanta, GA @ WTBS Studios (TV)
Buddy Landell beat Jimmy Backlund
Nikita Koloff beat Wayne Levinski
Black Bart beat Jason Walker
Ron Bass beat Randy Barber
Arn Anderson beat Adrian Bivins

9/8/85: Asheville, NC @ Civic Center
Little Coco beat Cowboy Lang
Starship Eagle draw Rising Sun #2
The Road Warriors beat Ivan Koloff & Krusher Khruschev by DQ
Sam Houston beat Joel Deaton
Ron Bass, Manny Fernandez & Magnum TA beat Ole Anderson, Arn Anderson & Tully Blanchard in a bunkhouse match
NWA World Champ Ric Flair NC with Ivan Koloff

9/8/85: Roanoke, VA @ Civic Center
Ivan Koloff & Krusher Khruschev vs. The Road Warriors
Tully Blanchard vs. Magnum TA
NWA World Champ Ric Flair vs. Buddy Landell

9/8/85: Marietta, GA @ Cobb County Civic Center
Italian Stallion beat Gerald Finley
Jimmy Valiant beat Paul Jones dog collar, chain match
Terry Taylor beat Black Bart by CO
The Barbarian beat Pez Whatley
Abdullah the Butcher beat Rocky King
Terry Taylor, Buzz & Brett Sawyer NC with The Midnight Express & Jim Cornette

9/9/85: Indianapolis, IN @ Market Square Arena
Boris Zhukov pinned Brad Rheingans
Billy Graham beat Pez Whatley
Steve Regal pinned Buck Zumhofe
Larry Hennig & Curt Hennig double by DQ Bill Irwin & Scott Irwin
Magnum TA beat Ivan Koloff via pinfall
Sgt. Slaughter beat Larry Zbyszko by DQ
Tully Blanchard DCO with Dusty Rhodes

9/9/85: Greenville, SC @ Memorial Auditorium
NWA World Champ Ric Flair beat Tully Blanchard
Dusty Rhodes & Magnum TA beat Ole & Arn Anderson by DQ
Rock & Roll Express draw The Midnight Express
Terry Taylor beat Joel Deaton
Sam Houston beat Abdullah the Butcher by DQ
The Barbarian beat Starship Eagle

9/9/85: Augusta, GA
Buzz Sawyer beat Billy Graham by DQ
Ronnie Garvin vs. Black Bart
Jimmy Valiant vs. Paul Jones in a dog collar match
Manny Fernandez & Pez Whatley vs. Ivan Koloff & Krusher Khruschev
Ron Bass vs. Buddy Landell
Stoney Burke vs. Mike Davis
Rocky King vs. Tommy Lane

9/10/85: Shelby, NC @ Recreation Center (TV)
Terry Taylor vs. Joel Deaton
Abdullah the Butcher vs. Lee Ramsey
Jimmy Valiant & Manny Fernandez vs. Jim Jeffers & Mark Fleming
Tully Blanchard, Ole & Arn Anderson vs. Ron Rossi, Gerald Finley & Vernon Deaton
Rock & Roll Express vs. Golden Terror & George South
The Midnight Express vs. Starship Eagle & Mac Jeffers
Rock & Roll Express vs. Mark Fleming & Lee Ramsey
The Midnight Express vs. Rocky King & Jim Jeffers
Magnum TA vs. Mac Jeffers
Buddy Landell vs. Ron Rossi
Billy Graham vs. Gerald Finley
Pez Whatley, Sam Houston & Ron Bass vs. Golden Terror, Gene Ligon & Vernon Deaton
Abdullah The Butcher vs. George South

9/12/85: Columbia, SC @ Township Auditorium
Joel Deaton beat Stoney Burke
Billy Graham beat Sam Houston
Krusher Khruschev beat Ricky Reeves
Buddy Landell beat Ron Bass by DQ
The Rock & Roll Express beat Abdullah The Butcher & The Barbarian by DQ
Dusty Rhodes, Manny Fernandez & Magnum TA beat Ole Anderson, Arn Anderson & Tully Blanchard

9/12/85: Wheeling, WV@ Civic Center
Pez Whatley beat Tommy Lane
Italian Stallion beat Mike Davis
The Midnight Express & Jim Cornette beat Buzz Sawyer, Brett Sawyer & Ron Garvin
Terry Taylor beat Black Bart by DQ

9/13/85: Norfolk, VA
Superstar Billy Graham beat Mark Fleming
Barbarian draw Ron Bass
Jimmy Valiant beat Buddy Landell
Manny Fernandez beat Abdullah the Butcher
Road Warriors beat Ivan Koloff & Krusher Kruschev DQ
Dusty Rhodes, Magnum TA & Sam Houston beat Ole & Arn Anderson & Tully Blanchard

9/14/85: Atlanta, GA @ WTBS Studios (TV)
No Wrestling

9/14/85: Columbus, GA @ Municipal Auditorium
Jim Jeffers draw Lee Ramsey
George South beat Mac Jeffers
Jim Jeffers beat Len Rossi
Arn Anderson beat Pez Whatley
Nikita Koloff beat Terry Taylor
The Midnight Express beat Buzz & Brett Sawyer in a loser leaves town, cage match

9/14/85: Charleston, WV @ Civic Center
Rocky King beat Tommy Lane
Mike Davis beat Ricky Reeves
Billy Graham beat Stoney Burke
Black Bart beat Ron Bass
Manny Fernandez beat Barbarian Texas death match
The Road Warriors beat Ivan Koloff & Krusher Khruschev by DQ
Magnum TA NC with Tully Blanchard

9/15/85: Norfolk, VA @ Scope
Billy Graham beat Mark Fleming
Starship Eagle & Stony Burke beat Joel Deaton & Golden Terror
Manny Fernandez beat Abdullah The Butcher
Jimmy Valiant beat Buddy Landell
The Road Warriors beat Krusher Khruschev & Ivan Koloff
Ron Bass draw The Barbarian
Dusty Rhodes, Magnum TA & Sam Houston beat Ole Anderson, Arn Anderson & Tully Blanchard in a bunkhouse match

9/15/85: Pensacola, FL
Buddy Landell beat Sam Houston
Manny Fernandez beat Krusher Khruschev
Brad Armstrong & Steve Armstrong beat Ole & Arn Anderson by DQ
Jimmy Valiant beat The Barbarian
The Rock & Roll Express beat The Midnight Express
Tommy Rich beat Adrian Street by DQ
Magnum TA NC with Tully Blanchard
The Road Warriors beat Ivan & Nikita Koloff
NWA World Champ Ric Flair beat Dusty Rhodes by DQ

9/15/85: College Park, GA
Black Bart vs. Ron Garvin
Buzz & Brett Sawyer vs. Billy Graham & Abdullah The Butcher
Denny Brown vs. Mike Davis
Starship Eagle vs. Tommy Lane
Italian Stallion vs. George South
Patrick Tanaka vs. Lee Ramsey

9/16/85: Fayetteville, NC
Gerald Finlay vs Superstar Billy Graham
Jimmy Valiant vs. Buddy Landell
Rock & Roll Express vs. Abdullah the Butcher & Barbarian
Dusty Rhodes, Magnum TA & Sam Houston vs. Ole Anderson, Arn Anderson & Tully Blanchard in a bunkhouse match

9/17/85: ?? (TV)
Magnum TA vs. Mac Jeffers
Jimmy Valiant & Rocky King vs. George South & Jim Jeffers
Ole & Arn Anderson vs. Brady Boone & Ricky Reeves
Tully Blanchard vs. Ricky Reeves
Abdullah The Butcher & The Barbarian vs. Mark Fleming & Ben Alexander
Terry Taylor vs. Ron Rossi
Terry Taylor vs. Mark Fleming
Sam Houston vs. Jim Jeffers
Abdullah The Butcher & The Barbarian vs. George South & Brady Boone
Billy Graham vs. Ricky Reeves
The Rock & Roll Express vs. Black Cat & Ben Alexander
Buddy Landell vs. ??

9/18/85: Raleigh, NC @ Dorton Arena
Joe Deaton beat Brady Boone
Billy Graham beat Gerald Finley
The Barbarian beat Rocky King
The Midnight Express beat Pat Tanaka & Italian Stallion
Jimmy Valiant beat Black Bart by DQ
The Rock & Roll Express draw Ole & Arn Anderson
Manny Fernandez beat Abdullah The Butcher in a cage match

9/19/85: Baltimore, MD @ Civic Center
Billy Robinson beat Jerry Oski
Brad Rheingans beat Kevin Kelly
Ron Garvin NC with Black Bart
Nick Bockwinkel & Larry Zbyszko beat Sgt. Slaughter & Greg Gagne by DQ
Dusty Rhodes draw Nikita Koloff
The Rock & Roll Express beat Ivan Koloff & Krusher Khruschev by DQ
NWA World Champ Ric Flair beat Magnum TA

9/20/85: Ft. Wayne, IN
Brad Rheingans draw Steve Regal
Bill Irwin & Scott Irwin beat Calypso Jim & Bobo Brazil
Billy Graham beat Pez Whatley
Larry Zbyszko beat Buck Zumhofe

Sgt. Slaughter beat Boris Zhukov by DQ
Magnum TA draw Tully Blanchard
Dusty Rhodes beat Ivan Koloff

9/20/85: Richmond, VA @ Coliseum
Mark Fleming beat Stoney Burke
Tommy Lane beat Brady Boone
Rocky King beat Mike Davis
The Barbarian beat Ricky Reeves
Terry Taylor beat Arn Anderson
Ron Bass beat Buddy Landell
Nikita Koloff & Krusher Khruschev beat The Rock & Roll Express chain match

9/20/85: Columbia, SC @ Township Auditorium
Pat Tanaka beat Rising Sun #1
Starship Eagle beat George South
Thunderfoot beat Italian Stallion
The Midnight Express beat Buzz Sawyer & Starship Eagle
Ron Garvin draw Black Bart

9/21/85: Atlanta, GA @ WTBS Studios (TV)
Ivan Koloff, Nikita Koloff & Krusher Khruschev vs. Ron Rossi, Mike Simani & Paul Garner
Buddy Landell vs. Larry Clark
Ole & Arn Anderson vs. Jim Jeffers & Mark Cooper
Ron Garvin vs. Black Cat
The Barbarian vs. Lee Ramsey
Denny Brown beat Gary Royal to win NWA World Junior Title
Magnum TA vs. Tony Zane
The Rock & Roll Express vs. Richard Dunn & Mac Jeffers
The Road Warriors vs. Terry Flynn & Vernon Deaton
The Midnight Express vs. Jimmy Backland & Italian Stallion

9/21/85: Greensboro, NC @ Coliseum
Thunderfoot beat Stoney Burke
Rocky King & Brady Boone beat Mike Davis & Tommy Lane
The Barbarian beat Pat Tanaka
Ron Garvin & Terry Taylor draw Ole & Arn Anderson
Ron Bass beat Buddy Landell in a bunkhouse match
Nikita Koloff & Krusher Khruschev beat The Rock & Roll Express chain match

9/22/85: Charlotte, NC @ Coliseum
Krusher Khruschev beat Gene Ligon
Ron Bass beat Billy Graham by DQ
Nikita Koloff beat Starship Eagle
Terry Taylor draw Buddy Landell
Jimmy Valiant beat Black Bart
The Rock & Roll Express beat The Midnight Express
Wahoo McDaniel, Dusty Rhodes & Magnum TA beat Ole Anderson, Arn Anderson & Tully Blanchard in a bunkhouse match

9/22/85: Atlanta, GA @ Omni
Terry Taylor beat Black Bart via pinfall to win NWA National Title

9/23/85: Greenville, SC @ Memorial Auditorium (TV)
Ron Bass beat Billy Graham by DQ
Billy Graham vs. Mark Fleming
The Midnight Express vs. Ricky Reeves & Mac Jeffers
Nikita Koloff vs. Stoney Burke
Terry Taylor vs. Ron Rossi
Ron Garvin vs. Gene Ligon
Tully Blanchard, Arn Anderson & Buddy Landell vs. Pez Whatley, Italian Stallion & Brady Boone

9/25/85: Queens, NY
Rocky King beat Mike Davis
Billy Graham beat Pez Whatley
Larry Zbyszko beat Baron Von Raschke
Bill Irwin & Scott Irwin beat Jerry Oski & Dominic DeNucci
Terry Taylor beat Black Bart
Jimmy Valiant beat Abdullah The Butcher by DQ

9/26/85: Harrisonburg, VA @ Harrisonburg H.S.
Johnny Weaver vs. Tommy Lane
Mark Fleming vs. Thunderfoot
Pat Tanaka vs. Buddy Landell
Starship Eagle & Buzz Sawyer vs. The Midnight Express
Tully Blanchard vs. Magnum TA

9/26/85: Staten Island, NY
Rocky King beat Mike Davis
Dominic DeNucci beat Joe Rodriguez
Billy Graham beat Pez Whatley
Terry Taylor beat Black Bart
Jimmy Valiant beat Abdullah The Butcher by DQ

9/27/85: Norfolk, VA @ Scope
NWA World Champ Ric Flair draw Magnum TA(60:00)
Tully Blanchard beat Dusty Rhodes by DQ
The Midnight Express beat Ron Garvin & Starship Eagle
Ivan & Nikita Koloff beat The Rock & Roll Express

9/28/85: Atlanta, GA @ WTBS Studios (TV)
Billy Graham vs. Mark Fleming

9/28/85: Mount Airy, NC
Dusty Rhodes vs. Tully Blanchard
Buzz Sawyer vs. Billy Graham
Starship Eagle vs. James J. Dillon
Mark Fleming vs. Lee Ramsey
Ron Rossi vs. Gene Ligon

9/28/85: Columbus GA @ Municipal Auditorium
Ricky Reeves beat George South
Ron Bass beat Ron Rossi
Stoney Burke beat Thunderfoot by DQ
Thunderfoot II beat Rocky King
Ron Bass NC with Buddy Landell
Ron Garvin beat Black Bart

9/29/85: Atlanta, GA @ Omni
Buddy Landell beat Denny Brown
Abdullah The Butcher beat Sam Houston
Ron Bass beat Black Bart by DQ
Ron Garvin & Terry Taylor draw Ole & Arn Anderson
Dusty Rhodes beat The Barbarian
The Rock & Roll Express beat Ivan Koloff & Krusher Khruschev by DQ
Magnum TA NC with Tully Blanchard
NWA World Champ Ric Flair beat Nikita Koloff cage match

9/29/85: Charlotte, NC @ Coliseum
Brady Boone beat Tommy Lane
Pez Whatley beat Mike Davis
Jimmy Valiant beat Billy Graham by DQ
The Rock & Roll Express beat Abdullah The Butcher & The Barbarian
Dusty Rhodes beat Arn Anderson
Magnum TA NC with Tully Blanchard
NWA World Champ Ric Flair beat Nikita Koloff

9/30/85: Forest City, NC

9/30/85: Norfolk, VA @ Scope
Brady Boone beat Tommy Lane
Arn Anderson beat Gene Ligon
Barbarian beat Pat Tanaka
Buddy Landell beat Italian Stallion
The Midnight Express beat Starship Eagle & Ron Garvin
Tully Blanchard beat Dusty Rhodes by DQ
Ivan & Nikita Koloff beat The Rock & Roll Express in a double chain match

9/30/85: Memphis, TN @ Mid-South Coliseum
Pez Whatley beat Buddy Landell
Billy Travis, Tommy Wright & Tojo Yamamoto defeated Buddy Wayne, Ron Sexton & Mr Class
Koko Ware beat Tom Pritchard by DQ
Ron Bass beat Tarus Bulba
Jimmy Valiant & Bill Dundee NC the Sheepheeders
Mongolain Stomper beat Phil Hickerson
The Fabulous Ones defeated the Freebirds
Magnum TA vs Tully Blanchard was a DDQ
Rock & Roll Express beat Ivan & Nikita Koloff to retain NWA World Tag Titles.
NWA World Champ Ric Flair beat Jerry Lawler by DQ (28:45)

10/1/85: Rick Hill, SC @ Winthrop Coliseum (TV)
The Rock & Roll Express vs. Ivan Koloff & Krusher Khrushchev
Tully Blanchard vs. Magnum TA
plus: Billy Graham, Ole Anderson, Arn Anderson, The Midnight Express, Buddy Landell, Abdullah the Butcher, Dusty Rhodes, Black Bart, The Barbarian
Billy Graham vs. Mac Jeffers
Ron Garvin vs. Jim Jeffers
Thunderfoot vs. Gene Ligon
Terry Taylor vs. Black Cat
The Midnight Express vs. Pez Whatley & Pat Tanaka
Ron Bass vs. Mike Lane
Tully Blanchard vs. Brady Boone

10/2/85: Mount Vernon, NY
Krusher Khruschev beat Pat Tanaka
Italian Stallion beat James J. Dillon
Billy Graham beat Sam Houston
The Midnight Express beat Brett Sawyer & Bulldog Brown
Buddy Landell beat Italian Stallion
Magnum TA beat Tully Blanchard by DQ

10/2/85: Raleigh, NC @ Dorton Arena
Ron Garvin beat Mike Davis
Arn Anderson beat Rocky King
Don Kernodle beat Tommy Lane
Thunderfoot beat Brady Boone
Jimmy Valiant beat Abdullah The Butcher
The Rock & Roll Express beat Ivan & Nikita Koloff DQ

10/3/85: Wheeling, WV @ Civic Center
Italian Stallion beat Tommy Lane
Denny Brown draw Mike Davis
Thunderfoot beat Brady Boone
Billy Graham beat Starship Eagle
Ron Garvin beat Black Bart
The Rock & Roll Express beat Ivan Koloff & Khrusher Khruschev

10/4/85: Hampton, VA @ Coliseum
Sam Houston beat Mike Davis
Italian Stallion beat Mark Fleming
Billy Graham beat Don Kernodle by DQ
Buddy Landell beat Pez Whatley
The Rock & Roll Express draw Ole & Arn Anderson
NWA World Champ Ric Flair beat Nikita Koloff

10/4/85: Albany, GA @ Civic Center
Brady Boone vs. Tommy Lane
Frank Dusek vs. Gerald Finley
Denny Brown vs. Thunderfoot
The Barbarian vs. Brett Sawyer
Ronnie Garvin & Rocky King vs. The Midnight Express
Terry Taylor vs. Black Bart

10/5/85: Atlanta, GA @ WTBS Studios (TV)
Billy Graham vs. Mac Jeffers

10/5/85: Greensboro, NC @ Coliseum
The Rock & Roll Express beat Ivan & Nikita Koloff
Rocky King & Jimmy Valiant beat The Midnight Express
Buddy Landell beat Terry Taylor
Krusher Khrushchev beat Pez Whatley
Thunderfoot beat Starship Eagle
Black Bart beat Stoney Burke
Rickey Reeves draw Tommy Lane

10/5/85: Philadelphia, PA @ Civic Center
Bulldog Brown draw Italian Stallion
Sam Houston beat Mike Davis
Billy Graham beat Starship Eagle
Manny Fernandez beat Arn Anderson
Magnum TA beat Tully Blanchard in a cage match

Ron Bass beat Abdullah The Butcher by DQ
Ron Garvin beat NWA World Champ Ric Flair by DQ

10/6/85: Atlanta, GA @ WTBS Studios (TV)
Ivan Koloff beat Don Turner
Billy Graham beat Brady Boone
Thunderfoot beat Mike Nicholls
Ronnie Garvin & Terry Taylor beat Jim & Mack Jeffers
Don Kernodle, Jimmy Valiant, & Pez Whatley beat Randy Barber, Jerry Garmon, & Paul Garner
Jimmy Valiant beat Tony Zane
Thunderfoot beat Brady Boone
Ole Anderson beat Brodie Chase
Billy Graham beat Randy Barber
NWA World Six-Man Tag Titles: Ivan & Nikita Koloff, & Krusher Khruschev (c) beat Ronnie Garvin, Don Kernodle, & Pez Whatley
Tully Blanchard beat Mike Nichols
Arn Anderson beat Mack Jeffers
Magnum TA beat Jerry Garmon
The Midnight Express beat Kent Glover & Don Turner

10/6/85: Cincinnati, OH @ Gardens
Starship Eagle beat Mike Davis
Denny Brown beat Pat Tanaka
Billy Graham beat Sam Houston
Terry Taylor beat Black Bart
The Rock & Roll Express beat Abdullah The Butcher & Thunderfoot by DQ
Arn Anderson beat Starship Eagle
Tully Blanchard beat Ron Garvin
NWA World Champ Ric Flair draw Magnum TA

10/7/85: Greenville, SC @ Memorial Auditorium
Buddy Landell beat Brady Boone
Don Kernodle, Manny Fernandez & Ron Bass beat Ivan Koloff, Nikita Koloff & Krusher Khruschev by DQ
Jimmy Valiant & Rocky King DCO Midnight Express

10/7/85: Canton, OH @ Civic Center
Denny Brown draw Pat Tanaka
Black Bart beat Starship Eagle
Terry Taylor beat Mike Davis
Arn Anderson beat Sam Houston
The Rock & Roll Express beat Abdullah The Butcher & Thunderfoot by DQ
Billy Graham beat Denny Brown
Magnum TA NC with Tully Blanchard
NWA World Champ Ric Flair beat Ron Garvin

10/8/85: Shelby, NC @ Recreation Center (TV)
Dennis Condrey & Bobby Eaton vs. Jimmy Valiant & Rocky King
Ivan Koloff, Nikita Koloff & Krusher Khruschev vs. Denny Brown, Starship Eagle & Ron Rossi
Don Kernodle vs. Jim Jeffers
Midnight Express vs. George South & Mark Fleming
Ron Garvin vs. Mac Jeffers
Tully Blanchard vs. Sam Houston

10/9/85: Raleigh, NC @ Dorton Arena
Billy Graham beat Brady Boone
Arn Anderson beat Ron Bass
Midnight Express beat Jimmy Valiant & Rocky King
The Rock & Roll Express & Don Kernodle beat Ivan Koloff, Nikita Koloff & Krusher Khruschev by DQ
Tully Blanchard beat Terry Taylor
Magnum TA beat NWA World Champ Ric Flair by DQ

10/10/85: Wheeling, WV @ Civic Center
Italian Stallion beat Tommy Lane
Denny Brown draw Mike Davis
Thunderfoot beat Brady Boone
Billy Graham beat Starship Eagle
Ron Garvin beat Black Bart in a taped fist match
The Rock & Roll Express beat Ivan Koloff & Krusher Khruschev

10/10/85: Norfolk, VA @ Scope
Pez Whatley beat Mark Fleming
Sam Houston beat Gene Ligon
Arn Anderson beat Manny Fernandez
Terry Taylor beat Buddy Landell
The Midnight Express beat Jimmy Valiant & Rocky King
Wahoo McDaniel beat Tully Blanchard by DQ
Magnum TA beat NWA World Champ Ric Flair by DQ

10/12/85: Atlanta, GA @ WTBS Studios (TV)
Jimmy Valliant vs. Tony Zane
Thunderfoot vs. Brady Boone
Ole Anderson vs. Brody Chase
Billy Graham vs. Randy Barber
Ivan & Nikita Koloff & Krusher Khruschev vs. Don Kernodle, Ron Garvin & Pez Whatley
Tully Blanchard vs. Mike Nichols
Arn Anderson vs. Mac Jeffers
Magnum T. A. vs. Jerry Garmon
Terry Taylor vs. Paul Garner
The Midnight Express vs. Don Turner & Kent Glover
Billy Graham beat John Burns

10/12/85: Nashville, TN
Pat Rose, Bota the Witch Doctor, Tom Branch & Taras Bulba beat Tojo Yamamoto, Billy Travis, Sean O'Reilly & Brian O'Reilly
Koko B. Ware beat Tom Prichard by DQ
Masked Superstar beat Phil Hickerson
Billy Graham beat Starship Eagle
Rocky Johnson beat Ron Sexton
Ron Garvin beat Black Bart
Bill Dundee beat Mongolian Stomper
Jimmy Valiant & Manny Fernandez beat The Midnight Express
Jackie Fargo beat Buddy Wayne
Stan Lane & Steve Keirn beat the Sheepherders in a hospital elimination match
The Rock & Roll Express beat Ivan & Nikita Koloff
AWA World Champ Rick Martel beat Jerry Lawler DQ

10/12/85: Jacksonville, FL @ Coliseum
Cocoa Samoa vs. Jack Hart
The Grappler vs. Hector Guerrero
Buddy Landell vs. Terry Taylor
Mike Graham vs. Rick Rude
Dusty Rhodes, Magnum & Ron Bass vs. Arn & Ole Anderson & Tully Blanchard
NWA World Champ Ric Flair vs. Wahoo McDaniel cage match

10/13/85: Atlanta, GA @ WTBS Studios (TV)
Jimmy Valiant beat Golden Terror
Black Bart beat Italian Stallion
Arn Anderson beat Ricky Reeves
The Midnight Express beat Brady Boone & Mack Jeffers
Tully Blanchard beat Ron Bass
Denny Brown beat Randy Barber
Abdullah the Butcher beat Jim Jeffers
Billy Graham beat John Barnes
Starship Eagle beat Thunderfoot

10/13/85: Asheville, NC @ Civic Center
NWA World Champ Ric Flair beat Magnum TA

10/13/85: Charlotte, NC @ Coliseum
Thunderfoot beat Rocky King
Terry Taylor beat Buddy Landell
Manny Fernandez beat Arn Anderson
Tully Blanchard beat Ron Garvin
Magnum TA beat NWA World Champ Ric Flair by DQ
Ivan & Nikita Koloff beat The Rock & Roll Express to win NWA World Tag Title
Jimmy Valiant & Don Kernodle beat The Midnight Express

10/14/85: Fayetteville, NC @ Cumberland County Civic Center
The Rock & Roll Express vs. Ivan & Nikita Koloff in a double chain match
Tully Blanchard vs. Manny Fernandez
Krusher Khruschev vs. Don Kernodle
The Midnight Express vs. Brett Sawyer & Italian Stallion
Billy Graham vs. Denny Brown

10/15/85: Greenwood, SC (TV)
The Rock & Roll Express beat The Midnight Express
The Rock & Roll Express vs. Golden Terror & Mac Jeffers
Krusher Khrushchev vs. Ricky Reeves
Billy Graham vs. Tommy Lane
Pez Whatley, Denny Brown & Brady Boone vs. Mike Davis, Gene Ligon & Tony Zane
Don Kernodle vs. Gerald Finley
Ivan & Nikita Koloff vs. Pat Tanaka & Stoney Burke

10/17/85: Columbia, SC @ Township Auditorium
The Rock & Roll Express vs. The Midnight Express
Manny Fernandez vs. Billy Graham
Nikita Koloff vs. Don Kernodle
Ivan Koloff vs. Pat Tanaka
Brett Sawyer vs. Krusher Khruschev

10/18/85: Charleston, SC @ County Hall
Denny Brown vs. Brady Boone
Italian Stallion vs. Tommy Lane
Golden Terror vs. Pat Tanaka
Brett Sawyer vs. Thunderfoot
Jimmy Valiant & Rocky King vs. The Midnight Express
Ron Bass vs. Black Bart in a taped fist match

10/18/85: Richmond, VA @ Coliseum
Pez Whatley beat Mike Davis
Billy Graham beat Starship Eagle
Terry Taylor beat Buddy Landell
Ron Garvin beat Abdullah The Butcher by DQ
Arn Anderson beat Manny Fernandez
The Rock & Roll Express & Don Kernodle beat Ivan Koloff, Nikita Koloff & Krusher Khruschev
Magnum TA beat Tully Blanchard in a cage match

10/19/85: Atlanta, GA @ WTBS Studios (TV)
NWA World Television Title vacated when Dusty Rhodes was injured
Billy Graham vs. Tommy Lane
Jimmy Valliant vs. Golden Terror
Black Bart vs. Italian Stallion
Arn Anderson vs. Ricky Reeves
The Midnight Express vs. Mac Jeffers & Brady Boone
Tully Blanchard vs. Ron Bass
Denny Brown vs. Randy Barber
Abdullah The Butcher vs. Jim Jeffers
Billy Graham vs. John Barnes
American Starship vs. Thunderfoot

10/19/85: Greensboro, NC @ Coliseum
Tully Blanchard NC with Magnum TA
The Rock & Roll Express beat Ole & Arn Anderson
Terry Taylor beat Black Bart
Billy Graham & Jimmy Valiant beat The Midnight Express
Don Kernodle beat Khrusher Khruschev
Ron Garvin beat Buddy Landell
Sam Houston beat Thunderfoot

10/20/85: Atlanta, GA @ WTBS Studios (TV)
Billy Graham beat Carl Styles(3:19) by DQ

10/20/85: Atlanta, GA @ Omni
Billy Graham beat Sam Houston
Thunderfoot beat Italian Stallion
Dennis Condrey beat Rocky King
Jimmy Valiant beat Bobby Eaton by DQ
Terry Taylor draw Buddy Landell
The Rock & Roll Express beat The Barbarian & Abdullah The Butcher by DQ
Wahoo McDaniel, Ron Garvin & Magnum TA beat Ole Anderson, Arn Anderson & Tully Blanchard in a bunkhouse match

10/21/85: Boiling Springs, NC
Jimmy Valiant & Manny Fernandez beat The Midnight Express

10/22/85: Mooresville, NC (TV)
The Rock & Roll Express beat The Midnight Express
The Rock & Roll Express vs. Tommy Lane & Mike Davis
Ivan Koloff, Nikita Koloff & Krusher Khruschev vs. Stoney Burke, Sam Houston & Brady Boone
Billy Graham vs. Mark Fleming
Arn Anderson vs. Mac Jeffers
The Midnight Express vs. Gene Ligon & Ron Rossi
Manny Fernandez vs. Jim Jeffers

10/25/85: Roanoke, VA @ Civic Center
Mike Davis draw Denny Brown
Thunderfoot beat Italian Stallion
Rocky King beat Tommy Lane
Barbarian beat Pez Whatley
Ronnie Garvin DDQ Abdullah the Butcher
Billy Graham & Jimmy Valiant beat The Midnight Express by DQ

10/26/85: Cleveland, OH @ Convention Center
Jerry Lawler beat Tony Viccaro
Pez Whatley draw Krusher Khruschev
Ole & Arn Anderson beat Jimmy Valiant & Sam Houston
The Rock & Roll Express beat Ivan & Nikita Koloff
Tully Blanchard beat Ron Garvin by DQ
Magnum TA beat NWA World Champ Ric Flair by DQ

10/26/85: Atlanta, GA @ WTBS Studios (TV)
Magnum TA vs. Tony Zane
Billy Graham vs. Carl Styles
The Midnight Express vs. Rocky King & Carl Styles
Buddy Landell vs. Richard Dunn
Wahoo McDaniel vs. Arn Anderson
The Rock & Roll Express vs. Randy Barber & Kent Glover
Ole Anderson vs. Mike Nichol
Sam Houston vs. Black Cat
Tully Blanchard vs. Italian Stallion

10/27/85: Charlotte, NC @ Coliseum
Billy Graham & Jimmy Valiant beat The Midnight Express by DQ

10/28/85: Greenville, SC @ Memorial Auditorium (TV)
Jimmy Valiant & Billy Graham beat The Midnight Express

10/29/85: Richburg, SC (TV)
The Midnight Express vs. Sam Houston & Pat Tanaka
Magnum TA vs. Tony Zane
Billy Jack Haynes vs. Vernon Deaton
Ole & Arn Anderson vs. Ben Alexander & Ron Rossi
Manny Fernandez vs. Jim Jeffers

11/2/85: Atlanta, GA @ WTBS Studios (TV)
Manny Fernandez beat Tommy Lane
Buddy Landell vs. Tony Zane
The Rock & Roll Express vs. Mike Davis & George South
Billy Jack Haynes vs. Black Cat
Magnum TA beat Keith Eric
Billy Graham beat Abdullah The Butcher by DQ
Pez Whatley beat Benny Traylor
Tully Blanchard vs. Denny Brown
Nikita Koloff vs. Mac Jeffers
Ivan Koloff & Krusher Khrushchev vs. Ricky Reeves & Jerry Garmon
Jimmy Valliant vs. Jimmy Black

11/2/85: Cincinnati, OH @ Gardens
Don Kernodle beat Jim Lancaster
Pez Whatley beat Thunderfoot
Ron Bass beat Buddy Landell in a Texas death match
The Midnight Express beat Sam Houston & Rocky King
Ivan Koloff & Krusher Khruschev beat The Rock & Roll Express chain match
Tully Blanchard beat Ronnie Garvin lumberjack match

11/3/85: Atlanta, GA @ Omni
The Barbarian beat Sam Houston
Dusty Rhodes beat Mike Davis
Billy Graham beat Abdullah The Butcher by DQ
Terry Taylor beat Buddy Landell
Ivan Koloff, Nikita Koloff & Krusher Khruschev beat Jimmy Valiant & The Rock & Roll Express by DQ
Tully Blanchard beat Ron Garvin by DQ
Magnum TA, Billy Jack Haynes & Dusty Rhodes beat Ole Anderson, Arn Anderson & Ric Flair

11/3/85: Asheville, NC @ Civic Center
Black Bart beat Pat Tanaka
Italian Stallion beat Stoney Burke
Don Kernodle beat Tommy Lane
Ron Bass beat Buddy Landell
Jimmy Valiant & Billy Graham beat The Midnight Express
NWA World Champ Ric Flair beat Magnum TA

11/4/85: Greenville, SC @ Memorial Auditorium
The Midnight Express beat Pez Whatley & Don Kernodle
Jimmy Valiant & Superstar Billy Graham defeated Abdullah the Butcher & the Barbarian

11/4/85: Lumberton, NC @ Recreation Center
Manny Fernandez & The Rock & Roll Express vs. Ivan Koloff, Nikita Koloff & Krusher Khrushchev
Buddy Landell vs. Tully Blanchard
The Barbarian vs. Don Kernodle
Terry Taylor vs. Black Bart
Pez Whatley vs. Mike Davis
Tommy Lane vs. Italian Stallion

11/5/85: Sumter, SC @ Exhibition Center (TV)
Jimmy Valiant & Billy Graham beat The Midnight Express by DQ
Manny Fernandez & Billy Jack Haynes vs. Mike Davis & Tommy Lane
Magnum TA vs. Doug Vines
Nikita Koloff vs. Tony Zane
Ole Anderson vs. Brady Boone
Tully Blanchard vs. Joe Malcom
The Rock & Roll Express vs. Golden Terror & ??

11/6/85: Raleigh, NC @ Dorton Arena
Magnum TA beat Arn Anderson
Ron Garvin beat Tully Blanchard
Manny Fernandez & ?? beat The Midnight Express DQ
Dusty Rhodes beat Mike Davis
Terry Taylor beat Black Bart
Ron Bass & Don Kernodle draw Buddy Landell & Thunderfoot

11/6/85: Setauket, NY
Billy Graham beat The Barbarian
The Rock & Roll Express beat Ivan Koloff & Krusher Khruschev

11/7/85: Comfort, SC
Jimmy Valiant & Billy Graham beat The Midnight Express by DQ

11/7/85: Norfolk, VA @ Scope
Magnum TA beat Arn Anderson
Tully Blanchard beat Terry Taylor
Ivan Koloff beat Rick Morton
Robert Gibson beat Nikita Koloff by DQ
Krusher Khruschev beat Ricky Reeves
Sam Houston beat Mike Davis
Pez Whatley beat Tommy Lane

11/8/85: Richmond, VA @ Coliseum
Tommy Lane vs. Pez Whatley
Terry Taylor vs. Mike Davis
the Rock & Roll Express vs. Ivan Koloff & Krusher Khruschev
Tully Blanchard vs. Ron Garvin
Billy Graham vs. Nikita Koloff
Dusty Rhodes, Magnum & Manny Fernandez beat Ric Flair, Ole & Arn Anderson

11/8/85: Columbus, GA @ Municipal Auditorium
Midnight Express beat Jimmy Valiant & Rocky King

11/9/85: Atlanta, GA @ WTBS Studios (TV)
Jimmy Valiant beat Tony Zane
Billy Jack Haynes beat Gerald Finley
Krusher Khruschev beat Larry Clark
Ron Bass beat Paul Garner
The Barbarian beat George South
Arn & Ole Anderson & Ric Flair beat Ronnie Garvin, Terry Taylor & Pez Whatley
The Road Warriors beat Jim Jeffers & Mack Jeffers
Tully Blanchard beat Jimmy Backlund
Magnum TA beat Joe Malcolm
Ivan & Nikita Koloff beat Adrian Bivins & Rocky King

11/9/85: Charlotte, NC @ Coliseum
Italian Stallion beat Mike Davis
Pez Whatley beat Tommy Lane
Abdullah the Butcher beat Sam Houston
Terry Taylor beat The Barbarian by DQ
The Midnight Express beat Billy Graham & Jimmy Valiant by CO
Tully Blanchard beat Ronnie Garvin
Dusty Rhodes, Magnum TA & Billy Jack Haynes beat Arn Anderson, Ole Anderson & Ric Flair

11/10/85: Charlotte NC
Midnight Express won by COR over Superstar Billy Graham & Jimmy Valiant

11/11/85: Fayetteville, NC @ Cumberland County Civic Center
Billy Graham & Jimmy Valiant vs. The Midnight Express
Manny Fernandez vs. Buddy Landell
George South vs. Don Kernodle
Pat Tanaka vs. Denny Brown

11/11/85: Saginaw, MI @ Civic Center
Tommy Lane beat Stoney Burke
Mike Davis beat Ricky Reeves
Krusher Khruschev beat Pez Whatley
Thunderfoot beat Italian Stallion
Ron Bass beat Black Bart
The Rock & Roll Express beat Ivan & Nikita Koloff DQ

11/12/85: Shelby, NC @ Recreation Center (TV)
Jimmy Valiant & Billy Graham beat The Midnight Express
The Midnight Express vs. George South & Brady Boone
Billy Jack Haynes vs. Golden Terror
Magnum TA vs. Gene Ligon
Tully Blanchard vs. Pat Tanaka
Jimmy Valiant, Billy Graham & Manny Fernandez vs. Vernon Deaton, Jim Jeffers & Mac Jeffers
Ole & Arn Anderson vs. Rocky King & Tony Zane
NWA World Champ Ric Flair vs. Sam Houston

11/13/85: Monroe, NC
Jimmy Valiant & Billy Graham beat The Midnight Express

11/14/85: Harrisonburg, VA @ Harrisonburg H.S.
Stoney Burke vs. Mark Fleming
Ricky Reeves vs. Tommy Lane
Italian Stallion vs. Mike Davis
Ron Bass vs. Black Bart in a Texas death match
The Rock & Roll Express & Manny Fernandez vs. Ivan Koloff, Nikita Koloff & Krusher Khrushchev

11/14/85: Columbia, SC @ Township Auditorium
Dusty Rhodes, Magnum TA & Billy Jack Haynes vs. Tully Blanchard, Ole & Arn Anderson
Jimmy Valiant & Billy Graham vs. The Midnight Express
Terry Taylor vs. Buddy Landell
Ron Garvin vs. The Barbarian
Starship Eagle vs. Jim Jeffers

11/15/85: Charleston, SC @ St. Andrews H.S. Gym
Billy Jack Haynes, Magnum TA & Dusty Rhodes vs. Ric Flair, Ole & Arn Anderson
Taped Fists: Tully Blanchard vs. Ron Garvin
Buddy Landell vs. Ron Bass
Pat Tanaka vs. Jim Jeffers
Sam Houston vs. Mike Davis

11/15/85: Misenheimer, NC
Jimmy Valiant & Billy Graham beat The Midnight Express

11/16/85: Atlanta, GA @ WTBS Studios (TV)
Jimmy Valiant vs. Tony Zane
Billy Jack Haynes vs. Gerald Finley
Krusher Khruschev vs. Larry Clark
Ron Bass vs. Paul Garner
The Barbarian vs. George South
Ric Flair, Ole & Arn Anderson beat Ron Garvin, Terry Taylor & Pez Whatley
The Road Warriors vs. Jim Jeffers & Mac Jeffers
Tully Blanchard vs. Jimmy Backlund
Magnum TA vs. Joe Malcom
Ivan & Nikita Koloff vs. Rocky King & Adrian Bivins
Billy Graham beat Tony Zane(3:19)

11/16/85: Cleveland, OH @ Convention Center
Dusty Rhodes, Billy Jack Haynes & Magnum TA beat Ric Flair, Ole & Arn Anderson
Tully Blanchard beat Ron Garvin
Manny Fernandez NC with Abdullah The Butcher
Ron Bass draw Buddy Landell
Sam Houston beat Mike Davis
Pez Whatley beat Tommy Lane

11/16/85: Conway, SC
Jimmy Valiant & Billy Graham beat The Midnight Express

11/17/85: Atlanta, GA @ WTBS Studios (TV)
Terry Taylor beat Black Cat
Don Kernodle beat Don Turner
The Barbarian beat Stoney Burke
Billy Graham beat Tony Zane
Manny Fernandez draw Buddy Landell
Black Bart beat Rocky King
Billy Jack Haynes beat Jim Jeffers
Ron Bass, Italian Stallion & Pez Whatley beat Larry Clark, Kent Glover & Carl Styles
Golden Terror beat Sam Houston by CO

11/18/85: Greenville, SC
The Barbarian defeated Superstar Billy Graham

11/18/85: Memphis, TN @ Mid-South Coliseum
Rip Morgan & Tarus Bulba beat Tojo Yamamoto & Billy Travis
The Fantastics (Bobby Fulton & Tommy Rogers) beat Pat Rose & Tom Pritchard
Jimmy Valiant beat Tony Falk
The Fabulous Ones beat the Midnight Express
Jerry Lawler, Magnum TA & Dusty Rhodes def Ole & arn Anderson & Tully Blanchard in a bunkhouse match
Ivan & Nikita Koloff beat Rock & Roll Express to retain NWA World Tag Titles
NWA World Champ Ric Flair beat Koko Ware

11/19/85: Greenwood, SC (TV)
Ron Bass & Don Kernodle vs. Jim Jeffers & Mac Jeffers
Billy Graham & Jimmy Valiant vs. Mike Davis & Tommy Lane
Billy Jack Haynes vs. Golden Terror
Manny Fernandez vs. Tony Zane
Buddy Landell vs. Pez Whatley
Ricky Morton & Robert Gibson vs. Gene Ligon & Mark Fleming
Tully Blanchard, Ole & Arn Anderson vs. Sam Houston, Denny Brown & Ricky Reeves

11/20/85: Canton, OH @ Civic Center
Terry Taylor beat Tully Blanchard by DQ
The Rock & Roll Express beat Ivan & Nikita Koloff
Manny Fernandez beat Buddy Landell
Krusher Khruschev beat Sam Houston
Don Kernodle beat Mike Davis
Pat Tanaka draw Tommy Lane

11/20/85: Raleigh, NC @ Dorton Arena
Dusty Rhodes beat Arn Anderson
Magnum TA beat Ole Anderson by DQ
The Midnight Express & Jim Cornette beat Rocky King, Jimmy Valiant & Billy Graham
Billy Jack Haynes beat Thunderfoot
The Barbarian beat Pez Whatley
Black Bart beat Italian Stallion
Denny Brown draw Brady Boone

11/21/85: Wheeling, WV @ Civic Center
Ivan Koloff & Khrusher Khruschev beat The Rock & Roll Express chain match
Terry Taylor beat Tully Blanchard
Manny Fernandez NC with Nikita Koloff
Buddy Landell beat Sam Houston
Don Kernodle beat Tommy Lane
Pat Tanaka draw Mike Davis

11/22/85: Hendersonville, NC
Billy Graham & Jimmy Valiant beat The Midnight Express by DQ
Billy Jack Haynes vs. The Barbarian
Ron Bass vs. Thunderfoot
Pez Whatley vs. Black Bart
Denny Brown vs. Brady Boone
Italian Stallion vs. Rocky King

11/22/85: Charleston, WV @ Civic Center
Dusty Rhodes & Magnum TA beat Arn Anderson & Ric Flair
Ivan & Nikita Koloff beat The Rock & Roll Express in a double chain match
Tully Blanchard beat Terry Taylor
Manny Fernandez beat Buddy Landell
Don Kernodle draw Krusher Khruschev
Mike Davis beat Pat Tanaka
Sam Houston beat Tommy Lane

11/23/85: Atlanta, GA @ WTBS Studios (TV)
Billy Graham & Jimmy Valiant vs. Mike Davis & Tommy Lane
Billy Graham vs. Tony Zane

11/23/85: Philadelphia, PA @ Civic Center
The Road Warriors & Dusty Rhodes beat Ole Anderson, Arn Anderson & Ric Flair
Billy Graham beat Krusher Khruschev by DQ
Ivan & Nikita Koloff beat The Rock & Roll Express
Terry Taylor draw Buddy Landell
Don Kernodle beat The Barbarian by DQ
Pez Whatley beat Mike Davis
Sam Houston beat Tommy Lane

11/24/85: Marietta, GA @ Cobb County Civic Center
The Rock & Roll Express beat The Midnight Express by DQ

11/24/85: Baltimore, MD @ Civic Center
Dusty Rhodes & The Road Warriors beat Arn & Ole Anderson & Tully Blanchard
Magnum TA beat Buddy Landell
Jimmy Valiant & Billy Graham NC Barbarian & Abdullah The Butcher
Rick Martel beat Kimala by DQ
Boris Zhukov beat Larry Winters
Mike Moore beat Bill Irwin

11/25/85: Easley, SC
The Rock & Roll Express beat The Midnight Express by DQ

11/26/85: ?? (TV)
Pez Whatley & Don Kernodle vs. Tommy Lane & Mike Davis
Abdullah The Butcher vs. Ron Rossi
Ole & Arn Anderson vs. Mark Fleming & Brady Boone
Billy Graham & Jimmy Valliant vs. Golden Terror & Gene Ligon
Black Bart vs. Ricky Reeves
The Barbarian vs. Tony Zane

11/26/85: Lincolnton, NC
The Rock & Roll Express beat Midnight Express by DQ

11/27/85: Raleigh, NC @ Dorton Arena
Jimmy Valiant & Billy Jack Haynes beat The Midnight Express
The Rock & Roll Express beat Tully Blanchard & The Barbarian by DQ
Manny Fernandez beat Mike Davis
Pez Whatley beat Golden Terror
Italian Stallion beat Tommy Lane
Sam Houston beat Gene Ligon

11/27/85: Miami, FL
Billy Graham beat Abdullah The Butcher by DQ
Dusty Rhodes, Magnum TA & Wahoo McDaniel beat Ric Flair, Ole & Arn Anderson in a bunkhouse match
Barry Windham beat Buddy Landell
Tyree Pride beat the Cubain Assassin
Mike Fever beat Red Menace
Lex Lugar beat Frankie Lann winning the Southern title

11/28/85: Greensboro, NC @ Coliseum; Atlanta, GA @ Omni
Starrcade: The Gathering
Atlanta:
Thunderfoot beat Italian Stallion via pinfall
Pez Whatley beat Mike Graham
Manny Fernandez beat Abdullah the Butcher in a Mexican death match
Billy Graham beat The Barbarian in a $10,000 arm wrestling contest
Billy Graham beat The Barbarian by DQ
Ole & Arn Anderson beat Wahoo McDaniel & Billy Jack Haynes(8:59)
Jimmy Valiant & Miss Atlanta Lively (Ron Garvin) beat The Midnight Express (6:36) in a street fight match
Dusty Rhodes beat NWA World Champ Ric Flair(22:06) by DQ

Greensboro:
Denny Brown beat Rocky King via pinfall
Don Kernodle beat Tommy Lane
Krusher Khruschev beat Sam Houston in tournament final to win vacant NWA Mid Atlantic Title
Ron Bass beat Black Bart via pinfall in a bullrope match
James J. Dillon beat Ron Bass via pinfall in a bullrope match
Buddy Landell beat Terry Taylor via pinfall to win NWA National Title
Magnum TA beat Tully Blanchard(15:00) in an I quit, steel cage match to win NWA United States Title
The Rock & Roll Express beat Ivan & Nikita Koloff(12:26) in a no time limit, No DQ, steel cage match to win NWA World Tag Title

11/29/85: St. Louis, MO
NWA World Champ Ric Flair NC with Dusty Rhodes
Khrusher Khruschev & Ivan & Nikita Koloff beat The Rock & Roll Express & Billy Jack Haynes
Magnum TA beat Arn Anderson
Jimmy Valiant & Billy Graham beat The Midnight Express by DQ
Jerry Blackwell beat Tarzan Goto(sub for Mr. Pogo)
Terry Taylor draw Buddy Landell
Tully Blanchard beat Art Crews

11/30/85: Atlanta, GA @ WTBS Studios (TV)
Billy Graham & Jimmy Valiant vs. Golden Terror & Gene Ligon
The Midnight Express vs. Rocky King & Italian Stallion
Manny Fernandez vs. Tommy Lane
The Road Warriors vs. Black Bart & Thunderfoot
Ron Garvin vs. Jim Jeffers

11/30/85: Macon, GA
Jimmy Valiant & Billy Graham beat The Midnight Express

11/30/85: Richmond, VA @ Coliseum
Dusty Rhodes & Magnum TA beat Ric Flair & Tully Blanchard elimination match
The Road Warriors NC with Nikita Koloff & Khrusher Khruschev

Arn Anderson beat Ron Bass
The Rock & Roll Express & Billy Jack Haynes beat Black Bart, James J. Dillon & Buddy Landell
Don Kernodle beat Mike Davis
Ivan Koloff beat Sam Houston
Denny Brown beat Brady Boone

12/1/85: Atlanta, GA @ WTBS Studios (TV)
The Rock & Roll Express beat Jim Jeffers & Mack Jeffers
Ronnie Garvin beat Tommy Lane
Nikita Koloff beat Italian Stallion
The Road Warriors beat Adrian Bivins & Paul Garner
Arn Anderson, Ole Anderson & Tully Blanchard beat Billy Jack Haynes, Sam Houston & Magnum TA
Jimmy Valiant beat Vernon Deaton
Terry Taylor beat Brodie Chase
The Barbarian beat George South
Buddy Landell beat Jeff Smith
Ivan Koloff & Krusher Khruschev beat Jimmy Backlund & Mark Cooper

12/1/85: Marietta, GA @ Cobb County Civic Center
Jimmy Valiant & Ron Garvin beat The Midnight Express by DQ

12/1/85: Asheville, NC @ Civic Center
Dusty Rhodes beat Arn Anderson in a bullrope match
Magnum TA beat Abdullah The Butcher by DQ
The Rock & Roll Express beat Tully Blanchard & Buddy Landell
Nelson Royal beat Tony Zane
Denny Brown beat Golden Terror
George South beat Gerald Finley

12/1/85: Columbia, SC @ Township Auditorium
Gene Ligon vs. Lee Ramsey
Stoney Burke vs. Pat Tanaka
Denny Brown vs. Rocky King
Ron Bass vs. James J. Dillon in a Texas bullrope match
Ivan & Nikita Koloff & Krusher Khruschev vs. Manny Fernandez, Billy Jack Haynes & Don Kernodle

12/2/85: Honea Path, SC
The Midnight Express beat Jimmy Valiant & Sam Houston

12/2/85: Lumberton, NC @ Recreation Center
Italian Stallion vs. Tommy Lane
Mike Davis vs. Pez Whatley
Black Bart vs. Terry Taylor
The Barbarian vs. Don Kernodle
Tully Blanchard vs. Buddy Landell
Manny Fernandez & The Rock & Roll Express vs. Ivan & Nikita Koloff, & Krusher Khruschev

12/3/85: Spartanburg, SC @ Memorial Auditorium (TV)
Ole & Arn Anderson vs. The Rock & Roll Express
The Road Warriors beat Vernon Deaton & ??(:38) via pinfall
The Midnight Express beat Mac Jeffers & Jim Jeffers(1:45) via pinfall
Tully Blanchard beat Italian Stallion(1:41) via pinfall
Ron Bass beat Golden Terror(1:06) via pinfall
The Rock & Roll Express beat Black Bart & Thunderfoot(6:35) via pinfall
Sam Houston & Pez Whatley beat Krusher Khruschev & Nikita Koloff DQ
Billy Jack Haynes beat Tommy Lane(:27) by submission

12/4/85: Raleigh, NC @ Dorton Arena
Road Warriors & Dusty Rhodes beat Ric Flair, Ole & Arn Anderson
Magnum TA beat Abdullah The Butcher by DQ
The Rock & Roll Express draw Buddy Landell & Tully Blanchard
Krusher Khruschev beat Terry Taylor
Manny Fernandez beat Thunderfoot
Ronnie Garvin beat Black Bart

12/5/85: Amelia, VA
The Rock & Roll Express beat Midnight Express DQ

12/6/85: Hampton, VA @ Coliseum
Jimmy Valiant, Miss Atlanta Lively & Ron Bass beat Jim Cornette & The Midnight Express

12/6/85: Albany, GA @ Civic Center
Ric Flair, Ole & Arn Anderson vs. Dusty Rhodes, Magnum & Manny Fernandez
Tully Blanchard vs. Terry Taylor
The Barbarian & Black Bart vs. The Rock & Roll Express
Tommy Lane vs. Sam Houston
Mike Davis vs. Denny Brown
Tony Zane vs. Pez Whatley

12/7/85: Atlanta, GA @ WTBS Studios (TV)
Billy Jack Haynes beat Tommy Lane
Terry Taylor beat George South
The Rock & Roll Express beat Larry Clark & Kent Glover
The Barbarian beat Mack Jeffers
Arn & Ole Anderson beat Italian Stallion & Jim Jeffers
Buddy Landell beat Bill Tabb
The Rock & Roll Express beat Jim & Mack Jeffers
Ron Garvin vs. Tommy Lane
Nikita Koloff vs. Italian Stallion
The Road Warriors vs. Adrian Bivins & Paul Garner
Magnum TA, Billy Jack Haynes & Sam Houston vs. Tully Blanchard, Ole & Arn Anderson
Jimmy Valiant vs. Vernon Deaton
Terry Taylor vs. Brodie Chase
The Barbarian vs. George South
Buddy Landell vs. Jeff Smith
Ivan Koloff & Krusher Khruschev vs. Mark Cooper & Jim Backlund

12/7/85: Cleveland, OH @ Convocation Center
Magnum TA won a Bunkhouse Stampede
Dusty Rhodes beat Arn Anderson Texas death match
The Road Warriors beat Nikita Koloff & Krusher Khruschev
Magnum TA beat Ole Anderson
Jimmy Valiant beat Black Bart
The Rock & Roll Express beat Abdullah The Butcher & The Barbarian
Ron Garvin draw Ivan Koloff

12/8/85: Atlanta, GA @ Omni
Ron Garvin beat NWA World Champ Ric Flair by DQ
The Road Warriors beat Ivan Koloff & Krusher Khruschev by DQ
Magnum TA won bunkhouse stampede
Dusty Rhodes beat Arn Anderson in a bullrope match
Magnum TA beat Ole Anderson in a Texas death match
Black Bart beat Italian Stallion
The Rock & Roll Express beat Buddy Landell & Tully Blanchard by DQ
The Barbarian beat Sam Houston

12/11/85: Rock Hill, SC @ Winthrop Coliseum (TV)
Dusty Rhodes & Magnum TA beat Tully Blanchard & Ric Flair via pinfall
The Barbarian beat George South
Ivan & Nikita Koloff & Krusher Khrushchev beat Ricky Reeves, Pat Tanaka & Stoney Burke
Arn Anderson beat Gene Ligon
Ricky Morton beat Mark Fleming
Manny Fernandez beat Ron Rossi
Magnum TA & Dusty Rhodes beat Jim Jeffers & Mac Jeffers
The Midnight Express beat Tommy Lane & Mike Davis
Ric Flair beat Vernon Deaton by submission
Ricky Morton beat Tommy Lane
Magnum TA & Dusty Rhodes beat Mark Fleming & Golden Terror
Krusher Khrushchev & Nikita Koloff beat Jim Jeffers & George South
Ric Flair beat Rocky King by submission
Tully Blanchard beat Mac Jeffers
Ole & Arn Anderson beat Mike Davis & Vernon Deaton by submission
The Rock & Roll Express vs. Jim Jeffers & Mac Jeffers
Tully Blanchard vs. Vernon Deaton
Ivan & Nikita Koloff vs. Pat Tanaka & George South
The Barbarian & Abdullah The Butcher vs. Ricky Reeves & Stoney Burke
Ole & Arn Anderson vs. Denny Brown & Ron Rossi

12/13/85: Richmond, VA @ Coliseum
20-man bunkhouse battle royal including Tully Blanchard, Ole Anderson, Arn nderson, Ivan Koloff, Nikita Koloff, Krusher Khruschev, Abdullah The Butcher, he Barbarian, Golden Terror, Ric Flair, Magnum TA, Dusty Rhodes, Billy Jack, he Rock & Roll Express, Don Kernodle, Pez Whatley, Manny Fernandez, Tommy ane, Denny Brown &
Dusty Rhodes & Magnum TA beat Ric Flair & Arn Anderson in a Texas bullrope match
Ivan Koloff, Nikita Koloff & Krusher Khruschev beat The Rock & Roll Express & Manny Fernandez
Tully Blanchard vs. Billy Jack
Abdullah The Butcher vs. Pez Whatley
Tommy Lane vs. Don Kernodle

12/14/85: Atlanta, GA @ WTBS Studios (TV)
The Rock & Roll Express beat Gerald Finley & George South
Magnum TA beat Vernon Deaton
Ivan & Nikita Koloff & Khruschev beat Richard Dunn, Kent Glover & Bill Tabb
Thunderfoot beat Don Turner
Black Bart beat Bob Wayne
The Barbarian beat Pablo Crenshaw
Ronnie Garvin beat Randy Mulkey

12/14/85: Fayetteville, NC @ Cumberland County Civic Center
Dusty Rhodes, & Magnum TA vs. Ric Flair & Tully Blanchard

12/14/85: Conway, SC
The Midnight Express beat Jimmy Valiant & Sam Houston

12/15/85: Atlanta, GA @ WTBS Studios (TV)
Sam Houston beat Tony Zane
The Midnight Express beat Mark Cooper & Josh Stroud
Arn Anderson beat George South
Rocky King beat Mac Jeffers
Black Bart beat Jim Jeffers
Magnum TA beat Ole Anderson
Ronnie Garvin beat NWA World Champ Ric Flair by DQ
Italian Stallion beat Pablo Crenshaw
Tully Blanchard beat Kent Glover
Magnum TA beat Josh Stroud
Black Bart beat George South
Arn & Ole Anderson beat Vernon Deaton & Bill Mulkey
Tully Blanchard beat Tony Zane
The Midnight Express beat Paul Garner & Bill Tabb
Ronnie Garvin beat Mike Nichols

12/15/85: Roanoke, VA @ Civic Center
Brady Boone draw Mark Fleming
Krusher Khruschev beat Don Kernodle
Jimmy Valiant beat The Barbarian by DQ
Manny Fernandez beat Krusher Khruschev
Ivan & Nikita Koloff beat Ricky Morton & Ron Bass

12/15/85: Greensboro, NC @ Coliseum
Dusty Rhodes won a 20-man Bunkhouse Battle Royal
Ric Flair, Ole & Arn Anderson beat Dusty Rhodes, Magnum TA & Manny Fernandez(14:00) via pinfall
Ron Bass beat J.J. Dillon in a Texas bullrope match
Ricky Morton beat The Barbarian
Krusher Khrushchev beat Pez Whatley
Jimmy Valiant beat Bobby Eaton by DQ
Don Kernodle draw Dennis Condrey(20:00)
Ivan & Nikita Koloff beat Ben Alexander & Gene Ligon
Tully Blanchard vs. Mac Jeffers

Ole & Arn Anderson vs. Mike Davis & Vernon Deaton
Ricky Morton vs. Tommy Lane
Nikita Koloff & Krusher Khruschev vs. George South & ??
Dusty Rhodes & Magnum TA vs. Mark Fleming & Golden Terror
NWA World Champ Ric Flair beat Rocky King(2:09)
Ole Anderson vs. Bob Wayne
Nikita Koloff vs. Tony Zane
The Barbarian vs. Richard Dunn
Krusher Khruschev vs. Bill Mulkey
Tully Blanchard vs. Vernon Deaton
Sam Houston vs. Kent Glover
Ron Garvin & Manny Fernandez vs. Black Bart & Thunderfoot
The Rock & Roll Express vs. Larry Clarke & Randy Mulkey
Magnum TA vs. George South
Arn Anderson vs. Joshua Stroud
Ivan Koloff vs. Don Turner

December 16 to December 24
No wrestling

12/25/85: Charlotte, NC @ Coliseum
Dusty Rhodes & Magnum TA beat Ric Flair & Tully Blanchard

12/25/85: Greenville, SC @ Memorial Auditorium
Jimmy Valiant & Miss Atlanta Lively beat The Midnight Express in a steel cage match

12/25/85: Atlanta, GA @ Omni
NWA World Champ Ric Flair beat Dusty Rhodes
Magnum TA beat Tully Blanchard by DQ
The Rock & Roll Express beat Ole & Arn Anderson by DQ
Jimmy Valiant & Billy Graham beat Black Bart & The Barbarian
Ron Garvin beat James J. Dillon
Sam Houston draw Krusher Khruschev
Manny Fernandez beat Thunderfoot

12/26/85: Norfolk, VA @ Scope
Magnum TA beat Tully Blanchard
Jimmy Valiant & Miss Atlanta Lively beat The Midnight Express
Ron Bass beat James J. Dillon
Denny Brown beat Tommy Lane
Don Kernodle beat Thunderfoot
Black Bart beat Mark Fleming
Pez Whatley beat Golden Terror

12/27/85: Columbia, SC @ Township Auditorium
Ron Garvin & Don Kernodle vs. Ivan Koloff & Krusher Khruschev
Jimmy Valiant & Miss Atlanta Lively vs. The Midnight Express Atlanta treet fight
Pez Whatley vs. Golden Terror
Billy Graha vs. The Barbarian
Italian Stallion vs. Ricky Reeves
Stoney Burke vs. Tommy Lane

12/27/85: Richmond, VA @ Coliseum
Sam Houston beat Mike Davis
Thunderfoot beat Pat Tanaka(sub for Pez Whatley)
Ron Bass beat Black Bart in a Texas bullrope match
Manny Fernandez beat The Barbarian(sub for Abdullah The Butcher) in a Mexican death match
Tully Blanchard beat Magnum TA in an I quit match
The Rock & Roll Express beat Ole & Arn Anderson by DQ
NWA World Champ Ric Flair DCO with Dusty Rhodes

12/28/85: Greensboro, NC @ Coliseum (TV)
Tully Blanchard beat Denny Brown
NWA World Champ Ric Flair beat Mac Jeffers
Manny Fernandez beat Thunderfoot
Magnum TA beat Mike Davis
Black Bart beat Pat Tanaka
The Rock & Roll Express beat Gene Ligon & George South
Ron Bass beat Tommy Lane
The Rock & Roll Express vs. Ole & Arn Anderson
Dusty Rhodes & Magnum TA beat Tully Blanchard & Ric Flair in an elimination match

12/28/85: Philadelphia, PA @ Civic Center
Dusty Rhodes won battle royal
Magnum TA & Dusty Rhodes beat Ric Flair & Tully Blanchard
Jimmy Valiant beat The Barbarian by DQ
Ole & Arn Anderson beat Ron Garvin & Sam Houston
Manny Fernandez beat Thunderfoot
Black Bart beat Pez Whatley
Don Kernodle draw Dennis Condrey

12/29/85: Asheville, NC @ Civic Center
Jimmy Valiant & Miss Atlanta Lively beat The Midnight Express in a steel cage match

12/29/85: Savannah, GA @ Civic Center
Jimmy Valiant & Miss Atlanta Lively beat The Midnight Express in a street fight match

12/29/85: East Rutherford, NJ @ Meadowlands
Ron Bass beat James J. Dillon
Little Tokyo beat Cowboy Lang
Sherri Martel beat Debbie Combs
Carlos Colon beat The Barbarian
Jake Roberts beat Paul Ellering by DQ
The Rock & Roll Express beat Bill Irwin & Scott Irwin
Sgt. Slaughter beat Chris Markoff & Boris Zhukov in a handicap match
Magnum TA beat Tully Blanchard
NWA World Champ Ric Flair beat Dusty Rhodes by DQ
The Road Warriors beat Ivan Koloff & Krusher Khruschev
Stan Hansen beat Rick Martel by submission to win AWA World Title

12/30/85: Baltimore, MD @ Civic Center
Sherri Martel beat Debbie Combs
Ron Bass beat James J. Dillon
Arn & Ole Anderson beat Wahoo McDaniel & Baron Von Raschke

Billy Graham beat The Barbarian in an arm wrestling match
Billy Graham beat The Barbarian by DQ
The Road Warriors beat Michael Hayes & Buddy Roberts
Rick Martel beat Stan Hansen by DQ
NWA World Champ Ric Flair beat Ron Garvin

12/30/85: Fayetteville, NC @ Cumberland County Civic Center
The Rock & Roll Express beat The Midnight Express by DQ

Chapter 7: 1986

1/1/86: St. Louis, MO @ Arena
NWA World Champion Ric Flair vs. Harley Race
The Road Warriors & Dusty Rhodes vs. Ivan & Nikita Koloff & Krusher Khruschev
Magnum TA vs. Tully Blanchard
Jimmy Valiant vs. Mr. Pogo
Cowboy Lang vs. Little Tokyo
Hacksaw Higgins vs. Art Crews
Brett Sawyer vs. Tarzan Goto
Brad Battan & Bart Battan vs. Sheik Abdullah & Akio Sato

1/1/86: Atlanta, GA @ Omni
Dusty Rhodes & The Road Warriors beat Ric Flair, Ole & Arn Anderson by DQ
Magnum TA beat Tully Blanchard by DQ
The Midnight Express(Bobby Eaton & Dennis Condrey) beat The Rock & Roll Express(Ricky Morton & Robert Gibson)
Ronnie Garvin beat Black Bart
Ron Bass beat Thunderfoot
Manny Fernandez beat Tony Zane
Sam Houston beat Jim Jeffers

1/2/86: Harrisonburg, VA @ H.S.
Denny Brown beat Brady Boone
Italian Stallion beat Mark Fleming
Shaska Whatley beat Golden Terror
The Barbarian vs. Jimmy Valiant
Arn Anderson vs. Ronnie Garvin
The Rock & Roll Express vs. The Midnight Express

1/3/86: Fredericksburg, VA @ Stafford H.S.
The Midnight Express beat The Rock & Roll Express
Arn Anderson vs. Jimmy Valiant
The Barbarian vs. Ronnie Garvin
Pez Whatley vs. Mark Fleming
Brady Boone vs. Denny Brown
Italian Stallion vs. Golden Terror

1/4/86: Atlanta, GA @ WTBS Studios (TV)
The Rock & Roll Express beat Jim Jeffers & Thunderfoot
Harley Race beat Tony Zane
Ron Bass beat Bill Tabb
Ronnie Garvin beat Mac Jeffers
The Road Warriors beat Mark Hawk, Gene Ligon & Josh Stroud handicap match
Manny Fernandez beat Larry Clark
Arn Anderson beat Kent Glover
Jimmy Valiant beat Adrian Bivins
Dennis Condrey beat Rocky King
Magnum TA beat The Barbarian
Sam Houston & Nelson Royal beat Pablo Crenshaw & Don Turner

1/4/86: Greensboro, NC @ Coliseum
NWA World Champion Ric Flair NC with Dusty Rhodes
Harley Race beat Magnum TA
Road Warrior Hawk beat Ivan Koloff
Ricky Morton beat Dennis Condrey

NWA World Television Title Tournament
1st Round
Black Bart DCO with Road Warrior Animal
Arn Anderson beat Jimmy Valiant
Wahoo McDaniel beat The Barbarian
Tully Blanchard beat Ron Bass

2nd Round
Arn Anderson received a bye
Wahoo McDaniel beat Tully Blanchard

Finals
Arn Anderson beat Wahoo McDaniel to win NWA World Television Title in tournament final

1/5/86: Asheville, NC @ Civic Center
Don Kernodle beat Pat Tanaka
Ronnie Garvin beat Thunderfoot
Jimmy Valiant beat Gene Ligon
The Midnight Express beat The Rock & Roll Express
Magnum TA beat Arn Anderson by DQ
The Road Warriors beat The Barbarian & Ivan Koloff
NWA World Champion Ric Flair beat Manny Fernandez

1/5/86: Charlotte, NC @ Coliseum
Arn Anderson beat Don Kernodle
The Rock & Roll Express beat The Barbarian & Black Bart
Road Warrior Hawk beat Thunderfoot
Road Warrior Animal beat Ivan Koloff
Magnum TA beat Tully Blanchard
NWA World Champion Ric Flair NC with Dusty Rhodes

1/6/86: Iva, SC
Jimmy Valiant & Miss Atlanta Lively(aka Ronnie Garvin) beat The Midnight Express

1/6/86: Fayetteville, NC @ Cumberland County Civic Center (TV)
Ron Bass & Don Kernodle beat Mark Fleming & George South
Ivan Koloff beat Mac Jeffers
The Barbarian beat Stoney Burke
Ronnie Garvin beat Gene Ligon
Tully Blanchard beat Rocky King
Arn Anderson beat Tony Zane
The Rock & Roll Express beat Ron Rossi & Pat Tanaka
Sam Houston & Nelson Royal vs. Tommy Lane & Mike Davis
Ron Bass vs. James J. Dillon
The Rock & Roll Express vs. The Barbarian & Black Bart
Magnum TA vs. Tully Blanchard in a no DQ match
NWA World Champion Ric Flair beat Dusty Rhodes

1/7/86: Spartanburg, SC @ Memorial Auditorium (TV)
Magnum TA vs. Tully Blanchard in a Texas death match
Ron Bass & Don Kernodle beat George South & Mark Fleming
Ivan Koloff beat Mack Jeffers
The Barbarian beat Stoney Burke
Ronnie Garvin beat Gene Ligon
Tully Blanchard beat Rocky King
Arn Anderson beat Tony Zane
The Rock & Roll Express beat ?? & ??

1/8/86: Raleigh, NC @ Dorton Arena
Sam Houston & Nelson Royal beat Gene Ligon & Pat Tanaka
Ron Bass beat Black Bart
Ronnie Garvin beat Thunderfoot
Pez Whatley beat Golden Terror
Magnum TA NC with Arn Anderson
Rock & Roll Express beat The Midnight Express by DQ

1/9/86: Canton, OH @ Civic Center
Sam Houston beat Jim Lancaster
Ron Bass draw The Barbarian
Arn Anderson beat Ronnie Garvin
Magnum TA NC with Tully Blanchard
The Rock & Roll Express beat The Midnight Express
NWA World Champion Ric Flair beat Dusty Rhodes by DQ

1/10/86: Norfolk, VA @ Scope
Denny Brown beat Pat Tanaka
Italian Stallion beat Ron Rossi
Arn Anderson beat Manny Fernandez
Krusher Khruschev beat Sam Houston
Jimmy Valiant & Ronnie Garvin beat The Midnight Express & Jim Cornette in a handicap match
Magnum TA beat Tully Blanchard
NWA World Champion Ric Flair beat Dusty Rhodes

1/10/86: Cincinnati, OH @ Gardens
Jim Lancaster beat Pat Tanaka
Black Bart beat Larry Wilson
Don Kernodle beat Thunderfoot
Pez Whatley beat Al Snow
Ron Bass NC with The Barbarian
The Rock & Roll Express beat Ivan & Nikita Koloff in a cage match

1/11/86: Atlanta, GA @ WTBS Studios (TV)
Ivan & Nikita Koloff beat Italian Stallion & Rocky King
Tully Blanchard beat Mac Jeffers
The Barbarian beat Art Pritts
Magnum TA beat Thunderfoot
Pez Whatley beat George South
Rock & Roll Express beat Vernon Deaton & Randy Mulkey
Ronnie Garvin beat Paul Garner
The Midnight Express beat Bill Mulkey & Bill Tabb
Sam Houston beat Krusher Khruschev to win NWA Mid Atlantic Title
Arn Anderson beat Mac Jeffers

1/11/86: Columbus, GA @ Municipal Auditorium
Rock & Roll Express beat The Midnight Express by DQ

1/11/86: Charleston, WV @ Civic Center
The Road Warriors vs. Ivan & Nikita Koloff

1/12/86: Cleveland, OH @ Convocation Center
Denny Brown beat Pat Tanaka
Robert Gibson beat Black Bart
Manny Fernandez beat The Barbarian
The Midnight Express beat Sam Houston & Jimmy Valiant
NWA World Champion Ric Flair beat Dusty Rhodes DQ
Magnum TA beat Tully Blanchard

1/13/86: Greenwood, SC (TV)
Rock & Roll Express beat The Midnight Express by DQ
Pez Whatley beat Tony Zane
Magnum TA beat Vernon Deaton
Manny Fernandez beat The Golden Terror
Jimmy Valiant beat George South
Tully Blanchard beat Mark Fleming
Ron Bass & Don Kernodle beat Gene Ligon & Stoney Burke
The Midnight Express beat Pat Tanaka & Jim Jeffers

1/14/86: Greenville, SC @ Memorial Auditorium
Tully Blanchard beat Pez Whatley
Ivan & Nikita Koloff & The Barbarian beat Don Kernodle, Ron Bass & Jimmy Valiant
Magnum TA beat Black Bart
Midnight Express beat The Rock & Roll Express by DQ
NWA World Champion Ric Flair NC with Dusty Rhodes

1/15/86: Columbia, SC @ Township Auditorium
Ron Bass beat Thunderfoot
Tully Blanchard beat Jimmy Valiant
The Rock & Roll Express beat Ivan Koloff & Baron Von Raschke
Magnum TA battled Nikita Koloff to a DCO
NWA World Champion Ric Flair beat Dusty Rhodes DQ

1/17/86: Richmond, VA @ Coliseum
Ronnie Garvin draw The Barbarian
Ron Bass beat Black Bart in a taped fist match
Ivan & Nikita Koloff beat Don Kernodle & Manny Fernandez
Midnight Express beat The Rock & Roll Express by DQ
Magnum TA beat Arn Anderson
Jimmy Valiant beat Tully Blanchard by DQ
NWA World Champion Ric Flair beat Dusty Rhodes

1/18/86: Atlanta, GA @ WTBS Studios (TV)
Ronnie Garvin beat Pablo Crenshaw
Ivan Koloff beat Benny Trailer
Jimmy Valiant beat Golden Terror
Baron Von Raschke beat Tony Zane
Sam Houston beat Art Pritts
The Barbarian beat Ray Traylor
Magnum TA beat Lee Peek
The Rock & Roll Express beat Larry Clark & Jerry Garmen
The Midnight Express beat Bill Tabb & Larry Vickery

Tully Blanchard beat Gene Ligon
Nikita Koloff beat Mac Jeffers

1/18/86: Philadelphia, PA @ Civic Center
Don Kernodle beat Mark Fleming
Jimmy Valiant beat Ramblin' Wreck
The Midnight Express beat Ron Bass & Pez Whatley
Baron Von Raschke beat Italian Stallion
The Barbarian beat Sam Houston
NWA World Champion Ric Flair beat Dusty Rhodes by DQ in a 2/3 falls match
The Road Warriors beat Ivan & Nikita Koloff by DQ in a Texas tornado match
Magnum TA beat Tully Blanchard in a I quit match

1/18/86: York, SC @ Cougar Den
Mac Jeffers vs. Rocky King
Jim Jeffers vs. Ricky Reeves
Denny Brown vs. Tommy Lane
Mike Davis vs. Ronnie Garvin
Arn Anderson vs. Manny Fernandez
The Rock & Roll Express vs. Black Bart & Thunderfoot

1/19/86: Roanoke, VA @ Civic Center
Denny Brown beat Mike Davis
The Barbarian beat Rocky King
Midnight Express beat The Rock & Roll Express DQ

1/19/86: Asheville, NC @ Civic Center
Jim Jeffers vs. Nelson Royal
Black Bart & Thunderfoot vs. Ricky Reeves & Pez Whatley
Krusher Khruschev vs. Sam Houston
Ron Bass & Don Kernodle vs. Ivan & Nikita Koloff
Arn Anderson vs. Manny Fernandez
Tully Blanchard vs. Jimmy Valiant

1/19/86: Atlanta, GA @ Omni
Baron Von Raschke beat Sam Houston
Manny Fernandez beat Black Bart
Ron Bass draw The Barbarian
Midnight Express beat The Rock & Roll Express by DQ
Tully Blanchard beat Jimmy Valiant
Magnum TA NC with Nikita Koloff
NWA World Champion Ric Flair draw Ronnie Garvin
Dusty Rhodes beat Arn Anderson in a Texas death, cage match

1/20/86: Greenville, SC @ Memorial Auditorium
The Road Warriors beat Ivan & Nikita Koloff
Tully Blanchard beat Jimmy Valiant by DQ
Ronnie Garvin beat The Barbarian by DQ
Baron Von Raschke beat Rocky King
Manny Fernandez beat Thunderfoot
Denny Brown & Black Bart beat Pez Whatley & Stoney Burke

1/20/86: Fayetteville, NC @ Cumberland County Civic Center
Jim Jeffers vs. Don Kernodle
Midnight Express beat The Rock & Roll Express by DQ
Magnum TA vs. Arn Anderson
NWA World Champion Ric Flair vs. Dusty Rhodes in a match with 2 referees

1/21/86: Shelby, NC @ Recreation Center (TV)
Jimmy Valiant beat Vernon Deaton
Baron Von Raschke beat Pat Tanaka
Black Bart beat George South
The Barbarian beat Italian Stallion
Ronnie Garvin & Manny Fernandez beat Mack Jeffers & Jeff Jeffers
The Rock & Roll Express beat Tony Zane & Thunderfoot
Tully Blanchard & Arn Anderson beat Pez Whatley & Rocky King

1/22/86: Raleigh, NC @ Dorton Arena
Nelson Royal & Sam Houston beat Leo Burke & Pat Tanaka
Ronnie Garvin beat The Barbarian
Tully Blanchard beat Jimmy Valiant
Italian Stallion beat Thunderfoot
Manny Fernandez draw Arn Anderson
The Rock & Roll Express beat The Midnight Express

1/23/86: Cheraw, SC
The Midnight Express beat Pez Whatley & Ronnie Garvin

1/24/86: Johnson City, TN
The Rock & Roll Express beat The Midnight Express

1/24/86: Norfolk, VA @ Scope
Nelson Royal beat Mark Fleming
Black Bart beat Gene Ligon
Ron Bass & Don Kernodle beat Ivan Koloff & Baron Von Raschke by DQ
Sam Houston beat Thunderfoot
Arn Anderson beat Ronnie Garvin
Magnum TA beat Nikita Koloff by DQ
Tully Blanchard beat Jimmy Valiant

1/25/86: Atlanta, GA @ WTBS Studios (TV)
The Barbarian vs. George South
Ron Bass vs. Mike Simani
Ivan Koloff vs. Pat Tanaka
Manny Fernandez vs. Tony Zane
The Rock & Roll Express vs. Bob Owens & Thunderfoot
Nikita Koloff vs. Bob Brown
Jimmy Valiant vs. Paul Garner
Bobby Eaton vs. Wee Willie Wilkens
Ronnie Garvin vs. Mark Hawk
Black Bart vs. ??
Baron Von Raschke vs. ??
Arn Anderson & Tully Blanchard vs. Don Kernodle & Italian Stallion

1/25/86: Greensboro, NC @ Coliseum
NWA World Champion Ric Flair beat Dusty Rhodes
Jimmy Valiant beat Tully Blanchard
Magnum TA beat Arn Anderson
Don Kernodle & Ron Bass beat Ivan & Nikita Koloff
Sam Houston draw Black Bart
Nelson Royal beat Jim Jeffries

1/25/86: Columbus, GA @ Municipal Auditorium
The Rock & Roll Express beat The Midnight Express

1/26/86: Marietta, GA @ Cobb County Civic Center
The Rock & Roll Express beat The Midnight Express

1/27/86: Greenville, SC @ Memorial Auditorium
The Barbarian beat Sam Houston
Manny Fernandez draw Arn Anderson
Jimmy Valiant beat Tully Blanchard in a taped fist match
Rock & Roll Express beat The Midnight Express by DQ
Magnum TA beat Baron Von Raschke by DQ
The Road Warriors beat Ivan & Nikita Koloff
Dusty Rhodes beat NWA World Champion Ric Flair by DQ

1/28/86: Rock Hill, SC @ Winthrop Coliseum (TV)
The Road Warriors beat Ivan & Nikita Koloff
The Rock & Roll Express beat Mac Jeffers & Jim Jeffers
Baron Von Raschke beat Tony Zane
The Barbarian beat Gene Ligon
The Road Warriors beat Thunderfoot & Golden Terror
The Midnight Express beat Rocky King & Pez Whatley
The Road Warriors beat George South & Mike Simani
Ronnie Garvin beat Tony Zane
Jimmy Valiant beat Jim Jeffers
Arn Anderson beat Ricky King
Baron Von Raschke, Ivan & Nikita Koloff beat Sam Houston, Italian Stallion & Pat Tanaka
Don Kernodle beat The Barbarian by DQ
The Rock & Roll Express beat Black Bart & Thunderfoot by DQ
Magnum TA DDQ Ivan Koloff

1/29/86: Raleigh, NC @ Dorton Arena
Ron Bass draw The Barbarian
Ronnie Garvin beat Black Bart
Don Kernodle beat Thunderfoot
Jimmy Valiant beat Baron Von Raschke
The Rock & Roll Express beat The Midnight Express
The Road Warriors beat Ivan & Nikita Koloff
Magnum TA beat Tully Blanchard in a no DQ match

1/30/86: Washington, DC @ Armory
Pez Whatley beat Pat Tanaka
Don Kernodle beat Gene Ligon
Ron Bass beat Black Bart
Manny Fernandez draw Arn Anderson
The Rock & Roll Express beat The Midnight Express

1/31/86: Beckley, WV
Rocky King beat Mark Fleming
Sam Houston beat Thunderfoot
Ronnie Garvin beat The Barbarian
Tully Blanchard beat Italian Stallion
Magnum TA beat Baron Von Raschke by DQ
The Road Warriors beat Ivan & Nikita Koloff

1/31/86: Columbia, SC @ Township Auditorium
The Rock & Roll Express beat The Midnight Express

2/1/86: Atlanta, GA @ WTBS Studios (TV)
Ivan Koloff & Baron Von Raschke beat Randy Mulkey & Josh Stroud
Nikita Koloff beat Tony Zane
The Midnight Express beat Mike Jackson & Bob Owens
Arn Anderson & Ric Flair beat Italian Stallion & Don Kernodle

2/1/86: Philadelphia, PA @ Civic Center
Italian Stallion beat Jim Jeffers
Ronnie Garvin beat Thunderfoot
Baron Von Raschke beat Pez Whatley
Dusty Rhodes beat Tully Blanchard
Rock & Roll Express beat The Midnight Express by DQ
NWA World Champion Ric Flair draw Magnum TA
The Road Warriors beat Ivan & Nikita Koloff in a cage match

2/2/86: Hamilton, Ontario @ Copps Coliseum
Joey War Eagle beat Jet Starr by DQ
Angelo Mosca, Jr. & Vic Rossitani NC with Pat Kelly & Mike Kelly
Sgt. Slaughter beat Danny Johnson
Jimmy Valiant NC with Abdullah The Butcher
Farmer Pete beat Frenchy Lamont
The Road Warriors beat Nikita Koloff & Baron Von Raschke
NWA World Champion Ric Flair beat Dusty Rhodes

2/2/86: Charlotte, NC @ Coliseum
Misty Blue beat Linda Dallas
Ron Bass & Nelson Royal beat Mac Jeffers & Jim Jeffers
Don Kernodle beat Thunderfoot
Sam Houston beat Black Bart
Magnum TA beat The Barbarian
Arn Anderson beat Manny Fernandez
Jimmy Garvin draw Tully Blanchard
The Rock & Roll Express beat The Midnight Express

2/2/86: Atlanta, GA @ Omni
Ron Bass draw The Barbarian
Baron Von Raschke beat Italian Stallion
Jimmy Valiant beat Arn Anderson by DQ
The Midnight Express beat The Rock & Roll Express(16:27) to win NWA World Tag Title
The Road Warriors beat Ivan & Nikita Koloff(6:55) by DQ
Dusty Rhodes draw Tully Blanchard(20:00)
NWA World Champion Ric Flair beat Ronnie Garvin(14:33)

2/3/86: Greenville, SC @ Memorial Auditorium
The Rock & Roll Express draw The Midnight Express(60:00)

2/3/86: Saginaw, MI
Misty Blue beat Linda Dallas
Denny Brown beat Pat Tanaka
Baron Von Raschke beat Pez Whatley
Tully Blanchard beat Jimmy Valiant
The Road Warriors beat Ivan & Nikita Koloff

NWA World Champion Ric Flair draw Ronnie Garvin

2/4/86: Spartanburg, SC @ Memorial Auditorium (TV)
Arn Anderson vs. Manny Fernandez
The Rock & Roll Express vs. Black Bart & The Barbarian

2/6/86: Boone, NC
Rock & Roll Express beat The Midnight Express by DQ

2/6/86: Canton, OH @ Civic Center
Pez Whatley beat Thunderfoot
Denny Brown beat Pat Tanaka
Don Kernodle beat Jim Lancaster
Misty Blue beat Linda Dallas
Ronnie Garvin beat Baron Von Raschke by DQ
Tully Blanchard beat Jimmy Valiant
The Road Warriors beat Ivan & Nikita Koloff

2/7/86: Norfolk, VA @ Scope @ Scope
The Rock & Roll Express draw The Midnight Express(60:00)

2/8/86: Atlanta, GA @ WTBS Studios (TV)
The Barbarian beat Tony Zane
The Midnight Express beat Mike Simani & Don Turner
Ivan Koloff beat Bill Mulkey
Baron Von Raschke beat George South
Arn Anderson beat Randy Mulkey
Nikita Koloff beat Bill Tabb

2/8/86: St. Louis, MO @ Arena
Rocky Johnson beat Tim Flowers
Debbie Combs beat Despina Montages
Jerry Blackwell beat Kareem Muhammad
Nick Bockwinkel beat Larry Zbyszko by DQ
Rock & Roll Express beat The Midnight Express by DQ
Tully Blanchard beat Jimmy Valiant
Harley Race beat NWA World Champion Ric Flair in a cage match

2/9/86: Asheville, NC @ Civic Center
Mac Jeffers vs. Teijo Khan
Denny Brown vs. Jim Jeffers
Nelson Royal vs. Thunderfoot
Sam Houston vs. The Barbarian
Arn Anderson vs. Manny Fernandez
Tully Blanchard vs. Jimmy Valiant in a taped fist match
NWA World Champion Ric Flair vs. Ronnie Garvin

2/9/86: Cleveland, OH @ Convocation Center
Black Bart beat Jim Lancaster
Ivan & Nikita Koloff & Baron Von Raschke beat Don Kernodle, Pez Whatley & Ron Bass
Manny Fernandez beat Ivan Koloff
The Rock & Roll Express beat The Midnight Express
Tully Blanchard beat Jimmy Valiant in a taped fist, boxing match
NWA World Champion Ric Flair beat Ronnie Garvin

2/10/86: Taylorsville, NC
Rock & Roll Express beat The Midnight Express by DQ

2/11/86: Rock Hill, SC @ Winthrop Coliseum (TV)
The Midnight Express beat Pez Whatley & Sam Houston
Dusty Rhodes & Magnum TA beat The Midnight Express by DQ
Also included Ronnie Garvin, Manny Fernandez, Jimmy Valiant, The Barbarian, Baron Von Raschke, Tully Blanchard, Sam Houston, Nikita Koloff & James J. Dillon

2/12/86: Raleigh, NC @ Dorton Arena
Don Kernodle beat Teijo Khan
Sam Houston beat The Barbarian
Baron Von Raschke beat Ron Bass
Ronnie Garvin draw Arn Anderson
Jimmy Valiant beat Tully Blanchard
Magnum TA beat Nikita Koloff
Rock & Roll Express beat The Midnight Express by DQ

2/13/86: Columbia, SC @ Township Auditorium
Rock & Roll Express beat The Midnight Express by DQ
Manny Fernandez vs. Ivan Koloff
Pez Whatley vs. Baron Von Raschke
Nelson Royal & Sam Houston vs. Thunderfoot & Black Bart
Denny Brown vs. Mac Jeffers

2/14/86: Cincinnati, OH @ Gardens
Rock & Roll Express beat The Midnight Express by DQ

2/14/86: Albany, GA @ Civic Center
Jim Jeffers vs. Rocky King
Don Kernodle vs. Thunderfoot
Teijo Khan vs. Pez Whatley
Manny Fernandez & Ronnie Garvin vs. Ivan Koloff & Baron Von Raschke
Magnum TA vs. Nikita Koloff
Arn Anderson vs. Dusty Rhodes

2/15/86: Atlanta, GA @ WTBS Studios (TV)
The Midnight Express beat Ron Bass & Don Kernodle

2/15/86: Norfolk, VA @ Scope
Don Kernodle beat Thunderfoot
Ivan Koloff beat Sam Houston
The Barbarian beat Ron Rossi
Nelson Royal draw Denny Brown
Tully Blanchard beat Jimmy Valiant
Magnum TA beat Nikita Koloff in a lumberjack match

2/15/86: Greensboro, NC @ Coliseum
NWA World Champion Ric Flair draw Ronnie Garvin
Dusty Rhodes beat Arn Anderson
The Rock & Roll Express beat The Midnight Express
Manny Fernandez beat Baron Von Raschke
Pistol Pez Whatley beat Teijo Khan
Black Bart beat Pat Tanaka
Rocky King beat Tony Zane

2/16/86: Charleston, SC @ St. Andrews H.S.
The Midnight Express beat The Rock & Roll Express(60:00+)

2/17/86: Fayetteville, NC @ Cumberland County Civic Center (TV)
The Rock & Roll Express beat Dave Dillinger & Ben Alexander
Tully Blanchard beat George South
Baron Von Raschke beat Ron Rossi
The Barbarian & Teijo Khan beat Rocky King & Italian Stallion
Ronnie Garvin, Manny Fernandez & Ron Bass beat Tony Zane, Jim Jeffers & Mac Jeffers
The Midnight Express beat Sam Houston & Nelson Royal by DQ
Arn Anderson beat Rocky Kernodle

2/18/86: Greenville, SC @ Memorial Auditorium
The Rock & Roll Express beat The Midnight Express in a 2/3 falls match

2/19/86: King of Prussia, PA @ Valley Forge Convention Center
Tully Blanchard beat Pez Whatley
The Rock & Roll Express beat The Midnight Express
Ron Bass draw Black Bart
Pez Whatley beat Teijo Khan
Baron Von Raschke, Ivan Koloff & The Barbarian beat Ronnie Garvin, Manny Fernandez & Sam Houston
Jimmy Valiant beat Tully Blanchard
Magnum TA beat Nikita Koloff by DQ

2/20/86: Baltimore, MD @ Civic Center
Scott Hall beat Boris Zhukov
Tully Blanchard beat Jimmy Valiant
Nick Bockwinkel NC with Larry Zbyszko
Magnum TA beat Baron Von Raschke
The Midnight Express beat The Rock & Roll Express
Sgt. Slaughter beat Stan Hansen by DQ
NWA World Champion Ric Flair beat Dusty Rhodes DQ
The Road Warriors beat Ivan & Nikita Koloff in a cage match

2/21/86: Richmond, VA @ Coliseum
Pez Whatley beat Mark Fleming
Denny Brown beat Mac Jeffers
Ronnie Garvin beat Teijo Khan
Manny Fernandez beat Baron Von Raschke
Magnum TA draw Arn Anderson
The Midnight Express beat The Rock & Roll Express
The Road Warriors NC with Ivan & Nikita Koloff
NWA World Champion Ric Flair beat Dusty Rhodes DQ

2/22/86: Atlanta, GA @ WTBS Studios (TV)
The Road Warriors vs. Carl Styles & Bill Mulkey
Tully Blanchard vs. Mike Jackson
Baron Von Raschke vs. Rocky King
Teijo Khan vs. George South
Ronnie Garvin vs. Bob Owens
Arn Anderson vs. Denny Brown
The Barbarian vs. Kent Glover
Ivan Koloff vs. Brodie Chase
The Midnight Express vs. Mike Simani & Larry Clark
The Rock & Roll Express vs. Black Bart & Thunderfoot
Magnum TA vs. Bill Tabb

2/22/86: Roanoke, VA @ Civic Center
Manny Fernandez & Ronnie Garvin beat The Midnight Express by DQ

2/23/86: Atlanta, GA @ WTBS Studios (TV)

2/23/86: Charlotte, NC @ Coliseum
Denny Brown draw Gary Royal
Sam Houston beat Teijo Khan
Don Kernodle beat Baron Von Raschke
Tully Blanchard beat Jimmy Valiant
The Midnight Express beat The Rock & Roll Express
NWA World Champion Ric Flair beat Magnum TA
Dusty Rhodes beat Arn Anderson in a cage match

2/24/86: East Rutherford, NJ @ Meadowlands
The Barbarian & Mongolian Stomper beat Marty Jannetty & Buck Zumhofe
Jimmy Valiant beat Tully Blanchard by DQ
Scott Hall & Curt Hennig beat The Long Riders(Scott Irwin & Bill Irwin)
Larry Zbyszko beat Nick Bockwinkel by DQ
The Road Warriors & Dusty Rhodes beat Ivan & Nikita Koloff & Baron Von Raschke
NWA World Champion Ric Flair beat Magnum T.A
Rock & Roll Express beat The Midnight Express by DQ
Stan Hansen DCO with Sgt. Slaughter

2/25/86: Greenwood, SC (TV)
The Rock & Roll Express beat Gene Ligon & Pat Tanaka
Arn Anderson beat Tony Zane
Jimmy Garvin beat George South
Leo Burke beat Mark Fleming
Thunderfoot beat Mike Simani
Tully Blanchard beat Italian Stallion
The Midnight Express beat Pez Whatley & Rocky King

2/26/86: North Wilkesboro, NC
Rock & Roll Express beat The Midnight Express by DQ

2/27/86: Bennettsville, SC
The Rock & Roll Express beat The Midnight Express

2/28/86: Hampton, VA @ Coliseum
Pat Tanaka beat Golden Terror
Italian Stallion beat Mark Fleming
Teijo Khan beat Pez Whatley
Sam Houston beat Black Bart
The Barbarian beat Ron Bass
Tully Blanchard beat Jimmy Valiant
The Road Warriors NC with Ivan & Nikita Koloff

2/28/86: Columbia, SC @ Township Auditorium
Dusty Rhodes vs. Arn Anderson in a Texas death, cage match
NWA World Champion Ric Flair vs. Magnum TA
The Midnight Express beat The Rock & Roll Express in a 2/3 falls match

Manny Fernandez vs. Baron Von Raschke
Denny Brown vs. Gary Royal
Don Kernodle vs. Thunderfoot

3/1/86: Atlanta, GA @ WTBS Studios (TV)
Jimmy Valiant beat Bob Owens
Baron Von Raschke beat George South
Ivan Koloff beat Rocky King
The Barbarian beat Tony Zane
Magnum TA beat Randy Mulkey
Tully Blanchard beat Bill Tabb
The Midnight Express beat Paul Garner & Alan Martin
The Rock & Roll Express beat Bill Mulkey & Mike Simani
Ronnie Garvin draw Arn Anderson
NWA World Champion Ric Flair beat Brodie Chase

3/1/86: Greensboro, NC @ Coliseum
NWA World Champion Ric Flair NC with Ronnie Garvin
The Midnight Express beat the Rock & Roll Express
Dusty Rhodes & The Road Warriors beat Ivan & Nikita Koloff & Baron Von Raschke

3/2/86: Charlotte, NC @ Coliseum
Don Kernodle beat Thunderfoot
Nelson Royal draw Denny Brown
Manny Fernandez beat Baron Von Raschke
The Midnight Express beat The Rock & Roll Express in a 2/3 falls match
Dusty Rhodes beat Arn Anderson in a Texas death match
NWA World Champion Ric Flair beat Magnum TA

3/2/86: St. Louis, MO @ Arena
Sam Houston draw Don Kernodle
Baron Von Raschke beat Italian Stallion
Jimmy Garvin beat Sam Houston
Magnum TA beat Nikita Koloff by DQ
Rock & Roll Express beat The Midnight Express by DQ
Dusty Rhodes beat Arn Anderson Texas Death Match
NWA World Champion Ric Flair beat Ronnie Garvin

3/3/86: Canton, OH @ Civic Center
Teijo Khan beat Jim Lancaster
Denny Brown draw Nelson Royal
The Barbarian & Black Bart beat Ron Bass & Don Kernodle
Manny Fernandez beat Baron Von Raschke
The Road Warriors beat Ivan & Nikita Koloff in a double chain match

3/3/86: Greenville, SC @ Memorial Auditorium
The Midnight Express beat The Rock & Roll Express in a 2/3 falls match

3/4/86: Wheeling, WV @ Civic Center
Denny Brown draw Gary Royal
Black Bart & The Barbarian beat Ron Bass & Don Kernodle
Ronnie Garvin beat Teijo Khan
Manny Fernandez beat Baron Von Raschke
The Road Warriors beat Ivan & Nikita Koloff in a double chain match

3/4/86: Spartanburg, SC @ Memorial Auditorium (TV)
Magnum TA beat Golden Terror
Thunderfoot beat Rocky King
Jimmy Valiant beat George South
The Midnight Express beat Gene Ligon & Mike Simani
Tully Blanchard beat Dusty Rhodes to win NWA National Title
The Midnight Express beat Pez Whatley & Rocky King
The Midnight Express beat Italian Stallion & Don Kernodle

3/5/86: Raleigh, NC @ Dorton Arena
Ben Alexander beat George South
Thunderfoot beat Italian Stallion
Jimmy Garvin beat Sam Houston
Arn Anderson beat Pez Whatley
Tully Blanchard beat Jimmy Valiant in a lumberjack match
The Midnight Express beat The Rock & Roll Express

3/6/86: Lenoir, NC
Rocky King beat George South
Nelson Royal draw Denny Brown
The Barbarian beat Italian Stallion
Ivan & Nikita Koloff beat Nelson Royal & Rocky King
Dusty Rhodes beat Tully Blanchard

3/6/86: Columbus, GA @ Municipal Auditorium
Ronnie Garvin & Magnum TA beat The Midnight Express by DQ

3/7/86: Charleston, SC @ St. Andrews H.S.
Tully Blanchard vs. Jimmy Valiant taped fist match
Ivan Koloff & Baron Von Raschke vs. Don Kernodle & Manny Fernandez
Leo Burke vs. Italian Stallion
Ron Bass vs. Black Bart
Denny Brown vs. Nelson Royal

3/7/86: Norfolk, VA @ Scope
Teijo Khan beat Rocky Kernodle
Black Bart beat Pez Whatley
The Midnight Express beat The Rock & Roll Express
Jimmy Garvin beat Sam Houston
Magnum TA beat Nikita Koloff in a cage match
Dusty Rhodes beat Ivan Koloff in a cage match
NWA World Champion Ric Flair NC with Ronnie Garvin

3/8/86: Atlanta, GA @ WTBS Studios (TV)
Ronnie Garvin beat Tony Zane
The Barbarian beat Bill Tabb
Leo Burke beat George South
Pez Whatley beat Art Pritts
The Midnight Express beat Brodie Chase & Mike Simani
The Road Warriors beat Carl Styles & Bill Mulkey
The Rock & Roll Express beat Bob Owens & Larry Clarke
Jimmy Garvin beat Rocky King
Black Bart beat Dr. X
Baron Von Raschke beat Mike Jackson

3/8/86: Columbus, GA @ Municipal Auditorium
Teijo Khan vs. Pez Whatley
Ron Bass vs. Thunderfoot
Sam Houston vs. Black Bart
The Midnight Express vs. Ronnie Garvin & Magnum TA
Arn Anderson vs. Jimmy Valiant

3/8/86: Cincinnati, OH @ Gardens
The Midnight Express beat The Rock & Roll Express in a 2/3 falls match

3/9/86: Atlanta, GA @ Omni
Dusty Rhodes beat Arn Anderson by DQ
Magnum TA beat Nikita Koloff
The Rock & Roll Express beat The Midnight Express
NWA World Champion Ric Flair NC with Ronnie Garvin
Rocky King beat Tony Zane
Nelson Royal draw Denny Brown
Ivan Koloff beat Sam Houston
Baron Von Raschke beat Pez Whatley

3/9/86: Roanoke, VA @ Civic Center
Mark Fleming beat Gene Ligon
Baron Von Raschke beat Pez Whatley
Ivan Koloff beat Sam Houston
Magnum TA beat Nikita Koloff
The Midnight Express beat The Rock & Roll Express
NWA World Champion Ric Flair beat Dusty Rhodes by DQ

3/10/86: Greenville, SC @ Memorial Auditorium (TV)
The Midnight Express beat George South & Don Kernodle
The Midnight Express beat Dusty Rhodes & Magnum TA by DQ

3/10/86: Fayetteville, NC @ Cumberland County Civic Center
Leo Burke beat Italian Stallion
Nelson Royal draw Denny Brown
Sam Houston NC with Black Bart
Manny Fernandez beat Teijo Khan
The Rock & Roll Express beat The Barbarian & Baron Von Raschke
NWA World Champion Ric Flair beat Ronnie Garvin

3/14/86: Bassett, VA
The Rock & Roll Express beat The Midnight Express

3/15/85 Atlanta, GA @ WTBS Studios (TV)
Tully Blanchard beat Don Turner
Jimmy Valiant beat Bob Owens
Jimmy Garvin beat Bill Mulkey
The Midnight Express beat Phil Brown & Lee Peak
Arn Anderson beat Mike Jackson
Manny Fernandez beat Tony Zane
Ronnie Garvin beat Kent Glover
Black Bart beat Carl Styles

3/15/86: Charleston, WV @ Civic Center
Rocky King beat Golden Terror
Leo Burke beat Italian Stallion
Black Bart beat Don Kernodle
Ivan Koloff beat Pez Whatley
Manny Fernandez beat Nikita Koloff by DQ
The Midnight Express beat The Rock & Roll Express

3/16/86: Asheville, NC @ Civic Center
The Midnight Express beat The Rock & Roll Express in a cage match

3/16/86: Cleveland, OH @ Convocation Center
Sam Houston beat Gene Ligon
Jimmy Valiant beat Golden Terror
Arn Anderson beat Dusty Rhodes by DQ
Leo Burke beat Pez Whatley
Jimmy Garvin beat Denny Brown
Magnum TA beat Tully Blanchard
The Midnight Express beat The Rock & Roll Express
NWA World Champion Ric Flair NC with Ronnie Garvin
The Road Warriors beat Ivan & Nikita Koloff in a double chain match

3/17/86: Greenville, SC @ Memorial Auditorium
The Rock & Roll Express beat The Midnight Express in a cage match

3/18/86: Mooresville, NC (TV)
Black Bart beat Sam Houston to win NWA Mid Atlantic Title
The Midnight Express beat Don Kernodle & Rocky Kernodle
The Midnight Express beat Ron Bass & Manny Fernandez
Tully Blanchard beat George South
Jimmy Garvin beat Rocky King

3/19/86: Raleigh, NC @ Dorton Arena
Sam Houston draw Black Bart
Jimmy Garvin beat Italian Stallion
Manny Fernandez beat George South
The Barbarian beat Ron Bass
Ronnie Garvin beat Tully Blanchard by DQ
The Rock & Roll Express beat The Midnight Express

3/20/86: Harrisonburg, VA @ H.S.
Jimmy Valiant vs. Baron Von Raschke
The Barbarian vs. Manny Fernandez
Ronnie Garvin vs. Teijo Khan
George South vs. Don Kernodle
Leo Burke vs. Denny Brown
Rocky King vs. Pat Tanaka

3/20/86: Macon, GA @ Coliseum
The Rock & Roll Express beat The Midnight Express

3/21/86: Huntington, WV @ Memorial Fieldhouse
The Midnight Express beat The Rock & Roll Express in a 2/3 falls match

3/22/86: Atlanta, GA @ WTBS Studios (TV)
Jimmy Valiant beat Kent Glover
The Midnight Express beat Ray Traylor & Phil Brown
Don Graves beat Leo Burke by DQ

Jimmy Garvin beat Bill Mulkey
Wahoo McDaniel beat Bob Owens
Baron Von Raschke & Teijo Khan beat Italian Stallion & Tony Zane
Rock & Roll Express beat Larry Clarke & Paul Garner
Arn Anderson & Tully Blanchard beat Mike Simani & Ron Rossi
Magnum TA beat Dave Dillinger
Ivan Koloff beat Rocky Kernodle
Ronnie Garvin beat Brodie Chase

3/22/86: Philadelphia, PA @ Civic Center
NWA World Champion Ric Flair beat Ronnie Garvin
Dusty Rhodes beat Arn Anderson
Magnum TA beat Nikita Koloff by DQ
Midnight Express beat The Rock & Roll Express by DQ
?? beat Ron Bass
Jimmy Garvin beat Sam Houston
Pez Whatley draw Leo Burke

3/23/86: Greenville, SC @ Memorial Auditorium (TV)
The Midnight Express vs. Magnum TA & Manny Fernandez
Tully Blanchard vs. Ronnie Garvin
Magnum TA beat Bobby Eaton
including Dusty Rhodes, Arn Anderson, Sam Houston, Jimmy Garvin, Nikita Koloff, Jimmy Valiant, Ivan Koloff & others

3/23/86: Columbia, SC @ Township Auditorium
Arn Anderson vs. Dusty Rhodes
Midnight Express beat The Rock & Roll Express by DQ
Tully Blanchard vs. Magnum TA
Nikita Koloff vs. Ronnie Garvin
Jimmy Garvin vs. Sam Houston
Italian Stallion vs. Ivan Koloff

3/24/86: Fayetteville, NC @ Cumberland County Civic Center
Leo Burke beat Italian Stallion
Don Kernodle beat Teijo Khan
The Barbarian beat Rocky King
Ivan Koloff & Baron Von Raschke beat Nelson Royal & Sam Houston
Arn Anderson beat Jimmy Valiant
Magnum TA NC with Nikita Koloff

3/24/86: New Orleans, LA
The Midnight Express beat The Rock & Roll Express

3/25/86: Rock Hill, SC @ Winthrop Coliseum (TV)
The Rock & Roll Express beat The Midnight Express
Magnum TA beat Baron Von Raschke
Arn Anderson beat Jimmy Valiant
Tully Blanchard DCO with Ronnie Garvin

3/26/86: Raleigh, NC @ Dorton Arena
Denny Brown draw Leo Burke
The Barbarian beat Rocky King
Baron Von Raschke beat Sam Houston
Jimmy Garvin beat Rocky Kernodle
Arn Anderson beat Don Kernodle
Ronnie Garvin draw Tully Blanchard
Magnum TA & The Rock & Roll Express beat The Midnight Express & Jim Cornette elimination match

3/27/86: Norfolk, VA @ Scope
Denny Brown beat George South
Leo Burke beat Italian Stallion
Jimmy Garvin beat Rocky Kernodle
Arn Anderson beat Pez Whatley
Rock & Roll Express beat Barbarian & Teijo Khan DQ
Ronnie Garvin beat Tully Blanchard by DQ
The Midnight Express beat Magnum TA & Dusty Rhodes by DQ

3/28/86: Richmond, VA @ Coliseum
Don Kernodle draw Black Bart
Jimmy Garvin beat Rocky Kernodle
Jimmy Valiant beat Teijo Khan
The Rock & Roll Express beat The Midnight Express & Jim Cornette in a handicap, cage match
Magnum TA beat Baron Von Raschke
Dusty Rhodes & Wahoo McDaniel beat Arn Anderson & Tully Blanchard in a bullrope, strap match
Road Warriors beat Ivan & Nikita Koloff cage match

3/29/86: Atlanta, GA @ WTBS Studios (TV)
Wahoo McDaniel beat Ron Rossi
The Midnight Express beat Phil Brown & Wee Willie Wilkens
Jimmy Garvin beat Don Turner
Ivan Koloff beat Ray Traylor
Ronnie Garvin beat Tony Zane
Magnum TA beat Bob Owens
Tully Blanchard beat Bill Tabb
The Rock & Roll Express beat Art Pitts & Kent Glover
Arn Anderson beat Dave Dillinger
The Road Warriors beat Larry Clarke & Paul Garner

3/29/86: Greensboro, NC @ Coliseum
Nelson Royal beat George South
Don Kernodle beat Thunderfoot
Jimmy Garvin beat Italian Stallion
The Rock & Roll Express beat The Midnight Express
Magnum TA beat Nikita Koloff
Dusty Rhodes & Wahoo McDaniel beat Arn Anderson & Tully Blanchard
NWA World Champion Ric Flair beat Ronnie Garvin

3/30/86: Savannah, GA @ Civic Center
Midnight Express beat The Rock & Roll Express by DQ

3/30/86: Atlanta, GA @ Omni
Hector Guerrero beat Thunderfoot
Jimmy Garvin beat Rocky Kernodle
Leo Burke beat Italian Stallion
The Rock & Roll Express & Nighthawk beat The Midnight Express & Jim Cornette
Magnum TA beat Nikita Koloff in a lumberjack match
Dusty Rhodes & Wahoo McDaniel beat Arn Anderson & Tully Blanchard in a chain, strap match
NWA World Champion Ric Flair beat Ronnie Garvin in a cage match

3/31/86: Baltimore, MD @ Civic Center
Mike Kahlua beat Tom Bradley
Jimmy Valiant beat Jimmy Garvin by DQ
Magnum TA draw Tully Blanchard
Midnight Express beat The Rock & Roll Express DQ
Paul Ellering & Animal beat Ivan & Nikita Koloff DQ
NWA World Champion Ric Flair beat Dusty Rhodes DQ

4/1/86: Spartanburg, SC @ Memorial Auditorium (TV)
NWA World Champion Ric Flair vs. Magnum TA

4/1/86: Canton, OH @ Civic Center
Don Kernodle draw Leo Burke
Thunderfoot beat Rocky Kernodle
Don Kernodle beat Teijo Khan
Black Bart beat Sam Houston
Jimmy Valiant beat The Barbarian bunkhouse match
Rock & Roll Express beat The Midnight Express by DQ

4/2/86: California, PA @ Harner Hall
Don Kernodle draw Leo Burke
Thunderfoot beat Rocky Kernodle
Don Kernodle beat Teijo Khan
Black Bart beat Sam Houston
The Barbarian beat Jimmy Valiant
Rock & Roll Express beat The Midnight Express by DQ in a 2/3 falls match

4/4/86: Roanoke, VA @ Civic Center
Denny Brown beat Thunderfoot
Jimmy Garvin beat Italian Stallion
Black Bart beat Sam Houston
Wahoo McDaniel beat Tully Blanchard by DQ
Magnum TA beat Nikita Koloff
The Midnight Express beat The Rock & Roll Express
NWA World Champion Ric Flair beat Dusty Rhodes DQ

4/5/86: Charleston, WV @ Civic Center
Thunderfoot beat Italian Stallion
Pez Whatley beat Nelson Royal
Sam Houston NC with Black Bart
Nighthawk beat Teijo Khan
The Barbarian beat Don Kernodle
The Rock & Roll Express beat The Midnight Express & Jim Cornette in a handicap, cage match

4/5/86: Atlanta, GA @ WTBS Studios (TV)
Wahoo McDaniel beat Ray Traylor
Nighthawk Coltrane beat Tony Zane
Manny Fernandez beat Bob Owens
Ivan Koloff beat Gene Ligon
Hector Guerrero beat Carl Styles
Baron Von Raschke, The Barbarian & Pez Whatley beat Rocky Kernodle, Brodie hase & Bill Tabb
The Rock & Roll Express beat Larry Clarke & Art Pitts
Magnum TA beat Randy Mulkey
Ronnie Garvin beat Arn Anderson by DQ
The Midnight Express beat Mike Simani & Denny Brown
The Rock & Roll Express beat Gene Ligon & Tony Zane
Ivan Koloff beat Carl Styles
Denny Brown beat Art Pritts
The Barbarian & Shaska Whatley beat Randy Mulkey & Mike Simani
Arn Anderson beat Rocky Kernodle
Jimmy Garvin beat Bob Owens
The Midnight Express beat Larry Clark & Paul Garner

4/6/86: Johnson City, TN
The Rock & Roll Express beat The Midnight Express

4/6/86: Savannah, GA @ Civic Center
The Rock & Roll Express beat The Midnight Express

4/7/86: Fayetteville, NC @ Cumberland County Civic Center
Nighthawk beat Teijo Khan
Pez Whatley beat Italian Stallion
The Barbarian beat Don Kernodle
Manny Fernandez draw Arn Anderson
Wahoo McDaniel beat Jimmy Garvin
The Road Warriors & Magnum TA beat Ivan & Nikita Koloff & Baron Von Raschke

4/7/86: Gaffney, SC
The Rock & Roll Express beat The Midnight Express

4/8/86: Spartanburg, SC @ Memorial Auditorium
The Midnight Express vs. The Rock & Roll Express
Magnum TA vs. Nikita Koloff
Tully Blanchard & Ric Flair vs. Dusty Rhodes & Wahoo McDaniel in a Texas bullrope & Indian strap match

4/8/86: Greenwood, SC (TV)
Sam Houston beat Dave Dillinger
Mid Atlantic Champ Black Bart beat Gene Ligon
Jimmy Garvin beat Rocky Kernodle
Baron Von Raschke & The Barbarian beat Gary Royal & Italian Stallion
Tully Blanchard & Arm Anderson beat George South & Denny Brown
The Midnight Express beat Mike Simani & Ron Rossi

4/9/86: Raleigh, NC @ Dorton Arena
Hector Guerrero beat Thunderfoot
Pez Whatley beat Sam Houston
Jimmy Garvin beat Denny Brown
Misty Blue beat Kat Laroux
The Rock & Roll Express beat The Barbarian & Baron Von Raschke
Wahoo McDaniel draw Arn Anderson
Magnum TA & Manny Fernandez beat The Midnight Express by DQ

4/9/86: ??
Don Kernodle vs. Teijo Khan
Black Bart beat Sam Houston

4/10/86: Hendersonville, NC
Dusty Rhodes vs. Arn Anderson
Magnum TA vs. Baron Von Raschke
Wahoo McDaniel vs. Jimmy Garvin
Ronnie Garvin vs. Teijo Khan
Linda Dallas vs. Misty Blue
Hector Guerrero vs. Thunderfoot

4/10/86: Kershaw, SC
The Rock & Roll Express beat The Midnight Express

4/11/86: Mount Airy, NC @ North Surry H.S.
The Midnight Express vs. Ronnie Garvin & Manny Fernandez
Denny Brown vs. Nelson Royal
Black Bart vs. Sam Houston
Don Kernodle vs. Leo Burke
Italian Stallion vs. Pistol Pez Whatley

4/11/86: Hampton, VA @ Coliseum
The Rock & Roll Express beat Ivan Koloff & Baron Von Raschke
Magnum TA beat Nikita Koloff
Misty Blue beat Linda Dallas
Arn Anderson beat Hector Guerrero
Wahoo McDaniel beat Tully Blanchard COR
NWA World Champion Ric Flair beat Dusty Rhodes DQ

4/12/86: Atlanta, GA @ WTBS Studios (TV)
Manny Fernandez & Hector Guerrero beat George South & Tony Zane
Black Bart beat Gene Ligon
Ivan & Nikita Koloff & Baron Von Raschke beat Italian Stallion, Nelson Royal & Denny Brown
Wahoo McDaniel beat Ron Rossi
Jimmy Garvin beat Rocky Kernodle
Arn Anderson beat Sam Houston
The Barbarian & Shaska Whatley beat Vernon Deaton & Randy Mulkey
The Rock & Roll Express vs. Ray Traylor & Carl Styles but Ric Flair arrived & challenged Ricky Morton to an impromptu match
Ricky Morton beat NWA World Champion Ric Flair after Gibson made the three count
The Midnight Express beat Paul Garner & Bob Owens
Black Bart beat George South
The Road Warriors beat Mark Fleming & Gene Ligon
Ricky Morton beat Tony Zane
Nighthawk Coltrane beat Vernon Deaton
The Barbarian beat Rocky King
Manny Fernandez & Hector Guerrero beat Golden Terror & Thunderfoot
Midnight Express beat Rocky Kernodle & Ron Rossi
Thunderfoot beat Larry Clark
Leo Burke beat Paul Garner
Ronnie Garvin beat Kent Glover
The Midnight Express beat Randy Mulkey & Lee Peek
Jimmy Garvin beat Bill Tabb
Shaska Whatley beat Ray Traylor

4/12/86: Charlotte, NC @ Coliseum
The Rock & Roll Express beat The Midnight Express

4/13/86: Atlanta, GA @ WTBS Studios (TV)
The Road Warriors vs. Bill Tabb & Ray Traylor
Nighthawk vs. Gene Ligon
Magnum TA vs. Paul Garner
Jimmy Garvin vs. George South
Ivan Koloff vs. Tony Zane
Arn Anderson vs. Manny Fernandez
The Midnight Express vs. Art Pritts & Bob Pearson

4/13/86: Atlanta, GA @ Omni
Nighthawk beat Teijo Khan
Manny Fernandez draw Arn Anderson
Jimmy Garvin beat Jimmy Valiant
Wahoo McDaniel, Dusty Rhodes & Magnum TA beat Ivan & Nikita Koloff & Baron Von Raschke by DQ
Tully Blanchard beat Ronnie Garvin
The Road Warriors beat Midnight Express by DQ
NWA World Champion Ric Flair draw Ricky Morton

4/14/86: Forest City, NC @ Chase H.S.
Gene Ligon beat Vernon Deaton
Rocky King beat George South
Manny Fernandez beat Leo Burke
Manny Fernandez beat Thunderfoot
The Rock & Roll Express beat The Midnight Express

4/14/86: Saginaw, MI
Rock & Roll Express beat The Midnight Express DQ

4/15/86: Lansing, MI
The Midnight Express beat Ricky Morton & Don Kernodle(sub for Robert Gibson)

4/15/86: Rock Hill, SC @ Winthrop Coliseum (TV)
Nikita Koloff DDQ Wahoo McDaniel
Leo Burke beat Ron Rossi
Sam Houston & Nelson Royal beat Gene Ligon & George South
Wahoo McDaniel & Manny Fernandez beat Ivan Koloff & Baron Von Raschke
Jimmy Valiant beat Vernon Deaton
Jimmy Garvin beat Mark Fleming
Pez Whatley beat George South
Baron Von Raschke beat Gene Ligon by submission
Manny Fernandez & Hector Guerrero beat Vernon Deaton & Tony Zane
Ivan Koloff beat Rocky Kernodle
Wahoo McDaniel beat Thunderfoot
Pez Whatley & Baron Von Raschke beat Denny Brown & Rocky Kernodle
Jimmy Garvin beat Tony Zane
Nighthawk beat Ron Rossi
Manny Fernandez, Hector Guerrero & Wahoo McDaniel beat Black Bart, Leo Burke & Thunderfoot

4/16/86: Raleigh, NC @ Dorton Arena
Ronnie Garvin beat Leo Burke
Hector Guerrero beat Black Bart by DQ
Magnum TA & Manny Fernandez draw The Midnight Express
Jimmy Garvin beat Wahoo McDaniel
The Rock & Roll Express & Jimmy Valiant beat Ivan & Nikita Koloff & Baron Von Raschke

4/17/86: Norfolk, VA @ Scope
Hector Guerrero beat Mark Fleming
Pez Whatley beat Italian Stallion
Manny Fernandez beat Tully Blanchard by DQ
Jimmy Garvin beat Wahoo McDaniel
Nikita Koloff beat Magnum TA Russian Chain match
Ric Flair beat Ronnie Garvin in a no DQ match

4/17/86: Bessemer City, NC
The Rock & Roll Express beat The Midnight Express

4/18/86: Philadelphia, PA @ Civic Center
The Rock & Roll Express beat The Midnight Express

4/19/86: Atlanta, GA @ WTBS Studios (TV)
The Road Warriors beat Ray Traylor & Bill Tabb
Nighthawk beat Gene Ligon
Wahoo McDaniel beat Vernon Deaton
Magnum TA beat Paul Garner
Jimmy Garvin beat George South
Ivan Koloff beat Tony Zane
Arn Anderson draw Manny Fernandez
The Midnight Express beat Art Pitts & Bob Pearson
Ronnie Garvin beat Brodie Chase

4/19/86: New Orleans, LA @ Superdome
Crockett Cup Tournament
1st Round
Wahoo McDaniel & Mark Youngblood beat Bobby Jaggers & Mike Miller (7:35)
Nelson Royal & Sam Houston beat Bart & Brad Battan
Jimmy Valiant & Manny Fernandez beat Baron Von Raschke & The Barbarian
Terry Taylor & Steve Williams beat Bill Dundee & Buddy Landell
The Sheepherders (Williams & Miller) beat Hector & Chavo Guerrero
Bobby Fulton & Tommy Rogers beat Stan Lane & Steve Keirn
Buzz Sawyer & Rick Steiner beat Koko Ware & Italian Stallion
Black Bart & Jimmy Garvin beat Brett Wayne & Dave Peterson

2nd Round
Road Warriors beat Wahoo McDaniel & Mark Youngblood
Midnight Express beat Sam Houston & Nelson Royal
Bobby Fulton & Tommy Rogers beat Arn Anderson & Tully Blanchard
Sheepherders beat The Rock & Roll Express by forfeit
Ivan & Nikita Koloff beat Jimmy Valiant & Manny Fernandez
Steve Williams & Terry Taylor beat Rick Martel & Dino Bravo
Magnum TA & Ronnie Garvin beat Buzz Sawyer & Rick Steiner
The Giant Baba & Tiger Mask beat Jimmy Garvin & Black Bart
Jim Duggan beat Dick Slater

3rd Round
The Road Warriors beat The Midnight Express
Bobby Fulton & Tommy Rogers DDQ The Sheepherders
Steve Williams & Terry Taylor draw Ivan & Nikita Koloff
Magnum TA & Ronnie Garvin beat the Giant Baba & Tiger Mask

NWA World Champion Ric Flair beat Dusty Rhodes DQ

Finals
The Road Warriors beat Magnum TA & Ronnie Garvin(9:49) to win Crocket Cup in tournament final

4/20/86: Greensboro, NC @ Coliseum
Hector Guerrero beat Italian Stallion
Black Bart beat Sam Houston
Ronnie Garvin beat Ivan Koloff
Baron Von Raschke beat Nighthawk
Jimmy Valiant beat Pez Whatley
Dusty Rhodes & The Rock & Roll Express beat Ric Flair, Tully Blanchard & Arn Anderson in an elimination match
Nikita Koloff beat Magnum TA in a Russian chain match

4/20/86: Savannah, GA @ Civic Center
Manny Fernandez & Rock & Roll Express beat Midnight Express & Jim Cornette

4/21/86: Fayetteville, NC @ Cumberland County Civic Center
Italian Stallion beat Mark Fleming
Thunderfoot beat Denny Brown
Black Bart beat Sam Houston
Manny Fernandez & Jimmy Valiant beat Pez Whatley & Baron Von Raschke
Nikita Koloff beat Magnum TA
NWA World Champion Ric Flair NC with Ricky Morton

4/21/86: Greenville, SC @ Memorial Auditorium (TV)

4/24/86: Columbia, SC @ Township Auditorium
Ronnie Garvin & The Rock & Roll Express beat Midnight Express & Jim Cornette
Jimmy Valiant & Nighthawk vs. Baron Von Raschke & Pez Whatley
Manny Fernandez vs. Nikita Koloff
Don Kernodle vs. Ivan Koloff
Rocky Kernodle vs. Tony Zane
Gene Ligon vs. Sam Houston

4/24/86: Harrisonburg, VA @ H.S.
Black Bart vs. Sam Houston
Don Kernodle vs. Teijo Khan
The Barbarian & Baron Von Raschke vs. Manny Fernandez & Hector Guerrero
Jimmy Valiant vs. Shaska Whatley
Tully Blanchard vs. Ronnie Garvin

4/25/86: Richmond, VA @ Coliseum
NWA World Champion Ric Flair DCO with Ricky Morton
Nikita Koloff beat Magnum TA
The Midnight Express beat The Road Warriors by DQ
Dusty Rhodes beat Tully Blanchard in a Texas death match
Wahoo McDaniel beat Arn Anderson
Jimmy Valiant beat Pez Whatley by DQ
Jimmy Garvin draw Robert Gibson
Hector Guerrero beat Black Bart

4/26/86: Atlanta, GA @ WTBS Studios (TV)
Jimmy Valiant beat Kent Glover
Manny Fernandez beat Art Pritts
Ronnie Garvin beat Paul Garner
The Road Warriors beat Randy Mulkey & Jeff Smith
Baron Von Raschke & Shaska Whatley beat Bill Tabb & Lee Peek
Wahoo McDaniel beat Jim Dawson
The Rock & Roll Express beat Ron Rossi & Bob Owens
The Midnight Express beat Rocky King & George South
Tully Blanchard beat Mike Simani
Arn Anderson beat Gene Ligon
Jimmy Garvin beat Lee Peek
Ivan & Nikita Koloff beat Jerry Garmen & Bob Owens
Manny Fernandez & Jimmy Valiant beat Larry Clark & Kent Glover
The Midnight Express beat Paul Garner & Art Pritts
Wahoo McDaniel beat Jeff Smith

4/26/86: Baltimore, MD @ Civic Center
The Road Warriors beat Ivan & Nikita Koloff in a Russian chain match
The Midnight Express beat Manny Fernandez & Hector Guerrero

4/26/86: Charlotte, NC @ Coliseum

4/27/86: Cleveland, OH @ Convocation Center
Teijo Khan beat Italian Stallion
Jimmy Valiant beat Pez Whatley by DQ
Black Bart beat Sam Houston
Magnum TA beat Baron Von Raschke
Dusty Rhodes & Wahoo McDaniel beat Arn Anderson & Tully Blanchard in a bullrope, Indian strap match
The Midnight Express beat The Road Warriors by DQ
NWA World Champion Ric Flair beat Ronnie Garvin

4/27/86: St. Louis, MO @ Arena
Manny Fernandez beat The Barbarian by DQ
Dusty Rhodes beat Thunderfoot
Tully Blanchard draw Ronnie Garvin
Magnum TA & The Road Warriors beat Ivan & Nikita Koloff & Baron Von Raschke
NWA World Champion Ric Flair beat Wahoo McDaniel

4/28/86: East Rutherford, NJ @ Meadowlands
Col. DeBeers beat Davey Gee
Mike Rotundo beat Doug Somers
Bruiser Brody beat Steve Olsonowski
Magnum TA beat Baron Von Raschke
Curt Hennig & Scott Hall beat The Barbarian & Boris Zhukov
Nick Bockwinkel beat Larry Zbyszko in a Texas death match
Tully Blanchard beat Ronnie Garvin by DQ
Stan Hansen beat Leon White
Dusty Rhodes beat Arn Anderson in a steel cage match
The Road Warriors beat Ivan & Nikita Koloff in a steel cage match

4/28/86: Greenville, SC @ Memorial Auditorium
Teijo Khan beat Rocky Kernodle
Todd Champion beat Golden Terror
Sam Houston beat Black Bart
Denny Brown draw Hector Guerrero
Sam Houston & Jimmy Valiant beat The Barbarian & Shaska Whatley
Wahoo McDaniel beat Jimmy Garvin by DQ

4/28/86: Forest City, NC
The Rock & Roll Express beat The Midnight Express

4/29/86: Macon, GA @ Coliseum
The Rock & Roll Express beat The Midnight Express

4/30/86: Raleigh, NC @ Dorton Arena
Baron Von Raschke beat Sam Houston
Arn Anderson beat Ronnie Garvin
Robert Gibson beat Bobby Eaton
Jimmy Valiant beat Pez Whatley
Nikita Koloff beat Magnum TA in a Russian chain match
Dusty Rhodes & Manny Fernandez beat Tully Blanchard & Jimmy Garvin
NWA World Champion Ric Flair beat Ricky Morton

5/1/86: Harrisonburg, VA @ H.S.
Tully Blanchard vs. Ronnie Garvin
Jimmy Valiant vs. Pez Whatley
The Barbarian & Baron Von Raschke vs. Manny Fernandez & Hector Guerrero
Teijo Khan vs. Don Kernodle
Sam Houston vs. Black Bart
Leo Burke vs. Denny Brown

5/1/86: Columbia, SC @ Township Auditorium
NWA World Champion Ric Flair vs. Ricky Morton
The Midnight Express beat Dusty Rhodes & Magnum TA by DQ
Jimmy Garvin vs. Robert Gibson
Arn Anderson vs. Wahoo McDaniel
Nikita Koloff vs. Nighthawk
Thunderfoot vs. Rocky Kernodle

5/2/86: Norfolk, VA @ Scope
Don Kernodle beat Mark Fleming
Leo Burke beat Denny Brown
Dusty Rhodes & Magnum TA beat Ivan & Nikita Koloff
Robert Gibson beat Tully Blanchard by DQ
Arn Anderson beat Ronnie Garvin
NWA World Champion Ric Flair draw Ricky Morton

5/3/86: Atlanta, GA @ WTBS Studios (TV)
The Barbarian, Pez Whatley & Baron Von Raschke vs. Lee Peek, Rocky King & Bill Mulkey
Frank & Jesse James(Dusty Rhodes & Magnum TA under masks) beat The Midnight Express(7:41)
Ronnie Garvin vs. David Dillinger
NWA World Champion Ric Flair vs. Tony Zane
Wahoo McDaniel vs. Bob Owens
Arn Anderson vs. Randy Mulkey
Ivan & Nikita Koloff vs. Mike Simani & Brodie Chase

5/3/86: Charleston, SC @ County Hall
Leo Burke beat Rocky Kernodle
Teijo Khan beat Denny Brown
Sam Houston beat Black Bart in a Texas death match
Jimmy Valiant beat Pez Whatley by DQ
The Barbarian & Baron Von Raschke beat Manny Fernandez & Hector Guerrero
Wahoo McDaniel NC with Jimmy Garvin

5/3/86: Greensboro, NC @ Coliseum
Nelson Royal beat Thunderfoot
Ivan Koloff beat Don Kernodle
Nikita Koloff beat Italian Stallion
Arn Anderson beat Nighthawk
Robert Gibson draw Tully Blanchard
The Midnight Express beat Dusty Rhodes & Magnum TA
NWA World Champion Ric Flair draw Ricky Morton

5/4/86: Asheville, NC @ Civic Center
The Midnight Express beat The Road Warriors by DQ

5/4/86: Philadelphia, PA @ Civic Center
Robert Gibson beat Thunderfoot
Black Bart beat Italian Stallion
Dusty Rhodes & Magnum TA NC with The Midnight Express
Ivan & Nikita Koloff & Baron Von Raschke beat Road Warriors & Paul Ellering
NWA World Champion Ric Flair NC with Ricky Morton
Wahoo McDaniel draw Arn Anderson
Ronnie Garvin beat Tully Blanchard by DQ

5/5/86: Fayetteville, NC @ Cumberland County Civic Center
Italian Stallion draw Thunderfoot
The Barbarian & Teijo Khan beat Nelson Royal & Sam Houston
Jimmy Garvin beat Hector Guerrero
Jimmy Valiant beat Pez Whatley
Tully Blanchard beat Ronnie Garvin
The Midnight Express beat Dusty Rhodes & Magnum TA

5/6/86: Spartanburg, SC @ Memorial Auditorium (TV)
The Road Warriors vs. The Midnight Express
Tully Blanchard beat Gene Ligon
Nikita Koloff beat Italian Stallion
Baron Von Raschke & Shaska Whatley beat Denny Brown & Rocky King
The Road Warriors beat George South & Thunderfoot
Ivan Koloff beat Randy Mulkey
The Rock & Roll Express beat David Dillinger & Don Kernodle
Sam Houston & Nelson Royal NC with Midnight Express
Wahoo McDaniel beat Thunderfoot

5/7/86: Wheeling, WV @ Civic Center
Nelson Royal beat Jim Lancaster
Sam Houston beat Al Snow
Manny Fernandez & Hector Guerrero beat Baron Von Raschke & Thunderfoot
Jimmy Valiant beat Pez Whatley by DQ
Ronnie Garvin beat Tully Blanchard by DQ
Nikita Koloff beat Magnum TA in a Russian chain match

5/7/86: Ronda, NC
The Rock & Roll Express beat The Midnight Express

5/8/86: Kannapolis, NC @ Northwest Cabarrus H.S.
Denny Brown beat Rocky King
Golden Terror vs. George South
Ivan & Nikita Koloff vs. The Rock & Roll Express
Arn Anderson vs. Dusty Rhodes

5/8/86: Whitmire, SC
The Midnight Express beat Rocky Kernodle & Italian Stallion

5/9/86: Richmond, VA @ Coliseum
Black Bart beat Todd Champion
Jimmy Garvin beat Denny Brown
Manny Fernandez & Ronnie Garvin draw Ivan & Nikita Koloff
Arn Anderson beat Wahoo McDaniel
Robert Gibson beat Tully Blanchard by DQ
The Midnight Express beat Dusty Rhodes & Magnum TA by DQ
Jimmy Valiant beat Pez Whatley by DQ
NWA World Champion Ric Flair beat Ricky Morton

5/10/86: Atlanta, GA @ WTBS Studios (TV)
Ronnie Garvin beat Maurice Cooper
Robert Gibson beat Dave Dillinger
Nikita Koloff beat Tony Zane
Tully Blanchard beat Rocky King
The Midnight Express beat Randy Mulkey & Bill Mulkey
Ric Flair & Arn Anderson beat Carl Styles & Bob Owens
Jimmy Valiant & Manny Fernandez beat Larry Clarke & Paul Garner
Baron Von Raschke, Shaska Whatley & The Barbarian beat Art Pritts, Kent lover & Butch Brannigan
Jimmy Garvin beat Jim Dawson

5/10/86: Charlotte, NC @ Coliseum
The Midnight Express beat Dusty Rhodes & Magnum TA by DQ

5/11/86: Atlanta, GA @ Omni
Pez Whatley beat Sam Houston
Wahoo McDaniel beat Jimmy Garvin by CO
Robert Gibson draw Arn Anderson
Ronnie Garvin beat Tully Blanchard in a taped fist match
Ivan & Nikita Koloff & Baron Von Raschke beat The Road Warriors & Paul Ellering
The Midnight Express beat Magnum TA & Dusty Rhodes by DQ
Ricky Morton beat NWA World Champion Ric Flair DQ

5/12/86: Greenville, SC @ Memorial Auditorium
Thunderfoot beat Rocky Kernodle
Black Bart draw Don Kernodle
Ronnie Garvin beat Ivan Koloff
Wahoo McDaniel beat Jimmy Garvin by DQ
Tully Blanchard & Arn Anderson NC with The Rock & Roll Express
Nikita Koloff beat Magnum TA Russian chain match

5/12/86: Oakwood, VA
The Midnight Express beat Manny Fernandez & Hector Guerrero

5/13/86: Richburg, SC (TV)
The Midnight Express beat Rocky Kernodle & Denny Brown
The Midnight Express beat Rocky King & Sam Houston

5/14/86: Raleigh, NC @ Dorton Arena
Baron Von Raschke beat Italian Stallion
Teijo Khan beat Denny Brown
The Barbarian beat Todd Champion
Jimmy Garvin beat Wahoo McDaniel in a Texas death match
Jimmy Valiant beat Pez Whatley in a lumberjack match
The Midnight Express beat Manny Fernandez & Hector Guerrero

5/14/86: Charleston, SC @ County Hall
Magnum TA vs. Nikita Koloff in a Russian chain match
The Rock & Roll Express vs. Arn Anderson & Tully Blanchard
Ronnie Garvin vs. Leo Burke
Black Bart vs. Sam Houston
Don Kernodle vs. Thunderfoot
Rocky Kernodle vs. Golden Terror

5/15/86: Lovington, VA
The Midnight Express beat Manny Fernandez & Hector Guerrero

5/17/86: Atlanta, GA @ WTBS Studios (TV)

5/17/86: Baltimore, MD @ Civic Center
Denny Brown draw Steve Regal
Black Bart beat Sam Houston
Manny Fernandez beat Leo Burke
The Rock & Roll Express beat The Midnight Express & Jim Cornette in a handicap, cage match
Ronnie Garvin beat Arn Anderson
Magnum TA NC with Tully Blanchard
Dusty Rhodes & The Road Warriors beat The Ivan & Nikita Koloff & Baron Von Raschke to win NWA World 6-Man Tag Title

5/19/86: Greenville, SC @ Memorial Auditorium
Hector Guerrero beat Leo Burke
Denny Brown draw Steve Regal
Ivan Koloff beat Sam Houston
Nikita Koloff beat Ronnie Garvin
The Rock & Roll Express beat Arn Anderson & Tully Blanchard in a Texas tornado match
Jimmy Garvin beat Wahoo McDaniel lumberjack match

5/19/86: Fayetteville, NC @ Cumberland County Civic Center
Midnight Express beat Dusty Rhodes & Magnum TA

5/20/86: Rock Hill, SC @ Winthrop Coliseum
Dusty Rhodes & Magnum TA beat The Midnight Express by DQ
Wahoo McDaniel beat Tully Blanchard by DQ
Arn Anderson beat Manny Fernandez
Baron Von Raschke, Ivan & Nikita Koloff beat The Rock & Roll Express & Sam Houston
Jimmy Valiant beat Pez Whatley by DQ
Jimmy Garvin beat Italian Stallion
The Barbarian beat Hector Guerrero
Denny Brown beat Leo Burke(sub for Steve Regal)

5/21/86: Taylorsville, NC
The Rock & Roll Express beat The Midnight Express

5/22/86: San Antonio, TX @ Hemisfair Arena
Ronnie Garvin beat The Barbarian
Manny Fernandez beat Baron Von Raschke
Wahoo McDaniel beat Jimmy Garvin by DQ
Jimmy Valiant beat Pez Whatley in a taped fist match
The Midnight Express beat The Rock & Roll Express
The Road Warriors beat Ivan & Nikita Koloff in a double Russian chain match
Magnum TA vs. Tully Blanchard
NWA World Champion Ric Flair vs. Dusty Rhodes

5/23/86: Norfolk, VA @ Scope
Hector Guerrero beat Mark Fleming
Denny Brown draw Steve Regal
Black Bart beat Sam Houston
Nelson Royal beat Thunderfoot
Ronnie Garvin beat Leo Burke
Magnum TA & The Road Warriors beat Ivan & Nikita Koloff & Baron Von Raschke
NWA World Champion Ric Flair NC with Ricky Morton

5/23/86: Columbia, SC @ Township Auditorium
Wahoo McDaniel vs. Jimmy Garvin
Robert Gibson beat Bobby Eaton
Pez Whatley vs. Jimmy Valiant in a lumberjack match
Manny Fernandez vs. The Barbarian
Dennis Condrey beat Todd Champion

5/24/86: Atlanta, GA @ WTBS Studios (TV)
Steve Regal beat George South
Jimmy Garvin beat Lee Peek
Nikita Koloff beat Bob Owens
Wahoo McDaniel beat Butch Cooper
The Rock & Roll Express beat Randy & Bill Mulkey
Shaska Whatley beat Dave Dillinger
The Midnight Express beat Mike Simani & Tony Zane
The Road Warriors beat Paul Garner & Larry Clarke
Ronnie Garvin beat Thunderfoot
Ric Flair & Arn Anderson beat Italian Stallion & Rocky Kernodle
The Barbarian beat Ron Rossi
Baron Von Raschke beat Rocky King

5/24/86: Cincinnati, OH @ Gardens
The Midnight Express beat The Road Warriors by DQ

5/25/86: Cleveland, OH @ Convocation Center
Denny Brown draw Steve Regal
Manny Fernandez beat Black Bart
Ricky Morton beat Thunderfoot
Magnum TA beat Baron Von Raschke
Dusty Rhodes beat Arn Anderson
The Road Warriors NC with The Midnight Express
NWA World Champion Ric Flair beat Robert Gibson

5/26/86: Greenville, SC @ Memorial Auditorium
Italian Stallion beat Thunderfoot
Baron Von Raschke beat Rocky Kernodle
Don Kernodle beat Black Bart by DQ
The Midnight Express beat Manny Fernandez & Hector Guerrero
Wahoo McDaniel beat Jimmy Garvin Texas death match
Dusty Rhodes & The Rock & Roll Express beat Ric Flair, Tully Blanchard & Arn Anderson in an elimination match

5/27/86: Greenwood, SC (TV)
Midnight Express beat Dusty Rhodes & Magnum TA

5/28/86: Raleigh, NC @ Dorton Arena
Don Kernodle beat Teijo Khan
Arn Anderson beat Italian Stallion
Ronnie Garvin beat Tully Blanchard in a taped fist match
Manny Fernandez & Jimmy Valiant beat The Barbarian & Pez Whatley
The Rock & Roll Express beat Ivan & Nikita Koloff
Wahoo McDaniel beat Jimmy Garvin in a combination death match
The Midnight Express beat Dusty Rhodes & Magnum TA by DQ

5/29/86: Amelia, VA
The Rock & Roll Express beat The Midnight Express

5/30/86: Hampton, VA @ Coliseum
Teijo Khan beat Mark Fleming
Wahoo McDaniel NC with Jimmy Garvin
Jimmy Valiant beat Pez Whatley
Nikita Koloff beat Magnum TA in a Russian chain match
The Rock & Roll Express beat The Midnight Express
Black Bart beat Sam Houston

5/31/86: Atlanta, GA @ WTBS Studios (TV)
Manny Fernandez & Hector Guerrero beat Thunderfoot & Bob Owens
Wahoo McDaniel beat Vernon Deaton
Shaska Whatley beat Bill Mulkey
The Midnight Express beat Art Pritts & Brodie Chase
The Rock & Roll Express beat David Dellinger & Paul Garner
Baron Von Raschke & The Barbarian beat Rocky King & Italian Stallion
Ronnie Garvin beat Kent Glover

5/31/86: Florence, SC
The Midnight Express beat Ronnie Garvin & Manny Fernandez by DQ

6/1/86: Charleston, SC @ County Hall
Denny Brown draw Steve Regal
Ivan Koloff beat Rocky Kernodle
Baron Von Raschke beat Italian Stallion
The Barbarian beat Sam Houston
The Midnight Express beat Manny Fernandez & Ronnie Garvin by DQ
Nikita Koloff beat Magnum TA in a Russian chain match
Dusty Rhodes & The Rock & Roll Express beat Arn Anderson, Ric Flair & Tully Blanchard in an elimination match

6/1/86: Greensboro, NC @ Coliseum
Ronnie Garvin beat Thunderfoot
Jimmy Garvin beat Hector Guerrero
Manny Fernandez beat Teijo Khan
Nikita Koloff beat Todd Champion
Jimmy Valiant beat Pez Whatley
Wahoo McDaniel beat Arn Anderson
Ric Flair & Tully Blanchard beat The Rock & Roll Express
The James Boys(aka Dusty Rhodes & Magnum TA) beat The Midnight Express in a lights out, bunkhouse match

6/2/86: Fayetteville, NC @ Cumberland County Civic Center
Rocky King beat George South
Steve Regal beat Rocky Kernodle
Todd Champion beat Thunderfoot
Ivan Koloff beat Italian Stallion
Wahoo McDaniel & Dusty Rhodes beat Tully Blanchard & Jimmy Garvin
Arn Anderson & Ric Flair beat The Rock & Roll Express

6/2/86: Greenup, KY
The Midnight Express beat Manny Fernandez & Hector Guerrero

6/3/86: Spartanburg, SC @ Memorial Auditorium (TV)
Ric Flair & Arn Anderson vs. The Rock & Roll Express

6/4/86: Raleigh, NC @ Dorton Arena
Denny Brown beat Steve Regal
Italian Stallion beat Zane Grey
Black Bart beat Todd Champion
Jimmy Garvin beat Hector Guerrero
The Midnight Express beat Wahoo McDaniel & Ronnie Garvin by DQ
Dusty Rhodes & The Rock & Roll Express beat Arn Anderson, Tully Blanchard & Ric Flair by DQ in an elimination match

6/4/86: Charleston, SC @ Arthur Ravenel Stadium
Magnum TA vs. Nikita Koloff
Sam Houston vs. Ivan Koloff

Jimmy Valiant & Manny Fernandez vs. Pez Whatley & The Barbarian
Nelson Royal vs. Teijo Khan
Rocky King vs. Dave Dellinger
Don Kernodle vs. Golden Terror

6/5/86: Columbus, GA @ Municipal Auditorium
The Midnight Express beat Dusty Rhodes & Magnum TA by DQ

6/6/86: Norfolk, VA @ Scope
Ronnie Garvin beat The Barbarian
Ivan Koloff beat Hector Guerrero
Manny Fernandez beat Teijo Khan
Jimmy Valiant beat Pez Whatley in a lumberjack match
Tully Blanchard beat Todd Champion
Wahoo McDaniel beat Nikita Koloff by DQ
Ric Flair & Arn Anderson beat The Rock & Roll Express
The James Boys beat The Midnight Express

6/7/86: Atlanta, GA @ WTBS Studios (TV)
Robert Gibson draw Arn Anderson

6/7/86: Roanoke, VA @ Civic Center
Italian Stallion beat Teijo Khan
The Barbarian & Black Bart beat Sam Houston & Italian Stallion
Jimmy Garvin beat Hector Guerrero
Manny Fernandez beat Ivan Koloff
Wahoo McDaniel beat Nikita Koloff by DQ
Ronnie Garvin & Rock & Roll Express beat Arn Anderson, Tully Blanchard & Ric Flair in an elimination match
The Midnight Express beat Dusty Rhodes & Magnum TA by DQ

6/8/86: Asheville, NC @ Civic Center
The Midnight Express beat Manny Fernandez & Hector Guerrero

6/8/86: Atlanta, GA @ Omni
Black Bart beat Rocky Kernodle
The Barbarian beat Hector Guerrero
Jimmy Garvin beat Don Kernodle
Jimmy Valiant beat Baron Von Raschke
Ronnie Garvin beat Nikita Koloff by DQ
Wahoo McDaniel beat Arn Anderson by CO
Tully Blanchard & Ric Flair & beat The Rock & Roll Express in a Texas tornado match
The James Boys beat The Midnight Express in a bunkhouse match

6/9/86: Greenville, SC @ Memorial Auditorium
Rocky Kernodle beat Rocky King
Denny Brown beat Steve Regal by DQ
Jimmy Garvin beat Todd Champion
The Rock & Roll Express beat Ivan Koloff & Baron Von Raschke
Tully Blanchard beat Wahoo McDaniel by DQ
The James Boys beat The Midnight Express in a bunkhouse match

6/10/86: Salisbury, NC (TV)

6/11/86: Mission, TX
The Midnight Express beat Dusty Rhodes & Magnum TA by DQ

6/12/86: San Antonio, TX @ Hemisfair Arena
The James Boys beat The Midnight Express in a bunkhouse match

6/14/86: Atlanta, GA @ WTBS Studios (TV)
The Rock & Roll Express vs. Ray Aaron & Mike Simani
Manny Fernandez & Jimmy Valiant vs. Pat Myers & Clement Fields
Ronnie Garvin vs. Vernon Deaton
Ole & Arn Anderson vs. Bill Mulkey & Randy Mulkey
NWA World Champion Ric Flair vs. Tony Zane

6/14/86: Baltimore, MD @ Civic Center
Sam Houston beat Teijo Khan
Jimmy Garvin beat Italian Stallion
The Barbarian beat Todd Champion
Black Bart beat Hector Guerrero
Manny Fernandez draw Arn Anderson
The Midnight Express beat Wahoo McDaniel & Ronnie Garvin by DQ
Magnum TA beat Tully Blanchard in a barbed wire match

6/15/86: Wilmington, NC @ Legion Stadium
The Midnight Express beat The Rock & Roll Express
Jimmy Valiant vs. Pez Whatley in a no DQ match
Wahoo McDaniel vs. Tully Blanchard
Also including Manny Fernandez & others

6/16/86: Greenville, SC @ Memorial Auditorium
Sam Houston & Denny Brown draw Black Bart & Steve Regal
The Warlord beat Italian Stallion
Baron Von Raschke beat Hector Guerrero
Manny Fernandez beat Jimmy Garvin by DQ
Wahoo McDaniel beat Ivan Koloff
The Rock & Roll Express beat Tully Blanchard & Arn Anderson
Dusty Rhodes & Magnum TA beat The Midnight Express in a lumberjack match

6/17/86: Greenwood, SC (TV)
Baron Von Raschke, Shaska Whatley & Teijo Khan beat Mark Fleming, Bill Mulkey & Randy Mulkey
The Warlord beat Mike Simani
The Midnight Express beat Todd Champion & Rocky Kernodle
Steve Regal beat George South
Hector Guerrero beat The Golden Terror
Don Kernodle beat Thunderfoot
The Barbarian beat Denny Brown
Arn Anderson & Tully Blanchard beat Sam Houston & Tony Zane

6/18/86: Raleigh, NC @ Dorton Arena
Don Kernodle beat Teijo Khan
The Warlord beat Rocky Kernodle
Magnum TA beat Ivan Koloff in a Texas death match
The Rock & Roll Express beat Arn Anderson & Tully Blanchard in a cage match
The Barbarian, Baron Von Raschke & Pez Whatley beat Hector Guerrero, Manny Fernandez & Jimmy Valiant
The Midnight Express beat Wahoo McDaniel & Ronnie Garvin by DQ

6/19/86: Hillsville, VA
The Midnight Express beat Manny Fernandez & Hector Guerrero
Jimmy Valiant beat Pez Whatley

6/20/86: Richmond, VA @ Coliseum
Black Bart beat Todd Champion
The Warlord beat Italian Stallion
Ole Anderson beat Hector Guerrero
Arn Anderson beat Ronnie Garvin
Magnum TA beat Ivan Koloff in a Texas death match
Tully Blanchard & Ric Flair beat The Rock & Roll Express Texas tornado match
The James Boys beat The Midnight Express in a bunkhouse match

6/21/86: Atlanta, GA @ WTBS Studios (TV)

6/21/86: Norfolk, VA @ Scope @ Scope
The Warlord vs. Italian Stallion
Jimmy Garvin vs. Todd Champion
Tully Blanchard vs. Wahoo McDaniel
Arn Anderson vs. Robert Gibson
NWA World Champion Ric Flair vs. Ricky Morton in a Texas death match
Dusty Rhodes & Magnum TA vs. The Midnight Express

6/22/86: Atlanta, GA @ Omni
Thunderfoot beat Rocky King
The Warlord beat Italian Stallion
Tully Blanchard beat Todd Champion
Ivan Koloff beat Hector Guerrero
The Midnight Express beat Dusty Rhodes & Magnum TA by DQ in a tennis racquet, lumberjack match
Ole & Arn Anderson beat Robert Gibson & Ronnie Garvin
NWA World Champion Ric Flair beat Ricky Morton in a cage match

6/22/86: Greensboro, NC @ Coliseum
Dusty Rhodes & Magnum TA beat The Midnight Express in a lumberjack match

6/23/86: Fayetteville, NC @ Cumberland County Civic Center (TV)
The Rock & Roll Express beat Mark Fleming & Ben Alexander
The Road Warriors beat Bill Mulkey & Randy Mulkey
Tully Blanchard beat Vernon Deaton
Magnum TA beat Brodie Chase
The Warlord beat Thunderfoot
Baron Von Raschke, Pez Whatley & Barbarian beat Mike Simani, George South & Tony Zane
Ole & Arn Anderson beat Sam Houston & Denny Brown

6/24/86: Rock Hill, SC @ Winthrop Coliseum (TV Taping)
The Midnight Express beat The Road Warriors by DQ
Jimmy Valiant & Manny Fernandez beat Baron Von Raschke & Pez Whatley
Jimmy Garvin & Wahoo McDaniel beat Black Bart & Teijo Khan
The Road Warriors beat Tony Zane & Vernon Deaton
The Warlord beat Randy Mulkey
Jimmy Garvin beat Gene Ligon
Krusher Khruschev, Ivan & Nikita Koloff beat Italian Stallion, Rocky King & George South
Ole Anderson beat Bill Mulkey by submission
The Rock & Roll Express beat Thunderfoot & Mark Fleming
The Rock & Roll Express beat Golden Terror & Thunderfoot
The Warlord beat Mark Fleming
Ole & Arn Anderson beat Don Kernodle & Rocky Kernodle
The Road Warriors beat Gene Ligon & Mike Simani
The Midnight Express beat Nelson Royal &Todd Champion
Nikita Koloff beat Tony Zane
The Barbarian & Baron Von Raschke beat Bill Mulkey & Randy Mulkey

6/26/86: Harrisonburg, VA @ H.S.
Wahoo McDaniel vs. Jimmy Garvin
Tully Blanchard vs. Ronnie Garvin
Baron Von Raschke, The Barbarian & Pez Whatley vs. Hector Guerrero, Manny Fernandez & Jimmy Valiant
Thunderfoot vs. Don Kernodle
Rocky Kernodle vs. The Warlord
Denny Brown vs. Steve Regal

6/26/86: Laurinburg, NC
The Rock & Roll Express beat The Midnight Express

6/27/86: Columbia, SC @ Township Auditorium
The James Boys beat The Midnight Express in a bunkhouse match
Ole & Arn Anderson vs. The Rock & Roll Express
Wahoo McDaniel vs. Tully Blanchard
Todd Champion vs. Black Bart
The Warlord vs. Golden Terror
Italian Stallion vs. Steve Regal

6/28/86: Atlanta, GA @ WTBS Studios (TV)
The Midnight Express beat Sam Houston & George South
Krusher Khruschev, Ivan & Nikita Koloff beat Vernon Deaton, Rocky King & Gene Ligon
The Warlord beat Mike Simani
Ole & Arn Anderson beat Tony Zane & Rocky Kernodle
The Rock & Roll Express beat Golden Terror & Thunderfoot

Baron Von Raschke & Pez Whatley beat Dave Spencer & Lee Peak
Tully Blanchard beat Italian Stallion
Ronnie Garvin & Wahoo McDaniel beat Paul Garner & Kent Glover

6/28/86: Albuquerque, NM
Hillbilly Tooter Dean beat Jackson Brody
Tom Reynosa beat Ted Heath
Dick Murdoch beat Steve Regal
Wahoo McDaniel NC with Tully Blanchard
Road Warriors & Paul Ellering beat Ivan & Nikita Koloff & Krusher Khruschev
The Midnight Express beat Dusty Rhodes & Magnum TA by DQ
NWA World Champion Ric Flair beat Ronnie Garvin

6/29/86: Gainesville, GA @ Georgia Mountain Center
Wahoo McDaniel & Ronnie Garvin beat The Midnight Express by DQ

6/29/86: Marietta, GA @ Cobb County Civic Center
The Midnight Express beat Wahoo McDaniel & Ronnie Garvin

6/30/86: Buckingham, VA
The Midnight Express beat Manny Fernandez & Hector Guerrero

7/1/86: Philadelphia, PA @ Veterans Stadium
The Barbarian beat Denny Brown
Black Bart beat Todd Champion
Manny Fernandez beat Pez Whatley bunkhouse match
Wahoo McDaniel beat Jimmy Garvin Indian strap match
Ronnie Garvin beat Tully Blanchard taped fist match
Jimmy Valiant beat Baron Von Raschke pole match
The Rock & Roll Express & Baby Doll beat The Midnight Express & Jim Cornette
Nikita Koloff beat Magnum TA in match #1 of the Best of 7 series
NWA World Champion Ric Flair beat Road Warrior Hawk by DQ
Dusty Rhodes & Road Warrior Animal beat Ole & Arn Anderson in a cage match

7/2/86:
No Wrestling

7/3/86: Washington, DC @ RFK Stadium
Baron Von Raschke beat Italian Stallion
Jimmy Garvin beat Todd Champion
Don Kernodle beat Thunderfoot
Ole Anderson beat Hector Guerrero
Wahoo McDaniel beat Arn Anderson Indian strap match
Manny Fernandez & Jimmy Valiant beat The Barbarian & Pez Whatley
Tully Blanchard beat Ronnie Garvin taped in a fist match
The Rock & Roll Express beat The Midnight Express in a cage match
Baby Doll beat Jim Cornette
NWA World Champion Ric Flair beat Dusty Rhodes
Road Warriors & Magnum TA beat Ivan & Nikita Koloff & Krusher Khruschev cage match

7/4/86: Memphis, TN @ Liberty Bowl
Hector Guerrero beat Thunderfoot
Wahoo McDaniel beat Jimmy Garvin
Manny Fernandez beat Pez Whatley in a bunkhouse match
Jimmy Valiant beat Baron Von Raschke in a pole match
The Rock & Roll Express draw Ole & Arn Anderson
Tully Blanchard beat Ronnie Garvin by DQ in a taped fist match
The Road Warriors beat Ivan Koloff & Krusher Khruschev indouble chain match
Black Bart beat Todd Champion
NWA World Champion Ric Flair beat Nikita Koloff
Dusty Rhodes, Magnum TA & Baby Doll beat The Midnight Express & Jim Cornette in a cage match

7/5/86: Charlotte, NC @ Independence Stadium
Denny Brown draw Steve Regal
Robert Gibson beat Black Bart
Ole & Arn Anderson beat Sam Houston & Nelson Royal
Manny Fernandez beat Baron Von Raschke
Wahoo McDaniel beat Jimmy Garvin in an Indian strap match
Ronnie Garvin beat Tully Blanchard in a boxing match
The Road Warriors beat Ivan & Nikita Koloff in a double chain match
Jimmy Valiant beat Pez Whatley in a hair vs. hair match
Dusty Rhodes, Magnum TA & Baby Doll beat The Midnight Express & Jim Cornette in a cage match
NWA World Champion Ric Flair beat Ricky Morton

7/6/86: Asheville, NC @ Civic Center
NWA World Champion Ric Flair vs. Ricky Morton

7/6/86: Raleigh, NC @ Civic Center (TV)
Ivan Koloff beat Rocky King
Ronnie Garvin beat Black Bart
The Warlord beat Gene Ligon
Magnum TA beat Nikita Koloff in a Texas death match
Dusty Rhodes & The Rock & Roll Express beat Ric Flair, Ole & Arn Anderson in a bunkhouse match
Wahoo McDaniel beat Tully Blanchard by reverse decision
The Road Warriors beat The Midnight Express by DQ

7/7/86: Rocky Mount, NC
Dusty Rhodes & The Rock & Roll Express beat Ric Flair, Ole & Arn Anderson

7/7/86: Greenville, SC @ Memorial Auditorium
Baby Doll beat Jim Cornette

7/8/86: Spartanburg, SC @ Memorial Auditorium (TV)
Arn & Ole Anderson beat Mark Fleming & Gene Ligon
Manny Fernandez beat Randy Mulkey
Don Kernodle beat Golden Terror
Ronnie Garvin beat Mike Simani
Jimmy Garvin beat Bill Mulkey
Baron Von Raschke & Shaska Whatley beat Italian Stallion & Rocky King
NWA World Champion Ric Flair beat Denny Brown
Dusty Rhodes, Magnum TA & The Rock & Roll Express vs. Ric Flair, Ole Anderson, Arn Anderson & Tully Blanchard

7/9/86: Cincinnati, OH @ Gardens
The Barbarian & Shaska Whatley beat Sam Houston & Nelson Royal
Chavo Guerrero beat Black Bart
Jimmy Garvin beat Todd Champion
Jimmy Valiant beat Baron Von Raschke in a pole match
Manny Fernandez & Ronnie Garvin draw Ivan Koloff & Krusher Khruschev
Tully Blanchard beat Wahoo McDaniel by DQ
Nikita Koloff beat Magnum TA
The Rock & Roll Express & Dusty Rhodes beat The Midnight Express & Jim Cornette
NWA World Champion Ric Flair beat Road Warrior Animal by DQ
Dusty Rhodes & Road Warrior Hawk beat Ole & Arn Anderson in a cage match

7/10/86: Charleston, WV @ Civic Center
Denny Brown beat Thunderfoot
Hector Guerrero beat Teijo Khan
Ole & Arn Anderson beat Don Kernodle & Italian Stallion
Jimmy Valiant & Manny Fernandez beat The Barbarian & Shaska Whatley
Ronnie Garvin beat Tully Blanchard
Robert Gibson beat Dennis Condrey in a bunkhouse match
Magnum TA & Baby Doll beat Bobby Eaton & Jim Cornette
Wahoo McDaniel beat Jimmy Garvin
The Road Warriors & Dusty Rhodes beat Ivan & Nikita Koloff & Krusher Khruschev in a cage match
NWA World Champion Ric Flair beat Ricky Morton

7/11/86: Roanoke, VA @ Civic Center
Ole & Arn Anderson beat Hector Guerrero & Denny Brown
Robert Gibson beat Dennis Condrey
Jimmy Valiant & Manny Fernandez beat Shaska Whatley & The Barbarian
Wahoo McDaniel beat Jimmy Garvin in an Indian strap match
Tully Blanchard beat Ronnie Garvin by CO
The Road Warriors & Paul Ellering beat Ivan Koloff, Baron Von Raschke & Krusher Khruschev
Nikita Koloff beat Magnum TA
Dusty Rhodes & Baby Doll beat Bobby Eaton & Jim Cornette
NWA World Champion Ric Flair beat Ricky Morton in a cage match

7/12/86: Atlanta, GA @ WTBS Studios (TV)
The Warlord vs. Gene Ligon
Ivan Koloff vs. Rocky King
Ronnie Garvin vs. Black Bart
Teijo Khan vs. Mark Fleming
Tully Blanchard vs. Wahoo McDaniel
Sam Houston vs. George South
The Road Warriors vs. The Midnight Express
Dusty Rhodes & The Rock & Roll Express vs. Ric Flair, Ole & Arn Anderson in a bunkhouse match

7/12/86: Jacksonville, FL @ Gator Bowl
Ronnie Garvin beat Tully Blanchard
Thunderfoot beat Ricky Santana
Jimmy Garvin beat Italian Stallion
Ole Anderson beat Hector Guerrero
Magnum TA beat Arn Anderson
The Rock & Roll Express beat The Midnight Express
Dusty Rhodes beat NWA World Champion Ric Flair by DQ
Wahoo McDaniel & The Road Warriors beat Ivan & Nikita Koloff & Krusher Khruschev in a cage match

7/13/86: San Antonio, TX @ Hemisfair Arena
Ken Fletcher beat Ken Johnson
Mr. Ebony beat Mike Williams
Hector Guerrero beat Mr. X
Denny Brown draw Steve Regal
Tully Blanchard beat Manny Fernandez by DQ
Wahoo McDaniel beat Jimmy Garvin
The Road Warriors beat The Midnight Express by DQ
NWA World Champion Ric Flair beat Magnum TA

7/13/86: Cleveland, OH @ Municipal Stadium
Held after a Cleveland Indians game
The Barbarian beat Todd Champion
Ronnie Garvin & Sam Houston vs. Arn Anderson & Krusher Khruschev
Jimmy Valiant beat Baron Von Raschke
The Rock & Roll Express beat Ivan & Nikita Koloff
Don Kernodle beat Black Bart

7/14/86: Wilmington, NC @ Legion Stadium
NWA World Champion Ric Flair vs. Ricky Morton
Dusty Rhodes & Magnum TA beat The Midnight Express

7/15/86: Gaffney, SC (TV)
Don Kernodle beat Mark Fleming
The Rock & Roll Express vs. The Barbarian & Teijo Khan
Jimmy Garvin & Steve Regal beat George South & Gene Ligon
Wahoo McDaniel beat Bill Mulkey
Ole & Arn Anderson beat Mike Simani & Randy Mulkey
The Midnight Express beat Hector Guerrero & Todd Champion
Krusher Khruschev beat Rocky Kernodle
The Midnight Express vs. Dusty Rhodes & Magnum TA

7/16/86: Charleston, SC @ Arthur Ravenel Stadium
The Rock & Roll Express vs. Ole & Arn Anderson
Wahoo McDaniel vs. Jimmy Garvin in an Indian strap match
Manny Fernandez vs. Shaska Whatley
Black Bart vs. Ronnie Garvin
Don Kernodle vs. The Barbarian
The Warlord vs. Rocky King

7/17/86: Kansas City, MO @ Kemper Arena
NWA World Champion Ric Flair beat Cousin Junior

7/17/86: Columbia, SC @ Township Auditorium (TV)
The Midnight Express beat Dusty Rhodes & Magnum TA by DQ
Tully Blanchard vs. Ronnie Garvin
Ivan Koloff vs. Todd Champion
The Warlord vs. Gene Ligon
Terror vs. Don Kernodle

7/18/86: Richmond, VA @ Coliseum
Steve Regal beat Italian Stallion
Teijo Khan & Shaska Whatley beat Sam Houston & Nelson Royal
Manny Fernandez beat The Barbarian
Jimmy Garvin beat Todd Champion
Tully Blanchard beat Ronnie Garvin by DQ in a taped fist match
The Rock & Roll Express draw Ole & Arn Anderson
Jimmy Valiant beat Baron Von Raschke
The Road Warriors beat Nikita Koloff & Krusher Khruschev
Dusty Rhodes, Magnum TA & Baby Doll beat The Midnight Express & Jim Cornette
NWA World Champion Ric Flair beat Wahoo McDaniel

7/19/86: Baltimore, MD @ Civic Center
Ivan Koloff & Krusher Khruschev beat Hector Guerrero & Manny Fernandez
Magnum TA beat Nikita Koloff
Steve Regal beat Rocky King
The Road Warriors beat The Midnight Express by DQ
Wahoo McDaniel beat Jimmy Garvin
Ronnie Garvin beat Tully Blanchard
Dusty Rhodes & The Rock & Roll Express beat Ric Flair, Ole & Arn Anderson

7/20/86: Greenville, SC @ Memorial Auditorium
The Rock & Roll Express vs. Ric Flair & Ole Anderson
Magnum TA & Baby Doll beat Bobby Eaton & Jim Cornette

7/21/86: Fayetteville, NC @ Cumberland County Civic Center
Hector Guerrero beat Sam Houston
Ricky Morton beat Baron Von Raschke in a pole match
Jimmy Valiant & Manny Fernandez beat Shaska Whatley & The Barbarian
Wahoo McDaniel beat Jimmy Garvin in an Indian strap match
The Road Warriors beat Ivan & Nikita Koloff in a steel cage match
Dusty Rhodes, Magnum TA & Baby Doll beat Jim Cornette & The Midnight Express in a steel cage match
Ronnie Garvin beat Tully Blanchard in a taped fist match
NWA World Champion Ric Flair beat Robert Gibson

7/22/86: Greenwood, SC (TV)
The Rock & Roll Express beat Bill Mulkey & Randy Mulkey
Nikita Koloff beat Vernon Deaton
Ronnie Garvin beat Gene Ligon
The Warlord beat George South
Don Kernodle beat Mike Simani
Baron Von Raschke & The Barbarian beat Sam Houston & Rocky Kernodle
Tully Blanchard, Ole & Arn Anderson beat Hector Guerrero, Rocky King & Denny Brown

7/23/86: Johnson City, TN
Dusty Rhodes, Magnum TA & Baby Doll beat The Midnight Express & Jim Cornette in a cage match

7/24/86: Hendersonville, NC
Jimmy Valiant & Manny Fernandez vs. Shaska Whatley & The Barbarian
Ronnie Garvin vs. Black Bart
Denny Brown vs. Steve Regal
Italian Stallion vs. Thunderfoot
George South vs. The Warlord
Todd Champion vs. Teijo Khan

7/25/86: Norfolk, VA @ Scope
Rocky Kernodle & Todd Champion beat Thunderfoot & Teijo Khan
Ronnie Garvin & Manny Fernandez beat Ivan & Nikita Koloff in a Texas tornado match
Jimmy Valiant beat Baron Von Raschke in a pole match
Black Bart beat Sam Houston in a taped fist match
Wahoo McDaniel beat Jimmy Garvin in an Indian strap match
The Rock & Roll Express & Baby Doll beat The Midnight Express & Jim Cornette
NWA World Champion Ric Flair beat Magnum TA by DQ
The Road Warriors & Dusty Rhodes beat Ole Anderson, Arn Anderson & Tully Blanchard
Denny Brown draw Steve Regal
Don Kernodle beat The Barbarian by DQ

7/26/86: Greensboro, NC @ Coliseum
Steve Regal beat Sam Houston
The Barbarian & Black Bart beat Denny Brown & Italian Stallion
Manny Fernandez beat Baron Von Raschke
Wahoo McDaniel beat Jimmy Garvin
Tully Blanchard beat Ronnie Garvin in a taped fist match
The Rock & Roll Express draw Ole & Arn Anderson
Paul Jones beat Jimmy Valiant
Magnum TA beat Nikita Koloff

The Road Warriors & Baby Doll beat The Midnight Express & Jim Cornette
Dusty Rhodes beat Ric Flair in a cage match to win NWA World Title

7/27/86: Atlanta, GA @ WTBS Studios (TV)

7/27/86: Dallas, TX @ Reunion Arena
The Road Warriors & Bill Watts beat Terry Gordy & Buddy Roberts by DQ
NWA World Champion Dusty Rhodes beat Ric Flair
Jim Duggan beat Kamala by DQ
Missing Link won a mini battle royal
Bobby Fulton & Tommy Rogers beat John Tatum & Jack Victory
Magnum TA beat Baron Von Raschke
Terry Taylor beat Eddie Gilbert
The Rock & Roll Express draw The Midnight Express
Chavo Guerrero beat Rick Steiner
One Man Gang beat Jeff Gaylord
Koko Ware beat Gustavo Mendoza
Sting beat Brett Sawyer

7/28/86: Wilmington, NC @ Legion Stadium
The Midnight Express beat Dusty Rhodes & Magnum TA by DQ
Ole & Arn Anderson vs. The Rock & Roll Express
Nikita Koloff vs. Todd Champion
Black Bart vs. Don Kernodle
Thunderfoot vs. The Warlord

7/29/86: Rock Hill, SC @ Winthrop Coliseum (TV Taping)
Dusty Rhodes & Rock & Roll Express beat Tully Blanchard, Ole & Arn Anderson
Ronnie Garvin & Wahoo McDaniel beat Randy & Bill Mulkey
The Rock & Roll Express beat George South & Ben Alexander
Nikita Koloff beat Mark Fleming
Jimmy Garvin beat Gene Ligon
Buddy Landell beat Rocky King by submission
Tully Blanchard beat Vernon Deaton
Ole & Arn Anderson beat Mike Simani & Vernon Deaton by submission
The Midnight Express beat Italian Stallion & Rocky Kernodle
Ivan Koloff & Krusher Khruschev beat Ron Rossi & Randy Mulkey by submission
The Warlord beat Mark Fleming
Buddy Landell beat George South by submission
Todd Champion beat Vernon Deaton
Magnum TA beat Thunderfoot
The Rock & Roll Express beat Ole & Arn Anderson DQ

7/30/86: Raleigh, NC @ Dorton Arena
Manny Fernandez draw Jimmy Garvin
Don Kernodle beat Black Bart by DQ
Steve Regal beat Italian Stallion
The Warlord beat Mark Fleming
Todd Champion beat Thunderfoot
Ole Anderson, Arn Anderson & Tully Blanchard beat The Rock & Roll Express & Magnum TA
The Midnight Express beat Ronnie Garvin & Wahoo McDaniel

7/31/86: Columbia, SC @ Township Auditorium
Dennis Condrey draw Ronnie Garvin(30:00)
Magnum TA & Baby Doll beat Bobby Eaton & Jim Cornette
Wahoo McDaniel vs. Steve Regal iIndian strap match
The Warlord vs. Teijo Khan
Ivan Koloff vs. Todd Champion
Denny Brown vs. Rocky King

8/1/86: San Antonio, TX @ Hemisfair Arena
The Rock & Roll Express & Baby Doll beat The Midnight Express & Jim Cornette

8/2/86: Atlanta, GA @ WTBS Studios (TV)
Krusher Khruschev, Ivan & Nikita Koloff vs. Randy Barber, Mike Simani & Vernon Deaton
The Midnight Express vs. The Road Warriors
Ronnie Garvin vs. Black Bart
Buddy Landell vs. George South
Dick Murdoch vs. Bill Mulkey

8/2/86: Atlanta, GA @ Fulton County Stadium
Steve Regal beat Denny Brown to win NWA Junior Title
Don Kernodle beat The Barbarian
Ivan Koloff, Khrusher Khruschev & Baron Von Raschke beat Manny Fernandez, Todd Champion & Sam Houston
Jimmy Valiant beat Shaska Whatley
Wahoo McDaniel beat Jimmy Garvin
Magnum TA beat Nikita Koloff
Tully Blanchard beat Ronnie Garvin in a brass knuckles match
The Rock & Roll Express beat Ole & Arn Anderson
The Road Warriors & Baby Doll beat The Midnight Express & Jim Cornette
NWA World Champion Dusty Rhodes beat Ric Flair

8/3/86: Greenville, SC @ Memorial Auditorium (TV)

8/7/86: Kansas City, MO @ Kemper Arena
NWA World Champion Dusty Rhodes beat Ric Flair by DQ
Rufus R. Jones beat Butch Reed
Giant Baba & Hiroshi Wajirna beat J.R. Hogg & Earthquake Ferris
Sam Houston vs. Buddy Landell
Joe Lightfoot & Billy Two Eagles beat Masked Apeman & Bob Owens
Dave Petersen beat Mike George
Moondog Moretti beat John Paul Demann

8/8/86: Richmond, VA @ Coliseum
Bill Dundee beat Denny Brown
Dennis Condrey beat Mark Fleming
Buddy Landell beat Italian Stallion
Dick Murdoch beat Khrusher Khruschev
Ronnie Garvin beat Shaska Whatley
Wahoo McDaniel beat Dennis Condrey

Bobby Eaton beat The Warlord
Magnum TA NC with Nikita Koloff

8/8/86: St. Joseph, MO @ Civic Arena
NWA World Champion Dusty Rhodes beat Ric Flair
Rufus R. Jones beat Butch Reed
Dave Petersen beat Bob Brown
Joe Lightfoot & Billy Two Eagles beat Moondog Moretti & Earthquake Ferris
Bob Owens beat John Paul
Cousin Junior beat JR Hogg

8/9/86: Atlanta, GA @ WTBS Studios (TV)
The Kansas Jayhawks(Dutch Mantell & Bobby Jaggers) vs. Bill Mulkey & Pat Myers
Jimmy Valiant vs. Tony Zane
The Warlord vs. George South
Nikita Koloff & Krusher Khruschev vs. Bill Bryant & Bill Tabb
Dick Murdoch vs. Vernon Deaton
Wahoo McDaniel & Sam Houston vs. Thunderfoot & Black Bart
Rocky King vs. Steve Regal
The Midnight Express vs. Darrin Evans & Tom Pittman
The Rock & Roll Express vs. Pablo Crenshaw & Bob Burroughs
Buddy Landell vs. Randy Barber

8/9/86: St. Louis, MO @ Arena
Cousin Junior beat Bob Owens
Rick McCord beat Ron Powers
Tully Blanchard beat Sam Houston
Wahoo McDaniel beat Jimmy Garvin in an Indian strap match
Magnum TA, Dick Murdoch & Baby Doll beat Jim Cornette & The Midnight Express in a steel cage match
Ric Flair beat Dusty Rhodes to win NWA World Title

8/10/86: Asheville, NC @ Civic Center
NWA World Champion Ric Flair beat Dusty Rhodes by DQ
The Rock & Roll Express & Dick Murdoch beat Ole Anderson, Arn Anderson & Tully Blanchard
Magnum TA beat Nikita Koloff in match #6 of best of 7 series
Jimmy Valiant beat Paul Jones
The Warlord beat Big Bubba by DQ
The Midnight Express draw The Kansas Jayhawks
Buddy Landell beat Rocky King
Bill Dundee beat Italian Stallion

8/11/86: Greenville, SC @ Memorial Auditorium
The Midnight Express draw The Rock & Roll Express(45:00)

8/11/86: Fayetteville, NC @ Cumberland County Civic Center
Hector Guerrero beat Thunderfoot
Black Bart beat Denny Brown
The Warlord beat Mark Fleming
The Barbarian & Shaska Whatley beat Ronnie Garvin & Sam Houston
Mexican Death: Manny Fernandez beat Baron Von Raschke in a Mexican death match
Jimmy Valiant beat Paul Jones in a lumberjack match
The Rock & Roll Express beat The Midnight Express 2/3 falls match

8/11/86: Camp Lejeune, NC @ Goettge Memorial Fieldhouse
Nikita Koloff vs. Ronnie Garvin
Ivan Koloff & Krusher Khrushchev vs. The Kansas Jayhawks
Baron Von Raschke vs. Manny Fernandez
The Barbarian vs. Italian Stallion
Black Bart vs. Todd Champion
Denny Brown vs. Hector Guerrero

8/12/86: Spartanburg, SC @ Memorial Auditorium
The Warlord vs. Teijo Khan
Sam Houston vs. Black Bart
The Kansas Jayhawks vs. Baron Von Raschke & The Barbarian
Jimmy Valiant vs. Paul Jones in a lumberjack match
Wahoo McDaniel & Dick Murdoch vs. Ivan Koloff & Krusher Khruschev
The Rock & Roll Express & Magnum TA vs. Arn Anderson, Ole Anderson & Tully Blanchard

8/13/86: Charleston, SC @ Arthur Ravenal Stadium
Jimmy Valiant vs. Paul Jones
Manny Fernandez vs. Shaska Whatley in a Mexican death match
The Kansas Jayhawks vs. The Barbarian & Teijo Khan
The Warlord vs. Black Bart
Thunderfoot vs. Denny Brown
Steve Regal vs. Rickey Lee Jones(aka Ricky Gibson)
Hector Guerrero vs. Tony Zane

8/13/86: Raleigh, NC @ Dorton Arena
Bill Dundee beat Italian Stallion
NWA World Champion Ric Flair beat Dusty Rhodes by DQ
Buddy Landell beat Sam Houston
Jimmy Garvin beat Todd Champion
Dick Murdoch & Don Kernodle beat Ivan Koloff & Khrusher Khruschev by DQ
Magnum TA draw Arn Anderson
Tully Blanchard beat Wahoo McDaniel in a no DQ match
The Midnight Express beat The Rock & Roll Express

8/14/86: Albany, GA @ Civic Center
The Midnight Express beat Ronnie Garvin & Manny Fernandez by DQ
Paul Jones vs. Jimmy Valiant in a lumberjack match
Shaska Whatley & The Barbarian vs. The Kansas Jayhawks
Baron Von Raschke vs. Hector Guerrero
Black Bart vs. Todd Champion
Ricky Lee Jones vs. Denny Brown

8/15/86: Columbia, SC @ Township Auditorium
Dusty Rhodes, Magnum TA & The Rock & Roll Express vs. Arn & Ole Anderson, Tully Blanchard & Ric Flair
Ronnie Garvin & Wahoo McDaniel vs. Nikita Koloff & Krusher Khrushchev
Dick Murdoch vs. Ivan Koloff
Baron Von Raschke vs. Todd Champion
Sam Houston vs. Buddy Landell
Italian Stallion vs. Bill Dundee

8/15/86: Hays, NC
Midnight Express beat Manny Fernandez & Hector Guerrero

8/16/86: Atlanta, GA @ WTBS Studios (TV)
The Kansas Jayhawks beat George South & Bill Mulkey
Road Warriors beat Pablo Crenshaw & Tom Pittman
Bill Dundee beat Vernon Deaton
Tully Blanchard, Ole & Arn Anderson beat Sam Houston, Todd Champion & Italian Stallion
Dick Murdoch beat Tony Zane
Krusher Khruschev, Ivan & Nikita Koloff beat Randy Barber, Clement Fields & Paul Garner
The Rock & Roll Express beat Bill Tabb & Art Pritts

8/16/86: Atlanta, GA @ Omni
The Warlord beat The Barbarian by DQ
Manny Fernandez beat Teijo Khan
Bill Dundee beat Sam Houston
Buddy Landell beat Todd Champion
Jimmy Valiant beat Paul Jones
The Road Warriors & Paul Ellering beat Ole & Arn Anderson & Tully Blanchard in an elimination match
NWA World Champion Ric Flair beat Dusty Rhodes DQ

8/16/86: Philadelphia, PA @ Civic Center
Magnum TA NC with Nikita Koloff in match #7 of best of 7 series with Bob Geigel as special referee
The Rock & Roll Express beat The Midnight Express in a 2/3 falls match to win the NWA World Tag Title
Ivan Koloff & Khrusher Khruschev draw The Kansas Jayhawks
Wahoo McDaniel beat Baron Von Raschke
Dick Murdoch beat Steve Regal

8/17/86: Huntington, WV @ Memorial Fieldhouse
Dusty Rhodes, Magnum TA & Baby Doll beat The Midnight Express & Jim Cornette in a cage match

8/17/86: Charlotte, NC @ Coliseum
Nikita Koloff beat Magnum TA in match #7 of best of7 series to win vacant NWA United States Title
The Rock & Roll Express beat The Midnight Express
Ole Anderson, Arn Anderson & Tully Blanchard beat Dick Murdoch, Ronnie Garvin & Wahoo McDaniel
Buddy Landell beat Sam Houston
The Kansas Jayhawks beat ?? & ??

8/18/86: Norfolk, VA @ Scope
Bill Dundee beat Italian Stallion
Buddy Landell beat Sam Houston
The Warlord beat Thunderfoot
Dick Murdoch & Don Kernodle beat Ivan Koloff & Krusher Khruschev
Nikita Koloff beat Wahoo McDaniel
Dusty Rhodes, The Rock & Roll Express & Magnum TA beat Ric Flair, Ole Anderson, Arn Anderson & Tully Blanchard

8/18/86: Fayetteville, NC @ Cumberland County Civic Center
Rock & Roll Express beat The Midnight Express by DQ

8/20/86: Indianapolis, IN @ State Fairgrounds
NWA World Champion Ric Flair vs. Dusty Rhodes
The Rock & Roll Express beat The Midnight Express
Nikita Koloff vs. Magnum TA
Tully Blanchard vs. Wahoo McDaniel
Arn Anderson vs. Manny Fernandez
Jimmy Valiant vs. Shaska Whatley
The Barbarian vs. Sam Houston
Jimmy Garvin vs. Todd Champion

8/21/86: Cincinnati, OH @ Riverfront Coliseum
Steve Regal beat Denny Brown
Khrusher Khruschev beat Italian Stallion
Ivan Koloff beat The Warlord
Jimmy Garvin beat Todd Champion
Ronnie Garvin beat Nikita Koloff
The Rock & Roll Express draw Ole & Arn Anderson
Tully Blanchard beat Wahoo McDaniel
The Midnight Express beat Dusty Rhodes & Magnum TA by DQ

8/22/86: Hampton, VA @ Coliseum
Todd Champion draw Italian Stallion
The Kansas Jayhawks beat The Barbarian & Teijo Khan
Ivan Koloff beat The Warlord
Wahoo McDaniel & Manny Fernandez beat The Midnight Express
Jimmy Valiant beat Shaska Whatley in a bunkhouse match
Dusty Rhodes beat Big Bubba in a cage match
Magnum TA beat Nikita Koloff in a Texas death match

8/22/86: Charleston, SC @ County Hall
Buddy Landell beat Rocky King
Steve Regal beat Denny Brown
Krusher Khruschev beat Rocky King
Jimmy Garvin beat Don Kernodle
Tully Blanchard beat Ronnie Garvin
Ole & Arn Anderson beat The Rock & Roll Express

8/23/86: Atlanta, GA @ WTBS Studios (TV)
The Rock & Roll Express vs. Mike Rose & Phil Brown
Tully Blanchard, Ole & Arn Anderson vs. Clement Fields, Paul Garner & Bill Tabb
Magnum TA vs. Art Pritts
The Road Warriors vs. Lee Peek & Kent Glover
The Midnight Express vs. Bill Mulkey & Randy Mulkey
Wahoo McDaniel vs. Randy Barber

8/23/86: Cleveland, OH @ Convocation Center
Buddy Landell beat Denny Brown

Krusher Khruschev NC with Ronnie Garvin
Dick Murdoch beat Ivan Koloff
The Kansas Jayhawks beat The Barbarian & Shaska Whatley
Jimmy Valiant beat Paul Jones
Paul Ellering & The Road Warriors beat The Midnight Express & Jim Cornette
Magnum TA beat Nikita Koloff
Dusty Rhodes beat Big Bubba in a cage match

8/24/86: Asheville, NC @ Civic Center
Bill Dundee beat Rocky King
Buddy Landell beat Todd Champion
Dennis Condrey beat The Warlord
Wahoo McDaniel beat Bobby Eaton
Ronnie Garvin beat Nikita Koloff
The Rock & Roll Express, Magnum TA & Dick Murdoch beat Ole Anderson, Arn Anderson, Tully Blanchard & James J. Dillon
Dusty Rhodes beat Big Bubba

8/24/86: Roanoke, VA @ Civic Center
Dusty Rhodes beat Big Bubba in a cage match
The Midnight Express beat Manny Fernandez & Hector Guerrero

8/25/86: Greenville, SC @ Memorial Auditorium
Steve Regal beat George South
Hector Guerrero beat Denny Brown
Black Bart beat Nelson Royal
Shaska Whatley beat Sam Houston
Jimmy Garvin beat Don Kernodle
Jimmy Valiant beat Paul Jones
Rock & Roll Express beat The Midnight Express by DQ in a 2/3 falls match

8/26/86: Rock Hill, SC @ Winthrop Coliseum (TV)
Magnum TA, Dusty Rhodes & The Rock & Roll Express beat Ric Flair, Arn Anderson, Tully Blanchard & James J. Dillon
Sam Houston beat Vernon Deaton
George South & Rocky King beat Randy & Bill Mulkey
Italian Stallion beat Tony Zane
The Kansas Jayhawks beat Thunderfoot & Mark Fleming
The Rock & Roll Express beat Bill Mulkey & Ron Rossi
Magnum TA beat Jack Jackson
Manny Fernandez beat Vernon Deaton
Baron Von Raschke beat George South by submission
Wahoo McDaniel & Ronnie Garvin beat Tony Zane & Colt Steele
NWA World Champion Ric Flair beat Rocky Kernodle
The Warlord beat Ron Rossi
The Midnight Express beat Vernon Deaton & Bill Mulkey
Jimmy Garvin beat Mitch Snow
Shaska Whatley beat George South
Arn Anderson beat Keith Patterson
Tully Blanchard beat Rocky Kernodle
Ivan Koloff & Krusher Khruschev beat Jack Jackson & Todd Champion
Nikita Koloff beat Sam Houston

8/28/86: Los Angeles, CA @ Olympic Auditorium
Hector Guerrero beat The Barbarian
Jimmy Valiant beat Shaska Whatley
Wahoo McDaniel beat Tully Blanchard to win NWA National Title
Dick Murdoch beat Arn Anderson
Road Warriors beat Ivan Koloff & Krusher Khruschev
Magnum TA NC with Nikita Koloff
The Rock & Roll Express beat The Midnight Express
NWA World Champ Ric Flair beat Dusty Rhodes by DQ

8/29/86: Norfolk, VA @ Scope
Denny Brown beat Mark Fleming
Bill Dundee beat Italian Stallion
Buddy Landell beat Hector Guerrero
Manny Fernandez beat Baron Von Raschke in a Texas death match
Jimmy Valiant beat Paul Jones in a lumberjack match
Magnum TA NC with Nikita Koloff
The Rock & Roll Express NC with The Midnight Express

8/29/86: Macon, GA @ Coliseum
Big Bubba DCO with The Warlord street fight match

8/30/86: Atlanta, GA @ WTBS Studios (TV)
Dick Murdoch vs. Mike Rose
The Kansas Jayhawks vs. Randy Barber & Alan Martin
Wahoo McDaniel vs. Tony Zane
The Rock & Roll Express vs. Phil Brown & Lee Peek
Bill Dundee & Buddy Landell vs. Rocky Johnson & Vernon Deaton
Jimmy Garvin vs. Rocky Kernodle
Jimmy Valiant vs. Art Pritts
Ole & Arn Anderson vs. Henry Rutley & Italian Stallion
NWA World Champion Ric Flair vs. Mike Jackson
Nikita Koloff vs. Dave Spencer
Baron Von Raschke, Shaska Whatley & Teijo Khan vs. Johnnie Cook, Charles Freeman & Mark Cooper

8/30/86: Greensboro, NC @ Coliseum
Nelson Royal beat Sam Houston
Bill Dundee beat Mark Fleming
Don Kernodle beat Black Bart
Buddy Landell beat Hector Guerrero
Big Bubba beat The Warlord in a Louisville street fight
Dick Murdoch & Wahoo McDaniel beat The Midnight Express
Dusty Rhodes, Magnum TA & Rock & Roll Express beat Ric Flair, Ole & Arn Anderson & Tully Blanchard

8/31/86: Atlanta, GA @ WTBS Studios (TV)

8/31/86: Atlanta, GA @ Omni
Dusty Rhodes beat Big Bubba in a cage match

8/31/86: Charlotte, NC @ Coliseum
Wahoo McDaniel & The Road Warriors vs. Tully Blanchard, Ole & Arn Anderson
The Rock & Roll Express beat The Midnight Express
Nikita Koloff vs. Ronnie Garvin
NWA World Champion Ric Flair vs. Dick Murdoch
Dusty Rhodes beat Big Bubba in a Louisville street fight in steel cage

9/1/86: Greenville, SC @ Memorial Auditorium
Rocky King beat George South
Misty Blue beat Linda Dallas
Denny Brown beat Steve Regal to win NWA World Junior Title
Buddy Landell beat Don Kernodle
Ivan Koloff & Krusher Khruschev beat Manny Fernandez & Hector Guerrero
Nikita Koloff beat Wahoo McDaniel
Ronnie Garvin beat Tully Blanchard

9/1/86: Fayetteville, NC @ Cumberland County Civic Center
Dusty Rhodes beat Big Bubba
Black Bart beat Rocky Kernodle
Nelson Royal beat Thunderfoot I
The Warlord beat Thunderfoot II
Arn Anderson beat Todd Champion
The Midnight Express beat The Kansas Jayhawks
Magnum TA beat Jimmy Garvin

9/2/86: Spartanburg, SC @ Memorial Auditorium (TV)
Magnum TA, Wahoo McDaniel & Ronnie Garvin vs. Ivan & Nikita Koloff & Krusher Khruschev
Ronnie Garvin beat Black Bart wins Mid Atlantic Title

9/3/86: Raleigh, NC @ Dorton Arena
Khrusher Khruschev beat The Warlord
Buddy Landell beat Hector Guerrero
Tully Blanchard beat Ronnie Garvin
Jimmy Valiant beat Jimmy Garvin
Dusty Rhodes beat Big Bubba in a cage match
Wahoo McDaniel NC with Nikita Koloff
The Midnight Express beat The Kansas Jayhawks
Misty Blue beat Linda Dallas
NWA World Champion Ric Flair beat Magnum TA

9/4/86: Kansas City, KS @ Memorial Hall
John Paul Demann draw The Assassin
Ric McCord beat Steve Estes
Sam Houston beat Bob Owens
Bob Brown & Butch Reed NC with Dave Peterson & Rufus R. Jones
Joe Lightfoot & Billy Two Eagles beat Chris Colt & Moondog Moretti

9/4/86: Albany, GA @ Civic Center
Hector Guerrero vs. Steve Regal
Denny Brown vs. Teijo Khan
The Barbarian vs. Don Kernodle
Sam Houston vs. Shaska Whatley
Big Bubba beat The Warlord by CO
Manny Fernandez vs. Jimmy Garvin
Wahoo McDaniel & Ronnie Garvin beat The Midnight Express by DQ

9/4/86: Cincinnati, OH @ Gardens
Misty Blue vs. Linda Dallas
Black Bart vs. Todd Champion
Buddy Landell vs. Jimmy Valiant
The Kansas Jayhawks vs. Ivan Koloff & Krusher Khruschev
Magnum TA vs. Nikita Koloff
Dusty Rhodes & The Road Warriors vs. Ole Anderson, Tully Blanchard & Ric Flair

9/5/86: Richmond, VA @ Coliseum
Denny Brown beat Mark Fleming
Italian Stallion beat George South
Misty Blue beat Linda Dallas
Shaska Whatley beat Todd Champion
The Midnight Express beat The Kansas Jayhawks
Buddy Landell beat The Warlord
Wahoo McDaniel & The Road Warriors beat Ole & Arn Anderson & Tully Blanchard
NWA World Champion Ric Flair beat Ronnie Garvin
Dusty Rhodes beat Big Bubba
9/6/86: Atlanta, GA @ WTBS Studios (TV)
Buddy Landell & Bill Dundee vs. Rocky King & Johnnie Cook
Ronnie Garvin & Dick Murdoch vs. Brodie Chase & Alan Martin
Wahoo McDaniel vs. Lee Peek
The Rock & Roll Express vs. ?? & ??
The Road Warriors vs. Art Pritts & Darrin Evans
The Kansas Jayhawks beat Ole & Arn Anderson by DQ
Nikita Koloff vs. Randy Barber
Tully Blanchard & Jimmy Garvin vs. ?? & ??
The Warlord vs. Jack Weathers

9/6/86: Baltimore, MD @ Civic Center
Denny Brown beat George South
Misty Blue beat Linda Dallas
Jimmy Garvin beat Sam Houston
The Warlord beat Thunderfoot I & Thunderfoot II in a handicap match
Baron Von Raschke beat Todd Champion
Ole & Arn Anderson beat The Rock & Roll Express
Tully Blanchard beat Ronnie Garvin
NWA World Champion Ric Flair beat Dusty Rhodes

9/6/86: Fayetteville, NC @ Cumberland County Civic Center
Tim Horner draw Bill Dundee
Rick Rude beat Alan West
Wahoo McDaniel beat Baron Von Raschke by DQ
The Kansas Jayhawks beat The Midnight Express
Magnum TA beat Jimmy Garvin
Dusty Rhodes beat Tully Blanchard

9/6/86: Philadelphia, PA @ Civic Center
Don Kernodle beat Steve Regal
Buddy Landell beat Italian Stallion
The Barbarian beat Dutch Mantell
Bobby Jaggers beat Shaska Whatley by DQ
Ivan Koloff & Khrusher Khruschev beat Manny Fernandez & Hector Guerrero
Jimmy Valiant beat Paul Jones in a lumberjack match
Wahoo McDaniel & Dick Murdoch beat The Midnight Express by DQ
Nikita Koloff beat Magnum TA in a cage match

9/7/86: Atlanta, GA @ WTBS Studios (TV)
The Rock & Roll Express beat The Midnight Express(20:00) by reverse decision

9/7/86: Marietta, GA @ Cobb County Civic Center
The Rock & Roll Express beat The Midnight Express
Dusty Rhodes beat Big Bubba in a street fight match

9/8/86: Wallace, SC
The Rock & Roll Express beat The Midnight Express

9/9/86: Columbia, SC @ Township Auditorium (TV)
Dusty Rhodes beat Arn Anderson to win NWA World Television Title
The Midnight Express beat The Kansas Jayhawks
NWA World Champion Ric Flair vs. Magnum TA
Ivan & Nikita Koloff & Krusher Khrushchev vs. The Rock & Roll Express & Wahoo McDaniel
also including The Warlord, Thunderfoot, Dick Murdoch, Sam Houston, Jimmy Garvin, Teijo Khan, Buddy Landell, Jimmy Valiant, Manny Fernandez & Hector Guerrero

9/11/86: Norfolk, VA @ Scope
Nikita Koloff beat Magnum TA by DQ
The Rock & Roll Express beat The Midnight Express in a 2/3 falls match
Dusty Rhodes beat Big Bubba by CO in a street fight match
Italian Stallion beat Mark Fleming
Misty Blue beat Linda Dallas
Buddy Landell beat Hector Guerrero
Arn Anderson beat The Warlord
Wahoo McDaniel beat Ivan Koloff
NWA World Champion Ric Flair beat Dick Murdoch by DQ

9/12/86: Charleston, SC @ County Hall
Dutch Mantell beat Thunderfoot II
Misty Blue beat Linda Dallas
Bobby Jaggers beat Thunderfoot I
Jimmy Garvin beat Sam Houston
Dick Murdoch & The Rock & Roll Express beat The Midnight Express & Big Bubba
Wahoo McDaniel beat Tully Blanchard
Magnum TA beat Nikita Koloff

9/13/86: Charlotte, NC @ Coliseum
Dusty Rhodes, The Rock & Roll Express beat The Midnight Express & Big Bubba

9/14/86: Atlanta, GA @ WTBS Studios (TV)
Baron Von Raschke vs. Tom Barrett
The Rock & Roll Express vs. Gene Ligon & Mike Simani
Arn Anderson vs. Jack Jackson
The Road Warriors vs. Vernon Deaton & Mike Simani
The Kansas Jayhawks vs. Pablo Crenshaw & Tony Zane
Dick Murdoch & Ronnie Garvin vs. Bill Mulkey & Randy Mulkey

9/14/86: Cleveland, OH @ Convocation Center
Bill Dundee beat Sam Houston
Ronnie Garvin draw Buddy Landell
Misty Blue beat Linda Dallas
Dick Murdoch beat Arn Anderson
Wahoo McDaniel beat Tully Blanchard by DQ
The Road Warriors & Paul Ellering beat Ivan Koloff, Krusher Khruschev & Baron Von Raschke
The Rock & Roll Express beat The Midnight Express
Nikita Koloff beat Magnum TA in a cage match

9/15/86:-9/17/86:
No wrestling due to annual NWA Convention

Note: Jim Crockett bought the Central States promotion in September of 1986: & ran the territory until February 1987, when he sold it back to Bob Geigel.

9/18/86: Kansas City, KS @ Memorial Hall
The Assassin, Tommy Sharpe & Billy Estes beat Joe Lightfoot, Billy Two Eagles & John Paul Demann in an elimination match
Sam Houston beat Chris Colt
Mike George beat Ric McCord
Bobby Jaggers beat Moondog Moretti
Sam Houston won a battle royal
Rufus R. Jones & Dave Peterson beat Bob Brown & Butch Reed by DQ in a Texas tornado, cage match

9/18/86: Green Bay, WI @ Brown County Arena
Ronnie Garvin beat Ole Anderson
Arn Anderson beat Baron Von Raschke by DQ
Jimmy Valiant beat Shaska Whatley
Paul Ellering beat James J. Dillon
Dick Murdoch beat Tully Blanchard by DQ
Wahoo McDaniel beat Jimmy Garvin in a strap match
The Rock & Roll Express beat The Midnight Express
Magnum TA DCO with Nikita Koloff
The Road Warriors beat Ivan Koloff & Krusher Khrushchev
NWA World Champion Ric Flair beat Dusty Rhodes

9/19/86: Bloomington, MN @ Met Center
Ronnie Garvin beat James J. Dillon
Baron Von Raschke beat Jimmy Garvin by DQ
Arn Anderson beat Jimmy Valiant
Dick Murdoch beat Shaska Whatley
Tully Blanchard beat Magnum TA by DQ
The Rock & Roll Express beat The Midnight Express
NWA World Champion Ric Flair beat Dusty Rhodes by DQ
The Road Warriors & Paul Ellering beat Ivan & Nikita Koloff & Khrusher Khruschev

9/20/86: Greensboro, NC @ Coliseum
The Kansas Jayhawks beat Bill Dundee & Buddy Landell
Mitch Snow beat Bill Mulkey
Krusher Khruschev beat Nelson Royal
Don Kernodle beat Baron Von Raschke
Dick Murdoch beat Jimmy Garvin
Dusty Rhodes beat Big Bubba
Ole & Arn Anderson beat The Rock & Roll Express by DQ
Nikita Koloff beat Magnum TA

9/21/86: Atlanta, GA @ WTBS Studios (TV)

9/21/86: Asheville, NC @ Civic Center
Tim Horner beat Mike Simani
Bill Dundee beat Joe Jackson
Ronnie Garvin beat Buddy Landell by DQ
The Kansas Jayhawks draw Ivan Koloff & Khrusher Khruschev
Wahoo McDaniel beat Tully Blanchard
Ole & Arn Anderson beat The Rock & Roll Express by DQ

9/21/86: Charlotte, NC @ Coliseum
The Midnight Express beat The Kansas Jayhawks
The Rock & Roll Express draw Ole & Arn Anderson

9/22/86: Greenville, SC @ Memorial Auditorium
Grudge Match: Tully Blanchard beat Dusty Rhodes DQ
US Title Match: Nikita Koloff(c) DCO Wahoo McDaniel
Magnum TA DDQ Jimmy Garvin
Ron Garvin DRAW Buddy Landell
Bill Dundee beat Rocky Kernodle
Manny Fernandez beat Tony Zane
Nelson Royal beat the Golden Terror

9/22/86: Saginaw, MI
The Rock & Roll Express beat The Midnight Express

9/23/86: Lansing, MI
The Rock & Roll Express beat The Midnight Express in a 2/3 falls match

9/23/86: Cincinnati, OH @ Gardens
Don Kernodle beat The Barbarian
Manny Fernandez & Jimmy Valiant beat Baron Von Raschke & Shaska Whatley
The Rock & Roll Express beat Ivan Koloff & Krusher Khruschev
Nikita Koloff beat Ronnie Garvin
NWA World Champion Ric Flair draw Dick Murdoch

9/24/86: Grand Rapids, MI
The Midnight Express beat The Kansas Jayhawks

9/25/86: Joplin, MO
Butch Reed & Bob Brown vs. Rufus R. Jones & Dave Peterson in a Texas tornado, cage match
13-man battle royal
Bobby Jaggers vs. Moondog Moretti
Mike George vs. Ric McCord
Sam Houston vs. Chris Colt
Billy Two Eagles, Joe Lightfoot & John Paul Demann vs. Bo Owens, Assassin & Steve Estes

9/25/86: Columbia, SC @ Township Auditorium
Dusty Rhodes vs. Arn Anderson
Jimmy Garvin vs. Magnum TA
The Midnight Express beat The Kansas Jayhawks
Wahoo McDaniel vs. Tully Blanchard

9/26/86: Kansas City, KS @ Memorial Hall
Sam Houston(sub for Mitch Snow) beat Mark Fleming
Jimmy Garvin beat Mitch Snow
Italian Stallion beat Colt Steele
The Mod Squad & Colt Steele beat George South, Rufus R. Jones & Mitch Snow
Italian Stallion beat Mark Fleming
Bill Dundee beat Rocky King
Denny Brown beat Teijo Khan
Thunderfoot I & Thunderfoot II beat Todd Champion & Dave Peterson
Sam Houston draw Buddy Landell
The Rock & Roll Express beat Big Bubba & The Warlord by DQ
Tully Blanchard beat Dusty Rhodes by DQ

9/26/86: Norfolk, VA @ Scope
The Midnight Express beat The Kansas Jayhawks

9/27/86: Macon, GA @ Coliseum (TV)

9/27/86: Mount Airy, NC
Jimmy Valiant vs. Shaska Whatley
Manny Fernandez & Hector Guerrero vs. The Barbarian & Baron Von Raschke
Don Kernodle vs. Krusher Khruschev
Nelson Royal vs. Golden Terror
Jack Jackson vs. Tony Zane

9/28/86: Atlanta, GA @ WTBS Studios (TV)
Jimmy Garvin vs. Vernon Deaton
Shaska Whatley & The Barbarian vs. Bill Mulkey & Randy Mulkey
Hector Guerrero & Manny Fernandez vs. Golden Terror & Tony Zane
Nikita Koloff vs. Bill Tabb
Jimmy Valiant vs. Brodie Chase
The Midnight Express vs. Art Pritts & Paul Garner

9/28/86: Atlanta, GA @ Omni
NWA United States Tag Title Tournament
1st Round
Ivan Koloff & Krusher Khruschev beat Tim Horner & Nelson Royal
Tully Blanchard & Jimmy Garvin beat Jimmy Valiant & Manny Fernandez
Dick Murdoch & Ronnie Garvin draw The Midnight Express
Dusty Rhodes & Magnum TA beat Baron Von Raschke & Shaska Whatley
Kansas Jayhawks beat Bill Dundee & Buddy Landell

Semifinals
Ivan Koloff & Khrusher Khruschev beat Dusty Rhodes & Magnum TA by DQ
Kansas Jayhawks beat Tully Blanchard & Jimmy Garvin

Finals
Ivan Koloff & Khrusher Khruschev beat The Kansas Jayhawks to win NWA nited States Tag Title
Ole & Arn Anderson beat The Rock & Roll Express by DQ
Nikita Koloff beat Wahoo McDaniel to win NWA National Title & unify it with NWA United States Title

9/29/86: Wichita, KS
Rufus R. Jones beat Mark Fleming
The Mod Squad beat Rocky King & George South
Denny Brown beat Thunderfoot I
Thunderfoot II beat Italian Stallion
Magnum TA draw Buddy Landell
Todd Champion & Dave Peterson beat Big Bubba & The Warlord by DQ
Sam Houston beat Teijo Khan
The Rock & Roll Express beat The Midnight Express
NWA World Champion Ric Flair beat Dusty Rhodes by DQ

9/30/86: Rock Hill, SC @ Winthrop Coliseum (TV)
NWA World Champion Ric Flair vs. Dusty Rhodes
The Kansas Jayhawks vs. The Midnight Express
Jimmy Garvin vs. Magnum TA
Ronnie Garvin vs. Ivan Koloff
Tim Horner vs. Hector Guerrero
Eddie Roberts vs. Danny Davis
Nelson Royal vs. Gary Royal
Ken Wayne vs. Allen West

9/30/86: St. Joseph, MO @ Civic Arena
Mitch Snow beat Colt Steele
Thunderfoot II beat Rufus R. Jones
Dennis Brown beat Thunderfoot I
Bill Dundee beat Mark Fleming
The Mod Squad beat George South & Rocky King
Sam Houston draw Buddy Landell
Dave Peterson & Todd Champion beat The Warlord & Big Bubba by DQ

10/1/86: Salina, KS @ Bicentennial Center
Rufus R. Jones vs. Big Bubba
Denny Brown vs. Mark Fleming
Italian Stallion vs. Teijo Khan
Dave Peterson & Todd Champion vs. Thunderfoot I & Thunderfoot II
Sam Houston vs. The Warlord
Jimmy Valiant vs. Shaska Whatley

10/1/86: Raleigh, NC @ Dorton Arena
The Kansas Jayhawks beat The Barbarian & Gary Royal
Manny Fernandez beat Baron Von Raschke
Wahoo McDaniel beat The Barbarian
Brad Armstrong beat Ivan Koloff
Magnum TA beat Jimmy Garvin by DQ
The Rock & Roll Express beat Ole & Arn Anderson
NWA World Champion Ric Flair beat Dick Murdoch

10/2/86: Des Moines, IA
Italian Stallion beat Teijo Khan
The Mod Squad beat Rocky King & George South
Jimmy Valiant beat Shaska Whatley
Todd Champion & Dave Peterson draw Thunderfoot I Thunderfoot II
Sam Houston beat The Warlord by DQ
The Rock & Roll Express beat Ole & Arn Anderson
NWA World Champion Ric Flair beat Dusty Rhodes

10/3/86: Kansas City, MO @ Kemper Arena
The Mod Squad beat Mitch Snow & Rocky King
Italian Stallion beat Teijo Khan
Denny Brown beat Mark Fleming
Todd Champion & Dave Peterson draw Thunderfoot I & Thunderfoot II
Sam Houston beat The Warlord by DQ
Jimmy Valiant beat Shaska Whatley
The Rock & Roll Express beat Ole & Arn Anderson
NWA World Champion Ric Flair beat Ronnie Garvin

10/3/86: Hampton, VA @ Coliseum
Midnight Express draw Kansas Jayhawks(20:00)

10/4/86: Albany, GA @ Civic Center
Danny Davis vs. Keith Patterson
Eddie Roberts vs. Gary Royal
Ken Wayne vs. Alan West
Nelson Royal vs. Shaska Whatley
Ivan Koloff vs. Jimmy Valiant
The Kansas Jayhawks beat The Midnight Express DQ

10/4/86: Charlotte, NC @ Coliseum
Tim Horner beat Grim Reaper
Rick Rude beat Alan West
Brad Armstrong beat The Barbarian
Shaska Whatley & Baron Von Raschke beat Manny Fernandez & Jimmy Valiant
Tully Blanchard beat Dick Murdoch
The Rock & Roll Express beat Ole & Arn Anderson
NWA World Champion Ric Flair beat Dusty Rhodes

10/5/86: Atlanta, GA @ WTBS Studios (TV)
Brad Armstrong beat Randy Mulkey
Rick Rude beat Bill Mulkey
Ronnie Garvin beat Brodie Chase
Manny Fernandez beat Lee Peek
The Midnight Express beat Clement Fields & Alan Martin
Magnum TA vs. Vernon Deaton
Manny Fernandez vs. Mike Simani
Tim Horner vs. Randy Mulkey
Tully Blanchard, Ole & Arn Anderson vs. Rocky Kernodle, Bill Tabb & Charles Freeman
Baron Von Raschke & Shaska Whatley vs. Bill Mulkey & Lee Peek
The Midnight Express vs. Randy Barber & Pablo Crenshaw
Ronnie Garvin vs. Gary Royal

10/5/86: Roanoke, VA @ Civic Center
Ricky Morton & Brad Armstrong beat The Midnight Express by DQ

10/6/86: Greenville, SC @ Memorial Auditorium
Shaska Whatley beat Eddie Roberts
Brad Armstrong beat Tony Zane
Hector Guerrero beat Gary Royal
Manny Fernandez beat Grim Reaper
Ronnie Garvin beat Ivan Koloff
Brad Armstrong & Ricky Morton beat Arn & Ole Anderson
NWA World Champion Ric Flair beat Dick Murdoch

10/6/86: Fayetteville, NC @ Cumberland County Civic Center
The Kansas Jayhawks beat The Midnight Express

10/7/86: Spartanburg, SC @ Memorial Auditorium (TV)
Magnum TA vs. Jimmy Garvin
NWA World Champion Ric Flair vs. Dusty Rhodes
Ole Anderson vs. Ricky Morton
The Midnight Express beat Gary Royal & Tony Zane
Brad Armstrong beat Eddie Roberts
Jimmy Garvin beat Ben Alexander
Rick Rude, Manny Fernandez & Baron Von Raschke beat Rocky Kernodle, Keith Patterson & ??
Tully Blanchard & Arn Anderson beat Nelson Royal & Tim Horner
Ricky Morton beat Gary Royal
Brad Armstrong beat Vernon Deaton
Ronnie Garvin beat Randy Mulkey
Rick Rude beat Keith Patterson
Bill Dundee beat Eddie Roberts
Wahoo McDaniel beat Mike Simani
Ole Anderson, Arn Anderson & Tully Blanchard beat Tony Zane, Ben Alexander & Bill Mulkey

10/8/86: Lenoir, NC
Magnum TA beat Jimmy Garvin
Ricky Morton & Brad Armstrong beat The Midnight Express

10/9/86: Baltimore, MD @ Civic Center
Ronnie Garvin beat Ivan Koloff
Jimmy Valiant beat Baron Von Raschke
Brad Armstrong beat Grim Reaper
Tim Horner draw Shaska Whatley
Dusty Rhodes beat Tully Blanchard
Ronnie Garvin & Ricky Morton beat Ole & Arn Anderson by DQ
NWA World Champion Ric Flair beat Dick Murdoch

10/9/86: Raleigh, NC @ Dorton Arena
Magnum TA beat Jimmy Garvin
Gary Royal beat Eddie Roberts
Rick Rude beat Allen West
Don Kernodle & Hector Guerrero beat Bill Mulkey & Randy Mulkey
Wahoo McDaniel beat Bill Dundee
The Kansas Jayhawks beat The Midnight Express in a bunkhouse match

10/10/86: Norfolk, VA @ Scope
Wahoo McDaniel beat Bobby Eaton by DQ

10/11/86: Charleston, SC @ County Hall
Wahoo McDaniel & Ronnie Garvin vs. Ole & Arn Anderson
Jimmy Valiant vs. Buddy Landell
Hector Guerrero vs. Bill Dundee
Nelson Royal vs. Grim Reaper
Allen West vs. Gary Royal
Eddie Roberts vs. Rob Patterson

10/11/86: Greensboro, NC @ Coliseum
Rick Rude beat Tim Horner
Brad Armstrong beat Ivan Koloff
Don Kernodle beat Baron Von Raschke
Magnum TA beat Jimmy Garvin
Ricky Morton & Brad Armstrong beat The Midnight Express by DQ
NWA World Champion Ric Flair beat Dick Murdoch
Tully Blanchard beat Dusty Rhodes by DQ

10/12/86: Atlanta, GA @ WTBS Studios (TV)
The Midnight Express vs. Paul Garner & Art Pritts
Brad Armstrong vs. Randy Barber
Tim Horner vs. Bill Tabb
Rick Rude vs. Lee Peek
Tully Blanchard vs. Tony Zane
Manny Fernandez vs. Randy Glover

10/12/86: St. Louis, MO @ Arena
Sam Houston beat The Warlord by DQ
Bill Dundee beat Italian Stallion
Denny Brown beat Colt Steele
Thunderfoot I & II beat Mark Fleming & Mitch Snow
Todd Champion & Dave Peterson draw The Mod Squad
Ricky Morton beat Ole & Arn Anderson
Dusty Rhodes beat Teijo Khan
NWA World Champion Ric Flair beat Dick Murdoch

10/12/86: Cincinnati, OH @ Gardens
The Kansas Jayhawks beat The Midnight Express

10/13/86: Greenville, SC @ Memorial Auditorium
Lumberjack Match: Magnum TA beat Jimmy Garvin
Bunkhouse Match: Kansas Jayhawks beat the Midnight Express
Dick Murdoch beat Rick Rude
Shaska Whatley beat Bill Mulky
Allen West beat Tony Zane
Manny Fernandez beat Hector Guerrero
Eddie Roberts beat Randy Mulky

10/14/86: Columbia, SC @ Township Auditorium (TV)
The Kansas Jayhawks beat The Midnight Express
The Midnight Express beat John Savage & Rocky Kernodle
Rick Rude, Manny Fernandez & Shaska Whatley beat Eddie Roberts, Alan West & Bill Mulkey
Brad Armstrong beat Vernon Deaton
Jimmy Garvin beat Randy Mulkey
Dick Murdoch beat Mike Simani
Rick Rude & Manny Fernandez beat Bill Mulkey & Randy Mulkey
Hector Guerrero beat John Savage
Brad Armstrong beat Mike Simani
Midnight Express beat Alan West & Vernon Deaton
Jimmy Garvin beat Eddie Roberts
Ric Flair & Jimmy Garvin vs. Magnum TA & Dusty Rhodes

*Magnum TA has serious car wreck that night and never wrestles again.

10/15/86: Grand Rapids, MI
Keith Patterson beat Grim Reaper
Nelson Royal draw Bill Dundee
Tim Horner beat Gary Royal
Ivan Koloff beat Keith Patterson
Ronnie Garvin beat Baron Von Raschke
Ricky Morton & Wahoo McDaniel beat Ole & Arn Anderson

10/16/86: Cambridge, MD
Ricky Morton & Brad Armstrong beat Midnight Express

10/17/86: Richmond, VA @ Coliseum
Tim Horner beat Grim Reaper
Ivan Koloff beat Eddie Roberts
Jimmy Valiant & Nelson Royal beat Baron Von Raschke & Shaska Whatley
Wahoo McDaniel beat Rick Rude by DQ
Jimmy Garvin beat Hector Guerrero(sub for Magnum TA)
The Midnight Express beat The Kansas Jayhawks DQ
Dick Murdoch beat James J. Dillon(1:30)
Brad Armstrong(sub for Robert Gibson) & Ricky Morton beat Ole & Arn Anderson

10/17/86: Kansas City, KS @ Memorial Hall
Rocky King beat Colt Steele
Mitch Snow beat Mark Fleming
Denny Brown & Italian Stallion draw The Mod Squad
Bill Dundee beat Rufus R. Jones
Sam Houston beat Teijo Khan
Todd Champion & Dave Peterson beat Thunderfoot I & Thunderfoot II by DQ
Ronnie Garvin beat The Warlord by DQ

10/18/86: Philadelphia, PA @ Civic Center
The Midnight Express beat Tim Horner & Don Kernodle
Ivan & Nikita Koloff & Krusher Khruschev beat Jimmy Valiant, Dick Murdoch & Wahoo McDaniel
Brad Armstrong beat Jimmy Garvin by DQ
Manny Fernandez beat Hector Guerrero
The Rock & Roll Express beat Ole & Arn Anderson DQ
Dusty Rhodes beat James J. Dillon

10/19/86: Atlanta, GA @ WTBS Studios (TV)
Ole & Arn Anderson vs. Keith Patterson & Vernon Deaton
Ronnie Garvin vs. Grim Reaper
Ivan Koloff vs. Mike Simani
Shaska Whatley, Rick Rude & Baron Von Raschke vs. Brad Armstrong & The Kansas Jayhawks
The Midnight Express vs. Alan West & Eddie Roberts

10/19/86: Charlotte, NC @ Coliseum
Dusty Rhodes & Nikita Koloff beat Ole Anderson & James J. Dillon(sub for Tully Blanchard) in a steel cage match

10/20/86: Fayetteville, NC @ Cumberland County Civic Center
Rocky Kernodle beat Eddie Roberts
Don Kernodle beat Keith Patterson
Rick Rude beat Hector Guerrero
Wahoo McDaniel beat Manny Fernandez
Jimmy Garvin beat Dick Murdoch
The Kansas Jayhawks beat The Midnight Express

10/20/86: Greenville, SC @ Memorial Auditorium
Steel Cage Match Dusty Rhodes & Nikita Koloff beat Ole & Arn Anderson
NWA World Tag Champs the Rock & Roll Express beat Ivan Koloff & Krusher Krushchev
Ron Garvin beat the Grim Reaper
Tim Horner beat Tony Zane
Brad Armstrong beat Randy Mulky
Gary Royal beat Alan West

10/21/86: Greenwood, SC (TV)
Brad Armstrong beat Gary Royal
Jimmy Garvin beat Keith Patterson
Ivan Koloff & Krusher Khruschev beat Rocky Kernodle & ??
Tully Blanchard, Ole & Arn Anderson beat John Savage, Tony Zane & Mike Simani
The Midnight Express beat Bill & Randy Mulkey
Rock & Roll Express beat Grim Reaper & Gary Royal
Ole & Arn Anderson beat Nelson Royal & Tim Horner
Rick Rude & Manny Fernandez beat Eddie Roberts & Alan West
Brad Armstrong beat Vernon Deaton
Wahoo McDaniel beat Tony Zane

10/23/86: Sumter, SC @ Exhibition Center
The Midnight Express beat The Kansas Jayhawks

10/23/86: Concordia, KS @ Bryant Gymnasium
Jimmy Valiant vs. Shaska Whatley
Sam Houston vs. The Warlord
Todd Champion & Dave Peterson vs. Ivan Koloff & Baron Von Raschke
Italian Stallion vs. Thunderfoot I
Denny Brown vs. Thunderfoot II
Mitch snow vs. Colt Steele
Rufus R. Jones, Rocky king & George South vs. The Mod Squad & Teijo Khan

10/24/86: Pittsburgh, PA @ Civic Arena
Rick Rude beat Tim Horner
Jimmy Garvin beat Hector Guerrero
Wahoo McDaniel beat Tully Blanchard by DQ
Ronnie Garvin & Dick Murdoch draw Midnight Express
Nikita Koloff beat Brad Armstrong
The Rock & Roll Express beat Ole & Arn Anderson
NWA World Champ Ric Flair beat Dusty Rhodes by DQ

10/24/86: Kansas City, KS @ Memorial Hall
Teijo Khan beat Mark Fleming
The Mod Squad beat Denny Brown & Mitch Snow
George South beat Colt Steele
Italian Stallion beat Baron Von Raschke
Rufus R. Jones beat The Assassin
Thunderfoot I & II beat Todd Champion & Dave Peterson Texas tornado match
Sam Houston beat Bill Dundee by DQ
Jimmy Valiant beat Shaska Whatley

10/25/86: Greensboro, NC @ Coliseum
Jimmy Valiant beat Gary Royal
Rick Rude beat Hector Guerrero
Tully Blanchard beat Tim Horner
Wahoo McDaniel beat Manny Fernandez
Dusty Rhodes & Nikita Koloff beat Ole & Arn Anderson in a cage match
The Rock & Roll Express beat The Midnight Express in a cage match

10/26/86: Atlanta, GA @ WTBS Studios (TV)
Brad Armstrong & Tim Horner vs. Bill Tabb & Brodie Chase
Jimmy Garvin vs. John Savage
Ole & Arn Anderson vs. Randy Barber & Clement Fields
Rick Rude & Manny Fernandez) vs. Kent Glover & Alan Martin

10/26/86: Atlanta, GA @ Omni
Rick Rude beat Nelson Royal
Tully Blanchard beat Rocky Kernodle
Ronnie Garvin beat Shaska Whatley
Manny Fernandez beat Hector Guerrero
Brad Armstrong & Tim Horner beat Ivan Koloff & Krusher Khruschev
The Rock & Roll Express & Wahoo McDaniel beat The Midnight Express & Big Bubba by DQ
Dusty Rhodes & Nikita Koloff beat Ole & Arn Anderson
NWA World Champion Ric Flair beat Dick Murdoch

10/26/86: St. Joseph, MO @ Civic Arena
Mitch Snow beat Colt Steele
George South beat Mark Fleming
The Mod Squad beat Rufus R. Jones & Rocky King
The Warlord beat Italian Stallion
Sam Houston beat Bill Dundee by DQ
Sgt. Slaughter beat Teijo Khan
Thunderfoot I & Thunderfoot II beat Todd Champion & Dave Peterson

10/27/86: Greenville, SC @ Memorial Auditorium
Dusty Rhodes & Nikita Koloff beat Tully Blanchard Bullrope match
Ole Anderson beat Dick Murdoch
Rock & Roll Express beat Manny Fernandez & Rick Rude
Wahoo McDaniel beat Shaska Whatley
Baron Von Raschke beat the Grim Reaper
Brad Armstrong beat Bill Dundee

10/27/86: Misenheimer, NC
The Midnight Express beat The Kansas Jayhawks

10/28/86: Rock Hill, SC @ Winthrop Coliseum (TV)
Rock & Roll Express & Dusty Rhodes beat Ric Flair, Ole & Arn Anderson cage match
The Midnight Express beat Eddie Roberts & Alan West
Tully Blanchard beat Rocky Kernodle
Jimmy Garvin beat Brodie Chase
Big Bubba beat Mike Simani & Vernon Deaton in a handicap match
Rick Rude & Manny Fernandez beat Tony Zane & Gary Royal
Brad Armstrong beat Grim Reaper
Ole & Arn Anderson beat John Savage & Bill Mulkey
Ivan Koloff & Krusher Khrushchev beat Rocky Kernodle & Keith Patterson
Rickie Lee Jones beat Tony Zane
Brad Armstrong beat John Savage
Big Bubba & Midnight Express beat Gary Royal, Keith Patterson & Mike Simani
Rick Rude & Manny Fernandez beat Bill & Randy Mulkey
The Kansas Jayhawks beat Alan West & Eddie Roberts

10/29/86: Boone, NC
The Kansas Jayhawks beat The Midnight Express

10/30/86: Charleston, WV @ Civic Center
Nelson Royal beat Alan West
Rocky Kernodle beat Gary Royal
Don Kernodle draw Shaska Whatley
Wahoo McDaniel beat Tully Blanchard by DQ
Jimmy Garvin beat Hector Guerrero
The Rock & Roll Express beat Ole & Arn Anderson in a double bullrope match
NWA World Champion Ric Flair beat Dusty Rhodes by DQ

10/31/86: Kansas City, KS @ Memorial Hall
No Wrestling

11/1/86: Atlanta, GA @ WTBS Studios (TV)
Brad Armstrong beat Gary Royal
Jimmy Garvin beat Alan West
Ivan Koloff & Krusher Khruschev beat Rocky Kernodle & Keith Patterson
Ole & Arn Anderson & Tully Blanchard beat John Savage, Mike S? & Tony Zane
The Midnight Express beat Bill Mulkey & Randy Mulkey
Brad Armstrong beat Alan West
Ivan Koloff & Krusher Khruschev beat Brodie Chase & Vernon Deaton
Tully Blanchard beat Eddie Roberts
Manny Fernandez & Rick Rude beat John Savage & Mike Simani
Rock & Roll Express beat Grim Reaper & Tony Zane
The Midnight Express & Big Bubba beat Pablo Crenshaw, Keith Patterson & Gary Royal

11/1/86: Philadelphia, PA @ Civic Center
Baron Von Raschke draw Shaska Whatley
Jimmy Garvin beat Tim Horner
Ivan Koloff & Krusher Khruschev beat Hector Guerrero & Don Kernodle
Brad Armstrong beat Rick Rude by DQ
Manny Fernandez beat Wahoo McDaniel
Dusty Rhodes & Nikita Koloff beat Ric Flair & Tully Blanchard
The Rock & Roll Express beat Ole & Arn Anderson
Midnight Express & Big Bubba beat Ronnie Garvin & Kansas Jayhawks

11/2/86: Omaha, NE @ Civic Auditorium
Mitch Snow beat Mark Fleming
Bill Dundee & The Mod Squad beat Rocky King, George South & Italian Stallion
Teijo Khan beat Denny Brown
Sam Houston beat The Warlord in a Texas death match
Thunderfoot I & Thunderfoot II beat Todd Champion & Dave Peterson
The Rock & Roll Express beat The Midnight Express
NWA World Champion Ric Flair beat Dusty Rhodes

11/3/86: Greenville, SC @ Memorial Auditorium
Rock & Roll Express & Brad Armstrong beat the Midnight Express & Big Bubba
US Tag Title Match: Ivan Koloff & Krusher Krushchev(c) DDQ Kansas Jayhawks
Jimmy Garvin beat Don Kernodle
Nelson Royal beat Bill Mulkey
Tim Horner beat randy Mulkey
Allen West beat Tony Zane

11/3/86: Fayetteville, NC @ Cumberland County Civic Center
Gary Royal beat Eddie Roberts
Rocky Kernodle beat Grim Reaper
Hector Guerrero draw Shaska Whatley
Baron Von Raschke beat Rick Rude by DQ
Manny Fernandez beat Wahoo McDaniel
Ronnie Garvin NC with Arn Anderson
Dusty Rhodes & Nikita Koloff beat Ric Flair & Tully Blanchard

11/3/86: Greenville, SC @ Memorial Auditorium
The Rock & Roll Express & Brad Armstrong beat The Midnight Express & Big Bubba by DQ

11/4/86: Spartanburg, SC @ Memorial Auditorium (TV)
Dusty Rhodes & The Rock & Roll Express beat The Midnight Express & Big Bubba by DQ
Jumbo Tsuruta & Genichiro Tenryu beat Brodie Chase & Tony Zane
Hiroshi Wajima beat Randy Mulkey
Tully Blanchard & Arn Anderson beat John Savage & Ron Rossi
Big Bubba & Midnight Express beat Alan West, Eddie Roberts & Tony Zane

11/4/86: Wheeling, WV @ Civic Center
Tim Horner beat Grim Reaper
Jimmy Valiant beat Bill Dundee
Wahoo McDaniel NC with Manny Fernandez
Kansas Jayhawks beat Ivan Koloff & Krusher Khruschev
NWA World Champion Ric Flair beat Brad Armstrong

11/5/86: Canton, OH @ Civic Center
The Rock & Roll Express beat The Midnight Express

11/6/86: Raleigh, NC @ Dorton Arena
Dusty Rhodes & Nikita Koloff beat Ric Flair & Tully Blanchard
Big Bubba & Midnight Express beat Ronnie Garvin & The Rock & Roll Express
Arn Anderson beat Wahoo McDaniel
Manny Fernandez beat Hector Guerrero
Baron Von Raschke beat Shaska Whatley
Brad Armstrong beat Rick Rude
Ricky Lee Jones beat Gary Royal

11/7/86: Kansas City, KS @ Memorial Hall
Mitch Snow beat Tommy Sharpe
Italian Stallion beat Mark Fleming
Mod Squad Spike beat George South
Mod Squad Basher beat Rocky King
Denny Brown beat Colt Steele
Todd Champion & Dave Peterson beat Thunderfoot I & II win NWA Central States Tag Title
Sam Houston & Rufus R. Jones NC with The Warlord & Bill Dundee

11/7/86: Roanoke, VA @ Civic Center
The Rock & Roll Express & Jimmy Valiant beat The Midnight Express & Big Bubba by DQ

11/8/86: Atlanta, GA @ WTBS Studios (TV)
The Midnight Express & Big Bubba beat Brodie Chase, Vernon Deaton & Tony Zane
Ivan Koloff & Krusher Khruschev beat John Savage & Mike Simani
Arn Anderson beat Eddie Roberts
Jimmy Garvin beat Pablo Crenshaw
Brad Armstrong beat Grim Reaper

11/8/86: Charlotte, NC @ Coliseum
Don Kernodle beat Tony Zane
Tim Horner beat Bill Dundee
Rick Rude beat Hector Guerrero
Rip Rogers & The Midnight Express beat The Rock & Roll Express & Brad Armstrong
Manny Fernandez beat Wahoo McDaniel
Road Warrior Animal beat Arn Anderson
Jumbo Tsuruta & Tenryu beat Grim Reaper & Art Pritts
Giant Baba & Hiroshi Wajima beat Gary Royal & Starship Eagle
Dusty Rhodes & Nikita Koloff beat Tully Blanchard & Ric Flair

11/9/86: Cincinnati, OH @ Gardens
Rick Rude beat Hector Guerrero
Manny Fernandez beat Wahoo McDaniel
The Rock & Roll Express & Brad Armstrong beat The Midnight Express & Big Bubba by DQ
Dusty Rhodes & Nikita Koloff beat Ric Flair & Tully Blanchard in a cage match

11/10/86: Greenville, SC @ Memorial Auditorium
Louisville Street Fight: Big Bubba beat Rick Morton
Manny fernandez beat Wahoo McDaniel
Robert Gibson beat Rick Rude
Midnight Express beat Brad Armstrong & Tim Horner
Bobby Jaggers beat Krusher Krushchev
Ivan Koloff beat Dutch Mantell
Baron Von Raschke beat Gary Royal

11/11/86: Columbia, SC @ Township Auditorium (TV)
The Road Warriors vs. Krusher Khrushchev & Ivan Koloff
The Rock & Roll Express & Brad Armstrong beat The Midnight Express & Big Bubba by DQ
Bill Dundee beat Randy Mulkey
Tully Blanchard beat Eddie Roberts
Ole & Arn Anderson beat Gary Royal & ??
The Midnight Express beat John Savage & Keith Patterson
Road Warrior Animal beat Tony Zane & Vernon Deaton
Rick Rude & Manny Fernandez beat Jack Johnson & John Savage
Midnight Express & Bubba Rogers beat Hector Guerrero, Ricky Lee Jones & Tim Horner
Road Warrior Animal beat Bill Mulkey & Randy Mulkey in a handicap match
Ole & Arn Anderson beat Brodie Chase & Vernon Deaton
The Kansas Jayhawks beat Eddie Roberts & Alan West
Wahoo McDaniel & Brad Armstrong beat Tony Zane & Keith Patterson

11/11/86: Hutchinson, KS @ Convention Hall
Mitch Snow vs. Mark Fleming
George South vs. Mod Squad Spike
Rocky King vs. Mod Squad Basher
Sam Houston & Italian Stallion vs. The Warlord & Teijo Khan
Denny Brown vs. Colt Steel
Todd Champion & Dave Peterson vs. Thunderfoot I & II

11/13/86: Norfolk, VA @ Scope
The Rock & Roll Express & Brad Armstrong beat The Midnight Express & Big Bubba by DQ

11/14/86: Kansas City, KS @ Memorial Hall
Sam Houston beat Mark Fleming
Jimmy Garvin beat Mitch Snow
Italian Stallion beat Colt Steele
Denny Brown draw Teijo Khan
Mod Squad beat Rocky King & George South by DQ
Mitch Snow beat Mark Fleming
Todd Champion & Dave Peterson beat Thunderfoot I & Thunderfoot II
Rufus R. Jones beat Colt Steele
Bob Brown beat George South
Sam Houston beat The Warlord
Rufus R. Jones & Jimmy Valiant NC with Bob Brown(sub for Jimmy Garvin) & Bill Dundee

11/14/86: Roanoke, VA @ Civic Center
Rocky Kernodle beat Eddie Roberts
Don Kernodle beat Grim Reaper
Tim Horner beat Tony Zane
Brad Armstrong beat Jimmy Garvin by DQ
Ronnie Garvin beat Shaska Whatley
The Rock & Roll Express & Jimmy Valiant beat The Midnight Express & Big Bubba

11/15/86: Washington DC @ Armory
The Barbarian beat Nelson Royal
Rick Rude beat Hector Guerrero
Ivan Koloff & Krusher Khruschev draw Tim Horner & Brad Armstrong(15:00)
Manny Fernandez beat Wahoo McDaniel
Road Warrior Animal & Paul Ellering beat The Midnight Express by DQ
The Rock & Roll Express beat Ole & Arn Anderson
Dusty Rhodes & Nikita Koloff beat on Ric Flair & Tully Blanchard(13:00) by DQ

11/15/86: Huntington, WV @ Memorial Fieldhouse
Road Warrior Animal & Paul Ellering beat The Midnight Express by DQ

11/15/86: Atlanta, GA @ WTBS Studios (TV)
Midnight Express & Bubba Rogers beat Vernon Deaton, Lee Peek & Alan West
Tim Horner & Ricky Lee Jones beat Bill Mulkey & Randy Mulkey
Tully Blanchard beat Keith Patterson
Brad Armstrong beat Tony Zane
Rick Rude beat Paul Garner

11/16/86: St. Louis, MO @ Arena
NWA World Champion Ric Flair beat Ricky Morton
Denny Brown & Italian Stallion beat Thunderfoot I & Thunderfoot II
Mitch Snow beat Mark Fleming
The Mod Squad & Colt Steele beat Rufus R. Jones, Rocky King & George South

NWA Central States Title Tournament
1st Round
Arn Anderson beat Dave Peterson
Sam Houston beat Tully Blanchard by DQ
Brad Armstrong draw Rick Rude
Bill Dundee beat Robert Gibson
Dusty Rhodes NC with The Warlord
Todd Champion beat Teijo Khan

Semifinals
Bill Dundee beat Todd Champion
Sam Houston beat Arn Anderson

Finals
Sam Houston beat Bill Dundee to win vacant NWA Central States Title in tournament final

11/16/86: Johnson City, TN
Road Warrior Animal & Paul Ellering beat The Midnight Express by DQ

11/17/86: Fayetteville, NC @ Cumberland County Civic Center
Brad Armstrong & The Rock & Roll Express beat Midnight Express & Big Bubba
Manny Fernandez beat Wahoo McDaniel
Jimmy Valiant beat Rick Rude by DQ
The Barbarian beat Keith Patterson
Bill Dundee beat Tony Zane

Don Kernodle beat John Savage

11/17/86: Greenville, SC @ Memorial Auditorium
Dusty Rhodes, Nikita Koloff, Paul Ellering & Road Warrior Animal beat Ric Flair, Ole & Arn Anderson & Tully Blanchard
Baron Von Raschke beat Shaska Whatley
Texas Tornado Death Match: Kansas Jayhawks beat Ivan Koloff & Krusher Krushchev
Jimmy Garvin beat Tim Horner
Hector Guerrero beat Gary Royal
Ricky Lee Jones beat Allen West
Nelson Royal beat Eddie Roberts

11/18/86: Lansing, MI
Road Warrior Animal & Paul Ellering beat The Midnight Express by DQ

11/18/86: Spartanburg, SC @ Memorial Auditorium
Bill Dundee & Jimmy Garvin vs. Don Kernodle & Jimmy Valiant
Hector Guerrero vs. Rick Rude
Manny Fernandez vs. Wahoo McDaniel
Brad Armstrong & The Rock & Roll Express vs. The Midnight Express & Big Bubba
Dusty Rhodes & Nikita Koloff vs. Tully Blanchard & Ric Flair

11/19/86: Green Bay, WI @ Brown County Arena
Dusty Rhodes & Nikita Koloff beat Ric Flair & Tully Blanchard
Wahoo McDaniel NC with Arn Anderson
The Rock & Roll Express & Brad Armstrong beat The Midnight Express & Big Bubba by DQ
Ivan Koloff & Krusher Khruschev beat Kansas Jayhawks
Jimmy Garvin beat Hector Guerrero
The Barbarian beat Alan West
Tim Horner draw Shaska Whatley

11/20/86: Grand Rapids, MI
Road Warrior Animal & Paul Ellering beat Bobby Eaton & Big Bubba

11/21/86: Saginaw, MI
Brad Armstrong beat Big Bubba by DQ
Road Warrior Animal beat Bobby Eaton

11/21/86: Kansas City, KS @ Memorial Hall
Italian Stallion draw The Warlord
Colt Steele beat George South
Mitch Snow beat Mark Fleming
Todd Champion & Dave Peterson beat Thunderfoot I & Thunderfoot II
Teijo Khan beat Denny Brown
Rufus R. Jones & Rocky King NC with The Mod Squad
Sam Houston beat Bob Brown in a lights out, Texas death match

11/22/86: Cleveland, OH @ Convocation Center
Nelson Royal beat Eddie Roberts
Shaska Whatley beat Alan West
Don Kernodle beat Bill Dundee by DQ
Ivan Koloff & Krusher Khruschev beat Tim Horner & Brad Armstrong
Wahoo McDaniel beat The Barbarian in an Indian Strap match
The Rock & Roll Express beat Manny Fernandez & Rick Rude by DQ

11/22/86: Baltimore, MD @ Civic Center
Larry Winters beat Ron Shaw
Ricky Lee Jones beat Rocky Kernodle
Jimmy Valiant beat Gary Royal
Ole & Arn Anderson beat The Kansas Jayhawks in a Texas tornado match
Road Warrior Animal & Paul Ellering beat The Midnight Express by DQ
Dusty Rhodes & Nikita Koloff beat Ric Flair & Tully Blanchard in a cage match

11/23/86: Atlanta, GA @ WTBS Studios (TV)

11/23/86: Asheville, NC @ Civic Center
Rocky Kernodle draw Gary Royal
The Barbarian beat Nelson Royal
Ricky Jones beat Shaska Whatley
Manny Fernandez beat Tim Horner
Brad Armstrong beat Rick Rude by DQ
The Midnight Express & Big Bubba beat The Kansas Jayhawks & Don Kernodle
The Rock & Roll Express beat Arn Anderson & Ric Flair

11/23/86: Topeka, KS @ Municipal Auditorium

11/24/86: Greenville, SC @ Memorial Auditorium (TV)
Rock & Roll Express vs Manny Fernandez & Rick Rude
The Road Warriors vs Ivan Koloff & Krusher Krushchev

11/25/86: Spartanburg, SC @ Memorial Auditorium
Jimmy Valiant & Don Kernodle vs. Jimmy Garvin & Bill Dundee
Hector Guerrero vs. Rick Rude
Wahoo McDaniel vs. Manny Fernandez
The Rock & Roll Express & Brad Armstrong vs. Midnight Express & Big Bubba
Dusty Rhodes & Nikita Koloff vs. Ric Flair & Tully Blanchard

11/26/86:
No wrestling

11/27/86: Kansas City, KS @ Memorial Hall
George South beat Colt Steele
Italian Stallion beat Thunderfoot II
Thunderfoot I beat Mitch Snow
The Mod Squad beat Rufus R. Jones & Rocky King
The Warlord beat Denny Brown
Todd Champion & Dave Peterson beat Bob Brown & Teijo Khan by DQ

11/27/86: Greensboro, NC @ Coliseum; Atlanta, GA @ Omni
Starrcade 86: Night of the Skywalkers
Atlanta:
Brad Armstrong draw Jimmy Garvin(15:08)
Krusher Khruschev & Ivan Koloff beat Kansas Jayhawks(7:51) no DQ match
Sam Houston beat Bill Dunde(10:21) by DQ at 10:21
Big Bubba beat Ronnie Garvin(11:50) in a street fight match
The Road Warriors beat The Midnight Express(7:07) in a scaffold match
NWA World Champion Ric Flair DDQ Nikita Koloff(19:12)

Greensboro:
Tim Horner & Nelson Royal beat Don Kernodle & Rocky Kernodle(7:30)
Hector Guerrero & Baron Von Raschke beat Shaska Whatley & Barbarian (7:30)
Wahoo McDaniel beat Rick Rude (9:05) in an Indian strap match
Jimmy Valiant beat Paul Jones (4:00) in a hair vs. hair match
Tully Blanchard beat Dusty Rhodes (8:41) first blood match, wins NWA World Television Title
The Rock & Roll Express beat Ole & Arn Anderson(19:03) in a steel cage match

11/28/86: Richmond, VA @ Coliseum
Hector Guerrero draw Bill Dundee
The Kansas Jayhawks beat Ivan Koloff & Krusher Khruschev
Brad Armstrong beat Jimmy Garvin by DQ
Wahoo McDaniel beat Manny Fernandez in an Indian strap match
Ole & Arn Anderson beat The Rock & Roll Express in a Texas tornado match
Road Warrior Animal & Paul Ellering beat The Midnight Express by DQ
Dusty Rhodes & Nikita Koloff beat Ric Flair & Tully Blanchard in a cage match

11/29/86: Bloomington, MN @ Met Center
Big Bubba vs. Tim Horner
The Midnight Express vs. Road Warrior Animal & Paul Ellering

11/29/86: Philadelphia, PA @ Civic Center
Hector Guerrero beat Allen West
Don Kernodle beat Gary Royal
Jimmy Valiant beat Tony Zane
Ronnie Garvin beat Bill Dundee by CO
Ivan Koloff & Krusher Khruschev beat The Kansas Jayhawks
Nikita Koloff beat Tully Blanchard
The Rock & Roll Express beat Rick Rude & Manny Fernandez by DQ

11/30/86: Peoria, IL
The Midnight Express & Big Bubba vs. The Road Warriors & Paul Ellering

11/30/86: St. Joseph, MO @ Civic Arena
Bob Brown beat Sam Houston(21:00) in a no DQ match
Rufus R. Jones, Rocky King & George South beat Mod Squad & Mark Fleming
Dave Peterson & Todd Champion beat The Warlord & Colt Steele
Mitch Snow beat Teijo Khan(12:00)
Italian Stallion & Denny Brown beat Thunderfoot I & Thunderfoot II

12/1/86: Fayetteville, NC @ Cumberland County Civic Center
Tim Horner beat Bill Dundee
Brad Armstrong draw Ivan Koloff
Krusher Khruschev beat Bobby Jaggers
Ronnie Garvin beat Bobby Eaton(sub for Big Bubba)
Dusty Rhodes & Nikita Koloff beat Tully Blanchard & Ric Flair
Road Warrior Animal won a bunkhouse battle royal

12/2/86: Rock Hill, SC @ Winthrop Coliseum (TV)
The Rock & Roll Express beat Manny Fernandez & Rick Rude by DQ
Big Bubba beat Ronnie Garvin by CO in a Louisville street fight match
Manny Fernandez & Rick Rude beat Allen West & Eddie Roberts
Barry Windham beat Mike Simani
Brad Armstrong beat Ron Rossi
Tully Blanchard beat John Savage
Wahoo McDaniel & Baron Von Raschke beat Tony Zane & Vernon Deaton
Arn Anderson beat Keith Patterson
Jimmy Garvin beat Randy Mulkey
The Midnight Express beat Nelson Royal & Tim Horner
Ronnie Garvin beat John Savage
Manny Fernandez & Rick Rude beat Ron Rossi & Vernon Deaton
Tully Blanchard & Arn Anderson beat Randy Mulkey & Keith Patterson
The Kansas Jayhawks beat Allen West & Eddie Roberts
Nikita Koloff beat Mike Simani

12/3/86: Raleigh, NC @ Dorton Arena
Big Bubba won a bunkhouse stampede
Dusty Rhodes & Nikita Koloff beat Tully Blanchard & Ric Flair in a chain/bullrope match
Dutch Mantell NC with Ivan Koloff
Brad Armstrong beat The Barbarian
Nelson Royal beat Shaska Whatley
Tim Horner beat Bill Dundee
Denny Brown beat Hector Guerrero

12/4/86: Columbus, GA @ Municipal Auditorium
The Midnight Express & Big Bubba vs. The Rock & Roll Express & Ronnie Garvin

12/5/86: Kansas City, KS @ Memorial Hall
Bob Brown beat Russell Sapp
Brad Batten & Bart Batten beat Thunderfoot I & Thunderfoot II

Rufus R. Jones beat Bill Dundee by DQ
Sam Houston beat Colt Steele
The Warlord won a bunkhouse stampede
Bob Brown beat Mitch Snow
Todd Champion & Dave Peterson beat The Barbarian & The Warlord
Italian Stallion beat Thunderfoot II
Sam Houston beat Jimmy Garvin by DQ
Wahoo McDaniel NC with Manny Fernandez

12/5/86: Hampton, VA @ Coliseum
Big Bubba vs. Ronnie Garvin in a street fight match
Bunkhouse Stampede Battle Royal

12/6/86: Atlanta, GA @ WTBS Studios (TV)
Tully Blanchard beat Mike Jackson
Brad Armstrong beat Vernon Deaton
Arn Anderson beat Alan Martin
The Midnight Express beat Art Pritts & Dave Spearman
Barry Windham beat Randy Barber
Rick Rude & Manny Fernandez beat The Rock & Roll Express(26:58) to win NWA World Tag Title

12/6/86: St. Louis, MO @ Arena

12/6/86: Cleveland, OH @ Convocation Center
Big Bubba beat Ronnie Garvin by CO
The Kansas Jayhawks beat Ivan Koloff & Krusher Khruschev in a Texas tornado match
Tully Blanchard beat Brad Armstrong by CO
Denny Brown draw Hector Guerrero
Ricky Lee Jones beat Super Destroyer
Jimmy Valiant & Baron Von Raschke beat Shaska Whatley & Gary Royal
Tim Horner beat Buddy Roberts

12/7/86: Des Moines, IA
Bunkhouse Stampede Battle Royal

12/8/86: Saginaw, MI
Big Bubba vs. Ronnie Garvin in a street fight match
The Midnight Express vs. Brad Armstrong & Tim Horner

12/8/86: Hutchinson, KS @ Convention Hall
Dave Peterson & Todd Champion beat The Warlord & Teijo Khan
Rufus R. Jones & Italian Stallion beat The Mod Squad by DQ
Sam Houston beat Bulldog Brown by DQ

12/8/86: Greenville, SC @ Memorial Auditorium
Indian Strap Match: Wahoo McDaniel vs Manny Fernandez
NWA World Tag Champs Rock & Roll Express vs Ivan Koloff & Krusher Krushchev
Baron Von Raschke vs Rick Rude
Jimmy Valiant vs Shaska Whatley
Hector Guerrero vs Denny Brown
Barry Windham vs Tony Zane
Kansas Jayhawks vs Thunderfoot 1 & 2

12/9/86: Spartanburg, SC @ Memorial Auditorium (TV)
The Rock & Roll Express vs. Rick Rude & Manny Fernandez)
Ronnie Garvin & Barry Windham beat Ivan Koloff & Krusher Khruschev to win NWA United States Tag Title

12/10/86: Asheville, NC @ Civic Center
Bunkhouse Stampede Battle Royal

12/11/86: Albany, GA @ Civic Center
Gary Royal vs. Alan West
Eddie Roberts vs. Tony Zane
Denny Brown vs. Hector Guerrero
Tim Horner vs. Thunderfoot
Brad Armstrong vs. Jimmy Garvin
Manny Fernandez & Rick Rude vs. The Rock & Roll Express

12/11/86: Norfolk, VA @ Scope
Big Bubba vs. Ronnie Garvin in a street fight match
Bunkhouse Stampede Battle Royal

12/12/86: Kansas City, KS @ Memorial Hall
Bart Batten & Brad Batten beat The Warlord & Teijo Khan by DQ
Pat Rose beat Joe Lightfoot
Dave Peterson & Todd Champion beat Pat Rose & Colt Steele
Porkchop Cash beat Mitch Snow
The Mod Squad beat Italian Stallion & Rufus R. Jones
Bob Brown beat Sam Houston

12/12/86: Charlotte, NC @ Coliseum (TV)
Ivan Koloff beat Rocky King
Denny Brown draw Hector Guerrero
The Road Warriors beat Randy Mulkey & Bill Mulkey
Barry Windham beat Art Pritts
Big Bubba beat Ronnie Garvin in a street fight match
The Midnight Express beat George South & Rocky King
Ronnie Garvin & Barry Windham beat Mike Simani & Vernon Deaton
Jimmy Valiant beat Tony Zane
The Rock & Roll Express beat Rick Rude & Manny Fernandez
Dusty Rhodes & Nikita Koloff beat Arn Anderson & Ric Flair

12/13/86: Atlanta, GA @ WTBS Studios (TV)
Dusty Rhodes & Nikita Koloff vs. Ric Flair & Arn Anderson bullrope/chain match

12/13/86: Philadelphia, PA @ Civic Center
Dusty Rhodes won a bunkhouse stampede
Nikita Koloff beat NWA World Champion Ric Flair by DQ
Dusty Rhodes & The Road Warriors beat The Midnight Express & Big Bubba
Barry Windham beat The Barbarian
Brad Armstrong & Tim Horner beat Ivan Koloff & Krusher Khruschev
Jimmy Valiant beat Shaska Whatley
Denny Brown beat Hector Guerrero

12/13/86: Baltimore, MD @ Civic Center
NWA World Champion Ric Flair beat Nikita Koloff
Dusty Rhodes won a bunkhouse stampede
The Road Warriors beat The Midnight Express
Big Bubba beat Ronnie Garvin
The Kansas Jayhawks beat Ivan Koloff & Krusher Khruschev
Brad Armstrong beat Shaska Whatley

12/14/86: Atlanta, GA @ WTBS Studios (TV)
The Midnight Express beat David Isley & Zane Smith
Ronnie Garvin beat Vernon Deaton
Brad Armstrong beat Brodie Chase
Ole & Arn Anderson beat Rocky King & George South by submission
Nikita Koloff beat Art Pritts
Barry Windham beat Tony Zane
The Road Warriors beat Larry Stevens & Butch Cooper
Ivan Koloff & Krusher Khruschev beat Bill Tabb & Al Garrett
Rick Rude & Manny Fernandez beat Bill Mulkey & Randy Mulkey
Tully Blanchard beat Randy Barber
Wahoo McDaniel beat Paul Garner

12/14/86: Rosemont, IL @ Rosemont Horizon
Dusty Rhodes & Nikita Koloff beat Tully Blanchard & Ric Flair
The Road Warriors won a bunkhouse stampede
The Road Warriors beat The Midnight Express
The Rock & Roll Express beat Ivan Koloff & Krusher Khruschev
Wahoo McDaniel beat Rick Rude by DQ
Jimmy Garvin draw Brad Armstrong
Tim Horner beat Shaska Whatley

12/14/86: Marysville, KS
Bart Batten & Brad Batten beat Porkchop Cash & Colt Steele
Pat Rose beat Mitch Snow
Todd Champion & Dave Peterson beat Teijo Khan & The Warlord
Italian Stallion & Rufus R. Jones beat The Mod Squad
Sam Houston NC with Bob Brown

12/15/86: Greenville, SC @ Memorial Auditorium (TV)
Big Bubba won a Bunkhouse Stampede Battle Royal
Hector Guerrero vs. Eddie Roberts
Barry Windham vs. Gary Royal
The Barbarian vs. Baron Von Raschke
Rick Rude vs. Robert Gibson
Dusty Rhodes & Nikita Koloff beat Ric Flair & Arn Anderson steel cage match

12/16/86:-12/24/86:
No Wrestling

12/25/86: Atlanta, GA @ Omni
The Road Warriors, Dusty Rhodes & Nikita Koloff beat Ric Flair, Tully Blanchard, Ole & Arn Anderson
The Midnight Express beat Brad Armstrong & Tim Horner
Ricky Morton NC with Manny Fernandez
Robert Gibson beat Rick Rude by DQ
Ronnie Garvin & Barry Windham beat Ivan Koloff & Khrusher Khruschev
Dick Murdoch beat Bobby Eaton
Denny Brown draw Nelson Royal

12/25/86: Greenville, SC @ Memorial Auditorium
The Midnight Express & Ivan Koloff beat the Kansas Jayhawks & Ronnie Garvin
Brad Armstrong beat Jimmy Garvin
The Kansas Jayhawks beat Ivan Koloff & Krusher Krushchev
Denny Brown DRAW Nelson Royal
Don Kernodle beat Ricky Lee Jones
Rocky Kernodle beat Allen West
Thunderfoot 1 & 2 beat George South & Rocky King

12/25/86: Charlotte, NC @ Coliseum
The Road Warriors, Dusty Rhodes & Nikita Koloff beat Ole Anderson, Arn Anderson, Tully Blanchard & Ric Flair
Robert Gibson draw Rick Rude
Ricky Morton beat Manny Fernandez
Jimmy Valiant beat Bill Dundee
Barry Windham beat Shaska Whatley
Barry Windham beat Gary Royal
Hector Guerrero beat Eddie Roberts

12/25/86: St. Joseph, MO @ Civic Arena
Dave Petersen beat The Warlord
Todd Champion beat Porkchop Cash
Ken Timbs beat Mitch Snow
Bart Batten & Brad Batten beat Teijo Khan & Pat Rose
Brady Boone beat Colt Steele
The Mod Squad DDQ Rufus R. Jones & Italian Stallion
Sam Houston draw Bob Brown
Bart Batten won a bunkhouse stampede

12/26/86: Kansas City, KS @ Memorial Hall
Brady Boone beat Teijo Khan
Bart Batten & Brad Batten beat Porkchop Cash & Colt Steele
Sam Houston beat Bob Brown by DQ
The Warlord beat Mitch Snow
Italian Stallion beat Mod Squad Basher(aka Mac Jeffers)
Dave Peterson & Todd Champion beat Pat Rose & Ken Timbs
Rufus R. Jones beat Mod Squad Spike in New Orleans death match

12/26/86: Charleston, WV @ Civic Center
Thunderfoot I & Thunderfoot II beat Alan West & Eddie Roberts
Nikita Koloff beat NWA World Champ Ric Flair by DQ
Denny Brown draw Nelson Royal
Jimmy Garvin NC with Brad Armstrong
Ricky Lee Jones beat Alan West
Manny Fernandez beat Hector Guerrero
Tim Horner & Don Kernodle beat Ivan Koloff & Krusher Khruschev

12/26/86: Richmond, VA @ Coliseum
Dusty Rhodes won a bunkhouse stampede
The Road Warriors beat The Midnight Express
Dick Murdoch draw Tully Blanchard
Robert Gibson beat Arn Anderson
Ricky Morton beat Rick Rude by DQ
Baron Von Raschke beat Shaska Whatley
Bill Dundee beat Mark Fleming

12/27/86: Atlanta, GA @ WTBS Studios (TV)
NWA Mid Atlantic Title retired when Ronnie Garvin gave up title
Dick Murdoch beat Brodie Chase
Ronnie Garvin & Barry Windham draw The Midnight Express
The Road Warriors beat Randy Mulkey & Bill Mulkey
Rick Rude & Manny Fernandez beat Pablo Crenshaw & Dave Spencer
Tully Blanchard beat Pat O'Brian
Bill Dundee beat Clement Fields
Ole & Arn Anderson beat Bill Tabb & Randy Barber
Brad Armstrong beat Mike Jackson
Jimmy Garvin beat Alan Martin

12/27/86: Minneapolis, MN @ Met Center
NWA World Champion Ric Flair vs. Nikita Koloff
Dusty Rhodes & The Road Warriors beat The Midnight Express & Jimmy Garvin (sub for Big Bubba)
Also included a bunkhouse Stampede

12/28/86: Greensboro, NC @ Coliseum
Big Bubba won a bunkhouse stampede
Dusty Rhodes & Nikita Koloff beat Arn Anderson & Ric Flair
Brad Armstrong & Barry Windham beat Ivan Koloff & Khrusher Khruschev
Ricky Morton NC with Manny Fernandez
Robert Gibson beat Rick Rude
Denny Brown draw Hector Guerrero
Tim Horner beat Shaska Whatley

12/28/86: Albuquerque, NM
Teijo Khan draw Italian Stallion
Todd Champion beat Pat Rose
Sam Houston beat The Warlord
Nikita Koloff beat Mod Squad Basher(sub for Big Bubba)(:29)
NWA World Champ Ric Flair beat Dusty Rhodes by DQ
The Road Warriors beat The Midnight Express(5:46)
Nikita Koloff won a Bunkhouse Stampede

12/29/86: Fayetteville, NC @ Cumberland County Civic Center
Rick Rude beat Jimmy Valiant
Tim Horner & Rufus R. Jones beat Tony Zane & Thunderfoot I
Denny Brown draw Hector Guerrero
Shaska Whatley beat Rocky King
Baron Von Raschke beat Shaska Whatley
Ronnie Garvin beat Bill Dundee
Jimmy Garvin beat Brad Armstrong
Kansas Jayhawks beat Krusher Khruschev & Ivan Koloff

12/29/86: Inglewood, CA @ Great Western Forum
Sam Houston beat Teijo Khan
Todd Champion beat Ken Timbs
Dick Murdoch beat The Warlord
The Rock & Roll Express beat Ole & Arn Anderson
Giant Baba & Hiroshi Wajima beat The Mod Squad
The Road Warriors beat The Midnight Express by DQ
Dusty Rhodes & Nikita Koloff beat Ric Flair & Tully Blanchard(20:00)
Road Warrior Hawk won a bunkhouse Stampede(7:30) by winning a coin flip between he & Road Warrior Animal after both men eliminated The Midnight Express; other participants included: The Rock & Roll Express, Manny Fernandez, Rick Rude, Ole Anderson, Arn Anderson, Teijo Khan, Ken Timbs, Italian Stallion, The Warlord, Sam Houston, Pat Rose, The Mod Squad, Dick Murdoch & Barry Windham

12/30/86: San Francisco, CA
NWA World Champion Ric Flair beat Dusty Rhodes by DQ
Nikita Koloff beat Tully Blanchard
Road Warrior Animal won a bunkhouse stampede
The Road Warriors beat The Midnight Express by DQ
The Rock & Roll Express beat Ole & Arn Anderson
Dick Murdoch beat The Warlord
Sam Houston beat Teijo Khan
Todd Champion beat Pat Rose

12/31/86:
No Wrestling

Chapter 8: 1987

1/1/87: Atlanta, GA @ Omni
Big Bubba won a bunkhouse stampede
Dusty Rhodes & Nikita Koloff beat Ric Flair & Tully Blanchard in a bullrope, chain match
The Road Warriors & Paul Ellering beat The Midnight Express(Dennis Condrey & Bobby Eaton) & Big Bubba
Manny Fernandez beat Denny Brown
Barry Windham beat Shaska Whatley
Baron Von Raschke beat Tony Zane
Tim Horner beat Bill Dundee

1/2/87: Johnson City, TN
The Rock & Roll Express(Ricky Morton & Robert Gibson) vs. Ole & Arn Anderson
Wahoo McDaniel vs. Manny Fernandez
Baron Von Raschke vs. Rufus R. Jones
Jimmy Garvin vs. Hector Guerrero
Nikita Koloff vs. Tully Blanchard
Bunkhouse Stampede

1/2/87: Kansas City, KS @ Memorial Hall
Bart Batten, Brad Batten & Brady Boone beat Colt Steele, Teijo Khan & The Warlord
Italian Stallion beat Ken Timbs by DQ
The Mod Squad(Basher & Spike) beat Dave Peterson & Todd Champion to win NWA Central States Tag Title
Pat Rose beat Mitch Snow
Porkchop Cash beat Mr. X(Russell Sapp)
The Mod Squad beat Bart Batten & Brad Batten
Bob Brown & Bill Dundee beat Sam Houston & Rufus R. Jones in a falls count anywhere, Texas death match

1/3/87: Atlanta, GA @ WTBS Studios (TV)
Brad Armstrong beat Kent Glover
The Rock & Roll Express beat Alan Martin & Tony Zane
Ronnie Garvin beat The White Knight
Barry Windham beat Randy Barber
Midnight Express beat Mike Jackson & George South
Tully Blanchard beat Tim Horner
Manny Fernandez & Rick Rude beat Eddie Roberts & Alan West
Vladimir Petrov beat Bill Mulkey, Randy Mulkey & Bill Tabb in a handicap match
Dick Murdoch beat Henry Rutley
Ole & Arn Anderson beat David Isley & Larry Stephens
Nikita Koloff beat Chance McQuade
Road Warriors beat Clement Fields & Dave Spearma

1/3/87: Amarillo, TX @ Sports Arena
NWA World Champ Ric Flair vs. Dusty Rhodes
Nikita Koloff vs. Tully Blanchard
Dick Murdoch vs. Ivan Koloff
The Midnight Express vs. The Road Warriors

1/3/87: Topeka, KS @ Municipal Auditorium
Bill Dundee beat Sam Houston to win NWA Central States Title

1/3/87: Charlotte, NC @ Coliseum
Ricky Morton beat Manny Fernandez by DQ
Barry Windham beat Shaska Whatley
Jimmy Valiant beat Bill Dundee
Dusty Rhodes, Nikita Koloff & The Road Warriors beat Ric Flair, Ole Anderson, Arn Anderson & Tully Blanchard

1/3/87: Columbia, SC @ Township Auditorium
Wahoo McDaniel vs. Jimmy Garvin
The Rock & Roll Express vs. Manny Fernandez & Rick Rude
Ronnie Garvin vs. Big Bubba
Barry Windham vs. Bill Dundee
Brad Armstrong vs. Gary Royal
Jimmy Valiant & Baron Von Raschke vs. Shaska Whatley & The Barbarian
Bobby Jaggers vs. Vladimir Petrov
Dutch Mantel vs. Thunderfoot I

1/4/87: Cincinnati, OH @ Gardens
Dusty Rhodes won a bunkhouse stampede
Rick Rude & Manny Fernandez beat Dick Murdoch & Tim Horner
Nikita Koloff beat NWA World Champ Ric Flair by DQ
Bobby Eaton beat Baron Von Raschke
Big Bubba beat Ronnie Garvin in a street fight match
Vladimir Petrov beat Jim Lancaster

1/4/87: Huntington, WV @ Memorial Fieldhouse
The Road Warriors vs. The Midnight Express in a scaffold match
Dusty Rhodes vs. Tully Blanchard
Nikita Koloff vs. Jimmy Garvin
Barry Windham vs. Shaska Whatley
Jimmy Valiant vs. Bill Dundee
Hector Guerrero vs. Denny Brown

1/4/87: St. Joseph, MO @ Civic Arena
6 matches in all

1/5/87: Baltimore, MD @ Civic Center
Jimmy Valiant beat Mark Fleming
Hector Guerrero beat Eddie Roberts
Bill Dundee beat Alan West
Jimmy Garvin beat Hector Guerrero
Big Bubba beat Ricky Lee Jones
The Midnight Express beat Ronnie Garvin & Dick Murdoch
The Rock & Roll Express beat Rick Rude & Manny Fernandez by DQ
Tully Blanchard draw Barry Windham

1/5/87: Greenville, SC @ Memorial Auditorium
NWA World Champ Ric Flair vs Brad Armstrong
Dusty Rhodes & Nikita Koloff vs Ivan Koloff & Krusher Krushchev
Baron Von Raschke vs Arn Anderson
Tim Horner vs Shaska Whatley
Kansas Jayhawks vs Thunderfoot 1 & 2
Rocky King vs Tony Zane
Nelson Royal vs Denny Brown

1/5/87: Rockport, MO
Todd Champion & D.J. Peterson beat Blue Demon & Teijo Khan
The Mod Squad beat Italian Stallion & Rufus R. Jones
Sam Houston beat Bob Brown by DQ

1/6/87: Spartanburg, SC @ Memorial Auditorium (TV)
Manny Fernandez & Rick Rude beat Keith Patterson & Mike Simani
Barry Windham beat Thunderfoot II
The Rock & Roll Express beat Gary Royal & Larry Stephens
Dick Murdoch beat Thunderfoot
Midnight Express & Big Bubba beat Tim Horner, Ricky Lee Jones & Rocky King
Vladimir Petrov beat Eddie Roberts, George South & Alan West
Brad Armstrong beat Brodie Chase
Jimmy Valiant beat Brodie Chase
The Midnight Express beat Vernon Deaton & Gary Royal
Brad Armstrong beat Larry Stephens
Tony Zane beat Vladimir Petrov by DQ
Nikita Koloff beat David Isley
Ronnie Garvin & Barry Windham beat Thunderfoot I & Thunderfoot II
Manny Fernandez & Rick Rude beat Bill Mulkey & Randy Mulkey
Nikita Koloff vs. Tully Blanchard

1/8/87: Raleigh, NC @ Dorton Arena
Brad Armstrong beat Bill Dundee
Jimmy Garvin beat Bobby Jaggers
Ivan Koloff beat Dutch Mantell
Vladimir Petrov beat Gary Royal
The Midnight Express beat Ronnie Garvin & Dick Murdoch
The Rock & Roll Express beat Rick Rude & Manny Fernandez by DQ
Tully Blanchard draw Barry Windham
Nikita Koloff beat NWA World Champ Ric Flair by DQ

1/9/87: Kansas City, KS @ Memorial Hall
Italian Stallion draw Teijo Khan
The Warlord beat Mitch Snow
Rufus R. Jones beat Ken Timbs by DQ
Brad & Bart Batten beat Porkchop Cash & Pat Rose
The Mod Squad beat Todd Champion & Dave Peterson
Sam Houston beat Bob Brown in a bullrope match

1/9/87: Norfolk, VA @ Scope
The Rock & Roll Express & Barry Windham beat The Midnight Express & Big Bubba by DQ

1/10/87: Atlanta, GA @ WTBS Studios (TV)
Jimmy Garvin beat Keith Vincent
Brad Armstrong beat Tommy Angel
Bill Dundee beat Randy Barber
Nikita Koloff beat Larry Stephens
Tully Blanchard beat Alan Martin
The Rock & Roll Express beat Eddie Roberts & West
The Road Warriors beat Rick Allen & David Isley
Ronnie Garvin & Barry Windham beat Bill Mulkey & Randy Mulkey
Vladimir Petrov beat Joel Deaton & George South in a handicap match
Ivan Koloff beat Zane Smith
Dick Murdoch beat Brody Chase

1/10/87: Philadelphia, PA @ Civic Center
Vladimir Petrov beat Tim Horner
Ronnie Garvin draw Ivan Koloff
Jimmy Garvin beat Brad Armstrong in a Texas death match
The Rock & Roll Express & Dick Murdoch beat Shaska Whatley, Rick Rude & Manny Fernandez
Tully Blanchard beat Dusty Rhodes by DQ
Barry Windham beat Arn Anderson
NWA World Champ Ric Flair NC with Nikita Koloff
The Road Warriors beat The Midnight Express in a scaffold match

1/11/87: Charlotte, NC @ Coliseum
Denny Brown draw Ricky Lee Jones
Brad Armstrong beat Bill Dundee
Barry Windham beat Arn Anderson
The Rock & Roll Express & Ronnie Garvin beat The Midnight Express & Big Bubba
Ivan Koloff & Vladimir Petrov beat Eddie Roberts & Hector Guerrero
The Road Warriors beat Manny Fernandez & Rick Rude by DQ
Tully Blanchard beat Dusty Rhodes
NWA World Champ Ric Flair beat Nikita Koloff

1/11/87: Atlanta, GA @ Omni
NWA World Champ Ric Flair draw Nikita Koloff
Dusty Rhodes & The Road Warriors beat Big Bubba & The Midnight Express
Rick Rude & Manny Fernandez beat Baron Von Raschke & Dick Murdoch
The Rock & Roll Express beat Ole & Arn Anderson
Brad Armstrong beat Jimmy Garvin

1/12/87: Greenville, SC @ Memorial Auditorium
Ricky Lee Jones beat Alan West
Tim Horner beat Thunderfoot I
Arn Anderson draw Ronnie Garvin
Road Warriors & Barry Windham beat The Midnight Express & Big Bubba
Manny Fernandez & Rick Rude beat The Rock & Roll Express
Tully Blanchard beat Dusty Rhodes
Nikita Koloff beat NWA World Champ Ric Flair by DQ

1/12/87: Raleigh, NC @ Dorton Arena
Ivan Koloff & Vladimir Petrov beat Brad Armstrong & Tim Horner

1/13/87: Columbia, SC @ Township Auditorium (TV)
Barry Windham beat Alan West
The Kansas Jayhawks beat Thunderfoot I & Thunderfoot II

The Rock & Roll Express beat Gary Royal & George South
Manny Fernandez & Rick Rude beat David Isley & Eddie Roberts
Big Bubba beat Vernon Deaton
Ronnie Garvin beat Larry Stephens
Arn Anderson, Tully Blanchard & Ric Flair beat Denny Brown, Hector Guerrero & Tim Horner
Barry Windham beat Ric Flair by DQ in a lumberjack match
The Rock & Roll Express vs. Mark Fleming & Brodie Chase
Rick Rude & Manny Fernandez vs. Gary Royal & Randy Mulkey
Vladimir Petrov vs. Rocky King
Ole Anderson vs. Bill Mulkey

1/13/87: Salina, KS @ Bicentennial Center
Brady Boone vs. Colt Steele
Mitch Snow vs. Porkchop Cash
Warlord & Teijo Khan vs. Dave Peterson & Todd Champion
Brad & Bart Batten beat Pat Rose & Ken Timbs
The Mod Squad beat Rufus R. Jones & Italian Stallion
Ivan Koloff & Vladimir Petrov beat Dick Murdoch & Baron Von Raschke
Bob Brown beat Sam Houston
Brad Armstrong & Jimmy Valiant beat Bill Dundee & Jimmy Garvin

1/14/87: Grand Rapids, MI
Barry Windham beat Ivan Koloff
The Midnight Express & Big Bubba beat The Road Warriors & Baron Von Raschke
The Rock & Roll Express beat Ole & Arn Anderson
Nikita Koloff beat NWA World Champ Ric Flair by DQ

1/15/87: Marquette, MI
The Midnight Express & Big Bubba beat Baron Von Raschke & The Road Warriors

1/16/87: Kansas City, KS @ Memorial Hall
Brady Boone beat Colt Steele
Brad & Bart Batten beat Teijo Khan & The Warlord
Porkchop Cash beat Mitch Snow
Rufus R. Jones & Italian Stallion draw Porkchop Cash & Bill Karchan
The Mod Squad beat Dave Peterson & Todd Champion
Bill Dundee beat Sam Houston

1/16/87: Hollywood, FL
The Rock & Roll Express beat Ivan Koloff & Vladimir Petrov by DQ

1/17/87: Atlanta, GA @ WTBS Studios (TV)
Rick Rude & Manny Fernandez vs. Rocky King & Bill Tabb
The Kansas Jayhawks vs. Allen West & Eddie Roberts
Barry Windham vs. Thunderfoot II
Dick Murdoch & Baron Von Raschke vs. Randy Barber & Gary Royal
Big Bubba & The Midnight Express vs. Larry Stephens, David Isley & Ronnie Angle
Vladimir Petrov vs. Zane Smith
Lex Luger vs. George South
Tim Horner vs. Thunderfoot I
Jimmy Garvin vs. Bill Mulkey
Brad Armstrong vs. Vernon Deaton
Tully Blanchard vs. Randy Mulkey

1/17/87: Charlotte, NC @ Coliseum
Barry Windham beat Alan West
Kansas Jayhawks beat Thunderfoot I & Thunderfoot II
The Rock & Roll Express beat George South & Gary Royal
Rick Rude & Manny Fernandez draw David Isley & Brodie Chase
Big Bubba beat Vernon Deaton
Ronnie Garvin beat Larry Stephens
Ric Flair, Tully Blanchard & Arn Anderson beat Tim Horner, Hector Guerrero & Denny Brown
Barry Windham beat NWA World Champ Ric Flair in a lumberjack match

1/17/87: Greensboro, NC @ Coliseum
NWA World Champ Ric Flair beat Nikita Koloff by DQ
Dusty Rhodes & The Road Warriors beat The Midnight Express & Big Bubba
The Rock & Roll Express beat Rick Rude & Manny Fernandez
Tully Blanchard beat Barry Windham
Ivan Koloff & Vladimir Petrov beat Dick Murdoch & Baron Von Raschke
Brad Armstrong beat Jimmy Garvin
Arn Anderson beat Tim Horner
Hector Guerrero beat Denny Brown

1/18/87: Asheville, NC @ Civic Center
NWA World Champ Ric Flair beat Nikita Koloff by DQ
The Rock & Roll Express DCO with Manny Fernandez & Rick Rude
Tully Blanchard draw Dick Murdoch
Jimmy Valiant beat Shaska Whatley
Denny Brown beat Gary Royal
Ricky Lee Jones & Hector Guerrero beat Eddie Roberts & Allen West

1/19/87: Chesterfield, SC
Big Bubba DCO with Dick Murdoch
The Midnight Express beat Ronnie Garvin & Baron Von Raschke

1/20/87: Fayetteville, NC @ Cumberland County Civic Center (TV)
NWA World Champ Ric Flair draw Barry Windham
Rock & Roll Express beat Mark Fleming & Brodie Chase
Rick Rude & Manny Fernandez beat Gary Royal & Randy Mulkey
Vladimir Petrov beat Rocky King
Ole Anderson beat Bill Mulkey

1/20/87: Hutchinson, KS @ Convention Hall
Brady Boone vs. Colt Steele
Bart Batten & Brad Batten vs. Ken Timbs & Pat Rose
Rufus R. Jones, Italian Stallion & Mitch Snow vs. The Warlord, Teijo Khan & Porkchop Cash
The Mod Squad vs. Todd Champion & Dave Peterson
Sam Houston vs. Bob Brown in a bullrope match

1/21/87: Jacksonville, FL @ Coliseum
Nikita Koloff beat NWA World Champ Ric Flair by DQ
Dusty Rhodes & The Road Warriors beat The Midnight Express & Big Bubba
Tully Blanchard beat Barry Windham by DQ
Denny Brown draw Hector Guerrero
Manny Fernandez & Rick Rude beat Dick Murdoch & Baron Von Raschke
The Kansas Jayhawks beat Jimmy Garvin & Bill Dundee by DQ

1/22/87: Raleigh, NC @ Dorton Arena
Note: The show took place during a blizzard
Ricky Lee Jones beat Thunderfoot I
Bill Dundee beat Gary Royal
Jimmy Garvin beat Eddie Roberts
Tully Blanchard beat Dusty Rhodes by DQ
Rick Rude & Manny Fernandez beat The Rock & Roll Express in a 2 out of 3 falls
Nikita Koloff DCO with NWA World Champ Ric Flair

1/22/87: Washington, DC @ Armory (Cancelled due to snowstorm)

1/23/87: Norfolk, VA @ Scope
Dusty Rhodes & The Road Warriors beat The Midnight Express & Big Bubba

1/23/87: Kansas City, KS @ Memorial Hall
Porkchop Cash beat Mitch Snow
Brady Boone beat The Warlord
Italian Stallion beat Colt Steele
Brad & Bart Batten beat Teijo Khan & Bob Brown
Rufus R. Jones beat Ken Timbs by DQ
The Mod Squad beat Todd Champion & Dave Peterson
Bill Dundee beat Sam Houston

1/24/87: Atlanta, GA @ WTBS Studios (TV)
Jimmy Valiant vs. Randy Barber
Dick Murdoch & Baron Von Raschke vs. Brodie Chase & Larry Stephens
Tully Blanchard vs. Zane Smith
Lex Luger vs. Randy Mulkey
Brad Armstrong vs. Gary Royal
The Rock & Roll Express vs. Eddie Roberts & David Isley
Rick Rude & Manny Fernandez vs. Tommy Angel & Chance McQuade
Vladimir Petrov vs. Alan Martin
Big Bubba & The Midnight Express vs. Denny Brown, Bill Mulkey & George South
Arn Anderson vs. Bill Tabb

1/24/87: Richmond, VA @ Coliseum
Nikita Koloff beat NWA World Champ Ric Flair by DQ
Tully Blanchard draw Dusty Rhodes
Road Warriors beat Rick Rude & Manny Fernandez DQ
Brad Armstrong beat Jimmy Garvin in a Texas death match
Ivan Koloff & Vladimir Petrov beat Dick Murdoch & Baron Von Raschke
The Rock & Roll Express & Barry Windham beat Midnight Express & Big Bubba
Arn Anderson beat Jimmy Valiant
Tim Horner beat Bill Dundee

1/24/87: Washington, DC @ Armory
The Road Warriors beat The Midnight Express in a scaffold match
Brad Armstrong beat Jimmy Garvin by DQ

1/25/87: St. Joseph, MO @ Civic Arena
Brady Boone beat The Warlord
Rufus R. Jones & Italian Stallion beat Ken Timbs & Korstia Korchinko by DQ
Bulldog Brown beat Sam Houston in a loser leaves town, bullrope match

1/27/87: Greenville, SC @ Memorial Auditorium
NWA World title match: Ric Flair vs Nikita Koloff
World TV Title Match Tully Blanchard vs Barry Windham
NWA World Tag Champs Manny Fernandez & Rick Rude vs Rock & Roll Express
Dick Murdoch vs Arn Anderson
Wahoo McDaniel & Brad Armstrong vs Midnight Express
Baron Von Raschke vs Jimmy Garvin
Jimmy Valiant vs Ivan Koloff
Tim Horner vs Shaska Whatley

1/27/87: Rock Hill, SC @ Winthrop Coliseum (TV)
Barry Windham beat Tully Blanchard by DQ
The Rock & Roll Express & Dick Murdoch beat The Midnight Express & Bib Bubba via pinfall
Tully Blanchard, Ole & Arn Anderson beat Tim Horner, Ricky Lee Jones & George South by submission
Jimmy Garvin beat Keith Vinson via pinfall
Rock & Roll Express beat Eddie Roberts & Tommy Angel
Manny Fernandez & Rick Rude beat Rocky King & David Isley via pinfall
Bill Dundee beat Gary Royal via pinfall
Vladimir Petrov beat Keith Patterson via pinfall
Barry Windham & Ronnie Garvin beat John Savage & Larry Stephens
Nikita Koloff beat Thunderfoot I via pinfall
Brad Armstrong beat David Isley via pinfall
Jimmy Garvin beat Tommy Angel via pinfall
Manny Fernandez & Rick Rude beat Gary Royal & Vernon Deaton via pinfall
Dick Murdoch vs. Keith Patterson
Barry Windham vs. Larry Stephens
Tully Blanchard vs. Rocky King

1/28/87: Odessa, TX
Ricky Romero beat Ted Heath

Ronnie Garvin draw Arn Anderson
Manny Fernandez & Rick Rude draw Barry Windham & Baron Von Raschke
Tully Blanchard beat Dick Murdoch by DQ
The Road Warriors & Dusty Rhodes beat Big Bubba & The Midnight Express
Nikita Koloff beat NWA World Champ Ric Flair by DQ

1/29/87: Inglewood, CA @ The Forum
Todd Champion beat Teijo Khan
Big Bubba beat Ronnie Garvin in a Louisville street fight match
Dusty Rhodes draw Tully Blanchard
Barry Windham NC with Arn Anderson
Rick Rude & Manny Fernandez beat Dick Murdoch & Baron Von Raschke
Nikita Koloff beat NWA World Champ Ric Flair by DQ
The Road Warriors beat The Midnight Express in a scaffold match

1/30/87: St. Louis, MO @ Kiel Auditorium
NWA World Champ Ric Flair beat Barry Windham DQ
Nikita Koloff beat Arn Anderson
Dusty Rhodes beat Tully Blanchard first blood match
Manny Fernandez & Rick Rude beat Dick Murdoch & Baron Von Raschke
The Midnight Express & Big Bubba beat Italian Stallion, Ronnie Garvin & Todd Champion
Bill Dundee beat Brady Boone
The Mod Squad beat Brad Batten & Bart Batten
Porkchop Cash beat Dave Peterson

1/31/87: Atlanta, GA @ WTBS Studios (TV)
Jimmy Garvin vs. George South
Ronnie Garvin vs. Gary Royal
Tully Blanchard vs. Brad Armstrong
Lex Luger vs. Tommy Angel
Ric Flair & Ole Anderson vs. Tim Horner & Eddie Roberts
Vladimir Petrov vs. Mike Simani
Rick Rude & Manny Fernandez vs. Rocky King & Kent Glover
The Midnight Express vs. Vernon Deaton & Larry Stephens
Arn Anderson vs. Tim Horner

1/31/87: Charleston, WV @ Civic Center
Kansas Jayhawks beat Thunderfoot I & Thunderfoot II
Baron Von Raschke beat Shaska Whatley
Ivan Koloff & Vladimir Petrov beat Ronnie Garvin & Tim Horner
Tully Blanchard beat Barry Windham by DQ
The Rock & Roll Express draw Manny Fernandez beat Rick Rude
NWA World Champ Ric Flair draw Nikita Koloff

1/31/87: Kansas City, KS @ Memorial Hall
Italian Stallion draw Bob Brown
Todd Champion beat The Warlord
Teijo Khan beat Mitch Snow
Brady Boone beat Ken Timbs
Brad & Bart Batten beat The Midnight Express by DQ
Mitch Snow, Rufus R. Jones & Brady Boone beat Ken Timbs, Teijo Khan & Colt Steele
Jimmy Valiant beat Arn Anderson by DQ
Dave Peterson beat Porkchop Cash by DQ
Brad Armstrong beat Bill Dundee by DQ
Dick Murdoch beat Big Bubba in a lights out, barbed wire match

2/1/87: Atlanta, GA @ Omni
Bill Dundee beat Dutch Mantell
Bob Armstrong beat Jimmy Garvin
Arn Anderson beat Brad Armstrong
Tully Blanchard beat Wahoo McDaniel
Robert Gibson & Ronnie Garvin beat The Midnight Express
Dusty Rhodes & Nikita Koloff beat Ivan Koloff & Vladimir Petrov
Road Warriors beat Manny Fernandez & Rick Rude DQ
NWA World Champ Ric Flair draw Barry Windham

2/2/87: Bassett, VA
Big Bubba DCO with Ronnie Garvin
The Rock & Roll Express beat The Midnight Express

2/2/87: Greenville, SC @ Memorial Auditorium
Shaska Whatley beat George South
Ivan Koloff & Vladimir Petrov beat Kansas Jayhawks
Lex Luger beat Baron Von Raschke
Arn Anderson beat Wahoo McDaniel
Nikita Koloff beat Tully Blanchard by DQ
Road Warriors beat Tick rude & Manny Fernandez DQ
NWA World Champ Ric Flair draw Barry Windham

2/2/87: Hutchinson, KS @ Convention Hall
Mitch Snow beat Colt Steele
Brady Boone vs. Teijo Khan
Bob Brown beat Dave Peterson
Porkchop Cash & The Warlord beat Italian Stallion & Rufus R. Jones
Bart Batten & Brad Batten beat The Mod Squad

2/3/87: Spartanburg, SC @ Memorial Auditorium (TV)
Tully Blanchard vs. Barry Windham
Rick Rude & Manny Fernandez vs. The Rock & Express
Barry Windham & Ronnie Garvin vs. Rocky King & George South
The Rock & Roll Express vs. ?? & ??
Bob Armstrong vs. Thunderfoot
Lex Luger vs. Eddie Roberts
Vladimir Petrov vs. Mike Simani
Arn Anderson vs. Tommy Angel
Rick Rude & Manny Fernandez vs. Tim Horner & Ricky Lee Jones
Jimmy Garvin vs. Rocky King
The Kansas Jayhawks vs. John Savage & Randy Mulkey
Vladimir Petrov vs. David Isley
Bob Armstrong vs. Vernon Deaton
The Midnight Express vs. Eddie Roberts & Tommy Angel
Lex Luger vs. George South
Barry Windham vs. Thunderfoot

2/3/87: Topeka, KS @ Municipal Auditorium
Bart Batten & Brad Batten beat The Mod Squad
Bob Brown beat Dave Peterson

2/4/87: Kenansville, NC
Ronnie Garvin & Tim Horner beat Big Bubba & Dennis Condrey

2/5/87: Harrisonburg, VA @ H.S.
Rocky King vs. Gary Royal
Denny Brown draw Hector Guerrero
Lex Luger beat Tim Horner
Brad Armstrong beat Arn Anderson
Bob Armstrong beat Jimmy Garvin
Ronnie Garvin & Bob Armstrong beat Midnight Express

2/6/87: Kansas City, KS @ Memorial Hall
Porkchop Cash beat Mitch Snow
Brady Boone beat Colt Steele
Ken Timbs & Bob Brown DDQ Rufus R. Jones & Italian Stallion
Todd Champion beat Teijo Khan
Dave Peterson beat The Warlord by DQ
Bart Batten & Brad Batten beat The Mod Squad
Brad Armstrong beat Bill Dundee in a no DQ match

2/6/87: Baltimore, MD @ Civic Center
Dutch Mantell beat Ricky Lee Jones
Baron Von Raschke beat Thunderfoot
Hector Guerrero draw Denny Brown
Bobby Jaggers beat Shaska Whatley
The Rock & Roll Express beat Manny Fernandez & Rick Rude by DQ
Lex Luger beat Wahoo McDaniel
Dusty Rhodes & The Road Warriors beat Midnight Express & Big Bubba
NWA World Champ Ric Flair NC with Nikita Koloff

2/6/87: Richmond, VA @ Coliseum
Ivan Koloff beat Gary Royal
Lex Luger beat Tim Horner
Road Warriors beat Rick Rude & Manny Fernandez DQ
Bob Armstrong beat Jimmy Garvin
NWA World Champ Ric Flair NC with Nikita Koloff
Dusty Rhodes beat Vladimir Petrov by DQ
Tully Blanchard beat Jimmy Valiant
Ronnie Garvin & Bob Armstrong beat Ole & Arn Anderson

2/7/87: Greensboro, NC @ Coliseum
Tim Horner beat Shaska Whatley
Jimmy Valiant beat Thunderfoot
Bob Armstrong beat Jimmy Garvin
Arn Anderson & Lex Luger beat Wahoo McDaniel & Baron Von Raschke
Ronnie Garvin & Barry Windham beat The Midnight Express
Tully Blanchard beat Dusty Rhodes by DQ
NWA World Champ Ric Flair NC with Nikita Koloff
Rick Rude & Manny Fernandez beat The Rock & Roll Express in a cage match

2/8/87: Cincinnati, OH @ Gardens
The Kansas Jayhawks beat Thunderfoot I & Thunderfoot II
Lex Luger beat Ricky Lee Jones
Bob Armstrong beat Jimmy Garvin
Ronnie Garvin, Dick Murdoch & Wahoo McDaniel beat The Midnight Express & Big Bubba
Tully Blanchard beat Barry Windham by DQ
Manny Fernandez & Rick Rude beat The Rock & Roll Express in a cage match
NWA World Champ Ric Flair draw Nikita Koloff

2/9/87: Greenville, SC @ Memorial Auditorium
NWA World Champ Ric Flair beat Barry Windham
Nikita Koloff beat Tully Blanchard
The Rock & Roll Express beat Manny Fernandez & Rick Rude
Big Bubba beat Ronnie Garvin
Lex Luger & Arn Anderson beat Bob Armstrong & Jimmy Valiant
The Midnight Express beat The Kansas Jayhawks
Dick Murdoch beat Thunderfoot
Bill Dundee beat Randy Mulkey

2/10/87: Spartanburg, SC @ Memorial Auditorium (TV)
Jimmy Garvin beat Rocky King
The Kansas Jayhawks beat Randy Mulkey & John Savage
Vladimir Petrov beat David Isley
Bob Armstrong beat Vernon Deaton
The Midnight Express beat Tommy Angel & Eddie Roberts
Lex Luger beat George South
Barry Windham beat Thunderfoot I

2/10/87: Columbia, SC @ Township Auditorium (TV)
Ole & Arn Anderson vs. Larry Stephens & Johnny Ace
Barry Windham vs. Thunderfoot II
Lex Luger vs. Vernon Deaton
Tully Blanchard vs. Gary Royal

2/11/87: Marion, NC
Ronnie Garvin & Barry Windham beat Midnight Express

2/12/87: St. Joseph, MO @ Civic Arena
Bart Batten & Brad Batten beat The Mod Squad(24:00)
Todd Champion beat Bill Dundee by DQ
Dave Peterson beat The Barbarian(11:00) by DQ in a bounty match
Porkchop Cash & Ken Timbs beat Italian Stallion & Rufus R. Jones via pinfall
Brady Boone beat Colt Steele(11:00)
Mitch Snow beat Teijo Khan(9:00)

2/12/87: Raleigh, NC @ Dorton Arena
The Rock & Roll Express beat Rick Rude & Manny Fernandez in a cage match
NWA World Champ Ric Flair beat Barry Windham
Lex Luger & Tully Blanchard beat Kansas Jayhawks

Bob Armstrong beat Gary Royal
Nikita Koloff beat Arn Anderson
Ricky Lee Jones beat Denny Brown
Wahoo McDaniel beat Shaska Whatley
Ivan Koloff & Vladimir Petrov beat Brad Armstrong & Tim Horner

2/13/87: Columbus, GA @ Municipal Auditorium
Ronnie Garvin & Barry Windham beat Midnight Express

2/13/87: Kansas City, KS @ Memorial all
Brady Boone & Italian Stallion beat Colt Steele & The Warlord
Teijo Khan beat Mitch Snow by forfeit
Rufus R. Jones beat Ken Timbs
Porkchop Cash beat Dave Peterson
The Barbarian beat Todd Champion
Brad & Bart Batten beat The Mod Squad by DQ
Bill Dundee beat Brad Armstrong

2/14/87: Charlotte, NC @ Coliseum (TV)
NWA World Champ Ric Flair beat Nikita Koloff
Brad Armstrong beat Thunderfoot I
Tully Blanchard beat Ricky Lee Jones
Dusty Rhodes beat Vladimir Petrov
Manny Fernandez & Rick Rude beat The Rock & Roll Express
Jimmy Garvin beat George South
Ivan Koloff & Dick Murdoch beat Keith Patterson & Brodie Chase
Tim Horner beat David Isley
Ronnie Garvin & Barry Windham beat The Midnight Express
Lex Luger beat Randy Mulkey

2/14/87: Atlanta, GA @ WTBS Studios (TV)
Jimmy Valiant beat Tommy Angel
Ronnie Garvin & Barry Windham beat Randy Barber & Jack Jackson
Lex Luger beat Kent Glover
Arn Anderson beat Zane Smith
Jimmy Garvin beat David Isley
The Midnight Express beat Larry Stephens & Rick Sullivan
Ivan Koloff, Dick Murdoch, Vladimir Petrov beat Alan Martin, Chance McQuade & Randy Mulkey
Big Bubba beat George South
Kansas Jayhawks beat Vernon Deaton & Keith Vincent
Bob Armstrong beat The Demon
Tully Blanchard & Lex Luger beat Tommy Angel & Zane Smith
Kansas Jayhawks beat Randy Barber & Jack Jackson
Bob Armstrong beat Keith Vincent
Tim Horner beat Alan Martin
Nikita Koloff beat Kent Glover
Dick Murdoch beat David Isley

2/15/87: Atlanta, GA @ WTBS Studios (TV)
Dick Murdoch, Dusty Rhodes & Nikita Koloff beat Ivan Koloff, Vladimir Petrov & Big Red Machine(Murdoch turns on his partners)

2/15/87: Toronto, Ontario @ Maple Leaf Gardens
Angelo Mosca, Jr. beat Shaska Whatley
Joey War Eagle beat Dan Johnson
Lex Luger beat Ricky Lee Jones
The Midnight Express beat Barry Windham & Hector Guerrero
Arn Anderson beat Tim Horner
Rick Rude & Manny Fernandez beat Bob Armstrong & Ricky Morton
Tully Blanchard beat Dusty Rhodes by DQ
Nikita Koloff beat NWA World Champ Ric Flair by DQ

2/16/87: Hutchinson, KS @ Convention Hall
Mod Squad vs. Brad & Bart Batten in a match w/Pat O'Connor as special referee
Bobby Jaggers vs. The Barbarian
The Warlord vs. Charles Dukes
Italian Stallion & Rufus R. Jones vs. Bill Dundee & Porkchop Cash
Ken Timbs vs. Brady Boone
Mitch Snow vs. Teijo Khan

2/16/87: Brantford, Ontario
Big Bubba beat Frank Marconi
Tully Blanchard beat Ricky Lee Jones
Nikita Koloff beat Eric The Red
Barry Windham beat Shaska Whatley
Midnight Express beat Troy Little Bear & Moondog Vachon
Rick Rude & Manny Fernandez beat Terry Morgan & Bob Armstrong
Lex Luger beat Ron Hutchinson
Arn Anderson beat Hector Guerrero
Tim Horner beat Silent Boyd
Nikita Koloff beat Tully Blanchard
Ricky Morton & Barry Windham beat The Midnight Express

2/17/87: Peterborough, Ontario
Ricky Lee Jones beat Lex Luger by DQ
Big Bubba beat Chico Fernandez
Arn Anderson beat Hector Guerrero
Rick Rude & Manny Fernandez beat Ricky Lee Jones & Bob Armstrong
Tully Blanchard NC with Barry Windham
Ricky Morton & Tim Horner beat The Midnight Express

2/20/87: Jacksonville, FL @ Coliseum
NWA World Champ Ric Flair NC with Nikita Koloff
The Rock & Roll Express beat Rick Rude & Manny Fernandez by DQ
Tully Blanchard NC with Barry Windham
Dusty Rhodes beat Big Bubba

2/20/87: Kansas City, KS @ Memorial Hall
Ken Timbs beat Brady Boone
The Warlord beat Colt Steele
Rufus R. Jones beat Porkchop Cash by DQ
Italian Stallion beat Teijo Khan
Bobby Jaggers DDQ Bill Dundee
The Mod Squad beat Ric McCord & Bart Batten

2/21/87: Atlanta, GA @ WTBS Studios (TV)
Jimmy Valiant beat Thunderfoot II(4:24) via pinfall
Brad Armstrong vs. Larry Stephens
Dick Murdoch, Ivan Koloff & Vladimir Petrov vs. Rick Sullivan, David Isley & Tommy Angel
Rick Rude & Manny Fernandez vs. Rikki Nelson & Alan Martin
Tim Horner vs. Randy Barber
Big Bubba vs. Kent Glover
The Midnight Express vs. Randy Mulkey & Zane Smith
Denny Brown vs. Rocky King
Baron Von Raschke vs. Brodie Chase
Tully Blanchard, Lex Luger, Ole & Arn Anderson vs. Bob Armstrong, Dutch Mantell, Eddie Roberts & Ricky Lee Jones

2/21/87: Philadelphia, PA @ Civic Center
Bob Armstrong beat Gary Royal
Arn Anderson beat Ricky Lee Jones
Lex Luger beat Eddie Roberts
Tully Blanchard beat Tim Horner
Wahoo McDaniel & Jimmy Garvin beat Midnight Express
Dusty Rhodes & Nikita Koloff beat Ivan Koloff & Vladimir Petrov by DQ
Rick Rude & Manny Fernandez beat Rock & Roll Express
NWA World Champ Ric Flair beat Barry Windham

2/22/87: Asheville, NC @ Civic Center
Tully Blanchard beat Barry Windham
Dick Murdoch & Ivan Koloff beat Bob Armstrong & Brad Armstrong
Lex Luger & Arn Anderson beat Denny Brown & Ricky Lee Jones
Vladimir Petrov beat Dutch Mantell
Jimmy Valiant beat Bill Dundee
Barbarian beat Hector Guerrero
Rick Rude & Manny Fernandez draw Rock & Roll Express

2/23/87: Greenville, SC @ Memorial Auditorium
Bob Armstrong & Brad Armstrong beat The Barbarian & Bill Dundee
Manny Fernandez beat Ricky Morton
Robert Gibson beat Rick Rude
The Midnight Express draw Baron Von Raschke & Wahoo McDaniel(20:00)
Jimmy Valiant beat Brodie Chase
Hector Guerrero beat Gary Royal
Rocky King & George South beat Randy Mulkey & Bill Mulkey

2/23/87: Fayetteville, NC @ Cumberland County Civic Center
Nelson Royal beat Thunderfoot I
Shaska Whatley beat Mark Fleming
Misty Blue beat Linda Dallas
Ivan Koloff & Dick Murdoch beat Dutch Mantell & Denny Brown
Lex Luger beat Ricky Lee Jones
Tully Blanchard beat Tim Horner
Jimmy Garvin beat Arn Anderson
NWA World Champ Ric Flair beat Barry Windham DQ

2/24/87: Rock Hill, SC @ Winthrop Coliseum (TV)
The Rock & Roll Express beat Manny Fernandez & Rick Rude in a steel cage
Ivan Koloff & Vladimir Petrov beat George South & Gary Royal
Jimmy Valiant beat Randy Mulkey via pinfall
Manny Fernandez & Rick Rude beat Tommy Angel & Rocky King via pinfall
The Rock & Roll Express beat Randy Mulkey & David Isley
Barry Windham beat Brodie Chase via pinfall
Arn Anderson, Tully Blanchard & Lex Luger beat Denny Brown, Eddie Roberts & Ricky Lee Jones by submission
Brad Armstrong beat Bill Mulkey via pinfall
Ivan Koloff, Vladimir Petrov & Dick Murdoch beat Rocky King, George South & Johnny Ace
Bob Armstrong beat Brodie Chase via pinfall
Tully Blanchard beat Gary Royal via pinfall
Ole & Arn Anderson beat Tommy Angel & Johnny Ace via pinfall
Barry Windham beat Thunderfoot II via pinfall
Lex Luger beat Vernon Deaton by submission
Tully Blanchard & Arn Anderson vs. Mitch Snow & Larry Stephens
Baron Von Raschke vs. Bill Mulkey
Rick Rude & Manny Fernandez vs. Chance McQuade & Randy Mulkey
Ivan Koloff & Dick Murdoch vs. George South & Gary Royal
Jimmy Valiant vs. Bill Mulkey
NWA Tag Team Champs Rick Rude & Manny Fernandez vs. Rocky King & Johnny Ace
Tully Blanchard, Arn Anderson & Lex Luger vs. Denny Brown, Chance McQuade & Eddie Roberts
Barry Windham vs. Brodie Chase
Rock & Roll Express vs. Randy Mulkey & David Isley

2/25/87: Hammond, IN
Dick Murdoch beat Ricky Lee Jones
Misty Blue beat Linda Dallas
Lex Luger beat Baron Von Raschke
Ronnie Garvin beat Arn Anderson by DQ
Tully Blanchard beat Tim Horner
The Rock & Roll Express beat Rick Rude & Manny Fernandez by DQ
NWA World Champ Ric Flair beat Barry Windham DQ

2/26/87: Minneapolis, MN
Dick Murdoch beat Ricky Lee Jones
Lex Luger, Ole & Arn Anderson beat Tim Horner, Baron Von Raschke & Wahoo McDaniel
Misty Blue beat Linda Dallas
Jimmy Garvin beat Big Bubba in a street fight match
The Rock & Roll Express beat Rick Rude & Manny Fernandez by DQ
Nikita Koloff beat Tully Blanchard
NWA World Champ Ric Flair beat Barry Windham

2/27/87: Albany, GA @ Civic Center
Rocky King & George South beat Randy Mulkey & John Savage
Misty Blue beat Linda Dallas
Denny Brown beat Thunderfoot II
Bob Armstrong beat Thunderfoot I
Arn Anderson beat Brad Armstrong
Barry Windham & Jimmy Garvin beat Bobby Eaton & Arn Anderson

2/27/87: Pittsburgh, PA @ Civic Center
Hector Guerrero draw Shaska Whatley
Vladimir Petrov beat Jim Lancaster
Dick Murdoch & Ivan Koloff beat Wahoo McDaniel & Dutch Mantell
Lex Luger beat Ricky Lee Jones
Tully Blanchard beat Tim Horner
Rick Rude & Manny Fernandez beat The Rock & Roll Express
Nikita Koloff beat NWA World Champ Ric Flair by DQ
Dusty Rhodes beat Big Bubba to win the Bunkhouse Stampede in a tournament final, cage match

2/27/87: Philadelphia, PA @ Civic Center

2/27/87: Kansas City, KS @ Memorial Hall
Bob Brown beat Bill Dundee to win NWA Central States Title loser leaves town
Rick McCord & Bart Batten beat Mod Squad win NWA Central States Tag Title
Karl Kovac beat Joe Lightfoot
Penny Mitchell beat Despina Montages
The Warlord beat Bobby Jaggers
Rufus R. Jones beat Ken Timbs

2/28/87: Atlanta, GA @ WTBS Studios (TV)
Tully Blanchard & Lex Luger vs. Ricky Sullivan & Chance McQuade
Barry Windham vs. Thunderfoot II
Brad Armstrong vs. Keith Vincent
Rick Rude & Manny Fernandez vs. Zane Smith & Jack Evans
Tim Horner vs. Kent Glover
Jimmy Garvin vs. Thunderfoot I
Bobby Eaton vs. Larry Stephens
Ronnie Garvin vs. Tommy Angel
Big Bubba vs. George South
Ole & Arn Anderson beat Alan Martin & Randy Mulkey via submission
Misty Blue vs. Linda Dallas

2/28/87: Taylorsville, NC
Rick Rude & Manny Fernandez vs. ?? & ??
Shaska Whatley vs. Ricky Lee Jones

2/28/87: Kingsport, TN
The Rock & Roll Express beat The Midnight Express

2/28/87: Baltimore, MD @ Civic Center

3/1/87: Richmond, VA @ Coliseum
The Kansas Jayhawks beat Ricky Lee Jones & Shaska Whatley
Jimmy Valiant draw Bobby Eaton
Lazertron(Hector Guerrero) beat Mark Fleming
Lex Luger beat Baron Von Raschke
Tully Blanchard beat Brad Armstrong
Rick Rude & Manny Fernandez NC with The Rock & Roll Express
Jimmy Garvin beat Big Bubba by CO
Dusty Rhodes & Nikita Koloff beat Ivan Koloff & Dick Murdoch by DQ
NWA World Champ Ric Flair beat Barry Windham

3/1/87: Atlanta, GA @ Omni
The Barbarian beat Italian Stallion
Bob Armstrong beat Thunderfoot I
Mike Rotundo beat Thunderfoot II
Lex Luger & Arn Anderson beat Tim Horner & Bob Armstrong
Rick Rude & Manny Fernandez NC with The Rock & Roll Express
Brad Armstrong beat Tully Blanchard by DQ
Jimmy Garvin beat Bobby Eaton
Dusty Rhodes & Nikita Koloff beat Ivan Koloff & Dick Murdoch
NWA World Champ Ric Flair beat Barry Windham

3/2/87: Greenville, SC @ Memorial Auditorium
Mike Rotundo beat Dennis Condrey by DQ
Jimmy Garvin beat Bobby Eaton
Ricky Lee Jones vs Bill Dundee
Bob Armstrong & Tim Horner vs Lex LUger & Arn Anderson
Rock & Roll Express & Brad Armstrong vs Manny Fernandez, Rick Rude & Paul Jones
Tully Blanchard vs Baron Von Raschke
Dusty Rhodes & Nikita Koloff vs Ivan Koloff & Dick Murdoch
NWA World title match 2/3 Falls Ric Flair vs Barry Windham

3/3/87: Spartanburg, SC @ Memorial Auditorium (TV)
Tully Blanchard & Lex Luger vs. The Rock & Roll Express
Barry Windham vs. Colt Steele
Jimmy & Ronnie Garvin vs. Vernon Deaton & ??
The Rock & Roll Express vs. Randy Mulkey & Gary Royal
Lazertron vs. Bill Mulkey
Lex Luger & Tully Blanchard vs. Chance McQuade & Eddie Roberts
Arn Anderson vs. Tommy Angel
Dick Murdoch, Ivan Koloff & Vladimir Petrov vs. George South, Mitch Snow & Italian Stallion
Lazertron vs. Keith Vincent
Dick Murdoch, Ivan Koloff & Vladimir Petrov vs. Randy Mulkey, ?? & ??
Bob Armstrong & Brad Armstrong vs. George South & Mark Fleming
Lex Luger vs. Gary Royal
Tully Blanchard & Arn Anderson vs. Brady Boone & Eddie Roberts

3/4/87: Wytheville, WV
The Kansas Jayhawks draw The Mod Squad
Baron Von Raschke beat Shaska Whatley
Lazertron beat Teijo Khan
Ivan Koloff & Vladimir Petrov beat Tim Horner & Italian Stallion
Wahoo McDaniel beat Dick Murdoch by DQ

3/4/87: Birmingham, AL @ Fairgrounds
Jimmy Valiant beat The Barbarian
Bob Armstrong, Ronnie & Jimmy Garvin beat The Midnight Express & Big Bubba
Brad Armstrong beat Bill Dundee
Barry Windham beat Lex Luger by DQ
Tully Blanchard beat Dusty Rhodes by DQ
Nikita Koloff beat Arn Anderson
Rick Rude & Manny Fernandez beat The Rock & Roll Express

3/5/87: Memphis, TN @ Mid-South Coliseum
The Barbarian draw Bob Armstrong
Brad Armstrong beat Big Bubba
Jimmy Valiant beat Arn Anderson
Jimmy & Ronnie Garvin beat The Midnight Express
Barry Windham beat Lex Luger by DQ
Nikita Koloff beat Tully Blanchard
Manny Fernandez & Rick Rude beat The Rock & Roll Express
Bill Dundee beat Dusty Rhodes in a King Of Tennessee match

Note: Champship Wrestling from Florida merged with Jim Crockett Promotions in March of 1987:, & lasted until November 1987: when the Florida promotion was shut down

3/6/87: Morganton, NC
Jimmy & Ronnie Garvin beat The Midnight Express

3/6/87: Winter Haven, FL @ Citrus Showcase

3/7/87: Atlanta, GA @ WTBS Studios (TV)
Lex Luger beat Rocky King
The Mod Squad beat Mitch Snow & George South
Mike Rotundo beat Thunderfoot I
Arn Anderson beat Mike Jackson
Lazertron beat Denny Brown to win NWA World Junior Title
Jimmy Valiant beat Tommy Angel
The Barbarian beat Randy Mulkey
Wahoo McDaniel & Baron Von Raschke beat Randy Barber & Rick Sullivan
Ivan Koloff, Dick Murdoch & Vladimir Petrov beat Cougar Jay, Alan Martin & Zane Smith
Barry Windham beat Chance McQuade
Jimmy & Ronnie Garvin beat Darryl Dalton & Larry Stephens
Tully Blanchard beat Brad Armstrong

3/7/87: Norfolk, VA @ Scope
Bobby Eaton draw Tim Horner(20:00)
Jimmy Garvin beat Bobby Eaton

3/7/87: Sarasota, FL @ Robarts Arena
The Southern Boys vs. New Breed
Ed Gantner vs. Mike Graham in a chain match
Bad News Allen & Scott Hall vs. Kevin Sullivan & Tombstone

3/8/87: Beckley, WV @ Civic Center
Ricky Morton & Brad Armstrong beat Rick Rude & Manny Fernandez
Wahoo McDaniel beat Arn Anderson
Mark Fleming beat Teijo Khan
Bobby Jaggers beat Gary Royal
Baron Von Raschke beat Shaska Whatley
Nelson Royal beat Johnny Ace
Bob Armstrong & Brad Armstrong beat Thunderfoot I & II

3/8/87: Greenville, SC @ Memorial Auditorium
Nikita Koloff beat Lex Luger
Dick Murdoch beat Dusty Rhodes
Barry Windham, Ronnie & Jimmy Garvin beat MIdnight Express & Big Bubba
Tully Blanchard beat Dutch Mantell
The Barbarian & Bill Dundee beat Jimmy Valiant & Brady Boone
Vladimir Petrov beat Denny Brown
The Mod Squad beat Rocky King & George South

3/8/87: Orlando, FL @ Eddie Graham Sports Complex
Dusty Rhodes vs. Big Bubba in a Louisville street fight match
Barry Windham & Nikita Koloff vs. Tully Blanchard & Arn Anderson
Jimmy Valiant vs. The Barbarian
Scott Hall, Mike Graham & Bad News Allen vs. Kevin Sullivan, Kareem Muhammad & Ed Gantner
The Southern Boys vs. New Breed
Mike Rotundo vs. Chic Donavan
Tombstone vs. Luis Astea & Scott Hodges in a handicap match
Ron Simmons vs. Bob Cook

3/9/87: Fayetteville, NC @ Cumberland County Civic Center (TV)
Lex Luger beat Gary Royal
Arn Anderson & Tully Blanchard beat Brady Boone & Eddie Roberts
Tully Blanchard, Arn Anderson & Lex Luger vs. Keith Anderson, Colt Steele & Italian Stallion
Wahoo McDaniel & Baron Von Raschke vs. Thunderfoot I & Thunderfoot II
The Rock & Roll Express vs. Larry Stephens & Tommy Angel
Rick Rude & Manny Fernandez vs. Bill & Randy Mulkey
Jimmy & Ronnie Garvin vs. Gary Royal & Johnny Ace
The Midnight Express vs. Brodie Chase & Mitch Snow

3/9/87: Fort Pierce, FL @ St. Lucie County Civic Center

3/10/87: Greenwood, SC
Jimmy & Ronnie Garvin beat The Midnight Express

3/10/87: Tampa, FL @ Spartan Sports Center
Mike Graham & Scott Hall beat Ed Gantner & Kevin Sullivan by DQ
The Southern Boys beat New Breed
Tombstone beat Jim Backlund
Ron Simmons beat Jack Hart
Kareem Muhammad beat Mark Sterling

3/11/87: Thomasville, NC
Ronnie Garvin beat Bobby Eaton
Brad Armstrong beat Dennis Condrey

3/11/87: Tampa, FL @ Sportatorium (TV)
Ed Gantner beat Mark Sterling
Bad News Allen beat Chris Champ
Mike Rotundo beat Sean Royal
Nikita Koloff beat Jack Hart
The Southern Boys beat New Breed by DQ
Bill Dundee & The Barbarian DDQ Stan Lane & Scott Hall

3/11/87: Homestead, FL @ H.S.
Scott Hall & Bad News Allen beat Kareem Muhammad & Kevin Sullivan
Ed Gantner beat Mark Sterling
Tombstone beat Jason Sterling
Ron Simmons beat Jack Hart
The Southern Boys beat New Breed

3/12/87: Sunrise FL @ Crystal River H.S.
Tully Blanchard beat Dusty Rhodes by DQ
Nikita Koloff beat Arn Anderson
Rick Rude & Manny Fernandez beat The Rock & Roll Express
Barry Windham draw Lex Luger
Jimmy Valiant beat The Barbarian
Chris Von Colt vs. Ron Simmons
Ed Gantner vs. Roberto Soto
New Breed vs. The Southern Boys
Bad News Allen & Scott Hall vs. Kareem Muhammad & Kevin Sullivan

3/12/87: Raleigh, NC @ Dorton Arena
Jimmy & Ronnie Garvin beat The Midnight Express
Vladimir Petrov beat Tim Horner
Ivan Koloff & Dick Murdoch beat Baron Von Raschke & Wahoo McDaniel
Big Bubba beat Brad Armstrong in a Louisville street fight match
Eddie Roberts & Brady Boone beat Thunderfoot I & Thunderfoot II
Bob Armstrong & Denny Brown beat The Mod Squad

3/13/87: Washington, DC @ Armory
Mark Fleming beat Teijo Khan
Tim Horner beat Johnny Ace
Lazertron beat Shaska Whatley
The Kansas Jayhawks beat The Mod Squad
Wahoo McDaniel beat Big Bubba by DQ
Jimmy Garvin beat Dennis Condrey by DQ
Ronnie Garvin beat Bobby Eaton
Rick Rude & Manny Fernandez beat The Rock & Roll Express in a cage match

3/13/87: Albany, GA @ Civic Center
Denny Brown beat Brady Boone
Thunderfoot I beat Rocky King
The Barbarian beat Italian Stallion
Vladimir Petrov beat Baron Von Raschke
Bob Armstrong & Brad Armstrong beat Lex Luger & Arn Anderson
Tully Blanchard beat Barry Windham by DQ
Dusty Rhodes & Nikita Koloff beat Ivan Koloff & Dick Murdoch by DQ

3/13/87: Plant City, FL @ Strawberry Festival

3/14/87: Atlanta, GA @ WTBS Studios (TV)
Jimmy Garvin beat Randy Barber(3:45) via pinfall
The Barbarian beat Zane Smith via pinfall
Ivan Koloff & Dick Murdoch beat Ronnie Garvin & Barry Windham (22:52) via pinfall to win NWA United States Tag Title
Brad Armstrong beat El Lobo
Arn Anderson, Tully Blanchard & Lex Luger beat Alan Martin, Bill Mulkey & Larry Stephens
Lazertron beat Tommy Angel
The Midnight Express beat Mike Jackson & Dexter Westcott
The Rock & Roll Express beat Darryl Dalton & Randy Mulkey
Lex Luger beat Bill Tabb
Manny Fernandez & Rick Rude beat Alan Martin & Rocky King
Denny Brown beat Mike Jackson
Barry Windham beat Thunderfoot
Mike Rotundo beat Vernon Deaton

3/14/87: Greensboro, NC @ Coliseum
Ole Anderson beat Big Bubba by DQ
The Kansas Jayhawks beat The Mod Squad
NWA World Champ Ric Flair beat Barry Windham
Baron Von Raschke beat Dennis Condrey
Ivan Koloff & Dick Murdoch beat Nikita Koloff & Dusty Rhodes
Jimmy Garvin beat Bobby Eaton in a Louisville street fight match
Tim Horner beat Lex Luger by DQ
Tully Blanchard beat Brad Armstrong
Wahoo McDaniel & The Rock & Roll Express beat Rick Rude, Manny Fernandez & Paul Jones

3/15/87: Atlanta, GA @ WTBS Studios (TV)

3/15/87: Bloomington, MN @ Met Center
The Kansas Jayhawks beat Thunderfoot I & Thunderfoot II
Jimmy Garvin beat Bobby Eaton
Lex Luger beat Baron Von Raschke
Nikita Koloff beat Vladimir Petrov
The Road Warriors beat Rick Rude & Manny Fernandez
NWA World Champ Ric Flair beat Barry Windham
Dusty Rhodes beat Big Bubba in a cage match

3/15/87: Daytona, FL @ Ocean Center
Mike Rotundo beat Ed Gantner to win NWA Florida Title
The Mod Squad beat The Southern Boys to win NWA Florida Tag Title
Jimmy Valiant beat The Barbarian
Scott Hall beat Tombstone
Kevin Sullivan beat Bad News Allen in a steel cage match
Adrian Street vs. Sir Oliver Humperdink
Ron Simmons vs. Colt Steele
Jason Sterling & Mark Sterling vs. New Breed

3/15/87: Jacksonville, FL @ Coliseum
New Breed vs. Jason Sterling & Mark Sterling
Colt Steele vs. Ron Simmons
Kareem Muhammad vs. Jimmy Valiant
Adrian Street vs. Sir Oliver Humperdink
The Mod Squad beat The Southern Boys
Mike Rotundo beat Ed Gantner
Scott Hall beat Tombstone
Kevin Sullivan beat Bad News Allen in a Thunderdome steel cage match

3/16/87: Lenoir, NC
Jimmy & Ronnie Garvin beat The Midnight Express

3/16/87: Greenville, SC @ Memorial Auditorium
NWA World title match 2/3 Falls Ric Flair beat Barry Windham
Ricky Morton beat Rick Rude Cage Match
US Title Match Nikita Koloff(c) DCO Lex Luger
Tim Horner, Bobby Jaggers beat Gary Royal & the Barbarian
Brad Armstrong beat Ivan Koloff
Bob Armstrong draw Vladimir Petrov
Tim Horner beat Italian Stallion

3/17/87: China Grove, NC @ South Rowan H.S. (TV)
Tim Horner beat Vernon Deaton
Barry Windham, Jimmy & Ronnie Garvin beat John Savage, Thunderfoot I & Thunderfoot II
Lazertron beat Rocky King
Jimmy Garvin beat Mark Fleming
Barry Windham beat John Savage
Wahoo McDaniel & Baron Von Raschke beat Gary Royal & Tommy Angel
Manny Fernandez & Rick Rude vs. The Rock & Roll Express

3/17/87: Tampa, FL @ Spartan Sports Center
Mike Rotundo draw Ed Gantner
Mulkey Brothers beat Kareem Muhammad & Colt Steele
Jimmy Valiant beat The Barbarian by DQ
New Breed beat Eddie Roberts & Brady Boone
The Mod Squad beat The Southern Boys
Pez Whatley beat Mitch Snow
Scott Hall, Stan Lane & Ron Simmons beat Tahitian Prince(aka Samu), Teijo Khan & Kevin Sullivan

3/18/87: Las Cruces, NM
Nikita Koloff beat NWA World Champ Ric Flair by DQ
The Rock & Roll Express beat Rick Rude & Manny Fernandez
Jimmy & Ronnie Garvin & Wahoo McDaniel beat The Midnight Express & Big Bubba
Barry Windham beat Arn Anderson
Dutch Mantell beat The Barbarian
Bobby Jaggers beat Thunderfoot II

3/18/87: Fort Lauderdale, FL @ War Memorial Auditorium

3/19/87: Inglewood, CA @ The Forum
Bobby Jaggers beat Thunderfoot II
Dutch Mantell beat The Barbarian
The Rock & Roll Express draw Lex Luger & Arn Anderson
Jimmy & Ronnie Garvin beat The Midnight Express in a bunkhouse match
Tully Blanchard beat Wahoo McDaniel by DQ
Manny Fernandez & Rick Rude beat Dusty Rhodes & Nikita Koloff by DQ
NWA World Champ Ric Flair beat Barry Windham
Road Warrior Animal beat Big Bubba in a Louisville street fight match

3/19/87: Okeechobee, FL @ Adventure Resort

3/20/87: Albuquerque, NM @ Tingley Coliseum
Bobby Jaggers beat Thunderfoot II
Dutch Mantell beat The Barbarian
Jimmy & Ronnie Garvin beat The Midnight Express
Wahoo McDaniel beat Lex Luger by DQ
Nikita Koloff & Road Warrior Animal beat Tully Blanchard & Arn Anderson
NWA World Champ Ric Flair beat Barry Windham
Rick Rude & Manny Fernandez beat The Rock & Roll Express
Dusty Rhodes beat Big Bubba in a chain match

3/21/87: Atlanta, GA @ WTBS Studios (TV)
Arn Anderson & Lex Luger beat Tommy Angel & Larry Stephens
Brad Armstrong beat Paul Garner
Tim Horner beat El Lobo
Wahoo McDaniel beat Randy Barber
Ronnie Garvin beat Dexter Westcott
Bobby Eaton beat Alan Fox
The Rock & Roll Express beat Darryl Dalton & Zane Smith
Barry Windham beat Bill Tabb

3/21/87: Chicago, IL @ UIC Pavilion
NWA World Champ Ric Flair NC with Nikita Koloff
The Road Warriors beat Rick Rude & Manny Fernandez by DQ
Tully Blanchard beat Dusty Rhodes by DQ
The Rock & Roll Express beat Ivan Koloff & Vladimir Petrov
Arn Anderson beat Baron Von Raschke
Bobby Jaggers beat Thunderfoot I
Tim Horner beat Ricky Lee Jones

3/21/87: Cincinnati, OH @ Gardens
Jimmy & Ronnie Garvin beat The Midnight Express in a cage match
Ole Anderson beat Big Bubba in a cage match
Barry Windham beat Lex Luger by DQ
Wahoo McDaniel beat Vladimir Petrov by CO
Brad Armstrong & Bob Armstrong beat Thunderfoot I & Gary Royal
Lazertron beat Denny Brown
Dutch Mantell beat Italian Stallion

3/21/87: Lakeland, FL @ Civic Center

3/22/87: Waco, TX
The Road Warriors beat The Midnight Express
Tully Blanchard beat Dusty Rhodes by DQ
Nikita Koloff beat NWA World Champ Ric Flair by DQ

3/22/87: Houston, TX @ Summit
Included NWA World Champ Ric Flair, Dusty Rhodes, The Rock & Roll Express & The Road Warriors

3/22/87: Orlando, FL @ Eddie Graham Sports Complex
Mitch Snow & Eddie Roberts beat New Breed
Kevin Sullivan beat Jimmy Valiant in a lights out match
Mike Rotundo draw Ed Gantner
Brady Boone beat Colt Steele
The Southern Boys beat The Mod Squad
The Barbarian beat Bill & Randy Mulkey in a handicap match
Ron Simmons, Stan Lane & Scott Hall NC with Teijo Khan, Tahitian Prince & Shaska Whatley

3/23/87: Fayetteville, NC @ Cumberland County Civic Center
Ronnie Garvin beat Bobby Eaton in a cage match
Jimmy Garvin beat Big Bubba in a street fight match
Brad Armstrong beat Dennis Condrey by DQ
Ivan Koloff & Vladimir Petrov beat Bob Armstrong & Tim Horner
Lazertron beat Denny Brown
Baron Von Raschke beat Mark Fleming
Nelson Royal beat Gary Royal

3/23/87: Greenville, SC @ Memorial Auditorium TV Taping
NWA World Tag Match: The Road Warriors beat Manny Fernandez & Rick Rude(c) by DQ
Rock & Roll Express draw Tully Blanchard & Lex Luger

3/24/87: Lincolnton, NC (TV)
The Kansas Jayhawks beat Tommy Angel & Ricky Nelson
Tully Blanchard & Lex Luger beat Tim Horner & Italian Stallion
Rick Rude & Manny Fernandez beat Mike Simani & Vernon Deaton
Arn Anderson beat John Savage
The Road Warriors beat Thunderfoot I & David Isley
Rick Rude & Manny Fernandez beat George South & Rocky King
Tully Blanchard, Arn Anderson & Lex Luger beat Ricky Lee Jones, Italian Stallion & Johnny Ace
Jimmy Ronnie Garvin beat The Midnight Express

Note: Dennis Condrey left the promotion after this event

3/24/87: Tampa, FL @ Spartan Sports Center

3/25/87: San Francisco, CA @ Civic Auditorium
Tim Horner beat Frank Dusek
Robert Gibson draw Rick Rude
Manny Fernandez beat Tim Horner
Barry Windham beat Big Bubba in a Louisville street fight match
Jimmy Garvin beat Bobby Eaton
Road Warriors & Dusty Rhodes beat Tully Blanchard, Lex Luger & Arn Anderson
Nikita Koloff beat NWA World Champ Ric Flair by DQ

3/25/87: Miami, FL @ Stadium

3/26/87: Amarillo, TX @ Civic Center
Included Dick Murdoch, Ivan Koloff, Nikita Koloff & Vladimir Petrov

3/26/87: Cocoa, FL @ H.S.

3/27/87: Norfolk, VA @ Scope
Jimmy Garvin beat Bobby Eaton

3/27/87: Atlanta, GA @ Omni
The Kansas Jayhawks beat Thunderfoot I & Thunderfoot II
Denny Brown beat George South
Tim Horner beat Gary Royal
The Barbarian beat Todd Champion
Tully Blanchard, Lex Luger & Arn Anderson beat Bob Armstrong, Barry Windham & Baron Von Raschke
NWA World Champ Ric Flair beat Brad Armstrong
Ole Anderson beat Big Bubba in a cage match
Dusty Rhodes & Nikita Koloff beat Ivan Koloff & Dick Murdoch in a cage match

3/28/87: Atlanta, GA @ WTBS Studios (TV)
Bill & Randy Mulkey beat The Gladiators

3/28/87: Philadelphia, PA @ Civic Center
Lazertron beat Denny Brown
Baron Von Raschke beat Gary Royal
Lex Luger beat Tim Horner
Nikita Koloff, Dusty Rhodes & Wahoo McDaniel beat Ivan Koloff, Vladimir Petrov & Dick Murdoch in a bunkhouse match
Ole Anderson beat Tully Blanchard by DQ
NWA World Champ Ric Flair beat Brad Armstrong
The Rock & Roll Express NC with Rick Rude & Manny Fernandez
Ronnie Garvin beat Bobby Eaton

3/28/87: Orlando, FL @ Eddie Graham Sports Complex
Kevin Sullivan beat Barry Windham in a lumberjack match
Mike Rotundo beat Ed Gantner
Jimmy Garvin beat The Barbarian
Scott Hall & Stan Lane draw Teijo Khan & Tahitian Prince
Pez Whatley beat Ron Simmons
Brady Boone beat Chic Donovan
Bill & Randy Mulkey beat Eddie Roberts & Colt Steele
The Mod Squad beat The Southern Boys

3/29/87: Asheville, NC @ Civic Center
Bob Armstrong beat Gary Royal
Ronnie Garvin beat Italian Stallion
The Kansas Jayhawks beat Thunderfoot I & Thunderfoot II
Nikita Koloff, Barry Windham & Wahoo McDaniel beat Tully Blanchard, Lex Luger & Arn Anderson
NWA World Champ Ric Flair beat Brad Armstrong
Jimmy Garvin beat Bobby Eaton
Ole Anderson beat Big Bubba in a Louisville street fight match

3/29/87: Charlotte, NC @ Coliseum
Tim Horner beat George South
Jimmy Garvin beat Rikki Nelson
Lex Luger & Arn Anderson beat Wahoo McDaniel & Brad Armstrong
Ole Anderson beat Tully Blanchard by DQ
Ronnie Garvin beat Bobby Eaton in a lights out match
Dusty Rhodes & Nikita Koloff beat Ivan Koloff & Dick Murdoch by DQ
NWA World Champ Ric Flair beat Barry Windham
Rick Rude & Manny Fernandez beat Rock & Roll Express

3/30/87: Greenville, SC @ Memorial Auditorium
Ronnie Garvin beat Bobby Eaton
Louisville Street fight: Ole Anderson beat Big Bubba
Tully Blanchard vs Ricky Morton
Robert Gibson vs Lex Luger
Tim Horner vs Arn Anderson
Lasertron vs Denny Brown
Italian Stallion vs Brody Chase

3/30/87: Punta Gorda, FL @ Charlotte County Memorial Auditorium

3/31/87: Gastonia, NC (TV)
NWA United States Tag Title vacated when Dick Murdoch was suspended
Jimmy Garvin vs. Tommy Angel
Bobby Jaggers vs. George South
Lazertron vs. Larry Stephens
Rick Rude & Manny Fernandez vs. Johnny Ace & Mike Force
Tully Blanchard & Lex Luger vs. Denny Brown & Nelson Royal
Rock & Roll Express vs. Vernon Deaton & Brodie Chase
Bobby Eaton & Big Bubba vs. Italian Stallion & Ricky Lee Jones

3/31/87: Eustis, FL @ H.S.

4/1/87: Sunrise, FL @ Music Theater
Tahitian Prince beat Eddie Roberts
Teijo Khan beat Mitch Snow
Ron Simmons beat Shaska Whatley by DQ
Wahoo McDaniel beat Ed Gantner
Steve Armstrong, Tracy Smothers & Scott Hall beat The Mod Squad & Bill Dundee
Mike Rotundo beat The Barbarian by DQ
Ole Anderson beat Arn Anderson by DQ
Dusty Rhodes & Nikita Koloff beat Tully Blanchard & Lex Luger

4/1/87: Laurinburg, NC
Big Bubba beat Brad Armstrong
Ronnie Garvin beat Bobby Eaton

4/2/87: Columbia, SC @ Township Auditorium
Ronnie Garvin beat Bobby Eaton

4/2/87: Hawthorne, FL L@ H.S.

4/3/87: Nassau, Bahamas @ Stadium
Ed Gantner vs. Mike Rotundo
Jimmy Valiant vs. Kevin Sullivan
The Southern Boys vs. The Mod Squad
Wahoo McDaniel vs. Bill Dundee

4/3/87: Albany, GA @ Civic Center
Big Bubba beat Bob Armstrong by CO
Ronnie Garvin beat Bobby Eaton

4/3/87: Greensboro, NC @ Coliseum
Bill & Randy Mulkey beat New Breed(Chris Champ & Sean Royal)
Lazertron beat Denny Brown
Nikita Koloff beat Vladimir Petrov by DQ
Rock & Roll Express beat Tully Blanchard & Lex Luger
Road Warriors beat Rick Rude & Manny Fernandez DQ
Ole Anderson beat Arn Anderson
Dusty Rhodes beat NWA World Champ Ric Flair by DQ
Baron Von Raschke beat John Savage
New Breed beat Bobby Jaggers & Tim Horner

4/4/87: Atlanta, GA @ WTBS Studios (TV)
Featured the introduction of Stan Lane into The Midnight Express
Jimmy & Ronnie Garvin beat Larry Clark & Mike Force
Manny Fernandez & Rick Rude beat Cougar Jay & Dexter Westcott
The Road Warriors beat Tommy Angel & Bill Tabb
Big Bubba beat Gary Royal
Lex Luger beat Italian Stallion
Ole Anderson beat Brodie Chase
Ivan Koloff & Vladimir Petrov beat Johnny Ace & Ricky Lee Jones
Tully Blanchard beat Larry Stephens
Arn Anderson beat Alan Martin
Bob Armstrong & Brad Armstrong beat Randy Barber & Mike Jackson

Barry Windham beat Chance McQuade
Tim Horner beat Thunderfoot I

4/4/87: Boston, MA @ Garden
Misty Blue beat Linda Dallas
Lex Luger beat Baron Von Raschke
Jimmy & Ronnie Garvin beat Thunderfoot I & Thunderfoot II
Ole Anderson beat Arn Anderson by DQ
Roll Express beat Ivan Koloff & Vladimir Petrov
The Road Warriors beat The Midnight Express(Bobby Eaton & Stan Lane)
Nikita Koloff beat Tully Blanchard
NWA World Champ Ric Flair beat Barry Windham
Dusty Rhodes beat Big Bubba in a cage match

4/4/87: St. Petersburg, FL @ Bayfront Center

4/5/87: Atlanta, GA @ WTBS Studios (TV)

4/5/87: Atlanta, GA @ Omni
Tim Horner beat Sean Royal
Lazertron beat Chris Champ
Baron Von Raschke beat Ricky Lee Jones
The Midnight Express beat Ronnie Garvin & Barry Windham
Road Warriors NC with Ivan Koloff & Vladimir Petrov
Ole Anderson beat Tully Blanchard
Dusty Rhodes beat Arn Anderson
Lex Luger beat Nikita Koloff by DQ
NWA World Champ Ric Flair beat Jimmy Garvin by DQ

4/5/87: Orlando, FL @ Eddie Graham Sports Complex
Kevin Sullivan beat Jimmy Valiant in a Texas death match
Bill & Randy Mulkey draw Colt Steele & Snake Brown
Rick Rude & Manny Fernandez beat Brad Armstrong & Wahoo McDaniel
Mike Rotundo beat The Barbarian
Scott Hall beat Ed Gantner
Teijo Khan & Tahitian Prince beat Brady Boone & Mitch Snow
The Southern Boys & Bob Armstrong beat Bill Dundee & The Mod Squad

4/6/87: Toccoa, GA
The Rock & Roll Express, Jimmy & Ronnie Garvin beat The Midnight Express, Big Bubba & Jim Cornette

4/7/87: Spartanburg, SC @ Memorial Auditorium (TV)
Rick Rude & Manny Fernandez vs. The Road Warriors
New Breed vs. George South & Rocky King
Jimmy Garvin vs. John Savage
Lex Luger vs. Todd Champion
The Midnight Express vs. Vernon Deaton & Gary Royal
The Road Warriors vs. Tommy Angel & Rikki Nelson

4/7/87: Tallahassee, FL @ Leon County Civic Center
NWA World Champ Ric Flair vs. Barry Windham
The Mod Squad vs. The Southern Boys
Mike Rotundo vs. Ed Gantner
Scott Hall, Ron Simmons & Stan Lane vs. Kevin Sullivan, Teijo Khan & Tahitian Prince
Brady Boone vs. Shaska Whatley
Randy Mulkey & Bill Mulkey vs. Eddie Roberts & Mitch Snow

4/8/87: Miami, FL @ Convention Center
Dusty Rhodes beat Big Bubba
Mike Rotundo beat The Barbarian
Jimmy Valiant beat Kevin Sullivan by DQ
The Mod Squad beat The Southern Boys
Scott Hall beat Ed Gantner
Ron Simmons beat Teijo Khan

Note: Jim Crockett bought UWF from Bill Watts on April 9, 1987:

4/9/87: Raleigh, NC @ Dorton Arena
Baron Von Raschke beat Thunderfoot I
Italian Stallion beat Thunderfoot II
Lazertron beat John Savage
Johnny Ace beat Mark Fleming
Wahoo McDaniel & Brad Armstrong beat Manny Fernandez & Rick Rude by DQ
New Breed beat Bobby Jaggers & Todd Champion
Jimmy & Ronnie Garvin, Baron Von Raschke & Robert Gibson beat Jim Cornette, Big Bubba & The Midnight Express

4/9/87: Johnstown, PA
Terry Gordy & Buddy Roberts beat Bill Irwin & Angel of Death
Savannah Jack beat Mt. Miller
Nickla Roberts(aka Baby Doll) won a catfight match
Sam Houston beat Jack Foley
Mt. Miller draw Troy Orndorff
Fido beat Hank Hudson

4/9/87: Gainesville, FL @ H.S.
Mike Rotundo vs. Ed Gantner
Colt Steele vs. Ron Simmons

4/10/87: Bloomington, MN @ Met Center
Steve Williams beat One Man Gang by DQ
Chris Adams & Terry Taylor beat Rick Steiner & Sting
Eddie Gilbert beat Sam Houston
Chris Adams beat King Parsons by CO
Missing Link beat Savannah Jack
Michael Hayes, Terry Gordy & Buddy Roberts beat Angel of Death, Bill Irwin & The Viking
The Terminators beat Top Guns
Chavo Guerrero beat Terminator Wolf
Nickla Roberts won a catfight match

4/10/87: Baltimore, MD @ Arena (Crockett Cup Day 1)
Crockett Cup Tournament
1st Round
Bob Armstrong & Brad Armstrong beat Arn Anderson & Kevin Sullivan
The Mod Squad beat Wahoo McDaniel & Baron Von Raschke

Denny Brown & Chris Champ beat Bill & Randy Mulkey
Steve Keirn & George South draw Mike Graham & Nelson Royal
Shaska Whatley & Teijo Khan beat Jimmy Valiant & Lazertron by DQ
Jimmy & Ronnie Garvin beat Ricky Lee Jones & Italian Stallion
Thunderfoot I & Thunderfoot II beat Rocky King & Bobby Jaggers
Bill Dundee & the Barbarian beat Tim Horner & Mike Rotundo via pinfall

2nd Round
Bob Armstrong & Brad Armstrong beat Ivan Koloff & Vladimir Petrov by DQ
Tully Blanchard & Lex Luger beat The Mod Squad
Giant Baba & Isao Takagi beat Denny Brown & Chris Champ
The Road Warriors beat Shaska Whatley & Teijo Khan
The Midnight Express beat Jimmy & Ronnie Garvin by CO
Rick Rude & Manny Fernandez beat Thunderfoot I & Thunderfoot II
Dusty Rhodes & Nikita Koloff beat Bill Dundee & The Barbarian
Ole Anderson beat Big Bubba via pinfall in a last man standing, steel cage match

4/11/87: Baltimore, MD @ Arena (Crockett Cup 87: Day 2)
Crockett Cup Tournament
Quarterfinals
Tully Blanchard & Lex Luger beat Bob Armstrong & Brad Armstrong via pinfall
Giant Baba & Isao Takagi beat The Rock & Roll Express via forfeit when it was announced Ricky Morton had sustained an eye injury two days before & could not compete
The Midnight Express beat The Road Warriors by DQ
Dusty Rhodes & Nikita Koloff beat Rick Rude & Manny Fernandez via pinfall

Semifinals
Tully Blanchard & Lex Luger beat Giant Baba & Isao Takagi
Dusty Rhodes & Nikita Koloff beat The Midnight Express via pinfall

Finals
Dusty Rhodes & Nikita Koloff beat Tully Blanchard & Lex Luger via pinfall to win Crockett Cup in tournament final
Also, NWA World Champ Ric Flair beat Barry Windham (26:01)

4/11/87: Atlanta, GA @ WTBS Studios (TV)
Ole Anderson vs. Ray Aaron
The Midnight Express vs. Larry Stephens & Tommy Angel
Arn Anderson vs. Zane Smith
The Road Warriors vs. Randy Barber & Thunderfoot II
Baron Von Raschke vs. Brodie Chase
Ivan Koloff vs. Dexter Westcott
Jimmy Garvin vs. Thunderfoot I
New Breed vs. Cougar Jay & Chance McQuade
Tully Blanchard vs. Alan Martin
Ronnie Garvin vs. Bill Tabb
Lex Luger vs. Larry Clarke
Tim Horner vs. Mike Force

4/11/87: New Orleans, LA @ Superdome
Steve Williams beat One Man Gang by DQ
Chris Adams & Terry Taylor beat Sting & Rick Steiner
Michael Hayes & Buddy Roberts beat Missing Link & Chavo Guerrero
Michael Hayes, Terry Gordy & Buddy Roberts beat Bill Irwin, Angel of Death & The Viking
Eddie Gilbert beat Sam Houston by CO
Nickla Roberts won a catfight match

4/12/87: Charlotte, NC @ Coliseum
Todd Champion beat Mark Fleming
Ivan Koloff beat Bobby Jaggers
Lazertron beat Gary Royal
The Road Warriors & Nikita Koloff beat Ric Flair, Lex Luger & Arn Anderson
Ronnie Garvin beat Rick Rude
Ole Anderson beat Tully Blanchard by DQ

4/12/87: Marietta, GA @ Cobb County Civic Center
Bobby Jaggers beat Thunderfoot I
Vladimir Petrov beat Baron Von Raschke
Brad Armstrong beat Rick Rude

4/12/87: Atlanta, GA @ Omni
Missing Link beat Jim Bryant
The Nightmares beat Ranger Ross & Shawn Michaels
The Assassin beat Randy Rose
Savannah Jack beat King Parsons Atlanta street fight
Grizzly Boone beat Mike Golden loser leaves town
Sting & Rick Steiner beat Terry Taylor & Chris Adams to win UWF Tag Title
Terry Gordy, Michael Hayes & Buddy Roberts beat Bill Irwin, The Viking & Angel of Death badstreet match
Steve Williams beat One Man Gang by DQ
Nickla Roberts won a cat fight match

4/12/87: Orlando, FL @ Eddie Graham Sports Complex
Bill & Randy Mulkey beat Colt Steele & Jack Hart
Denny Brown beat Mitch Snow
Teijo Khan beat Ed Roberts
Tahitian Prince beat Brady Boone
Pez Whatley & Ed Gantner beat Ron Simmons & Scott Hall
Jimmy Valiant & The Southern Boys draw The Mod Squad & Bill Dundee
Mike Rotundo beat The Barbarian
Wahoo McDaniel NC with Kevin Sullivan

4/13/87: Marion, VA
Jimmy Valiant beat Big Bubba by DQ
Ronnie & Jimmy Garvin beat The Midnight Express

4/13/87: West Palm Beach, FL @ Auditorium

4/13/87: Greenville, SC @ Memorial Auditorium
Italian Stallion beat George South
Bobby Jaggers beat Todd Champion
Ivan Koloff beat Nelson Royal
Bob Armstrong & Brad Armstrong draw New Breed
Arn Anderson & Lex Luger beat Tim Horner & Baron Von Raschke
US Title Match Nikita Koloff(c) beat Vladimir Petrov
Lights Out Match: Ole Anderson beat Tully Blanchard
Dusty Rhodes beat NWA World Champ Ric Flair by DQ

4/14/87: Salisbury, NC (TV)
Jimmy Garvin vs. Tommy Angel
Barry Windham vs. Denny Brown
Nikita Koloff vs. John Savage
New Breed vs. Bobby Jaggers & Todd Champion
The Midnight Express vs. Italian Stallion & Nelson Royal
Bob Armstrong & Brad Armstrong vs. Gary Royal & Vernon Deaton
Lex Luger vs. Rocky King

4/14/87: Dallas, TX @ Reunion Arena
Michael Hayes, Terry Gordy & Buddy Roberts beat One Man Gang, Bill Irwin & Kareem Muhammad
Rick Steiner & Sting beat Chris Adams & Terry Taylor
Steve Williams beat One Man Gang by DQ
King Parsons beat Savannah Jack in a street fight match
Gary Young beat Chavo Guerrero by DQ
Sam Houston & Nickla Roberts beat Buddy Roberts & Sunshine by DQ
Steve Cox beat The Ninja
Mike George beat Jeff Raitz
Eddie Gilbert beat Sam Houston

4/14/87: Tampa, FL @ Spartan Sports Center
Colt Steele & Jack Hart vs. Bill & Randy Mulkey
Denny Brown vs. Eddie Roberts
Mitch Snow vs. Tahitian Prince
Brady Boone vs. Teijo Khan
Ed Gantner & Shaska Whatley vs. Scott Hall & Ron Simmons
The Mod Squad vs. The Southern Boys in a no DQ match
Mike Rotundo vs. The Barbarian
Wahoo McDaniel vs. Kevin Sullivan

4/15/87: Tampa, FL @ Sportatorium (TV)
Mike Rotundo beat Ed Gantner

4/15/87: Jacksonville, FL @ Coliseum

4/16/87: Harrisonburg, VA @ H.S.
Italian Stallion beat Gary Royal
Bruce Bonner beat John Savage
Ricky Lee Jones beat Thunderfoot II
Lazertron beat George South
Todd Champion beat Thunderfoot
New Breed beat Bobby Jaggers & Nelson Royal
Jimmy Valiant beat The Barbarian

4/16/87: Athens, GA @ Coliseum
Ronnie Garvin, Wahoo McDaniel, Jimmy Garvin & Barry Windham vs. Big Bubba, Jim Cornette & The Midnight Express
Bob Armstrong vs. Ivan Koloff
Baron Von Raschke vs. Rick Rude
Brad Armstrong vs. Arn Anderson
Ole Anderson vs. Tully Blanchard
NWA World Champ Ric Flair vs. Dusty Rhodes

4/16/87: Galveston, TX @ Moody Center
Terry Gordy & Michael Hayes vs. The Viking & Angel of Death in a badstreet rules match
Buddy Roberts vs. Bill Irwin in a whip on a pole match
Chavo Guerrero vs. Gary Young in a no DQ match
Steve Williams & Steve Cox vs. One Man Gang & Scandor Akbar
plus two other matches featuring Sam Houston, King Parsons, Savannah Jack, Eddie Gilbert & Super Ninja

4/16/87: Port St. Richey, FL @ Southland Roller Palace

4/17/87: Fort Myers, FL @ Lee County Civic Center

4/17/87: Richmond, VA @ Coliseum
Johnny Ace beat Mark Fleming
The Barbarian beat Italian Stallion
Lazertron beat Thunderfoot I
Ivan Koloff beat Baron Von Raschke
Nikita Koloff beat Rick Rude
Wahoo McDaniel beat Vladimir Petrov by DQ
Ole Anderson beat Tully Blanchard by DQ
Dusty Rhodes & The Road Warriors beat Ric Flair, Arn Anderson & Lex Luger

4/17/87: Macon, GA @ Coliseum
Ronnie & Jimmy Garvin beat The Midnight Express

4/18/87: Atlanta, GA @ WTBS Studios (TV)
The Midnight Express vs. Dave Diamond & Alan Martin
Ivan Koloff & Vladimir Petrov vs. Mike Force & Russ Taylor
Brad Armstrong vs. Randy Barber
Ronnie Garvin vs. Tony Beason
The Road Warriors vs. Dexter Westcott & Rick Sullivan
Lex Luger vs. Larry Clarke
New Breed vs. Chance McQuade & Larry Stephens
Ole Anderson & Tim Horner vs. Bill Tabb & Vernon Deaton
Arn Anderson vs. Italian Stallion
NWA World Champ Ric Flair vs. Brodie Chase
Lazertron vs. Darrell Dalton
Jimmy Garvin vs. Billy Moore
The Barbarian vs. Clement Fields

4/18/87: Roanoke, VA @ Civic Center
Ronnie & Jimmy Garvin beat The Midnight Express

4/18/87: Lakeland, FL @ Civic Center

4/18/87: Fort Worth, TX @ Cowtown Coliseum
King Parsons beat Savannah Jack in a loser gets 10 lashes match
Chavo Guerrero beat Bob Bradley
Steve Cox beat Gary Young
Big Bubba beat Mike Reed & Glassman in a handicap match
Angel of Death beat Buddy Roberts
Eddie Gilbert beat Savannah Jack
Steve Williams beat The Viking
Steve Williams beat Bob Bradley
King Parsons beat Glassman
Eddie Gilbert beat Sam Houston
Michael Hayes drew Angel of Death
Terry Gordy drew One Man Gang

4/19/87: Muskogee, OK @ Civic Center
Big Bubba beat One Man Gang(12:03) via pinfall to win UWF Title
Chris Adams & Terry Taylor beat Bob Bradley & The Red Devil(3:25) via pinfall
Steve Cox beat Super Ninja(1:13) via pinfall
Chavo Guerrero beat Mike Boyette(2:18) via pinfall
Rick Steiner & Sting beat Jeff Raitz & Mike Reed(1:27) via pinfall
King Parsons beat Jeff Raitz(2:25) via pinfall
Chris Adams beat Terry Taylor(13:04) by CO
Big Bubba beat Steve Cox
Angel of Death beat Mike Reed(1:29) via pinfall
Steve Williams beat Bill Irwin(5:14) via pinfall

4/19/87: Huntington, WV @ Memorial Fieldhouse
Brad Armstrong beat Stan Lane by DQ
Ronnie Garvin beat Bobby Eaton in a bunkhouse match

4/19/87: Orlando, FL @ Eddie Graham Sports Complex
Brady Boone beat Mitch Snow
Scott Hall & Denny Brown beat Colt Steele & Teijo Khan
Ron Simmons beat Shaska Whatley
The Southern Boys & Kendall Windham beat The Mod Squad & Bill Dundee
Jimmy Valiant beat Vladimir Petrov
Baron Von Raschke beat Ivan Koloff
Dusty Rhodes & Barry Windham beat Kevin Sullivan & Tahitian Prince
NWA World Champ Ric Flair beat Mike Rotundo

4/20/87: Fayetteville, NC @ Cumberland County Civic Center
Lazertron beat Gary Royal
Ivan Koloff beat Tim Horner
Vladimir Petrov beat Baron Von Raschke
Ole Anderson beat James J. Dillon
Barry Windham beat Lex Luger by DQ
Nikita Koloff beat Rick Rude
Dusty Rhodes beat NWA World Champ Ric Flair by DQ

4/20/87: Greenville, SC @ Memorial Auditorium
Ronnie & Jimmy Garvin beat the Midnight Express Lights Out Bunkhouse Match
Rock & Roll Express draw the New Breed
Big Bubba beat Bob Armstrong
Jimmy Valiant beat Thunderfoot #2
Todd Champion beat Thunderfoot #1
Nelson Royal beat Johnny Ace
Italian Stallion beat John Savage

4/20/87: St. Louis, MO @ Kiel Auditorium
Terry Gordy beat One Man Gang
Buddy Roberts & Michael Hayes beat Bill Irwin & Angel of Death
Terry Taylor won a 6-man first blood elimination match
Steve Williams beat The Viking
Eddie Gilbert beat Sam Houston
Nickla Roberts beat Sunshine
Super Ninja beat Ken Massey
Chavo Guerrero & Steve Cox beat Mike George & Gary Young
Bob Bradley beat Mike Boyette

4/21/87: Columbia, SC @ Township Auditorium (TV)
Brad Armstrong & Barry Windham draw Ric Flair & Lex Luger
Ivan Koloff & Vladimir Petrov beat George South & Tommy Angel
Tully Blanchard beat Bob Armstrong
Rock & Roll Express beat Rikki Nelson & Gary Royal
The Midnight Express beat Mike Force & Rocky King
New Breed beat Brodie Chase & Tommy Angel
Rock & Roll Express beat Verne Deaton & Johnny Ace
Brad Armstrong beat George South
Lex Luger beat Rikki Nelson
Jimmy Valiant & Lazertron beat Thunderfoot II & Dexter Westcott
The Midnight Express beat Gary Royal & Todd Champion
Jimmy Garvin vs. Mike Force

4/21/87: Melbourne, FL @ City Auditorium
The Mod Squad vs. The Southern Boys
Mike Rotundo vs. Tahitian Prince
Ron Simmons vs. Shaska Whatley
Scott Hall vs. Ed Gantner
Brady Boone vs. Colt Steele
Kendall Windham vs. Teijo Khan

4/22/87: Inglewood, CA @ The Forum
Baron Von Raschke beat The Barbarian
Bob Armstrong draw Ivan Koloff
Jimmy Garvin beat Bobby Eaton by DQ
Ronnie Garvin beat Stan Lane in a taped fist match
The Road Warriors & Nikita Koloff beat Rick Rude, Manny Fernandez & Paul Jones
NWA World Champ Ric Flair beat Brad Armstrong
Ole Anderson beat Tully Blanchard by DQ

4/22/87: Miami, FL @ Convention Center
Brady Boone, Denny Brown & Mitch Snow vs. Colt Steele, Bill & Randy Mulkey
Ed Gantner vs. Eddie Roberts
Ron Simmons vs. Shaska Whatley
Teijo Khan vs. Kendall Windham
Kevin Sullivan vs. Barry Windham
Mod Squad vs. The Southern Boys in a no DQ match

4/23/87: San Francisco, CA @ Civic Auditorium
Baron Von Raschke beat The Barbarian
Bob Armstrong draw Ivan Koloff
Jimmy & Ronnie Garvin beat The Midnight Express by DQ
Ole Anderson beat Tully Blanchard by DQ
Road Warriors & Brad Armstrong beat Rick Rude, Manny Fernandez & Paul Jones
NWA World Champ Ric Flair NC with Nikita Koloff

4/23/87: Raleigh, NC @ Dorton Arena
Lazertron beat Nelson Royal
Ricky Morton beat Lex Luger by DQ
John Savage beat Gary Royal
Tim Horner beat Thunderfoot II
Todd Champion beat Thunderfoot I
New Breed beat Italian Stallion & Bobby Jaggers

4/23/87: Springfield, MO
Steve Williams beat One Man Gang
Chris Adams, Terry Taylor & Sam Houston beat Eddie Gilbert, Sting & Rick teiner
Michael Hayes beat Angel of Death
King Parsons beat Savannah Jack
Steve Cox beat Bill Irwin
Chavo Guerrero beat Gary Young
Sam Houston & Nickla Roberts beat Buddy Roberts & Sunshine
Bob Bradley beat Super Ninja
Mike George beat Mike Boyette

4/23/87: Memphis, TN @ Mid-South Coliseum
The Shadow beat Ken Massey
Steve Cox beat Mike George
Iceman Parsons beat Savannah Jack in a loser gets 10 lashes match
Eddie Gilbert beat Sam Houston via pinfall
Terry Taylor & Chris Adams beat Sting & Rick Steiner by DQ
One Man Gang beat Steve Cox by CO
Michael Hayes & Buddy Roberts beat Angel of Death & Bill Irwin via pinfall

4/24/87: Chicago, IL @ UIC Pavilion
Tully Blanchard beat Tim Horner
Brad Armstrong beat Barbarian
Ivan Koloff beat Baron Von Raschke
Ole Anderson beat James J. Dillon bunkhouse match
Rick Rude & Manny Fernandez beat Rock & Roll Express
Road Warriors & Nikita Koloff beat Arn Anderson, Lex Luger & Tully Blanchard
NWA World Champ Ric Flair beat Dusty Rhodes by DQ

4/24/87: Columbus, GA @ Municipal Auditorium
Jimmy Garvin beat Stan Lane

4/24/87: Arcadia, FL @ National Guard Armory

4/25/87: Atlanta, GA @ WTBS Studios (TV)
Ronnie Garvin & Barry Windham beat Ivan Koloff & Vladimir Petrov by DQ

4/25/87: Greensboro, NC @ Coliseum
NWA World Champ Ric Flair beat Jimmy Garvin by DQ
Dusty Rhodes beat Ivan Koloff
Lex Luger beat Nikita Koloff by DQ
Brad Armstrong beat The Barbarian
Ronnie Garvin, Bob Armstrong & Barry Windham beat Midnight Express & Big Bubba
The Rock & Roll Express beat New Breed
Lazertron beat Gary Royal
Nelson Royal beat Johnny Ace

4/25/87: Philadelphia, PA @ Civic Center
The Road Warriors beat Manny Fernandez & Rick Rude by DQ
Ole Anderson beat Arn Anderson
Tully Blanchard beat Tim Horner
Italian Stallion & Bobby Jaggers beat Thunderfoot I & Thunderfoot II
Todd Champion beat John Savage
Ricky Lee Jones beat Mark Fleming

4/25/87: Sarasota, FL @ Robarts Arena
Mike Rotundo vs. Tahitian Prince

4/26/87: Rock Hill SC @ Winthrop Coliseum (TV)
The Road Warriors & Nikita Koloff beat Ric Flair, Arn Anderson & Lex Luger
Ole Anderson beat Tully Blanchard by DQ
The Road Warriors beat Tommy Angel & Brodie Chase via pinfall
Lazertron beat Rocky King via pinfall
Jimmy Garvin beat George South via pinfall
Ronnie Garvin beat Thunderfoot II via pinfall
The Rock & Roll Express beat David Isley & Bill Mulkey
The Midnight Express beat Todd Champion & Rikki Nelson via pinfall
Tully Blanchard & Lex Luger beat Rikki Nelson & Todd Champion via pinfall
Ric Flair, Tully Blanchard & Lex Luger beat Bob & Brad Armstrong & Tim Horner
Nikita Koloff beat Gary Royal via pinfall
Lex Luger beat Brodie Chase via pinfall
Manny Fernandez & Rick Rude beat Rikki Nelson & Tommy Angel via pinfall
Lex Luger beat Tommy Angel
Manny Fernandez & Rick Rude beat Nelson Royal & David Isley
Ivan Koloff & Vladimir Petrov beat Johnny Ace & Italian Stallion via pinfall
Ronnie Garvin beat George South via pinfall
Jimmy Garvin beat Rocky King via pinfall
The Midnight Express beat Gary Royal & Dexter Westcott via pinfall
Tully Blanchard beat Nelson Royal

4/26/87: Daytona, FL @ Ocean Center
The Road Warriors, Dusty Rhodes & Nikita Koloff beat Ric Flair, Arn Anderson, Tully Blanchard & Lex Luger
Mike Graham & Steve Keirn beat The Mod Squad to win NWA Florida Tag Title

4/26/87: Lubbock, TX
Terry Taylor & Chris Adams beat Sting & Rick Steiner by DQ
Chavo Guerrero beat Gary Young in a Texas death match
Buddy Roberts beat Bill Irwin
Eddie Gilbert beat Sam Houston
King Parsons beat Savannah Jack
Nickla Roberts beat Sunshine by CO
Steve Cox beat Mike Boyette
Bob Bradley draw The Terminator

4/26/87: Albuquerque, NM @ Tingley Coliseum
Chavo Guerrero beat Gary Young Texas death match
Michael Hayes & Terry Gordy beat Bill Irwin & Angel Of Death
Steve Williams beat One Man Gang
Sting & Rick Steiner beat Chris Adams & Terry Taylor by DQ
Eddie Gilbert beat Sam Houston
Nickla Roberts beat Sunshine
King Parsons beat Savannah Jack
Sam Houston & Steve Cox beat The Terminator & Mike Boyette
Bob Bradley beat Super Ninja

4/27/87: Phoenix, AZ
The Rock & Roll Express beat The Midnight Express

4/27/87: Lake City, FL @ Community Center

4/28/87: Tampa, FL @ Spartan Sports Center
Mike Rotundo & Dusty Rhodes beat Kevin Sullivan & Teijo Khan

4/28/87: El Paso, TX
The Rock & Roll Express beat The Midnight Express
Barry Windham beat NWA World Champ Ric Flair DQ

4/29/87: Marion, NC
Ronnie Garvin beat Stan Lane
Jimmy Garvin beat Bobby Eaton by DQ

4/29/87: Sunrise, FL @ Music Theater

4/29/87: Fort Lauderdale, FL @ War Memorial Auditorium
Ed Gantner, Scott Hall & Kendall Windham vs. Teijo Khan, Tahitian Prince & Sir Oliver Humperdink
Ron Simmons vs. Shaska Whatley in a no DQ match
The Mod Squad vs. The Southern Boys in a no DQ match
Kevin Sullivan vs. Barry Windham Texas death match
NWA World Champ Ric Flair vs. Mike Rotundo

4/30/87: Pembroke, NC @ Jones PE Center
Ronnie & Jimmy Garvin vs. The Midnight Express
Jimmy Valiant vs. Big Bubba
Baron Von Raschke vs. Thunderfoot I
New Breed vs. The Kansas Jayhawks
Gary Royal vs. Denny Brown
Johnny Ace vs. John Savage

4/30/87: Ocala, FL @ Central Florida Community College
Scott Hall beat Kevin Sullivan
Barry & Kendall Windham(sub for Ed Gantner) beat Teijo Khan & Tahitian Prince
Mike Rotundo beat Shaska Whatley
Kendall Windham & Ron Simmons beat The Mod Squad
Brady Boone beat Colt Steele
The Southern Boys beat Randy & Bill Mulkey

4/30/87: Birmingham, AL @ Boutwell Auditorium
Dusty Rhodes beat NWA World Champ Ric Flair by DQ
Nikita Koloff beat Tully Blanchard
Brad Armstrong beat The Barbarian
Ole Anderson & Tim Horner beat Arn Anderson & Lex Luger
The Rock & Roll Express & Bob Armstrong beat Paul Jones, Manny Fernandez & Rick Rude

5/1/87: Atlanta, GA @ Omni
New Breed beat Jeff Sampson & Jeff Belk
Baron Von Raschke beat Thunderfoot I
Vladimir Petrov beat Jimmy Valiant
The Midnight Express beat Bob Armstrong & Brad Armstrong
Barry Windham beat Lex Luger by DQ
Arn Anderson & Tully Blanchard beat Ole Anderson & Tim Horner
Nikita Koloff beat Ivan Koloff in a chain match
NWA World Champ Ric Flair beat Jimmy Garvin

5/1/87: Nassau, Bahamas @ Stadium

5/2/87: Atlanta, GA @ WTBS Studios (TV)
Lazertron & Jimmy Valiant beat Randy Barber & Alan Martin
Lex Luger beat Jeff Belk
New Breed beat Bob Armstrong & Brad Armstrong in NWA United States Tag Title tournament
Ivan Koloff & Vladimir Petrov beat Cougar Jay & Jerry Sampson
The Midnight Express beat Larry Clarke & Bill Tabb
The Road Warriors beat David Isley & Mike Force
Ronnie Garvin beat Larry Stephens
Jimmy Garvin beat Paul Garner

5/2/87: Chattanooga, TN @ Memorial Auditorium
Bob Armstrong & Brad Armstrong beat The Midnight Express by DQ

5/2/87: Freeport, Bahamas

5/2/87: Lakeland, FL @ Civic Center

5/2/87: Fort Worth, TX @ Cowtown Coliseum (TV)
Barry Windham beat Super Ninja(2:35) via pinfall
Rick Steiner & Sting beat Glassman & Hank Wilburn(2:27) via pinfall
Vladimir Petrov beat Ken Massey(1:13) via pinfall
Chris Adams beat Craig Whitford(3:05) via pinfall
King Parsons beat Jeff Raitz(3:21) via pinfall
Steve Williams beat Mike Boyette(1:35) via pinfall
Big Bubba beat David Price & Johnny Stewart(2:560 via pinfall in a handicap match
Vladimir Petrov beat Jeff Raitz(:52) via pinfall
Barry Windham beat Gary Young(4:01) via pinfall
Chris Adams beat Thunderbird(2:36) via pinfall
Steve Cox beat Super Ninja(2:23) via pinfall
Big Bubba beat Johnny Stewart & ??(1:36) via pinfall in a handicap match
Rick Steiner & Sting beat Glassman & Bobby Howell(1:18) via pinfall
Steve Williams beat Ron Ellis(1:47) via pinfall

5/3/87: Cincinnati, OH @ Gardens
Baron Von Raschke beat Jim Lancaster
Ivan Koloff beat Tim Horner
Lazertron beat Denny Brown
The Midnight Express beat Bob Armstrong & Brad Armstrong
Ole Anderson NC with Arn Anderson
The Road Warriors NC with Lex Luger & Tully Blanchard
NWA World Champ Ric Flair beat Jimmy Garvin by DQ

5/3/87: Charleston, WV @ Civic Center
New Breed beat Rocky King & Italian Stallion
Jimmy Valiant beat Thunderfoot I
Lazertron beat Nelson Royal
The Midnight Express beat Bob Armstrong & Brad Armstrong
Ole Anderson beat Arn Anderson by DQ
Lex Luger & Tully Blanchard NC with Road Warriors
NWA World Champ Ric Flair beat Jimmy Garvin by DQ

5/3/87: Orlando, FL @ Eddie Graham Sports Complex

5/3/87: Tulsa, OK @ Convention Center
Barry Windham beat Bob Bradley
Vladimir Petrov beat Bobby Howell
Terry Taylor beat Chris Adams by CO
Rick Steiner & Sting beat Glassman & Bobby Howell
Barry Windham beat Mike Boyette
Steve Cox draw Iceman Parsons
Big Bubba beat Ron Ellis
Terry Taylor beat Jeff Raitz
Vladimir Petrov beat Ken Massey
Big Bubba beat Barry Windham by CO
Ted DiBiase & Steve Williams beat Rick Steiner & Sting by DQ

5/4/87: Fayetteville, NC @ Cumberland County Civic Center
Dusty Rhodes beat Dick Murdoch
Todd Champion beat Italian Stallion
Rocky King beat Tommy Angel
Bob Armstrong & Brad Armstrong beat Ivan Koloff & Vladimir Petrov
The Road Warriors beat New Breed
Lex Luger NC with Barry Windham

5/4/87: Greenville, SC @ Memorial Auditorium
Thunderfoot I beat George South
Gary Royal beat Johnny Ace
The Barbarian beat Denny Brown
Lazertron beat Nelson Royal by DQ
Jimmy Valiant beat John Savage
Arn Anderson & Tully Blanchard beat Ole Anderson & Tim Horner
Rock & Roll Express beat The Midnight Express by CO
NWA World Champ Ric Flair beat Jimmy Garvin

5/4/87: Fort Pierce, FL @ St. Lucie County Civic Center

5/5/87: Spartanburg SC @ Memorial Auditorium (TV)
The Road Warriors beat Dexter Westcott & Mike Force
Barry Windham beat Tommy Angel
Lex Luger beat David Isley
The Rock & Roll Express beat Mike Simani & Vernon Deaton
New Breed beat Rocky King & Brodie Chase
Jimmy Garvin beat Thunderfoot II
New Breed beat Mike Force & Rikki Nelson
Midnight Express beat Rocky King & Larry Stephens
Ronnie Garvin beat Tommy Angel
Barry Windham beat Thunderfoot II
The Rock & Roll Express beat The Gladiators
Tully Blanchard beat Chance McQuade
Lex Luger beat Mike Simani

5/5/87: Green Cove Springs, FL @ H.S.

5/6/87: Cheraw, SC
The Midnight Express beat Tim Horner & Baron Von Raschke

5/6/87: Miami, FL @ Convention Center
NWA World Champ Ric Flair beat Jimmy Garvin by DQ
Mike Rotundo & Dusty Rhodes beat Kevin Sullivan & Teijo Khan
The Rock & Roll Express beat The Mod Squad by DQ
Ron Simmons beat Shaska Whatley in an African death match
Ed Gantner beat Sam Bass
Jimmy Valiant beat Colt Steele
Jerry Grey beat Jim Backlund
The Southern Boys beat Randy Mulkey & Bill Mulkey

5/7/87: Spring Hill, FL @ Springstead H.S. Football Field
Mike Rotundo & Ed Gantner vs. Kevin Sullivan & Tahitian Prince
The Mod Squad vs. The Southern Boys(Tracy Smothers & Steve Armstrong) in bunkhouse match
Pez Whatley vs. Ron Simmons

5/7/87: Waldorf, MD @ Thomas Stone H.S.
New Breed beat Ron Shaw & ??
Arn Anderson beat Larry Winters
Dick Murdoch beat Baron Von Raschke
Bob Armstrong beat Ivan Koloff
Jimmy & Ronnie Garvin beat Manny Fernandez & Rick Rude by DQ
NWA World Champ Ric Flair beat Brad Armstrong
Lex Luger beat Tim Horner

5/7/87: Raleigh, NC @ Dorton Arena
Tully Blanchard beat Ole Anderson in a cage match
Thunderfoot I & Thunderfoot II beat Ricky Lee Jones & Mark Fleming
Italian Stallion beat John Savage
Denny Brown beat Johnny Ace
Lazertron beat Nelson Royal by DQ
Jimmy Valiant beat Gladiator #2
The Rock & Roll Express beat The Midnight Express

5/8/87: Baltimore, MD @ Civic Center
Jimmy Garvin beat NWA World Champ Ric Flair by DQ
Bob Armstrong & Brad Armstrong draw New Breed
Arn Anderson beat Tim Horner
Vladimir Petrov beat Baron Von Raschke
Lex Luger beat Ronnie Garvin by DQ
Road Warriors beat Rick Rude & Manny Fernandez DQ
Dick Murdoch beat Dusty Rhodes in a Texas Death Match
Nikita Koloff beat Ivan Koloff in a chain match

5/8/87: Norfolk, VA @ Scope
The Rock & Roll Express beat The Midnight Express

5/8/87: Sebring, FL @ Fairgrounds Pavilion

5/9/87: Atlanta, GA @ WTBS Studios (TV)
The Midnight Express beat The Rock & Roll Express by DQ in NWA United States Tag Title tournament

5/9/87: St. Petersburg, FL @ Bayfront Center
NWA World Champ Ric Flair beat Dusty Rhodes by DQ
Barry Windham & Ed Gantner beat Dory Funk, Jr. & Tahitian Prince
Manny Fernandez & Rick Rude beat Road Warriors by DQ
Jimmy Garvin beat Teijo Khan
Mike Rotundo beat Kevin Sullivan
Mike Graham beat Dory Funk, Jr.
Bob Armstrong & Brad Armstrong beat The Mod Squad
Jimmy Valiant beat Colt Steele

5/9/87: Charlotte, NC @ Coliseum
Ronnie Garvin beat Jim Cornette in a cage match
The Rock & Roll Express beat Vladimir Petrov & Dick Murdoch
Nikita Koloff beat Lex Luger by DQ
Tully Blanchard beat Ole Anderson
Lazertron beat Nelson Royal
Baron Von Raschke beat Thunderfoot
New Breed beat Rocky King & Italian Stallion
Ivan Koloff beat Todd Champion

5/10/87: Orlando, FL @ Eddie Graham Sports Complex
Bill & Randy Mulkey vs. Mitch Snow & Kendall Windham
Colt Steele vs. Jimmy Garvin
Bob Armstrong & Brad Armstrong vs. The Mod Squad
Jimmy Valiant vs. Shaska Whatley
Dory Funk, Jr., Kevin Sullivan & Tahitian Prince vs. Ed Gantner, Dusty Rhodes & Barry Windham
Manny Fernandez & Rick Rude vs. The Rock & Roll Express in a Texas tornado match
NWA World Champ Ric Flair vs. Mike Rotundo

5/11/87: Punta Gorda, FL @ Charlotte County Memorial Auditorium

5/11/87: Newton, NC
Ronnie & Jimmy Garvin beat The Midnight Express

5/11/87: Greenville, SC @ Memorial Auditorium
Nikita Koloff beat Ivan Koloff Russian Chain Match
Ric Flair & Arn Anderson beat Ole Anderson & Tim Horner
Lex Luger beat Brad Armstrong
NWA World Jr Title Match: Lazor-Tron(c) beat Nelson Royal
New Breed Chris Champ beat Italian Stallion
New Breed Sean Royal draw Bob Armstrong
Denny Brown beat Jeff Sampson

5/12/87: Columbia, SC @ Township Auditorium (TV)
Arn Anderson beat Jeff Sampson
Tully Blanchard beat Robert Gibson(17:00) by DQ
The Midnight Express beat David Isley & Tommy Angel
Ric Flair & Lex Luger beat Italian Stallion & Todd Champion
Jimmy Garvin beat Johnny Ace
Jimmy Valiant beat Jeff Sampson
Ronnie Garvin & Barry Windham beat Vernon Deaton & Brodie Chase
Manny Fernandez & Rick Rude beat Italian Stallion & Tim Horner
Sean Royal beat George South
Arn Anderson, Tully Blanchard & Lex Luger beat Todd Champion, Tommy Angel & David Isley

5/13/87: Westminster, SC
The Rock & Roll Express beat The Midnight Express

5/13/87: Sunrise, FL @ Music Theater
NWA World Champ Ric Flair beat Jimmy Garvin
Kendall Windham & Ed Gantner beat Kevin Sullivan & Tahitian Prince
Mike Rotundo beat Dory Funk, Jr. by DQ
Ron Simmons beat Shaska Whatley

5/14/87: Hartwell, GA
Jimmy Garvin beat Stan Lane by DQ
Ronnie Garvin beat Bobby Eaton

5/14/87: Melbourne, FL @ Civic Auditorium

5/15/87: Albany, GA @ Civic Center
The Midnight Express beat Bob Armstrong & Brad Armstrong

5/15/87: Mount Dora, FL @ H.S.

5/16/87: Atlanta, GA @ WTBS Studios (TV)
The Midnight Express beat Barry Windham & Ronnie Garvin to win vacant NWA United States Tag Title in tournament final

5/16/87: Chesterfield, SC
The Midnight Express beat Ronnie Garvin & Bob Armstrong

5/16/87: Greensboro, NC @ Coliseum
NWA World Champ Ric Flair beat Jimmy Garvin
Dusty Rhodes beat Dick Murdoch
Nikita Koloff beat Ivan Koloff in a Russian chain match
Ricky Morton draw Tully Blanchard
The Road Warriors beat Lex Luger & Arn Anderson
Jimmy Valiant & Lazertron beat New Breed
Robert Gibson beat Thunderfoot II
Nelson Royal beat Rikki Nelson

5/16/87: Shreveport, LA (TV)
Barry Windham beat Mike Reed(1:44) via pinfall
Steve Cox beat Terry Taylor(2:360 by DQ
Davey Haskins beat Gary Young(2:36) by DQ
Brad Armstrong & Tim Horner beat Bob Bradley & The Red Devil (5:30)
Big Bubba beat Steve Welles (1:06)
Rick Steiner, Sting & Eddie Gilbert beat Bobby Howell, Craig Whitford & Hank Wilburn (3:52)
Angel of Death beat Ron Ellis via pinfall
Brad Armstrong & Tim Horner beat Mike Boyette & The Red Devil (5:32)
Chris Adams beat Hank Wilburn(3:23) via pinfall
Black Bart beat Bobby Howell(2:36) via pinfall
Chris Adams vs. Terry Taylor

5/16/87: Sarasota, FL @ Robarts Arena

5/17/87: Asheville, NC @ Civic Center
Stan Lane beat Todd Champion
Ronnie Garvin beat Bobby Eaton

5/17/87: Daytona, FL @ Ocean Center
The Rock & Roll Express beat The Midnight Express
Steve Keirn & Mike Graham beat The Mod Squad

5/17/87: Tulsa, OK @ Convention Center (TV)
Steve Williams beat Eddie Gilbert via pinfall
Barry Windham beat The Red Devil(2:44) via pinfall
Davey Haskins beat Terry Taylor(4:41) by DQ
Barry Windham beat Ron Ellis(4:04) via pinfall
Brad Armstrong & Tim Horner beat Sting & Rick Steiner to win UWF Tag Title

5/18/87: Greenville, SC @ Memorial Auditorium
Rock & Roll Express beat Ric Flair & Lex Luger
Tully Blanchard beat Bob Armstrong
Jimmy Valiant & Lazor-Tron beat The New Breed
Rick Rude beat Johnny Ace
Baron Von Raschke beat Thunderfoot #2
Thunderfoot #1 beat John Savage
Italian Stallion beat Gary Royal

5/18/87: Fayetteville, NC @ Cumberland County Civic Center
Denny Brown beat Larry Stephens
Rocky King beat Mark Fleming
Vladimir Petrov beat Todd Champion
Ronnie & Jimmy Garvin beat The Midnight Express
Nikita Koloff beat Ivan Koloff

5/19/87: Raleigh, NC @ Dorton Arena (TV)
The Rock & Roll Express beat Gene Ligon & John Savage
Jimmy Garvin beat Gladiator #1
Ronnie Garvin beat Gladiator #2
Ivan Koloff & Vladimir Petrov beat Rikki Nelson & Italian Stallion
Dusty Rhodes & Nikita Koloff beat Ric Flair & Lex Luger(5:26) by DQ
New Breed beat Rocky King & John Savage
Barry Windham beat Gladiator #1
Midnight Express beat Gene Ligon & Dexter Westcott
Bob Armstrong beat Mark Fleming
Vladimir Petrov beat Italian Stallion
Arn Anderson vs. Tommy Angel
Rock & Roll Express vs. Rikki Nelson & Gary Young

5/19/87: Tampa, FL @ Spartan Sports Center (TV)
Johnny Ace beat Colt Steele
Teijo Khan beat Jerry Gray
Kendall Windham beat Shaska Whatley
The Southern Boys beat The Mod Squad by DQ
The Sheepherders beat Randy & Bill Mulkey
Rick Steiner & Sting beat Mike Rotundo & Ron Simmons
Big Bubba DCO with Ed Gantner
Road Warriors beat Kevin Sullivan & Tahitian Prince

5/20/87: Hillsville, VA
Jimmy Valiant & Italian Stallion beat New Breed by DQ
Vladimir Petrov beat Todd Champion
Italian Stallion beat Larry Stephens
Nelson Royal beat Rocky King
Gary Royal beat Mark Fleming
Denny Brown beat John Savage
Mark Fleming beat David Diamond

5/20/87: Miami, FL @ Stadium
Big Bubba beat Ed Gantner(5:29)
Mike Rotundo beat Dory Funk, Jr.(11:49)
Steiner & Sting beat Ron Simmons & Johnny Ace(sub for Mike Graham)(12:03)
Kendall Windham beat Shaska Whatley(10:24)
The Sheepherders beat Randy & Bill Mulkey(7:31)
Mitch Snow vs. Teijo Khan(cancelled)
Johnny Ace beat Colt Steele(10:45)
Teijo Khan beat Jerry Gray(6:12)
The Southern Boys beat The Mod Squad(15:14)

5/20/87: Savannah, GA @ Civic Center
Ronnie Garvin & Barry Windham beat Midnight Express

5/21/87: Salisbury, MD @ Wicomico Youth & Civic Center
Baron Von Raschke beat Mark Fleming
Vladimir Petrov beat Brad Armstrong
Ivan Koloff beat Tim Horner
Jimmy & Ronnie Garvin beat The Midnight Express
Nikita Koloff beat Tully Blanchard
Rick Rude & Manny Fernandez beat The Rock & Roll Express

5/21/87: Tallahassee, FL @ Leon County Civic Center
Dusty Rhodes beat NWA World Champ Ric Flair by DQ
Kendall Windham DDQ Lex Luger
Terry Gordy & Michael Hayes beat Sting & Rick Steiner
Big Bubba DCO with Ed Gantner

5/22/87: Richmond, VA @ Coliseum
The Rock & Roll Express NC with The Midnight Express & Jim Cornette in a handicap match
Nikita Koloff beat Ivan Koloff in a chain match
Rick Rude & Manny Fernandez beat Brad Armstrong & Bob Armstrong
Jimmy Valiant beat Sean Royal by DQ
Lazertron draw Chris Champ
Vladimir Petrov beat Baron Von Raschke
Tim Horner beat Mark Fleming
Todd Champion & Denny Brown beat Thunderfoot I & Thunderfoot II

5/22/87: Jacksonville, FL @ Coliseum
Ric Flair beat Mike Rotundo
Dusty Rhodes beat Big Bubba by DQ
Terry Gordy & Buddy Roberts beat Sting & Rick Steiner

5/23/87: Atlanta, GA @ WTBS Studios (TV)
Michael Hayes & Terry Gordy beat ?? & ??

5/23/87: Columbus, GA @ Municipal Auditorium
Ronnie & Jimmy Garvin beat The Midnight Express-bunkhouse match

5/23/87: Fort Myers, FL @ Lee County Civic Center

5/24/87: Roanoke, VA @ Civic Center
The Road Warriors beat Ric Flair & Lex Luger by DQ
Nikita Koloff beat Ivan Koloff in a chain match
Tully Blanchard beat Bob Armstrong
New Breed beat Lazertron & Jimmy Valiant
Tim Horner vs. Gary Royal
Jeff Sampson vs. Ricky Lee Jones
Baron Von Raschke vs. Nelson Royal
Jeff Belk vs. Italian Stallion

5/24/87: Orlando, FL @ Eddie Graham Sports Complex

5/24/87: Chicago, IL @ UIC Pavilion
Tim Horner draw Eddie Gilbert
Terry Gordy & Buddy Roberts beat Sting & Rick Steiner
Terry Taylor NC with Chris Adams
The Rock & Roll Express beat The Midnight Express
Michael Hayes beat Big Bubba by DQ
Manny Fernandez & Vladimir Petrov beat Barry Windham & Brad Armstrong
Nikita Koloff beat Ivan Koloff in a chain match
The Road Warriors & Dusty Rhodes beat Lex Luger, Ric Flair & Tully Blanchard

5/25/87: Fort Pierce, FL @ St. Lucie County Civic Center

5/25/87: Greenville, SC @ Memorial Auditorium
May 25, 1987: Greenville, SC @ Memorial Auditorium
Nikita Koloff beat Vladimir Petrov
Midnight Express & Jim Cornette beat Barry Windham & Brad Armstrong
Ronnie Garvin beat Ivan Koloff
Manny Fernandez beat Baron Von Raschke
Jimmy Valiant & Lazor-Tron beat Thunderfoot #1 & 2
Nelson Royal beat John Savage
Italian Stallion beat Brody Chase

5/26/87: Greenwood, SC (TV)
Nikita Koloff beat Gladiator #1
The Midnight Express beat Bill & Randy Mulkey
Barry Windham beat Brodie Chase
Tully Blanchard beat George South
Manny Fernandez & Ivan Koloff beat Larry Stephens & Rikki Nelson
Lex Luger beat Dexter Westcott
Lex Luger beat David Isley
The Midnight Express beat George South & Vernon Deaton
Vladimir Petrov beat Rikki Nelson
New Breed beat Italian Stallion & Billy Mulkey
Tully Blanchard beat Randy Mulkey
The Rock & Roll Express beat Thunderfoot I & Thunderfoot II

5/27/87: Tampa, FL @ Sportatorium (TV)
Mike Rotundo beat Dory Funk, Jr. by DQ

5/27/87: Fort Lauderdale, FL @ War Memorial Auditorium
Bob Armstrong & Brad Armstrong beat The Mod Squad
The Southern Boys beat Krusher Knopf & Sam Bass
Jim Garvin beat Teijo Khan
Mike Graham beat Dory Funk, Jr. by DQ
Barry Windham & Ed Gantner beat Tahitian Prince & Teijo Khan
Barry Windham & Ed Gantner beat Dory Funk, Jr. & Tahitian Prince
Road Warriors beat Rick Rude & Manny Fernandez DQ

5/27/87: Oklahoma City, OK @ Myriad
Chris Adams vs. Terry Taylor
Nikita Koloff vs. Lex Luger

Barry Windham vs. Big Bubba
The Road Warriors vs. Rick Rude & Manny Fernandez
NWA World Champ Ric Flair vs. Jimmy Garvin

5/28/87: Siler City, NC
Midnight Express beat Italian Stallion & Todd Champion

5/28/87: Tulsa, OK @ Fairgrounds Pavilion (TV)
Terry Taylor beat Ron Ellis(1:05) by submission
Brad Armstrong & Tim Horner beat Gary Young & Mike Boyette(4:30) via pinfall
The Enforcers beat Bobby Howell & Craig Whitford(2:52) via pinfall
Black Bart beat Jeff Raitz(2:42) via pinfall
Terry Gordy beat Dick Murdoch(13:42) by DQ
Chris Adams beat The Red Devil via pinfall
Rick Steiner beat Bobby Howell(2:53) via pinfall
Chavo Guerrero beat Mike Boyette(4:23) via pinfall
Steve Cox beat Big Bubba(2:01) by DQ
Dick Murdoch & Eddie Gilbert beat Craig Whitford & Hank Wilburn via pinfall
Brad Armstrong, Tim Horner & Davey Haskins beat The Enforcers & Angel of Death(3:49) by DQ
Terry Gordy beat Bob Bradley(:58) via pinfall

5/29/87: Gainesville, FL @ Stephen C. O'Connell Center
NWA World Champ Ric Flair vs. Dusty Rhodes
Nikita Koloff vs. ??(sub for Rick Rude)
The Road Warriors & Ed Gantner vs. Tahitian Prince, Dory Funk, Jr. & Kevin Sullivan
Manny Fernandez vs. Mike Rotundo
Kendall Windham vs. Teijo Khan
Steve Keirn vs. Jerry Grey
Ron Simmons vs. Shaska Whatley
The Southern Boys & ?? vs. Randy Mulkey, Bill Mulkey & Colt Steele

5/29/87: Beckley, WV @ Civic Center
The Rock & Roll Express beat The Midnight Express

5/30/87: Atlanta, GA @ WTBS Studios (TV)
The Rock & Roll Express ware awarded NWA World Tag Title after Rick Rude left promotion

5/30/87: Florence, SC
Note: The show was to have seen The Rock & Roll Express defeat NWA Tag eam Champs Rick Rude & Manny Fernandez to regain the titles but Rude had already left the promotion

5/30/87: Philadelphia, PA @ Civic Center
Denny Brown beat Thunderfoot II(Joel Deaton)
Baron Von Raschke beat Mark Fleming
Todd Champion beat Thunderfoot I(Gene Ligon)
The Midnight Express draw Ronnie Garvin & Barry Windham
Lex Luger, Arn Anderson & Tully Blanchard beat The Road Warriors & Dusty Rhodes by DQ
Nikita Koloff beat Ivan Koloff in a chain match
NWA World Champ Ric Flair beat Jimmy Garvin by DQ

5/30/87: Sarasota, FL @ Robarts Arena

5/31/87: Orlando, FL @ Eddie Graham Sports Complex
Mike Rotundo vs. Dory Funk, Jr. NWA FL Title held up

5/31/87: Asheville, NC @ Civic Center
Nikita Koloff beat NWA World Champ Ric Flair by DQ
The Rock & Roll Express beat New Breed
Barry Windham DCO with Tully Blanchard
Lex Luger beat Todd Champion
Jimmy Garvin beat Ivan Koloff by DQ
Ronnie Garvin draw Vladimir Petrov
Baron Von Raschke beat George South
Jimmy Valiant & Lazertron beat The Thunderfoot I & Thunderfoot II

5/31/87: Little Rock, AR @ Barton Coliseum
Brad Armstrong & Tim Horner beat Bob Bradley & Ron Ellis
Terry Taylor beat Sting via pinfall
Black Bart beat Bobby Howell via pinfall
Dick Murdoch beat Steve Cox via pinfall
Terry Gordy & Michael Hayes beat Angel of Death & Mike Boyette
Dick Murdoch beat Jeff Raitz via pinfall
The Enforcers & Shaska Whatley beat Bobby Howell, Ken Massey & Hank Wilburn
Chris Adams beat Mike Boyette via pinfall
Big Bubba beat Craig Whitford via pinfall
Sting beat Ron Ellis via pinfall
Rick Steiner DCO with Chavo Guerrero(3:48)
Brad Armstrong & Tim Horner beat Bob Bradley & Gary Young
Eddie Gilbert & Terry Taylor beat Steve Cox & Davey Haskins

6/1/87: West Palm Beach, FL @ Auditorium
The Sheepherders vs. The Southern Boys
Mike Graham & Steve Keirn vs. Dory Funk, Jr. & Tahitian Prince
Ed Gantner vs. Kevin Sullivan
NWA World Champ Ric Flair vs. Mike Rotundo

6/2/87: Spartanburg, SC @ Memorial Auditorium (TV)
Midnight Express vs. Ronnie Garvin & Barry Windham
Tully Blanchard vs. Ricky Morton
Lex Luger vs. Gene Ligon
New Breed vs. Mike Force & Cougar Jay
The Midnight Express vs. John Savage & Rikki Nelson
Ivan Koloff & Vladimir Petrov vs. Tommy Angel & Rocky King
Tully Blanchard vs. Todd Champion
Arn Anderson & Tully Blanchard vs. Rikki Nelson & Tommy Angel
Jimmy Valiant & Lazertron vs. ?? & ??
Ivan Koloff & Vladimir Petrov vs. Italian Stallion & Todd Champion
Nikita Koloff vs. Cougar Jay
Jimmy & Ronnie Garvin vs. Mike Force & John Savage
Kendall Windham vs. Thunderfoot I
The Midnight Express vs. George South & Gary Royal

6/3/87: Winter Haven, FL @ Citrus Showcase
Mike Rotundo vs. Dory Funk, Jr.
Steve Keirn vs. Tahitian Prince
The Southern Boys vs. The Sheepherders
Ed Gantner vs. Kevin Sullivan
Ron Simmons vs. Shaska Whatley
Randy Mulkey & Bill Mulkey vs. The Mod Squad
Teijo Khan vs. Johnny Ace

6/4/87: Raleigh, NC @ Dorton Arena
The Midnight Express beat Todd Champion & Italian Stallion
Nikita Koloff beat Lex Luger by DQ
Ricky Morton draw Tully Blanchard
Robert Gibson beat Arn Anderson
Kendall Windham beat Gary Royal
Ronnie Garvin & Barry Windham beat Ivan Koloff & Vladimir Petrov

6/4/87: Ocala, FL @ Central Florida Community College
Mike Rotundo vs. Dory Funk, Jr.

6/5/87: Richmond, VA @ Coliseum
New Breed beat Baron Von Raschke & Denny Brown
Vladimir Petrov beat Italian Stallion
Arn Anderson beat Todd Champion
The Midnight Express beat Lazertron & Jimmy Valiant
Tully Blanchard beat Kendall Windham
Ivan Koloff & Vladimir Petrov beat The Rock & Roll Express by DQ
Ric Flair & Lex Luger beat Dusty Rhodes & Nikita Koloff
Ronnie Garvin beat Jim Cornette in a cage match

6/5/87: Nassau, Bahamas @ Stadium

6/6/87: Atlanta, GA @ WTBS Studios (TV)

6/6/87: St. Petersburg, FL @ Bayfront Center (TV)
The Midnight Express beat The Southern Boys

6/6/87: Greensboro, NC @ Coliseum
Tully Blanchard beat Dusty Rhodes by CO
Ric Flair & Lex Luger beat The Rock & Roll Express
Nikita Koloff beat Dick Murdoch
Barry Windham beat Big Bubba by DQ
Terry Gordy & Michael Hayes beat Rick Steiner & Sting by DQ
Terry Taylor NC with Chris Adams
Ivan Koloff & Vladimir Petrov beat Ronnie Garvin & Baron Von Raschke
Eddie Gilbert beat Kendall Windham

6/7/87: Atlanta, GA @ Omni
New Breed beat Jimmy Valiant & Lazertron
Eddie Gilbert beat Kendall Windham
Rick Steiner & Sting beat Todd Champion & Baron Von Raschke
Terry Taylor DCO with Chris Adams
The Rock & Roll Express beat Ivan Koloff & Vladimir Petrov
Barry Windham beat Big Bubba by DQ
Ric Flair, Tully Blanchard & Lex Luger beat Terry Gordy, Michael Hayes & Buddy Roberts
Nikita Koloff beat Dick Murdoch in a cage match

6/7/87: Orlando, FL @ Eddie Graham Sports Complex
Mike Rotundo beat Dory Funk, Jr. to win held up NWA Florida Title
Steve Keirn & Jimmy Garvin beat Kevin Sullivan & Tahitian Prince
The Southern Boys & Johnny Ace beat The Mod Squad & Shaska Whatley
The Midnight Express beat Ron Simmons & Ed Gantner
Arn Anderson beat Jerry Grey
The Sheepherders beat Randy Mulkey & Bill Mulkey

6/8/87: Greenville, SC @ Memorial Auditorium
NWA World TV Title Match: Tully Blanchard beat Ricky Morton by CO
US Tag Title Match Barry windham & Ronnie Garvin beat Midnight Express(c) dq
US Title Match: Nikita Koloff(c) beat Manny Fernandez
Lex Luger & Arn Anderson beat Jimmy Garvin & Kendall Windham
Italian Stallion beat Thunderfoot #1
Vladimir Petrov beat Todd Champion
New Breed beat Jimmy Valiant & Lazor-Tron
Denny Brown beat Gary Royal

6/8/87: Fort Pierce, FL @ St. Lucie County Civic Center

6/9/87: Columbia, SC @ Township Auditorium (TV)
The Midnight Express beat Rikki Nelson & John Savage
Barry Windham beat Brodie Chase
The Rock & Roll Express beat Gene Ligon & Larry Stephens
The Midnight Express beat Vernon Deaton & Chance McQuade
Arn Anderson, Tully Blanchard & Lex Luger beat David Isley, Rikki Nelson & John Savage
The Midnight Express vs. John Savage & Rikki Nelson

6/9/87: Starke, FL @ Bradford County H.S.
Mike Rotundo vs. Dory Funk, Jr.
The Southern Boys vs. The Sheepherders
Ed Gantner vs. Tahitian Prince
The Mod Squad vs. Bill & Randy Mulkey
Teijo Khan vs. Jerry Grey
The Cuban Connection vs. Jim Backlund & Colt Steele
Ron Simmons vs. ??

6/10/87: Sunrise, FL @ Music Theater
Bill & Randy Mulkey vs. The Mod Squad
Mike Rotundo vs. Teijo Khan
Ed Gantner & Ron Simmons vs. Kevin Sullivan & Tahitian Prince
The Sheepherders vs. The Southern Boys
Dory Funk, Jr. vs. Steve Keirn

6/11/87: Albany, GA @ Civic Center
The Rock & Roll Express vs. Manny Fernandez & Vladimir Petrov
New Breed vs. Jimmy Valiant & Lazertron
Gladiator #1 vs. Nelson Royal
Gladiator #2 vs. Denny Brown
Larry Stephens vs. Dexter Westcott
Rikki Nelson vs. John Savage

6/11/87: Thibodeaux, LA
Black Bart beat Scott Sanders
Michael Hayes, Terry Gordy & Buddy Roberts beat Mike Boyette, The Enforcer & Shaska Whatley
Brad Armstrong & Tim Horner beat Steve Cox & Davey Haskins
Dick Murdoch & Rick Steiner beat Shane Douglas & Jeff Raitz
Sting beat The Red Devil
Chris Adams beat Bob Bradley
Barry Windham beat Angel of Death
Chris Adams beat Dick Murdoch by DQ
Michael Hayes & Buddy Roberts beat Black Bart & Rick Steiner

6/11/87: Cincinnati, OH @ Gardens
Thunderfoot I beat Jim Lancaster
Rocky King beat Thunderfoot II
The Midnight Express beat Italian Stallion & Kendall Windham
Tully Blanchard beat Todd Champion
Nikita Koloff beat Arn Anderson by DQ
Ronnie Garvin beat Jim Cornette in a cage match
NWA World Champ Ric Flair beat Jimmy Garvin in a cage match

6/11/87: Melbourne, FL @ City Auditorium

6/12/87: Norfolk, VA @ Scope
NWA World Champ Ric Flair beat Jimmy Garvin in a cage match
Ronnie Garvin beat Jim Cornette in a cage match
Arn Anderson & Lex Luger beat Dusty Rhodes & Nikita Koloff
The Midnight Express beat Kendall Windham & Mark Fleming
Mark Fleming beat Cougar Jay
John Savage beat Gladiator #1
Tommy Angel beat Gladiator #2

6/12/87: Lake Charles, LA
Chris Adams beat Rick Steiner
Black Bart beat Steve Cox
Eddie Gilbert, Dick Murdoch & Rick Steiner beat Shane Douglas, Ken Massey & Jeff Raitz
Black Bart beat Bob Bradley
Brad Armstrong & Tim Horner beat The Enforcer & Shaska Whatley
Barry Windham beat Davey Haskins
Steve Cox beat Mike Boyette

6/12/87: Palmetto, FL @ Manatee Civic Center

6/12/87: Charleston, WV @ Civic Center
New Breed beat Jimmy Valiant & Lazertron
Manny Fernandez beat Robert Gibson in a lumberjack match
Tully Blanchard draw Ricky Morton

6/13/87: Atlanta, GA @ WTBS Studios (TV)
Kendall Windham vs. Art Pritts
Jimmy Garvin vs. Rick Sullivan
Arn Anderson, Tully Blanchard & Lex Luger vs. Mike Force, Cougar Jay & Chance McQuade

6/13/87:
Note: New Breed(Chris Champ & Sean Royal) were injured in a car wreck driving from the television studio in Atlanta to Florence, SC. The car hydroplaned in rain, with both men being thrown through the windshield before the car exploded. Royal suffered major burns while Champ's arm was broken in two places.

6/13/87: Florence, SC

6/13/87: Baltimore, MD @ Civic Center
Italian Stallion beat Thunderfoot I
Todd Champion beat Mark Fleming
Arn Anderson beat Kendall Windham
Manny Fernandez beat Rocky King
The Midnight Express beat The Southern Boys(Tracy Smothers & Steve Armstrong)
Tully Blanchard beat Ronnie Garvin
Nikita Koloff beat Lex Luger by DQ
NWA World Champ Ric Flair beat Jimmy Garvin

6/13/87: New Orleans, LA @ Superdome
Shane Douglas beat Shaska Whatley
Buddy Roberts beat Mike Boyette
Steve Cox beat Gary Young
Michael Hayes & Terry Gordy beat The Enforcer & The Terminator
The Rock & Roll Express beat Vladimir Petrov & Angel of Death
Tim Horner & Brad Armstrong beat Rick Steiner & Sting
Big Bubba beat Barry Windham
Bart Batten beat Chris Adams
Steve Williams beat Dick Murdoch

6/14/87: Orlando, FL @ Eddie Graham Sports Complex
Johnny Ace beat Jim Backlund
Cuban Assassin #1 beat Jerry Grey
Cuban Assassin #2 beat Colt Steele
The Sheepherders beat Randy Mulkey & Bill Mulkey
Steve Keirn & Ron Simmons beat Tahitian Prince & Teijo Khan
Mike Rotundo beat Kevin Sullivan
Steve Keirn & Mike Rotundo beat Dory Funk, Jr. & Kevin Sullivan Texas death match

6/14/87: Charlotte, NC @ Coliseum
The Mod Squad draw The Southern Boys
Lazertron & Jimmy Valiant beat The Gladiators
Arn Anderson beat Kendall Windham
Manny Fernandez & Vladimir Petrov beat Ronnie Garvin & Todd Champion
The Rock & Roll Express beat The Midnight Express
Lex Luger NC with Nikita Koloff
Dusty Rhodes beat Tully Blanchard Texas death match
NWA World Champ Ric Flair beat Jimmy Garvin

6/14/87: Fort Worth, TX @ Cowtown Coliseum
Jeff Raitz draw Bob Bradley
Chris Adams beat Black Bart by DQ
Steve Cox beat Bob Bradley
Big Bubba beat Michael Hayes in a badstreet match
Tim Horner & Brad Armstrong beat Rick Steiner & Sting
Steve Williams & Terry Gordy beat Dick Murdoch & Eddie Gilbert

6/15/87: Greenville, SC @ Memorial Auditorium
NWA World Tag Champs Rock & Roll Express beat Lex Luger & Arn Anderson
NWA World TV Title Match: Tully Blanchard(c) beat Barry Windham
The Midnight Express DCO Ronnie & Jimmy Garvin
Manny Fernandez beat Todd Champion
Vladimir Petrov beat Denny Brown
Kendall Windham beat Gladiator #1
Lazor-Tron beat Gladiator #2
The Mod Squad beat Southern Boys

6/15/87: Dallas, TX @ Reunion Arena
Steve Williams & Terry Gordy beat Dick Murdoch & Eddie Gilbert
Tim Horner & Brad Armstrong beat Rick Steiner & Sting
Big Bubba beat Michael Hayes
Steve Cox beat Bob Bradley
Chris Adams beat Black Bart by DQ
Jeff Raitz draw Bob Bradley

6/15/87: Leesburg, FL @ H.S.

6/16/87: Fayetteville, NC @ Cumberland County Civic Center (TV)
Jimmy & Ronnie Garvin vs. John Savage & David Isley
Tracy Smothers & Steve Armstrong vs. Cougar Jay & Tommy Angel
Barry Windham vs. Thunderfoot II
Manny Fernandez, Ivan Koloff & Vladimir Petrov vs. Italian Stallion, Rocky King & Todd Champion
Nikita Koloff vs. Gladiator #1
Tully Blanchard vs. Rikki Nelson
The Midnight Express vs. Nelson Royal & Mike Force

6/17/87: Atlanta, GA @ WTBS Studios (TV)
Barry Windham draw Tully Blanchard(15:00)

6/18/87: Atlanta, GA @ WTBS Studios (TV)
The Mod Squad vs. Alan Martin & El Negro
Arn Anderson vs. Dexter Westcott
Ric Flair & Lex Luger DDQ Jimmy & Ronnie Garvin
Ricky Morton vs. Freddy Smith
Nikita Koloff vs. Brodie Chase
Barry Windham vs. Gary Phelps
Tully Blanchard vs. Hal Moore
The Midnight Express vs. Mike Force & Larry Stephens
Thunderfoot II vs. Darrel Dalton

6/18/87: Alexandria, LA @ Rapides Parish Coliseum
Shane Douglas vs. Gary Young
Mike Boyette vs. The Terminator
Sting vs. Steve Cox
Big Bubba vs. Davey Haskins
Shaska Whatley & The Enforcer vs. Brad Armstrong & Tim Horner
Chris Adams vs. Terry Taylor
Steve Williams, Terry Gordy, Michael Hayes & Buddy Roberts vs. Dick Murdoch, Eddie Gilbert, Rick Steiner & Angel of Death

6/18/87: Port St. Richey, FL @ Southland Roller Palace

6/19/87: Tallahassee, FL @ Leon County Civic Center
The Midnight Express beat Ronnie & Jimmy Garvin

6/20/87: Houston, TX @ The Summit
Steve Cox won pole battle royal
Brad Armstrong & Tim Horner beat The Terminator & The Enforcer
The Rock & Roll Express beat Angel Of Death & Big Bubba
NWA World Champ Ric Flair beat Michael Hayes
Steve Williams & Dusty Rhodes beat Dick Murdoch & Eddie Gilbert in a bunkhouse, tornado match

NWA Western States Heritage Title tournament
1st Round
Shaska Whatley beat Buddy Roberts
Black Bart beat Sting
Rick Steiner DDQ Terry Gordy
Barry Windham beat Chris Adams
Semifinals
Barry Windham beat Shaska Whatley
Black Bart received a bye
Finals
Barry Windham beat Black Bart to win NWA Western States Heritage Title in tournament final

6/20/87: Lakeland, FL @ Civic Center
Nikita Koloff vs. Lex Luger
The Midnight Express beat Ronnie & Jimmy Garvin
Tully Blanchard vs. Mike Rotundo
Steve Keirn & Mike Graham vs. Tahitian Prince & Dory Funk, Jr. steel cage
The Mod Squad vs. The Sheepherders
Big Ed Gantner vs. The Cuban Connection #1
The Cuban Connection #2 vs. Colt Steele
The Southern Boys vs. Arn Anderson & Kevin Sullivan

6/21/87: Greensboro, NC @ Coliseum
Kendall Windham beat Denny Brown
Jimmy Valiant & Lazertron draw The Mod Squad
Manny Fernandez beat Italian Stallion
Ivan Koloff beat Todd Champion
Midnight Express beat Jimmy & Ronnie Garvin by DQ
Nikita Koloff beat Arn Anderson
Dusty Rhodes beat Tully Blanchard
Rock & Roll Express beat Ric Flair & Lex Luger by DQ

6/21/87: Orlando, FL @ Eddie Graham Sports Complex

6/22/87: Greenville, SC @ Memorial Auditorium (TV)
Midnight Express beat Ronnie & Jimmy Garvin by DQ
The Rock & Roll Express beat Gladiator #2 & Thunderfoot II
Barry Windham vs. Larry Stephens
Arn Anderson & Tully Blanchard vs. Tommy Angel & Rikki Nelson
The Midnight Express vs. Rocky King & David Isley
Manny Fernandez vs. Italian Stallion
Jimmy & Ronnie Garvin vs. Cougar Jay & Thunderfoot

6/23/87: Tampa, FL @ USF Sun Dome (TV)
The Sheepherders beat Mike Graham & Steve Keirn to win NWA Florida Tag Title
Ed Gantner NC with Kevin Sullivan
Steve Williams beat Tahitian Prince
Barry Windham beat Teijo Khan
The Rock & Roll Express beat Arn Anderson & Lex Luger by DQ
Nikita Koloff beat Dory Funk, Jr.
NWA World Champ Ric Flair beat Mike Rotundo

6/24/87: Sunrise, FL @ Music Theater

6/25/87: Macon, GA @ Coliseum
Rock & Roll Express beat The Midnight Express by DQ

6/25/87: Fort Myers, FL @ Lee County Civic Center

6/26/87: Greenville, NC
Ronnie & Jimmy Garvin beat Midnight Express by DQ

6/26/87: Jacksonville, FL @ Coliseum

6/27/87: Philadelphia, PA @ Civic Center
Todd Champion beat Thunderfoot II
Italian Stallion beat Thunderfoot I
Kendall Windham beat Mark Fleming
Barry Windham beat Ivan Koloff
The Rock & Roll Express beat The Midnight Express by DQ in a 2 of 3 falls
Nikita Koloff NC with Lex Luger
Dusty Rhodes beat Tully Blanchard
NWA World Champ Ric Flair beat Jimmy Garvin

6/27/87: Fayetteville, NC @ Cumberland County Civic Center
Italian Stallion beat Thunderfoot I
Barbarian beat Todd Champion
Paul Ellering beat Paul Jones
Lazertron beat The Mod Squad Basher
Jimmy Valiant beat The Mod Squad Spike
Midnight Express beat Barry & Kendall Windham
Rock & Roll Express beat Tully Blanchard & Arn Anderson
The Road Warriors beat Ivan Koloff & Manny Fernandez in a double chain match
Ronnie Garvin beat NWA World Champ Ric Flair by DQ
Nikita Koloff beat Lex Luger by DQ

6/27/87: Sarasota, FL @ Robarts Arena

6/28/87: Rock Hill, NC @ Winthrop Coliseum (TV)
Nikita Koloff draw Lex Luger
Jimmy Garvin beat Thunderfoot II
Barry Windham beat Larry Stephens
Rock & Roll Express beat Rick Sullivan & Gladiator #2
Ivan Koloff beat Tommy Angel
Nikita Koloff beat Chance McQuade
John Savage beat Lex Luger
Tully Blanchard & Arn Anderson beat Ricky Morton & Dexter Westcott
Lex Luger beat Larry Stephens
Jimmy Garvin beat Gladiator #2
Nikita Koloff beat Dexter Westcott
The Rock & Roll Express beat The Midnight Express

6/28/87: Wilmington, NC @ Legion Stadium
The Rock & Roll Express vs. The Midnight Express

6/28/87: Orlando, FL @ Eddie Graham Sports Complex

6/29/87: Greenville, SC @ Memorial Auditorium
NWA World Tag Champs Rock & Roll Express draw Tully Blanchard & Arn Anderson
Barry Windham beat Lex Luger
US Tag title Match The Midnight Express beat Jimmy Valiant & Lazor-Tron
Italian Stallion beat Brody Chase
Nelson Royal beat Gladiator #1
Denny Brown vs David Diamond

6/29/87: Fort Pierce, FL @ St. Lucie County Civic Center

6/30/87: Columbia, SC @ Township Auditorium
The Midnight Express vs. Ronnie & Jimmy Garvin

7/1/87: Russellville, AR @ Tucker Coliseum
Sting beat Mike Boyette
Dick Murdoch beat Bob Bradley
Big Bubba beat Davey Haskins
Shane Douglas NC with Steve Cox
Chris Adams beat Eddie Gilbert by DQ
Brad Armstrong & Tim Horner beat Enforcer & Gary Young
Sting beat Black Bart
Steve Williams beat Dick Murdoch coward waves the flag match

7/1/87: Lakeland, FL @ Civic Center (TV)
Dusty Rhodes beat NWA World Champ Ric Flair by DQ in a 2 of 3 falls match
Tully Blanchard draw Barry Windham
Mike Rotundo beat The Barbarian
Bugsy McGraw, Ed Gantner & Blackjack Mulligan beat Dory Funk, Jr., Black Assassin & Sir Oliver Humperdink in a bunkhouse match
Nikita Koloff beat Lex Luger
The Rock & Roll Express beat Midnight Express by DQ
Jimmy Garvin draw Arn Anderson
Steve Keirn & Mike Graham DCO with The Sheepherders
Buddy Roberts & Terry Gordy beat The Mod Squad
Ron Simmons beat Tahitian Prince
The Cuban Connection beat Bill & Randy Mulkey
Jerry Grey(sub for Buddy Roberts) vs. Black Assassin

7/2/87: Landover, MD @ Capital Centre
Kendall Windham beat Thunderfoot I(3:28) via pinfall
Rocky King beat Thunderfoot II(6:30) via pinfall
Terry Gordy & Buddy Roberts beat Paul Jones & Ivan Koloff via pinfall
Dick Murdoch beat Steve Williams(10:51) in a Texas Death Match
Big Bubba beat Barry Windham(7:15) by CO
Eddie Gilbert beat Mark Fleming(3:27) via pinfall
The Rock & Roll Express beat The Midnight Express by reverse decision
Dusty Rhodes, Nikita Koloff & The Road Warriors beat Ric Flair, Arn Anderson, Tully Blanchard & Lex Luger(18:00) via pinfall in a steel cage match

7/3/87: Richmond, VA @ Coliseum
Misty Blue beat Kat Laroux
Italian Stallion beat Mark Fleming
The Barbarian beat Todd Champion
Eddie Gilbert beat Kendall Windham
Terry Gordy, Michael Hayes & Buddy Roberts beat Ivan Koloff, Manny Fernandez & Vladimir Petrov
Steve Williams beat Dick Murdoch
Barry Windham beat Big Bubba by CO in a street fight match
The Rock & Roll Express beat Midnight Express by DQ in a 2 of 3 falls match
Nikita Koloff beat Arn Anderson
The Road Warriors beat Ric Flair & Lex Luger by DQ
Dusty Rhodes beat Tully Blanchard I quit, cage match

7/3/87: Nassau, Bahamas @ Stadium
Kevin Sullivan & Blackjack Mulligan vs. Dory Funk, Jr. & Sir Oliver Humperdink
Mike Rotundo vs. Tahitian Prince
Bugsy McGraw vs. Johnny Ace
Bill & Randy Mulkey vs. The Sheepherders

7/4/87: Atlanta, GA @ Omni
Dusty Rhodes, Road Warriors, Paul Ellering & Nikita Koloff beat James J. Dillon, Lex Luger, Ric Flair, Arn Anderson & Tully Blanchard in War Games
Steve Williams beat Dick Murdoch
The Rock & Roll Express beat Midnight Express DQ
Terry Gordy, Michael Hayes & Buddy Roberts beat Paul Jones, Ivan Koloff & Manny Fernandez
Chris Adams beat Black Bart by DQ
Brad Armstrong & Tim Horner beat Big Bubba & Angel of Death
Jimmy & Ronnie Garvin beat Vladimir Petrov & The Barbarian
Barry Windham beat Rick Steiner
Jimmy Valiant beat The Mod Squad Basher
Lazertron beat The Mod Squad Spike
Sting beat Thunderfoot I
Kendall Windham beat Gladiator #1

7/5/87: Greenville, SC @ Memorial Auditorium
The Road Warriors beat Tully Blanchard & Arn Anderson
NWA World Tag Champs Rock & Roll Express beat Ivan Koloff & Manny Fernandez
Nikita Koloff beat Lex Luger
Jimmy Valiant beat Mod Squad #1
Lazor-Tron beat Mod Squad #2
Nelson Royal beat Clark?
Rocky King beat John Savage

7/5/87: Charleston, WV @ Civic Center
Italian Stallion beat Gladiator #2
Kendall Windham beat Thunderfoot I
Misty Blue beat Kat Laroux
The Barbarian beat Todd Champion
Mike Rotundo draw Dory Funk, Jr.
Jimmy Garvin beat Ivan Koloff
Ronnie Garvin beat Manny Fernandez by DQ
Barry Windham beat Vladimir Petrov
The Road Warriors beat The Midnight Express
NWA World Champ Ric Flair beat Dusty Rhodes by DQ
Nikita Koloff & Rock & Roll Express beat Lex Luger, Arn Anderson & Tully Blanchard in a cage match

7/6/87: Inglewood, CA @ The Forum
Misty Blue beat Kat Laroux
Mike Rotundo draw Dory Funk, Jr.
Chris Adams beat Black Bart by DQ
Barry Windham beat Big Bubba in a street fight match
Jimmy & Ronnie Garvin beat Ivan Koloff & Manny Fernandez
The Rock & Roll Express beat Midnight Express by DQ
Steve Williams beat Dick Murdoch
Dusty Rhodes beat Tully Blanchard in a cage match
The Road Warriors & Nikita Koloff beat Ric Flair, Arn Anderson & Lex Luger in a cage match

7/7/87: San Francisco, CA @ Cow Palace
Dusty Rhodes beat Tully Blanchard in a cage match
The Rock & Roll Express beat Ric Flair & Lex Luger
The Road Warriors beat The Midnight Express
Nikita Koloff beat Arn Anderson
Dick Murdoch beat Steve Williams
Jimmy & Ronnie Garvin beat Ivan Koloff & Manny Fernandez
Mike Rotundo draw Dory Funk, Jr.
Barry Windham beat Black Bart
Big Bubba beat Chris Adams
Misty Blue beat Kat Laroux

7/8/87: Atlanta, GA @ WTBS Studios (TV)

7/9/87: Cincinnati, OH @ Gardens
Lazertron & Kendall Windham beat Ivan Koloff & Paul Jones
Misty Blue beat Kat Laroux
Jimmy Valiant beat The Mod Squad Basher
Ronnie Garvin beat The Mod Squad Spike
Michael Hayes & Buddy Roberts beat Big Bubba & Angel of Death
Jimmy Garvin beat Manny Fernandez by DQ
The Rock & Roll Express beat Midnight Express DQ
Barry Windham beat The Barbarian
Steve Williams & Terry Gordy beat Dick Murdoch & Eddie Gilbert
Nikita Koloff, The Road Warriors & Dusty Rhodes beat Lex Luger, Ric Flair, Tully Blanchard & Arn Anderson in a cage match

7/10/87: Pittsburgh, PA @ Civic Center
Misty Blue beat Kat Laroux
Sting & Chris Adams beat Barbarian & Thunderfoot I
Black Bart beat Italian Stallion
Buddy Roberts beat Jerry Jackson
Tim Horner & Brad Armstrong beat Rick Steiner & Eddie Gilbert
Jimmy Garvin beat Big Bubba by DQ
Michael Hayes & Terry Gordy beat The Mod Squad
Steve Williams beat Dick Murdoch
Ronnie Garvin & Barry Windham beat The Midnight Express by DQ
Nikita Koloff, The Road Warriors & Dusty Rhodes beat Ric Flair, Lex Luger, Arn Anderson & Tully Blanchard

7/10/87: Fort Myers, FL @ Lee County Civic Center

7/11/87: Atlanta, GA @ WTBS Studios (TV)
The Rock & Roll Express vs. ?? Phelps & ?? Long
Steve Williams vs. Alan Martin
Bugsy McGraw vs. Dexter Westcott
Barry Windham vs. Clement Fields
Michael Hayes, Buddy Roberts & Terry Gordy vs. David Isley, Cougar Jay & Larry Stephens
Ron Simmons vs. Tommy Angel
The Midnight Express vs. Mike Jackson & Ricky Lee Jones
Misty Blue Simms vs. Kat Laroux

7/11/87: Greensboro, NC @ Coliseum
Lex Luger beat Nikita Koloff to win NWA US Title
NWA World Champ Ric Flair beat Jimmy Garvin in a cage match
Arn Anderson & Tully Blanchard beat The Rock & Roll Express by DQ
Ole Anderson beat The Barbarian
Michael Hayes & Buddy Roberts draw Manny Fernandez & Ivan Koloff
The Mod Squad beat Jimmy Valiant & Lazertron
Nelson Royal beat Thunderfoot II
Kendall Windham beat Thunderfoot I

7/11/87: Oklahoma City, OK @ Myriad
Tim Horner & Brad Armstrong beat Gary Young & The Terminator
Davey Haskins & Shane Douglas beat The Enforcer & Bob Bradley
Steve Cox won a 6-man pole battle royal
Terry Gordy NC with Black Bart in a taped fist match
The Road Warriors beat The Midnight Express
Sting, Chris Adams & Dusty Rhodes beat Angel of Death, Rick Steiner & Eddie Gilbert bunkhouse brawl
Barry Windham draw Dick Murdoch
Steve Williams beat Big Bubba to win UWF Title

7/12/87: Baltimore, MD @ Civic Center
Misty Blue beat Kat Laroux
Terry Gordy beat Thunderfoot I
Rick Steiner beat Sting
Jimmy Garvin beat Manny Fernandez by DQ
Midnight Express beat Michael Hayes & Buddy Roberts
Barry Windham beat Big Bubba
Miss Atlanta Lively(aka Ronnie Garvin) beat Bobby Eaton
Steve Williams beat Dick Murdoch
The Road Warriors & Nikita Koloff beat Ric Flair, Lex Luger & Arn Anderson
Dusty Rhodes beat Tully Blanchard barbed wire match

7/12/87: Orlando, FL @ Eddie Graham Sports Complex
Lazertron beat Jerry Grey
Ed Gantner & Bugsy McGraw beat Black Assassin & Incubus
The Rock & Roll Express beat The Cuban Connection
Kevin Sullivan beat Tahitian Prince
Mike Rotundo beat Ivan Koloff
The Sheepherders beat Mike Graham & Steve Keirn
Blackjack Mulligan & Kevin Sullivan beat Dory Funk, Jr. & Sir Oliver Humperdink

7/13/87: West Palm Beach, FL @ Auditorium
Jimmy Valiant beat Ricky Santana
Cuban Assassin #1(David Sierra) beat Bill Mulkey
Ron Simmons & Scott Hall beat Black Assassin & Incubus
The Sheepherders beat Steve Keirn & Ed Gantner
Mike Rotundo beat Ivan Koloff
Jimmy & Ronnie Garvin beat Arn Anderson & Tully Blanchard
Lex Luger draw Nikita Koloff
The Rock & Roll Express beat The Midnight Express
Blackjack Mulligan & Bugsy McGraw beat Oliver Humperdink & Dory Funk, Jr.
NWA World Champ Ric Flair beat Dusty Rhodes

7/13/87: Salisbury MD @ Convention Center
Steve Williams beat Dick Murdoch
Barry Windham beat Big Bubba
Sting beat Rick Steiner
Michael Hayes & Buddy Roberts beat The Mod Squad
Eddie Gilbert beat Mark Fleming
Terry Gordy beat Thunderfoot II
Misty Blue beat Kat Laroux

7/14/87: Gaffney, SC @ Timken Gymnasium (TV)
Jimmy & Ronnie Garvin vs. Manny Fernandez & The Barbarian
Sean Royal vs. Todd Champion
Nelson Royal vs. Colt Steele
Barry Windham vs. Tully Blanchard
also including Jimmy Valiant, Manny Fernandez, Thunderfoot I & Thunderfoot II

7/14/87: Key West, FL

7/14/87: Baton Rouge, LA @ Centroplex
Dave Haskins & Shane Douglas draw The Enforcer(Doug Gilbert) & Gary Young
Angel of Death beat Buddy Roberts
Shaska Whatley beat Steve Cox
Michael Hayes beat The Terminator
Brad Armstrong & Tim Horner beat Ivan Koloff & Paul Jones
Chris Adams & Sting beat Rick Steiner & Black Bart
Barry Windham beat Big Bubba by DQ
Robert Gibson & Brad Armstrong beat The Midnight Express by DQ
Steve Williams & Terry Gordy beat Dick Murdoch & Eddie Gilbert in a bunkhouse match

7/15/87: Little Rock, AR @ Barton Coliseum
Robert Gibson & Barry Windham beat The Midnight Express by DQ

7/16/87: Johnson City, TN
Ronnie & Jimmy Garvin beat Midnight Express by DQ

7/17/87: Norfolk, VA @ Scope
Mark Fleming beat Gladiator #1
Nelson Royal beat Thunderfoot II
Lazertron beat Thunderfoot I
The Mod Squad beat Italian Stallion & Todd Champion
Manny Fernandez beat Rocky King
Barbarian beat Kendall Windham
Paul Ellering beat Paul Jones in a bunkhouse match
Robert Gibson beat Sean Royal
Jimmy & Ronnie Garvin beat The Midnight Express by DQ
The Road Warriors, Dusty Rhodes & Nikita Koloff beat Ric Flair, Lex Luger, Arn Anderson & Tully Blanchard in a cage match

7/17/87: Tallahassee, FL @ Leon County Civic Center

7/18/87: Atlanta, GA @ WTBS Studios (TV)
Ron Simmons vs. Gladiator #1
The Mod Squad vs. Alan Martin & Long
Jimmy Valiant vs. Gladiator #2
Kendall Windham vs. Thunderfoot II
Todd Champion & Italian Stallion vs. Force & David Isley
Lex Luger vs. Rocky King
Ronnie Garvin vs. El Negro

7/18/87: Charlotte, NC @ Independence Stadium
Jimmy Valiant, Lazertron & Kendall Windham beat The Gladiators & Sean Royal
Vladimir Petrov beat Todd Champion
Jimmy & Ronnie Garvin beat Manny Fernandez & Ivan Koloff by DQ
Barry Windham beat Big Bubba
Michael Hayes & Buddy Roberts beat The Midnight Express by DQ
Road Warrior Animal beat Arn Anderson in a taped fist match
Terry Gordy & Steve Williams beat Eddie Gilbert & Dick Murdoch bunkhouse match
The Rock & Roll Express beat The Mod Squad
Black Bart beat Chris Adams
NWA World Champ Ric Flair beat Road Warrior Hawk by DQ
Lex Luger beat Nikita Koloff by DQ
Dusty Rhodes beat Tully Blanchard in a barbed wire, fence match

7/18/87: Sarasota, FL @ Robarts Arena

7/19/87: Roanoke, VA @ Civic Center
Italian Stallion beat Gene Ligon
Barbarian beat Kendall Windham
Jimmy Valiant & Lazertron beat Thunderfoot II & Sean Royal
Jimmy Garvin beat Manny Fernandez by DQ
Ronnie Garvin beat Ivan Koloff in a chain match
Rock & Roll Express beat The Midnight Express by DQ
Sean Royal beat Rocky King
The Barbarian beat Italian Stallion
Barry Windham beat Thunderfoot II
Mike Rotundo draw Dory Funk, Jr.
The Road Warriors, Nikita Koloff & Dusty Rhodes beat Ric Flair, Lex Luger, Arn Anderson & Tully Blanchard in a cage match

7/19/87: Chicago, IL @ UIC Pavilion
Ivan Koloff beat Todd Champion
Sting beat Rick Steiner
Michael Hayes & Buddy Roberts beat The Mod Squad
Black Bart beat Chris Adams
Brad Armstrong & Tim Horner beat Big Bubba & Angel of Death
Terry Gordy & Steve Williams beat Dick Murdoch & Eddie Gilbert
Lex Lugar NC with Road Warrior Hawk
Nikita Koloff beat Arn Anderson
Rock & Roll Express beat The Midnight Express by DQ
Road Warrior Animal beat NWA World Champ Ric Flair by DQ
Dusty Rhodes beat Tully Blanchard barbed wire match

7/20/87: Greenville, SC @ Memorial Auditorium
Cage Match: Dusty Rhodes beat Tully Blanchard
Cage Match: Nikita Koloff & the Road Warriors beat Ric Flair, Lex Luger & Arn Anderson
Paul Ellering beat Paul Jones
NWA World Tag Champs the Rock & Roll Express beat the Midnight Express

Barry Windham beat Manny Fernandez
Jimmy Valiant & Lazor-Tron beat the Mod Squad
Ronnie & Jimmy Garvin beat Thunderfoot 1 & 2
Ivan Koloff beat Todd Champion
Barbarian beat Kendall Windham
Sean Royal beat Rocky King

7/21/87: Jackson, MS
Brad Armstrong & Tim Horner beat Killer Khalifa & The Red Devil
Big Bubba beat Chief White Eagle
Shane Douglas draw Davey Haskins
Michael Hayes & Buddy Roberts beat Mike Boyette & Bob Bradley
Steve Cox beat Rick Steiner by DQ
Sting beat Gary Young by DQ
Shaska Whatley beat Chief White Eagle
Sting beat Bob Bradley
The Enforcer beat Steve Cox by CO
Brad Armstrong & Tim Horner NC with Eddie Gilbert & Dick Murdoch
Brad Armstrong & Tim Horner beat Big Bubba & The Terminator
Chris Adams & Sting beat Black Bart & Eddie Gilbert
Steve Williams beat Dick Murdoch in a bunkhouse match

7/22/87: Atlanta, GA @ WTBS Studios (TV)

7/22/87: Columbus, GA @ Municipal Auditorium
The Rock & Roll Express beat Midnight Express by DQ

7/23/87: Harrisonburg VA @ H.S.
The Rock & Roll Express beat Ivan Koloff & The Barbarian
Ronnie Garvin beat The Mod Squad Basher
Jimmy Valiant & Lazertron beat Thunderfoot I & Thunderfoot II
Jimmy Garvin beat The Mod Squad Spike
Todd Champion beat John Savage
Italian Stallion beat Gladiator #2
Kendall Windham beat Gladiator #1

7/23/87: Dallas, TX @ Reunion Arena
Black Bart & Eddie Gilbert beat Barry Windham & Chris Adams
Shane Douglas won a pole battle royal
Rick Steiner beat Sting
Brad Armstrong & Tim Horner beat The Midnight Express by DQ
Terry Gordy, Michael Hayes & Buddy Roberts beat Big Bubba, The Terminator & Angel of Death
Steve Williams beat Dick Murdoch
The Road Warriors beat Arm Anderson & Lex Luger
Dusty Rhodes beat Tully Blanchard
NWA World Champ Ric Flair beat Nikita Koloff

7/24/87: Houston, TX @ The Summit
Shane Douglas & Davey Haskins beat Shaska Whatley & The Enforcer
Buddy Roberts beat The Terminator
Steve Cox beat Angel of Death
Sting beat Rick Steiner
Barry Windham DDQ Tully Blanchard
Chris Adams beat Black Bart by DQ
Brad Armstrong & Tim Horner beat Arn Anderson & Lex Luger by DQ
NWA World Champ Ric Flair DDQ Dusty Rhodes
Michael Hayes, Terry Gordy & Rock & Roll Express DDQ vs Eddie Gilbert, Midnight Express & Big Bubba
Steve Williams beat Dick Murdoch barbed wire cage match

7/24/87: St. Petersburg, FL @ Bayfront Center

7/25/87: Atlanta, GA @ WTBS Studios (TV)
Arn Anderson & Tully Blanchard vs. Tommy Angel & Larry Stephens
Barry Windham vs. Alan Martin
The Midnight Express vs. Mike Jackson & Cougar Jay
The Rock & Roll Express vs. Keith Steinborn & Ricky Lee Jones
Ronnie Garvin vs. Art Pritts

7/25/87: Philadelphia, PA @ Civic Center
Kendall Windham & Todd Champion beat Mod Squad
Lazertron beat Nelson Royal
Sean Royal beat Italian Stallion
Mike Rotundo draw Dory Funk, Jr.
The Barbarian beat Jimmy Valiant
Terry Gordy, Michael Hayes & Buddy Roberts beat Manny Fernandez, Ivan Koloff & Vladimir Petrov by DQ
Barry Windham NC with Arn Anderson
Jimmy Garvin & Precious beat Dark Journey & Paul Jones
Steve Williams beat Dick Murdoch bunkhouse match
The Rock & Roll Express beat The Midnight Express in a lumberjack with tennis racquets match
Dusty Rhodes & Ronnie Garvin beat Ric Flair & Tully Blanchard via pinfall in a double cage match
Nikita Koloff beat Lex Luger by DQ in a cage match

7/25/87: Alexandria, LA @ Rapides Parish Coliseum
Eddie Gilbert beat Davey Haskins
Big Bubba beat Bobby Howell & Craig Whitford in a handicap match
Black Bart & The Terminator beat Bob Bradley & Ron Ellis
Sting beat Mike Boyette
Rick Steiner beat Bobby Howell
Big Bubba beat Ron Ellis & Craig Whitford
Brad Armstrong beat Eddie Gilbert by DQ

7/26/87: Cleveland, OH @ Municipal Stadium(After Cleveland Indians Game)
Ronnie Garvin beat The Barbarian
Jimmy Valiant beat Ivan Koloff
Tully Blanchard draw Jimmy Garvin
The Rock & Roll Express beat The Midnight Express

7/26/87: Daytona, FL @ Ocean Center
The Road Warriors vs. The Sheepherders
Blackjack Mulligan & Kevin Sullivan vs. Dory Funk, Jr. & Sir Oliver Humperdink in a barbed wire match
NWA World Champ Ric Flair vs. Mike Rotundo

7/27/87: Fayetteville, NC @ Cumberland County Civic Center
Italian Stallion beat Thunderfoot I
The Barbarian beat Todd Champion
Paul Ellering beat Paul Jones
Lazertron beat The Mod Squad Basher
Jimmy Valiant beat The Mod Squad Spike
The Midnight Express beat Barry Windham & Kendall Windham
Rock & Roll Express beat Tully Blanchard & Arn Anderson
Road Warriors beat Manny Fernandez & Ivan Koloff
Ronnie Garvin beat NWA World Champ Ric Flair
Nikita Koloff beat Lex Luger

7/28/87: Rock Hill, SC @ Winthrop Coliseum
The Rock & Roll Express beat Tully Blanchard & Arn Anderson
Lex Luger beat Barry Windham
Jimmy & Ronnie Garvin draw The Midnight Express
Jimmy Valiant beat Ivan Koloff by DQ
Todd Champion & Italian Stallion beat Thunderfoot I & Thunderfoot II
The Barbarian beat Lazertron
Manny Fernandez beat Kendall Windham

7/28/87: Lubbock, TX
David Haskins beat Mike Boyette
Shaska Whatley draw Buddy Roberts
Eddie Gilbert beat Shane Douglas
The Terminator beat Steve Cox
Gary Young beat Bob Bradley
Terry Gordy beat Rick Steiner
Tim Horner & Brad Armstrong beat Big Bubba & Angel of Death
Chris Adams & Sting beat Eddie Gilbert & Black Bart by DQ
Steve Williams beat Dick Murdoch

7/29/87: Atlanta, GA @ WTBS Studios (TV)
Sean Royal vs. Rocky King
The Barbarian vs. Italian Stallion
Barry Windham vs. Thunderfoot II
Italian Stallion vs. Gene Ligon
Kendall Windham vs. the Barbarian
Jimmy Valiant & Lazertron vs. Sean Royal & Thunderfoot I
Jimmy Garvin vs. Manny Fernandez

7/30/87: Tampa, FL @ Sportatorium (TV)
Dory Funk, Jr. NC with Mike Rotundo

7/30/87: Jacksonville, FL @ Coliseum
Rock & Roll Express beat The Midnight Express DQ

7/31/87: Miami, FL @ Orange Bowl
Steve Keirn & Bugsy McGraw beat The Cuban Connection (David Sierra & Ricky Santana)
Manny Fernandez beat Randy Mulkey & Bill Mulkey in a handicap match
Scott Hall beat Bob Cook
Barry Windham beat Incubus via pinfall
The Sheepherders DDQ Jimmy & Ronnie Garvin
Mike Rotundo beat Ivan Koloff via pinfall
Kevin Sullivan beat Dory Funk, Jr. Texas death match
The Rock & Roll Express beat The Midnight Express(10:15) by DQ
Dusty Rhodes, Nikita Koloff, The Road Warriors & Paul Ellering beat Ric Flair, Arn Anderson, Tully Blanchard, Lex Luger & War Machine(Big Bubba) (sub. for James J. Dillon)(19:38) by submission in a war games, cage match

7/31/87: Albuquerque, NM @ Tingley Coliseum
David Haskins draw Shane Douglas
The Terminator beat Mike Boyette
Gary Young beat Steve Cox
Rick Steiner DCO with Sting
Tim Horner & Brad Armstrong beat The Enforcers
Michael Hayes, Terry Gordy & Buddy Roberts beat Dick Murdoch, Angel of Death & Scandor Akbar
Chris Adams beat Black Bart
Steve Williams beat Eddie Gilbert in a cage match

8/1/87: Atlanta, GA @ WTBS Studios (TV)
The Midnight Express vs. George South & Cougar Jay
Jimmy Garvin vs. Thunderfoot II
Nikita Koloff vs. David Isley
Barry Windham vs. Dave Spearman
Arn Anderson & Tully Blanchard vs. Dexter Westcott & ?? Patterson
Sean Royal vs. Rikki Nelson
Ronnie Garvin vs. Thunderfoot I
Lex Luger vs. Alan Martin
Ivan Koloff vs. Dale Laperouse
Ricky Morton vs. Tully Blanchard

8/1/87: Richmond, VA @ Coliseum
Thunderfoot I & Sean Royal beat Italian Stallion & Nelson Royal
Ivan Koloff beat Todd Champion
Barbarian beat Kendall Windham
Jimmy Valiant & Bugsy McGraw beat The Mod Squad
Jimmy Garvin beat Manny Fernandez
Nikita Koloff beat Lex Luger by DQ
The Rock & Roll Express beat Arn Anderson & Tully Blanchard by DQ
Ronnie Garvin beat NWA World Champ Ric Flair by DQ

8/1/87: New Orleans, LA @ Superdome
Shane Douglas beat Gary Young
David Haskins beat Mike Boyette
Terry Gordy beat Angel of Death
Terry Taylor beat Steve Cox
Barry Windham beat Shaska Whatley
Rick Steiner beat Chris Adams in a taped fist match
Sting beat The Enforcer
Brad Armstrong & Tim Horner beat The Midnight Express by reverse decision
Dusty Rhodes & Steve Williams beat Eddie Gilbert & Dick Murdoch in a Texas bullrope match
Michael Hayes, Terry Gordy & Buddy Roberts beat Black Bart, Big Bubba & The Terminator in a steel cage, first blood, elimination match

8/1/87: Sarasota, FL @ Robarts Arena
Blackjack Mulligan & Kevin Sullivan vs. The Sheepherders

8/2/87: Huntington, WV @ Memorial Fieldhouse
The Rock & Roll Express beat The Midnight Express

8/2/87: Charlotte, NC @ Coliseum
Nelson Royal beat Keith Patterson
Nikita Koloff beat Arn Anderson
Lex Luger beat Dusty Rhodes by DQ
The Rock & Roll Express beat The Midnight Express in a bunkhouse match

8/2/87: Orlando, FL @ Eddie Graham Sports Complex
The Sheepherders beat The Cuban Connection

8/3/87: Morgan City, LA
Buddy Roberts beat The Terminator by DQ
Chris Adams beat Mike Boyette
Rick Steiner & Terry Taylor beat Shane Douglas & David Haskins
Brad Armstrong & Tim Horner beat Big Bubba & The Terminator by DQ
Gary Young beat Chief White Eagle
Steve Cox beat The Red Devil
Buddy Roberts beat Mike Boyette
Shane Douglas beat Eddie Gilbert to win UWF Television Title
Chris Adams beat Terry Taylor

8/3/87: Greenville, SC @ Memorial Auditorium
NWA World Champ Ric Flair DCO Ronnie Garvin
US Title Match: Lex Luger(c) beat Barry Windham
NWA World TV Title Match: Tully Blanchard(c) beat Nikita Koloff
Rock & Roll Express beat the Barbarian
Jimmy Garvin beat Manny Fernandez
Jimmy Valiant & Bugsy Mcgraw beat the Mod Squad
Sean Royal beat Italian Stallion
Lazor-Tron beat Gladiator #1

8/4/87: Spartanburg, SC @ Memorial Auditorium (TV)
The Midnight Express beat David Isley & Rikki Nelson
Jimmy Garvin & Barry Windham beat Thunderfoot I & Thunderfoot II
Ronnie Garvin beat Gladiator #2
Arn Anderson & Tully Blanchard beat Mike Force & John Savage
Bugsy McGraw beat Tommy Angel
Nikita Koloff beat Gary Royal
NWA World Champ Ric Flair beat Rocky King
Bugsy McGraw & Jimmy Valiant beat Thunderfoot I & Thunderfoot II
Rock & Roll Express beat Rikki Nelson & Gary Royal
Barry Windham beat Mike Force
Barbarian & Ivan Koloff beat Tommy Angel & David Isley
Tully Blanchard beat Colt Steele
Arn Anderson beat Brodie Chase
Midnight Express beat George South & Larry Stephens
Rock & Roll Express vs. Arn Anderson & Tully Blanchard
Nikita Koloff vs. Arn Anderson
Lex Luger vs. Dusty Rhodes

8/5/87: Atlanta, GA @ WTBS Studios (TV)

8/5/87: Tampa, FL @ Sportatorium (TV)

8/7/87: St. Louis, MO @ Kiel Auditorium
NWA World Champ Ric Flair beat Michael Hayes
Dusty Rhodes & Steve Williams beat Dick Murdoch & Eddie Gilbert in a bunkhouse match
Barry Windham beat Big Bubba
Lex Luger beat Nikita Koloff by CO
Midnight Express beat Jimmy & Ronnie Garvin by DQ
Terry Gordy beat Black Bart
Ron Simmons beat Ivan Koloff
Sting draw Rick Steiner

8/7/87: Springfield, MO
Shane Douglas beat Mike Boyette
Steve Cox & David Haskins beat Shaska Whatley & Gary Young
Buddy Roberts beat The Enforcer
Chris Adams, Brad Armstrong & Tim Horner beat Angel of Death, Terry Taylor & The Terminator
Shane Douglas & David Haskins beat Mike Boyette & The Enforcer
Steve Cox beat Gary Young by DQ
Buddy Roberts draw Shaska Whatley
Brad Armstrong & Tim Horner beat Angel of Death & The Terminator
Chris Adams NC with Terry Taylor

8/7/87: Nassau, Bahamas @ Stadium

8/8/87: Kansas City, MO @ Kemper Arena
The Midnight Express beat Michael Hayes & Terry Gordy by DQ

8/8/87: Pittsburgh, PA @ Civic Center
Denny Brown beat Jimmy Jackson
Italian Stallion & Nelson Royal beat Thunderfoot II & Gladiator #1
Sean Royal beat Kendall Windham
Jimmy Valiant & Lazertron beat The Mod Squad
Ronnie Garvin beat Thunderfoot I
Jimmy Garvin beat Manny Fernandez
Rock & Roll Express beat Tully Blanchard & Arn Anderson
Nikita Koloff beat Lex Luger by DQ

8/8/87: Sarasota, FL @ Robarts Arena

8/9/87: Ocala, FL @ Jai Alai Fronton
Bugsy McGraw, Blackjack Mulligan & Kevin Sullivan vs. The Sheepherders & Johnny Ace
Dory Funk, Jr. vs. Mike Rotundo
Steve Keirn & Mike Graham vs. Incubus & Black Assassin
The Untouchables vs. Randy Mulkey & Bill Mulkey
Black Magic vs. Jerry Gray

8/9/87: Orlando, FL @ Eddie Graham Sports Complex
Mike Rotundo beat Terry Funk
Kevin Sullivan beat Dory Funk, Jr. by DQ
The Sheepherders DCO with The Cuban Connection
Bugsy McGraw beat Black Assassin
Johnny Ace beat Bob Cook
Mike Graham & Steve Keirn beat Samurai Warriors
Incubus beat Bill Mulkey
Jerry Grey beat Black Magic

8/9/87: Atlanta, GA @ Omni
Denny Brown beat George South
Ron Simmons beat Teijo Khan
Barry Windham beat Dick Murdoch
The Midnight Express draw Terry Gordy & Buddy Roberts
Steve Williams beat Big Bubba
Nikita Koloff NC with Ivan Koloff
Dusty Rhodes beat Lex Luger by DQ
Rock & Roll Express beat Arn Anderson & Tully Blanchard
NWA World Champ Ric Flair beat Ronnie Garvin by DQ

8/9/87: Asheville, NC @ Civic Center
Rocky King beat John Savage
Rock & Roll Express beat The Midnight Express
Tully Blanchard beat Nikita Koloff
Barry Windham beat Arn Anderson
Mod Squad beat Kendall Windham & Italian Stallion
Manny Fernandez beat Colt Steele
Sean Royal beat Lazertron

8/10/87: Buckingham, VA
Ronnie & Jimmy Garvin beat Midnight Express by DQ

8/10/87: Stockton, CA
Ron Simmons beat Shaska Whatley
Michael Hayes beat The Terminator
Terry Taylor beat Chris Adams by DQ
Brad Armstrong & Tim Horner beat Big Bubba & Black Bart
Sting & Robert Gibson beat Arn Anderson & Tully Blanchard
Nikita Koloff beat Lex Luger by DQ
Steve Williams & Terry Gordy beat Eddie Gilbert & Dick Murdoch in a bunkhouse match

8/10/87: West Palm Beach, FL @ Auditorium

8/11/87: San Jose, CA
Buddy Roberts beat Steve Pardee
Sting & Ron Simmons draw Shaska Whatley & Rick Steiner
Michael Hayes beat The Terminator
Brad Armstrong & Tim Horner beat Big Bubba & Black Bart by DQ
Chris Adams beat Terry Taylor by DQ
Nikita Koloff beat Eddie Gilbert
Terry Gordy NC with Dick Murdoch
Steve Williams & The Rock & Roll Express beat Tully Blanchard, Arn Anderson & Lex Luger

8/11/87: Columbia, SC @ Township Auditorium (TV)
The Midnight Express beat Ronnie & Jimmy Garvin
Jimmy Valiant & Bugsy McGraw vs. Thunderfoot I & Thunderfoot II
The Rock & Roll Express vs. Rikki Nelson & Gary Royal
Barry Windham vs. Mike Force
Ivan Koloff & The Barbarian vs. David Isley & Tommy Angel
Tully Blanchard vs. Colt Steele
Arn Anderson vs. Brodie Chase
Midnight Express vs. George South & Larry Stephens

8/12/87: Inglewood, CA @ The Forum (TV)
Chris Adams beat Terry Taylor
Buddy Roberts beat Tau Lugo
Ron Simmons beat Rodney Anoai
Rock & Roll Express beat Big Bubba & Black Bart DQ
Tully Blanchard draw Michael Hayes
Shaska Whatley beat Tim Patterson
Terry Taylor & Eddie Gilbert beat Harry Hell & Billy Anderson
Arn Anderson beat Brad Armstrong
Tim Horner beat The Terminator
Eddie Gilbert & Dick Murdoch beat Terry Gordy & Steve Williams
Nikita Koloff beat Lex Luger by DQ

8/12/87: Tampa, FL @ Sportatoriuim (TV)
Mike Rotundo beat Terry Funk by DQ

8/12/87: Atlanta, GA @ WTBS Studios (TV)
Mike Rotundo vs. Alan Martin
Jimmy Valiant vs. El Negro
Kendall Windham & Lazertron vs. Dexter Westcott & Dale Laperouse
Brad Armstrong & Tim Horner vs. Tommy Angel & Cougar Jay
Terry Taylor vs. Italian Stallion
Ivan Koloff & Manny Fernandez vs. George South & Rocky King
Chris Adams vs. Colt Steele
Ronnie Garvin vs. Keith Steinborn
Kevin Sullivan vs. Larry Stephens
Bugsy McGraw vs. Terry Jones
Note: Beginning with this television taping, World Champship Wrestling was taped the Wednesday prior to the Saturday's airing.

8/13/87: Raleigh, NC @ Dorton Arena
NWA World Champ Ric Flair DCO with Ronnie Garvin
Barry Windham & Jimmy Garvin beat The Midnight Express by DQ in a 2 of 3 falls match
Jimmy Valiant & Lazertron beat The Barbarian & Ivan Koloff
Denny Brown beat Thunderfoot I
Italian Stallion beat Colt Steele
The Mod Squad Spike beat Rocky King
Nelson Royal draw The Mod Squad Basher

8/13/87: Sebring, FL @ Fairgrounds Pavilion

8/14/87: Norfolk, VA @ Scope
The Mod Squad draw Italian Stallion & Lazertron
NWA World Champ Ric Flair beat Ronnie Garvin by DQ
The Rock & Roll Express beat Tully Blanchard & Arn Anderson
Sean Royal beat Colt Steele
Dusty Rhodes beat Lex Luger by DQ
Ivan Koloff beat Kendall Windham
Nikita Koloff & Barry Windham beat The Midnight Express by DQ
Jimmy Garvin beat Manny Fernandez

8/14/87: Melbourne, FL @ City Auditorium

8/15/87: Baltimore, MD @ Civic Center
Steve Cox beat Thunderfoot I
Lazertron draw Nelson Royal
Jimmy Valiant beat Angel of Death
Sting beat Eddie Gilbert by DQ
Michael Hayes & Terry Gordy beat Manny Fernandez & Shaska Whatley
The Road Warriors beat Ivan Koloff & The Barbarian
NWA World Champ Ric Flair draw Ronnie Garvin(50:00)

8/15/87: Charlotte, NC @ Coliseum
Tully Blanchard & Lex Luger vs. The Rock & Roll Express
The Midnight Express draw Barry Windham & Jimmy Garvin(30:00)

8/15/87: Westville, OK @ Westville H.S. Football Field
Shane Douglas vs. The Enforcer
David Haskins vs. Gary Young
Ron Simmons vs. Mike Boyette
Buddy Roberts vs. Rick Steiner
Brad Armstrong & Tim Horner vs. Black Bart & The Terminator
Chris Adams vs. Terry Taylor in a no DQ match with Jim Ross as special referee

8/15/87: Sarasota, FL @ Robarts Arena

8/16/87: Kingsport, TN
The Rock & Roll Express beat The Midnight Express

8/16/87: Chicago, IL @ UIC Pavilion
Ronnie Garvin, Dusty Rhodes, The Road Warriors & Nikita Koloff beat Ric Flair, Lex Luger, Arn Anderson, Tully Blanchard & James J. Dillon in a war games, cage match
Ivan Koloff beat Italian Stallion
Sting beat Black Bart
Ron Simmons beat Sean Royal
Barry Windham beat Rick Steiner
The Rock & Roll Express beat The Midnight Express
Steve Williams beat Eddie Gilbert

8/16/87: Orlando, FL @ Eddie Graham Sports Complex

8/17/87: Denver, CO @ City Auditorium
Ron Simmons beat Rick Steiner
Sting beat Black Bart
Barry Windham beat Big Bubba
The Rock & Roll Express beat The Midnight Express
Steve Williams beat Dick Murdoch
The Road Warriors & Nikita Koloff beat Lex Luger & Arn Anderson & Tully Blanchard
NWA World Champ Ric Flair beat Dusty Rhodes by DQ

8/19/87: Fayetteville, NC @ Cumberland County Civic Center (TV)
Jimmy Valiant vs. John Savage
Dusty Rhodes vs. Colt Steele
Italian Stallion vs. The Mod Squad Basher
Ivan Koloff & The Barbarian vs. George South & Rocky King
Sean Royal vs. Rikki Nelson
Kendall Windham vs. Denny Brown
Barry Windham & Jimmy Garvin vs. Teijo Khan & Cougar Jay
Dusty Rhodes vs. Gladiator #1
The Mod Squad vs. George South & Rocky King
Manny Fernandez, The Barbarian & Ivan Koloff vs. Denny Brown, Rikki Nelson & Larry Stephens
The Midnight Express beat Jimmy & Ronnie Garvin

8/19/87: Forest City, NC
Ronnie Garvin & Barry Windham beat Midnight Express by DQ

8/19/87: Jacksonville, FL @ Coliseum

8/20/87: Pennington Gap, VA
The Midnight Express beat Jimmy Valiant & Lazertron

8/20/87: Cincinnati, OH @ Gardens
Kendall Windham beat Jim Lancaster
Rocky King beat Teijo Khan
Denny Brown beat Gladiator #1
Sean Royal beat Italian Stallion
Jimmy Garvin beat Colt Steele
Barry Windham beat Ivan Koloff
Lex Luger NC with Nikita Koloff
The Rock & Roll Express beat Arn Anderson & Tully Blanchard
NWA World Champ Ric Flair beat Ronnie Garvin by DQ

8/20/87: Jackson, MS

8/20/87: Tampa, FL @ Al Lopez Field

8/21/87: Charleston, WV @ Civic Center
Mark Fleming beat Cougar Jay
Teijo Khan beat Keith Patterson
Colt Steele beat Rikki Nelson
Sean Royal beat Denny Brown
Barry Windham beat Ivan Koloff by DQ
The Rock & Roll Express beat Tully Blanchard & Arn Anderson

8/21/87: Macon, GA @ Coliseum
Jimmy Valiant & Jimmy Garvin beat The Midnight Express by DQ in a 2 of 3 falls match

8/21/87: Fort Lauderdale, FL @ War Memorial Auditorium
Jimmy Backlund beat Rex King
The Samurai Warriors beat Bill Mulkey & Rick Rider
Mike Graham & Steve Keirn draw The Mighty Yankees
Blackjack Mulligan beat Incubus
The Sheepherders DDQ The Cuban Connection
Mike Rotundo beat Dory Funk, Jr.
Kevin Sullivan DDQ Terry Funk in a Boston street fight match

8/22/87: Atlanta, GA @ WTBS Studios (TV)
Dusty Rhodes beat The Gladiator
Mike Rotundo beat Alan Martin
Jimmy Valiant beat El Negro
Lazertron & Kendall Windham beat Dale Laperouse & Dexter Westcott
Brad Armstrong & Tim Horner beat Tommy Angel & Cougar Jay
Terry Taylor beat Italian Stallion
Manny Fernandez & Ivan Koloff beat Rocky King & George South
Chris Adams beat Colt Steele
Ronnie Garvin beat Keith Steinborn
Kevin Sullivan beat Larry Stephens
Bugsy McGraw beat Terry Jones
Michael Hayes & Buddy Roberts beat Thunderfoot I & Thunderfoot II

8/22/87: Greensboro, NC @ Coliseum
Kendall Windham beat Teijo Khan
Colt Steele beat Rikki Nelson
Italian Stallion beat Larry Stephens
Rocky King beat Gladiator #1
Dusty Rhodes beat Lex Luger by DQ
The Rock & Roll Express beat Arn Anderson & Tully Blanchard
Chris Adams & Sting beat Eddie Gilbert & Terry Taylor
NWA World Champ Ric Flair beat Ronnie Garvin

8/22/87: Philadelphia, PA @ Civic Center
The Mod Squad beat Italian Stallion & Denny Brown
Lazertron beat Gladiator #1(George South)
Jimmy Valiant beat Sean Royal by DQ
Jimmy Garvin beat Manny Fernandez
Steve Williams beat Big Bubba
Nikita Koloff & Barry Windham beat The Midnight Express by DQ
The Road Warriors beat Ivan Koloff & The Barbarian

8/22/87: Sarasota, FL @ Robarts Arena

8/22/87: Fort Worth, TX @ Cowtown Coliseum

8/23/87: Ocala, FL @ Jai Alai Fronton
Mike Rotundo vs. Dory Funk, Jr.
The Mighty Yankees vs. Steve Keirn & Mike Graham
The Sheepherders vs. Bugsy McGraw & Kevin Sullivan
The Cuban Connection vs. The Samurai Warriors
Black Assassin vs. Bill Mulkey
Sam Bass vs. Incubus

8/23/87: Orlando, FL @ Eddie Graham Sports Complex
The Cuban Connection #1 beat Ric McCord
Black Magic beat Sam Bass
Bill Mulkey beat Krusher Knopf
The Mighty Yankees beat Black Assassin & Incubus
Mike Rotundo, Steve Keirn & Mike Graham beat The Samurai Warriors & Hiro Matsuda
The Sheepherders NC with Bugsy McGraw & Blackjack Mulligan
Kevin Sullivan beat Dory Funk, Jr. in a thunderdome cage match

8/23/87: Chattanooga, TN @ Memorial Auditorium
Denny Brown beat Gladiator #1
Colt Steele beat Larry Stephens
Lazertron draw The Mod Squad Basher
The Mod Squad Spike beat Rocky King
Manny Fernandez beat Jimmy Valiant
Lex Luger NC with Nikita Koloff
The Rock & Roll Express beat Tully Blanchard & Arn Anderson
NWA World Champ Ric Flair beat Jimmy Garvin

8/23/87: Bloomington, MN @ Met Center
The Road Warriors, Dusty Rhodes & Nikita Koloff beat Ric Flair, Lex Luger, Arn Anderson & Tully Blanchard
The Rock & Roll Express beat Bobby Eaton & The Barbarian
Steve Williams beat Big Bubba
Chris Adams beat Terry Taylor by DQ
Ivan Koloff beat Jimmy Garvin
Ronnie Garvin beat Sean Royal
Barry Windham beat Eddie Gilbert

8/24/87: Greenville, SC @ Memorial Auditorium
NWA World Title No DQ Match: Ric Flair beat Ronnie Garvin
US Title Match: Dusty Rhodes beat Lex LUger(c) by DQ
#1 Contendor's Match: Tully Blanchard & Arn Anderson beat Barry Windham & Jimmy Garvin
Barbarian beat Rocky King
Ivan Koloff & Manny Fernandez beat Kendall Windham & Jimmy.Valiant
Italian Stallian beat Colt Steele
Mod Squad 1 beat Larry Stephens

8/24/87: Weslaco, TX
The Rock & Roll Express beat The Midnight Express

8/25/87: Rock Hill, SC @ Winthrop Coliseum (TV)
Barry Windham beat Arn Anderson
Lex Luger & Tully Blanchard beat The Road Warriors
Barry Windham beat Ivan Koloff
Jimmy & Ronnie Garvin beat Manny Fernandez & The Barbarian by DQ
Teijo Khan beat John Savage

Barry Windham beat Vernon Deaton
The Road Warriors beat Cougar Jay & The Gladiator
Arn Anderson & Tully Blanchard beat Italian Stallion & Denny Brown
Ivan Koloff beat Ricky King
The Mod Squad beat David Isley & Rikki Nelson
Jimmy Valiant beat Brodie Chase
Lex Luger beat John Savage
The Road Warriors beat Larry Stephens & Brodie Chase
Ronnie Garvin beat Vernon Deaton
Sean Royal beat Cougar Jay
The Mod Squad vs. Denny Brown & Italian Stallion

8/25/87: Corpus Christi, TX
The Rock & Roll Express beat The Midnight Express

8/26/87: Miami, FL @ Convention Center
Johnny Ace beat Luis Astea
Ricky Santana beat Robbie Idol
Jimmy Backlund beat Rick Rider
The Samurai Warriors beat Rex King & Bill Mulkey
Mike Graham & Steve Keirn beat The Sheepherders
Mike Rotundo beat Black Assassin
Barry Windham beat Ivan Koloff
Kevin Sullivan & Bugsy McGraw beat The Mighty Yankees by DQ
Blackjack Mulligan beat Dory Funk, Jr.
The Road Warriors beat Arn Anderson & Tully Blanchard
NWA World Champ Ric Flair DCO with Ronnie Garvin

8/26/87: Galveston, TX
The Rock & Roll Express beat The Midnight Express

8/26/87: Atlanta, GA @ WTBS Studios (TV)
Lex Luger vs. Cougar Jay
Jimmy Garvin vs. John Savage
The Mod Squad vs. Kendall Windham & Italian Stallion
Jimmy Valiant vs. Tim Hardy
The Barbarian vs. Rocky King
Denny Brown vs. Mike Jackson

8/27/87: Amarillo, TX @ Sports Arena
Brad Armstrong & Tim Horner beat The Midnight Express

8/27/87: Tallahassee, FL @ Leon County Civic Center

8/28/87: Hampton, VA @ Coliseum
The Rock & Roll Express beat The Midnight Express

8/28/87: Daytona, FL @ Ocean Center
Johnny Ace vs. Kevin Sullivan in a taped fist match
The Road Warriors vs. The Sheepherders in a steel cage match

8/29/87: Houston, TX The Summit
Misty Blue beat Comrade Orca
Shane Douglas beat Shaska Whatley
Ron Simmons beat The Enforcer
Steve Cox beat Gary Young by DQ
Brad Armstrong & Tim Horner beat The Terminator & Black Bart
Terry Taylor beat Chris Adams
Steve Williams beat Big Bubba
Dusty Rhodes beat Lex Luger by DQ
Sting beat Eddie Gilbert
The Rock & Roll Express beat Tully Blanchard & Arn Anderson in a Texas tornado match
NWA World Champ Ric Flair beat Barry Windham

8/29/87: St. Petersburg, FL @ Bayfront Center
The Road Warriors beat The Midnight Express
Mike Graham & Steve Keirn beat The Sheepherders to win NWA Florida Tag Title

8/30/87: Charlotte, NC @ Coliseum
Kendall Windham beat Gladiator #1
Denny Brown beat Colt Steele
Arn Anderson draw Robert Gibson
The Midnight Express beat Barry Windham & Nikita Koloff by DQ
Tully Blanchard beat Ricky Morton
The Road Warriors beat Ivan Koloff & Barbarian
Dusty Rhodes beat Lex Luger by DQ
NWA World Champ Ric Flair beat Ronnie Garvin

8/30/87: Atlanta, GA @ Omni
The Mod Squad Basher draw Italian Stallion
Teijo Khan beat Denny Brown
Barry Windham beat Manny Fernandez
Nikita Koloff beat Sean Royal
The Midnight Express NC with Barry Windham & Michael Hayes
Jimmy Garvin beat Ivan Koloff
The Road Warriors & Dusty Rhodes beat Arn Anderson, Lex Luger & Tully Blanchard

8/30/87: Orlando, FL @ Eddie Graham Sports Complex

8/31/87: Savannah, GA @ Civic Center
Jimmy Garvin & Jimmy Valiant beat The Midnight Express by DQ

9/1/87: Spartanburg, SC @ Memorial Auditorium (TV)
Barry Windham vs. Arn Anderson
Ivan Koloff vs. Kendall Windham
Nikita Koloff beat Tully Blanchard(16:00)l to win NWA World Television Title
Arn Anderson vs. George South
Lazertron vs. Gladiator #2
The Midnight Express vs. Greg Stevens & David Isley
The Rock & Roll Express vs. Dexter Westcott & ??
Lex Luger vs. Mike Force
Jimmy Valiant vs. Brodie Chase
The Mod Squad vs. Rikki Nelson & David Isley
Ivan Koloff vs. Rocky King
Arn Anderson & Tully Blanchard vs. Italian Stallion & Denny Brown
The Road Warriors vs. Gladiator #1 & Cougar Jay
Barry Windham vs. Vernon Deaton
Teijo Khan vs. John Savage

9/2/87: Atlanta, GA @ WTBS Studios (TV)
Nikita Koloff vs. Alan Martin
Lex Luger vs. Keith Steinborn
Tully Blanchard vs. Ed Franks
Arn Anderson vs. Mike Jackson
Ronnie Garvin vs. Terry Jones
The Midnight Express vs. Barry Windham & Kendall Windham

9/2/87: Lafayette, LA @ Cajun Dome (TV)
Terry Taylor beat Shane Douglas to win UWF Television Title
The Jive Tones(Shaska Whatley & Tiger Conway, Jr.) beat Brad Armstrong & Tim Horner
Chris Adams & Sting beat Eddie Gilbert & Terry Taylor by DQ
Chris Adams beat Eddie Gilbert by DQ
Brad Armstrong & Tim Horner beat Big Bubba & The Terminator
Steve Williams beat Black Bart

9/3/87: Anderson, SC @ Recreation Center
The Midnight Express beat Bill & Randy Mulkey

9/4/87: Columbus, OH @ Ohio Center
Steve Cox & Shane Douglas beat Rick Steiner & Gary Young
Sting beat The Terminator
Ron Simmons beat Black Bart
Brad Armstrong & Tim Horner beat The Midnight Express by DQ
Chris Adams NC with Terry Taylor
Barry Windham beat Rick Steiner
Steve Williams beat Big Bubba

9/4/87: Richmond, VA @ Coliseum
Denny Brown beat David Isley
Sean Royal beat Kendall Windham
The Road Warriors beat Ivan Koloff & Gladiator #1
The Rock & Roll Express beat Tully Blanchard & Arn Anderson
Lex Luger beat Jimmy Garvin
NWA World Champ Ric Flair beat Ronnie Garvin

9/4/87: Albany, GA @ Civic Center
Ricky Nelson vs. Colt Steele
John Savage vs. Dexter Westcott
Gladiator #2 vs. Larry Stephens
Rocky King vs. Lazertron
Todd Champion & Italian Stallion vs. The Mod Squad
Teijo Khan vs. Jimmy Valiant
The Barbarian & Manny Fernandez vs. Michael Hayes & Buddy Robrets

9/5/87: Nassau, Bahamas @ Stadium
Johnny Ace vs. Tyree Pride
Bugsy McGraw & Mike Rotundo vs. The Sheepherders
Dory Funk, Jr. vs. Kevin Sullivan

9/5/87: Philadelphia, PA @ Civic Center
Lazertron beat Mark Fleming
Denny Brown beat The Mod Squad Basher
The Mod Squad Spike beat Italian Stallion
Lazertron beat Gladiator
NWA World Champ Ric Flair beat Ronnie Garvin
Kendall Windham & Jimmy Valiant beat Teijo Khan & Sean Royal
The Rock & Roll Express beat Tully Blanchard & Arn Anderson
Jimmy Garvin beat Manny Fernandez

9/5/87: Baltimore, MD @ Civic Center
Ron Simmons beat The Barbarian
Midnight Express beat Brad Armstrong & Tim Horner
Sting & Chris Adams beat Rick Steiner & Terry Taylor
Barry Windham beat Eddie Gilbert
Steve Williams beat Ivan Koloff by DQ
Lex Luger NC with Nikita Koloff
The Road Warriors & Dusty Rhodes beat Ric Flair, Arn Anderson & Tully Blanchard in a cage match

9/6/87: Asheville, NC @ Civic Center (TV)
Sean Royal vs. Larry Stephens
Ivan Koloff vs. George South
Barry Windham vs. Vernon Deaton
Midnight Express vs. Dexter Westcott & Rikki Nelson
Nikita Koloff vs. Colt Steele
The Mod Squad vs. Rocky King & John Savage
Midnight Express vs. Nikita Koloff & Barry Windham
The Warlord vs. George South
Lex Luger vs. Larry Stephens
Jimmy Garvin vs. Teijo Khan
Manny Fernandez vs. Colt Steele
Sean Royal vs. Rikki Nelson

9/6/87: Orlando, FL @ Eddie Graham Sports Complex
Gary Fitzpatrick beat Rick Ryder
Jim Backlund beat Rex King
Incubus beat Bill Mulkey
Black Assassin beat Black Magic
Samurai Warriors beat Ricky Santana & Robbie Idol
Mike Graham & Steve Keirn beat The Mighty Yankees
Mike Rotundo, Kevin Sullivan & Bugsy McGraw beat The Sheepherders & Dory Funk, Jr.

9/7/87: Wilmington, NC & Legion Stadium(Cancelled due to rain)

9/7/87: West Palm Beach, FL @ Auditorium
Johnny Ace vs. Ricky Santana
Mike Rotundo vs. Dory Funk, Jr.
Bugsy McGraw & Kevin Sullivan vs. The Sheepherders

9/7/87: Greenville, SC @ Memorial Auditorium
NWA World ChampRic Flair beat Ronnie Garvin No DQ Match
Russian Chain Match Lex Luger beat Nikita Koloff
Western States Title Match: Barry Windham(c) DCO Arn Anderson
Kendall Windham beat Teijo Khan
Denny Brown beat Gladiator #2
Colt Steele beat David Isley
John Savage beat Brody Chase

9/8/87: Amherst, VA
Ronnie & Jimmy Garvin beat The Midnight Express DQ

9/8/87: Tampa, FL @ Fairgrounds Special events Center
The Mighty Yankees(Bob Cook & Jerry Grey) beat Mike Graham & Steve Keirn to win NWA Florida Tag Title

9/9/87: Atlanta, GA @ WTBS Studios (TV)
Sean Royal vs. Alan Martin
Nikita Koloff vs. Bobby Eaton
Barry Windham vs. Arn Anderson
Stan Lane vs. Mike Jackson
The Barbarian vs. Colt Steele
Lex Luger vs. Barry Windham
Ivan Koloff vs. George South
Jimmy Valiant vs. Tommy Angel
Jimmy Garvin vs. John Savage
Nikita Koloff vs. David Isley
Rock & Roll Express vs. Arn Anderson & Tully Blanchard

9/9/87: New Orleans, LA @ UNO Lakefront Arena
The Sheepherders beat Bobby Howell & Ken Massey
Terry Taylor beat Davey Haskins
Sting beat Mike Boyette
Brad Armstrong & Tim Horner beat The Jive Tones DQ
Eddie Gilbert & Terry Taylor beat Shane Douglas & Sting

9/9/87: Miami, FL @ Convention Center

9/10/87: Jackson, MS
Ken Massey beat Killer Khalifa
Davey Haskins beat The Enforcer
The Terminator beat Mike Boyette
Brad Armstrong & Tim Horner beat The Jive Tones by DQ
Steve Cox beat Gary Young
Ron Simmons beat Rick Steiner
The Midnight Express beat Michael Hayes & Shane Douglas
Sting beat Eddie Gilbert & Terry Taylor by DQ in a handicap match
Steve Williams beat Black Bart by DQ

9/11/87: Memphis, TN @ Mid-South Coliseum
Davey Haskins won a pole battle royal
Tim Horner beat Tiger Conway, Jr.
Brad Armstrong draw Shaska Whatley
Steve Cox beat Gary Young
Ron Simmons beat Rick Steiner
Michael Hayes & Shane Douglas beat Black Bart & The Terminator
The Road Warriors & Steve Williams beat Midnight Express & Big Bubba
Sting & Steve Williams beat Eddie Gilbert & Terry Taylor in a steel cage match

9/11/87: Sumter, SC @ Exhibition Center
Barry Windham vs. Ivan Koloff
Jimmy Garvin vs. Manny Fernandez
Jimmy Valiant vs. The Barbarian
Kendall Windham vs. Sean Royal
Rocky King vs. The Gladiator
Teijo Khan vs. Larry Stephens

9/11/87: Charleston, WV @ Civic Center
George South beat Mark Fleming
Lazertron beat Denny Brown
The Mod Squad beat Italian Stallion & Keith Patterson
Arn Anderson beat Robert Gibson
Ricky Morton beat Tully Blanchard in a Texas death match
Lex Luger beat Nikita Koloff by DQ
NWA World Champ Ric Flair beat Ronnie Garvin

9/11/87: Tallahassee, FL @ Leon County Civic Center

9/12/87: Greensboro, NC @ Coliseum
Denny Brown beat Gladiator #1
The Barbarian beat George South
Italian Stallion beat Teijo Khan
Mod Squad & Sean Royal beat Lazertron, Jimmy Valiant & Kendall Windham
Barry Windham beat Ivan Koloff
Jimmy Garvin beat Manny Fernandez
Lex Luger beat Nikita Koloff by DQ
The Rock & Roll Express draw Arn Anderson & Tully Blanchard(60:00)

9/12/87: St. Louis, MO @ Kiel Auditorium
Ron Simmons beat The Enforcer
Rick Steiner beat Shane Douglas
Michael Hayes & Sting beat Eddie Gilbert & Terry Taylor
Black Bart & The Terminator beat Steve Cox & Shane Douglas
Tim Horner draw Tiger Conway, Jr.
Tim Horner beat Shaska Whatley by DQ
Road Warrior Hawk & Dusty Rhodes beat The Midnight Express
Steve Williams beat Dory Funk, Jr.
NWA World Champ Ric Flair DCO with Ronnie Garvin

9/12/87: Sarasota, FL @ Robarts Arena

9/13/87: Dallas, TX @ Reunion Arena (TV)
NWA World Champ Ric Flair NC with Ronnie Garvin
Steve Williams beat Black Bart
Dusty Rhodes beat Lex Luger by DQ
Barry Windham beat Eddie Gilbert
Ron Simmons beat Big Bubba by CO
Sting beat Terry Taylor by DQ
Ron Simmons beat The Enforcer
Brad Armstrong, Tim Horner, Michael Hayes & Shane Douglas beat Shaska Whatley, Tiger Conway, Jr., The Terminator & The Enforcer
Ron Simmons beat The Enforcer(unmasked as Rick Steiner) by CO
Gary Young beat Steve Cox

9/13/87: Cincinnati, OH @ Gardens
The Midnight Express beat Jimmy Valiant & Kendall Windham

9/13/87: Orlando, FL @ Eddie Graham Sports Complex

9/14/87: to 9/17/87:
No wrestling due to annual NWA Convention

9/18/87: Pittsburgh, PA @ Civic Center
Sean Royal beat Jimmy Jackson
Denny Brown beat Colt Steele
The Barbarian beat Rocky King
Ivan Koloff beat Kendall Windham
Midnight Express draw Barry Windham & Jimmy Garvin
Lex Luger beat Nikita Koloff by DQ
Rock & Roll Express beat Arn Anderson & Tully Blanchard
NWA World Champ Ric Flair beat Ronnie Garvin

9/18/87: Kansas City, MO @ Kemper Arena
Rick Steiner beat David Haskins
Shane Douglas beat The Enforcer
Steve Cox beat Gary Young
Tim Horner & Brad Armstrong draw Shaska Whatley & Tiger Conway, Jr.
Shane Douglas beat Terry Taylor by DQ
Ron Simmons beat The Terminator
Michael Hayes beat Big Bubba by CO in a street fight
Steve Williams beat Black Bart
Sting beat Eddie Gilbert in a cage match

9/19/87: Charlotte, NC @ Coliseum (TV)
Nikita Koloff & Barry Windham beat The Midnight Express by DQ
The Warlord beat George South
Lex Luger beat Larry Stephens
Jimmy Garvin beat Teijo Khan
Manny Fernandez beat Colt Steele
Sean Royal beat Rikki Nelson
Barry Windham beat Larry Stephens
Midnight Express beat Rikki Nelson & George South
Jimmy Valiant beat John Savage
Dusty Rhodes & Road Warrior Animal beat Arn Anderson & Lex Luger in a ouble bullrope match
Ricky Morton beat Tully Blanchard by CO in a Texas death match
NWA World Champ Ric Flair beat Ronnie Garvin

9/19/87: Lubbock, TX
Davey Haskins beat The Enforcer
Steve Cox beat Gary Young
Ron Simmons beat Shaska Whatley
Brad Armstrong & Tim Horner draw Shaska Whatley & Tiger Conway, Jr.
Steve Williams beat Black Bart
Shane Douglas, Michael Hayes & Sting beat Big Bubba, Rick Steiner & The Terminator in a first blood, elimination, steel cage match

9/20/87: Chicago, IL @ UIC Pavilion
Rick Steiner draw Ron Simmons
Jimmy Valiant beat Sean Royal
Barry Windham beat Black Bart
Brad Armstrong & Tim Horner beat Shaska Whatley & Tiger Conway, Jr.
Terry Taylor beat Shane Douglas
Eddie Gilbert beat Sting
Steve Williams beat Ivan Koloff
Lex Luger beat Dusty Rhodes by DQ
NWA World Champ Ric Flair NC with Ronnie Garvin

9/20/87: Atlanta, GA @ Omni
Teijo Khan beat Larry Clarke
Todd Champion beat Gladiator #2
The Mod Squad beat Denny Brown & Rocky King
Italian Stallion beat Gladiator #1
Manny Fernandez beat Kendall Windham
Nikita Koloff beat Big Bubba
Michael Hayes & Jimmy Garvin beat The Midnight Express by DQ
The Rock & Roll Express beat Tully Blanchard & Arn Anderson by DQ

9/20/87: Roanoke, VA @ Civic Center
NWA World Champ Ric Flair beat Ronnie Garvin
The Rock & Roll Express beat Tully Blanchard & Arn Anderson
Lex Luger beat Barry Windham
Nikita Koloff beat Ivan Koloff
Jimmy Garvin beat Manny Fernandez
The Warlord beat Rikki Nelson
Colt Steele beat John Savage

9/21/87: ?? (TV)
Mike Rotundo vs. Bobbie Idol
Steve Keirn & Mike Graham vs. The Masked Yankees
Lex Luger vs. Jim Backlund
Nikita Koloff vs. the Black Assassin
Barry Windham vs. Masked Villain
Bugsy McGraw vs. Rick Ryder
Kevin Sullivan vs. Rex King
The Sheepherders vs. Bill Mulkey & Rick McCord

9/21/87: Winnsboro, SC @ Fairfield Central H.S.
Barry Windham vs. Ivan Koloff
Jimmy Garvin vs. Manny Fernandez
Lazertron & Todd Champion vs. The Mod Squad
Cougar Jay vs. Rikki Nelson
Italian Stallion vs. Gladiator #1
Gladiator #2 vs. Larry Stephens

9/21/87: Greenville, SC @ Memorial Auditorium
NWA World Champ Ric Flair beat Ronnie Garvin Steel Cage
Texas Death Match: Ricky Morton beat Tully Blanchard
Lex LUger & Arn Anderson beat Dusty Rhodes & Nikita Koloff
Robert Gibson beat the Barbarian
Jimmy Valiant & Kendall Windham beat Sean Royal & Teijo Khan
Colt Steele beat Rocky King
Denny Brown beat John Savage

9/22/87: Fayetteville, NC @ Cumberland County Civic Center
The Rock & Roll Express beat Arn Anderson & Tully Blanchard
Jimmy Valiant beat Manny Fernandez
The Barbarian beat Kendall Windham
Denny Brown & Italian Stallion beat The Mod Squad
Tommy Angel beat Gladiator #1
Gladiator #2 beat Larry Stephens
Teijo Khan beat Rocky King

9/22/87: Tampa, FL @ USF Sun Dome
Mike Rotundo beat Robbie Idol
Mike Graham & Steve Keirn beat The Mighty Yankees
Lex Luger beat Jimmy Backlund
Nikita Koloff beat The Black Assassin
Barry Windham beat ??
Bugsy McGraw beat Rick Rider
Kevin Sullivan beat Rex King
The Sheepherders beat Rick McCord & Bill Mulkey
NWA World Champ Ric Flair beat Ronnie Garvin
Dusty Rhodes beat Lex Luger
Kevin Sullivan & Bugsy McGraw beat Dory Funk, Jr. & Incubus
Mike Graham & Steve Keirn beat The Sheepherders loser leaves town match

9/23/87: Atlanta, GA @ WTBS Studios (TV)
Rock & Roll Express vs. Tommy Angel & Mike Force
Kevin Sullivan vs. Larry Stephens
Arn Anderson vs. Art Pritts
Tully Blanchard vs. The Menace
Mike Rotundo vs. Dave Spearman
Arn Anderson & Tully Blanchard vs. Mike Force & Mike Jackson
Mike Rotundo vs. Tommy Angel

9/23/87: Inglewood, CA @ The Forum
Steve Cox beat Gary Young
Brad Armstrong, Tim Horner & Shane Douglas beat Shaska Whatley, Tiger Conway, Jr. & The Enforcer
Michael Hayes & Ron Simmons beat The Terminator & Big Bubba
Barry Windham beat Rick Steiner
Terry Taylor & Eddie Gilbert beat Shane Douglas & Sting
Steve Williams beat Black Bart
Lex Luger beat Nikita Koloff
NWA World Champ Ric Flair NC with Ronnie Garvin

9/24/87: Las Vegas, NV @ Cashman Field
NWA World Champ Ric Flair beat Ronnie Garvin
Steve Williams beat Black Bart
Terry Taylor beat Shane Douglas
Sting beat Eddie Gilbert
Brad Armstrong & Tim Horner beat Shaska Whatley & Tiger Conway, Jr.
Lex Luger beat Nikita Koloff by DQ
Barry Windham beat Rick Steiner
Michael Hayes & Ron Simmons beat Big Bubba & The Terminator
Steve Cox beat Gary Young

9/24/87: Harrisonburg, VA @ Harrisonburg H.S.
Rikki Nelson vs. Teijo Khan
Colt Steele vs. John Savage
Rocky King vs. Chris Champ
Italian Stallion vs. Sean Royal
Todd Champion vs. Manny Fernandez
The Midnight Express vs. Ronnie & Jimmy Garvin

9/25/87: Detroit, MI @ Cobo Arena
The Barbarian beat Shane Douglas
Tiger Conway Jr. beat Gary Young
Sting beat Eddie Gilbert
Barry Windham beat Rick Steiner
Nikita Koloff beat Ivan Koloff
Rock & Roll Express beat The Midnight Express by DQ
Michael Hayes beat The Terminator
Terry Taylor beat Brad Armstrong
Steve Williams beat Big Bubba
Dusty Rhodes & The Road Warriors beat Lex Luger, Arn Anderson & Tully Blanchard in a steel cage match
Ronnie Garvin beat Ric Flair steel cage match to win NWA World Title

9/26/87: Jacksonville, FL @ Coliseum
The Road Warriors vs. The Sheepherders
Kevin Sullivan vs. Dory Funk, Jr. Texas bullrope match
Chris Adams & Sting vs. Terry Taylor & Eddie Gilbert
Michael Hayes & Terry Gordy vs. Big Bubba & Black Bart
Bugsy McGraw vs. The Black Assassin
Ron Simmons vs. Rick Steiner
Steve Keirn vs. Ricky Santana
Randy Mulkey & Bill Mulkey vs. The Samurai Warriors

9/26/87: Norfolk, VA @ Scope
Dusty Rhodes & Nikita Koloff beat Midnight Express by DQ

9/27/87: Greensboro, NC @ Coliseum
Nikita Koloff, Dusty Rhodes & The Road Warriors beat Ric Flair, Lex Luger, Arn Anderson & Tully Blanchard in a cage match
NWA World Champ Ronnie Garvin beat Big Bubba
Ricky Morton beat Bobby Eaton
Robert Gibson beat Stan Lane
Steve Williams beat Black Bart
Sting beat Eddie Gilbert
Jimmy Garvin beat Manny Fernandez
Kendall Windham & Lazertron beat The Mod Squad

9/29/87: Misenheimer, NC @ Pfeffer Gym (TV)
NWA World Champ Ronnie Garvin vs. Tommy Angel
The Warlord vs. David Isley
Sean Royal vs. Gary Royal
Barry Windham beat Gary Royal
Kevin Sullivan beat Rikki Nelson
Sean Royal beat John Savage
Arn Anderson & Lex Luger draw Ronnie Garvin & Nikita Koloff
Ronnie Garvin beat Tommy Angel
The Warlord beat David Isley
Arn Anderson & Tully Blanchard beat the Rock & Roll Express for NWA Tag Titles

9/29/87: Greenville, SC @ Memorial Auditorium
NWA World Champ Ronnie Garvin beat Arn Anderson
Dusty Rhodes & Robert Gibson beat Ric Flair & Lex Luger
Ricky Morton beat Bobby Eaton
Stan Lane beat Denny Brown
Italian Stallion & Todd Champion draw the Mod Squad
Denny Brown beat Gladiator #1
Teijo Khan beat Larry Stephens
Thunderfoot #1 beat Rocky King

9/30/87: Charleston, SC @ St. Andrew's H.S.
Barry Windham & Jimmy Garvin vs. The Midnight Express
Jimmy Valiant vs. Manny Fernandez
Kendall Windham vs. Teijo Khan
Lazertron vs. Denny Brown
Italian Stallion & Todd Champion vs. The Mod Squad
Rocky King vs. Warlord

9/30/87: Atlanta, GA @ WTBS Studios (TV)
The Road Warriors vs. Clement Fields & ?? Franks
Terry Taylor vs. Terry Jones
Arn Anderson & Tully Blanchard vs. Force & Tommy Angel
Lex Luger vs. Max MacGyver
Ivan Koloff & The Warlord vs. Keith Steinborn & Rusty Riddle
Nikita Koloff vs. El Negro

10/1/87: Raleigh, NC @ Dorton Arena
Arn Anderson beat Jimmy Garvin in a cage match
Robert Gibson beat Tully Blanchard in a cage match
The Mod Squad draw The Cuban Connection(Ricky Santana & David Sierra)
Todd Champion beat John Savage
Lazertron beat Denny Brown
The Samurai Warriors beat Kendall Windham & Italian Stallion
Jimmy Valiant beat Thunderfoot I
Mike Rotundo beat Ivan Koloff

10/2/87: Richmond, VA @ Coliseum
Rick Steiner beat Lazertron
The Mod Squad Spike draw Ricky Santana
Denny Brown beat Colt Steele
Sting beat John Savage
Michael Hayes & Jimmy Garvin beat Eddie Gilbert & Terry Taylor
Mike Rotundo NC with Dick Murdoch
The Road Warriors beat The Midnight Express by DQ
Tully Blanchard & Arn Anderson beat The Rock & Roll Express in a cage match

10/3/87: Pittsburgh, PA @ Civic Center
The Warlord & Teijo Khan beat The Cuban Connection
Bugsy McGraw beat The Mod Squad Spike
Todd Champion beat Samurai Warrior #1
Mike Rotundo beat Samurai Warrior #2
Ron Simmons beat The Terminator
Jimmy Garvin beat Dory Funk, Jr. by DQ
Barry Windham draw Dick Murdoch
The Road Warriors beat The Midnight Express by DQ

10/3/87: Charlotte, NC @ Coliseum
Dusty Rhodes beat Lex Luger
Tully Blanchard & Arn Anderson beat The Rock & Roll Express
NWA World Champ Ronnie Garvin beat Ivan Koloff
Sting beat Eddie Gilbert
Michael Hayes beat Terry Taylor by DQ
New Breed beat Italian Stallion & Kendall Windham
Kevin Sullivan beat Thunderfoot I
Lazertron beat Denny Brown

10/4/87: Asheville, NC @ Civic Center
Robert Gibson beat Bobby Eaton

10/4/87: Macon, GA @ Coliseum
Robert Gibson & Jimmy Valiant beat The Midnight Express

10/5/87: Greenville, SC @ Memorial Auditorium
Ronnie Garvin beat Tully Blanchard
US Title Match: Lex Luger(c) beat Barry Windham
NWA World Tag Champs The Rock & Roll Express beat the Midnight Express
Kendall Windham & Lazor-Tron beat Thunderfoot #1 & Gladiator #1
Bugsy McGraw draw The Warlord
Kevin Sullivan beat Teijo Khan
Ricky Santana beat Colt Steele

10/6/87: Spartanburg, SC @ Memorial Auditorium (TV)
Rock & Roll Express & Dusty Rhodes vs. Arn Anderson, Lex Luger & JJ Dillon
NWA World Champ Ronnie Garvin vs. Tully Blanchard

10/7/87: Atlanta, GA @ WTBS Studios (TV)
Lex Luger vs. Rikki Nelson
Arn Anderson & Tully Blanchard vs. Alan Martin & Rusty Riddle
The Road Warriors vs. Larry Stephens & David Isley
Eddie Gilbert vs. The Menace
Ivan Koloff vs. Mike Jackson
The Canadian Kodiaks vs. Rocky King & Terry Jones
Kevin Sullivan vs. George South
NWA World Champ Ronnie Garvin vs. Mike Force
The Sheepherders vs. Keith Steinborn & Franks
The Warlord vs. Max MacGyver
Terry Taylor vs. Tommy Angel

10/7/87: Cleveland, OH @ Convocation Center (TV)
The Canadian Kodiaks beat Bob Morgan & Curtis Thompson
Kevin Sullivan beat David Isley
The Road Warriors beat Joe Lynn & Mac McGyver
Ric Flair, Lex Luger, Arn Anderson & Tully Blanchard beat Brad Armstrong, Tim Horner, Mike Rotundo & Barry Windham by DQ
Sting beat Colt Steele
The Road Warriors beat Mike Force & Bob Morgan
Jimmy Garvin & Michael Hayes beat Black Bart & Rick Steiner by DQ
Sheepherders beat Shane Douglas & Ron Simmons

Barry Windham beat Eddie Gilbert by DQ
NWA World Champ Ronnie Garvin beat Tully Blanchard by DQ
Dusty Rhodes & The Road Warriors beat Arn Anderson, Ric Flair & Lex Luger in a steel cage match

10/8/87: Pasadena, TX(Show cancelled)

10/8/87: North Wilkesboro, NC
Dusty Rhodes vs. ??

10/8/87: Hammond, IN
NWA World Champ Ronnie Garvin beat Ric Flair
The Road Warriors beat Lex Luger & Tully Blanchard

10/9/87: Charleston, WV @ Civic Center
Nelson Royal beat Teijo Khan by DQ
The Warlord beat Larry Stephens
Denny Brown beat John Savage
Kevin Sullivan beat Samurai Warrior #2
Mike Rotundo beat Samurai Warrior #1
Michael Hayes & Jimmy Garvin beat Teijo Khan & The Mod Squad Spike
Robert Gibson beat Arn Anderson
Tully Blanchard beat Ricky Morton

10/9/87: St. Louis, MO @ Kiel Auditorium
The Canadian Kodiaks beat Kendall Windham & Italian Stallion
Rick Steiner beat Shane Douglas
Bugsy McGraw beat The Terminator
Jimmy Valiant beat Black Bart
Ron Simmons NC with Ivan Koloff
The Road Warriors beat Sheepherders
Barry Windham draw Terry Taylor
NWA World Champ Ronnie Garvin beat Ric Flair

10/9/87: Albany, GA @ Civic Center
The Gladiator vs. Bill Mulkey
Gladiator #2 vs. Randy Mulkey
Lazertron vs. Thunderfoot
The Cuban Connection vs. The Mod Squad
Todd Champion vs. Mighty Wilbur
The Midnight Express vs. New Breed
Big Bubba beat George South
Bobby Eaton beat Chris Champ

10/10/87: Denver, CO @ City Auditorium
Rick Steiner beat Shane Douglas
The Canadian Kodiaks beat Kendall Windham & Italian Stallion
Bugsy McGraw beat The Terminator
Jimmy Valiant NC with Black Bart
Terry Taylor draw Ron Simmons
Michael Hayes & Jimmy Garvin beat Sheepherders DQ
Barry Windham beat Ivan Koloff
The Road Warriors beat Stan Lane & Big Bubba

10/10/87: Greensboro, NC @ Coliseum
NWA Champ Ronnie Garvin beat Ric Flair
Tully Blanchard beat Ricky Morton in a lumberjack match
Robert Gibson beat Arn Anderson
Lex Luger beat Sting
Kevin Sullivan beat The Mod Squad Basher via pinfall
New Breed beat Teijo Khan & The Warlord
Mike Rotundo beat Mighty Wilbur
Teijo Khan beat Rocky King

10/11/87: Columbus, OH @ Ohio Center
Barry Windham beat Dick Murdoch by DQ
Black Bart beat Jimmy Valiant
The Canadian Kodiaks beat Italian Stallion & Kendall Windham
The Midnight Express draw Michael Hayes & Jimmy Garvin
Terry Taylor beat Ron Simmons
Tim Horner & Brad Armstrong beat The Sheepherders
NWA World Champ Ronnie Garvin beat Ric Flair

10/11/87: Cincinnati, OH @ Gardens
Jimmy Valiant beat The Terminator
The Canadian Kodiaks beat Kendall Windham & Italian Stallion
Black Bart beat Bugsy McGraw by DQ
Terry Taylor beat Ron Simmons
The Midnight Express draw Michael Hayes & Jimmy Garvin
Barry Windham beat Dick Murdoch by DQ
Brad Armstrong & Tim Horner beat The Sheepherders
NWA World Champ Ronnie Garvin beat Ric Flair

10/11/87: Jacksonville, FL @ Coliseum
Bill Mulkey vs. The Warlord
Mike Graham & Steve Keirn vs. The Mighty Yankees
Eddie Gilbert vs. Sting
Mighty Wilbur vs. Kevin Sullivan
Lex Luger vs. Mike Rotundo
The Road Warriors vs. Dory Funk, Jr. & Ivan Koloff
Arn Anderson & Tully Blanchard vs. The Rock & Roll Express

10/11/87: Orlando, FL @ Eddie Graham Sports Complex
Arn Anderson & Tully Blanchard vs. The Road Warriors

10/12/87: Marion, VA
The Midnight Express beat Barry& Kendall Windham

10/12/87: West Palm Beach, FL @ Auditorium

10/12/87: Greenville, SC @ Memorial Auditorium
Ric Flair & Lex Luger beat Ronnie Garvin & Robert Gibson
Bunkhouse Match: the Road Warriors beat Tully Blanchard & Arn Anderson
Mike Rotunda beat Colt Steele
Lazor-Tron beat Teijo Khan
Mighty Wilbur beat Italian Stallion
Warlord beat Todd Champion

10/13/87: Shelby, NC @ Recreation Center (TV)
New Breed beat The Midnight Express by DQ

10/13/87: Spartanburg, SC @ Memorial Auditorium (TV)
Arn Anderson & Tully Blanchard beat Rocky King & George South
Barry Windham beat Colt Steele
Lex Luger beat Larry Stephens
Bugsy McGraw & Jimmy Valiant beat Cougar Jay & The Gladiator
Ronnie Garvin beat Thunderfoot
The Road Warriors beat Brodie Chase & Thunderfoot II
The Midnight Express beat David Isley & John Savage
Ronnie Garvin beat Colt Steele
Ivan Koloff & Mighty Wilbur beat Rocky King & George South
Lex Luger beat Brodie Chase
The Road Warriors beat Thunderfoot I & II
Midnight Express beat Italian Stallion & Kendall Windham
Bugsy McGraw & Jimmy Valiant beat Tommy Angel & David Isley

10/14/87: Atlanta, GA @ WTBS Studios (TV)

10/14/87: Philadelphia, PA @ Civic Center
Bugsy McGraw beat Teijo Khan
Mighty Wilbur beat Ivan Koloff by DQ
Jimmy Valiant beat The Warlord
Sting beat Eddie Gilbert
Jimmy Garvin & Michael Hayes draw Sheepherders
Mike Rotundo beat Rick Steiner
The Midnight Express beat New Breed
Ric Flair beat Nikita Koloff by DQ

10/15/87: Atlanta, GA @ WTBS Studios (TV)

10/16/87: Norfolk, VA @ Scope
Sean Royal draw The Mod Squad Basher
Bugsy McGraw beat The Mod Squad Spike
Kendall Windham beat Samurai Warrior #1
Mike Rotundo beat Samurai Warrior #2
Kevin Sullivan NC with The Warlord
New Breed beat The Midnight Express by DQ
Lex Luger beat Barry Windham
Tully Blanchard & Arn Anderson beat The Rock & Roll Express in a cage match

10/16/87: Kansas City, MO @ Kemper Arena (TV)
NWA World Champ Ronnie Garvin beat Ric Flair in a 2 of 3 falls match
Eddie Gilbert & Terry Taylor beat Sting & Shane Douglas in a bunkhouse match
Michael Hayes & Jimmy Garvin beat Sheepherders DQ
Ron Simmons beat Black Bart by DQ
The Sheepherders beat Brad Armstrong & Tim Horner to win UWF Tag Title
The Canadian Kodiaks beat ?? & ??
Sting & Shane Douglas beat Shaska Whatley & Tiger Conway, Jr.

10/17/87: Baltimore, MD @ Arena
Italian Stallion draw Samurai Warrior #2
Kendall Windham beat Samurai Warrior #1
Mike Rotundo beat Black Bart
Sting beat The Terminator
The Midnight Express beat Brad Armstrong & Tim Horner
Tully Blanchard & Arn Anderson beat The Rock & Roll Express
NWA World Champ Ronnie Garvin beat Ric Flair

10/17/87: Lakeland, FL @ Civic Center
Mike Graham & Steve Keirn beat The Mighty Yankees to win NWA Florida Tag Title

10/18/87: Roanoke, VA @ Civic Center
Gary Royal & Colt Steele beat Larry Stephens & John Savage
Mighty Wilbur beat Thunderfoot I
Kendall Windham beat George South
Robert Gibson beat Thunderfoot II
Nikita Koloff beat Big Bubba
New Breed beat The Midnight Express
Ricky Morton beat Tully Blanchard by DQ

10/18/87: Atlanta, GA @ Omni
David Sierra, Kendall Windham & Nelson Royal beat The Samurai Warriors & Black Assassin
Kevin Sullivan beat Teijo Khan
Bugsy McGraw & Jimmy Valiant beat The Mod Squad
Sting beat Terry Taylor by DQ
The Midnight Express beat New Breed
Nikita Koloff beat Eddie Gilbert
Tully Blanchard beat Ricky Morton in a lumberjack strap match

10/18/87: Detroit, MI @ Cobo Arena
Shaska Whatley beat Italian Stallion
Tim Horner beat Tiger Conway, Jr.
Brad Armstrong draw Rick Steiner
Mike Rotundo beat Dory Funk, Jr. by DQ
Michael Hayes & Jimmy Garvin beat Ivan Koloff & Warlord
Barry Windham NC with Arn Anderson
Ric Flair & Lex Luger beat Dusty Rhodes & Ronnie Garvin

10/19/87: New Orleans, LA @ UNO Lakefront Arena (TV)

10/19/87: Greenville, SC @ Memorial Auditorium
Lights Out Bunkhouse Match: Ricky Morton beat Tully Blanchard
US Tag Title Match: Midnight Express beat New Breed
Taped Fist Match: Arn Anderson beat Robert Gibson
Jimmy Valiant & Bugsy McGraw beat the Mod Squad
Nelson Royal beat Denny Brown
Mighty Wilbur beat Teijo Khan
Kendall Windham & Italian Stallion draw the Cuban Connection

10/20/87: Fayetteville, NC @ Cumberland County Civic Center (TV)
Jimmy Valiant & Bugsy McGraw vs. George South & John Savage

Mike Rotundo vs. Gladiator #1
Kevin Sullivan vs. Rocky King
Barry Windham vs. Samurai Warrior #1
Ivan Koloff, Warlord & Mighty Wilbur vs. Ricky Santana, David Sierra & Rikki Nelson
Arn Anderson & Tully Blanchard vs. Kendall Windham & Italian Stallion
The Midnight Express vs. New Breed
Arn Anderson & Tully Blanchard vs. John Savage & Rocky King
Barry Windham vs. George South
The Rock & Roll Express vs. Thunderfoot I & Thunderfoot II
The Midnight Express vs. Rikki Nelson & David Isley
Lex Luger vs. Kendall Windham
Mighty Wilbur vs. Tommy Angel

10/21/87: Greenwood, SC
New Breed beat The Midnight Express by DQ

10/21/87: Atlanta, GA @ WTBS Studios (TV)
Jimmy Valiant & Bugsy McGraw vs. ?? & ??
Barry Windham vs. John Savage
The Mighty Wilbur vs. David Isley
New Breed vs. Bob Riddle & Gladiator #1
Ivan Koloff & The Warlord vs. Rick Ryder & Rex King
Michael Hayes & Jimmy Garvin vs. Rick Idol & Thunderfoot I
Kevin Sullivan vs. Terry Jones
Arn Anderson & Tully Blanchard vs. Keith Steinborn & Rikki Nelson
Mike Rotundo vs. Alan Martin
Rock & Roll Express vs. Larry Stephens & Tony Suber
Midnight Express vs. George South & Italian Stallion

10/22/87: West Palm Beach, FL @ Auditorium
Bill Mulkey vs. Mighty Yankee #2
Mike Graham vs. Mighty Yankee #1
Steve Keirn beat Ivan Koloff
New Breed draw The Midnight Express(30:00)
Robert Gibson beat Dory Funk, Jr. by DQ
Ricky Morton beat Tully Blanchard in a Texas death match
Dusty Rhodes, Nikita Koloff & Kevin Sullivan beat Ric Flair, Lex Luger & Arn Anderson

10/23/87: Charlotte, NC @ Coliseum
The Midnight Express beat New Breed

10/23/87: Tallahassee, FL @ Leon County Civic Center

10/24/87: St. Petersburg, FL @ Bayfront Center (TV)
Dick Murdoch vs. Kendall Windham
Kevin Sullivan vs. Big Bubba
Dusty Rhodes vs. Lex Luger
Tully Blanchard & Arn Anderson vs. The Rock & Roll Express
also included Steve Keirn, Mike Graham, Bugsy McGraw, Jimmy Valiant, Mighty Yankees & Ivan Koloff

10/24/87: Philadelphia, PA @ Civic Center
Bugsy McGraw beat Teijo Khan
Mike Rotundo beat Rick Steiner
Jimmy Valiant beat The Warlord by DQ
Michael Hayes & Jimmy Garvin draw Luke Williams & Johnny Ace
Mighty Wilbur beat Ivan Koloff by CO
Sting beat Eddie Gilbert
The Midnight Express beat New Breed
Ric Flair beat Nikita Koloff by DQ

10/25/87: Greensboro, NC @ Coliseum
Ricky Santana beat The Mod Squad Basher
Kendall Windham beat The Mod Squad Spike
Mighty Wilbur beat Thunderfoot I
Ivan Koloff NC with Kevin Sullivan
Dusty Rhodes beat Hiro Matsuda
The Midnight Express beat New Breed
Barry Windham beat Arn Anderson
Ric Flair, Lex Luger & Tully Blanchard beat The Rock & Roll Express & Nikita Koloff

10/25/87: Jonesboro, AR
David Haskins draw The Terminator
Steve Cox beat Gary Young
The Canadian Kodiaks beat Ken Massey & The Enforcer
Tim Horner beat Black Bart
David Haskins beat Terry Taylor
Brad Armstrong & Tim Horner beat Shaska Whatley & Tiger Conway, Jr.

10/26/87: Greenville, SC @ Memorial Auditorium
Rock & Roll Express beat Ric Flair & Lex Luger
Tully Blanchard DCO Nikita Koloff
Western States Title Match: Barry Windham(c) beat Arn Anderson
Us Tag Title Match: the Midnight Express(c) beat the New Breed
Mike Rotunda beat Ivan Koloff
Kendall Windham & Italian Stallion beat Mod Squad
John Savage beat David Sierra

10/27/87: Columbia, SC @ Township Auditorium (TV)
Ivan Koloff & The Warlord vs. David Isley & Larry Stephens
NWA World Champ Ronnie Garvin vs. George South
Arn Anderson & Tully Blanchard vs. Ricky Santana & Cougar Jay
Mighty Wilbur vs. Thunderfoot II
Nikita Koloff vs. Gladiator #2
Jimmy Valiant & Bugsy McGraw vs. Chance McQuade & Tommy Angel
The Midnight Express vs. the Texas Cowboys(aka The Rock & Roll Express)

10/28/87: Atlanta, GA @ WTBS Studios (TV)

10/29/87: Atlanta, GA @ WTBS Studios (TV)

10/29/87: Harrisonburg, VA @ H.S.
Cuban Assassin I vs. Samurai Warrior #2
The Warlord vs. Cuban Assassin II
Denny Brown beat David Sierra
Italian Stallion beat Thunderfoot I
Jimmy Valiant beat Teijo Khan
Mighty Wilbur beat Ivan Koloff by DQ
The Rock & Roll Express beat Tully Blanchard & Arn Anderson by DQ

10/30/87: Norfolk, VA @ Scope
Nikita Koloff, Ronnie Garvin & The Rock & Roll Express beat Ric Flair, Lex Luger, Arn Anderson & Tully Blanchard by DQ
Barry Windham beat Ivan Koloff
The Midnight Express beat Chris Champ & Sean Royal
Jimmy Garvin & Michael Hayes beat Teijo Khan & The Warlord
Kevin Sullivan beat Denny Brown
Mike Rotundo beat Nelson Royal

11/1/87: Salisbury, MD @ Wicomico Youth & Civic Center (TV)
Nikita Koloff vs. David Isley
Arn Anderson & Tully Blanchard vs. Cougar Jay & Gary Royal
Mike Rotundo vs. Thunderfoot I
Ricky Santana vs. Rikki Nelson
Lex Luger & Hiro Matsuda vs. Italian Stallion & Larry Stephens
Kevin Sullivan vs. George South
Dusty Rhodes vs. Hiro Matsuda
Mighty Wilbur & The Rock & Roll Express vs. Thunderfoot II, Ivan Koloff & The Warlord
New Breed vs. Thunderfoot I & Thunderfoot II
Lex Luger vs. Larry Stephens
Hiro Matsuda vs. Rocky King
The Midnight Express vs. George South & Gary Royal
Barry Windham & Ricky Santana vs. Ivan Koloff & The Warlord
Shane Douglas & Tim Horner vs. ?? & ??
Ric Flair & Lex Luger vs. Dusty Rhodes & Ronnie Garvin

11/1/87: Asheville, NC @ Civic Center
The Rock & Roll Express beat The Midnight Express in a bunkhouse match

11/1/87: Orlando, FL @ Eddie Graham Sports Complex
Kendall Windham beat Bill Mulkey
Jimmy Valiant beat Thunderfoot II
Bugsy McGraw beat Thunderfoot
Mike Graham & Rex King beat The Barbarian & Dory Funk, Jr.
Kevin Sullivan beat Big Bubba by CO in a Louisville street fight match
Arn Anderson & Tully Blanchard beat Nikita Koloff & Barry Windham
The Rock & Roll Express beat The Midnight Express in a lights out, bunkhouse match

11/2/87: Fayetteville, NC @ Cumberland County Civic Center
Rick Steiner beat Cuban Assassin
Sting beat The Terminator
Mighty Wilbur beat Black Bart
Brad Armstrong & Tim Horner beat Luke Williams & Johnny Ace
Nikita Koloff beat Eddie Gilbert
Ric Flair beat Jimmy Garvin
Dusty Rhodes & Johnny Weaver beat Lex Luger & JJ Dillon

11/2/87: Greenville, SC @ Memorial Auditorium (TV)
Barry Windham beat Arn Anderson in a Texas death match
The Rock & Roll Express beat The Midnight Express in a bunkhouse match
Ronnie Garvin beat the Warlord
Bugsy McGraw & Jimmy Valiant vs Ivan Koloff & Barbarian
Sean Royal vs Mod Squad #1
Todd Champion vs Larry Zbyszko
Chris Champ vs Mod Squad #2

11/3/87: Rock Hill, SC @ Winthrop Coliseum (TV)
Johnny Weaver vs. James J. Dillon

11/3/87: Winston-Salem, NC @ Memorial Coliseum
The Rock & Roll Express beat The Midnight Express in a bunkhouse match

11/3/87: Columbia, SC @ Township Auditorium (TV)
New Breed beat Thunderfoot I & Thunderfoot II
Lex Luger beat Larry Stephens
Hiro Matsuda beat Rocky King
The Midnight Express beat Gary Royal & George South
Ricky Santana & Barry Windham beat Ivan Koloff & The Warlord by DQ
Nikita Koloff beat David Isley
Arn Anderson & Tully Blanchard beat Cougar Jay & Gary Royal
Mike Rotundo beat Thunderfoot
Ricky Santana beat Rikki Nelson
Lex Luger & Hiro Matsuda beat Italian Stallion & Larry Stephens
Kevin Sullivan beat George South
Mighty Wilbur & The Rock & Roll Express beat Ivan Koloff, Thunderfoot II & The Warlord

11/4/87: Monroe, NC
The Midnight Express beat New Breed

11/4/87: Portsmouth, VA @ Grant Middle School
Ron Simmons vs. Larry Zbyszko
Brad Armstrong & Tim Horner vs. The Sheepherders
Sting vs. Terry Taylor
Tully Blanchard vs. Michael Hayes
Ric Flair & Lex Luger vs. Ronnie Garvin & Nikita Koloff

11/5/87: Raleigh, NC @ Dorton Arena
Rick Steiner beat Denny Brown
Italian Stallion & John Savage beat The Canadian Kodiaks
Jimmy Valiant beat The Terminator
Bugsy McGraw beat The Barbarian
Mighty Wilbur beat Terry Taylor by DQ
Michael Hayes, Jimmy Garvin & Mike Rotundo beat James J. Dillon, Tully Blanchard & Lex Luger
Nikita Koloff beat Eddie Gilbert
The Rock & Roll Express beat The Midnight Express

11/5/87: Portsmouth, OH @ Grant Middle School
Ronnie Garvin & Nikita Koloff vs. Lex Luger & Ric Flair
Tully Blanchard vs. Michael Hayes
Terry Taylor vs. Sting
Brad Armstrong & Tim Horner vs. The Sheepherders
Larry Zbyszko vs. Ron Simmons

11/5/87: Cocoa, FL @ Brevard County Fair

11/6/87: Marion, NC
The Midnight Express beat New Breed

11/7/87: Akron, OH
Kendall Windham beat Thunderfoot I
Bugsy McGraw & Jimmy Valiant beat The Canadian Kodiaks
Mike Rotundo beat Big Bubba by DQ
Jimmy Garvin & Mighty Wilbur beat The Barbarian & The Warlord via pinfall
Michael Hayes beat Ivan Koloff via pinfall
The Rock & Roll Express beat The Midnight Express via pinfall in a bunkhouse match
Dusty Rhodes beat Lex Luger by DQ

11/8/87: Atlanta, GA @ Omni
Rick Steiner draw Kevin Sullivan
Michael Hayes beat The Warlord
Mighty Wilbur beat Barbarian by DQ
Ivan Koloff beat Mike Rotundo
NWA World Champ Ronnie Garvin beat The Gladiators in a handicap match
Ric Flair beat Kendall Windham & Italian Stallion in a handicap match
Hiro Matsuda beat Johnny Weaver
Lex Luger beat Jimmy Garvin
Dusty Rhodes & Nikita Koloff beat Terry Taylor & Eddie Gilbert
The Midnight Express, Tully Blanchard & Arn Anderson NC with The Rock & Roll Express & New Breed

11/8/87: Anaheim, CA @ Convention Center
The Road Warriors beat Luke Williams & Johnny Ace
Larry Zbyszko draw Barry Windham
The Terminator beat Golden Bear
Shaska Whatley beat Samoan Tau
Brad Armstrong & Tim Horner beat The Canadian Kodiaks
Steve Williams beat Dory Funk, Jr. by DQ
Ron Simmons beat Black Bart

11/9/87: San Francisco, CA @ Civic Auditorium
Shaska Whatley beat George Wells
Ron Simmons beat Black Bart
Brad Armstrong & Tim Horner beat The Canadian Kodiaks
Nikita Koloff beat Eddie Gilbert
Barry Windham NC with Larry Zbyszko
The Road Warriors beat Luke Williams & Johnny Ace
Steve Williams beat Dory Funk, Jr. by DQ
Jimmy & Ronnie Garvin beat Ric Flair & Lex Luger

11/9/87: Toccoa, GA
The Rock & Roll Express beat The Midnight Express

11/10/87: Jacksonville, NC
The Midnight Express beat New Breed

11/10/87: Spartanburg, SC @ Memorial Auditorium (TV)
Sting beat Tommy Angel
Larry Zbyszko beat Curtis Thompson
Eddie Gilbert & Terry Taylor beat Rocky King & Rikki Nelson
Barry Windham beat Rick Steiner by DQ
Ron Simmons beat Tommy Angel
Arn Anderson, Tully Blanchard & Lex Luger beat Cougar Jay, David Isley & Rikki Nelson
Ronnie Garvin beat Larry Stephens
Larry Zbyszko beat Kendall Windham
Rick Steiner beat Rocky King
Michael Hayes & Sting beat Cougar Jay & Gene Ligon
Eddie Gilbert vs. Nikita Koloff
Ric Flair & Lex Luger vs. Jimmy Garvin & Ronnie Garvin

11/11/87: Atlanta, GA @ WTBS Studios (TV)

11/12/87: Atlanta, GA @ WTBS Studios (TV)

11/13/87: Hampton, VA @ Coliseum
Ronnie Garvin & Nikita Koloff beat Ric Flair & Tully Blanchard
The Road Warriors beat Ivan Koloff & The Warlord
Dusty Rhodes & Johnny Weaver beat Hiro Matsuda & Lex Luger
Terry Taylor beat Mark Fleming
Ricky Morton beat Arn Anderson lumberjack match
Robert Gibson beat The Barbarian by DQ
Mike Rotundo beat Thunderfoot I
Rick Steiner draw Ricky Santana

11/13/87: West Palm Beach, FL @ Auditorium
Mike Graham, Kevin Sullivan & Rocky King beat The Midnight Express & Big Bubba

11/14/87: Sarasota, FL @ Robarts Arena
The Midnight Express beat Mike Graham & Rocky King

11/15/87: Oklahoma City, OK @ Myriad
Bobby Eaton beat ??
Big Bubba beat ??
Kevin Sullivan beat Stan Lane

11/15/87: Tulsa, OK @ Convention Center (TV)
Barry Windham beat Larry Zbyszko by DQ
Dusty Rhodes & Nikita Koloff beat Terry Taylor & Eddie Gilbert

11/16/87: Inglewood, CA @ Great Western Forum
Shaska Whatley & Tiger Conway Jr. beat Billy Anderson & Tim Patterson
Ron Simmons beat The Terminator via pinfall
Sting beat Black Bart via pinfall
Brad Armstrong & Tim Horner beat Luke Williams & Johnny Ace
Michael Hayes beat Terry Taylor by DQ
Barry Windham DCO with Larry Zbyszko
Nikita Koloff beat Eddie Gilbert
Ric Flair & Lex Luger beat Ronnie Garvin & Steve Williams elimination match

11/16/87: Greenville, SC @ Memorial Auditorium
US Tag Title Match: Midnight Express(c) beat New Breed
The Rock & Roll Express & Mighty Wilbur beat Ivan Koloff, Warlord & Barbarian
Kevin Sullivan beat Hiro Matsuda
Rick Steiner & Denny Brown draw Rocky King & Italian Stallion
John Savage beat Thunderfoot #1
Rick Nelson draw Larry Stephens

11/17/87: Columbia, SC @ Township Auditorium (TV)
The Midnight Express beat Larry Stephens & John Savage(1:56) via pinfall
Mike Rotundo beat David Isley(2:02) via pinfall
Mighty Wilbur beat Gene Ligon(:49) via pinfall
Ricky Santana beat Thunderfoot I(Joel Deaton)(3:55) via pinfall
Nelson Royal beat Denny Brown via pinfall to win vacant NWA World Junior Title
Rick Steiner beat George South(2:28) via pinfall
Barbarian, Warlord & Ivan Koloff beat Curtis Thompson, Max MacGyver & Chance McQuadel
Jimmy Valiant & Bugsy McGraw beat George South & Thunderfoot I
Ricky Santana beat Gary Royal via pinfall
Rick Steiner beat Tommy Angel(3:20) via pinfall
The Midnight Express beat The Rock & Roll Express by DQ
Larry Zbyszko vs. David Isley
Arn Anderson & Tully Blanchard vs. Mike Rotundo & Ricky Santana
The Rock & Roll Express vs. Tony Suber & Max MacGyver
Nikita Koloff vs. Eddie Gilbert

11/18/87: Lincolnton, NC
The Midnight Express beat New Breed

11/19/87: Troy, OH
The Midnight Express vs. The Rock & Roll Express

11/20/87: Williamson, WV @ Fieldhouse
Ric Flair vs. Nikita Koloff
The Midnight Express vs. The Rock & Roll Express in a bunkhouse match
Lex Luger vs. Barry Windham
Michael Hayes vs. Larry Zbyszko
Also including Black Bart, Sting, Brad Armstrong, Terry Taylor & others

11/20/87: Bluefield, WV @ Brushfork Armory Civic Center
Arn Anderson & Tully Blanchard vs. Ronnie & Jimmy Garvin
Kendall Windham vs. Rick Steiner
Denny Brown vs. John Savage
Mighty Wilbur vs. Ivan Koloff
New Breed vs. The Warlord & The Barbarian
Cuban Assassin(aka David Sierra) vs. Samurai Warrior #2
Ricky Santana vs. Samurai Warrior #1

11/21/87: Washington, DC @ Armory
Dusty Rhodes beat Lex Luger in a bullrope match
Road Warriors beat Ric Flair & Tully Blanchard by DQ
The Rock & Roll Express beat The Midnight Express in a bunkhouse match
NWA World Champ Ronnie Garvin beat Arn Anderson
Michael Hayes & Jimmy Garvin beat Eddie Gilbert & Terry Taylor
Steve Williams beat Rick Steiner
Sting beat Larry Zbyszko by DQ
Kevin Sullivan draw The Barbarian

11/22/87: Johnstown, PA
Eddie Gilbert beat Jimmy Jackson
Big Bubba beat John Gavin
Kevin Sullivan draw Rick Steiner
Paul Ellering beat James J. Dillon
Arn Anderson beat Robert Gibson
Ricky Morton beat Tully Blanchard
The Road Warriors beat The Midnight Express

11/22/87: Boone, NC
The Rock & Roll Express beat The Midnight Express

11/23/87: Greenville, SC @ Memorial Auditorium
Road Warriors & Paul Ellering vs Ric Flair, Tully Blanchard & JJ Dillon
Johnny Weaver vs Hiro Matsuda
Nikita Koloff vs Eddie Gilbert
Barry Windham vs Rick Steiner
New Breed vs Black Bart & Barbarian
John savage vs Nelson Royal

11/23/87: Bennettsville, SC
The Rock & Roll Express beat The Midnight Express by DQ
Bugsy McGraw & Jimmy Valiant beat George South & Thunderfoot I
Ricky Santana beat Gary Royal
Rick Steiner beat Tommy Angel

11/24/87: Hillsville, VA
John Savage beat Gladiator #1
Ricky Santana beat Rocky King
Mike Rotundo beat Thunderfoot I
Kevin Sullivan beat Eddie Gilbert
Rick Steiner beat Kendall Windham
Jimmy Valiant, Bugsy McGraw & Mighty Wilbur beat The Barbarian, The Warlord, Ivan Koloff by DQ
Barry Windham beat Arn Anderson

11/24/87: Columbia, SC @ Township Auditorium (TV)
The Midnight Express beat John Savage & Larry Stephens
Mike Rotundo beat David Isley
Mighty Wilbur beat Gene Ligon
Ricky Santana beat Thunderfoot
Nelson Royal beat Denny Brown
Rick Steiner beat George South
Ivan Koloff, The Barbarian & The Warlord beat Max McGyver, Chance McQuade & Curtis Thompson

11/25/87: Uniondale, NY @ Nassau Coliseum
Sting & Ron Simmons draw Terry Taylor & The Barbarian
Larry Zbyszko beat Kevin Sullivan
Jimmy Valiant, Bugsy McGraw & Mighty Wilbur beat Black Bart, The Warlord & Ivan Koloff
Michael Hayes & Jimmy Garvin beat Shaska Whatley & Tiger Conway, Jr.
Steve Williams beat Rick Steiner
The Sheepherders beat Brad Armstrong & Tim Horner
Nikita Koloff beat Eddie Gilbert
The Road Warriors beat Ric Flair & Lex Luger by DQ
Ronnie Garvin, Dusty Rhodes, Barry Windham & The Rock & Roll Express beat Big Bubba, Arn Anderson, Tully Blanchard & The Midnight Express by submission

11/26/87: Chicago, IL @ UIC Pavilion
Starrcade 87: Chi-Town Heat
Michael Hayes, Jimmy Garvin & Sting draw Eddie Gilbert, Rick Steiner & Larry Zbyszko (15:00)
Steve Williams beat Barry Windham
Rock & Roll Express beat The Midnight Express (9:00) in a scaffold match
Nikita Koloff beat Terry Taylor to win UWF Television Title & unify it with NWA World Television Title
Arn Anderson & Tully Blanchard beat The Road Warriors (13:24) by DQ
Dusty Rhodes beat Lex Luger(16:24) Cage Match wins NWA United States Title
Ric Flair beat Ronnie Garvin (17:38) to win NWA World Title in cage match

11/26/87: Greensboro, NC @ Coliseum
The Warlord beat Ricky Santana
Mike Rotundo beat Black Bart
Misty Blue won a 7-woman, $15,000 battle royal that also included Kat Laroux, Linda Dallas, Jamie West, Venus, Mad Dog Debbie & Whitney Hansen
Kevin Sullivan beat Hiro Matsuda
Mighty Wilbur beat Ivan Koloff

11/26/87: New Orleans, LA @ UNO Lakefront Arena
Bugsy McGraw & Jimmy Valiant beat The Jive Tones
Ron Simmons beat Johnny Ace
Sean Royal beat Killer Khalifa
Sheepherders beat Brad Armstrong & Tim Horner DQ

11/28/87: Atlanta, GA @ WTBS Studios (TV)

11/28/87: St. Petersburg, FL @ Bayfront Center
NWA World Champ Ric Flair beat Ronnie Garvin
Dusty Rhodes & The Road Warriors beat Lex Luger, Tully Blanchard & Arn Anderson by DQ
The Rock & Roll Express beat The Midnight Express
Barry Windham draw Larry Zbyszko
Nikita Koloff beat Eddie Gilbert
Michael Hayes, Jimmy Garvin & Sting beat Ivan Koloff, Warlord & Barbarian
Bugsy McGraw beat Mighty Yankee #1
Mighty Yankee #2 beat Rick Ryder

12/1/87: Monroe, LA (TV)
Steve Williams beat The Red Devil
The Midnight Express beat Tug Taylor & Bob War
Barry Windham beat Black Bart
The Road Warriors beat Ron Ellis & Jerry Newton
NWA World Champ Ric Flair beat Kendall Windham
Mike Rotundo beat Tug Taylor
The Rock & Roll Express beat The Shadow & Phil Wiley
Lex Luger beat Jerry Newton
Ron Simmons, Sting & Steve Williams beat Terry Hayes, Chan Torres & Bob War
Bunkhouse Stampede battle royal
Steve Williams vs. Tug Taylor
Michael Hayes vs. ??
Larry Zbyszko vs. Ron Ellis
The Road Warriors vs. Terry Hays & Chan Torrez
The Rock & Roll Express vs. Jerry Newton & Craig Wintford
Michael Hayes & Jimmy Garvin vs. Arn Anderson & Tully Blanchard

12/2/87: Miami, FL @ Convention Center
Lex Luger won a bunkhouse stampede
Note: During this battle royal, Luger turned on the Four Horsemen
NWA World Champ Ric Flair beat Michael Hayes
Barry Windham draw Larry Zbyszko

12/3/87: Atlanta, GA @ WTBS Studios (TV)
Barry Windham vs. Larry Zbyszko
The Warlord & The Barbarian vs. ?? Towers & Robbie Idol
Steve Williams vs. Jerry Grey
Sting vs. Bob Cook
Stan Lane vs. Kendall Windham
Arn Anderson & Tully Blanchard vs. Gary Royal & Italian Stallion
Nikita Koloff vs. Mark Starr
Kevin Sullivan vs. Rick Ryder
Bobby Eaton vs. Rex King
Mike Rotundo vs. Thunderfoot I
NWA World Champ Ric Flair vs. Michael Hayes

12/4/87: Hampton, VA @ Coliseum (TV)
Michael Hayes & Jimmy Garvin vs. Cougar Jay & David Isley
The Warlord & The Barbarian vs. Tommy Angel & ??
Nikita Koloff vs. John Savage
Mighty Wilbur vs. ??
The Midnight Express beat Ricky Santana & Mike Rotundo
Bunkhouse Stampede battle royal

12/4/87: Alexandria, LA @ Rapides Parish Coliseum
Larry Zbyszko beat Brad Armstrong
Tim Horner beat Black Bart
Jimmy Valiant & Bugsy McGraw beat Shaska Whatley & Tiger Conway, Jr. by DQ
Steve Williams draw Barry Windham
The Sheepherders beat Chris Champ & Ron Simmons
Sting won a bunkhouse stampede that also included Tiger Conway, Jr., Steve Williams, The Sheepherders, Johnny Ace, Larry Zbyszko, Barry Windham, Eddie Gilbert, Brad Armstrong, Jimmy Valiant, Ron Simmons, Tim Horner, Black Bart, Chris Champ, Bugsy McGraw, Terry Taylor & Shaska Whatley

12/6/87: Atlanta, GA @ Omni
Bugsy McGraw draw The Barbarian
Larry Zbyszko beat Ricky Santana
The Sheepherders draw Brad Armstrong & Tim Horner
Sting beat Terry Taylor
Steve Williams & Ron Simmons beat Kevin Sullivan & Black Assassin
Nikita Koloff beat Eddie Gilbert in a chain match
The Road Warriors beat Ric Flair & Arn Anderson by DQ
Arn Anderson, Tully Blanchard & The Midnight Express beat The Rock & Roll Express & New Breed in a cage match

12/6/87: Charlotte, NC @ Coliseum (TV)
Eddie Gilbert & Terry Taylor beat Denny Brown & John Savage
The Rock & Roll Express beat Rikki Nelson & Keith Jackson
Sting beat Gladiator #2
The Road Warriors beat Thunderfoot I & Gladiator II
Larry Zbyszko beat Rocky King
Mighty Wilbur beat Arn Anderson
Bobby Knight beat Italian Stallion
Ivan Koloff & The Warlord beat Rocky King & Jason McGraw
Mike Rotundo beat John Savage
Nikita Koloff beat Thunderfoot II
Steve Williams beat Gladiator #2
Larry Zbyszko beat Italian Stallion
The Midnight Express DDQ Michael Hayes & Jimmy Garvin
The Road Warriors & Paul Ellering beat Tully Blanchard, Arn Anderson & James J. Dillon
NWA World Champ Ric Flair beat Sting

12/7/87: Lafayette, LA @ Cajundome
Mike Rotundo beat Kendall Windham
Ron Simmons beat Tiger Conway Jr.
Jimmy Garvin & Michael Hayes draw The Sheepherders
Ronnie Garvin & Nikita Koloff beat Eddie Gilbert & Terry Taylor
NWA World Champ Ric Flair beat Sting
Nikita Koloff won a 26-man Bunkhouse Stampede battle royal

12/7/87: Greenville, SC @ Memorial Auditorium
#1 Contender for US Tag Titles: Ivan Koloff & Warlord beat the New Breed
Barbarian beat Bugsy McGraw
Jimmy Valiant beat Thunderfoot #1
Rocky King beat John Savage
Nelson Royal beat Italian Stallion
Denny Brown beat Ricky Nelson

12/8/87: Baton Rouge, LA @ Centroplex
Jimmy Garvin & Michael Hayes beat Don Brown & David Spencer
Bobby Eaton beat Terry Jones
Larry Zbyszko beat Tim Horner
Ronnie Garvin beat Alan Martin
Sting beat Steve Atkinson
The Road Warriors beat The Maniac & Lee Peek
The Rock & Roll Express beat The Sheepherders by DQ
Sting beat Gene Miller
Steve Williams beat Keith Steinborn
Larry Zbyszko beat Ed Franks
Nikita Koloff beat Mike Rotundo
Big Bubba won a Bunkhouse Stampede battle royal

12/9/87: Atlanta, GA @ WTBS Studios (TV)

12/10/87: Raleigh, NC @ Dorton Arena
Michael Hayes won a Bunkhouse Stampede battle royal
NWA World Champ Ric Flair NC with Jimmy Garvin
Dusty Rhodes & Nikita Koloff beat The Midnight Express by DQ

12/11/87: Houston, TX @ The Summit
Mighty Wilbur beat Shaska Whatley
Larry Zbyszko beat Tim Horner
Michael Hayes beat Black Bart
Ron Simmons & Steve Williams beat The Sheepherders
NWA World Champ Ric Flair beat Sting
Steve Williams won a Bunkhouse Stampede battle royal

12/12/87: Atlanta, GA @ WTBS Studios (TV)
Brad Armstrong & Tim Horner beat Cougar Jay & Gary Royal
Barry Windham beat Trent Knight
Jimmy Garvin & Michael Hayes beat David Isley & John Savage
Steve Williams beat Gladiator #2
Ronnie Garvin beat Larry Stephens
Mighty Wilbur & Ricky Santana beat Brown & Lynn
Sting beat Tommy Angel

Larry Zbyszko beat Rocky King
Nikita Koloff beat Thunderfoot
The Midnight Express beat Italian Stallion & George South

12/12/87: Baltimore, MD @ Arena
Road Warrior Hawk won a bunkhouse stampede
Michael Hayes beat NWA World Champ Ric Flair by DQ
Steve Williams beat Terry Taylor
Eddie Gilbert beat Nikita Koloff by DQ
Sting draw The Barbarian
Larry Zbyszko beat Mighty Wilbur

12/12/87: Greensboro, NC @ Coliseum
Lex Luger won a 25-man Bunkhouse Stampede
NWA World Champ Ric Flair beat Sting
Kevin Sullivan beat Rocky King
Steve Williams beat Tommy Salvage
The Warlord beat George South
Ricky Morton bested Mike Force
Ronnie Garvin topped Thunderfoot I
Sting beat Thunderfoot II
Eddie Gilbert beat George South
Nikita Koloff & Dusty Rhodes beat Tully Blanchard & Arn Anderson
The Midnight Express beat Mike Force & Cougar Jay
Tully Blanchard & Arn Anderson beat Gary Royal & John Salvage
The Road Warriors beat Chance McQuade & Larry Stephens
The Midnight Express & Big Bubba beat Mighty Wilbur, Italian Stallion & Kendall Windham

12/13/87: Albany GA @ Civic Center (TV)
Ivan Koloff beat Chris Champ
The Midnight Express beat Denny Brown & George South
Dusty Rhodes & Nikita Koloff beat Tully Blanchard & Arn Anderson by DQ
NWA World Champ Ric Flair beat Ronnie Garvin
Tully Blanchard won a bunkhouse stampede
Nikita Koloff vs. Thunderfoot II
Ivan Koloff & the Warlord vs. Rocky King & Jessie McClain
Mike Rotundo vs. John Savage
Steve Williams vs. Gladiator #1
Larry Zbyszko vs. Italian Stallion
Michael Hayes & Jimmy Garvin vs Midnight Express
The Sheepherders vs. The Rock & Roll Express
Sting vs. Gene Miller
Steve Williams vs. Keith Steinborn
Larry Zbyszko vs. Ed Franks
Nikita Koloff vs. Mike Rotundo

12/13/87: Cincinnati, OH @ Gardens
Tully Blanchard & Arn Anderson draw Dusty Rhodes & Nikita Koloff
Steve Williams beat Jim Lancaster
Ivan Koloff beat Mike Rotundo
Larry Zbyszko beat Mighty Wilbur by CO
NWA World Champ Ric Flair beat Sting
Mighty Wilbur won a Bunkhouse Stampede battle royal

12/14/87: to 12/24/87:
No wrestling due to Christmas break

12/25/87: Greenville, SC @ Memorial Auditorium
$20,000 25 Man Bunkhouse Stampede
-Barbarian
Nelson Royal draw Kendall Windham
Ricky Santana beat Thunderfoot #1
Mike Rotundo beat Italian Stallion
Shaska Whatley beat Rocky King
Lightning Express beat the Barbarian & John King

12/25/87: Atlanta, GA @ Omni
Lex Luger won a Bunkhouse Stampede battle royal

12/25/87: Charlotte, NC @ Coliseum
Bunkhouse Stampede battle royal

12/26/87: Richmond, VA @ Coliseum (TV)
Bunkhouse Stampede battle royal
Michael Hayes & Jimmy Garvin vs. Dave Spencer & ??
Bobby Eaton vs. Randy Mulkey
Larry Zbyszko vs. Tim Horner
Ronnie Garvin vs. Alan Martin
Sting vs. Steve Atkinson
The Road Warriors vs. The Menace & ??
Ronnie Garvin & Mighty Wilbur vs. Chance McQuade & Tommy Angel
The Road Warriors vs. Bob Emory & Trent Knight
Larry Zbyszko vs. Rikki Nelson
Sting vs. Mark Fleming
Steve Williams vs. Curtis Thompson
Eddie Gilbert vs. George South
Michael Hayes vs. Larry Stephens
The Midnight Express vs. Dusty Rhodes & Nikita Koloff
Mike Rotundo vs. David Isley

12/26/87: Detroit, MI @ Cobo Arena
Black Bart draw Tim Horner
Mike Rotundo beat Italian Stallion
Jimmy Garvin beat Ivan Koloff
Nikita Koloff draw Dick Murdoch
Road Warrior Hawk won Bunkhouse Stampede battle royal

12/26/87: Philadelphia, PA @ Civic Center
The Barbarian beat Ricky Santana
The Warlord beat Ronnie Garvin by CO
Barry Windham draw Bobby Eaton
Dusty Rhodes beat Tully Blanchard by DQ
NWA World Champ Ric Flair beat Sting
The Warlord won a 20-man Bunkhouse Stampede battle royal

12/27/87: Charleston, WV @ Civic Center (TV)
Road Warrior Animal won a Bunkhouse Stampede battle royal
NWA World Champ Ric Flair beat Michael Hayes
Barry Windham & Sting beat Tully Blanchard & Arn Anderson by DQ
Bobby Eaton beat Chris Champ
Kendall Windham beat Gary Royal

The Sheepherders beat David Isley & Tommy Angel(4:18) via pinfall
Bobby Eaton beat Mark Fleming(3:41) via pinfall
Mike Rotundo beat Chance McQuade(1:53) via pinfall
Shaska Whatley & Tiger Conway, Jr. beat Mike Force & Gene Ligon
Black Bart beat George South(3:15) via pinfall
Tully Blanchard & Arn Anderson beat Larry Stephens & Kendal Windham

12/27/87: Norfolk, VA @ Scope
Bobby Eaton draw Barry Windham(20:00)

12/28/87: St. Louis, MO @ Kiel Auditorium (TV)
Ronnie Garvin beat Arn Anderson by DQ
Dusty Rhodes & The Road Warriors beat The Warlord, Barbarian & Ivan Koloff
Michael Hayes & Jimmy Garvin beat Arn Anderson & Tully Blanchard by DQ
NWA World Champ Ric Flair beat Sting
Steve Williams won a Bunkhouse Stampede battle royal
Ricky Morton vs. Mike Force
Ronnie Garvin vs. Thunderfoot I
Eddie Gilbert vs. George South
Dusty Rhodes & Nikita Koloff vs. Arn Anderson & Tully Blanchard
Big Bubba & The Midnight Express vs. Kendall Windham, Italian Stallion & Mighty Wilbur

12/29/87: Savannah, GA @ Civic Center
Bunkhouse Stampede battle royal

12/30/87: Chicago, IL @ UIC Pavilion
Jimmy Garvin beat Eddie Gilbert
Ron Simmons beat Johnny Ace
Barry Windham beat Larry Zbyszko by DQ
Nikita Koloff draw Dick Murdoch
NWA World Champ Ric Flair beat Sting
Road Warrior Animal won a Bunkhouse Stampede battle royal

12/31/87: Atlanta, GA @ WTBS Studios (TV)
Michael Hayes & Jimmy Garvin vs. ?? Bradley & Alan Martin
Lex Luger vs. Keith Steinborn
Dick Murdoch vs. Jason Walker
Eddie Gilbert vs. Steve Atkinson
The Midnight Express vs. Mike Jackson & Mark Starr
Larry Zbyzsko vs. Lee Peak
Nikita Koloff vs. The Menace
Arn Anderson vs. Ronnie Garvin
Dusty Rhodes & The Road Warriors vs. Ivan Koloff, The Warlord & The Barbarian

Chapter 9: 1988

1/1/88: Atlanta, GA @ Omni
Dusty Rhodes won a bunkhouse battle royal
NWA World Champ Ric Flair beat Michael Hayes
Lex Luger & Ole Anderson beat Tully Blanchard & Arn Anderson
Road Warrior Animal beat The Warlord
Barry Windham draw Larry Zbyszko
The Sheepherders (Luke Williams & Butch Miller) beat Robert Gibson & Ricky Santana
Ron Garvin beat Eddie Gilbert
Sting, Jimmy Garvin & Ricky Santana beat Terry Taylor, Mike Rotundo & Kevin Sullivan

1/2/88: Asheville, NC @ Civic Center
Stan Lane beat Chris Champ
Nikita Koloff beat Bobby Eaton

1/2/88: Greensboro, NC @ Coliseum
NWA World Champ Ric Flair beat Michael Hayes by DQ
Lex Luger beat Arn Anderson
Dusty Rhodes beat Larry Zbyszko by DQ
The Road Warriors beat The Warlord & Ivan Koloff
Tully Blanchard beat Jimmy Garvin in a Texas death match
The Sheepherders beat Ricky Santana & Robert Gibson
Brad Armstrong & Tim Horner beat The Gladiators
Dick Murdoch beat Italian Stallion

1/3/88: Baltimore, MD @ Civic Center (TV)
Dick Murdoch draw Nikita Koloff (20:00)
Michael Hayes & Jimmy Garvin vs. ?? & ??
Kevin Sullivan vs. George South
Dick Murdoch vs. ??
Barry Windham vs. ??
Eddie Gilbert vs. ??
Nikita Koloff vs. Tommy Angel
Ric Flair, Arn Anderson & Tully Blanchard vs. ??
Sting vs. The Warlord
NWA World Champ Ric Flair beat Michael Hayes

1/3/88: Greenville, SC @ Memorial Auditorium
Lex Luger beat Arn Anderson
Ric Flair beat Michael Hayes NWA World title match
Steve Williams beat Dick Murdoch
Tully Blanchard beat Jimmy Garvin
Sting beat Eddie Gilbert
Ricky Santana beat Terry Taylor
Lightning Express beat Italian Stallion & Chris Champ
Shaska Whatley beat Jimmy Valiant

1/4/88: Macon, GA @ Coliseum

1/5/88: Spartanburg, SC @ Memorial Auditorium
The Rock & Roll Express (Ricky Morton & Robert Gibson) vs. The Sheepherders
Ron Simmons & Sting vs. The Midnight Express (Bobby Eaton & Stan Lane)
Mighty Wilbur vs. Dick Murdoch
Italian Stallion vs. Larry Zbyszko
Sean Royal vs. Tim Horner
Chris Champ vs. Brad Armstrong

1/5/88: Albany, GA @ Civic Center
Ronnie Garvin vs. Terry Taylor
Black Bart vs. Lex Luger
Ivan Koloff & The Warlord vs. The Road Warriors
Arn Anderson & Tully Blanchard vs. Jimmy Garvin & Michael Hayes
NWA World Champ Ric Flair vs. Nikita Koloff

1/6/88: Atlanta, GA @ WTBS Studios (TV)
Sting & Barry Windham beat Tommy Angel & Alan Martin
The Midnight Express beat Mac McGyver & Lee Peek
Nikita Koloff beat Jeff Crews
The Barbarian beat Steve Atkins
Ron Simmons beat David Isley
Larry Zbyszko beat Cougar Jay
Brad Armstrong & Tim Horner beat Trent Knight & Rusty Riddle
The Warlord beat Larry Stevens
Lex Luger beat Curtis Thompson
Dick Murdoch beat Ricky Nelson
The Road Warriors beat Ken Bolin & Dale Laperouse
The Sheepherders beat Italian Stallion & Mike Jackson
Black Bart beat Ricky Nelson (3:42) via pinfall
Eddie Gilbert & Terry Taylor beat Italian Stallion & Tommy Angel (4:24)
Dick Murdoch beat David Isley (4:22)
Warlord & Barbarian beat Larry Stephens & Trent Knight
Sting beat Lee Peak (:27) by submission
Midnight Express beat Mike Jackson & Alan Martin

1/7/88: Jacksonville, FL @ Veterans Memorial Coliseum

1/8/88: Newton, NC (Card cancelled due to snow)

1/9/88: Huntington, WV @ Civic Center
Dusty Rhodes & Nikita Koloff beat The Midnight Express in a steel cage match

1/10/88: Greenville, SC @ Memorial Auditorium
Ron Garvin & Sting beat The Midnight Express by DQ
Nikita Koloff beat Tully Blanchard
Robert Gibson beat Luke Williams
Mike Rotundo beat Ricky Santana
The Warlord beat the Italian Stallion
Ron Simmons beat Kevin Sullivan
Jimmy Valiant beat Black Bart
Kendall Windham beat Johnny Ace
Chris Champ beat John Savage

1/10/88: Charlotte, NC @ Coliseum
Dick Murdoch & Midnight Express beat Italian Stallion, Brad_Armstrong & Tim Horner
Midnight Express NC with Dusty Rhodes & Nikita Koloff steel cage match

1/10/88: Columbus, OH @ Ohio Center
NWA World Champ Ric Flair beat Michael Hayes
Lex Luger beat Arn Anderson
Barry Windham NC with The Barbarian
Road Warrior Hawk beat Ivan Koloff
Jimmy Garvin beat Al Snow
Brad Armstrong beat Jim Lancaster

1/11/88: Fayetteville, NC @ Cumberland County Civic Center
Ron Simmons beat Black Bart
Stan Lane beat Jimmy Valiant
Sting, Ron & Jimmy Garvin beat Kevin Sullivan, Dick Murdoch & Mike Rotundo
Tully Blanchard draw Nikita Koloff
The Rock & Roll Express beat The Sheepherders
Lex Luger beat Arn Anderson

1/12/88: North Wilkesboro, NC
Ron Garvin & Sting beat The Midnight Express

1/12/88: Sumter, SC @ Exhibition Center
The Rock & Roll Express vs. Barbarian & Warlord
Barry Windham vs. Larry Zbyszko
Ivan Koloff vs. Ron Simmons
Brad Armstrong & Tim Horner vs. Shaska Whatley & Tiger Conway, Jr.
Chris Champ vs. The Gladiator
Jimmy Valiant vs. Black Bart
Italian Stallion vs. John Savage
Nelson Royal vs. Denny Brown

1/13/88: Atlanta, GA @ WTBS Studios (TV)
Jimmy Garvin & Michael Hayes beat George South & Tony Suber
The Warlord & The Barbarian beat Clement Fields & Keith Steinborn
Ron Simmons beat Cody Starr
Rock & Roll Express beat Steve Atkinson & Alan Martin
Arn Anderson & Tully Blanchard beat Ed Franks & Lee Peek
Mike Rotundo beat Larry Wayne
Dick Murdoch beat Larry Spencer
Ivan Koloff beat Dave Spencer

1/14/88: Fisherville, VA
Ivan Koloff beat Jimmy Valiant
Brad Armstrong & Tim Horner beat Shaska Whatley & Tiger Conway, Jr.
Eddie Gilbert beat Ron Simmons
Rick Steiner beat Italian Stallion
Chris Champ beat Rocky King
Ricky Santana beat John Savage

1/14/88: Norfolk, VA @ Scope (TV)
Arn Anderson & Tully Blanchard beat Tommy Angel & Cougar Jay (3:15)
The Warlord & The Barbarian beat Larry Stephens & Trent Knight (3:01)
Black Bart beat Mark Cruz (3:20) via pinfall
The Rock & Roll Express beat George South & Gene Ligon (2:32)
Sting beat Mark Fleming (2:56) by submission
Mike Rotundo beat Bob Riddle (1:06) via pinfall
Barry Windham beat Larry Zbyzsko via pinfall
The Road Warriors DDQ The Warlord & The Barbarian
Nikita Koloff beat Mike Rotundo by DQ
Lex Luger beat Arn Anderson via pinfall
NWA World Champ Ric Flair beat Dusty Rhodes in a steel cage match

1/15/88: Richmond, VA @ Coliseum (TV)
Stan Lane & Dick Murdoch beat ?? & ??
NWA World Champ Ric Flair beat Michael Hayes
Dusty Rhodes & Nikita Koloff beat Dick Murdoch (sub Eaton) & Stan Lane in a cage match
The Road Warriors beat Ivan Koloff & The Warlord
Lex Luger beat Arn Anderson
Barry Windham DDQ Tully Blanchard (27:00)
Steve Williams vs. Mark Fleming
The Road Warriors vs. ?? & ??
Ivan Koloff, The Warlord & The Barbarian vs. ??
Mike Rotundo vs. Bob Riddle
Sting & Barry Windham vs. Arn Anderson & Tully Blanchard

1/16/88: Philadelphia, PA @ Civic Center
NWA World Champ Ric Flair beat Michael Hayes
Lex Luger beat Arn Anderson
Dusty Rhodes beat Stan Lane
The Road Warriors NC with Warlord & Barbarian
Nikita Koloff beat Mike Rotundo by DQ
Tully Blanchard draw Ron Garvin
Dick Murdoch, Eddie Gilbert & Kevin Sullivan beat Kendall Windham, Sting & Ron Simmons
Jimmy Garvin beat Black Bart

1/17/88: Charleston, WV @ Civic Center (TV)
Rock & Roll Express vs. Tommy Angel & Cougar Jay
Sting vs. Gladiator #1
Ivan Koloff & The Warlord vs. Mark Fleming & Bob Riddle
The Sheepherders vs. Larry Stevens & Trent Knight
Stan Lane & Dick Murdoch vs. Andrew Bellamy & Jeff Crews
Arn Anderson vs. George South
Ron Garvin vs. Gene Ligon
Barry Windham vs. Tully Blanchard

1/17/88: St. Louis, MO @ Arena
NWA World Champ Ric Flair beat Michael Hayes in a cage match
Lex Luger beat Arn Anderson
Dusty Rhodes beat Dick Murdoch by DQ
Nikita Koloff draw Tully Blanchard
Sting beat Larry Zbyszko
Mike Rotundo beat Kendall Windham
Rock & Roll Express beat Gary Royal & Max MacGyver

1/18/88: Columbia, SC @ Township Auditorium
Sting beat Dick Murdoch by DQ

1/20/88: Georgetown, SC
Ron Garvin & Jimmy Valiant beat The Midnight Express by DQ

1/20/88: Honolulu, HI
NWA World Champ Ric Flair beat Nikita Koloff
Dusty Rhodes beat Tully Blanchard
Lex Luger beat Arn Anderson
The Road Warriors beat The Warlord & The Barbarian
Barry Windham & Rock & Roll Express beat Midnight Express & Larry Zbyszko
Michael Hayes beat Kevin Sullivan by DQ
Barry Windham beat Larry Zbyszko
Farmer Boy Ipo beat Kinipopo
Super Fly Tui beat Mighty Milo

1/21/88: Inglewood, CA @ The Forum
NWA World Champ Ric Flair beat Michael Hayes
Dusty Rhodes beat Larry Zbyszko by DQ
Lex Luger beat Arn Anderson
The Road Warriors NC with The Warlord & The Barbarian
Tully Blanchard draw Nikita Koloff
Kevin Sullivan beat Hurricane Kid
Barry Windham beat Samoan Tau

1/21/88: Chesterfield, SC
Jimmy & Ron Garvin beat Midnight Express by DQ

1/22/88: Elberton, GA
Barry Windham & Robert Gibson beat The Midnight Express by DQ

1/23/88: Lakeland, FL
Barry Windham & Ron Garvin beat The Midnight Express by DQ
Dusty Rhodes vs. Dick Murdoch

1/23/88: Cincinnati, OH @ Gardens
Sting (sub for Michael Hayes) beat NWA World Champ Ric Flair by DQ
Lex Luger beat Arn Anderson
Nikita Koloff draw Larry Zbyszko
Ivan Koloff & The Warlord beat The Rock & Roll Express
Tully Blanchard beat Jimmy Garvin by countout
Jimmy Valiant beat Jim Lancaster

1/24/88: Orlando, FL @ Orange County Convention Center
Ron Garvin beat Dick Murdoch in a cage match
Brad Armstrong & Ricky Santana beat Eddie Gilbert & The Terminator
Bugsy McGraw beat Mighty Yankee#1 (Jerry Grey)
Ron Simmons beat Yankee #2 (Bob Cook)
Ricky Santana beat Black Bart
Shaska Whatley beat Robbie Idol
Tiger Conway, Jr. beat Rex King

1/24/88: Uniondale, NY @ Nassau Coliseum
Sting & Jimmy Garvin (subs for The Rock & Roll Express) beat The Sheepherders by DQ
Nikita Koloff draw Bobby Eaton (20:00)
Larry Zbyzsko beat Barry Windham (19:16) via pinfall to win NWA Western States Heritage Title
Road Warrior Hawk beat NWA World Champ Ric Flair (22:40) by DQ
Dusty Rhodes won a $500,000 8-man Bunkhouse Stampede by last eliminating The Barbarian at 26:20

1/25/88: Greenville, SC @ Memorial Auditorium
NWA World Champ Ric Flair beat Barry Windham in a steel cage match
Jan 25, 1988: Greenville, SC @ Memorial Auditorium
NWa World title match Ric Flair beat Barry windham
Nikita Koloff draw Mike Rotundo
Dick Murdoch & Black Bart beat Ricky Santana & Italian Stallion
Sting beat the Barbarian
Ron Simmons DCOR the Warlord
Ivan Koloff beat Jimmy Valiant
Luke Williams beat Larry Stevens
Butch Miller beat George South

1/25/88: Fayetteville, NC @ Cumberland County Civic Center
Nelson Royal beat John Savage
Tiger Conway, Jr. beat Rocky King
Shaska Whatley beat Chris Champ
Larry Zbyszko beat Gary Royal
Arn Anderson beat Kendall Windham
Jimmy Garvin & Ronnie Garvin beat The Midnight Express by DQ
Lex Luger beat Tully Blanchard

1/26/88: Raleigh, NC @ Dorton Arena (TV)
Bobby Eaton beat Dusty Rhodes by DQ
Mike Rotundo beat Nikita Koloff (13:00) via pinfall to win NWA World Television Title
Dick Murdoch & The Midnight Express beat Kendall Windham, Italian Stallion & Tommy Angel
Ricky Santana beat Bob Emory
The Warlord & The Barbarian beat George South & Rocky King
Butch Miller beat David Isley
Barry Windham beat David Isley
Sting beat Bob Emory
Larry Zbyszko beat George South

1/27/88: Atlanta, GA @ WTBS Studios (TV)
The Midnight Express beat Dale Laperouse & El Negro
Larry Zbyszko beat Alan Martin
Shaska Whatley & Tiger Conway, Jr. beat Italian Stallion & Kendall Windham
Jimmy Garvin & Ronnie Garvin beat Charles Ryan & Tony Suber
Sting & Barry Windham beat Mike Jackson & Gary Royal
The Warlord & The Barbarian beat Ed Franks & Max McGyver

1/28/88: Hammond, IN @ Civic Center
Nikita Koloff beat Larry Zbyszko
The Road Warriors & Paul Ellering beat Ivan Koloff, The Warlord & Paul Jones
Lex Luger beat Arn Anderson
Dusty Rhodes beat Tully Blanchard
NWA World Champ Ric Flair beat Jimmy Garvin

1/28/88: Harrisonburg, VA @ JMU Center
Barry Windham & Ron Garvin beat The Sheepherders
Brad Armstrong & Tim Horner beat Midnight Express
Kendall Windham beat Shaska Whatley
Rick Steiner beat John Savage
Black Bart beat Italian Stallion
Eddie Gilbert beat Mark Fleming

1/29/88: Pittsburgh, PA @ Civic Center
Sting beat NWA World Champ Ric Flair by DQ
Dusty Rhodes beat Bobby Eaton
Lex Luger beat Arn Anderson
Road Warrior Hawk & Paul Ellering beat Ivan Koloff & The Barbarian
Nikita Koloff beat Mike Rotundo by DQ
Tully Blanchard beat Jimmy Garvin
Stan Lane beat Ricky Santana
Warlord beat Jimmy Jackson

1/30/88: Greensboro, NC @ Coliseum (TV)
Arn Anderson beat Kendall Windham
Mike Rotundo & Rick Steiner beat Gary Royal & George South
Lex Luger & Barry Windham beat Tommy Angel & Trent Knight
Black Bart beat Curtis Thompson
Dick Murdoch beat Joe Cruz
Jimmy & Ronnie Garvin beat Bob Emory & Bob Riddle
Dusty Rhodes beat Bobby Eaton no DQ match by pinning Jim Cornette
Lex Luger & Barry Windham beat Cougar Jay & ??
Arn Anderson & Tully Blanchard beat Tommy Angel & Gary Royal
Kevin Sullivan beat Joe Cruz
Dusty Rhodes & Nikita Koloff beat The Midnight Express in a double bullrope match
NWA World Champ Ric Flair beat Barry Windham
Bench press contest between The Road Warriors & The Warlord & The Barbarian

1/31/88: Atlanta, GA @ Omni
Mike Rotundo beat Nikita Koloff via pinfall
Road Warrior Hawk & Paul Ellering beat The Warlord & The Barbarian in a $50,000 ladder match
Dusty Rhodes beat Larry Zbyzsko by DQ
Lex Luger & Ole Anderson beat Arn Anderson & Tully Blanchard by DQ
NWA World Champ Ric Flair beat Sting via pinfall

2/1/88: Newton, NC
Sting & Barry Windham beat Midnight Express by DQ

2/2/88: Spartanburg, SC @ Memorial Auditorium
Sting, Brad Armstrong & Tim Horner vs. The Midnight Express & Dick Murdoch
Arn Anderson vs. Steve Williams
Jimmy Valiant vs. Chris Champ
Ron Simmons vs. Shaska Whatley
Italian Stallion vs. Tiger Conway
Kendall Windham vs. Black Bart
Ricky Santana vs. The Terminator

2/2/88: Miami, FL @ James L. Knight Center
Dusty Rhodes & Lex Luger beat Ric Flair & Tully Blanchard
Road Warrior Hawk & Paul Ellering beat Ivan Koloff & The Warlord
Nikita Koloff beat Mike Rotundo by DQ
Barry Windham draw Larry Zbyszko
Ricky Santana beat Kevin Sullivan by DQ
Bugsy McGraw beat Mighty Yankee #1

2/3/88: Atlanta, GA @ WTBS Studios (TV)
Sting beat David Isley
Tim Horner beat The Gladiator
Dick Murdoch beat Bob Emory
Arn Anderson & Tully Blanchard beat Max McGyver & John Savage
Italian Stallion beat Gene Ligon
Lex Luger & Barry Windham beat Bob Riddle & Tony Suber
Mike Rotundo & Rick Steiner beat Andrew Bellamy & Dave Spearman
Kevin Sullivan beat Ryan Wagner
The Midnight Express beat Mike Jackson & Alan Martin
Mike Rotundo beat Ryan Wagner (2:42) via pinfall
Joe Cruz beat Kevin Sullivan (1:51) by DQ
Lex Luger & Barry Windham beat David Isley & Tommy Angel
Warlord & Barbarian beat Dave Spearman & Bob Riddle
Arn Anderson & Tully Blanchard beat Alan Martin & Larry Stephens

2/3/88: Jacksonville, FL @ Memorial Coliseum

2/4/88: Chattanooga, TN @ UTC Arena
The Midnight Express beat Jimmy Garvin & Mike Jackson
Nikita Koloff beat Dick Murdoch

2/6/88: Charlotte, NC @ Coliseum
Nikita Koloff beat Dick Murdoch in a Texas barbed wire, bunkhouse match

2/7/88: Fayetteville, NC @ Cumberland County Civic Center

2/7/88: Columbia, SC @ Township Auditorium
Sting & Jimmy Garvin beat The Midnight Express by DQ

2/8/88: Macon, GA @ Coliseum
Barry Windham, Brad Armstrong & Tim Horner beat Jim Cornette & The Midnight Express

2/9/88: Albany, GA @ Civic Center
Sting & Barry Windham beat Midnight Express by DQ
Jimmy Garvin beat Black Bart
Brad Armstrong & Tim Horner beat The Sheepherders
Eddie Gilbert beat Ron Garvin
Jimmy Valiant beat Tiger Conway, Jr.
Shaska Whatley beat Rocky King

2/10/88: Atlanta, GA @ WTBS Studios (TV)
Arn Anderson beat John Savage
Eddie Gilbert beat David Isley
Road Warrior Hawk beat Keith Steinborn & Ryan Wagner in a handicap match
Mike Rotundo beat Rocky King
Sting beat Bob Riddle
Ivan Koloff, Warlord & Barbarian beat Steve Atkinson, Randy Hogan & Gene Miller
Jimmy & Ronnie Garvin beat Joe Cruz & Red Raider
Shane Douglas beat George South
Mike Rotundo & Rick Steiner beat John Savage & David Isley (3:04)
Eddie Gilbert beat Joe Cruz (2:57) via pinfall
Sting, Lex Luger & Barry Windham beat George South, Gary Royal & Tommy Angel (3:22)
Black Bart beat Randy Hogan (1:22) via pinfall
The Midnight Express beat Bob Riddle & Curtis Thompson (1:44)
Shane Douglas beat Alan Martin (:57)

2/10/88: Johnson City, TN @ Freedom Hall
Sting beat NWA World Champ Ric Flair by DQ

2/11/88: Columbus, GA @ Municipal Auditorium
Ron & Jimmy Garvin beat The Midnight Express by DQ

2/11/88: Raleigh, NC @ Dorton Arena
Lex Luger & Barry Windham beat Ric Flair & Tully Blanchard by DQ
The Warlord & The Barbarian NC with Nikita Koloff & Road Warrior Hawk
Mike Rotundo beat Ricky Santana
Arn Anderson beat Italian Stallion
Jimmy Valiant beat The Terminator
Chris Champ beat Black Bart
Rick Steiner beat Rocky King

2/12/88: Baltimore, MD @ Civic Center
Dusty Rhodes, Nikita Koloff, Barry Windham & Misty Blue beat The Midnight Express, Dick Murdoch & Jim Cornette
Lex Luger & Ron Garvin beat Ric Flair & Tully Blanchard by DQ
Hawk & Paul Ellering NC with Warlord & Barbarian
Mike Rotundo draw Jimmy Garvin
Arn Anderson beat Kendall Windham
Ron Simmons beat The Terminator

2/13/88: Philadelphia, PA @ Civic Center (TV)
Shane Douglas beat Curtis Thompson
Tully Blanchard & Arn Anderson beat Tom Marker & Bob Emory
Sting beat Tony Super
Barry Windham beat Steve Sampson
Mike Rotundo beat Joe Cruz
Jimmy & Ron Garvin beat Midnight Express by DQ
Nikita Koloff beat Dick Murdoch
Barry Windham & Lex Luger beat Ric Flair & Tully Blanchard by DQ
Barbarian & Warlord beat Tony Super & Tom Marker
Ric Flair, Tully Blanchard & Arn Anderson beat Curtis Thompson, Steve Sampson & Joe Cruz
Shane Douglas beat Jimmy Miller
Dusty Rhodes beat Bobby Eaton
Warlord, Barbarian & Ivan Koloff beat Dusty Rhodes, Paul Ellering & Hawk to win NWA World 6-Man Title

2/14/88: Greenville, SC @ Memorial Auditorium
Lightning Express beat the Sheepherders
Ron Simmons beat Ivan Koloff
Jimmy Valiant beat Eddie Gilbert
Rocky King beat the Gladiator
Jive Tones beat Kendall Windham and Italian Stallion
Misty Blue beat Lat Laroux
Shane Douglas draw Rick Steiner
The Terminator beat George South

2/14/88: Chicago, IL @ UIC Pavilion
Lex Luger beat Arn Anderson in a cage match
Road Warrior Hawk & Paul Ellering beat Warlord & Barbarian in a ladder match
Dusty Rhodes beat Larry Zbyszko by DQ
Mike Rotundo beat Nikita Koloff
Barry Windham, Ron & Jimmy Garvin draw The Midnight Express & Dick Murdoch
Tully Blanchard beat Ricky Santana
J.T. The Spider beat Catfish Charlie

2/14/88: Atlanta, GA @ Omni
NWA World Champ Ric Flair beat Sting
Tully Blanchard & Arn Anderson beat Lex Luger & Ole Anderson
Road Warrior Hawk & Paul Ellering beat Warlord & Barbarian in a ladder match
Ron & Jimmy Garvin & Barry Windham beat Midnight Express & Dick Murdoch
Mike Rotundo beat Nikita Koloff
Ivan Koloff beat Ron Simmons

2/15/88: Atlanta, GA @ WTBS Studios (TV)
Mike Rotundo & Rick Steiner vs. Curtis Thompson & Max MacGyver
Shane Douglas vs. Thunderfoot II
Ron Simmons vs. David Isley
Eddie Gilbert vs. George South
Larry Zbyzsko vs. Trent Knight
Warlord, Barbarian & Ivan Koloff vs. Mike Jackson, The Raider & Steve Atkinson
Arn Anderson & Tully Blanchard vs. Larry Stevens & Tony Suber
Lex Luger & Barry Windham vs. Bear Collie & Cougar Jay
Ricky Santana vs. Keith Steinborn
Shaska Whatley & Tiger Conway, Jr. vs. Alan Martin & Bob Riddle

2/16/88: Albuquerque, NM
Dusty Rhodes, Lex Luger & Barry Windham beat Ric Flair, Tully Blanchard & Arn Anderson
Road Warrior Hawk & Paul Ellering beat Warlord & Barbarian
The Midnight Express draw Sting & Jimmy Garvin
Ricky Santana beat Kevin Sullivan
Larry Zbyszko beat Tim Chappa
Dick Murdoch beat Hillbilly Tooter

2/17/88: Inglewood, CA @ The Forum
Lex Luger & Barry Windham beat Ric Flair & Tully Blanchard by DQ
Dusty Rhodes beat Larry Zbyszko
Hawk & Paul Ellering beat Warlord & Barbarian
The Midnight Express draw Sting & Jimmy Garvin
Dick Murdoch beat Billy Anderson
Arn Anderson beat Tim Patterson
Ricky Santana beat Hurricane Kid

2/18/88: Sioux City, IA
NWA World Champ Ric Flair beat Dusty Rhodes by DQ
Lex Luger beat Arn Anderson
Road Warrior Hawk, Sting & Paul Ellering beat Paul Jones, The Warlord & The Barbarian
Barry Windham beat Tully Blanchard
Midnight Express draw Jimmy Garvin & Ricky Santana
Dick Murdoch beat J.T. The Spider
Larry Zbyszko beat Richard Starling

2/19/88: Hillsville, VA
Brad Armstrong & Tim Horner beat Sheepherders DQ
Ron Garvin beat Dick Murdoch
Jimmy Valiant beat Black Bart
Ron Simmons beat The Terminator
Chris Champ beat Gladiator #1
Italian Stallion beat John Savage

2/19/88: Richmond, VA @ Coliseum (TV)
Sting, Road Warrior Hawk & Paul Ellering beat The Warlord, The Barbarian & Ivan Koloff
Dusty Rhodes beat Larry Zbyszko by DQ
Lex Luger & Ole Anderson beat Arn Anderson & Tully Blanchard in a cage match
Jimmy Garvin beat Kevin Sullivan
Midnight Express beat Barry Windham & Ron Garvin

2/20/88: Charleston, WV @ Civic Center

2/20/88: Norfolk, VA @ Scope
Ole Anderson, Lex Luger & Dusty Rhodes beat Ric Flair, Arn Anderson & Tully Blanchard
Midnight Express beat Barry Windham & Jimmy Garvin
Larry Zbyszko beat Sting
Rick Steiner beat Kendall Windham
Shane Douglas beat Shaska Whatley

2/21/88: Charlotte, NC @ Coliseum

2/21/88: Uniondale, NY @ Nassau Coliseum
Stan Lane draw Ron Simmons (20:00)
Misty Blue beat Linda Dallas via pinfall
Bobby Eaton beat Ricky Santana via pinfall
Sting draw Mike Rotundo
Ron Garvin beat Kevin Sullivan
Barry Windham beat Larry Zbyzsko by countout
Road Warrior Hawk & Paul Ellering beat The Warlord & The Barbarian in a $50,000 ladder match by DQ
Dusty Rhodes & Lex Luger beat Ric Flair & Tully Blanchard by DQ

2/22/88: Poughkeepsie, NY
The Midnight Express beat Ron Garvin & Ron Simmons

2/23/88: Savannah, GA @ Civic Center

2/23/88: Elizabeth, NJ (Cancelled due to almost no advance sales)
Barry Windham vs. Larry Zbyzsko

2/24/88: Atlanta, GA @ WTBS Studios (TV)
Sting vs. John Savage
Shane Douglas & Ricky Santana vs. Cruel Connection
The Sheepherders vs. Brad Armstrong & Tim Horner
Midnight Express vs. Curtis Thompson & Cody Starr
Lex Luger & Barry Windham vs. Gene Ligon & Riki Ataki
Jimmy & Ron Garvin vs. David Isley & Brodie Lee
The Warlord, The Barbarian & Ivan Koloff vs. Joe Cruz, Mike Jackson & Alan Martin
Ron Simmons vs. Ryan Wagner
Mike Rotundo & Rick Steiner vs. Trent Knight & Gary Phelps
Arn Anderson & Tully Blanchard vs. Bear Collie & Tony Suber
Larry Zbyzsko vs. Max MacGyver

2/25/88: Akron, OH @ James Rhodes Arena
Brad Armstrong & Tim Horner beat The Sheepherders
Ron Simmons beat Rick Steiner by DQ
Jimmy Valiant beat Ivan Koloff
Sting beat Mike Rotundo when Sting pinned Kevin Sullivan
Larry Zbyszko DCO with Barry Windham
Warlord & Barbarian beat Road Warriors in a Chicago street fight match

2/25/88: Columbia, SC @ Township Auditorium
Ron & Jimmy Garvin beat The Midnight Express by DQ

2/26/88: Cincinnati, OH @ Gardens (TV)
Sting beat The Terminator (:15)
Barry Windham beat Mike Rotundo by DQ
Shane Douglas beat ??
The Warlord & The Barbarian beat Max MacGyver & ??
Tully Blanchard & Arn Anderson beat George Cox & ??
Lex Luger beat ??
Lex Luger & Ole Anderson beat Arn Anderson & Tully Blanchard by DQ
Lex Luger & Barry Windham beat Tony Super & Terminator
Mike Rotundo & Rick Steiner beat Max MacGyver & ??
Ron Simmons beat David Isley
Larry Zbyszko beat George Cox
Shane Douglas beat ??
Sting beat Bob Emory
Tully Blanchard & Arn Anderson beat Joe Cruz & ??
The Warlord & The Barbarian beat Trent Knight & Curtis Thompson
NWA World Champ Ric Flair beat Sting (17:00)

2/26/88: Lynchburg, VA @ City Armory
Jimmy & Ron Garvin beat The Midnight Express

2/27/88: Greensboro, NC @ Coliseum
Dusty Rhodes, Lex Luger & Ole Anderson beat Ric Flair, Tully Blanchard & Arn Anderson
Road Warrior Hawk & Paul Ellering beat The Warlord & The Barbarian in a ladder match
Barry Windham beat Mike Rotundo by DQ
Sting beat Larry Zbyszko by DQ
Ron Garvin beat Ivan Koloff
Jimmy Garvin beat Kevin Sullivan
Brad Armstrong & Tim Horner beat The Sheepherders
Ricky Santana beat Black Bart
Jimmy Valiant beat John Savage

2/28/88: Atlanta, GA @ Omni
Dusty Rhodes, Lex Luger & Ole Anderson beat Ric Flair, Arn Anderson & Tully Blanchard
TWarlord & Barbarian DDQ Hawk & Paul Ellering
Barry Windham beat Mike Rotundo by DQ
Sting beat Larry Zbyszko by DQ
The Midnight Express beat Jimmy & Ron Garvin
Shaska Whatley & Tiger Conway, Jr. beat Kendall Windham & Ron Simmons
Rick Steiner beat Italian Stallion
Ricky Santana beat Black Bart

2/29/88: Greenville, SC @ Memorial Auditorium
Lex Luger & Barry Windham beat Tully Blanchard & Arn Anderson
Sting beat Mike Rotundo
Lightning Express beat Johnny Ace & Luke Williams
Rick Steiner beat John Savage
Ron Simmons beat Gladiator #1
Shane Douglas beat Terminator

2/29/88: Washington, DC @ Armory
Jimmy & Ron Garvin beat Midnight Express by DQ

3/1/88: Gainesville, GA @ Georgia Mountain Center
Jimmy & Ron Garvin beat The Midnight Express

3/2/88: Atlanta, GA @ WTBS Studios (TV)
Shane Douglas beat Gene Ligon
Mike Rotundo draw Ricky Santana
Barry Windham beat Gary Phelps
Larry Zbyszko beat Randy Hogan
Shaska Whatley & Tiger Conway, Jr. beat Keith Steinborn & Ryan Wagner
Rick Steiner & Kevin Sullivan beat Steve Atkinson & Alan Martin
The Road Warriors beat Bob Riddle & Riki Ataki
Tony Suber beat Super Destroyer
Arn Anderson, Tully Blanchard & Ric Flair beat Mike Jackson, Rocky King & Trent Knight

3/3/88: Harrisonburg, VA @ High School
George South vs. The Terminator
Ron Simmons vs. John Savage
Shane Douglas vs. Black Bart
Jimmy Valiant vs. Green Machine
Ron Garvin vs. Ivan Koloff
Larry Zbyszko vs. Barry Windham

3/4/88: Pittsburgh, PA @ Civic Arena
The Road Warriors beat The Warlord & The Barbarian
Lex Luger & Ole Anderson beat Tully Blanchard & Arn Anderson by DQ
Brad Armstrong & Tim Horner beat The Sheepherders
Ricky Santana draw Ivan Koloff
Chris Champ beat Shaska Whatley
Jimmy Valiant beat Jerry Jackson
Green Machine beat Italian Stallion

3/4/88: Houston, TX @ The Summit
NWA World Champ Ric Flair beat Sting
The Midnight Express beat Jimmy & Ron Garvin
Dusty Rhodes beat Larry Zbyszko
Barry Windham beat Mike Rotundo by DQ
Ron Simmons beat Rick Steiner
Shane Douglas beat Tiger Conway, Jr.
Kendall Windham draw Black Bart
Linda Dallas won a girls battle royal

3/5/88: Louisville, KY @ Convention Center (TV)

3/6/88: St. Louis, MO @ Arena
Kendall Windham beat Johnny Ace via pinfall
Shane Douglas beat Mr. Missouri
Ricky Santana draw Rick Steiner (20:00)
Brad Armstrong & Tim Horner beat The Sheepherders
Dusty Rhodes beat Mike Rotundo by DQ
Lex Luger & Barry Windham beat Arn Anderson & Tully Blanchard by DQ
NWA World Champ Ric Flair beat Sting

3/6/88: Raleigh, NC @ Dorton Arena
Road Warriors beat Warlord & Barbarian in street fight
Jimmy & Ron Garvin beat Midnight Express by DQ
Ron Simmons beat Tiger Conway, Jr.
Green Machine beat Jimmy Valiant
Black Bart beat Italian Stallion
Ivan Koloff beat Tommy Angel
Chris Champ beat Shaska Whatley

3/7/88: Macon, GA @ Coliseum
Shaska Whatley & Tiger Conway, Jr. vs. Chris Champ & Italian Stallion
Nelson Royal DCO with George South
7-woman battle royal included Misty Blue, Kat Laroux, Linda Dallas, Venus, Comrade Olga, Wendy Whitney Hensen & Mad Dog Debbie
Ron Garvin vs. Ivan Koloff
The Sheepherders vs. Brad Armstrong & Tim Horner
The Road Warriors vs. The Warlord & The Barbarian

3/7/88: Greenville, SC @ Memorial Auditorium
Sting beat Ric Flair by DQ in a NWA World Title Match
Lex Luger & Barry Windham beat Tully Blanchard & JJ Dillon
Jimmy Garvin beat Mike Rounda DQ
Green Machine beat Jimmy Valiant
Shane Douglas beat Gary Royal
Ron Simmons beat Black Bart
Rick Steiner beat Rocky King
Kendall Windham beat John Savage

3/8/88: Spartanburg, SC @ Memorial Auditorium
Shane Douglas vs. Eddie Gilbert
Italian Stallion & Ricky Santana vs. The Sheepherders
Kendall Windham vs. Rick Steiner
Jimmy Valiant vs. Green Machine
Mike Rotundo vs. Jimmy Garvin
The Midnight Express vs. Brad Armstrong & Tim Horner

3/9/88: Atlanta, GA @ WTBS Studios (TV)
The Road Warriors beat Gary Phelps & Keith Steinborn
Shaska Whatley & Tiger Conway, Jr. beat Rocky King & Gene Ligon
Midnight Express beat Trent Knight & Curt Thompson
Ricky Santana beat Bob Riddle
Lex Luger beat Dale Laperhouse
The Warlord & The Barbarian beat Randy Hogan & ??
Mike Rotundo beat Jimmy Garvin
Arn Anderson & Tully Blanchard beat Steve Atkinson & Dave Spearman
Rick Steiner beat Gary Royal

3/9/88: Wadesboro, NC
Lightning Express beat The Midnight Express by DQ

3/10/88: Marion, VA
Lightning Express beat The Midnight Express

3/10/88: Baltimore, MD @ Civic Center
NWA World Champ Ric Flair beat Sting
The Road Warriors beat The Warlord & The Barbarian in a ladder match
Lex Luger & Barry Windham beat Tully Blanchard & Arn Anderson by DQ
Jimmy Garvin beat Mike Rotundo by DQ
Shane Douglas beat Black Bart
Rick Steiner beat Kendall Windham
Ricky Santana beat Gary Royal

3/11/88: Lenoir, NC
Brad Armstrong & Tim Horner beat The Midnight Express

3/12/88: Norfolk, VA @ Scope (TV)
Arn Anderson & Tully Blanchard beat Lex Luger & Barry Windham
Dusty Rhodes beat Larry Zbyzsko
Sting beat NWA World Champ Ric Flair (12:00) by DQ
The Fantastics (Bobby Fulton & Tommy Rogers) beat The Midnight Express (27:00) via pinfall

3/13/88: Columbus, GA @ Municipal Auditorium
Mickey Doyle beat Ben Patrick
Jim Lancaster beat Al Snow
Shane Douglas & Ricky Santana beat The Midnight Express by DQ
Larry Zbyszko DCO with Ron Garvin
The Road Warriors & Paul Ellering beat The Warlord, The Barbarian & Paul Jones (6:06) via pinfall in a Chicago street fight match
Sting beat NWA World Champ Ric Flair by DQ

3/13/88: Atlanta, GA @ Omni
Sting beat NWA World Champ Ric Flair by DQ
The Warlord & The Barbarian beat Dusty Rhodes & Road Warrior Hawk
Tully Blanchard & Arn Anderson beat Lex Luger & Barry Windham
Mike Rotundo beat Jimmy Garvin
The Midnight Express beat Brad Armstrong & Tim Horner
Ron Garvin beat Larry Zbyszko by DQ
Gary Royal beat Rick Steiner

3/14/88: Atlanta, GA @ WTBS Studios (TV)
Mike Rotundo & Rick Steiner vs. Keith Steinborn & Ryan Wagner
Shane Douglas vs. Barry Collie
Sting vs. Joe Cruz
Warlord & Barbarian vs. Bob Riddle & Max MacGyver
Ron Simmons vs. Trent Knight
The Road Warriors vs. Steve Atkinson & El Negro
Lex Luger vs. Andrew Bellamy
Al Perez vs. Tony Suber
The Midnight Express vs. Mike Jackson & Alan Martin

3/15/88: Reno, NV
NWA World Champ Ric Flair beat Sting

3/15/88: Columbia, SC @ Township Auditorium
Stan Lane beat Shane Douglas
Dusty Rhodes beat Bobby Eaton

3/16/88: Atlanta, GA @ WTBS Studios (TV)
Mike Rotundo & Rick Steiner beat Keith Steinborn & Ryan Wagner
Shane Douglas beat Bear Collie
Sting beat Joe Cruz
Warlord & Barbarian beat Max McGyver & Bob Riddle
Ron Simmons beat Trent Knight
The Road Warriors beat Steve Atkinson & El Negro
Lex Luger beat Andrew Bellamy
Al Perez beat Tony Suber
The Midnight Express beat Mike Jackson & Gary Martin

3/16/88: San Francisco, CA @ Cow Palace
NWA World Champ Ric Flair beat Sting
The Road Warriors beat The Warlord & The Barbarian
Barry Windham & Lex Luger beat Tully Blanchard & Arn Anderson by DQ
Larry Zbyszko beat Jimmy Garvin
Rick Steiner beat Rex Farmer
George Wells NC with Earthquake Ferris

3/17/88: Inglewood, CA @ The Forum
NWA World Champ Ric Flair beat Sting
The Road Warriors beat The Warlord & The Barbarian
Lex Luger & Barry Windham beat Arn Anderson & Tully Blanchard by DQ
Mike Rotundo draw Jimmy Garvin
Larry Zbyszko beat Ron Garvin
Rick Steiner beat Pistol Pete
Mando Guerrero draw Tony Rocco

3/18/88: Cincinnati, OH @ Riverfront Coliseum (TV)
NWA Champ Ric Flair NC with Sting
Road Warriors beat Barbarian & Warlord lumberjack match
Jimmy & Ronnie Garvin beat Mike Rotundo & Rick Steiner by DQ
Arn Anderson & Tully Blanchard beat Lex Luger & Barry Windham by DQ

3/13/88: Columbus, OH @ Ohio Center
Jimmy & Ronnie Garvin beat Rick Steiner & Mike Rotundo by DQ
Arn Anderson & Tully Blanchard beat Lex Luger & Barry Windham by DQ
NWA World Champ Ric Flair NC with Sting
Paul Ellering & Road Warriors beat Paul Jones, Warlord & Barbarian (6:06) via pinfall in a lumberjack match

3/19/88: Chicago, IL @ UIC Pavilion
Ivan Koloff beat Shane Douglas via pinfall
Rick Steiner beat Kendall Windham via pinfall
Arn Anderson DDQ Barry Windham
The Midnight Express beat Jimmy & Ron Garvin
Lex Luger beat Tully Blanchard
Dusty Rhodes beat Mike Rotundo by DQ
NWA World Champ Ric Flair beat Sting via pinfall
The Road Warriors & Paul Ellering beat Paul Jones, Warlord & Barbarian in a Chicago street fight match

3/20/88: Charleston, WV @ Civic Center
Dusty Rhodes beat Bobby Eaton
Lex Luger & Barry Windham beat Tully Blanchard & James J. Dillon
Mike Rotundo beat Jimmy Garvin
Shaska Whatley, Tiger Conway & Green Machine beat Jimmy Valiant, Chris Champ & Italian Stallion
Stan Lane draw Shane Douglas
Rick Steiner beat Kendall Windham

3/20/88: Peoria, IL @ Civic Center
NWA World Champ Ric Flair beat Sting
Paul Ellering & The Road Warriors beat Paul Jones, The Warlord & The Barbarian by DQ
Ron Garvin beat Ivan Koloff
Steve Regal beat Spike Huber
Larry Cameron bat Johnny Love

3/20/88: Charlotte, NC @ Coliseum
Midnight Express beat Shane Douglas & Ricky Santana

3/21/88: Atlanta, GA @ WTBS Studios (TV)
The Sheepherders vs. Tony Borman & Ryan Wagner
The Fantastics vs. Gene Ligon & Steve Atkinson
Mike Rotundo & Rick Steiner vs. Tommy Angel & Italian Stallion
Ron Simmons vs. David Diamond
Sting vs. Max MacGyver
Midnight Express vs. Kendall Windham & Bear Collie
Green Machine vs. El Negro
Jimmy Garvin & Shane Douglas vs. Mike Jackson & Art Pritts

3/22/88: Sumter, SC @ Exhibition Center
NWA World Champ Ric Flair vs. Sting
Mike Rotundo vs. Dusty Rhodes
Brad Armstrong, Tim Horner & Shane Douglas vs. Barbarian,Warlord & Ivan Koloff
Ricky Santana vs. The Terminator
Kevin Sullivan vs. Italian Stallion
Sheepherders vs. Kendall Windham & Ron Simmons

3/22/88: Athens, GA
Ron & Jimmy Garvin beat The Midnight Express by DQ

3/23/88: Atlanta, GA @ WTBS Studios (TV)
The Sheepherders beat Tony Borman & Ryan Wagner
Al Perez beat Alan Martin
The Fantastics beat Steve Atkinson & Gene Ligon
Mike Rotundo & Rick Steiner beat Tommy Angel & Italian Stallion
Ron Simmons beat David Diamond
Sting beat Max McGyver
Midnight Express beat Bear Collie & Kendall Windham
Green Machine beat El Negro
Shane Douglas & Jimmy Garvin beat Mike Jackson & Art Pritts

3/23/88: Gastonia, NC
Stan Lane beat Shane Douglas
Ron Garvin beat Bobby Eaton

3/24/88: Columbia, SC @ Township Auditorium
Shane Douglas beat Doug Savage via pinfall
Chris Champ draw The Terminator
Ricky Santana beat Johnny Ace
Black Bart beat Italian Stallion
Arn Anderson beat Kendall Windham via pinfall
Jimmy & Ron Garvin beat Midnight Express by DQ
Lex Luger beat Tully Blanchard via pinfall

3/25/88: Raleigh, NC @ Dorton Arena (TV)

3/25/88: Biscoe, NC
Jimmy & Ron Garvin beat Midnight Express by DQ

3/26/88: Richmond, VA @ Coliseum
Ricky Santana beat Rick Steiner
The Fantastics beat Mark Fleming & John Savage
Midnight Express beat Jimmy Garvin & Ronnie Garvin
Mike Rotundo draw Barry Windham
Lex Luger beat Tully Blanchard
Ivan Koloff, The Warlord & The Barbarian beat Dusty Rhodes & The Road Warriors
NWA World Champ Sting beat Ric Flair by DQ

3/27/88: Greensboro, NC @ Coliseum
Mike Rotundo beat Jimmy Garvin via pinfall in an amateur wrestling match
Midnight Express beat The Fantastics reverse decision
Dusty Rhodes & The Road Warriors beat Ivan Koloff, Warlord & Barbarian (4:00) in a barbed wire match
Lex Luger & Barry Windham beat Arn Anderson & Tully Blanchard (9:33) to win NWA World Tag Title
NWA World Champ Ric Flair draw Sting (39:14)
Larry Zbyszko beat Shane Douglas

3/28/88: Greenville, SC @ Memorial Auditorium
NWA World title match - NO DQ- Ric Flair beat Sting
The Fantastics beat the Midnight Express DQ
Larry Zbyszko beat Shane Douglas
Ron Simmons beat Shaska Whatley
Kendall Windham beat Tiger Conway Jr.
Nelson Royal beat George South
Tully Blanchard & Arn Anderson beat Rocky King & John Savage

3/29/88: North Wilkesboro, NC
Ron & Jimmy Garvin beat The Midnight Express

3/30/88: Atlanta, GA @ WTBS Studios (TV)
The Fantastics beat Alan Martin & Keith Steinborn
Sting beat Bear Collie
The Sheepherders beat Rocky King & Larry Stevens
Arn Anderson beat Art Pritts
The Road Warriors beat Joe Cruz & El Negro
Jimmy & Ronnie Garvin beat Steve Atkinson & Ryan Wagner
Al Perez beat Mike Jackson
Midnight Express beat Trent Knight & Tony Suber
Mike Rotundo, Rick Steiner & Kevin Sullivan beat Larry Davis, Bob Riddle & George South
Ivan Koloff beat Curtis Thompson

3/31/88: Spartanburg, SC @ Memorial Auditorium (TV)
Ric Flair, Tully Blanchard & Arn Anderson beat Barry Windham, Lex Luger & Sting (13:00) via pinfall
Dusty Rhodes beat Ivan Koloff (6:38) via pinfall
The Road Warriors beat Super Destroyer (sub for Black Bart) & Larry Zbyszko (3:23) via pinfall
The Warlord & The Barbarian beat Tim Horner & Italian Stallion(5:00) via pinfall
Steve Williams DCO with Arn Anderson (9:46)
Barry Windham beat Tully Blanchard (15:34) via pinfall

4/1/88: Norfolk, VA @ Scope
NWA World Champ Ric Flair beat Sting cage match
Tully Blanchard & Arn Anderson beat Lex Luger & Barry Windham by DQ
Dusty Rhodes beat Mike Rotundo by DQ
The Midnight Express draw The Fantastics
Steve Williams beat Rick Steiner
Tim Horner beat Tiger Conway, Jr.
Shaska Whatley beat Mark Fleming

4/2/88: Charlotte, NC @ Coliseum (TV)

4/2/88: Bluefield, WV @ Armory
The Fantastics beat The Midnight Express by DQ

4/3/88: Atlanta, GA @ Omni
NWA World Champ Ric Flair beat Sting
The Road Warriors beat The Warlord & The Barbarian
Lex Luger beat Mike Rotundo by DQ
Barry Windham beat Tully Blanchard
The Midnight Express beat Nikita Koloff & Steve Williams by DQ
The Fantastics beat The Sheepherders
Arn Anderson beat Italian Stallion
Tiger Conway beat Brad Armstrong
Tim Horner beat Shaska Whatley
Rick Steiner beat Ricky Santana

4/4/88: Hartwell, GA
The Fantastics beat The Midnight Express by DQ

4/5/88: Gaffney, SC (TV)
The Sheepherders beat Italian Stallion & Nelson Royal
Green Machine beat Jimmy Valiant
Cruel Connection beat Rock Riddle
Nikita Koloff beat The Warlord
The Fantastics beat The Midnight Express by DQ

4/5/88: Macon, GA @ Coliseum

4/6/88: Atlanta, GA @ WTBS Studios (TV)
The Fantastics beat Bear Collie & Art Pritts
Al Perez & Larry Zbyszko beat Tommy Angel & Ricky Santana
Steve Williams beat Alan Martin
Nikita Koloff beat Ryan Wagner
Arn Anderson & Tully Blanchard beat Mike Jackson & Kendall Windham
Sting beat Super Destroyer
Ronnie Garvin beat Bob Emory
Mike Rotundo & Kevin Sullivan beat Tony Borman & El Negro

4/7/88: Kings Mountain, NC
The Fantastics beat The Midnight Express

4/8/88: Richmond, VA @ Coliseum
Tiger Conway beat Kendall Windham via pinfall
Ricky Santana beat Shaska Whatley via pinfall
Steve Williams & Ron Garvin beat Kevin Sullivan & Rick Steiner via pinfall
Mike Rotundo draw Nikita Koloff
The Fantastics beat The Midnight Express by DQ
Dusty Rhodes beat Larry Zbyzsko via pinfall
NWA World Champ Ric Flair beat Sting via pinfall

4/8/88: Uniondale, NY @ Nassau Coliseum
Mighty Wilbur beat The Terminator
Ron Simmons beat Johnny Ace via pinfall
Jimmy Valiant beat Green Machine (Bugsy McGraw)
Brad Armstrong & Tim Horner beat The Sheepherders
Dick Murdoch beat Shane Douglas via pinfall
Lex Luger & Barry Windham beat Arn Anderson & Tully Blanchard by DQ
The Road Warriors beat The Warlord & The Barbarian

4/8/88: Houston, TX @ Sam Houston Coliseum
Ricky Santana & Kendall Windham beat The Sheepherders by DQ
Nikita Koloff beat Tiger Conway, Jr.
Arn Anderson & Tully Blanchard draw Steve Williams & Barry Windham

4/9/88: Philadelphia, PA @ Civic Center
Ron Simmons beat the Terminator via pinfall
Jimmy Valiant draw Green Machine

The Road Warriors beat The Warlord & The Barbarian
Sting beat NWA World Champ Ric Flair by DQ
Ron Garvin DCO with Dick Murdoch
Brad Armstrong & Tim Horner beat The Sheepherders
Steve Williams beat Larry Zbyzsko (5:00)
Lex Luger & Barry Windham beat Arn Anderson & Tully Blanchard via pinfall

4/9/88: Baltimore, MD @ Arena
NWA World Champ Ric Flair beat Sting
The Warlord, The Barbarian & Ivan Koloff beat The Road Warriors & Dusty Rhodes by DQ
The Fantastics beat The Midnight Express by DQ
Mike Rotundo draw Nikita Koloff
Rick Steiner & Kevin Sullivan beat Ricky Santana & Kendall Windham
Shaska Whatley beat Italian Stallion
Tiger Conway, Jr. draw Chris Champ

4/10/88: Roanoke, VA @ Civic Center (TV)

4/10/88: Salisbury, MD
The Fantastics beat The Midnight Express by DQ

4/11/88: Fayetteville, NC @ Cumberland County Civic Center
The Fantastics beat The Midnight Express by DQ

4/12/88: Kingstree, SC
The Fantastics beat The Midnight Express by DQ

4/13/88: Atlanta, GA @ WTBS Studios (TV)
NWA US Title vacated when Dusty Rhodes was suspended
Midnight Express beat Trent Knight & George South
Dick Murdoch beat Larry Stevens
Lex Luger beat Art Pritts
Warlord & Barbarian beat Steve Atkinson & Bob Riddle
Rick Steiner & Mike Rotundo beat Dave Spearman & Cody Starr
Arn Anderson & Tully Blanchard beat Tony Borman & ?
Nikita Koloff beat El Negro
Jimmy Garvin beat Larry Davis
The Fantastics beat Alan Martin & Keith Steinborn
Al Perez beat Ryan Wagner

4/14/88: Greenwood, SC (TV)
Ricky Santana & Kendall Windham beat The Sheepherders (9:04) by DQ
Nikita Koloff beat Tiger Conway, Jr. via pinfall
Arn Anderson & Tully Blanchard draw Steve Williams & Barry Windham (14:23)
Sting beat Shaska Whatley (5:51) via pinfall
Ricky Santana & Kendall Windham beat The Sheepherders (9:21) via pinfall
Nikita Koloff beat Al Perez (14:08) by DQ

4/14/88: Columbia, SC @ Township Auditorium
The Fantastics beat The Midnight Express by DQ

4/15/88: Boston, MA @ Garden
The Road Warriors beat The Warlord & The Barbarian
Mike Rotundo draw Steve Williams
The Fantastics beat The Midnight Express by DQ
Nikita Koloff beat Larry Zbyszko Dusty Rhodes, Sting, Barry Windham & Lex Luger beat Ric Flair, Tully Blanchard, Arn Anderson & Ivan Koloff
Rick Steiner & Kevin Sullivan beat Kendall Windham & Italian Stallion

4/16/88: Chicago, IL @ UIC Pavilion
Shaska Whatley & Tiger Conway, Jr. beat The Rebel & Mike Tolos
Ron Simmons beat The Terminator
The Sheepherders beat Brad Armstrong & Tim Horner
Dick Murdoch beat Ricky Santana
Lex Luger & Barry Windham beat Arn Anderson & Tully Blanchard by DQ
The Road Warriors & Steve Williams beat The Warlord, The Barbarian & Paul Jones
NWA World Champ Ric Flair vs. Sting

4/16/88: Rock Hill, SC @ Winthrop Coliseum
Johnny Ace, Ricky Santana, & Kendall Windham vs. Rip Morgan & The Sheepherders

4/16/88: Cincinnati, OH @ Gardens
The Fantastics beat The Midnight Express by DQ

4/17/88: Asheville, NC @ Civic Center (TV)
Sting vs. David Isley
The Fantastics vs. Larry Stevens & ?? Watson
Steve Williams vs. Bob Riddle
The Midnight Express vs. Tommy Angel & Rocky King
The Warlord & The Barbarian & Ivan Koloff vs. Max MacGyver, Bob Emory & Curtis Thompson
Al Perez vs. Larry Stevens
Nikita Koloff vs. Krusher Knoff
Mike Rotundo vs. Sam Bass

4/17/88: Charlotte, NC @ Coliseum
The Fantastics beat The Midnight Express by DQ
Shaska Whatley & Tiger Conway, Jr. vs. Road Warriors
Tully Blanchard vs. Midnight Rider
Lex Luger & Barry Windham vs. Arn Anderson & Ric Flair

4/18/88: West Palm Beach, FL @ Auditorium
Rick Steiner beat Kendall Windham via pinfall
Kevin Sullivan NC with Jimmy Garvin
The Fantastics beat The Midnight Express by DQ
Barry Windham draw Mike Rotundo
Midnight Rider (Dusty Rhodes), Sting & Lex Luger beat Ric Flair, Arn Anderson Tully Blanchard (14:00)

4/19/88: Miami, FL @ James L. Knight Center
Ricky Santana beat Rocky King via pinfall
Bugsy McGraw beat Crusher Balboa via pinfall
Rick Steiner beat Kendall Windham via pinfall
The Fantastics beat The Midnight Express by DQ
Kevin Sullivan beat Jimmy Garvin via pinfall
Lex Luger beat Arn Anderson by countout
Midnight Rider beat Tully Blanchard by DQ
Sting beat NWA World Champ Ric Flair by DQ

4/20/88: Jacksonville, FL @ Coliseum (TV)
Mike Rotundo beat Sam Bass
Sting beat David Isley
The Fantastics beat Kelly Stevens & Snake Watson
Steve Williams beat Bob Riddle
The Midnight Express beat Tommy Angel & Rocky King
Ivan Koloff, The Warlord & The Barbarian beat Bob Emory, Max McGyver & Curtis Thompson
Al Perez beat Larry Stevens
Nikita Koloff beat ??
Arn Anderson & Tully Blanchard beat Lex Luger & Barry Windham via pinfall to win NWA World Tag Title when Windham turned on Luger & joined the Horseman

4/21/88: Sumter, SC @ Exhibition Center
The Fantastics beat The Midnight Express by DQ

4/21/88: Harrisonburg, VA @ Harrisonburg H.S.
Chris Champ vs. Cruel Connection II
Johnny Ace vs. Cruel Connection I
Brad Armstrong & Tim Horner vs. The Sheepherders
Jimmy Valiant vs. Green Machine
Barry Windham & Ron Garvin vs. Rick Steiner & Al Perez
Jimmy Garvin vs. Mike Rotundo

4/22/88: Greenville, SC @ Memorial Auditorium (Crockett Cup Day 1)
Crockett Cup
1st Round
Kendall Windham & Italian Stallion beat the Green Machine &Terminator
Dick Murdoch & Ivan Koloff beat Jimmy Valiant & Mighty Wilbur (6:14)
Tiger Conway, Jr. & Shaska Whatley beat Rocky King & Nelson Royal (6:05)
Chris Champ & Mark Starr beat The Twin Devils (Curtis Thompson & Gene Ligon in red outfits) (7:46)
Brad Armstrong & Tim Horner beat Johnny Ace & John Savage
The Sheepherders beat Cruel Connection (Gary Royal & George South) (7:20)
Larry Zbyzsko & Al Perez beat Ricky Santana & Joe Cruz
Mike Rotundo & Rick Steiner beat Steve Williams & Ron Simmons (9:20)
Jimmy Garvin beat Kevin Sullivan in a blindfold match

2nd Round
Arn Anderson & Tully Blanchard beat Kendall Windham & Italian Stallion (6:24)
Lex Luger & Sting beat Dick Murdoch & Ivan Koloff (9:41)
The Road Warriors beat Shaska Whatley & Tiger Conway, Jr. (5:26)
Warlord & Barbarian beat Chris Champ & Mark Starr (8:04)
The Sheepherders beat Brad Armstrong & Tim Horner
The Fantastics beat Larry Zbyzsko & Al Perez (5:03)
The Midnight Express beat The Sheepherders (4:44)

4/23/88: Greensboro, NC @ Coliseum (Crockett Cup Day 2)
Crockett Cup
Quarter Finals
Tommy Rogers & Bobby Fulton beat Mike Rotundo & Rick Steiner (27:20) via pinfall
Sting & Lex Luger beat The Midnight Express (13:40)
Warlord & Barbarian beat The Road Warriors by DQ
Midnight Rider (Dusty Rhodes) beat James J. Dillon (4:10)Texas bullrope match

Semi Finals
Sting & Lex Luger beat Warlord & Barbarian (6:50)
Arn Anderson & Tully Blanchard beat The Fantastics
Nikita Koloff beat NWA World Champ Ric Flair DQ

Finals
Sting & Lex Luger beat Arn Anderson & Tully Blanchard (16:05) via pinfall to win Crockett Cup in tournament final

4/24/88: Charleston, WV @ Civic Center (TV)
Jimmy Garvin beat Mike Rotundo by DQ
The Fantastics DDQ The Midnight Express
Sting & Lex Luger beat Arn Anderson & Tully Blanchard in a steel cage match

4/24/88: Atlanta, GA @ Omni
The Road Warriors & Paul Ellering beat Paul Jones, The Warlord & The Barbarian in a cage match
Ric Flair & Tully Blanchard beat Sting & Lex Luger
Jimmy Garvin beat Dick Murdoch
Arn Anderson beat Midnight Rider by DQ
The Midnight Express NC with The Fantastics
Ivan Koloff beat Jimmy Valiant
Lightning Express draw Rick Steiner & Mike Rotundo
Ron Garvin beat Terminator

4/25/88: Nashville, TN @ Municipal Auditorium
Road Warrior Hawk vs. ?? (sub. for NWA World Champ Ric Flair)
The Midnight Express DCO with The Fantastics
Arn Anderson & Tully Blanchard vs. Dusty Rhodes & Road Warrior Animal

Note: NWA World Champ Ric Flair did not appear as scheduled; refunds were offered as a result

4/26/88: Chattanooga, TN @ UTC Arena (TV)
Sting beat John Savage
Ivan Koloff beat Joe Cruz
The Sheepherders beat Brad Armstrong & Tim Horner
Barry Windham beat George South
Arn Anderson & Tully Blanchard beat Tommy Angel & Trent Knight
The Fantastics beat Andrew Bellamy & Bob Riddle
Shaska Whatley beat Larry Stevens
Shaska Whatley & Tiger Conway, Jr. beat Tommy Angel & John Savage
The Fantastics beat The Midnight Express (40:00) via pinfall to win NWA United States Tag Title

Note: NWA World Champ Ric Flair did not appear as scheduled; refunds were offered as a result

4/27/88: Atlanta, GA @ WTBS Studios (TV)
Al Perez beat George South
Ivan Koloff beat Larry Davis
The Sheepherders beat Tommy Angel & Larry Stevens
Jimmy Garvin beat Alan Martin
Rick Steiner & Mike Rotundo beat Andrew Bellamy & Joe Cruz
Sting beat Steve Atkinson
Nikita Koloff beat Trent Knight
The Warlord & The Barbarian beat Jerry Price & Keith Steinborn
Rip Morgan beat Ryan Wagner

Note: NWA World Champ Ric Flair did not appear as scheduled

4/28/88: Rock Hill, SC @ Winthrop Coliseum (TV)
Steve Williams beat The Terminator (4:51) via pinfall
The Sheepherders & Rip Morgan beat Ricky Santana, Kendall Windham & Johnny Ace (9:38) via pinfall
Lex Luger beat Arn Anderson (10:00) by DQ
Sting & Steve Williams draw Mike Rotundo & Rick Steiner (15:00)
Kevin Sullivan beat Ricky Santana (1:16) via pinfall
Lex Luger beat Bobby Eaton (9:30) via pinfall

Note: NWA World Champ Ric Flair did not appear as scheduled; refunds were offered as a result

4/29/88: Washington, DC @ Armory
Jimmy Valiant beat Mark Fleming
Ron Simmons beat The Terminator
The Sheepherders beat Brad Armstrong & Tim Horner
Nikita Koloff beat Ivan Koloff
Al Perez beat Chris Champ
The Midnight Express DCO with The Fantastics
Steel Cage: The Road Warriors beat The Warlord & The Barbarian in a steel cage match

4/29/88: Norfolk, VA @ Scope
Ric Flair & Arn Anderson beat Lex Luger & Sting
Midnight Rider beat Tully Blanchard barbed wire match
Steve Williams beat Larry Zbyszko
Jimmy & Ron Garvin beat Kevin Sullivan & Rick Steiner
Mike Rotundo & Kevin Sullivan beat Ricky Santana & ?
Shaska Whatley & Tiger Conway, Jr. beat Kendall Windham & Italian Stallion
Green Machine beat Gene Ligon

4/29/88: Miami, FL @ James L. Knight Center
Sting beat NWA World Champ Ric Flair by DQ
Midnight Rider beat Tully Blanchard by DQ
Lex Luger beat Arn Anderson by CO
Barry Windham draw Mike Rotundo
Kevin Sullivan beat Jimmy Garvin
The Fantastics beat The Midnight Express by DQ
Rick Steiner beat Kendall Windham
Bugsy McGraw beat Crusher Balboa
Ricky Santana beat Rocky King

4/30/88: Detroit, MI @ Cobo Hall
The Road Warriors beat The Warlord & The Barbarian
Sting beat NWA World Champ Ric Flair by DQ
Mike Rotundo draw Steve Williams
Kevin Sullivan & Rick Steiner NC with Jimmy & Ron Garvin
Larry Zbyszko beat Ron Simmons
The Sheepherders beat Brad Armstrong & Tim Horner
Ivan Koloff beat Jimmy Valiant

4/30/88: Laurinburg, NC
Midnight Rider & Lex Luger beat Arn Anderson, Tully Blanchard & James J. Dillon in a handicap match
The Fantastics beat The Midnight Express
Nikita Koloff beat Al Perez by DQ
Barry Windham beat Rocky King
Shaska Whatley beat Kendall Windham
Chris Champ draw The Terminator
Ricky Santana beat Green Machine

5/1/88: Indianapolis, IN @ Market Square Arena
Jimmy Garvin beat Kevin Sullivan
Brad Armstrong & Tim Horner beat The Midnight Express
Steve Williams beat Arn Anderson
The Road Warriors beat The Warlord & The Barbarian
Lex Luger & Nikita Koloff beat The Sheepherders
Dusty Rhodes DCO with Tully Blanchard
NWA World Champ Ric Flair beat Sting via pinfall

5/2/88: Bishopville, SC
The Fantastics beat The Midnight Express

5/2/88: Greenville, SC @ Memorial Auditorium
Dusty Rhodes reinstated by the NWA.
Dusty Rhodes & Dr Death Steve Williams beat Tully Blanchard & Arn Anderson
Lex Luger & Sting beat the Sheepherders
Nikita Koloff DCO Dick Murdoch
Mighty Wilbur beat Terminator
Barry Windham beat Italian Stallion
Shaska Whatley beat Johnny Ace
Tiger Conway Jr beat John Savage

5/4/88: Atlanta, GA @ WTBS Studios (TV)
The Midnight Express vs. Jerry Price & Cody Starr
Sting vs. Bob Emory
Al Perez vs. Gary Royal
The Warlord & The Barbarian vs. Curtis Thompson & ?
Steve Williams vs. Keith Steinborn
Kevin Sullivan vs. Robbie Aumen
Barry Windham vs. Larry Davis
The Fantastics vs. ?? Strickland & Tony Borman
Ivan Koloff vs. David Isley

5/5/88: Raleigh, NC @ Dorton Arena (TV)
Rick Steiner & Kevin Sullivan beat Tommy Angel & Bob Emory
Barry Windham beat Italian Stallion
Nikita Koloff & Steve Williams beat Cruel Connection
Arn Anderson beat Chris Champ
The Midnight Express beat Joe Cruz & Tony Suber
Al Perez beat Rob Riddle
The Fantastics beat Bear Collie & Larry Stevens
Dusty Rhodes, Lex Luger & Nikita Koloff vs. Ric Flair, Barry Windham & Tully Blanchard
The Fantastics beat The Midnight Express by DQ

5/5/88: Johnstown, PA
The Road Warriors beat The Warlord & The Barbarian
Sting beat Larry Zbyzsko
The Fantastics beat The Midnight Express by DQ
Mighty Wilbur beat Luke Williams by DQ
Butch Miller draw Johnny Ace
Rip Morgan beat Jimmy Jackson
Sy Youngblood beat Johnny Rotten

5/6/88: Pittsburgh, PA @ Civic Arena
Road Warriors beat Warlord & Barbarian cage match
Steve Williams beat NWA World Champ Ric Flair DQ
Al Perez NC with Nikita Koloff
The Fantastics beat The Midnight Express
Barry Windham & Arn Anderson beat Brad Armstrong & Tim Horner
Dusty Rhodes beat Tully Blanchard bullrope match
Sting beat Dick Murdoch
The Sheepherders beat Johnny Ace & Mighty Wilbur

5/7/88: Baltimore, MD @ Civic Center
NWA World Champ Ric Flair beat Sting
Steve Williams & Dusty Rhodes beat Tully Blanchard & Arn Anderson by DQ
The Road Warriors beat The Sheepherders
Al Perez NC with Nikita Koloff
The Fantastics beat The Midnight Express
Barry Windham beat Tim Horner
Dick Murdoch beat Mighty Wilbur
Larry Zbyszko beat Johnny Ace

5/8/88: Roanoke, VA @ Civic Center
NWA World Champ Ric Flair beat Sting in a cage match
The Warlord, The Barbarian & Ivan Koloff beat Nikita Koloff & The Road Warriors
Steve Williams beat Kevin Sullivan
The Fantastics beat The Midnight Express by DQ
Ron Garvin beat Larry Zbyszko by DQ
Jimmy Garvin beat Rick Steiner
The Sheepherders beat Johnny Ace & Bugsy McGraw
Al Perez beat Ricky Santana
Barry Windham beat Italian Stallion

5/9/88: Greenville, SC @ Memorial Auditorium
Steve Williams beat Ric Flair DQ NWA World title match
Nikita Koloff beat Al Perez
Road Warriors & Jimmy Garvin beat the Varsity Club & Larry Zbyszko
Ron Simmons beat cruel Connection #1
Bugsy McGraw beat Terminator
Brad Armstrong beat Chris Champ

5/9/88: Fayetteville, NC @ Cumberland County Civic Center (TV)
The Fantastics beat The Midnight Express
Arn Anderson vs. Ronnie Garvin
The Fantastics vs. Ivan Koloff & The Warlord

5/10/88: Cherryville, NC
The Fantastics beat The Midnight Express

5/11/88: Miami, FL @ James L. Knight Center
Steve Williams beat NWA World Champ Ric Flair DQ
Dusty Rhodes & Sting NC Tully Blanchard & Barry Windham
Road Warriors beat The Warlord & The Barbarian
Rick Steiner & Mike Rotundo beat Jim & Ron Garvin
Arn Anderson beat Ricky Santana
Al Perez beat Bobby Brooks

5/12/88: Tallahassee, FL @ Leon County Civic Center (TV)
Dusty Rhodes beat Tully Blanchard bullrope match
Road Warriors beat Warlord & Barbarian by DQ
The Fantastics vs. Robbie Aumen & Jerry Price
Steve Williams vs. Gary Phelps
Mike Rotundo & Rick Steiner vs. Jimmy & Ron Garvin
Al Perez vs. Russ Mosley
Ricky Santana vs. Mike Jackson
Arn Anderson vs. Ryan Wagner
Barry Windham vs. Keith Steinborn

5/12/88: Walterboro, SC
The Fantastics beat The Midnight Express

5/13/88: Hammond, IN @ Civic Center
The Fantastics beat The Midnight Express

5/13/88: Houston, TX @ Sam Houston Coliseum
NWA United States Title tournament
1st Round
Lex Luger NC with Al Perez
Barry Windham beat Midnight Rider (Italian Stallion)
Nikita Koloff beat Ivan Koloff
Larry Zbyszko beat Rudy Gonzales

Semifinals
Barry Windham received a bye
Nikita Koloff beat Tully Blanchard

Finals
Barry Windham beat Nikita Koloff to win vacant NWA United States Title
The Road Warriors beat The Warlord & The Barbarian
Steve Williams beat Arn Anderson
NWA World Champ Ric Flair beat Sting cage match

5/14/88: Chicago, IL @ UIC Pavilion
Sting beat NWA World Champ Ric Flair by DQ
The Road Warriors beat The Midnight Express
Al Perez DCO with Nikita Koloff

Mike Rotundo beat Jimmy Garvin
Ricky Santana & Mighty Wilbur beat Max Blue & Harley Matson
Rick Steiner beat Bugsy McGraw
Larry Zbyszko draw Ron Garvin
The Fantastics beat The Sheepherders

5/15/88: Wilmington, NC
The Fantastics beat The Midnight Express
The Warlord vs. Tim Horner
The Sheepherders vs. Mighty Wilbur & Johnny Ace
Ron Garvin vs. Arn Anderson

5/15/88: Asheville, NC @ Civic Center (TV)
Larry Zbyszko & Al Perez beat Italian Stallion & Tommy Angel by submission
Barry Windham beat Mighty Wilbur (9:22) by countout
Ron Garvin beat Mike Rotundo (12:30) by DQ
The Fantastics beat The Midnight Express
Sting & The Road Warriors vs. Ric Flair, Arn Anderson & Tully Blanchard

5/16/88: Greenville, SC @ Memorial Auditorium
Ronnie Garvin, Sting & Lex Luger beat Ric Flair, Barry Windham & Tully Blanchard by DQ
Mike Rotundo beat Jimmy Garvin
Road Warriors beat Midnight Express
The Fantastics beat the Sheepherders
Arn Anderson beat Italian Stallion
Ron Simmons beat Shaska Whatley
Bugsy McGraw beat Tiger Conway Jr.

5/17/88: West Jefferson, NC
The Fantastics beat The Midnight Express

5/19/88: Fisherville, VA
Lex Luger beat Tully Blanchard
Mike Rotundo draw Jimmy Garvin
The Warlord & The Barbarian beat Kendall Windham & Italian Stallion
Ron Simmons beat Chris Champ
Jimmy Valiant & Bugsy McGraw beat Cruel Connection
Mighty Wilbur beat Tommy Angel
Rick Steiner beat Mark Fleming

5/20/88: Norfolk, VA @ Scope (TV)
Tim Horner vs. Rip Morgan
Kevin Sullivan vs. Italian Stallion
The Fantastics vs. Ivan Koloff & The Warlord
Bugsy McGraw & Ron Simmons beat Kevin Sullivan & Rick Steiner by DQ
Nikita Koloff beat Larry Zbyszko by DQ
Mike Rotundo beat Jimmy Garvin via pinfall
Dusty Rhodes, Lex Luger, Sting & Nikita Koloff beat Ric Flair, Barry Windham, Arn Anderson & Tully Blanchard by DQ

5/21/88: Atlanta, GA @ WTBS Studios (TV)
Arn Anderson vs. David Isley
Mike Rotundo vs. Trent Knight
Sting vs. Max MacGyver
Barry Windham vs. Ryan Wagner
Al Perez vs. Keith Steinborn
Tully Blanchard vs. Dave Spearman
Mike Rotundo & Rick Steiner vs. Rick Allen & ?
Nikita Koloff vs. Bob Riddle

5/21/88: Richmond, VA @ Coliseum
NWA World Champ Ric Flair beat Sting
Dusty Rhodes, Lex Luger & Nikita Koloff NC with Barry Windham, Tully Blanchard & Arn Anderson
Mike Rotundo beat Steve Williams by DQ
Jimmy Garvin beat Rick Steiner
Al Perez beat Chris Champ
Ron Simmons & Bugsy McGraw beat Cruel Connection
The Sheepherders beat Mighty Wilbur & Gary Royal

5/22/88: Atlanta, GA @ Omni
Steve Williams beat NWA World Champ Ric Flair DQ
Dusty Rhodes, Sting & Lex Luger NC with Barry Windham, Tully Blanchard & Arn Anderson
The Fantastics beat The Midnight Express
The Road Warriors beat The Sheepherders
Nikita Koloff beat Al Perez by DQ
Jimmy & Ron Garvin beat Kevin Sullivan & Mike Rotundo
Warlord, Barbarian & Ivan Koloff beat Tim Horner, Italian Stallion & Bugsy McGraw
Larry Zbyszko draw Brad Armstrong
Rick Steiner beat Kendall Windham

5/23/88: Hartsville, SC
The Fantastics beat The Midnight Express

5/24/88: Elberton, GA
The Fantastics beat The Midnight Express

5/24/88: Hillsville, VA
Lex Luger & Nikita Koloff beat Tully Blanchard & Arn Anderson
Jimmy Garvin beat Mike Rotundo by DQ
Al Perez beat Chris Champ
Rip Morgan beat Rocky King
The Sheepherders beat George South & Gary Royal

5/26/88: Louisville, KY @ Convention Center
The Midnight Express DCO with The Fantastics

5/27/88: St. Louis, MO @ Arena
Steve Williams beat NWA World Champ Ric Flair DQ
Dusty Rhodes & Lex Luger NC with Barry Windham & Tully Blanchard
Road Warriors beat Warlord & Barbarian cage match
The Fantastics beat The Midnight Express
Sting beat Mike Rotundo
Nikita Koloff beat Al Perez by DQ
The Sheepherders beat Bugsy McGraw & Gary Royal

5/28/88: Atlanta, GA @ WTBS Studios (TV)
The Fantastics vs. Larry Stevens & Trent Knight
Sting, Nikita Koloff & Steve Williams vs. Ryan Wagner, Dale Laperouse & Gary Phelps
Al Perez vs. Bob Riddle
Arn Anderson vs. Keith Steinborn
Ron Garvin & Mighty Wilbur vs. Robbie Aumen & Jed Grundy

5/28/88: Charleston, WV @ Civic Center
Steve Williams beat NWA World Champ Ric Flair DQ
Lex Luger NC with Barry Windham
Dusty Rhodes beat Tully Blanchard bullrope match
The Fantastics beat The Midnight Express
Larry Zbyszko beat Ron Garvin by countout
Ivan Koloff beat Kendall Windham
Arn Anderson beat Italian Stallion
Ron Simmons draw Tiger Conway, Jr.

5/29/88: Greensboro, NC @ Coliseum
Warlord & Barbarian beat Road Warriors & Sting DQ
Steve Williams beat NWA World Champ Ric Flair DQ
Dusty Rhodes & Lex Luger beat Tully Blanchard & Barry Windham
Nikita Koloff beat Al Perez by DQ
Mike Rotundo & Rick Steiner beat Kendall Windham & Bugsy McGraw
Arn Anderson beat Italian Stallion
The Sheepherders draw Ron Simmons & Mighty Wilbur

5/30/88: Union, SC
The Fantastics beat The Midnight Express

5/30/88: Savannah, GA @ Civic Center (TV)
Barry Windham beat Larry Stevens
Brad Armstrong & Tim Horner & Mighty Wilbur beat Bear Collie, Bob Riddle, & Curtis Thompson
Jimmy Garvin beat David Isley
Sting beat Tony Suber
Kevin Sullivan beat Curtis Thompson
Nikita Koloff & Steve Williams beat Joe Cruz & Trent Knight
Al Perez & Larry Zbyszko beat Tommy Angel & Bob Emory
Dusty Rhodes vs. Barry Windham in a lumberjack match

5/31/88: Sumter, SC @ Exhibition Center (TV)
Bobby Eaton beat Tommy Rogers (12:51) via pinfall
Sting beat Stan Lane (8:47) via pinfall
Lex Luger beat Arn Anderson (8:07) by DQ
Bobby Fulton beat Al Perez (5:30) by DQ
Barry Windham & Tully Blanchard beat Ron Garvin & Mighty Wilbur
Nikita Koloff & Steve Williams DCO Midnight Express
Arn Anderson beat Tommy Angel (2:00) via pinfall
Midnight Express beat Kendall Windham & Italian Stallion
Tommy Rogers & Bobby Fulton beat Larry Zbyzsko & Al Perez

6/2/88: Raleigh, NC @ Dorton Arena
Lex Luger NC with Barry Windham
Nikita Koloff & Steve Williams beat Tully Blanchard & Arn Anderson by DQ
The Warlord, The Barbarian & Ivan Koloff beat Mighty Wilbur, Chris Champ & Kendall Windham
Jimmy Garvin beat Kevin Sullivan
Rick Steiner beat Gary Royal
Jimmy Valiant beat Tiger Conway, Jr.
Bugsy McGraw beat John Savage

6/2/88: Bluefield, WV @ Armory
The Fantastics beat The Midnight Express
Sting beat Mike Rotundo by DQ
Ron Garvin beat Al Perez by DQ
Brad Armstrong & Tim Horner draw The Sheepherders
Larry Zbyszko beat Italian Stallion
Ron Simmons beat Cruel Connection II
Rip Morgan beat Rocky King

6/3/88: Richmond, VA @ Coliseum
Lex Luger NC with Barry Windham
Sting & Nikita Koloff beat Tully Blanchard & Arn Anderson by DQ
Mike Rotundo beat Steve Williams by countout
Warlord & Barbarian beat Brad Armstrong & Tim Horner
Ivan Koloff beat Kendall Windham
Larry Zbyszko beat Chris Champ
Ron Simmons beat Tiger Conway, Jr.
Mighty Wilbur beat Cruel Connection
Al Perez beat Mark Fleming

6/4/88: Atlanta, GA @ WTBS Studios (TV)
Ron Garvin vs. Russ Tyler
The Fantastics vs. Keith Steinborn & Dave Spearman
Mike Rotundo vs. Trent Knight
Barry Windham vs. Curtis Thompson
Nikita Koloff & Steve Williams vs. Bob Riddle & Bob Emory
The Warlord, Barbarian & Ivan Koloff vs. Tony Suber, ?? Paradise & Cody Starr
Kevin Sullivan & Rick Steiner vs. Jerry Price & Grundy
Jimmy Garvin vs. Bobby Rose
Larry Zbyzsko & Al Perez vs. Gary Phelps & Dale Laperouse
Sting vs. Tommy Royal
Arn Anderson & Tully Blanchard vs. Rick Allen & Robbie Aumen

6/4/88: Charlotte, NC @ Coliseum
Midnight Express beat Brad Armstrong & Tim Horner

6/5/88: Roanoke, VA @ Civic Center (TV)
Arn Anderson & Tully Blanchard beat Bear Collie & Curtis Thompson
Al Perez beat Mark Fleming
Ivan Koloff, The Warlord & The Barbarian beat Tommy Angel, Joe Cruz & Trent Knight
Ronnie Garvin beat George South
Barry Windham beat Lex Luger

6/5/88: Columbus, OH @ Ohio Center
The Fantastics beat The Midnight Express

6/6/88: Greenville, SC @ Memorial Auditorium
Lex Luger DCO Barry Windham
Bobby Fulton beat Bobby Eaton
Powers of Pain & Ivan Koloff beat Ronnie & Jimmy Garvin & Mighty Wilbur
Larry Zbyszko beat Trent Knight
Jimmy Valiant & Italian Stallion beat Tiger Conway Jr & John Savage
Cruel Connection #1 beat Tony Suber

6/7/88: Columbia, SC @ Township Auditorium
Bobby Eaton beat Tim Horner

6/7/88: Gainesville, FL @ Stephen O'Connell Center
Jimmy & Ronnie Garvin vs. Rick Steiner & Kevin Sullivan
Arn Anderson & Tully Blanchard vs. Nikita Koloff & Sting
Mike Rotundo vs. Steve Williams
Dusty Rhodes & Lex Luger vs. Ric Flair & Barry Windham

6/8/88: Miami, FL @ James L. Knight Center
Barry Windham beat Brad Armstrong (13:56) via pinfall
Tommy Rogers & Bobby Fulton beat Sheepherders
Jimmy & Ron Garvin beat Mike Rotundo & Rick Steiner (13:14)
Nikita Koloff beat Al Perez (11:50) by DQ at 11:50
Sting & Dusty Rhodes DDQ Arn Anderson & Tully Blanchard (11:01)

6/9/88: Dunn, NC @ Triton H.S.
Chris Champ beat Cruel Connection II
Cruel Connection I beat Larry Stevens
Rip Morgan beat Gene Ligon
Rocky King & Bugsy McGraw beat Tiger Conway, Jr. & Tony Suber
Rick Steiner beat Jimmy Valiant
Jimmy Garvin beat Mike Rotundo by countout
Brad Armstrong & Tim Horner beat Sheepherders DQ

6/9/88: Tallahassee, FL @ Leon County Civic Center

6/10/88: Houston, TX @ Sam Houston Coliseum
Dusty Rhodes beat Tully Blanchard barbed wire match
Lex Luger, Nikita Koloff & Steve Williams NC with Ric Flair, Arn Anderson & Barry Windham
Sting beat Mike Rotundo by DQ
Al Perez beat Jimmy Garvin
The Fantastics beat The Midnight Express
The Warlord, The Barbarian & Ivan Koloff beat Ron Garvin, Mighty Wilbur & Kendall Windham
Larry Zbyszko beat Chris Champ
Rick Steiner beat Randy Hogan
Kevin Sullivan beat ??

6/11/88: Atlanta, GA @ WTBS Studios (TV)
Sting vs. Rick Allen
Barry Windham beat Curtis Thompson (3:11) via pinfall
Steve Williams vs. Trent Knight
Tully Blanchard vs. Dave Spearman
Kevin Sullivan vs. Bob Riddle
Arn Anderson vs. Tommy Angel
The Midnight Express vs. Ryan Wagner & Bob Emory
The Fantastics vs. The Grappler & Joe Cruz

6/11/88: Baltimore, MD @ Civic Center
Lex Luger & Dusty Rhodes NC with Ric Flair & Barry Windham
Sting & Nikita Koloff beat Tully Blanchard & Arn Anderson by DQ
Mike Rotundo draw Steve Williams
The Warlord & The Barbarian beat Ron Garvin & Mighty Wilbur
Al Perez beat Mark Fleming
Ivan Koloff beat Larry Winters
Brad Armstrong beat Bounty Hunter

6/11/88: Florence, SC @ Civic Center
Fantastics beat Midnight Express in a steel cage match

6/12/88: Asheville, NC @ Civic Center
The Fantastics beat The Midnight Express

6/12/88: Albany, GA @ Civic Center (TV)
Steve Williams beat Joe Cruz
Barry Windham beat Trent Knight
Arn Anderson & Tully Blanchard beat ?
Sting beat Agent Steele
The Midnight Express beat Curtis Thompson & ??
The Fantastics beat Tommy Angel & Bob Riddle
The Midnight Express draw Sting & Steve Williams
The Fantastics beat The Midnight Express
Lex Luger NC with Barry Windham
Nikita Koloff & Sting beat Tully Blanchard & Ric Flair by DQ

6/13/88: Columbus, GA @ Municipal Auditorium
The Fantastics beat The Midnight Express

6/14/88: Spartanburg, SC @ Memorial Auditorium
The Fantastics vs. The Sheepherders
Ron Garvin vs. Ivan Koloff
Midnight Express beat Tim Horner & Brad Armstrong
Bugsy McGraw vs. Shaska Whatley
Ron Simmons vs. Tiger Conway, Jr.
Italian Stallion vs. Rip Morgan
Kendall Windham vs. Rick Steiner

6/16/88: Harrisonburg, VA @ Harrisonburg H.S.
The Road Warriors beat Rick Steiner & Mike Rotundo
Ron Garvin & Mighty Wilbur beat Ivan Koloff & Larry Zbyszko
Jimmy Garvin beat Kevin Sullivan
Ivan Koloff beat Mark Fleming
Kendall Windham beat Cruel Connection I
Italian Stallion beat Cruel Connection II

6/16/88: Albany, GA @ Civic Center

6/17/88: Charleston, WV @ Civic Center
Bugsy McGraw beat Chris Champ
Ron Garvin beat Gary Royal
Jimmy Garvin beat Cruel Connection I
Al Perez beat Mighty Wilbur
Sting & Steve Williams beat Larry Zbyzsko & Cruel Connection II
The Fantastics beat The Midnight Express
The Road Warriors beat Mike Rotundo & Rick Steiner

6/18/88: Atlanta, GA @ WTBS Studios (TV)
The Fantastics beat Agent Steel & Curtis Thompson
Nikita Koloff & Steve Williams beat Mac McGyver & Rusty Riddle
The Road Warriors beat Robbie Aumen & J.C. Wilde
Al Perez beat Dark Star
Russian Assassin beat Italian Stallion
Ronnie Garvin beat Jerry Price
Arn Anderson & Tully Blanchard beat Tommy Angel & Jed Grundy
Kevin Sullivan beat Ryan Wagner
The Midnight Express & The Sheepherders beat Jimmy Garvin, Brad Armstrong, Tim Horner & Mighty Wilbur

6/18/88: Philadelphia, PA @ Civic Center
Dusty Rhodes & Lex Luger NC with Ric Flair & Barry Windham
Sting & Nikita Koloff beat Arn Anderson & Tully Blanchard by DQ
Paul Ellering beat Paul Jones by countout
The Road Warriors beat Kevin Sullivan & Rick Steiner
Steve Williams beat Larry Zbyszko
Mike Rotundo beat Jimmy Garvin
The Midnight Express beat Brad Armstrong & Tim Horner
Al Perez beat Kendall Windham

6/19/88: Johnson City, TN @ Freedom Hall (TV)
Al Perez beat Max MacGyver via pinfall
Sting, Nikita Koloff & Steve Williams beat Joe Cruz, Doug Savage & Mark Starr
The Road Warriors beat Arn Anderson & Tully Blanchard by DQ
Lex Luger DCO with Barry Windham

6/20/88: Montgomery, AL @ Garrett Coliseum
Italian Stallion beat Ron Simmons
Rick Steiner beat Kendall Windham
Mike Rotundo draw Brad Armstrong
Ivan Koloff beat Tim Horner
The Road Warriors beat The Sheepherders
Sting, Steve Williams & Brad Armstrong beat Ric Flair, Arn Anderson & Tully Blanchard
Lex Luger NC with Barry Windham

6/21/88: Birmingham, AL @ Civic Center

6/22/88: Atlanta, GA @ WTBS Studios (TV)
Sting beat Jerry Price
Ivan Koloff & Russian Assassin beat Robbie Aumen & Keith Steinborn
Brad Armstrong & Tim Horner & Kendall Windham beat The Cruel Connection & Mac McGyver
Scott Putski beat David Isley
The Road Warriors beat Gary Royal & J.C. Wilde
Nikita Koloff beat Ryan Wagner
The Sheepherders beat Allen & Italian Stallion
Arn Anderson & Tully Blanchard beat Bowen & Joe Cruz
Steve Williams beat Bear Collie
Barry Windham beat Bobby Rose

6/23/88: Nashville, TN @ Municipal Auditorium
The Fantastics beat The Midnight Express

6/24/88: Charlottesville, VA @ University Hall
Midnight Express beat Brad Armstrong & Tim Horner
Arn Anderson & Tully Blanchard vs. Nikita Koloff & Sting

6/26/88: Orlando, FL @ Arena
Dusty Rhodes, Lex Luger, The Road Warriors & Paul Ellering beat James J. Dillon, Ric Flair, Tully Blanchard, Arn Anderson & Barry Windham
Al Perez beat Nikita Koloff in a Texas death match
Sting beat Mike Rotundo by DQ
Steve Williams beat Kevin Sullivan by DQ
The Fantastics beat The Midnight Express
The Rock & Roll Express beat The Sheepherders
Ivan Koloff & Russian Assassin beat Jimmy & Ron Garvin
Larry Zbyszko beat Bugsy McGraw

6/27/88: Greenville, SC @ Memorial Auditorium (TV)
Italian Stallion & Kendall Windham vs Al Perez & Larry Zbyszko
Chris Champ vs Shaska Whatley
Jimmy & Ronnie Garvin vs Kevin Sullivan & Rick Steiner
Mighty Wilbur vs Ivan Koloff
The Lightning Express vs the Midnight Express
The Fantastics vs the Sheepherders
Mike Rotundo vs Dr Death Steve williams
Lex Luger, Sting, Nikta Koloff & Dusty Rhodes vs Ric Flair Tully Blanchard, Barry Windham & Arn Anderson
Road Warriors vs Powers of Pain

6/28/88: Columbia, SC @ Township Auditorium (TV)
The Fantastics beat Jim Cornette & The Midnight Express bunkhouse match

6/29/88: Atlanta, GA @ WTBS Studios (TV)
Ronnie Garvin beat Larry Stevens
Sting beat Gary Phelps
Al Perez beat George South
Jimmy Garvin beat Agent Steele
Mike Rotundo beat Tony Suber
The Fantastics beat Mike Jackson & Curtis Thompson
The Rock & Roll Express beat Joe Cruz & Bob Riddle
Ivan Koloff & Russian Assassin beat Larry Davis & Keith Steinborn
Steve Williams beat Ryan Wagner
The Sheepherders beat Danny Little & J.C. Wilde

7/1/88: Norfolk, VA @ Scope
Bugsy McGraw & Italian Stallion beat Tiger Conway, Jr. & Rip Morgan
Ronnie Garvin beat Larry Zbyszko
Ivan Koloff, Rick Steiner & Russian Assassin beat Brad Armstrong, Tim Horner & Mighty Wilbur
The Rock & Roll Express beat The Sheepherders
Jimmy Garvin beat Kevin Sullivan in a prince of darkness match

Mike Rotundo beat Steve Williams by DQ
Russian Chain: Nikita Koloff beat Al Perez
The Fantastics beat The Midnight Express & Jim Cornette bunkhouse match
Dusty Rhodes beat Tully Blanchard in an I quit match
Lex Luger, The Road Warriors & Sting beat Arn Anderson, Ric Flair, Barry Windham & James J. Dillon in a steel cage match

7/2/88: Charlotte, NC @ Coliseum
Dusty Rhodes, Nikita Koloff, Lex Luger, Sting & Paul Ellering beat Ric Flair, Barry Windham, Arn Anderson, Tully Blanchard & James J. Dillon War Games
The Road Warriors beat Russian Assassin & Ivan Koloff in a scaffold match
Steve Williams beat Mike Rotundo by DQ
The Fantastics beat The Midnight Express & Jim Cornette in a bunkhouse match
Jimmy Garvin beat Kevin Sullivan in a prince of darkness match
The Rock & Roll Express beat The Sheepherders
Ron Garvin beat Rick Steiner
Al Perez beat Mighty Wilbur
Larry Zbyszko beat Kendall Windham
Brad Armstrong, Tim Horner & Bugsy McGraw beat Cruel Connection, Chris Champ & Tiger Conway, Jr.

7/3/88: Amarillo, TX @ Civic Center
Brad Armstrong & Tim Horner draw The Sheepherders
Larry Zbyszko beat Bugsy McGraw
The Rock & Roll Express beat Rick Steiner & Kevin Sullivan
Ronnie Garvin DCO with Dick Murdoch
Mike Rotundo beat Jimmy Garvin
The Fantastics beat The Midnight Express & Jim Cornette in a handicap, street fight match
Nikita Koloff beat Al Perez in a Russian chain match
Sting & Steve Williams beat Arn Anderson & Tully Blanchard by DQ
Dusty Rhodes & Lex Luger beat Ric Flair & Barry Windham in a Texas bullrope match
The Road Warriors beat Ivan Koloff & Russian Assassin in a scaffold match

7/4/88: Dallas, TX @ Reunion Arena
Lex Luger & Dusty Rhodes beat Ric Flair & Barry Windham
The Road Warriors beat Ivan Koloff & Russian Assassin in a scaffold match
The Fantastics beat Jim Cornette & The Midnight Express in a handicap, bunkhouse match

7/5/88: Miami, FL @ James L. Knight Center
The Road Warriors beat Russian Assassin & Ivan Koloff in a scaffold match
Dusty Rhodes & Lex Luger beat Ric Flair & Barry Windham by countout
Sting & Steve Williams beat Tully Blanchard & Arn Anderson by DQ
The Fantastics beat The Midnight Express & Jim Cornette in a bunkhouse match
Ron Garvin draw Dick Murdoch
Jimmy Garvin beat Kevin Sullivan
The Rock & Roll Express beat The Sheepherders
Mike Rotundo beat Kendall Windham

7/6/88: Atlanta, GA @ WTBS Studios (TV)
Brad Armstrong beat Mike Jackson
The Rock & Roll Express beat Phelps & Gary Royal
Sting beat Larry Stevens
The Midnight Express beat Little & Ryan Wagner
Steve Williams beat Joe Cruz
Rick Steiner & Mike Rotundo beat Rick Allen & George South
Arn Anderson & Tully Blanchard beat Tony Suber & J.C. Wilde
Barry Windham beat Max McGyver
The Sheepherders beat Tommy Angel & Keith Steinborn

7/6/88: Tampa, FL @ Stadium
Al Perez beat Kendall Windham
Ronnie Garvin, Ron Simmons & Sting beat Ivan Koloff, Russian Assassin & Larry Zbyszko
The Rock & Roll Express beat The Sheepherders
The Fantastics beat The Midnight Express & Jim Cornette in a handicap match
Jimmy Garvin draw Dick Murdoch
Mike Rotundo beat Steve Williams by DQ
Dusty Rhodes, Nikita Koloff, Lex Luger & Road Warriors beat Ric Flair, Arn Anderson, Tully Blanchard, Barry Windham & Kevin Sullivan in war games

7/7/88: Raleigh, NC @ Dorton Arena
Lex Luger, Sting, Nikita Koloff & Dusty Rhodes beat Ric Flair, Arn Anderson, Tully Blanchard & Barry Windham
The Road Warriors beat Russian Assassin & Ivan Koloff
The Fantastics beat The Midnight Express & Jim Cornette in a bunkhouse match
Mike Rotundo beat Steve Williams by DQ
The Rock & Roll Express beat The Sheepherders
Jimmy Garvin beat Dick Murdoch
Ron Garvin & Mighty Wilbur beat Larry Zbyszko & Al Perez
Kendall Windham draw Rick Steiner
Brad Armstrong beat Cruel Connection I

7/8/88: Pittsburgh, PA @ Civic Arena
Lex Luger & Dusty Rhodes beat Ric Flair & Barry Windham
The Fantastics beat The Midnight Express in a scaffold match
The Road Warriors beat Tully Blanchard & Arn Anderson by DQ
Sting, Nikita Koloff & Steve Williams beat Ivan Koloff, Assassin & Dick Murdoch
Mike Rotundo beat Jimmy Garvin
The Rock & Roll Express beat The Sheepherders
Ron Garvin beat Rick Steiner
Al Perez & Larry Zbyszko beat Brad Armstrong & Tim Horner
Rip Morgan NC with Bugsy McGraw
Chris Champ draw Kendall Windham

7/9/88: Chicago, IL @ UIC Pavilion
The Road Warriors & Dusty Rhodes beat Ric Flair, Arn Anderson & Tully Blanchard in a cage match to win vacant NWA World 6-man Tag Title
Lex Luger beat Barry Windham in a Texas death match
The Fantastics beat Midnight Express & Jim Cornette in a bunkhouse match
Sting & Nikita Koloff beat Ivan Koloff & Dick Murdoch
The Rock & Roll Express beat The Sheepherders
Jimmy Garvin beat Kevin Sullivan
Ron Garvin NC with Mike Rotundo
Steve Williams beat Al Perez by DQ
Rick Steiner draw Tim Horner
Russian Assassin beat Kendall Windham

7/10/88: Baltimore, MD @ Arena
Rick Steiner & Dick Murdoch beat Tim Horner & Kendall Windham (7:00)
Nikita Koloff & Sting draw Arn Anderson & Tully Blanchard (20:07)
The Midnight Express beat The Fantastics via pinfall to win NWA US tag Title
Jimmy & Ron Garvin, Road Warriors & Steve Williams beat Kevin Sullivan, Mike Rotundo, Al Perez, Russian Assassin & Ivan Koloff in a Tower of Doom match
Barry Windham beat Dusty Rhodes via pinfall
NWA World Champ Ric Flair beat Lex Luger via blood stoppage

7/11/88: Salisbury MD (TV)
The Road Warriors beat Ivan Koloff & Russian Assassin in a scaffold match
Ric Flair & Barry Windham NC with Lex Luger & Sting
Steve Williams & Nikita Koloff beat Arn Anderson & Tully Blanchard by DQ
The Fantastics beat The Midnight Express & Jim Cornette bunkhouse match
Rick Steiner draw Kendall Windham

7/12/88: Huntsville, AL @ Von Braun Civic Center
The Road Warriors, Sting, Lex Luger & Nikita Koloff beat Ric Flair, Barry Windham, Tully Blanchard, Arn Anderson & James J. Dillon in a War Games
The Fantastics beat The Midnight Express & Jim Cornette
Mike Rotundo beat Steve Williams by DQ
The Rock & Roll Express beat The Sheepherders
Ivan Koloff, Russian Assassin & Dick Murdoch beat Chris Champ, Ron Simmons & Mighty Wilbur
Brad Armstrong & Tim Horner beat Tiger Conway, Jr. & Rip Morgan
Ron Garvin beat Italian Stallion
Al Perez beat Kendall Windham
Larry Zbyszko beat Bugsy McGraw

7/13/88: Louisville, KY @ Convention Center
The Fantastics beat The Midnight Express & Jim Cornette bunkhouse match

7/14/88: Chattanooga, TN @ UTC Arena
The Road Warriors, Sting, Lex Luger & Steve Williams beat James J. Dillon, Ric Flair, Barry Windham, Arn Anderson & Tully Blanchard in a war games
Fantastics beat Midnight Express in a scaffold match
Nikita Koloff beat Al Perez in a chain match
Mike Rotundo beat Brad Armstrong
The Rock & Roll Express beat The Sheepherders
Dick Murdoch, Ivan Koloff & Russian Assassin beat Chris Champ, Mighty Wilbur & Kendall Windham
Ron Garvin beat Italian Stallion
Tim Horner beat Larry Zbyszko

7/15/88: Richmond, VA @ Coliseum
The Road Warriors, Sting, Lex Luger & Nikita Koloff beat Barry Windham, Tully Blanchard, Arn Anderson, Ric Flair & James J. Dillon in a War Games
Fantastics beat Midnight Express in a scaffold match
Steve Williams beat Mike Rotundo by DQ
The Rock & Roll Express beat The Sheepherders
Dick Murdoch, Russian Assassin & Ivan Koloff beat Ron Simmons, Jimmy Garvin & Mighty Wilbur
Al Perez beat Brad Armstrong
Larry Zbyszko beat Tim Horner
Bugsy McGraw beat Rip Morgan
Kevin Sullivan & Rick Steiner beat Italian Stallion & Kendall Windham
Ron Garvin beat Chris Champ

7/16/88: Atlanta, GA @ WTBS Studios (TV)
Sting & Steve Williams beat Green Hornet & Dale Laperhouse
Brad Armstrong beat Larry Stevens
Dick Murdoch beat Curtis Thompson
Arn Anderson & Tully Blanchard beat Tommy Angel & Trent Knight
Al Perez beat Agent Steele
The Road Warriors beat Rick Allen & Gary Phelps
The Midnight Express beat ?? Spearman & J.C. Wilde
Nikita Koloff beat Gary Royal

7/16/88: Greensboro, NC @ Coliseum
Dusty Rhodes, Lex Luger, Nikita Koloff, Paul Ellering & Steve Williams beat Ric Flair, Barry Windham, Tully Blanchard, Arn Anderson & James J. Dillon War Games
The Road Warriors beat Ivan Koloff & Russian Assassin in a scaffold match
The Fantastics beat The Midnight Express & Jim Cornette in a handicap, bunkhouse match
Sting beat Mike Rotundo by DQ
Al Perez beat Brad Armstrong
The Rock & Roll Express beat The Sheepherders
Jimmy Garvin beat Rick Steiner
Dick Murdoch beat Gary Royal
Ron Garvin beat Italian Stallion
Bugsy McGraw & Tim Horner beat Rip Morgan & Larry Zbyszko

7/17/88: Charleston, WV @ Civic Center
Sting, Lex Luger, Nikita Koloff & Steve Williams beat Ric Flair, Barry Windham, Arn Anderson & Tully Blanchard in a scaffold match

The Road Warriors beat Ivan Koloff & Russian Assassin in a scaffold match
Jimmy Garvin beat Kevin Sullivan in a prince of darkness match
Ron Garvin beat Mighty Wilbur in a bunkhouse match
The Fantastics beat The Midnight Express
Al Perez beat Brad Armstrong
The Rock & Roll Express beat The Sheepherders
Mike Rotundo beat Bugsy McGraw
Tim Horner beat Larry Zbyszko

7/18/88: Columbus, GA @ Municipal Auditorium (TV)
Sting beat Mike Rotundo by DQ
The Fantastics beat Jim Cornette & The Midnight Express in a handicap, bunkhouse match
Dusty Rhodes, Nikita Koloff & Steve Williams NC with Ric Flair, Barry Windham & Tully Blanchard
The Road Warriors beat Ivan Koloff & Russian Assassin in a scaffold match

7/19/88: Atlanta, GA @ WTBS Studios (TV)
Russian Assassin vs. Trent Knight
The Fantastics vs. Chris Champ & Sean Royal
Ron Garvin vs. Tommy Angel
Rock & Roll Express vs. Agent Steele & George South
The Road Warriors vs. Rick Allen & J.C. Wilde
Tully Blanchard vs. Ryan Wagner
Lex Luger vs. Keith Steinborn
Sting, Nikita Koloff & Steve Williams vs. Green Hornet, Larry Stevens & Cruel Connection II
NWA World Champ Ric Flair vs. Curtis Thompson

7/19/88: Macon, GA @ Coliseum (TV)
The Fantastics beat The Midnight Express & Jim Cornette in a handicap, bunkhouse match

7/21/88: Cincinnati, OH @ Riverfront Coliseum
Sting, Lex Luger, The Road Warriors & Nikita Koloff beat Ric Flair, Arn
Anderson, Barry Windham, Tully Blanchard & James J. Dillon in a War Games
Mike Rotundo NC with Steve Williams
The Fantastics beat The Midnight Express & Jim Cornette in a handicap, bunkhouse match
Jimmy Garvin & Mighty Wilbur beat Ivan Koloff & Russian Assassin
The Rock & Roll Express beat The Sheepherders
Ron Garvin beat Chris Champ
Al Perez beat Tim Horner
Rick Steiner beat Ron Simmons
Bugsy McGraw beat Rip Morgan

7/22/88: St. Louis, MO @ Arena
Nikita Koloff, Dusty Rhodes, Lex Luger & Steve Williams beat Ric Flair, Arn Anderson, Tully Blanchard & Barry Windham in a War Games
The Road Warriors beat Ivan Koloff & Russian Assassin in a scaffold match
The Fantastics beat The Midnight Express & Jim Cornette in a handicap, bunkhouse match
Sting draw Mike Rotundo
Bugsy McGraw beat Rip Morgan
Al Perez & Larry Zbyszko beat Jimmy Garvin & Kendall Windham
The Rock & Roll Express beat The Sheepherders
Ron Garvin beat Mighty Wilbur

7/23/88: Philadelphia, PA @ Civic Center
Nikita Koloff, Lex Luger, Dusty Rhodes & The Road Warriors beat Barry Windham, Arn Anderson, Ric Flair, Tully Blanchard & JJ Dillon in a War Games
Sting beat Mike Rotundo by DQ
The Fantastics beat The Midnight Express & Jim Cornette bunkhouse match
Steve Williams & Jimmy Garvin beat Ivan Koloff & Russian Assassin
Al Perez beat Mighty Wilbur
The Rock & Roll Express beat The Sheepherders
Rick Steiner beat Kendall Windham
Larry Zbyszko beat Bugsy McGraw
Ron Garvin beat Italian Stallion

7/24/88: Roanoke, VA @ Civic Center
The Fantastics beat The Midnight Express & Jim Cornette in a handicap, bunkhouse match

7/24/88: Johnson City, TN @ Freedom Hall
Italian Stallion vs. Cruel Connection II
Bugsy McGraw vs. Cruel Connection I
The Rock & Roll Express vs. Al Perez & Larry Zbyzsko
The Fantastics vs. Jim Cornette & The Midnight Express in a handicap, bunkhouse match
Steve Williams vs. Mike Rotundo
Lex Luger, Sting, Nikita Koloff & The Road Warriors vs. Ric Flair, Barry Windham, Arn Anderson & Tully Blanchard & James J. Dillon in a War Games

7/25/88: Atlanta, GA @ WTBS Studios (TV)
Barry Windham & Ron Garvin vs. Tommy Angel & Dale Laperouse
Arn Anderson & Tully Blanchard vs. J.C. Wilde & Trent Knight
Sting vs. Rick Allen
The Fantastics vs. Mike Jackson & Stevens
Mike Rotundo & Rick Steiner vs. Brad Holiday & Bob Emory
The Sheepherders vs. Tony Suber & Brett Holiday
Brad Armstrong vs. Joe Cruz
Kevin Sullivan vs. J.C. Wilde
Mike Jackson & Curtis Thompson vs. Tommy Angel & Bob Riddle
Chris Champ vs. Don Valentine
Bobby Eaton vs. Gary Phelps
Al Perez vs. Rick Allen
Rip Morgan vs. Bear Collie

7/25/88: Fayetteville, NC @ Cumberland County Civic Center
The Fantastics beat The Midnight Express & Jim Cornette in a handicap, bunkhouse match

7/26/88: Savannah, GA @ Civic Center (TV)
The Fantastics beat The Midnight Express in a scaffold match

7/27/88: Jacksonville, FL @ Memorial Coliseum (TV)
The Fantastics beat The Midnight Express & Jim Cornette in a handicap, bunkhouse match
Rick Steiner beat Kendall Windham (5:30) via pinfall
The Rock & Roll Express & The Fantastics beat Mike Rotundo, Rick Steiner, Ivan Koloff & Russian Assassin via pinfall

7/28/88: Daytona, FL @ Ocean Center
The Road Warriors, Sting, Dusty Rhodes & Nikita Koloff beat Ric Flair, Arn Anderson, Tully Blanchard, Kevin Sullivan & James J. Dillon in a War Games Texas Death Match
Lex Luger beat Barry Windham Texas death match
Steve Williams NC with Mike Rotundo
The Fantastics beat The Midnight Express
Ricky Morton, Tim Horner & Brad Armstrong beat Dick Murdoch, Russian Assassin & Ivan Koloff
Al Perez beat Kendall Windham
Rick Steiner beat Italian Stallion
Bugsy McGraw beat Larry Zbyszko
Ron Garvin beat Will Clifford

7/29/88: Houston, TX @ Sam Houston Coliseum
The Fantastics beat The Midnight Express & Jim Cornette in a handicap, bunkhouse match

7/30/88: Landover, MD @ Capital Centre
Tim Horner beat Rick Steiner
Bugsy McGraw draw Larry Zbyszko
Dick Murdoch beat Rip Morgan
Russian Assassin beat Mighty Wilbur
Brad Armstrong & Ricky Morton beat The Sheepherders
The Fantastics beat The Midnight Express & Jim Cornette in a handicap, bunkhouse match
Mike Rotundo DCO with Steve Williams
Tower of Doom: Dusty Rhodes, Lex Luger, The Road Warriors, Sting & Paul Ellering beat Ric Flair, Arn Anderson, Tully Blanchard, Barry Windham, Kevin Sullivan & James J. Dillon in a tower of doom match

7/31/88: Detroit, MI @ Cobo Hall
Dusty Rhodes & The Sheik beat Kevin Sullivan & Dick Murdoch
Sting, Lex Luger & The Road Warriors beat Ric Flair, Tully Blanchard, Barry Windham & Arn Anderson
Fantastics beat Midnight Express in a scaffold match
Nikita Koloff beat Al Perez
Rick Steiner beat Kendall Windham
Ricky Morton & Brad Armstrong beat The Sheepherders
Ron Garvin beat Tim Horner
Jimmy Garvin beat Ivan Koloff
Larry Zbyszko draw Bugsy McGraw

8/1/88: Milwaukee, WI @ City Auditorium
Dusty Rhodes, Sting, Lex Luger & The Road Warriors beat Ric Flair, Tully Blanchard, Arn Anderson, Barry Windham & James J. Dillon in a War Games
Mike Rotundo beat Nikita Koloff
The Fantastics beat The Midnight Express in a bunkhouse match
Dick Murdoch beat Russian Assassin
Jimmy Garvin beat Rick Steiner
Ricky Morton & Brad Armstrong beat The Sheepherders
Larry Zbyszko beat Tim Horner
Bugsy McGraw beat Rip Morgan
Al Perez beat Kendall Windham

8/2/88: Sioux City, IA
Sting, Steve Williams & Nikita Koloff beat Ric Flair, Arn Anderson & Tully Blanchard
Lex Luger beat Barry Windham
The Fantastics beat The Midnight Express & Jim Cornette
Road Warriors beat Ivan Koloff & Russian Assassin
Al Perez beat Jimmy Garvin
Ron Garvin draw Dick Murdoch
Mike Rotundo beat Kendall Windham
Larry Zbyszko beat Ed Tossel

8/3/88: Seattle, WA
Lex Luger, Nikita Koloff & The Road Warriors beat Barry Windham, Tully Blanchard, Ric Flair & Arn Anderson in a steel cage match
Steve Williams DCO with Mike Rotundo
Jimmy Garvin beat Kevin Sullivan in a taped fist match
Sting & Dick Murdoch beat Ivan Koloff & Ron Garvin
Al Perez beat Mighty Wilbur via forfeit
The Fantastics beat The Midnight Express & Jim Cornette in a handicap, bunkhouse match
Larry Zbyszko beat Kendall Windham
Steve Doll & Scott Peterson beat Buddy Rose & Col. DeBeers
Mike Golden beat The Grappler by DQ
Avalanche (aka Paul Neu) beat Billy Two Eagles
Note: Card co-promoted with Don Owen

8/4/88: Las Vegas, NV @ Thomas & Mack center
Dusty Rhodes & Lex Luger beat Ric Flair & Barry Windham
Sting & Nikita Koloff beat Arn Anderson & Tully Blanchard by DQ
The Road Warriors beat Ivan Koloff & Russian Assassin in a scaffold match
Kendall Windham beat Mike Rotundo by DQ
The Fantastics beat The Midnight Express & Jim Cornette in a handicap, bunkhouse match
Ron Garvin draw Dick Murdoch
Al Perez beat Kendall Windham
Jimmy Garvin beat Larry Zbyszko

8/5/88: Inglewood, CA @ The Forum
Dusty Rhodes, Lex Luger, The Road Warriors & Paul Ellering beat Ric Flair, Tully Blanchard, Arn Anderson, Barry Windham & James J. Dillon in a War Games
The Fantastics beat The Midnight Express & Jim Cornette in a handicap, bunkhouse match
Nikita Koloff beat Al Perez in a chain match
Steve Williams beat Rick Steiner
Sting beat Mike Rotundo by DQ

Dick Murdoch beat Larry Zbyszko
Jimmy Garvin beat Kevin Sullivan
Rick Steiner beat Mike Starr
Ron Garvin beat Riki Ataki

8/6/88: Atlanta, GA @ WTBS Studios (TV)
Rick Steiner & Mike Rotundo beat Bob Emory & Brett Holiday
The Sheepherders beat Brad Holiday & Tony Suber
Brad Armstrong beat Joe Cruz
Kevin Sullivan beat J.C. Wilde
Mike Jackson & Curtis Thompson beat Tommy Angel & Rusty Riddle
Chris Champ beat Don Valentine
Bobby Eaton beat Gary Phelps
Al Perez beat Rick Allen
Rip Morgan beat Bear Collie

8/6/88: Oakland, CA @ Kaiser Convention Center
Dusty Rhodes, Lex Luger, The Road Warriors & Paul Ellering beat Ric Flair, Barry Windham, Arn Anderson, Tully Blanchard & James J. Dillon in a War Games
The Fantastics beat The Midnight Express by DQ
Mike Rotundo NC with Steve Williams
Sting beat Larry Zbyszko
Ron Garvin draw Dick Murdoch
Nikita Koloff beat Al Perez in a chain match
Jimmy Garvin beat Kevin Sullivan
Ivan Koloff beat Kendall Windham

8/7/88: Kansas City, MO @ Kemper Arena
Dusty Rhodes, Dick Murdoch & Lex Luger beat Ric Flair, Tully Blanchard & Barry Windham
The Road Warriors beat Ivan Koloff & Russian Assassin in a scaffold match
Steve Williams beat Arn Anderson
Sting beat Mike Rotundo by DQ
The Fantastics beat The Midnight Express by DQ
Ron Garvin beat Kendall Windham
Jimmy Garvin beat Kevin Sullivan
Al Perez beat J.R. Hogg
Rick Steiner draw Larry Zbyszko

8/10/88: Atlanta, GA @ WTBS Studios (TV)
Ricky Morton vs. Lee Ramsey
Kevin Sullivan, Mike Rotundo & Rick Steiner vs. Don Valentine, Rick Allen & Gary Phelps
Brad Armstrong vs. Dave Spearman
Al Perez vs. Max MacGyver
Barry Windham vs. Curtis Thompson
The Fantastics vs. Brad Holiday & Brett Holiday

8/12/88: Norfolk, VA @ Scope (TV)
Lex Luger beat NWA World Champ Ric Flair by DQ
Tully Blanchard & Arn Anderson NC Midnight Express
Barry Windham beat Nikita Koloff
Brad Armstrong beat Al Perez by DQ
Mike Rotundo beat Kendall Windham

8/13/88: Macon, GA @ Coliseum
Midnight Express DDQ Arn Anderson & Tully Blanchard

8/17/88: Atlanta, GA @ WTBS Studios (TV)
Al Perez beat Jerry Price
The Fantastics beat Jim Boss & The Menace
Russian Assassin beat Robbie Aumen
Ricky Morton beat Dave Spearman
Italian Stallion & Kendall Windham beat Keith Steinborn & Don Valentine
Rick Steiner beat Tony Suber
Brad Armstrong beat Max McGyver
The Midnight Express beat Bear Collie & The Shadow
Mike Rotundo beat Rick Allen
Nikita Koloff beat Russ Tyler
The Sheepherders beat Brad Holiday & Brett Holiday
Barry Windham beat Lee Ramsey

8/18/88: Raleigh, NC @ Dorton Arena
Lex Luger beat NWA World Champ Ric Flair by DQ
Arn Anderson NC with Stan Lane
The Road Warriors beat Rick Steiner & Mike Rotundo
Ricky Morton beat Barry Windham by DQ
Sting beat Al Perez
The Fantastics beat The Sheepherders
Brad Armstrong beat Ivan Koloff
Russian Assassin beat Italian Stallion

8/19/88: Richmond, VA @ Coliseum
Lex Luger beat NWA World Champ Ric Flair by DQ
The Midnight Express NC with Arn Anderson & Tully Blanchard
Dusty Rhodes beat Russian Assassin
Barry Windham beat Steve Williams by countout
The Road Warriors beat Mike Rotundo & Rick Steiner
Sting beat Al Perez
Ricky Morton, Nikita Koloff & Brad Armstrong beat The Sheepherders & Rip Morgan
Ron Simmons draw Larry Zbyszko

8/20/88: Philadelphia, PA @ Civic Center
The Road Warriors beat The Midnight Express by DQ
Dusty Rhodes beat Russian Assassin
Barry Windham beat Nikita Koloff by countout
Sting, Steve Williams, Ricky Morton & Brad Armstrong beat Arn Anderson, Tully Blanchard, Larry Zbyszko & Al Perez
The Fantastics beat The Sheepherders
Ron Simmons & Brad Armstrong draw Rick Steiner & Mike Rotundo

8/21/88: Cincinnati, OH @ Gardens
The Fantastics beat Mike Rotundo & Rick Steiner
Sting beat Al Perez via pinfall
Steve Williams beat Russian Assassin via pinfall
The Midnight Express beat Ricky Morton & Brad Armstrong (sub for Robert Gibson)
Barry Windham beat Nikita Koloff by countout
The Road Warriors beat Arn Anderson & Tully Blanchard by DQ
Lex Luger beat NWA World Champ Ric Flair by DQ

8/22/88: Sumter, SC @ Exhibition Center (TV)
The Midnight Express DDQ Arn Anderson & Tully Blanchard

8/24/88: Atlanta, GA @ WTBS Studios (TV)
Nikita Koloff & Ricky Morton beat Mac McGyver & Jerry Price
Russian Assassin beat Brett Holiday
Rick Steiner beat Keith Steinborn
Al Perez beat Gary Royal
Arn Anderson & Tully Blanchard beat Brad Holiday & Lee Ramsey
Brad Armstrong beat Gary Phelps
Sting beat Cruel Connection
Steve Williams beat The Menace
Jimmy Garvin beat Agent Steele
Mike Rotundo beat Eddie Sweat

8/25/88: Columbus, GA @ Municipal Auditorium
Nikita Koloff beat Al Perez by DQ
The Fantastics beat Kevin Sullivan & Mike Rotundo
Italian Stallion beat Kendall Windham
Ron Simmons beat Rip Morgan via pinfall
Steve Williams beat Rick Steiner via pinfall
Midnight Express DDQ Arn Anderson & Tully Blanchard
Lex Luger & Sting beat Ric Flair & Barry Windham DQ

8/26/88: Atlanta, GA @ Omni
Ricky Morton, Brad Armstrong, Nikita Koloff, Steve Williams & Jimmy Garvin beat Mike Rotundo, Rick Steiner, Ivan Koloff, Al Perez & Kevin Sullivan in a tower of doom match
Lex Luger beat NWA World Champ Ric Flair by DQ
The Road Warriors beat Tully Blanchard & Arn Anderson by DQ
Dusty Rhodes beat Russian Assassin
Barry Windham draw Sting
The Fantastics beat The Sheepherders
Italian Stallion beat Kendall Windham
Ron Simmons beat Rip Morgan

8/27/88: Charlotte, NC @ Coliseum
Lex Luger beat NWA World Champ Ric Flair by DQ
Jimmy Garvin, Brad Armstrong, Steve Williams & The Road Warriors beat Kevin Sullivan, Rick Steiner, Mike Rotundo, Ivan Koloff & Russian Assassin in a tower of doom match
Midnight Express NC Arn Anderson & Tully Blanchard
Dusty Rhodes & Sting beat Barry Windham & Larry Zbyszko
Nikita Koloff beat Al Perez
Ricky Morton beat Cruel Connection I
Rip Morgan & The Sheepherders beat Kendall Windham, Ron Simmons & Italian Stallion

8/28/88: Greensboro, NC @ Coliseum (TV)
Sting & The Road Warriors beat Kevin Sullivan, Mike Rotundo & Rick Steiner by DQ
Barry Windham beat Steve Williams by CO
The Midnight Express NC with Arn Anderson & Tully Blanchard
Lex Luger & Dusty Rhodes beat Ric Flair & Al Perez

8/28/88: Daytona, FL @ Ocean Center
Dusty Rhodes, The Road Warriors, Paul Ellering & Nikita Koloff vs. Ric Flair, Arn Anderson, Tully Blanchard, JJ. Dillon & Kevin Sullivan War Games
Barry Windham vs. Lex Luger
Mike Rotundo vs. Steve Williams
The Fantastics vs. The Midnight Express
Jimmy Garvin & The Rock & Roll Express vs. Russian Assassin, Ivan Koloff & Dick Murdoch
Kendall Windham vs. Al Perez
Brad Armstrong vs. Rick Steiner
Tim Horner vs. Larry Zbyszko
Bugsy McGraw vs. Krusher Knoff

8/29/88: Greenville, SC @ Memorial Auditorium
NWA World Tag Champs Tully Blanchard & Arn Anderson DDQ Midnight Express
Ricky Morton, Sting & the Fantastics beat The Russian Assassin, Ivan Koloff. Luke Williams & Rip Morgan
Mike Rotundo & rick Steiner beat Brad Armstrong & Ron Simmons
Al Perez beat Chris Champ
Kevin Sullivan beat Italian Stallion

8/30/88: Savannah, GA @ Civic Center (TV)
The Midnight Express DDQ Arn Anderson & Tully Blanchard

8/31/88: Atlanta, GA @ WTBS Studios (TV)
The Fantastics vs. George South & Keith Steinborn
The Midnight Express vs. Mike Jackson & Gary Royal
Mike Rotundo vs. Bob Emory
Barry Windham vs. Italian Stallion
Ron Simmons vs. Joe Cruz
Ricky Morton & Steve Williams vs. The Menace & Jerry Price
Ivan Koloff & Russian Assassin vs. ?? Jones & J.C. Wilde
Arn Anderson & Tully Blanchard vs. Tommy Angel & Trent Knight
Al Perez vs. Rick Allen

9/1/88: Raleigh, NC @ Dorton Arena
Arn Anderson & Tully Blanchard NC with The Midnight Express
Barry Windham beat Steve Williams by countout
Al Perez & Kevin Sullivan beat Sting & Nikita Koloff
Dick Murdoch beat Larry Zbyszko
Brad Armstrong, Ricky Morton & The Fantastics beat Mike Rotundo, Rick Steiner, The Sheepherders
Russian Assassin beat Chris Champ
Ivan Koloff beat George South
Italian Stallion beat Gary Royal

9/2/88: Norfolk, VA @ Scope (TV)
Lex Luger beat NWA World Champ Ric Flair by countout
Tully Blanchard & Arn Anderson beat The Midnight Express
Sting beat Barry Windham by DQ
Ricky Morton beat Russian Assassin
Steve Williams, Dick Murdoch & Nikita Koloff beat Kevin Sullivan, Mike Rotundo & Al Perez
The Fantastics beat The Sheepherders
Mike Rotundo beat Italian Stallion
Larry Zbyszko beat Mark Fleming

9/3/88: Baltimore, MD @ Civic Center
Lex Luger beat NWA World Champ Ric Flair by DQ
Tully Blanchard & Arn Anderson NC with The Midnight Express
Dusty Rhodes & Sting beat Al Perez & Barry Windham
Dick Murdoch beat Kevin Sullivan by DQ
Mike Rotundo beat Steve Williams by DQ
Nikita Koloff beat Rip Morgan
The Fantastics beat Ivan Koloff & Russian Assassin
Ricky Morton, Ron Simmons & Brad Armstrong beat The Sheepherders & Larry Zbyszko

9/4/88: Detroit, MI @ Cobo Hall
Lex Luger beat NWA World Champ Ric Flair by DQ
The Midnight Express NC with Tully Blanchard & Arn Anderson
Dusty Rhodes & Dick Murdoch beat Kevin Sullivan & Larry Zbyszko
Barry Windham beat Sting by DQ
Steve Williams beat Ivan Koloff
The Fantastics & Brad Armstrong beat The Sheepherders & Mike Rotundo
Rick Steiner beat Italian Stallion
Ron Simmons beat Rip Morgan

9/5/88: Covington, GA
George South beat Rip Morgan
Ron Simmons & Italian Stallion beat The Sheepherders in a 2 out of 3 falls match
Brad Armstrong beat Ivan Koloff via pinfall

9/7/88: Albany, GA @ Civic Center
Brad Armstrong draw Mike Rotundo (20:00)
Nikita Koloff & Steve Williams beat The Sheepherders via pinfall
Dusty Rhodes beat Kevin Sullivan (7:00) by pinning an interfering Gary Hart Ricky Morton beat Ivan Koloff in a Russian chain match
Sting beat Barry Windham by DQ

9/7/88: Atlanta, GA @ WTBS Studios (TV)
Sting beat Tommy Angel
Ron Simmons beat Rusty Riddle
The Fantastics beat Jerry Price & Lee Scott
Russian Assassin beat Keith Steinborn
Brad Armstrong & Ricky Morton beat Agent Steele & The Menace
Rick Steiner & Mike Rotundo beat David Isley & Larry Stevens
Steve Williams beat Don Valentine
Larry Zbyszko beat Tony Suber
Al Perez beat Mike Justice

9/9/88: Houston, TX @ Sam Houston Coliseum
Lex Luger beat NWA World Champ Ric Flair by DQ
The Midnight Express NC with Tully Blanchard & Arn Anderson
Steve Williams & Dusty Rhodes beat Al Perez & Kevin Sullivan
Barry Windham beat Sting by countout
Nikita Koloff beat Russian Assassin I
Ricky Morton beat Rip Morgan
Brad Armstrong beat Rick Steiner
The Fantastics beat Tug Taylor & Rip Morgan

9/10/88: Philadelphia, PA @ Civic Center
Lex Luger beat NWA World Champ Ric Flair by DQ
Dusty Rhodes beat Kevin Sullivan in a dog collar match
The Road Warriors beat Rip Morgan & Russian Assassin I
The Midnight Express beat Tully Blanchard & Arn Anderson to win NWA World Tag Title
Sting beat Barry Windham by DQ
Mike Rotundo beat Nikita Koloff by DQ
The Fantastics & Brad Armstrong beat Rick Steiner, Larry Zbyszko & Al Perez
Ricky Morton beat Curtis Thompson
Ron Simmons beat Agent Steele

9/11/88: Fayetteville, NC @ Cumberland County Civic Center (TV)
NWA United States Tag Title vacated when The Midnight Express won NWA World Tag Title
Also included The Midnight Express

9/11/88: Greensboro, NC @ Coliseum
Lex Luger beat NWA World Champ Ric Flair by DQ
Sting beat Barry Windham by DQ
Dusty Rhodes beat Al Perez in a dog collar match
The Road Warriors beat The Sheepherders
Russian Assassins beat Ricky Morton & Nikita Koloff by DQ
Steve Williams beat Rip Morgan
Mike Rotundo & Rick Steiner beat Brad Armstrong & Italian Stallion
The Midnight Express beat The Fantastics

9/12/88: Greenville, SC @ Memorial Auditorium
Brad Armstrong beat Luke Williams
Russian Assassin #1 beat Italian Stallion
Ricky Morton beat Al Perez
Nikita Koloff beat Rip Morgan
The Road Warriors & Steve Williams beat the Varsity Club & Kevin Sullivan
The Midnight Express beat The Fantastics
Sting beat Barry Windham by DQ

9/12/88: ??
Sting beat Barry Windham by DQ
Ricky Morton beat Ivan Koloff in a chain match
Dusty Rhodes beat Kevin Sullivan
Steve Williams & Nikita Koloff beat The Sheepherders
Brad Armstrong draw Mike Rotundo

9/13/88: Columbia, SC @ Township Auditorium (TV)
The Midnight Express beat The Fantastics

9/14/88: Atlanta, GA @ WTBS Studios (TV)

9/15/88: Atlanta, GA @ WTBS Studios (TV)

9/16/88: Richmond, VA @ Coliseum
NWA World Champ Ric Flair NC with Lex Luger
Sting beat Barry Windham by DQ
Dusty Rhodes beat Kevin Sullivan dog collar match
The Midnight Express beat The Fantastics
Road Warriors & Steve Williams beat Mike Rotundo, Rick Steiner & Larry Zbyszko
Russian Assassins beat Nikita Koloff & Italian Stallion
The Sheepherders beat Chris Champ & Mark Fleming
Ivan Koloff beat Rip Morgan

9/17/88: Charleston, SC @ Civic Center
The Road Warriors beat The Midnight Express

9/18/88: Roanoke, VA @ Civic Center
Lex Luger beat NWA World Champ Ric Flair by DQ
Sting beat Barry Windham by DQ
The Midnight Express beat The Fantastics
The Road Warriors beat Mike Rotundo & Rick Steiner
Russian Assassins beat Nikita Koloff & Italian Stallion
The Sheepherders beat Chris Champ & Mark Fleming
Larry Zbyszko beat Curtis Thompson

9/21/88: Atlanta, GA @ WTBS Studios (TV)
The Road Warriors beat The Menaces
Barry Windham beat Agent Steele
Sting beat Jerry Price
The Midnight Express beat Cruel Connection & Curtis Thompson
The Fantastics beat ?? Griffin & Mike Justice
Nikita Koloff beat Eddie Sweat
Brad Armstrong & Steve Williams beat ?? Jones & Keith Steinborn
Kevin Sullivan, Mike Rotundo & Rick Steiner beat ?? Hollis, Bill Mulkey & Gary Royal
Al Perez beat Max McGyver
Russian Assassins beat Italian Stallion & ?? Miles

9/23/88: Frederick, MD @ Community College Fieldhouse
Ric Flair & Barry Windham vs. Sting & Lex Luger
The Midnight Express vs. ?? & ??
Mike Rotundo vs. Steve Williams
The Sheepherders vs. The Fantastics
Nikita Koloff vs. Russian Assassin I
Russian Assassin II vs. Brad Armstrong
Al Perez vs. Ricky Morton

9/24/88: Washington, DC @ Armory
Al Perez beat Italian Stallion
Russian Assassins beat The Sheepherders
Mike Rotundo draw Steve Williams
Sting DCO with Barry Windham
Dusty Rhodes beat Kevin Sullivan
The Midnight Express beat The Fantastics
Lex Luger beat NWA World Champ Ric Flair by DQ

9/25/88: Atlanta, GA @ Omni
Lex Luger beat NWA World Champ Ric Flair by DQ
Sting beat Barry Windham by DQ
Dusty Rhodes beat Kevin Sullivan dog collar match
The Midnight Express beat The Fantastics
Russian Assassin II beat Ivan Koloff
Mike Rotundo, Rick Steiner & Al Perez beat Steve Williams, Nikita Koloff & Italian Stallion
Dick Murdoch beat Larry Zbyszko
Luke Wlliams beat Curtis Thompson

9/26/88: Greenville, SC @ Memorial Auditorium
Barry Windham beat Sting
Steve Williams & Dick Murdoch beat Midnight Express(c) by DQ in NWA Worl Tag Team Title match
Al Perez beat Ron Simmons
Italion Stallion beat Mike Rotundo
The Fantastics beat Rick Steiner & Larry Zbyszko
Assassin #1 beat George South
Assassin #2 beat Curtis Thompson
Gary Royal draw Agent Steele

9/27/88: Columbus, GA @ Municipal Auditorium (TV)
The Midnight Express beat The Fantastics

9/28/88: Atlanta, GA @ WTBS Studios (TV)
Ron Simmons vs. Eddie Sweat
Ivan Koloff vs. Agent Steele
Rick Steiner vs. Italian Stallion
Bam Bam Bigelow vs. Trent Knight
The Fantastics vs. The Menace & The Nightmare
Barry Windham vs. George South
Steve Williams vs. Joe Cruz
Sting vs. Terry Jones
The Midnight Express vs. Gary Royal & Jerry Price
Dick Murdoch vs. J.C. Wilde
Larry Zbyzsko & Al Perez vs. Mike Jackson & Keith Steinborn

9/30/88: Winnipeg, Manitoba @ Arena
Lex Luger beat NWA World Champ Ric Flair by DQ
The Midnight Express beat The Sheepherders
Barry Windham NC with Sting
Ivan Koloff & Nikita Koloff beat Russian Assassins by DQ
The Fantastics beat Larry Zbyszko & Rick Steiner
Mike Rotundo beat Italian Stallion
Rip Morgan beat Masked Invader

10/1/88: Brandon, Manitoba
Sting & Lex Luger beat Ric Flair & Barry Windham DQ
The Midnight Express beat The Fantastics
Nikita Koloff beat Russian Assassin I by DQ
Ivan Koloff beat Russian Assassin II
The Sheepherders beat Ron Ritchie & Bill Cody
Mike Rotundo beat Italian Stallion
Rick Steiner beat Larry Zbyszko

10/2/88: Chicago, IL @ UIC Pavilion
NWA World Champ Ric Flair draw Lex Luger
Sting beat Barry Windham by DQ
Russian Assassins beat Ivan Koloff & Nikita Koloff DQ
The Fantastics beat The Sheepherders
Midnight Express draw Dick Murdoch & Dusty Rhodes
Mike Rotundo beat Italian Stallion
Ron Simmons beat Rip Morgan

10/4/88: Macon, GA @ Coliseum (TV)
Barry Windham beat Dick Murdoch
Lex Luger beat NWA World Champ Ric Flair by DQ

10/5/88: Atlanta, GA @ WTBS Studios (TV)
The Road Warriors vs. Rick Allen & ?? Jones
Ron Simmons vs. the Menace
The Fantastics vs. Keith Steinborn & Jerry Price
Dick Murdoch vs. Cruel Connection I
Russian Assassin I vs. Brett Holiday
The Sheepherders vs. Mike Justice & J.C. Wilde
Rick Steiner vs. Curtis Thompson
The Midnight Express vs. Agent Steele & Mike Jackson
Barry Windham vs. Gary Royal
Nikita Koloff vs. Blue Demon
Larry Zbyzsko vs. Eddie Sweat

10/6/88: Raleigh, NC @ Dorton Arena
Lex Luger & Sting beat Ric Flair & Barry Windham
Nikita Koloff NC with Russian Assassin I
Midnight Express beat Kevin Sullivan & Rick Steiner
The Road Warriors beat Al Perez & Larry Zbyszko
Mike Rotundo beat Ron Simmons
Bobby Fulton beat Luke Williams
Italian Stallion beat Rip Morgan

10/7/88: Richmond, VA @ Coliseum (TV)
Sting & The Road Warriors vs. Mike Rotundo, Rick Steiner & Kevin Sullivan
Larry Zbyzsko beat Italian Stallion
Russian Assassins beat Ivan Koloff & Nikita Koloff DQ
Ric Flair & Barry Windham beat Lex Luger & Ron Simmons.
Kevin Sullivan vs. Bear Collie
Sting & Steve Williams vs. Mike Rotundo & Rick Steiner
Nikita Koloff vs. Al Perez

10/8/88: Charlotte, NC @ Coliseum

10/9/88: Greensboro, NC @ Coliseum
Lex Luger beat NWA World Champ Ric Flair by DQ
Russian Assassins beat Ivan Koloff & Nikita Koloff
Sting NC with Barry Windham
The Road Warriors beat Al Perez & Larry Zbyszko
Mike Rotundo beat Ron Simmons
The Fantastics beat Rick Steiner & Kevin Sullivan
The Sheepherders beat Chris Champ & Italian Stallion
Rip Morgan beat Curtis Thompson

10/10/88: Greenville, SC @ Memorial Auditorium
NWA World Tag Champs Midnight Express beat the Road Warriors by DQ
The Russian Assassins beat Ivan & Nikita Koloff
Mike Rotundo beat Italian Stallion
The Fantastics beat Al Perez & Larry Zbyszko
Dick Murdoch beat Kevin Sullivan
Rick Steiner beat Agent Steele
The Sheepherders beat Gary Royal & Chris Champ
Ron Simmons beat Rip Morgan

10/11/88: Fayetteville, NC @ Cumberland County Civic Center (TV)
The Road Warriors vs. The Midnight Express

10/12/88: Atlanta, GA @ WTBS Studios (TV)
Larry Zbyzsko & Al Perez vs. David Isley & Mike Justice
Bam Bam Bigelow vs. George South
Nikita Koloff vs. Russian Assassin II
Ron Simmons vs. John Savage
Eddie Gilbert vs. Trent Knight
Sheepherders vs. Curtis Thompson & Tommy Angel
Mike Rotundo & Rick Steiner vs. Gene Ligon & Joe Cruz
Kevin Sullivan vs. Bob Emory
Dick Murdoch vs. Agent Steele
The Midnight Express vs. George South & Gary Royal

10/13/88: Sumter, SC @ Exhibition Center (TV)
The Midnight Express beat The Road Warriors by DQ

10/14/88: Norfolk, VA @ Scope
The Midnight Express beat The Road Warriors by DQ

10/??/88: Charleston, SC @ Civic Center
Sheepherders beat Italian Stallion & Curtis Thompson
Steve Williams beat Rip Morgan via pinfall
Nikita Koloff beat Russian Assassin I via pinfall
The Fantastics beat the Mike Rotundo & Rick Steiner
The Road Warriors beat The Midnight Express
Lex Luger & Sting beat Ric Flair & Barry Windham DQ

10/15/88: Philadelphia, PA @ Civic Center
James J. Dillon beat Jim Cornette in a cage match
The Midnight Express beat The Fantastics
Barry Windham beat Sting by countout
Russian Assassins beat Ivan Koloff & Nikita Koloff
Road Warriors beat Rick Steiner & Mike Rotundo by countout
Kevin Sullivan beat Eddie Gilbert
Al Perez draw Ron Simmons
Larry Zbyszko beat Italian Stallion

10/16/88: Baltimore, MD @ Civic Center
Rick Steiner beat NWA World Champ Ric Flair by DQ
Russian Assassins beat Ivan Koloff & Nikita Koloff
The Midnight Express beat The Road Warriors by DQ
Barry Windham beat Sting by countout
The Fantastics beat Kevin Sullivan & Rick Steiner by DQ
Larry Zbyszko draw Eddie Gilbert
Al Perez beat Ron Simmons
Mike Rotundo beat Italian Stallion

10/17/88: Atlanta, GA @ WTBS Studios (TV)
Ron Simmons vs. Keith Steinborn
Russian Assassins vs. Jerry Price & Rick Allen
The Midnight Express vs. Mike Jackson & ?? Jones
Dick Murdoch vs. Larry Stevens
Ivan Koloff & Nikita Koloff vs. The Menaces
Larry Zbyzsko vs. Tony Suber
Eddie Gilbert vs. Gary Royal
Mike Rotundo vs. Eddie Sweat

10/19/88: Lansing, MI (TV)
Road Warrior Animal & Paul Ellering (sub for Road Warrior Hawk) beat The Midnight Express (3:39) by DQ
Brad Armstrong beat Al Perez (10:47) by DQ

10/20/88: Saginaw, MI (TV)
Sting (sub for Lex Luger) beat NWA World Champ Ric Flair by DQ
The Midnight Express vs. Mike Jackson & ?? Bruce
Eddie Gilbert & Ron Simmons beat Larry Zbyzsko & Al Perez via pinfall in NWA United States Tag Title tournament
The Sheepherders vs. ?? & ??
Ivan Koloff vs. ??
The Sheepherders vs. ?? & ??
Russian Assassins DDQ Ivan Koloff & Nikita Koloff in NWA United States Tag Title tournament
Eddie Gilbert vs. ??
Larry Zbyszko vs. ??
Kevin Sullivan & Rick Steiner vs. Randy Hogan & ??
The Road Warriors beat The Midnight Express by DQ

10/21/88: Detroit, MI @ Cobo Arena
The Sheepherders beat Ron Simmons & Tony Zon (9:45)
The Fantastics beat Larry Zbyzsko & Rip Morgan
Mike Rotundo beat Italian Stallion via pinfall
Eddie Gilbert beat Kevin Sullivan (3:32) by reverse decision
The Midnight Express beat The Road Warriors (6:30) by DQ
Ivan Koloff & Nikita Koloff beat Russian Assassins via pinfall
Sting (sub for Lex Luger) beat NWA World Champ Ric Flair (21:05) by DQ

10/22/88: Cincinnati, OH @ Gardens
Ric Flair & Barry Windham beat Sting & Ron Simmons (sub for Lex Luger)
The Midnight Express beat The Road Warriors by DQ

10/23/88: Charleston, WV @ Civic Center
The Midnight Express beat The Road Warriors by DQ

10/24/88: Little Rock, AR
The Midnight Express beat The Road Warriors by DQ

10/25/88: Jackson, TN
The Midnight Express beat The Road Warriors by DQ

10/26/88: Atlanta, GA @ WTBS Studios (TV)
The Midnight Express vs. Mike Justice & David Isley
Eddie Gilbert vs. Tommy Angel
Barry Windham vs. Bob Riddle
The Fantastics vs. Jerry Price & Mike Jackson
Mike Rotundo & Rick Steiner vs. Brad Holiday & Brett Holiday
Larry Zbyzsko & Al Perez vs. Keith Sweat & Rick Allen
Ivan Koloff vs. The Executioner
Italian Stallion vs. Gary Royal
Russian Assassins vs. Bob Emory & Keith Steinborn
The Sheepherders vs. ?? Hollis & ?? Jones
Ron Simmons vs. George South

10/26/88: Greenwood, MS
The Midnight Express beat The Road Warriors by DQ

10/27/88: Jackson, MS
The Midnight Express beat The Road Warriors by DQ
Lex Luger & Nikita Koloff beat Ric Flair & Al Perez
Dusty Rhodes beat Kevin Sullivan by DQ
Barry Windham beat Dick Murdoch
Ivan Koloff beat Russian Assassin II by DQ
Mike Rotundo beat Italian Stallion
The Fantastics & Ron Simmons beat The Sheepherders & Rip Morgan
Eddie Gilbert beat Larry Zbyszko

10/28/88: Baton Rouge, LA
The Midnight Express beat The Road Warriors by DQ

10/29/88: New Orleans, LA @ Municipal Auditorium
Lex Luger beat NWA World Champ Ric Flair by DQ
The Road Warriors beat The Midnight Express to win NWA World Tag Title
Steve Williams beat Larry Zbyszko
Kevin Sullivan beat Dusty Rhodes by DQ

10/30/88: Alexandria, LA
The Road Warriors beat The Midnight Express
Nikita Koloff & Lex Luger beat Ric Flair & Al Perez
Barry Windham NC with Sting
Steve Williams beat Larry Zbyszko
Eddie Gilbert beat Russian Assassin I by DQ
Mike Rotundo beat Italian Stallion
Ivan Koloff beat Russian Assassin II
The Fantastics & Ron Simmons beat The Sheepherders & Rip Morgan

11/1/88: Savannah, GA @ Civic Center (TV)
The Road Warriors beat The Midnight Express
The Sheepherders beat Ron Simmons & Eddie Gilbert

11/2/88: Jim Crockett Promotions was officially sold to Ted Turner, and renamed World Champship Wrestling

Check Out Mark James' Entire Line Of Books At
www.memphiswrestlinghistory.com
www.memphiswrestlingbook.com

Rags, Paper & Pins:
The Merchandising of
Memphis Wrestling

by
Jim Cornette
& Mark James

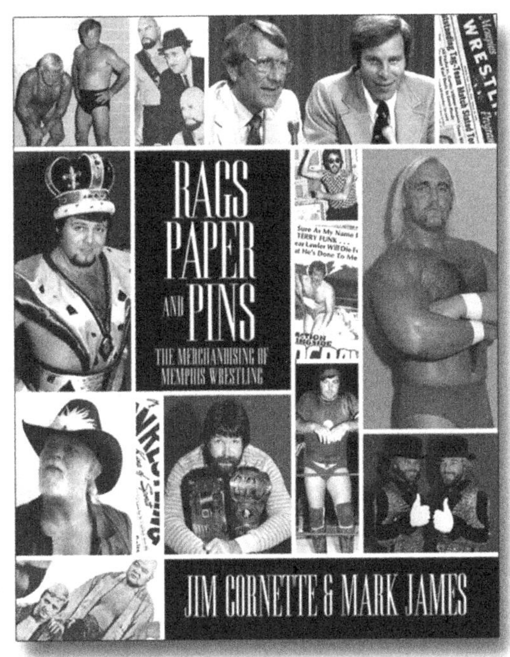

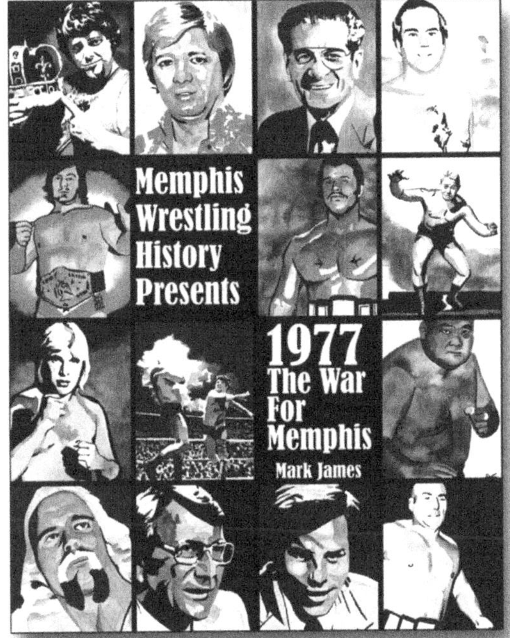

Memphis Wrestling History
Presents 1977

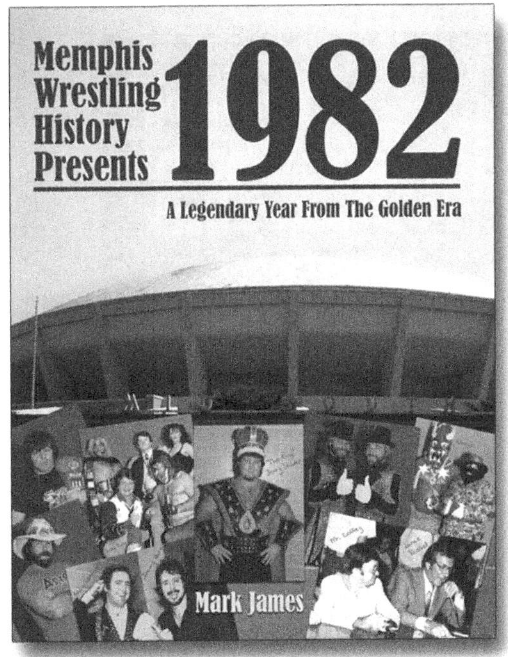

Memphis Wrestling History
Presents 1982

Check Out Mark James' Entire Line Of Books At
www.memphiswrestlinghistory.com
www.memphiswrestlingbook.com

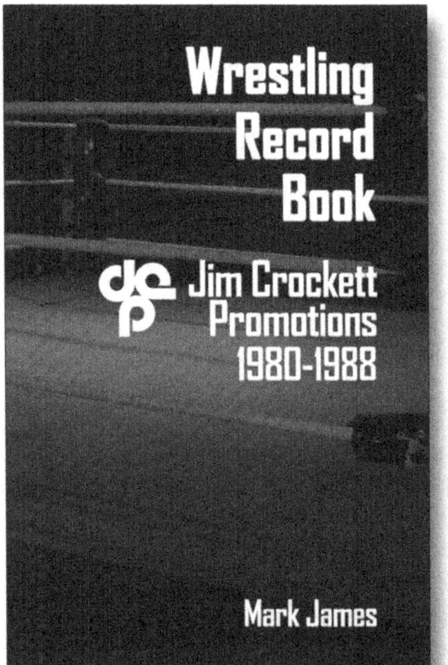

Wrestling Record Book: Jim Crockett Promotions 1980-1988

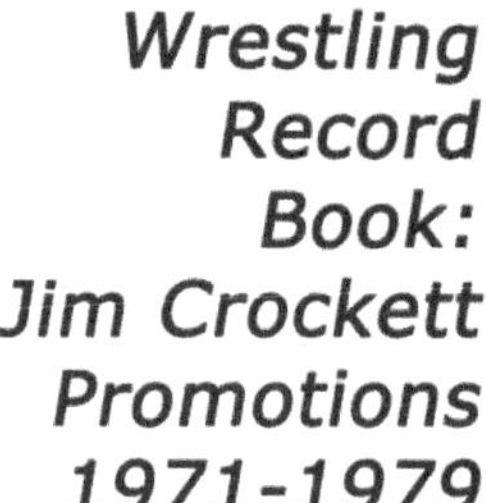

Wrestling Record Book: Jim Crockett Promotions 1971-1979

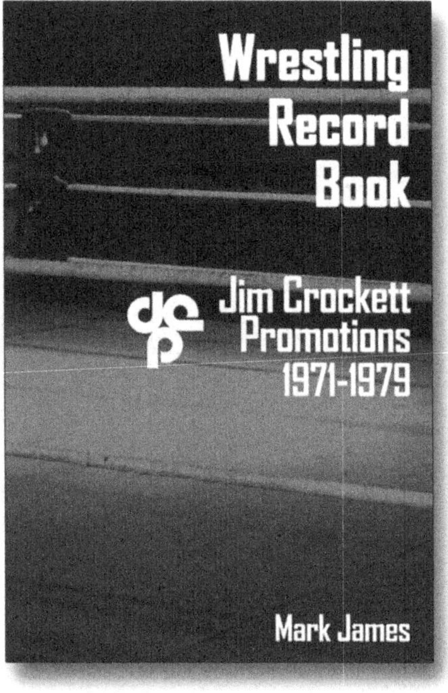

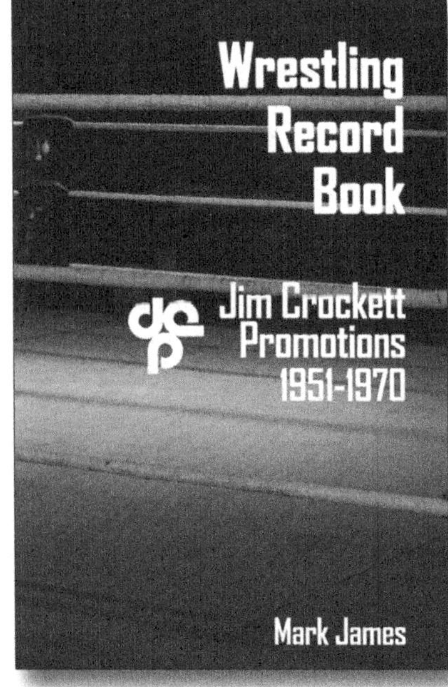

Wrestling Record Book: Jim Crockett Promotions 1951-1970

Check Out Mark James' Entire Line Of Books At
www.memphiswrestlinghistory.com
www.memphiswrestlingbook.com

Memphis Wrestling History: Tennesse Record Book 1980-1989

Memphis Wrestling History: Tennesse Record Book 1973-1979

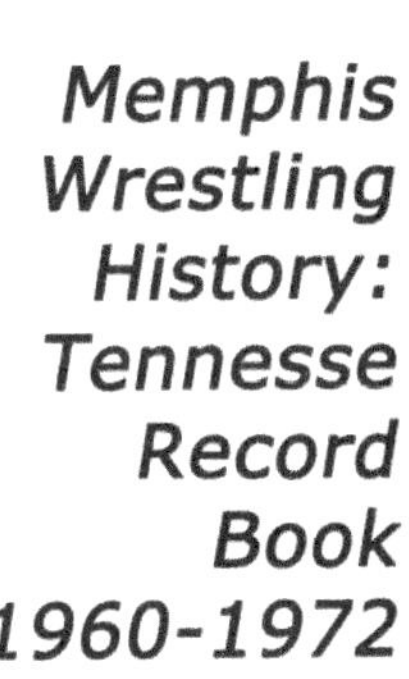
Memphis Wrestling History: Tennesse Record Book 1960-1972

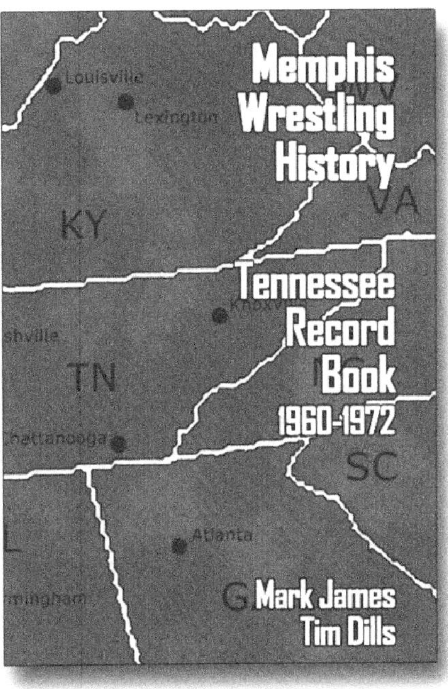

Check Out Mark James' Entire Line Of Books At
www.memphiswrestlinghistory.com
www.memphiswrestlingbook.com

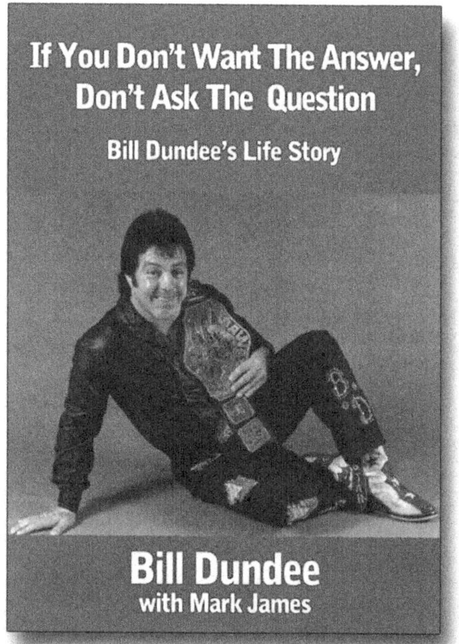

If You Don't Want The Answer, Don't Ask The Question
Bill Dundee's Autobiography

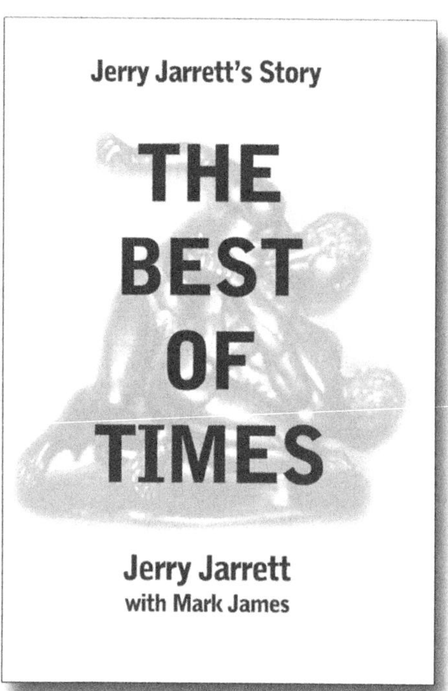

The Best Of Times
Jerry Jarrett's Autobiography

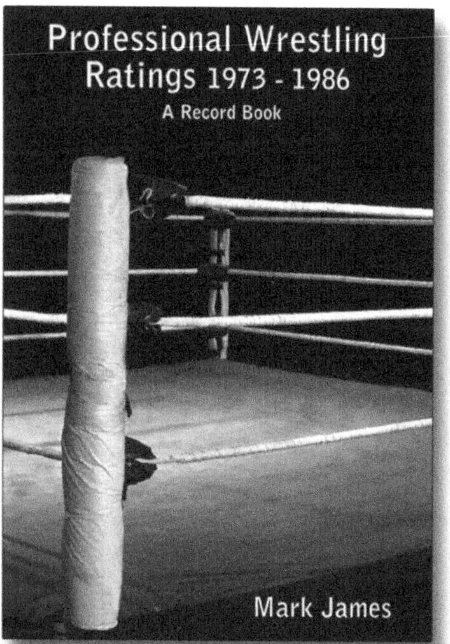

Professional Wrestling Ratings 1973-1986: A Record Book

Check Out Mark James' Entire Line Of Books At
www.memphiswrestlinghistory.com
www.memphiswrestlingbook.com

Memphis Wrestling History Presents The 1950s

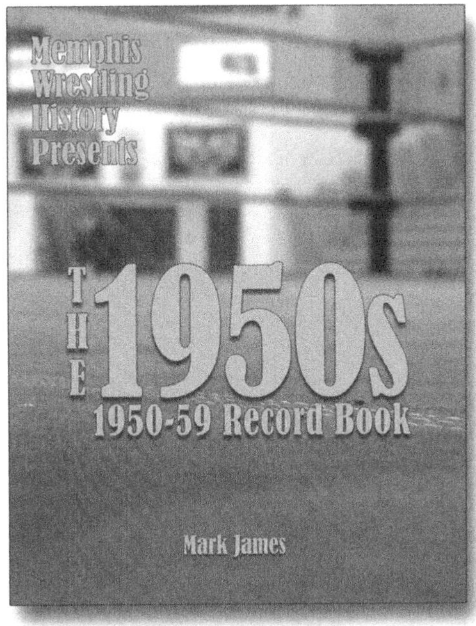

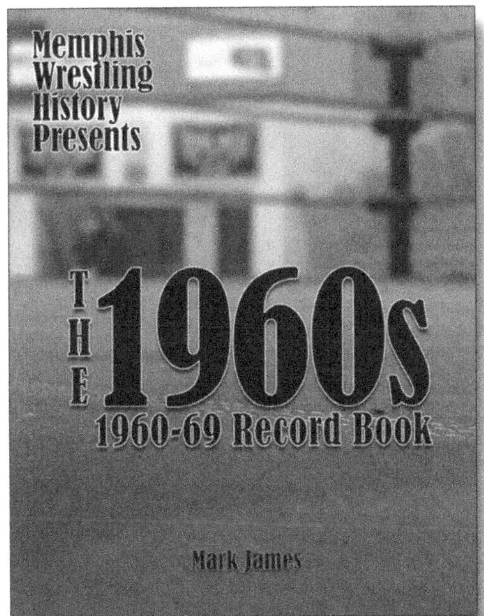

Memphis Wrestling History Presents The 1960s

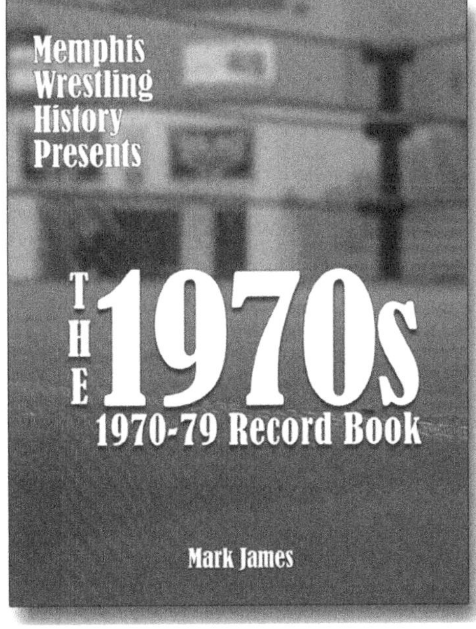

Memphis Wrestling History Presents The 1970s

Check Out Mark James' Entire Line Of Books At
www.memphiswrestlinghistory.com
www.memphiswrestlingbook.com

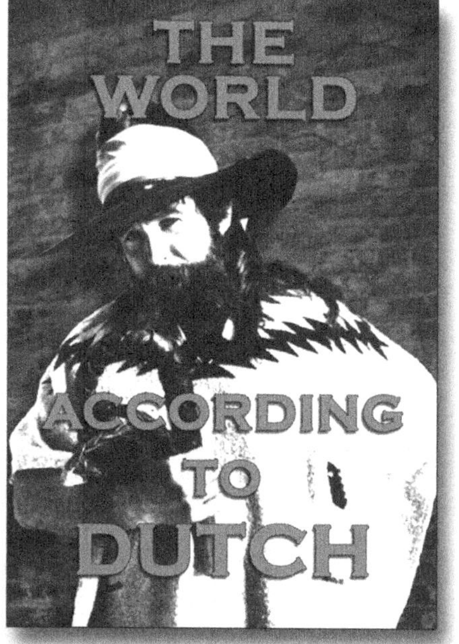

The World According To Dutch

Great Wrestling Stories From Dutch Mantell

Tales From A Dirt Road

More Wrestling Stories From Dutch Mantell

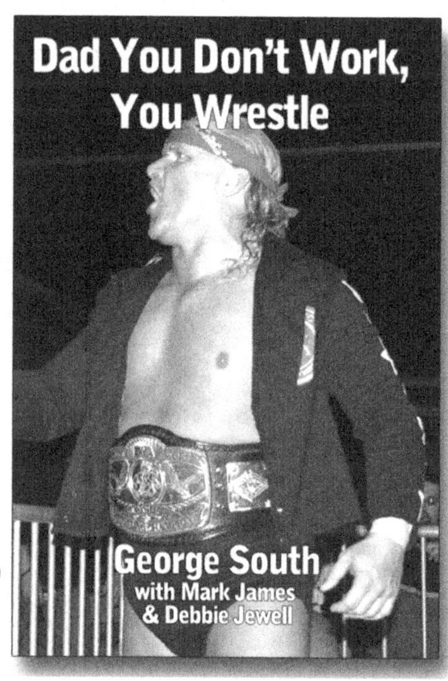

Dad You Don't Work, You Wrestle

George South's Autobiography

Check Out Mark James' Entire Line Of Books At
www.memphiswrestlinghistory.com
www.memphiswrestlingbook.com

Wrestling Record Book

Nashville Programs 1951-1952

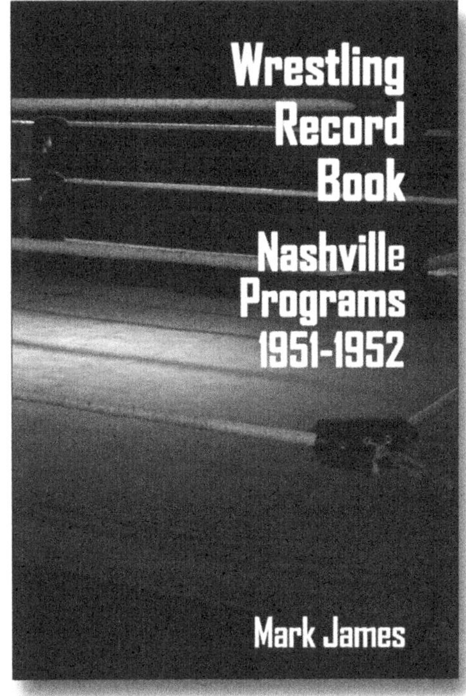

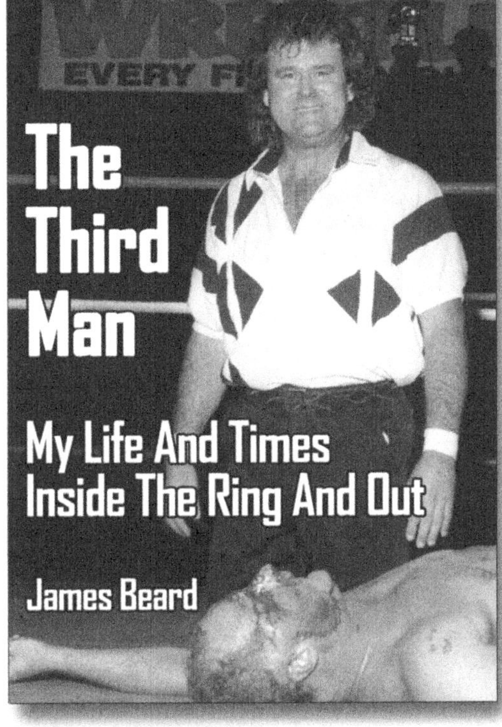

James Beard's
The Third Man

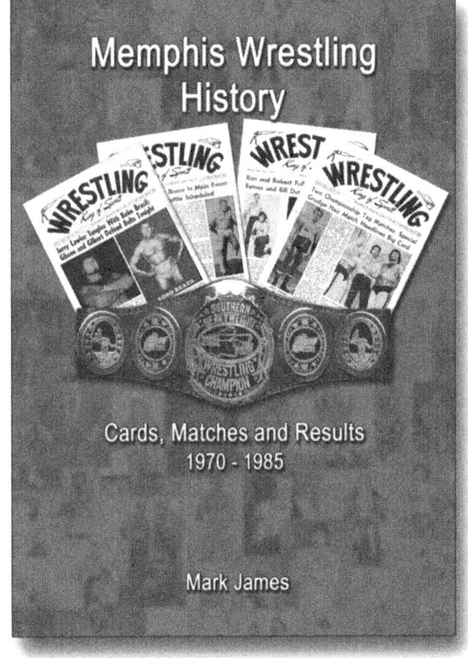

Memphis Wrestling History: Cards, Matches & Results 1970 - 1985

21468301R00216

Made in the USA
Middletown, DE
13 December 2018